PHILIP'S

NAVIGATOR Britain

www.philips-maps.co.uk

First published in 1994 by Philip's,
a division of Octopus Publishing Group Ltd
www.octopusbooks.co.uk
Endeavour House, 189 Shaftesbury Avenue,
London WC2H 8JY
An Hachette UK Company
www.hachette.co.uk

Eleventh edition 2014
First impression 2014

ISBN 978-1-84907-317-2

Cartography by Philip's
Copyright © 2014 Philip's

This product includes mapping data licensed from
Ordnance Survey®, with the permission of the Controller of
Her Majesty's Stationery Office. © Crown copyright 2014.
All rights reserved. Licence number 100011710

Data for the speed cameras provided by
PocketGPSWorld.com Ltd.

Data for the caravan sites provided by The Camping and
Caravanning Club.

Information for the selection of Wildlife Trust nature reserves
provided by The Wildlife Trusts.

Information for National Parks, Areas of Outstanding Natural
Beauty, National Trails and Country Parks in Wales supplied
by the Countryside Council for Wales.

Information for National Parks, Areas of Outstanding Natural
Beauty, National Trails and Country Parks in England
supplied by Natural England. Data for Regional Parks, Long
Distance Footpaths and Country Parks in Scotland provided
by Scottish Natural Heritage.

Information for Forest Parks supplied by the
Forestry Commission

Information for the RSPB reserves provided by the RSPB

Gaelic name forms used in the Western Isles provided by
Comhairle nan Eilean.

Data for the National Nature Reserves in England provided
by Natural England. Data for the National Nature Reserves in
Wales provided by Countryside Council for Wales. Darparwyd
data'n ymwneud â Gwarchodfeydd Natur Cenedlaethol
Cymru gan Gyngor Cefn Gwlad Cymru.

Information on the location of National Nature Reserves in
Scotland was provided by Scottish Natural Heritage.

Data for National Scenic Areas in Scotland provided by
the Scottish Executive Office. Crown copyright material is
reproduced with the permission of the Controller of HMSO
and the Queen's Printer for Scotland. Licence number
C02W0003960.

Printed in China

Contents

Road map symbols

M25	Motorway
16 — 17	Motorway junctions – full access, restricted access
	Toll motorway
Pease Pottage Services	Motorway service area
	Motorway under construction
S	Primary route – dual, single carriageway, services – under construction, narrow
Cardiff	Primary destination
25 — 26	Numbered junctions – full, restricted access
	A road – dual, single carriageway – under construction, narrow
	B road – dual, single carriageway – under construction, narrow
	Minor road – dual, single carriageway
	Drive or track
	Urban side roads
	Roundabout, multi-level junction
2	Distance in miles
	Tunnel
Toll	Toll, steep gradient – points downhill
40 40	Speed camera – single, multiple
CLEVELAND WAY	National trail – England and Wales
GREAT GLEN WAY	Long distance footpath – Scotland
YATTON	Railway with station, level crossing, tunnel
ROPLEY	Preserved railway with level crossing, station, tunnel
	Tramway
	National boundary
	County or unitary authority boundary
	Car ferry, catamaran
	Passenger ferry, catamaran
CALAIS 1:30	Ferry destination, journey time – hours: minutes
	Hovercraft
V P	Internal ferry – car, passenger
	Principal airport, other airport or airfield
MENDIP HILLS	Area of outstanding natural beauty, National Forest – England and Wales, Forest park, National park, National scenic area – Scotland, Regional park
	Woodland
	Beach – sand, shingle
KENNET AND AVON CANAL	Navigable river or canal
6 6	Lock, flight of locks, canal bridge number
Ç CF CS LS	Caravan or camping sites – CCC* Club Site, Camping in the Forest Site – CCC Certificated Site, Listed Site *Categories defined by the Camping and Caravanning Club of Great Britain
☼ P&R ▲965	Viewpoint, park and ride, spot height – in metres
	Linear antiquity
29	Adjoining page number
SY 80 70	Ordnance Survey National Grid reference – see page 402

Road map scale 1:100 000 or 1.58 miles to 1 inch

0   1   2   3 miles
0   1   2   3   4   5 km

Road map scale (Isle of Man and parts of Scotland)
1:200 000 or 3.15 miles to 1 inch

0   1   2   3   4   5   6 miles
0 1 2 3 4 5 6 7 8 9 10 km

Tourist information

BYLAND ABBEY	Abbey or priory		Marina
WOODHENGE	Ancient monument	SILVERSTONE	Motor racing circuit
SEALIFE CENTRE	Aquarium or dolphinarium		Nature reserves
CITY MUSEUM AND ART GALLERY	Art collection or museum	HOLTON HEATH	– National nature reserve
TATE ST IVES	Art gallery	BOYTON MARSHES	– RSPB reserve
1644	Battle site and date	DRAYCOTT SLEIGHTS	– Wildlife Trust reserve
ABBOTSBURY SWANNERY	Bird sanctuary or aviary		Picnic area
BAMBURGH CASTLE	Castle	WEST SOMERSET RAILWAY	Preserved railway
YORK MINSTER	Cathedral	THIRSK	Racecourse
SANDHAM MEMORIAL CHAPEL	Church of interest	LEAHILL TURRET	Roman antiquity
SEVEN SISTERS	Country park – England and Wales	THRIGBY HALL	Safari park
LOCHORE MEADOWS	– Scotland	FREEPORT BRAINTREE	Shopping village
ROYAL BATH & WEST SHOWGROUND	County show ground	MILLENNIUM STADIUM	Sports venue
MONK PARK FARM	Farm park	ALTON TOWERS	Theme park
HILLIER GARDENS AND ARBORETUM	Garden, arboretum		Tourist information centres – open all year – open seasonally
ST ANDREWS	Golf course – 18-hole		
TYNTESFIELD	Historic house	NATIONAL RAILWAY MUSEUM	Transport collection
SS GREAT BRITAIN	Historic ship	LEVANT MINE	World heritage site
HATFIELD HOUSE	House and garden	HELMSLEY	Youth hostel
CUMBERLAND PENCIL MUSEUM	Museum	MARWELL	Zoo
MUSEUM OF DARTMOOR LIFE	– Local	SUTTON BANK VISITOR CENTRE	Other place of interest
NAT MARITIME MUSEUM	– Maritime or military	GLENFIDDICH DISTILLERY	

Approach map symbols

M6	Motorway
	Toll motorway
6 5	Motorway junction – full, restricted access
S	Service area
	Under construction
A6	Primary route – dual, single carriageway
S	Service area
	Multi-level junction
	roundabout
	Under construction
A195	A road – dual, single carriageway
B1288	B road – dual, single carriageway
	Minor road – dual, single carriageway
	Ring road
3	Distance in miles
COSELEY	Railway with station
LOXDALE	Tramway with station
M	Underground or metro station
	Congestion charge area

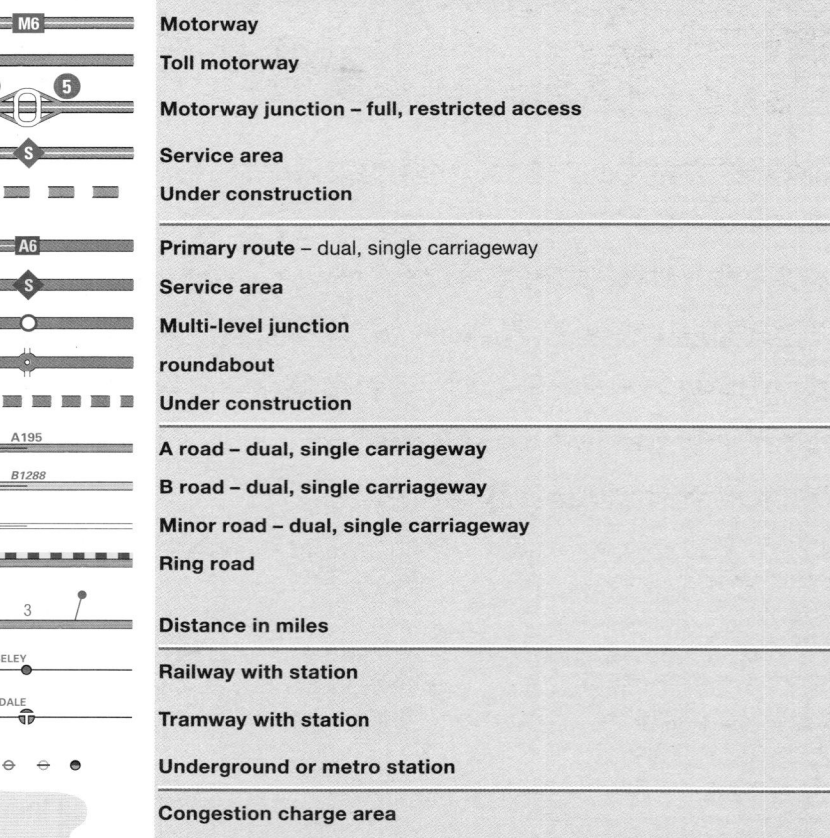

Speed Cameras

Fixed camera locations are shown using the 40 symbol. In congested areas the 40 symbol is used to show that there are two or more cameras on the road indicated.

Due to the restrictions of scale the camera locations are only approximate and cannot indicate the operating direction of the camera. Mobile camera sites, and cameras located on roads not included on the mapping are not shown. Where two or more cameras are shown on the same road, drivers are warned that this may indicate that a SPEC system is in operation. These cameras use the time taken to drive between the two camera positions to calculate the speed of the vehicle. At the time of going to press, some local authorities were considering decommissioning their speed cameras.

The Death of the Full English?

A Motorway pile up you'll want to avoid

by Stephen Mesquita,
Philip's On The Road Correspondent

Now come on. Be honest. When you're away from home and on the road early, haven't you been tempted by a Full English? Live it up. Put the new diet on hold. Build up your strength for the day ahead. Won't have to eat again till dinner. (A full list of excuses may be available on our web site).

shutterstock

One Full English can be a struggle. But, on a hot and sunny day last August, your intrepid Philip's On The Road Correspondent, ably assisted by his right-hand man Stuart the Sales Supremo, consumed eight of them. Our location: a typical stretch of Middle England – otherwise known as Milton Keynes. Our guide: The Philip's atlas, dotted with Post-it notes for each location (we won't mention the sat-nav). Our mission: to see if the hungry early-morning motorist is adequately catered for.

I'm sad to report that, in my view, The Full English for the motorist in a hurry has become an endangered species. Here are a few of the threats to one of our great traditions:

- **Low-quality ingredients** – most of the sausages and bacon served up seem to be from the 'we've got something cheaper out the back' counter.

- **Sausages have more than one side** – the striped sausage reigns supreme, burnt on two sides.

- **Baked Beans** – OK for the Full American but they alter the taste of the Full English. They should be offered as an option only.

- **Triangles of frozen Hash Browns** – these have no place in the Full English and should not be allowed through Passport Control.

- **Bring back the Fried Bread, please** – it may be horribly unhealthy but it's the forbidden pleasure of the Full English, the apple in the Garden of Eden. Where is it now?

- **Tinned tomatoes** – some people may prefer them but we don't. We like a lightly cooked ripe tomato, not one that's been refrigerated for six months and then burnt.

- **Cold, lukewarm or barely warm?** These seem to be the thermal options. None of the breakfasts were piping hot and many were stone cold.

- **Value for money** – not a concept understood by Motorway Service Areas.

So here is what we thought of what we tasted – a bite-by-bite account of the whole gory episode:

1 Moto Toddington Services Eat and Drink Company 🕒 6.20am

Price: £8.49

The Highlights

- Eggs cooked to order and cover provided (but still not hot)
- **Fried bread** (hurrah – the only one)
- **A decent amount for your money** (but needs to be for £8.49)
- Sausages like rubber
- Bacon unappetising
  - **Hash browns superfluous and tasted of frozen goo**
    - **Black pudding** – a terrible mistake
    Verdict: 5 out of 10
    Comment: a reasonable attempt let down by less than adequate ingredients.

▼ 6.20am Moto Toddington, Stuart decides

2 Premier Inn ⏱ 7.30am

Price: £8.25

The Highlights
- **Egg** – rubbery and covered in grease (with an extra greasy bit thrown in)
- **Tomato** – unripe
- **Sausage** –not a disaster but rather sweet
- **Bacon** – mainly salt
- **Mushrooms** – a bit chewy
- **Swamped** by baked beans
- **Intrusive drivel** from local radio station

Comment: Lovely location, pity about the breakfast. We liked the windmill.

Verdict: 4 out of 10

3 Toby Carvery, Travel Lodge ⏱ 8.05am

Price: £3.99

The Highlights
- **Egg** –beyond repair
- **Sausage** – seemed to be a veteran of many campaigns
- **Bacon** – tasted like 99% salt
- **Hash brown** – completely tasteless pancake
- **Tomato** – unripe
- **2 orange juices** cost nearly as much as the breakfast

Comment: The unseemly mess highlighted by the arrow is a triumph of innovation over taste. Overall, this breakfast was not what you want to be faced with first thing in the morning.

Verdict: 2 out of 10

4 Comfort Inn Milton Keynes Hotel ⏱ 8.45am

Price: £7.50 but didn't accept credit cards or have change so accepted £6.70 (all the change we had)

The Highlights
- **An unspeakable experience**
- **Mushrooms** – like cardboard filings, late 20th Century
- **Eggs** – greasy and unappetising
- **Sausage** – tasted as if it had made only passing contact with meat.
- **Tomato** – a quarter, slightly burnt

Comment: The website says this hotel is an unrivalled experience. That's true.

Verdict: 1 out of 10

5 McDonald's

Price: Big Breakfast £3.39 including OJ/ Sausage and Egg McMuffin £3.29 including OJ

The Highlights:
- **The Full American** – not really an English breakfast as we know it
- **You can't fault the price**
- **Couldn't look more unappetising**
- **Hash brown slab mainly fat**
- **A confession:** the sausage burger's quite nice
- **Stick to the scrambled egg in the Big Breakfast** – the flying saucer in the Egg McMuffin is dire
- **Here's what the others don't tell you:** the Big Breakfast is 550 calories

Verdict: 4 out of 10

Comment: It doesn't pretend to be an English breakfast but you know what you're getting.

6 Super Sausage A5 Towcester ⏱ 9.50am

The Price: £6.20

The Highlights
- **Tasty sausages** (bravo!)
- **Good value for money**
- **Egg** – nicely cooked and not too greasy
- **Bacon** –tasted of bacon
- **A bit let down by some of the extras** (hash browns were tasteless, except slightly burnt)
- **Excellent service**

Comment: not a classic Full English but by some way the best we tasted. Great for families as well as motorists.

Verdict: 7 out of 10

7 Jack's Hill Café A5/A43 ⏱ 10.20am

The Price: £4.50

The Highlights
- **Excellent value for money**
- **Reasonably tasty**
- **Ingredients** – you get what you pay for

Comment: you expect truck stops to be cheap and filling and this fits the bill. You won't (and we didn't) get a gourmet experience.

Verdict: 6 out of 10

8 Road Chef Watford Gap Services Fresh Food Cafe ⏱ 11.00am

The Price:

The Highlights
- **Arrived in 1 minute**
- **All lukewarm**
- **Egg** – cooked both sides (not asked for)
- **Bacon** – like salty mdf
- **Hash Brown** – a fried mush
- **A real mushroom (hurrah)** but rubbery and watery
- **Comment:** As Julius Caesar said, 'We Came, We Saw, We Left'.

Verdict: 3 out of 10

9 Welcome Break Newport Pagnell Services ⏱ 11.55

The Price: £7.99

The Highlights
- **Mushrooms** –a bit wizened
- **Bacon** – tough, cold and horrible, with watery white residue
- **3 sausages** with the designer 'zebra' look
- **Hash brown** – like a fishcake without the fish
- **Tomatoes** – lukewarm
- **Egg specially cooked (hurrah!)** – two cooked, only one put on plate. Where did it go?

Comment: sausages would win a 'Find the Meat' competition

Verdict: 3 out of 10

10 Home – the £2 Challenge

The Price: £1.98

I've been impolite about almost all the breakfasts we tasted – so it seems only fair that I have a go myself.

And to make things harder, I set myself a stiff challenge. To create a Full English with the best ingredients I could find for no more than £2.

Why £2? Because then I could sell it for a four times mark up for £7.99. That's a reasonable price for good breakfast. And – I'm sure you'll agree, beleaguered consumers and travellers, a more than generous profit margin for me as the supplier. I'm sure that most of the breakfasts we ate on the road were making substantially more profit – great for them but not so good for us.

Part 1: The shopping

Off to the market in my local town of Halesworth in Suffolk and the tension is mounting. Armed with a calculator, I was asking the big question: could I buy the ingredients for my Under £2 Full English and bring it in under budget?

First stop – the local farm for absolutely fresh, speckled eggs, laid in the last 24 hours. Then to the Wednesday market stall for the tomatoes and mushrooms. Next the Farmhouse Bakery for a small granary loaf and – last stop – Allen's The Butcher for the meat (best Suffolk pork, of course).

That was the easy bit. Now the fun really started, as I retired to Frapa's for a cup of their excellent coffee and agonised over the costings with a calculator. The ingredients were great: fresh, wholesome and local. But could I bring it in on budget?

The shopping list – in the best traditions of male shopping, created on a spreadsheet – reveals all.

▲ Allen's Butchers Halesworth

▼ Halesworth Market

Ingredients	Price per portion	Notes
Eggs (2)	£0.33	Six farm-laid eggs £1.00
Bacon (1)	£0.30	Best Suffolk Pork Smoked Bacon £10.99 per kilo £1.21 for 4 rashers
Sausages (2)	£0.84	Best Suffolk Pork Sausages £6.99 per kilo £1.68 for 4
Tomato (1)	£0.145	Ripe English vine tomatoes £0.60 per lb
Mushrooms (4)	£0.28	Fresh mushrooms £1.20 per lb
Bread (1)	£0.085	Granary loaf £0.95 for 11 slices
Total	**£1.98**	

The spreadsheet

The total cost: £1.98. Just 2p to spare! I'd done it! Now I had to cook it.

Part 2: The Preparation

◄ The picture says it all

Part 3: The Cooking

I took the view that a Full English shouldn't pretend to be 100% healthy – but my personal preference was for something not too cholesterol-soaked. So the sausages, bacon and tomatoes were cooked in the oven, the bread was toasted not fried and the eggs fried in almost no olive oil. Here are the results:

Part 4: The Eating

It may sound immodest to say this – but this was the most pleasurable 10 minutes of the whole exercise. Actually, it isn't immodest because the pleasure had almost nothing to do with my cooking and almost everything to do with the ingredients. They were yummy. Where do I start?

- **The eggs were as good as they looked**
- **The sausages tasted of meat and were not too salty.**
- **The bacon was lean and beautifully flavoured**
- **The tomatoes were ripe and succulent**
- **The mushrooms were juicy and nicely flavoured**
- **Even the toast had a pleasant aroma**

This Full English actually tasted quite healthy (all right – the bacon and sausage were a bit of an indulgence) and didn't require 3 litres of water to recover from it. All for £1.98.

Restricted motorway junctions

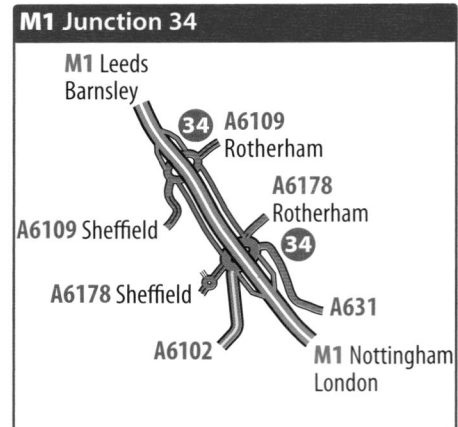

M1 Junction 34

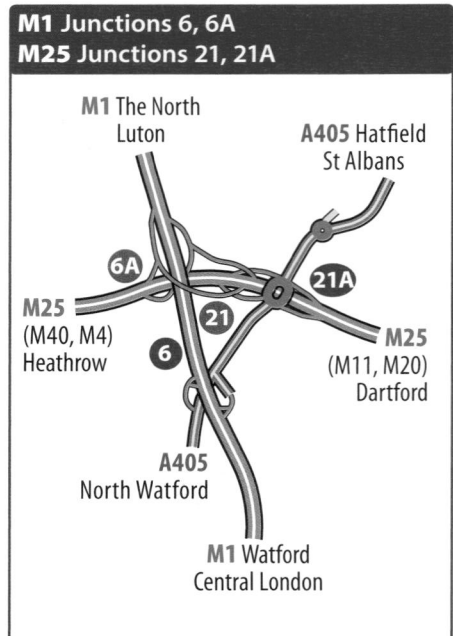

M1 Junctions 6, 6A
M25 Junctions 21, 21A

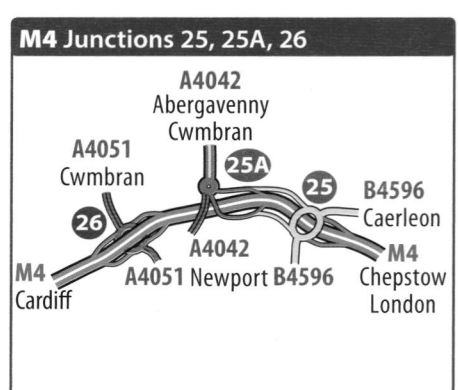

M4 Junctions 25, 25A, 26

M8 Junctions 8, 9 · M73 Junctions 1, 2 · M74 Junctions 2A, 3, 3A, 4

M1	Northbound	Southbound
2	No exit	No access
4	No exit	No access
6A	No exit. Access from M25 only	No access. Exit to M25 only
7	No exit. Access from A414 only	No access. Exit to A414 only
17	No access. Exit to M45 only	No exit. Access from M45 only
19	No exit to A14	No access from A14
21A	No access	No exit
23A		Exit to A42 only
24A	No exit	No access
35A	No access	No exit
43	No access. Exit to M621 only	No exit. Access from M621 only
48	No exit to A1(M) southbound	

M3	Eastbound	Westbound
8	No exit	No access
10	No access	No exit
13	No access to M27 eastbound	
14	No exit	No access

M4	Eastbound	Westbound
1	Exit to A4 eastbound only	Access from A4 westbound only
2	Access from A4 eastbound only	Access to A4 westbound only
21	No exit	No access
23	No access	No exit
25	No exit	No access
25A	No exit	No access
29	No exit	No access
38		No access
39	No exit or access	No exit
41	No access	No exit
41A	No exit	No access
42	Access from A483 only	Exit to A483 only

M5	Northbound	Southbound
10	No exit	No access
11A	No access from A417 eastbound	No exit to A417 westbound

M6	Northbound	Southbound
3A	No access. Exit to M42 northbound only	No exit. Access from M6 eastbound only
4A	No exit. Access from M42 southbound only	No access. Exit to M42 only
5	No access	No exit
10A	No access. Exit to M54 only	No exit. Access from M54 only
11A	No exit. Access from M6 Toll only	No access. Exit to M6 Toll only
20	No exit to M56 eastbound	No access from M56 westbound
24	No exit	No access
25	No access	No exit
30	No exit. Access from M61 northbound only	No access. Exit to M61 southbound only
31A	No access	No exit
45	No access	No exit

M6 Toll	Northbound	Southbound
T1		No exit
T2	No exit, no access	No access
T5	No exit	No access
T7	No access	No exit
T8	No access	No exit

M8	Eastbound	Westbound
8	No exit to M73 northbound	No access from M73 southbound
9	No access	No exit
13	No exit southbound	Access from M73 southbound only
14	No access	No exit
16	No exit	No access
17	No exit	No access
18		No exit
19	No exit to A814 eastbound	No access from A814 westbound
20	No exit	No access
21	No access from M74	No exit
22	No exit. Access from M77 only	No access. Exit to M77 only
23	No exit	No access
25	Exit to A739 northbound only. Access from A739 southbound only	Access from A739 southbound only
25A	No exit	No access
28	No exit	No access
28A	No exit	No access

M9	Eastbound	Westbound
1A	No exit	No access
2	No access	No exit
3	No exit	No access
6	No access	No exit
8	No exit	No access

M5 Junction 11A

M11	Northbound	Southbound
4	No exit	No access
5	No access	No exit
9	No access	No exit
13	No access	No exit
14	No exit to A428 westbound	No exit. Access from A14 westbound only

M20	Eastbound	Westbound
2	No access	No exit
3	No exit Access from M26 eastbound only	No access Exit to M26 westbound only
11A	No access	No exit

M23	Northbound	Southbound
7	No exit to A23 southbound	No access from A23 northbound
10A	No exit	No access

M25	Clockwise	Anticlockwise
5	No exit to M26 eastbound	No access from M26 westbound
19	No access	No exit
21	No exit to M1 southbound. Access from M1 southbound only	No exit to M1 southbound. Access from M1. southbound only
31	No exit	No access

M27	Eastbound	Westbound
10	No exit	No access
12	No access	No exit

M40	Eastbound	Westbound
3	No exit	No access
7	No exit	No access
8	No exit	No access
13	No exit	No access
14	No access	No exit
16	No access	No exit

M42	Northbound	Southbound
1	No exit	No access
7	No access Exit to M6 northbound only	No exit Access from M6 northbound only
7A	No access. Exit to M6 southbound only	No exit
8	No exit. Access from M6 southbound only	Exit to M6 northbound only. Access from M6 southbound only

M45	Eastbound	Westbound
M1 J17	Access to M1 southbound only	No access from M1 southbound
With A45	No access	No exit

M48	Eastbound	Westbound
M4 J21	No exit to M4 westbound	No access from M4 eastbound
M4 J23	No access from M4 westbound	No exit to M4 eastbound

M49	Southbound	Northbound
18A	No exit to M5 northbound	No access from M5 southbound

M53	Northbound	Southbound
11	Exit to M56 eastbound only. Access from M56 westbound only	Exit to M56 eastbnd only. Access from M56 westbound only

M56	Eastbound	Westbound
2	No exit	No access
3	No access	No exit
4	No exit	No access
7		No access
8	No exit or access	No exit
9	No access from M6 northbound	No access to M6 southbound
15	No exit to M53	No access from M53 northbound

M57	Northbound	Southbound
3	No exit	No access
5	No exit	No access

M58	Eastbound	Westbound
1	No exit	No access

M60	Clockwise	Anticlockwise
2		
3	No exit to A34 northbound	No exit to A34 northbound
4	No access from M56	No exit to M56
5	No exit to A5103 southbound	No exit to A5103 northbound
14	No exit	No access
16	No exit	No access
20	No access	No exit
22		No access
25	No access	
26		No exit or access
27	No exit	No access

M61	Northbound	Southbound
2	No access from A580 eastbound	No exit to A580 westbound
3	No access from A580 eastbound. No access from A666 southbound	No exit to A580 westbound
M6 J30	No exit to M6 southbound	No access from M6 northbound

M62	Eastbound	Westbound
23	No access	No exit

M65	Eastbound	Westbound
9	No access	No exit
11	No access	No access

M66	Northbound	Southbound
1	No access	No exit

M67	Eastbound	Westbound
1A	No access	No exit
2	No exit	No access

M69	Northbound	Southbound
2	No access	No access

M73	Northbound	Southbound
2	No access from M8 or A89 eastbound. No exit to A89	No exit to M8 or A89 westbound. No access from A89

M74	Northbound	Southbound
3	No access	No exit
3A	No exit	No access
7	No exit	No access
9	No exit or access	No access
10		No exit
11	No exit	No access
12	No access	No exit

M77	Northbound	Southbound
4	No exit	No access
6	No exit	No access
7	No exit or access	
8	No access	No access

M80	Northbound	Southbound
4A	No access	No exit
6A	No exit	
8	Exit to M876 northbound only. No access	Access from M876 southbound only. No exit

M90	Northbound	Southbound
2A	No access	No exit
7	No exit	No access
8	No access	No exit
10	No access from A912	No exit to A912

M180	Eastbound	Westbound
1	No access	No exit

M621	Eastbound	Westbound
2A	No exit	No access
4	No exit	
5	No exit	No access
6	No access	No exit

M876	Northbound	Southbound
2	No access	No exit

A1(M)	Northbound	Southbound
2	No access	No exit
3		No access
5	No exit	No access
14	No exit	No access
40	No access	No access
43	No exit. Access from M1 only	No access. Exit to M1 only
57	No access	No access
65	No access	No exit

A3(M)	Northbound	Southbound
1	No exit	No access
4	No access	No exit

A38(M) with Victoria Rd, (Park Circus) Birmingham

Northbound	No exit
Southbound	No access

A48(M)	Northbound	Southbound
M4 Junc 29	Exit to M4 eastbound only	Access from M4 westbound only
29A	Access from A48 eastbound only	Exit to A48 westbound only

A57(M)	Eastbound	Westbound
With A5103	No access	No exit
With A34	No access	No exit

A58(M)		Southbound
With Park Lane and Westgate, Leeds		No access

A64(M)	Eastbound	Westbound
With A58 Clay Pit Lane, Leeds	No access	No exit
With Regent Street, Leeds	No access	No access

A74(M)	Northbound	Southbound
18	No access	No exit
22		No exit

A194(M)	Northbound	Southbound
A1(M) J65 Gateshead Western Bypass	Access from A1(M) northbound only	Exit to A1(M) southbound only

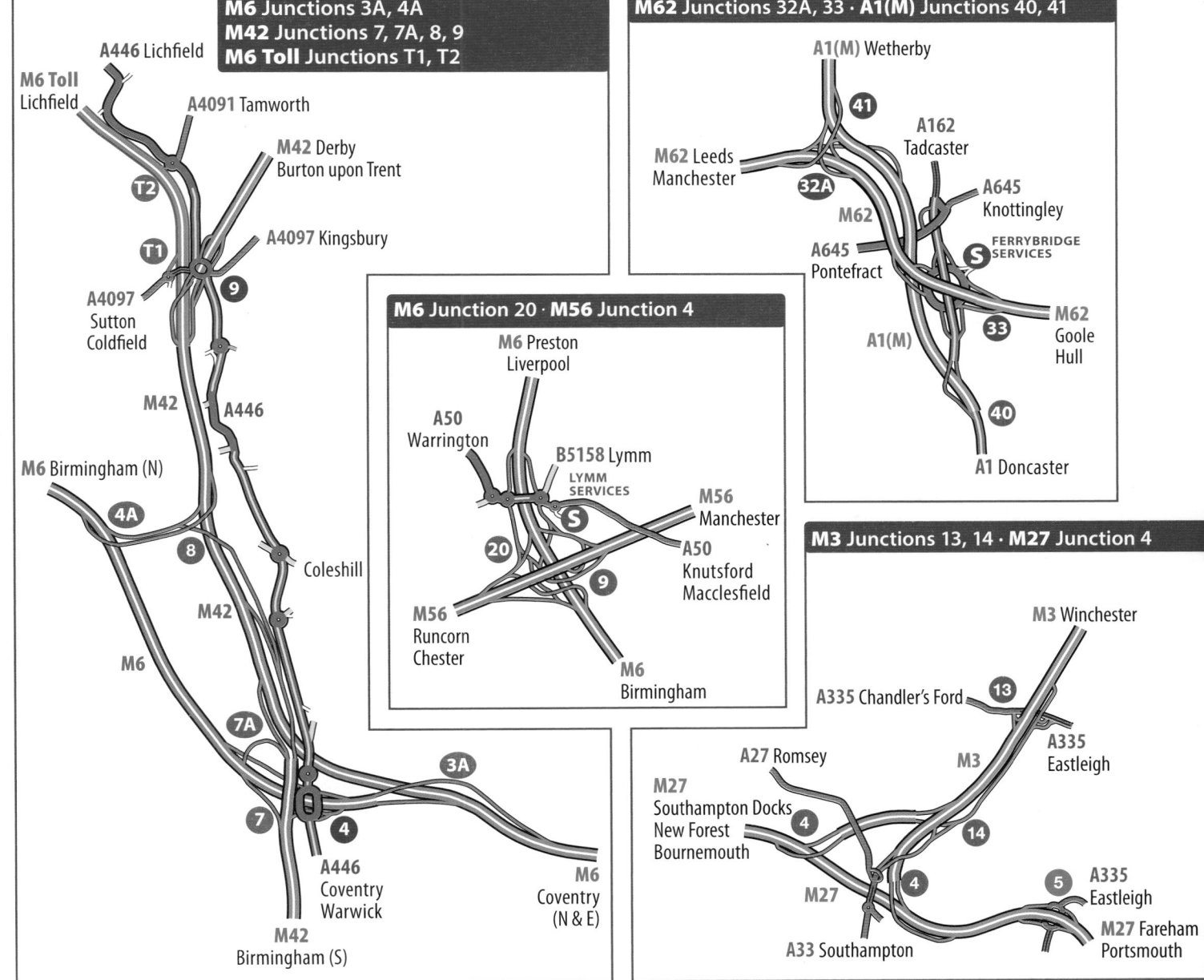

M6 Junctions 3A, 4A
M42 Junctions 7, 7A, 8, 9
M6 Toll Junctions T1, T2

M62 Junctions 32A, 33 · A1(M) Junctions 40, 41

M6 Junction 20 · M56 Junction 4

M3 Junctions 13, 14 · M27 Junction 4

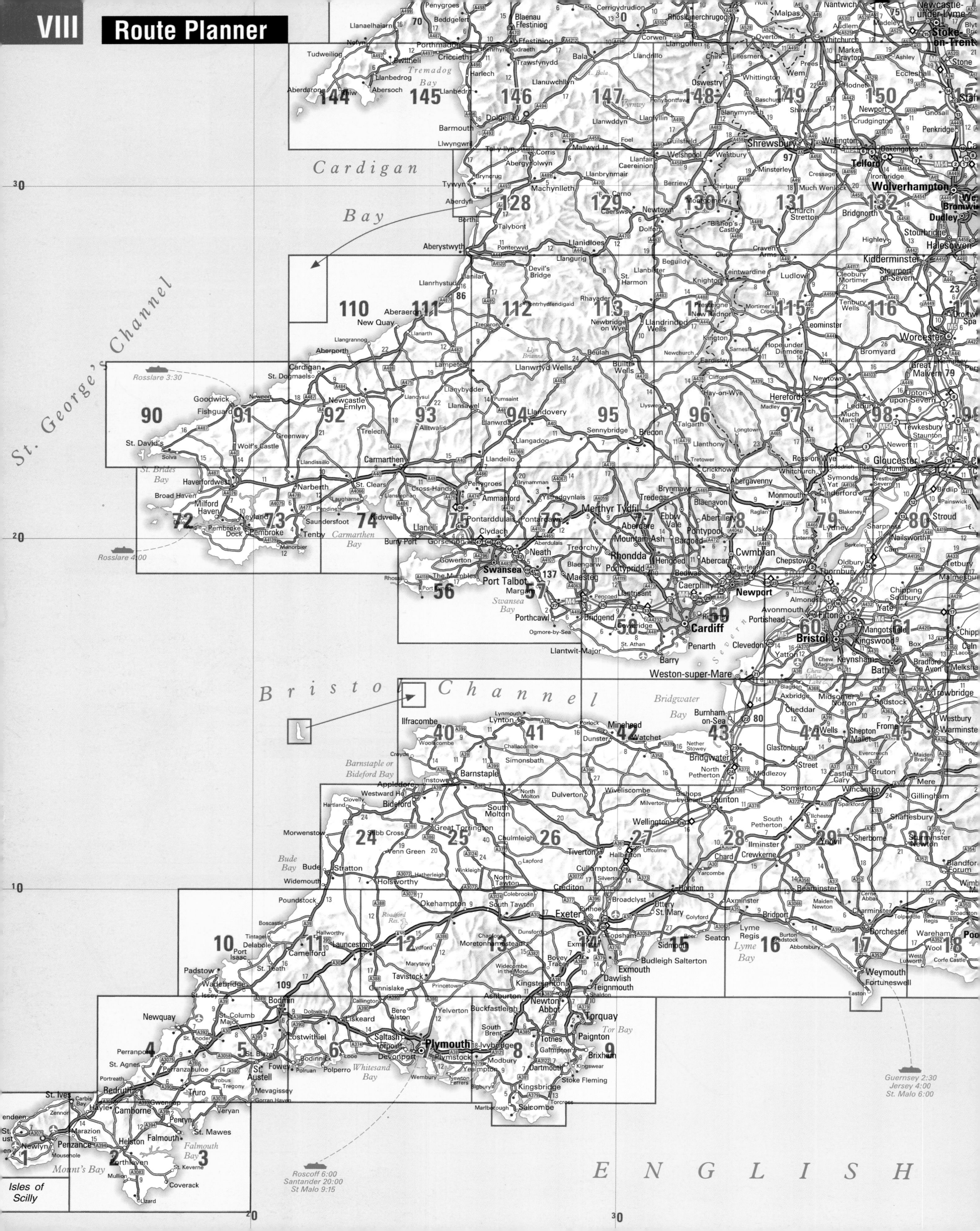

Scale 1:1 000 000   1cm = 10km   1 inch = 15.78 miles

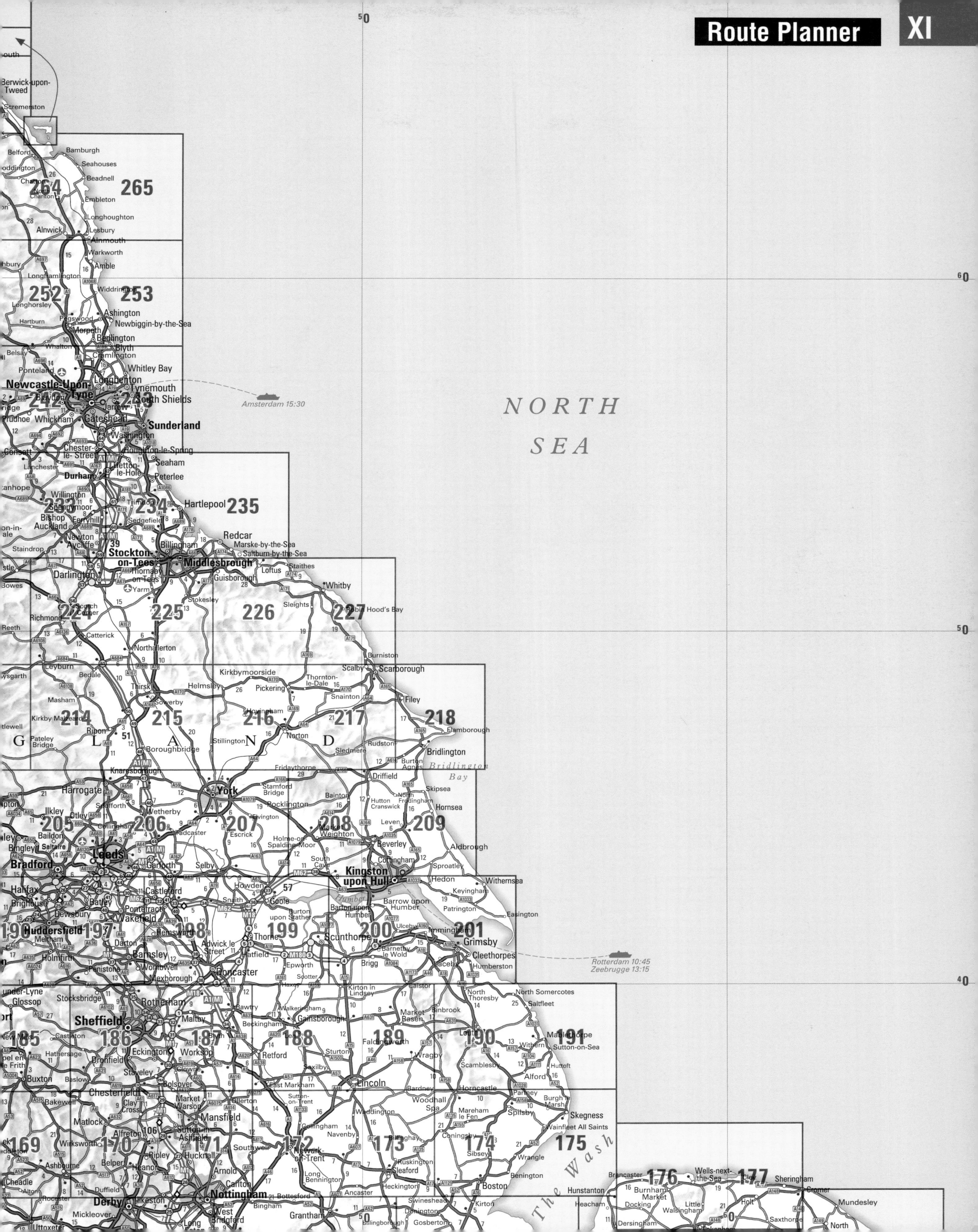

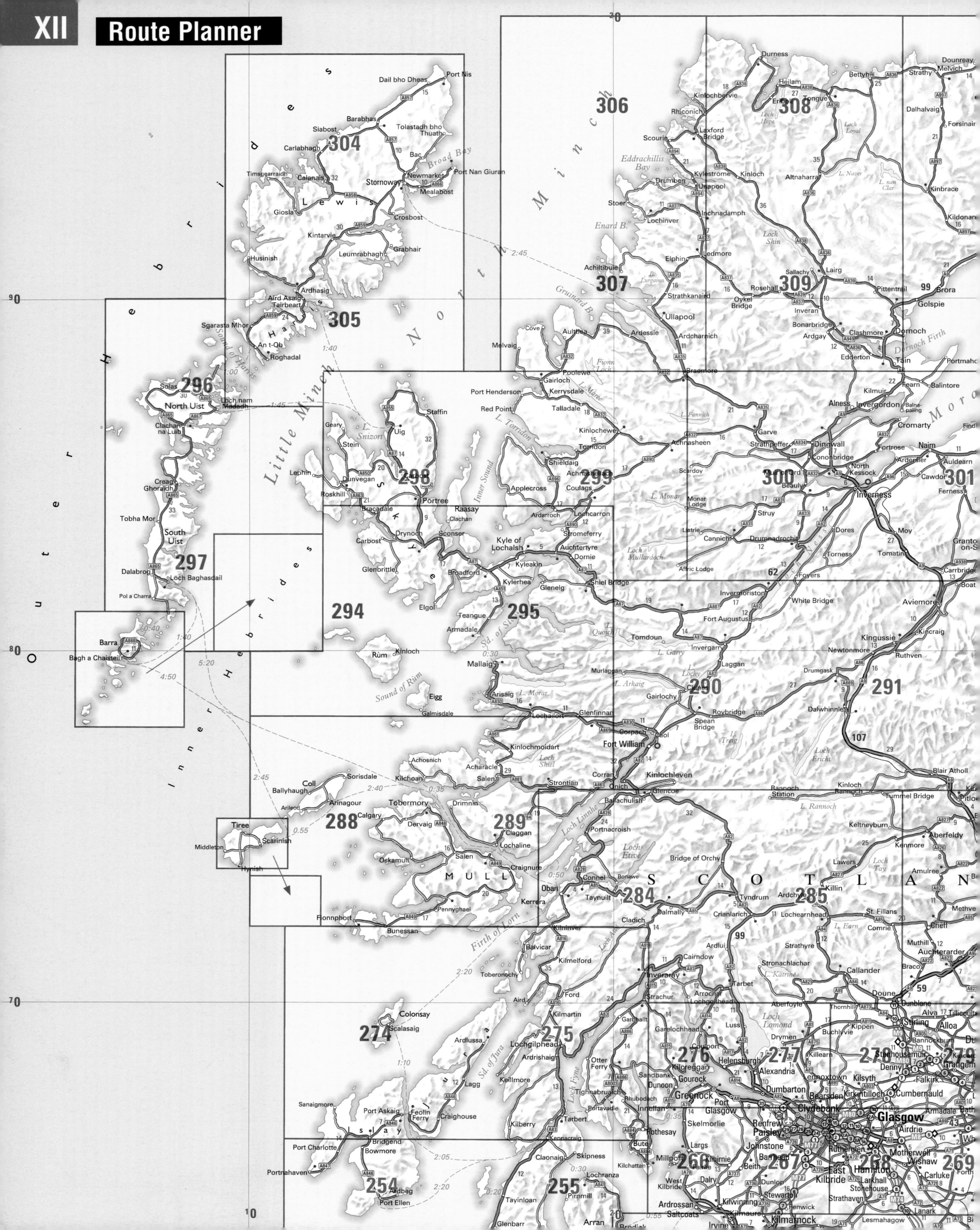

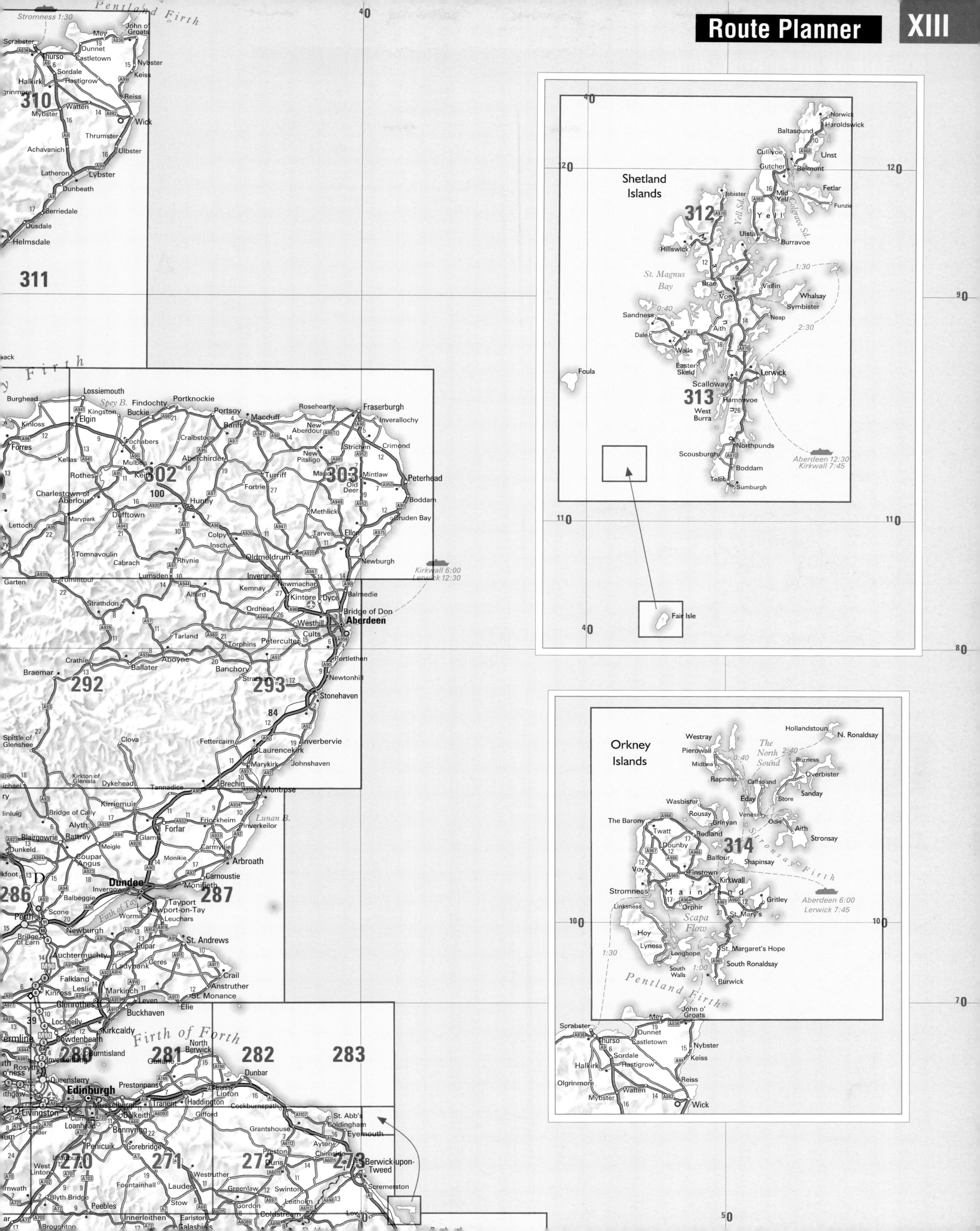

Pentland Firth

Stromness 1:30

Mey
John o'
Groats
Sprabster
Thurso
Castletown
Dunnet
Nybster
Sordale
Keiss
Halkirk
Hastigrow
Reiss
grinmore
310
Watten
Wick
Mybster
Thrumster
Achavanich
Ulbster
Latheron
Lybster
Dunbeath
Berriedale
Ousdale
Helmsdale

311

Shetland Islands

Norwick
Haroldswick
Baltasound
Cullivoe
Unst
Gutcher
Belmont
312
Isbister
Mid
Yell
Fetlar
Hillswick
Funzie
Ulsta
Burravoe
St. Magnus Bay
Brae
Voe
Vidlin
1:30
Sandness
Whalsay
Dale
Aith
Symbister
Neap
Walls
Easter
Skeld
Lerwick
Foula
Scalloway
313
Hamnavoe
West
Burra
Northpunds
Scousburgh
Aberdeen 12:30
Kirkwall 7:45
Boddam
Tolob
Sumburgh

Fair Isle

Firth

Burghead
Lossiemouth
Portknockie
Rosehearty
Fraserburgh
Spey B.
Findochty
Buckie
Portsoy
Macduff
Inverallochy
Kinloss
Kingston
Banff
New
Aberdour
Crimond
Elgin
Fochabers
Aberchirder
New
Pitsligo
Strichen
Forres
Mulben
Craibstone
Aberchirder
Maud
Mintlaw
Kellas
Keith
Turriff
Old
Deer
Peterhead
Rothes
302
Huntly
Fortrie
Boddam
Lettoch
Dufftown
Methlick
Cruden Bay
Marypark
Rhynie
Colpy
Tarves
Ellon
Tomnavoulin
Cabrach
Insch
Oldmeldrum
Newburgh
Garten
Lumsden
Inverurie
Tomintoul
Alford
Kemnay
Newmachar
Strathdon
Kintore
Dyce
Balmedie
Ordhead
Bridge of Don
Westhill
Aberdeen
Tarland
Cults
Torphins
Peterculter
Braemar
Crathie
Aboyne
Portlethen
Ballater
Banchory
Newtonhill
292
293
Strachan
Stonehaven
Spittle of
Glenshee
Clova
Inverbervie
Fettercairn
Laurencekirk
Johnshaven
Kirkton of
Glenisla
Marykirk
Dykehead
Tannadice
Brechin
Montrose
Bridge of Cally
Kirriemuir
Alyth
Forfar
Friockheim
Inverkeilor
Blairgowrie
Rattray
Glamis
Lunan B.
Dunkeld
Meigle
Carnoustie
Coupar
Angus
Monikie
Arbroath
Invergowrie
Monifieth
286
Dundee
287
Scone
Tayport
Balbeggie
Newport-on-Tay
Perth
Newburgh
Wormit
Bridge of Earn
Auchtermuchty
Leuchars
Kinross
Cupar
St. Andrews
Ladybank
Ceres
Falkland
Leslie
Markinch
Crail
Lochgelly
Leven
Anstruther
Cowdenbeath
Buckhaven
St. Monance
Kirkcaldy
Elie
Burntisland
North
Berwick
280
281
Gullane
282
283
Queensferry
Prestonpans
Dunbar
Edinburgh
Musselburgh
Tranent
Haddington
Dalkeith
East
Linton
Cockburnspath
Livingston
Bonnyrigg
Gifford
St. Abb's
Coldingham
Penicuik
Gorebridge
Grantshouse
Eyemouth
Ayton
270
271
Preston
Chirnside
Duns
Berwick-upon-Tweed
West
Linton
Lauder
Westruther
Greenlaw
Swinton
Blyth Bridge
Fountainhall
Stow
Gordon
Leitholm
Coldstream
Screnerston
Peebles
Innerleithen
Earlston
Broughton
Galashiels

Orkney Islands

Westray
Hollandstoun
N. Ronaldsay
Pierowall
The
North
Sound
Burriess
Midbea
Rapness
Calfsound
Overbister
Wasbister
Eday
Store
Sanday
The Barony
Rousay
Brinyan
Odie
Aith
Twatt
Veness
Stronsay
Redland
Shapinsay
314
Dounby
Balfour
Finstown
Voy
Kirkwall
Aberdeen 6:00
Lerwick 7:45
Stromness
Mainland
Gritley
Linksness
Orphir
St. Mary's
Hoy
Scapa
Flow
Lyness
Longhope
St. Margaret's Hope
South
Walls
South Ronaldsay
Burwick
Pentland Firth

Scrabster
Mey
John o'
Groats
Thurso
Dunnet
Castletown
Halkirk
Sordale
Nybster
Olgrinmore
Hastigrow
Keiss
Reiss
Mybster
Watten
Wick

Kirkwall 6:00
Lerwick 12:30

Distances and journey times

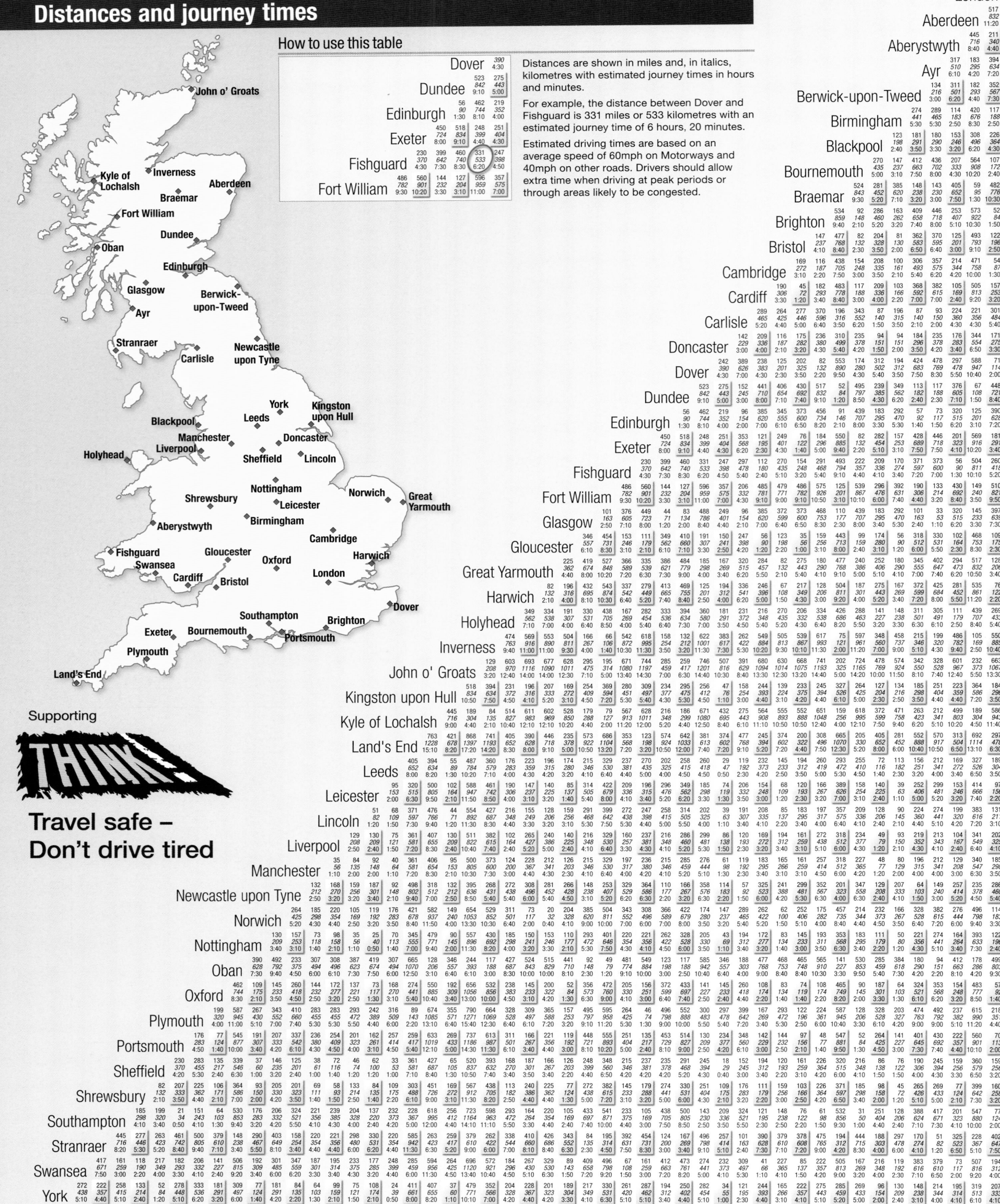

How to use this table

Distances are shown in miles and, in italics, kilometres with estimated journey times in hours and minutes.

For example, the distance between Dover and Fishguard is 331 miles or 533 kilometres with an estimated journey time of 6 hours, 20 minutes.

Estimated driving times are based on an average speed of 60mph on Motorways and 40mph on other roads. Drivers should allow extra time when driving at peak periods or through areas likely to be congested.

Supporting

THINK!

Travel safe –
Don't drive tired

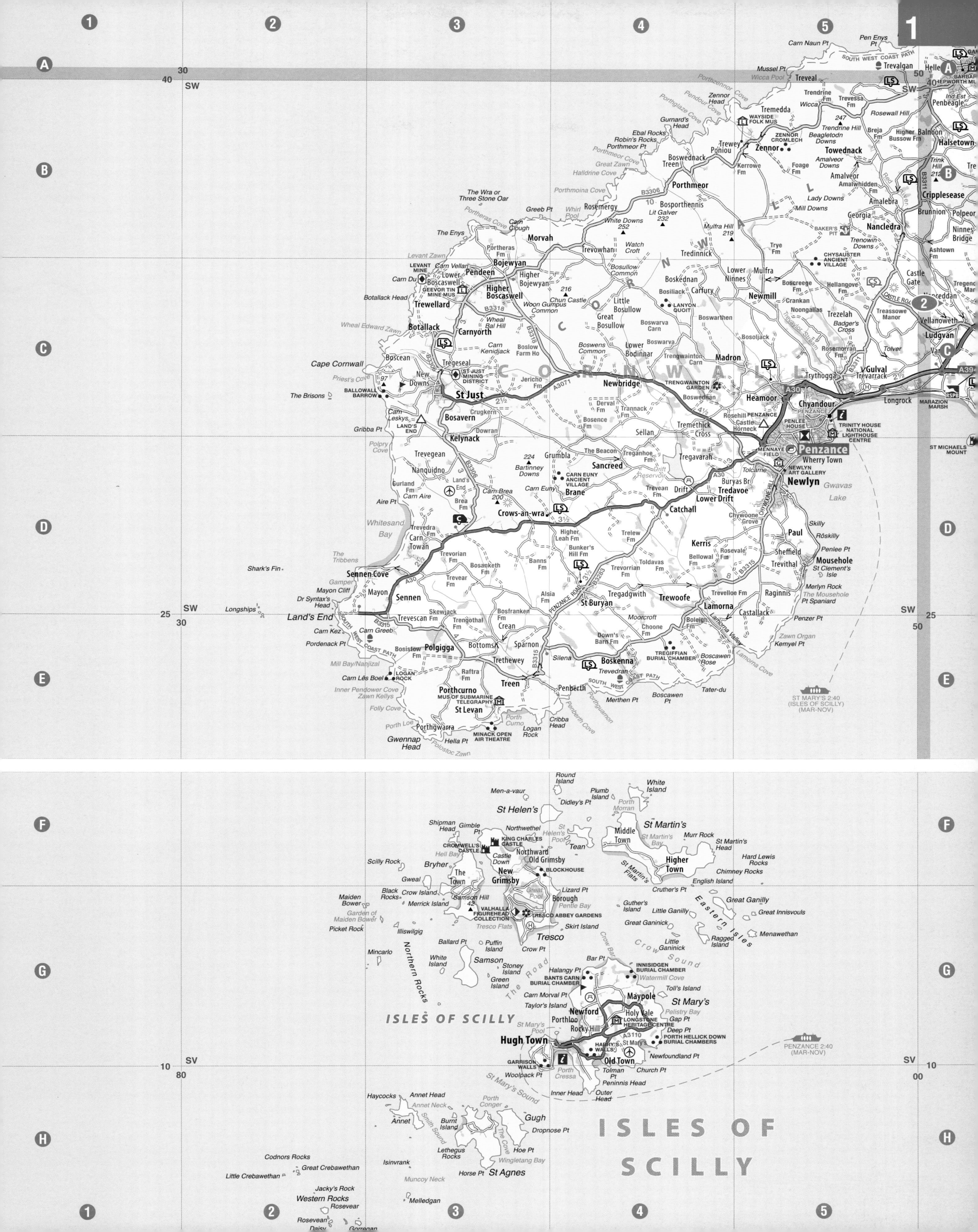

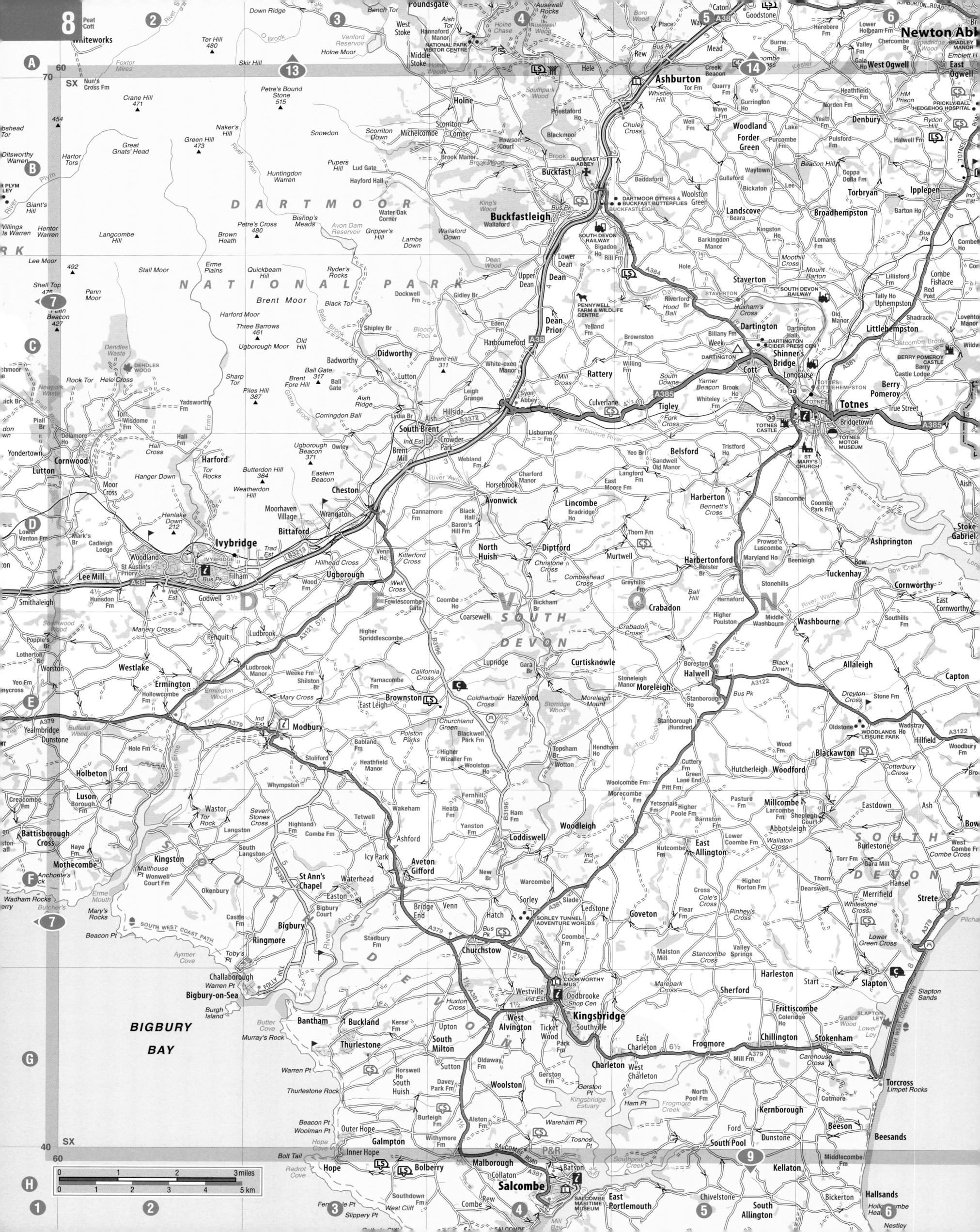

A

80
00
SW

B

C

D

The Island
Tintagel Head
Glebe
Dunderhole Pt
TINTAGEL
Penhallic Pt

Tre
Trebarw
Stra
Gull Rock
Port William
Dennis Pt
Backways Cove
Start Pt

E

Trerubies Cove
Tregardock Cliff
Jacket's Pt
Crookmoyle Rock
Delabole Pt
West
Dannonchapel
Port Isaac Bay
Barrett's Zawn
Ranie Pt

Newland
Rumps Pt
The Mouls
Kellan Head
Scarnor
Varley Head
Lobber Pt
Tresungers Pt
Port Gaverne
Port Isaac
Trewetha
Treore
Fm

Pentire Pt
83
Pentire Fm
Com Head
Port Quin Bay
Doyden
Reedy Cliff
Carnweather Pt
Trevan Fm
Port Quin

Pentireglaze Haven
Padstow Bay
Scarrabine Fm
LONG CROSS VICTORIAN GDNS
Plain Street
Trelights
St Endellion
Pendoggett
B3267

New Polzeath
Hayle Bay
Trenant
Porteath
Carruan
Gunvenna

Poltreworgey
Trelill
Pennytinney
Lanow
Tregellist
Trevine
Trewethern

Gulland Rock
Pepper Hole
Stepper Pt
The Narrows
Polzeath
Shilla Mill
Trebetherick
Pityme
St Minver
Tredrizzick
Tregurrin
Treglyn Down
Rooke Fm
Chapel Amble
Carclaze
Trequite
St Kew
Greater Brighter Fm
Hendra

F

Butter Hole
Gunver Head
Harbour Cove
Daymer Bay
Trebetherick Pt
Gun Pt
Crugmeer
Tregirls Fm
Splatt
Penmayne
Trefresa
Treglyn
Blakes Keiro
Penpont Fm
Lower Amble
Trewornan
St Kew Highway
Trevisqu
Trehaveral
Manor
Trevose Head
Merope Rocks
Round Hole
Mother Ivey's or Polventon Bay
Stinking Cove
Dinas Head
Porthmissen Bridge
Trevone Bay
Round Hole
Trethillick
Rock
Stoptide
Porthilly
Trelver
Gutt Bridge
Cross
Hill
Trega

Quies
Toll
Harlyn Bay
Trevone
Harlyn
Treator
PRIDEAUX PLACE
PADSTOW MUSEUM
Town Bar
Porthilly Cove
Cant Cove
River Camel
Tregorden
Kelly
Rocksea
Dinham's Br
Booby's Bay
Constantine Bay
Constantine Bay
B3276
Padstow
Ind Est
Dinas
NATIONAL LOBSTER HATCHERY
Trevelver
Tregunna
Burniere Fm
Trevanson
Bodieve
Ball
A39
Three Holes Cross
St Mabyn
Treyarnon Pt
Windmill
Trewithen Fm
A389
Oldtown
Oldtown Cove
Bodellick
Dunveth
Ind Est
Trenant
Hingham Mill
Trevilder

Trethias Island
Warren Cove
Pepper Cove
Fox Cove
TREYARNON BAY
Treyarnon
Towan
St Merryn
Treraval Fm
Sea Mills
Dennis Hill
Tregonce
Trevorrick
Trevilgus Fm
Perlees Fm
Whitecross
Penhale
Wadebridge
St Breock
Egloshayle
Clapper
Sladesbridge
Lower Croan
Croanford

G

Minnows Islands
Trehemborne
Carnevas
Trevorrick
Trevean
Highlanes
Burgois
Tregonna
CORNWALL
ROYAL CORNWALL SHOWGROUND
PENCARROW HOUSE

Will's Rock
Shop
Edmonton
Trescore Islands
Porth Mear
Porthcothan
Trevothan
Little Petherick
Mellingey
St Issey
Trevance
3
A389
Trelyl Fm
Polmorla
Tredannick
6½

High Cove
Park Head
Diggory's Island
Trevemedar
Treburrick
Penrose
Lewidden Lane
Treglinnick
Trevio
St Merryn Airfield (disused)
Tregingey Fm
Trefeigh Fm
Pentruse Fm
Trenance
Blable Ho
Treveal Fm
Tredruston Fm
Hay
A389
Trellow Downs
Pengelly Fm
Bishop's Wood
Costislost
Bozion Fm
Costislost Plantn
Polgeel Wood
Park
Trescowe Brake
Tredannick
6½

H

Queen Bess Rock
BEDRUTHEN STEPS
Tregona
Gollan
Trerair Fm
St Ervan
Rumford
St Jidgey
Cannalidgey
Pawton Manor Fm
Burlawn
Polbrock
Washaway
Lane-end
Tregoose
Brocton

0   1   2   3miles
0 1   2   3   4   5 km

Downhill
Trevisker Fm
Bogee Fm
CREALY GREAT ADVENTURE PARK
Burlorne
Penaligon Downs
Mount Charles

1

Trenance Pt
High Cove

St Eval Airfield (disused)
Bear's Downs
St Eval
Long Stone
Bogee Common
Trelow Downs
Scotland Corner
208
Higher Cransworth
Great Grogley

Trenance

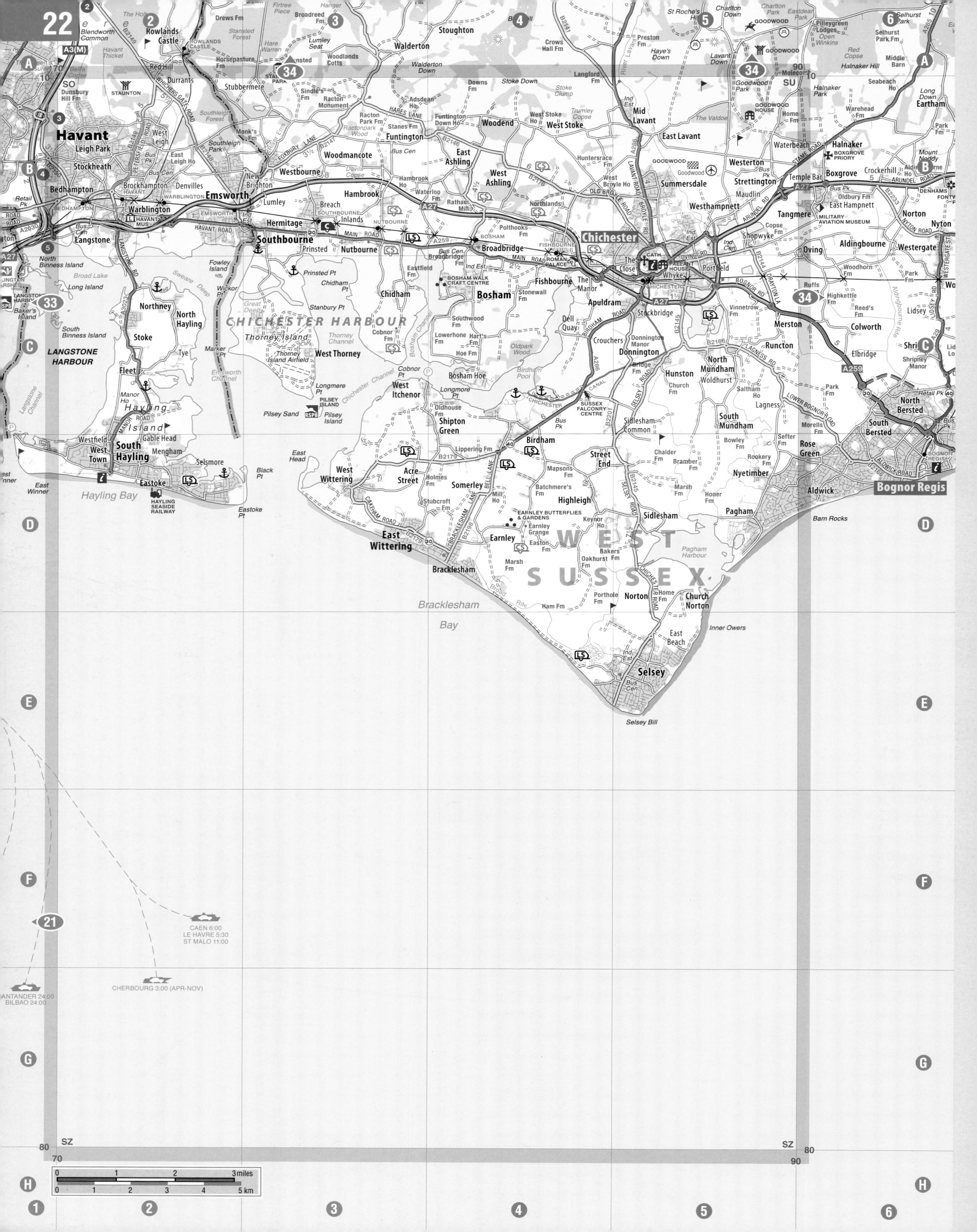

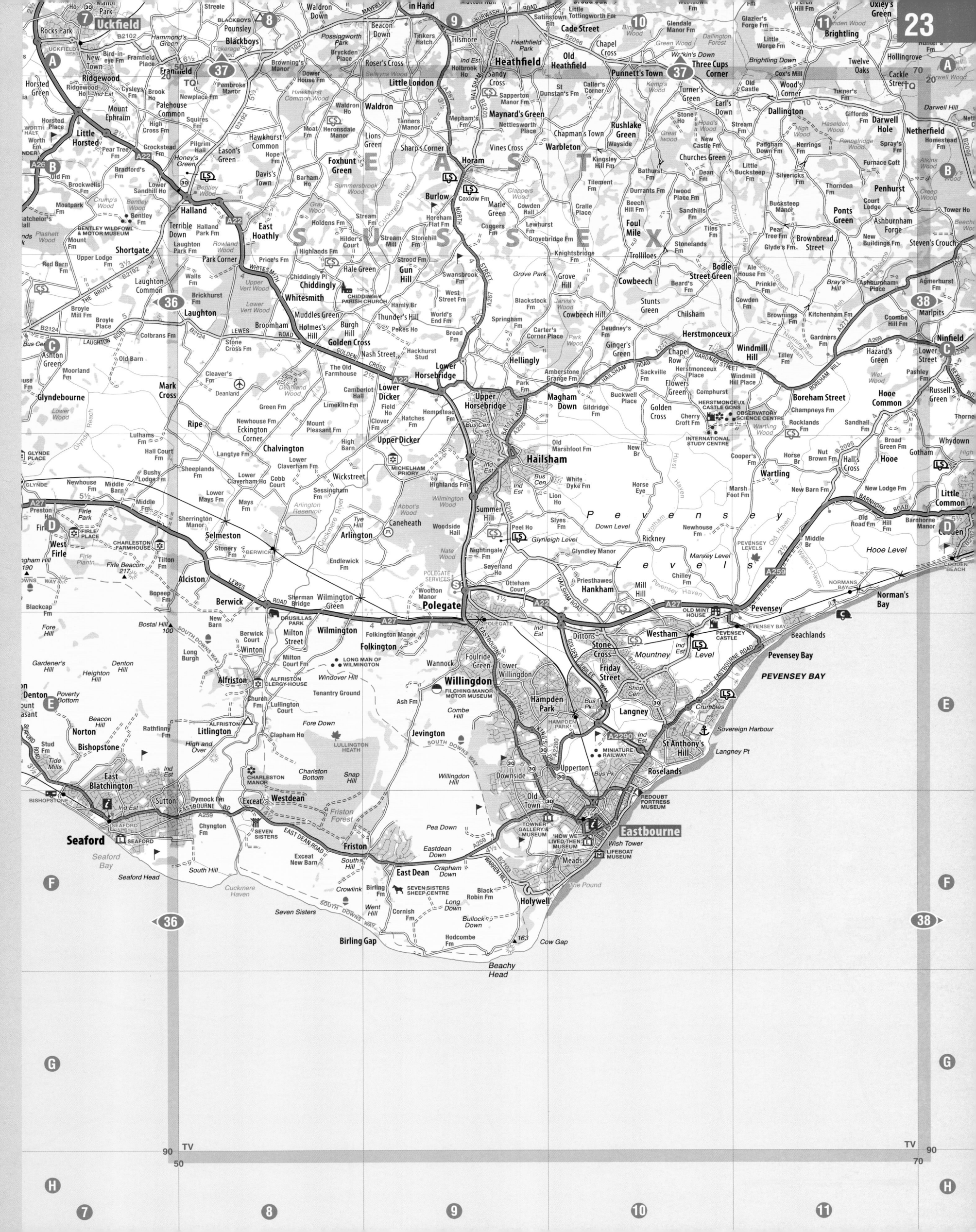

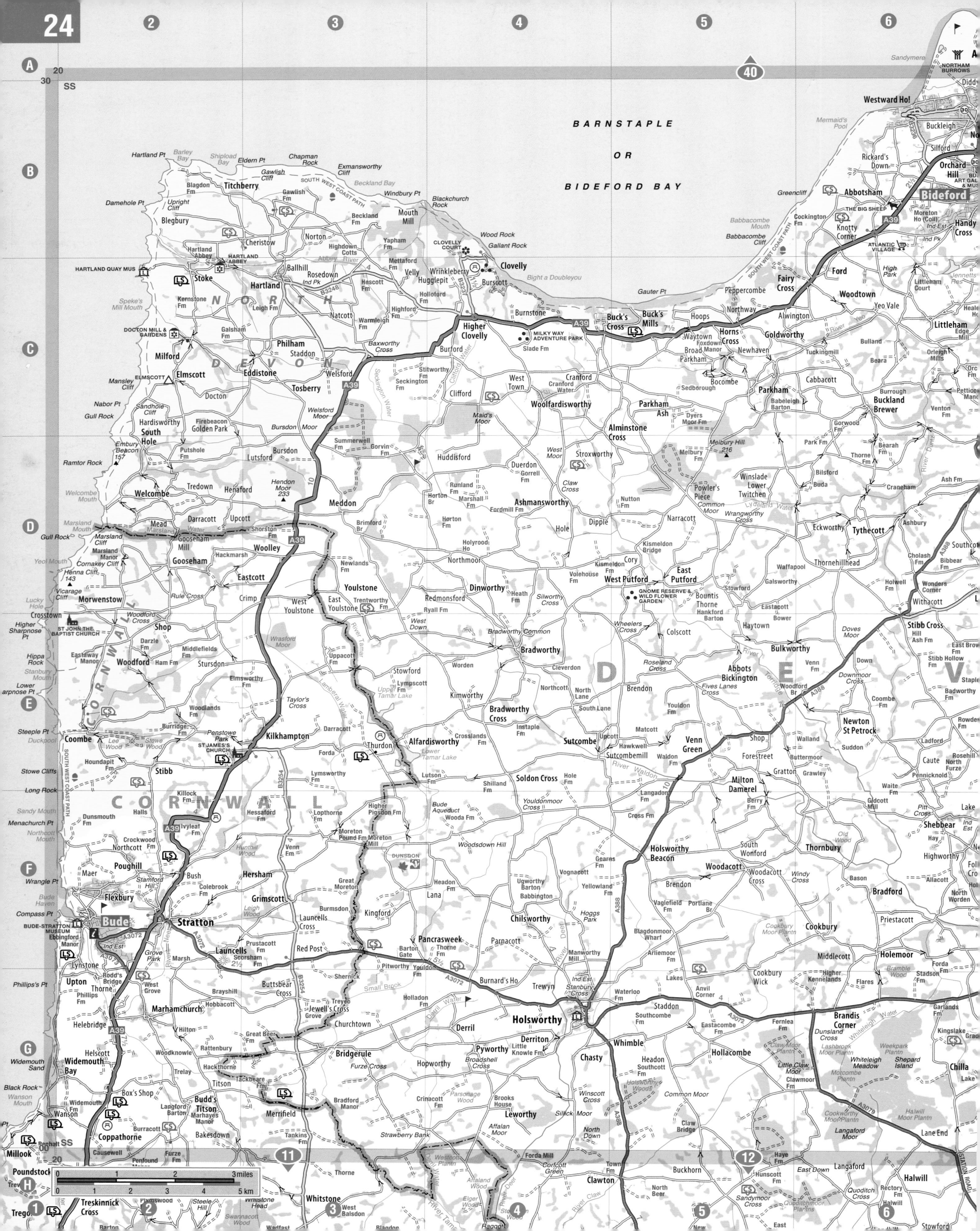

DEVON

South Molton • North Molton • Heasley Mill • Brinsworthy • Twitchen • Molland • Hawkridge • Dulverton • Battleton • Brushford • Exebridge

Bishops Nympton • Newtown • Bish Mill • Ash Mill • Knowstone • Roachill • Oakfordbridge • Oakford • Stoodleigh

George Nympton • Alswear • Mariansleigh • Rose Ash • Creacombe • Rackenford • Loxbeare • Washfield

Romansleigh • Meshaw • Ash Moor • Queen Dart • Templeton Bridge • Templeton • Calverleigh

Week • Lutworthy • Drayford • West Worlington • East Worlington • Witheridge • Nomansland • Cruwys Morchard • Withleigh

Cheldon • Thelbridge Barton • Washford Pyne • Puddington • Pennymoor • Way Village • Well Town • Little Silver

Chawleigh • Filleigh • Black Dog • Woolfardisworthy • Poughill • Upham • Cadeleigh

Eggesford Station • Eastington • Lapford • Morchard Bishop • Kennerleigh • Stockleigh English • Cheriton Fitzpaine • Cadbury

Nymet Rowland • Coldridge • Oldborough • Newbuildings • East Village • Upton Hellions • Stockleigh Pomeroy • Thorverton

West Leigh • East Leigh • Zeal Monachorum • Down St Mary • Ash Bullayne • West Sandford • Sandford • Efford • Shobrooke

Bow • Copplestone • Knowle • Coleford • Colebrooke • Crediton • Sweetham • Shute • Brampford Speke • Up Exe

Nymet Tracey • Hillerton • Yeoford • Hookway • Newton St Cyres • Nether Exe • Stoke Canon

Scale: 0 — 3 miles / 0 — 5 km

Grid references: A B C D E F G H — 1 2 3 4 5 6
Motorway junctions: 25, 41, 42, 13, 14
Roads: A361, A377, A3072, B3137, B3226, B3227, B3096, B3042

River Exe • River Yeo • River Mole • River Dalch • River Taw • River Creedy • River Culm

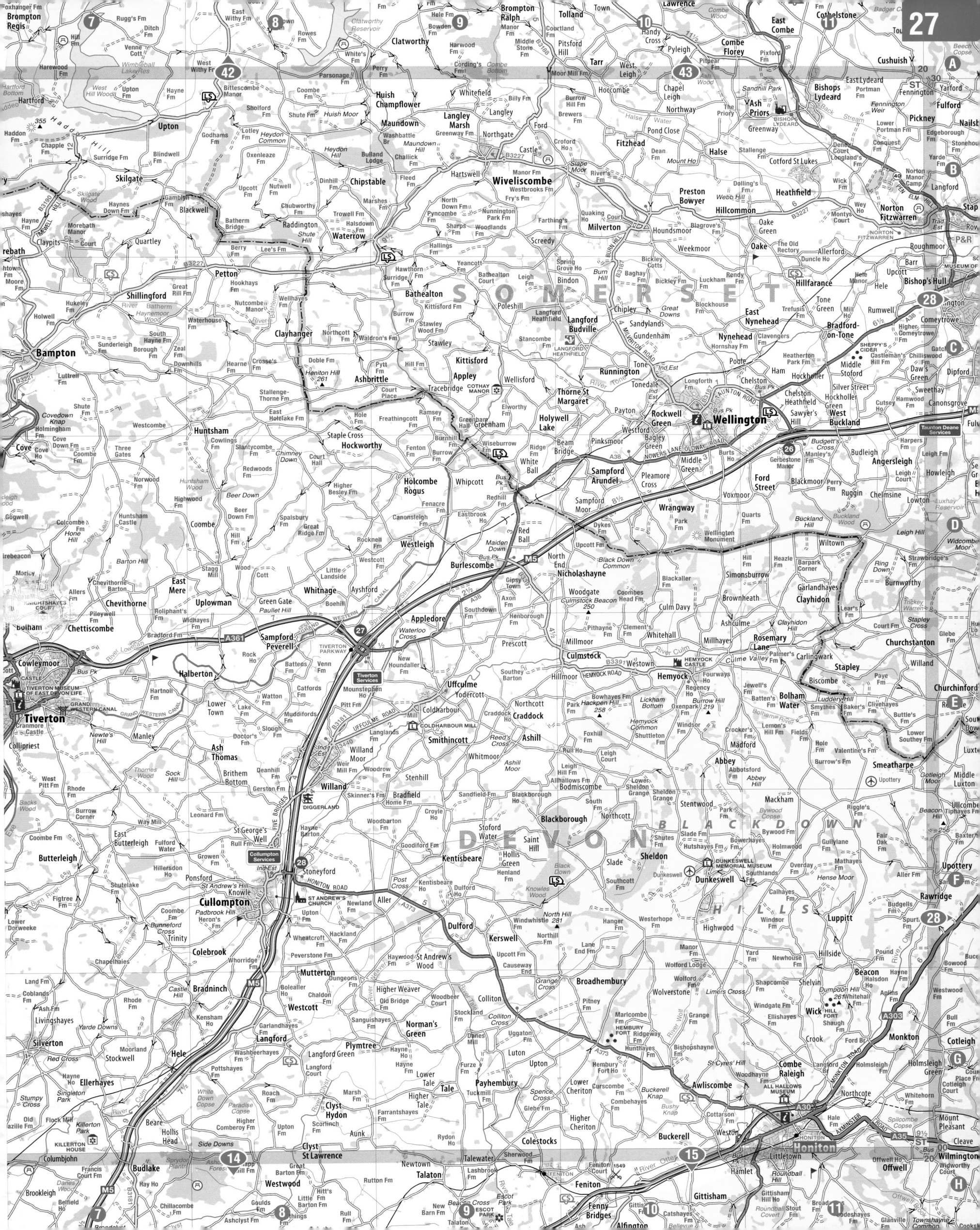

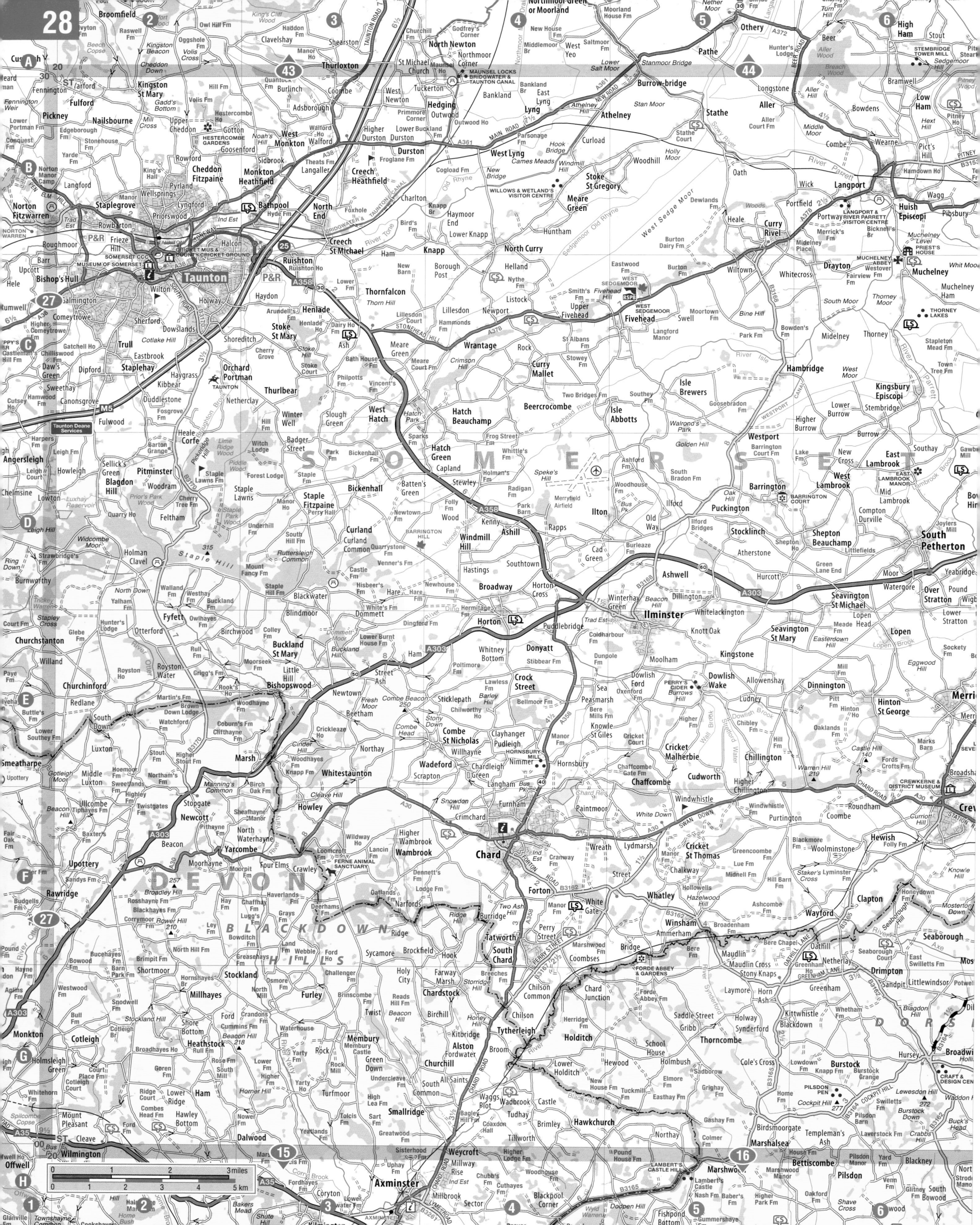

Park
Hill
HORNE'S
PLACE CHAPEL
The Dowels

Corner
Thrift
Cott
Higham
Fm

Johnson's
Corner

Wey Street
Fm

Will's
Fm

Ho

Forty Acre
Cott

Burmarsh

Donkey
Street

7
8
9
Newchurch
Brooker
Fm
Manor
Fm
Norwood
Fm
New
Barn Fm
Gammon's
Fm
Orgarswick
Fm
Chapel
Cottage Fm
HYTHE
ROAD
10

B2080
APPLEDORE
dore
Bridge Fm

54
Snave
Poplar Ho

Romney
Lodgeland
Fm
Willow
Pickney
Bush Fm
Blackmanstone
Br
DYMCHURCH
Sellinge Fm
Sutton
Fm
A259
Dymchurch Wall
55
DYMCHURCH
MARTELLO TOWER
20
30
TR
A

Ham
Fm
Whitehall
Fm
Hope
Fm

Brenzett
Green
Moat
Ho
New
House Fm
Poplar
Fm

M a r s h
North Fording
Bungalow
Haffenden
Fm

Dymchurch

A259

Snargate
Priory
Fm
A2070
Spring
Fm
Melon Fm
ROMNEY, HYTHE &
DYMCHURCH RAILWAY
St Mary in
the Marsh
ST MARY'S
BAY
St Mary's Bay

B

Ivychurch

Fairfield
Court
Becket
Barn Fm
Brattle Ho
Brenzett
Brenzett Place
AERONAUTICAL
MUSEUM
Blue House Fm
Yoakes
Court
Fm
Beechcroft
Fm
Honeychild
Manor
Brodnyx
ROMNEY WARREN
COUNTRY PARK
ROMNEY
WARREN
HALT
ROMNEY
MARSH
B2071

Fairfield
Poplar
Hall
Old
Hall Fm
Rheewall
Fm
New
Sewer

New
Buildings Fm
Dean
Court
A259
Brookland
Bush Fm
A259
Sycamore
Fm
Old
Romney
New Romney
i
NEW
ROMNEY
30
B2071
Warren Fm

C
Whitehouse
Fm
Hook Ho
Coldharbour
Fm
LYDD ROAD
Phoenix
Caisson
Littlestone-on-Sea
Romney Sands

ffen's
Fm
Court
eford
Blue
House Fm
Old Cheyne
Court
Court
Lodge
Hammonds
Corner
Kemp's
Hill
Romney Sands

GUILDFORD LANE
7½
White Kemp Sewer
Midley
Cotts
Hawthorn
Corner
Coldicott
Fm
Belgar Fm
Greatstone-on-Sea

W a l l a n d
Guldeford
Lane Corner
Baynham
Fm
Newland Fm
Westbrook
Fm
Footway Fm
B2075

M a r s h
Little
Cheyne Court
Westbroke
Ho
Jack's
Court
3½

Kent Ditch
Little
Scotney
Lydd
(London Ashford)
Lade
Lydd-on-Sea

Barn Fm
Pigwell
Lydd
Denge Marsh
Halfway Bush

Point
Fm
Red
Ho
Scotney
Court
LYDD INTERNATIONAL
RACEWAY
RSPB
DUNGENESS
Boulderwall
Fm
DUNGENESS

Camber
Jury's
Gap
Holmstone
Lydd Ranges
West
Ripe
Manor
Fm
Open
Pits

Camber Sands
Broomhill Level
Danger
area
South Brooks
Danger
area
Brickwall
Fm
Dungeness
Power Sta
DUNGENESS

Broomhill Sands
Danger
area
THE OLD
LIGHTHOUSE
Dungeness

RYE BAY
D

E

F

G

TR
00
20
H

7
8
9
10
11

Lundy (inset map)

Hen & Chickens
North West Pt
Seals' Rock
North East Pt
Gannets' Rock
Gannets' Bay
St James's Stone
Tibbetts Hill 138
Tibbett's Pt
LUNDY MARINE NATURE RESERVE
Jenny's Cove
Lundy
BIDEFORD 2:00 (MAR-OCT)
ILFRACOMBE 2:00 (MAR-OCT)
Dead Cow Pt
Ackland's Moor 142
Lundy Roads
Halftide Rock
Beacon Hill
Castle Hill
Rat Island
South West Pt
Surf Pt
15
45
15
SS

40
60
SS

56
56

Main map

Samson's Bay
Water Mouth
WATERMOUTH CASTLE
LUNDY 2:00 (MAR-OCT)
Capstone Pt
Hele Bay
Rawn's Rocks
Blackstone Pt
Elwill Bay
Trentishoe
SOUTH WEST COAST PATH
Little Hangman 218
Gt Hangman 318
Holdstone Down 349
South Dean Fm
Ilfracombe
Hele
Hangman Pt
Hole Fm
MUSEUM
Chambercombe
OLD CORN MILL
Hole Fm
Goosewell
Lester Cliff
Girt Fm
Girt Down
Holdstone Down
Trentishoe Down
Walner
Shag Pt
Flat Pt
Bull Pt
Pensport Rock
Lee Bay
CHAMBERCOMBE MANOR
Kitstone Hill
Berrynarbor
Lee
Combe Martin
Knap Down
Verwill
Tattiscombe
Stony Corner
Lincombe
Higher Slade
NORTH DEVON
Sterridge
Warmscombe Fm
Ruggaton Fm
Stoneditch Hill
Nutcombe Fm
Truckham
Dean
Higher Warcombe
Whitestone
Lower Slade
Oakridge Fm
Two Pots
Bowden Fm
Smythen
Hampster
Henstridge
WILDLIFE & DINOSAUR PARK
LONG LANE
South Ley
Cowley Wood
Kentisbury
Morte Pt
North Morte Fm
Shaftsboro Fm
Campscott Fm
Slade Resrs
3½
Hore Down
2 A3123
Stapleton Fm
Berry Fm
Berry Down Cross
LONG LANE
Bugford
Stonecombe
Higher Week Fm
Preston Ho
Kentisbury Down
Rockham Bay
Mortehoe
Little Shelfin Fm
Manor Fm
B3343
Ind Est
Outer Narracott Fm
Hillcrest Fm
Berry Down
5
CS
Highlands
Cleave Fm
Patchole
Northcote Fm
Bridwick
Borough Cross
Trimstone
Cheglinch
Century Fm
Collacott Fm
Bittadon
Wigmore Fm
Kentisbury Ford
Halls Cross
East Down
Wistlandpound Reservoir
Hallsdown
Woolacombe
Mill Rock
Ossaborough
Willingcott
Dean
Dean Cross
Higher Aylescott
Fullabrook
Burland Fm
Little Silver
Bowden Corner
Ford Fm
Clifton
Churchill
Arlington Beccott
Arlington
Huckham
Besshill
EXE
Grunta Pool
Ivycott
Roadway
West Down
Fullabrook Down
Metcombe Fm
Hewish Down
Whitefield Down
Churchill Down
ARLINGTON COURT
White Cawsey
Tidicombe Fm
Rye Park
Black Rock
Pickwell Down
Spreacombe Manor
North Downs
Stoneyard Wood
River Caen
Okewill Cross
Garman's Down
Deerpark Wood
Putsborough Sand
Bradwell
Buckland Down
Castle Street Fm
Halsinger Down Ho
Winsham Down
Beara Down
Swindon Down
Viveham Fm
Woolley Wood
Loxhore
Baggy Pt
Vention
Putsborough
SOUTH WEST COAST PATH
North Buckland
Gipsy Corner
Milltown
Plaistow Barton
South Woolley
Croyde Bay
Ora Hill
Forda
Georgeham
Nethercott
Halsinger
Winsham
Whiddon
Crockers Fm
Higher Muddiford
Plaistow Mill
Muddiford
Loxhore Cott
The Warren
Chilbridge
Croyde Bay
Croyde
Darracott
Cross
Upcott
Incledon Fm
South Hole Fm
Knowle
Beara
Middle Marwood
Marwood
MARWOOD HILL
Guineaford
Kingsheanton
Lower Loxhore
Saunton Sands
Lobb
Buckland Manor
Boode
Pippacott
Luscott Barton
Whitehall
BROOMHILL SCULPTURE GARDENS
Prixford
South Hill
Shirwell Cross
Shirwell
Brat Flem
CROYDE ROAD
SAUNTON
ROAD 4½
B3231
Saunton
Sandy Lane
CS
Braunton
Waterlake
Mainstone
Varley Fm
Springfield Cross
Waytown
SHIRWELL ROAD
Sepscott Fm
Bratton Cross
Birch
Shop Cen
Braunton Down
Knowl Water
West Ashford
Brightlycott Fm
Youlston Wood
Stoke Rivers
ELLIOT GALLERY
Velator
Heanton Punchardon
A361
Ashford
Burridge
Kingdon's Gardens
Northleigh Fm
Chelfham Horridge
Hakeford
NON
Wrafton
Braunton Marsh
Braunton Down
Bradiford
Raleigh
Pitt Fm
Snapper
Goodleigh
Middle Dean Fm
Hutcherton Down
Stone Cross
Braunton Burrows
Chivenor
Penhill Pt
Allen's Rock
SOUTH WEST COAST PATH
Pilton
Pottington Ind Est
Derby
Waytown
Youlden Fm
Coombe Willesleigh
Dean Head
Airy Pt
Horsey Island
Saltpill Duck Pond
Penhill
ST ANNE'S CHAPEL & MUSEUM
Barnstaple
MUSEUM OF BARNSTAPLE & NORTH DEVON
Westacott
Gunn
LUNDY 2:00 (MAR-OCT)
River Taw
Broad Sands
Lower Yelland
BICKINGTON ROAD
Sticklepath
Newport
Portmor
60
Harford
Sandick Cross
Crow Pt
Yelland
B3233
'Ind Est
Lake
1½
P&R
A361
Landkey
Accott
Crow Rock
WEST YELLAND
Fremington
Combrew
Bickington
Upcott Fm
Roundswell
Rumsam
Landkey Newland
Harford
Hurscott
Sandymere
Instow Sands
The Quay
Worlington
Brynsworthy
A39
Swimbridge Newland
Yeoland Ho
Riverton
Yarnacott
NORTHAM BURROWS
N DEVON MARITIME MUSEUM
Appledore
Instow
Bickleton
Myrtle Cott
Collacott Fm
CS
Hollamoor Clump
Bishops Tawton
Swimbridge
Kerscott
Diddywell
24
Huish
St John's Chapel
Eastacombe
A377
NORTH DEVON FARM PARK
Tawstock
25
Downrew Ho
Horswell
Hannaford
Westleigh
TAPELEY PARK GARDENS
Coombe Fm
Trayhill
Huish Moor
Stonyland
Uppacott
Hangman's Hill
Bydown Fm
Lane End Fm
SS
30
40
0 1 2 3 miles
0 1 2 3 4 5 km
Silford
Northam
6½
Holmacott
Horwood
Prospect Corner
Halmpstone Manor
Summer

1 2 3 4 5 6

A 90
60 SS
◄ 41

B

C
BRISTOL CHANNEL

D
Hurlstone Pt   Selworthy Sand
Bossington   Selworthy Beacon
Lynch   308   Greenaleigh Pt
EXMOOR FALCONRY   SOUTH WEST COAST PATH   Moor Wood
Porlock   Allerford   Memorial Hut   **Minehead**
Doverhay   Selworthy   Wydon Fm   Woodcombe   Higher Town   Madbrain Sands   Warren Pt
Glen Lodge   West Luccombe   Hindon   Holnicote   Bratton   BUTLINS
Horner   Brandish Street   A39   Blackford   Periton   Alcombe
317   Troytes   HOPCOTT ROAD
Ley Hill   Luccombe   Tivington   Great Headon Plantn   Staunton Plantn   Dunster Beach
Horner Wood   Luccombe Hill   Knowle Top   Tivington Knowle   Periton Hill 295   Penny Hill   Ellicombe   DUNSTER   Blue Anchor Bay
Water   Huntscott   Wootton Courtenay   Knowle Hill   Marsh Street   Quantock's Head
Robin How 428   MINEHEAD   DOLL MUSEUM   Dunster   Blue Anchor   HOME FARM   Watchet   St Audrie's Bay   Blue Ben   East Quantoxhead
E   Dunkery   Brockwell   DUNKERY VINEYARD   DUNSTER WATERMILL   DUNSTER CASTLE GARDENS   BLUE ANCHOR   EASTBURY ROAD   Warren Bay   Black Rock   Parkhouse   East Wood   Higher Street
Dunkery Beacon 519   Fairgarden   Burrow   Well Fm   Cowbridge   Whits Wood   Carhampton   Marshwood Chapel   Cleeve   Old Cleeve   Bye   Kentsford   St Decumans   Doniford   Perry Fm   Kilve Court
Dunkery Gate 387   Elsworthy   Timberscombe   Bickham   Broadwood Fm   Aller Hill   Withycombe   Binham   WEST SOMERSET RAILWAY   RAILWAY MUS   Five Bells   Egrove Fm 2½   Rydon   West Wood   West Quantoxhead   Pardlestone   Pardlestone Hill
Croydon Ho   Gupworthy Fm   Combe Fm   Bilbrook   WASHFORD   TROPIQUARIA ANIMAL & ADVENTURE PARK   Williton   High Bridge   Wibble Fm   Staple   West Hill Beacon Hill 310   Staple Plantn
West Harwood Fm   OAKTROW WOOD   Croydon Hill   Black Hill 353   Hungerford   CLEEVE ABBEY   Torre   Washford Cross   Sampford Brett   Torweston   Lower Weacombe   Weacombe   Bicknoller Post
Ford Fm   EXMOOR   365   Rodhuish Common   381 Rodhuish Hill   Escott   CIDER FARM   Beggearn Huish   Fair Cross   Orchard Wyndham   Woolston   Bicknoller
F   Cutcombe   Stowey   Well   Rodhuish   Golsoncott   Lower Roadwater   Yarde   Black Down Wood   Capton   Quantock Moor Fm   Thorncombe Hill   Thorncombe Ho
Luckwell Bridge   Wheddon Cross   Kersham Hill 361   Nurcott Fm   Churchtown   Monkham Hill   Croydon Hall   Woodford   Yellow Wood   Newton   A358   Chilcombe   Halsway Manor
Torre Fm   Hoe Fm   Triscombe   White Moor   Couple Cross   Slowley Wood   Slowley Fm   Tacker Street   Roadwater   Nettlecombe Court   Rowdon   Escott Wayshill   Kingswood   Halsway   Black Hill 358
Kemps   Great Scott   Honeywell Ho   Luxborough   Kingsbridge   Washford River   Monksilver   Vellow Wood   Vellow   Hurley   Crowcombe Park
41 ►   Lype Hill 423   Colly Hill   Newcombe Fm   Poolton   Langridge Wood   Woodadvent Fm   Birchanger Fm   Coombe Cross   Catford Cott   Crowcombe Court   Crowcombe
G   South Quarme Fm   390 Quarme Hill   Chargot Wood   Langham   Chapman's Fm   Leighland Chapel   Chidgley   Stogumber   Wood Fm   THE CHURCH HOUSE
Winsford   Coppleham   Witheridge   Exton Hill 348   Weekfield Fm   Langham Hill   Stamborough   Sticklepath   Colton Fm   Pond Wood   Lower Vexford   Lawford
Burrow Wood   West Howetown   Kendle Fm   Leigh Fm   Ford Fm   Brendon Hill   Treborough   Hook Hill Fm   Bird's Hill   Elworthy   Higher Vexford   Triscc
The Allotment   Yellowcombe   Summerway   Combeshead Fm   Withiel   Eastcott   Burrow Fm   Brendon Hills Common   WITHIEL HILL   Sminhays Corner   Eastern Wood   Ralegh's Cross Inn   Holcombe Water Fm   Hartrow Manor   Willett Ho   Rexton   Crowcombe Heathfield   Flaxpo
Draydon Knap   Exton   King's Brompton Fm   Blagdon Hill   Swansea Fm   Tone Fm   Brendon Hill Fm   Tripp Bottom   Fryan Fm   Colwell Fm   Willett   Coleford Water   Rich's Holford   Nethercott
326 South Hill   Bridgetown   Howetown   Kings Brompton Forest   Withiel Florey   Cophole   Middleton Bottom   Rook's Nest   Willett Hill   New Marsh   Coursley Fm   Westowe
Ashw   Hollam Fm   Higher Foxhanger Fm   Rugg's Fm   Ditch Fm   Tripp Fm   Broadway Head Fm   Battin's Fm   Coleford   Emble Fm   Whitmoor   Tret Hol
G   Draydon Fm   Mounsey Castle   Broford Fm   Kents   Daws Fm   Brompton Regis   Hill Fm   Venne Cott   East Withy Fm   Week Fm   Hele Fm   Bowden Fm   Brompton Ralph   Tolland   Courtland   Pitsford Hill   Lydeard St Lawrence   Combe Wood
Halscombe   Chilly Bridge   Redcross   Harewood Fm   WIMBLEBALL LAKE/RES   Rowes Fm   Clatworthy   Harwood Fm   Manor Fm   Middle Stone   Handy Cross   The Priory
316   Lyncombe Fm   Hartford Bottom   Clatworthy Reservoir   Perry Fm   Cording's Combe   Tarr   West Leigh   Pyleigh   Homelea   Ash Fm
H   SS 30   90   Court   26   Hartford   West Hill Wood   Upton   Hayne   Bittescombe Manor   Coombe   Huish Champflower   Whitefield   27   Burrow Hill Fm   Chapel Leigh   Northway   Pond Close
355   Sholford   Shute Fm   Huish Moor   Maundown   Langley Marsh   Langley   Brewers   Hoccombe   Fitzhea
Draydon   Old Berry   Dulverton   Hele Br   Haddon Fm   Chapple   Godhams Fm   Lotley Hey Corn   Washbattle   Maundown Hill   Greenway   Northgate   Ford   Croford Fm   Com Flor   Castle
1   2   3   Upton   Blindwell   4   Heydon   5   6

0   1   2   3 miles
0   1   2   3   4   5 km

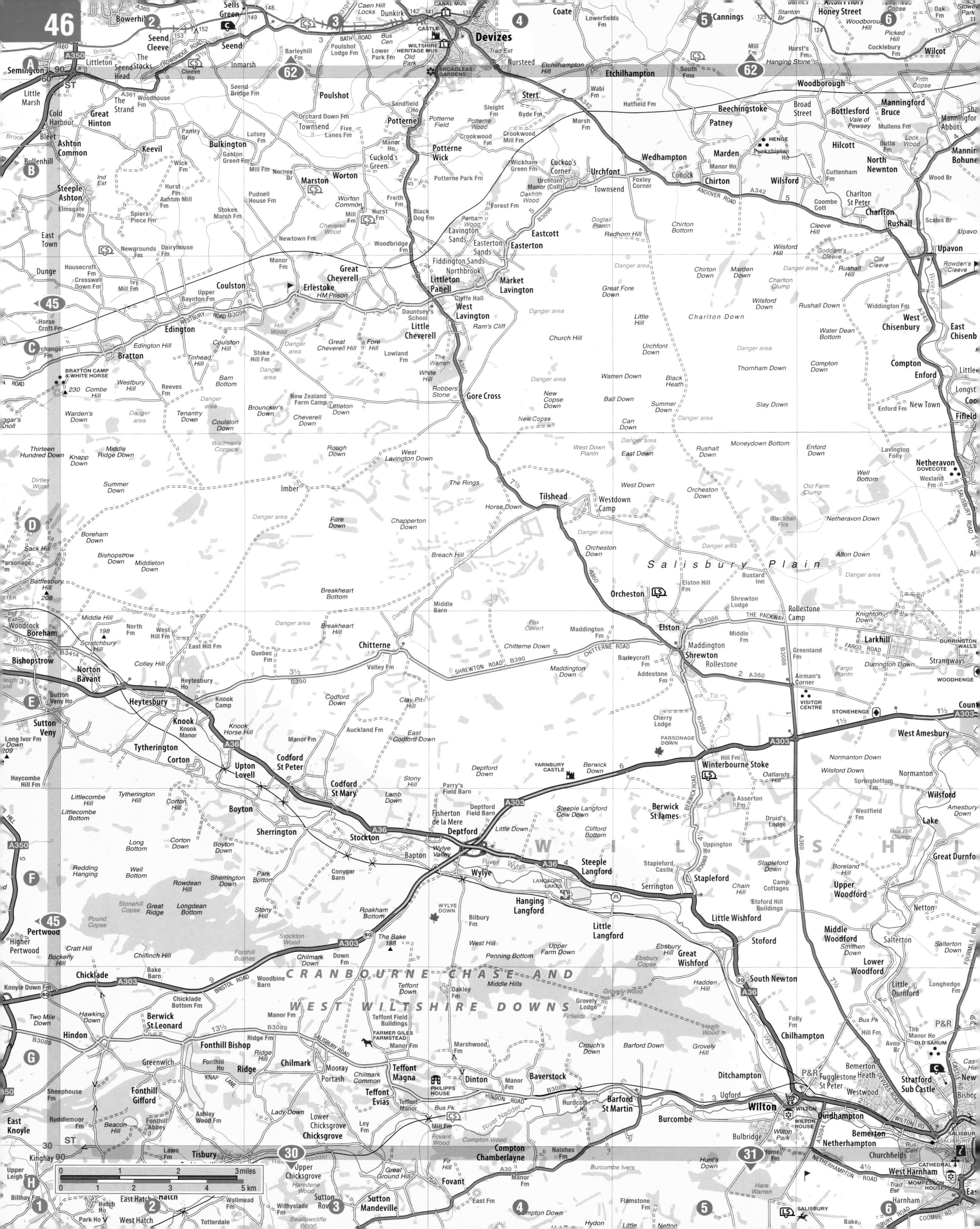

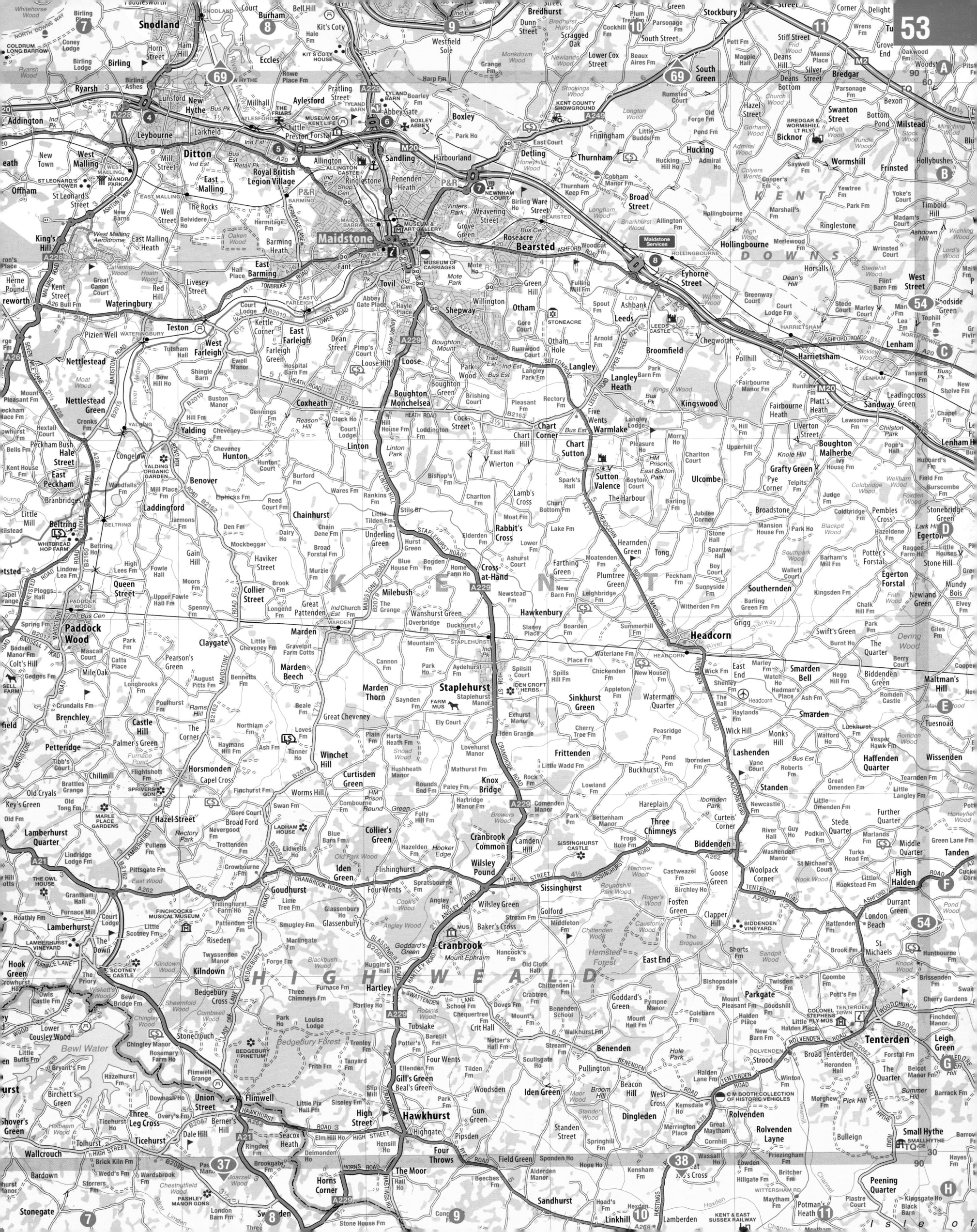

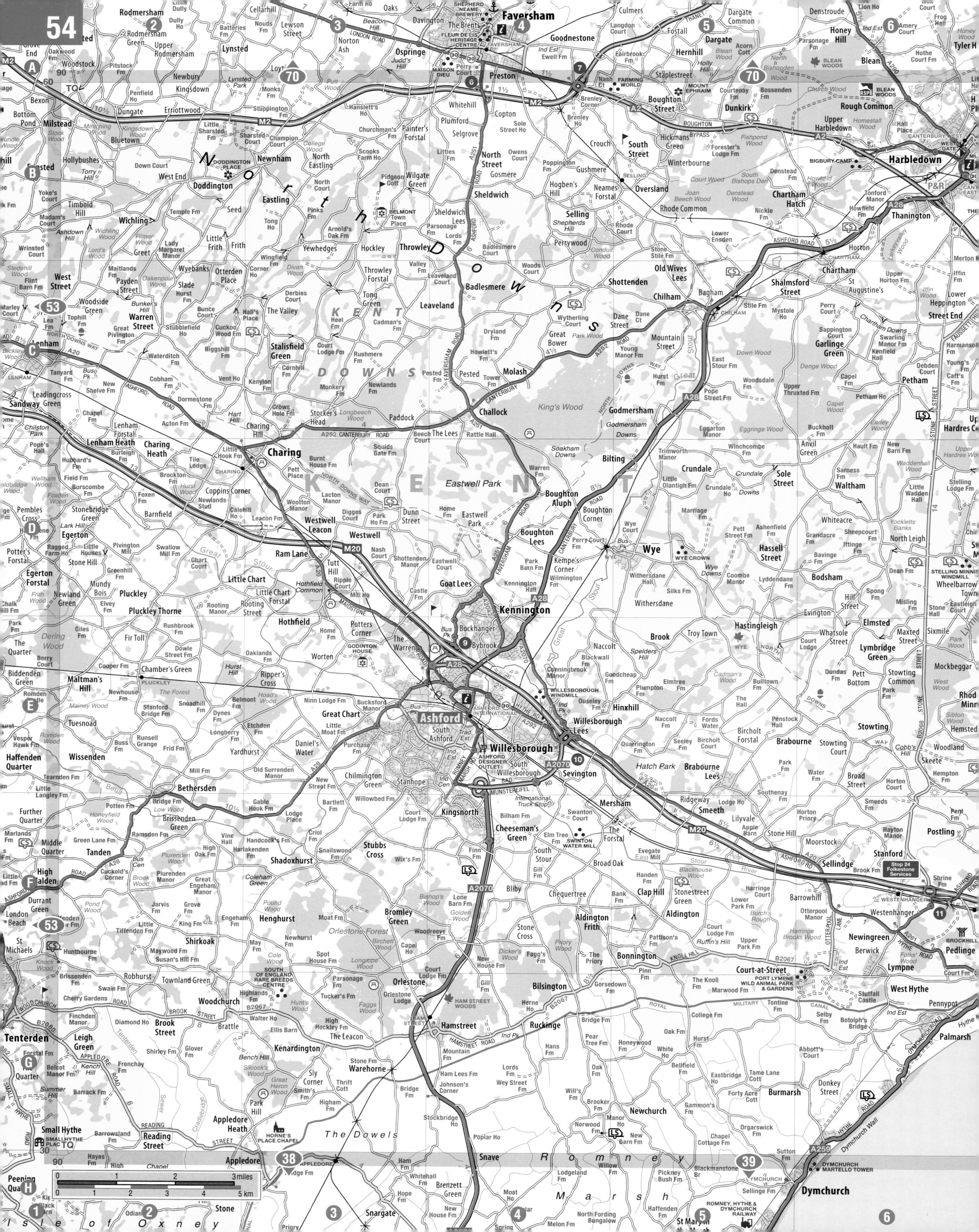

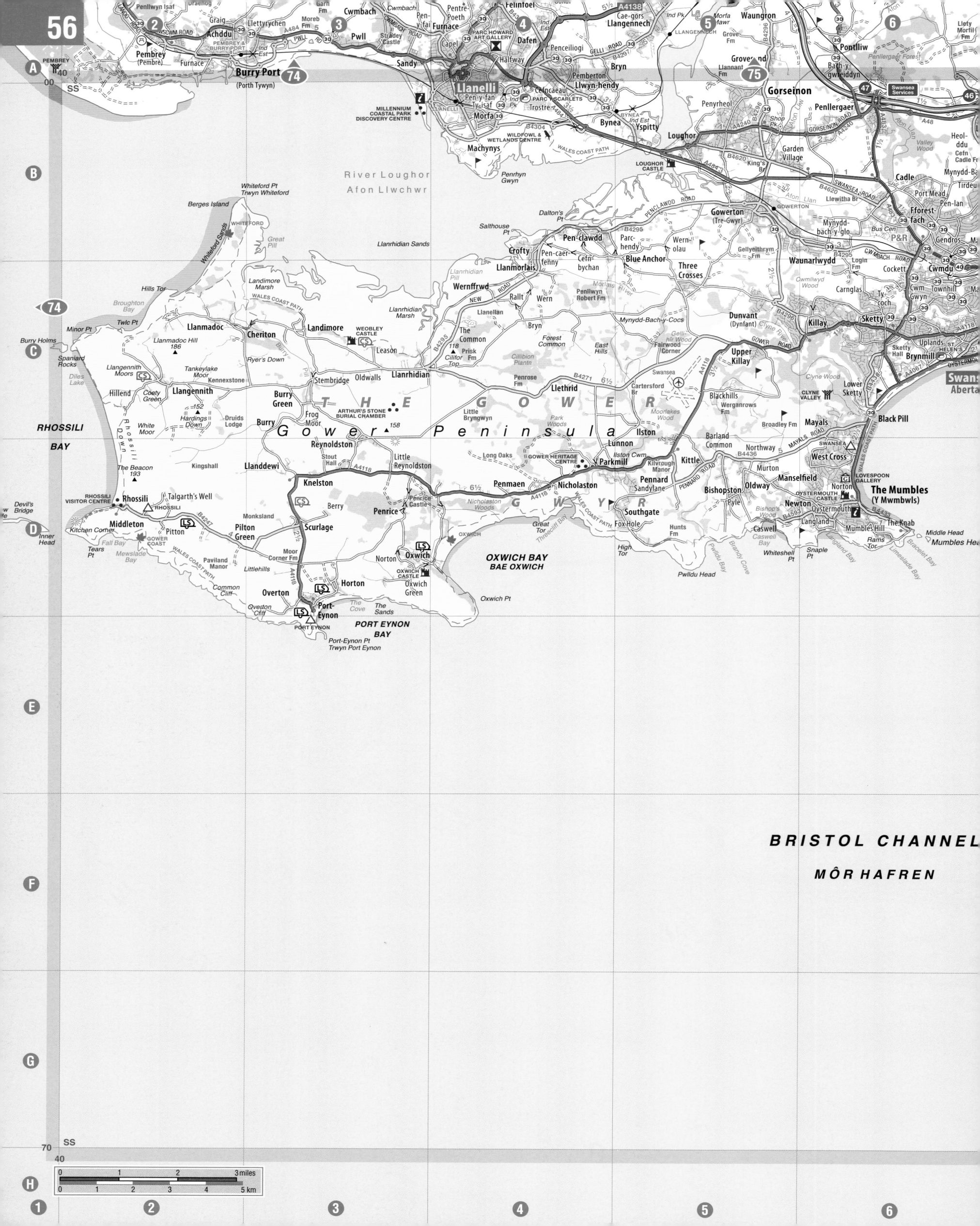

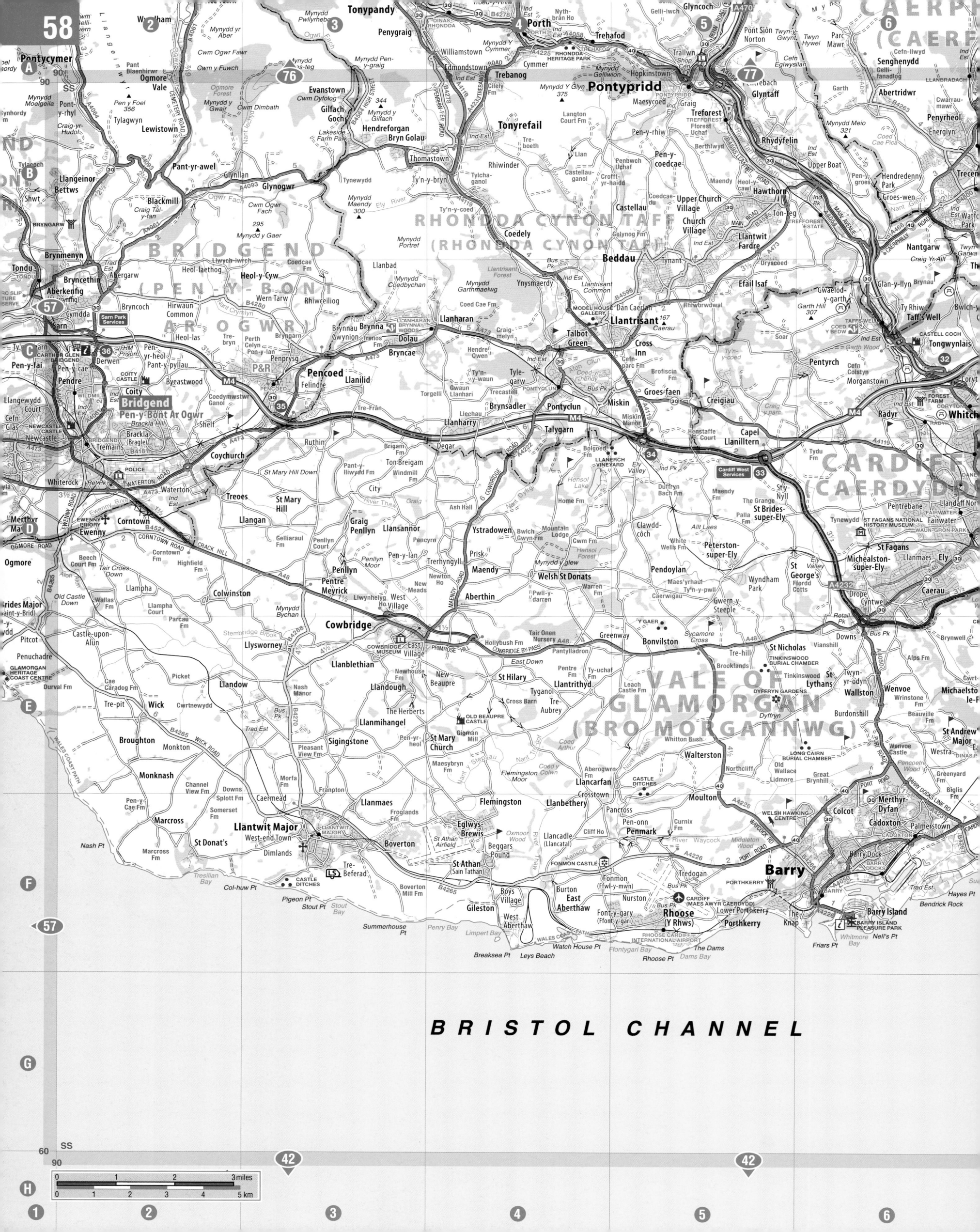

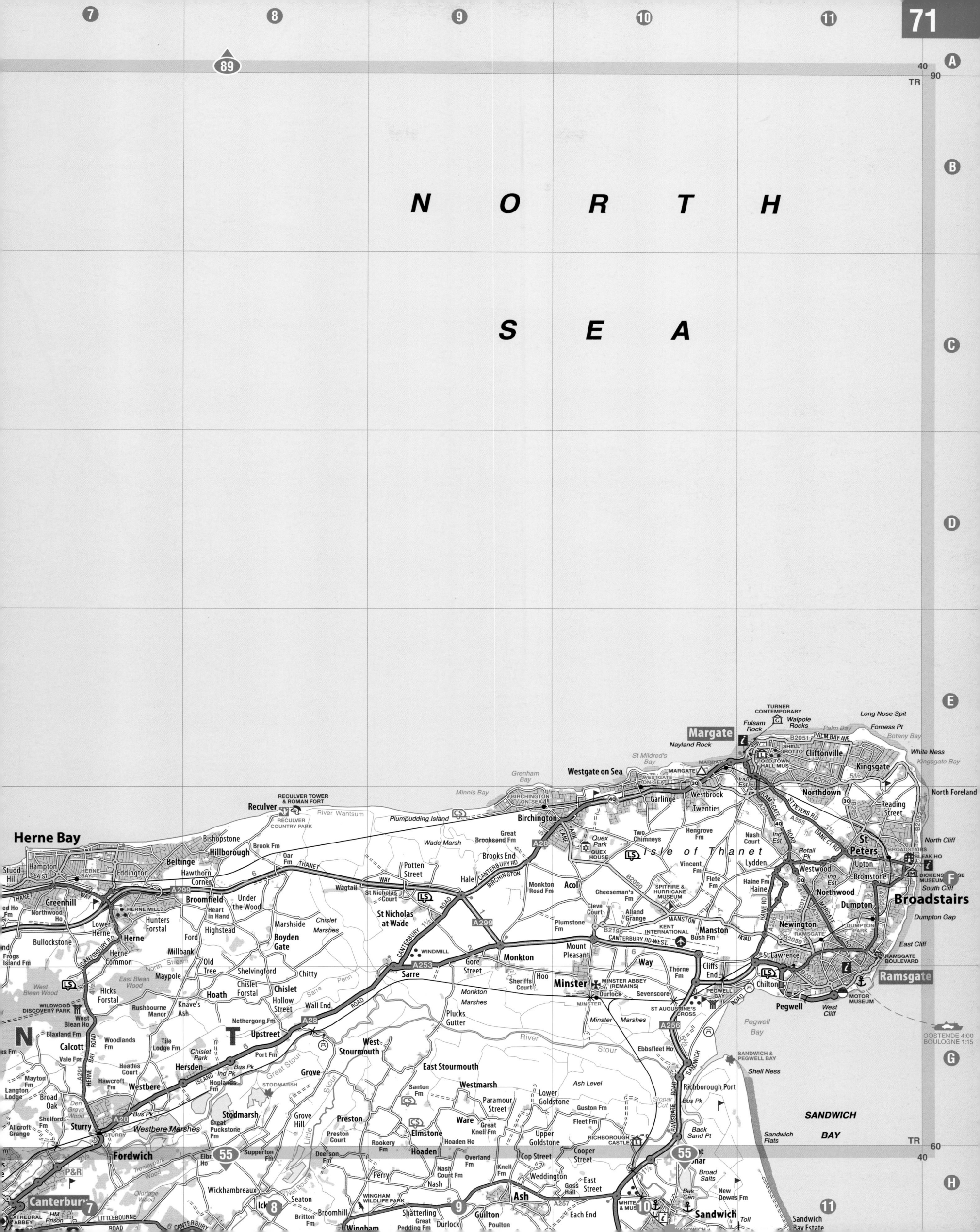

NORTH

SEA

Herne Bay

Margate

Westgate on Sea

Broadstairs

Ramsgate

Canterbury

SANDWICH
BAY

ST BRIDES BAY

BAIE SAIN FFRAID

PEMBROKESHIRE COAST

NATIONAL PARK

PEMBROKESHIRE

COAST NATIONAL PARK

Skomer Island
Ynys Skomer

Skokholm Island
Ynys Skokholm

Broad Sound

Milford Haven
Aberdaugleddyf

Milford Haven
Aberdaugleddau

Angle Bay
Bae Angle

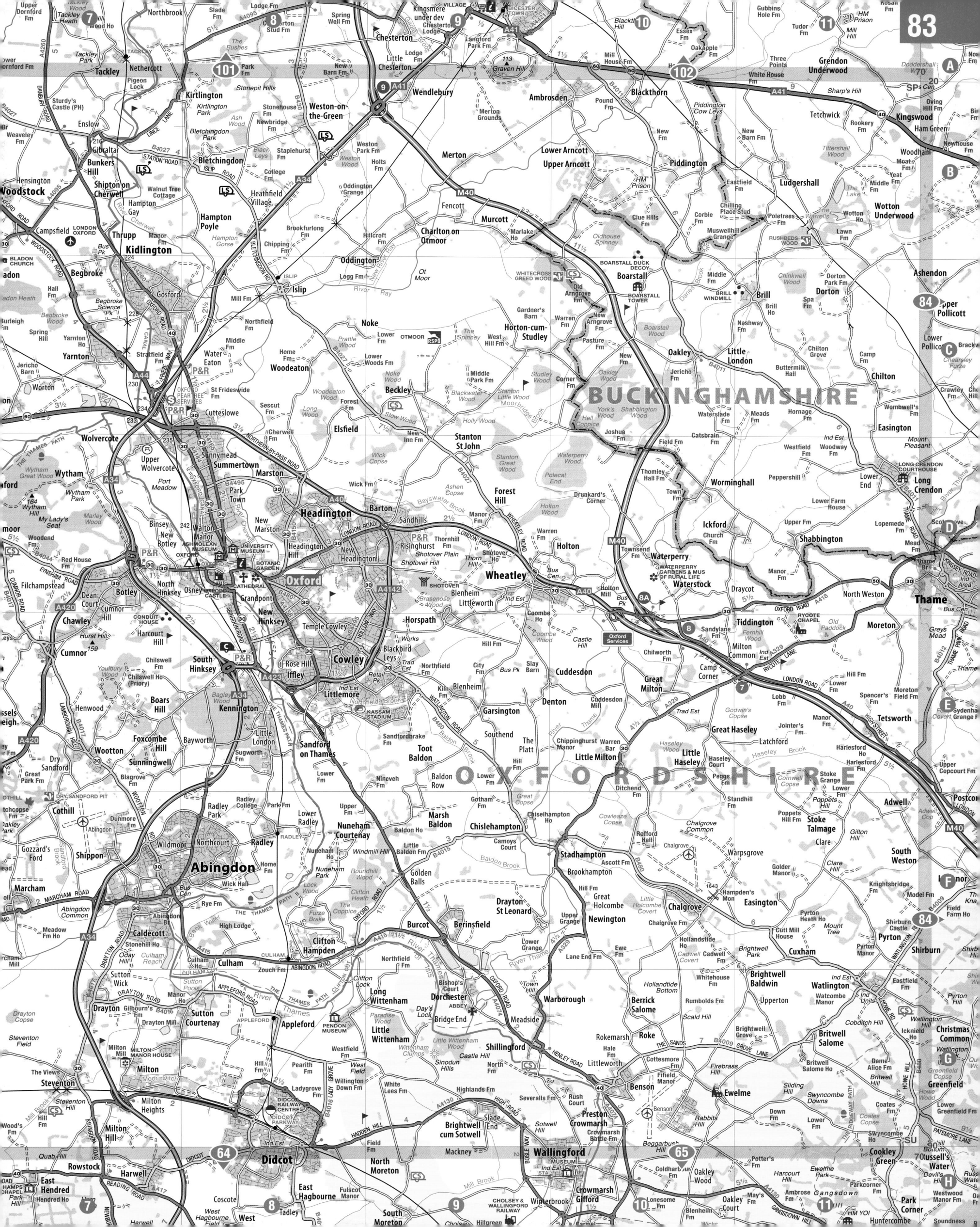

IRISH SEA

MÔR IWERDDON

Ynys Deullyn

Pwll Whiting
CARRE
SAMPSO
Pwll Llong
Pwll Olfa
Porth-gain
Trwyn Llwyd
Aber Draw
Trefin
(Trevine)

Penclegyr
Porth Dwfn
Porth Egr
Porthgain
TREFIN
(TREVINE)

Trwyncastell
Barry
Island Fm
Felindre
Ho
Binchurn
Fm
Llanrhian Llanon
Pe
Abereiddi
Bay
Abereiddy Portheiddy
Mesur-y-dorth

Aberdinas
Cwmwdig
Water
Bank Ho

Porth Tre-wen
Croes-goch
A487
Peqys
Fm

Berea
Trefochlyd
Fm
Trevigan
Trenewydd
Fawr
Tremich
Loch

Dduallt
Carn Treliwyd
Waun
Beddau
Tretio
Tretio Common
Spite
Moor
Treglemais
Waun
Fawr
Treffynnon

Penllechwen
Gesail-fawr
Porthgwyn
PEMBROKESHIRE COAST PATH LLWYBR ARFORDIR PENFR
Carnhedryn
Uchaf
Carn
Treglemaes
Abernant

Llechenhinen
WALES COAST PATH
Carn Llidi
181
PEMBROKESHIRE COAST
Carnhedryn

North Bishop
St David's Head
Penmaen Dewi
ST
DAVID'S
Carn
Hen
Llanhowel
Skyfog
Llanddinog

Porthmelgan
**Treleddyd-
fawr**
Hendre

Rhodiad
Porth Lleuog
B4583
Dowrog
Common
Caerforiog

Whitesands Bay Porth-mawr
Caerfarchell
Tremaenhir
Paran

Porthselau
Penarthur
Fm
Mynydd du
A487
NATIONAL PARK
Tremoch
Loch

Carreg
Rhoson
Tresswny
Moor
Middle Mill
Rickeston
Hall

Trwyn-Siôn-Owen
Point St John
BISHOP'S
PALACE
CATHEDRAL
St David's
(Tyddewi)
Vachelich
Whitchurch

Rhosson
St Justinian
Nine Wells
Prendergast
Solva (Solfach)
Mount
Fm
Brawdy
Airfield
(disused)

Bishops and Clerks
Trwyn-drain-du
Carnysgubor
Summer only
ST NON'S
CHAPEL
Llandruidion
Morfa Common
Upper
Solva
Lower
Solva

Daufraich
Porthstinian
Treginnis
St Non's
Bay
Caer Bwdy Bay
PEMBROKESHIRE
Pointz
Castle
A487
PENFRO

Aber Mawr
RAMSEY ISLAND
RSPB
**RAMSEY
ISLAND**
Porth Clais
Aber-west
COAST PATH LLWYBR ARFOR
Bus Pk

South Bishop/Em-sger
Aberfelin
Rhod Isaf
136
**Ramsey
Island**
Ynys Dewi
Porthllisky
Green
Scar
Dinas Fawr
Pwll March
Newgale

Trwynmynachdy
Penrhyn Twll
Carreg Fran
Black Scar
Dinas Fach
Porthmynnydd

Bay Dillyn
Meini Duon
Newgale Sa

ST BRIDES BAY
72

BAIE SAIN FFRAID
Rickets M

0 1 2 3miles
0 1 2 3 4 5 km

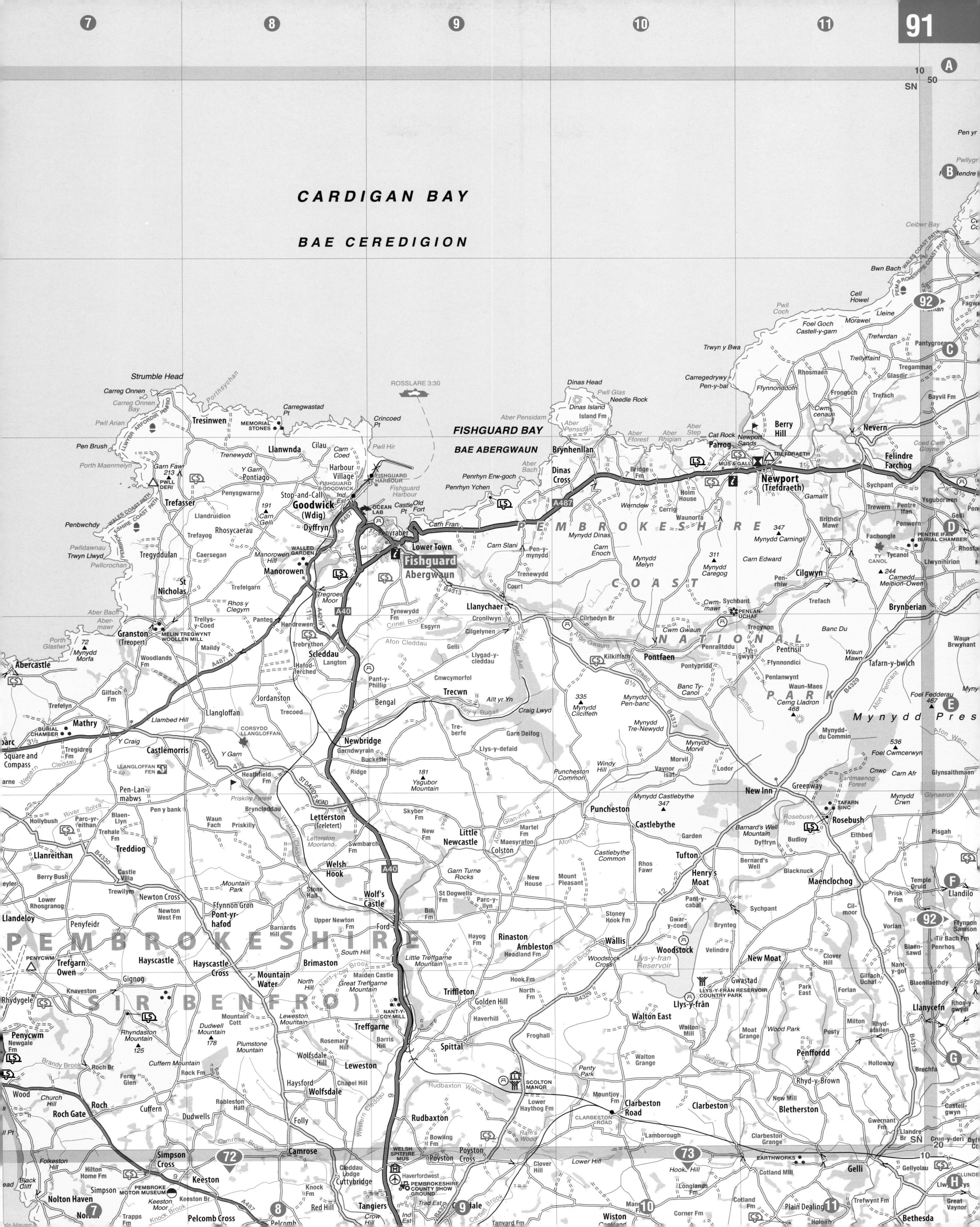

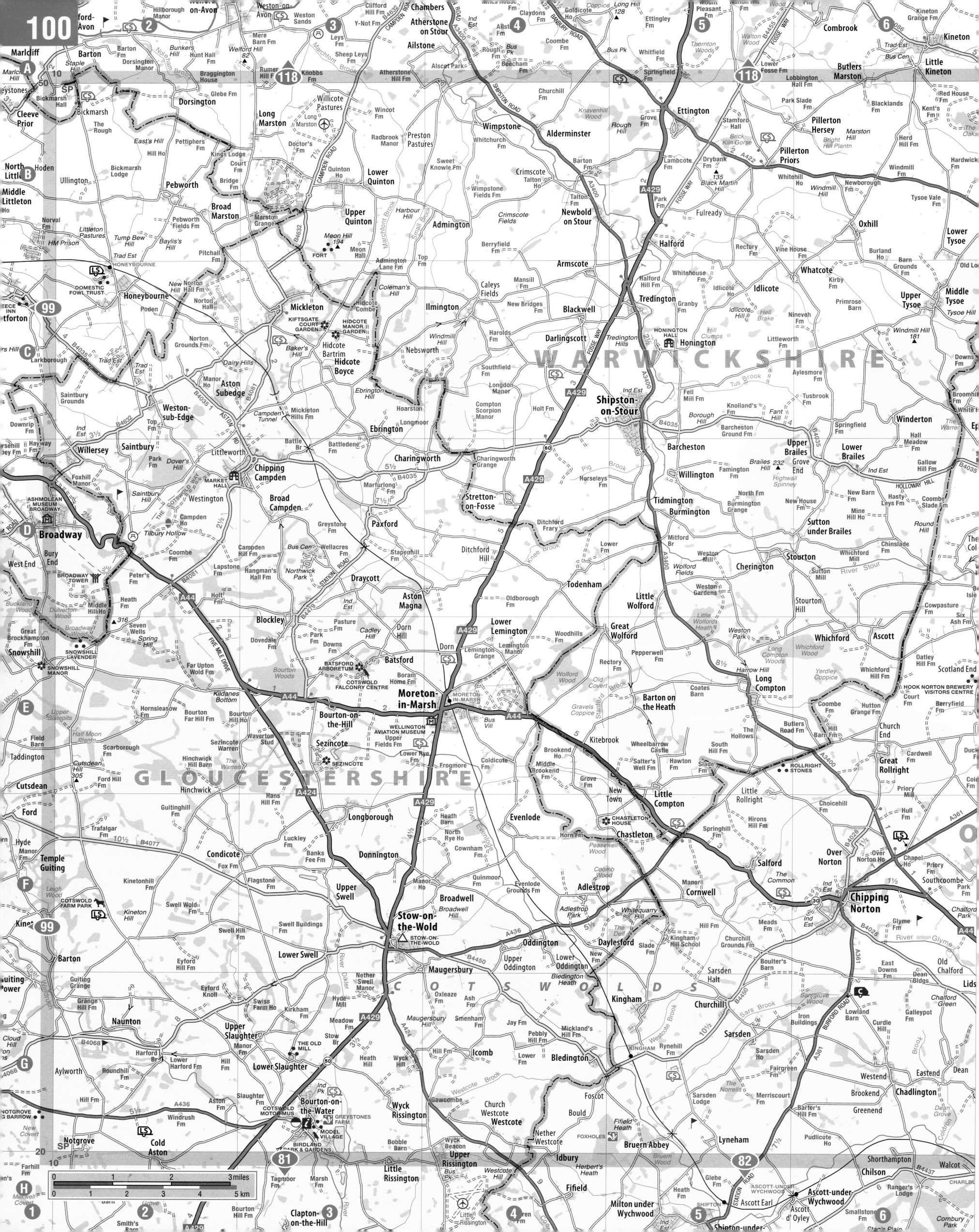

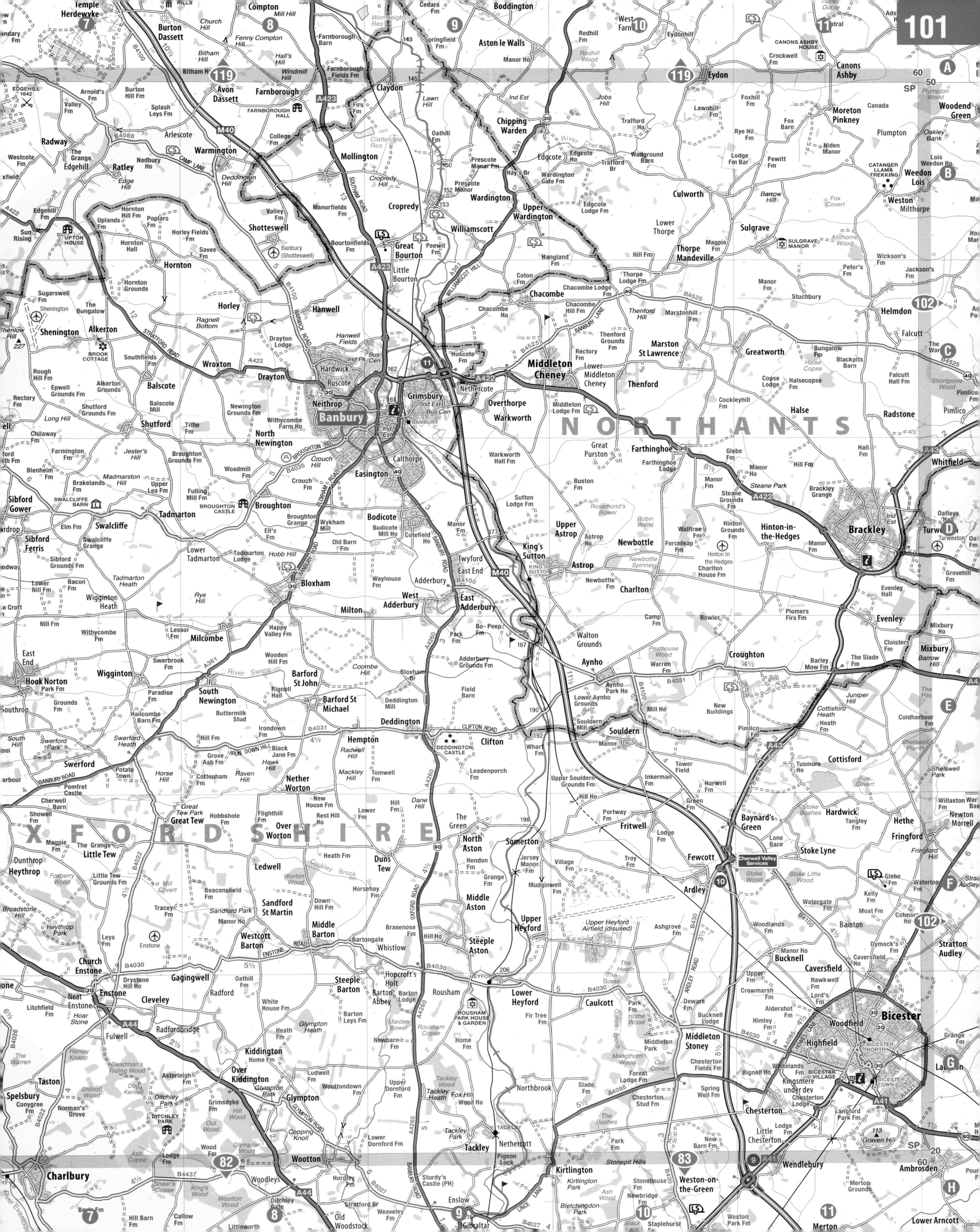

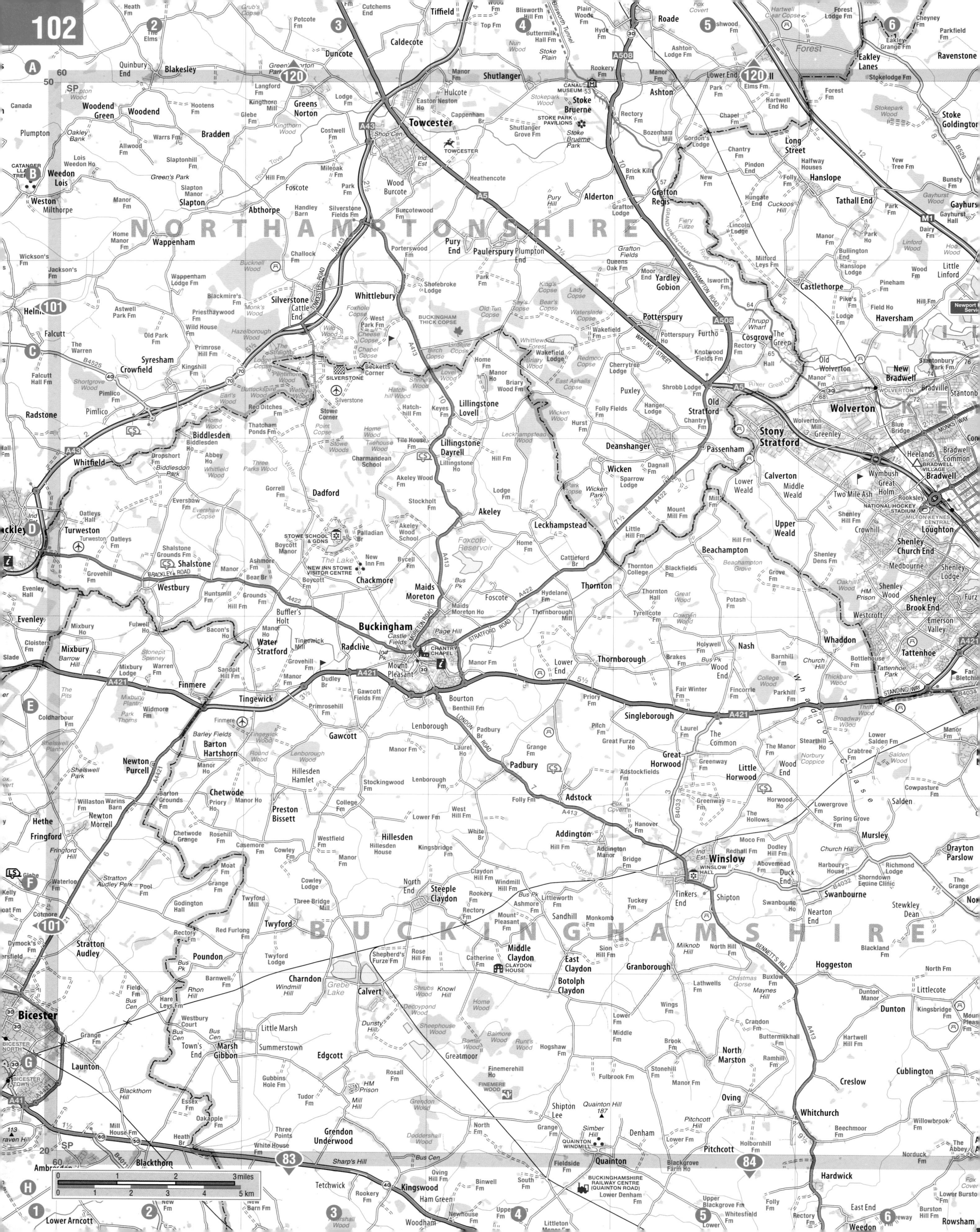

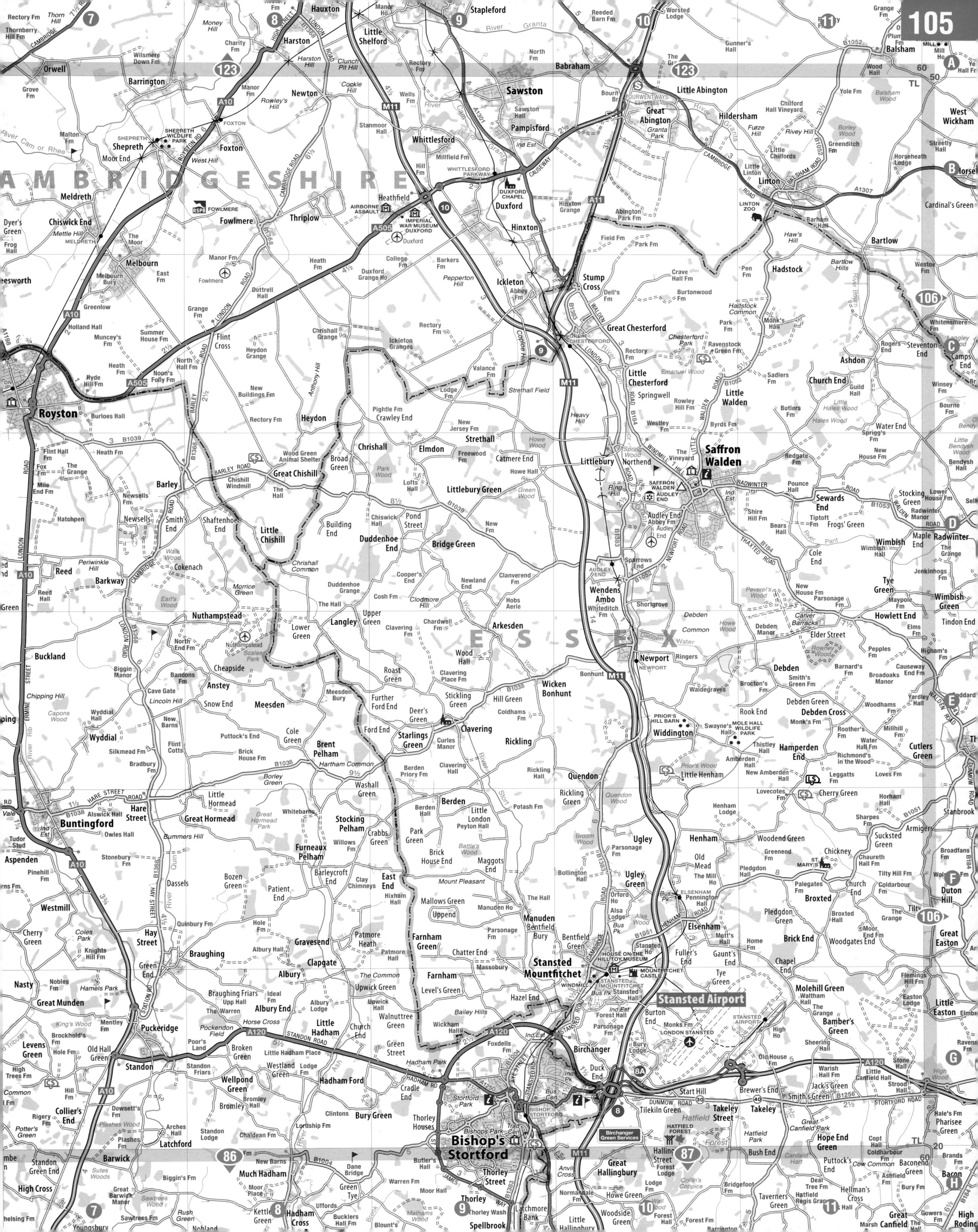

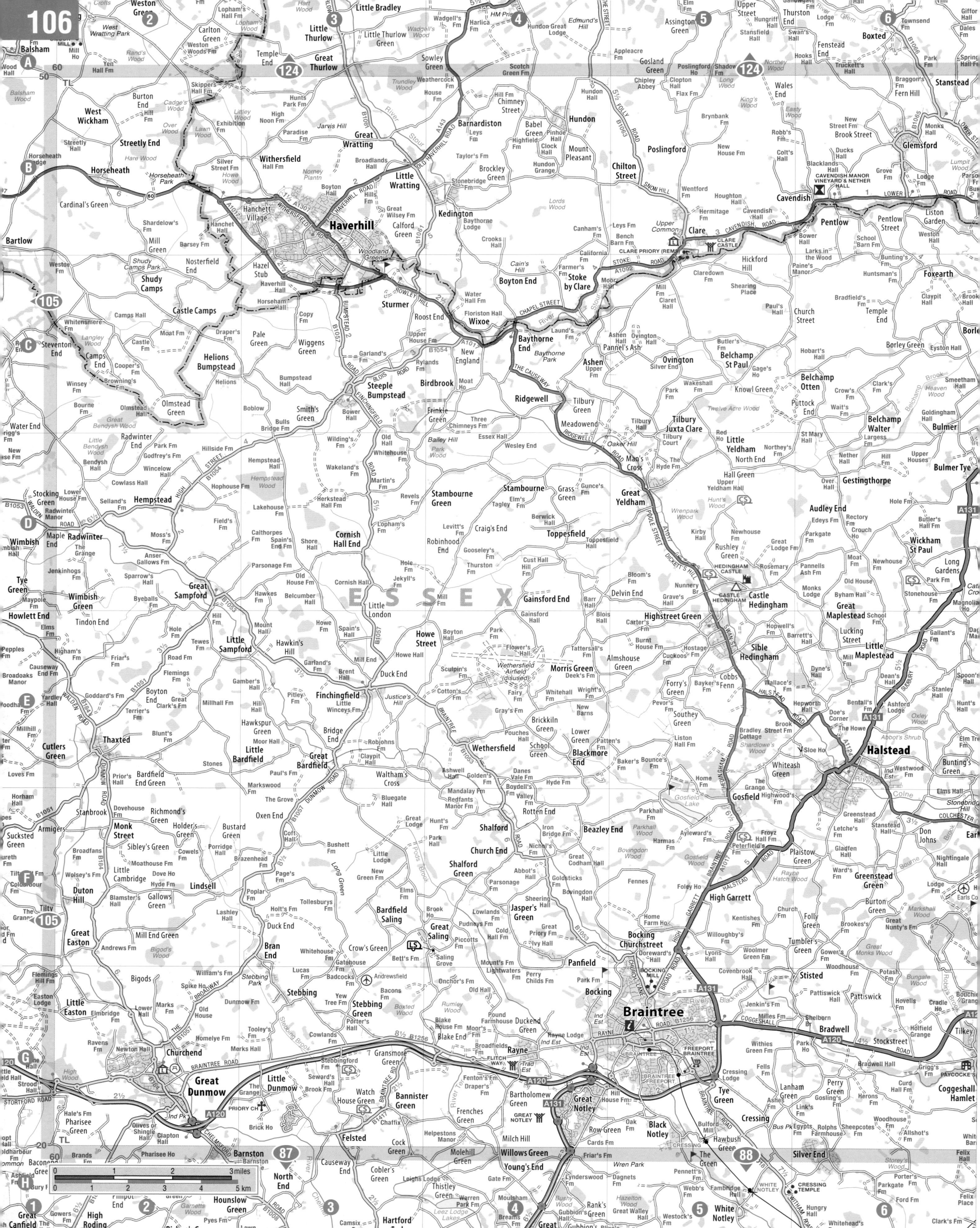

N O R T H

S E A

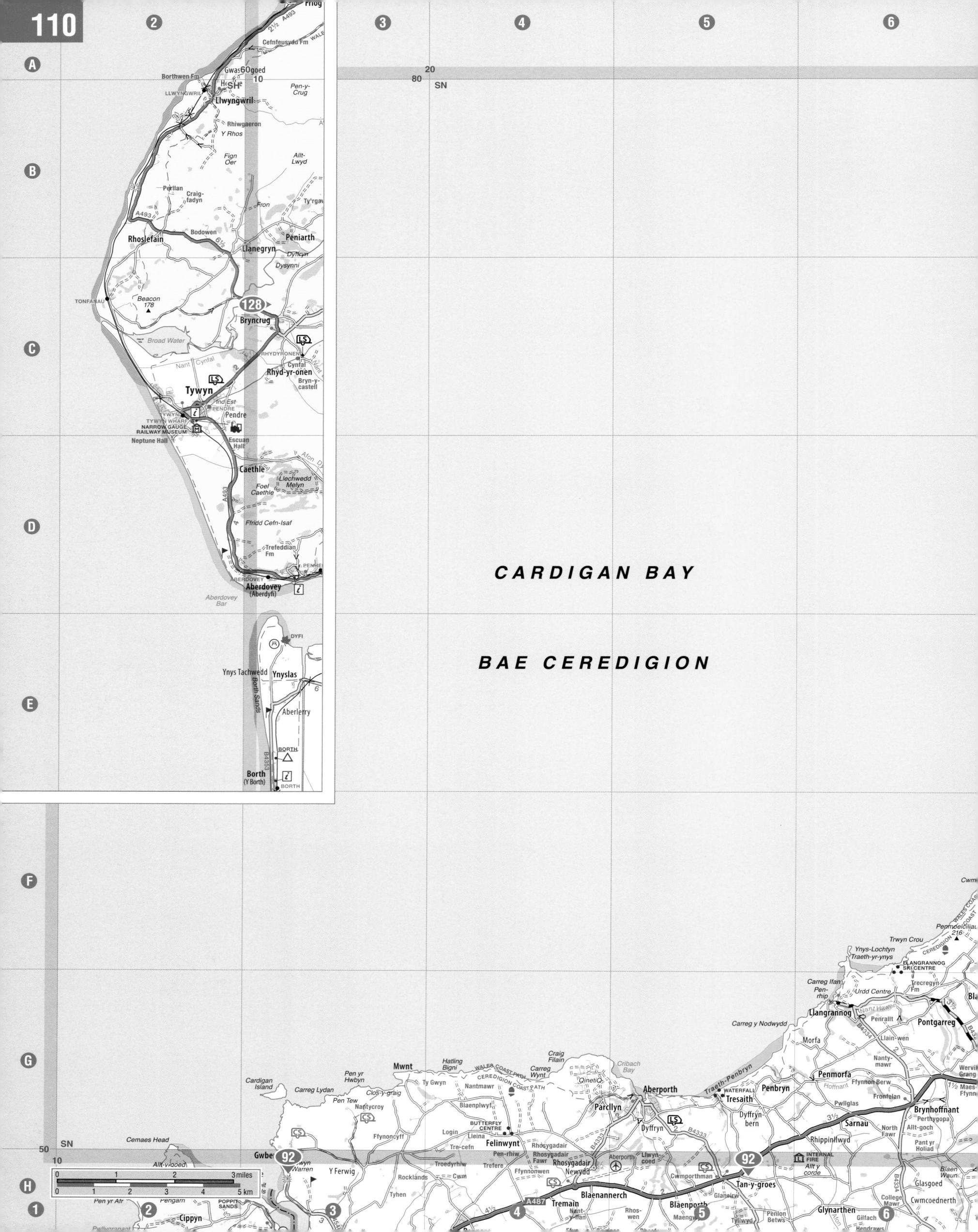

CARDIGAN BAY

BAE CEREDIGION

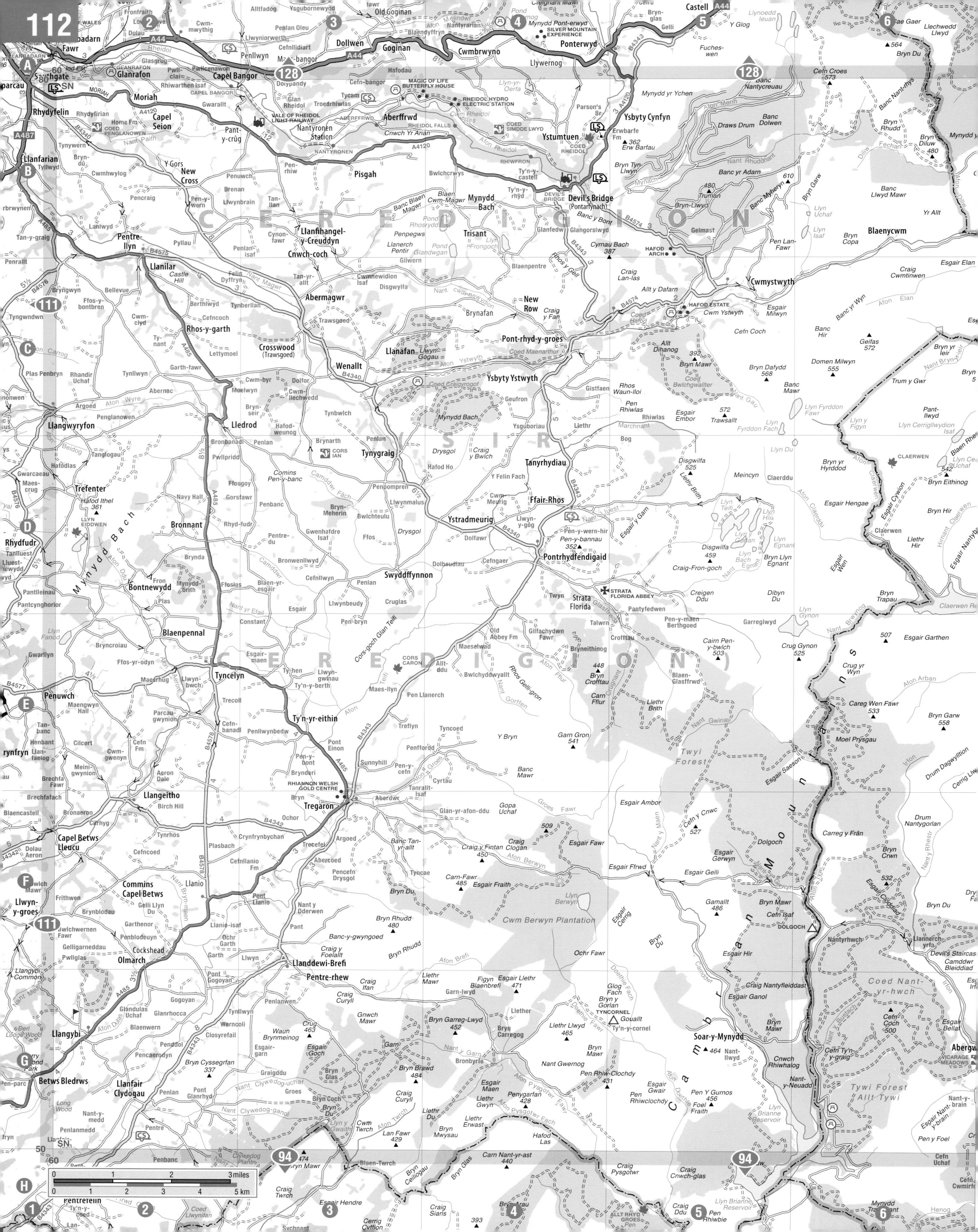

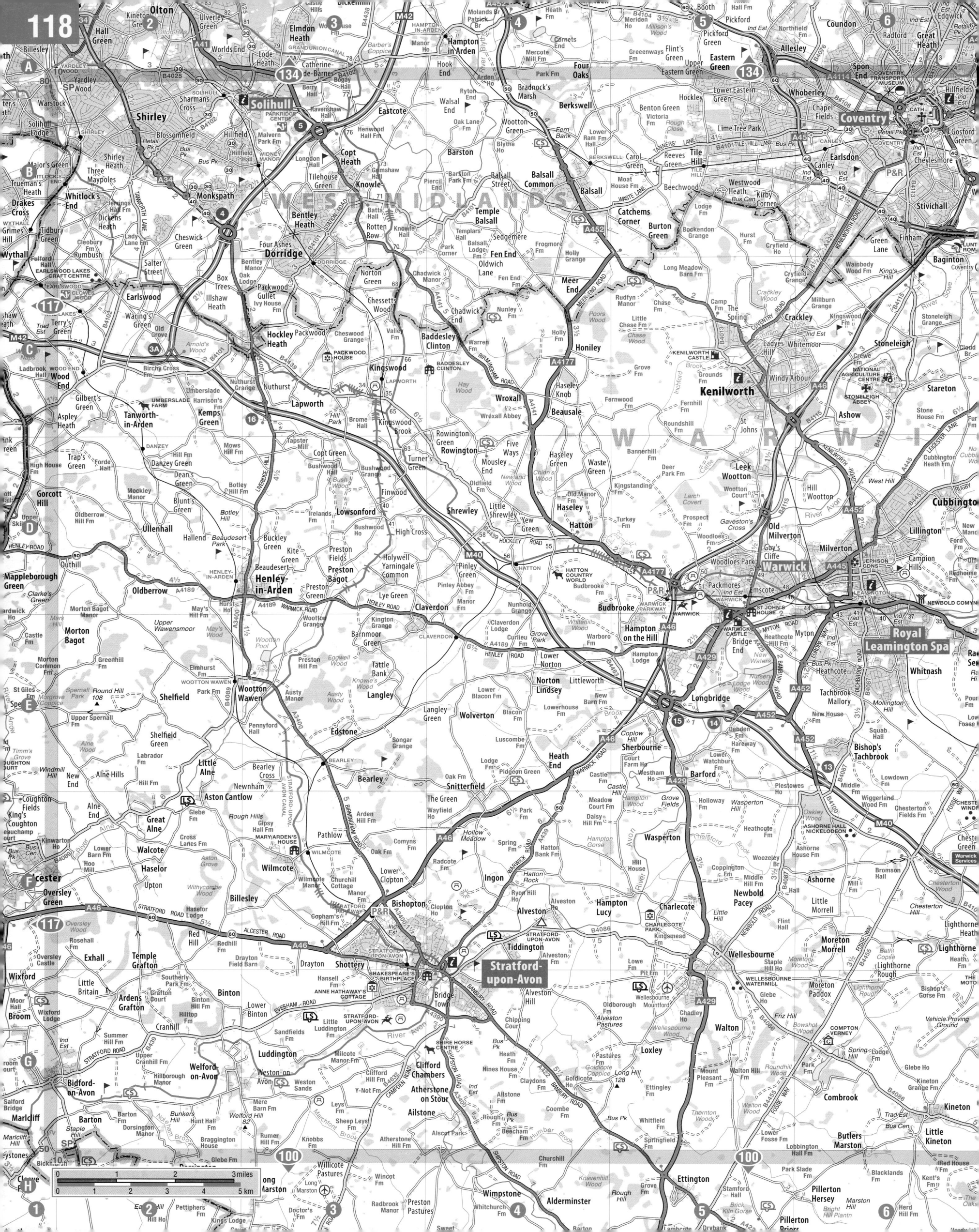

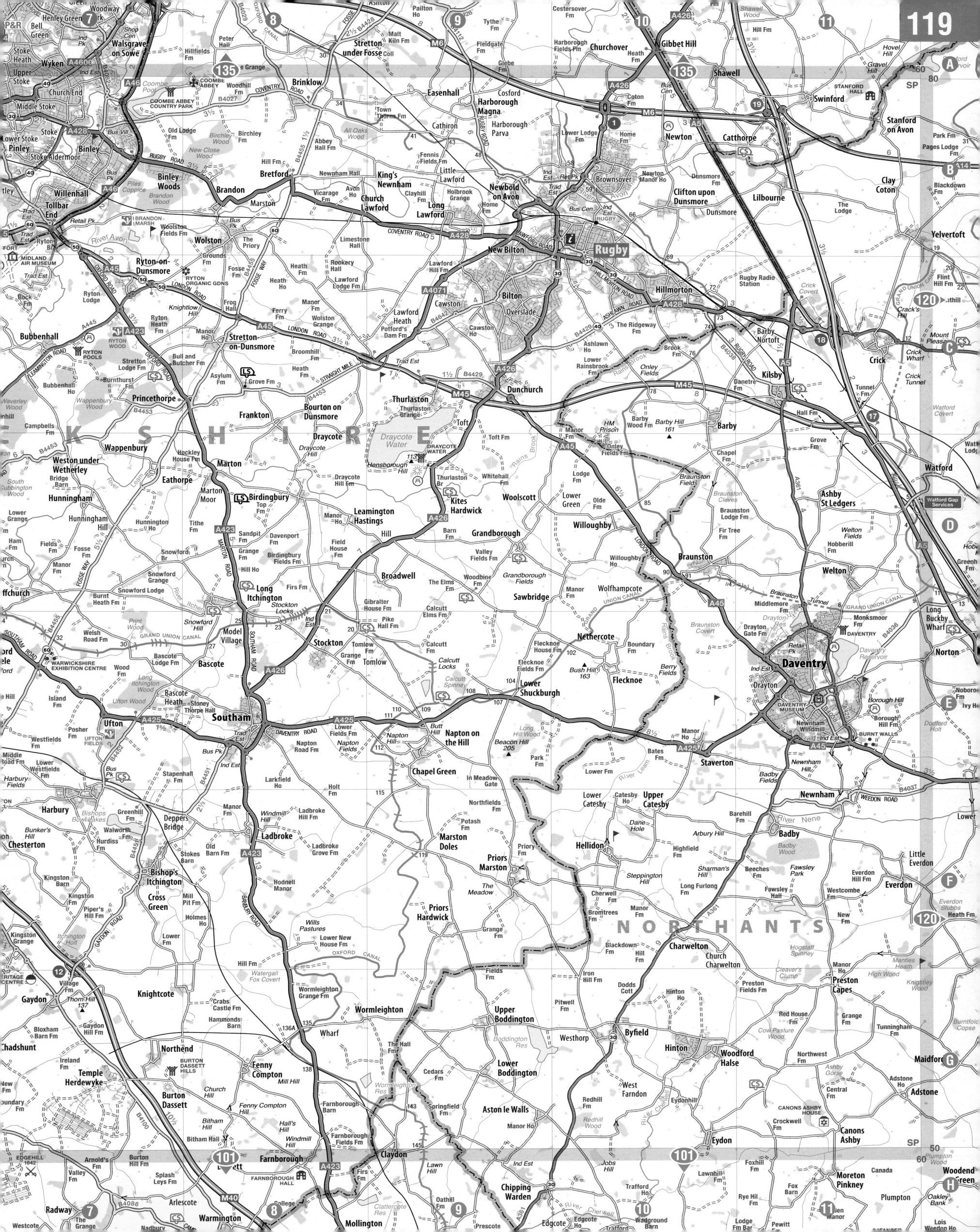

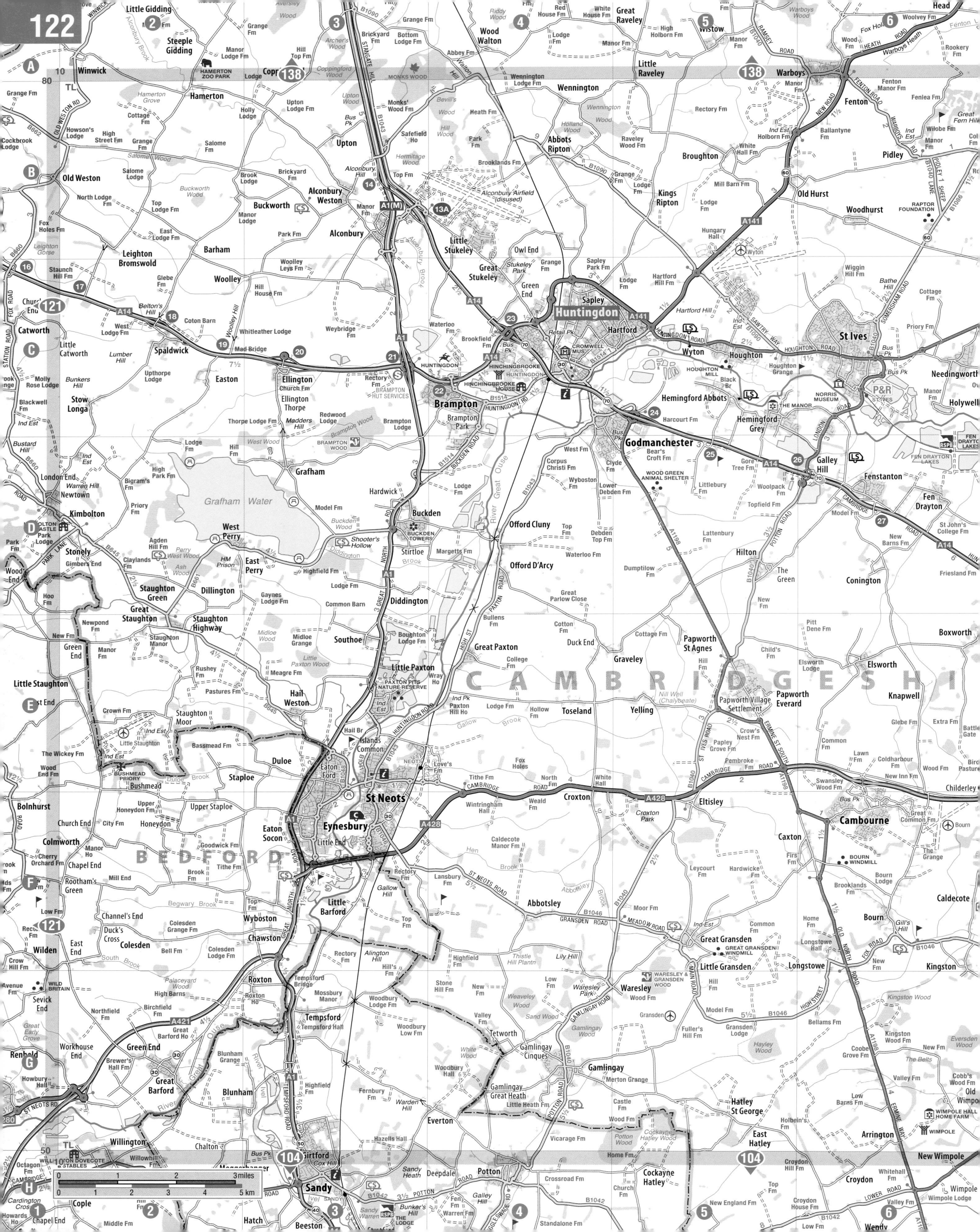

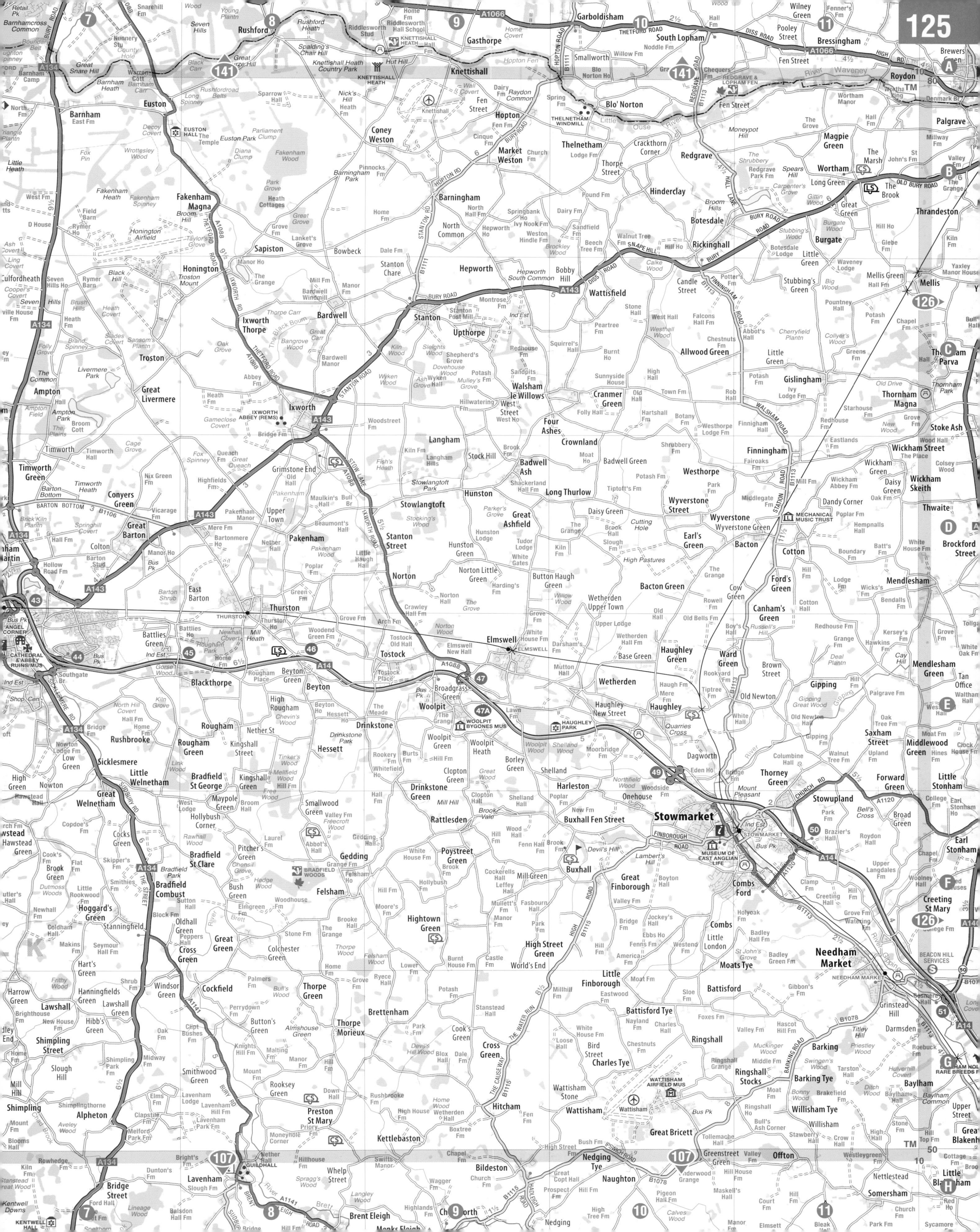

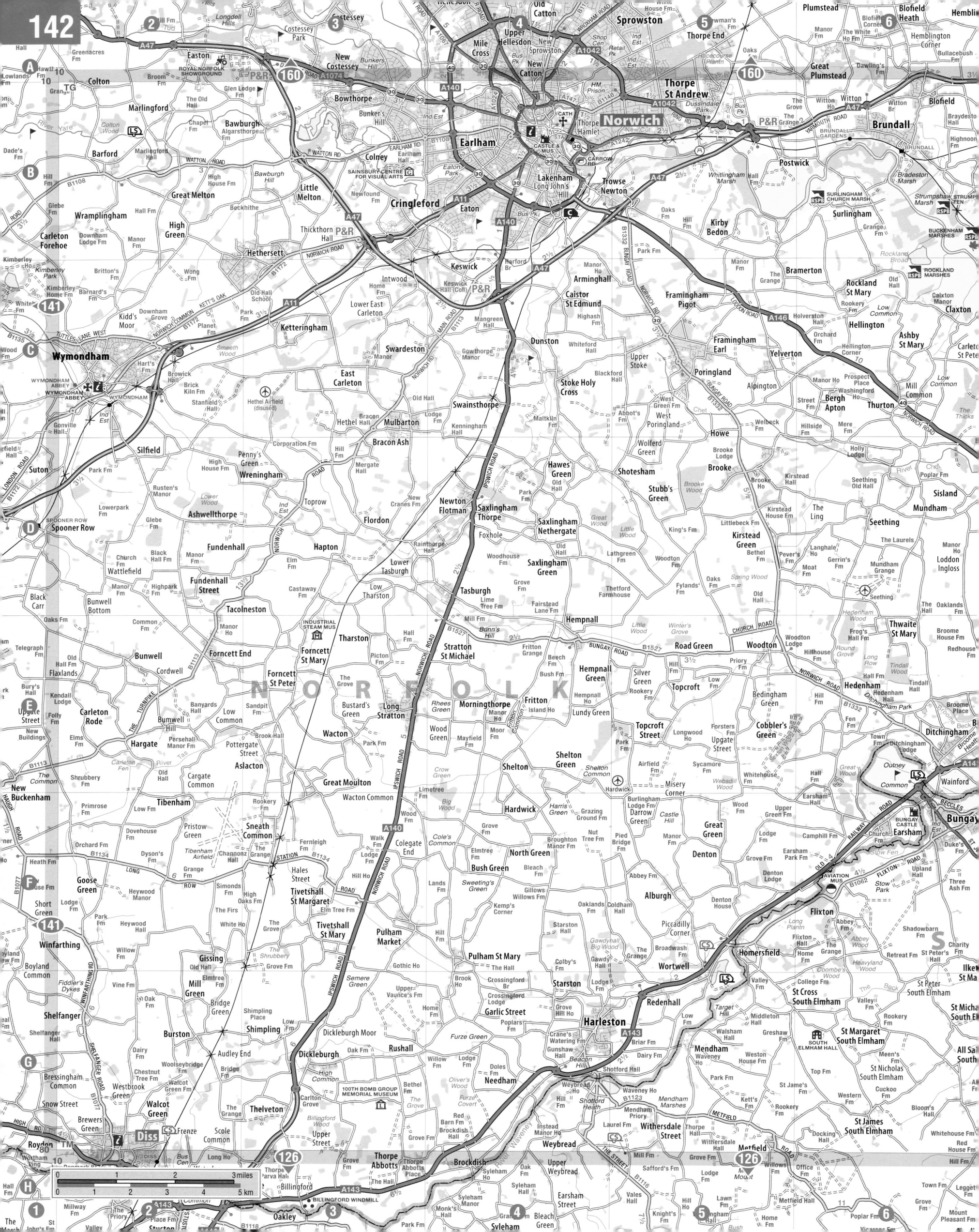

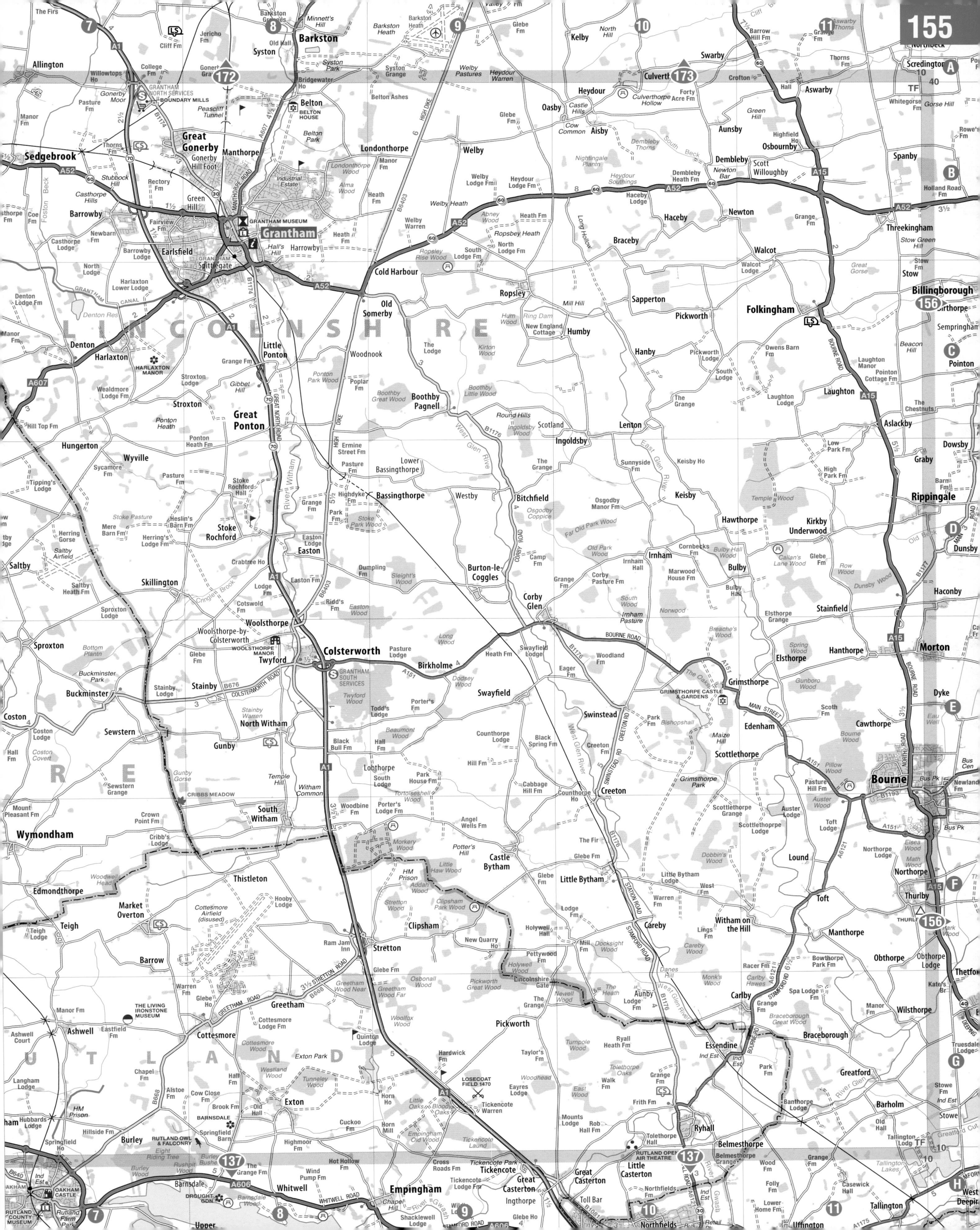

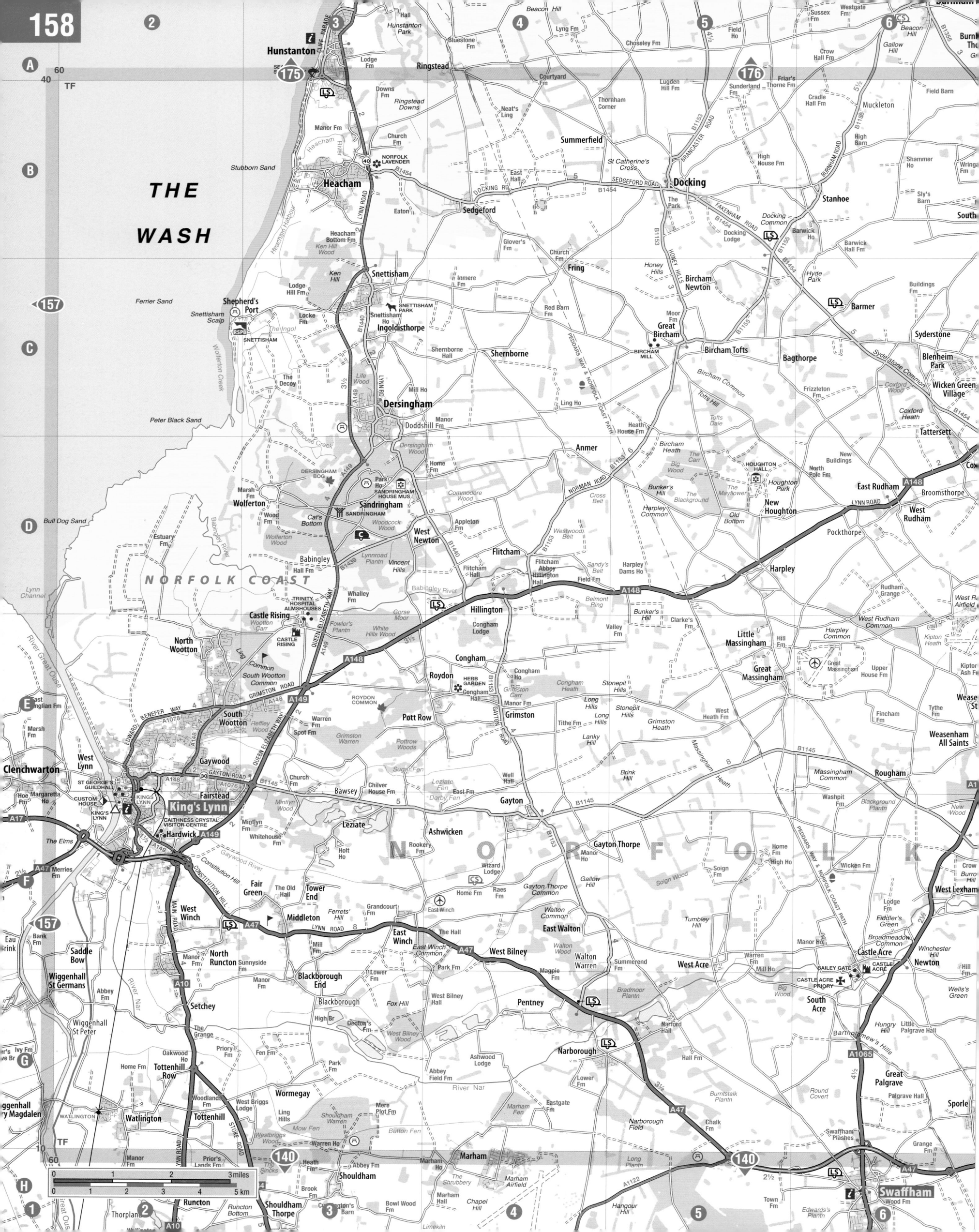

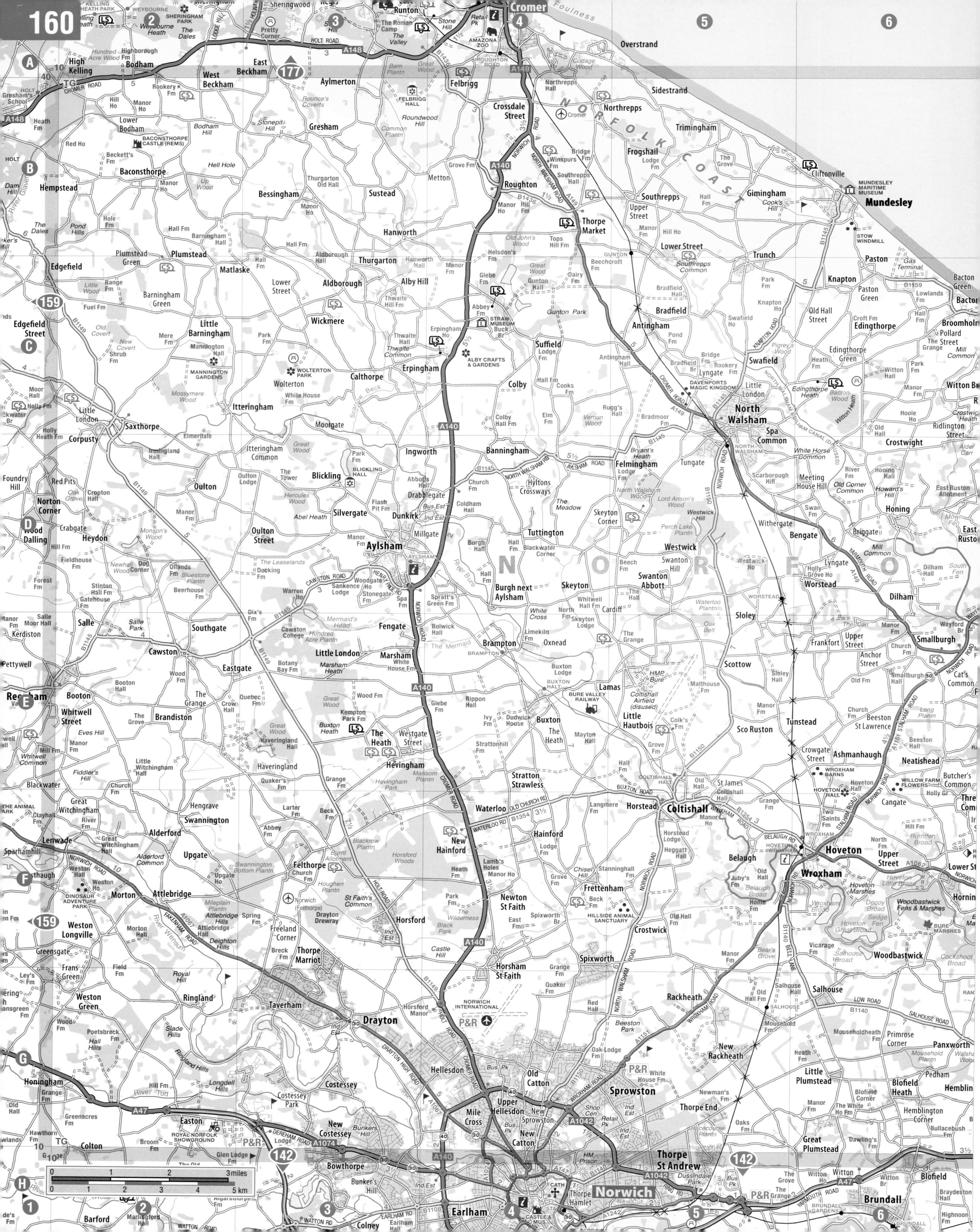

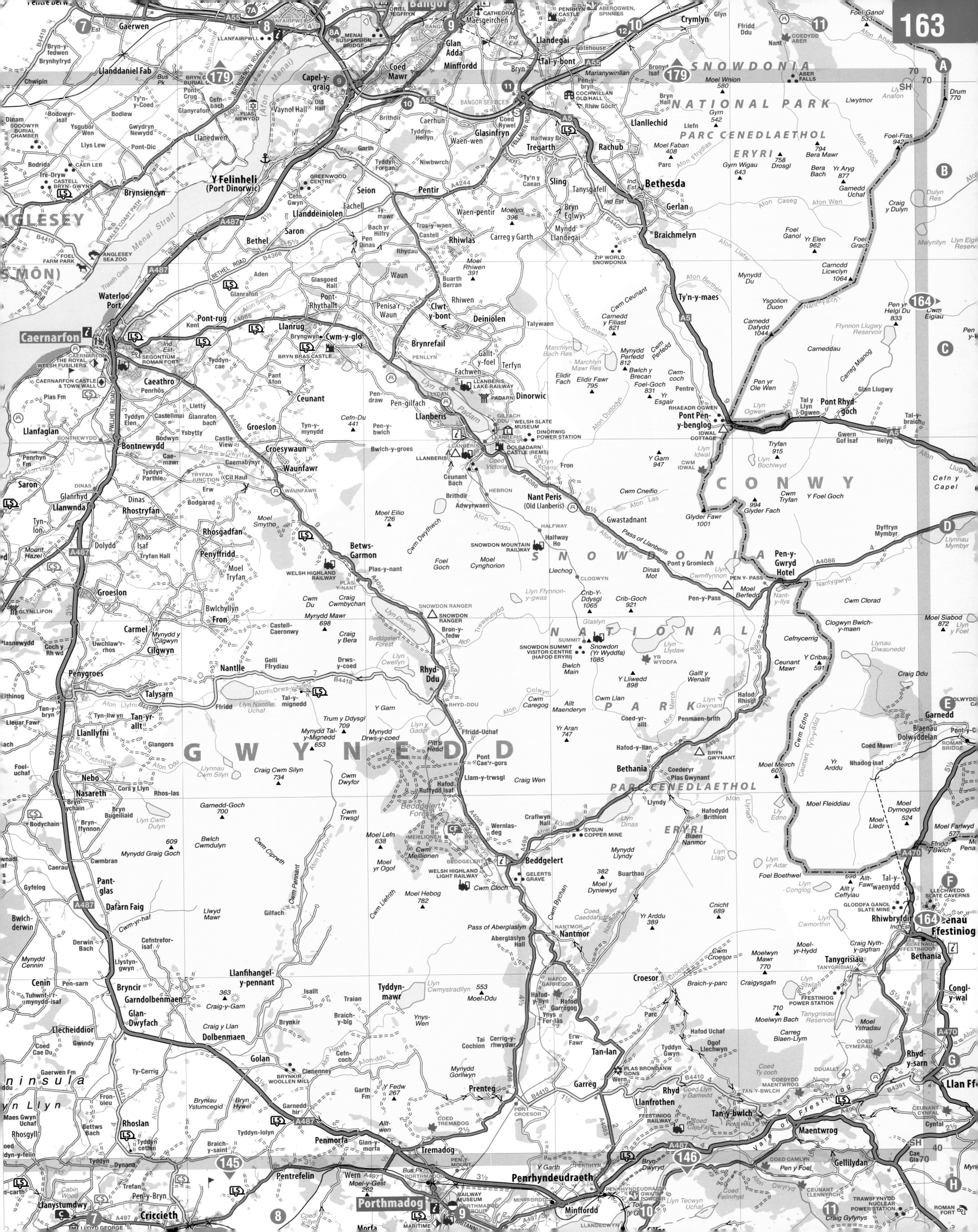

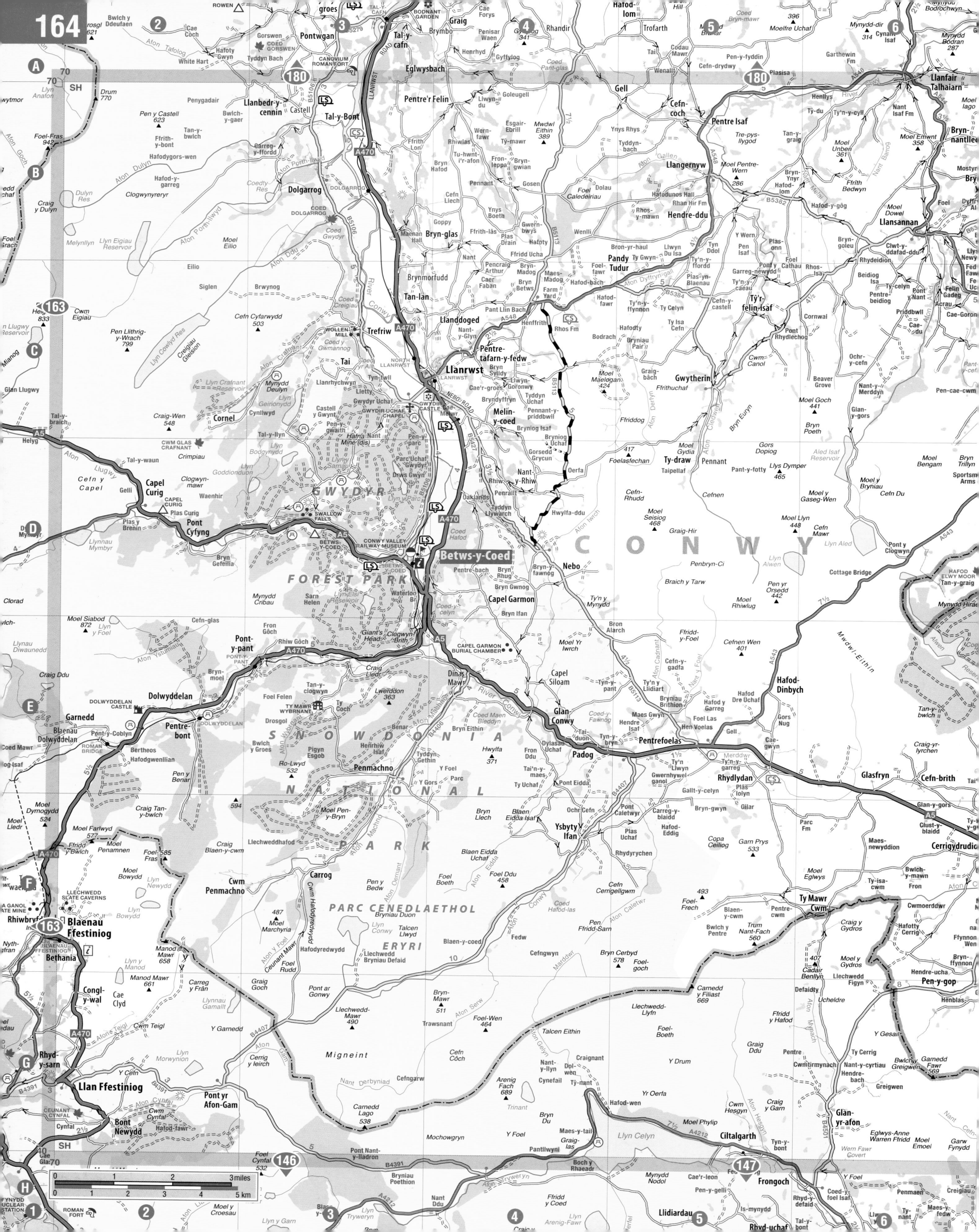

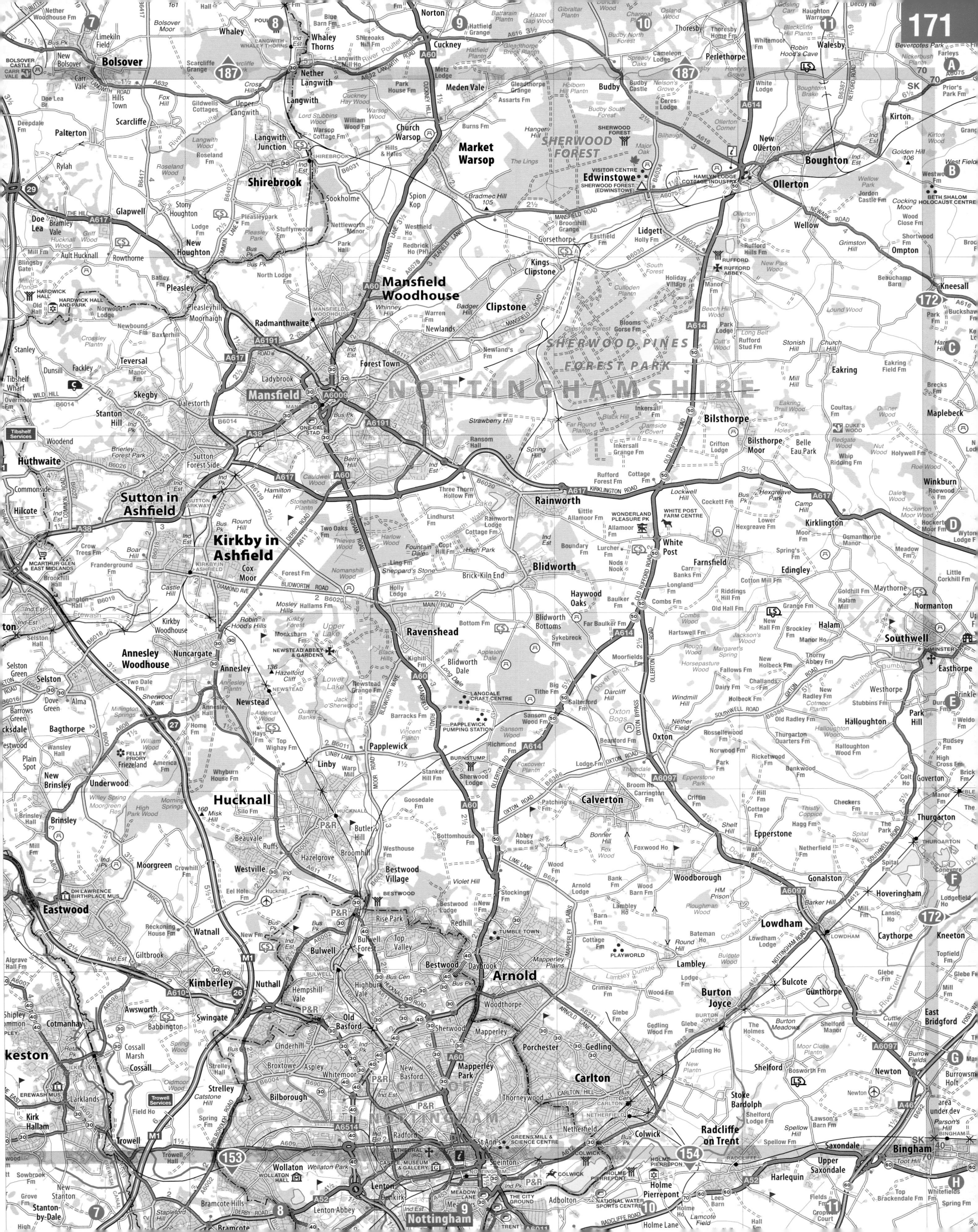

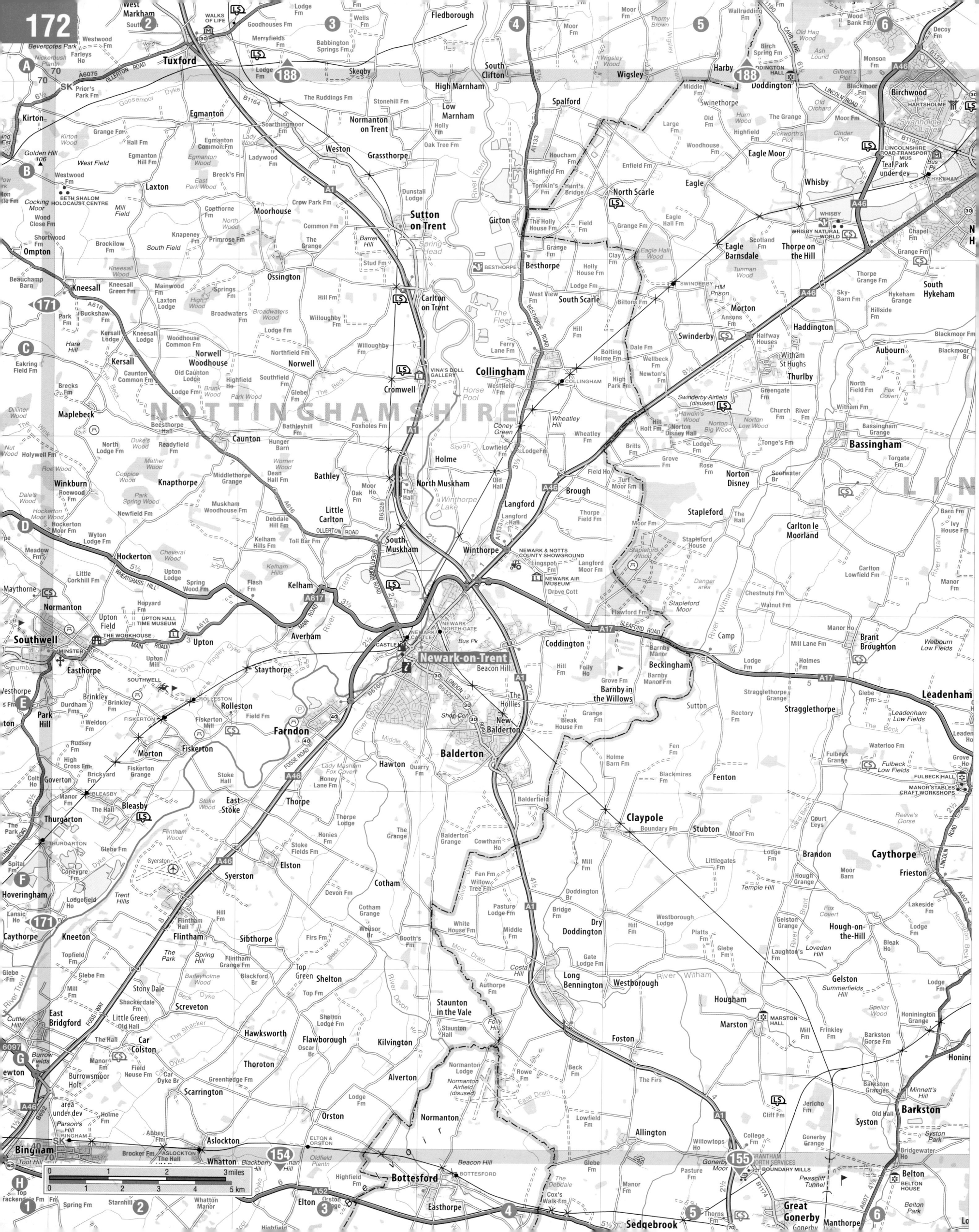

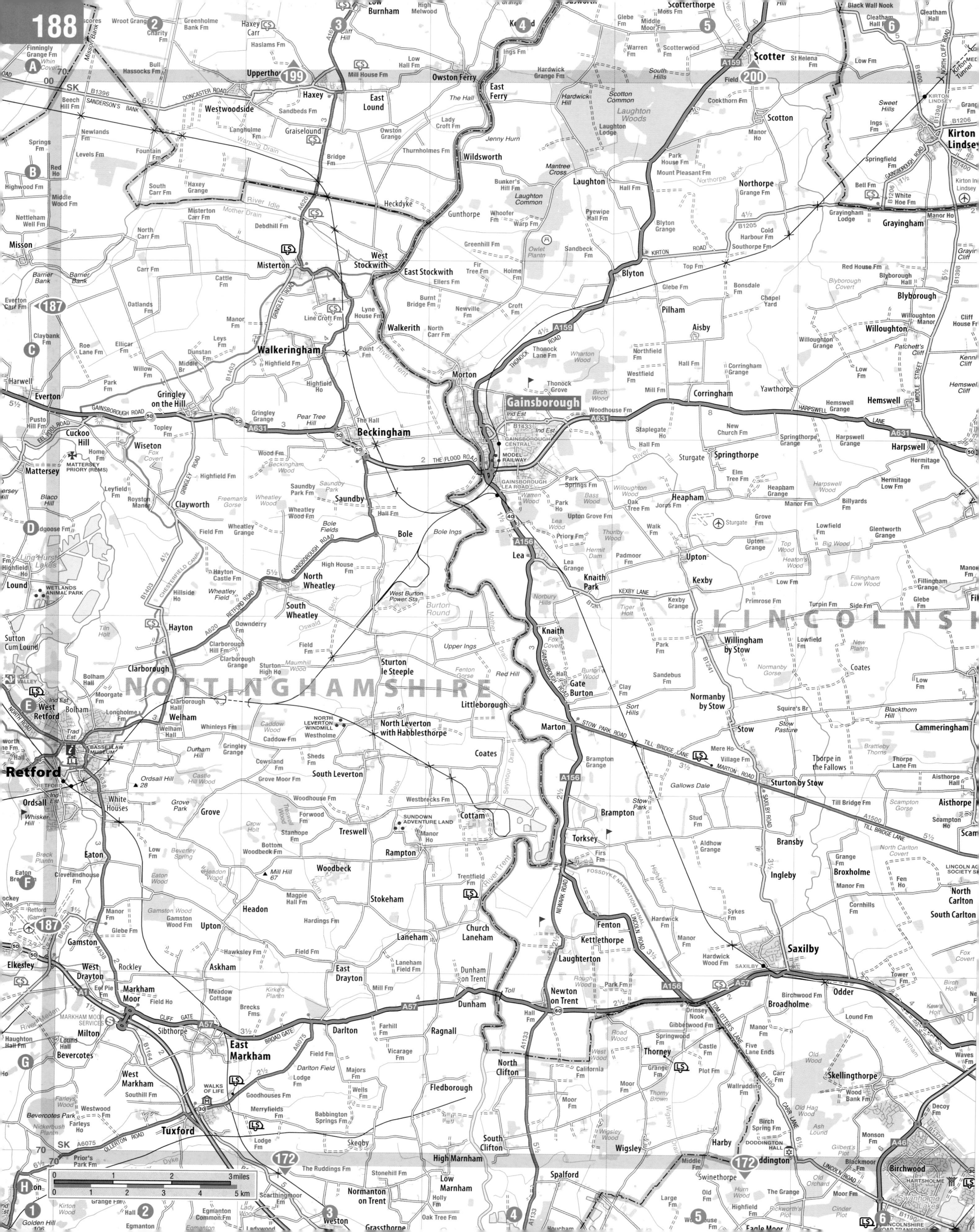

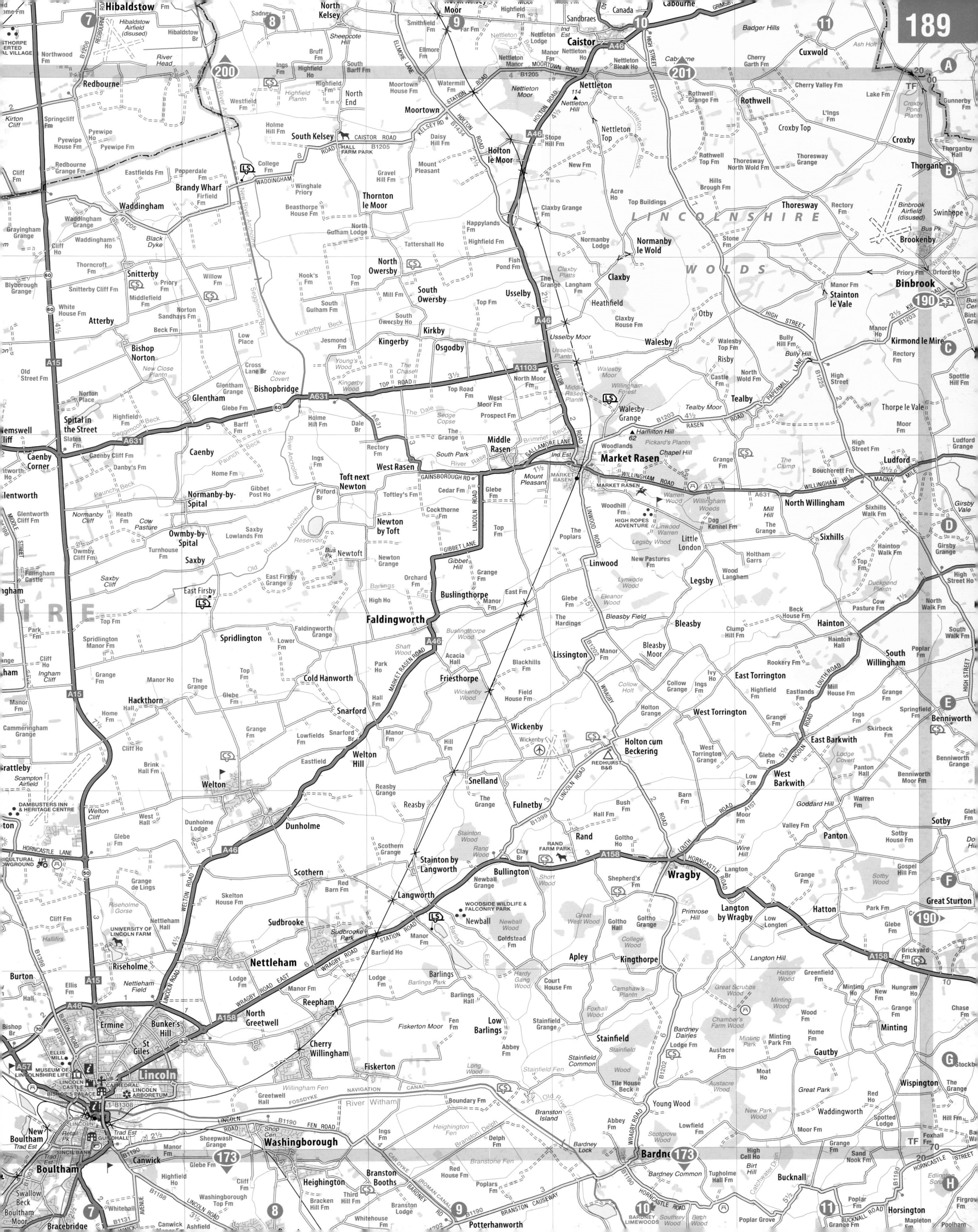

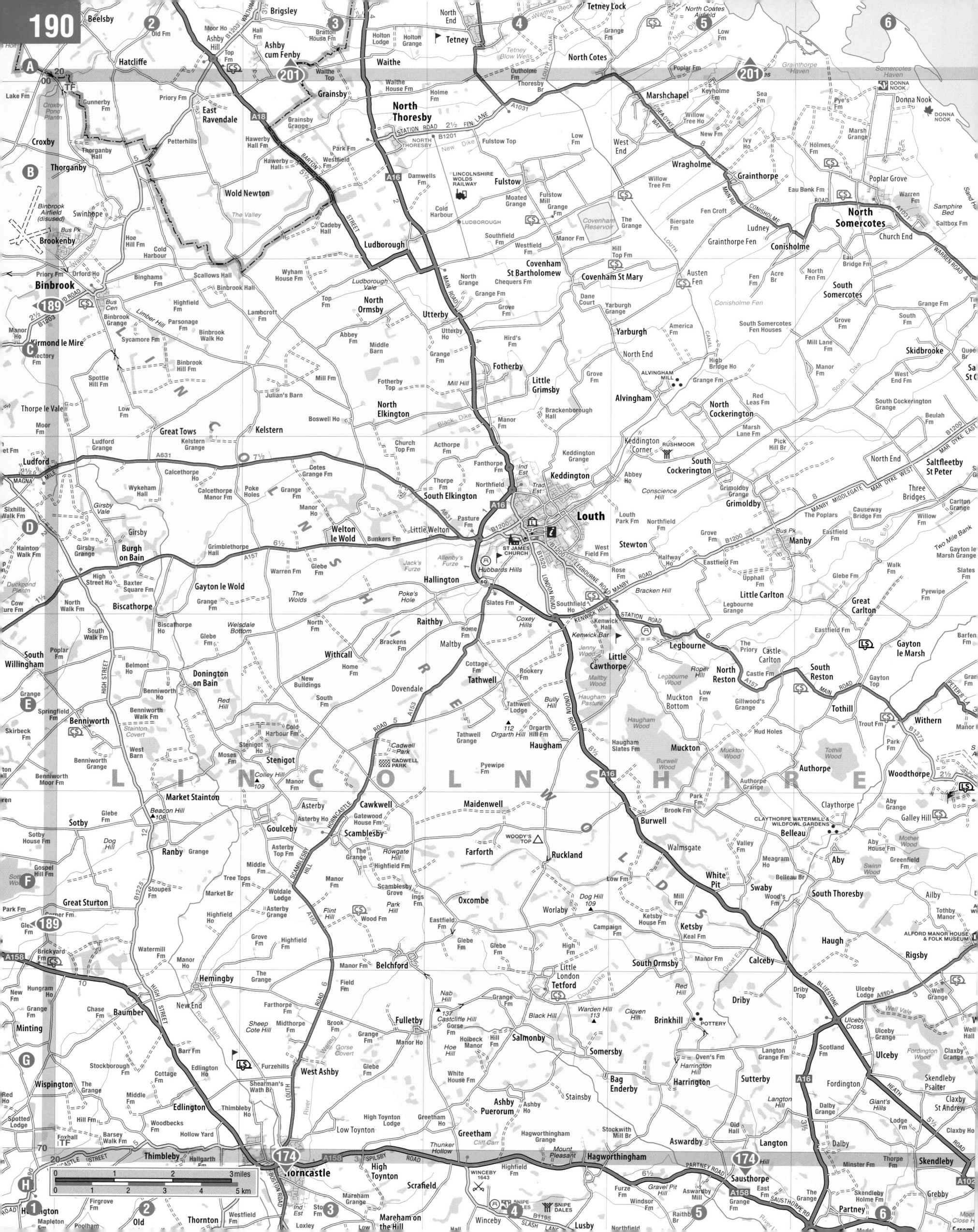

A
B
C
D
E
F
G
H

7   8   9   10   11

70
TF 00

Toby's Hill
Saltfleet
Saltfleet Haven
Sea View Fm
Rimac
eetby ments
SALTFLEETBY THEDDLETHORPE
Saltfleetby All Saints
SALTFLEET ROAD
Lodge Fm
eetby nge
Manor Ho
Theddlethorpe St Helen
Hall Fm
MABLETHORPE RD
Gayton Engine
Theddlethorpe All Saints
Will Row
High Gate
A1031
Gas Terminal
North End
THE SEAL SANCTUARY & NATURE CENTRE
Westfield Fm
Stain Hill
Meers Bank
Mablethorpe Hall
FUN FAIR
Mablethorpe
THEDDLETHORPE RD
Strubby Grange
Earl's Br
Grange Fm
A1104
ALFORD ROAD
Poplar Fm
Trusthorpe
A52
Bamber's Br
Willow Fm
SUTTON ROAD
Strubby
A157
Thorpe
Trusthorpe Hall
ALFORD ROAD
Sutton on Sea
Maltby le Marsh
Manor Ho
Sandilands
BEESBY ROAD
Mill Hill
Poplar Lodge Fm
Beesby
Abbey Fm
Beesby Grange
Manor Fm
Washdyke Br
Hagnaby
HUTTOFT ROAD
Sea Bank Fm
Hannah
America Fm
Cob Hill
A1104
Saleby
Glebe Fm
Priory Fm
Markby
The Grange
Saleby Manor
College Fm
Asserby
Black House Fm
Asserby Turn
Willow Fm
SUTTON ROAD
Thoresthorpe
Bilsby
Dryby Fm
Moat Ho
Huttoft
Manor Fm
Anderby Creek
EAST ST
The Grange
The Manor
MUMBY ROAD
LONG LANE
Anderby
Alford
Thurlby
B1449
Wolla Bank
Bilsby Field
Farlesthorpe Fen
ON YOUR MARQUES
Langham Fm
Chapel Six Marshes
Well Fm
Farlesthorpe
School Fm
Mumby
Manor Ho
Manor Fm
l Vale
Main Drain
Mill Hill
Authorpe Row
Chapel Pt
Mawthorpe
Elsom Fm
Cumberworth
Cherry Fm
Mickleberry Hill
Chapman's Fm
Bonthorpe
Manor Fm
Helsey
Croft Fm
B1196
Listoft
Hogsthorpe
Chapel St Leonards
Willoughby
Poplar Fm
Willoughby High Drain
Claxby
Willoughby Wood
A52
Sloothby
Hogsbeck Ho
Boothby
B1196
Welton Low Wood
Hasthorpe
Howlet Ho
Slackholme End
Hope Fm
Beeches Fm
SKEGNESS ROAD
TF 70
70
Welton High Wood
175
Welbourne Fm
HARDY'S ANIMAL FARM
175
Highfield Fm
Thwaite Hall
Habertoft
North Drain
Ingoldmells
Candlesby Hill
Rookery
Welton Marsh
Boothby Hall
Addlethorpe
Manor Fm
FANTASY ISLAND
Ingoldmells Pt
Boothby Grange
Whitehouse Corner

7   8   9   10   11

N O R T H

S E A

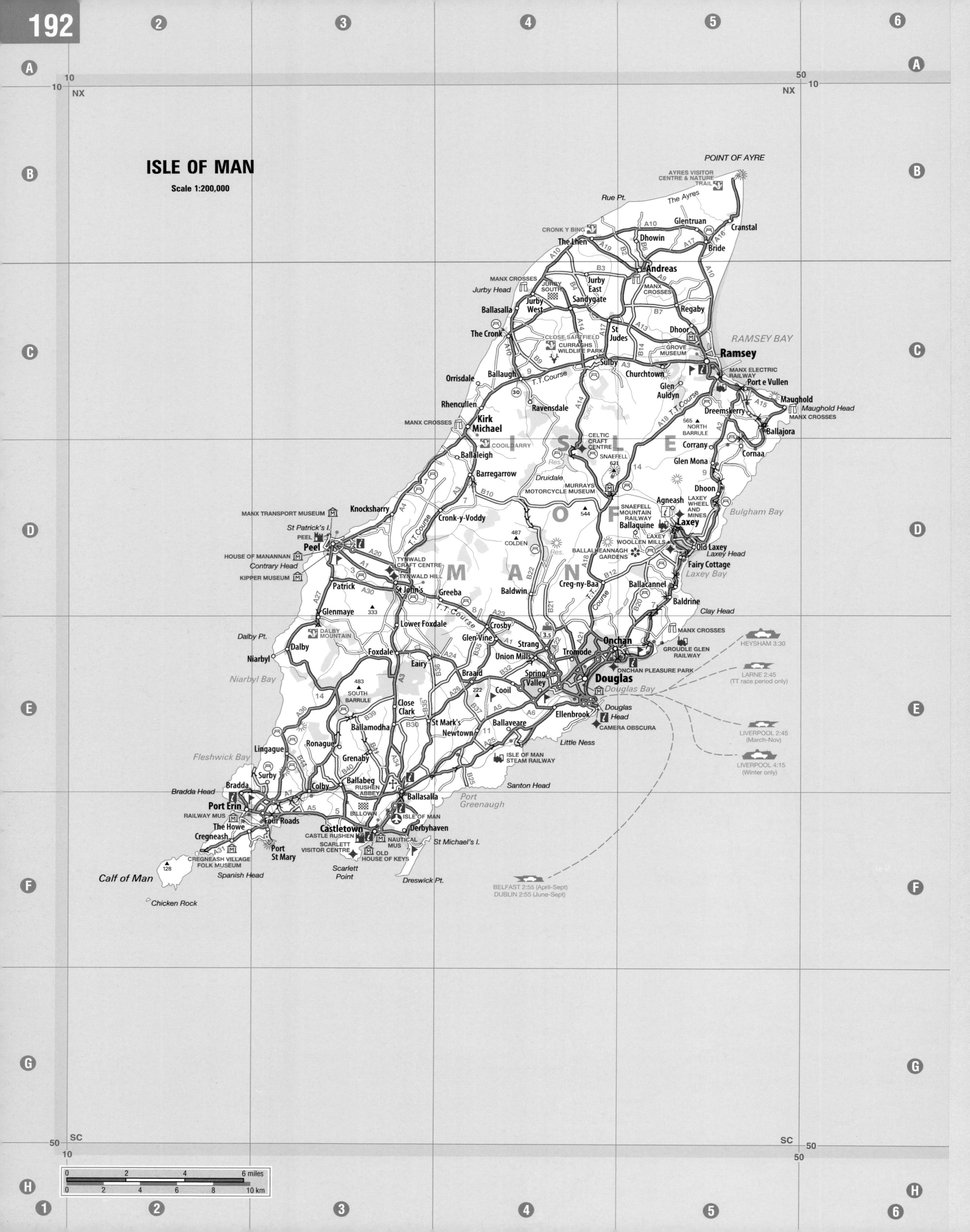

ISLE OF MAN

Scale 1:200,000

POINT OF AYRE

AYRES VISITOR
CENTRE & NATURE
TRAIL

Rue Pt.

The Ayres

CRONK Y BING

Glentruan

Cranstal

The Lhen

Dhowin

Bride

MANX CROSSES

Andreas

Jurby Head

Jurby
South

Jurby
East

Sandygate

Regaby

Ballasalla

Jurby
West

MANX
CROSSES

Dhoor

The Cronk

St
Judes

RAMSEY BAY

CLOSE SARTFIELD
CURRAGHS WILDLIFE PARK

GROVE
MUSEUM

Sulby

Ramsey

Orrisdale

Ballaugh

Churchtown

MANX ELECTRIC
RAILWAY

Port e Vullen

Glen
Auldyn

Rhencullen

Maughold

Ravensdale

Dreemskerry

Maughold Head
MANX CROSSES

MANX CROSSES

**Kirk
Michael**

CELTIC
CRAFT
CENTRE

565 ▲
NORTH
BARRULE

Corrany

Ballajora

COOILDARRY

Ballaleigh

ISLE

Glen Mona

Cornaa

Barregarrow

SNAEFELL
621

14

9

Dhoon

Druidale

MURRAYS
MOTORCYCLE MUSEUM

SNAEFELL
MOUNTAIN
RAILWAY

Agneash

LAXEY
WHEEL
AND
MINES

OF

487 ▲
COLDEN

544 ▲

Ballaquine

Laxey

Bulgham Bay

Knocksharry

MANX TRANSPORT MUSEUM

Cronk-y-Voddy

St Patrick's I.

PEEL

BALLALHEANNAGH
GARDENS

LAXEY
WOOLLEN MILLS

Old Laxey

Laxey Head

Peel

HOUSE OF MANANNAN

A20

TYNWALD
CRAFT CENTRE

Baldwin

Creg-ny-Baa

MAN

Fairy Cottage

Laxey Bay

Contrary Head

KIPPER MUSEUM

TYNWALD HILL

St John's

Greeba

B22

Ballacannel

Patrick

333 ▲

A23

Baldrine

Glenmaye

Lower Foxdale

Crosby

3.5

Clay Head

Dalby Pt.

DALBY
MOUNTAIN

Glen Vine

Strang

MANX CROSSES

Niarbyl

Dalby

Foxdale

Eairy

Union Mills

Tromode

Onchan

GROUDLE GLEN
RAILWAY

HEYSHAM 3:30

Braaid

Spring
Valley

Douglas

LARNE 2:45
(TT race period only)

Niarbyl Bay

483 ▲
SOUTH
BARRULE

14

Cooil

ONCHAN PLEASURE PARK

Douglas Bay

Close
Clark

222 ▲

Ellenbrook

*Douglas
Head*

LIVERPOOL 2:45
(March-Nov)

Lingague

Ballamodha

St Mark's
Newtown

Ballaveare

CAMERA OBSCURA

Little Ness

Ronague

Grenaby

11

LIVERPOOL 4:15
(Winter only)

Fleshwick Bay

Surby

Colby

Ballabeg

ISLE OF MAN
STEAM RAILWAY

Bradda

RUSHEN
ABBEY

Ballasalla

*Port
Greenaugh*

Santon Head

Bradda Head

Port Erin

Four Roads

BILLOWN

ISLE OF MAN

The Howe

RAILWAY MUS

Castletown

OLD
HOUSE OF KEYS

Derbyhaven

Cregneash

CASTLE RUSHEN

NAUTICAL
MUS

St Michael's I.

SCARLETT VISITOR CENTRE

Port
St Mary

CREGNEASH VILLAGE
FOLK MUSEUM

128 ▲

*Scarlett
Point*

Calf of Man

Spanish Head

Dreswick Pt.

° *Chicken Rock*

BELFAST 2:55 (April-Sept)
DUBLIN 2:55 (June-Sept)

0   2   4   6 miles

0   2   4   6   8   10 km

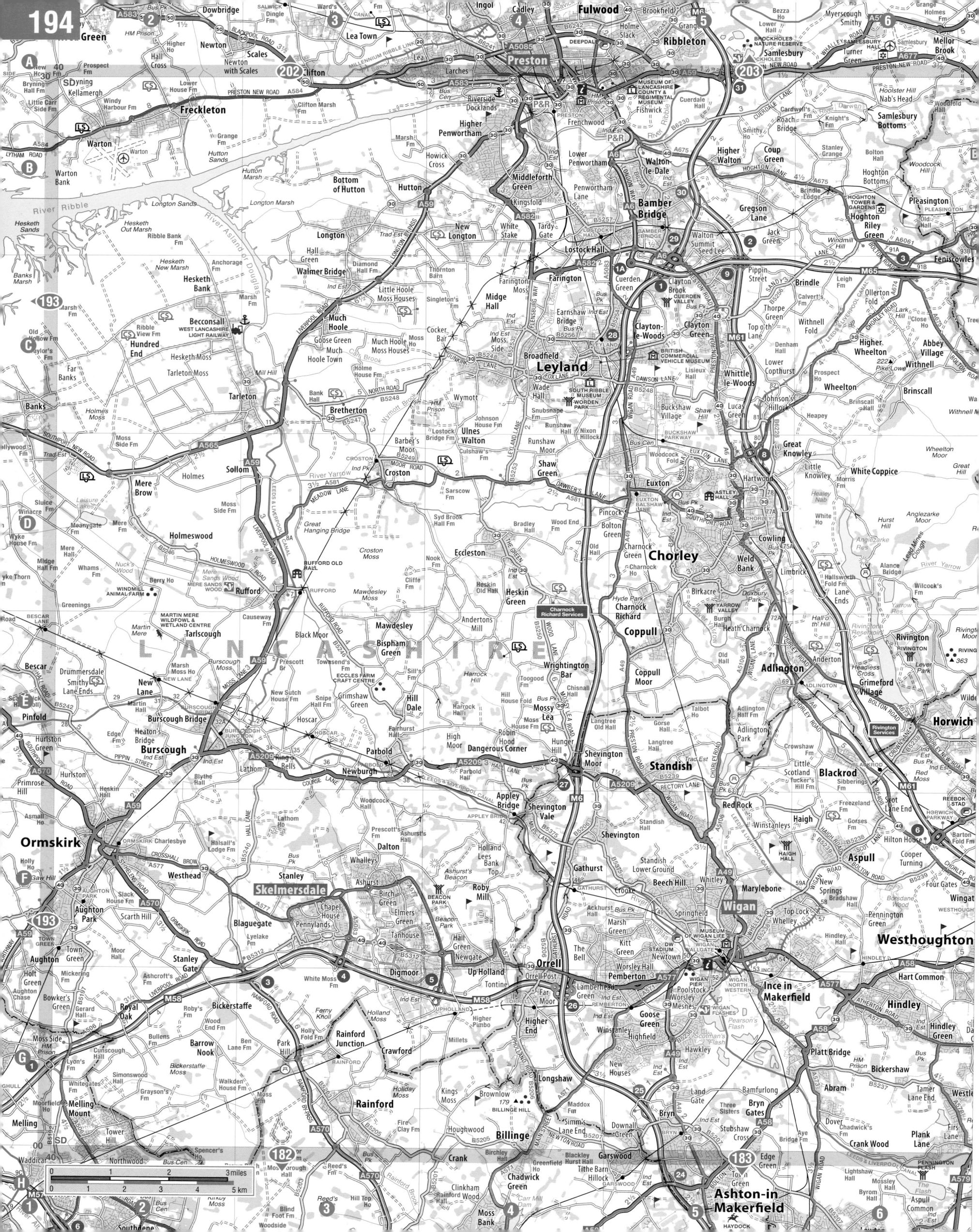

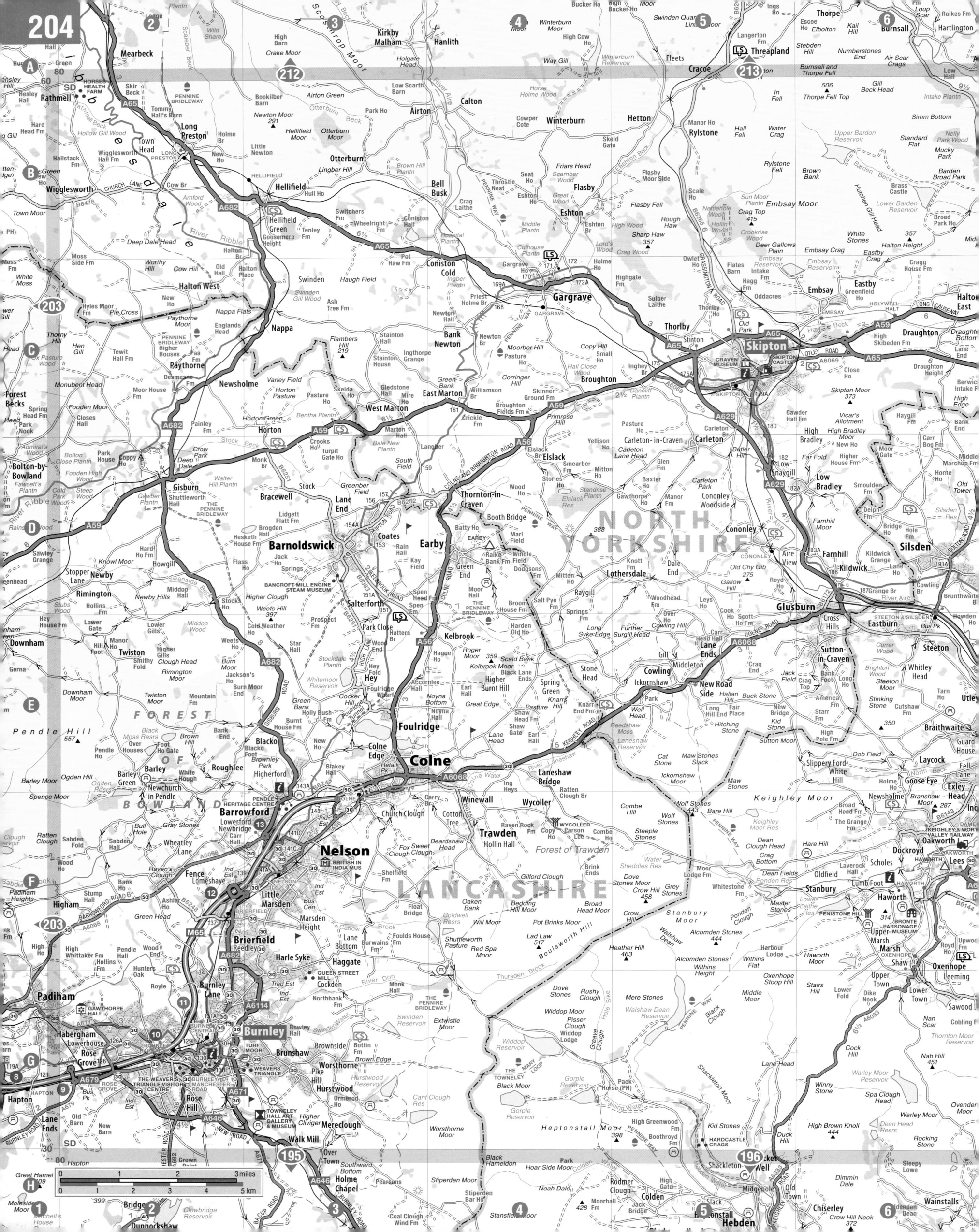

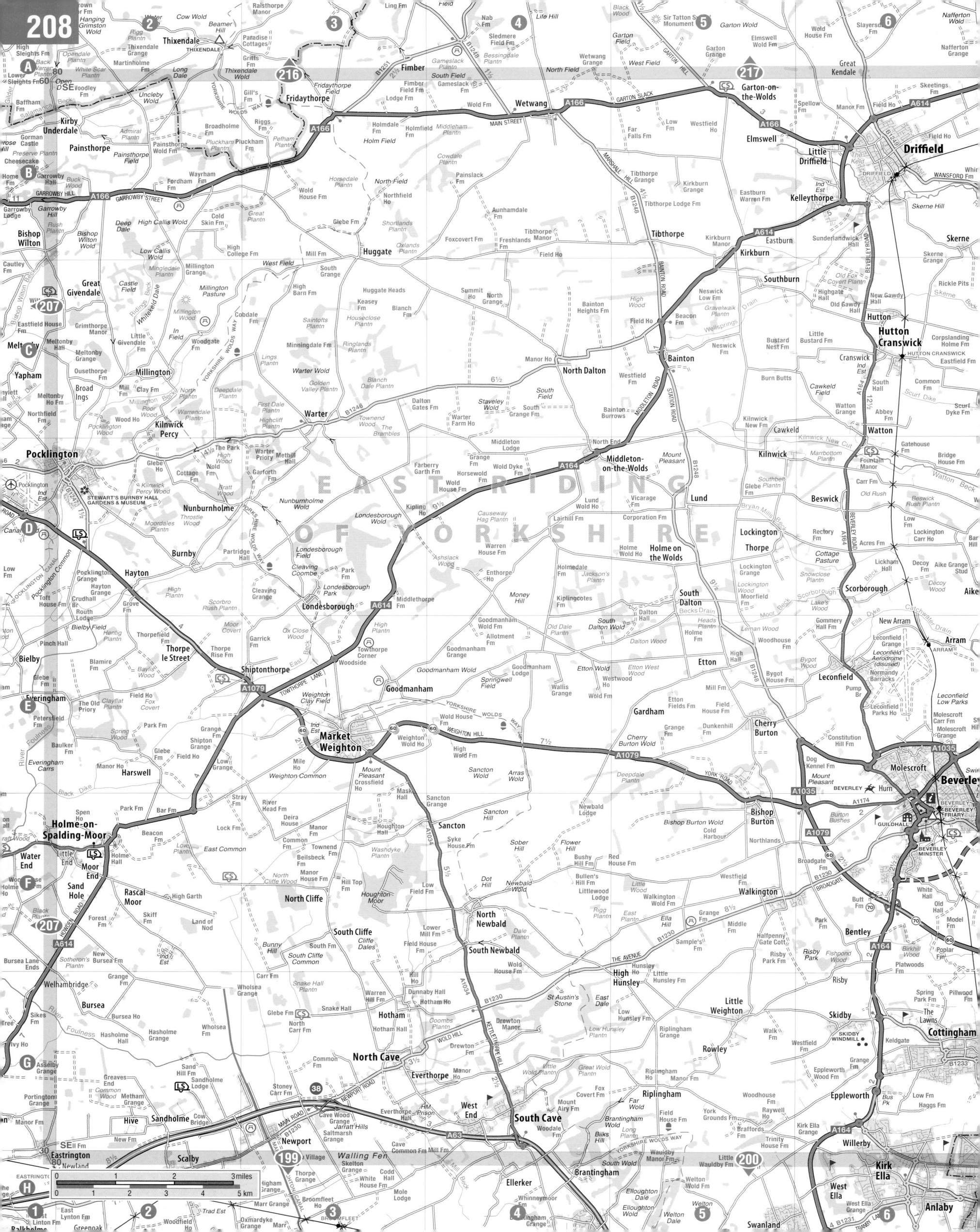

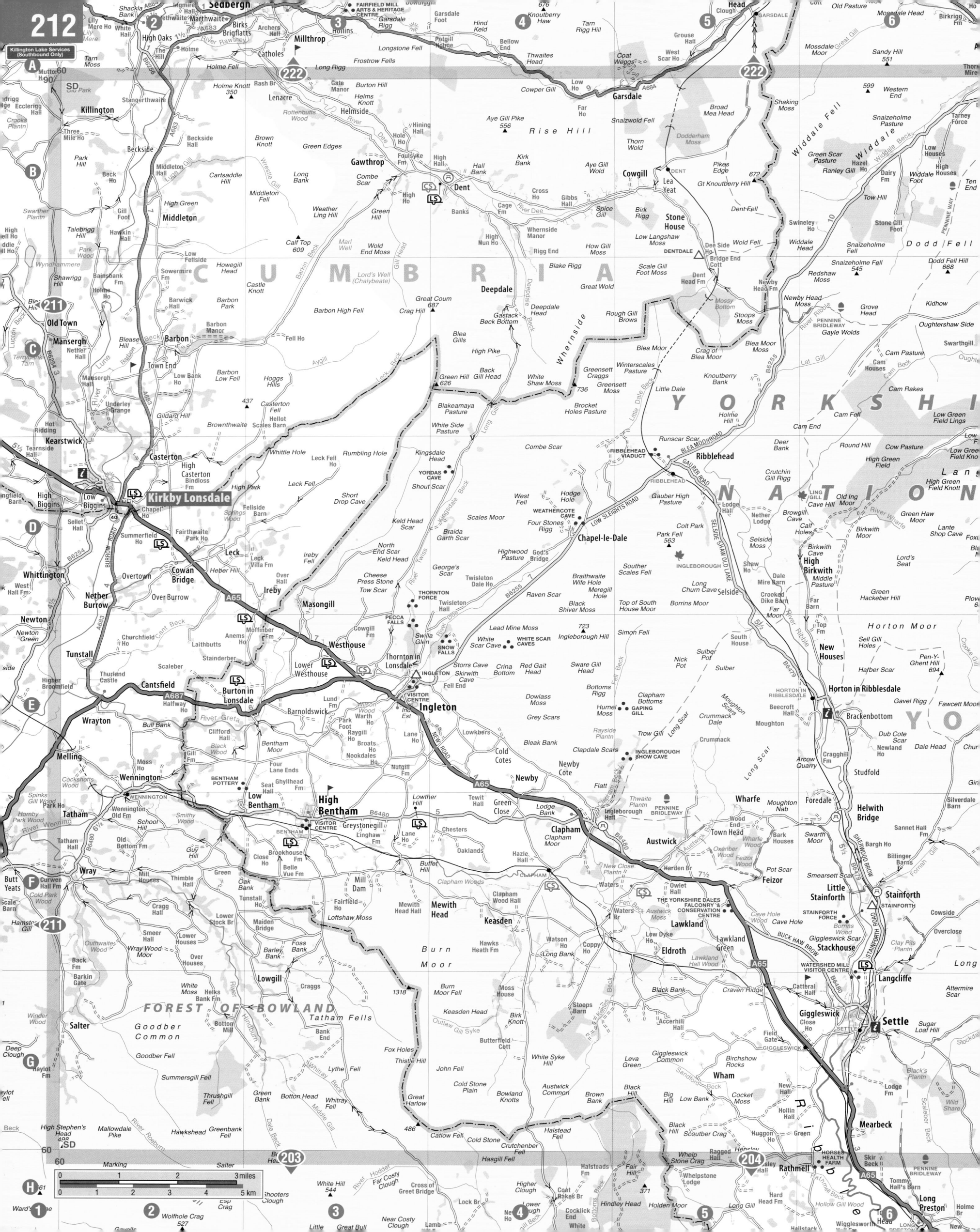

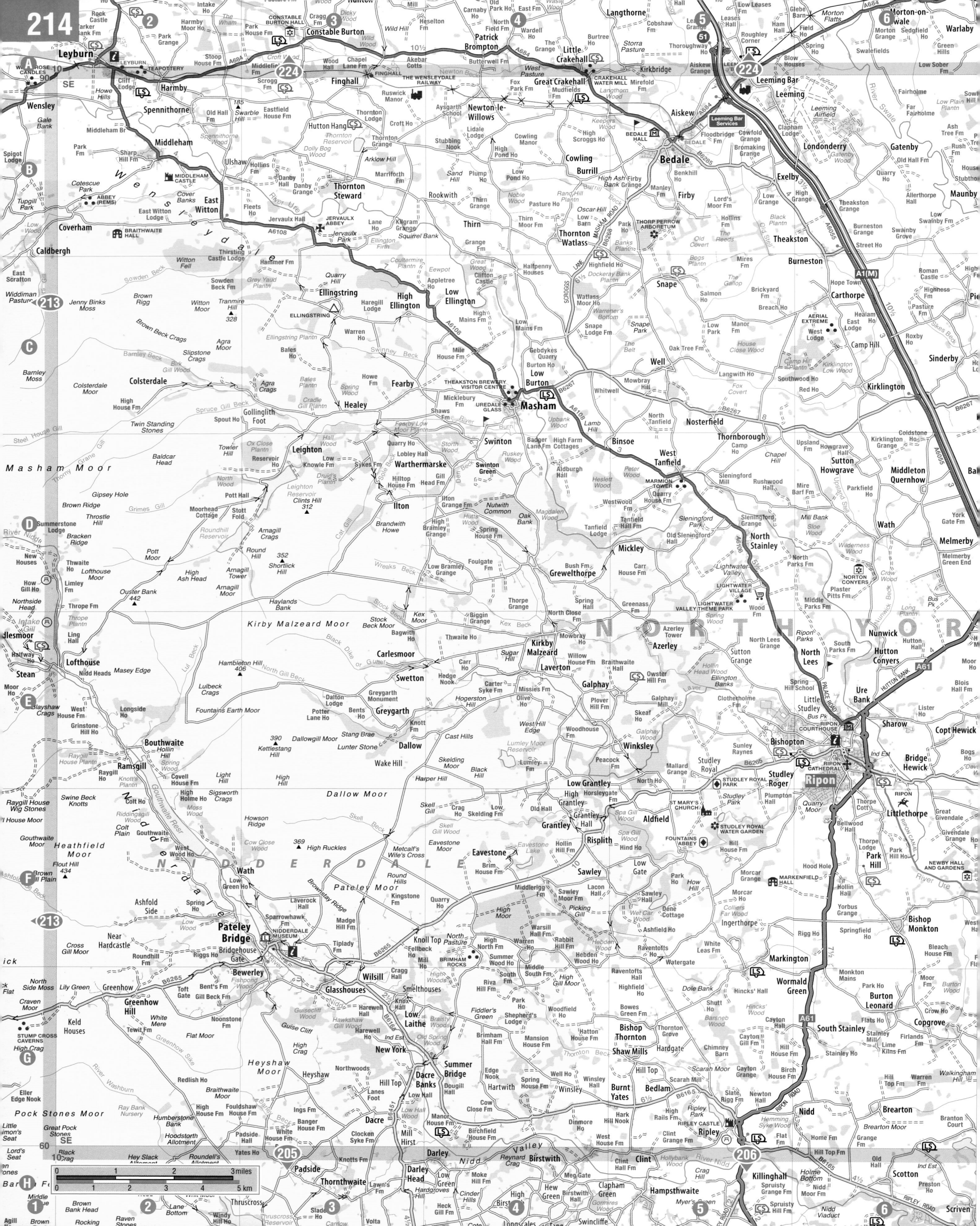

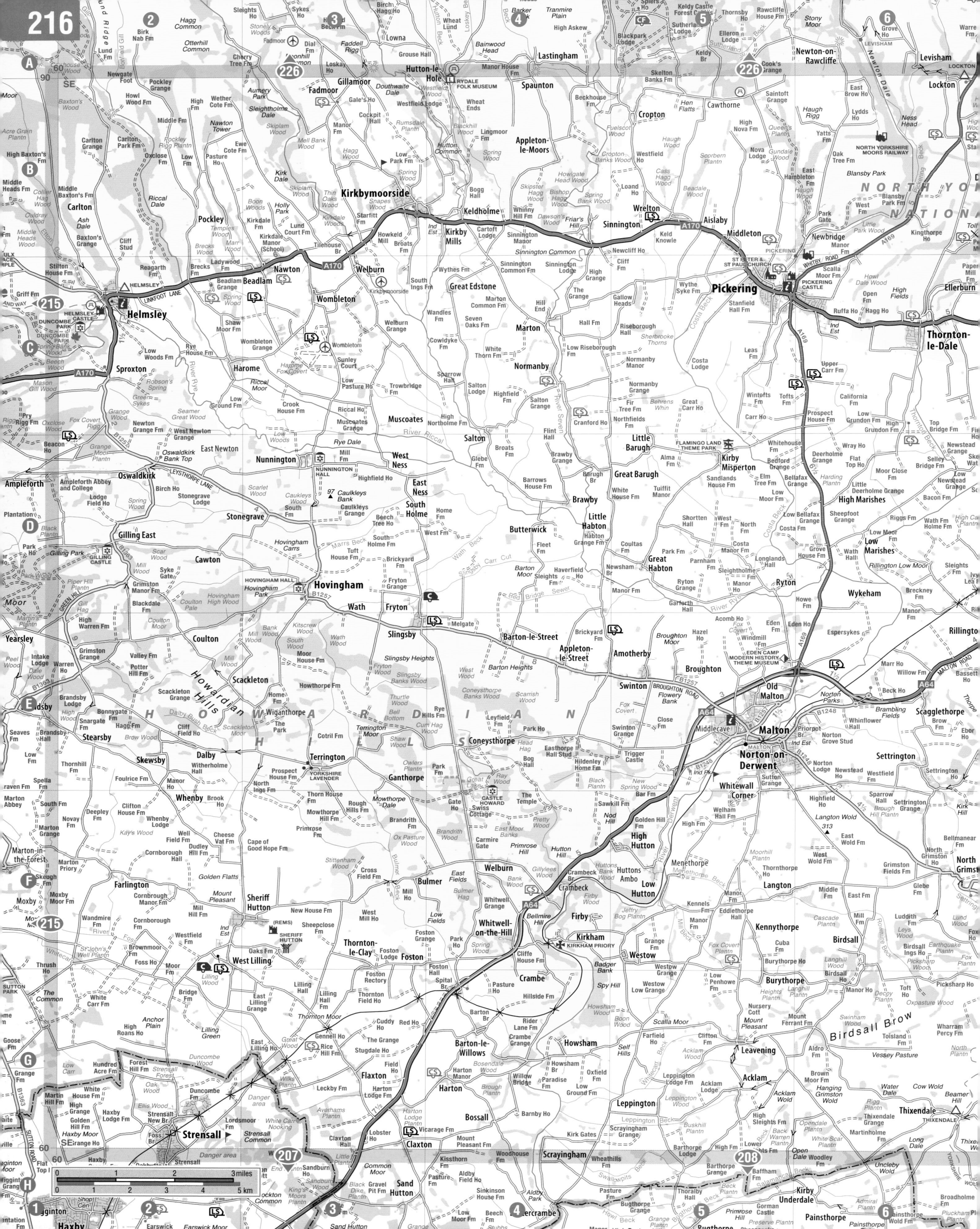

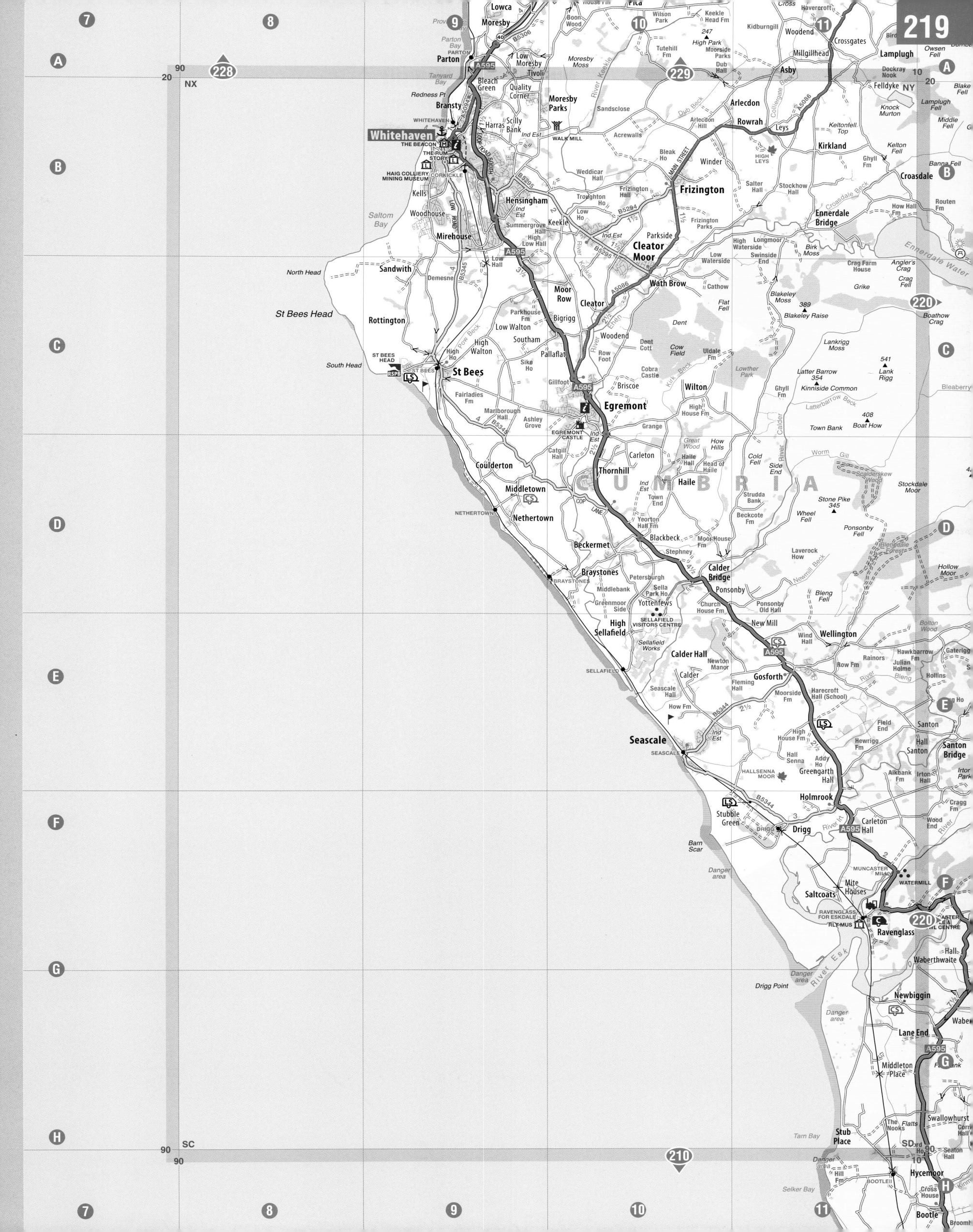

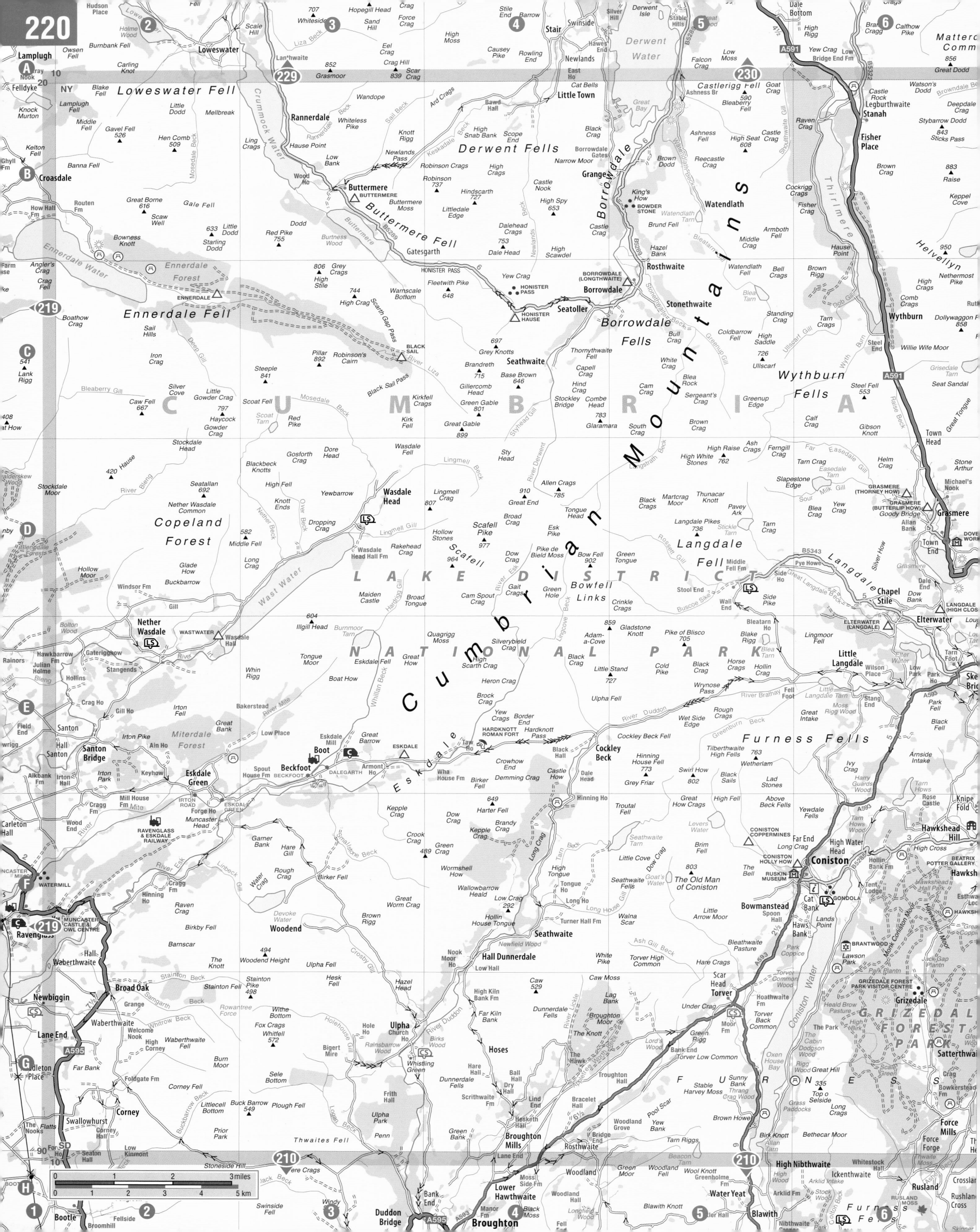

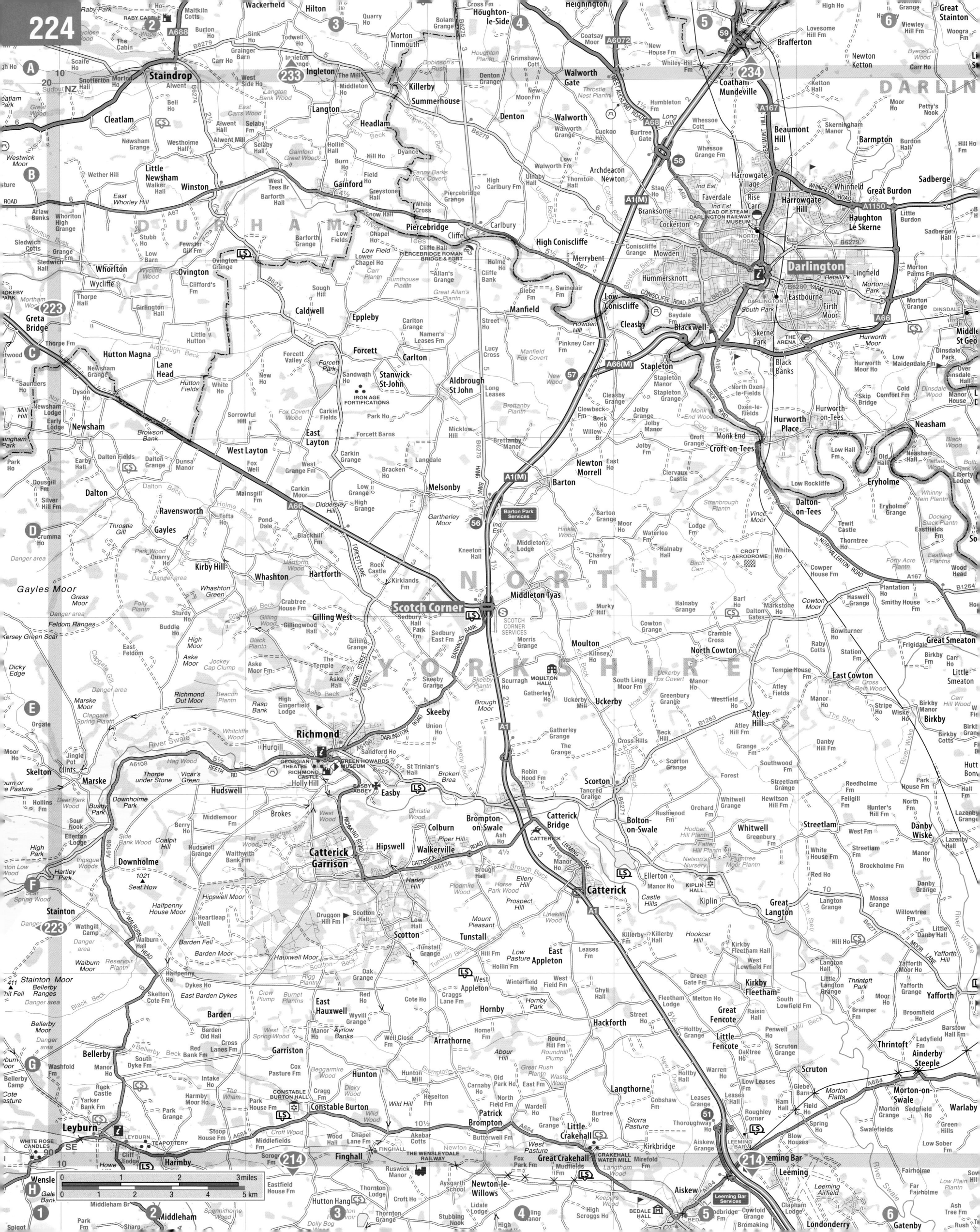

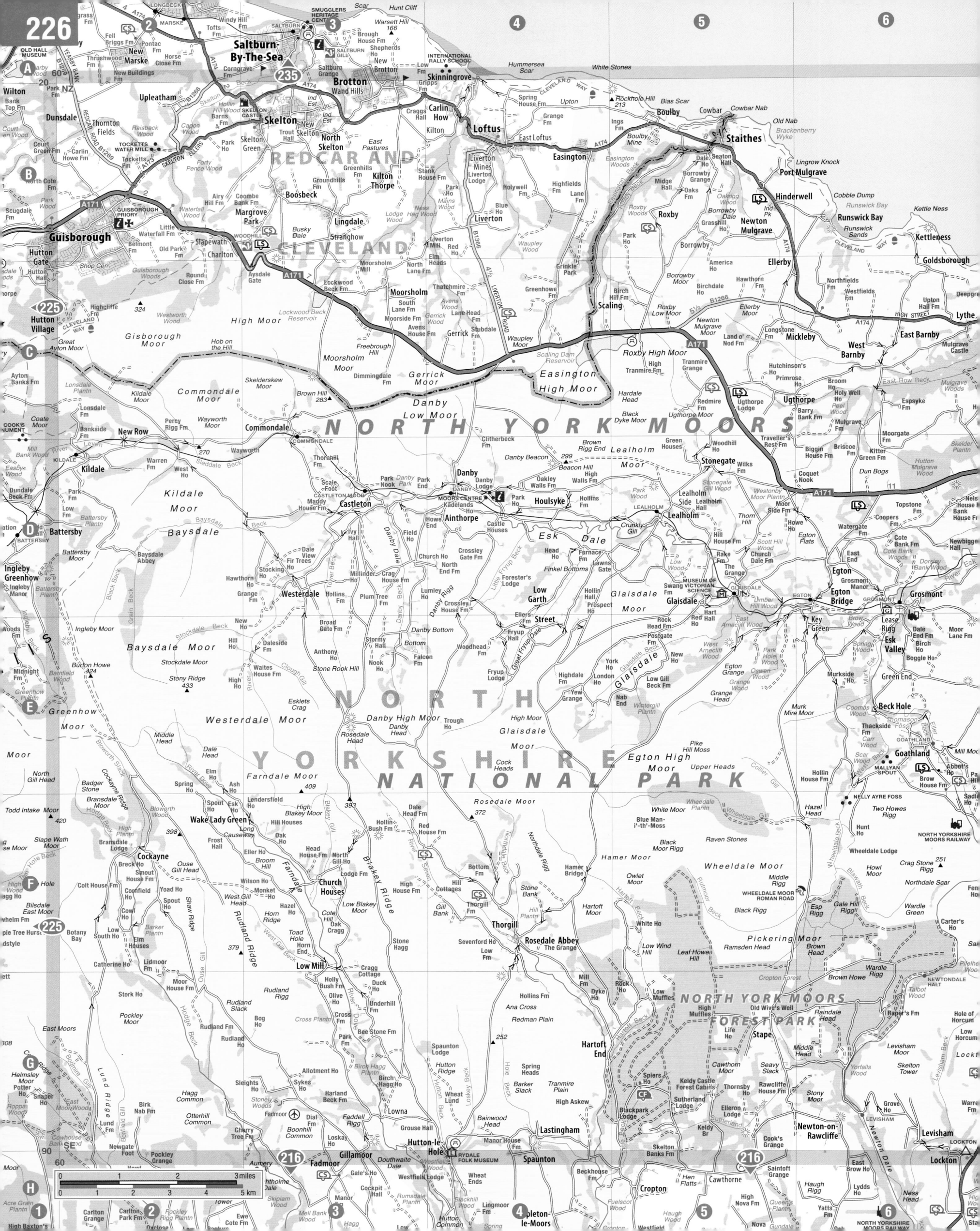

East STEWARTRY COAST

Drungans

Auchencairn

Auchencairn Bay

Moyl

White Port
Almorness Pt

Hestan Island

Cairn Hill

Auchencairn Ho

Airds Cott

Balcary Bay

NX

Balcary Pt

Airds

Airds Pt

Nether Hazelfield

Rascarrel

Rascarrel Bay

Castle Muir Pt

Barlocco Bay

237

237

Bank End

SENHOUSE ROMAN MUSEUM

LAKE DISTRICT COAST AQUARIUM

MARITIME MUS.

Maryport

THE WAVE CENTRE

Maryport Ind Est

Netherton

Ewanrigg

Ellenb

Risehow Fm

Risehow

Fothergill

Woodside

Ind Est

FLIMBY

Flimby

Standings

St Helens

Camerton Grange

MAIN ROAD

A596

Siddick

Seaton

Stud Fm

Camerton

Camerton Hall

Ribton Hall

Bus Pk

North Side
Hawk Hill

Salmon Hall

Barepot

Stainburn Hall Fm

Clifton Hall

Great Clifton

WORKINGTON

WORKINGTON HALL

Stainburn

Workington

HELENA THOMPSON MILL MUSEUM

Schoose

A66

Close End

2½

Quarry Hill

Moorclose

Mossbay

A596

East Town End Fm

A595

Westfield

2½

Winscales

Lucy Close Fm

Moss Bay

Salterbeck

Wythemoor Ho

Lostrigg Beck

Harrington

Gale Ho

HARRINGTON

High Harrington

Grayson Green

Lillyhall Industrial Estate

West Ghyll End Fm

Distington Works

Kelmore Hill Fm

Branthwaite Row Fm

Wythemoor Head

Harrington Parks

Park Ho

Cunning Pt

Barngill Fm

Distington

Common End

Gilgarran

High House Fm

Pica

Lowca

Moresby

B5306

Boon Wood

Wilson Park

Keekle Head Fm

Moorside Parks

Providence Bay

40

247

High Park

Dub Hall

Tutehill Fm

Parton Bay

PARTON

Low Moresby

Moresby Moss

River Keekle

Dub Beck

NX

A595

Tivoli

Tanyard Bay

Bleng Gre ality

219

Moresby Corner

Moresby Parks

Sandsciose

Arlecdon Fm

Redness Pt

Parton

Bransty

Acreway

WHITEHAVEN

Scilly Bank

Harras

WALK MILL

Bleak

THE BEACON

5

THE RUM

0   1   2   3miles

0   1   2   3   4   5 km

7   8   9   10   11

A
80
50
NZ

B

C

D

E

N O R T H   S E A

TEES BAY

F

Bran
Sands

Coatham Sands

West Scar   Salt Scar

Grangetown
Works

COATHAM
MARSH

Coatham

Redcar
Rocks   The Flashes

REDCAR CENTRAL

Warrenby

Redcar
Mill Howle

BRITISH STEEL
REDCAR

TRUNK ROAD

Westfield

REDCAR
RACECOURSE

REDCAR EAST

COAST ROAD

Scanbeck Howle

Dormanstown

REDCAR

REDCAR LANE

B1269

**Marske-by-
the-Sea**

Stone Gap

A1042

CS   3 A1085

Saltburn
Scar   Hunt Cliff

G

Kirkleatham

Grewgrass
Fm

A174

LONGBECK

MARSKE

Windy Hill
Fm

Tofts
Fm

SMUGGLERS
HERITAGE
CENTRE

Warsett Hill
166

Wilton
Chemical Works

Fell
Briggs Fm

Pontac
Fm

SALTBURN

SALTBURN
GILL

Brough
House Fm

Shepherds
Ho

OLD HALL
MUSEUM

Yearby

Horse
Close Fm

**Saltburn-
By-The-Sea**

SALTBURN
GRANGE

New
Brotton

INTERNATIONAL
RALLY SCHOOL

**New
Marske**

CS

Thrushwood

Corngrave
Fm

Low
Fm

Hummersea
Scar

White Stones

Lazenby

Yearby
Bank

B1269

New Buildings
Fm

Brotton
Wand Hills

Skinningrove

Gripps

NZ
20
80

Getown

A1053

Wilton

Lackenby

Wilton
Castle

Wilton
Bank

Park
Fm

225

Upleatham

A174

B1268

Ind
Est

**Carlin
How**

Spring
House Fm

WAY

226

Upton

Rockhole Hill
213

Bias Scar

H

Dunsdale

Thornton
Fields

Raisbeck
Wood

Capon
Wood

SKELTON
CASTLE

Hollin
Hill Wood

Skelton
Wood

Skelton

Ind
Est

Craggs
Hall

Kilton

Grange
Fm

Loftus

Ings
Fm

Boulby
Mine

Boulby

Cowbar   Cowbar Nab

Old Nab

242

7

Wilton Moor
Plantns

Court
Green Wood

TOCKETTS
WATER MILL

8

Court
Fm

Carlin
Howe Fm

Skelton
Green

Park
Ho

New
Skelton

Trout
Hall

9

North
Skelton

East
Pastures

REDCAR AND

Liverton

East Loftus   10

Easington

11   **Staithes**

Brackenberry
Wyke

A701

NY 00

Lockerbie
Rosebank
B7068
Bankshill
Northburn
Grange Hill

Ladyward
Millhill
Scroggs
The Linns
Birrens Hill
Grange Fell

Priesthead
Long Plantn
Castle Loch
Mounthoolie
Tundergarth Mains
Powhaffet
Risp Hill

Shaw's Hill
Moss
Blackrig
Parkfoot
Kirk Loch
LOCHMABEN CASTLE Castle Mains
A709
South Tummuln Plantn
Blackford
Westwood
Minantee
Coursiein
Torbeckhill Res
Crossbank

248

Whitelaird
Rye Muir
Heck
Hightae Mill Loch
A74(M)
18
Well Springs Plantn
Burnswark
Howat's Hill
248

Hempland Hill
Branetrigg
Beacon Hill
Parkend
Greenhill
Pilmuir Common
Hallmuir
Blackcross Plantn
BURNSWARK HILL FORT
Burnswark
Gilmartin

Tinwald Parks
Tinwald
The Broom
Corsegreen
Millriggs
Skairfield
Greenhth
B723
Gummenbie
Stockbridge
Darlawhill
Grainhall
Craighouse

Glenclair Hill
Woodlands
West Roucan
Hightae
Muirfield
Castlemilk
Cowdens
Haregills
Douglashall
Relief
Whitenill
Stoneybeck
Dockenflat

Downs Bank
Torthorwald
A709
Muirsburn
Mossburn
Kettleholm
Glenholm
Axletreewell
Paulsland
Orchard
Langdyke
Middlebie
Ashyards Gate

AVIATION MUS
Ind Est Lochar Moss
Rammerscales
Smallholm
Woodlands
Middleshaw
Hunter's Gate
Nether Collinhirst
Ecclefechan
THOMAS CARLYLE'S BIRTHPLACE
Burnfoot Mill
BIRRENS FORT
Johnstone Hall
The Braes
B722
Eaglesfield

The Grove
B
Greystone
Gasstown
A75
Barton's House
Hazelshaw Hill
Holmains Moor
Range Castle 217
Almagill
Kirkwood
Dormont
Kirkwood Mains
Sorrysike Moor
HODDOM
Buckie Cott
Hoddom Mill
19
Donkins
Allerbeck
Burnhead

ANNAN ROAD
Georgetown
A780
Isle of Man
Collin
Greenlea
Woodside
Elizafield
Racks
Druminuir
Mid Dargavel
Nether Dargavel
Rockhall Mains
Mouswald Banks
Newton
Dalton
Dalton Green
Waterside
Hoddom Mains
20
Whins
Quarry Park
Breconbeds
Kirtlebridge
Langs
Robgill Tower

237
Cairn of Craigs
Craigs Moss
Brocklehirst
Cleughbrae
B724
Mouswald Grange
Townhead Fm
Hallidayhill
Meikle Dyke
Isle of Dalton
Phyllis Park
Oakbank
Hoddom
Mains
Woodcock Air
Greycraig
Brydekirk Mains
Dumbretton
East Bretton
Robgill Mains

C
Kelton Ho
Keltonbank
Kelton
Barnkin of Craigs
Bush of Craigs
Ironhirst
West Raffles
East Raffles
Carrutherstown
Denbie Mains
Stenries
Nether Stenries
Brydekirk
Windyknowe
Johnstonlee
Creca
Creca Hall

B725
Boreland
Kirkblane
Ballieknowe
Mabie Forest
Ironhirst Moss
Horseholm
Holmhead Moss
Straggleringwath Plantn
Langdyke
Fostermeadowfoot
Gillbrae
Upper Mains
B720
Nether Stenries
Wintersheugh Plantn
Millside Plantn
Park
Power Sta
Allalea

Horseholm
Black Grain
Longbridge Muir
Longbridgemuir
Comlongon Mains
Long Plantn Mains Cotts
Plans
Denbieyett
Clarencefield
Newfield Plantn
Cocklicks
Wintersheugh
Outerford
Charlesfield
Limekilns
Mount Annan
Creca Hall

D
Glencaple
Highmains Hill
Highmains Fm
Bankend
Bankend Hill
Byres Fm
Comlongon Wood
RUTHWELL CROSS
Newfield
Holly Bush Wood
Beetylands Park
Burnside
Spittalriddinghill
Preston Hall
Stapleton Grange
B6357
Tulliesfield
Woodhall

Willo Dockridding Wood
Cockpool Plantn
Brow Well
B725
Ruthwell
DUNCAN SAVINGS BANK MUSEUM
Mackwhinny Park
Hitchill
Greenhill Plantn
Justenlees
Newbie Mill
A75
Topping Hall
Hardrigg Lodge
Woodhall

Airds Pt
Scar Pt
Shearington
Mains
Southfield
Lochar Water
Priestside
Priestside Flow
Cummertrees
Powfoot
Croftheads Cotts
Annan
Welldale
Watchill
Dornock
Low

Airds
Bowhouse
Blackshaw
Eastpark
SALTCOT HILLS
WILDFOWL & WETLAND CENTRE
Nethertown
Newbie
Shawhill
East

CAERLAVEROCK CASTLE
Merse
NITH ESTUARY
Newbie Mains
Barnkirk Pt

Overton
Burnfoot
Blackshaw Bank

E
Dru Bay
Bowness-on-Solway
Herd Hill
Biglands Ho
Bowness Hall
VALLUM (COURSE OF)
Port Ca

Carse Bay
RSPB CAMPFIELD MARSH
BOWNESS ON SOLWAY
Glasson Moss
Gla

SOLWAY FIRTH
Cardurnock Flats
Bowness Common
Low Flow

Carsethorn
Hogus Pt
Borron Pt
Cardurnock
Herd Hill
Anthorn
Longcroft
Whitrigg

F
ARBIGLAND GARDENS
JOHN PAUL JONES COTTAGE MUSEUM
Channel of River Wampool
Angerton
Whitriggle

237
Grune Pt
Skinburness
Skinburness Marsh
Starry Hill
Newton Arlosh
Newton Marsh
Kirkbride
Powhill

Skinburness
Border
Longlands Head
Shaw Ho

Calvo
Salt Coates
Watch Hill
Kirkbride

Silloth
Ind Est
Meadow Lodge
Seaville
Moss Side
SOUTH SOLWAY MOSSES
Lawrencehalme
Low Eskrigg
Grassing

Greenrow
Causewayhead
Orchard Ho
Blackdyke
Raby Grange
Raby
High Ho
Corbet Houses

G
Blitterlees
B5300
Parkhead
Flagstaff
Sleightholme
Wedholme
Wedholme Hill
Midd

Heather Bank
Wolsty Hall
Dryholme
Kingside Hill
Abbey Town
Kelsick
River Waver
Oulton
Oul

NY 50

228
Beckfoot
Newtown
Peluthe Grange
Wolsty
Highlaws
Lowsay Fm
Aldoth
The Hill
Weary Fm
East Hill
THORNHILL MOSS & MEADOW
Kelsickhouse Hall
Dundraw
Moor Row
Lessonhall
229

H
0 1 2 3 miles
0 1 2 3 4 5 km

1   2   3   4   5   6

F I R T H

O F

C L Y D E

Culzean Bay

CULZEAN CASTLE
CULZEAN
Glasson Rock
Barwhin Pt
Maidenhead Bay
Morriston
Birniehill
Thomas
Balvaird

Port Murray
Castle Port
Maidens
Turnberry Pt
Turnberry
Minnybae
Broadshear

Kirkoswald
SOUTE
COTTA

Turnberry Bay
Brest Rocks
Turnberry

Milton Burn
High Park
Hallowshean

Balkenna Isle
Littleton Fm
Macawston Fm
Chapelton Burn
Chapelton

Townhead
High McGownston
Braehead
Drummuck

Dowhill
Blair

Wright's Island
Ladybank
High Craighead
Bargany Mains
Kilg

Dipple
Burnside Fm
Barneil
Barnweil
Burnhead

A77
Chaperdonan
Ladywell
Macrindlestone
Robstone
BARGAN
GARDEN

Ind Est.
Camregan
B734
Old Dailly

Girvan Mains
Girvan
Camregan Hill
Penkill

Girvan
Houdston
Saugh Hill
Tralorg Hill
Penwhapple Burn

Glendoune
Doune Hill
Troweir Hill
High Tralorg

Horse Rock
Dow Hill
High Troweir

Woodland Bay
A714
Byne Hill
Laggan Hill
Tormitchell

Ardmillan Castle
Dalfask Hill

Ardwell
Pinminnoch
Pinmacher
Benan Hill
Kirkland Hill

Kilranny
Fell Hill
Cairn Hill
Pinmacher
Daldowie Hill
Kirkland

Kennedy's Pass
297
Grey Hill
Bynehill
Knocklaugh Lodge
Laigh Letterpin
Merkland

Pinbain Hill
Knocklaugh
Pinmore

Pinbain Burn
Currarie
Lendal Lodge
Fell Hill
Aldons Hill
Pinmore Mains

10½
Straid
Cundry Mains
B734

Carleton Bay
CARLETON CASTLE
Bargain Hill

Lendalfoot
Whilk Isle
Holmhead

Balsalloch Hill
Knockdaw Hill
Breaker Hill
Glake

Games Loup
Craig Hill
Glessal Hill
Dochernel Burn

Balcreuchan Port
Troax
Lochton Hill
Craig Fm
Poundland
Pinwherry
Bellamore

Port Vad
Little Bennane
South Ballaird
Balhamie Hill
Clauchanton Hill
Craig Ho.
Spenceston
Garleffin Fm

Bennane Head
Littleton Hill
Kirkhill Ho
Alticane
Liglartrie

Bennane Lea
Bougang Fm
Belhamie Hill
Colmonell
Dalreoch Hill
Pinwherry Hill
Sixpence
Barbae Hill
Craigcannochie Hill

A77
Knockdolian
Milwharran Hill
Glenduisk
Ballochmorrie

B734
265
Polcardoch
Craigneil Hill
Ford Hill
Reuchal
Drumskeoch
Craigbrae
Ballochmorrie Fm

Corseclays Fm
Cairn Hill
Knockdhu
Farden Hill
Bents
Glenwhask

Balig Fm
Laggan Ho.
Heronsford
Craig Wood
Kildonan

Park End
11½
Shiel Hill
Scaurhead White Cairn
Barrhill

Ballantrae
MAINS ROAD
Cosses
Balkissock
Little Fell
Donald Hill
Eldridge Hill
Loch Hill
Cairnlea

Garleffin
Crailloch Burn
Water of Tig

Sgavoch Rock
17
Balkissock Hill
Millmore
Water of Tig
Eyes

Downan Pt
Glenapp Castle
Smyrton
Strawarren Fell

Downan
Auchencrosh
Smyrton Hill
Beneraird 439
Kilmoray
Wee Fell
Knockshin

Currarie Fm
Auchencrosh Hill
Lear
Benaw

Ailsa Craig area:
Swine Cave
338
Foreland Pt
Stranny Pt
AILSA CRAIG
Ailsa Craig
RSPB

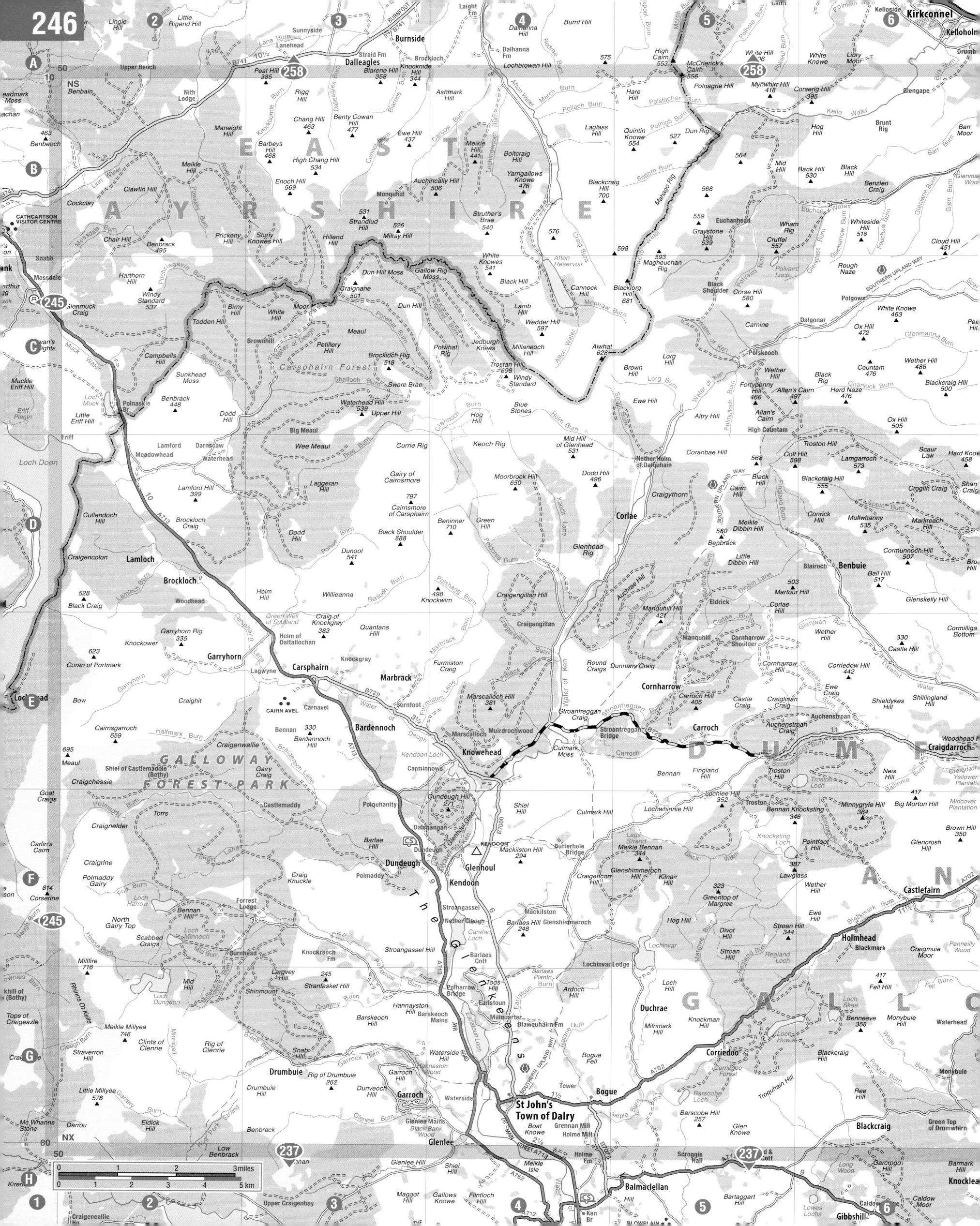

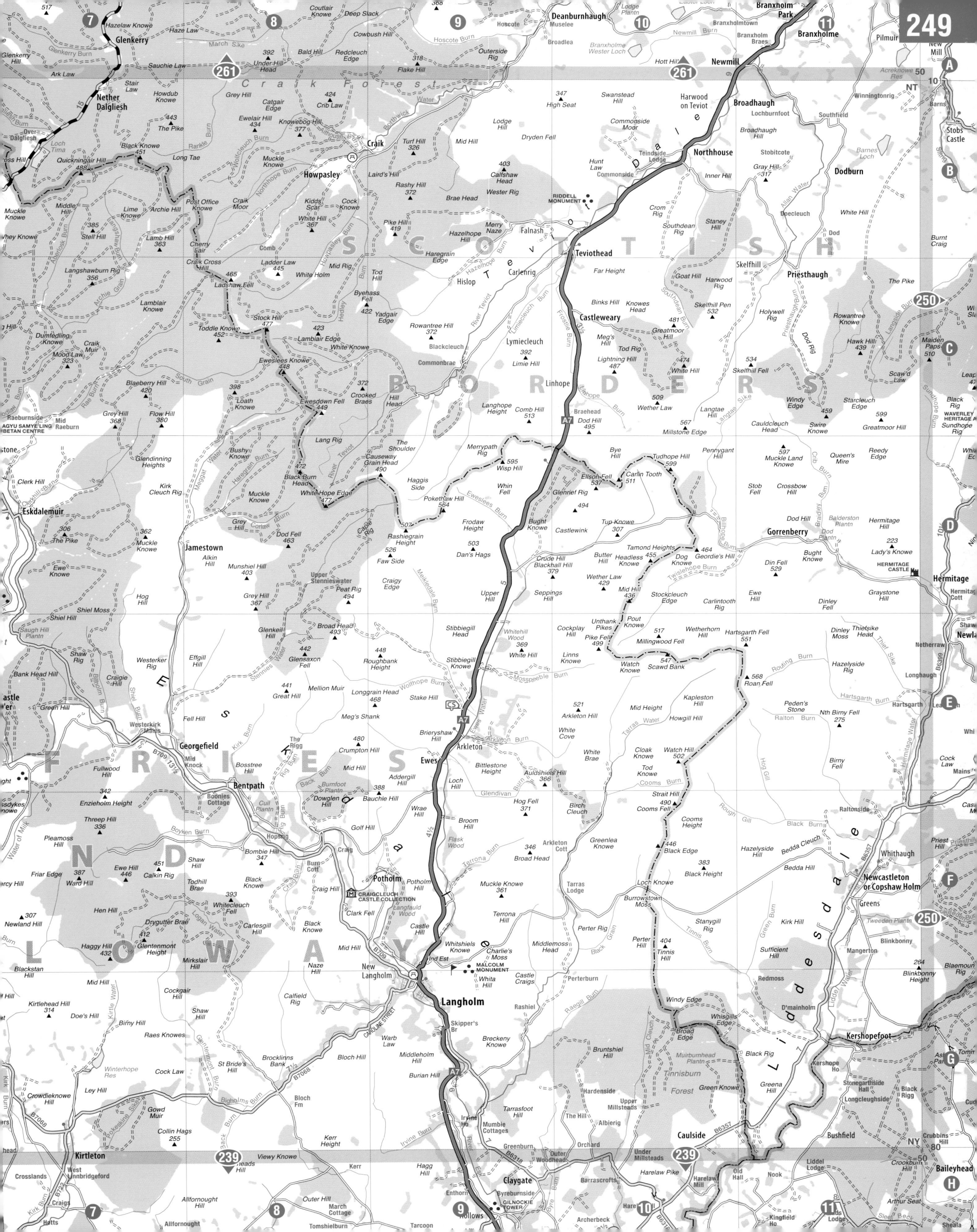

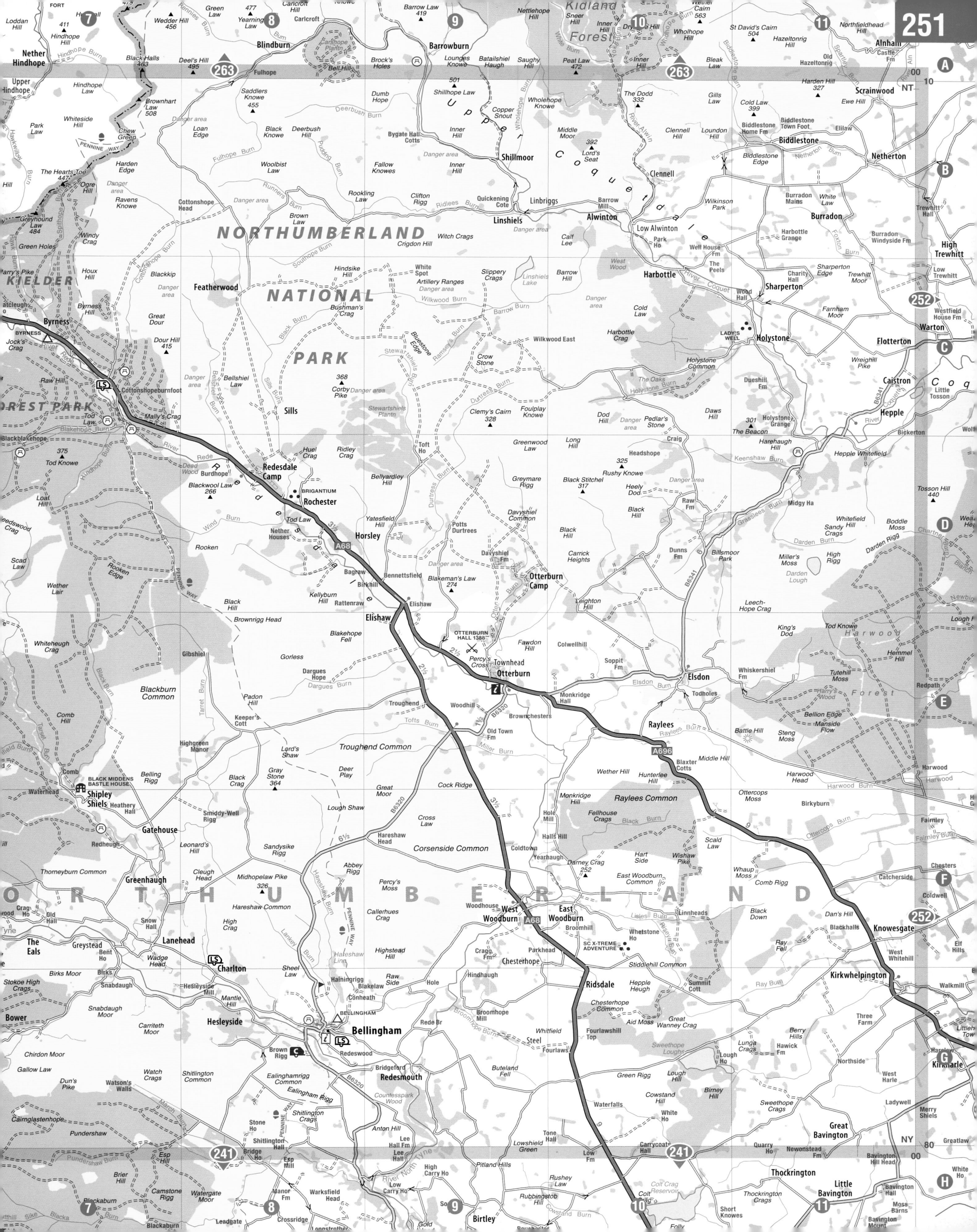

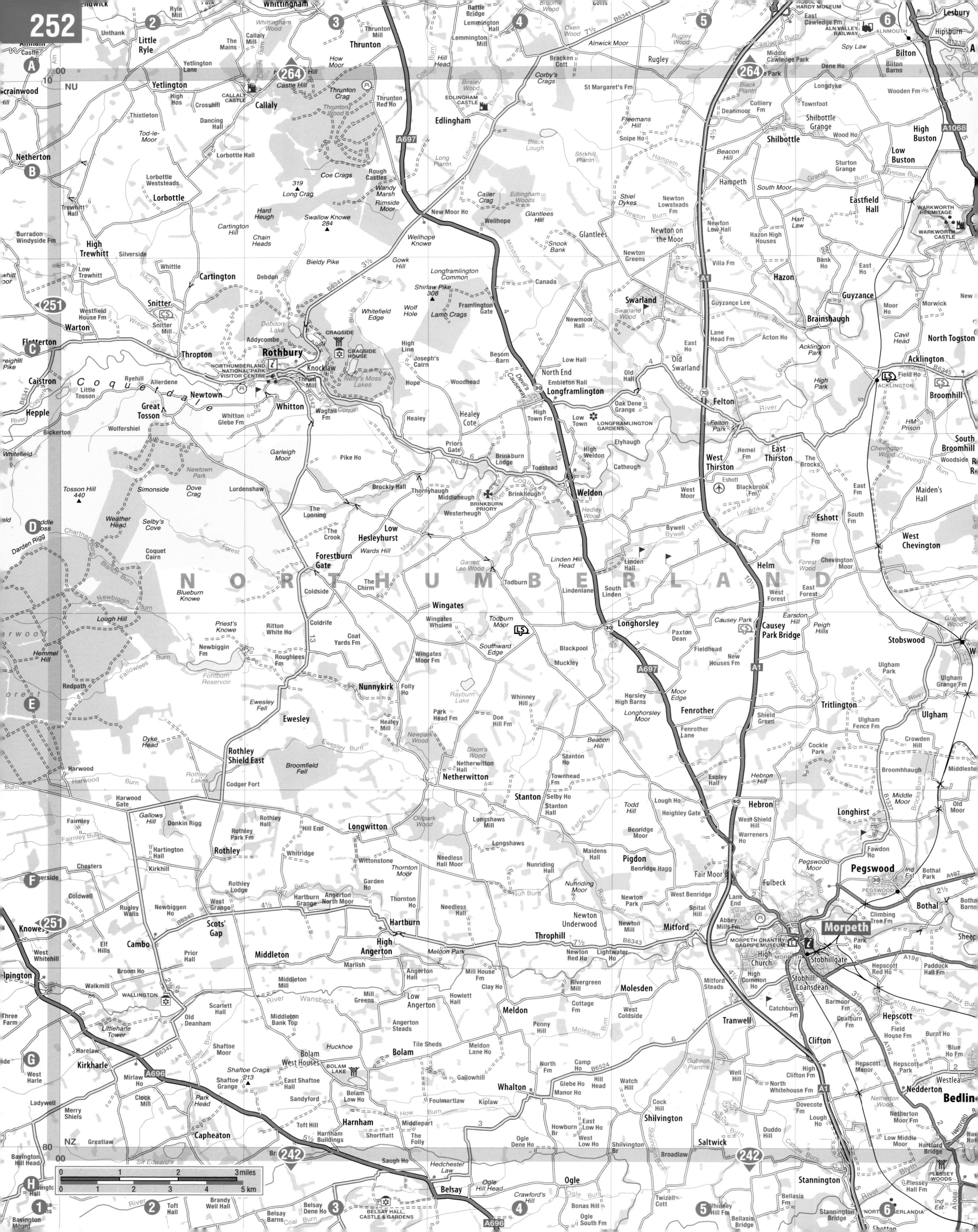

NORTH

SEA

Marden Rocks

mouth
Alnmouth
Bay

Birling

Warkworth

Gloster
Hill
Amble

Moorhouse
Fm
High Hauxley

Togston
Hall
Radcliffe
Low Hauxley
HAUXLEY

Togston
Barns
Togston
East Fm

gston

Danger
area
Ladyburn
Lake

Hadston
DRURIDGE
BAY

Druridge
Bay

Whitefield
Ho

Chibburn
Fm

High Chibburn

Widdrington

Hemscott Hill

INGTON

drington
ation

Highthorn
Cresswell

Warkworthlane
Cott

North
ton Fm
Hagg
House

Ellington

Cresswell
Home Fm

Linton
Lynemouth

Potland
Fm
East
Moor Fm

LINTON LANE

Potland Burn

Works

QUEEN
ELIZABETH II
Woodhorn

WOODHORN
COLLIERY MUS
WOODHORN
CHURCH MUS

Bus Cen

Woodbridge

Ashington
Newbiggin-by-the-Sea

Hirst
North
Seaton
Newbiggin Bay

WANSBECK

River
North Seaton
Colliery

Stakeford
Wansbeck

West
Sleekburn

STAKEFORD LANE

Guide Post

Scotland
Gate
Bomarsund
Bus Cen
Cambois

Choppington
East
Sleekburn

Bedlington
Station

Mount
Pleasant Fm
North Blyth

ton
STEAD

Bebside
Cowpen
Blyth

Isabella
Pit

East
Hartford
New Delaval
Low
Horton Fm
Newsh
South
Beach

Humford
Mill

LAVEROCK HALL ROAD
South
Newsham
Gloucester
Lodge Fm

Shankhouse
Lysdon
Fm

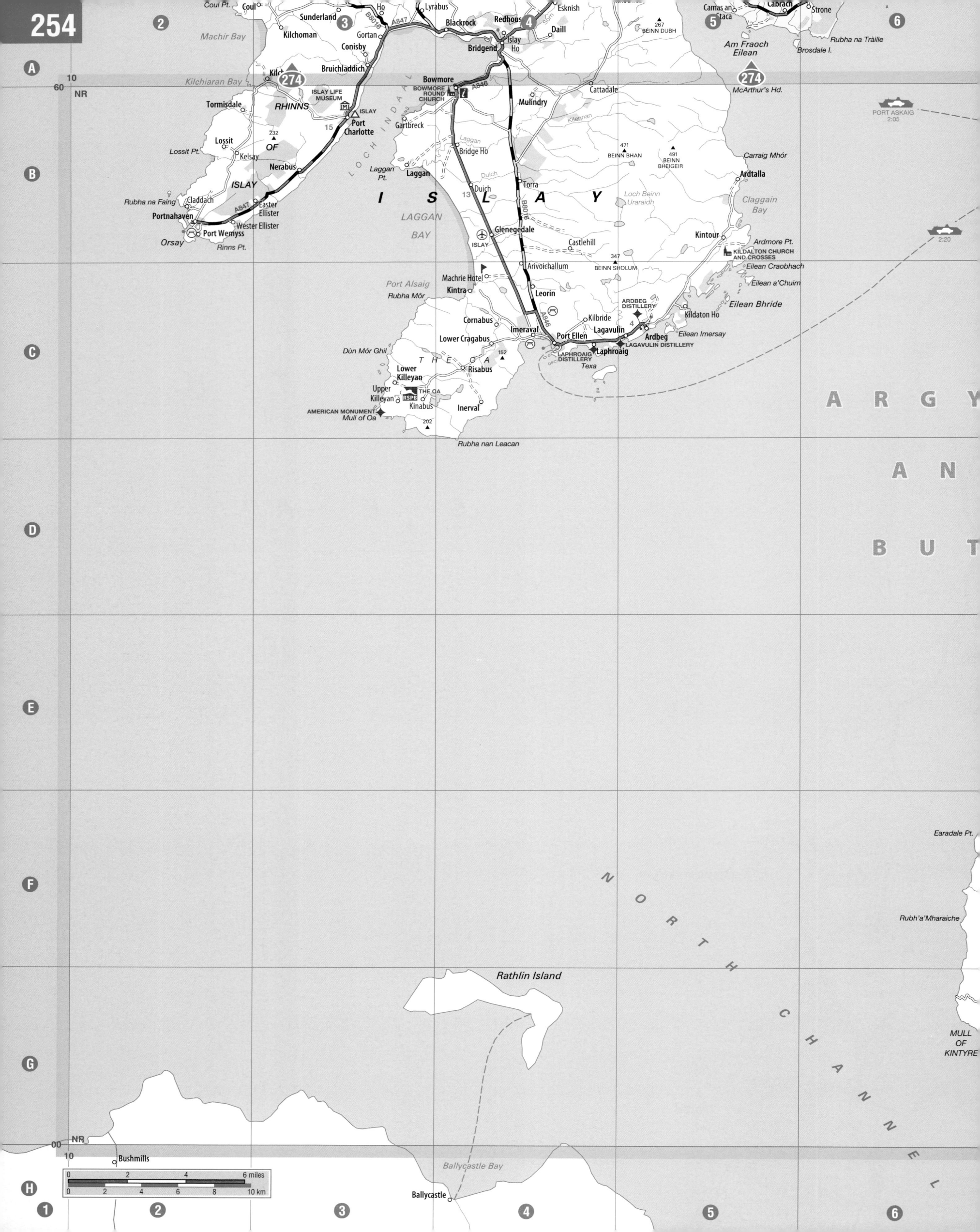

Coul Pt.
Coul
Sunderland
Ho
Lyrabus
Esknish
Labrach
Strone
Kilchoman
B808
A847
Blackrock
Redhouse
Camas an
Staca
Gortan
Conisby
Bridgend
Islay
Ho
Daill
BEINN DUBH
267
Rubha na Tràille
Brosdale I.
Machir Bay
Kilchiaran Bay
Kilcl
274
Bruichladdich
Bowmore
BOWMORE ROUND CHURCH
A846
Am Fraoch
Eilean
274
McArthur's Hd.
60
10
NR
Tormisdale
RHINNS
ISLAY LIFE MUSEUM
Mulindry
Cattadale
PORT ASKAIG
2:05
Lossit
Port Charlotte
ISLAY
Gartbreck
BEINN BHAN
471
BEINN BHEIGEIR
491
Carraig Mhór
Lossit Pt.
Kelsay
OF
Bridge Ho
Laggan
Loch Beinn
Uraraidh
Ardtalla
Nerabus
Laggan Pt.
Laggan
Duich
Torra
B8016
Claggain
Bay
Rubha na Faing
Claddach
ISLAY
I S L A Y
Duich
2:20
Portnahaven
Easter Ellister
Wester Ellister
LAGGAN
BAY
Glenegedale
ISLAY
Kintour
Ardmore Pt.
KILDALTON CHURCH AND CROSSES
Port Wemyss
Castlehill
Orsay
Rinns Pt.
Arivoichallum
BEINN SHOLUM
347
Eilean Craobhach
Port Alsaig
Machrie Hotel
Leorin
Eilean a'Chuirn
Rubha Mòr
Kintra
ARDBEG DISTILLERY
Eilean Bhride
Cornabus
Kilbride
Kildaton Ho
A R G Y
Lower Cragabus
Imeraval
Port Ellen
Lagavulin
Ardbeg
Eilean Imersay
Dùn Mòr Ghil
T H E   O A
152
LAPHROAIG DISTILLERY
Laphroaig
LAGAVULIN DISTILLERY
Risabus
Lower Killeyan
Texa
A N
Upper Killeyan
RSPB
THE OA
Kinabus
Inerval
AMERICAN MONUMENT
Mull of Oa
202
B U T
Rubha nan Leacan

Earadale Pt.

N O R T H

Rubh'a'Mharaiche

Rathlin Island

C H A N

MULL OF KINTYRE

60
10
NR
Bushmills
E L

0   2   4   6 miles
0 2 4 6 8 10 km
Ballycastle Bay
Ballycastle

A B C D E F G H
1 2 3 4 5 6

Kilberry
SCULPTURED STONES
Torinturk
Carse Ho.
Dunmore
Kennacraig
Redhouse
CNOC A'BHAILESHIOS
Ardroscadale
Rothesay
Straad
Woodend Ho.
Tiennan
Ardlamont Pt.
ISLAND
Loch Storn
Ardpatrick
Kilchamaig
Whitehouse
Northpark
Kerrylamont
Scoulag
NS
Ardpatrick Ho.
Rubha Leathan
Midpark
MOUNT STUART HOUSE AND GARDEN
Portachoillan
Gartnagrenach
Scalpsie
OF
Ardpatrick Pt.
Eilean Tràighe
Glenreasdell Mains
Skipness
SKIPNESS CASTLE
Ardscalpsie Pt.
Scalpsie Bay
BUTE
Piperhall
Kingarth
Ronachan Pt.
Clachan
Claonaig
Skipness Pt.
Skipness Bay
Kilchattan Bay
Ronachan Ho.
CRUACH NAM FIADH
Claonaig Bay
SOUND OF BUTE
St Blane's Chapel
Eilean Garbh
Loch Ciaran
Balochroy
Crossaig Glen
Crossaig
Cock of Arran
West Tarbert Bay
CRUACH MHIC GOUGAN
Loch Garasdale
Tarbert
East Tarbert Bay
Gigha Island
Ardailly
Rhunahaorine
Gortinanane
Cour Bay
Cour
Garroch Hd.
Ardminish
ACHAMORE GARDENS
Ardminish Bay
Ardlamey
BEINN BHREAC
LOCHRANZA CASTLE
Lochranza
Catacol Bay
Catacol
LOCHRANZA
ISLE OF ARRAN DISTILLERY
Millstone Pt.
Gigalum I.
Tayinloan
CNOC NAN CRAOBH
Braids
Auchenbreck
Grogport
Fairhaven
NORTH
MEALL NAN DAMH
Cara Island
Killean
CRUACH MHIC-AN T-SAOIR
Thundergay
Pirnmill
Loch Tanna
Sannox
Sannox Bay
Beacharr
Achaglass
CRUACH NAN GABHAR
Brackley
ARRAN
CIR MHOR
GOAT FELL
Corrie
Muasdale
Rhonadale
Carradale
Whitefarland
BEINN BHARRAIN
BEINN TARSUINN
ISLE
Port Righ
Amod
Bridgend
Waterfoot
Imachar
Glen Iorsa
Glenrosa
Merkland
Glenacardoch Pt.
BEINN BHREAC
Torrisdale-Square
Balliekine
BRODICK
Belloch
Torrisdale Castle
Carradale Pt.
Dougarie
BRODICK CASTLE
Glenbarr
CLAN MACALISTER CENTRE
Killegruer
BEINN AN TUIRC
Carradale Bay
Machrie Bay
Auchencar
OF
Machrie Water
ARRAN AROMATICS
Cleongart
Saddell Glen
Auchagallon
Glenloig
ISLE OF ARRAN HERITAGE MUSEUM
Brodick
Brodick Bay
Bellochantuy Bay
Saddell
SADDELL ABBEY
Saddell Ho.
Machrie
A'CHRUACH
Glen Cloy
Strathwhillan
North Corriegills
Bellochantuy
A'CHRUACH
Saddell Bay
ARRAN
Tormore
MACHRIE MOOR STANDING STONES
South Corriegills
Killocraw
Corrylach
Lussa Loch
KING'S CAVE
BALMICHAEL VISITOR CENTRE
Balmichael
Clauchlands Pt.
Ugadale
Blairbeg
Margnaheglish
Westport
Tangy Loch
SGREADAN HILL
Torbeg
Shiskine
Lamlash
Lamlash Bay
Tangy
Skeroblingarry
Birchburn
North Feorline
Cordon
Holy Island
Kilchenzie
Glenlussa Ho.
Kilkeddan
Black Bay
Drumadoon Pt.
Blackwaterfoot
Kilpatrick
KILPATRICK DUN
Kingscross Pt.
Peninver
Ardnacross Bay
Drumadoon Bay
Corriecravie Moor
Glenree
TIGHVEIN
Auchencairn
Kingscross
West Darlochan
Kilmichael
Corriecravie
Knockenkelly
North Kiscadale
Whiting Bay
CAMPBELTOWN
CAMPBELTOWN HERITAGE CENTRE
Low Smerby
Brown Hd.
CARN BAN
Clachaig
Auchareoch
GLENASHDALE FALLS
South Kiscadale
Largymore
Machrihanish Bay
Machrihanish
Trodigal
Drumore
Sliddery
Lagg
Levencorroch
Largybeg
Largymeanoch
Dippin
Ballygroggan
LS
Drumlemble
Stewarton
CAMPBELTOWN BUCKHOUSE
Moy
Kilkerran
Kildalloig
DAVAAR ISLAND CAVE PAINTING
Island Davaar
Shannochie
Kilmory
TORRYLINN CAIRN
Bennan
Bennan Hd.
Kildonan
Dippin Head
Whiting Bay
High Tirfergus
Knocknaha
BEINN GHUILEAN
Achinhoan Hd.
ARDROSSAN 2:40 (MAY-SEPT)
Pladda
Sound of Pladda
THE SLATE
Lochorodale
Woodbank
CNOC MOY
Largiebaan
Johnston's Pt.
Feochaig
CNOC ODHAR
Knockstapplemore
Keprigan
Polliwilline
Strone
North Carrine
Macharioch
Mill Park
Polliwilline Bay
Carskiey
Southend
Cove Pt.
Rubha Chlachan
Brunerican Bay
Port Mean
Sheep I.
Sanda Island
Ailsa Craig

FIRTH

OF

CLYDE

Isle
of
Arran

NORTH

AYRSHIRE

Brodick
BRODICK CASTLE
Cladach
Old Quay
ARRAN AROMATICS VISITOR CENTRE
ISLE OF ARRAN HERITAGE MUSEUM

Merkland
Merkland Wood
Merkland Pt
Wine Port

Maol Donn
368

Glenshant Hill
Creag Rosa
Glenrosa
Torr Breac
Glen Shurig
THE STRING

Strathwhillan
Corriegills Pt
North Corriegills
South Corriegills
Fairy Glen
Dun Dubh
Clauchland Hills
Clauchlands Fm
Clauchlands Pt
Kerr's Port
Hamilton Isle
Cnoc Dubh
Meall Buidhe
Margnaheglish
Clauchlands
Blairbeg
Lamlash
Benlister Glen
The Ross
311
Monamore Br
Cordon
Monamore Glen
Gortonallister
White Pt
Mullach Beag
Holy Island
314
Mullach Mòr
Pillar Rock Pt

The Knowe Fm
Cnoc Dubh
Urie Loch
Auchencairn
Kingscross Pt
Kingscross
Knockenkelly
Sandbraes
Glas Choirein
Borrach
North Kiscadale
Cnoc Donn
Cnoc an Fheidh
Cnoc Mòr
South Kiscadale
Whiting Bay
Auchareoch
GLENASHDALE FALLS
Largymore
Kilmory Water
Cnoc Craobhach
Cnoc na Garbad
Cnoc na Comhairle
Largymeanoch
Largybeg
Largybeg Pt
Port na Gaillin
Torr a' Mheannain
Margenaish Fm
Levencorroch Hill
Dippin Head
Dippin
Southbank
East Bennan
Levencorroch
Auchenhew
Drumla
Porta Leacach
West Bennan
STRUEY ROCKS
Port a'Ghillie Ghlais
Porta Buidhe
Port Dearg
Kildonan
Bennan Head

Sound of Pladda
Pladda

ARDROSSAN 0:55

BRODICK 0:55
CAMPBELTOWN
(May-Sept) 2:40
Saltcoats
South Bay
ARDROSSAN HARBOUR
NORTH AYRSHIRE MUSEUM
Outer Nebbock

Broad Craig
Dun

CULZEAN CASTLE
Culzean Bay
Glasson Rock
Barwhin Pt
Maidenhead Bay
Swan Pond
Thoma
Birnichill
Morriston
Balvaird
Port Mutray
A719

A841
B880

255
255
255
255
266
244
244

0   1   2   3miles
0 1 2 3 4 5 km

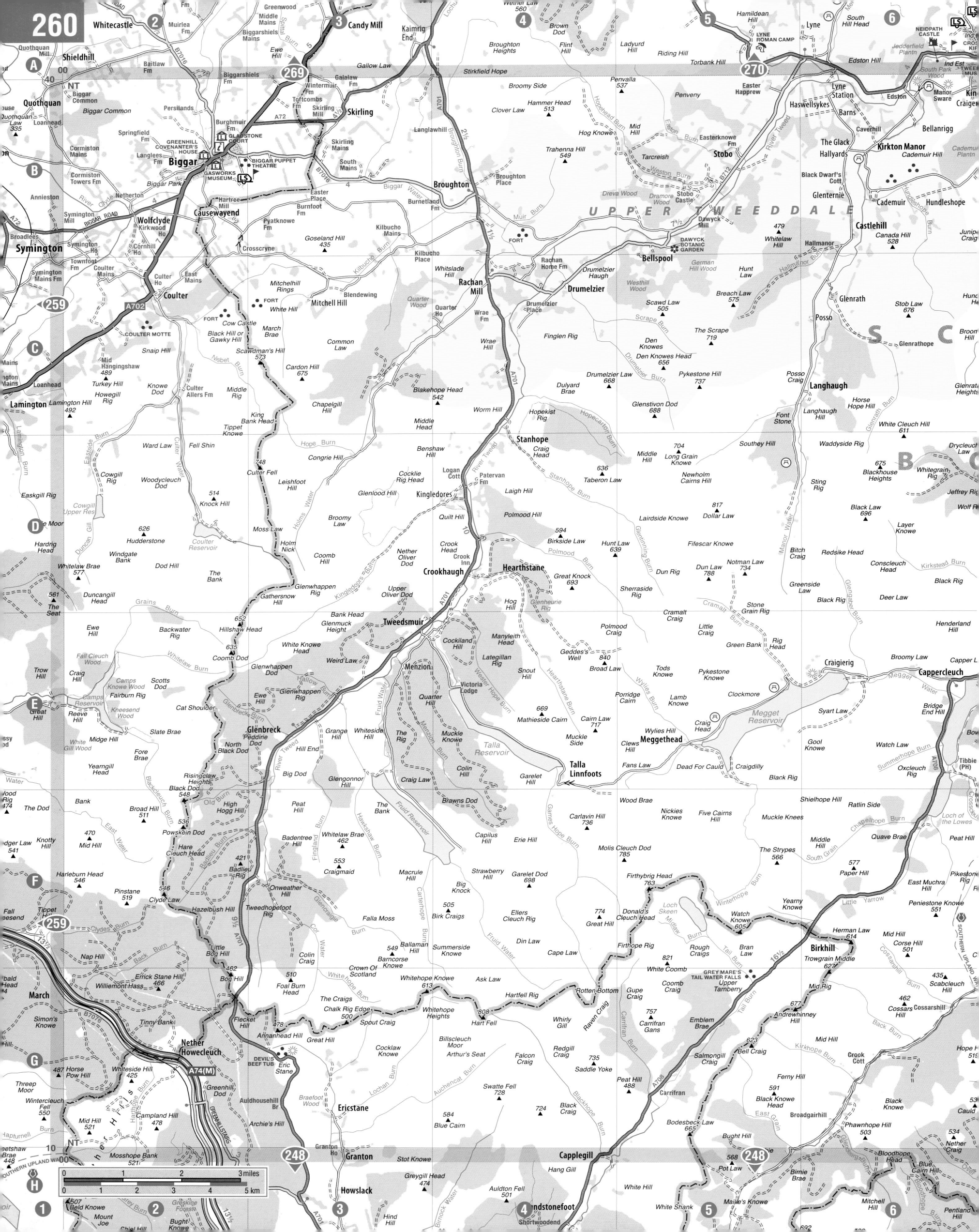

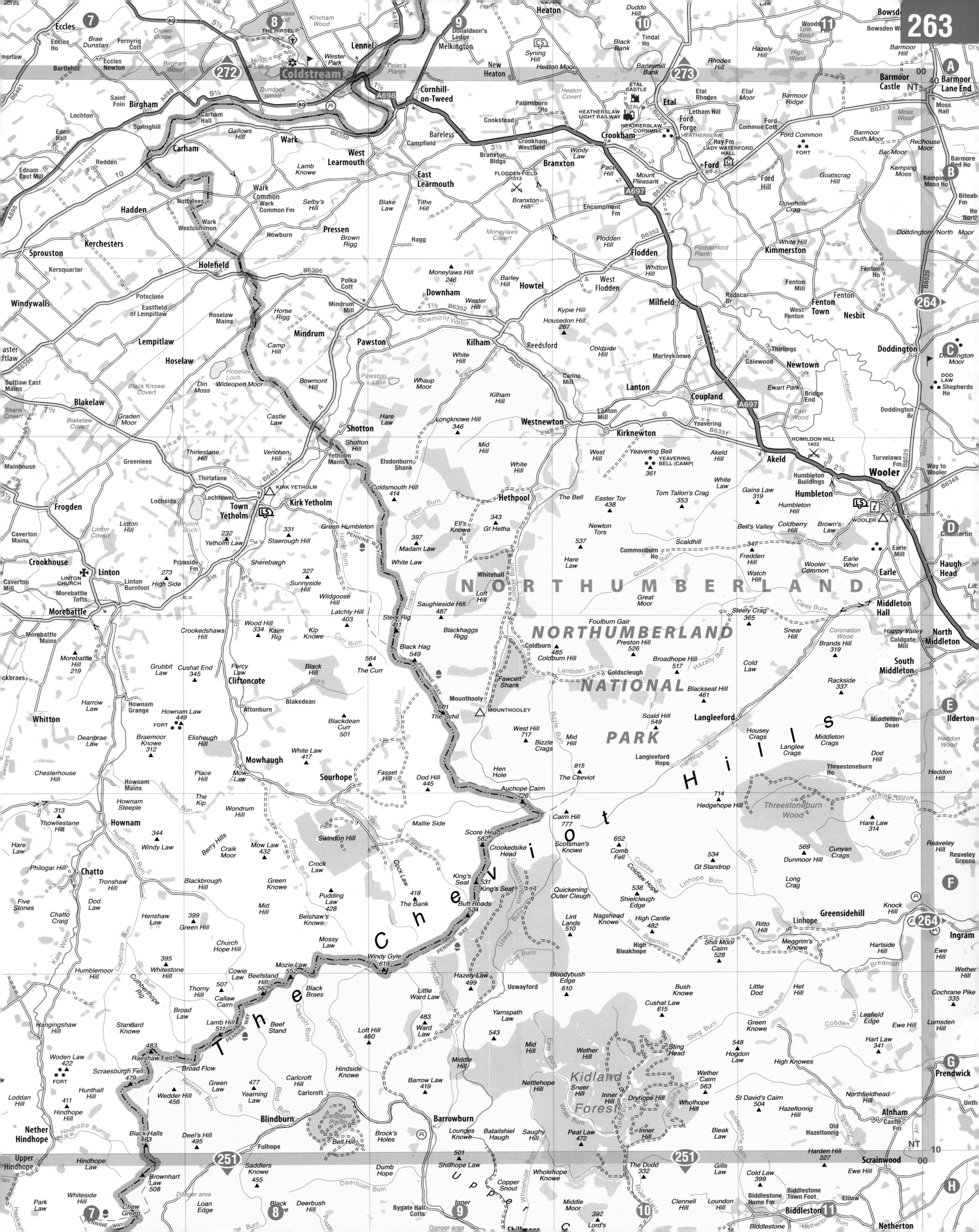

7   8   9   10   11

A
50
40
NU

B

C

D

N O R T H

S E A

E

Embleton
Bay

Castle Pt
BUNSTANBURGH
CASTLE
Queen
Margaret's Cove

Craster

Cullernose Pt

Howick

F

Rumbling Kern

Red
Stead

Howick
Haven

Sugar Sands

Low
Stead

Howdiemont Sands

ghoughton

Red Ends

Boulmer

Boulmer
Haven

Field
Ho

G

Seaton Pt

Marden Rocks

nmouth

Alnmouth
Bay

NU
10
50

253   253

H

7   8   9   10   11

ngstone
ar

wton Pt

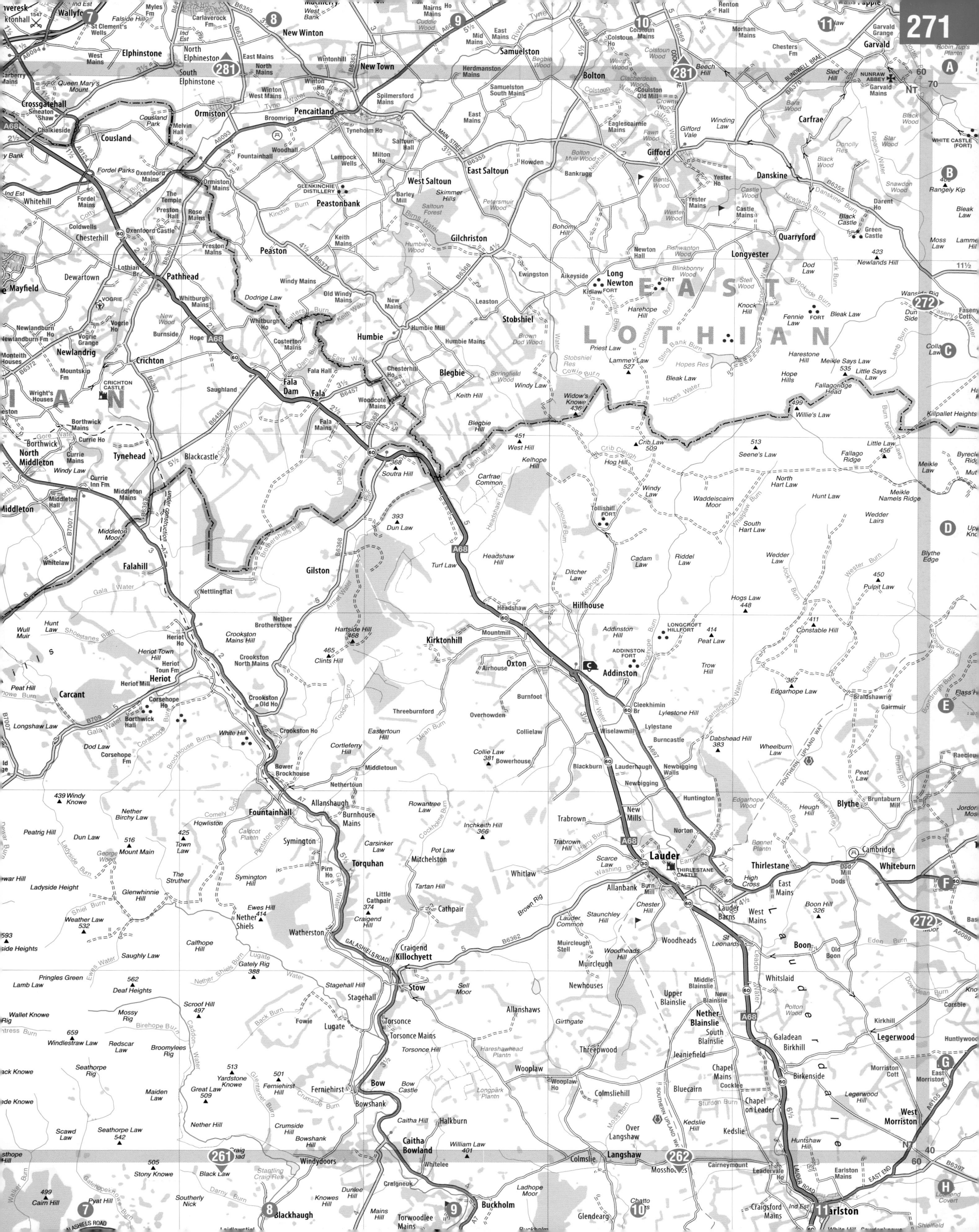

A

10
00
NT

B

C

D

E

F

G

Fast Castle
Head　Wheat Stack

Telegraph
Hill　FAST
CASTLE

Oatlee Hill
Dowlaw Burn

Lumsdaine

Coldingham
Common

Lumsdaine
Moor

⑦

Cross
Law

Moorside

273

St Abb's Head

ST ABB'S HEAD
Horsecastle Bay

Mire
Loch

Bell
Hill

Starney Bay

273

NT
70
10

H

A
B
C
D
E
F
G
H

7
8
9
10
11

Tressait
Trinafour
B847
Auchleeks Ho.
GLEN ERROCH
Tummel Forest
Water
Errochty
B847
Bridge of
Ericht
Craiganor
Lodge
Kinloch
Rannoch
Tummel
Bridge
B8019
TUMMEL
LOCH
Craiganor
Lodge
290
291
80
60
Killichonan
19
Dunalastair
Water
Dunalastair
Tullochroisk
Foss
B846
Rannoch Station
Rannoch
Lodge
Carie
Inverhadden
Crossmount
B846
515
SRON BHEAG
Finnart
Bridge
of Gaur
Camghouran
Rannoch
Black Wood of Rannoch
891
BEN A'CHUALLAICH
477
Bhac
477
80
60
Black Corries
Lodge
739
STOB NA CRUAICHE
Loch
Eigheach
Gaur
Dall
Burn
Allt na
Bogair
Allt Mor
K
1083
SCHIEHALLION
GLENGOULANDIE
DEER PARK
Glengoulandie
CASTLE
MENZIES
RANNOCH MOOR
547
Loch
Laidon
Loch Bà
PERTH
TUMMEL FOREST
LOCH PARK
RANNOCH
1042
CARN MAIRG
13
Garth
Keltneyburn
Camserney
Dull
BOLFRACKS
GARDEN
745
MEALL A'MHUIC
1029
CARN GORM
Camusvrachan
Invervar
Carnbahn
St FILLAN'S
CHURCH &
FORTINGALL
YEW
Comrie
286
Croftmoraig
Loch na
14
931
MEALL BUDHIE
AND
Balnahanaid
Fortingall
Taymouth
Castle
566
907
MEALL BUIDHE
KINROSS
GLEN LYON
GALLERY
Innerwick
GLEN
LYON
Bridge
of Lyon
Kenmore
SCOTTISH CRANNOG CENTRE
RANNOCH
Achállader
1081
BEINN A'
CHREACHAIN
Meggernie
Castle
Gallin
Bridge of
Balgie
SLYON
Fearnan
Acharn
Remony
Falls of Acharn
1004
BEINN AN DOTHAIDH
953
BEINN MHANACH
Pubil
Cashlie
Stronuich
Reservoir
Loch
Lyon
1118
1214
BEN LAWERS
Ben Lawers
Ardradnaig
716
BEINN BHREAC
Garrow
Quaich
1076
BEINN DÒRAIN
Beinn Heasgarnich
1076
960
STUCHD AN
LOCHAIN
780
MEALL NAN
TARMACHAN
1043
BEN LAWERS
VISITOR CENTRE
Lawers
A827
888
805
MEALL NAM
MARAN
Auch
A82
6
1047
CREAG MHOR
Kenknock
Glen
Lochay
Duncroisk
Milton
Morenish
Kiltyrie
Carie
Ardtalnaig
Claggan
901
BEINN ODHAR
Batavaime
FALLS OF LOCHAY
AND FISH LIFT
Boreland
MOIRLANICH
LONGHOUSE
Finlarig
Morenish
LS
Ardeonaig
Auchnafree
1025
BEN CHALLUM
937
BEINN CHEATHAICH
Killin
Monemore
Achmore
637
679
CREAG UCHDAG
Clifton
Tyndrum
Dalrigh
Auchtertyre
Bovain
Auchlyne
Lix Toll
Wester
Lix
A827
Falls of Dochart
931
BEN CHONZIE
Loch
Turret
Reservoir
GLEN DOCHART
A85
Ledcharrie
Ardchyle
5
Invergeldie
Funtullich
Carroglen
Auchessan
Lochdochart
House
11
852
Dalveich
Ardveich
1174
BEN MORE
Inverhaggernie
Loch Dochart
Benmore
Portnellan
A85
13
St Fillans
MELVILLE
MONUMENT
FALLS
TURRET
E
Loch Turret
Crianlarich
CRIANLARICH
WEST HIGHLAND WAY
978
DUBHCHRAIG
1165
STOB BINNEIN
Lochearnhead
Craggan
Derry
LOCH EARN
RIVER
Dunira
Ochtertyre
Comrie
Quoig
A82
Derrydaroch
Edinchip
Ardvorlich
Ardtrostan
Dundurn
EARN
Dalchonzie
Comrie Croft
Lawers
985
BEN VORLICH
Edinample
Balquhidder
ROB ROY'S GRAVE
Auchtubh
Balquhidder Station
Glenample
678
EDINAMPLE FALLS
Dalchruin
Tullybannocher
EARTHQUAKE HOUSE
Ross
Dalginross
Glascorrie
Lochlane
Monachylemore
Craigruie
Aberuchill
Castle
811
BEINN EACH
Strathyre
Forest
533
BEN CLACH
Langside
Inverlochlarig
Ballimore
Stronvar
Ardoch
A84
Strathyre
Immervoulin
13
AUCHINGARRICH
WILDLIFE & HIGHLAND
CATTLE CENTRE
Forest of
Glenartney
Dalchruin
Glen Artney
Tigh-na-Blair
Ochtermuthill
TROSSACHS
865
STOB A'CHOIN
Portnellan
940
BEINN A'CHROIN
687
BEINN BHREAC
771
820
BENVANE
Ardchullarie
More
Loch
Lubnaig
Auchinner
Auchnashelloch
Culloch
Torlum
Wood
Strath Gartney
STIRLING
Drumardoch
Anie
665
UAMH BHEAG
Glenlichorn
286
B827
770
16
Rob Roy's
Cave
Stronachlachar
Brenachoile
Lodge
LOCH KATRINE
Glen Finglas
Res.
879
BEN LEDI
Coirea-
chrombe
FALLS OF LENY
Pass of
Leny
Leny Ho.
ROB ROY AND TROSSACHS
VISITOR CENTRE
Bracklinn Falls
The Bows
Braco
Castle
NATIONAL
Inversnaid
Hotel
Garrison
RSPB
Loch Arklet
WEST HIGHLAND WAY
The
Trossachs
TROSSACHS PIER COMPLEX
SS SIR WALTER SCOTT
Trossachs
Hotel
Brig o'Turk
Kilmahog
Bochastle
Callander
Easter
Brackland
Drumloist
Muckle Burn
Wester Feddal
B8003
Cailness
Ben Venue
727
598
Duncraggan
Lendrick
Lodge
Coilantogle
Callandrode
Auchenlaich
Braes of Doune
Dalbrack
Kinbuck
Idle
Sheriff
Muir
1715
Frenich
Loch Achray
THE TROSSACHS
Invertrossachs
Loch Venachar
9
A821
Callandrode
Burn of
Cambus
Lanrick
Ashfield
Kilbryde
Castle
Tarbet
Inverbeg
Gallery
LOCH PARK
LOMOND
974
BEN LOMOND
Kinlochard
Altskeith
Drumlean
Milton
Achray
Forest
D. MARSHALL LODGE
VISITOR CENTRE
Menteith
Hills
Loch
Rusky
Torrie Forest
Drumvaich
Doune
CATHEDRAL
Dunblane
Pisgah
LEIGHTON LIBRARY
Stronmachair
Mill of Chon
Couligartan
Loch Chon
SCOTTISH WOOL CENTRE
TROSSACHS
DISCOVERY CENTRE
Port of
Menteith
Lake of
Menteith
DUNAVERIG
FARMLIFE CENTRE
Brae of
Boquhapple
18
Deanston
Blair
Drummond
Easter
Row
Badgergate
Ptarmigan Lodge
681
Loch Ard Forest
Aberfoyle
Kirkton
Balleich
INCHMAHOME
PRIORY
Ruskie
A873
Thornhill
278
Blair Drummond
BLAIR DRUMMOND
SAFARI PARK
Sunnylaw
NN
Bridge of A
Firkin
277
Rowardennan
Lodge
596
BEINN UIRD
577
BEINN BHREAC
Cobleland
Gartmore Ho.
Bigram
B826
Blairdrummond
Moss
Blairlogie
ROWARDENNAN
HOTEL
Gartmore
Malling
Lochend
Ho.
Gartur
FLANDERS MOSS
Flanders Moss
M9
NAT WALLACE
MONUMENT
Inverbeg
Inverbeg
Gallery
FOREST PARK
Rowardennan
Forest
Dalmary
Balleich
Ballochleam
Dykehead
Forth
B8031
Drip
Moss
P&R
Causeway-head
7
8
9
10
11

SOUND OF EIGG

RUM 1:10
AN SGURR 393
Galmisda
Eilea

Eilean nan Each
0:35

294   294   Gallanach
Port Mor
Muck   137

Sanna Point
Sanna Bay   Sanna
Portuairk   Achnaha
Point of   Achosnich
Ardnamurchan
ARDNAMURCHAN LIGHTHOUSE
An Acairseid   Ormsaigmore   Kilchoa
Ormsaigbeg   i
Kilchoan
Bay

Rubha Mor   Eilean Mor
Bousd   Sorisdale
Cairns of Coll
Cornaigmore
Cliad Bay   Ardmore Bay   Ardmore Pt.
Arnabost   Gallanach   Bloody
Grishipoll   B8072
Clabhach   B8071   COLL   OBAN 2:40   Glengorm
Ballyhaugh   73   Castle   MULL MUSEUM
Hogh Bay   104   B8070   Quinish Pt.
RSPB   Arinagour   Rubha   Tobermory
COLL   an Aird   Cuin   'S AIRDE-BEINN
Totronald   Eilean   Caliach Pt.   MULL   292
Arileod   Uig Acha   Ornsay   Caliach Mornish   Sunipol   THEATRE Achnadrish
Feall   LS   Croig Penmore Dervaig
Bay   Breachacha   Friesland   Mill West THE OLD BYRE
Castle   Calgary   Ardhu HERITAGE CENTRE
CASTLEBAY 2:45   Calgary Bay   Druimnacroish
(Summer only) Calgary Pt.   Lev
Gunna   Crossapol   Loch   Ensay   342
Bay   Soa Breachacha   CARN MOR Kengharair Achnacraig
TIREE   Vaul   Rubha Dubh   Haunn   390   Druimnacroish
Balephetrish Bay Vaul Bay Salum Caolas   Rubh a'Chaoil   Burg Kilninian
Cornaigmore   Vaul   0:55   Achleck
moluaig Cornaigbeg Kirkapol   Ruaig   23 Fanmore   390
Kenovay   Gott   Ruaig Soa   EAS FORS
Moss   TIREE   Scarinish Gott Bay   Treshnish Isles WATERFALL BEINN NA DRISE 424
Heylipol   Baugh   Lagganulva
Balinoe Crossapol Heanish   Fladda   Ardalum Oskamull
B8067   Rubha Traigh Hynish Bay   Eilean Dioghlum Baligortan Ho Ulva Killien
Balemartine   an Duin   Bearnus 313 Ulva House
141 Mannal   Gometra   Gometra   LOCH NA KEAL
West   Ho   Eorsa
Hynish Hynish   Bac Mor   Little   INCH KENNETH ISLE OF
Colonsay   CHAPEL
Staffa STAFFA   Inch
FINGAL'S CAVE   Kenneth Balnahard
Erisgeir   MACKINNON'S CAVE
Balmeanach   561
519   Glen Sellisdeir
BEINN NA SREINE
ARDMEANACH   Ki
Tiroran

0   2   4   6 miles
0   2   4   6   8   10 km

MACLEAN'S CROSS   Eilean
Annraidh
IONA ABBEY AND   Rubha nan Cearc
CATHEDRAL   Kintra
Iona   100   ST COLUMBA EXHIBITION Achnahard Knokan Torrans
Baile Mor   & WELCOME CENTRE   18
Stac an   Aridhglas Eorabus
Aoineidh Sligneach   Lower   LOCH SCRIDAIN
Fionnphort A849 Tiraghoil Ardtun Lee
Fidden   Bunessan   376
CRUACHAN MIN
Gunna   ROS OF MULL 274
Erraid   Errald   Knockvologan   Ardlanish Uisken Scoor
Soa I.   Ardchiavaig 125
Eilean a'Chalmain   Rubha nam Malcolm's Pt.
Braithean
Rubh' Ardalanish

TIREE
Vaul Bay Salum
Sraid Cornaigmore Vaul Caolas
Ruadh   Rubha Dubh.
Balevullin   Kirkapol
Hough Kilmoluaig Cornaigbeg Kenovay Ruaig
Gott Soa
Kilkenneth   Moss   Gott Bay
Middleton Heylipol TIREE Scarinish
rt Mor Baugh Heanish CASTLEBAY 2:45
Barrapol Crossapol Rubha Traigh (Summer only)
Balinoe an Duin COLL 0:55
Loch B8067
a'Phuill Balemartine Hynish Bay
141 Mannal
Balephuil
Balephuil West
Bay Hynish Hynish
Port Snoig

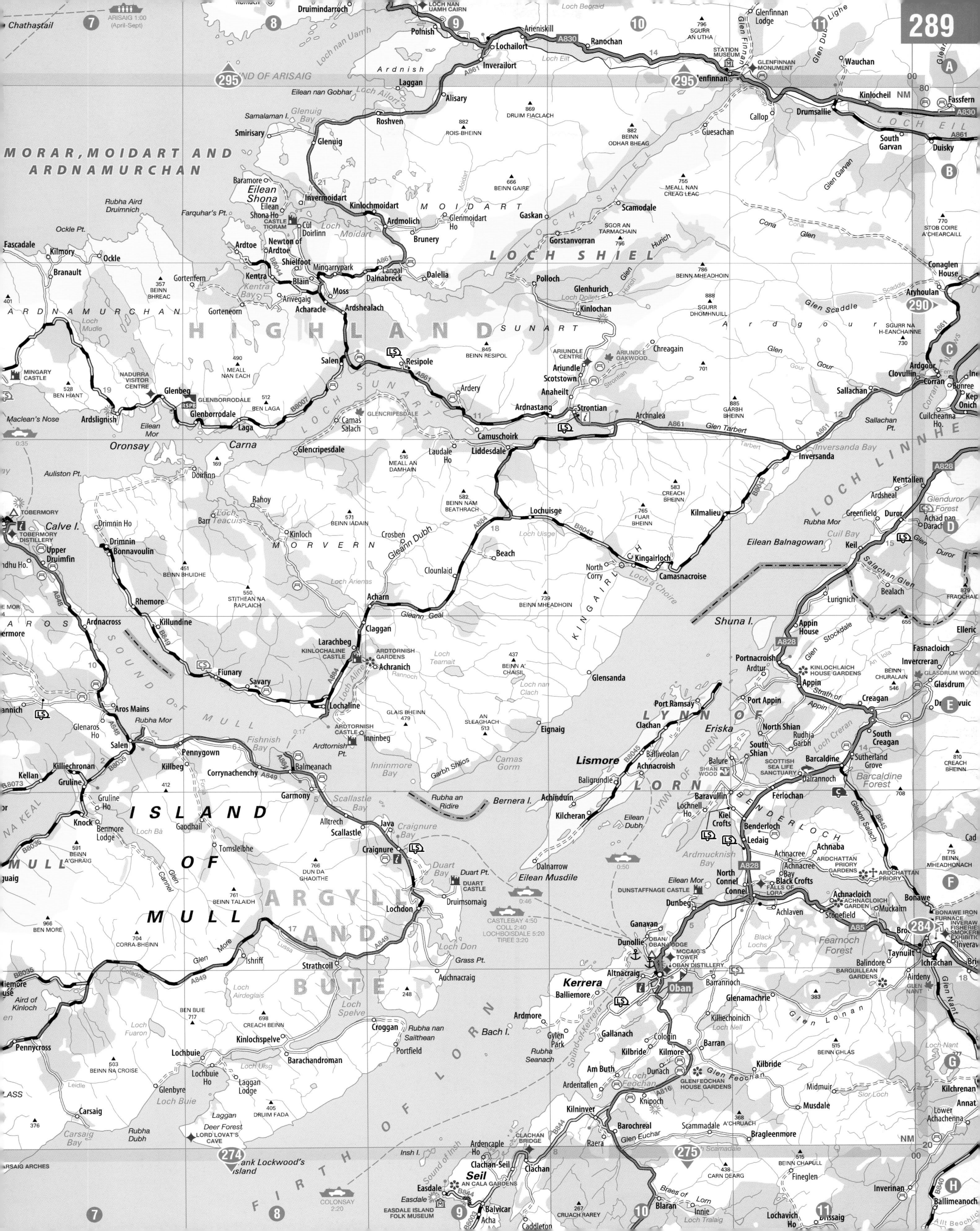

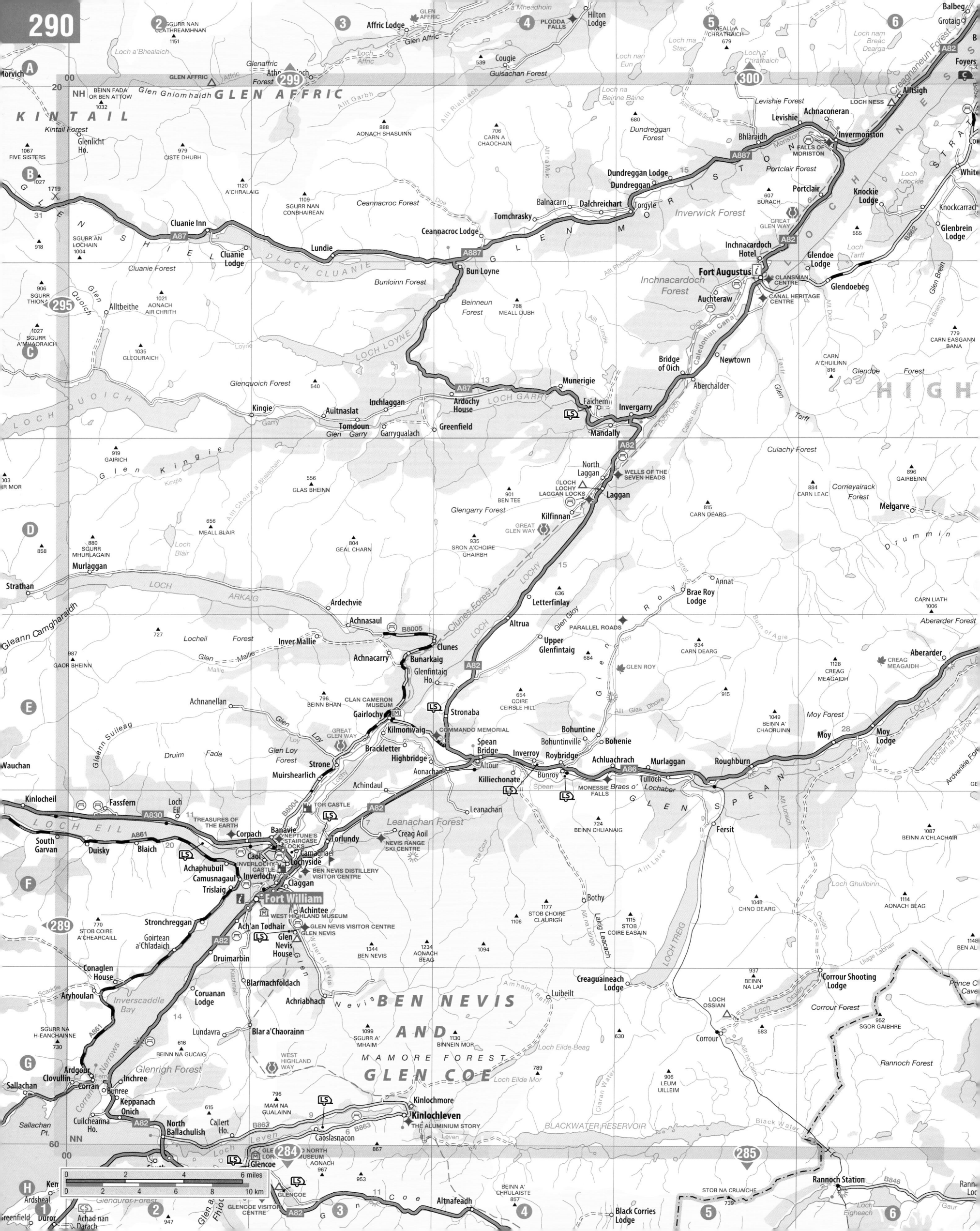

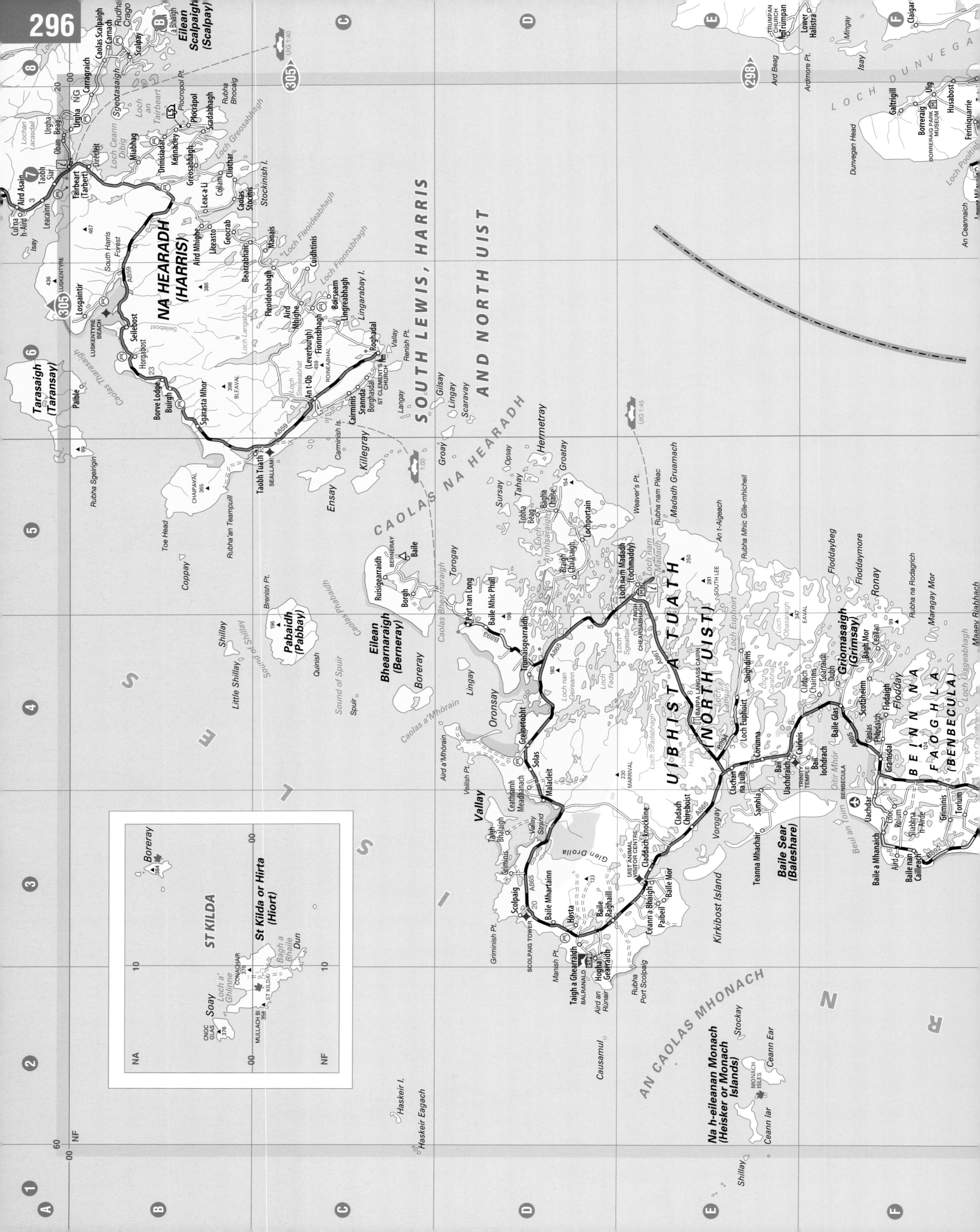

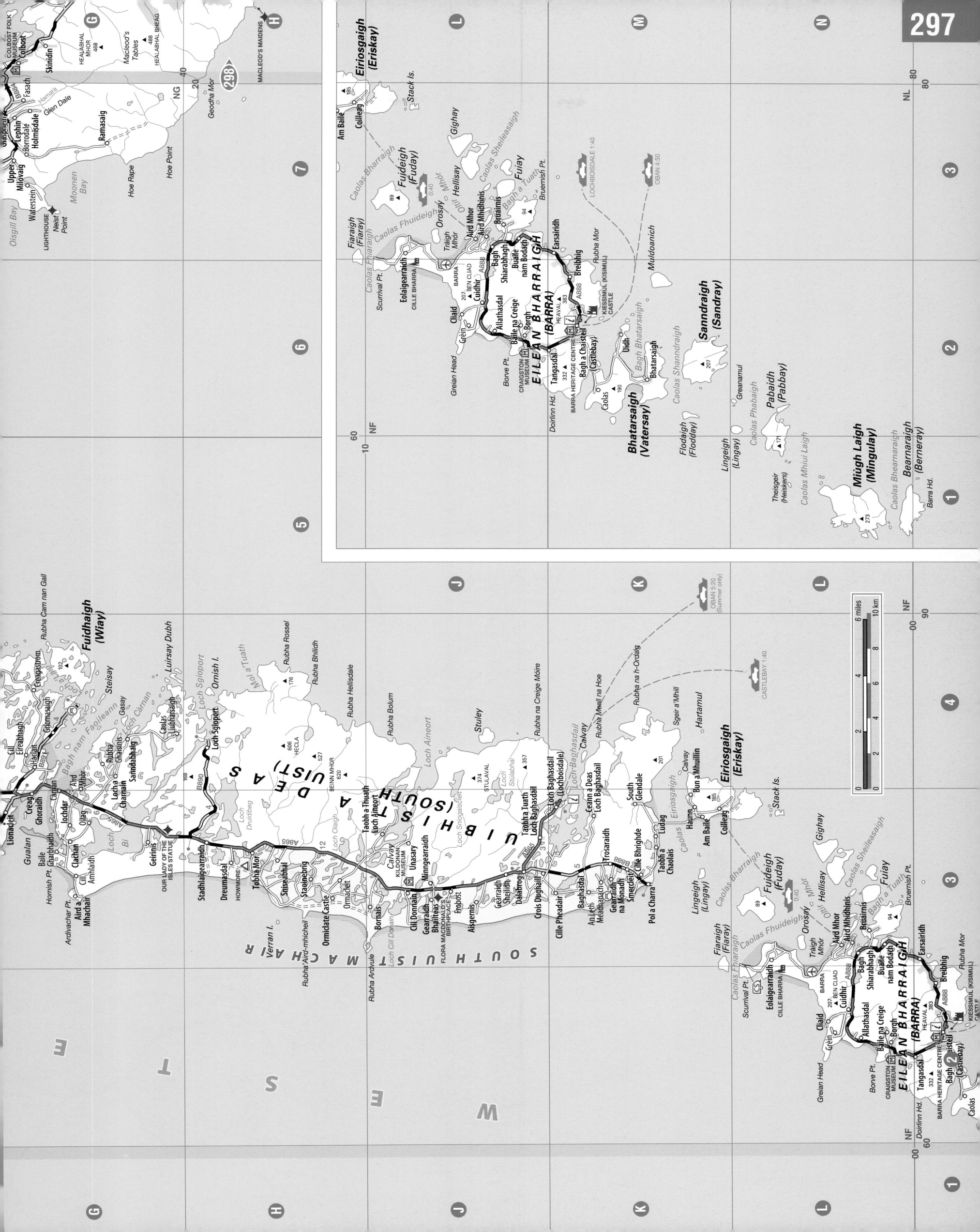

Eiriosgaigh (Eriskay)

Fuidheigh (Fuday)

Fiaraigh (Fiaray)

Caolas Bharraigh

Caolas Fhuideigh

Caolas Phiaraigh

Gighay

Orosay Mhòr

Oitir Hellisay

Caolas Sheileasaigh

Hellisay

Bàgh a Tuath

Bruernish Pt.

Aird Mhor

Aird Mhidhinis

Brutainnis

Traigh Mhòr

LOCHBOISDALE 1:40

OBAN 4:50

Eolaigearraidh

BEN CLAD

A888

Bàgh Shiarabhagh

Buaile nam Bodach

Earsairidh

CILLE BHARRA

Clad

Cuidhir

Borgh

Breibhig

Muldoanich

EILEAN BHARRAIGH (BARRA)

HEAVAL ▲ 383

Grein

Allathasdal

Baile na Creige

Balla

Sanndraigh (Sandray)

Greian Head

Borve Pt.

CRAIGSTON MUSEUM

BARRA HERITAGE CENTRE

Tangasdal 332

Bàgh a Chaisteil (Castlebay)

KIESSIMUL (KISIMUL) CASTLE

Uidh

Bàgh Bhatarsaigh

Bhatarsaigh

Caolas Shanndraigh

Doirlinn Hd.

Caolas

190

Pabaidh (Pabbay)

Caolas Phabaidh

Bhatarsaigh (Vatersay)

Flodaigh (Flodday)

Lingeigh (Lingay)

Greanamul

171

Bearnaraigh (Berneray)

Caolas Mhiul Laigh

Theisgeir (Heiskeir)

Caolas Bhearnaraigh

Barra Hd.

Miùgh Laigh (Mingulay)

273

Fuidhaigh (Wiay)

Rubha Cam nan Gall

Creagastrom

102

Steisay

Gasay

Luirsay Dubh

Loch Sgioport

Ornish I.

Mol a Tuath

Rubha Rossel

176

Rubha Bhilidh

Rubha Hellisdale

Rubha Bolum

Stuley

Rubha na Creige Mòire

OBAN 5:20 (Summer only)

CASTLEBAY 1:40

Rubha na h-Ordaig

Calvay

Sgeir a'Mhill

Hartamul

Eiriosgaigh (Eriskay)

Cill

Eireabhal

Cnocan

Gualan

Baile

Creag Ghoraidh

Aird a' Mhachair

Hornish Pt.

Clachan

Lionacleit

Iochdar

Olgag

Cill Amhlaidh

Ardivachar Pt.

Rubha Ardvule

OUR LADY OF THE ISLES STATUE

Geirinis

Stadhlaigearraidh

HOWMORE

Dreumasdal

Tobha Mòr

Staoinebrig

Snaiseabhal

Verran I.

Ormidate Castle

Rubha Aird-mhichiel

Loch Bì

A865

Loch Druidibeg

HECLA 606

627

Loch Sgioport

188

B890

Loch a Charnain

Locha Charnain

Sanndabhaig

Rubha Ghasinis

Aird Mhor

Loch Aineort

BENN MHOR 620

UIBHIST A DEAS (SOUTH UIST)

STULAVAL 374

357

Loch Stùlabhal

Loch Sniogaisdeil

Taobh a Thuath Loch Aineort

Taobh a Deas Loch Baghasdail

Loch Baghasdail (Lochboisdale)

Bornais

Ormaclait

Aisgernis

KILDONAN MUSEUM

Calvay

Unasary

Minngearraidh

Geàrraidh Sheilidh

Dalabrog

FLORA MACDONALD'S BIRTHPLACE

Probost

Gearraidh na Mònadh

An Leth Meadhanach

Smeircleit

Baghasdail

Ludag

Cille Pheadair

Cille Bhrighde

Crois Dùghaill

Trosaraidh

Pol a Charra

Taobh a Chaolais

Caolas Eriosgaigh

Haunn

Am Baile

Coilleag

Bun a'Mhuillin

South Glendale

Rubha Meall na Hoe

Calvay

201

Stack Is.

185

Fuidheigh (Fuday)

Fiaraigh (Fiaray)

Lingeigh (Lingay)

89

Orosay Mhòr

Oitir Hellisay

Caolas Fhuideigh

Caolas Phiaraigh

Hellisay

Bàgh a Tuath

Bruernish Pt.

Aird Mhor

Aird Mhidhinis

Brutainnis

94

Traigh Mhòr

Eolaigearraidh

BEN CLAD

Scurrival Pt.

CILLE BHARRA

Clad

Cuidhir

A888

Bàgh Shiarabhagh

Buaile nam Bodach

Earsairidh

Grein

Borgh

Breibhig

EILEAN BHARRAIGH (BARRA)

HEAVAL ▲ 383

Allathasdal

Baile na Creige

A888

Greian Head

Borve Pt.

CRAIGSTON MUSEUM

BARRA HERITAGE CENTRE

Tangasdal 332

Bàgh a Chaisteil (Castlebay)

KIESSIMUL (KISIMUL) CASTLE

Doirlinn Hd.

Caolas

SOUTH UIST MACHAIR

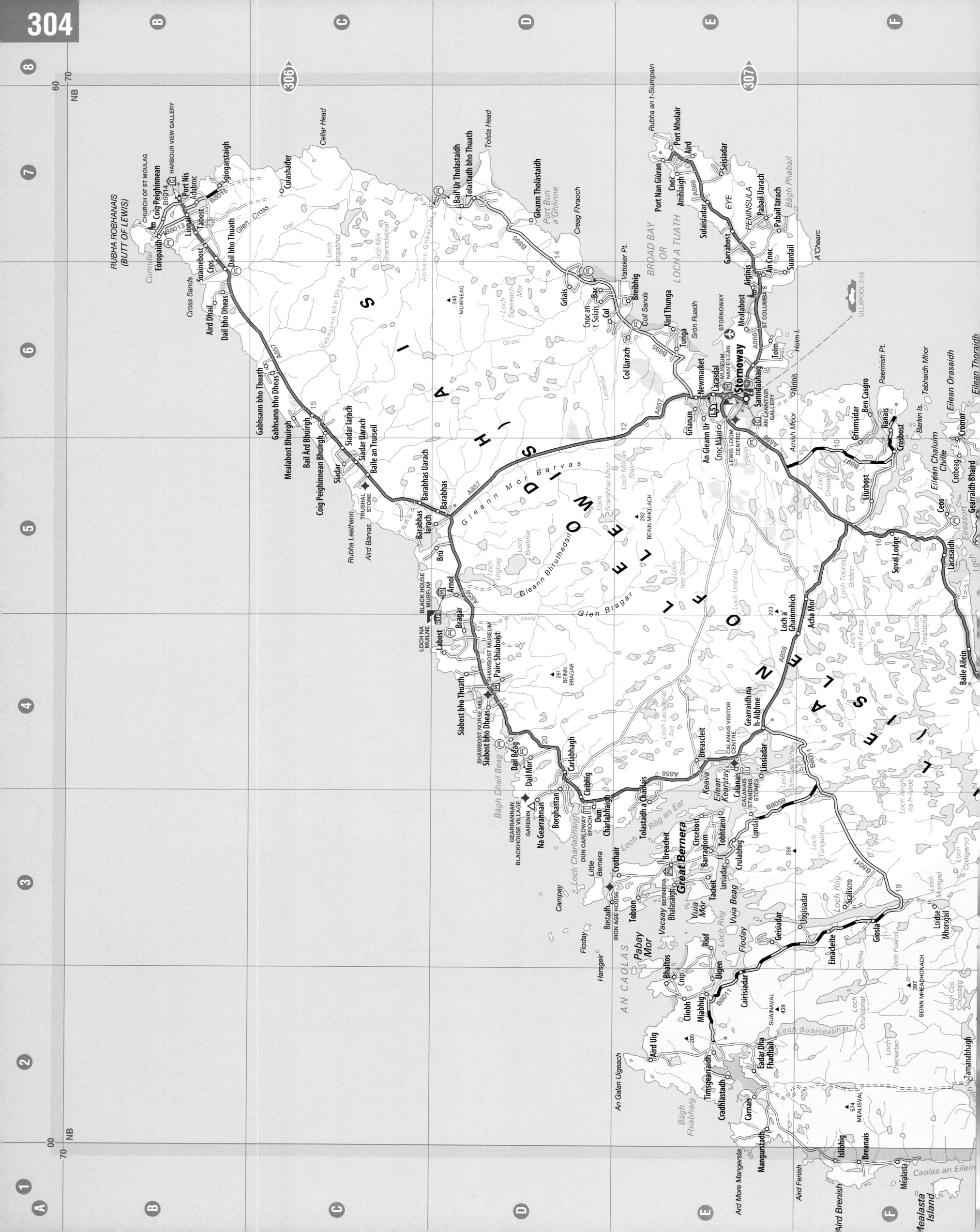

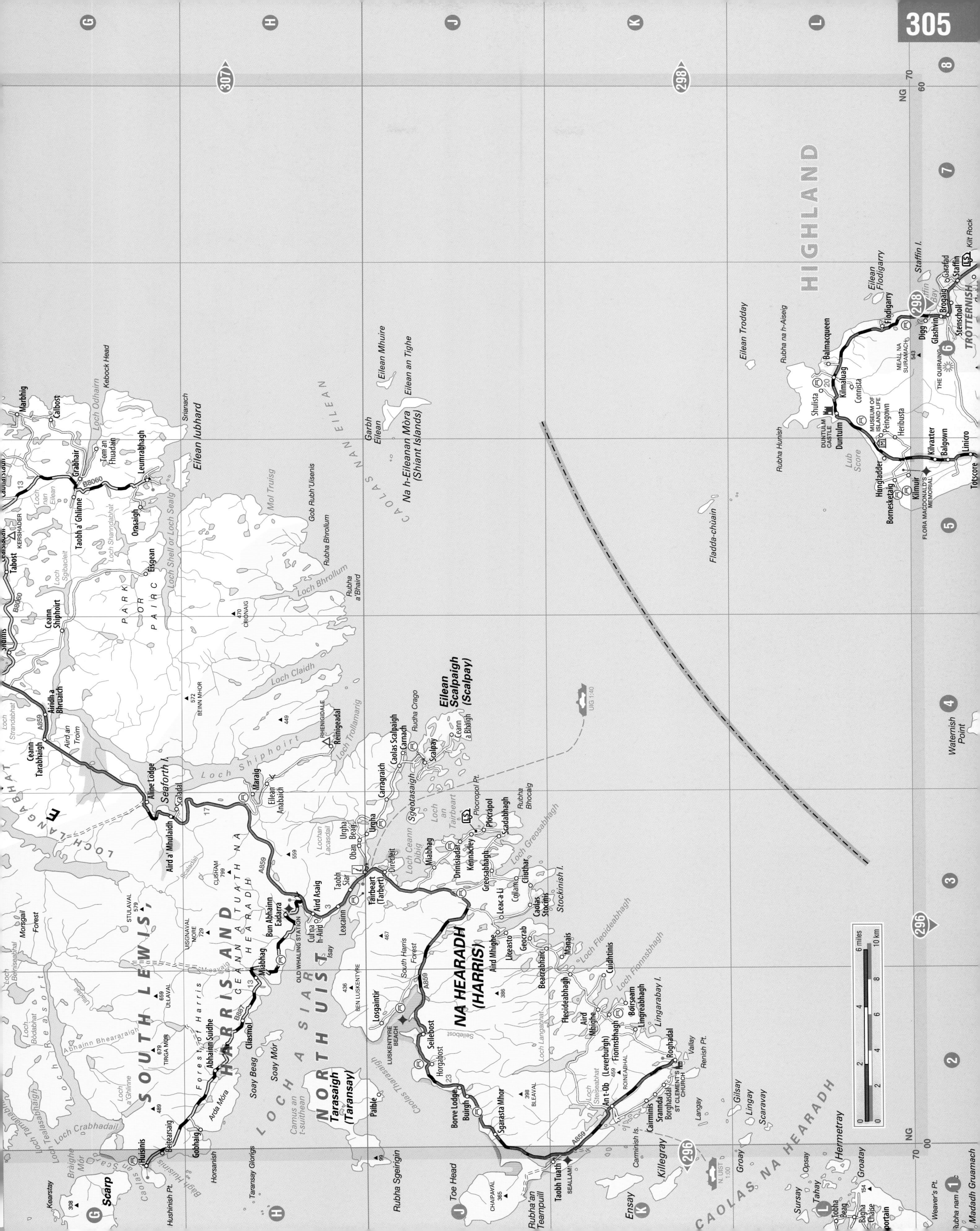

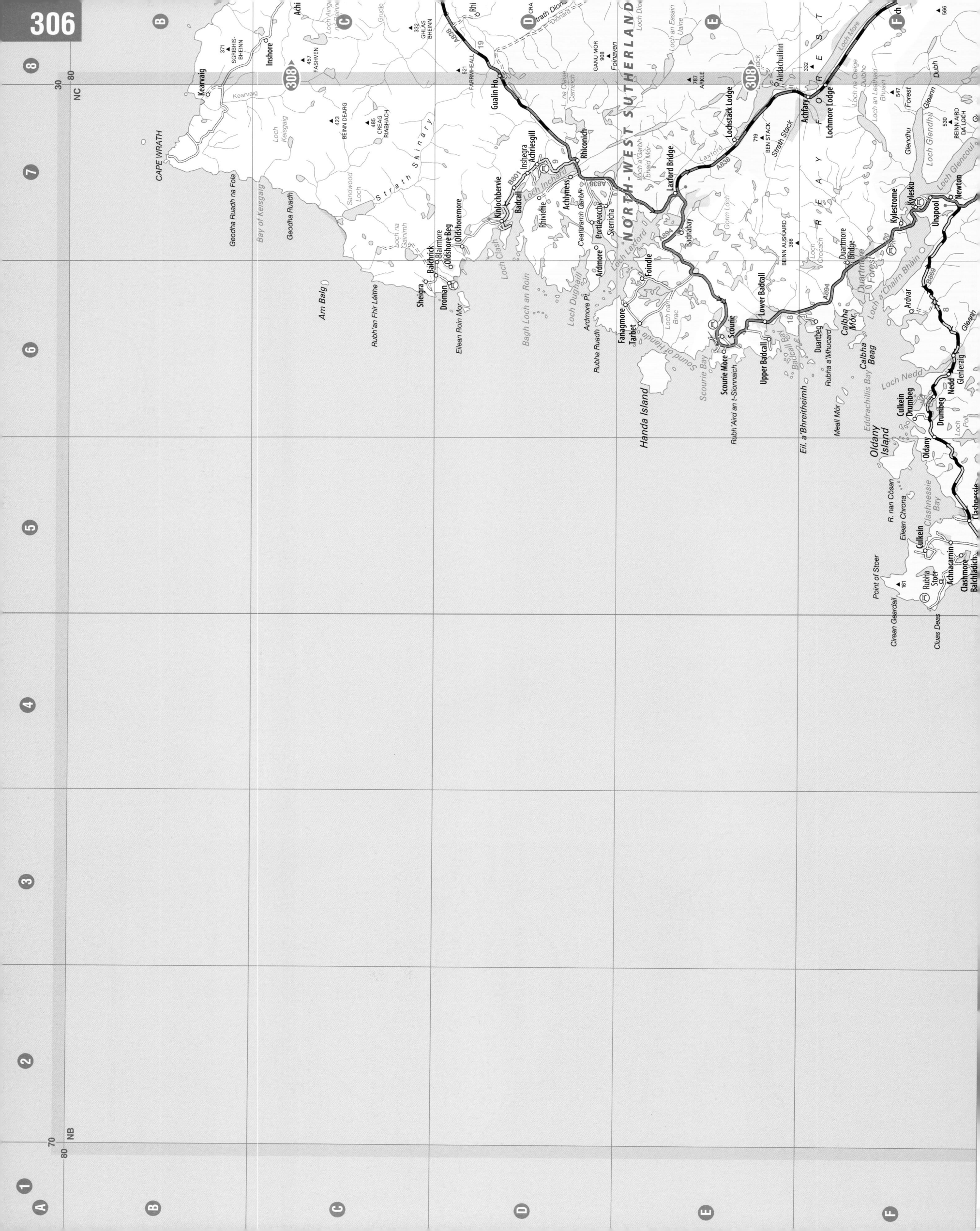

CAPE WRATH

NORTH-WEST SUTHERLAND

Kearvaig
Inshore
SGRIBHIS-BHEINN
GHLAS BHEINN
FASHVEN
BEINN DEARG
CREAG RIABHACH
Gualin Ho
Achriesgill
Inshegra
Rhiconich
Kinlochbervie
Badcall
Achlyness
Rhividhe
Oldshoremore
Oldshore Beg
Blairmore
Balchrick
Sheigra
Droman
Am Balg
Rubh'an Fhir Léithe
Eilean Roin Mor
Strath Shinary
Bay of Keisgaig
Loch Keisgaig
Geodha Ruadh na Fola
Geodha Ruadh
Sandwood Loch
loch na Gainimh
Loch Clash
Loch Inchard
Ceathramh Garbh
Ardmore
Portlevorchy
Skerricha
Foindle
Laxford Bridge
Laxford Forest
Lochstack Lodge
BEN STACK
Strath Stack
ARKLE
Achfary
Lochmore Lodge
Airdachuilinn
Loch More
BEINN AIRD DA LOCH
Loch Glencoul
Newton
Unapool
Kylesku
Kylestrome
Duartmore Bridge
Calbha Mór
Calbha Beg
Loch a'Chairn Bhain
Ardvar
Duartbeg
Upper Badcall
Lower Badcall
Scourie
Scourie More
Fanagmore
Tarbet
Handa Island
Sound of Handa
Scourie Bay
Eddrachillis Bay
Oldany Island
Oldany
Culkein Drumbeg
Drumbeg
Nedd
Glenleraig
Loch Nedd
Culkein
Clashnessie
Clashnessie Bay
Clashmore
Balchladich
Achnacarnin
Rubha Stoer
Point of Stoer
Cluas Deas
Cirean Geardail
Eilean Chrona
R. nan Còsan
Gleann
Loch Glendhu
Glendhu
BEINN AIRD DA LOCH
Loch na Creige Duibhe
Loch na Leathaid Bhuain

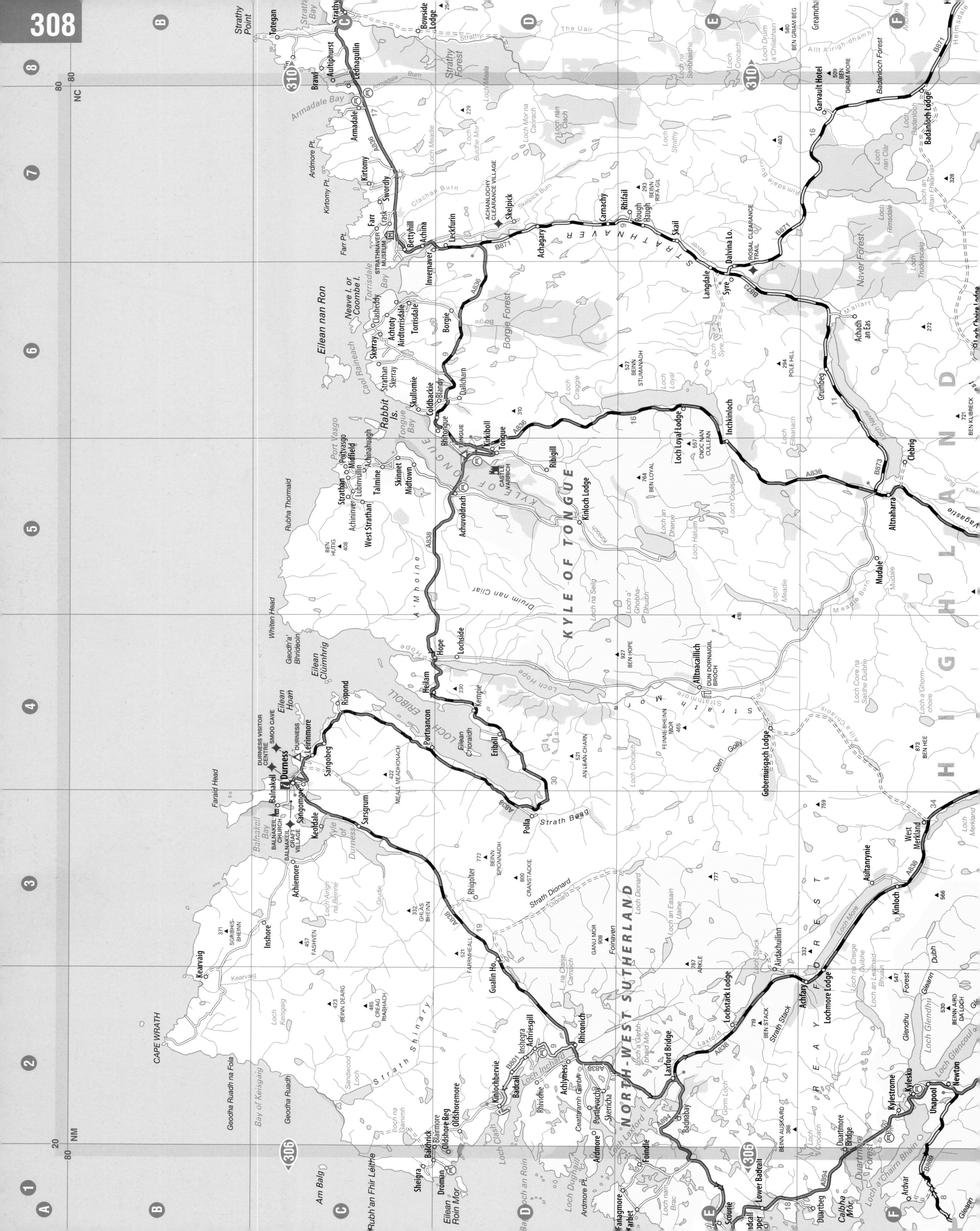

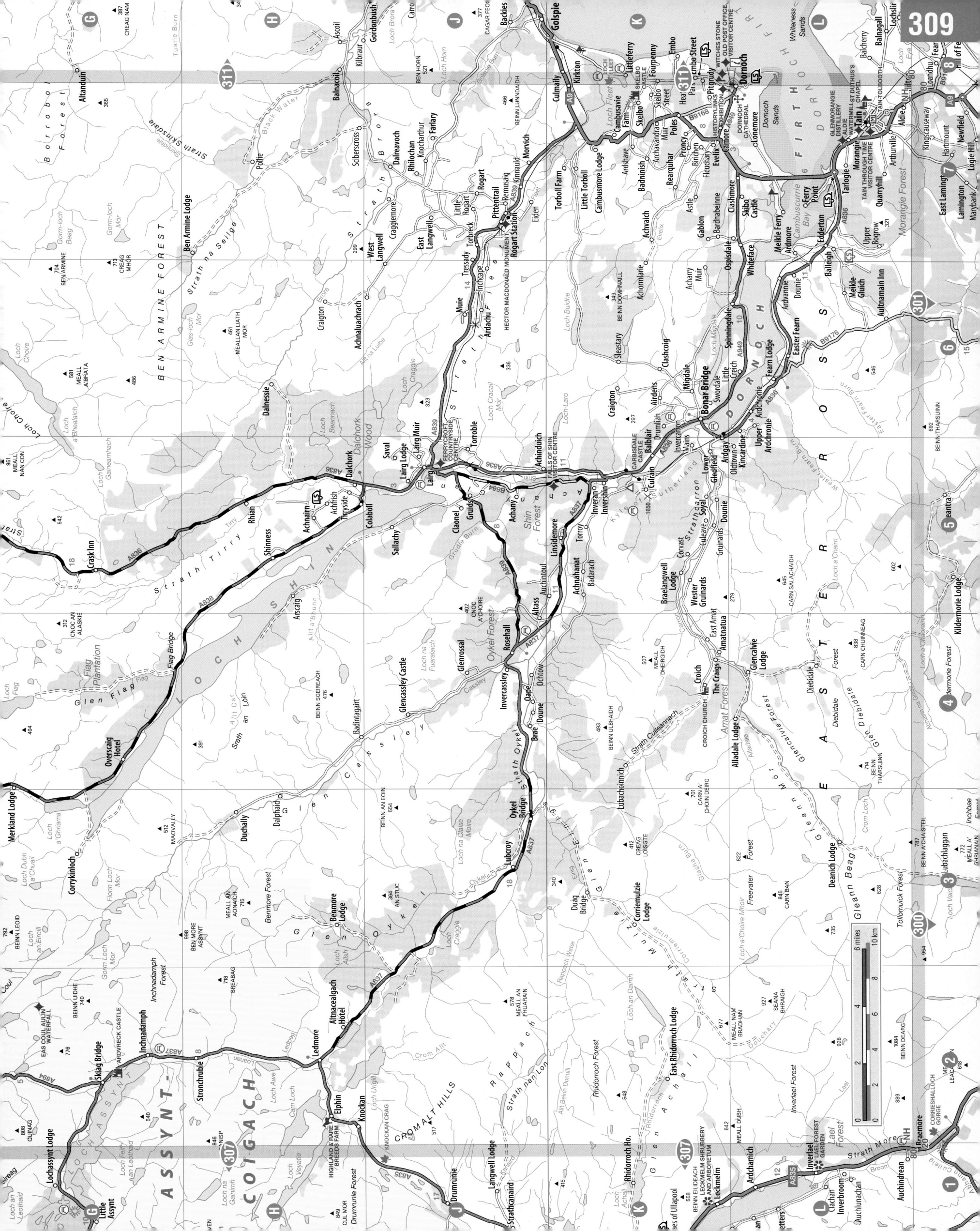

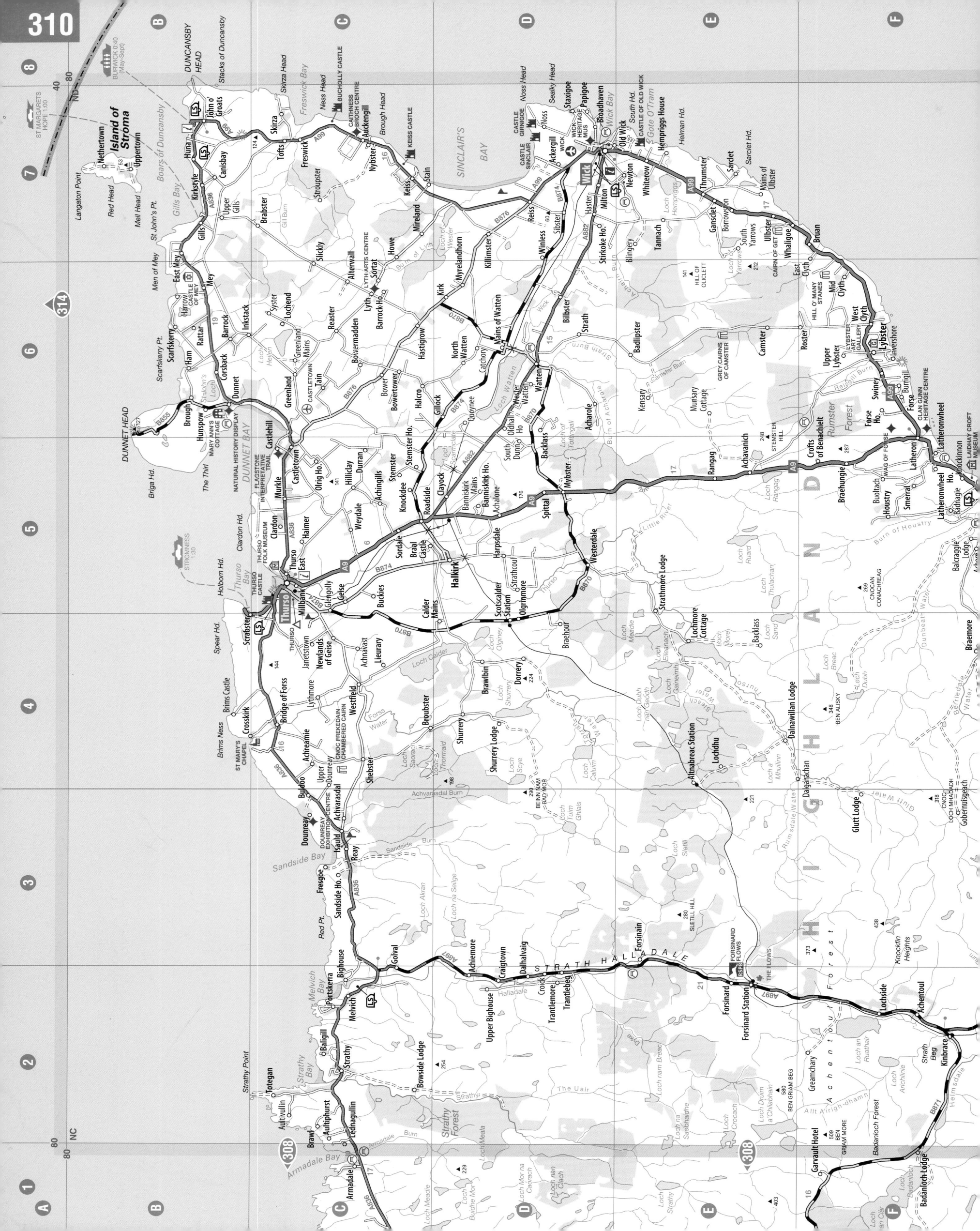

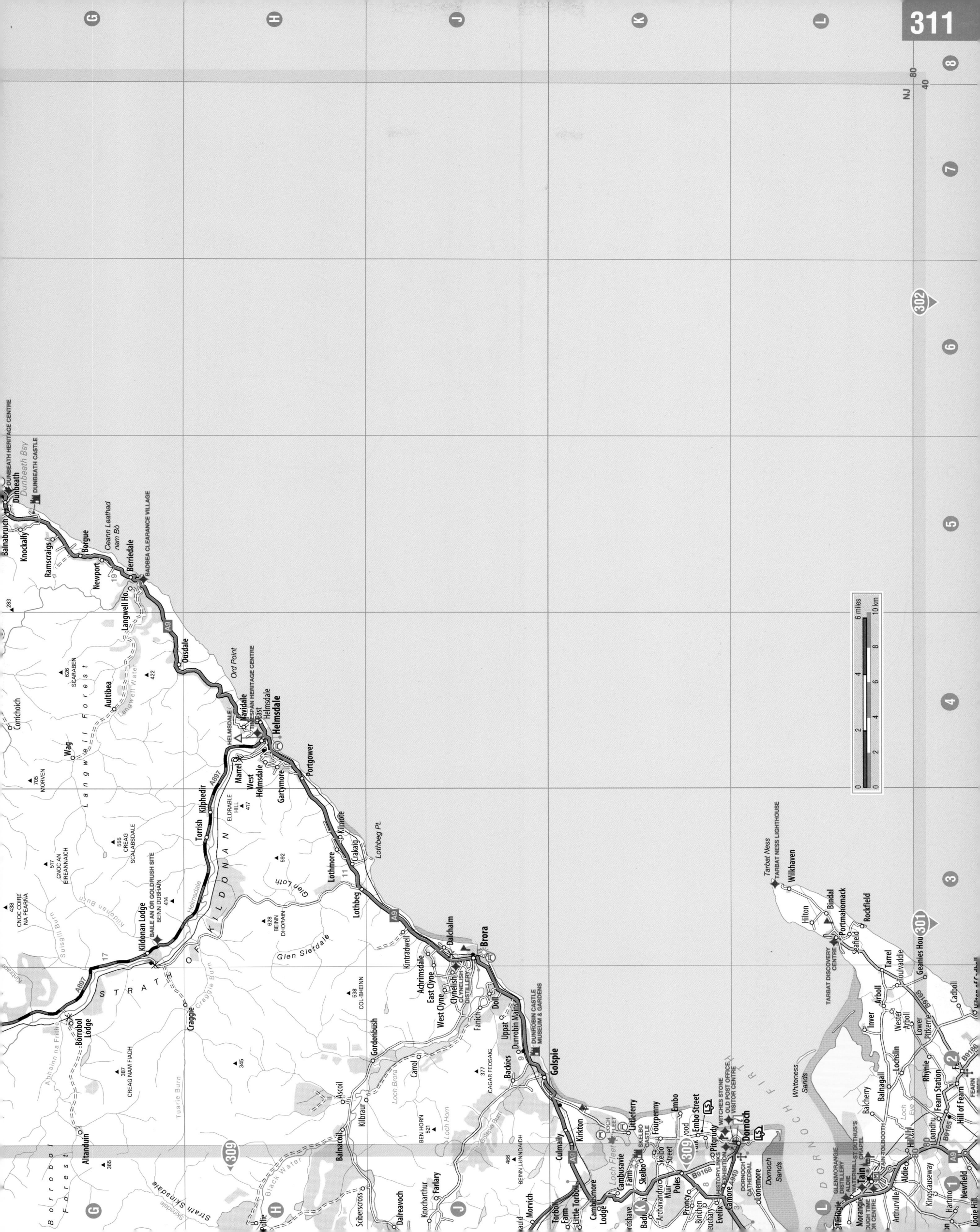

G　　　　H　　　　J　　　　K　　　　L

NJ 80
40

8

7

302

6

5

6 miles
10 km

4

2

4

6

8

2

4

6

8

0

0

4

Tarbat Ness
TARBAT NESS LIGHTHOUSE
Wilkhaven

3

Hilton
Bindal
Portmahomack
Rockfield
TARBAT DISCOVERY
CENTRE
Seafield

301

DUNBEATH HERITAGE CENTRE
Dunbeath
Dunbeath Bay
DUNBEATH CASTLE

Balnabruaich
Knockally
Borgue
Ramscraigs
Ceann Leathad
nam Bò
Newport
Berriedale
BADBEA CLEARANCE VILLAGE
Langwell Ho

283

Langwell Forest
SCARABEN
626
Aultibea
422
Corrichoich
Wag
MORVEN
705
517
CNOC AN
EIREANNAICH
555
CREAG
SCALABSDALE

Ousdale

Ord Point
TIMESPAN HERITAGE CENTRE
Navidale
East
Helmsdale
Helmsdale
HELMSDALE
Helmsdale
Portgower

A9

A897

Marrel
West
Helmsdale
Gartymore
ELDRABLE
HILL
417
Torrish
Kilphedir

Kilmote
Crakaig
Lothbeg Pt.

438
CNOC COIRE
NA PEARNA

Kildonan Lodge
BAILE AN OR GOLDRUSH SITE
BEINN DUBHAIN
414

592
Lothmore
11
Glen Loth

628
BEINN
DHORAIN
Lothbeg

STRATH OF KILDONAN
Helmsdale

387
CREAG NAM FIADH
345

538
COL-BHEINN
Borrobol
Lodge

466
BEINN LUNNDAIDH

Altanduin
365

Borrobol
Forest

A897
17

Craggie
Craggie Burn

Kintradwell
Achrimsdale
East Clyne
Clynelish
CLYNELISH
DISTILLERY
West Clyne
Fanich
Uppat
Doll

Dalchalm
Brora

DUNROBIN CASTLE
MUSEUM & GARDENS

Gordonbush
Glen Sletdale

Carrol
CAGAR FEOSAIG
377
Backies
9
Golspie

Loch Brora

BEN HORN
521

Ascoil
Kilbraur
Loch Horn

309

Balnacoil
STRATH BROAN

Craigton

DORNOCH
FIRTH

Whiteness
Sands

Inver
Wester
Arboll
Lower
Pitkerrie
Cadboll
Arboll
Tarrel
Geanies Hou
B9165
Balchery
B9168

Lochslin
Rhynie
Balnagall

Loandhu
Hilton of Cadboll

Fearn
2
Hill of Fearn
Cambuscurrie
FEARN

1
GLENMORANGIE
DISTILLERY

Abhainn na Fridh

Suisgill Burn

Kildonan Burn

Tuarie Burn

WITCHES STONE
OLD POST OFFICE
VISITOR CENTRE

LOCH FLEET
Littleferry
Foupenny
Embo
Embo Street

Culmaily
Kirkton
SKELBO
CASTLE
wood

DORNOCH
CATHEDRAL

Dornoch
Dornoch
Sands

HISTORYLINKS
EXHIBITION

Morvich
Torboll
Cambusavie
Pronay
Skelbo
Farm
Skelbo
Muie
Poles
Pitgrudy

309

Knockarthur
Farlary
Little Torboll
Torboll
Farm

Dalreavoch
Sciberscross

Badninish
Archavandra
Evelix
Birichen
Clashmore
Cambusmore
Lodge
Kirkton
Torrangie
Morangie
Tain
WATERMILL
PICTISH
CHAPEL
Meikle
Ferry
Arthurville
Aldie
Newfield

TAIN
TOLBOOTH

Loch
Evelix
B9176

Lonemore
Camore

A9

A9

309

A9

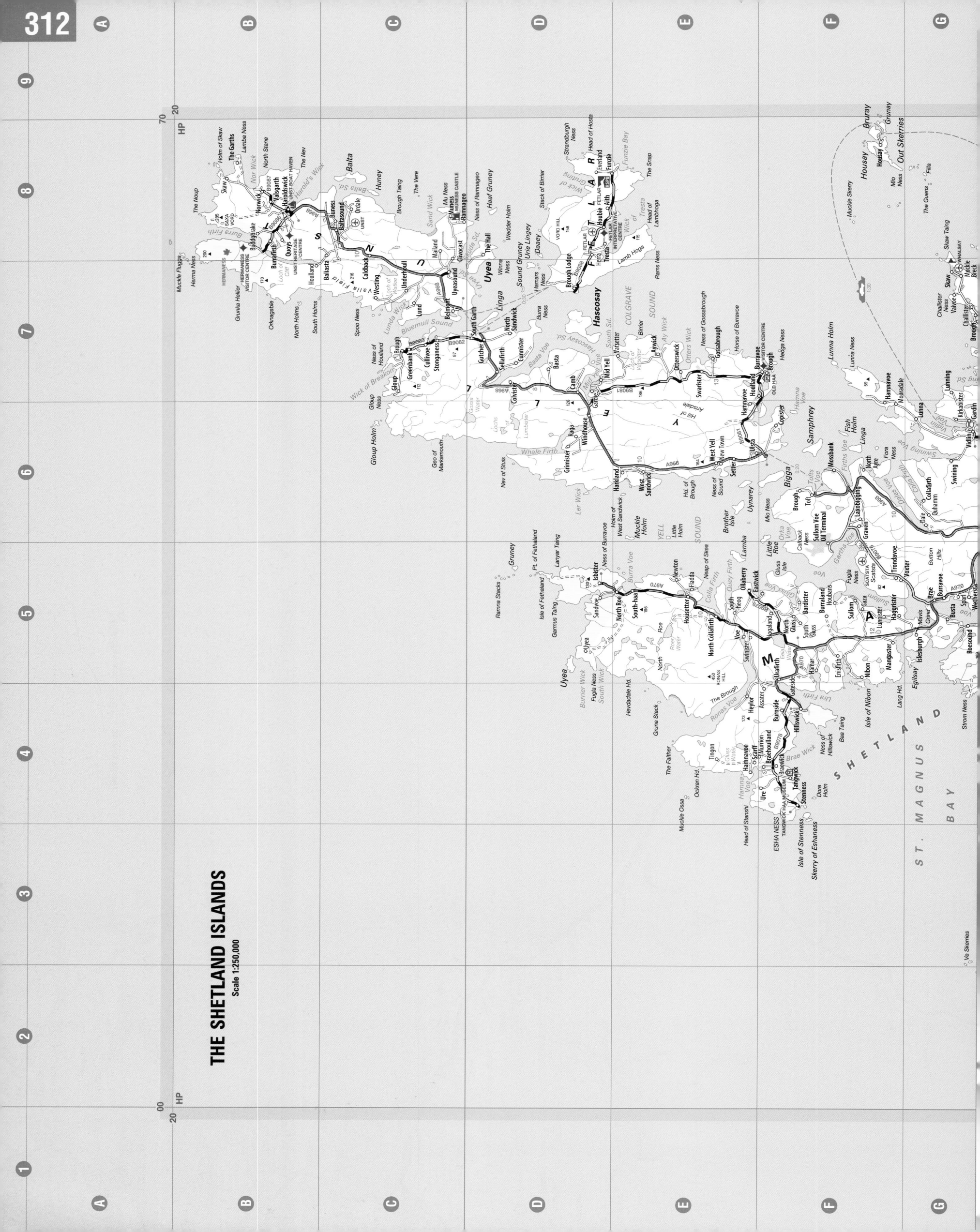

THE SHETLAND ISLANDS

Scale 1:250,000

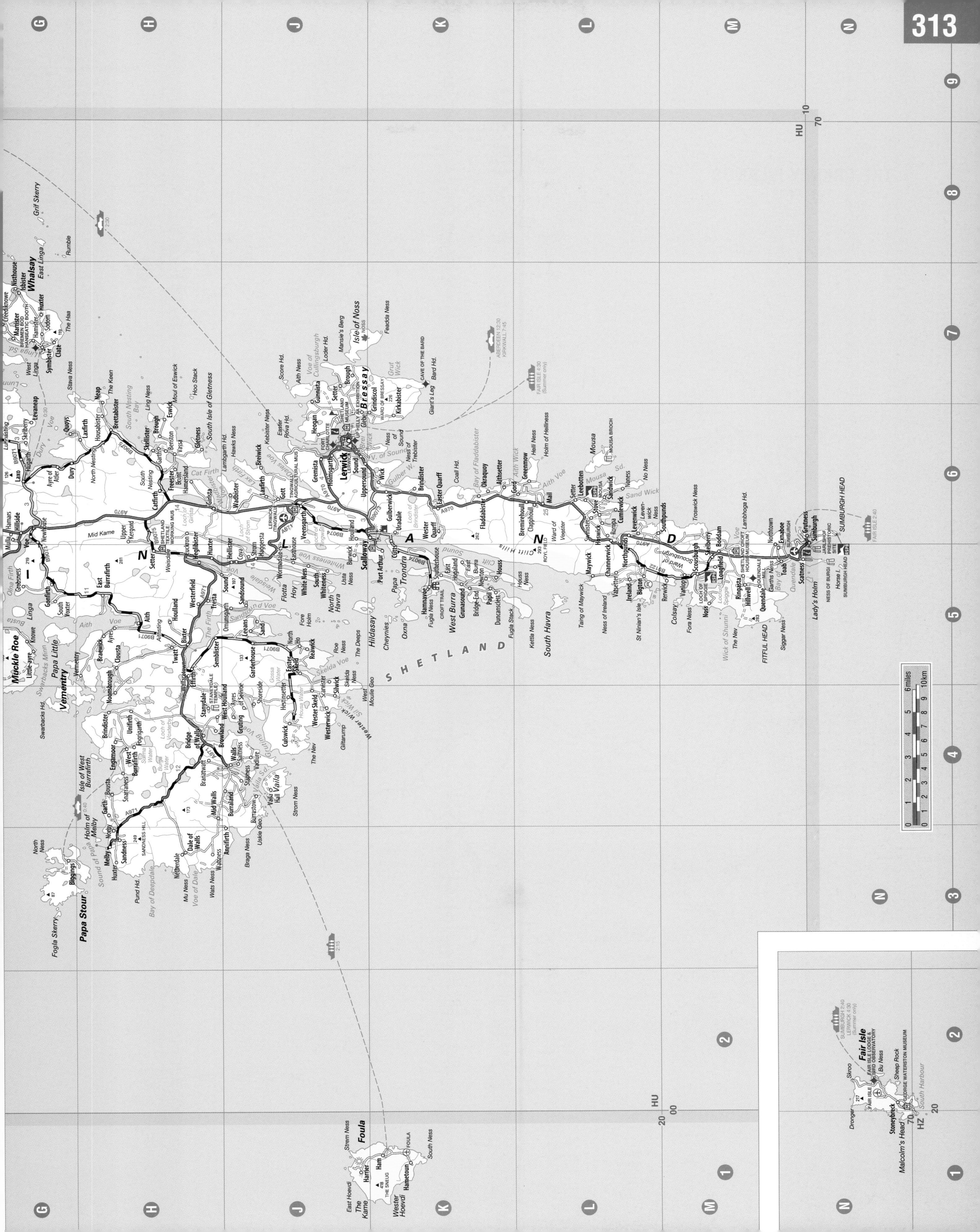

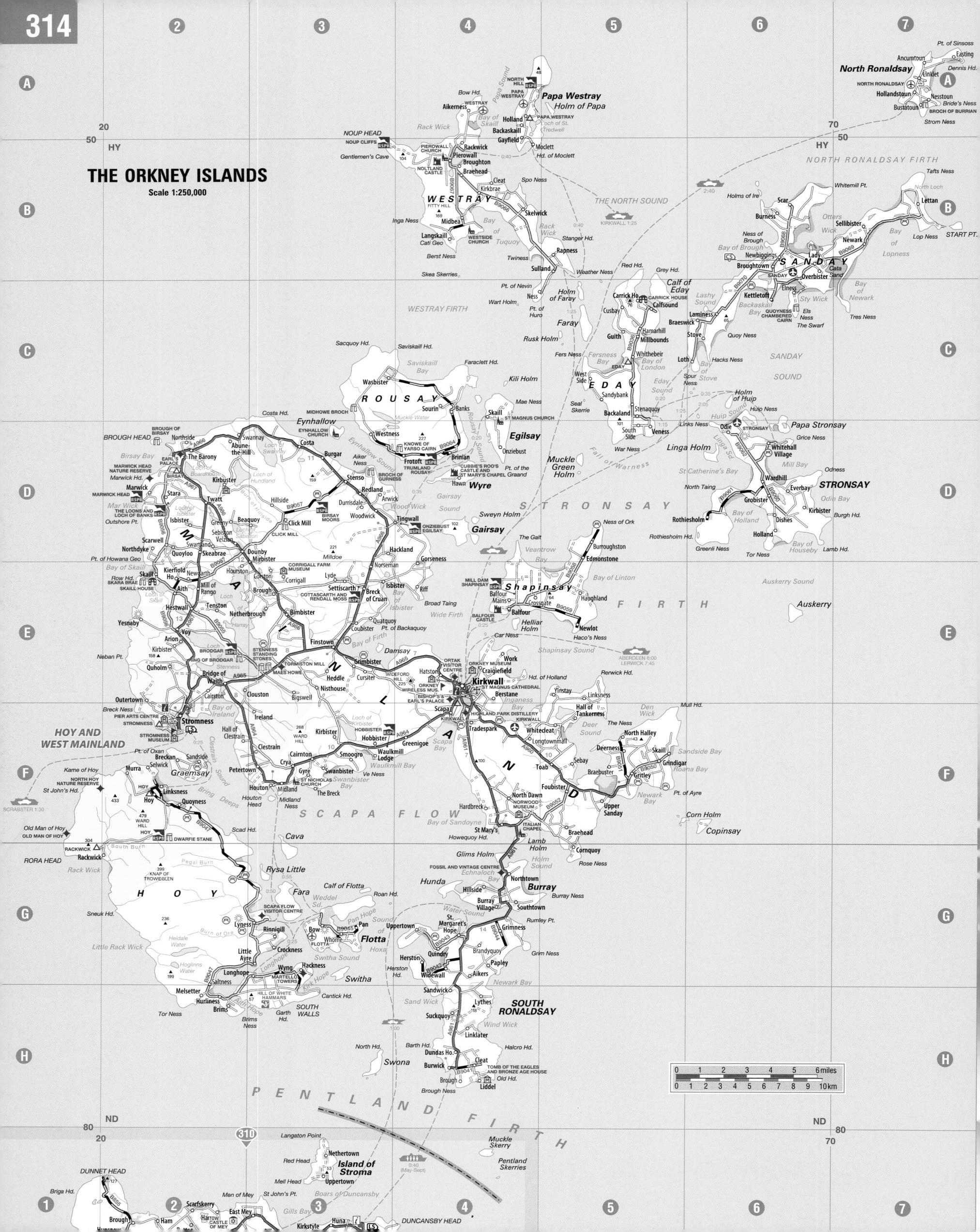

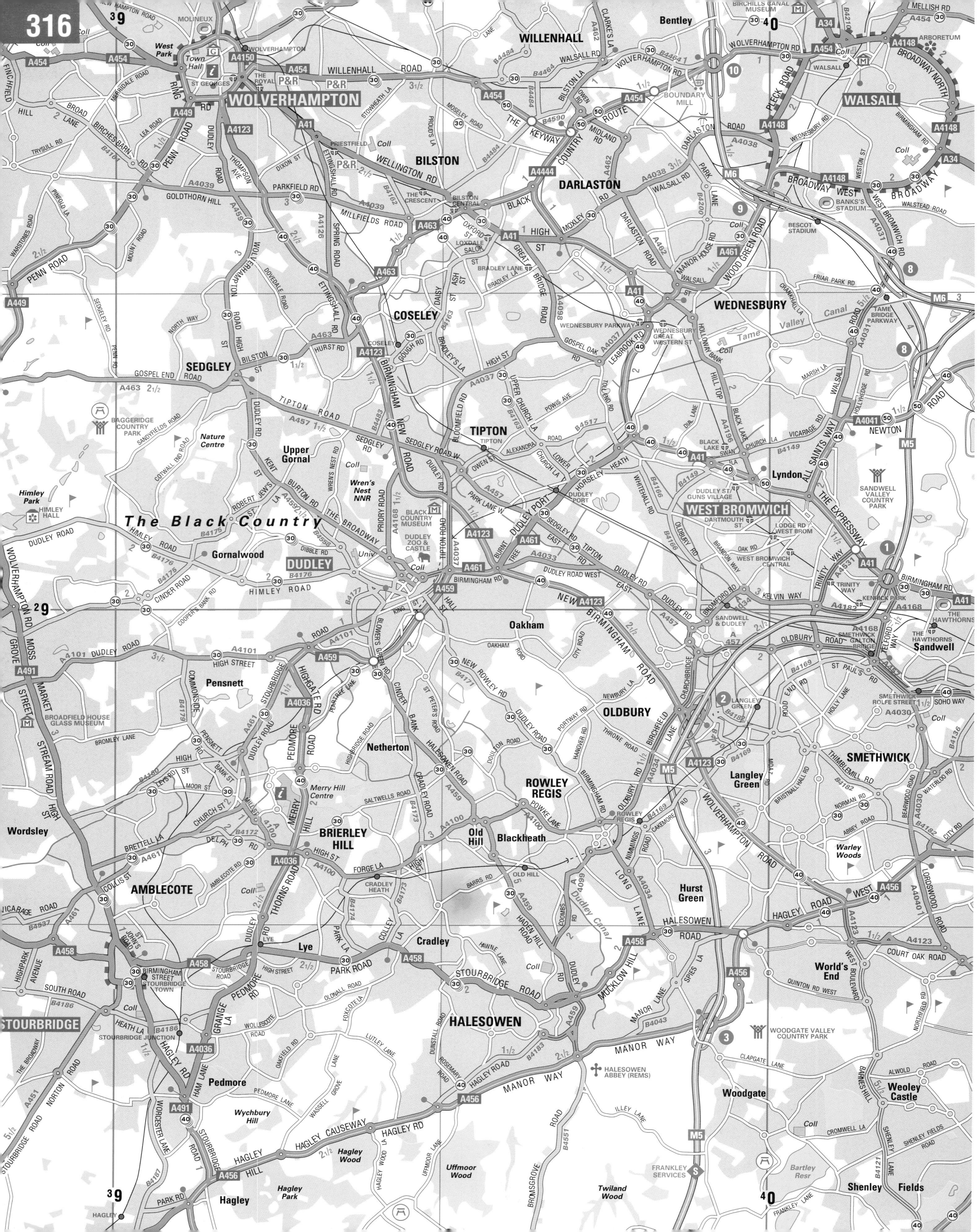

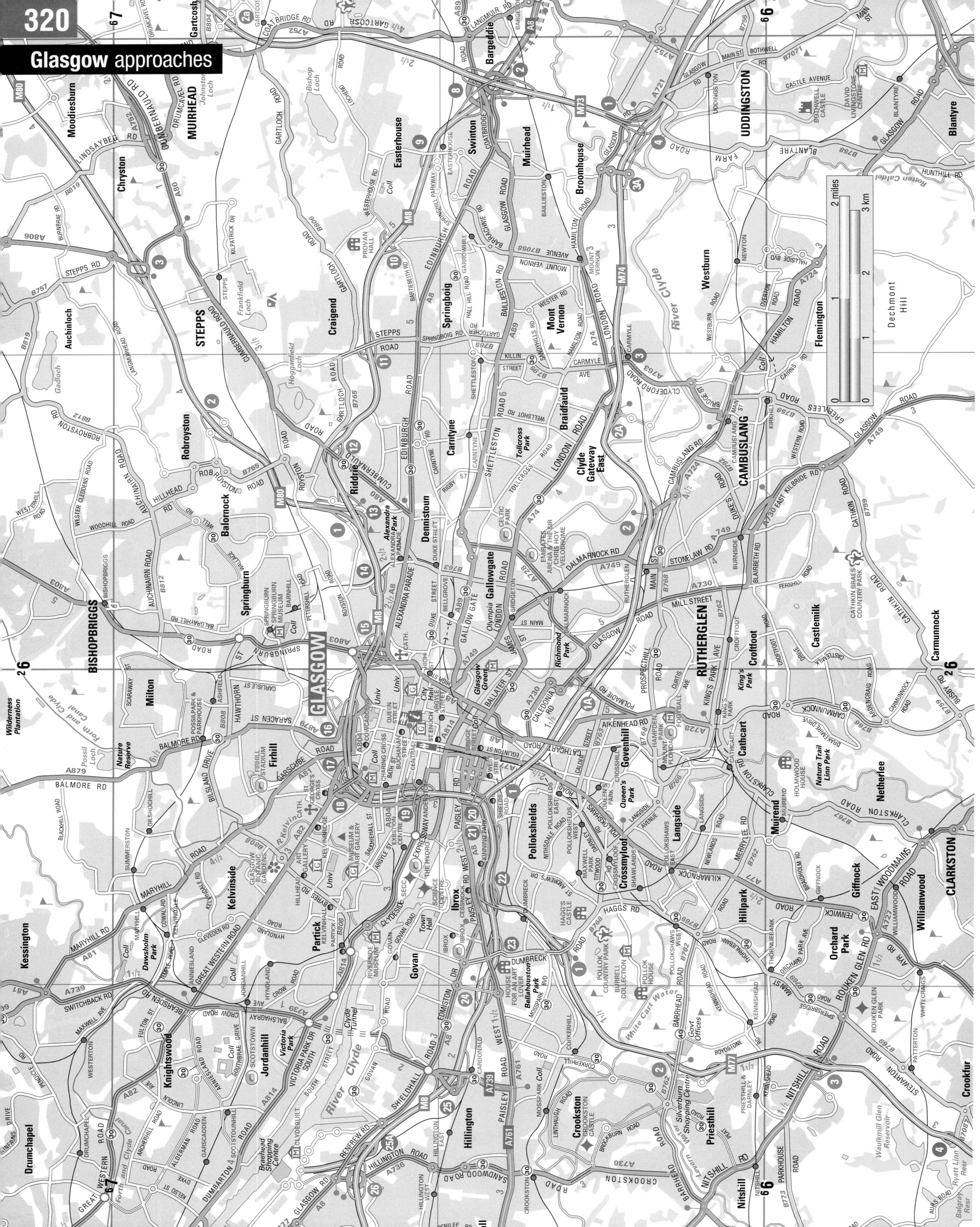

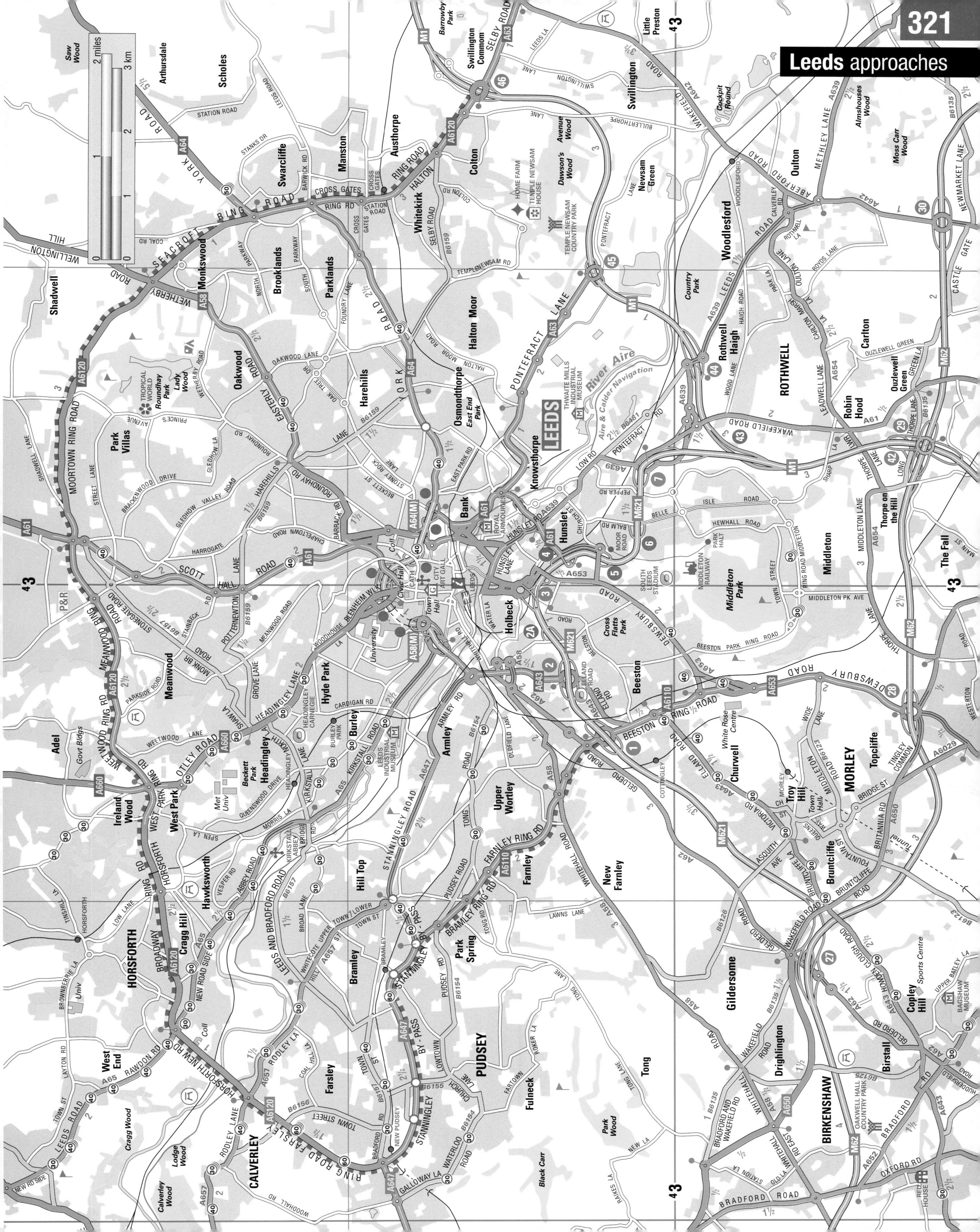

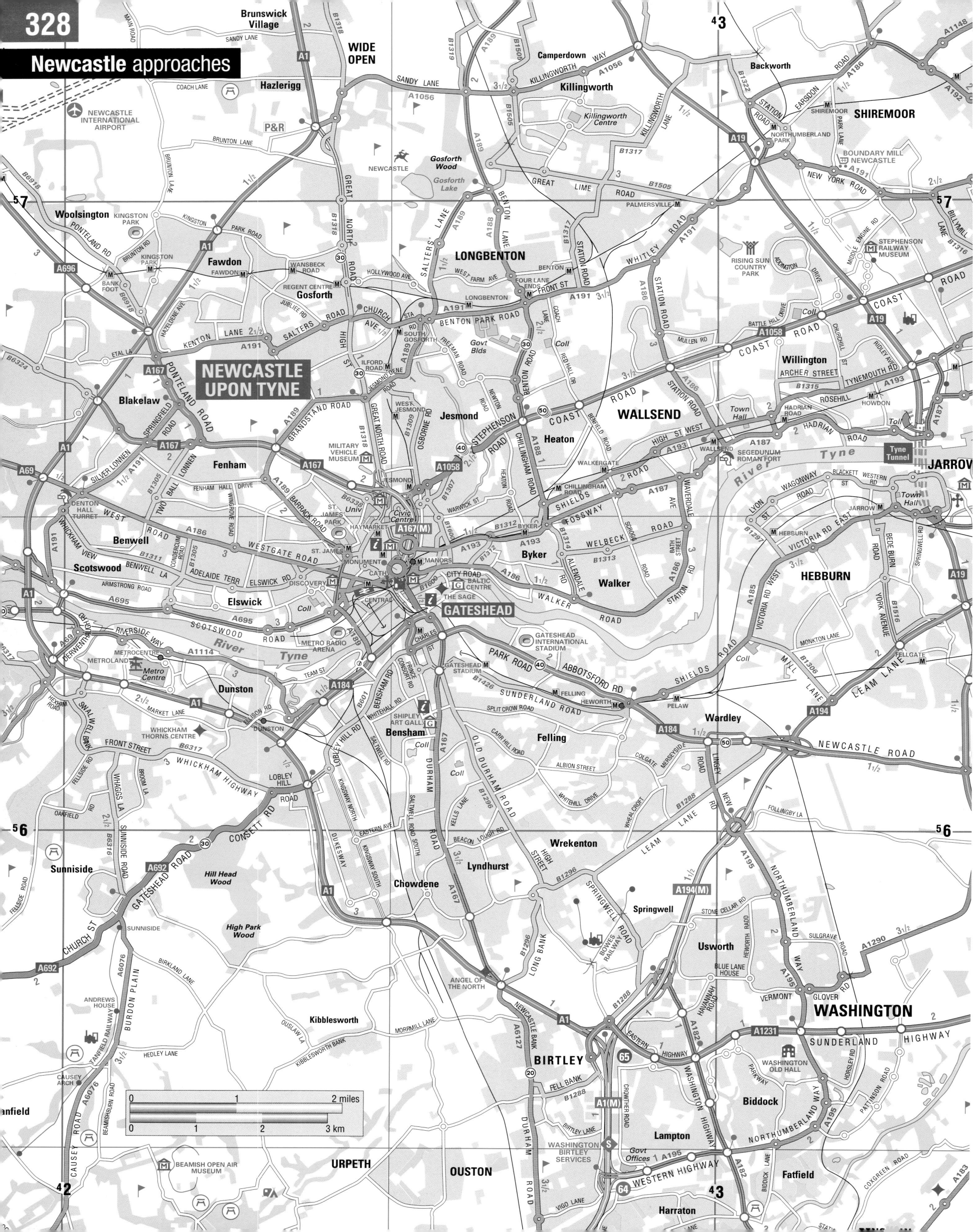

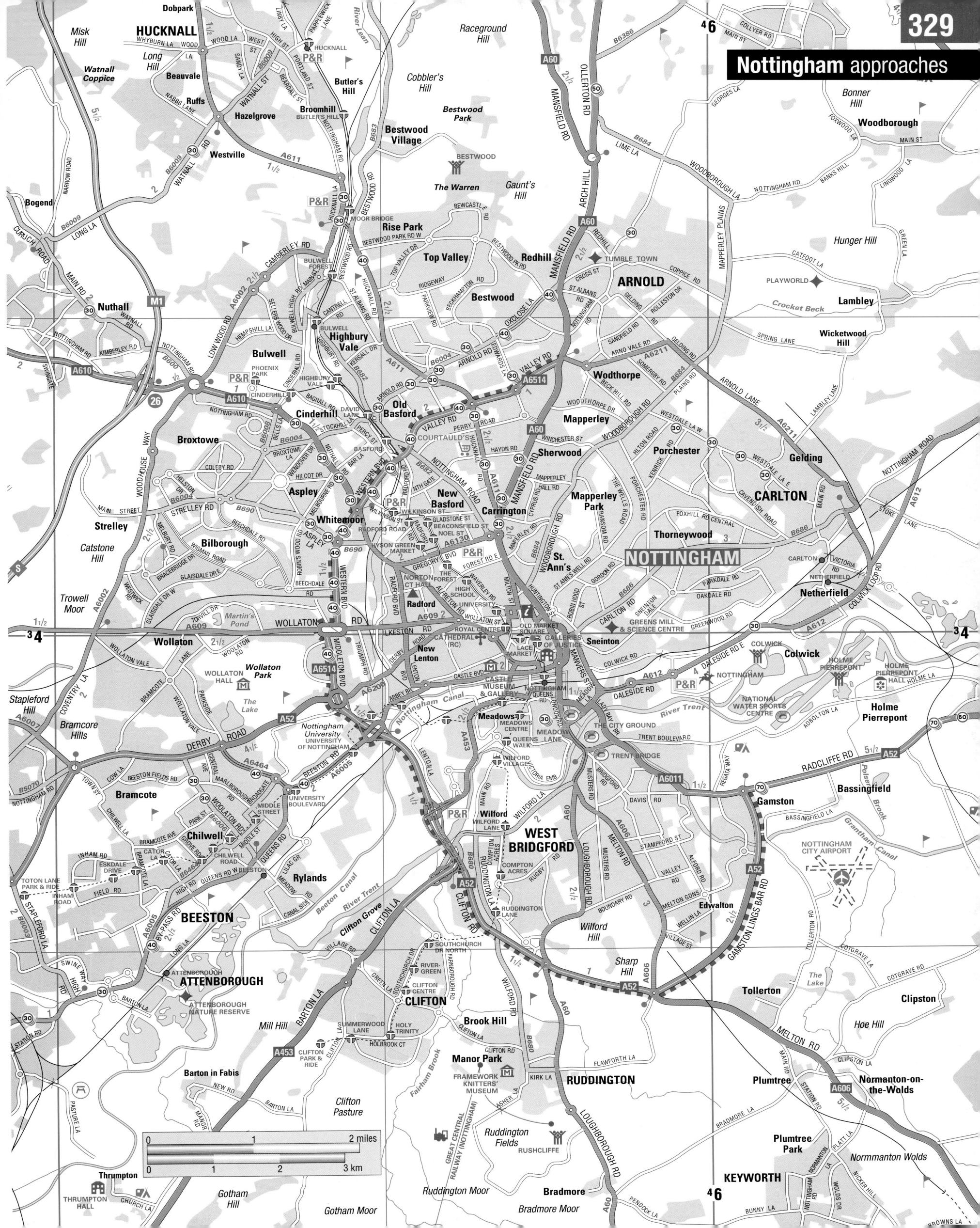

Aberdeen page 293 ● Aberystwyth page 128 ● Ashford page 54 ● Ayr page 257 ● Bangor page 179 ● Barrow-in-Furness page 210 ● Bath page 61 ● Berwick-upon-Tweed page 273

331

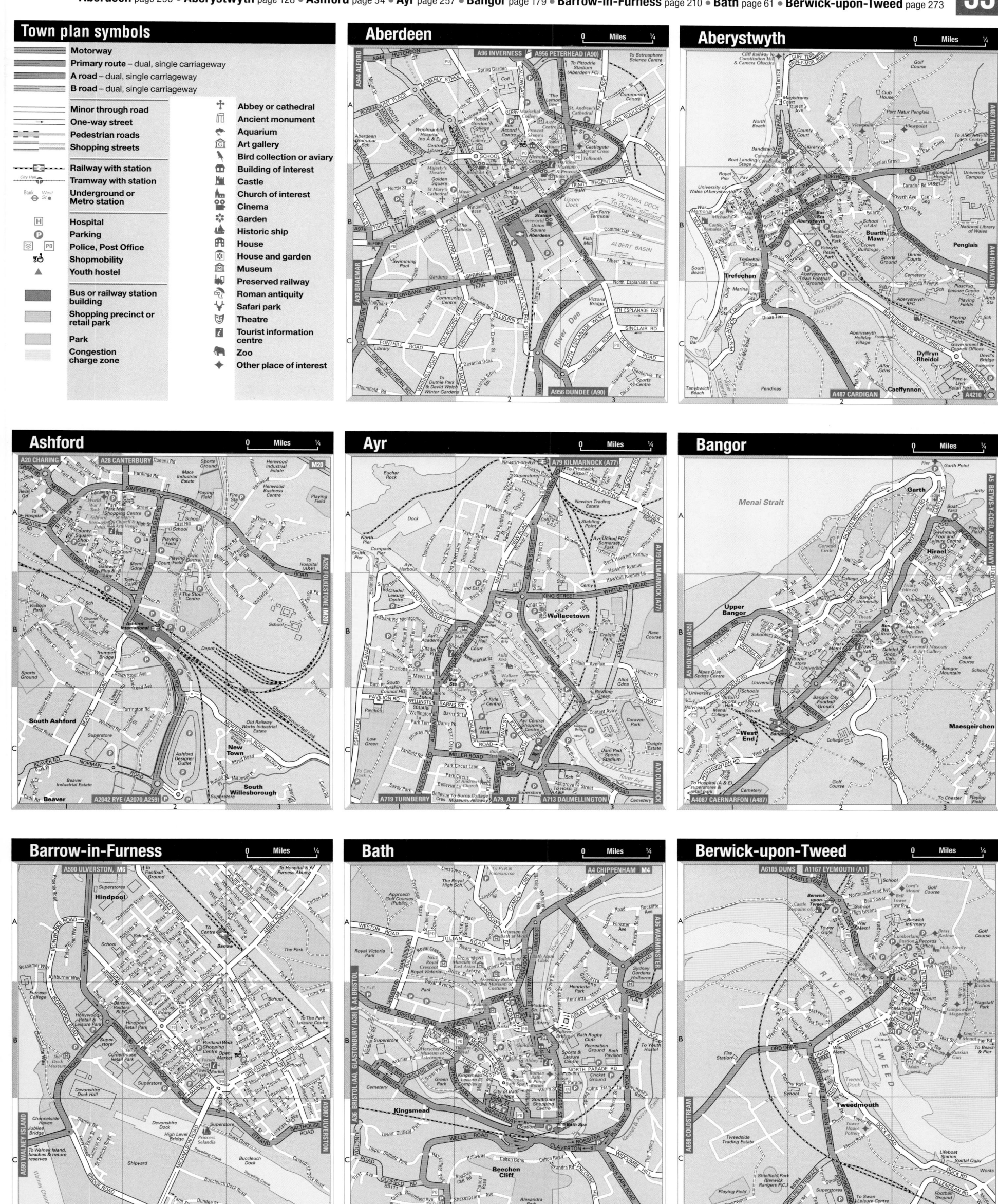

Birmingham

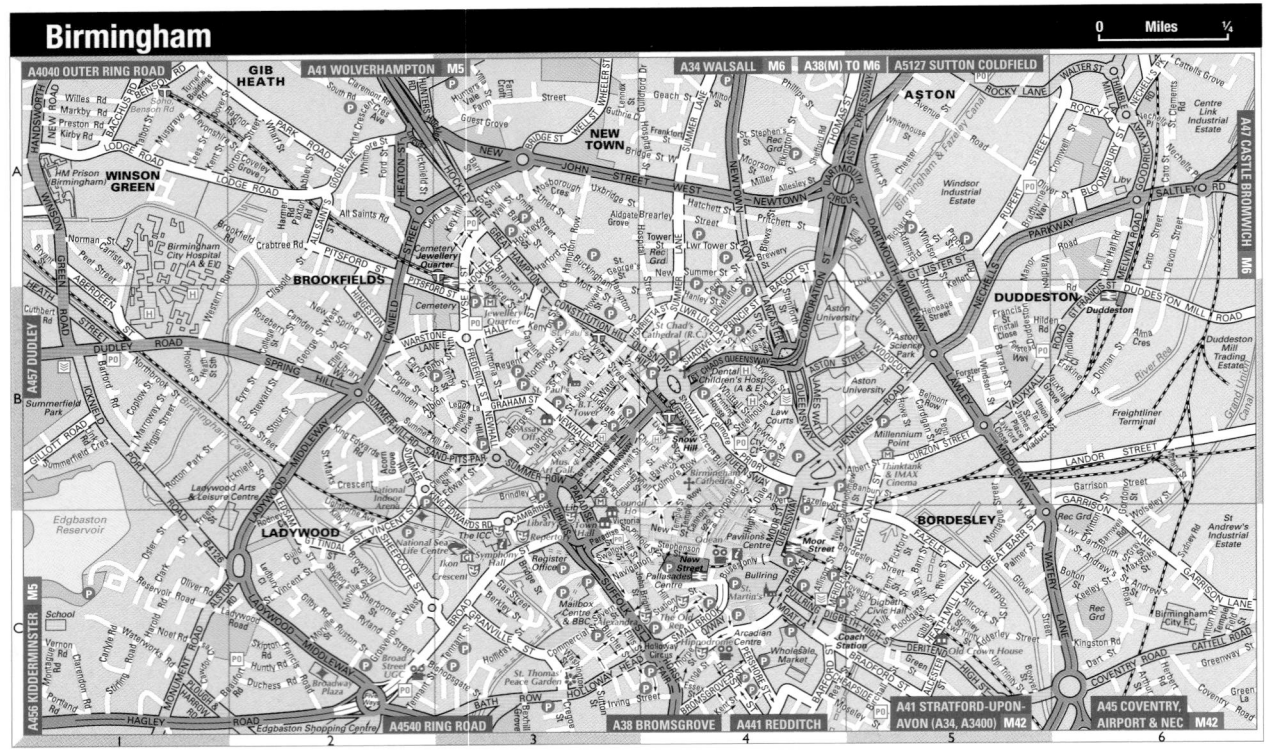

Blackpool

Bournemouth

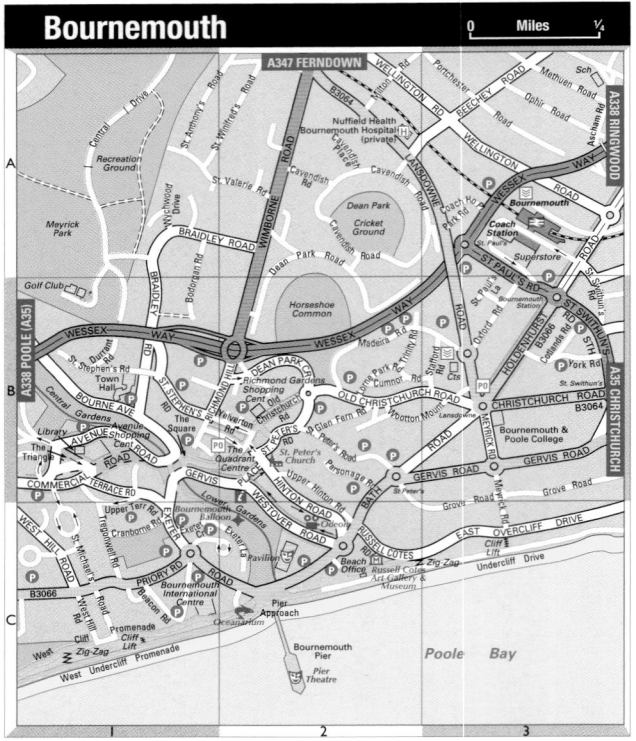

Bradford

Brighton

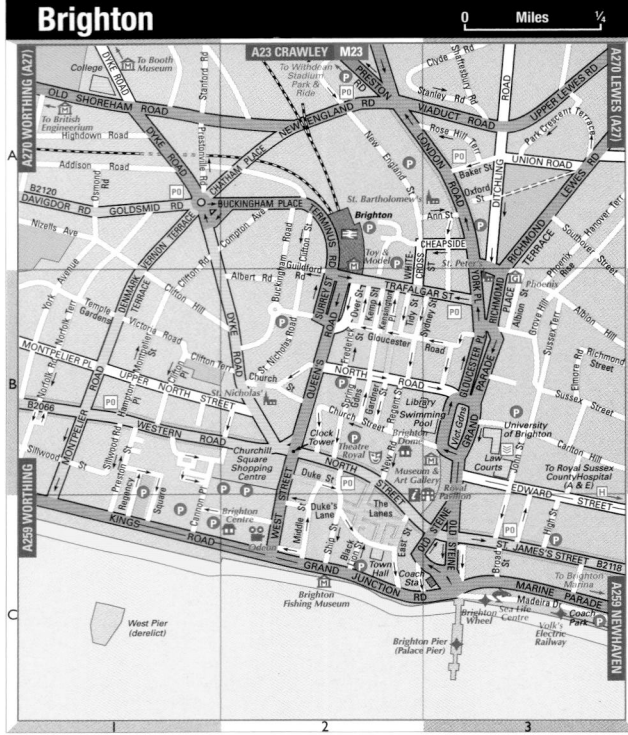

Bristol

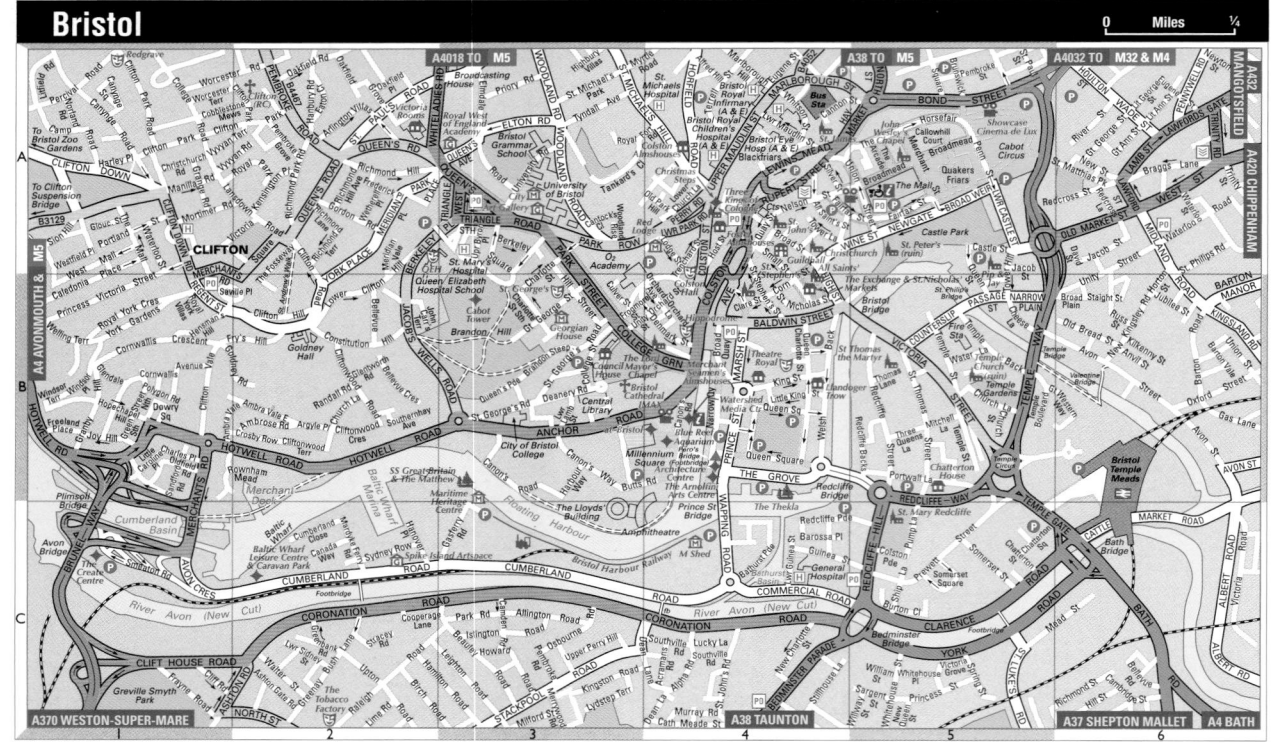

Bury St Edmunds

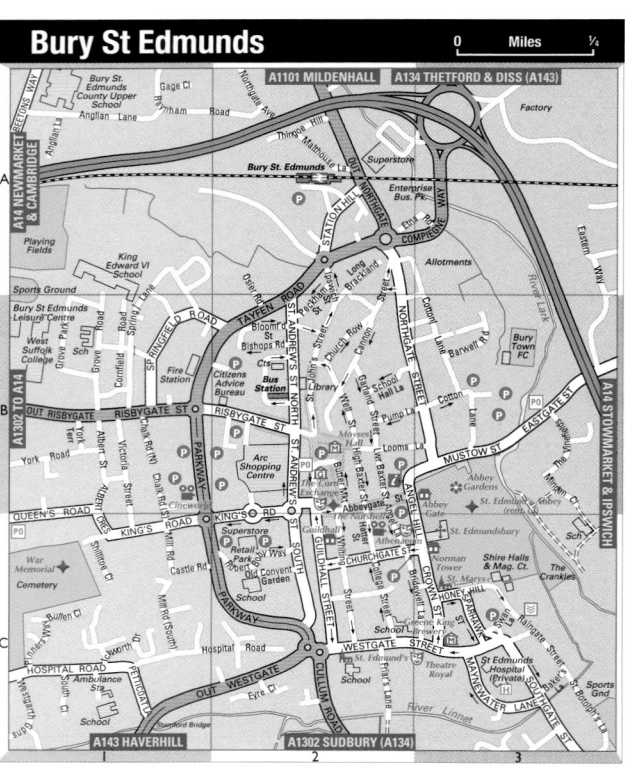

Cambridge page 123 ● Canterbury page 54 ● Cardiff page 59 ● Carlisle page 239 ● Chelmsford page 88 ● Cheltenham page 99 ● Chester page 166 ● Chichester page 22 ● Colchester page 107

333

334

Coventry page 118 ● **Derby** page 153 ● **Dorchester** page 17 ● **Dumfries** page 237 ● **Dundee** page 287 ● **Durham** page 233 ● **Edinburgh** page 280 ● **Exeter** page 14

Coventry

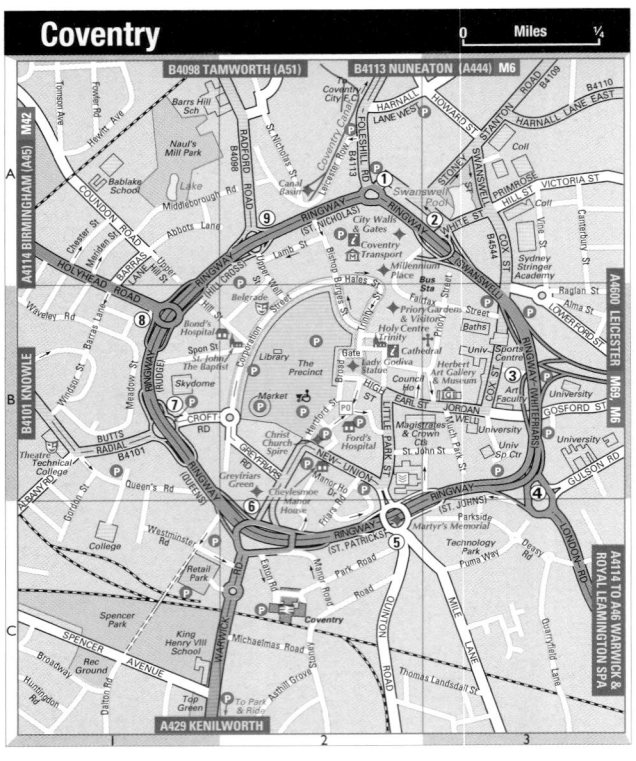

Derby

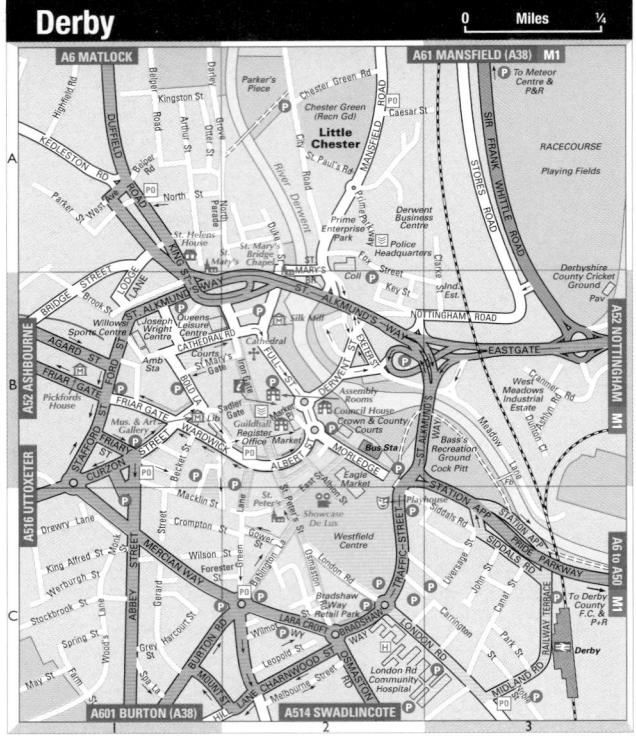

Dorchester

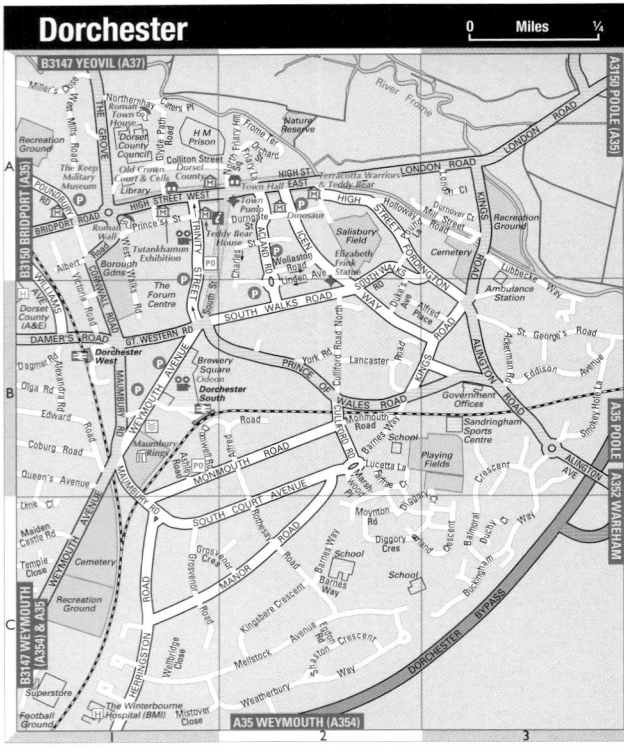

Dumfries

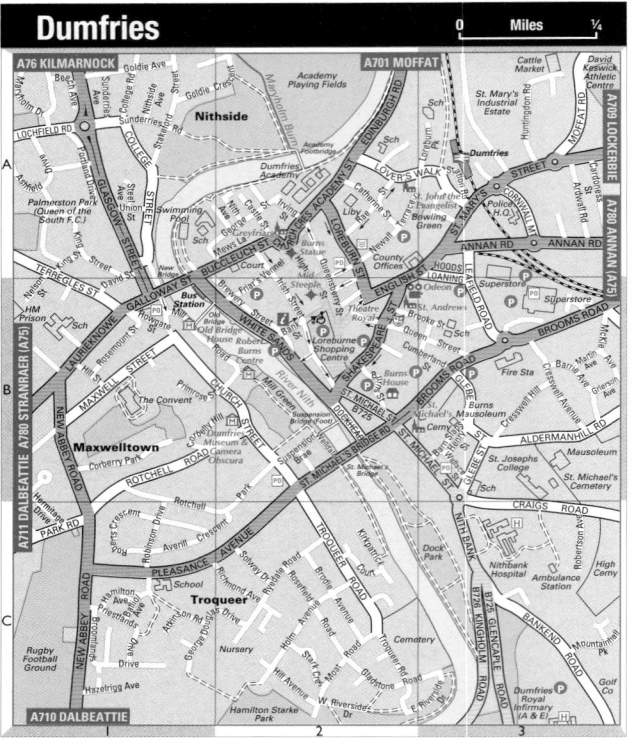

Dundee

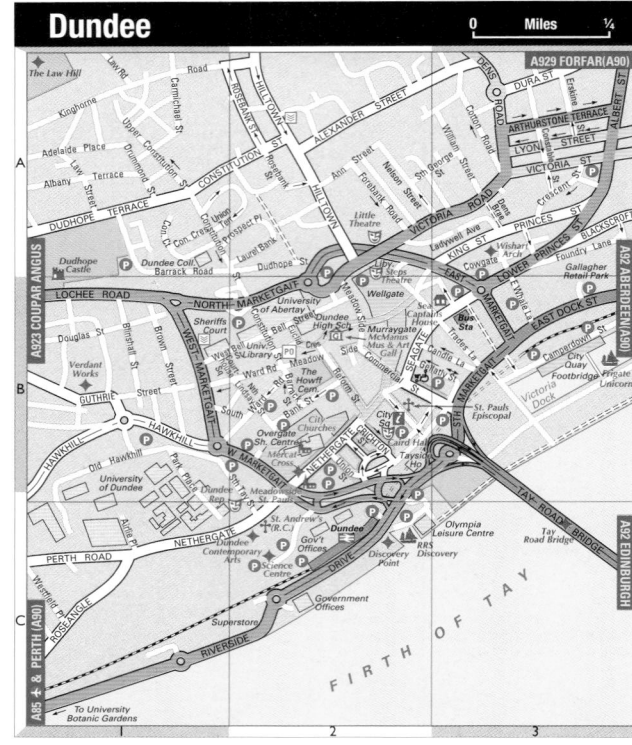

Durham

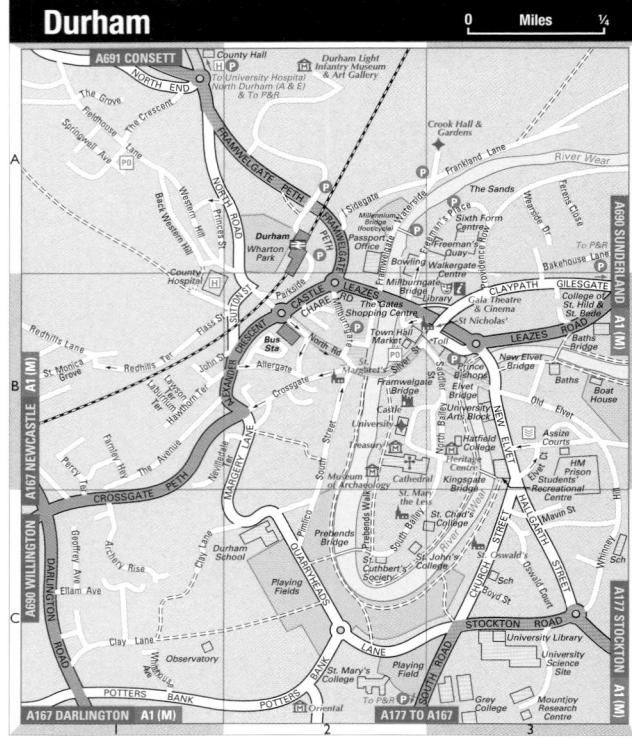

Edinburgh

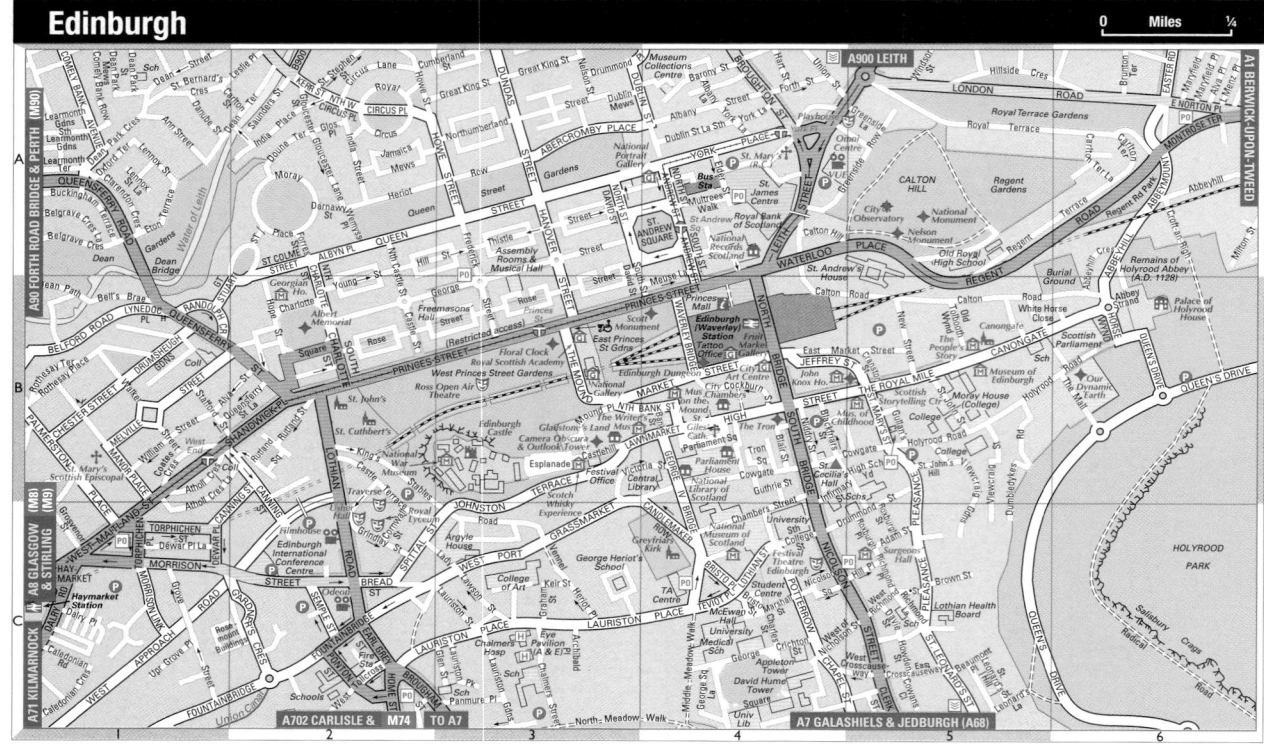

Exeter

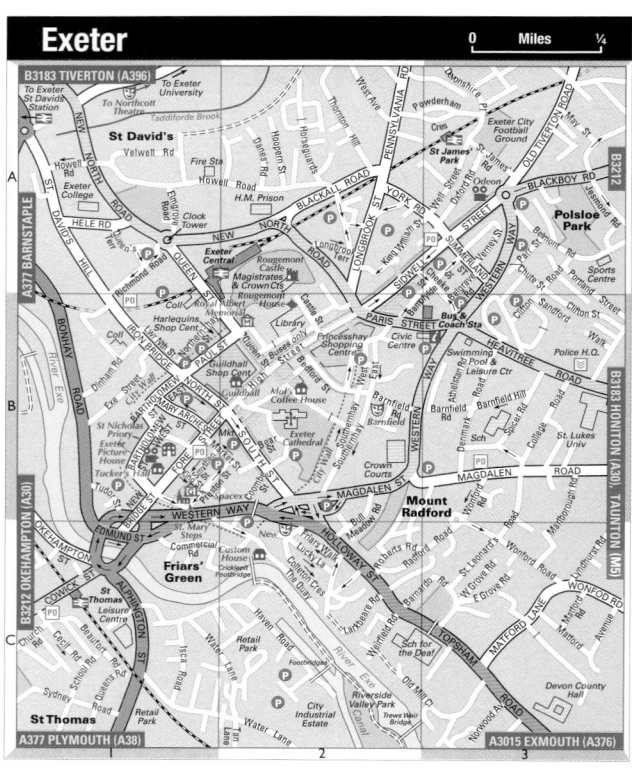

Fort William

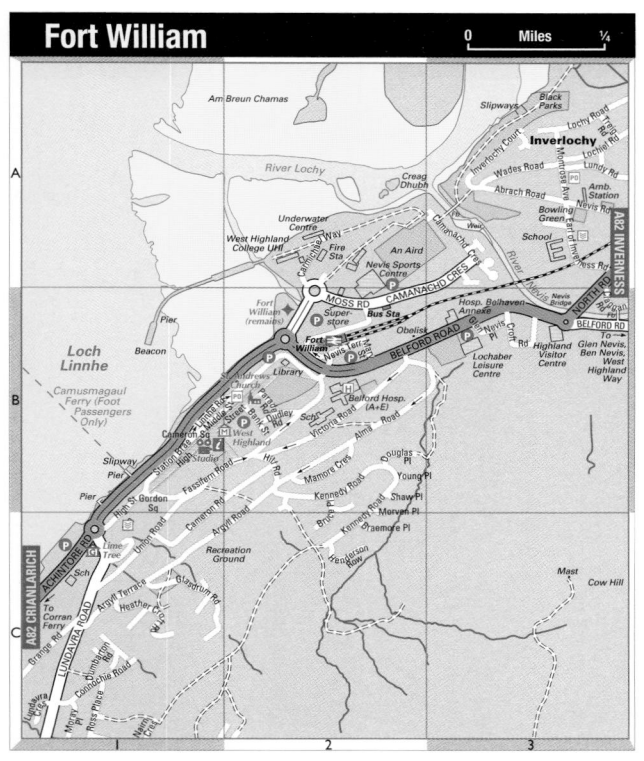

Glasgow

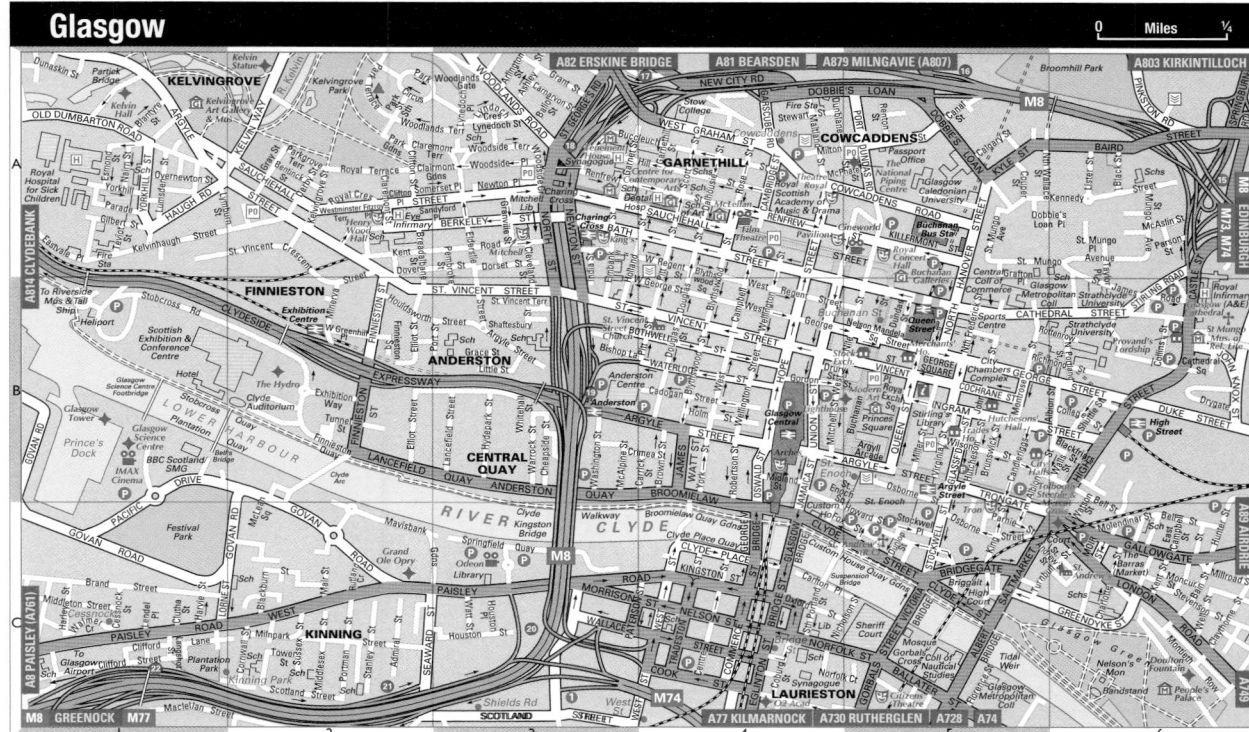

Gloucester

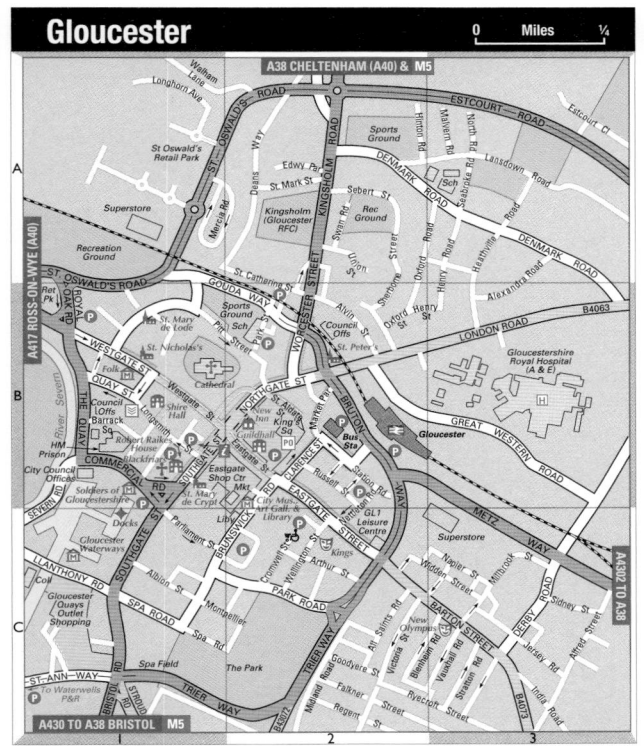

Grimsby

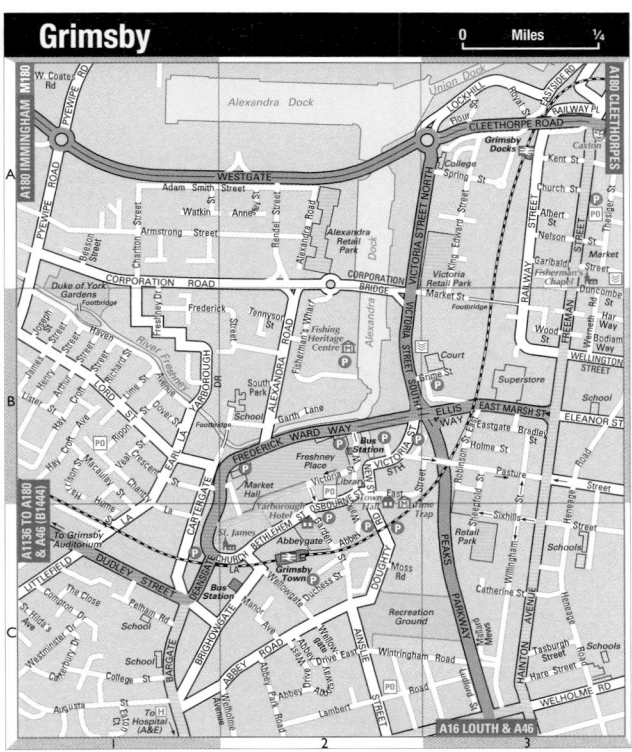

Hanley (Stoke-on-Trent)

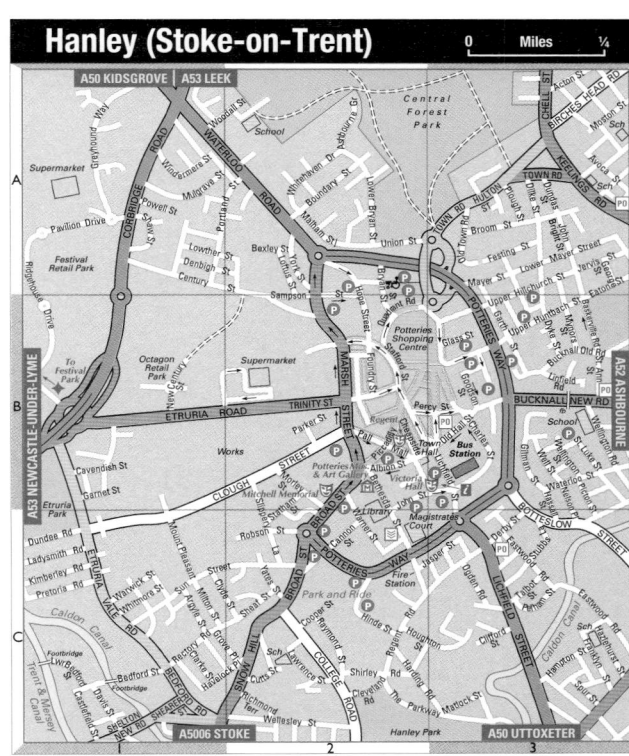

Harrogate

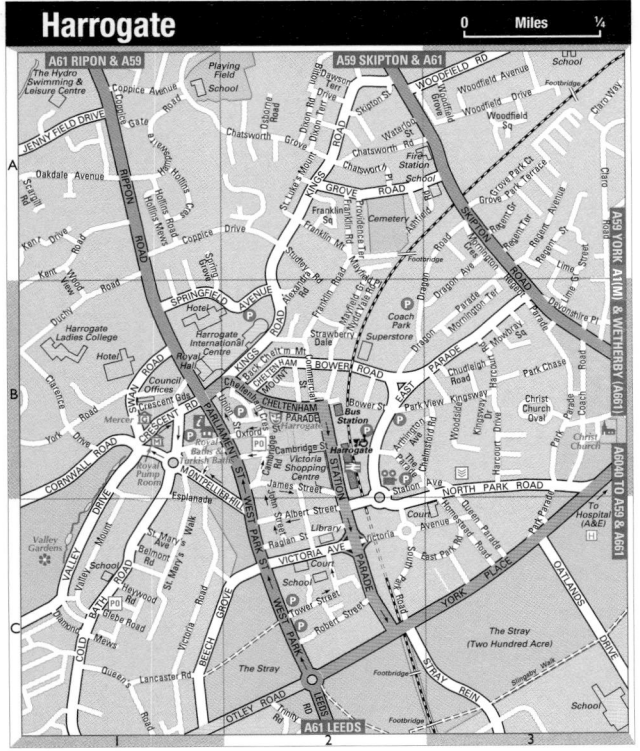

Holyhead / Caergybi

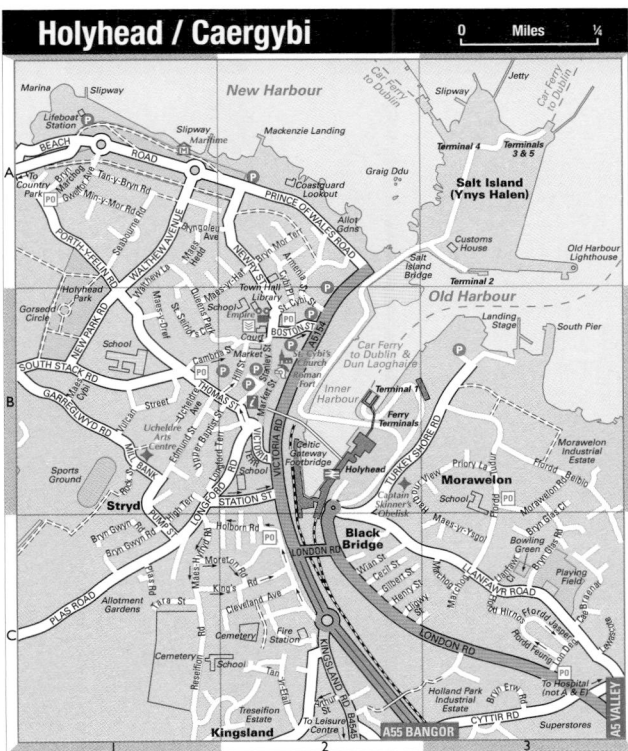

Hull

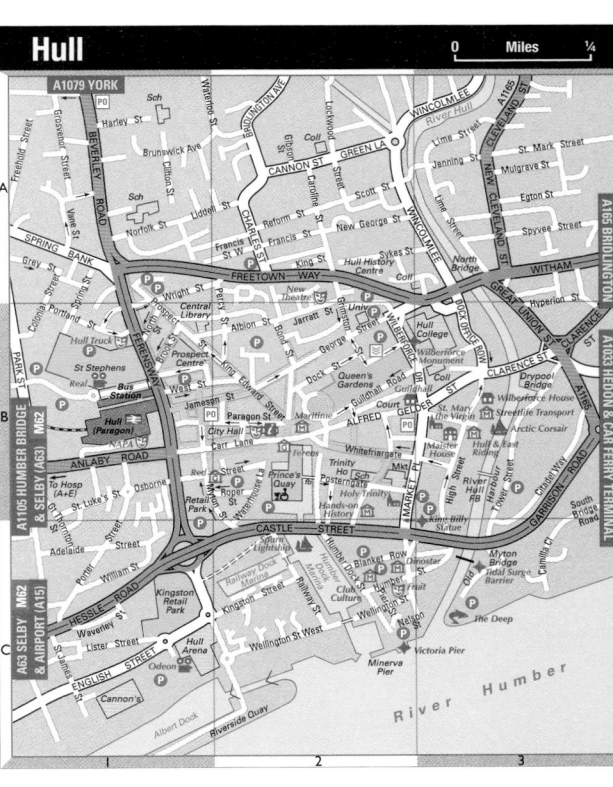

Inverness

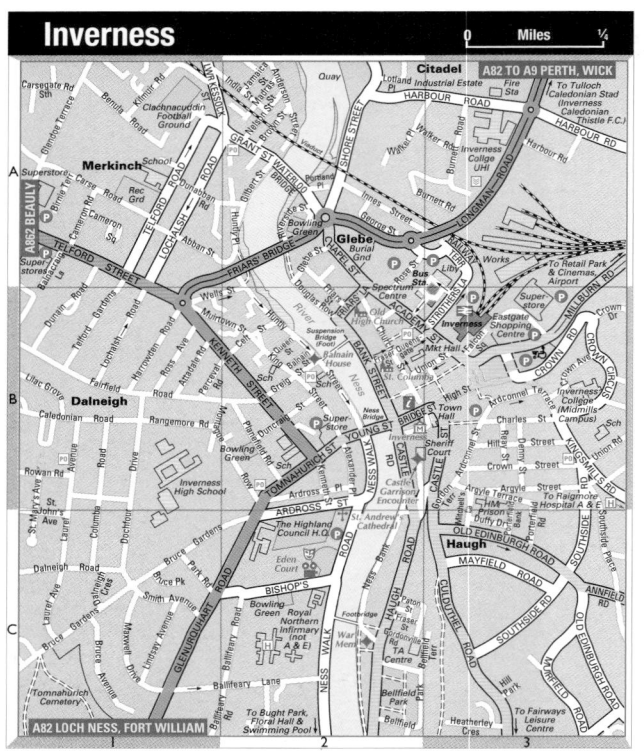

Ipswich

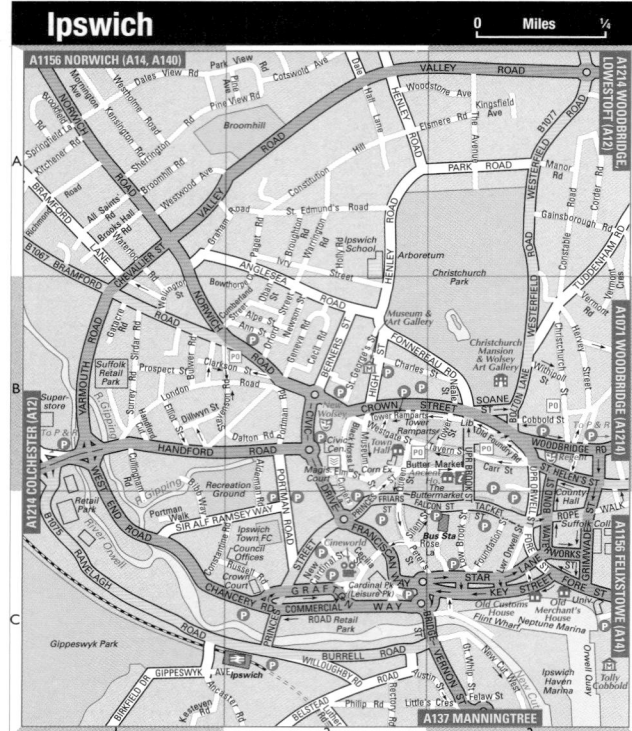

Kendal

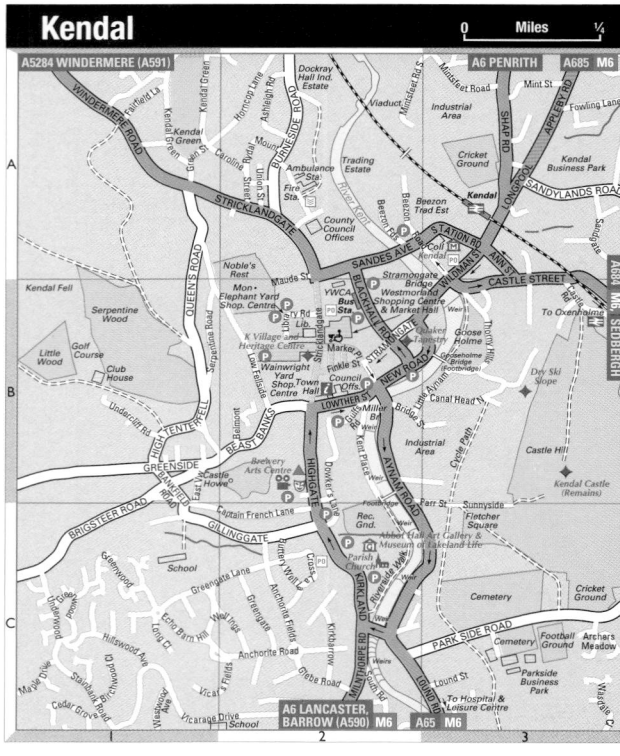

King's Lynn

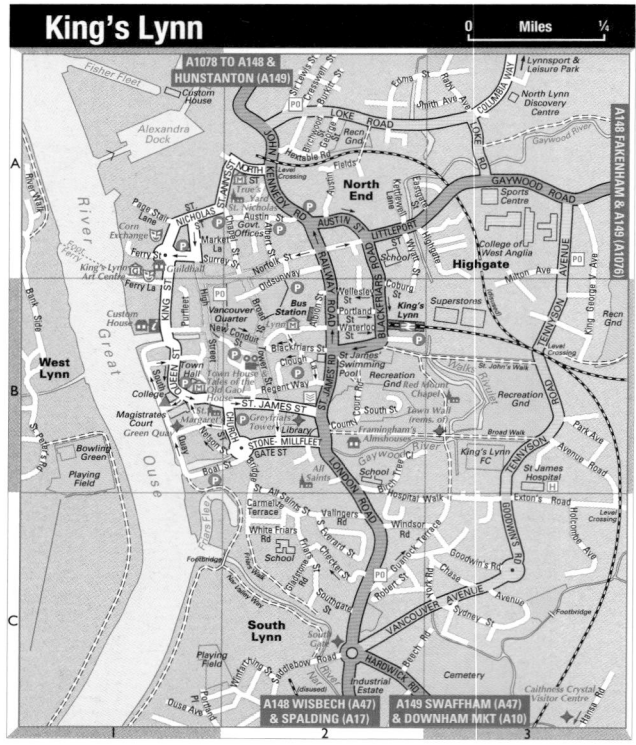

Leeds

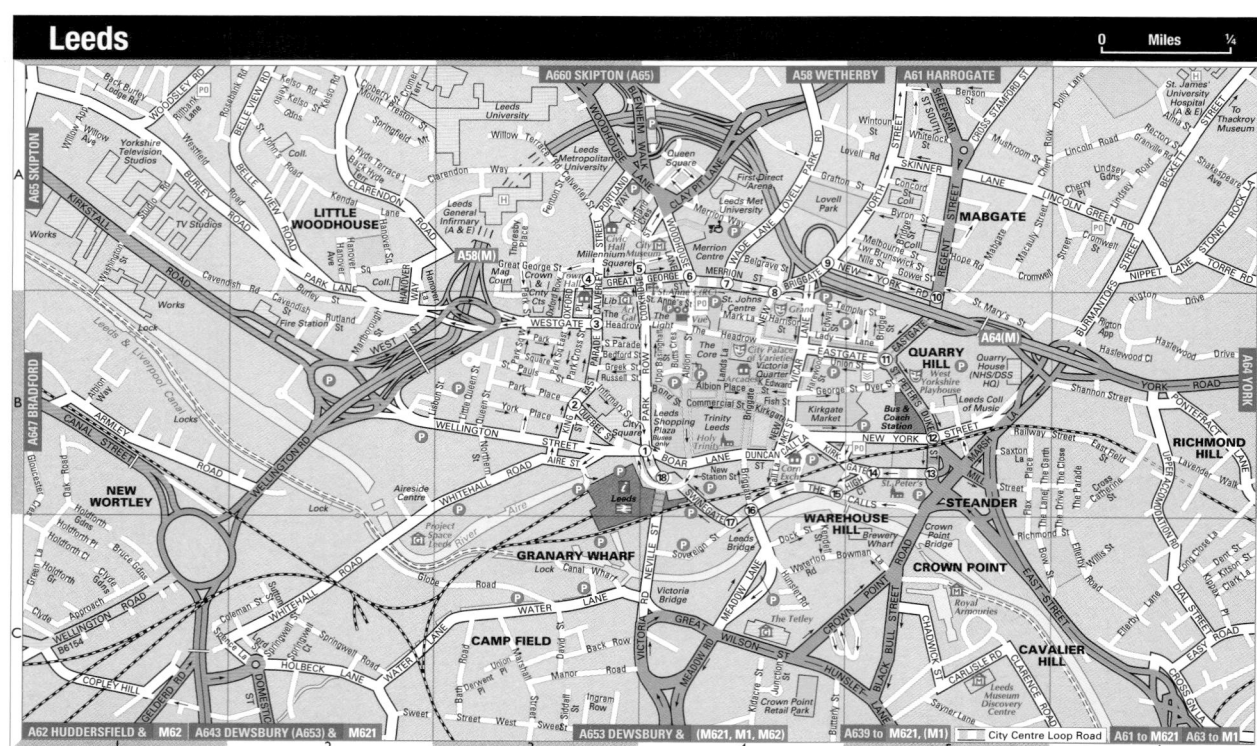

Lancaster

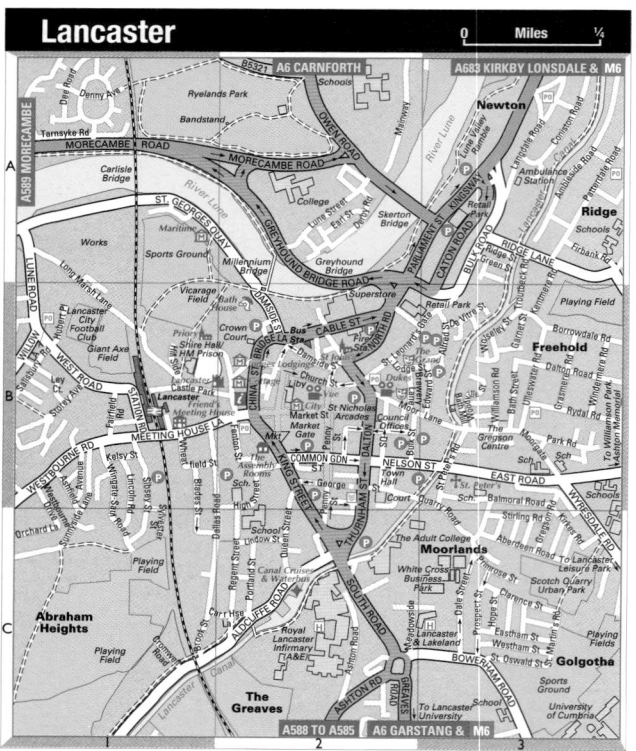

Leicester

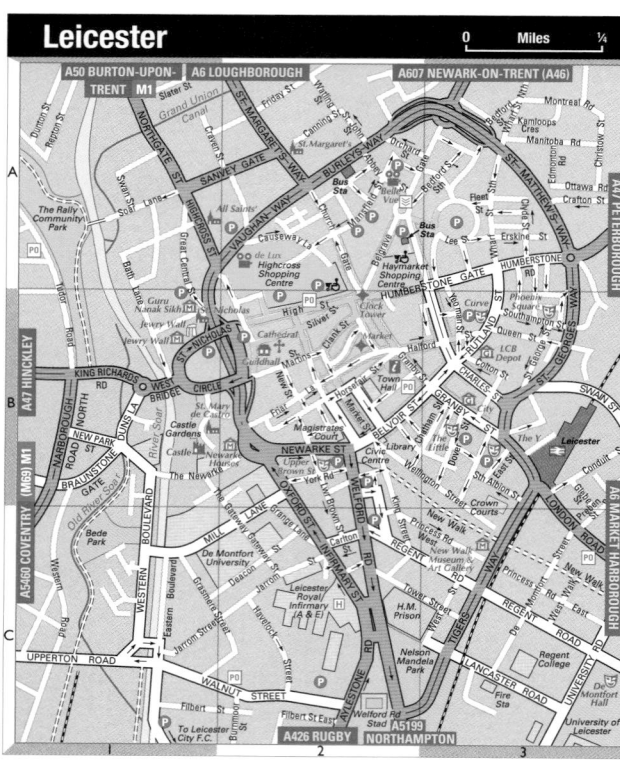

Lewes

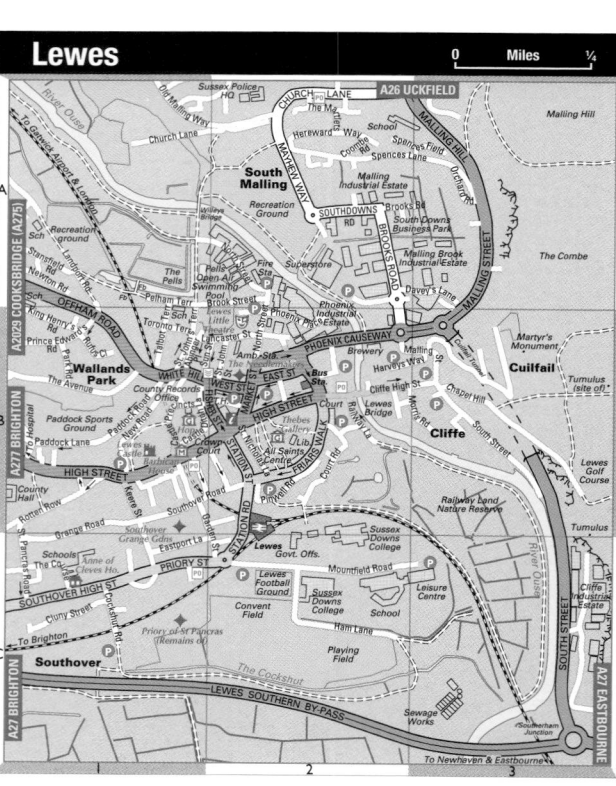

Lincoln page 189 ● **Liverpool** page 182 ● **Llandudno** page 180 ● **Llanelli** page 56 ● **Luton** page 103 ● **Macclesfield** page 184 ● **Manchester** page 184

337

Lincoln

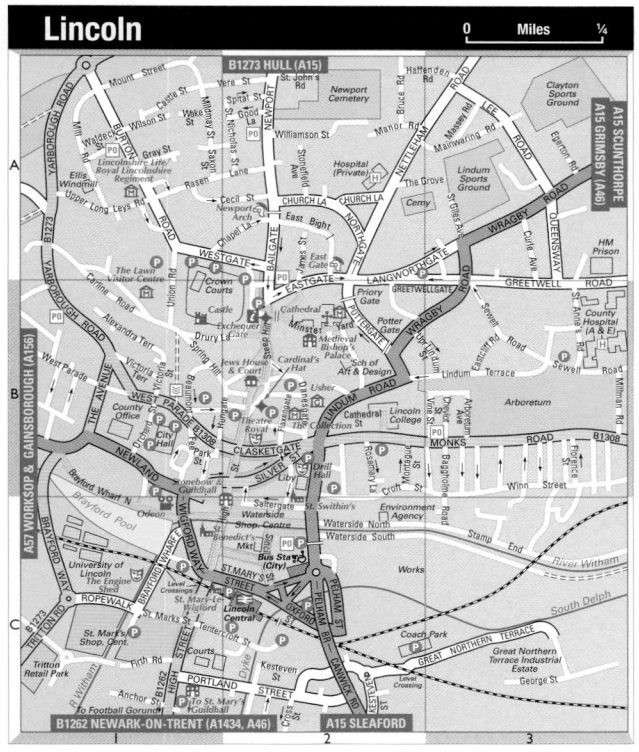

Liverpool

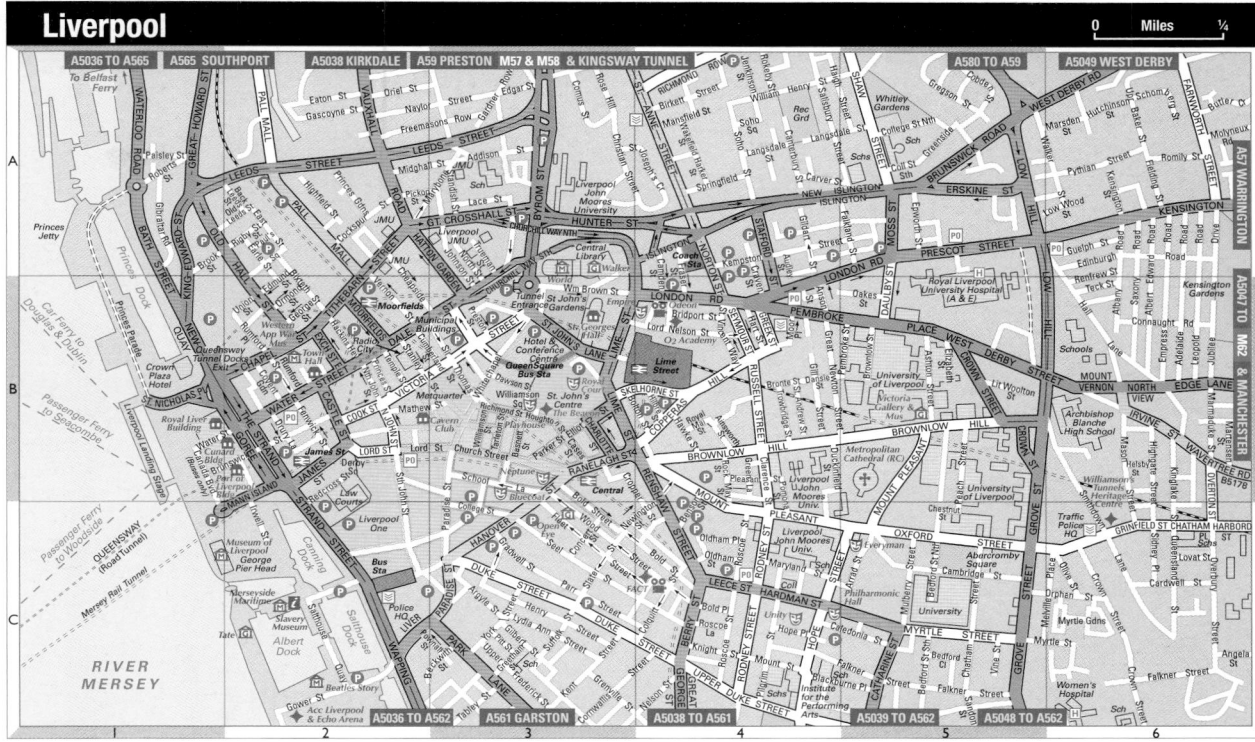

Llandudno

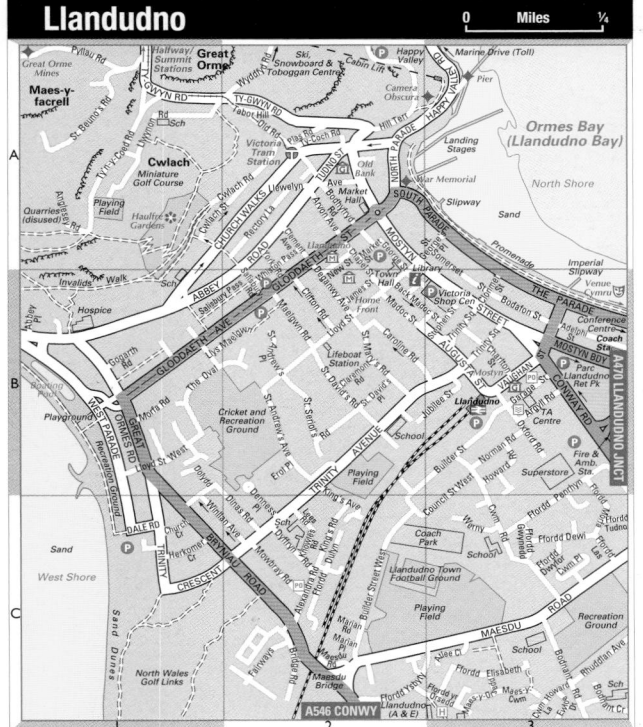

Llanelli

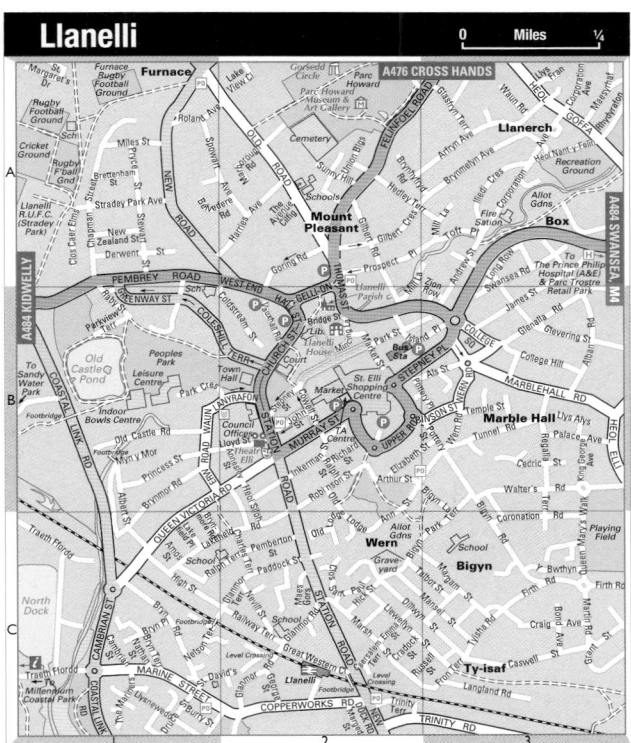

Luton

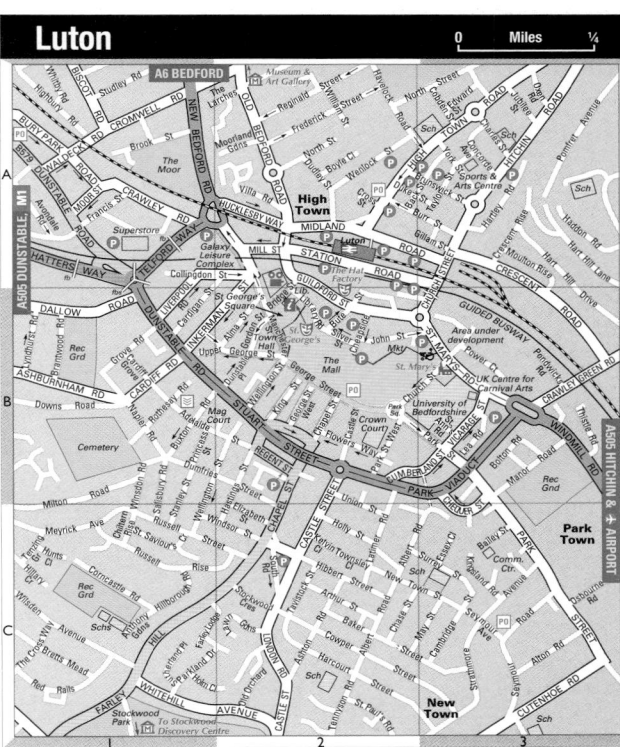

Macclesfield

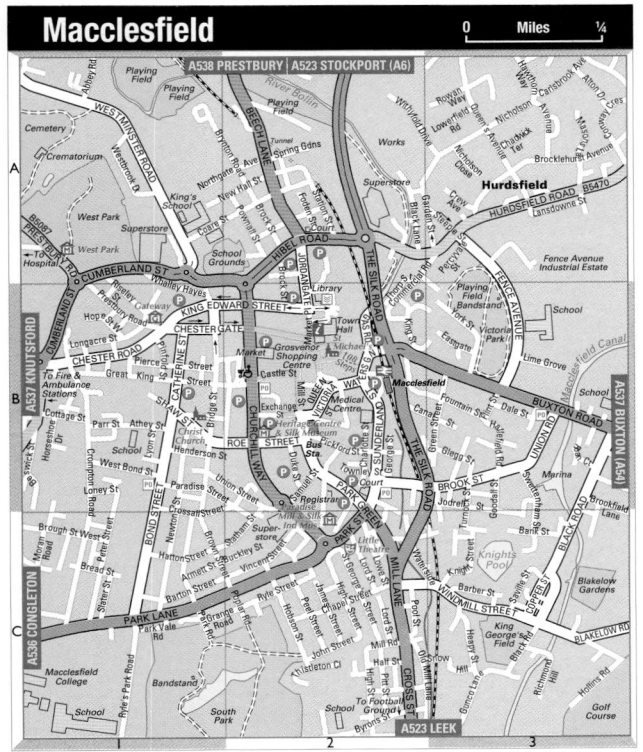

Manchester

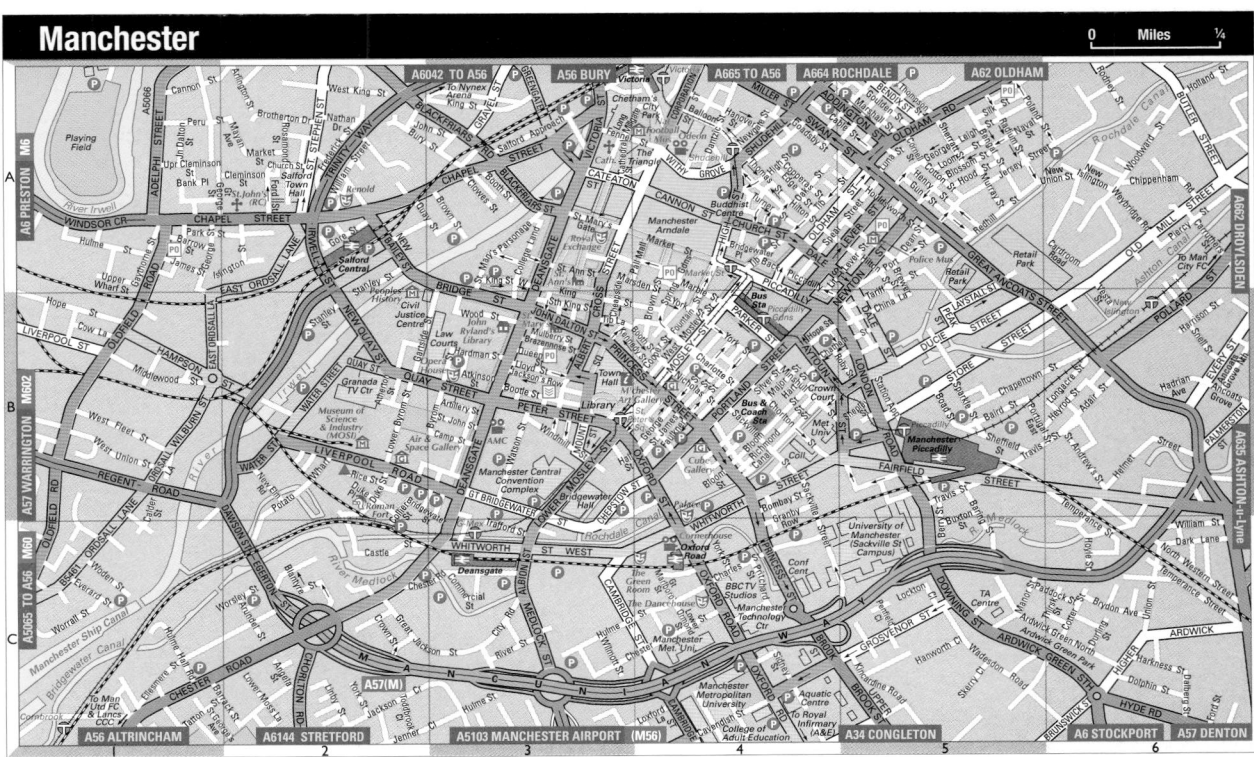

Maidstone

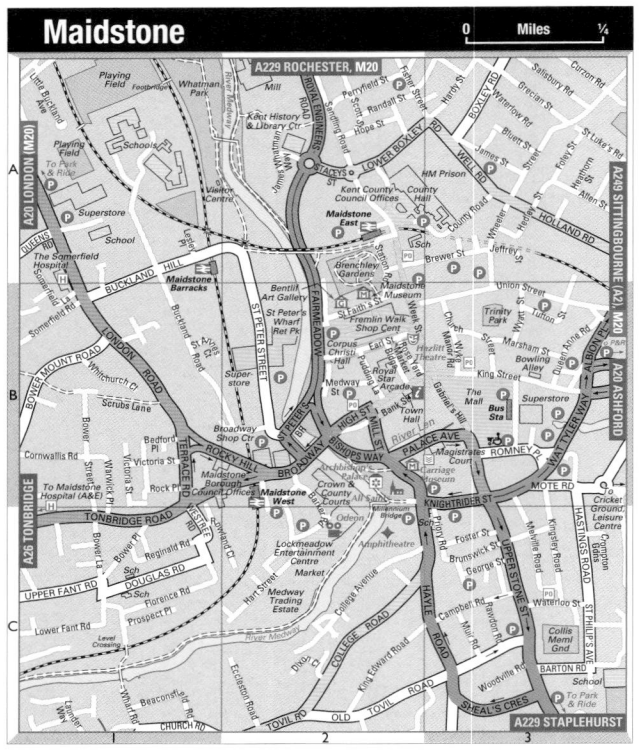

Merthyr Tydfil / Merthyr Tudful

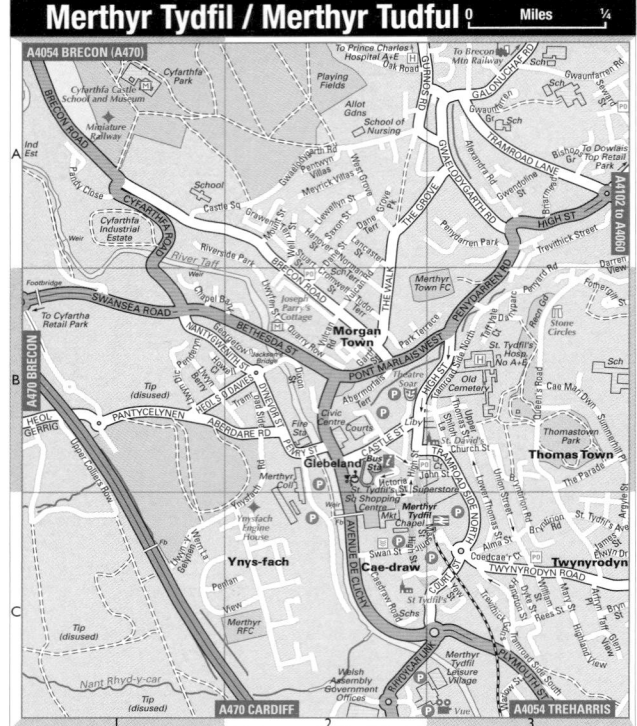

Middlesbrough

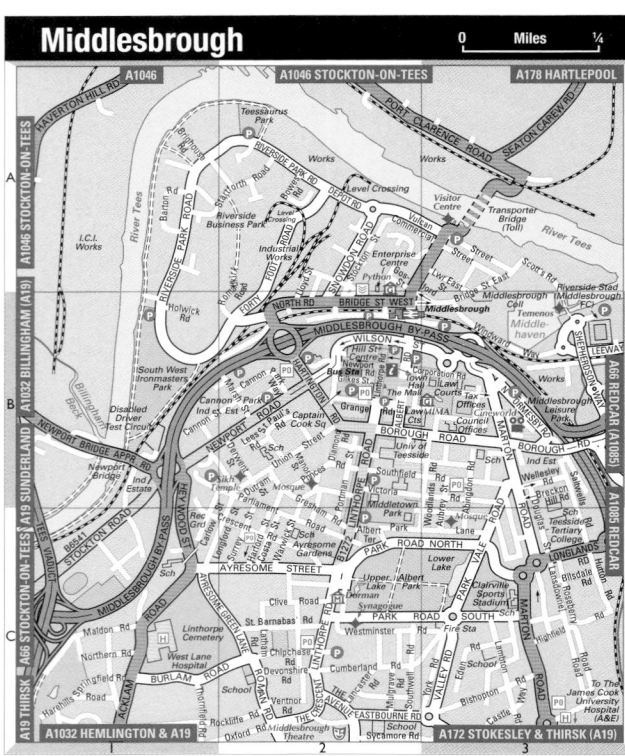

Milton Keynes

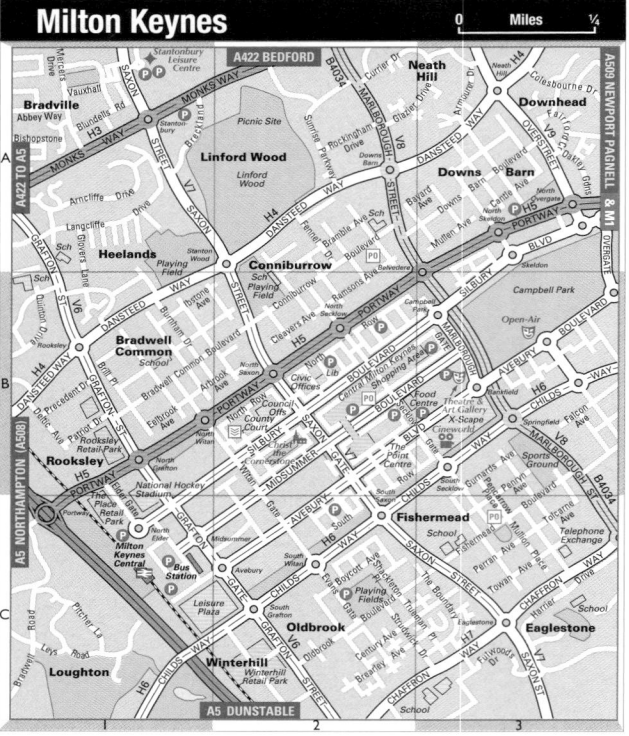

Newcastle upon Tyne

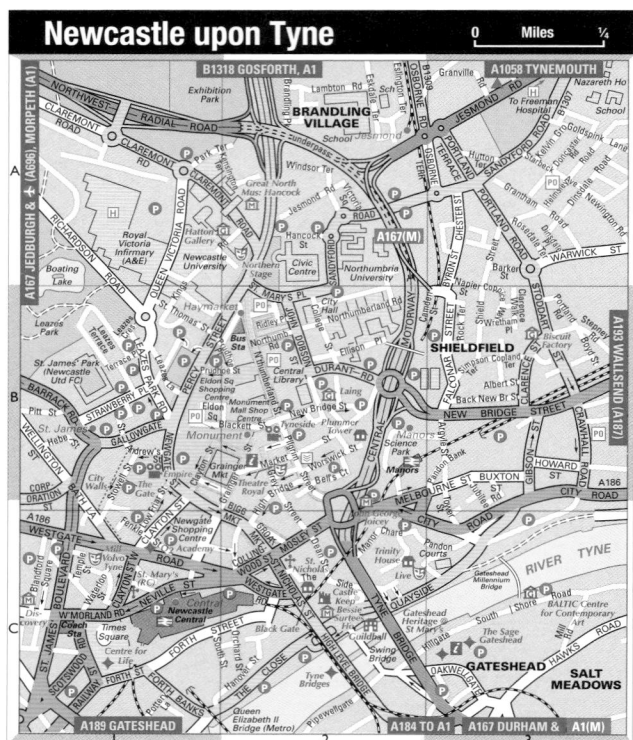

Newport / Casnewydd

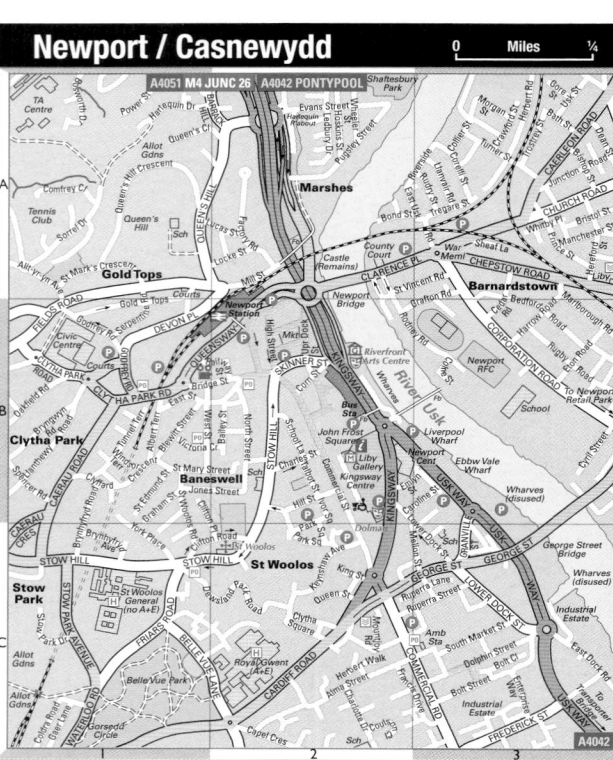

Newquay

Newtown / Y Drenewydd

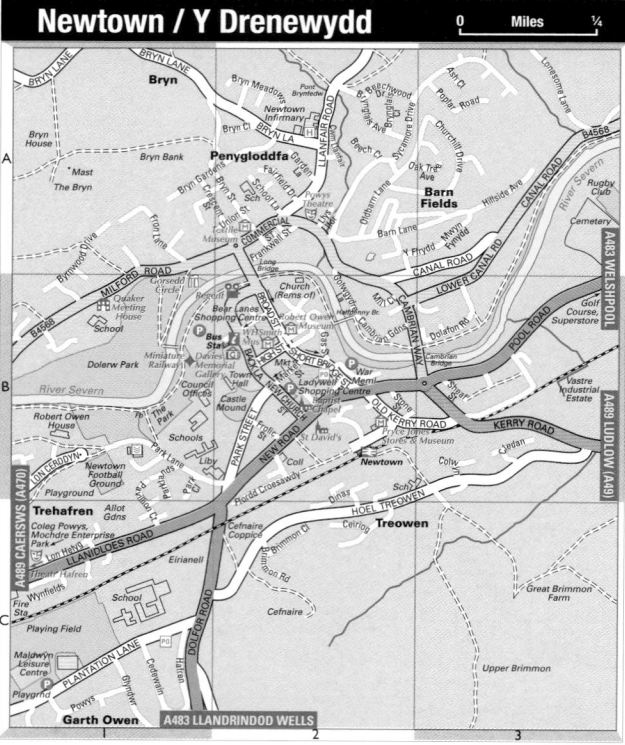

Northampton

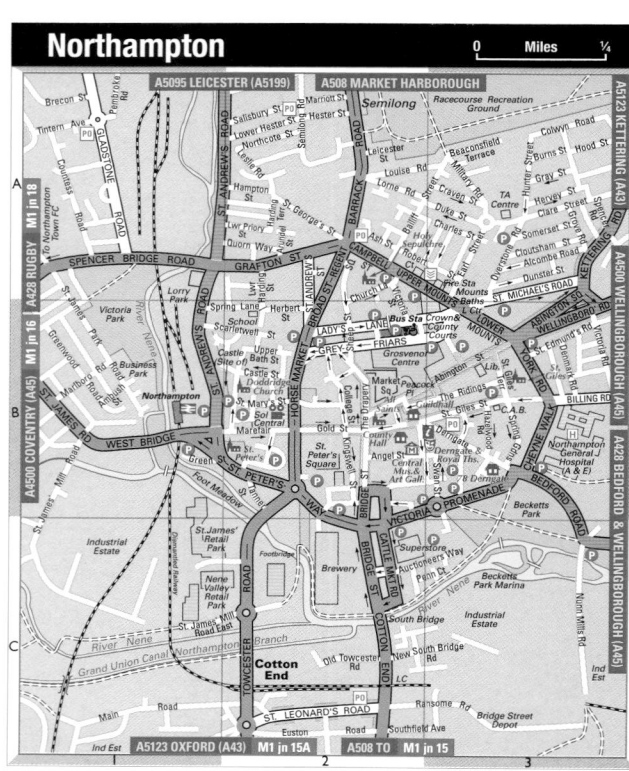

Norwich

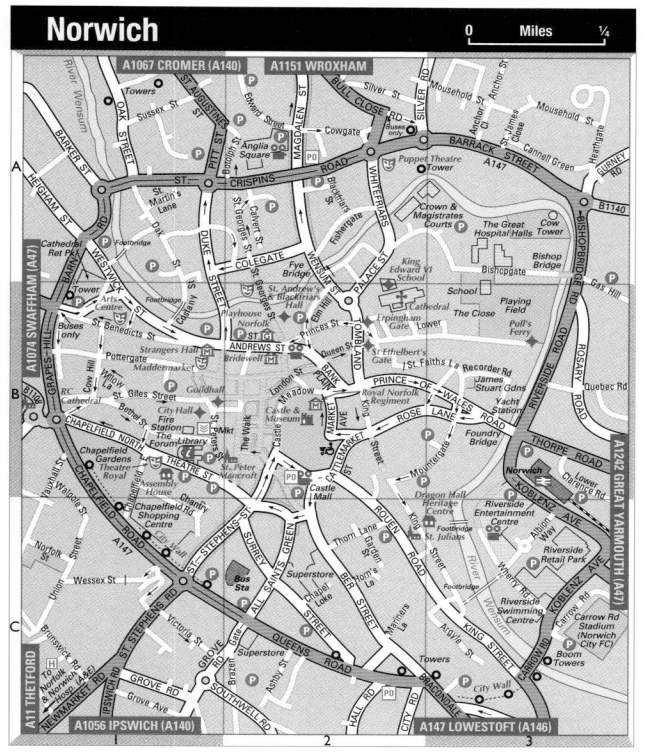

Nottingham

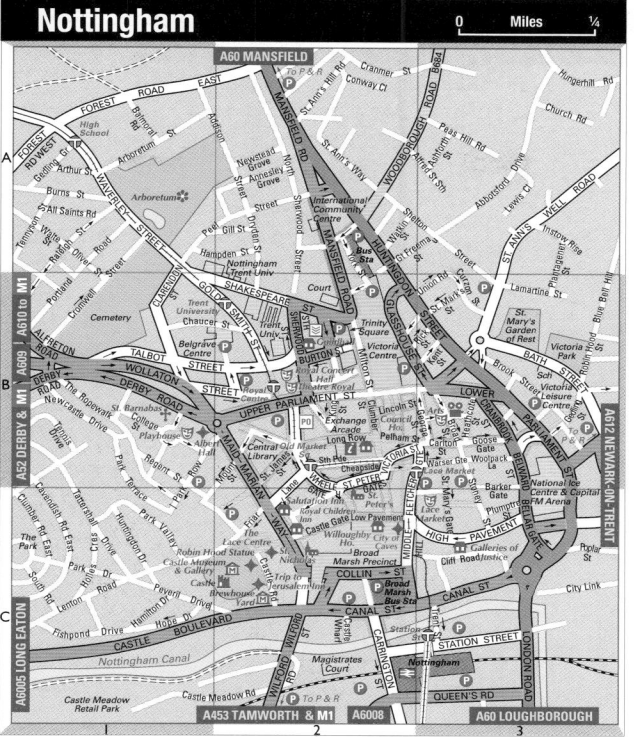

Oban

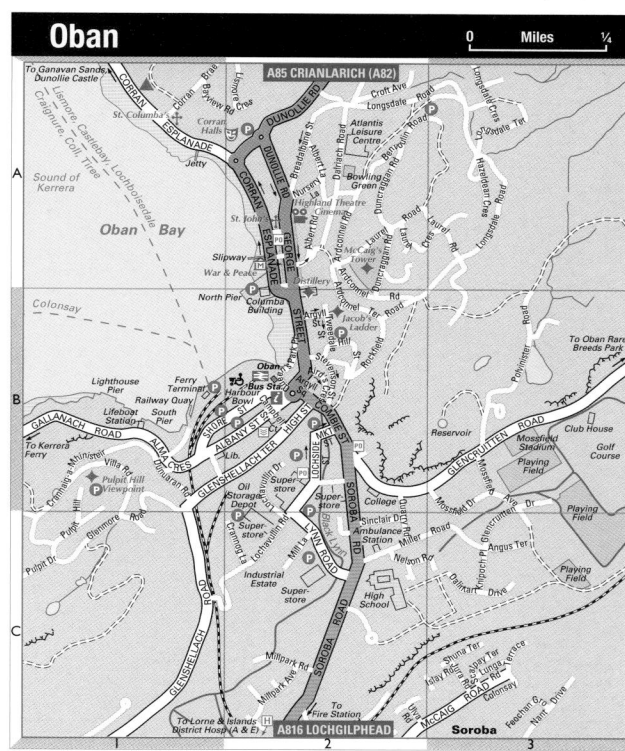

Oxford

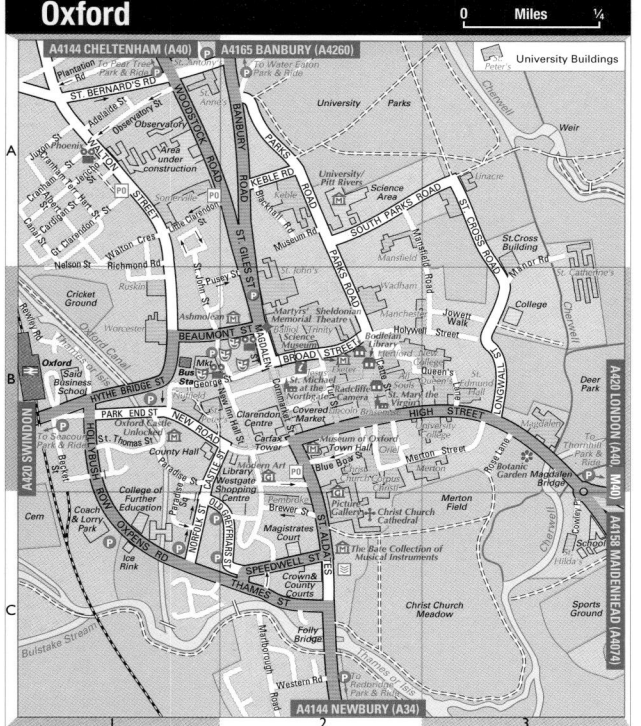

Perth

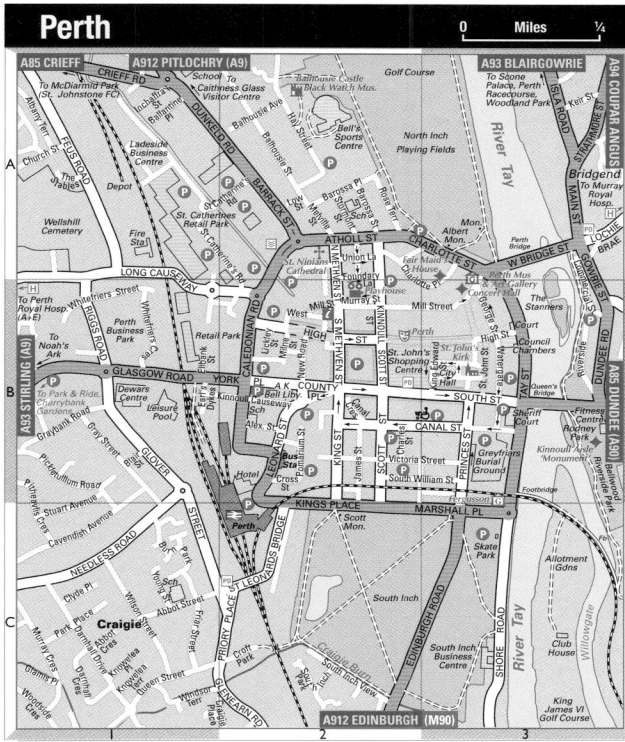

Peterborough

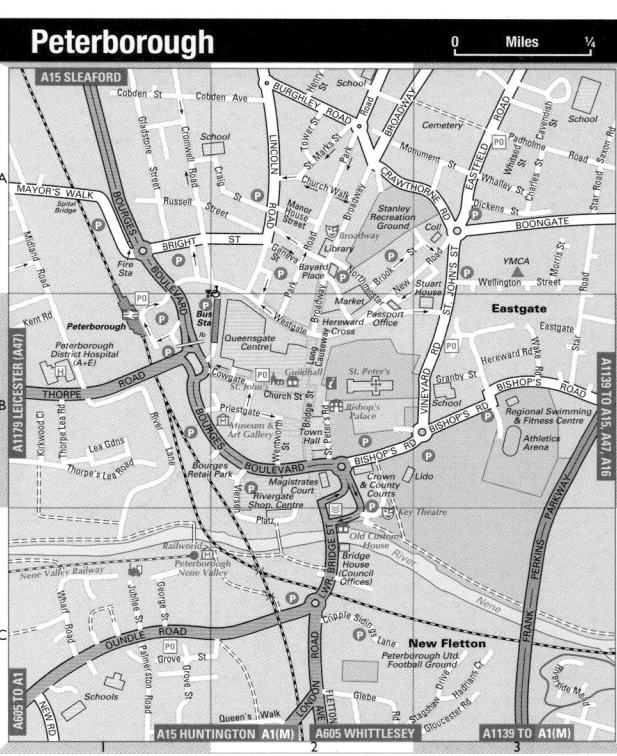

Plymouth

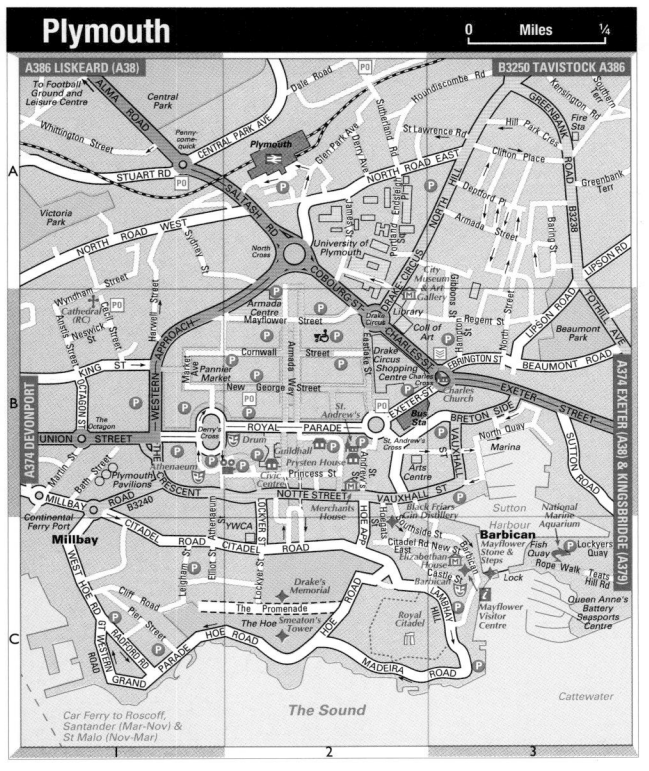

Poole

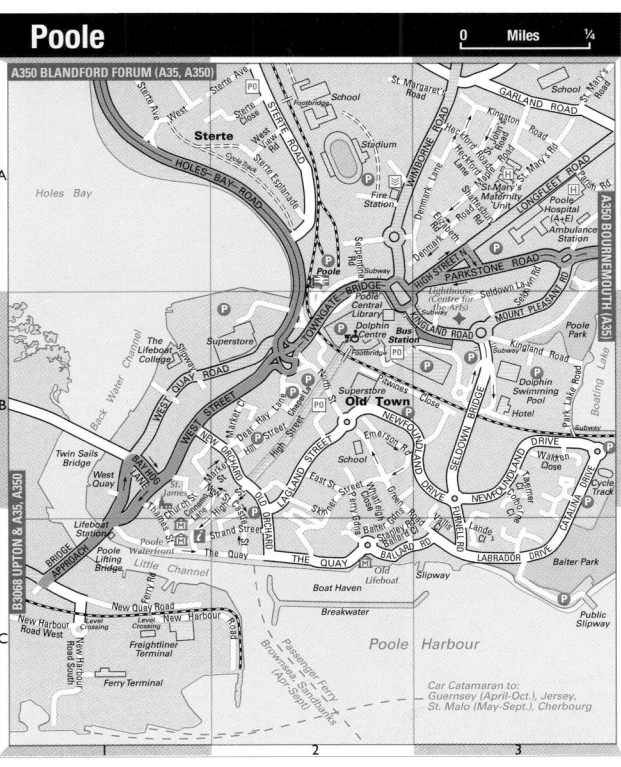

Portsmouth

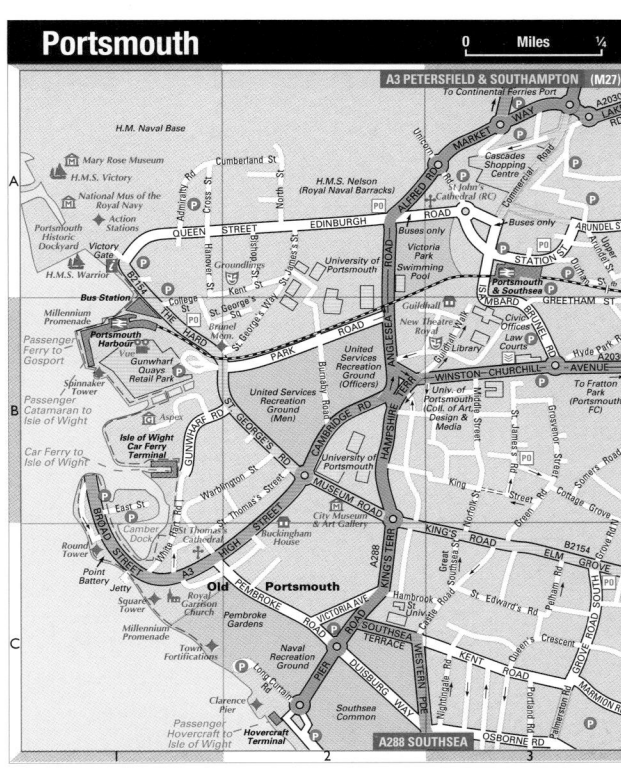

Preston
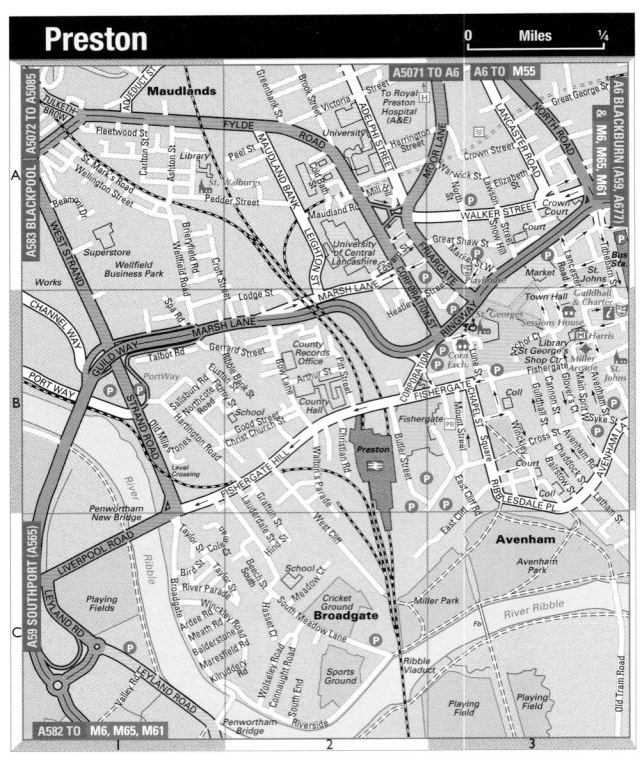

Reading
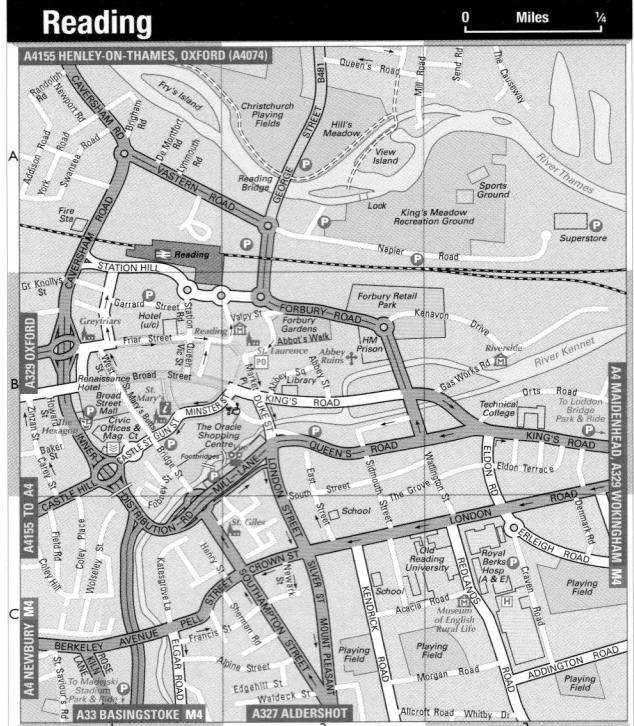

St Andrews
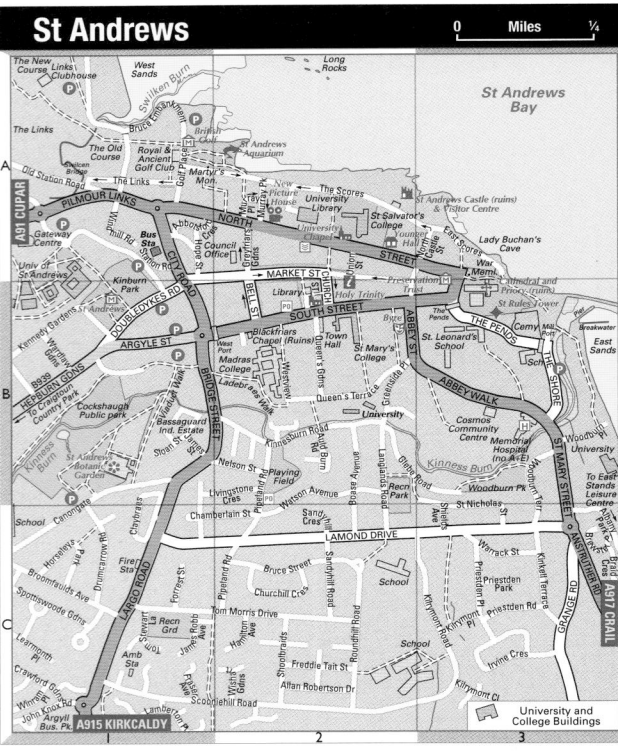

Salisbury
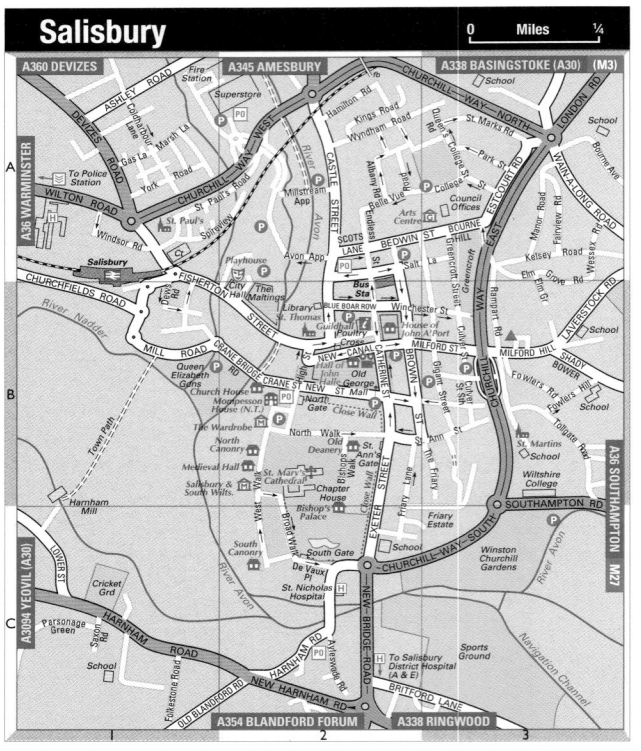

Scarborough
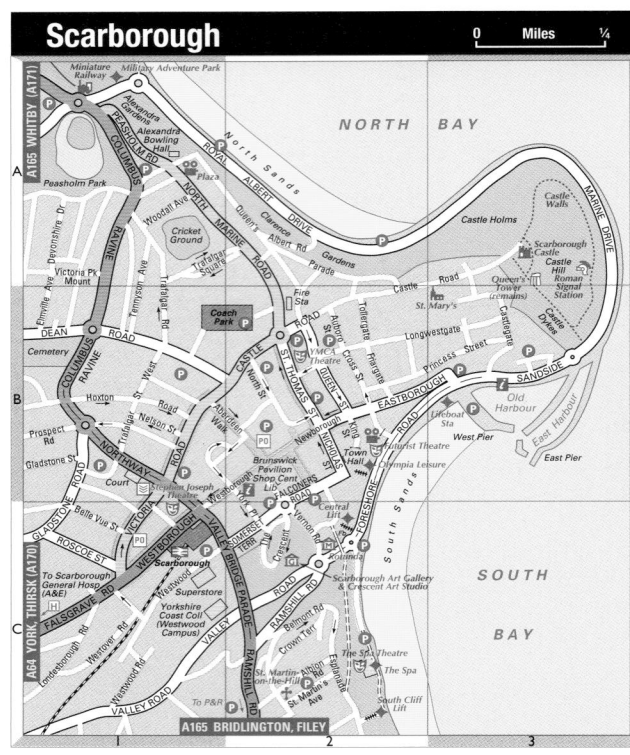

Shrewsbury
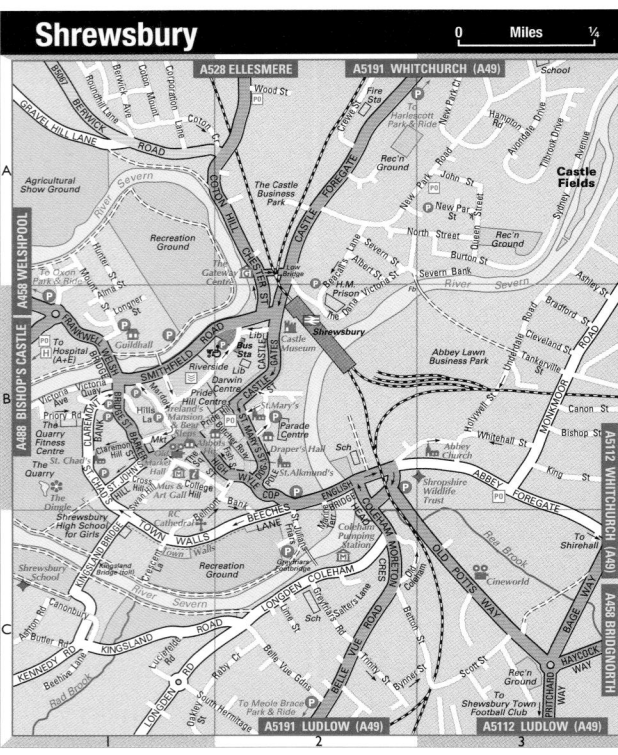

Sheffield
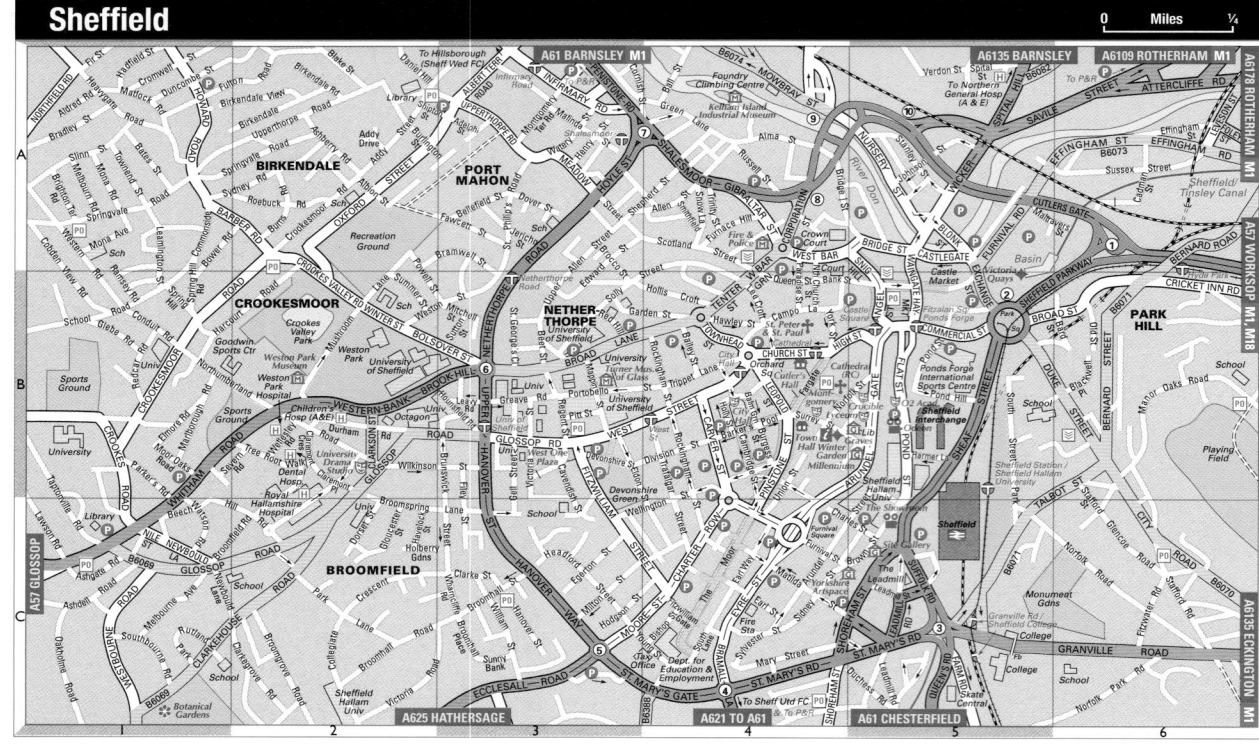

Southampton
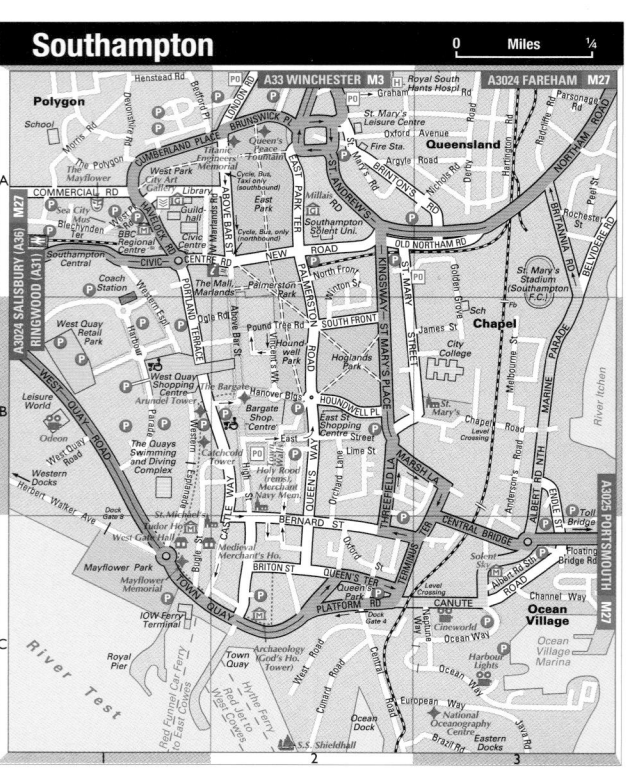

Southend page 69 ● Stirling page 278 ● Stoke page 168 ● Stratford-upon-Avon page 118 ● Sunderland page 243 ● Swansea page 56 ● Swindon page 63 ● Taunton page 28 ● Telford page 132

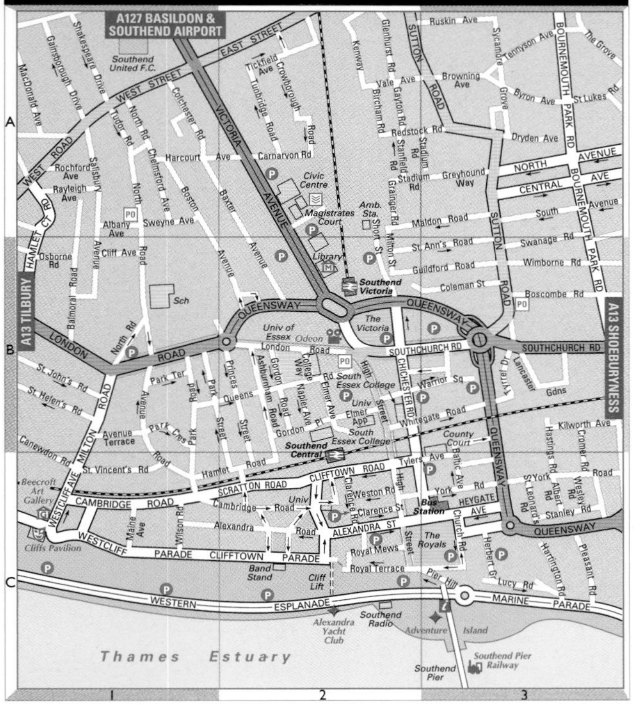

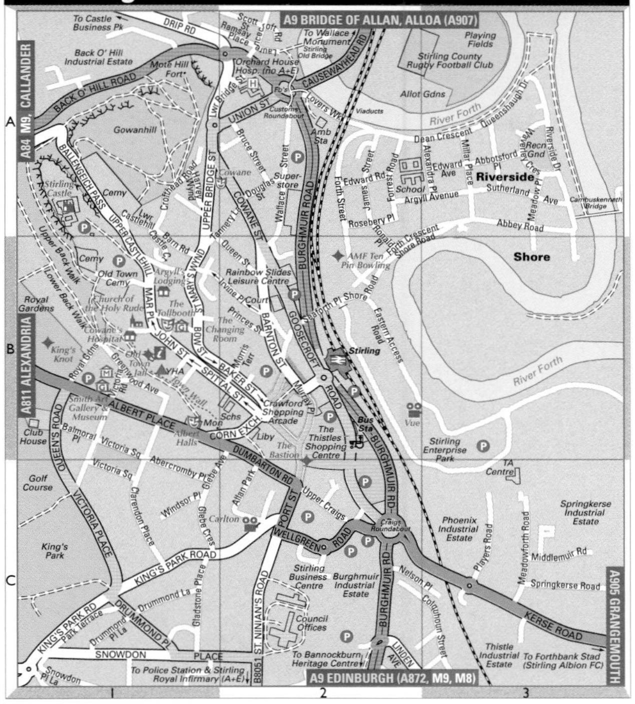

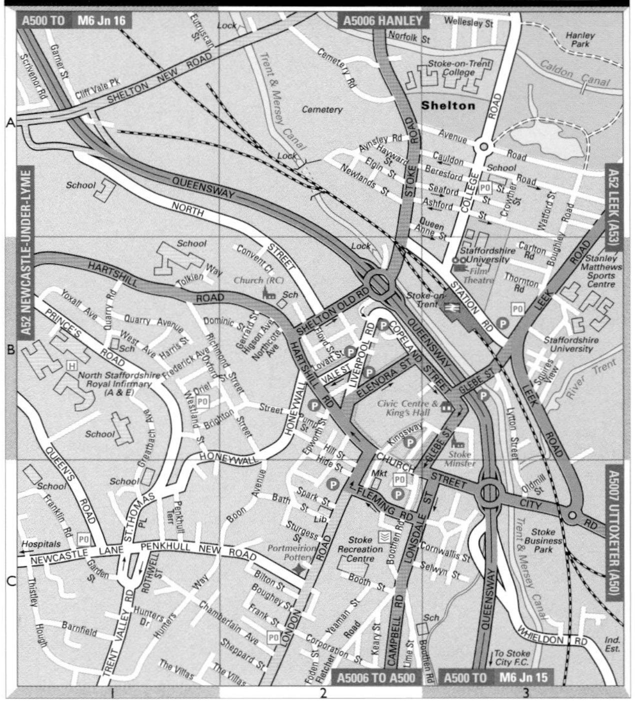

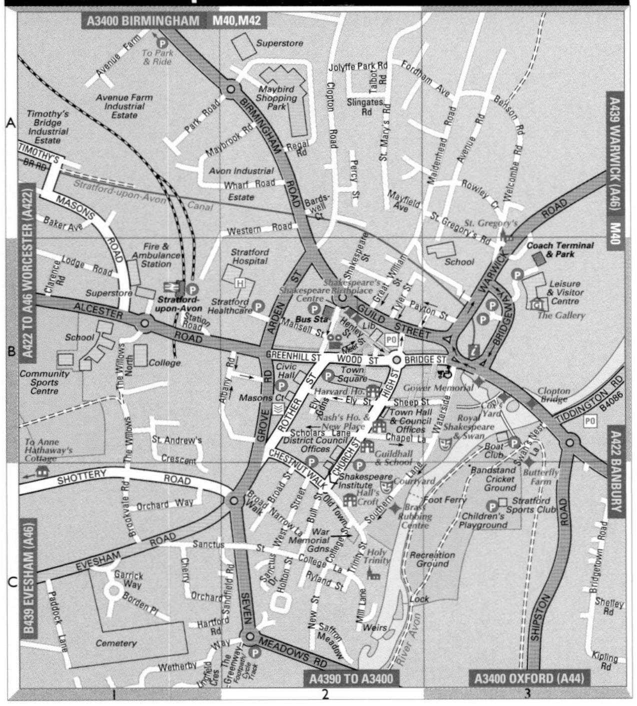

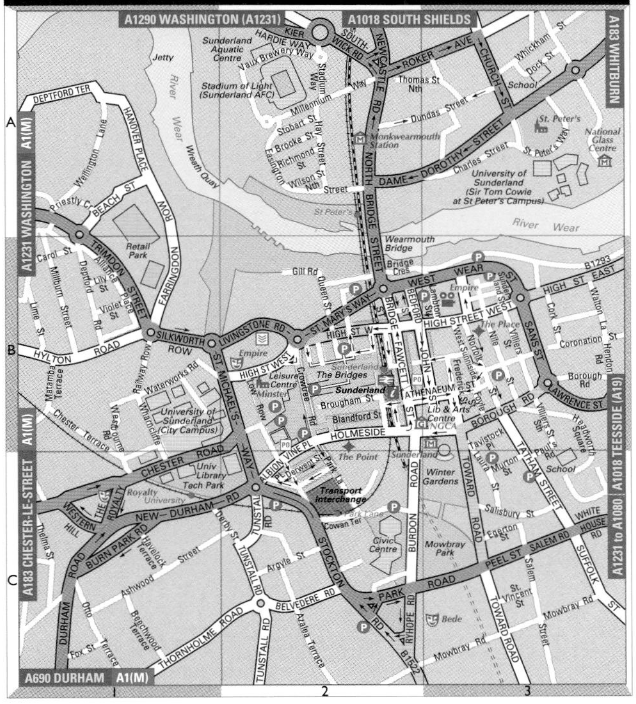

343

Southend-on-Sea

Stirling

Stoke

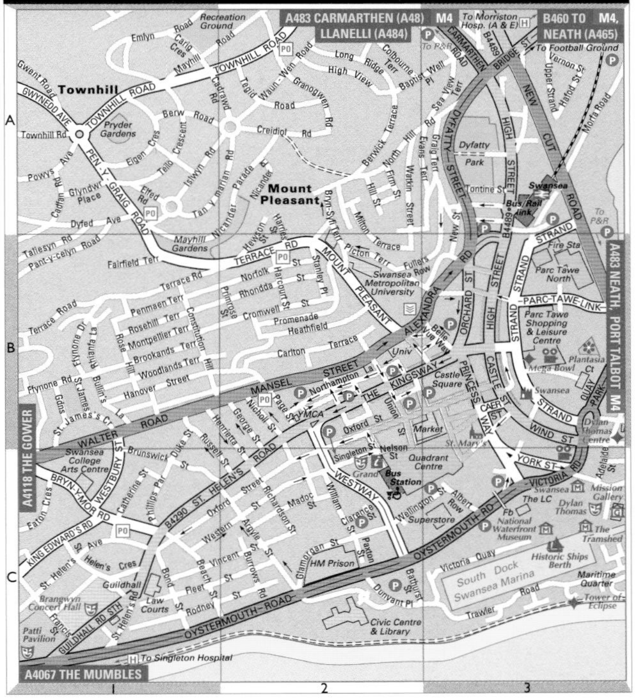

Stratford-upon-Avon

Sunderland

Swansea / Abertawe

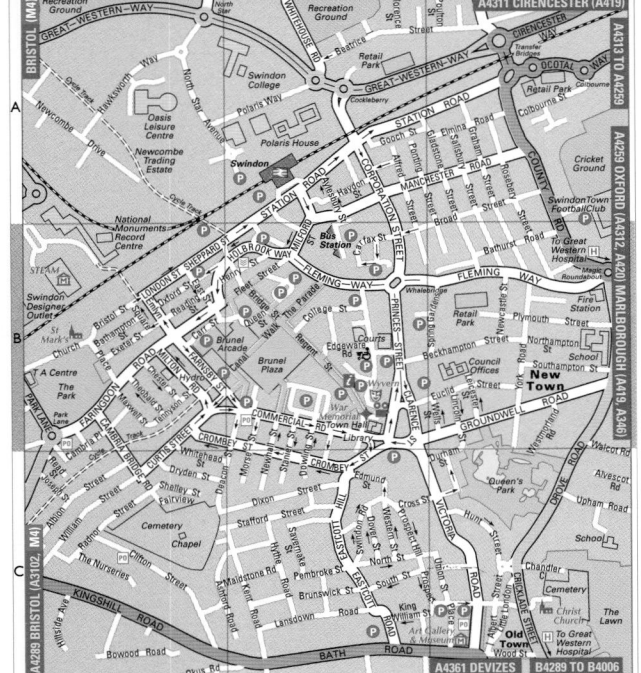

Swindon

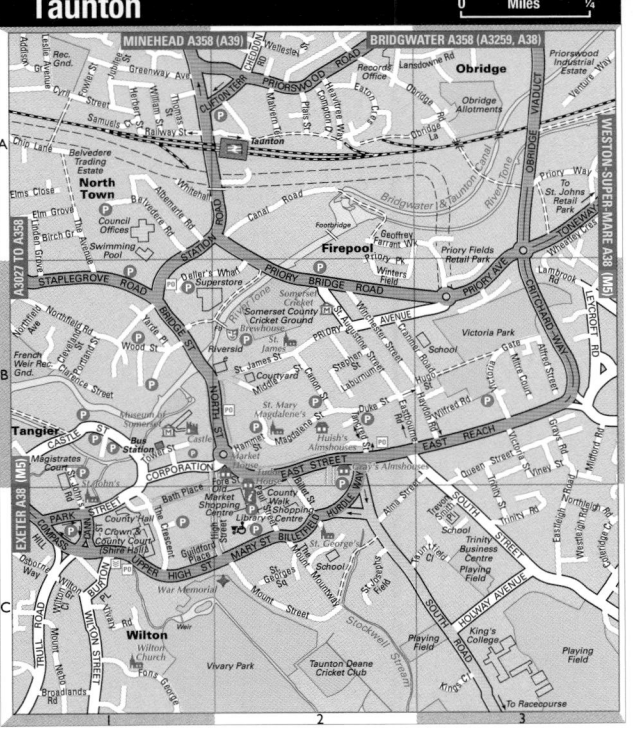

Taunton

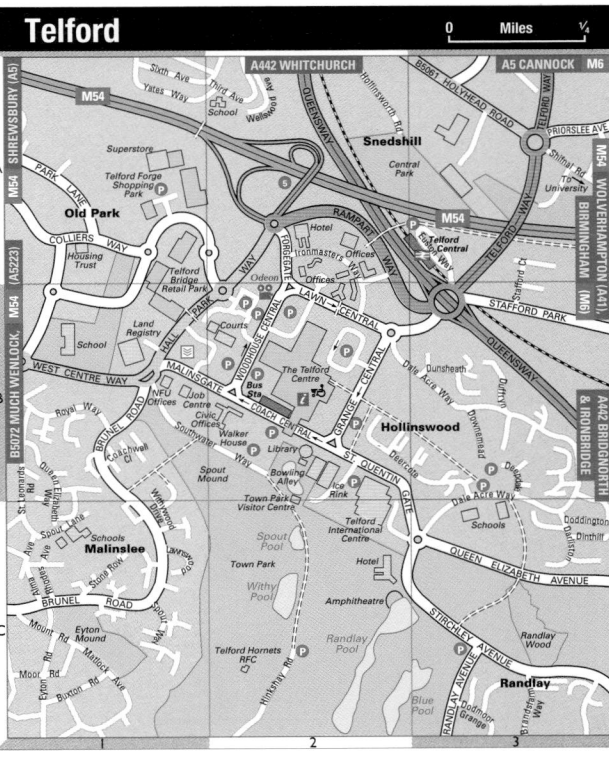

Telford

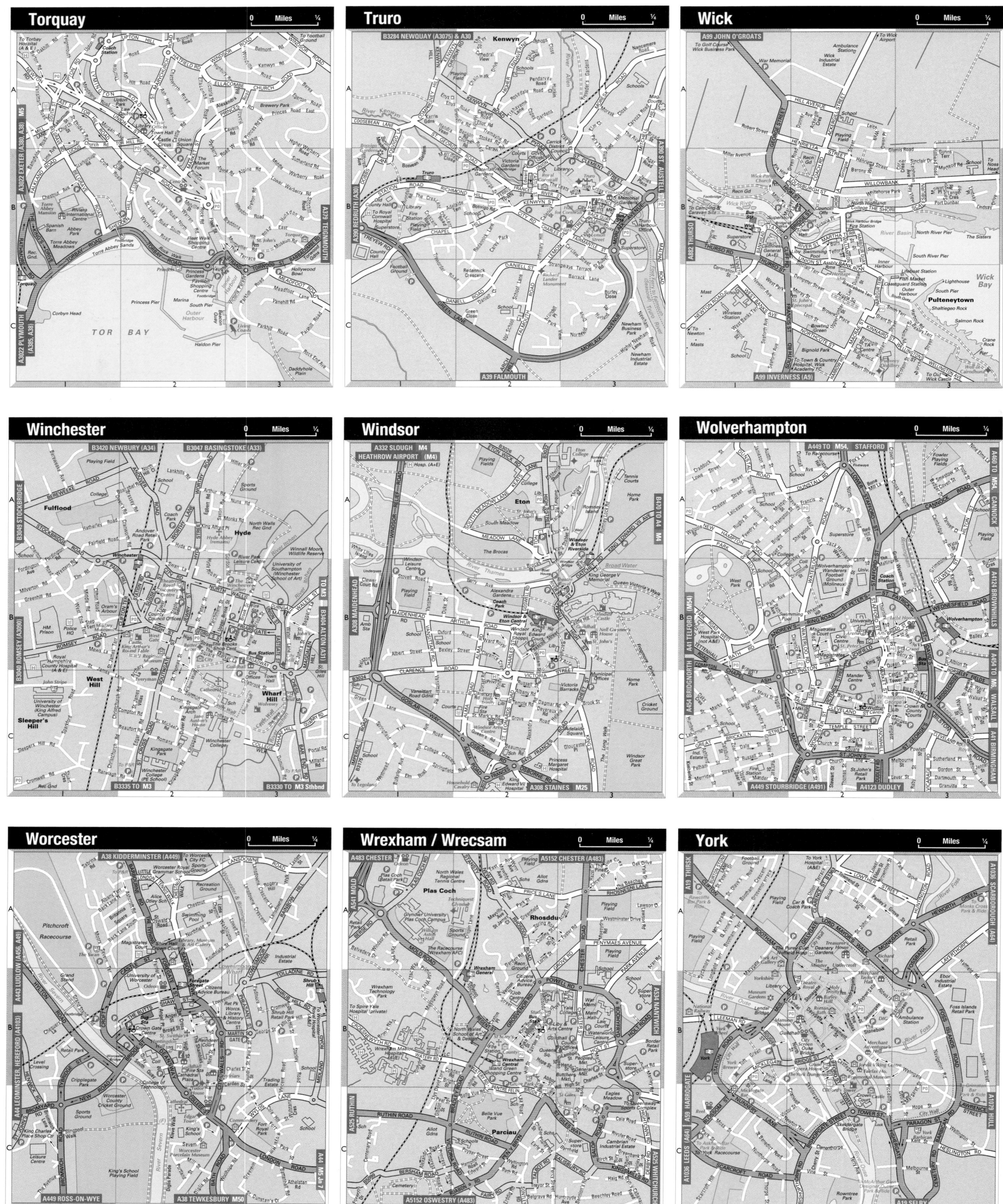

Town plan indexes

Canon's Rd B3/B4
Canon's Way B3
Cantock's Cl A3
Canynge Rd A1
Canynge Sq A1
Castle Park A5
Castle St A5
Catherine Meade St C4
Cattle Market Rd C6
Central Library B3
Charles Pl B1
Charlotte St B3
Charlotte St South B3
Chatterton House B5
Chatterton Sq C5
Chatterton St C5
Cheese La B5
Christchurch A4
Christchurch Rd A1
Christmas Steps A4
Church La B2/B5
Church St B5
City Museum A3
City of Bristol College B3
Clare St B4
Clarence Rd C5
Cliff Rd C1
Clift House Rd C1
Clifton Cath (RC) A2
Clifton Down A1
Clifton Down Rd A1
Clifton Hill B2
Clifton Park A1/A2
Clifton Park Rd A1
Clifton Rd A2
Cliftonwood Cr B2
Cliftonwood Rd B2
Cliftonwood Terr B2
Clifton Vale B1
Cobblestone Mews A1
College Green B3
College Rd A1
College St B3
Colston Almshouses A4
Colston Ave B4
Colston Hall B4
Colston Parade C5
Colston St A4
Commercial Rd C4
Commonwealth Museum B5
Constitution Hill B2
Cooperage La C2
Corn St B4
Cornwallis Ave B1
Cornwallis Cr B1
Coronation Rd C2/C4
Council House B3
Counterslip B5
Courts A4
Create Centre, The C1
Crosby Row B2
Culver St B3
Cumberland Basin C1
Cumberland Cl C2
Cumberland Rd C2/C3
David St A6
Dean La C4
Deanery Rd B3
Denmark St B4
Dowry Sq B1
Eaton Cr A2
Elmdale Rd A3
Elton Rd A3
Eugene St A4/A6
Exchange, The and St Nicholas' Mkts B4
Fairfax St A4
Fire Station B5
Floating Harbour C3
Foster Almshouses A4
Frayne Rd C1
Frederick Pl A2
Freeland Pl B1
Frogmore St B3
Fry's Hill B2
Gas La B6
Gasferry Rd C3
General Hospital C4
Georgian House B3
Glendale B1
Glentworth Rd B2
Gloucester St A1
Goldney Hall B2
Goldney Rd B1
Gordon Rd A2
Granby Hill B1
Grange Rd A1
Great Ann St A6
Great George St A6/B3
Great George Rd B3
Great Western Way B6
Green St North B1
Green St South B1
Greenay Bush La C2
Greenbank Rd C2
Greville Smyth Park C1
Guildhall A4
Guinea St C4
Hamilton Rd C3
Hanbury Rd A2
Hanover Pl C2
Harbour Way B3
Harley Pl A1
Haymarket A5
Hensman's Hill B1
High St B4
Highbury Villas A3
Hill St B3
Hill St C6
Hippodrome B4
Hopechapel Hill B1
Horfield Rd A4
Horton St B6
Host St A4
Hotwell Rd B1/B2
Houlton St A6
Howard Rd C3
IMAX Cinema B4
Information Ctr B4
Islington Rd C3
Jacob St A5/A6
Jacob's Wells Rd B2
John Carr's Terr B2
John Wesley's Chapel A5
Joy Hill B1
Jubilee St B6
Kensington Pl A2
Kilkenny St B6
King St B4
Kingsland Rd B6
Kingston Rd C3
Lamb St A6
Lansdown Rd A2
Lawford St A6
Lawfords Gate A6
Leighton Rd C3
Lewins Mead A4
Lime Rd C2
Little Ann St A6
Little Caroline Pl B1
Little George St A6
Little King St B4
Litfield Rd A1
Llandoger Trow B4
Lloyds' Building, The C3
Lodge St A4
Lord Mayor's Chapel, The B4
Lower Castle St A5
Lower Church La A4
Lower Clifton Hill B2
Lower Guinea St C4
Lower Lamb St B3
Lower Maudlin St A4
Lower Park Rd A4
Lower Sidney St C2
Lucky La C4
Lydstep Terr C3
Mall (Galleries Shopping Centre), The A5
Manilla Rd A1
Mardyke Ferry Rd C2
Maritime Heritage Centre B3
Marlborough Hill A4
Marlborough St A4
Marsh St B4
Mead St C5
Merchant Dock B2
Merchant Seamen's Almshouses B4
Merchant St A5
Merchants Rd A1
Merchants Rd C1
Meridian Pl A2
Meridian Vale A2
Merrywood Rd C3
Midland Rd A6
Milford St C3
Millennium Sq B3
Mitchell La B5
Mortimer Rd A1
M Shed C4
Murray Rd C4
Myrtle Rd A3
Narrow Plain B5
Narrow Quay B4
Nelson St A4
New Charlotte St C4
New Kingsley Rd B6
New Queen St C5
New St A6
Newgate A5
Newton St A6
Norland Rd A1
North St C2
O2 Academy B3
Oakfield Gr A2
Oakfield Pl A2
Oakfield Rd A2
Old Bread St B6
Old Market St A6
Old Park Hill A4
Oldfield Rd B1
Orchard Ave B4
Orchard La B4
Orchard St B4
Osbourne Rd C3
Oxford St B6
Park Pl A2
Park Rd C3
Park Row A3
Park St A3
Passage St B5
Pembroke Gr A2
Pembroke Rd A2
Pembroke Rd C3
Pembroke St A5
Penn St A5
Pennywell Rd A6
Percival Rd A1
Pero's Bridge B4
Perry Rd A4
Pip & Jay A5
Plimsoll Bridge B1
Police Sta A4/A6
Polygon Rd B1
Portland St A1
Portwall La B5
Post Office A1/A3/A4/A5/A6/B1/B4/C4/C5
Prewett St C5
Prince St B4
Prince St Bridge C4
Princess St C5
Princess Victoria St B1
Priory Rd A3
Pump La C5
QEH Theatre A2
Queen Charlotte St B4
Quakers Friars A5
Quay St A4
Queen Elizabeth Hospital School B2
Queen Sq B4
Queen St A5
Queen's Ave A3
Queen's Parade B3
Queen's Rd A2/A3
Raleigh Rd C2
Randall Rd B2
Redcliffe Backs B5
Redcliffe Bridge B4
Redcliffe Hill C5
Redcliffe Parade C4
Redcliffe St B5
Redcliffe Way B5
Redcross St A6
Redgrave Theatre A1
Red Lodge A4
Regent St B1
Richmond Hill A2
Richmond Hill Ave A2
Richmond La A2
Richmond Park Rd A2
Richmond St C6
Richmond Terr A2
River St A6
Rownham Mead B2
Royal Fort Rd A3
Royal Park A2
Royal West of England Academy A3
Royal York Cr B1
Royal York Villas B1
Rupert St A4
Russ St B6
St Andrew's Walk B2
St George's B3
St George's Rd B3
St James A4
St John's A4
St John's Rd C4
St Luke's Rd C5
St Mary Redcliffe C5
St Mary's Hospital A3
St Matthias Park A6
St Michael's Hill A3
St Michael's Hospl A4
St Michael's Park A3
St Nicholas St B4
St Paul St A5
St Paul's Rd A2
St Peter's (ruin) A5
St Philip's Bridge B5
St Philips Rd A6
St Stephen's B4
St Stephen's St B4
St Thomas St B5
St Thomas the Martyr B5
Sandford Rd B1
Sargent St C5
Saville Pl B1
Ship La C5
Showcase Cinema de Lux A5
Silver St A4
Sion Hill A1
Small St A4
Smeaton Rd C1
Somerset Sq C5
Somerset St C5
Southernhay Ave B2
Southville Rd C4
Spike Island Artspace C2
Spring St C5
SS Great Britain and The Matthew B2
Stackpool Rd C3
Staight St B6
Stillhouse La C4
Stracey Rd C2
Sydney Row C2
Tankard's Cl A3
Temple Back B5
Temple Boulevard B5
Temple Bridge B5
Temple Church B5
Temple Circus B5
Temple Gate C5
Temple St B5
Temple Way B5
Terrell St A4
The Arcade A5
The Fosseway A2
The Grove B4
The Horsefair A5
The Mall A1
Theatre Royal B4
Thekla The B4
Thomas La B5
Three Kings of Cologne A4
Three Queens La B5
Tobacco Factory, The C2
Tower Hill B5
Tower La A4
Trenchard St A4
Triangle South A3
Triangle West A3
Trinity Rd A6
Trinity St A6
Tyndall Ave A3
Union St A5
Union St B6
Unity St A6
Unity St B3
University of Bristol A3
University Rd A3
Upper Maudlin St A4
Upper Perry Hill C3
Upper Byron Pl A3
Upton Rd C2
Valentine Bridge B6
Victoria Gr C5
Victoria Rd C6
Victoria Rooms A2
Victoria Sq A2
Victoria St B5
Vyvyan Rd A1
Vyvyan Terr A1
Wade St A6
Walter St C2
Wapping Rd C4
Water La B5
Waterloo Rd A6
Waterloo St A1
Waterloo St A6
Watershed Media Centre B4
Welling Terr B1
Welsh Back B4
West Mall A1
West St A6
Westfield Pl A1
Wetherell Pl A2
Whitehouse Pl C5
Whitehouse St C5
Whiteladies Rd A2
Whitson St A4
William St C5
Willway St C5
Windsor Pl B1
Windsor Terr B1
Wine St A4
Woodland Rise A3
Woodland Rd A3
Worcester Rd A1
Worcester Terr A1
YHA B4
York Gdns B1
York Pl A2
York Rd C5

Bury St Edmunds 332

Abbey Gardens B3
Abbey Gate B3
Abbeygate St B2
Albert Cr B1
Albert St B1
Ambulance Sta C1
Angel Hill B2
Angel La B2
Anglian Lane A1
Arc Shopping Centre B2
Athenaeum C2
Baker's La C3
Barwell Rd B3
Beetons Way A1
Bishops Rd B2
Bloomfield St B2
Bridewell La C2
Bullen Cl C1
Bury St Edmunds ≥ A2
Bury St Edmunds County Upper School A1
Bury St Edmunds L Ctr B1
Bury Town FC B3
Bus Station B2
Butter Mkt B2
Cannon St B2
Castle Rd C1
Cemetery C1
Chalk Rd (N) B1
Chalk Rd (S) B1
Church Row B2
Churchgate St C2
Cineworld B1
Citizens Advice Bureau B2
College St C2
Compiegne Way A3
Corn Exchange, The B2
Cornfield Rd B1
Cotton Lane B3
Courts B2
Covent Garden C2
Crown St C3
Cullum Rd C2
Eastern Way A3
Eastgate St B3
Enterprise Bsns Park A2
Etna Rd A2
Eyre Cl C2
Fire Station B1
Friar's Lane C2
Gage Cl A1
Garland St B2
Greene King Brewery C3
Grove Park B1
Grove Rd B1
Guildhall C2
Guildhall St C2
Hatter St C2
High Baxter St B2
Honey Hill C3
Hospital Rd C1/C2
Ickworth Dr C1
Information Ctr B2
Ipswich St A2
King Edward VI Sch A1
King's Rd C1/B2
Library B2
Long Brackland A2
Looms La B2
Lwr Baxter St B2
Malthouse La A2
Maynewater La C3
Mill Rd C1
Mill Rd (South) C1
Minden Close B3
Moyses Hall B2
Mustow St B3
Norman Tower C3
Northgate Ave A2
Northgate St B2
Nutshell, The B2
Osier Rd A2
Out Northgate A2
Out Risbygate B1
Out Westgate C2
Parkway B1/C2
Peckham St B2
Petticoat La C1
Phoenix Day Hospl C1
Pinners Way C1
Police Station C3
Post Office B2/B3
Pump La B2
Queen's Rd B1
Raingate St C3
Raynham Rd A1
Retail Park C2
Risbygate St B1/B2
Robert Boby Way C2
St Andrew's St North B2
St Andrew's St South B2
St Botolph's La C3
St Edmunds Hospital (private) C3
St Edmund's C2
St Edmund's Abbey (Remains) B3
St Edmundsbury C3
St John's St B2
St Marys C3
School Hall La B2
Shillitoe Cl C1
Shire Halls & Magistrates Ct C3
South Cl C1
Southgate St C3
Sparhawk St C3
Spring Lane B1
Springfield Rd B1
Station Hill A2
Swan La C3
Tayfen Rd B2
The Vinefields B3
Theatre Royal C3
Thingoe Hill A2
Victoria St B1
War Memorial C1
Well St B2
West Suffolk College B1
Westgarth Gdns C1
Westgate St C2
Whiting St C2
York Rd B1
York Terr B1

Cambridge 333

Abbey Rd A3
ADC A2
Anglia Ruskin Univ B3
Archaeology & Anthropology B2
Art Gallery A1
Arts Picture House B2
Arts Theatre B1
Auckland Rd A3
Bateman St C2
BBC C3
Benet St B1
Bradmore St B3
Bridge St A1
Broad St B3
Brookside C2
Brunswick Terr A3
Burleigh St B3
Bus Station B2
Butt Green A2
Cambridge Contemporary Art Gallery B1
Castle Mound A1
Castle St A1
Cemetery B3
Chesterton La A1
Christ's (Coll) B2
Christ's Lane B2
Christ's Pieces B2
City Rd B3
Clare (Coll) B1
Clarendon St B2
Coe Fen C2
Coronation St C2
Corpus Christi (Coll) B1
Council Offices C3
Cross St C3
Crusoe Bridge C1
Darwin (Coll) C1
Devonshire Rd C3
Downing (Coll) C2
Downing St B2
Earl St B2
East Rd B3
Eden St B3
Elizabeth Way A3
Elm St B2
Emery St B3
Emmanuel (Coll) B2
Emmanuel Rd B2
Emmanuel St B2
Fair St A3
Fenners Physical Education Centre C3
Fire Station B3
Fitzroy St A3
Fitzwilliam Mus C2
Fitzwilliam St C2
Folk Museum A1
Glisson Rd C3
Gonville & Caius (Coll) B1
Gonville Place C2
Grafton Centre A3
Grand Arcade B2
Gresham Rd C3
Green St B1
Guest Rd B3
Guildhall B2
Harvey Rd C3
Hills Rd C3
Hobson St B2
Hughes Hall (Coll) B3
Information Ctr B2
James St A3
Jesus (Coll) A2
Jesus Green A2
Jesus La A2
Jesus Terr B3
John St B3
Kelsey Kerridge Sports Centre B3
King St A2
King's (Coll) B1
King's Coll Chapel B1
King's Parade B1
Lammas Land Rec Gd C1
Lensfield Rd C2
Library B2
Lion Yard B2
Little St Mary's La B1
Lyndewod Rd C3
Magdalene (Coll) A1
Magdalene St A1
Maid's Causeway A3
Malcolm St A2
Market Hill B1
Market St B1
Mathematical Bridge B1
Mawson Rd C3
Midsummer Common A3
Mill La B1
Mill Rd B3
Mill St C3
Mumford B3
Napier St A3
New Square A2
Newmarket Rd A3
Newnham Rd C1
Norfolk St B3
Northampton St A1
Norwich St C2
Orchard St B2
Panton St C2
Paradise Nature Reserve C1
Paradise St B3
Park Parade A1
Park St A2
Park Terr B2
Parker St B2
Parker's Piece B2
Parkside B3
Parkside Pools B3
Parsonage St A3
Pemberton Terr C2
Pembroke (Coll) B2
Pembroke St B1
Perowne St B3
Peterhouse (Coll) C1
Petty Cury B2
Police Station B3
Post Office A1/A3/B2/B3/C1/C2/C3
Queens' (Coll) B1
Queen's La B1
Queen's Rd B1
Regent St B2
Regent Terr B2
Ridley Hall (Coll) C1
Riverside A3
Round Church, The A1
Russell St C2
St Andrew's St B2
St Benet's B1
St Catharine's (Coll) B1
St Eligius St C2
St John's (Coll) A1
St Mary's B1
St Paul's Rd C3
Saxon St C2
Scott Polar Institute & Museum C2
Sedgwick Museum B2
Sheep's Green C1
Shire Hall A1
Sidgwick Ave C1
Sidney St A1
Sidney Sussex (Coll) A2
Silver St B1
Station Rd C3
Tenison Ave C3
Tenison Rd C3
Tennis Court Rd B2
The Backs B1
The Fen Causeway C1
Thompson's La A1
Trinity (Coll) A1
Trinity Hall (Coll) B1
Trinity St B1
Trumpington Rd C2
Trumpington St B1
Union Rd C2
University Botanic Gardens C2
Victoria Ave A2
Victoria St B2
Warkworth St B3
Warkworth Terr B3
Wesley House (Coll) A2
West Rd B1
Westcott House (Coll) A2
Westminster (Coll) A1
Whipple B2
Willis Rd B3
Willow Walk A2

Canterbury 333

Artillery St B2
Barton Mill Rd A3
Beaconsfield Rd A1
Beaney The B2
Beverley Rd A1
Bingley's Island B1
Black Griffin La B1
Broad Oak Rd A2
Broad St B2
Brymore Rd A3
Burgate B2
Bus Station C2
Canterbury College C3
Canterbury East C1
Canterbury Tales, The B2
Canterbury West A1
Castle C1
Castle Row C1
Castle St C1
Cathedral B2
Chaucer Rd A3
Christ Church Univ B3
Christchurch Gate B2
City Council Offices A3
City Wall B2
Coach Park A2
College Rd B3
Cossington Rd C2
Court B2
Craddock Rd A3
Crown & County Courts B3
Dane John Gdns C2
Dane John Mound C1
Deanery B2
Dover St C2
Duck La B2
Eastbridge Hospl B1
Edgar Rd B3
Ersham Rd C3
Ethelbert Rd C3
Fire Station C2
Forty Acres Rd A1
Gordon Rd C1
Greyfriars B1
Guildford Rd C1
Havelock St B2
Heaton Rd C1
High St B2
HM Prison B3
Information Ctr A2/B2
Ivy La B2
Ivy Pl C1
King St B2
King's School B2/B3
King's School Leisure Facilities A2
Kingsmead Leisure Ctr A2
Kingsmead Rd A2
Kirby's La B1
Lansdown Rd C2
Lime Kiln Rd C1
Longport B3
Lower Chantry La C3
Mandeville Rd A1
Market Way A2
Marlowe Arcade B2
Marlowe Ave C2
Marlowe Theatre B2
Martyrs Field Rd C1
Mead Way B1
Military Rd B2
Monastery St B2
Mus of Canterbury (Rupert Bear Mus) B1
New Dover Rd C3
Norman Rd C2
North Holmes Rd B3
North La B1
Northgate A2
Nunnery Fields C2
Nunnery Rd C2
Oaten Hill C2
Odeon Cinema C2
Old Dover Rd C2
Old Palace B2
Old Ruttington La B2
Old Weavers B2
Orchard St B1
Oxford Rd C1
Palace St B2
Pilgrims Way C3
Pin Hill C1
Pine Tree Ave A1
Police Station C2
Post Office B2/C1/C2
Pound La B1
Puckle La C2
Raymond Ave C2
Registry Office A2
Rheims Way B1
Rhodaus Cl C2
Rhodaus Town C2
Roman Museum B2
Roper Gateway A1
Roper Rd A1
Rose La B2
St Augustine's Abbey (remains) B3
St Augustine's Rd C3
St Dunstan's A1
St Dunstan's St A1
St George's Pl C2
St George's St B2
St George's Tower B2
St Gregory's Rd B3
St John's Hospital A2
St Margaret's St B2
St Martin's B3
St Martin's Ave B3
St Martin's Rd B3
St Michael's Rd A1
St Mildred's C1
St Peter's Gr B1
St Peter's La B2
St Peter's Pl B1
St Peter's St B1
St Radigunds St B2
St Stephen's Ct A1
St Stephen's Path A1
St Stephen's Rd A2
Salisbury Rd A1
Simmonds Rd C1
Spring La C3
Station Rd West B1
Stour St B1
Sturry Rd A3
The Causeway A2
The Friars B2
Tourtel Rd A3
Tudor Rd C1
Union St B2
University for the Creative Arts C3
Vernon Pl C2
Victoria Rd C1
Watling St B2
Westgate Gdns B1
Westgate Towers B1
Whitefriars B2
Whitehall Gdns B1
Whitehall Rd B1
Wincheap C1
York Rd C1
Zealand Rd C2

Cardiff Caerdydd 333

Adam St B3
Alexandra Gdns A2
Allerton St C1
Arran St A3
ATRiuM (University of Glamorgan) C3
Beauchamp St C1
Bedford St A3
Blackfriars Priory (rems) B1
Boulevard De Nantes B2
Brains Brewery C2
Brook St B1
Bus Station C2
Bute Park B1
Bute St C2
Bute Terr C3
Callaghan Sq C2/C3
Capitol Sh Ctr, The B3
Cardiff Arms Park (Cardiff RFC) B1
Cardiff Bridge B1
Cardiff Castle B2
Cardiff Central Sta C2
Cardiff Ctr Trading Est C3
Cardiff Univ A1/A2/B3
Cardiff University Student's Union A2
Caroline St C2
Castle Green B2
Castle Mews A1
Castle St (Heol y Castell) B1
Cathays Station A2
Celerity Drive C3
Central Library C2
Central Sq C2
Charles St (Heol Siarl) B3
Churchill Way B3
City Hall A2
City Rd A3
Clare Rd C1
Clare St C1
Coburn St A3
Coldstream Terr B1
College Rd A1
Colum Rd A1
Court C2
Court Rd C1
Craiglee Drive C3
Cranbrook St A3
Customhouse St C2
Cyfartha St A3
Despenser Place C1
Despenser St C1
Dinas St C1
Duke St (Heol y Dug) B2
Dumfries Place B3
East Grove A3
Ellen St C3
Fire Station B3
Fitzalan Place B3
Fitzhamon Emb C1
Fitzhamon La C1
g39 B2
Gloucester St C1
Glynrhondda St A2
Gordon Rd A3
Gorsedd Gdns B2
Green St B1
Greyfriars Rd B2
HM Prison B3
Hafod St C1
Herbert St C3
High St B2
Industrial Estate C3
John St C3
Jubilee St C1
King Edward VII Ave A1
Kingsway (Ffordd y Brenin) B2
Knox Rd B3
Law Courts B2
Llanbleddian Gdns A2
Llantwit St A2
Lloyd George Ave C3
Lower Cathedral Rd B1
Lowther Rd A3
Magistrates Court B3
Mansion House A3
Mardy St C1
Mark St B1
Market B2
Mary Ann St C3
Merches Gdns C1
Mill La C2
Millennium Bridge B1
Millennium Plaza Leisure Complex C1
Millennium Stadium C1
Millennium Stadium Tours (Gate 3) B2
Miskin St A2
Monmouth St C1
Motorpoint Arena Cardiff C3
Museum Ave A2
Museum Place A2
National Museum of Wales A2
National War Meml A2
Neville Place C1
New Theatre B2
Newport Rd B3
Northcote La A3
Northcote St A3
Park Grove A4
Park Place A2
Park St C2
Penarth Rd C2
Pendyris St C1
Plantaganet St C1
Quay St B2
Queen Anne Sq A1
Queen St (Heol y Frenhines) B2
Queen St Station B3
Regimental Museums B2
Rhymney St A3
Richmond Rd A3
Royal Welsh College of Music and Drama A1
Russell St A3
Ruthin Gdns A2
St Andrews Place A2
St David's B2
St David's 2 C2
St David's Centre B2
St David's Hall B2
St John The Baptist B2
St Mary St (Heol Eglwys Fair) B2
St Peter's St A3
Salisbury Rd A3
Sandon St B3
Schooner Way C3
Scott Rd C2
Scott St C2
Senghennydd Rd A2
Sherman Theatre A2
Sophia Gardens A1
South Wales Baptist College A3
Stafford Rd C1
Station Terr B3
Stuttgarter Strasse B2
Sussex St C1
Taffs Mead Emb C1
Talworth St A3
Temple of Peace & Health A1
The Cardiff Story B2
The Friary B2
The Hayes B2
The Parade A3
The Walk A3
Treharris St A3
Trinity St B2
Tudor La C1
Tudor St C1
Welsh Assembly Offices A1
Welsh Inst of Sport A1
West Grove A3
Westgate St (Heol y Porth) B2
Windsor Place B3
Womanby St B2
Wood St C2
Working St B2
Wyeverne Rd A2

Carlisle 333

Abbey St A1
Aglionby St B3
Albion St C3
Alexander St C3
AMF Bowl C2
Annetwell St A1
Bank St B2
Bitts Park A1
Blackfriars St B2
Blencome St C1
Blunt St C1
Botchergate B2
Boustead's Grassing C2
Bowman St B3
Broad St B3
Bridge St A1
Brook St C3
Brunswick St B2
Bus Station B2
Caldew Bridge A1
Caldew St C1
Carlisle (Citadel) Station B2
Carlisle College A2
Castle A1
Castle St A1
Castle Way A1
Cathedral A1
Cecil St B2
Chapel St A2
Charles St B3
Charlotte St B1
Chatsworth Square A2
Chiswick St B2
Citadel, The B2
City Walls A1
Civic Centre A2
Clifton St C1
Close St B3
Collingwood St C1
Colville St C1
Colville Terr C1
Court B2
Court St B2
Crosby St B2
Crown St C2
Currock Rd C2
Dacre Rd A1
Dale St C1
Denton St C1
Devonshire Walk A1
Duke's Rd A2
East Dale St C1
East Norfolk St C1
Eden Bridge A2
Edward St B3
Elm St B1
English St B2
Fire Station A2
Fisher St A1
Flower St B3
Freer St C1
Fusehill St B3
Georgian Way A2
Gloucester Rd C3
Golf Course A2
Graham St C1
Grey St B3
Guildhall Museum A2
Halfey's La B3
Hardwicke Circus A2
Hart St B3

348 Chelmsford • Cheltenham • Chester • Chichester • Colchester • Coventry • Derby • Dorchester

Hewson St C2
Howard Pl A3
Howe St B3
Information Ctr A2
James St B2
Junction St B1
King St B2
Lancaster St B2
Lanes Shopping Ctr B2
Laserquest B2
Library A2/B1
Lime St B1
Lindisfarne St C3
Linton St B3
Lismore Pl A3
Lismore St B3
London Rd C3
Lonsdale Rd B2
Lord St C3
Lorne Cres B1
Lorne St B1
Lowther St B2
Market Hall A2
Mary St B2
Memorial Bridge A3
Metcalfe St C1
Milbourne St B1
Myddleton St B3
Nelson St C1
Norfolk St C1
Old Town Hall A2
Oswald St C3
Peter St A2
Petteril St B3
Police Station A2
Portland Pl B2
Portland Sq B2
Post Office A2/B2/B3/C1/C3
Princess St C2
Pugin St B1
Red Bank Terr C2
Regent St C3
Richardson St C1
Rickerby Park A3
Rickergate A2
River St B3
Rome St C2
Rydal St B3
St Cuthbert's B2
St Cuthbert's La B2
St James' Park C1
St James' Rd C1
St Nicholas St C3
Sands Centre A2
Scotch St A2
Shaddongate B1
Sheffield St B1
South Henry St B3
South John St C2
South St B3
Spencer St B2
Sports Centre A2
Strand Rd A2
Swimming Baths B2
Sybil St B3
Tait St B2
Thomas St B1
Thomson St C3
Trafalgar St C1
Tullie Ho Museum A1
Tyne St C3
University of Cumbria B3
Viaduct Estate Rd B1
Victoria Pl A2
Victoria Viaduct B2
Vue B2
Warwick Rd B2
Warwick Sq B3
Water St B2
West Walls B1
Westmorland St C1

Chelmsford 333

Ambulance Station B1
Anchor St C1
Anglia Ruskin Univ A2
Arbour La A3
Baddow Rd B2/C3
Baker St C1
Barrack Sq B2
Bellmead B2
Bishop Hall La A2
Bishop Rd A2
Bond St B2
Boswells Dr B3
Boudicca Mews C2
Bouverie Rd C2
Bradford St C1
Braemar Ave C1
Brook St A2
Broomfield Rd A1
Burns Cres C2
Bus Station B1
Can Bridge Way B2
Cedar Ave A1
Cedar Ave West A1
Cemetery A1
Cemetery A2
Cemetery C1
Central Park B1
Chelmsford B2
Chelmsford A1
Chichester Dr A3
Chinery Cl A3
Cinema B2
Civic Centre A1
Civic Theatre B1
College C1
Cottage Pl A2
County Cricket Gd B2
County Hall B2
Coval Ave B1
Coval La B1
Coval Wells B1
Crown Court B2
Duke St B2
Elm Rd C1
Elms Dr A1
Essex Record Office, The B3
Fairfield Rd B1
Falcons Mead B1
George St C2
Glebe Rd A1
Godfrey's Mews C2
Goldlay Ave C3
Goldlay Rd C2
Grove Rd C2
HM Prison A3
Hall St C2
Hamlet Rd C2
Hart St C1
Henry Rd A2
High Bridge Rd B2
High Chelmer Sh Ctr B2
High St B2
Hill Cres B3
Hill Rd Sth B3
Hill Rd B3
Hillview Rd A3
Hoffmans Way A2
Hospital B2
Lady La C2
Langdale Gdns C3
Legg St B2
Library B2
Library C2
Lionfield Terr A3
Lower Anchor St C1
Lynmouth Ave C2
Lynmouth Gdns C3
Magistrates Court B2
Maltese Rd A1
Manor Rd C2
Marconi Rd A2
Market B2
Market Rd B2
Marlborough Rd C1
Meadows Sh Ctr, The B2
Meadowside A3
Mews Ct C2
Mildmay Rd C2
Moulsham Dr C2
Moulsham Mill C3
Moulsham St C1/C2
Navigation Rd B3
New London Rd B2/C1
New St A2/B2
New Writtle St C1
Nursery Rd C2
Orchard St C2
Park Rd B1
Parker Rd C2
Parklands Dr A3
Parkway A1/B1/B2
Police Station A2
Post Office A3/B2/C2
Primrose Hill A1
Prykes Dr B1
Queen St C1
Queen's Rd B3
Railway St A1
Rainsford Rd A1
Ransomes Way A2
Rectory La A2
Regina Rd A2
Riverside Ice & L Ctr B2
Riverside Retail Park A3
Rosebery Rd C2
Rothesay Ave C1
St John's Rd C2
Sandringham Pl B3
Seymour St B1
Shrublands Cl B3
Southborough Rd C1
Springfield Basin B3
Springfield Rd A3/B2/B3
Stapleford Cl C1
Swiss Ave A1
Telford Pl A3
The Meades B1
Tindal St B2
Townfield St A1
Trinity Rd B3
University B1
Upper Bridge Rd C1
Upper Roman Rd C2
Van Dieman's Rd C3
Viaduct Rd B1
Vicarage Rd C1
Victoria Rd A2
Victoria Rd South B2
Vincents Rd C2
Waterloo La B2
Weight Rd B3
Westfield Ave A1
Wharf Rd B3
Writtle Rd C1
YMCA A2
York Rd C1

Cheltenham 333

Albert Rd A3
Albion St B3
All Saints Rd B3
Ambrose St B2
Andover Rd C1
Art Gallery & Mus B2
Axiom Centre B3
Back Montpellier Terr C2
Bandstand C2
Bath Pde B2
Bath Rd C2
Bays Hill Rd C1
Beechwood Sh Ctr B3
Bennington St B2
Berkeley St B3
Brewery The A2
Brunswick St South A2
Bus Station B2
CAB B2
Carlton St B3
Central Cross Road A3
Cheltenham College C2
Cheltenham FC A3
Cheltenham General (A&E) C3
Christchurch Rd B1
Cineworld A2
Clarence Rd A2
Clarence Sq A2
Clarence St B2
Cleeveland St A1
Coach Park A2
College Baths Road C3
College Rd C2
Colletts Dr A1
Corpus St C3
Devonshire St A2
Douro Rd B1
Duke St B3
Dunalley Pde A2
Dunalley St A2
Everyman B2
Evesham Rd A3
Fairview Rd B3
Fairview St B3
Fire Station C3
Folly La A2
Gloucester Rd A1
Grosvenor St B3
Grove St A1
Gustav Holst A3
Hanover St A2
Hatherley St C1
Henrietta St A2
Hewlett Rd B3
High St B2/B3
Hudson St A2
Imperial Gdns C2
Imperial La B2
Imperial Sq C2
Information Ctr B2
Keynsham Rd C3
King St A2
Knapp Rd B2
Ladies College B2
Lansdown Cr C1
Lansdown Rd C1
Leighton Rd B3
Library B2
London Rd C3
Lypiatt Rd C1
Malvern Rd B1
Manser St A2
Market St A1
Marle Hill Pde A2
Marle Hill Rd A2
Millbrook St A1
Milsom St A2
Montpellier Gdns C2
Montpellier Gr C2
Montpellier Pde C2
Montpellier Spa Rd C2
Montpellier St C1
Montpellier Terr C2
Montpellier Walk C2
New St B2
North Pl B2
Old Bath Rd C3
Oriel Rd B2
Overton Park Rd B1
Overton Rd B1
Oxford St C3
Parabola Rd B1
Park Pl C1
Park St A1
Pittville Circus A3
Pittville Cr A3
Pittville Lawn A3
Pittville Park A2
Playhouse B2
Police Station B1/C1
Portland St B3
Post Office B2/C2
Prestbury Rd A3
Prince's Rd C1
Priory St B3
Promenade B2
Queen St A1
Recreation Ground A2
Regent Arcade B2
Regent St B2
Rodney Rd B2
Royal Cr B2
Royal Wells Rd B2
St George's Pl B2
St Georges Rd B1
St Gregory's B2
St James St B3
St John's Ave B3
St Luke's Rd C2
St Margarets Rd A2
St Mary's B2
St Matthew's B2
St Paul's La A2
St Paul's Rd A2
St Paul's St A2
St Stephen's Rd C1
Sandford Lido C3
Sandford Mill Road C3
Sandford Park C3
Sandford Rd C2
Selkirk St A3
Sherborne Pl B3
Sherborne St B3
Suffolk Pde C2
Suffolk Rd C1
Suffolk Sq C1
Sun St A1
Swindon Rd B2
Sydenham Villas Rd C3
Tewkesbury Rd A1
The Courtyard B1
Thirlstaine Rd C2
Tivoli Rd C1
Tivoli St C1
Town Hall & Theatre B2
Townsend St A1
Trafalgar St C2
Union St B3
Univ of Gloucestershire (Francis Cl Hall) A2
Univ of Gloucestershire (Hardwick) A1
Victoria Pl B3
Victoria St A2
Vittoria Walk C2
Wel Pl B2
Wellesley Rd A2
Wellington Rd A3
Wellington Sq A3
Wellington St B2
West Drive A3
Western Rd B1
Winchcombe St B3
Winston Churchill Memorial Gardens A1

Chester 333

Abbey Gateway A2
Appleyards La C3
Bedward Row B1
Beeston View C3
Bishop Lloyd's Pal B2
Black Diamond St A2
Bottoms La C3
Boughton B3
Bouverie St A1
Bridge St B2
Bridgegate C2
British Heritage Ctr B2
Brook St A3
Brown's La C2
Bus Station B2
Cambrian Rd A1
Canal St A2
Carrick Rd C1
Castle C2
Castle Dr C2
Cathedral B2
Catherine St A1
Chester A3
Cheyney Rd A1
Chichester St A1
City Rd A3
City Walls B1/B2
City Walls Rd B1
Cornwall St A2
County Hall C2
Cross Hey C3
Cuppin St B2
Curzon Park North C1
Curzon Park South C1
Dee Basin A1
Dee La B3
Delamere St A2
Dewa Roman Experience B2
Duke St B2
Eastgate B2
Eastgate St B2
Eaton Rd C2
Edinburgh Way C3
Elizabeth Cr B3
Fire Station A2
Foregate St B2
Frodsham St B2
Gamul House B2
Garden La A1
Gateway Theatre B2
George St A2
Gladstone Ave A1
God's Providence House B2
Gorse Stacks A2
Greenway St C2
Grosvenor Bridge C1
Grosvenor Museum B2
Grosvenor Park B3
Grosvenor Precinct B2
Grosvenor Rd C1
Grosvenor St B2
Groves Rd B3
Guildhall Museum B1
Handbridge C2
Hartington St C3
Hoole Way A2
Hunter St B2
Information Ctr B2
King Charles' Tower A2
King St A2
Leisure Centre A2
Library B2
Lightfoot St A3
Little Roodee C2
Liverpool Rd A2
Love St B3
Lower Bridge St B2
Lower Park Rd B3
Lyon St A2
Magistrates Court B2
Meadows La C3
Military Museum C2
Milton St A3
New Crane St B1
Nicholas St B2
Northgate A2
Northgate St A2
Nun's Rd B1
Old Dee Bridge C2
Overleigh Rd C2
Park St B2
Police Station B2
Post Office A2/A3/B2/C2
Princess St B2
Queen St B2
Queen's Park Rd C3
Queen's Rd A3
Race Course B1
Raymond St A1
River La C2
Roman Amphitheatre & Gardens B2
Roodee, The (Chester Racecourse) B1
Russell St A3
St Anne St A2
St George's Cr C3
St Martin's Gate A1
St Martin's Way B1
St Oswalds Way A2
Saughall Rd A1
Sealand Rd A1
South View Rd A1
Stanley Palace B1
Station Rd A3
Steven St A3
The Bars B3
The Cross B2
The Groves B3
The Meadows B3
Tower Rd B1
Town Hall B2
Union St B3
Vicar's La B2
Victoria Cr C3
Victoria Rd A2
Walpole St A1
Water Tower St A1
Watergate B1
Watergate St B2
Whipcord La A1
White Friars B2
York St B3

Chichester 333

Adelaide Rd A3
Alexandra Rd A3
Arts Centre B2
Ave de Chartres B1/B2
Barlow Rd A1
Basin Rd C2
Beech Ave B1
Bishops Pal Gardens B2
Bishopsgate Walk A3
Bramber Rd C3
Broyle Rd A2
Bus Station B2
Caledonian Rd B3
Cambrai Ave B3
Canal Wharf C2
Canon La B2
Cathedral B2
Cavendish St A1
Cawley Rd B2
Cedar Dr A1
Chapel St A2
Cherry Orchard Rd C3
Chichester By-Pass C2/C3
Chichester Cinema B3
Chichester Festival A2
Chichester B2
Churchside A2
Cineworld C1
City Walls B2
Cleveland Rd B3
College La A2
Coll of Science & Technology B1
Cory Cl C2
Council Offices B2
County Hall B2
Courts B2
District B2
Duncan Rd A1
Durnford Cl A1
East Pallant B2
East Row B2
East St B2
East Walls B3
Eastland Rd C3
Ettrick Cl B3
Ettrick Rd B3
Exton Rd C3
Fire Station A2
Football Ground A2
Franklin Pl A2
Friary (Rems of) A2
Garland Cl C3
Green La A3
Grove Rd C3
Guilden Rd B3
Guildhall A2
Hawthorn Cl A1
Hay Rd C3
Henty Gdns B1
Herald Dr C3
Information Ctr B2
John's St B2
Joys Croft A3
Jubilee Pk A3
Jubilee Rd A3
Juxon Cl B2
Kent Rd A3
King George Gdns A2
King's Ave C2
Kingsham Ave C3
Kingsham Rd C2
Laburnum Gr B2
Leigh Rd C1
Lennox Rd A3
Lewis Rd A3
Library B2
Lion St B2
Litten Terr A3
Little London B2
Lyndhurst Rd B3
Market B3
Market Ave B2
Market Cross B2
Market Rd B3
Martlet Cl C2
Melbourne Rd A3
Mount La B1
New Park Rd A3
Newlands La A1
North Pallant B2
North St A2
North Walls A2
Northgate A2
Oak Ave A1
Oak Cl A1
Oaklands Park A2
Oaklands Way A2
Orchard Ave A1
Orchard St A1
Ormonde Ave B3
Pallant House B2
Parchment St A1
Parklands Rd A1/B1
Peter Weston Pl B3
Police Station C2
Post Office A1/B2/B3
Priory La A2
Priory Park A2
Priory Rd A2
Queen's Ave C1
Riverside A3
Roman Amphitheatre B3
St Cyriacs A2
St Pancras A3
St Paul's Rd A2
St Richard's Hospital (A&E) A3
Shamrock Cl A3
Sherbourne Rd A1
Somerstown A2
South Bank C2
South Downs Planetarium C2
South Pallant B2
South St B2
Southgate B2
Spitalfield La A3
Stirling Rd B3
Stockbridge Rd C1/C2
Swanfield Dr A3
Terminus Ind Est C1
Terminus Rd C1
The Hornet B3
The Litten A3
Tower St A2
Tozer Way A3
Turnbull Rd A3
Upton Rd C1
Velyn Ave B3
Via Ravenna B1
Walnut Ave A1
West St B2
Westgate B1
Westgate Fields B1
Westgate Leisure Ctr B1
Weston Ave C1
Whyke Cl C3
Whyke La B3
Whyke Rd C3
Winden Ave B3

Colchester 333

Abbey Gateway C2
Albert St A1
Albion Grove C2
Alexandra Rd C1
Artillery St C3
Arts Centre B1
Balkerne Hill B1
Barrack St C3
Beaconsfield Rd C1
Beche Rd C3
Bergholt Rd A1
Bourne Rd C3
Brick Kiln Rd A1
Bristol Rd B2
Broadlands Way A3
Brook St B3
Bury Cl B2
Bus Sta B2
Butt Rd C1
Camp Folley North C2
Camp Folley South C2
Campion Rd C2
Cannon St C3
Canterbury Rd C2
Castle B2
Castle Park B2
Castle Rd B2
Catchpool Rd A1
Causton Rd B1
Cavalry Barracks C1
Chandlers Row C3
Circular Rd East C2
Circular Rd North C1
Circular Rd West C1
Clarendon Way A1
Claudius Rd C2
Colchester Camp Abbey Field C1
Colchester Institute B1
Colchester A1
Colchester Town C2
Colne Bank Ave A1
Colne View Retail Pk A2
Compton Rd A3
Cowdray Ave A1/A2
Cowdray Centre, The A2
Crouch St B1
Crowhurst Rd B1
Culver Square Sh Ctr B1
Culver St East B2
Culver St West B1
Dilbridge Rd A3
East Hill B2
East St B3
East Stockwell St B1
Eld La B1
Essex Hall Rd A1
Exeter Dr B2
Fairfax Rd C2
Fire Station A2
Flagstaff Rd C1
George St B2
Gladstone Rd C2
Golden Noble Hill C2
Goring Rd A3
Granville Rd C3
Greenstead Rd B3
Guildford Rd B2
Harsnett Rd C3
Harwich Rd B3
Head St B1
High St B1/B2
High Woods Ctry Park A2
Hollytrees B2
Hythe Hill C3
Information Ctr B2
Ipswich Rd A3
Jarmin Rd A2
Kendall Rd C2
Kimberley Rd C3
King Stephen Rd C3
Le Cateau Barracks C1
Leisure World A2
Library B1
Lincoln Way B2
Lion Walk Sh Ctr B1
Lisle Rd C2
Lucas Rd C2
Magdalen Green C3
Magdalen St C2
Maidenburgh St B2
Maldon Rd C1
Manor Rd B1
Margaret Rd A1
Mason Rd A2
Mercers Way A1
Mercury B1
Mersea Rd C2
Meyrick Cr C2
Mile End Rd A1
Military Rd C2
Mill St C2
Minories B2
Moorside B3
Morant Rd C3
Napier Rd C2
Natural History B2
New Town Rd C2
Norfolk Cr A3
North Hill B1
North Station Rd A1
Northgate St B1
Nunns Rd B1
Odeon B1
Old Coach Rd B3
Old Heath Rd C3
Osborne St B2
Petrolea Cl A1
Police Station C1
Popes La B1
Port La C3
Post Office B1/B2/C2
Priory St B2
Queen St B2
Rawstorn Rd B1
Rebon St C3
Recreation Rd C3
Ripple Way A3
Roman Rd B2
Roman Wall B2
Romford Cl A3
Rosebery Ave B2
St Andrews Ave B3
St Andrews Gdns B3
St Botolph St B2
St Botolphs B2
St John's Abbey (site of) C2
St John's St B1
St Johns Walk Sh Ctr B1
St Leonards Rd C3
St Marys Fields B1
St Peters B1
St Peter's St B1
Salisbury Ave C1
Serpentine Walk A1
Sheepen Pl B1
Sheepen Rd B1
Sir Isaac's Walk B1
Smythies Ave B2
South St C1
South Way C1
Sports Way A2
Suffolk Cl A3
Town Hall B1
Valentine Dr A3
Victor Rd C3
Wakefield Cl B2
Wellesley Rd C1
Wells Rd B2/B3
West St C1
West Stockwell St B1
Weston Rd C3
Westway A1
Wickham Rd C1
Wimpole Rd C3
Winchester Rd C2
Winnock Rd C2
Wolfe Ave C2
Worcester Rd B2

Coventry 334

Abbots La A1
Albany Rd B1
Alma St B3
Art Faculty B3
Asthill Grove C2
Bablake School A1
Barras La A1/B1
Barrs Hill School A1
Belgrade B2
Bishop Burges St A2
Bond's Hospital B1
Broad Gate B2
Broadway C1
Bus Station A3
Butts Radial B1
Canal Basin A2
Canterbury St A3
Cathedral B3
Chester St A1
Cheylesmore Manor House B2
Christ Church Spire B2
City Walls & Gates A2
Corporation St B2
Council House B2
Coundon Rd A1
Coventry Station C2
Coventry Transport Museum A2
Cox St A3
Croft Rd B1
Dalton Rd C1
Deasy Rd C3
Earl St B2
Eaton Rd C2
Fairfax St B2
Foleshill Rd A2
Ford's Hospital B2
Fowler Rd A1
Friars Rd C2
Gordon St C1
Gosford St B3
Greyfriars Green B2
Greyfriars Rd B2
Gulson Rd B3
Hales St A2
Harnall Lane East A3
Harnall Lane West A2
Herbert Art Gallery & Museum B3
Hertford St B2
Hewitt Ave A1
High St B2
Hill St B1
Holy Trinity B2
Holyhead Rd A1
Howard St A3
Huntingdon Rd C1
Information Ctr B2
Jordan Well B3
King Henry VIII Sch C1
Lady Godiva Statue B2
Lamb St A2
Leicester Row A2
Library B2
Little Park St B2
London Rd C3
Lower Ford St B3
Magistrates & Crown Courts B2
Manor House Drive B2
Manor Rd C2
Market B2
Martyr's Memorial C2
Meadow St B1
Meriden St A1
Michaelmas Rd C2
Middleborough Rd A1
Mile La C3
Millennium Place A2
Much Park St B3
Naul's Mill Park A1
New Union B2
Park Rd C2
Parkside C3
Post Office B2
Primrose Hill St A3
Priory Gardens & Visitor Centre B2
Priory St B3
Puma Way C3
Quarryfield La C3
Queen's Rd B1
Quinton Rd C2
Radford Rd A2
Raglan St B3
Retail Park C1
Ringway (Hill Cross) A1
Ringway (Queens) B1
Ringway (Rudge) B1
Ringway (St Johns) B3
Ringway (St Nicholas) A2
Ringway (St Patricks) C2
Ringway (Swanswell) A2
Ringway (Whitefriars) B3
St John St B2
St John The Baptist B2
St Nicholas St A2
Skydome B1
Spencer Ave C1
Spencer Park C1
Spon St B1
Sports Centre B3
Stoney Rd C2
Stoney Stanton Rd A3
Swanswell Pool A3
Sydney Stringer Acad A3
Technical College B1
Technology Park C3
The Precinct B2
Theatre B1
Thomas Landsdail St C2
Tomson Ave A1
Top Green C1
Trinity St B2
University B3
University Sports Ctr B3
Upper Hill St A1
Upper Well St A2
Victoria St A3
Vine St A3
Warwick Rd C2
Waveley Rd B1
Westminster Rd C1
White St A3
Windsor St B1

Derby 334

Abbey St C1
Agard St B1
Albert St B2
Albion St B2
Ambulance Station B1
Arthur St A1
Ashlyn Rd B3
Assembly Rooms B2
Babington La C2
Becket St B1
Belper Rd A1
Bold La B1
Bradshaw Way C2
Bradshaw Way Ret Pk C2
Bridge St B1
Brook St B1
Burton Rd C1
Bus Station B2
Caesar St A2
Canal St C3
Carrington St C3
Cathedral B2
Cathedral Rd B1
Charnwood St C2
Chester Green Rd A2
City Rd A2
Clarke St A3
Cock Pitt B3
Council House B2
Courts B1
Cranmer Rd B3
Crompton St C1
Crown & County Courts B2
Curzon St B1
Darley Grove A1
Derby C3
Derbyshire County Cricket Ground B3
Derwent Bsns Centre A2
Derwent St B2
Drewry La C1
Duffield Rd A1
Duke St A2
Dunton Cl B3
Eagle Market C2
Eastgate B3
East St B2
Exeter St B2
Farm St C1
Ford St B1
Forester St C1
Fox St A2
Friar Gate B1
Friary St B1
Full St B2
Gerard St C1
Gower St C2
Green La C2
Grey St C1
Guildhall B2
Harcourt St C1
Highfield Rd A1
Hill La C2
Information Ctr B2
Iron Gate B2
John St C3
Joseph Wright Centre B1
Kedleston Rd A1
Key St B2
King Alfred St C1
King St A1
Kingston St A1
Lara Croft Way C2
Leopold St C2
Library B1
Liversage St C3
Lodge La B1
London Rd C2
London Rd Community Hospital C2
Macklin St C1
Mansfield Rd A2
Market B2
Market Pl B2
May St C1
Meadow La B3
Melbourne St C2
Mercian Way C1
Midland Rd C3
Monk St C1
Morledge B2
Mount St C1
Mus & Art Gallery B1
Noble St C3
North Parade A1
North St A1
Nottingham Rd B3
Osmaston Rd C2
Otter St A1
Park St C3
Parker St A1
Pickfords House B1
Playhouse C2
Police HQ A2
Police Station B2
Post Office A1/A2/B1/B2/C2/C3
Prime Enterprise Park A2
Pride Parkway C3
Prime Parkway A2
Queens Leisure Centre B1
Racecourse A3
Railway Terr C3
Register Office B2
Sadler Gate B1
St Alkmund's Way B1/B2
St Helens House A1
St Mary's A1
St Mary's Bridge A2
St Mary's Bridge Chapel A2
St Mary's Gate B1
St Paul's Rd A2
St Peter's C2
St Peter's St C2
Showcase De Lux C2
Siddals Rd C3
Silk Mill B2
Sir Frank Whittle Rd A3
Spa La C1
Spring St C1
Stafford St B1
Station Approach C3
Stockbrook St C1
Stores Rd A3
Traffic St C2
Wardwick B1
Werburgh St C1
West Ave A1
Westfield Centre C2
West Meadows Ind Est B3
Wharf Rd A2
Wilmot St C2
Wilson St C1
Wood's La C1

Dorchester 334

Ackerman Rd B3
Acland Rd A2
Albert Rd A1
Alexandra Rd B1
Alfred Place B3
Alfred Rd B2
Alington Ave B3
Alington Rd B3
Ambulance Station B3
Ashley Rd B1
Balmoral Cres C3

Barnes Way B2/C2
Borough Gdns A1
Brewery Sq B1
Bridport Rd A1
Buckingham Way C3
Caters Place A1
Cemetery A3/C1
Charles St A2
Coburg Rd B1
Colliton St A1
Cornwall Rd A1
Cromwell Rd B1
Culliford Rd B2
Culliford Rd North B2
Dagmar Rd B1
Damer's Rd B1
Diggory Cres C2
Dinosaur Museum A2
Dorchester Bypass C2
Dorchester South Station B1
Dorchester West Station B1
Dorset County Council Offices A1
Dorset County (A&E) B1
Dorset County Mus A1
Duchy Close C3
Duke's Ave B2
Durngate St A2
Durnover Court A3
Eddison Ave B3
Edward Rd B1
Egdon Rd C2
Elizabeth Frink Statue B2
Farfrae Cres B2
Forum Centre, The B1
Friary Hill A2
Friary Lane A2
Frome Terr A2
Garland Cres C3
Glyde Path Rd A1
Government Offices B3
Gt Western Rd B1
Grosvenor Cres C1
Grosvenor Rd C1
H M Prison A1
Herringston Rd C1
High St East A2
High St Fordington A2
High Street West A1
Holloway Rd A2
Icen Way A2
Keep Military Museum, The A1
Kings Rd A3/B3
Kingsbere Cres C2
Lancaster Rd B2
Library A1
Lime Cl C1
Linden Ave B2
London Cl A3
London Rd A2/A3
Lubbecke Way A3
Lucetta La B2
Maiden Castle Rd C1
Manor Rd C2
Marshwood Pl B2
Maumbury Rd B1
Maumbury Rings B1
Mellstock Ave C2
Mill St A3
Miller's Cl A1
Mistover Cl C1
Monmouth Rd B1/B2
Moynton Rd C2
Nature Reserve A2
North Sq A2
Northernhay A1
Odeon B1
Old Crown Court & Cells A1
Olga Rd B1
Orchard St A2
Police Station B1
Post Office A1/B1
Pound Lane A2
Poundbury Rd A1
Prince of Wales Rd B2
Prince's St A1
Queen's Ave B1
Roman Town House A1
Roman Wall A1
Rothesay Rd C2
St George's Rd B3
Salisbury Field A2
Sandringham Sports Centre B3
Shaston Cres C2
Smokey Hole La B3
South Court Ave C1
South St B1
South Walks Rd B2
Superstore C3
Teddy Bear House A1
Temple Cl C1
Terracotta Warriors & Teddy Bear Mus A2
The Grove A1
Town Hall A2
Town Pump A2
Trinity St A1
Tutankhamun Ex A1
Victoria Rd B1
Weatherbury Way C2
Wellbridge Cl C1
West Mills Rd A1
West Walks Rd A1
Weymouth Ave C1
Williams Ave B1
Winterbourne (BMI) C1
Wollaston Rd A2
York Rd B2

Dumfries 334

Academy St A2
Aldermanhill Rd B3
Ambulance Station C3
Annan Rd A3
Ardwall Rd A3
Ashfield Dr A1
Atkinson Rd C1
Averill Cres C1
Balliol Ave C1
Bank St B2
Bankend Rd C3
Barn Slaps B3
Barrie Ave B3
Beech Ave A1
Bowling Green A3
Brewery St B2
Brodie Ave C2
Brooke St B2
Broomlands Dr C1
Brooms Rd B3
Buccleuch St A2
Burns House B2
Burns Mausoleum B3
Burns St B2
Burns Statue A2
Bus Station B1
Cardoness St A3
Castle St A2
Catherine St A2
Cattle Market A3
Cemetery B3
Cemetery C2
Church Cres A2
Church St B2
College Rd A1
College St A1
Corbelly Hill B1
Convent, The B1
Corberry Park B1
Cornwall Mt A3
County Offices A2
Court A2
Craigs Rd C3
Cresswell Ave B3
Cresswell Hill B3
Cumberland St B3
David Keswick Athletic Centre A3
David St B1
Dock Park C3
Dockhead B2
Dumfries A3
Dumfries Academy A2
Dumfries Museum & Camera Obscura B2
Dumfries Royal Infirmary (A&E) C3
East Riverside Dr C3
Edinburgh Rd A2
English St B2
Fire Station B3
Friar's Vennel A2
Galloway St B1
George Douglas Dr C1
George St A2
Gladstone Rd C2
Glasgow St A1
Glebe St B3
Glencaple Rd C3
Goldie Ave A1
Goldie Cres A1
Golf Course C3
Greyfriars A2
Grierson Ave B3
HM Prison B1
Hamilton Ave C1
Hamilton Starke Park C2
Hazelrigg Ave C1
Henry St B3
Hermitage Dr C1
High Cemetery C3
High St A2
Hill Ave C2
Hill St B1
Holm Ave C2
Hoods Loaning A3
Howgate St B1
Huntingdon Rd A3
Information Ctr B2
Irish St B2
Irving St A2
King St A2
Kingholm Rd C3
Kirkpatrick Ct C2
Laurieknowe B1
Leafield Rd B3
Library A2
Lochfield Rd A1
Loreburn Pk A3
Loreburn St A2
Loreburne Sh Ctr B2
Lover's Walk A2
Martin Ave B3
Maryholm Dr A1
Mausoleum B3
Maxwell St B1
McKie Ave B3
Mews La A2
Mid Steeple B2
Mill Green B2
Mill Rd B1
Moat Rd C2
Moffat Rd A3
Mountainhall Pk C3
Nelson St B1
New Abbey Rd B1/C1
New Bridge B1
Newall Terr A2
Nith Ave A2
Nith Bank C3
Nithbank Hospital C3
Nithside Ave A1
Odeon B2
Old Bridge B1
Old Bridge House B1
Palmerston Park (Queen of the South FC) A1
Park Rd C1
Pleasance Ave C1
Police HQ A3
Police Station A2
Portland Dr A1
Post Office A2/B1/B2/B3/B3
Priestlands Dr C1
Primrose St B1
Queen St B3
Queensberry St A2
Rae St A2
Richmond Ave C2
Robert Burns Ctr B2
Roberts Cres C1
Robertson Ave C3
Robinson Dr C1
Rosefield Rd C2
Rosemount St B1
Rotchell Park C1
Rotchell Rd B1
Rugby Football Gd C1
Ryedale Rd C2
St Andrews B2
St John the Evangelist A2
St Josephs College B3
St Mary's Ind Est A3
St Mary's St A3
St Michael St B2
St Michael's B2
St Michael's Bridge B2
St Michael's Bridge Rd B2
St Michael's Cemetery B3
Shakespeare St B2
Solway Dr C2
Stakeford St A1
Stark Cres C2
Station Rd A3
Steel Ave A1
Sunderries Ave A1
Sunderries Rd A1
Suspension Brae B2
Swimming Pool A1
Terregles St B1
Theatre Royal B2
Troqueer Rd C2
Union St A1
Wallace St B3
Welldale B2
West Riverside Dr C2
White Sands B2

Dundee 334

Adelaide Pl A1
Airlie Pl C1
Albany Terr A1
Albert St A3
Alexander St A2
Ann St A2
Arthurstone Terr A3
Bank St B2
Barrack Rd A1
Barrack St B2
Bell St B2
Blackscroft A3
Blinshall St B1
Brown St B1
Bus Station B3
Caird Hall B2
Camperdown St B3
Candle La B3
Carmichael St A1
City Churches B2
City Quay B3
City Sq B2
Commercial St B2
Constable St A3
Constitution Ct A1
Constitution Cres A1
Constitution St A1/B2
Cotton Rd A3
Courthouse Sq B1
Cowgate A3
Crescent St A3
Crichton St B2
Dens Brae A3
Dens Rd A3
Discovery Point C2
Douglas St B1
Drummond St A1
Dudhope Castle A1
Dudhope St A2
Dudhope Terr A1
Dundee C2
Dundee College A1
Dundee Contemporary Arts C2
Dundee High School B2
Dundee Repertory C2
Dura St A3
East Dock St B3
East Whale La B3
East Marketgait B3
Erskine St A3
Euclid Cr B2
Forebank Rd A2
Foundry La A3
Frigate Unicorn B3
Gallagher Retail Park B3
Gellatly St B3
Government Offices C2
Guthrie St B1
Hawkhill B1
Hilltown A2
Howff Cemetery, The B2
Information Ctr B2
King St A3
Kinghorne Rd A1
Ladywell Ave A3
Laurel Bank A2
Law Hill, The A1
Law Rd A1
Law St A1
Library A2
Little Theatre A2
Lochee Rd B1
Lower Princes St A3
Lyon St A3
McManus Museum & Art Gallery B2
Meadow Side B2
Meadowside St Pauls B2
Mercat Cross B2
Murraygate B2
Nelson St A2
Nethergate B2/C1
North Marketgait B2
North Lindsay St B2
Old Hawkhill B1
Olympia Leisure Ctr C3
Overgate Shopping Centre B2
Park Pl B1
Perth Rd C1
Police Station A2/B1
Post Office B2
Princes St A3
Prospect Pl A2
Reform St B2
Riverside Dr C2
Roseangle C1
Rosebank St A2
RRS Discovery C2
St Andrew's C2
St Pauls Episcopal B3
Science Centre C2
Seagate B2
Sheriffs Court B1
South George St A2
South Marketgait B3
South Tay St B2
South Ward Rd B2
Steps A2
Tay Road Bridge C3
Tayside House B2
Trades La B3
Union St B2
Union Terr A1
University Library B2
University of Abertay B2
University of Dundee B1
Upper Constitution St A1
Verdant Works B1
Victoria Dock B3
Victoria Rd A2
Victoria St A3
West Marketgait B1/B2
Ward Rd B1
Wellgate B2
West Bell St B1
Westfield Pl C1
William St A3
Wishart Arch A3

Durham 334

Alexander Cr B2
Allergate B2
Archery Rise C1
Assize Courts B3
Back Western Hill A1
Bakehouse La A3
Baths B3
Baths Bridge B3
Boat House B3
Bowling A2
Boyd St C3
Bus Station B2
Castle B2
Castle Chare B2
Cathedral B2
Church St C3
Clay La C1
Claypath B3
College of St Hild & St Bede B3
County Hall A1
County Hospital B1
Crook Hall & Gardens A3
Crossgate B2
Crossgate Peth C1
Darlington Rd C1
Durham A2
Durham Light Infantry Mus & Arts Gallery A2
Durham School C2
Ellam Ave C1
Elvet Bridge B3
Elvet Court B3
Farnley Hey B1
Ferens Cl A3
Fieldhouse La A1
Flass St B1
Framwelgate A2
Framwelgate Bridge B2
Framwelgate Peth A2
Framwelgate Waterside A2
Frankland La A3
Freeman's Pl A3
Freeman's Quay L Ctr A3
Gala Theatre & Cinema B3
Gates Sh Ctr, The B2
Geoffrey Ave C1
Gilesgate B3
Grey College C3
Hallgarth St C3
Hatfield College B3
Hawthorn Terr B1
Heritage Centre B3
HM Prison B3
Information Ctr B3
John St B1
Kingsgate Bridge B3
Laburnum Terr B1
Lawson Terr B1
Leazes Rd B2/B3
Library B2
Margery La B2
Market B2
Mavin St C3
Millburngate B2
Millburngate Bridge B2
Millennium Bridge (foot/cycle) A2
Mountjoy Research Centre C3
Mus of Archaeology B2
Nevilledale Terr B1
New Elvet B3
New Elvet Bridge B3
North Bailey B3
North End A1
North Rd A1/B2
Observatory C1
Old Elvet B3
Oriental Museum C2
Oswald Court C3
Parkside B2
Passport Office A2
Percy Terr B1
Pimlico C2
Police Station B3
Post Office A1/B2
Potters Bank C1/C2
Prebends Bridge C2
Prebends Walk C2
Prince Bishops Sh Ctr B3
Princes St A1
Providence Row A3
Quarryheads La C2
Redhills La B1
Redhills Terr B1
Saddler St B3
St Chad's College C3
St Cuthbert's Society C2
St John's College C2
St Margaret's B2
St Mary The Less C2
St Mary's College C2
St Monica Grove B1
St Nicholas' B3
St Oswald's C3
Sidegate A2
Silver St B2
Sixth Form Centre (Durham Gilesgate) A3
South Bailey C2
South Rd C3
South St B2
Springwell Ave A1
Stockton Rd C3
Students' Rec Centre B3
Sutton St B2
The Avenue B1
The Crescent A1
The Grove A1
The Sands A3
Town Hall B2
Treasury Museum B2
University B2
University Arts Block B3
University Library C3
Univ Science Site C3
Walkergate Centre A3
Wearside Dr A3
Western Hill A1
Wharton Park A2
Whinney Hill C3
Whitehouse Ave C1

Edinburgh 334

Abbey Strand B6
Abbeyhill A6
Abbeyhill Cr B6
Abbeymount A6
Abercromby Pl A3
Adam St C5
Albany La A4
Albany St A4
Albert Memorial B2
Albyn Pl A2
Alva Pl A6
Alva St B1
Ann St A1
Appleton Tower C4
Archibald Pl C3
Argyle House C3
Assembly Rooms & Musical Hall A3
Atholl Cr B1
Atholl Crescent La C1
Bank St B4
Barony St A4
Beaumont Pl C5
Belford Rd B1
Belgrave Cr A1
Belgrave Crescent La A1
Bell's Brae B1
Blackfriars St B4
Blair St B4
Bread St C2
Bristo Pl C4
Bristo St C4
Brougham St C2
Broughton St A4
Brown St C5
Brunton Terr A6
Buckingham Terr A1
Burial Ground A6
Bus Station A4
Caledonian Cr C1
Caledonian Rd C1
Calton Hill A4
Calton Hill A5
Calton Rd B4
Camera Obscura & Outlook Tower B3
Candlemaker Row C4
Canning St B2
Canongate B5
Canongate B5
Carlton St A1
Carlton Terr A6
Carlton Terrace La A6
Castle St B2
Castle Terr B2
Castlehill B3
Central Library B4
Chalmers Hospital C3
Chalmers St C3
Chambers St C4
Chapel St C4
Charles St C4
Charlotte Sq B2
Chester St B1
Circus La A2
Circus Pl A2
City Art Centre B4
City Chambers B4
City Observatory A5
Clarendon Crescent A1
Clerk St C5
Coates Crescent B1
Cockburn St B4
College of Art C3
Comely Bank Ave A1
Comely Bank Row A1
Cornwall St C2
Cowans Cl C5
Cowgate B4
Cranston St B5
Crichton St C4
Croft-An-Righ A6
Cumberland St A2
Dalry Pl C1
Dalry Rd C1
Danube St A1
Darnawy St A2
David Hume Tower C4
Davie St C5
Dean Bridge A1
Dean Gdns A1
Dean Park Cr A1
Dean Park Mews A1
Dean Park St A1
Dean Path B1
Dean St A1
Dean Terr A1
Dewar Pl C1
Dewar Place La C1
Doune Terr A2
Drummond Pl A3
Drummond St C5
Drumsheugh Gdns B1
Dublin Mews A3
Dublin St A4
Dublin Street La South A4
Dumbiedykes Rd B5
Dundas St A3
Earl Grey St C2
East Crosscauseway C5
East Market St B4
East Norton Pl A6
East Princes St Gdns B3
Easter Rd A6
Edinburgh (Waverley) B4
Edinburgh Castle B3
Edinburgh Dungeon B4
Edinburgh International Conference Ctr C2
Elder St A4
Esplanade B3
Eton Terr A1
Eye Pavilion C3
Festival Office B3
Festival Theatre Edinburgh C4
Filmhouse C2
Fire Station C2
Floral Clock B3
Forres St A2
Forth St A4
Fountainbridge C2
Frederick St A3
Freemasons' Hall B3
Fruit Market B4
Gardner's Cr C2
George Heriot's School C3
George IV Bridge B4
George Sq C4
George Sq La C4
George St B3
Georgian House B2
Gladstone's Land B3
Glen St C3
Gloucester La A2
Gloucester Pl A2
Gloucester St A2
Graham St C3
Grassmarket C3
Great King St A3
Great Stuart B1
Greenside La A5
Greenside Row A5
Greyfriars Kirk C4
Grindlay St C2
Grosvenor St C1
Grove St C1
Gullan's Cl B5
Guthrie St B4
Hanover St A3
Hart St A4
Haymarket C1
Haymarket Station C1
Heriot Pl C3
Heriot Row A2
High School Yard B5
High St B4
Hill Pl C5
Hill St A2
Hillside Cr A5
Holyrood Park C6
Holyrood Rd B5
Home St C2
Hope St B2
Horse Wynd B6
Howden St C5
Howe St A2
India Pl A2
India St A2
Infirmary St B4
Information Ctr B4
Jamaica Mews A2
Jeffrey St B4
John Knox House B4
Johnston Terr C3
Keir St C3
Kerr St A2
King's Stables Rd B2
Lady Lawson St C3
Lauriston Gdns C3
Lauriston Park C3
Lauriston Pl C3
Lauriston St C3
Lawnmarket B3
Learmonth Gdns A1
Learmonth Terr A1
Leith St A4
Lennox St A1
Lennox St La A1
Leslie Pl A2
London Rd A5
Lothian Health Board C5
Lothian Rd B2
Lothian St C4
Lower Menz Pl A6
Lynedoch Pl B1
Manor Pl B1
Market St B4
Marshall St C4
Maryfield A6
Maryfield Pl A6
McEwan Hall C4
Medical School C4
Melville St B1
Meuse La B4
Middle Meadow Walk C4
Milton St A6
Montrose Terr A6
Moray House (college) B5
Moray Place A2
Morrison Link C1
Morrison St C1
Mound Pl B3
Multrees Walk A4
Mus Collections Ctr A4
Mus of Childhood B5
Mus of Edinburgh B5
Mus on the Mound B4
National Gallery B3
National Library of Scotland B4
National Monument A5
National Museum of Scotland C4
National Portrait Gallery B4
National Records Scotland A4
Nelson Monument A5
Nelson St A3
New St B5
Nicolson Sq C4
Nicolson St C4
Niddry St B4
North Bridge B4
North Meadow Walk C3
North Bank St B3
North Castle St A2
North Charlotte St A2
North St Andrew St A4
North St David St A3
North West Circus Pl A2
Northumberland St A3
Odeon C2
Old Royal High School A5
Old Tolbooth Wynd B5
Omni Centre A4
Our Dynamic Earth B6
Oxford Terr A1
Pal of Holyrood Ho B6
Palmerston Pl B1
Panmure Pl C3
Parliament House B4
Parliament Sq B4
People's Story, The B5
Playhouse Theatre A4
Pleasance C5
Police Station A4
Ponton St C2
Post Office A3/A4/B5/C1/C2/C4/C5
Potterrow C4
Princes Mall B4
Princes St B3
Princes St B3
Queen St A2
Queen Street Gdns A3
Queen's Dr B6/C6
Queensferry Rd A1
Queensferry St B1
Queensferry Street La B2
Radical Rd C6
Randolph Cr B1
Regent Gdns A5
Regent Rd B5
Regent Rd Park A6
Regent Terr A5
Remains of Holyrood Abbey (AD 1128) A6
Richmond La C5
Richmond Pl C5
Rose St B2
Rosemount Bldgs C1
Ross Open Air Theatre B3
Rothesay Pl B1
Rothesay Terr B1
Roxburgh Pl C5
Roxburgh St C5
Royal Bank of Scotland A4
Royal Circus A2
Royal Lyceum C2
Royal Scottish Acad B3
Royal Terr A5
Royal Terrace Gdns A5
Rutland Sq B2
Rutland St B2
St Andrew Sq A4
St Andrew Sq A4
St Andrew's House A4
St Bernard's Cr A1
St Cecilia's Hall B4
St Colme St A2
St Cuthbert's B2
St Giles' B4
St James Centre A4
St John St B5
St John's B2
St John's Hill B5
St Leonard's Hill C5
St Leonard's La C5
St Leonard's St C5
St Mary's A4
St Mary's Scottish Episcopal B1
St Mary's St B5
St Stephen St A2
Salisbury Crags C6
Saunders St A2
Scotch Whisky Experience B3
Scott Monument B4
Scottish Parliament B6
Scottish Storytelling Centre B5
Semple St C2
Shandwick Pl B2
South Bridge B4
South Charlotte St B2
South College St C4
South Learmonth Gdns A1
South St Andrew St A4
South St David St A3
Spittal St C2
Stafford St B1
Student Centre C4
Surgeons' Hall C5
TA Centre C4
Tattoo Office B4
Teviot Pl C4
The Mall B6
The Mound B3
The Royal Mile B5
The Writer's Mus B4
Thistle St A3
Torphichen Pl C1
Torphichen St C1
Traverse Theatre B2
Tron Sq B4
Tron, The B4
Union St A4
University C4
University Library C4
Upper Grove Pl C1
Usher Hall C2
Vennel C3
Victoria St B4
Viewcraig Gdns B5
Viewcraig St B5
VUE A4
Walker St B1
Waterloo Pl A4
Waverley Bridge B4
Wemyss Pl A2
West Approach Rd C1
West Crosscauseway C5
West End B1
West Maitland St C1
West of Nicholson St C4
West Port C3
West Princes St Gdns B3
West Richmond St C5
West Tollcross C2
White Horse Cl B5
William St B1
Windsor St A5
York La A4
York Pl A4
York Pl A4
Young St B2

Exeter 334

Alphington St C1
Athelstan Rd B3
Bampfylde St B2
Barnardo Rd C3
Barnfield Hill B3
Barnfield Rd B2/B3
Barnfield Theatre B2
Bartholomew St East B1
Bartholomew St West B1
Bear St B2
Beaufort Rd C1
Bedford St B2
Belgrave Rd A3
Belmont Rd A3
Blackall Rd A2
Blackboy Rd A3
Bonhay Rd B1
Bull Meadow Rd C2
Bus & Coach Sta B3
Castle St B2
Cecil Rd C1
Cheeke St A3
Church Rd C1
Chute St A3
City Industrial Estate C2
City Wall B1/B2
Civic Centre B2
Clifton Rd B3
Clifton St B3
Clock Tower A1
College Rd B3
Colleton Cr C2
Commercial Rd C1
Coombe St B2
Cowick St C1
Crown Courts B2
Custom House C2
Danes' Rd A2
Denmark Rd B3
Devon County Hall C3
Devonshire Pl A3
Dinham Rd B1
East Grove Rd C3
Edmund St C1
Elmgrove Rd A1
Exe St B1
Exeter Cathedral B2
Exeter Central Sta A1
Exeter City Football Ground A3
Exeter College A1
Exeter Picture Ho B1
Fire Station A1
Fore St B1
Friars Walk C2
Guildhall B2
Guildhall Shopping Ctr B2
Harlequins Sh Ctr B1
Haven Rd C2
Heavitree Rd B3
Hele Rd A1
High St B2
HM Prison A2
Holloway St C2
Hoopern St A2
Horseguards A2
Howell Rd A1
Information Ctr B3
Iron Bridge B1
Isca Rd C1
Jesmond Rd A3
King William St A2
King St B1
Larkbeare Rd C2
Leisure Centre C1
Library B2
Longbrook St A2
Longbrook Terr A2
Lower North St B1
Lucky La C2
Lyndhurst Rd C3
Magdalen Rd B3
Magdalen St B2
Magistrates & Crown Courts A2
Market B2
Market St B2
Marlborough Rd C3
Mary Arches St B1
Matford Ave C3
Matford La C3
Matford Rd C3
May St A3
Mol's Coffee House B2
New Theatre C2
New Bridge St B1
New North Rd A1/A2
North St B1
Northernhay St B1
Norwood Ave C3
Odeon A3
Okehampton St C1
Old Mill Cl C2
Old Tiverton Rd A3
Oxford Rd A3
Paris St B2
Parr St A3
Paul St B1
Pennsylvania Rd A2
Police HQ B3
Portland Street A3
Post Office A3/B1/B3/C1
Powderham Cr A3
Preston St B1
Princesshay Sh Ctr B2
Queen St A1
Queens Rd C1
Queen's Terr A1
Radford Rd C2
Richmond Rd A1
Roberts Rd C2
Rougemont Castle A2
Rougemont House B2
Royal Albert Memorial Museum B2
St David's Hill A1
St James' Pk Sta A3
St James' Rd A3
St Leonard's Rd C3
St Lukes University B3
St Mary Steps C1
St Nicholas Priory B1
St Thomas Station C1
Sandford Walk B3
School for the Deaf C2
School Rd C1
Sidwell St A2
Smythen St B1
South St B2
Southernhay East B2
Southernhay West B2
Spacex Gallery B1
Spicer Rd B3
Sports Centre A3
Summerland St A3
Swimming Pool & Leisure Centre B3
Sydney Rd C1
Tan La C2
The Quay C2
Thornton Hill A2
Topsham Rd C3
Tucker's Hall B1
Tudor St B1
Velwell Rd A1
Verney St A3
Water La C1/C2
Weirfield Rd C2
Well St A3
West Ave A2
West Grove Rd C3
Western Way A3/B1/B2
Wonford Rd B3/C3
York Rd A2

Fort William 335

Abrach Rd A3
Achintore Rd C1
Alma Rd B2
Am Breun Chamas A2
Ambulance Station A3
An Aird A2
Argyll Rd C1
Argyll Terr C1
Bank St B2
Belford Hospital B2
Belford Rd B2/B3
Black Parks A3
Braemore Pl C2
Bruce Pl C2
Bus Station B2
Camanachd Cr A3/B2
Cameron Rd C1

Cameron Sq B1
Carmichael Way A2
Claggan Rd B3
Connochie Rd C1
Cow Hill C3
Creag Dhubh A2
Croft Rd B3
Douglas Pl B2
Dudley Rd B2
Dumbarton Rd C1
Earl of Inverness Rd A3
Fassifern Rd B1
Fire Station A2
Fort William B2
Fort William (Remains) B2
Glasdrum Rd C1
Glen Nevis Pl B3
Gordon Sq B1
Grange Rd C1
Heather Croft Rd C1
Henderson Row C2
High St B1
Highland Visitor Ctr B3
Hill Rd B2
Hospital Belhaven Annexe B3
Information Ctr A3
Inverlochy Ct A3
Kennedy Rd B2/C2
Library B2
Lime Tree Gallery C1
Linnhe Rd B1
Lochaber Leisure Ctr B3
Lochiel Rd A3
Lochy Rd A3
Lundavra Cres C1
Lundavra Rd C1
Lundy Rd A3
Mamore Cr B2
Mary St B2
Middle St B1
Montrose Ave A3
Moray Pl C1
Morven Pl C2
Moss Rd B2
Nairn Cres C1
Nevis Bridge B3
Nevis Rd A3
Nevis Sports Centre A2
Nevis Terr B2
North Rd B3
Obelisk B2
Parade Rd B2
Police Station A3/C1
Post Office A3/B2
Ross Pl C1
St Andrews B2
Shaw Pl B2
Station Brae B1
Studio B1
Treig Rd A3
Underwater Centre A2
Union Rd C1
Victoria Rd B2
Wades Rd A3
West Highland B2
West Highland Collge UHI A2
Young Pl B2

Glasgow 335

Admiral St C2
Albert Bridge C5
Albion St B5
Anderston B3
Anderston Centre B3
Anderston Quay B3
Arches B4
Argyle St A1/A2/B3/B4/B5
Argyle Street B5
Argyll Arcade B5
Arlington St A3
Arts Centre B3
Ashley St A3
Bain St C6
Baird St A6
Baliol St A3
Ballater St C5
Barras, The (Market) C6
Bath St A3
BBC Scotland/SMG B1
Bell St C6
Bell's Bridge B1
Bentinck St A2
Berkeley St A3
Bishop La B3
Black St A6
Blackburn St C2
Blackfriars St B6
Blantyre St A1
Blythswood Sq A4
Blythswood St B4
Bothwell St B4
Brand St C1
Breadalbane St A2
Bridge St C4
Bridge St C4
Bridgegate C5
Briggait C5
Broomhill Park A6
Broomielaw B4
Broomielaw Quay Gdns B3
Brown St B4
Brunswick St B5
Buccleuch St A3
Buchanan Bus Station A5
Buchanan Galleries A5
Buchanan St B5
Buchanan St B5
Cadogan St B4
Caledonian University A5
Calgary St A5
Cambridge St A4
Canal St A5
Candleriggs B5
Carlton Pl C4
Carnarvon St A3
Carrick St B4
Castle St B6
Cathedral Sq B6
Cathedral St B5
Central College of Commerce B5
Ctr for Contemporary Arts A4
Centre St C4
Cessnock C1
Cessnock St C1
Charing Cross A3
Charlotte St C6
Cheapside St B3
Cineworld A5
Citizens' Theatre C5
City Chambers Complex B5
City Halls B5
Clairmont Gdns A2
Claremont St A2
Claremont Terr A2
Claythorne St C6
Cleveland St A3
Clifford La C1
Clifford St C1
Clifton Pl A2
Clifton St A2
Clutha St C1
Clyde Arc B2
Clyde Auditorium B2
Clyde Pl C4
Clyde Place Quay C4
Clyde St C5
Clyde Walkway C3
Clydeside Expressway B2
Coburg St C4
Cochrane St B5
College of Nautical Studies C5
College St B6
Collins St B6
Commerce St C4
Cook St C4
Cornwall St C2
Couper St A5
Cowcaddens A4
Cowcaddens Rd A4
Crimea St B3
Custom House C4
Custom Ho Quay Gdns C4
Dalhousie St A4
Dental Hospital A4
Derby St A2
Dobbie's Loan A4/A5
Dobbie's Loan Pl A5
Dorset St A3
Douglas St B4
Doulton Fountain C6
Dover St A2
Drury St B4
Drygate B6
Duke St B6
Dunaskin St A1
Dunblane St A4
Dundas St B5
Dunlop St C5
East Campbell St C6
Eastvale Pl A1
Eglinton St C4
Elderslie St A3
Elliot St B2
Elmbank St A3
Esmond St A1
Exhibition Centre B2
Exhibition Way B2
Eye Infirmary A2
Festival Park C1
Film Theatre A4
Finnieston Quay B2
Finnieston Sq B2
Finnieston St B2
Fitzroy Pl A2
Florence St C5
Fox St C5
Gallowgate C6
Garnet St A3
Garnethill St A4
Garscube Rd A4
George Sq B5
George St B5
George V Bridge C4
Gilbert St A1
Glasgow Bridge C4
Glasgow Cathedral B6
Glasgow Central B4
Glasgow Green C6
Glasgow Metropolitan College B5/C5
Glasgow Tower B1
Glasgow Science Centre B1
Glasgow Science Centre Footbridge B1
Glassford St B5
Glebe St A6
Gorbals Cross C5
Gorbals St C5
Gordon St B4
Govan Rd B1/C1/C2
Grace St B3
Grand Ole Opry C2
Grafton Pl A5
Grant St A3
Granville St A3
Gray St A2
Greendyke St C6
Grey Eagle St B7
Harley St C1
Harvie St C1
Haugh Rd A1
Heliport B1
Henry Wood Hall A2
High Court C5
High St B6
High Street B6
Hill St A3
Holland St A3
Holm St B4
Hope St A5
Houldsworth St B2
Houston Pl C3
Houston St C3
Howard St C5
Hunter St C6
Hutcheson St B5
Hutchesons Hall B5
Hydepark St B3
Hydro The B2
Imax Cinema B1
India St A3
Information Ctr B5
Ingram St B5
Jamaica St B4
James Watt St B4
John Knox St B6
John St B5
Kelvin Hall A1
Kelvin Statue A2
Kelvin Way A2
Kelvingrove Art Gallery & Museum A1
Kelvingrove Park A2
Kelvingrove St A2
Kelvinhaugh St A1
Kennedy St A6
Kent Rd A2
Killermont St A5
King St B5
King's A3
Kingston Bridge C3
Kingston St C4
Kinning Park C2
Kyle St A5
Lancefield Quay B2
Lancefield St B3
Langshot St C1
Lendel Pl C1
Lighthouse B4
Lister St A6
Little St B3
London Rd C6
Lorne St C1
Lower Harbour B1
Lumsden St A1
Lymburn St A1
Lyndoch Cr A3
Lynedoch Pl A3
Lynedoch St A3
Maclellan St C1
Mair St C2
Maitland St A4
Mansell St C7
Mavisbank Gdns C2
Mcalpine St B3
Mcaslin St A6
McLean Sq C2
McLellan Gallery A4
McPhater St A4
Merchants' House B5
Middlesex St C2
Middleton St C1
Midland St B4
Miller St B5
Millroad St C6
Milnpark St C2
Milton St A4
Minerva St B2
Mitchell Library A3
Mitchell St West B4
Mitchell Theatre A3
Modern Art Gallery B5
Moir St C6
Molendinar St C6
Moncur St C6
Montieth Row C6
Montrose St B5
Morrison St C3
Mosque C5
Nairn St A1
Nelson Mandela Sq B5
Nelson St C4
Nelson's Monument C6
New City Rd A4
Newton St A3
Newton Pl A3
Nicholson St C4
Nile St B5
Norfolk Court C4
Norfolk St C4
North Frederick St B5
North Hanover St B5
North Portland St B6
North St A3
North Wallace St A5
O2 Academy C4
Odeon C3
Old Dumbarton Rd A1
Osborne St B5/C5
Oswald St B4
Overnewton St A1
Oxford St C4
Pacific Dr B1
Paisley Rd C3
Paisley Rd West C1
Park Circus A2
Park Gdns A2
Park St South A2
Park Terr A2
Parkgrove Terr A2
Parnie St C5
Parson St A6
Partick Bridge A1
Passport Office A5
Pavilion Theatre A4
Pembroke St A3
People's Palace C6
Pinkston Rd A6
Piping Centre, The National A5
Pitt St A4/B4
Plantation Park C1
Plantation Quay B1
Police Sta A4/A6/B5
Port Dundas Rd A5
Port St B2
Portman St C2
Prince's Dock B1
Princes Sq B5
Provand's Lordship B6
Queen St B5
Queen Street B5
Renfrew St A3/A4
Renton St A5
Richmond St B5
Robertson St B4
Rose St A4
Rottenrow B5
Royal Concert Hall A5
Royal Cr A2
Royal Exchange Sq B5
Royal Highland Fusiliers Museum A3
Royal Hospital For Sick Children A1
Royal Infirmary B6
Royal Scottish Academy of Music & Drama A4
Royal Terr A2
Rutland Cr C2
St Kent St C6
St Andrew's (RC) C5
St Andrew's C6
St Andrew's St C5
St Enoch B5
St Enoch Shopping Ctr B5
St Enoch Sq B4
St George's Rd A3
St James Rd B6
St Mungo Ave A5/A6
St Mungo Museum of Religious Life B6
St Mungo Pl A6
St Vincent Cr A2
St Vincent Pl B5
St Vincent St B3/B4
St Vincent Street Church B4
St Vincent Terr B3
Saltmarket C5
Sandyford Pl A3
Sauchiehall St A2/A4
School of Art A4
Sclater St B7
Scotland St C2
Scott St A4
Scottish Exhibition & Conference Centre B1
Seaward St C2
Shaftesbury St B3
Sheriff Court C5
Shields Rd C3
Shuttle St B6
Somerset Pl A2
South Portland St C4
Springburn Rd A6
Springfield Quay C3
Stanley St C2
Stevenson St C6
Stewart St A4
Stirling Rd B6
Stirling's Library B5
Stobcross Quay B1
Stobcross Rd B1
Stock Exchange B5
Stockwell Pl C5
Stockwell St B5
Stow College A4
Strathclyde University B6
Sussex St C2
Synagogues A3/C4
Taylor Pl A6
Tenement House A3
Teviot St A1
Theatre Royal A4
Tolbooth Steeple & Mercat Cross C6
Tower St C2
Trades House B5
Tradeston St C4
Transport Museum A1
Tron C5
Trongate B5
Tunnel St B2
Turnbull St C5
Union St B4
Victoria Bridge C5
Virginia St B5
West Greenhill Pl B2
West Regent St A4
Wallace St C3
Walls St B6
Walmer Cr C1
Warrock St B3
Washington St B3
Waterloo St B4
Watson St B6
Watt St C3
Wellington St B4
West Campbell St B4
West George St B4
West Graham St A4
West Regent St B4
West St C4
West St C4
Westminster Terr A2
Whitehall St B3
Wilkes St C7
Wilson St B5
Woodlands Gate A3
Woodlands Rd A3
Woodlands Terr A2
Woodside Cr A3
Woodside Pl A3
Woodside Terr A3
York St B4
Yorkhill Pde A1
Yorkhill St A1

Gloucester 335

Albion St C1
Alexandra Rd B3
Alfred St C3
All Saints Rd C2
Alvin St B2
Arthur St C2
Barton St C2
Barrack Square B1
Blackfriars B1
Blenheim Rd C2
Bristol Rd C1
Brunswick Rd C2
Bruton Way B2
Bus Station B2
City Council Offices B1
City Mus, Art Gall & Library B2
Clarence St B2
Commercial Rd B1
Cromwell St C2
Deans Way A2
Denmark Rd A3
Derby Rd C3
Docks C1
Eastgate Shopping Ctr B1
Eastgate St B2
Edwy Pde A2
Estcourt Cl A3
Estcourt Rd A3
Falkner St C2
Folk Museum B1
GL1 Leisure Centre C2
Gloucester Cath B1
Gloucester Quays Outlet Shopping C1
Gloucester Station B2
Gloucestershire Royal Hospital (A&E) B3
Gloucester Waterways C1
Goodyere St C2
Gouda Way A1
Great Western Rd B3
Guildhall B2
Heathville Rd A3
Henry Rd B3
Henry St B2
Hinton Rd A2
HM Prison B1
India Rd C3
Information Ctr B1
Jersey Rd C3
King's C2
King's Sq B2
Kingsholm (Gloucester RFC) A2
Kingsholm Rd A2
Lansdown Rd A3
Library C2
Llanthony Rd C1
London Rd B3
Longhorn Ave A1
Longsmith St B1
Malvern Rd A3
Market Pde B2
Mercia Rd A1
Metz Way C3
Midland Rd C2
Millbrook St C3
Market B2
Montpellier C1
Napier St C3
Nettleton Rd C2
New Inn B2
New Olympus C3
North Rd A3
Northgate St B2
Oxford Rd A2
Oxford St B2
Pk & Ride Gloucester A1
Park Rd C2
Park St B2
Parliament St C1
Pitt St B1
Police Station B1
Post Office B2
Quay St B1
Recreation Gd A1/A2
Regent St C2
Robert Raikes Ho B1
Royal Oak Rd B1
Russell St B2
Ryecroft St C2
St Aldate St B2
St Ann Way C1
St Catherine St A2
St Mark St A2
St Mary de Crypt B1
St Mary de Lode B1
St Nicholas's B1
St Oswald's Rd A1
St Oswald's Retail Pk A1
St Peter's B2
Seabroke Rd A3
Sebert St A2
Severn Rd C1
Sherborne St B2
Shire Hall B1
Sidney St C3
Soldiers of Gloucestershire B1
Southgate St B1/C1
Spa Field C1
Spa Rd C1
Sports Ground A2/B2
Station Rd B2
Stratton Rd C3
Stroud Rd C1
Superstore A1
Swan Rd A2
The Park C2
The Quay B1
Trier Way C1/C2
Union St A2
Vauxhall Rd C3
Victoria St C2
Walham Lane A1
Wellington St C2
Westgate Retail Park B1
Westgate St B1
Widden St C2
Worcester St B2

Grimsby 335

Abbey Drive East C2
Abbey Drive West C2
Abbey Park Rd C2
Abbey Rd C2
Abbey Walk C2
Abbeygate Sh Ctr C2
Abbotsway C2
Adam Smith St A1/A2
Ainslie St C2
Albert St A3
Alexandra Dock A2/B2
Alexandra Retail Park A2
Alexandra Rd A2/B2
Annesley St A2
Armstrong St A1
Arthur St B1
Augusta St C1
Bargate C1
Beeson St A1
Bethlehem St C2
Bradley St B3
Brighowgate C1/C2
Bus Station B2/C2
Canterbury Dr C1
Cartergate B1/C1
Catherine St C3
Caxton A3
Chantry La B1
Charlton St A1
Church La C2
Church St A3
Cleethorpe Rd A3
College C2
College St C1
Compton Dr C1
Corporation Bridge A2
Corporation Rd A1
Court B3
Crescent St B1
Deansgate C1
Doughty Rd C2
Dover St B1
Duchess St C2
Dudley St C1
Duke of York Gardens B1
Duncombe St B3
Earl La B1
East Marsh St B3
East St B2
Eastgate B3
Eastside Rd A3
Eaton Ct C1
Eleanor St B3
Ellis Way B3
Fisherman's Chapel A3
Fisherman's Wharf B2
Fishing Heritage Centre B2
Flour Sq A3
Frederick St B3
Frederick Ward Way B2
Freeman St A3/B3
Freshney Dr B1
Freshney Pl B2
Garden St C2
Garibaldi St A3
Garth La B2
Grime St B3
Grimsby Docks Sta A3
Grimsby Town Sta C2
Hainton Ave C3
Har Way B3
Hare St C3
Harrison St B1
Haven Ave B1
Hay Croft Ave B1
Hay Croft St B1
Heneage Rd B3/C3
Henry St B1
Holme St B3
Hume St C1
James St B1
Joseph St B1
Kent St A3
King Edward St A3
Lambert Rd C2
Library B2
Lime St B1
Lister St B1
Littlefield La C1
Lockhill A3
Lord St B1
Ludford St C3
Macaulay St B1
Mallard Mews C3
Manor Ave C2
Market A3
Market Hall B2
Market St B3
Moss Rd C2
Nelson St A3
New St B2
Osbourne St B2
Pasture St B3
Peaks Parkway C3
Pelham Rd C1
Police Station A3
Post Office B1/B2/C2
Pyewipe Rd A1
Railway Pl A3
Railway St A3
Recreation Ground C2
Rendel St A2
Retail Park B3
Richard St B1
Ripon St B1
Robinson St East B3
Royal St A3
St Hilda's Ave C1
St James C2
Sheepfold St B3/C3
Sixhills St C3
South Park B2
Spring St A3
Superstore B3
Tasburgh St C3
Tennyson St B2
The Close C1
Thesiger St A3
Time Trap C2
Town Hall B2
Veal St B1
Victoria Retail Park A3
Victoria St North A2
Victoria St South B2
Victoria St West B2
Watkin St A1
Welholme Ave C2
Welholme Rd C3
Wellington St B3
Wellowgate C2
Werneth Rd B3
West Coates Rd A1
Westgate A2
Westminster Dr C1
Willingham St C3
Wintringham Rd C2
Wood St B3
Yarborough Dr B1
Yarborough Hotel C2

Hanley 335

Acton St A3
Albion St B2
Argyle St C1
Ashbourne Gr A2
Avoca St A3
Baskerville Rd B3
Bedford Rd C1
Bedford St C1
Bethesda St B2
Bexley St A2
Birches Head Rd A3
Botteslow St C3
Boundary St A2
Broad St C2
Broom St A3
Bryan St A2
Bucknall New Rd B3
Bucknall Old Rd B3
Bus Station B3
Cannon St C2
Castlefield St C1
Hanley Park C2
Cavendish St B1
Central Forest Pk A2
Charles St B3
Cheapside B2
Chell St A3
Clarke St C1
Cleveland Rd C2
Clifford St C3
Clough St B2
Clyde St C1
College Rd C2
Cooper St C2
Corbridge Rd A1
Cutts St C2
Davis St C1
Denbigh St A1
Derby St C3
Dilke St A3
Dundas St A3
Dundee Rd C1
Dyke St B3
Eastwood Rd C3
Eaton St A3
Etruria Park B1
Etruria Rd B1
Etruria Vale Rd C1
Festing St A3
Festival Retail Park A1
Fire Station C2
Foundry St B2
Franklyn St C3
Garnet St B1
Garth St B3
George St C3
Gilman St B3
Glass St B3
Goodson St B3
Greyhound Way A1
Grove Pl C1
Hampton St C3
Hanley Park C2
Harding Rd C2
Hassall St B3
Havelock Pl C1
Hazlehurst St C3
Hinde St C2
Hope St B2
Houghton St C2
Hulton St A3
Information Ctr B3
Jasper St C2
Jervis St A3
John Bright St A3
John St B2
Keelings Rd A3
Kimberley Rd C1
Ladysmith Rd C1
Lawrence St C2
Leek Rd C3
Library C2
Lichfield St C3
Linfield Rd B3
Loftus St A2
Lower Bedford St C1
Lower Bryan St A2
Lower Mayer St A3
Lowther St A1
Magistrates Court C2
Malham St A2
Marsh St B2
Matlock St C3
Mayer St A3
Milton St C1
Mitchell Memorial Theatre B2
Morley St B2
Moston St A3
Mount Pleasant C1
Mulgrave St A1
Mynors St B3
Nelson Pl B3
New Century St B1
Octagon Retail Park B1
Ogden Rd C3
Old Hall St B3
Old Town Rd A3
Pall Mall B2
Palmerston St C3
Park and Ride C2
Parker St B2
Pavilion Dr A1
Pelham St C3
Percy St B2
Piccadilly B2
Picton St B3
Plough St A3
Police Station C2
Portland St A1
Post Office A3/B3/C3
Potteries Museum & Art Gallery B2
Potteries Sh Ctr B2
Potteries Way C2
Powell St A1
Pretoria Rd C1
Quadrant Rd B2
Ranelagh St C2
Raymond St C2
Rectory Rd C1
Regent Rd C2
Regent Theatre B2
Richmond Terr C2
Ridgehouse Dr A1
Robson St C2
St Ann St B3
St Luke St B3
Sampson St B2
Shaw St A1
Sheaf St C2
Shearer St C1
Shelton New Rd C1
Shirley Rd C2
Slippery La B2
Snow Hill C2
Spur St C3
Stafford St B2
Statham St B2
Stubbs La C3
Sun St C1
Supermarket A1/B2
Talbot St C3
The Parkway C2
Town Hall B2
Town Rd A3
Trinity St B2
Union St A2
Upper Hillchurch St A3
Upper Huntbach St B3
Victoria Hall Theatre B3
Warner St C2
Warwick St C1
Waterloo Rd A1
Waterloo St B3
Well St B3
Wellesley St C2
Wellington Rd B3
Wellington St B3
Whitehaven Dr A2
Whitmore St C1
Windermere St A1
Woodall St A1
Yates St C2
York St A2

Harrogate 335

Albert St C2
Alexandra Rd B2
Arthington Ave B2
Ashfield Rd A2
Back Cheltenham Mount B2
Beech Grove C1
Belmont Rd C1
Bilton Dr A2
Bower Rd B2
Bower St B2
Bus Station B2
Cambridge Rd B2
Cambridge St B2
Cemetery A2
Chatsworth Pl A2
Chatsworth Grove A2
Chatsworth Rd A2
Chelmsford Rd B3
Cheltenham Cr B2
Cheltenham Mt B2
Cheltenham Pde B2
Christ Church B3
Christ Church Oval B3
Chudleigh Rd B3
Clarence Dr B1
Claro Rd A3
Claro Way A3
Coach Park B2
Coach Rd B3
Cold Bath Rd C1
Commercial St B2
Coppice Ave A1
Coppice Dr A1
Coppice Gate A1
Cornwall Rd B1
Council Offices B1
Court C3
Crescent Gdns B1
Crescent Rd B1
Dawson Terr A2
Devonshire Pl B3
Diamond Mews C1
Dixon Rd A2
Dixon Terr A2
Dragon Ave B3
Dragon Parade B2
Dragon Rd B2
Duchy Rd B1
East Parade B2
East Park Rd C3
Esplanade B1
Fire Station A2
Franklin Mount A2
Franklin Rd B2
Franklin Square A2
Glebe Rd C1
Grove Park Ct A3
Grove Park Terr A3
Grove Rd A2
Hampswaite Rd A1
Harcourt Dr B3
Harcourt Rd B3
Harrogate B2
Harrogate Int Ctr B1
Harrogate Ladies Coll B1
Harrogate Theatre B2
Heywood Rd C1
Hollins Cr A1
Hollins Mews A1
Hollins Rd A1
Homestead Rd C3
Hydro Leisure Ctr, The A1
Information Ctr B1
James St B2
Jenny Field Dr A1
John St B2
Kent Dr A1
Kent Rd A1
Kings Rd A2
Kingsway B3
Kingsway Dr B3
Lancaster Rd C1
Leeds Rd C2
Lime Grove B3
Lime St A3
Mayfield Grove B2
Mayfield Pl A2
Mercer B1
Montpellier Hill B1
Mornington Cr A3
Mornington Terr B3
Mowbray Sq B3
North Park Rd B3
Nydd Vale Rd B2
Oakdale Ave A1
Oatlands Dr C3
Odeon B2
Osborne Rd A2
Otley Rd C2
Oxford St B2
Park Chase B3
Park Parade B3
Park View B2
Parliament St B1
Police Station B3
Post Office B2/C1
Providence Terr A2
Queen Parade C3
Queen's Rd C1
Raglan St C2
Regent Ave A3
Regent Grove A3
Regent Parade A3
Regent St A3
Regent Terr A3
Rippon Rd A1
Robert St C2
Royal Baths & Turkish Baths B1
Royal Pump Room B1
St Luke's Mount A2
St Mary's Ave C1
St Mary's Walk C1
Scargill Rd A1
Skipton Rd A3
Skipton St A2
Slingsby Walk C3
South Park Rd C2
Spring Grove A1
Springfield Ave B1
Station Ave B2
Station Parade B2
Strawberry Dale B2
Stray Rein C3
Studley Rd A2
Superstore B2
Swan Rd B1
The Parade B2
The Stray C2/C3
Tower St C2
Trinity Rd C2
Union St B2
Valley Dr C1
Valley Gardens C1
Valley Mount C1
Victoria Ave C2
Victoria Rd C1
Victoria Shopping Ctr B2
Waterloo St A2
West Park C2
West Park St C2
Wood View A1
Woodfield Ave A3
Woodfield Dr A3
Woodfield Grove A3
Woodfield Rd A3
Woodfield Square A3
Woodside B3
York Pl C3
York Rd B1

Holyhead *Caergybi* 335

Armenia St A2
Arthur St C2
Beach Rd A1
Boston St B2
Bowling Green C3
Bryn Erw Rd C3
Bryn Glas Cl C3
Bryn Glas Rd C3
Bryn Gwyn Rd C1
Bryn Marchog A1
Bryn Mor Terr A2
Bryngoleu Ave A1
Cae Braenar C3
Cambria St B1
Captain Skinner's Obelisk B2
Cecil St C2
Celtic Gateway Footbridge B2
Cemetery C1/C2
Cleveland Ave C2

Coastguard Lookout . . A2
Court B2
Customs House. A3
Cybi Pl C3
Cyttir Rd. C3
Edmund St B1
Empire 😕 B2
Ferry Terminals B2
Fford Beibio C3
Fford Feurig C3
Fford Hirnos B3
Fford Jasper B3
Fford Tudur. B3
Fire Station C2
Garreglwyd Rd B2
Gilbert St C3
Gorsedd Circle B2
Gwelfor Ave. A1
Harbour View B2
Henry St. C1
High Terr C1
Hill St B2
Holborn Rd C3
Holland Park Ind Est . . C3
Holyhead Park B1
Holyhead Station ≥ . . B2
Information Ctr ℹ B2
King's Rd C3
Kingsland Rd. C3
Lewascote C3
Library B1
Lifeboat Station A1
Llanfawr Cl C3
Llanfawr Rd. C3
Lligwy St C2
Lon Deg B3
London Rd C3
Longford Rd B1
Longford Terr B1
Maes Cybi B2
Maes Hedd A1
Maes-Hyfryd Rd C1
Maes-y-Dref B3
Maes-yr-Haf A2/B1
Maes-yr-Ysgol C3
Marchog C3
Marina A2
Maritime Museum 🏛 . . A1
Market B2
Market St B2
Mill Bank B2
Min-y-Mor Rd A1
Morawelon Ind Est . . . B3
Morawelon Rd. B3
Moreton Rd B1
New Park Rd B1
Newry St A2
Old Harbour
 Lighthouse A3
Plas Rd C1
Police Station ◼ B2
Porth-y-Felin Rd A1
Post Office
 �◼ . . A1/B1/B2/B3/C2/C3
Prince of Wales Rd. . . . B3
Priory La B3
Pump St C1
Queens Park C1
Reseifion Rd C1
Rock St. B2
Roman Fort 🏛 B2
St Cybi St B2
St Cybi's Church ♱ . . . B2
St Seiriol's Cl. C1
Salt Island Bridge. . . . A2
Seabourne Rd A1
South Stack Rd B1
Sports Ground B1
Stanley St. B2
Station St. B2
Tan-y-Bryn Rd C3
Tan-yr-Efail C1
Tara St C1
Thomas St B1
Town Hall. B2
Treseifion Estate C2
Turkey Shore Rd A2
Ucheldre Arts Ctr ♦ . . B1
Ucheldre Ave. B1
Upper Baptist St B1
Victoria Rd. B1
Victoria Terr B1
Vulcan St C2
Walthew Ave A1
Walthew La A1
Wian St. C2

Hull 335

Adelaide St C1
Albert Dock C1
Albion St B2
Alfred Gelder St B2
Anlaby Rd. B1
Arctic Corsair ♦ B3
Beverley Rd A1
Blanket Row C2
Bond St B2
Bridlington Ave. A1
Brook St B1
Brunswick Ave A1
Bus Station B1
Camilla Cl A3
Cannon St A2
Cannon's C1
Caroline St. A2
Carr La B1
Castle St. C2
Central Library B1
Charles St A2
Citadel Way. B3
City Hall B1
City Hall Theatre B1
Clarence St B3
Cleveland St A3
Clifton St. A1
Club Culture 🏛 C1
Colonial St. B1
Court B2
Deep, The ⚓ C3

Dock Office Row. B3
Dock St. B2
Dinostar 🏛 C1
Drypool Bridge. B3
Egton St A3
English St C1
Ferens Gallery 🏛 B2
Ferensway. B1
Francis St A2
Francis St West. A1
Freehold St A1
Freetown Way A1
Fruit Theatre 🎭 C2
Garrison Rd B3
George St. B2
Gibson St A3
Great Thornton St . . . B1
Great Union St A3
Green La A2
Grey St. A1
Grimston St B2
Grosvenor St A1
Guildhall B2
Guildhall Rd. B2
Hands-on History 🏛 . . B3
Harley St A1
Hessle Rd C1
High St. B3
Holy Trinity ♱ B2
Hull & East Riding
 Museum 🏛 B3
Hull Arena C1
Hull College. B3
Hull History Centre . . . A2
Hull (Paragon) Sta ≥ . . B1
Hull Truck Theatre . . . B1
Humber Dock Marina . . C2
Humber Dock St C2
Humber St C2
Hyperion St A3
Information Ctr ℹ B2
Jameson St B1
Jarratt St B2
Jenning St A3
King Billy Statue ♦ . . . C2
King Edward St B1
King St C2
Kingston Retail Park . . C1
Kingston St C2
Liddell St A1
Lime St A3
Lister St C1
Lockwood St A2
Maister House 🏛 B3
Maritime Museum 🏛 . . B2
Market B2
Market Place. C2
Minerva Pier C2
Mulgrave St A3
Myton Bridge C3
Myton St. B1
NAPA (Northern Acad of
 Performing Arts) 🎭 . . B1
Nelson St C2
New Cleveland St A3
New George St A2
New Theatre 🎭 B2
Norfolk St A1
North Bridge A3
North St B1
Odeon 😕 C1
Old Harbour C3
Osborne St. B1
Paragon St B1
Park St B1
Percy St A1
Pier St. C2
Police Station ◼ B2
Post Office ⌖ . . A1/B1/B2
Porter St C1
Portland St. B1
Posterngate B2
Prince's Quay C2
Prospect Centre B1
Prospect St B1
Queen's Gdns B2
Railway Dock Marina. . C2
Railway St C2
Real 😕 B1
Red Gallery 🏛 B1
Reform St A2
Retail Park. B1
River Hull Footbridge . . B3
Riverside Quay C2
Roper St B2
St James St C1
St Luke's St B1
St Mark St A3
St Mary the Virgin 🏛 .
St Stephens Sh Ctr. . . . B1
Scott St A2
South Bridge Rd B3
Spring Bank. A1
Spring St B1
Spurn Lightship ♦ C2
Spyvee St A3
Streetlife Transport
 Museum 🏛 B3
Sykes St A2
Tidal Surge Barrier ♦ . C3
Tower St. B3
Trinity House. B2
University B2
Vane St. A1
Victoria Pier ♦ C2
Waterhouse La B1
Waterloo St A1
Waverley St C1
Wellington St C2
Wellington St West . . . B1
West St. B1
Whitefriargate B2
Wilberforce Dr C2
Wilberforce House 🏛 . B3
Wilberforce Mon ♦ . . . B3
William St B1
Wincolmlee A3
Witham A3
Wright St A1

Inverness 336

Abban St A1
Academy St B2
Alexander Pl B2
Anderson St A2
Annfield Rd C3
Ardconnel St B3
Ardconnel Terr B3
Ardross Pl B2
Ardross St B2
Argyle St B3
Argyle Terr B3
Attadale Rd B1
Ballifeary La C2
Balliferay Rd C1/C2
Balnacraig La A1
Balnain House ♦ B2
Balnain St B2
Bank St. B2
Bellfield Park C2
Bellfield Terr. C3
Benula Rd A1
Birnie Terr A1
Bishop's Rd C2
Bowling Green A2
Bowling Green B2
Bowling Green B3
Bridge St B2
Brown St A2
Bruce Ave. C1
Bruce Gdns C1
Bruce Pk C1
Burial Ground A2
Burnett Rd A3
Bus Station B3
Caledonian Rd B1
Cameron Rd A1
Cameron Sq A1
Carse Rd. A1
Carsegate Rd Sth A1
Castle Garrison
 Encounter ♦ B2
Castle Rd B2
Castle St. B3
Celt St B2
Chapel St A2
Charles St B3
Church St. B2
Clachnacuddin
 Football Ground A1
Columba Rd B1/C1
Crown Ave B3
Crown Circus B3
Crown Dr B3
Crown Rd B3
Crown St B3
Culduthel Rd C3
Dalneigh Cres C1
Dalneigh Rd C1
Denny St. B3
Dochfour Dr B1/C1
Douglas Row B2
Duffy Dr C3
Dunabban Rd A1
Dunain Rd B1
Duncraig St B2
Eastgate Shopping Ctr . B3
Eden Court 🎭 C2
Fairfield Rd B1
Falcon Sq. B3
Fire Station A3
Fraser St B2
Fraser St C2
Friars' Bridge A2
Friars' La B2
Friars' St B2
George St. A2
Gilbert St A2
Glebe St A2
Glendoe Terr. A1
Glenurquhart Rd C1
Gordon Terr. C2
Gordonville Rd C2
Grant St A2
Greig St B2
HM Prison B3
Harbour Rd A3
Harrowden Rd. B1
Haugh Rd. C2
Heatherley Cres C3
High St B3
Highland Council HQ,
 The C2
Hill Park C3
Hill St B3
Huntly Pl B1
Huntly St. B2
India St. A2
Industrial Estate. A3
Information Ctr ℹ B2
Innes St B3
Inverness 😕 B2
Inverness College
 (Midmills Campus) . . B3
Inverness College UHI . A2
Inverness High School . B1
Inverness Museum 🏛 . B2
Jamaica St. A2
Kenneth St. B2
Kilmuir Rd A1
King St B2
Kingsmills Rd B3
Laurel Ave B1/C1
Library C2
Lilac Gr. C3
Lindsay Ave C1
Lochalsh Rd A1/B1
Longman Rd A3
Lotland Pl. B2
Lower Kessock St. A1
Madras St. A2
Market Hall B3
Maxwell Dr C1
Mayfield Rd C3
Millburn Rd B3
Mitchell's La C3
Montague Row B2
Muirfield Rd B3
Muirtown St B1

Nelson St A2
Ness Bank C2
Ness Bridge B2
Ness Walk B2/C2
Old Edinburgh Rd. C3
Old High Church 🏛 . . . B2
Park Rd C2
Paton St B3
Perceval Rd B1
Planefield Rd B1
Police Station ◼ A3
Porterfield Bank C3
Porterfield Rd. C3
Portland Pl A3
Post Office
 ⌖ A2/B1/B2/B3
Queen St B2
Queensgate. B2
Railway Terr A3
Rangemore Rd B1
Reay St B3
Riverside St A2
Rose St A2
Ross Ave. B1
Rowan Rd C1
Royal Northern
 Infirmary 🏥 C2
St Andrew's Cath ♱ . . . C2
St Columba 😕 B2
St John's Ave. C1
St Mary's Ave B1
Sheriff Court. B3
Shore St A2
Smith Ave. C1
Southside Pl C3
Southside Rd C3
Spectrum Centre B2
Strothers La B3
Superstore C2
TA Centre C2
Telford Gdns B1
Telford Rd A1
Telford St A1
Tomnahurich
 Cemetery C1
Tomnahurich St B2
Town Hall B3
Union Rd B3
Union St B3
Walker Pl A3
Walker Rd A3
War Memorial ♦ C2
Waterloo Bridge. A2
Wells St B2
Young St B2

Ipswich 336

Alderman Rd B2
All Saints' Rd A1
Alpe St B2
Ancaster Rd. C1
Ancient House 🏛 B3
Anglesea Rd A2
Ann St A2
Arboretum A2
Austin St C2
Belstead Rd C1
Berners St B2
Bibb Way B1
Birkfield Dr C1
Black Horse La B2
Bolton La B3
Bond St. C3
Bowthorpe Cl A1
Bramford La A1
Bramford Rd. A1
Bridge St C2
Brookfield Rd A1
Brooks Hall Rd A1
Broomhill. A1
Broomhill Rd. A1
Broughton Rd A2
Bulwer Rd B1
Burrell Rd C2
Butter Market B2
Buttermarket Shopping
 Centre, The B3
Cardinal Park L Park . . C2
Carr St B3
Cecil St B2
Cecilia St C2
Chancery Rd C2
Charles St B2
Chevallier St A1
Christchurch Mansion &
 Wolsey Art Gallery 🏛 . A3
Christchurch Park A3
Christchurch St B3
Cineworld 😕 C2
Civic Centre. B2
Civic Dr. B2
Clarkson St B1
Cobbold St B3
Commercial Rd. C2
Constable Rd. A3
Constantine Rd. C1
Constitution Hill. A3
Corder Rd A3
Corn Exchange B2
Cotswold Ave A1
Council Offices. B2
County Hall. B3
Crown Court B2
Crown St B2
Cullingham Rd B1
Cumberland St A2
Curriers La. B2
Dale Hall La A2
Dales View Rd A1
Dalton Rd A2
Dillwyn St B1
Elliot St C1
Elm St B2
Elsmere Rd A3
Falcon St C2
Felaw St C2
Flint Wharf C3
Fonnereau Rd B2
Fore St C3

Kendal 336

Abbot Hall Art Gallery &
 Museum of Lakeland
 Life 🏛 C2
Ambulance Station . . . A2

Foundation St C3
Franciscan Way C2
Friars St C2
Gainsborough Rd B1
Gatacre Rd. B1
Geneva Rd A2
Gippeswyk Ave C1
Gippeswyk Park C1
Grafton Way C2
Graham Rd A1
Grimwade St B3
Great Whip St C3
Handford Cut B1
Handford Rd B1
Henley Rd A2
Hervey St A3
High St. B2
Holly Rd A2
Information Ctr ℹ B3
Ipswich Haven
 Marina C3
Ipswich School A2
Ipswich Station ≥ C2
Ipswich Town FC
 (Portman Road) C2
Ivry St A2
Kensington Rd A1
Kesteven Rd C1
Key St C3
Kingsfield Ave. A3
Kitchener Rd. A1
Magistrates Court . . . B2
Little's Cr C2
London Rd B1
Low Brook St C3
Lower Orwell St C3
Luther Rd C2
Manor Rd A3
Mornington Ave A1
Mus & Art Gallery 🏛 . . B2
Museum St B2
Neale St. B3
New Cardinal St C2
New Cut East C3
New Cut West C3
New Wolsey 😕 B2
Newson St. B2
Norwich Rd A1/B1
Oban St. A1
Old Customs House 🏛 . C3
Old Foundry Rd B3
Old Merchant's Ho 🏛 . C3
Orford St A2
Paget Rd A2
Park Rd A2
Peter's St C2
Philip Rd C1
Pine Ave A2
Pine View Rd A2
Police Station ◼ B2
Portman Rd C2
Portman Walk. C1
Post Office ⌖ . . B2/B2/B3
Princes St C2
Prospect St B1
Queen St B2
Ranelagh Rd C1
Recreation Ground . . . B1
Rectory Rd. A1
Regent Theatre 🎭 . . . B3
Retail Park. B1
Retail Park. C2
Richmond Rd. A1
Rope Walk B3
Rose La B2
Russell Rd B2
St Edmund's Rd. A2
St George's La A1
St Helen's St B3
Sherrington Rd A1
Silent St. C2
Sir Alf Ramsey Way . . . C1
Sirdar Rd. A1
Soane St B3
Springfield La A1
Star La C3
Stevenson Rd A1
Suffolk College C3
Suffolk Retail Park. . . . C2
Superstore C2
Surrey Rd. B1
Tacket St B3
Tavern St B2
The Avenue A3
Tolly Cobbold Mus 🏛 . C3
Tower Ramparts B2
Tower Ramparts
 Shopping Centre B2
Tower St B2
Tuddenham Rd A3
Upper Brook St B3
Upper Orwell St B3
University C3
Valley Rd A2
Vermont Cr A3
Vermont Rd A3
Vernon St C3
Warrington Rd A2
Waterloo Rd A1
Waterworks St B3
Wellington St B2
West End Rd B1
Westerfield Rd A3
Westgate St. B2
Westholme Rd A1
Westwood Ave C1
Willoughby Rd C1
Withipoll St B3
Woodbridge Rd A3
Woodstone Ave A1
Yarmouth Rd A1

Anchorite Fields C2
Anchorite Rd. C2
Ann St A3
Appleby Rd A3
Archers Meadow C3
Ashleigh Rd A2
Aynam Rd. C3
Bankfield Rd B1
Beast Banks B2
Beezon Fields A3
Beezon Rd A3
Beezon Trad Est A3
Belmont B2
Birchwood Cl B1
Blackhall Rd B2
Brewery Arts Ctr 😕♦ . B2
Bridge St B3
Brigsteer Rd C1
Burneside Rd A2
Buttery Well La. C2
Canal Head North B3
Captain French La C2
Caroline St. A2
Castle Hill B3
Castle Howe B2
Castle Rd B3
Castle St. A3/B3
Cedar Gr. C1
Chapel St B2
Chase Ave C3
Checker St B2
Church St. B2
Clough La. B2
Coburg St C3
College of West Anglia . A3
Columbia Way. A3
Corn Exchange 🏛 A1
County Court Rd B2
Cresswell St A2
Custom House 🏛 A1
Eastgate St A2
Edma St A2
Exton's Rd C3
Ferry La A1
Ferry St A1
Framingham's
 Almshouses B2
Friars St. B2
Friars Walk B2
Gaywood Rd A3
George St. B2
Gladstone Rd C2
Goodwin's Rd C3
Green Quay ♦ B1
Greengate C2
Greengate La C1/C2
Greenside B2
Greenwood C1
Gulfs Rd B2
High Tenterfell C1
Highgate B2
Hillswood Ave C1
Horncop La A2
Information Ctr ℹ B2
K Village and Heritage
 Centre ♦ C3
Kendal Business Park . . A3
Kendal Castle
 (Remains) ♦ B3
Kendal Fell B1
Kendal Green A1
Kendal ≥ A3
Kendal Station ≥ A3
Kent Pl A2
Kirkbarrow. C2
Kirkland C2
Library B2
Library Rd B2
Little Aynam B3
Little Wood B1
Long Cl C1
Longpool A3
Lound Rd B3
Lound St. C3
Low Fellside B2
Lowther St B2
Maple Dr A3
Market Pl. B2
Maude St B2
Miller Bridge. B2
Milnthorpe Rd. C2
Mint St A3
Mintsfeet Rd A3
Mintsfeet Rd South . . . A2
New Rd B2
Noble's Rest B2
Parish Church ♱ B3
Park Side Rd C3
Parkside Bsns Park . . . C3
Parr St B3
Police Station ◼ A2
Post Office ⌖ . A3/B2/C2
Quaker Tapestry ♦ . . . A2
Queen's Rd C1
Riverside Walk C2
Rydal Mount C1
Sandes Ave A2
Sandgate C3
Sandylands Rd A3
Serpentine Rd. B1
Serpentine Wood B1
Shap Rd A3
South Rd C2
Stainbank Rd. C1
Station Rd. A3
Stramongate. B2
Stramongate Bridge . . B2
Stricklandgate . . . A2/B2
Sunnyside C2
Thorny Hills B3
Town Hall. B2
Underbarrow Rd B1
Underwood C1
Union St A3
Vicar's Fields C1
Vicarage Dr C1/C2
Wainwright Yd Sh Ctr . B2
Wasdale Cl. B1
Well Ings C2
Westmorland Shopping
 Centre & Market Hall . B2

King's Lynn 336

Albert St. C2
Albion St A2
All Saints 😕 B2
All Saints St B2
Austin Fields A2
Austin St B2
Avenue Rd C2
Bank Side. B1
Beech St C2
Birch Tree Cl B3
Birchwood St A2
Blackfriars Rd. B2
Blackfriars St B2
Boal St B1
Bridge St B2
Broad St B2
Broad Walk A2
Burkitt St A2
Bus Station B2
Carmelite Terr C2
Chapel St A2
Checker St C2
Church St B2
Clough La. B2
Coburg St C3
College of West Anglia . A3
Columbia Way A3
Corn Exchange 🏛 A1
County Court Rd B2
Cresswell St A2
Custom House 🏛 A1
Eastgate St A2
Edma St A2
Exton's Rd C3
Ferry La A1
Ferry St A1
Framingham's
 Almshouses B2
Friars St. B2
Friars Walk B2
Gaywood Rd A3
George St. B2
Gladstone Rd C2
Goodwin's Rd C3
Green Quay ♦ B1
Greengate C2
Greengate La C1/C2
Greenside B2
Greenwood C1
Gulfs Rd B2
High Tenterfell C1
Highgate B2
Hillswood Ave C1
Horncop La A2
Information Ctr ℹ B2

Town Ho & Tales of The
 Old Gaol Ho 🏛 B1
Town Wall
 (Remains) ♦ B3
True's Yard Mus 🏛 . . . A2
Valingers Rd C2
Vancouver Ave C2
Vancouver Quarter . . . B2
Waterloo St B1
Wellesley St C2
White Friars Rd. C2
Windsor Rd C2
Winfarthing St C2
Wyatt St B2
York Rd. C3

Lancaster 336

Aberdeen Rd. C3
Adult College, The C3
Aldcliffe Rd C2
Alfred St B3
Ambleside Rd B2
Ambulance Sta A3
Ashfield Ave B1
Ashton Rd C2
Assembly Rooms,
 The B2
Balmoral Rd B3
Bath House 🏛 B3
Bath Mill La B3
Bath St B3
Blades St B2
Borrowdale Rd C3
Bowerham Rd C3
Brewery La B3
Bridge La B2
Brook St C3
Bulk Rd A3
Bulk St B3
Bus Station B2
Cable St B2
Canal Cruises &
 Waterbus ♦ C3
Carlisle Bridge A1
Carr House La C3
Castle 😕 B1
Castle Park B2
Caton Rd A3
China St B2
Church St. B2
City Museum 🏛 B2
Clarence St C3
Common Gdn St B2
Coniston Rd. C3
Cottage Museum 🏛 . . B2
Council Offices. B2
Court B2
Cromwell Rd C2
Crown Court B2
Dale St C2
Dallas Rd B1/C2
Dalton Rd. B3
Dalton Sq. B2
Damside St B2
De Vitre St B3
Dee Rd A3
Denny Ave. A3
Derby Rd A3
Dukes 😕 B2
Earl St A3
East Rd B3
Eastham St C3
Edward St B3
Fairfield Rd B1
Fenton St B2
Firbank Rd A3
Fire Station A3
Friend's Meeting Ho 🏛 . B1
Garnet St B3
George St. B2
Giant Axe Field B1
Grand, The 😕 B2
Grasmere Rd B3
Greaves Rd C2
Green St A3
Gregson Centre, The . . C3
Gregson Rd C3
Greyhound Bridge A2
Greyhound Bridge Rd . . A2
High St B2
Hill Side C2
Hope St C3
Hubert Pl A3
Information Ctr ℹ B2
Judges Lodgings 🏛 . . . B2
Kelsy St A3
Kentmere Rd. B3
King St B2
Kingsway A3
Kirkes St C3
Lancaster &
 Lakeland 😕
Lancaster City
 Football Club B1
Lancaster Station ≥ . . . B1
Langdale Rd A3
Ley Ct A3
Library B2
Lincoln Rd B3
Lindow St. C2
Lodge St. A3
Long Marsh La B1
Lune Rd A2
Lune St A3
Lune Valley Ramble . . . A3
Mainway A2
Maritime Museum 🏛 . . A1
Market St B2
Mkt Gate Shopping Ctr . B2
Meadowside C3
Meeting House La B1
Millennium Bridge . . . A2
Moor La. B3
Moorgate B3
Morecambe Rd A1/A2
Nelson St B3
North Rd B2
Orchard La. C1
Owen Rd A2

Park Rd B3
Parliament St A3
Patterdale Rd A3
Penny St. B2
Police Station ◼ B2
Portland St C2
Post Office
 ⌖ . A3/B1/B2/B3/C3
Primrose St C3
Priory 😕 B1
Prospect St C3
Quarry Rd C3
Queen St C2
Regent St C2
Ridge La. B3
Ridge St. A3
Royal Lancaster
 Infirmary (A&E) 🏥 . . . C2
Rydal Rd B3
Ryelands Park. A1
St Georges Quay. A1
St John's 🏛 B2
St Leonard's Gate B2
St Martin's Rd C2
St Nicholas Arcades
 Shopping Centre B2
St Oswald St C3
St Peter's ♱ B3
Salisbury Rd B1
Scotch Quarry
 Urban Park C3
Shire Hall/HM Prison . . B1
Sibsey St B1
Skerton Bridge A2
South Rd C2
Station Rd B1
Stirling Rd C3
Storey Ave A1
Sunnyside La C1
Sylvester St C1
Tarnsyke Rd. A1
Thurnham St C2
Town Hall. B2
Troutbeck Rd B3
Ulleswater Rd B3
University of Cumbria . C3
Vicarage Field B1
Vue 😕 B2
West Rd B1
Westbourne Dr C1
Westbourne Rd. C1
Westham St C3
White Cross Bsns Park . C2
Wheatfield St B1
Williamson Rd. C3
Willow La A2
Windermere Rd B3
Wingate-Saul Rd B1
Wolseley St B3
Woodville St C3
Wyresdale Rd C3

Leeds 336

Aire St B3
Aireside Centre B2
Albion Pl B4
Albion St B4
Albion Way B1
Alma St A6
Arcades 🏛 B4
Armley Rd B1
Back Burley Lodge Rd . . A1
Back Hyde Terr A2
Back Row C3
Bath Rd. C3
Beckett St A6
Bedford St B4
Belgrave St A4
Belle View Rd A2
Benson St A5
Black Bull St C5
Blenheim Walk A3
Boar La. B4
Bond St. B4
Bow St C5
Bowman La C4
Brewery ♦ C4
Bridge St A5/B5
Briggate B4
Bruce Gdns C1
Burley Rd A1
Burley St A2
Burmantofts St B6
Bus & Coach Station . . B5
Butterly St C4
Butts Cr B4
Brewery Wharf C5
Byron St A5
Call La B4
Calverley St A3/B3
Canal St B1
Canal Wharf C3
Carlisle Rd C5
Cavendish Rd A1
Cavendish St A2
Chadwick St C5
Cherry Pl A6
Cherry Row A5
City Museum 🏛 B4
City Pal of Varieties 😕 . B4
City Sq B3
Civic Hall 🏛 A3
Clarence Road C5
Clarendon Rd A2
Clarendon Way A3
Clark La C6
Clay Pit La A4
Cloberry St A2
Clyde Approach C1
Clyde Gdns. C1
Coleman St C2
Commercial St B4
Concord St A5
Cookridge St A4
Copley Hill C1
Corn Exchange 🏛 B4
Cromer Terr A3
Cromwell St A5

Cross Catherine St B6
Cross Green La C6
Cross Stamford St A5
Crown & County Courts A3
Crown Point Bridge C5
Crown Point Retail Pk C4
Crown Point Rd C4
David St C3
Dent St C6
Derwent Pl C3
Dial St C6
Dock St C4
Dolly La A6
Domestic St C2
Duke St B5
Duncan St B4
Dyer St B5
East Field St B6
East Pde B3
East St C5
Eastgate B5
Easy Rd C6
Edward St B4
Ellerby La C6
Ellerby Rd C6
Fenton St A3
Fire Station B2
First Direct Arena A4
Fish St B4
Flax Pl B5
Gelderd Rd C1
George St B4
Globe Rd C2
Gloucester Cr B1
Gower St A5
Grafton St A4
Grand Theatre B4
Granville Rd A6
Great George St A3
Great Wilson St C4
Greek St B3
Green La C1
Hanover Ave A2
Hanover La A2
Hanover Sq A2
Hanover Way A2
Harewood St B4
Harrison St B4
Haslewood Cl B6
Haslewood Drive B6
High Court B5
Holbeck La C2
Holdforth Cl C1
Holdforth Gdns B1
Holdforth Gr C1
Holdforth Pl C1
Holy Trinity B4
Hope Rd A5
Hunslet La C4
Hunslet Rd C4
Hyde Terr A2
Infirmary St B3
Information Ctr B3
Ingram Row C3
Junction St C4
Kelso Gdns A2
Kelso Rd A2
Kelso St A2
Kendal La A2
Kendell St C4
Kidacre St C4
King Edward St B4
King St B3
Kippax Pl C6
Kirkgate B4
Kirkgate Market B4
Kirkstall Rd A1
Kitson St C6
Lady La B4
Lands La B4
Lavender Walk B6
Leeds Art Gallery B3
Leeds Bridge C4
Leeds Coll of Music B5
Leeds General Infirmary (A&E) A3
Leeds Metropolitan University A3/A4
Leeds Museum Discovery Centre C5
Leeds Shopping Plaza B4
Leeds Station B3
Leeds University A3
Library B3
Lincoln Green Rd A6
Lincoln Rd A6
Lindsey Gdns A6
Lindsey Rd A6
Lisbon St B3
Little Queen St B3
Long Close La C6
Lord St C2
Lovell Park A4
Lovell Park Rd A4
Lovell Rd A5
Lower Brunswick St A5
Mabgate A5
Macauly St A5
Magistrates Court A3
Manor Rd C3
Mark La B4
Marlborough St B2
Marsh La B5
Marshall St C3
Meadow La C4
Meadow Rd C4
Melbourne St A5
Merrion Centre A4
Merrion St A4
Merrion Way A4
Mill St B5
Millennium Sq A3
Mount Preston St A2
Mushroom St A5
Neville St C4
New Briggate A4/B4
New Market St B4
New Station St B4
New York Rd A5
New York St B5
Nile St A5
Nippet La A6
North St A4
Northern St B3
Oak Rd B1
Oxford Pl B3
Oxford Row A3
Park Cross St B3
Park La A2
Park Pl B3
Park Row B4
Park Sq B3
Park Sq East B3
Park Sq West B3
Park St B3
Police Station B5
Pontefract La B6
Portland Cr A3
Portland Way A3
Post Office B4/B5
Project Space Leeds C2
Quarry House (NHS/DSS Headquarters) B5
Quebec St B3
Queen St B3
Railway St B5
Rectory St A6
Regent St A5
Richmond St C5
Rigton Approach B6
Rigton Dr B6
Rillbank La A1
Rosebank Rd A1
Royal Armouries C5
Russell St B3
Rutland St B2
St Anne's Cath (RC) A4
St Anne's St B4
St James' Hospital A6
St Johns Centre B4
St John's Rd A2
St Mary's St B5
St Pauls St B3
St Peter's B5
Saxton La B5
Sayner La C5
Shakespeare Ave A6
Shannon St B6
Sheepscar St South A5
Siddall St C3
Skinner La A5
South Pde B3
Sovereign St C4
Spence La C2
Springfield Mount A2
Springwell Ct C2
Springwell Rd C2
Springwell St C2
Stoney Rock La A6
Studio Rd A1
Sutton St C2
Sweet St C3
Sweet St West C3
Swinegate B4
Templar St B5
The Calls B5
The Close B6
The Core B4
The Drive B6
The Garth B5
The Headrow B3/B4
The Lane B5
The Light B4
The Parade B6
Thoresby Pl A3
Torre Rd A6
Town Hall A3
Union Pl C3
Union St B5
Upper Accomodation Rd B6
Upper Basinghall St B4
Vicar La B4
Victoria Bridge C4
Victoria Quarter B4
Victoria Rd C4
Vue B4
Wade La A4
Washington St A1
Water La C3
Waterloo Rd C4
Wellington Rd B2/C1
Wellington St B3
West St B2
West Yorkshire Playhouse B5
Westfield Rd A1
Westgate B3
Whitehall Rd B3/C2
Whitelock St A5
Willis St C6
Willow Approach A1
Willow Ave A1
Willow Terrace Rd A3
Wintoun St A5
Woodhouse La A3/A4
Woodsley Rd A1
York Pl B3
York Rd B6
Yorkshire Television Studios A1

Leicester 336

Abbey St A2
All Saints' A1
Aylestone Rd C2
Bath La A1
Bede Park C1
Bedford St A3
Bedford St South A3
Belgrave Gate A2
Belle Vue A2
Belvoir St B2
Braunstone Gate B1
Burleys Way A2
Burnmoor St C2
Bus Station A2
Canning St A2
Carlton St C2
Castle B1
Castle Gardens B1
Cathedral B2
Causeway La A2
Charles St B3
Chatham St B2
Christow St A3
Church Gate A2
City Gallery B3
Civic Centre B2
Clank St B2
Clock Tower ✦ B2
Clyde St A3
Colton St B3
Conduit St B3
Crafton St A3
Craven St A1
Crown Courts B3
Curve B3
De Lux A2
De Montfort Hall C3
De Montfort St C3
De Montfort Univ C1
Deacon St C2
Dover St B3
Duns La B1
Dunton St A1
East St B3
Eastern Boulevard C1
Edmonton Rd A3
Erskine St A3
Filbert St C1
Filbert St East C2
Fire Station C3
Fleet St A3
Friar La B2
Friday St A2
Gateway St C2
Glebe St B3
Granby St B3
Grange La C2
Grasmere St C1
Great Central St A1
Guildhall B2
Guru Nanak Sikh Museum B1
Halford St B2
Havelock St C2
Haymarket Sh Ctr A2
High St A2
Highcross St A1
Highcross Sh Ctr A2
HM Prison C2
Horsefair St B2
Humberstone Gate B2
Humberstone Rd A3
Infirmary St C2
Information Ctr B2
Jarrom St C2
Jewry Wall B1
Kamloops Cr A3
King Richards Rd B1
King St B2
Lancaster Rd C3
LCB Depot B3
Lee St A3
Leicester Royal Infirmary (A&E) C2
Leicester Station B3
Library B2
Little Theatre, The B3
London Rd C3
Lower Brown St B2
Magistrates Court B2
Manitoba Rd A3
Mansfield St A2
Market ✦ B2
Market St B2
Mill La C2
Montreal Rd A3
Narborough Rd North B1
Nelson Mandela Park C2
New Park St B1
New St B2
New Walk C3
New Walk Museum & Art Gallery C3
Newarke Houses B2
Newarke St B2
Northgate St A1
Orchard St A2
Ottawa Rd A3
Oxford St C2
Upper Brown St B2
Phoenix Square B3
Police Station A3
Post Office A1/B2/C2/C3
Prebend St C3
Princess Rd East C3
Princess Rd West C3
Queen St B3
Regent College C3
Regent Rd C2/C3
Repton St A1
Rutland St B3
St Georges St B3
St Georges Way B3
St John St A2
St Margaret's A2
St Margaret's Way A2
St Martins B2
St Mary de Castro B1
St Matthew's Way A3
St Nicholas B1
St Nicholas Circle B1
Sanvey Gate A2
Silver St B2
Slater St A1
Soar La A1
South Albion St B3
Southampton St B3
Swain St B3
Swan St A1
The Gateway C2
The Newarke B1
The Rally Com Park A2
Tigers Way C3
Tower St C3
Town Hall B2
Tudor Rd B1
University of Leicester C3
University Rd C3
Upperton Rd C1
Vaughan Way A2
Walnut St C2
Watling St A2
Welford Rd B2
Welford Rd Stadium C2
Wellington St B2
West Bridge B1
West St C3
West Walk C3
Western Boulevard C1
Western Rd C1
Wharf St North A3
Wharf St South A3
Y' Theatre, The B3
Yeoman St B3
York Rd B2

Lewes 336

Abinger Pl B1
All Saints Centre B2
Ambulance Station B2
Anne of Cleves Ho C1
Barbican Ho Mus B1
Brewery B2
Brook St A2
Brooks Rd A2
Bus Station B2
Castle Ditch La B1
Castle Precincts B1
Chapel Hill B3
Church La A1/A2
Cliffe High St B2
Cliffe Industrial Est C3
Cluny St C1
Cockshut Rd C1
Convent Field C2
Coombe Rd A2
County Hall B1
County Records Office B1
Court B2
Court Rd B2
Crown Court B2
Cuilfail Tunnel B3
Davey's La A3
East St B2
Eastport La C1
Fire Station B2
Fisher St B2
Friars Walk B2
Garden St B1
Government Offices C2
Grange Rd B1
Ham La C2
Harveys Way B2
Hereward Way A2
High St B1/B2
Hop Gallery B2
Information Ctr B2
Keere St B1
King Henry's Rd B1
Lancaster St B2
Landport Rd A1
Leisure Centre C3
Lewes Bridge B2
Lewes Castle B1
Lewes Football Gd C2
Lewes Golf Course B3
Lewes Southern By-Pass C2
Lewes Station B2
Library B2
Malling Ind Est A2
Malling Brook Ind Est A3
Malling Hill A3
Malling St A3/B3
Market St B2
Martyr's Monument B3
Mayhew Way A2
Morris Rd B3
Mountfield Rd C2
New Rd B1
Newton Rd A1
North St A2/B2
Offham Rd B1
Old Malling Way A1
Orchard Rd A3
Paddock La B1
Paddock Rd B1
Paddock Sports Gd B1
Park Rd B1
Pelham Terr A1
Pells Open Air Swimming Pool A1
Phoenix Causeway B2
Phoenix Ind Est B2
Phoenix Pl B2
Pinwell Rd B2
Police Station B1
Post Office A2/B1/B2/C1
Prince Edward's Rd B1
Priory St C1
Priory of St Pancras (remains of) ✦ C1
Railway La B2
Railway Land Nature Reserve B3
Rotten Row B1
Rufus Cl B1
St Pancras Rd C1
St John St B2
St John's Terr B2
St Nicholas La B2
Sewage Works C3
South Downs Bsns Pk A3
South St B3/C3
Southdowns Rd A2
Southerham Junction C3
Southover Grange Gdns ✦ B1
Southover High St C1
Southover Rd B1
Spences Field A3
Spences La A2
Stansfield Rd A1
Station Rd B2
Station St B2
Sun St B1
Sussex Downs College C2
Sussex Police HQ A2
Talbot Terr B1
The Avenue B1
The Course C1
The Martlets A2
The Needlemakers ✦ B2
The Pells A1
Thebes Gallery B2
Toronto Terr B1
Town Hall B2
West St B2
White Hill B1
Willeys Bridge A1

Lincoln 337

Alexandra Terr B1
Anchor St C1
Arboretum B3
Arboretum Ave B3
Baggholme Rd B3
Bailgate A2
Beaumont Fee B1
Brayford Way C1
Brayford Wharf East C1
Brayford Wharf North B1
Bruce Rd A2
Burton Rd A1
Bus Station (City) C2
Canwick Rd C2
Cardinal's Hat ✦ B2
Carline Rd B1
Castle B1
Castle St A1
Cathedral B2
Cathedral St B2
Cecil St A2
Chapel La A2
Cheviot St B3
Church La A2
City Hall B1
Clasketgate B2
Clayton Sports Gd A3
Coach Park C2
Collection, The B2
County Hospital (A&E) B3
County Office B1
Courts C1
Croft St B2
Cross St C2
Crown Courts B1
Curle Ave A3
Danesgate B2
Drill Hall B2
Drury La B1
East Bight A2
East Gate A2
Eastcliff Rd B3
Eastgate B2
Egerton Rd A3
Ellis Windmill A1
Engine Shed, The C1
Environment Agency C2
Exchequer Gate ✦ B2
Firth Rd C1
Flaxengate B2
Florence St B3
George St C3
Good La A2
Gray St A1
Great Northern Terr C3
Great Northern Terrace Industrial Estate C3
Greetwell Rd B3
Greetwellgate B3
Haffenden Rd A2
High St B2/C1
HM Prison A3
Hospital (Private) A2
Hungate B2
James St A2
Jews House & Ct B2
Kesteven St C2
Langworthgate A2
Lawn Visitor Centre, The B1
Lee Rd A3
Library B2
Lincoln College B2
Lincoln Central Sta C2
Lincolnshire Life/Royal Lincolnshire Regiment Museum A1
Lindum Rd B2
Lindum Sports Ground A3
Lindum Terr B3
Mainwaring Rd A3
Manor Rd A2
Market C2
Massey Rd A3
Medieval Bishop's Palace B2
Mildmay St A1
Mill Rd A1
Millman Rd B3
Minster Yard B2
Monks Rd B3
Montague St B2
Mount St A1
Nettleham Rd A2
Newland B1
Newport A2
Newport Arch A2
Newport Cemetery A2
Northgate A2
Odeon C1
Orchard St B1
Oxford St C2
Park St B1
Pelham Bridge C2
Pelham St C2
Police Station B1
Portland St C2
Post Office A1/A2/B1/B3/C2
Potter Gate B2
Priory Gate B2
Queensway A3
Rasen La A1
Ropewalk C1
Rosemary La B2
St Anne's Rd B3
St Benedict's C1
St Giles Ave A3
St John's Rd A2
St Marks St C1
St Mark's Sh Ctr C1
St Mary-Le-Wigford C1
St Mary's St C2
St Nicholas St A2
St Swithin's B2
Saltergate C1
Saxon St A1
Sch of Art & Design B2
Sewell Rd B3
Silver St B2
Sincil St C2
Spital St A2
Spring Hill B1
Stamp End C3
Steep Hill B2
Stonebow & Guildhall C2
Stonefield Ave A2
Tentercroft St C1
The Avenue B1
The Grove A3
Theatre Royal B2
Tritton Retail Park C1
Tritton Rd C1
Union Rd B1
University of Lincoln C1
Upper Lindum St B3
Upper Long Leys Rd A1
Usher B2
Vere St A2
Victoria St B1
Victoria Terr B1
Vine St B3
Wake St A1
Waldeck St A1
Waterside Sh Ctr C2
Waterside North C2
Waterside South C2
West Pde B1
Westgate A2
Wigford Way C1
Williamson St A2
Wilson St A1
Winn St B3
Wragby Rd A3
Yarborough Rd A1

Liverpool 337

Abercromby Sq C5
Acc Liverpool ✦ C2
Addison St A3
Adelaide Rd B6
Ainsworth St B4
Albany Rd B6
Albert Dock C2
Albert Edward Rd B6
Angela St C6
Anson St B4
Archbishop Blanche High School B6
Argyle St C3
Arrad St C4
Ashton St B5
Audley St A4
Back Leeds St A2
Basnett St B3
Bath St A1
Beatles Story C2
Beckwith St C3
Bedford Close C5
Bedford St North C5
Bedford St South C5
Benson St C4
Berry St C4
Birkett St A4
Bixteth St B2
Blackburne Place C4
Bluecoat B3
Bold Place C4
Bold St C4
Bolton St B3
Bridport St B4
Bronte St B4
Brook St A1
Brownlow Hill B4/B5
Brownlow St B5
Brunswick Rd A5
Brunswick St B1
Bus Station C2
Butler Cr A6
Byrom St A3
Caledonia St C4
Cambridge St C5
Camden St A4
Canada Blvd B1
Canning Dock C2
Canterbury St A4
Cardwell St C6
Carver St A4
Cases St B3
Castle St B2
Catherine St C5
Cavern Club B3
Central Library A3
Central Station B3
Chapel St B2
Charlotte St B3
Chatham Place C6
Chatham St C5
Cheapside B2
Chestnut St C5
Christian St A3
Church St B3
Churchill Way North A3
Churchill Way South B3
Clarence St B4
Coach Station A4
Cobden St A5
Cockspur St A2
College St C3
College St North A5
College St South A5
Colquitt St C4
Comus St A3
Concert St C3
Connaught Rd B6
Cook St B2
Copperas Hill B4
Cornwallis St C3
Covent Garden B2
Craven St A4
Cropper St B3
Crown St B5/C6
Cumberland St B2
Cunard Building B1
Dale St B2
Dansie St B4
Daulby St B5
Dawson St B3
Derby Sq B2
Drury La B2
Duckinfield St B4
Duke St C3
Earle St A2
East St A2
Eaton St A2
Edgar St A3
Edge La B6
Edinburgh Rd A6
Edmund St B2
Elizabeth St B5
Elliot St B3
Empire Theatre B4
Empress Rd B6
Epworth St A5
Erskine St A5
Everyman Theatre C5
Exchange St East B2
Fact Centre, The ✦ C4
Falkland St A5
Falkner St C5/C6
Farnworth St A6
Fenwick St B2
Fielding St A6
Fleet St C3
Fraser St A4
Freemasons Row A2
Gardner Row A3
Gascoyne St A2
George Pier Head C1
George St B2
Gibraltar Road A1
Gilbert St C3
Gildart St A4
Gill St B4
Goree B2
Gower St C2
Gradwell St C3
Great Crosshall St A3
Great George St C4
Great Howard St A1
Great Newton St B4
Greek St B4
Green La B4
Greenside A5
Greetham St C3
Gregson St A5
Grenville St C3
Grinfield St C6
Grove St C5
Guelph St A6
Hackins Hey B2
Haigh St A4
Hall La B6
Hanover St B3
Harbord St C6
Hardman St C4
Harker St A4
Hart St B4
Hatton Garden A2
Hawke St B4
Helsby St B6
Henry St C3
HM Customs & Excise National Museum C2
Highfield St A2
Highgate St B6
Hilbre St B4
Hope Place C4
Hope St C4
Houghton St B3
Hunter St A3
Hutchinson St A6
Information Ctr C2
Institute For The Performing Arts C4
Irvine St B6
Irwell St B2
Islington A4
James St B2
James St Station B2
Jenkinson St A4
Johnson St A3
Jubilee Drive B6
Kempston St A4
Kensington A6
Kensington Gdns B6
Kensington St A6
Kent St C3
King Edward St A1
Kinglake St B6
Knight St C4
Lace St A3
Langsdale St A4
Law Courts C2
Leece St C4
Leeds St A2
Leopold Rd B6
Lime St B3
Lime St Station B4
Little Woolton St B5
Liver St C2
Liverpool John Moores University A3/B4/C4
Liverpool Landing Stage B1
Liverpool One C2
London Rd A4/B4
Lord Nelson St B4
Lord St B2
Lovat St C6
Low Hill A5
Low Wood St A6
Lydia Ann St C3
Mansfield St A4
Marmaduke St B6
Marsden St A6
Martensen St B6
Marybone A3
Maryland St C4
Mason St B6
Mathew St B2
May St B4
Melville Place C6
Merseyside Maritime Museum C2
Metquarter B3
Metropolitan Cathedral (RC) B5
Midghall St A2
Molyneux Rd A6
Moor Place B4
Moorfields B2
Moorfields Station B2
Moss St A5
Mount Pleasant B4/B5
Mount St C4
Mount Vernon B6
Mulberry St C5
Municipal Buildings B2
Mus of Liverpool C2
Myrtle Gdns C6
Myrtle St C5
Naylor St A2
Nelson St C4
Neptune Theatre B3
New Islington A4
New Quay B1
Newington St C3
North John St B2
North St A3
North View B6
Norton St A4
Oakes St B5
O2 Academy
Odeon B4
Old Hall St A1
Old Leeds St A2
Oldham Place C4
Oldham St C4
Olive St C6
Open Eye Gallery C3
Oriel St A2
Ormond St B2
Orphan St C6
Overbury St C6
Overton St B6
Oxford St C5
Paisley St A1
Pall Mall A2
Paradise St C3
Park La C3
Parker St B3
Parr St C3
Peach St B5
Pembroke Place B4
Pembroke St B5
Philharmonic Hall C5
Pickop St A2
Pilgrim St C4
Pitt St C3
Playhouse Theatre B3
Pleasant St B4
Police HQ C2
Police Station A4/B4
Pomona St B4
Port of Liverpool Building B2
Post Office A2/A4/A5/A6/B2/B3/B4/C4
Pownall St C2
Prescot St A5
Preston St B3
Princes Dock A1
Princes Gdns A2
Princes Jetty A1
Princes Pde B1
Princes St B2
Pythian St A6
Queen Sq Bus Station B3
Queensland St C6
Queensway Tunnel (Docks exit) B1
Queensway Tunnel (Entrance) B3
Radio City B2
Ranelagh St B3
Redcross St B2
Renfrew St B6
Renshaw St B4
Richmond Row A4
Richmond St B3
Rigby St A2
Roberts St A1
Rock St B4
Rodney St C4
Rokeby St A4
Romily St A6
Roscoe La C4
Roscoe St C4
Rose Hill A3
Royal Court Theatre B3
Royal Liver Building B1
Royal Liverpool Hospital (A&E) B5
Royal Mail St B4
Rumford Place B2
Rumford St B2
Russell St B4
St Andrew St B4
St Anne St A4
St Georges Hall B3
St John's Centre B3
St John's Gdns B3
St John's La B3
St Joseph's Cr A4
St Minishull St B5
St Nicholas Place B1
St Paul's Sq A2
St Vincent Way B4
Salisbury St A4
Salthouse Dock C2
Salthouse Quay C2
Sandon St C5
Saxony Rd B6
Schomberg St A6
School La B2
Seel St C3
Seymour St B4
Shaw St A5
Sidney Place C6
Sir Thomas St B3
Skelhorne St B4
Slater St C3
Slavery Museum C2
Smithdown La B6
Soho Sq A4
Soho St A4
South John St B2
Springfield A4
Stafford St A4
Standish St A3
Stanley St B2
Strand St C2
Suffolk St C3
Tabley St C3
Tarleton St B3
Tate Gallery C2
Teck St B6
Temple St B2
The Beacon ✦ B3
The Strand B2
Tithebarn St B2
Town Hall B2
Traffic Police HQ C6
Trowbridge St B4
Trueman St A3
Union St B2
Unity Theatre C4
University C5
University of Liverpool B5
Upper Duke St C4
Upper Frederick St C3
Upper Baker St A6
Vauxhall Rd A2
Vernon St B2
Victoria Gallery & Museum B5
Victoria St B2
Vine St C5
Wakefield St A4
Walker Art Gallery A3
Walker St A6
Wapping C2
Water St B1/B2
Waterloo Rd A1
Wavertree Rd B6
West Derby Rd A6
West Derby St B5
Whitechapel B3
Western Approaches War Museum B2
Whitley Gdns A5
William Brown St B3
William Henry St A4
Williamson Sq B3
Williamson St B3
Williamson's Tunnels Heritage Centre ✦ C6
Women's Hospital C6
Wood St B3
World Museum, Liverpool A3
York St C3

Llandudno 337

Abbey Pl B1
Abbey Rd B1
Adelphi St B3
Alexandra Rd C2
Anglesey Rd A1
Argyll Rd B3
Arvon Ave A2
Atlee Cl C3
Augusta St B3
Back Madoc St B2
Bodafon St B3
Bodhyfryd Rd A2
Bodnant Cr C3
Bodnant Rd C3
Bridge Rd C2
Bryniau Rd C1
Builder St B3
Builder St West C2
Cabin Lift A2
Camera Obscura ✦ A3
Caroline Rd B2
Chapel St A2
Charlton St B3
Church Cr C1
Church Walks A2
Claremont Rd B2
Clement Ave A2
Clifton Rd B2
Clonmel St B3
Coach Station B3
Conway Rd B3
Council St West C3
Cricket and Rec Gd B2
Cwlach Rd A2
Cwlach St A1
Cwm Howard La C3
Cwm Pl C3
Cwm Rd C3
Dale Rd C1
Deganwy Ave B2
Denness Pl C2
Dinas Rd C2
Dolydd B1
Erol Pl B2
Ewloe Dr C3
Fairways C2

Royal Festival Hall 🎭 D5
Royal London Hospital for Integrated Medicine Ⓗ C5
Royal Marsden Hospital Ⓗ F1
Royal National Theatre 🎭 D6
Royal National Throat, Nose and Ear Hospital Ⓗ B5
Royal Opera House 🎭 D5
Rushworth St E6
Russell Sq B4
Russell Square ⊖ B5
Rutland Gate E2
Sackville St D4
Sadlers Wells 🎭 B6
Saffron Hill C6
Sale Pl C2
Sancroft St F5
Savile Row D4
Savoy Pl D5
Savoy St D5
School of Hygiene & Tropical Medicine C4
Science Mus 🏛 E1
Scrutton St B8
Sekforde St B6
Serpentine Gallery 🖼 E1
Serpentine Rd D2
Seven Dials C5
Seward St B6
Seymour Pl C2
Seymour St C2
Shad Thames D8/E8
Shaftesbury Ave D4
Shakespeare's Globe Theatre 🎭 D7
Shepherd Market D3
Sherwood St D4
Shoe La C6
Shoreditch High St B8
Shoreditch High St ⊖ B8
Shorts Gdns C5
Shouldham St C2
Sidmouth St B5
Silk St C7
Sir John Soane's Museum 🏛 C5
Skinner St B6
Sloane Ave F2
Sloane Sq F2
Sloane Square ⊖ F3
Sloane St E2
Snow Hill C6
Soho Sq C4
Somerset House ⌂ D5
South Audley St D3
South Carriage Dr E2
South Eaton Pl F3
South Kensington ⊖ F1
South Molton St C3
South Parade F1
South Pl C7
South St D3
South Terr F2
South Wharf Rd C1
Southampton Row C5
Southampton St D5
Southwark ⊖ D6
Southwark Bridge D7
Southwark Bridge Rd D7
Southwark Cath ✝ D7
Southwark Park Rd F8
Southwark St D7
Spa Rd E8
Speakers' Corner D2
Spencer St B6
Spital Sq C8
Spring St C1
St Alban's St D4
St Andrew St C6
St Barnabas St F3
St Bartholomew's Hospital Ⓗ C6
St Botolph St C8
St Bride St C6
St George's Circus F6
St George's Dr F4
St George's Rd E6
St George's Sq F4
St Giles High St C4
St James's Palace ⌂ D4
St James's Park ⊖ E4
St James's St D4
St John St B6
St John's Wood Rd B1
St Margaret St E5
St Mark's Hosp Ⓗ B6
St Martin's La D5
St Martin's Le Grand C7
St Mary Axe C8
St Mary's Hosp Ⓗ C1
St Pancras Int ⇌ A5
St Paul's ⊖ C7
St Paul's Cath ✝ C7
St Paul's Churchyard C6
St Thomas' Hosp Ⓗ E5
St Thomas St D7
Stamford St D6
Stanhope St B4
Stanhope Terr D1
Stephenson Way B4
Stock Exchange C6
Stoney St D7
Strand C6
Strathearn Pl D2
Stratton St D3
Sumner St D6
Sussex Gdns C1
Sussex Pl C1
Sussex Sq D1
Sussex St F3
Sutton's Way B7
Swan St E7
Swanfield St B8
Swinton St B5
Sydney Pl F1
Sydney St F2
Tabard St E7
Tabernacle St B7
Tachbrook St F4
Tanner St E8
Tate Britain 🖼 F5
Tate Modern 🖼 D7
Tavistock Pl B5
Tavistock Sq B4
Tea & Coffee Mus 🏛 D7
Temple ⊖ D6
Temple Ave D6
Temple Pl D5
Terminus Pl E3
Thayer St C3
The Barbican Centre for Arts C7
The Brunswick Sh Ctr B5
The Cut E6
The Mall E4
Theobald's Rd C5
Thorney St F5
Threadneedle St C7
Throgmorton St C7
Thurloe Pl F1
Thurloe Sq F2
Tonbridge St B5
Tooley St D8
Torrington Pl B4
Tothill St E4
Tottenham Court Rd B4
Tottenham Ct Rd ⊖ C4
Tottenham St C4
Tower Bridge ✦ D8
Tower Bridge App D8
Tower Bridge Rd E8
Tower Hill D8
Tower Hill ⊖ D8
Tower of London, The 🏰 D8
Toynbee St C8
Trafalgar Square D4
Trinity Sq D8
Trinity St E7
Trocadero Centre D4
Tudor St D6
Turin St B9
Turnmill St C6
Tyers St F5
Ufford St E6
Union St D6
Univ Coll Hospl Ⓗ B4
University of London C4
Univ of Westminster C3
University St B4
Upper Belgrave St E3
Upper Berkeley St C2
Upper Brook St D3
Upper Grosvenor St D3
Upper Ground D6
Upper Montague St C2
Upper St Martin's La D5
Upper Thames St D7
Upper Wimpole St C3
Upper Woburn Pl B4
Vauxhall Bridge Rd F4
Vauxhall St F5
Vere St C3
Vernon Pl C5
Vestry St B7
Victoria ⇌⊖ E3
Victoria and Albert Mus 🏛 E1
Victoria Coach Station F3
Victoria Embankment D5
Victoria Pl Sh Ctr F3
Victoria St E4
Villiers St D5
Vincent Sq F4
Vinopolis City of Wine 🏛 D7
Virginia Rd B8
Wakley St B6
Walbrook C7
Walcot Sq F6
Wallace Collection 🖼 C3
Walnut Tree Walk F6
Walton St F2
Walworth Rd F7
Wardour St C4/D4
Warner St B6
Warren St ⊖ B4
Warren St B4
Warwick Sq F4
Warwick Way F3
Waterloo ⇌⊖ E6
Waterloo Bridge D5
Waterloo East ⇌ D6
Waterloo Rd E6
Watling St C7
Webber St E6
Welbeck St C3
Wellington Arch ✦ E3
Wellington Mus 🏛 E3
Wellington Rd B2
Wellington Row B9
Wells St C4
Wenlock St A7
Wentworth St C8
West Carriage Dr D2
West Smithfield C6
West Sq E6
Westbourne St D1
Westbourne Terr C1
Westminster ⊖ E5
Westminster Abbey ✝ E5
Westminster Bridge E5
Westminster Bridge Rd E6
Westminster Cathedral (RC) ✝ E4
Westminster City Hall E4
Westminster Hall ⌂ E5
Weston St E7
Weymouth St C3
Wharf Rd A7
Wharton St B5
Whitcomb St D4
White Cube 🖼 B8
White Lion Hill D6
White Lion St A6
Whitechapel Rd C9
Whitecross St B7
Whitefriars St C6
Whitehall D5
Whitehall Pl D5
Wigmore Hall C3
Wigmore St C3
William IV St D5
Willow Walk F8
Wilmington Sq B6
Wilson St C7
Wilton Cres E3
Wilton Rd F4
Wimpole St C3
Winchester St F3
Wincott St F6
Windmill Walk D6
Woburn Pl B5
Woburn Sq B4
Wood St C7
Woodbridge St B6
Wootton St D6
Wormwood St C8
Worship St B7
Wren St B5
Wynyatt St B6
York Rd E5
York St C2
York Terrace East B3
York Terrace West B3

Luton 337

Adelaide St B1
Albert Rd C2
Alma St B2
Alton Rd C3
Anthony Gdns C1
Arthur St C2
Ashburnham Rd B1
Ashton Rd C2
Avondale Rd A1
Back St A2
Bailey St C3
Baker St C2
Biscot Rd A1
Bolton Rd B3
Boyle Cl A2
Brantwood Rd B1
Bretts Mead C1
Bridge St B2
Brook St A1
Brunswick St A3
Burr St A3
Bury Park Rd A1
Bute St B2
Buxton Rd B2
Cambridge St C3
Cardiff Grove B1
Cardiff Rd B1
Cardigan St A2
Castle St B2/C2
Chapel St C2
Charles St A3
Chase St C2
Cheapside B2
Chequer St C3
Chiltern Rise C1
Church St B2/B3
Cinema 🎬 A2
Cobden St A3
Collingdon St A1
Community Centre C3
Concorde Ave A3
Corncastle Rd C1
Cowper St C2
Crawley Green Rd B3
Crawley Rd A1
Crescent Rise A3
Crescent Rd A3
Cromwell Rd A1
Cross St A2
Crown Court B2
Cumberland St B2
Cutenhoe Rd C3
Dallow Rd B1
Downs Rd B1
Dudley St A2
Duke St A2
Dumfries St B1
Dunstable Place B2
Dunstable Rd A1/B1
Edward St A3
Elizabeth St C2
Essex Cl C3
Farley Hill C1
Farley Lodge C1
Flowers Way B2
Francis St A1
Frederick St A2
Galaxy L Complex A2
George St B2
George St West B2
Gillam St A3
Gordon St B2
Grove Rd B1
Guildford St A2
Haddon Rd A3
Harcourt St C2
Hart Hill Drive A3
Hart Hill Lane A3
Hartley Rd A3
Hastings St B2
Hat Factory, The 🎭 B2
Hatters Way A1
Havelock Rd A2
Hibbert St C2
High Town Rd A3
Highbury Rd A1
Hightown Community Sports & Arts Centre A3
Hillary Cres C1
Hillborough Rd C1
Hitchin Rd A3
Holly St C2
Holm C1
Hucklesby Way A2
Hunts Cl C1
Information Ctr ℹ B2
Inkerman St A2
John St B2
Jubilee St A3
Kelvin Cl C2
King St B2
Kingsland Rd C3
Latimer Rd C2
Lawn Gdns C2
Lea Rd B3
Library B2
Library Rd B2
Liverpool Rd B1
London Rd C2
Luton Station ⇌ A2
Lyndhurst Rd B1
Magistrates Court B2
Mall, The B2
Manchester St B2
Manor Rd B3
May St C3
Meyrick Ave C1
Midland Rd A2
Mill St A2
Milton Rd B1
Moor St A1
Moor, The A1
Moorland Gdns A2
Moulton Rise A3
Museum & Art Gallery 🏛🖼 A2
Napier Rd B1
New Bedford Rd A1
New Town St C2
North St A3
Old Bedford Rd A2
Old Orchard C2
Osbourne Rd C3
Oxen Rd A3
Park Sq B2
Park St B3/C3
Park St West B2
Park Viaduct B3
Parkland Drive C1
Police Station 🚓 B1
Pomfret Ave A3
Pondwicks Rd B3
Post Office ✉ A1/A2/B2/C3
Power Court B3
Princess St B1
Red Rails C1
Regent St B2
Reginald St A2
Rothesay Rd B1
Russell Rise C1
Russell St C1
St Ann's Rd B3
St George's 🎭 B2
St George's Square B2
St Mary's ⛪ B3
St Marys Rd B3
St Paul's Rd C2
St Saviour's Cres C1
Salisbury Rd B1
Seymour Ave C3
Seymour Rd C3
Silver St B2
South Rd C2
Stanley St B1
Station Rd A2
Stockwood Cres C2
Stockwood Park C1
Strathmore Ave C2
Stuart St B2
Studley Rd A1
Surrey St C3
Sutherland Place C1
Tavistock St C2
Taylor St A3
Telford Way A1
Tennyson Rd C2
Tenzing Grove C1
The Cross Way C1
The Larches A2
Thistle Rd B3
Town Hall B2
Townsley Cl C2
UK Centre for Carnival Arts ✦ B3
Union St B2
Univ of Bedfordshire B3
Upper George St B2
Vicarage St B3
Villa Rd A2
Waldeck Rd A1
Wellington St B1/B2
Wenlock St A2
Whitby Rd A1
Whitehill Ave C1
William St A2
Wilsden Ave C1
Windmill Rd B3
Windsor St C2
Winsdon Rd B1
York St A3

Macclesfield 337

108 Steps B2
Abbey Rd A1
Alton Dr A3
Armett St C1
Athey St B1
Bank St C3
Barber St C3
Barton St C1
Beech La A2
Beswick St B1
Black La A2
Black Rd C3
Blakelow Gardens C3
Blakelow Rd C3
Bond St B1/C1
Bread St C1
Bridge St B1
Brock St A2
Brocklehurst Ave A3
Brook St B3
Brookfield La B3
Brough St West C1
Brown St C1
Brynton Rd A2
Buckley St C2
Bus Station B2
Buxton Rd B3
Byrons St C2
Canal St B3
Carlsbrook Ave A3
Castle St B2
Catherine St B1
Cemetery A1
Chadwick Terr A3
Chapel St C2
Charlotte St B2
Chester Rd B1
Chestergate B1
Christ Church ⛪ B1
Churchill Way B2
Coare St A1
Commercial Rd B2
Conway Cres A3
Copper St C3
Cottage St B1
Court A2
Court B2
Crematorium A1
Crew Ave A3
Crompton Rd B1/C1
Cross St C2
Crossall St C1
Cumberland St A1/B1
Dale St B3
Duke St B2
Eastgate B3
Exchange St B2
Fence Ave B3
Fence Ave Ind Est A3
Flint St B3
Foden St A2
Fountain St B3
Gateway Gallery ✦ B1
Garden St A3
Gas Rd B2
George St B2
Glegg St B3
Golf Course C3
Goodall St B3
Grange Rd C1
Great King St B1
Green St B3
Grosvenor Sh Ctr B2
Gunco La C3
Half St C2
Hallefield Rd B3
Hatton St C1
Hawthorn Way A3
Heapy St C3
Henderson St B1
Heritage Centre & Silk Museum 🏛 B2
Hibel Rd A2
High St C2
Hobson St C2
Hollins Rd C3
Hope St West B1
Horseshoe Dr B1
Hurdsfield Rd A3
Information Ctr ℹ B2
James St C2
Jodrell St B3
John St C2
Jordangate A2
King Edward St B2
King George's Field C3
King St B2
King's School A1
Knight Pool C3
Knight St C3
Lansdowne St A3
Library B2
Lime Gr B3
Little Theatre 🎭 C2
Loney St B1
Longacre St B1
Lord St C2
Lowe St C2
Lowerfield Rd A3
Lyon St B1
Macclesfield College C1
Macclesfield Sta ⇌ B2
Marina B3
Market B2
Market Pl B2
Masons La A3
Mill La C2
Mill Rd C2
Mill St B2
Moran Rd C1
New Hall St A2
Newton St C1
Nicholson Ave A3
Nicholson Cl A3
Northgate Ave A2
Old Mill La C2
Paradise Mill 🏛 C2
Paradise St B1
Park Green B2
Park La C1
Park Rd C1
Park St C2
Park Vale Rd C1
Parr St B1
Peel St C2
Percyvale St A3
Peter St C1
Pickford St B2
Pierce St B1
Pinfold St B1
Pitt St C2
Police Station 🚓 B2
Pool St C2
Poplar Rd C2
Post Office ✉ B1/B2/B3
Pownall St A2
Prestbury Rd A1/B1
Queen Victoria St B2
Queen's Ave A3
Registrar B2
Richmond Hill C3
Riseley St B1
Roan Ct B3
Roe St B2
Rowan Way A3
Ryle St C2
Ryle's Park Rd C1
St George's St C2
St Michael's ⛪ B2
Samuel St B2
Saville St C3
Shaw St B1
Slater St C1
Snow Hill C3
South Park C1
Spring Gdns A2
Statham St C2
Station St A2
Steeple St A3
Sunderland St B2
Superstore A1/A2/C2
Swettenham St B3
The Silk Rd A2/B2
Thistleton Cl C2
Thorp St B2
Town Hall B2
Townley St B2
Turnock St C3
Union Rd B3
Union St B2
Victoria Park B3
Vincent St C2
Waters Green B2
Waterside C2
West Bond St B1
West Park A1
West Park Museum 🏛 A1
Westbrook Dr A1
Westminster Rd A1
Whalley Hayes B1
Windmill St C3
Withyfold Dr A2
York St B3

Maidstone 340

Albion Pl B3
All Saints ⛪ B2
Allen St A3
Amphitheatre ✦ C2
Archbishop's Pal ⌂❁ B2
Bank St B2
Barker Rd C2
Barton Rd C3
Beaconsfield Rd C1
Bedford Pl B1
Bentlif Art Gallery 🖼 B2
Bishops Way B2
Bluett St A3
Bower La C1
Bower Mount Rd B1
Bower Pl C1
Bower St B1
Bowling Alley B3
Boxley Rd A3
Brenchley Gardens A2
Brewer St A3
Broadway B2
Broadway Sh Ctr B2
Brunswick St C3
Buckland Hill A1
Buckland Rd B1
Bus Station B3
Campbell Rd C3
Carriage Museum 🏛 B2
Church Rd C1
Church St B3
Cinema 🎬 C2
College Ave C2
College Rd C2
Collis Memorial Gdn C3
Cornwallis Rd B1
Corpus Christi Hall B2
County Hall A2
County Rd A3
Crompton Gdns C3
Crown & County Courts B2
Curzon Rd A3
Dixon Cl C2
Douglas Rd C1
Earl St B2
Eccleston Rd C2
Fairmeadow B2
Fisher St A2
Florence Rd C1
Foley St A3
Foster St C3
Fremlin Walk Sh Ctr B2
Gabriel's Hill B3
George St C3
Grecian St A3
Hardy St A3
Hart St C2
Hastings Rd C3
Hayle Rd C3
Hazlitt Theatre 🎭 B2
Heathorn St A3
Hedley St A3
High St B2
HM Prison A3
Holland Rd A3
Hope St A2
Information Ctr ℹ B2
James St A3
James Whatman Way A2
Jeffrey St A3
Kent County Council Offices A2
Kent History & Liby Ctr A2
King Edward Rd C2
King St B3
Kingsley Rd C3
Knightrider St B3
Launder Way C1
Lesley Pl A1
Little Buckland Ave A1
Lockmeadow Leisure Complex C2
London Rd B1
Lower Boxley Rd A2
Lower Fant Rd C1
Magistrates Court B3
Maidstone Barracks Station ⇌ A1
Maidstone Borough Council Offices B1
Maidstone East Sta ⇌ A2
Maidstone Museum 🏛 B2
Maidstone West Sta ⇌ B2
Market C2
Market Buildings B2
Marsham St B3
Medway St B2
Medway Trading Est C2
Melville Rd C3
Mill St B2
Millennium Bridge C2
Mote Rd B3
Muir Rd C3
Old Tovil Rd C2
Palace Ave B3
Perryfield St A2
Police Station 🚓 B3
Post Office ✉ A2/B2/B3/C3
Priory Rd C3
Prospect Pl C1
Pudding La B2
Queen Anne Rd B3
Queens Rd A1
Randall St A2
Rawdon Rd C3
Reginald Rd C1
Rock Pl B1
Rocky Hill B1
Romney Pl B3
Rose Yard B2
Rowland Cl C1
Royal Engineers' Rd A2
Royal Star Arcade B2
St Annes Ct B1
St Faith's St B2
St Luke's Rd A3
St Peter's Br B2
St Peter's Wharf Retail Park B2
St Peter St B2
St Philip's Ave C3
Salisbury Rd A3
Sandling Rd A2
Scott St A2
Scrubs La B1
Sheal's Cres C3
Somerfield La B1
Somerfield Rd B1
Staceys St A2
Station Rd A2
Superstore A1/B2/B3
Terrace Rd B1
The Mall B3
The Somerfield Hospital Ⓗ A1
Tonbridge Rd C1
Tovil Rd C2
Town Hall B2
Trinity Park B3
Tufton St B3
Union St B3
Upper Fant Rd C1
Upper Stone St C3
Victoria St B1
Visitor Centre A1
Warwick Pl B1
Wat Tyler Way B3
Waterloo St C3
Waterlow Rd A3
Week St B2
Well Rd A3
Westree Rd C1
Wharf Rd C1
Whatman Park A1
Wheeler St A3
Whitchurch Cl B1
Woodville Rd C3
Wyatt St B3
Wyke Manor Rd B3

Manchester 337

Adair St B6
Addington St A5
Adelphi St A1
Air & Space Gallery 🖼 B2
Albert Sq B3
Albion St C3
AMC Great Northern 🎬 B3
Ancoats Gr B6
Ancoats Gr North B6
Angela St C2
Aquatic Centre C4
Ardwick Green Park C5
Ardwick Green North C5
Ardwick Green South C5
Arlington St A2
Artillery St B3
Arundel St C2
Atherton St B2
Atkinson St B3
Aytoun St B4
Back Piccadilly A4
Baird St B5
Balloon St A4
Bank Pl A1
Baring St B5
Barrack St C1
Barrow St A1
BBC TV Studios C4
Bendix St A5
Bengal St A5
Berry St C5
Blackfriars Rd A3
Blackfriars St A3
Blantyre St C2
Bloom St B4
Blossom St A5
Boad St B5
Bombay St B4
Booth St A3
Booth St B4
Bootle St B3
Brazennose St B3
Brewer St A5
Bridge St A3
Bridgewater Hall B3
Bridgewater Pl A4
Bridgewater St B2
Brook St C4
Brotherton Dr A2
Brown St A3
Brown St B4
Brunswick St C6
Brydon Ave C6
Buddhist Centre A4
Bury St A2
Bus & Coach Station B4
Bus Station B4
Butler St A6
Buxton St C5
Byrom St B3
Cable St A5
Calder St B1
Cambridge St C3/C4
Camp St B3
Canal St B4
Cannon St A1
Cannon St A4
Cardroom Rd A6
Carruthers St A6
Castle St C2
Cateaton St A3
Cathedral ✝ A3
Cathedral St A3
Cavendish St C4
Chapel St A1/A3
Chapeltown St B5
Charles St C4
Charlotte St B4
Chatham St B4
Cheapside A3
Chepstow St B3
Chester Rd C1/C2
Chester St C4
Chetham's (Dept Store) A3
China La B5
Chippenham Rd A6
Chorlton Rd C2
Chorlton St B4
Church St A2
Church St A4
City Park A4
City Rd C3
Civil Justice Centre B2
Cleminson St A2
Clowes St A3
College Land A3
Coll of Adult Ed C4
Collier St B2
Commercial St C3
Conference Centre C4
Cooper St B4
Copperas St A4
Cornbrook 🚊 C1
Cornell St A5
Cornerhouse 🎬 C4
Corporation St A4
Cotter St C6
Cotton St A5
Cow La B1
Cross St B3
Crown Court B4
Crown St C2
Cube Gallery 🖼 B4
Dalberg St C6
Dale St A4/B5
Dancehouse, The 🎭 C4
Dantzic St A4
Dark La C6
Dawson St C2
Dean St A5
Deansgate A3/B3
Deansgate Station ⇌ C3
Dolphin St C6
Downing St C5
Ducie St B5
Duke Pl B2
Duke St B2
Durling St C6
East Ordsall La A2/B1
Edge St A4
Egerton St C2
Ellesmere St C1
Everard St C1
Every St B6
Fairfield St B5
Faulkner St B4
Fennel St A3
Ford St A2
Ford St C6
Fountain St B4
Frederick St A2
Gartside St B2
Gaythorne St A1
George Leigh St A5
George St A1
George St B4
G-Mex 🚊 C3
Goadsby St A4
Gore St A2
Goulden St A5
Granada TV Centre B2
Granby Row B4
Gravel St A3
Great Ancoats St A5
Great Bridgewater St B3
Great George St A1
Great Jackson St C2
Great Marlborough St C4
Greengate A3
Green Room, The 🎭 C4
Grosvenor St C5
Gun St A5
Hadrian Ave B6
Hall St B3
Hampson St B1
Hanover St A4
Hanworth Cl C5
Hardman St B3
Harkness St C6
Harrison St B6
Hart St B4
Helmet St B6
Henry St A5
Heyrod St B6
High St A4
Higher Ardwick C6
Hilton St A4/A5
Holland St A6
Hood St A5
Hope St B1
Hope St B4
Houldsworth St A5
Hoyle St C6
Hulme Hall Rd C1
Hulme St A1
Hulme St C3
Hyde Rd C6
Information Ctr ℹ B3
Irwell St A2
Islington St A2
Jackson Cr C2
Jackson's Row B3
James St A1
Jenner Cl C2
Jersey St A5
John Dalton St A1
John Dalton St B3
John Ryland's Liby ⌂ B3
John St A2
Kennedy St B3
Kincardine Rd C5
King St A3
King St West A3
Law Courts B3
Laystall St B5
Lever St A5
Library B3
Linby St C2
Little Lever St A4
Liverpool Rd B2
Liverpool St B1
Lloyd St B3
Lockton Cl C5
London Rd B5
Long Millgate A3
Longacre St B6
Loom St A5
Lower Byrom St B2
Lower Mosley St B3
Lower Moss La C2
Lower Ormond St C4
Loxford La C4
Luna St A5
Major St B4
Manchester Arndale A4
Manchester Art Gallery 🖼 B4
Manchester Central Convention Complex B3
Manchester Metropolitan University B4/C4
Manchester Piccadilly Station ⇌ B5
Manchester Technology Centre C4
Mancunian Way C3
Manor St C5
Marble St A4
Market St A2
Market St A4
Market St 🚊 A4
Marsden St A3
Marshall St A5
Mayan Ave A2
Medlock St C3
Middlewood St B1
Miller St A4
Minshull St B4
Mosley St A4
Mount St B3
Mulberry St B3
Murray St A5
Museum of Science & Industry (MOSI) 🏛 B2
Nathan Dr A2
National Football Mus 🏛 A4
Naval St A5
New Bailey St A2
New Elm Rd B2
New Islington A6
New Islington Station 🚊 B6
New Quay St B2
New Union St A6
Newgate St A4
Newton St A5
Nicholas St B4
North Western St C6
Oak St A4
Odeon 🎬 A4
Old Mill St A6
Oldfield Rd A1/C1
Oldham Rd A5
Oldham St A4
Opera House 🎭 B3
Ordsall La C1
Oxford Rd C4
Oxford Rd ⇌ C4
Oxford St B4
Paddock St C6
Palace Theatre 🎭 B4
Pall Mall A3
Palmerston St B6
Park St A1
Parker St B4
Peak St B5
Penfield Cl C5
Peoples' History Museum 🏛 B2
Peru St A1
Peter St B3
Piccadilly A4
Piccadilly 🚊 B5
Piccadilly Gdns 🚊 B4
Piercy St A6
Poland St A5
Police Museum 🏛 A5
Police Station 🚓 B3/B5
Pollard St B6

Port St A5
Portland St B4
Portugal St East B5
Post Office A1/A4/A5/B3
Potato Wharf B2
Princess St B3/C4
Pritchard St C4
Quay St A2
Quay St B2
Queen St B3
Radium St A5
Redhill St A5
Regent Rd B1
Renold Theatre A2
Retail Park A5
Rice St B2
Richmond St B4
River St C3
Roby St B5
Rodney St A6
Roman Fort B2
Rosamond St A2
Royal Exchange A3
Sackville St B4
St Andrew's St B6
St Ann St A3
St Ann's A3
St George's Ave C1
St James St B4
St John St B3
St John's Cath (RC) A2
St Mary's B3
St Mary's Gate A3
St Mary's Parsonage A3
St Peter's Sq B3
St Stephen St A2
Salford Approach A3
Salford Central A2
Sheffield St B5
Shepley St B5
Sherratt St A5
Shudehill A4
Shudehill A4
Sidney St C4
Silk St A5
Silver St B4
Skerry Cl C5
Snell St B6
South King St B3
Sparkle St B5
Spear St A4
Spring Gdns A4
Stanley St A2/B2
Station Approach B5
Store St B5
Swan St A4
Tariff St B5
Tatton St C1
Temperance St B6/C6
The Triangle A4
Thirsk St C6
Thomas St A4
Thompson St A5
Tib La B3
Tib St A4
Town Hall (Manchester) B3
Town Hall (Salford) A2
Trafford St C3
Travis St B5
Trinity Way A2
Turner St A4
Union St C6
University of Manchester (Sackville Street Campus) C5
Upper Brook St C5
Upper Cleminson St A1
Upper Wharf St A1
Vesta St B6
Victoria A4
Victoria Station A4
Victoria St A3
Wadesdon Rd C5
Water St B2
Watson St B3
West Fleet St B1
West King St A2
West Mosley St B4
West Union St B1
Weybridge Rd A6
Whitworth St B4
Whitworth St West C3
Wilburn St B1
William St A2
William St C6
Wilmott St C3
Windmill St B3
Windsor Cr A1
Withy Gr A4
Woden St C1
Wood St B3
Woodward St A6
Worrall St C1
Worsley St C2
York St B4
York St C2
York St C4

Merthyr Tydfil 340
Merthyr Tudful

Aberdare Rd B2
Abermorlais Terr B2
Alexandra Rd A3
Alma St C3
Arfryn Pl C3
Argyle St C3
Avenue De Clichy C2
Bethesda St B2
Bishops Gr A3
Brecon Rd A1/B2
Briarmead A3
Bryn St C3
Bryntirion Rd B3/C3
Bus Station B2
Caedraw Rd C2
Cae Mari Dwn B3
Castle Sq A1
Castle St B2
Chapel C2
Chapel Bank B1
Church St B3
Civic Centre B2
Coedcae'r Ct C3
Court B3
Courts B2
Court St C3
Cromwell St B2
Cyfarthfa Castle School and Museum A1
Cyfarthfa Ind Est A1
Cyfarthfa Park A1
Cyfarthfa Rd A1
Dane St A2
Dane Terr A2
Danyparc B3
Darren View A3
Dixon St B2
Dyke St C3
Dynevor St B2
Elwyn Dr C3
Fire Station B2
Fothergill St B3
Galonuchaf Rd A3
Garth St B2
Georgetown B2
Grawen Terr A2
Grove Pk A2
Gurnos Rd A2
Gwaelodygarth Rd A2/A3
Gwaunfarren Gr A3
Gwaunfarren Rd A3
Gwendoline St A3
Hampton St C3
Hanover St A2
Heol S O Davies B1
Heol-Gerrig B1
Highland View C3
High St A3/B2/B3/C2
Howell Cl B1
Information Ctr B2
Jackson's Bridge B2
James St C3
John St B3
Joseph Parry's Cott B2
Lancaster St A2
Library B2
Llewellyn St A2
Llwyfen St B2
Llwyn Berry B1
Llwyn Dic Penderyn B1
Llwyn-y-Gelynen C1
Lower Thomas St B3
Market C2
Mary St C3
Masonic St C2
Merthyr RFC C2
Merthyr College B2
Merthyr Town FC B3
Merthyr Tydfil Leisure Village C3
Merthyr Tydfil Sta C3
Meyrick Villas A2
Miniature Railway A1
Mount St A2
Nantygwenith St B1
Norman Terr B2
Oak Rd A2
Old Cemetery B3
Pandy Cl A1
Pantycelynen B1
Park Terr B2
Penlan View C2
Penry St B2
Pentwyn Villas A2
Penyard Rd B3
Penydarren Park A3
Penydarren Rd B3
Plymouth St C3
Police Station C2
Pont Marlais West B2
Post Office A3/B2/C3
Quarry Row B2
Queen's Rd B3
Rees St C3
Rhydycar Link C2
Riverside Park A1
St David's B3
St Tydfil's C2
St Tydfil's Ave C3
St Tydfil's Hospital (No A&E) B3
St Tydfil's Sq Sh Ctr C2
Saxon St A2
School of Nursing A2
Seward St A3
Shiloh La B3
Stone Circles B3
Stuart St A2
Summerhill Pl B3
Superstore B3
Swan St C2
Swansea Rd B1
Taff Glen View C3
Taff Vale Ct B3
Theatre Soar B2
The Grove A2
The Parade B3
The Walk B2
Thomastown Park B3
Tramroad La A3
Tramroad Side B2
Tramroad Side North B3
Tramroad Side South C3
Trevithick Gdns C3
Trevithick St A3
Tudor Terr B2
Twynyrodyn Rd C3
Union St B3
Upper Colliers Row B1
Upper Thomas St B3
Victoria St B2
Vue C3
Vulcan Rd B2
Warlow St C3
Well St A2
Welsh Assembly Government Offices C2
Wern La C1
West Gr A2
William St C3
Yew St C3
Ynysfach Engine House C2
Ynysfach Rd C2

Middlesbrough 340

Abingdon Rd C3
Acklam Rd C1
Albert Park C2
Albert Rd B2
Albert Terr C2
Aubrey St C3
Ayresome Gdns C2
Ayresome Green La C1
Ayresome St C2
Barton Rd A1
Bilsdale Rd C3
Bishopton Rd C3
Borough Rd B2/B3
Bowes Rd A2
Breckon Hill Rd B3
Bridge St East B3
Bridge St West B2
Brighouse Rd A1
Burlam Rd C1
Bus Station B2
Cannon Park B1
Cannon Park Way B2
Cannon St B1
Captain Cook Sq B2
Carlow St C1
Castle Way C3
Chipchase Rd C2
Cineworld B3
Clairville Sports Stadium C3
Cleveland Centre B2
Clive Rd C2
Commercial St A2
Corporation Rd B2
Costa St C2
Council Offices B3
Crescent Rd C2
Cumberland Rd C2
Depot Rd A2
Derwent St B2
Devonshire Rd C2
Diamond Rd B2
Disabled Driver Test Circuit B1
Dorman Museum C2
Douglas St B3
Eastbourne Rd C2
Eden Rd C3
Enterprise Centre A2
Forty Foot Rd A2
Gilkes St B2
Gosford St A2
Grange Rd B2
Gresham Rd B2
Harehills Rd C1
Harford St C2
Hartington Rd B2
Haverton Hill Rd A1
Hey Wood St B1
Highfield Rd C3
Hill St Centre B2
Holwick Rd B1
Hutton Rd C3
ICI Works A1
Information Ctr B2
Lambton Rd C3
Lancaster Rd C2
Lansdowne Rd C3
Latham Rd C2
Law Courts B2/B3
Lees Rd B2
Leeway B3
Linthorpe Cemetery C1
Linthorpe Rd B2
Lloyd St B2
Longford St C2
Longlands Rd C3
Lower East St A3
Lower Lake C3
Maldon Rd C1
Manor St B2
Marsh St B2
Marton Rd B3
Middlehaven B3
Middlesbrough By-Pass B2/C1
Middlesbrough Coll B3
Middlesbrough L Park B3
Middlesbrough Sta B2
Middlesbrough Theatre C2
Middletown Park C2
MIMA B3
Mosque B2
Mosque C3
Mulgrave Rd C2
North Ormesby Rd B3
Newport Bridge B1
Newport Bridge Approach Rd B1
Newport Rd B2
North Rd B2
Northern Rd C1
Outram St B2
Oxford Rd C2
Park La C2
Park Rd North C2
Park Rd South C2
Park Vale Rd C3
Parliament Rd B1
Police Station A2
Port Clarence Rd A3
Portman St B2
Post Office B3/C1/C2/C3
Princes Rd B2
Python A2
Riverside Bsns Park A2
Riverside Park Rd A1
Riverside Stadium (Middlesbrough FC) B3
Rockliffe Rd C2
Romaldkirk Rd B1
Roman Rd C2
Roseberry Rd C3
St Barnabas' Rd C2
St Paul's Rd B2
Saltwells Rd B3
Scott's Rd A3
Seaton Carew Rd A3
Shepherdson Way B3
Sikh Temple B2
Snowdon Rd A2
South West Ironmasters Park B1
Southfield Rd B2
Southwell Rd C2
Springfield Rd C1
Startforth Rd A2
Stockton Rd C1
Stockton St A2
Surrey St C2
Sycamore Rd C2
Synagogue C2
Tax Offices B3
Tees Viaduct C1
Teessaurus Park A2
Teesside Tertiary College C3
Temenos B3
The Avenue C2
The Crescent C2
Thornfield Rd C1
Town Hall B2
Transporter Bridge (Toll) A3
Union St B2
University of Teesside B2
Upper Lake C2
Valley Rd C3
Ventnor Rd C2
Victoria Rd B2
Visitor Centre A3
Vulcan St A2
Warwick St C2
Wellesley Rd B3
West Lane Hospital C1
Westminster Rd C2
Wilson St B2
Windward Way B3
Woodlands Rd B2
York Rd C3

Milton Keynes 340

Abbey Way A1
Arbrook Ave B1
Armourer Dr A3
Arncliffe Dr A1
Avebury C2
Avebury Blvd C2
Bankfield B3
Bayard Ave A2
Belvedere A2
Bishopstone A1
Blundells Rd A1
Boycott Ave C2
Bradwell Comm Blvd B1
Bradwell Rd C1
Bramble Ave A2
Brearley Ave C2
Breckland A1
Brill Place B1
Burnham Dr B1
Bus Station C1
Campbell Park B3
Cantle Ave A3
Central Milton Keynes Shopping Area B2
Century Ave C2
Chaffron Way C3
Childs Way C1
Christ the Cornerstone B2
Cineworld B2
Civic Offices B2
Cleavers Ave B2
Colesbourne Dr A3
Conniburrow Blvd B2
County Court B2
Currier Dr A2
Dansteed Way A2/A3/B1
Deltic Ave B1
Downs Barn A2
Downs Barn Blvd A3
Eaglestone C3
Eelbrook Ave B1
Elder Gate B1
Evans Gate C2
Fairford Cr A3
Falcon Ave B3
Fennel Dr A2
Fishermead Blvd C3
Food Centre B3
Fulwoods Dr C3
Glazier Dr A2
Glovers La A1
Grafton Gate C1
Grafton St A1/C2
Gurnards Ave B3
Harrier Dr C3
Ibstone Ave B1
Langcliffe Dr A1
Leisure Plaza C1
Leys Rd C1
Library B2
Linford Wood A2
Marlborough Gate B3
Marlborough St A2/B3
Mercers Dr A1
Midsummer C2
Midsummer Blvd B2
Milton Keynes Central C1
Monks Way A1
Mullen Ave A3
Mullion Pl C3
National Hockey Stadium B1
Neath Hill A3
North Elder C1
North Grafton B1
North Overgate A3
North Row B2
North Saxon B2
North Secklow B2
North Skeldon A3
North Witan B1
Oakley Gdns A3
Oldbrook Blvd C2
Open-Air Theatre B3
Overgate A3
Overstreet A3
Patriot Dr B1
Pencarrow Pl B3
Penryn Ave B3
Perran Ave C3
Pitcher La C1
Place Retail Park, The C1
Point Centre, The B2
Police Station B2
Portway B2
Post Office A2/B2/C3
Precedent Dr B1
Quinton Dr B1
Ramsons Ave B2
Rockingham Dr A2
Rooksley B1
Rooksley Retail Park C1
Saxon Gate B2
Saxon St A1/C3
Secklow Gate B2
Shackleton Pl C2
Silbury Blvd B2
Skeldon A3
South Grafton C2
South Row C2
South Saxon C2
South Secklow B3
South Witan C2
Springfield B3
Stanton Wood A1
Stantonbury A1
Stantonbury L Ctr A1
Strudwick Dr C2
Sunrise Parkway A2
Telephone Exchange C3
The Boundary C3
Theatre & Art Gallery B3
Tolcarne Ave C3
Towan Ave C3
Trueman Pl C2
Vauxhall A1
Winterhill Retail Park C2
Witan Gate B2
X-Scape B3

Newcastle upon Tyne 340

Albert St B3
Argyle St B3
Back New Bridge St B3
BALTIC Centre for Contemporary Art C3
Barker St A3
Barrack Rd B1
Bath La B1
Bell's Court B2
Bessie Surtees Ho C2
Bigg Market C2
Biscuit Factory B3
Black Gate C2
Blackett St B2
Blandford Sq C1
Boating Lake A1
Boyd St B3
Brandling Park A2
Bus Station B2
Buxton St B3
Byron St A3
Camden St B2
Castle Keep C2
Central C1
Central Library B2
Central Motorway B2
Chester St A3
City Hall B2
City Rd B3/C3
City Walls C1
Civic Centre A2
Claremont Rd A1
Clarence St B3
Clarence Walk B3
Clayton St C1/B1
Clayton St West C1
Coach Station C1
College St B2
Collingwood St C2
Copland Terr B3
Coppice Way B3
Corporation St B1
Courts C3
Crawhall Rd B3
Dean St C2
Discovery C1
Dinsdale Pl A3
Dinsdale Rd A3
Doncaster Rd A3
Durant Rd B2
Eldon Sq B1
Eldon Square Shopping Centre B2
Ellison Pl B2
Empire B1
Eskdale Terr A2
Eslington Terr A2
Exhibition Park A1
Falconar St B3
Fenkle St C1
Forth Banks C1
Forth St C1
Gallowgate B1
Gateshead Heritage @ St Mary's C3
Gateshead Millennium Bridge C3
Gibson St B3
Goldspink La A3
Grainger Market B2
Grainger St B2
Grantham Rd A3
Granville Rd A3
Great North Mus:Hancock A2
Grey St B2
Groat Market C2
Guildhall C2
Hancock St A2
Hanover St C2
Hatton Gallery A1
Hawks Rd C3
Haymarket B2
Heber St B1
Helmsley Rd A3
High Bridge B2
High Level Bridge C2
Hillgate C3
Howard St B3
Hutton Terr A3
Information Ctr C3
Jesmond A2
Jesmond Rd A2/A3
John Dobson St B2
John George Joicey Museum C2
Jubilee Rd B3
Kelvin Gr A3
Kensington Terr A2
Laing Gallery B2
Lambton Rd A2
Leazes Cr B1
Leazes La B1
Leazes Park B1
Leazes Park Rd B1
Leazes Terr B1
Live C2
Low Friar St C1
Manor Chare C2
Manors B2
Manors Station B2
Market St B2
Melbourne St B2
Mill Rd C3
Mill Volvo Tyne C1
Monument B2
Monument Mall Sh Ctr B2
Morpeth St A2
Mosley St C2
Napier St A3
Nazareth House A3
New Bridge St B2/B3
Newcastle Central Station C1
Newcastle University A1
Newgate Shopping Ctr C1
Newgate St B1
Newington Rd A3
Northern Stage Theatre A2
Northumberland Rd B2
Northumberland St B2
Northumbria Univ A2
Northwest Radial Rd A1
O2 Academy C1
Oakwellgate C3
Orchard St C2
Osborne Rd A2
Osborne Terr A3
Pandon C3
Pandon Bank B3
Park Terr A1
Percy St B1
Pilgrim St B2
Pipewellgate C2
Pitt St B1
Plummer Tower A2
Police Station B2
Portland Rd A3/B3
Portland Terr A3
Post Office A3/B1/B2/B3
Pottery La C1
Prudhoe Pl B1
Prudhoe St B1
Quayside C2
Queen Elizabeth II Bridge C2
Queen Victoria Rd A1
Richardson Rd A1
Ridley Pl B2
Rock Terr B3
Rosedale Terr A3
Royal Victoria Infirmary A1
Sage Gateshead, The C3
St Andrew's St B1
St James B1
St James' Blvd C1
St James' Park (Newcastle Utd FC) B1
St Mary's (RC) C1
St Mary's Place B2
St Nicholas C2
St Nicholas St C2
St Thomas' St B1
Sandyford Rd A2/A3
Science Park B2
Shield St B3
Shieldfield B3
Simpson Terr B3
South Shore Rd C3
South St C1
Starbeck Ave A3
Stepney Rd B3
Stoddart St B3
Stowell St B1
Strawberry Pl B1
Swing Bridge C2
Temple St C1
Terrace Pl B1
The Close C2
The Gate C1
The Side C2
Theatre Royal B2
Times Sq C1
Tower St B3
Trinity House C2
Tyne Bridge C2
Tyne Bridges C2
Tyneside B2
Victoria Sq A2
Warwick St A3
Waterloo St C1
Wellington St B1
Westgate Rd C1/C2
Windsor Terr A2
Worswick St B2
Wretham Pl B3

Newport 340
Casnewydd

Albert Terr B1
Allt-yr-Yn Ave A1
Alma St C2
Ambulance Station C3
Bailey St B2
Barrack Hill A2
Bath St A3
Bedford Rd B3
Belle Vue La C1
Belle Vue Park C1
Bishop St A3
Blewitt St B1
Bolt Cl C3
Bolt St C3
Bond St A2
Bosworth Dr A1
Bridge St B1
Bristol St A3
Bryngwyn Rd B1
Brynhyfryd Ave C1
Brynhyfryd Rd C1
Bus Station B2
Caerau Cres C1
Caerau Rd B1
Caerleon Rd A3
Capel Cres C2
Cardiff Rd C2
Caroline St B3
Castle (Remains) A2
Cedar Rd B3
Charles St B2
Charlotte Dr C2
Chepstow Rd A3
Church Rd A3
City Cinema B1
Civic Centre B1
Clarence Pl A2
Clifton Pl B1
Clifton Rd C1
Clyffard Cres B1
Clytha Park Rd B1
Clytha Sq C2
Coldra Rd C1
Collier St A3
Colne St B3
Comfrey Cl A1
Commercial Rd C3
Commercial St B2
Corelli St A3
Corn St B2
Corporation Rd B3
Coulson Cl C2
County Court A2
Courts A1
Courts B1
Crawford St A3
Cyril St B3
Dean St A3
Devon Pl B1
Dewsland Park Rd C2
Dolman B2
Dolphin St C3
East Dock Rd C3
East St B1
East Usk Rd A3
Ebbw Vale Wharf B3
Emlyn St B2
Enterprise Way C3
Eton Rd B3
Evans St A2
Factory Rd A2
Fields Rd B1
Francis Dr C2
Frederick St C3
Friars Rd C1
Gaer La C1
George St C3
George Street Bridge C3
Godfrey Rd B1
Gold Tops B1
Gore St A3
Gorsedd Circle C1
Grafton Rd A3
Graham St B1
Granville St C3
Harlequin Dr A1
Harrow Rd B3
Herbert Rd A3
Herbert Walk C2
Hereford St A3
High St B2
Hill St B2
Hoskins St A2
Information Ctr B2
Ivor Sq B2
John Frost Sq B2
Jones St B1
Junction Rd A3
Keynshaw Ave C2
King St C2
Kingsway B2
Kingsway Centre B2
Ledbury Dr A2
Library A3
Library, Museum & Art Gallery B2
Liverpool Wharf B3
Llanthewy Rd B1
Llanvair Rd A3
Locke St A2
Lower Dock St C3
Lucas St A2
Manchester St A3
Market B2
Marlborough Rd B3
Mellon St C3
Mill St A2
Morgan St A3
Mountjoy Rd C2
Newport Bridge A2
Newport Ctr B2
Newport RFC B3
Newport Station B2
North St B2
Oakfield Rd B1
Park Sq C2
Police Station A3/C2
Post Office B1/B2/C1/C3
Power St A1
Prince St A3
Pugsley St A2
Queen St C2
Queen's Cl A1
Queen's Hill A1
Queen's Hill Cres A1
Queensway B2
Railway St B2
Riverfront Arts Centre B2
Riverside A3
Rodney Rd B2
Royal Gwent (A&E) C2
Rudry St A3
Rugby Rd B3
Ruperra La C3
Ruperra St C3
St Edmund St B1
St Mark's Cres A1
St Mary St B1
St Vincent Rd A3
St Woolos C2
St Woolos General (no A&E) C1
St Woolos Rd B1
School La B2
Serpentine Rd B1
Shaftesbury Park A2
Sheaf La A3
Skinner St B2
Sorrel Dr A1
South Market St C3
Spencer Rd B1
Stow Hill B2/C1/C2
Stow Park Ave C1
Stow Park Dr C1
TA Centre A1
Talbot St B2
Tennis Club A1
Tregare St A3
Trostrey St A3
Tunnel Terr B1
Turner St A3
Upper Dock St B2
Usk St A3
Usk Way B3/C3
Victoria Cr B1
War Memorial A3
Waterloo Rd C1
West St B1
Wharves B2
Wheeler St A2
Whitby Pl A3
Windsor Terr B1
York Pl C1

Newquay 340

Agar Rd B2
Alma Pl B1
Ambulance Station B2
Anthony Rd C1
Atlantic Hotel A1
Bank St B1
Barrowfields A3
Bay View Terr B2
Beachfield Ave B1
Beach Rd B1
Beacon Rd A1
Belmont Pl A1
Berry Rd B2
Blue Reef Aquarium B1
Boating Lake C2
Bus Station B1
Chapel Hill B1
Chester Rd A3
Cheviot Rd C1/C2
Chichester Cres C2
Chynance Dr C1
Chyverton Cl C1
Cliff Rd B2
Coach Park B2
Colvreath Rd A3
Council Offices B1
Crantock St B1
Criggar Rocks A3
Dale Cl C3
Dale Rd C3
Dane Rd A1
East St B2
Edgcumbe Ave B3
Edgcumbe Gdns B3
Eliot Gdns B3
Elm Cl C3
Ennor's Rd B1
Fernhill Rd B1
Fire Station B1
Fore St B1
Gannel Rd C2
Golf Driving Range B3
Gover La B1
Great Western Beach A2
Grosvenor Ave B2
Harbour A1
Hawkins Rd C2
Headleigh Rd B2
Hilgrove Rd A3/B3
Holywell Rd B3
Hope Terr B1
Huer's House, The A1
Information Ctr B1
Island Cres B2
Jubilee St B1
Kew Cl C3
Killacourt Cove A2
King Edward Cres A1
Lanhenvor Ave B2
Library B1
Lifeboat Station A1
Linden Ave C2
Listry Rd C2
Lusty Glaze Beach A3
Lusty Glaze Rd A3
Manor Rd B1
Marcus Hill B2
Mayfield Rd B2
Meadowside C3
Mellanvrane La C2
Michell Ave B2
Miniature Golf Course C3
Miniature Railway B3
Mount Wise B1
Mowhay Cl C3
Narrowcliff A3
Newquay B2
Newquay Hospital (no A&E) B2
Newquay Town Football Ground B1
Newquay Zoo B3
North Pier A1
North Quay Hill A1
Oakleigh Terr B2
Pargolla Rd B2
Pendragon Cres C3
Pengannel Cl C1
Penina Ave C3
Police Sta & Courts B2
Post Office B1/B2
Quarry Park Rd B3
Rawley La C2
Reeds Way B1
Robartes Rd B2
St Anne's Rd A3
St Aubyn Cres B3
St George's Rd B1
St John's Rd B1
St Mary's Rd B1
St Michael's B1
St Michael's Rd B1
St Thomas' Rd B2
Seymour Ave B2
South Pier A1
South Quay Hill A1
Sweet Briar Cres C3
Sydney Rd A1
The Crescent B1
Tolcarne Beach A2
Tolcarne Point A2
Tolcarne Rd B2
Tor Rd B2
Towan Beach A1
Towan Blystra Rd B3
Tower Rd A1
Trebarwith Cres B2
Tredour Rd C2
Treforda Rd C3
Tregoss Rd B3
Tregunnel Hill B1/C1
Tregunnel Saltings C1
Trelawney Rd B2
Treloggan La C3
Treloggan Rd C3
Trembath Cres C1
Trenance Ave B2
Trenance Gardens B2
Trenance La C2
Trenance Leisure Park B3
Trenance Rd B2
Trenarth Rd B2
Treninnick Hill C3
Tretherras Rd B3
Trethewey Way C1
Trevemper Rd C2
Tunnels Through Time B1
Ulalia Rd B3
Vivian Cl B2
Waterworld B3
Whitegate Rd B3
Wych Hazel Way C3

Newtown 340
Y Drenewydd

Ash Cl A3
Back La B2
Baptist Chapel B2
Barn La A2
Bear Lanes Sh Ctr B2
Beech Cl A2
Beechwood Dr A2
Brimmon Cl C2
Brimmon Rd C2
Broad St B2
Bryn Bank A1
Bryn Cl A2
Bryn Gdns A1
Bryn House A1
Bryn La A1/A2
Bryn Meadows A2
Bryn St A2
Brynglais Ave A2
Brynglais Cl A2
Bus Station B2
Byrnwood Dr A1
Cambrian Bridge B3
Cambrian Gdns B2
Cambrian Way B2
Canal Rd A3
Castle Mound B2
Cedewain C1
Cefnaire C2
Cefnaire Coppice C2
Ceiriog C2
Cemetery A2
Church (Remains of) B2
Churchill Dr A3
Cledan B3

Colwyn B3
Commercial St A2
Council Offices B1
Crescent St A1
Cwm Llanfair A2
Davies Memorial Gallery B2
Dinas B2
Dolafon Rd B3
Dolerw Park B1
Dolfor Rd C1
Eirianell C1
Fairfield Dr A2
Ffordd Croesawdy B2
Fire Station C1
Frankwell St A2
Frolic St B2
Fron La A1
Garden La A2
Gas St B2
Glyndwr C1
Golwgydre La B2
Gorsedd Circle B1
Great Brimmon Farm C3
Hafren C1
Halfpenny Bridge B2
High St B2
Hillside Ave A3
Hoel Treowen C1
Information Ctr B2
Kerry Rd B3
Ladywell Shopping Ctr B2
Library B1
Llanfair Rd A2
Llanidloes Rd C1
Llys Ifor A2
Lon Cerddyn B1
Lonesome La A3
Long Bridge A2
Lon Helyg C1
Lower Canal Rd B3
Maldwyn Leisure Ctr C1
Market B2
Market St B2
Milford Rd B1
Mill Cl B2
Miniature Railway B1
Mwyn Fynydd A3
New Church St B2
New Rd B2
Newtown Football Gd B1
Newtown Infirmary A2
Newtown Station B2
Oak Tree Ave A3
Old Kerry Rd B2
Oldbarn La A2
Park Cl B1
Parklands B1
Park La B1
Park St B2
Pavillion Ct C1
Plantation La C1
Police Station B1
Pont Brynfedw A2
Pool Rd B3
Poplar Rd A3
Post Office B2/C1
Powys C1
Powys Theatre A2
Pryce Jones Stores & Museum B2
Quaker Meeting Ho B1
Regent B2
Robert Owen House B1
Robert Owen Mus B2
Rugby Club A3
St David's B2
School La A2
Sheaf St B3
Short Bridge St B2
Stone St B2
Sycamore Dr A2
Textile Museum A2
The Bryn A1
The Park B1
Town Hall B2
Union St A2
Upper Brimmon C3
Vastre Industrial Est B3
War Memorial B2
WHSmith Museum B2
Wynfields C1
Y Ffrydd A3

Northampton 340

78 Derngate B3
Abington Sq B3
Abington St B3
Alcombe St A3
All Saints' B2
Ambush St B1
Angel St B2
Arundel St A2
Ash St A2
Auctioneers Way C2
Bailiff St A2
Barrack Rd A2
Beaconsfield Terr A3
Becketts Park C3
Becketts Park Marina C3
Bedford Rd B3
Billing Rd B3
Brecon St A1
Brewery C2
Bridge St C2
Broad St B2
Burns St A3
Bus Station B2
Campbell St A2
Castle (Site of) B2
Castle St B2
Cattle Market Rd C2
Central Museum & Art Gallery B2
Charles St A3
Cheyne Walk B3
Church La A2
Clare St A3
Cloutsham St A3
College St B2
Colwyn Rd A3
Cotton End C2
Countess Rd A1
County Hall B2
Court A2
Craven St A3
Crown & County Courts B3
Denmark Rd B3
Derngate B3
Derngate & Royal Theatres B3
Doddridge Church B2
Duke St A3
Dunster St A3
Earl St A3
Euston Rd C2
Fire Station A3
Foot Meadow B2
Gladstone Rd A1
Gold St B2
Grafton St A2
Gray St A3
Green St B1
Greenwood Rd B1
Greyfriars B2
Grosvenor Centre B2
Grove Rd A3
Guildhall B2
Hampton St A2
Harding Terr A2
Hazelwood Rd B3
Herbert St B2
Hervey St A3
Hester St A2
Holy Sepulchre A2
Hood St A3
Horse Market B2
Hunter St A3
Information Ctr B1
Kettering Rd A3
Kingswell St B2
Lady's La B2
Leicester St A2
Leslie Rd A2
Library B3
Lorne Rd A2
Lorry Park A1
Louise Rd A2
Lower Harding St A2
Lower Hester St A2
Lower Mounts B3
Lower Priory St A2
Main Rd C1
Marefair B2
Market Sq B2
Marlboro Rd B1
Marriott St A2
Military Rd A3
Mounts Baths Leisure Centre A3
Nene Valley Retail Pk C1
New South Bridge Rd C2
Northampton General Hospital (A&E) B3
Northampton Sta B1
Northcote St A2
Nunn Mills Rd C3
Old Towcester Rd C2
Overstone Rd A3
Peacock Pl B2
Pembroke Rd A1
Penn Court C2
Police Station B3
Post Office A1/A2/B3/C2
Quorn Way A2
Ransome Rd C3
Regent Sq A2
Robert St A2
St Andrew's Rd B1
St Andrew's St A2
St Edmund's Rd B3
St George's St A2
St Giles B3
St Giles St B3
St Giles' Terr B3
St James' Mill Rd B1
St James' Mill Rd East C1
St James Park Rd B1
St James Retail Park C1
St James Rd B1
St Leonard's Rd C2
St Mary's St B2
St Michael's Rd A3
St Peter's B2
St Peter's Square Shopping Precinct B2
St Peter's Way B2
Salisbury St A2
Scarletwell St B2
Semilong Rd A2
Sheep St B2
Sol Central (Leisure Centre) B2
Somerset St A3
South Bridge C2
Southfield Ave C2
Spencer Bridge Rd A1
Spencer Rd A3
Spring Gdns B3
Spring La B2
Swan St B3
TA Centre A3
Tanner St B2
The Drapery B2
The Ridings B3
Tintern Ave A1
Towcester Rd C2
Upper Bath St B2
Upper Mounts A2
Victoria Park A1
Victoria Promenade B2
Victoria Rd B3
Victoria St A2
Wellingborough Rd B3
West Bridge B1
York Rd B3

Norwich 341

Albion Way C3
All Saints Green C2
Anchor Cl A3
Anchor St A3
Anglia Sq A2
Argyle St C3
Arts Centre B1
Ashby St C2
Assembly House B1
Bank Plain B2
Barker St A1
Barn Rd A1
Barrack St A3
Ber St C2
Bethel St B1
Bishop Bridge A3
Bishopbridge Rd A3
Bishopgate A3
Blackfriars St A2
Botolph St A2
Bracondale C3
Brazen Gate C2
Bridewell B2
Brunswick Rd C1
Bull Close Rd A2
Bus Station C2
Calvert St A2
Cannell Green A3
Carrow Rd C3
Castle Mall B2
Castle Meadow B2
Castle & Museum B2
Cathedral B2
Cathedral Retail Park A1
Cattlemarket St B2
Chantry Rd C1
Chapel Loke C2
Chapelfield East B1
Chapelfield Gdns B1
Chapelfield North B1
Chapelfield Rd B1
Chapelfield Sh Ctr C1
City Hall B1
City Rd C2
City Wall C1/C3
Colegate A2
Coslany St B1
Cow Hill B1
Cow Tower A3
Cowgate A2
Crown & Magistrates Courts A2
Dragon Hall Heritage Centre C3
Duke St A1
Edward St A2
Elm Hill B2
Erpingham Gate B2
Fire Station B1
Fishergate A2
Foundry Bridge B3
Fye Bridge A2
Garden St C2
Gas Hill B3
Grapes Hill B1
Great Hospl Halls, The A3
Grove Ave C1
Grove Rd C1
Guildhall B1
Gurney Rd A3
Hall Rd C2
Heathgate A3
Heigham St A1
Horn's La C2
Information Ctr B1
Ipswich Rd C1
James Stuart Gdns B3
King Edward VI School B2
King St B2
King St C3
Koblenz Ave C3
Library B1
London St B2
Lower Clarence Rd B3
Lower Cl B3
Maddermarket B1
Magdalen St A2
Mariners La C2
Market B2
Market Ave B2
Mountergate B3
Mousehold St A3
Newmarket Rd C1
Norfolk Gallery B2
Norfolk St C1
Norwich City FC C3
Norwich Station B3
Oak St A1
Palace St A2
Pitt St A1
Playhouse B2
Post Office A2/B2/C2
Pottergate B1
Prince of Wales Rd B2
Princes St B2
Pull's Ferry B3
Puppet Theatre A2
Quebec Rd B3
Queen St B2
Queens Rd C2
RC Cathedral B1
Recorder Rd B3
Riverside Entertainment Centre C3
Riverside Swimming Centre C3
Riverside Retail Park C3
Riverside Rd B3
Rosary Rd B3
Rose La B2
Rouen Rd C2
Royal Norfolk Regiment Museum B2
St Andrew's & Blackfriars Hall B2
St Andrews St B2
St Augustines St A1
St Benedicts St B1
St Ethelbert's Gate B2
St Faiths La B3
St Georges St A2
St Giles St B1
St James Cl A3
St Julians C2
St Martin's La A1
St Peter Mancroft B2
St Peters St B1
St Stephens Rd C1
St Stephens St C1
Silver Rd A2
Silver St A2
Southwell Rd C2
Strangers Hall B1
Superstore C2
Surrey St C2
Sussex St A1
The Close B3
The Forum B1
The Walk B2
Theatre Royal B1
Theatre St B1
Thorn La C2
Thorpe Rd B3
Tombland B2
Union St C1
Vauxhall St B1
Victoria St C1
Walpole St B1
Wensum St A2
Wessex St C1
Westwick St A1
Wherry Rd C3
Whitefriars A2
Willow La B1
Yacht Station B3

Nottingham 341

Abbotsford Dr A3
Addison St A1
Albert Hall B1
Alfred St South A3
Alfreton Rd B1
All Saints Rd A1
Annesley Gr A2
Arboretum A1
Arboretum St A1
Arthur St A1
Arts Theatre B3
Ashforth St A3
Balmoral Rd A1
Barker Gate B3
Bath St B3
Belgrave Centre B1
Bellar Gate B3
Belward St B3
Blue Bell Hill Rd B3
Brewhouse Yard C2
Broad Marsh Bus Sta C2
Broad Marsh Precinct C2
Broad St B3
Brook St B3
Burns St A1
Burton St B2
Bus Station A2
Canal St C2
Carlton St B3
Carrington St C2
Castle Blvd C1
Castle C2
Castle Gate C2
Castle Mdw Retail Pk C1
Castle Meadow Rd C1
Castle Museum & Gallery C2
Castle Rd C2
Castle Wharf C2
Cavendish Rd East C1
Cemetery B1
Chaucer St B1
Cheapside B2
Church Rd A3
City Link C3
City of Caves C2
Clarendon St B1
Cliff Rd C3
Clumber Rd East C1
Clumber St B2
College St B1
Collin St C2
Conway Cl A2
Council House B2
Court B2
Cranbrook St B3
Cranmer St A2
Cromwell St B1
Curzon St B3
Derby Rd B1
Dryden St A2
Exchange Arcade B2
Fishpond Dr C1
Fletcher Gate B3
Forest Rd East A1
Forest Rd West A1
Friar La C2
Galleries of Justice C3
Gedling Gr A1
Gedling St B3
George St B3
Gill St A2
Glasshouse St B2
Goldsmith St B2
Goose Gate B3
Great Freeman St A2
Guildhall B2
Hamilton Dr C1
Hampden St A1
Heathcote St B3
High Pavement C3
High School A1
Holles Cr C1
Hope Dr C1
Hungerhill Rd A3
Huntingdon Dr C1
Huntingdon St A2
Information Ctr B2
Instow Rise A3
International Com Ctr A2
Kent St B3
King St B2
Lace Centre, The C2
Lace Market B3
Lace Mkt Theatre C3
Lamartine St B3
Lenton Rd C1
Lewis Cl A3
Lincoln St B2
London Rd C3
Long Row B2
Low Pavement C2
Lower Parliament St B3
Magistrates Court C2
Maid Marian Way B2
Mansfield Rd A2/B2
Middle Hill C2
Milton St B2
Mount St B2
National Ice Centre C3
Newcastle Dr B1
Newstead Gr A2
North Sherwood St A2
Nottingham Arena C3
Nottingham Station C3
Nottingham Trent University A2/B2
Old Market Square B2
Oliver St A1
Park Dr C1
Park Row C1
Park Terr B1
Park Valley C1
Peas Hill Rd A3
Peel St A1
Pelham St B2
Peveril Dr C1
Plantagenet St A3
Playhouse Theatre B1
Plumptre St C3
Police Station B2
Poplar St C3
Portland Rd B1
Post Office B2
Queen's Rd C3
Raleigh St A1
Regent St B1
Rick St B3
Robin Hood Statue C2
Robin Hood St B3
Royal Centre B2
Royal Children Inn C2
Royal Concert Hall B2
St Ann's Hill Rd A2
St Ann's Way A2
St Ann's Well Rd A3
St Barnabas B1
St James' St B2
St Mark's St B3
St Mary's Gdn of Rest B3
St Mary's Gate B3
St Nicholas C2
St Peter's C2
St Peter's Gate B2
Salutation Inn C2
Shakespeare St B2
Shelton St A2
South Pde B2
South Rd C1
South Sherwood St B2
Station St C3
Station Street C3
Stoney St B3
Talbot St B1
Tattershall Dr C1
Tennis Dr B1
Tennyson St A1
The Park C1
The Ropewalk B1
Theatre Royal B2
Trent St C3
Trent University B2
Trinity Square Sh Ctr B2
Trip To Jerusalem Inn C2
Union Rd B3
Upper Parliament St B2
Victoria Centre B2
Victoria Leisure Ctr B3
Victoria Park B3
Victoria St B2
Walter St A1
Warser Gate B3
Watkin St A2
Waverley St A1
Wheeler Gate B2
Wilford Rd C2
Wilford St C2
Willoughby House C2
Wollaton St B1
Woodborough Rd A2
Woolpack La B3
York St A2

Oban 341

Aird's Cres B2
Albany St B2
Albert La A2
Albert Rd A2
Alma Cres B1
Ambulance Station C2
Angus Terr C3
Ardconnel Rd A2
Ardconnel Terr B2
Argyll Sq B2
Argyll St B2
Atlantis Leisure Ctr A2
Bayview Rd A1
Benvoulin Rd A2
Bowling Green A2
Breadalbane St A2
Bus Station B2
Campbell St B2
College B2
Colonsay Terr C3
Columba Building B2
Combie St B2
Corran Brae A1
Corran Esplanade A1/A2
Corran Halls A2
Court B2
Crannaig-a-Mhinisteir B1
Crannog La C2
Croft Ave A2
Dalintart Dr C3
Dalriach Rd A2
Distillery B2
Drummore Rd C2
Duncraggan Rd A2
Dunollie Rd A2
Dunuaran Rd B1
Feochan Gr C3
Ferry Terminal B1
Gallanach Rd B1
George St A2
Glencruitten Dr C3
Glencruitten Rd B3
Glenmore Rd C1
Glenshellach Rd C1
Glenshellach Terr B2
Harbour Bowl B2
Hazeldean Cres A3
High St B2
Highland Theatre Cinema A2
Hill St B2
Industrial Estate C2
Information Ctr B2
Islay Rd C3
Jacob's Ladder B2
Jura Rd C3
Knipoch Pl C3
Laurel Cres A2
Laurel Rd A2/A3
Library B1
Lifeboat Station B1
Lighthouse Pier B1
Lismore Cres A2
Lochavullin Dr B2
Lochavullin Rd C2
Lochside St B2
Longsdale Cres A3
Longsdale Rd A2/A3
Longsdale Terr A3
Lunga Rd C3
Lynn Rd C2
Market St B2
McCaig Rd C3
McCaig's Tower A2
Mill La C2
Miller Rd C2
Millpark Ave C2
Millpark Rd C2
Mossfield Ave B3
Mossfield Dr B3
Mossfield Stadium B3
Nant Dr C3
Nelson Rd C2
North Pier B2
Nursery La A2
Oban B2
Police Station B2
Polvinister Rd B3
Post Office A2/B2
Pulpit Dr C1
Pulpit Hill C1
Pulpit Hill Viewpoint B1
Quarry Rd C2
Queen's Park Pl C2
Railway Quay B1
Rockfield Rd B2
St Columba's A1
St John's A2
Scalpay Terr C3
Shore St B1
Shuna Terr C3
Sinclair Dr C2
Soroba Rd B2/C2
South Pier B1
Stevenson St B2
Tweedale St B2
Ulva Rd C2
Villa Rd B1
War & Peace A2

Oxford 341

Adelaide St A1
Albert St A1
All Souls (Coll) B2
Ashmolean Mus B2
Balliol (Coll) B2
Banbury Rd A2
Bate Collection of Musical Instruments C2
Beaumont St B1
Becket St B1
Blackhall Rd A2
Blue Boar St B2
Bodleian Library B2
Botanic Garden B3
Brasenose (Coll) B2
Brewer St C2
Broad St B2
Burton-Taylor Theatre B2
Bus Station B1
Canal St A1
Cardigan St A1
Carfax Tower B2
Castle B1
Castle St B1
Catte St B2
Cemetery C1
Christ Church (Coll) B2
Christ Church Cath C2
Christ Church Mdw C2
Clarendon Centre B2
Coach & Lorry Park C1
College B3
Coll of Further Ed C1
Cornmarket St B2
Corpus Christi (Coll) B2
County Hall B1
Covered Market B2
Cowley Pl C3
Cranham St A1
Cranham Terr A1
Cricket Ground B1
Crown & County Courts C2
Deer Park B3
Exeter (Coll) B2
Folly Bridge C2
George St B1
Great Clarendon St A1
Hart St A1
Hertford (Coll) B2
High St B3
Hollybush Row B1
Holywell St B2
Hythe Bridge St B1
Ice Rink C1
Information Ctr B2
Jericho St A1
Jesus (Coll) B2
Jowett Walk B3
Juxon St A1
Keble (Coll) A2
Keble Rd A2
Library B2
Linacre (Coll) A3
Lincoln (Coll) B2
Little Clarendon St A1
Longwall St B3
Magdalen (Coll) B3
Magdalen Bridge B2
Magdalen St B2
Magistrate's Court C2
Manchester (Coll) B2
Manor Rd B3
Mansfield (Coll) A2
Mansfield Rd A3
Market B1
Marlborough Rd C2
Martyrs' Memorial B2
Merton Field B3
Merton (Coll) B3
Merton St B2
Mus of Modern Art B2
Museum of Oxford B2
Museum Rd A2
New College (Coll) B3
New Inn Hall St B2
New Rd B1
New Theatre B2
Norfolk St C1
Nuffield (Coll) B1
Observatory A1
Observatory St A1
Odeon B1/B2
Old Fire Station B1
Old Greyfriars St C2
Oriel (Coll) B2
Oxford Station B1
Oxford Story, The B2
Oxford University Research Centres A1
Oxpens Rd C1
Paradise Sq C1
Paradise St B1
Park End St B1
Parks Rd A2/B2
Pembroke (Coll) C2
Phoenix A1
Picture Gallery C2
Plantation Rd A1
Playhouse B2
Police Station C2
Post Office A1/B2
Pusey St B1
Queen's La B3
Queen's (Coll) B3
Radcliffe Camera B2
Rewley Rd B1
Richmond Rd A1
Rose La B3
Ruskin (Coll) B1
Saïd Business School B1
St Aldates C2
St Anne's (Coll) A1
St Antony's (Coll) A1
St Bernard's Rd A1
St Catherine's (Coll) B3
St Cross Building A3
St Cross Rd A3
St Edmund Hall (Coll) B3
St Giles St A2
St Hilda's (Coll) C3
St John St B2
St John's (Coll) B2
St Mary the Virgin B2
St Michael at the Northgate B2
St Peter's (Coll) B1
St Thomas St B1
Science Area A2
Science Museum B2
Sheldonian Theatre B2
Somerville (Coll) A1
South Parks Rd A2
Speedwell St C2
Sports Ground C3
Thames St C2
Town Hall B2
Trinity (Coll) B2
Turl St B2
University Coll (Coll) B3
Univ Mus & Pitt Rivers Mus A2
University Parks A2
Wadham (Coll) B2
Walton Cr A1
Walton St A1
Western Rd C2
Westgate Sh Ctr B2
Woodstock Rd A1
Worcester (Coll) B1

Perth 341

A K Bell Library B2
Abbot Cres C1
Abbot St C1
Albany Terr A1
Albert Monument A3
Alexandra St B2
Atholl St A2
Balhousie Ave A2
Balhousie Castle Black Watch Museum A2
Balhousie St A2
Ballantine Pl A1
Barossa Pl A2
Barossa St A2
Barrack St A2
Bell's Sports Centre A2
Bellwood B3
Blair St B1
Burn Park C1
Bus Station B2
Caledonian Rd B2
Canal Cres B2
Canal St B3
Cavendish Ave C1
Charles St B2
Charlotte Pl A2
Charlotte St A3
Church St A1
City Hall B3
Club House C3
Clyde Pl C1
Commercial St A3
Concert Hall B3
Council Chambers B3
County Pl B2
Court B3
Craigie Pl C2
Crieff Rd A1
Croft Park C2
Cross St B2
Darnhall Cres C1
Darnhall Dr C1
Dewars Centre B1
Dundee Rd B3
Dunkeld Rd A1
Earl's Dykes B1
Edinburgh Rd C3
Elibank St B1
Fair Maid's House A3
Fergusson B3
Feus Rd A1
Fire Station A1
Fitness Centre B3
Foundary La A2
Friar St C2
George St B3
Glamis Pl C1
Glasgow Rd B1
Glenearn Rd C2
Glover St B1/C1
Golf Course A2
Gowrie St A3
Gray St B1
Graybank Rd B1
Greyfriars Burial Grnd B3
Hay St A2
High St B2/B3
Hotel B2
Inchaffray St A1
Industrial/Retail Park B1
Information Ctr B2
Isla Rd A3
James St B2
Keir St A3
King Edward St B3
King James VI Golf Course C3
King St B2
Kings Pl C2
Kinnoull Causeway B2
Kinnoull Aisle 'Monument' B3
Kinnoull St B2
Knowelea Pl C1
Knowelea Terr C1
Ladeside Bsns Centre A1
Leisure Pool B1
Leonard St B2
Lickley St B2
Lochie Brae A3
Long Causeway A1
Low St A2
Main St A3
Marshall Pl C3
Melville St A2
Mill St B3
Milne St B2
Murray Cres C1
Murray St B2
Needless Rd C1
New Rd B2
North Inch A3
North Methven St A2
Park Pl C1
Perth B2
Perth Bridge A3
Perth Business Park B1
Perth Museum & Art Gallery B3
Perth Station C2
Pickletulllum Rd B1
Pitheavlis Cres C1
Playhouse B2
Police Station A2
Pomarium St B2
Post Office A3/B2/C2
Princes St B3
Priory Pl C2
Queen St C1
Queen's Bridge B3
Riggs Rd B1
Riverside B3
Riverside Park B3
Rodney Park B3
Rose Terr A2
St Catherines Ret Pk A1
St Catherine's Rd A1/A2
St John St B3
St John's Kirk B3
St John's Shopping Ctr B2
St Leonards Bridge C2
St Ninians Cathedral A2
Scott Monument C2
Scott St B2
Sheriff Court B3
Shore Rd C3
Skate Park C3
South Inch C2
South Inch Bsns Ctr C3
South Inch Park C2
South Inch View C2
South Methven St B2
South St B3
South William St B2
Stormont St A2
Strathmore St A3
Stuart Ave C1
Tay St B3
The Stables A1
The Stanners B3
Union La A2
Victoria St B2
Watergate B3
Wellshill Cemetery A1
West Bridge St A3
West Mill St B2
Whitefriers Cres B1
Whitefriers St B1
Wilson St C1
Windsor Terr C1
Woodside Cres C1
York Pl B2
Young St C1

Peterborough 341

Athletics Arena B3
Bishop's Palace B2
Bishop's Rd B2/B3
Boongate A3
Bourges Boulevard A1
Bourges Retail Pk B1/B2
Bridge House (Council Offices) C2
Bridge St B2
Bright St A1
Broadway A2
Broadway A2
Brook St A2
Burghley Rd A2
Bus Station B2
Cavendish St A3
Charles St A3
Church St B2
Church Walk A2
Cobden Ave A1
Cobden St A1
Cowgate B2
Craig St A2
Crawthorne Rd A2
Cripple Sidings La C2
Cromwell Rd A1
Dickens St A3
Eastfield Rd A3
Eastgate B3
Fire Station A1
Fletton Ave C2
Frank Perkins Parkway C3
Geneva St A2
George St C1
Gladstone St A1
Glebe Rd C2
Gloucester Rd C3
Granby St B3
Grove St C1
Guildhall B2
Hadrians Ct C3
Henry St A2
Hereward Cross (Sh) B2
Hereward Rd B3
Information Ctr B2
Jubilee St C1
Key Theatre C2
Kent Rd B1
Kirkwood Cl B1
Lea Gdns B1
Library A2
Lincoln Rd A2
London Rd C2
Long Causeway B2
Lower Bridge St C2
Magistrates Court B2
Manor House St A2
Mayor's Walk A1
Midland Rd A1
Monument St A2
Morris St A3
Mus & Art Gallery B2
Nene Valley Railway C1
New Rd A2
New Rd C1
Northminster A2
Old Customs House C2
Oundle Rd C1
Padholme Rd A3
Palmerston Rd C1
Park Rd A2
Passport Office B2
Peterborough District Hospital (A&E) B1
Peterborough Sta B1
Peterborough Nene Valley C1
Peterborough United FC C2
Police Station B2
Post Office A3/B1/B2/B3/C1
Priestgate B2
Queen's Walk C2
Queensgate Centre B2
Railworld C1
Regional Swimming & Fitness Centre B3
River La B1
Rivergate Sh Ctr B2
Riverside Mead C3
Russell St A1
St John's B2
St John's St A3
St Marks St A2
St Peter's B2

Plymouth • Poole • Portsmouth • Preston • Reading • St Andrews • Salisbury • Scarborough • Sheffield 357

St Peter's Rd B2
Saxon Rd A3
Spital Bridge A1
Stagshaw Dr C3
Star Rd B3
Thorpe Lea Rd B1
Thorpe Rd B1
Thorpe's Lea Rd B1
Tower St B1
Town Hall B2
Viersen Platz B2
Vineyard Rd B3
Wake Rd B3
Wellington St A3
Wentworth St B2
Westgate B2
Whalley St A3
Wharf Rd C2
Whitsed St A3
YMCA A3

Plymouth 341

Alma Rd A1
Anstis St B1
Armada Centre B2
Armada St A3
Armada Way B2
Arts Centre B2
Athenaeum B1
Athenaeum St C1
Barbican C3
Barbican C3
Baring St A3
Bath St B1
Beaumont Park B3
Beaumont Rd B3
Black Friars Gin Distillery C2
Breton Side B3
Bus Station B2
Castle St C3
Cathedral (RC) B1
Cecil St B1
Central Park A1
Central Park Ave A2
Charles Church B3
Charles Cross B3
Charles St B2
City Museum & Art Gallery B2
Citadel Rd C2
Citadel Rd East C2
Civic Centre B2
Cliff Rd C1
Clifton Pl A3
Cobourg St A2
College of Art B2
Continental Ferry Port B1
Cornwall St B2
Dale Rd A2
Deptford Pl A3
Derry Ave A2
Derry's Cross B1
Drake Circus B2
Drake Cir Sh Ctr B2
Drake's Memorial C2
Drum B2
Eastlake St B2
Ebrington St B3
Elizabethan House C3
Elliot St C1
Endsleigh Pl A2
Exeter St B3
Fire Station A3
Fish Quay C3
Gibbons St A3
Glen Park Ave A2
Grand Pde C1
Great Western Rd C1
Greenbank Rd A3
Greenbank Terr A3
Guildhall B2
Hampton St B3
Harwell St B1
Hill Park Cr A3
Hoe Approach B2
Hoe Rd C2
Hoegate St C2
Houndiscombe Rd A2
Information Ctr C3
James St A2
Kensington Rd A3
King St B1
Lambhay Hill C3
Leigham St C1
Library B2
Lipson Rd A3/B3
Lockyer St C2
Lockyers Quay C3
Madeira Rd C2
Marina B3
Market Ave B1
Martin St B1
Mayflower Stone & Steps C3
Mayflower St B2
Mayflower Visitor Centre C3
Merchants House B2
Millbay Rd B1
National Marine Aquarium C3
Neswick St B1
New George St B2
New St C3
North Cross A2
North Hill A3
North Quay B2
North Rd East A2
North Rd West A1
North St B3
Notte St B2
Octagon St B1
Pannier Market B1
Pennycomequick A1
Pier St C1
Plymouth Pavilions B1
Plymouth Station A2
Police Station B3
Portland Sq A2
Post Office A1/B1/B2
Princess St B2
Prysten House B2
Queen Anne's Battery Seasports Centre C3
Radford Rd C1
Regent St B3
Rope Walk C3
Royal Citadel C2
Royal Pde B2
St Andrew's B2
St Andrew's Cross B2
St Andrew's St B2
St Lawrence Rd A2
Saltash Rd A2
Smeaton's Tower C2
Southern Terr A3
Southside St C2
Stuart Rd A1
Sutherland Rd A2
Sutton Rd B3
Sydney St A1
Teats Hill Rd C3
The Crescent B1
The Hoe C2
The Octagon B1
The Promenade C2
Tothill Ave B3
Union St B1
Univ of Plymouth A2
Vauxhall St B2/3
Victoria Park A1
West Hoe Rd C1
Western Approach B1
Whittington St A1
Wyndham St B1
YMCA B2
YWCA C2

Poole 341

Ambulance Station A3
Baiater Gdns C2
Baiter Park C3
Ballard Cl C2
Ballard Rd C2
Bay Hog La B1
Bridge Approach C1
Bus Station B2
Castle St B2
Catalina Dr B3
Chapel La B2
Church St B1
Cinnamon La B1
Colborne Cl B3
Dear Hay La B2
Denmark La A3
Denmark Rd A3
East St B2
Elizabeth Rd A3
Emerson Rd B2
Ferry Rd C1
Ferry Terminal C1
Fire Station A2
Freightliner Terminal C1
Furnell Rd B3
Garland Rd A3
Green Rd B2
Heckford La A3
Heckford Rd A3
High St B2
High St North A3
Hill St B2
Holes Bay Rd A1
Hospital (A&E) A3
Information Ctr C2
Kingland Rd B3
Kingston Rd A3
Labrador Dr C3
Lagland St B2
Lander Cl C3
Old Lifeboat C2
Lighthouse -Poole Centre for the Arts B3
Longfleet Rd A3
Maple Rd A3
Market Cl B2
Market St B2
Mount Pleasant Rd B3
New Harbour Rd C1
New Harbour Rd South C1
New Harbour Rd West C1
New Orchard B1
New Quay Rd C1
New St B2
Newfoundland Dr B2
North St B2
Old Orchard B2
Parish Rd A3
Park Lake Rd B3
Parkstone Rd A3
Perry Gdns B2
Pitwines Cl B2
Police Station A2
Poole Central Library B2
Poole Lifting Bridge C1
Poole Park B2
Poole Station A2
Poole Waterfront Museum C1
Post Office A2/B2
St John's Rd A3
St Margaret's Rd A2
St Mary's Maternity Unit A3
St Mary's Rd A3
Seldown Bridge B3
Seldown La B3
Seldown Rd B3
Serpentine Rd A2
Shaftesbury Rd A3
Skinner St B2
Slipway B1
Stanley Rd C2
Sterte Ave A2
Sterte Ave West A1
Sterte Cl A2
Sterte Esplanade A2
Sterte Rd A2
Strand St C2
Swimming Pool B3
Taverner Cl B3
Thames St B1
The Lifeboat College B2
The Quay C2
Towngate Bridge B2
Vallis Cl C3
Waldren Cl B3
West Quay B1
West Quay Rd B1
West St B1
West View Rd A2
Whatleigh Cl B2
Wimborne Rd A3

Portsmouth 341

Action Stations C1
Admiralty Rd A1
Alfred Rd A2
Anglesea Rd B2
Arundel St B3
Aspex B1
Bishop St A2
Broad St C1
Buckingham House C2
Burnaby Rd B2
Bus Station B1
Camber Dock C1
Cambridge Rd B2
Car Ferry to Isle of Wight B1
Cascades Sh Ctr A3
Castle Rd C3
City Museum & Art Gallery B2
Civic Offices B3
Clarence Pier C2
College St B1
Commercial Rd A3
Cottage Gr B3
Cross St A1
Cumberland St A2
Duisburg Way C2
Durham St A3
East St B1
Edinburgh Rd A2
Elm Gr C3
Great Southsea St C3
Green Rd B3
Greetham St B3
Grosvenor St B3
Groundlings A2
Grove Rd North C3
Grove Rd South C3
Guildhall B3
Guildhall Walk B3
Gunwharf Quays Retail Park B1
Gunwharf Rd B1
Hambrook St C2
Hampshire Terr B2
Hanover St A1
High St C2
HM Naval Base A1
HMS Nelson (Royal Naval Barracks) A2
HMS Victory A1
HMS Warrior A1
Hovercraft Terminal C2
Hyde Park Rd B3
Information Ctr A1/B3
Isambard Brunel Rd B3
Isle of Wight Car Ferry Terminal B1
Kent Rd C3
Kent St A2
King St B3
King's Rd C3
King's Terr C2
Lake Rd A3
Law Courts B3
Library B3
Long Curtain Rd C2
Market Way A3
Marmion Rd C3
Mary Rose Museum A1
Middle St B3
Millennium Prom B1/C1
Museum Rd B2
National Museum of the Royal Navy A1
Naval Recreation Gd C2
Nightingale Rd C3
Norfolk St B3
North St A2
Osborne Rd C3
Park Rd B2
Passenger Catamaran to Isle of Wight B1
Passenger Ferry to Gosport B1
Pelham Rd C3
Pembroke Gdns C2
Pier Rd C2
Point Battery C1
Police Station B3
Portsmouth & Southsea A3
Portsmouth Harbour B1
Portsmouth Historic Dockyard A1
Post Office A2/A3/B1/B3/C3
Queen St A1
Queen's Cr C3
Round Tower C1
Royal Garrison Church C1
St Edward's Rd C3
St George's Rd B2
St George's Sq B1
St George's Way B2
St James's Rd B3
St James's St A2
St John's Cath (RC) A3
St Thomas's Cath C1
St Thomas's St B2
Somers Rd B3
Southsea Common C2
Southsea Terr C2
Spinnaker Tower B1
Square Tower C1
Station St A3
Swimming Pool A2
The Hard B1
Town Fortifications C1
Unicorn Rd A2
United Services Recreation Ground B2
University of Portsmouth A2/B2
University of Portsmouth – College of Art, Design & Media B3
Upper Arundel St A3
Victoria Ave C2
Victoria Park A2
Victory Gate A1
Vue B1
Warblington St B1
Western Pde C2
White Hart Rd C1
Winston Churchill Ave B3

Preston 342

Adelphi St A2
Anchor Ct B3
Aqueduct St A1
Ardee Rd C1
Arthur St B2
Ashton St A1
Avenham La B3
Avenham Park C3
Avenham Rd B3
Avenham St B3
Bairstow St B3
Balderstone Rd C1
Beamont Dr A1
Beech St South C2
Bird St C1
Bow La B2
Brieryfield Rd A1
Broadgate C1
Brook St A2
Bus Station A3
Butler St B2
Cannon St B3
Carlton St A1
Chaddock St B3
Channel Way B1
Chapel St B3
Christ Church St B2
Christian Rd B2
Cold Bath St A2
Coleman Ct C1
Connaught Rd C2
Corn Exchange B3
Corporation St A2/B2
County Hall B2
County Records Office B2
Court A3
Court B3
Cricket Ground C2
Croft St A1
Cross St B3
Crown Court A3
Crown St A3
East Cliff C3
East Cliff Rd B3
Edward St A2
Elizabeth St A3
Euston St B1
Fishergate B2/B3
Fishergate Hill B2
Fishergate Sh Ctr B2
Fitzroy St B1
Fleetwood St A1
Friargate A3
Fylde Rd A1/A2
Gerrard St B2
Glover's Ct B3
Good St B2
Grafton St B2
Great George St A3
Great Shaw St A3
Greenbank St A2
Guild Way B1
Guildhall & Charter B3
Guildhall St B3
Harrington St A2
Harris Museum B3
Hartington Rd B1
Hasset Cl C2
Heatley St B2
Hind St C2
Information Ctr B3
Kilruddery Rd C1
Lancaster Rd A3/B3
Latham St B3
Lauderdale St C2
Lawson St A3
Leighton St A2
Leyland Rd C1
Library A1
Library B3
Liverpool Rd C1
Lodge St B2
Lune St B3
Main Sprit West B3
Maresfield Rd C1
Market St West A3
Marsh La B1/B2
Maudland Bank A2
Maudland Rd A2
Meadow Ct C2
Meath Rd C1
Mill Hill A2
Miller Arcade B3
Miller Park C3
Moor La A3
Mount St B3
North Rd A3
North St A3
Northcote Rd B1
Old Milestones B1
Old Tram Rd C3
Pedder St A1/A2
Peel St A2
Penwortham Bridge C2
Penwortham New Bridge C1
Pitt St B2
Playhouse A3
Police Station A3
Port Way B1
Post Office B3
Preston Station B2
Ribble Bank St B2
Ribble Viaduct C2
Ribblesdale Pl B3
Ringway B3
River Parade C1
Riverside C2
St Georges B3
St George's Sh Ctr B3
St Johns B3
St Johns Shopping Ctr A3
St Mark's Rd A1
St Walburges A1
Salisbury Rd B1
Sessions House B3
Snow Hill A3
South End C2
South Meadow La C2
Spa Rd B1
Sports Ground C2
Strand Rd B1
Syke St B3
Talbot Rd B1
Taylor St C1
Tithebarn St A3
Town Hall B3
Tulketh Brow A1
University of Central Lancashire A2
Valley Rd C1
Victoria St A2
Walker St A3
Walton's Parade B2
Warwick St A3
Wellfield Bsns Park A1
Wellfield Rd A1
Wellington St A1
West Cliff C2
West Strand A1
Winckley Rd C1
Winckley Square B3
Wolseley Rd C2

Reading 342

Abbey Ruins B2
Abbey Sq B2
Abbey St B2
Abbot's Walk B2
Acacia Rd C2
Addington Rd C3
Addison Rd A1
Allcroft Rd C3
Alpine St C2
Baker St B1
Berkeley Ave C1
Bridge St B1
Brigham Rd A1
Broad St B1
Broad Street Mall B1
Carey St B1
Castle Hill C1
Castle St B1
Caversham Rd A1
Christchurch Playing Fields A2
Civic Offices & Magistrate's Court B1
Coley Hill C1
Coley Pl C1
Craven Rd C3
Crown St C2
De Montfort Rd A1
Denmark Rd C3
Duke St B2
East St B2
Edgehill St C2
Eldon Rd B3
Eldon Terr B3
Elgar Rd C1
Erleigh Rd C3
Field Rd C1
Fire Station A1
Fobney St B1
Forbury Gdns B2
Forbury Retail Park B2
Forbury Rd B2
Francis St C1
Friar St B1
Garrard St B1
Gas Works Rd B3
George St A2
Great Knollys St B1
Greyfriars B1
Gun St B1
Henry St C1
Hexagon Theatre, The B1
Hill's Meadow A2
HM Prison B2
Howard St B1
Information Ctr B1
Inner Distribution Rd B1
Katesgrove La C1
Kenavon Dr B2
Kendrick Rd C2
King's Meadow Rec Gd A2
King's Rd B2
Library B2
London Rd C3
London St B2
Lynmouth Rd A1
Market Pl B2
Mill La B2
Mill Rd A2
Minster St B1
Morgan Rd C3
Mount Pleasant C2
Museum of English Rural Life C3
Napier Rd A2
Newark St C2
Newport Rd A1
Old Reading Univ C3
Oracle Sh Ctr, The B1
Orts Rd B3
Pell St C1
Queen Victoria St B1
Queen's Rd A2
Queen's Rd B2
Police Station B1
Post Office B2
Randolph Rd A1
Reading Bridge A2
Reading Station A1
Redlands Rd C3
Renaissance Hotel B1
Riverside Museum B3
Rose Kiln La C1
Royal Berks Hospital (A&E) C3
St Giles C2
St Laurence B2
St Mary's B1
St Mary's Butts B1
St Saviour's Rd C1
Send Rd A3
Sherman Rd C2
Sidmouth St B2
Silver St C2
South St B2
Southampton St C2
Station Hill A1
Station Rd B1
Superstore A3
Swansea Rd A1
Technical College B3
The Causeway A3
The Grove B2
Valpy St B2
Vastern Rd A1
Vue B2
Waldeck St C2
Watlington St B3
West St B1
Whitby Dr C3
Wolseley St C1
York Rd A1
Zinzan St B1

St Andrews 342

Abbey St B2
Abbey Walk B3
Abbotsford Cres A1
Albany Pk C3
Allan Robertson Dr C2
Ambulance Station C1
Anstruther Rd C3
Argyle St B1
Argyll Business Park C1
Auld Burn Rd B2
Bassaguard Ind Est B1
Bell St B2
Blackfriars Chapel (Ruins) B2
Boase Ave B2
Braid Cres C3
Brewster Pl C3
Bridge St B1
British Golf Mus A1
Broomfaulds Ave C1
Bruce Embankment A1
Bruce St C2
Bus Station A1
Byre B2
Canongate C1
Cathedral and Priory (Ruins) B3
Cemetery B1
Chamberlain St C1
Church St B2
Churchill Cres C2
City Rd A1
Claybraes C1
Cockshaugh Public Pk B1
Cosmos Com Centre B3
Council Office A2
Crawford Gdns C1
Doubledykes Rd B1
Drumcarrow Rd C1
East Sands B3
East Scores A3
Fire Station C1
Forrest St C1
Fraser Ave C1
Freddie Tait St C2
Gateway Centre A1
Glebe Rd B2
Golf Pl A1
Grange Rd C3
Greenside Pl B2
Greyfriars Gdns A2
Hamilton Ave C2
Hepburn Gdns B1
Holy Trinity B2
Horseleys Park C1
Information Ctr B2
Irvine Cres C3
James Robb Ave C1
James St B1
John Knox Rd C1
Kennedy Gdns B1
Kilrymont Cl C3
Kilrymont Pl C3
Kilrymont Rd C3
Kinburn Park B1
Kinkell Terr C3
Kinnesburn Rd B2
Ladebraes Walk B2
Lady Buchan's Cave A3
Lamberton Pl C1
Lamond Dr C2
Langlands Rd B2
Largo Rd C1
Learmonth Pl C1
Library B2
Links Clubhouse A1
Links, The A1
Livingstone Cres B2
Long Rocks A2
Madras College B2
Market St A2
Martyr's Monument A1
Memorial Hospital (No A&E) B3
Murray Pk A2
Murray Pl A2
Nelson St B2
New Course, The A1
New Picture House A2
North Castle St A3
North St A2
Old Course, The A1
Old Station Rd A1
Pends, The B3
Pilmour Links A1
Pipeland Rd B2/C2
Police Station A2
Post Office B2
Preservation Trust B2
Priestden Pk C3
Priestden Pl C3
Priestden Rd C3
Queen's Gdns B2
Queen's Terr B2
Roundhill Rd C2
Royal & Ancient Golf Club A1
St Andrews B1
St Andrews Aquarium A2
St Andrews Botanic Garden B1
St Andrews Castle (Ruins) & Visitor Centre A2
St Leonard's School B3
St Mary St B3
St Mary's College B2
St Nicholas St C3
St Rules Tower B3
St Salvator's College A2
Sandyhill Cres C2
Sandyhill Rd C2
Scooniehill Rd C2
Shields Ave C3
Shoolbraids C2
Sloan St B1
South St B2
Spottiswoode Gdns C1
Station Rd A1
Swilcen Bridge A1
The Scores A2
The Shore B3
Tom Morris Dr C2
Tom Stewart La C1
Town Hall B2
Union St A2
University Chapel A2
University Library A2
Univ of St Andrews A1
Viaduct Walk B1
War Memorial A3
Wardlaw Gdns B1
Warrack St C3
Watson Ave B2
West Port B2
West Sands A1
Westview B2
Windmill Rd A1
Winram Pl C1
Wishart Gdns C2
Woodburn Pk B3
Woodburn Pl B3
Woodburn Terr B3
Younger Hall A2

Salisbury 342

Albany Rd A2
Arts Centre A3
Ashley Rd A1
Avon Approach A2
Ayleswade Rd C2
Bedwin St A2
Belle Vue A2
Bishop's Palace C2
Bishops Walk B2
Blue Boar Row B2
Bourne Ave A3
Bourne Hill A3
Britford La C2
Broad Walk C2
Brown St B2
Bus Station B2
Castle St A2
Catherine St B2
Chapter House B2
Church House B2
Churchfields Rd B1
Churchill Way East B3
Churchill Way North A3
Churchill Way South C2
Churchill Way West A1
City Hall B2
Close Wall B2
Coldharbour La A1
College St A3
Council Offices A3
Court A1
Crane Bridge Rd B2
Crane St B2
Cricket Ground C1
Culver St South B3
De Vaux Pl C2
Devizes Rd A1
Dews Rd B1
Elm Grove B3
Elm Grove Rd A3
Endless St A2
Estcourt Rd A3
Exeter St C2
Fairview Rd A3
Fire Station A1
Fisherton St A1
Folkestone Rd C1
Fowlers Hill B3
Fowlers Rd B3
Friary Estate C3
Friary La B2
Gas La A1
Gigant St B3
Greencroft B3
Greencroft St A3
Guildhall B2
Hall of John Halle B2
Hamilton Rd A2
Harnham Mill B1
Harnham Rd C1/C2
High St B2
Hospital A1
Ho of John A'Port B2
Information Ctr B2
Kelsey Rd A3
King's Rd A2
Laverstock Rd B3
Library B2
London Rd A3
Lower St C1
Maltings, The B2
Manor Rd A3
Marsh La A1
Medieval Hall B2
Milford Hill B3
Milford St B3
Mill Rd B1
Millstream Approach A2
Mompesson House (NT) B2
New Bridge Rd C2
New Canal B2
New Harnham Rd C2
New St B2
North Canonry B2
North Gate B2
North Walk B2
Old George Hall B2
Old Blandford Rd C1
Old Deanery B2
Park St A3
Parsonage Green C1
Playhouse Theatre A2
Post Office A2/B2/C2
Poultry Cross B2
Queen Elizabeth Gdns B1
Queen's Rd A3
Rampart Rd B3
St Ann's Gate B2
St Ann St B2
St Marks Rd A3
St Martins B3
St Mary's Cathedral B2
St Nicholas Hospital C2
St Paul's A1
St Paul's Rd A1
St Thomas B2
Salisbury & South Wiltshire Museum B2
Salisbury General Hospital (A&E) C2
Salisbury Station A1
Salt La A3
Saxon Rd C1
Scots La A2
Shady Bower B3
South Canonry C2
South Gate C2
Southampton Rd B2
Spire View A1
Sports Ground C3
The Friary B3
Tollgate Rd B3
Town Path B1
Wain-a-Long Rd A3
Wardrobe, The B2
Wessex Rd A3
West Walk C2
Wilton Rd A1
Wiltshire College B3
Winchester St B3
Windsor Rd A1
Winston Churchill Gdns C3
Wyndham Rd A2
YHA B3
York Rd A1

Scarborough 342

Aberdeen Walk B2
Albert Rd A2
Albion Rd C2
Alexandra Bowling Hall A1
Alexandra Gardens A1
Auborough St B2
Belle Vue St C1
Belmont Rd C2
Brunswick Pavilion Shopping Centre B2
Castle Dykes B3
Castlegate B3
Castle Holms A3
Castle Hill A3
Castle Rd B2
Castle Walls A3
Cemetery B1
Central Lift C2
Clarence Gardens A2
Coach Park B1
Columbus Ravine A1
Court B1
Cricket Ground A1
Cross St B2
Crown Terr C2
Dean Rd B1
Devonshire Dr A1
East Harbour B3
East Pier B3
Eastborough B2
Elmville Ave B1
Esplanade C2
Falconers Rd B2
Falsgrave Rd C1
Fire Station B2
Foreshore Rd B2
Friargate B2
Futurist Theatre B2
Gladstone Rd B1
Gladstone St B1
Hoxton Rd B1
Information Ctr B2/B3
King St B2
Library B2
Lifeboat Station B3
Londesborough Rd C1
Longwestgate B3
Marine Dr A3
Military Adventure Pk A1
Miniature Railway A1
Nelson St B1
Newborough B2
Nicolas St B2
North Marine Rd A1
North St B2
Northway B1
Old Harbour B3
Olympia Leisure B2
Peasholm Park A1
Peasholm Rd A1
Plaza A1
Police Station B1
Post Office B2/C1
Princess St B3
Prospect Rd B1
Queen St B2
Queen's Parade A2
Queen's Tower (Remains) A3
Ramshill Rd C2
Roman Signal Sta A3
Roscoe St C1
Rotunda Museum C2
Royal Albert Dr A2
St Martin-on-the-Hill C2
St Martin's Ave C2
St Mary's B3
St Thomas St B2
Sandside B3
Scarborough Art Gallery and Crescent Art Studio C2
Scarborough Castle A3
Scarborough C1
Somerset Terr C2
South Cliff Lift C2
Spa, The C2
Spa Theatre, The C2
Stephen Joseph Theatre B1
Tennyson Ave B1
The Crescent C2
Tollergate B2
Town Hall B2
Trafalgar Rd B1
Trafalgar Square A1
Trafalgar St West B1
Valley Bridge Parade C2
Valley Rd C1
Vernon Rd C2
Victoria Park Mount A1
Victoria Rd B1
West Pier B3
Westbourough C1
Westover Rd C1
Westwood C1
Woodall Ave A1
YMCA Theatre B2
York Pl B2
Yorkshire Coast College (Westwood Campus) C1

Sheffield 342

Addy Dr A2
Addy St A2
Adelphi St A3
Albert Terrace Rd A3
Albion St A2
Aldred Rd A1
Allen St A4
Alma St A4
Angel St B5
Arundel Gate B5
Arundel St C4
Ashberry Rd A2
Ashdell Rd C1
Ashgate Rd C1
Athletics Centre B2
Attercliffe Rd A6
Bailey St B4
Ball St A4
Balm Green B4
Bank St B4
Barber Rd A2
Bard St B5
Barker's Pool B4
Bates St A1
Beech Hill Rd C1
Beet St B3
Bellefield St A3
Bernard Rd A6
Bernard St B6
Birkendale A2
Birkendale Rd A2
Birkendale View A1
Bishop St C4
Blackwell Pl B6
Blake St A2
Blonk St A5
Bolsover St B2
Botanical Gdns C1
Bower Rd A1
Bradley St A1
Bramall La C4
Bramwell St A3
Bridge St A4/A5
Brighton Terrace Rd A1
Broad La B3
Broad St B6
Brocco St A3
Brook Hill B3
Broomfield Rd C1
Broomgrove Rd C2
Broomhall Pl C3
Broomhall Rd C2

358 Shrewsbury • Southampton • Southend-on-Sea • Stirling • Stoke • Stratford-upon-Avon

Broomhall St C3
Broomspring La C2
Brown St C5
Brunswick St B3
Burgess St B4
Burlington St A2
Burns Rd A2
Cadman St A6
Cambridge St B4
Campo La B4
Carver St B4
Castle Market B5
Castle Square B5
Castlegate A5
Cathedral (RC) † B4
Cathedral B4
Cavendish St B3
Charles St C4
Charter Row C4
Children's Hospital (A&E) B2
Church St B4
City Hall B4
City Hall B4
City Rd C6
Claremont Cr B2
Claremont Pl B2
Clarke St C3
Clarkegrove Rd C2
Clarkehouse Rd C1
Clarkson St B2
Cobden View Rd A1
Collegiate Cr C2
Commercial St B5
Commonside A1
Conduit Rd B1
Cornish St A3
Corporation St A4
Court B4
Cricket Inn Rd B6
Cromwell St A1
Crookes Rd B1
Crookes Valley Park B2
Crookes Valley Rd B2
Crookesmoor Rd A2
Crown Court A4
Crucible Theatre B5
Cutlers Gate A6
Cutler's Hall B4
Daniel Hill A2
Dental Hospital B2
Dept for Education & Employment C4
Devonshire Green B3
Devonshire St B3
Division St B4
Dorset St C2
Dover St A3
Duchess Rd C5
Duke St B5
Duncombe St A1
Durham Rd B2
Earl St C4
Earl Way C4
Ecclesall Rd C3
Edward St B3
Effingham Rd A6
Effingham St A6
Egerton St C3
Eldon St B3
Elmore Rd B1
Exchange St B5
Eyre St C4
Fargate B4
Farm Rd C5
Fawcett St A3
Filey St B3
Fire & Police Mus A4
Fire Station C4
Fir St A1
Fitzalan Sq/ Ponds Forge B5
Fitzwater Rd C6
Fitzwilliam Gate C4
Fitzwilliam St B3
Flat St B5
Foley St A6
Foundry Climbing Ctr A4
Fulton Rd A1
Furnace Hill A4
Furnival Rd A5
Furnival Sq C4
Furnival St C4
Garden St B3
Gell St B3
Gibraltar St A4
Glebe Rd B1
Glencoe Rd C6
Glossop Rd B2/B3/C1
Gloucester St C2
Granville Rd C6
Granville Rd/ Sheffield College C5
Graves Gallery B5
Greave Rd B3
Green La A4
Hadfield St A1
Hanover St C3
Hanover Way C3
Harcourt Rd B1
Harmer La B5
Havelock St C2
Hawley St B4
Haymarket B5
Headford St C3
Heavygate Rd A1
Henry St A3
High St B4
Hodgson St C3
Holberry Gdns C2
Hollis Croft B4
Holly St B4
Hounsfield Rd B3
Howard Rd A1
Hoyle St A3
Hyde Park A6
Infirmary Rd A3
Infirmary Rd A3
Information Ctr B4
Jericho St A3
Johnson St A5
Kelham Island Industrial Museum A4
Lawson Rd C1
Leadmill Rd C5
Leadmill St C5
Leadmill, The C5
Leamington St A1
Leavy Rd B3
Lee Croft B4
Leopold St B4
Leveson St A6
Library A2
Library B5
Library C1
Lyceum Theatre B5
Malinda St A3
Maltravers St A5
Manor Oaks Rd B6
Mappin St B3
Marlborough Rd B1
Mary St C4
Matilda St C4
Matlock Rd A1
Meadow St A3
Melbourn Rd A1
Melbourne Ave C1
Millennium Galleries B5
Milton St C3
Mitchell St B3
Mona Ave A1
Mona Rd A1
Montgomery Terr Rd A3
Montgomery Theatre B4
Monument Gdns C6
Moor Oaks Rd B1
Moore St C3
Mowbray St A4
Mushroom La B2
Netherthorpe Rd B3
Netherthorpe Rd B3
Newbould La C1
Nile St C1
Norfolk Park Rd C6
Norfolk Rd C6
Norfolk St B4
North Church St B4
Northfield Rd A1
Northumberland Rd B1
Nursery St A5
O2 Academy B5
Oakholme Rd C1
Octagon B2
Odeon B5
Old St B6
Orchard Square B4
Oxford St A2
Paradise St B4
Park La C2
Park Sq B5
Parker's Rd B1
Pearson Building (Univ) C2
Penistone Rd A3
Pinstone St B4
Pitt St B3
Police Station A4/B5
Pond Hill B5
Pond St B5
Ponds Forge Int Sports Ctr B5
Portobello St B3
Post Office A1/A2/B3/B4/B5/B6/C1/C3/C4/C6
Powell St A2
Queen St B4
Queen's Rd C5
Ramsey Rd B1
Red Hill B3
Redcar Rd B1
Regent St B3
Rockingham St B4
Roebuck Rd A2
Royal Hallamshire Hospital C2
Russell St A4
Rutland Park C1
St George's Cl B3
St Mary's Gate C3
St Mary's Rd C4/C5
St Peter & St Paul Cathedral † B4
St Philip's Rd A3
Savile St A5
School Rd B1
Scotland St A4
Severn Rd B1
Shalesmoor A4
Shalesmoor A3
Sheaf St B5
Sheffield Hallam Univ B5
Sheffield Ice Sports Ctr – Skate Central C5
Sheffield Interchange B5
Sheffield Parkway A6
Sheffield Station C5
Sheffield Sta/ Sheffield Hallam Univ B5
Sheffield University B2
Shepherd St A3
Shipton St A2
Shoreham St C4
Showroom, The C5
Shrewsbury Rd C5
Sidney St C4
Site Gallery C5
Slinn St A1
Smithfield A4
Snig Hill A5
Snow La A4
Solly St B3
Southbourne Rd C1
South La C4
South Street Park B5
Spital Hill A5
Spital St A5
Spring Hill B1
Spring Hill Rd B1
Springvale Rd A1
Stafford Rd C6
Stafford St B6
Stanley St A5
Suffolk Rd C5
Summer St B2
Sunny Bank C3
Surrey St B4
Sussex St A6
Sutton St B3
Sydney Rd A2
Sylvester St C4
Talbot St B5
Taptonville Rd B1
Tax Office C4
Tenter St B4
The Moor C4
Town Hall B4
Townend St A1
Townhead St B4
Trafalgar St B4
Tree Root Walk B2
Trinity St A4
Trippet La B4
Turner Mus of Glass B3
Union St B4
Univ Drama Studio B2
Univ of Sheffield B3
Upper Allen St A3
Upper Hanover St B3
Upperthorpe Rd A2/A3
Verdon St A5
Victoria Quays B5
Victoria Rd C2
Victoria St B3
Waingate B5
Watery St A3
Watson Rd C1
Wellesley Rd B2
Wellington St C3
West Bar A4
West Bar Green A4
West One Plaza B3
West St B3
West St B4
Westbourne Rd C1
Western Bank B2
Western Rd A1
Weston Park B2
Weston Park Hospl B2
Weston Park Mus B2
Weston St B2
Wharncliffe Rd C3
Whitham Rd B1
Wicker A5
Wilkinson St B2
William St C3
Winter Garden B4
Winter St B2
York St B4
Yorkshire Artspace C5
Young St C4

Shrewsbury 342

Abbey Church B3
Abbey Foregate B3
Abbey Lawn Bsns Park B3
Abbots House B2
Agricultural Show Gd A1
Albert St A2
Alma St B1
Ashley St A3
Ashton Rd C1
Avondale Dr A3
Bage Way C3
Barker St B1
Beacall's La A2
Beeches La C2
Beehive La C1
Belle Vue Gdns C2
Belle Vue Rd C2
Belmont Bank C1
Berwick Ave A1
Berwick Rd A1
Betton St C2
Bishop St B3
Bradford St B3
Bridge St B1
Bus Station B2
Butcher Row B2
Burton St A3
Butler Rd C1
Bynner St C2
Canon St B3
Canonbury C1
Castle Bsns Park, The A2
Castle Foregate A2
Castle Gates B2
Castle Museum B2
Castle St B2
Cathedral (RC) † C1
Chester St A2
Cineworld C3
Claremont Bank B1
Claremont Hill B1
Cleveland St B3
Coleham Head B2
Coleham Pumping Station C2
College Hill B1
Corporation La A1
Coton Cres A1
Coton Hill A2
Coton Mount A1
Crescent La C1
Crewe St A2
Cross Hill B1
Darwin Centre B2
Dingle, The B1
Dogpole B2
Draper's Hall B2
English Bridge B2
Fish St B2
Frankwell B1
Gateway Ctr, The A2
Gravel Hill La A1
Greyfriars Rd C2
Guildhall B1
Hampton Rd A3
Haycock Way C3
HM Prison B2
High St B1
Hills La B1
Holywell St B3
Hunter St A1
Information Ctr B1
Ireland's Mansion & Bear Steps B1
John St A3
Kennedy Rd C1
King St B3
Kingsland Bridge C1
Kingsland Bridge (toll) C1
Kingsland Rd C1
Library B2
Lime St C2
Longden Coleham C2
Longden Rd C1
Longner St B1
Luciefelde Rd C1
Mardol B1
Market B1
Marine Terr C2
Monkmoor Rd B3
Moreton Cr C2
Mount St A1
New Park Cl A3
New Park Rd A2
New Park St A3
North St A2
Oakley St C1
Old Coleham C2
Old Market Hall B1
Old Potts Way C3
Parade Centre B2
Police Station B1
Post Office A2/B1/B2/B3
Pride Hill B1
Pride Hill Centre B1
Priory Rd B1
Pritchard Way C3
Queen St A2
Raby Cr C2
Rad Brook C1
Rea Brook C3
Riverside B1
Roundhill La A1
St Alkmund's B2
St Chad's B1
St Chad's Terr B1
St John's Hill B1
St Julians Friars C2
St Mary's B2
St Mary's St B2
Salters La C2
Scott St C3
Severn Bank A3
Severn St A2
Shrewsbury B2
Shrewsbury High School for Girls C1
Shrewsbury Mus & Art Gall B1
Shrewsbury School C1
Shropshire Wildlife Trust B3
Smithfield Rd B1
South Hermitage C1
Swan Hill B1
Sydney Ave A3
Tankerville St B3
The Dana B2
The Quarry B1
The Square B1
Tilbrook Dr A3
Town Walls C1
Trinity St C2
Underdale Rd B3
Victoria Ave B1
Victoria Quay B1
Victoria St B2
Welsh Bridge B1
Whitehall St B3
Wood St A2
Wyle Cop B2

Southampton 342

Above Bar St A2
Albert Rd North B3
Albert Rd South C3
Anderson's Rd B3
Archaeology Mus (God's Ho Tower) C2
Argyle Rd A2
Arundel Tower B1
Bargate, The B2
Bargate Shopping Ctr B2
BBC Regional Centre A1
Bedford Pl A1
Belvidere Rd A3
Bernard St C2
Blechynden Terr A1
Brazil Rd C3
Brinton's Rd A2
Britannia Rd A3
Briton St C2
Brunswick Pl A2
Bugle St C1
Canute Rd C3
Castle Way C2
Catchcold Tower B1
Central Bridge C3
Central Rd C2
Channel Way C3
Chapel Rd B3
Cineworld C3
City Art Gallery A1
City College B3
Civic Centre A1
Civic Centre Rd A1
Coach Station B1
Commercial Rd A1
Cumberland Pl A1
Cunard Rd C2
Derby Rd A3
Devonshire Rd A1
Dock Gate 4 C2
Dock Gate 8 B1
East Park A2
East Park Terr A2
East St B2
East St Shopping Ctr B2
Endle St B3
European Way C2
Fire Station A2
Floating Bridge Rd C3
Golden Gr A3
Graham Rd A2
Guildhall A1
Hanover Bldgs B2
Harbour Lights C3
Harbour Pde B1
Hartington Rd A3
Havelock Rd A1
Henstead Rd A1
Herbert Walker Ave B1
High St B2
Hoglands Park B2
Holy Rood (Rems), Merchant Navy Memorial B2
Houndwell Park B2
Houndwell Pl B2
Hythe Ferry C2
Information Ctr A1
Isle of Wight Ferry Terminal C1
James St B3
Java Rd C3
Kingsway A2
Leisure World B1
Library A1
Lime St B2
London Rd A2
Marine Pde B3
Marsh La B2
Mayflower Meml C1
Mayflower Park C1
Mayflower Theatre, The A1
Medieval Merchant's House C1
Melbourne St B3
Millais A2
Morris Rd A1
National Oceanography Centre C3
Neptune Way C3
New Rd A2
Nichols Rd A3
North Front A2
Northam Rd A3
Ocean Dock C2
Ocean Village Marina C3
Ocean Way C3
Odeon B1
Ogle Rd B1
Old Northam Rd A2
Orchard La B2
Oxford Ave A2
Oxford St C2
Palmerston Park A2
Palmerston Rd A2
Parsonage Rd A3
Peel St A3
Platform Rd C2
Police Station A1
Portland Terr B1
Post Office A2/A3/B2
Pound Tree Rd B2
Quays Swimming & Diving Complex, The B1
Queen's Park C2
Queen's Peace Fountain A2
Queen's Terr C2
Queen's Way B2
Radcliffe Rd A3
Rochester St A3
Royal Pier C1
Royal South Hants Hospital A2
Sea City Mus A1
St Andrew's Rd A2
St Mary St A2
St Mary's B3
St Mary's Leisure Ctr A2
St Mary's Pl B2
St Mary's Rd A2
St Mary's Stadium (Southampton FC) A3
St Michael's C1
Solent Sky C3
South Front B2
Southampton Central Station A1
Southampton Solent University A2
SS Shieldhall C2
Terminus Terr C2
The Mall, Marlands A1
The Polygon A1
Threefield La B2
Titanic Engineers' Memorial A2
Town Quay C1
Town Walls B2
Tudor House C1
Vincent's Walk B2
West Gate Hall C1
West Marlands Rd A1
West Park A1
West Park Rd A1
West Quay Rd B1
West Quay Retail Park B1
West Quay Sh Ctr B1
West Rd C2
Western Esplanade B1
Winton St A2

Southend-on-Sea 343

Adventure Island C3
Albany Ave A1
Albert Rd C3
Alexandra Rd C2
Alexandra St C2
Alexandra Yacht Club C2
Ashburnham Rd B2
Ave Rd B1
Avenue Terr B1
Balmoral Rd B1
Baltic Ave B3
Baxter Ave A2/B2
Beecroft Art Gallery C1
Bircham Rd A2
Boscombe Rd B3
Boston Ave A1/B2
Bournemouth Park Rd A3
Browning Ave A3
Bus Station C3
Byron Ave A3
Cambridge Rd C1/C2
Canewdon Rd B1
Carnarvon Rd A2
Central Ave A3
Chelmsford Ave A1
Chichester Rd B2
Church Rd C3
Civic Centre A2
Clarence Rd C2
Clarence St C2
Cliff Ave B1
Cliffs Pavilion C1
Clifftown Parade C2
Clifftown Rd C2
Colchester Rd A1
College Way B2
Coleman St B3
County Court B3
Cromer Rd B3
Crowborough Rd A2
Dryden Ave A3
East St A2
Elmer App B2
Elmer Ave B2
Gainsborough Dr A1
Gayton Rd A2
Glenhurst Rd A2
Gordon Pl B2
Gordon Rd B2
Grainger Rd A2
Greyhound Way A3
Guildford Rd B3
Hamlet Ct Rd B1
Hamlet Rd C1
Harcourt Ave A1
Hartington Rd C3
Hastings Rd B3
Herbert Gr C3
Heygate Ave C3
High St B2/C2
Information Ctr C3
Kenway A2
Kilworth Ave B3
Lancaster Gdns B3
Library B2
London Rd B1
Lucy Rd C3
MacDonald Ave A1
Magistrates Court A2
Maldon Rd A2
Maine Ave C1
Marine Rd C1
Marine Parade C3
Milton Rd B1
Milton St B2
Napier Ave B2
North Ave A3
North Rd A1/B1
Odeon B2
Osborne Rd B1
Park Cres B1
Park Rd B1
Park St B1
Park Terr B1
Pier Hill C3
Pleasant Rd C3
Police Station A2
Post Office B2/B3
Princes St B2
Queens Rd B2
Queensway B2/B3/C3
Rayleigh Ave A1
Redstock Rd A2
Rochford Ave A1
Royal Mews C2
Royal Terr C2
Royals Sh Ctr, The C3
Ruskin Ave A3
St Ann's Rd B3
St Helen's Rd B1
St John's Rd B1
St Leonard's Rd C3
St Lukes Rd A3
St Vincent's Rd C1
Salisbury Ave A1/B1
Scratton Rd C2
Shakespeare Dr A1
Short St A2
South Ave A3
Southchurch Rd B3
South Essex College B2
Southend Central B2
Southend Pier Railway C3
Southend Radio C2
Southend United FC A1
Southend Victoria B2
Stadium Rd A2
Stanfield Rd A2
Stanley Rd C3
Sutton Rd A3/B3
Swanage Rd B3
Sweyne Ave A1
Sycamore Gr A3
Tennyson Ave A3
The Grove A3
Tickfield Ave A2
Tudor Rd A1
Tunbridge Rd A2
Tylers Ave B3
Tyrrel Dr B3
Univ of Essex B2/C2
Vale Ave A2
Victoria Ave A2
Victoria Sh Ctr, The B2
Warrior Sq B3
Wesley Rd C3
West Rd A1
West St A1
Westcliff Ave C1
Westcliff Parade C1
Western Esplanade C1
Weston Rd C2
Whitegate Rd B3
Wilson Rd C1
Wimborne Rd B3
York Rd C3

Stirling 343

Abbey Rd A3
Abbotsford Pl A3
Abercromby Pl C1
Albert Halls B1
Albert Pl B1
Alexandra Pl A3
Allan Park C2
Ambulance Station A2
AMF Ten Pin Bowling B2
Argyll Ave A3
Argyll's Lodging B1
Back O' Hill Ind Est A1
Back O' Hill Rd A1
Baker St B2
Ballengeich Pass A1
Balmoral Pl B1
Barn Rd B1
Barnton St B2
Bow St B1
Bruce St A2
Burghmuir Ind Est C2
Burghmuir Rd A2/B2/C2
Bus Station B2
Cambuskenneth Bridge A3
Carlton C2
Castle Ct B1
Causewayhead Rd A2
Cemetery A1
Church of the Holy Rude B1
Clarendon Pl C1
Club House B1
Colquhoun St C3
Corn Exchange B2
Council Offices C2
Court B2
Cowane B2
Cowane St A2
Cowane's Hospital B1
Crawford Sh Arc B2
Crofthead Rd A1
Dean Cres A3
Douglas St A2
Drip Rd A1
Drummond La C1
Drummond Pl C1
Drummond Pl La C1
Dumbarton Rd C2
Eastern Access Rd B2
Edward Ave A3
Edward Rd A2
Forrest Rd A2
Fort A1
Forth Cres B2
Forth St A2
Gladstone Pl C1
Glebe Ave C1
Glebe Cres C1
Golf Course C1
Goosecroft Rd B2
Gowanhill A1
Greenwood Ave B1
Harvey Wynd A1
Information Ctr B1
Irvine Pl B2
James St A2
John St B1
Kerse Rd C3
King's Knot B1
King's Park C1
King's Park Rd C1
Laurencecroft Rd A2
Leisure Pool B2
Library B2
Linden Ave C2
Lovers Wk A2
Lower Back Walk B1
Lower Bridge St A2
Lower Castlehill A1
Mar Pl B1
Meadow Pl A3
Meadowforth Rd C3
Middlemuir Rd C3
Millar Pl A3
Morris Terr B2
Mote Hill A1
Murray Pl B2
Nelson Pl C2
Old Town Cemetery B1
Old Town Jail B1
Orchard House Hospital (No A&E) C2
Park Terr C1
Phoenix Industrial Est C3
Players Rd C3
Port St C2
Princes St B2
Queen St B2
Queen's Rd B1
Queenshaugh Dr A3
Rainbow Slides B2
Ramsay Pl A2
Riverside Dr A3
Ronald Pl A1
Rosebery Pl A2
Royal Gardens B1
Royal Gdns B1
St Mary's Wynd B1
St Ninian's Rd C2
Scott St A2
Seaforth Pl B2
Shore Rd B2
Smith Art Gallery & Museum B1
Snowdon Pl C1
Snowdon Pl La C1
Spittal St B2
Springkerse Ind Est C3
Springkerse Rd C3
Stirling Bsns Centre C2
Stirling Castle A1
Stirling County Rugby Football Club A3
Stirling Enterprise Pk B3
Stirling Old Bridge A2
Stirling Station B2
Superstore A2
Sutherland Ave A3
TA Centre C3
Tannery La A2
The Bastion C2
The Changing Room B1
Thistle Industrial Est C3
Thistles Sh Ctr, The B2
Tollbooth, The B1
Town Wall B1
Union St A2
Upper Back Walk B1
Upper Bridge St A1
Upper Castlehill B1
Upper Craigs C2
Victoria Pl C1
Victoria Rd B1
Victoria Sq B1/C1
Vue B2
Wallace St A2
Waverley Cres A3
Wellgreen Rd C2
Windsor Pl C1
YHA B1

Stoke 343

Ashford St A3
Avenue Rd A3
Aynsley Rd A2
Barnfield C1
Bath St C2
Beresford St A3
Bilton St C3
Boon Ave C2
Booth St C2
Boothen Rd C2/C3
Boughey St C2
Boughley Rd B3
Brighton St B1
Campbell Rd C2
Carlton Rd B3
Cauldon Rd A3
Cemetery A2
Cemetery Rd A2
Chamberlain Ave C1
Church (RC) B2
Church St C2
City Rd C3
Civic Centre & King's Hall B3
Cliff Vale Pk A1
College Rd A3
Convent Cl B2
Copeland St B2
Cornwallis St C3
Corporation St C2
Crowther St A3
Dominic St B1
Elenora St B2
Elgin St B2
Epworth St A3
Etruscan St A1
Film Theatre B3
Fleming Rd C2
Fletcher Rd C2
Floyd St B2
Foden St C2
Frank St C2
Franklin Rd C1
Frederick Ave B1
Garden St C1
Garner St A1
Gerrard St B2
Glebe St B3
Greatbach Ave B1
Hanley Park A3
Harris St B1
Hartshill Rd B1
Hayward St A2
Hide St B2
Higson Ave B2
Hill St B2
Honeywall B2
Hunters Dr C1
Hunters Way C1
Keary St C2
Kingsway B2
Leek Rd B3
Library C2
Lime St C2
Liverpool Rd B2
London Rd C2
Lonsdale St C2
Lovatt St B2
Lytton St B3
Market C2
Newcastle La C1
Newlands St A2
Norfolk St A2
North St A1/B2
North Staffordshire Royal Infirmary (A&E) B1
Northcote Ave B2
Oldmill St C3
Oriel St B1
Oxford St B1
Penkhull New Rd C1
Penkhull St C1
Police Station C2
Portmeirion Pottery C2
Post Office A3/B1/B3/C1/C2
Prince's Rd B1
Pump St B2
Quarry Ave B1
Quarry Rd B1
Queen Anne St A3
Queen's Rd C1
Queensway A1/B2/C3
Richmond St B1
Rothwell St C1
St Peter's B3
St Thomas Pl C1
Scrivenor Rd A1
Seaford St A3
Selwyn St C3
Shelton New Rd A1
Shelton Old Rd B2
Sheppard St C2
Spark St C2
Spencer Rd B3
Spode St C2
Squires View B3
Staffordshire Univ B3
Stanley Matthews Sports Centre B3
Station Rd B3
Stoke Business Park C3
Stoke Recreation Ctr C2
Stoke Rd A2
Stoke-on-Trent Coll A3
Stoke-on-Trent Sta B3
Sturgess St C2
The Villas C1
Thistley Hough C1
Thornton Rd B3
Tolkien Way B1
Trent Valley Rd C1
Vale St B2
Watford St A3
Wellesley St A3
West Ave B1
Westland St B1
Yeaman St C2
Yoxall Ave B1

Stratford-upon-Avon 343

Albany Rd B1
Alcester Rd B1
Ambulance Station B1
Arden St B2
Avenue Farm A1
Ave Farm Ind Est A1
Avenue Rd A3
Avon Industrial Estate A2
Baker Ave A1
Bandstand C3
Benson Rd A3
Birmingham Rd A2
Boat Club B3
Borden Pl C1
Brass Rubbing Ctr C2
Bridge St B2
Bridgetown Rd C3
Bridgeway B3
Broad St C2
Broad Walk C2
Brookvale Rd C1
Bull St C2
Bus Station B2
Butterfly Farm C3
Cemetery C1
Chapel La B2
Cherry Orchard C1
Chestnut Walk B2
Children's Playground C3
Church St C2
Civic Hall B2
Clarence Rd B1
Clopton Bridge B3
Clopton Rd A2
Coach Terminal & Park B3
College B1
College La C2
College St C2
Com Sports Centre B1
Council Offices (District) B2
Courtyard C2
Cox's Yard B3
Cricket Ground C3
Ely Gdns B2
Ely St B2
Evesham Rd C1
Fire Station B1
Foot Ferry C3
Fordham Ave A2
Gallery, The B3
Garrick Way C1
Gower Memorial B3
Great William St B2
Greenhill St B2
Grove Rd B2
Guild St B2
Guildhall & School B2
Hall's Croft C2
Hartford Rd C1
Harvard House B2
Henley St B2
High St B2
Holton St C2
Holy Trinity C2
Information Ctr B3
Jolyffe Park Rd A2
Kipling Rd C3
Leisure & Visitor Ctr B3
Library B2
Lodge Rd B1
Maidenhead Rd A3
Mansell St B2
Masons Court B2
Masons Rd A1
Maybird Shopping Pk A2
Maybrook Rd A1
Mayfield Ave A2
Meer St B2
Mill La C2
Moat House Hotel B3

Sunderland • Swansea • Swindon • Taunton • Telford • Torquay • Truro • Wick 359

Narrow La C2
Nash's Ho & New Pl B2
New St C2
Old Town C2
Orchard Way C1
Paddock La C1
Park Rd A1
Payton St B2
Percy St A2
Police Station B2
Post Office B2/B3
Recreation Ground C2
Regal Road B2
Rother St B2
Rowley Cr A3
Royal Shakespeare Theatre B3
Ryland St C2
Saffron Meadow C2
St Andrew's Cr B1
St Gregory's A3
St Gregory's Rd A3
St Mary's Rd A2
Sanctus Dr C2
Sanctus St C1
Sandfield Rd C2
Scholars La B1
Seven Meadows Rd C2
Shakespeare Ctr B2
Shakespeare Institute C2
Shakespeare St B2
Shakespeare's Birthplace B2
Sheep St B2
Shelley Rd C3
Shipston Rd C3
Shottery Rd C1
Slingates Rd A2
Southern La C2
Station Rd B1
Stratford Healthcare B2
Stratford Hospital B2
Stratford Sports Club B1
Stratford-upon-Avon Station B1
Swan's Nest La B3
Swan Theatre B3
Talbot Rd A2
The Greenway C2
The Willows B1
The Willows North B1
Tiddington Rd B3
Timothy's Bridge Industrial Estate A1
Timothy's Bridge Rd A1
Town Hall & Council Offices B2
Town Sq B2
Trinity St C2
Tyler St B2
War Memorial Gdns B3
Warwick Rd B3
Waterside B3
Welcombe Rd A3
West St C2
Western Rd A2
Wharf Rd A2
Wood St B2

Sunderland 343

Albion Pl C2
Alliance Pl B1
Argyle St C2
Ashwood St C1
Athenaeum St B2
Azalea Terr C2
Beach St A1
Bede Theatre C3
Bedford St B2
Beechwood Terr C1
Belvedere Rd C2
Blandford St B2
Borough Rd B3
Bridge Cr B2
Bridge St B2
Brooke St A2
Brougham St B2
Burdon Rd C2
Burn Park C1
Burn Park Rd C1
Burn Park Tech Park C1
Carol St B1
Charles St A3
Chester Rd C1
Chester Terr B1
Church St A3
Civic Centre C2
Cork St B3
Coronation St B3
Cowan Terr C2
Crowtree Rd B2
Dame Dorothy St A2
Deptford Rd B1
Deptford Terr A1
Derby St C2
Derwent St C2
Dock St A3
Dundas St A2
Durham Rd C1
Easington St A2
Egerton St C3
Empire B3
Empire Theatre B2
Farringdon Row B1
Fawcett St B2
Fox St C1
Foyle St B3
Frederick St B3
Gill Rd B2
Hanover Pl A1
Havelock Terr C1
Hay St A2
Headworth Sq B3
Hendon Rd B3
High St East B3
High St West B2/B3
Holmeside B2
Hylton Rd B1
Information Ctr B2
John St B3
Kier Hardie Way A2
Lambton St B3
Laura St C3
Lawrence St B3
Leisure Centre B2
Library & Arts Centre B3
Lily St B1
Lime St B1
Livingstone Rd B2
Low Row B2
Matamba Terr B1
Millburn St B1
Millennium Way A2
Minster B2
Monkwearmouth Station Museum A2
Mowbray Park C3
Mowbray Rd C3
Murton St C3
National Glass Ctr A3
New Durham Rd C1
Newcastle Rd A2
Nile St B3
Norfolk St B3
North Bridge St A2
Northern Gallery for Contemporary Art B3
Otto Terr C1
Park La C2
Park Lane C2
Park Rd C2
Paul's Rd B3
Peel St C3
Police Station B2
Post Office B2
Priestly Cr A1
Queen St B2
Railway Row B1
Retail Park B1
Richmond St A2
Roker Ave A2
Royalty Theatre C1
Ryhope Rd C2
St Mary's Way B2
St Michael's Way B2
St Peter's A3
St Peter's A2
St Peter's Way A3
St Vincent St C3
Salem Rd C3
Salem St C3
Salisbury St C3
Sans St B3
Silkworth Row B1
Southwick Rd A2
Stadium of Light (Sunderland AFC) A2
Stadium Way A2
Stobart St A2
Stockton Rd C2
Suffolk St C3
Sunderland Aquatic Centre A2
Sunderland B2
Sunderland Mus B3
Sunderland Station B2
Sunderland St B3
Tatham St C3
Tavistock Pl B3
The Bridges B2
The Place B3
The Royalty C1
Thelma St C1
Thomas St North A2
Thornholme Rd C1
Toward Rd C3
Transport Interchange C2
Trimdon St Way B1
Tunstall Rd C2
University C1
University Library C1
University of Sunderland (City Campus) B1
University of Sunderland (Sir Tom Cowie at St Peter's Campus) A3
Vaux Brewery Way A2
Villiers St B3
Villiers St South B3
Vine Pl C2
Violet St B1
Walton La B3
Waterworks Rd B1
Wearmouth Bridge B2
Wellington La A1
West Sunniside B3
West Wear St B3
Westbourne Rd B1
Western Hill C1
Wharncliffe B1
Whickham St A3
White House Rd C3
Wilson St North A2
Winter Gdns C3
Wreath Quay A1

Swansea 343
Abertawe

Adelaide St C3
Albert Row C3
Alexandra Rd B3
Argyle St C1
Baptist Well Pl A2
Beach St C1
Belle Vue Way B3
Berw Rd A1
Berwick Terr A2
Bond St C1
Brangwyn Concert Hall C1
Bridge St A3
Brookands Terr B1
Brunswick St C1
Bryn-Syfi Terr A2
Bryn-y-Mor Rd C1
Bullins La B1
Burrows Rd C1
Bus/Rail link A3
Bus Station C2
Cadfan Rd A1
Cadrawd Rd A1
Caer St B3
Carig Cr A1
Carlton Terr B2
Carmarthen Rd A3
Castle Square B3
Castle St B3
Catherine St C1
Cinema C3
Civic Centre & Library C2
Clarence St C2
Colbourne Terr A2
Constitution Hill B1
Court B3
Creidiol Rd A2
Cromwell St B2
Duke St B1
Dunvant Pl C2
Dyfatty Park A3
Dyfatty St A3
Dyfed Ave A1
Dylan Thomas Ctr B3
Dylan Thomas Theatre C3
Eaton Cr C1
Eigen Cr A1
Elfed Rd A1
Emlyn Rd A1
Evans Terr A3
Fairfield Terr B1
Ffynone Dr B1
Ffynone Rd B1
Fire Station B3
Firm St A2
Fleet St C1
Francis St C1
Fullers Row B2
George St B2
Glamorgan St C2
Glyndwr Pl A1
Graig Terr A3
Grand Theatre C2
Granogwen Rd A2
Guildhall C1
Guildhall Rd South C1
Gwent Rd A1
Gwynedd Ave A1
Hafod St A3
Hanover St B1
Harcourt St B2
Harries St A2
Heathfield B2
Henrietta St B1
Hewson St B2
High St A3/B3
High View A2
Hill St A2
Historic Ships Berth C3
HM Prison C2
Information Ctr C2
Islwyn Rd A1
King Edward's Rd C1
Law Courts C1
Long Ridge A2
Madoc St C2
Mansel St B2
Maritime Quarter C3
Market B3
Mayhill Gdns B1
Mayhill Rd A1
Mega Bowl B3
Milton Terr A2
Mission Gallery C3
Montpellier Terr B1
Morfa Rd A3
Mount Pleasant B2
National Waterfront Museum C3
Nelson St C2
New Cut Rd A3
New St A3
Nicander Pde A2
Nicander Pl A2
Nicholl St B2
Norfolk St B2
North Hill Rd A2
Northampton La B2
Orchard St B3
Oxford St B2
Oystermouth Rd C1
Page St B2
Pant-y-Celyn Rd B1
Parc Tawe Link B3
Parc Tawe North B3
Parc Tawe Sh & L Ctr B3
Patti Pavilion C1
Paxton St C2
Penmaen Terr B1
Pen-y-Graig Rd A1
Phillips Pde C1
Picton Terr B2
Plantasia B3
Police Station B2
Post Office A1/A2/B2/C1
Powys Ave A1
Primrose St B2
Princess Way B3
Promenade B2
Pryder Gdns A1
Quadrant Centre C2
Quay Park B3
Rhianfa La B1
Rhondda St B2
Richardson St C2
Rodney St C1
Rose Hill B1
Rosehill Terr B1
Russell St B1
St Helen's Ave C1
St Helen's Cr C1
St Helen's Rd C1
St James Gdns B1
St James's Cr B1
St Mary's B3
Sea View Terr A3
Singleton St C2
South Dock C3
Stanley Pl B2
Strand B3
Swansea Castle B3
Swansea Coll Arts Ctr C1
Swansea Metropolitan University B2
Swansea Museum C3
Swansea Station A3
Taliesyn Rd B1
Tan y Marian Rd A1
Tegid Rd A2
Teilo Cr A1
Terrace Rd B1/B2
The Kingsway B2
The LC C3
Tontine St A3
Tower of Eclipse C3
Townhill Rd A1
Tramshed The C3
Trawler Rd C3
Union St B2
Upper Strand A3
Vernon St A3
Victoria Quay C3
Victoria Rd B3
Vincent St C1
Walter Rd B1
Watkin St A2
Waun-Wen Rd A2
Wellington St C2
Westbury St C1
Western St C1
Westway C2
William St C2
Wind St B3
Woodlands Terr B1
YMCA B2
York St C3

Swindon 343

Albert St C3
Albion St C1
Alfred St A2
Alvescot Rd C3
Art Gallery & Mus C3
Ashford Rd C1
Aylesbury St A2
Bath Rd C2
Bathampton St B1
Bathurst Rd B3
Beatrice St A2
Beckhampton St B3
Bowood Rd C1
Bristol St B1
Broad St A3
Brunel Arcade B2
Brunel Plaza B2
Brunswick St C2
Bus Station B2
Cambria Bridge Rd B1
Cambria Place B1
Canal Walk B2
Carfax St B2
Carr St B1
Cemetery C1/C3
Chandler Cl C3
Chapel C1
Chester St B1
Christ Church C3
Church Place B1
Cirencester Way A3
Clarence St B2
Clifton St C1
Cockleberry A2
Colbourne A3
Colbourne St A3
College St B2
Commercial Rd B2
Corporation St A2
Council Offices B3
County Rd A3
Courts B2
Cricket Ground A3
Cricklade Street C3
Crombey St B1/C2
Cross St C2
Curtis St B1
Deacon St C1
Designer Outlet (Great Western) B1
Dixon St C2
Dover St C2
Dowling St C2
Drove Rd C3
Dryden St C1
Durham St C3
East St B1
Eastcott Hill C2
Eastcott Rd C2
Edgeware Rd B2
Edmund St C2
Elmina Rd A3
Emlyn Square B1
Euclid St B3
Exeter St B1
Fairview C1
Faringdon Rd B1
Farnsby St B1
Fire Station B3
Fleet St B2
Fleming Way B2/B3
Florence St A2
Gladstone St A3
Gooch St A2
Graham St A3
Great Western Way A1/A2
Groundwell Rd B3
Hawksworth Way A1
Haydon St A2
Henry St B2
Hillside Ave C1
Holbrook Way B2
Hunt St C3
Hydro B1
Hythe Rd C2
Information Ctr B2
Joseph St C1
Kent Rd C2
King William St C2
Kingshill Rd C1
Lansdown Rd C2
Leicester St B3
Library B2
Lincoln St B3
Little London C3
London St B1
Magic B3
Maidstone Rd C2
Manchester Rd A3
Maxwell St B1
Milford St B2
Milton Rd B1
Morse St C2
National Monuments Record Centre B1
Newcastle St B3
Newcombe Drive A1
Newcombe Trading Estate A1
Newhall St C2
North St C2
North Star Ave A1
North Star A1
Northampton St B3
Oasis Leisure Centre A1
Ocotal Way A3
Okus Rd C1
Old Town C3
Oxford St B1
Park Lane B1
Park Lane B1
Pembroke St C2
Plymouth St B3
Polaris House A2
Polaris Way A2
Police Station B2
Ponting St A2
Post Office B1/B2/C1/C3
Poulton St A3
Princes St B2
Prospect Hill C2
Prospect Place C2
Queen St B2
Queen's Park C3
Radnor St C1
Read St C1
Reading St B1
Regent St B2
Retail Park A2/A3/B3
Rosebery St A3
St Mark's B1
Salisbury St A3
Savernake St C2
Shelley St C1
Sheppard St B1
South St C2
Southampton St B3
Spring Gardens B3
Stafford Street C2
Stanier St C2
Station Road A2
STEAM B1
Swindon College A2
Swindon Rd C2
Swindon Station A2
Swindon Town Football Club A3
T A Centre B1
Tennyson St B1
The Lawn C3
The Nurseries C1
The Parade B2
The Park B1
Theobald St B1
Town Hall B2
Transfer Bridges A3
Union St C2
Upham Rd C3
Victoria Rd C3
Walcot Rd B3
War Memorial B2
Wells St B3
Western St C2
Westmorland Rd B3
Whalebridge B2
Whitehead St C1
Whitehouse Rd A2
William St C1
Wood St C3
Wyvern Theatre & Arts Centre B2
York Rd B3

Taunton 343

Addison Gr A1
Albemarle Rd A1
Alfred St B3
Alma St C2
Bath Pl C1
Belvedere Rd A1
Billet St B2
Billetfield C2
Birch Gr A1
Brewhouse Theatre B2
Bridge St B1
Bridgwater & Taunton Canal A2
Broadlands Rd C1
Burton Pl C1
Bus Station B1
Canal Rd A2
Cann St C1
Canon St B2
Castle B1
Castle St B1
Cheddon Rd A2
Chip Lane A1
Clarence St B1
Cleveland St B1
Clifton Terr A2
Coleridge Cres C3
Compass Hill C1
Compton Cl A2
Corporation St B1
Council Offices A1
County Walk Sh Ctr C2
Courtyard B2
Cranmer Rd B2
Critchard Way B3
Cyril St A1
Deller's Wharf B1
Duke St B2
East Reach B3
East St B3
Eastbourne Rd B2
Eastleigh Rd C3
Eaton Cres A2
Elm Gr A1
Elms Cl A1
Fons George C1
Fore St B2
Fowler St A1
French Weir Rec Grd B1
Geoffrey Farrant Wk A2
Gray's Almshouses B2
Grays Rd B3
Greenway Ave A1
Guildford Pl C1
Hammet St B2
Haydon Rd B3
Heavitree Way A2
Herbert St A1
High St C2
Holway Ave C3
Hugo St B3
Huish's Almshouses B2
Hurdle Way C2
Information Ctr C2
Jubilee St A1
King's College C3
Kings Cl C3
Laburnum St B2
Lambrook Rd B3
Lansdowne Rd A3
Leslie Ave A1
Leycroft Rd B3
Library C2
Linden Gr A1
Magdalene St B2
Magistrates Court B1
Malvern Terr A2
Market House B2
Mary St C2
Middle St B2
Midford Rd B3
Mitre Court B3
Mount Nebo C1
Mount St C2
Mountway C2
Mus of Somerset B1
North St B2
Northfield Ave B1
Northfield Rd B1
Northleigh Rd C3
Obridge Allotments A3
Obridge Lane A3
Obridge Rd A3
Obridge Viaduct A3
Old Mkt Shopping Ctr C2
Osborne Way C1
Park St C1
Paul St C2
Plais St A2
Playing Field C3
Police Station C1
Portland St B1
Post Office B1/B2/C1
Priorswood Ind Est A3
Priorswood Rd A2
Priory Ave B2
Priory Bridge Rd B2
Priory Fields Retail Pk A3
Priory Park A2
Priory Way A3
Queen St B3
Railway St A1
Records Office A2
Recreation Grd A1
Riverside Place B2
St Augustine St B2
St George's C2
St Georges Sq C2
St James B2
St James St B2
St John's C1
St John's Rd B1
St Josephs Field C2
St Mary Magdalene B2
Samuels Ct A1
Shire Hall & Law Courts C1
Somerset County Cricket Ground B2
Somerset County Hall C1
Somerset Cricket B2
South Rd C3
South St C3
Staplegrove Rd B1
Station Rd A1
Stephen St B2
Swimming Pool A1
Tancred St B2
Tauntfield Cl C3
Taunton Deane Cricket Club C2
Taunton Station A2
The Avenue A1
The Crescent C1
The Mount C2
Thomas St A1
Toneway A3
Tower St B1
Trevor Smith Pl C3
Trinity Bsns Centre C3
Trinity Rd C3
Trinity St B3
Trull Rd C1
Tudor House B2
Upper High St C1
Venture Way A3
Victoria Gate B3
Victoria Park B3
Victoria St B3
Viney St B3
Vivary Park C2
Vivary Rd C1
War Memorial C1
Wellesley St A2
Wheatley Cres A3
Whitehall A1
Wilfred Rd B3
William St A1
Wilton Church C1
Wilton Cl C1
Wilton Gr C1
Wilton St C1
Winchester St B2
Winters Field B2
Wood St B1
Yarde Pl B1

Telford 343

Alma Ave C1
Amphitheatre C2
Bowling Alley B2
Brandsfarm Way C3
Brunel Rd B1
Bus Station B2
Buxton Rd C1
Central Park A2
Civic Offices B2
Coach Central B2
Coachwell Cl B1
Colliers Way A1
Courts B2
Dale Acre Way B3
Darliston C3
Deepdale B3
Deercote B2
Dinthill C3
Doddington C3
Dodmoor Grange C3
Downemead B3
Duffryn B3
Dunsheath B3
Euston Way A3
Eyton Mound C1
Eyton Rd C1
Forgegate A2
Grange Central B2
Hall Park Way B1
Hinkshay Rd C2
Hollinsworth Rd A2
Holyhead Rd A3
Housing Trust A1
Ice Rink B2
Information Ctr B2
Ironmasters Way A2
Job Centre B1
Land Registry B1
Lawn Central B2
Lawnswood C1
Library B2
Malinsgate B1
Matlock Ave C1
Moor Rd C1
Mount Rd C1
NFU Offices B1
Odeon B2
Park Lane A1
Police Station B1
Priorslee Ave A3
Queen Elizabeth Ave C3
Queen Elizabeth Way B1
Queensway A2/B3
Rampart Way A2
Randlay Ave C3
Randlay Wood C3
Rhodes Ave C1
Royal Way B1
St Leonards Rd B1
St Quentin Gate B2
Shifnal Rd A3
Sixth Ave A1
Southwater Way B1
Spout Lane C1
Spout Mound B1
Spout Way C1
Stafford Court B3
Stafford Park B3
Stirchley Ave C3
Stone Row C1
Telford Bridge Ret Pk A1
Telford Central Sta A3
Telford Centre, The B2
Telford Forge Sh Pk A1
Telford Hornets RFC C2
Telford Int Ctr C2
Telford Way A3
Third Ave A2
Town Park C2
Town Park Visitor Ctr B2
Walker House B2
Wellswood Ave A2
West Centre Way B1
Withywood Drive C1
Woodhouse Central B2
Yates Way A1

Torquay 344

Abbey Rd B2
Alexandra Rd A2
Alpine Rd B3
Ash Hill Rd A2
Babbacombe Rd B3
Bampfylde Rd B1
Barton Rd A1
Beacon Quay C2
Belgrave Rd A1/B1
Belmont Rd A3
Berea Rd A3
Braddons Hill Rd East B3
Brewery Park A3
Bronshill Rd A2
Castle Circus A2
Castle Rd A2
Cavern Rd A3
Central B2
Chatsworth Rd A2
Chestnut Ave B1
Church St A1
Civic Offices A2
Coach Station A1
Corbyn Head C1
Croft Hill B1
Croft Rd B1
Daddyhole Plain C3
East St A1
Egerton Rd A3
Ellacombe Church Rd A3
Ellacombe Rd A2
Falkland Rd B1
Fleet St B2
Fleet Walk Sh Ctr B2
Grafton Rd B3
Haldon Pier C2
Hatfield Rd A2
Highbury Rd A2
Higher Warberry Rd A3
Hillesdon Rd B3
Hollywood Bowl C3
Hoxton Rd A3
Hunsdon Rd B3
Information Ctr B2
Inner Harbour C3
Kenwyn Rd A3
Laburnum St A1
Law Courts A2
Library A2
Lime Ave B1
Living Coasts C3
Lower Warberry Rd B3
Lucius St B1
Lymington Rd A1
Magdalene Rd A1
Marina C2
Market Forum The B2
Market St B2
Meadfoot Lane C3
Meadfoot Rd C3
Melville St B2
Middle Warberry Rd B3
Mill Lane A1
Montpellier Rd B3
Morgan Ave A1
Museum Rd B3
Newton Rd A1
Oakhill Rd A1
Outer Harbour C2
Parkhill Rd C3
Pavilion Shopping Ctr C2
Pimlico B2
Police Station A1
Post Office A1/B2
Princes Rd A3
Princes Rd East A3
Princes Rd West A3
Princess Gdns C2
Princess Pier C2
Princess Theatre C2
Rathmore Rd B1
Recreation Grd B1
Riviera Int Ctr B1
Rock End Ave C3
Rock Rd B2
Rock Walk B2
Rosehill Rd A3
St Efride's Rd A1
St John's B3
St Luke's Rd B2
St Luke's Rd North B2
St Luke's Rd South B2
St Marychurch Rd A2
Scarborough Rd B1
Shedden Hill B2
South Pier C2
South St A1
Spanish Barn B1
Stitchill Rd B3
Strand B3
Sutherland Rd B3
Teignmouth Rd A1
Temperance St B2
The King's Drive B1
The Terrace B3
Thurlow Rd A1
Tor Bay B1
Tor Church Rd A1
Tor Hill Rd A1
Torbay Rd B2
Torquay Museum B3
Torquay Station C1
Torre Abbey Mansion B1
Torre Abbey Meadows B1
Torre Abbey Sands B1
Torwood Gdns B3
Torwood St C3
Town Hall A2
Union Square A2
Union St A1
Upton Hill A2
Upton Park A1
Upton Rd A1
Vanehill Rd C3
Vansittart Rd A1
Vaughan Parade C2
Victoria Parade C3
Victoria Rd A2
Warberry Rd West B2
Warren Rd B2
Windsor Rd A2/A3
Woodville Rd A3

Truro 344

Adelaide Ter B1
Agar Rd B3
Arch Hill C2
Arundell Pl C2
Avondale Rd B1
Back Quay B3
Barrack La C3
Barton Meadow A1
Benson Rd A2
Bishops Cl A2
Bosvean Gdns B1
Bosvigo Gardens B1
Bosvigo La A1
Bosvigo Rd B2
Broad St A3
Burley Cl C3
Bus Station B3
Calenick St B2
Campfield Hill B3
Carclew St B3
Carew Rd A2
Carey Park B2
Carlyon Rd A2
Carvoza Rd A3
Castle St B2
Cathedral View A2
Chainwalk Dr A2
Chapel Hill B1
Charles St B2
City Hall B3
City Rd B2
Coinage Hall B3
Comprigney Hill A1
Coosebean La A1
Copes Gdns A2
County Hall B1
Courtney Rd A2
Crescent Rd B1
Crescent Rise B1
Daniell Court C2
Daniell Rd C2
Daniell St C2
Daubuz Cl A2
Dobbs La B1
Edward St B2
Eliot Rd A2
Elm Court A3
Enys Cl A1
Enys Rd A1
Fairmantle St B3
Falmouth Rd C2
Ferris Town B2
Fire Station B1
Frances St B2
George St B2
Green Cl C2
Green La C1
Grenville Rd A2
Hall For Cornwall B3
Hendra Rd A2
Hendra Vean A1
High Cross B3
Higher Newham La C3
Higher Trehaverne A2
Hillcrest Ave B1
Hospital B2
Hunkin Cl A2
Hurland Rd C3
Infirmary Hill B2
James Pl B3
Kenwyn Church Rd A1
Kenwyn Hill A1
Kenwyn Rd A2
Kenwyn St B2
Kerris Gdns A1
King St B3
Lemon Quay B3
Lemon St Gallery B3
Library B1/B3
Malpas Rd B3
Market
Memorial Gdns B3
Merrifield Close B1
Mitchell Hill A3
Moresk Cl A3
Moresk Rd A3
Morlaix Ave C3
Nancemere Rd A3
Newham Bsns Park C3
Newham Industrial Est C3
Newham Rd C3
Northfield Dr C3
Oak Way A3
Old County Hall B1
Pal's Terr A3
Park View C2
Pendarves Rd A2
Plaza Cinema B3
Police Station B3
Post Office B2/B3
Prince's St B3
Pydar St A2
Quay St B3
Redannick Cres C2
Redannick La B2
Richard Lander Monument C2
Richmond Hill B1
River St B2
Rosedale Rd A2
Royal Cornwall Mus B2
St Aubyn Rd C3
St Clement St B3
St George's Rd A1
School La C2
Station Rd B1
Stokes Rd A2
Strangways Terr C3
Tabernacle St B3
The Avenue A3
The Crescent B1
The Leats B2
The Spires A2
Trehaverne La A2
Tremayne Rd A2
Treseder's Gdns A3
Treworder Rd B1
Treyew Rd B1
Truro Cathedral B3
Truro Harbour Office B3
Truro Station B3
Union St B2
Upper School La C2
Victoria Gdns B2
Waterfall Gdns B2

Wick 344

Ackergill Cres A2
Ackergill St A2
Albert St C2
Ambulance Station C2
Argyle Sq C2
Assembly Rooms C2

361

Index to road maps of Britain

W Isles
Highland
Moray
Aberds
Aberdeen
Perth and Kinross
Angus
Dundee
Argyll and Bute
Stirling
Fife
Glasgow
Edin
E Loth
N Ayrs
S Lanark
Midloth
E Ayrs
Borders
S Ayrs
Dumfries and Galloway
Northumberland
Tyne and Wear
Hartlepool
Redcar and Cleveland
Middlesbrough
Darlington
Stockton-on-Tees
Cumbria
Durham
IoM
North Yorkshire
York
E Yorks
Blackpool
Lancs
W Yorks
N Lincs
NE Lincs
Gtr Man
S Yorks
Mers
Anglesey
Conwy
Flint
Denb
Wrex
Ches
Derbys
Notts
Lincolnshire
Gwyn
Staffs
Telford
Leics
Rutland
Norfolk
Shrops
W Mid
Ceredigion
Powys
Worcs
Warks
Northants
Cambs
Hereford
Bedford
Suffolk
C Beds
Pembs
Carms
Mon
Glos
Bucks
Herts
Essex
Swansea
Cardiff
Bristol
Oxon
W Berks
London
Southend
Medway
Wilts
Surrey
Kent
Somerset
Hants
Devon
Dorset
Soton
W Sus
E Sus
IoW
Ptsmouth
Brighton
Cornwall
Torbay
Bmouth
Poole
Plymouth
Scilly

Abbreviations used in the index

Aberdeen	Aberdeen City
Aberds	Aberdeenshire
Ald	Alderney
Anglesey	Isle of Anglesey
Angus	Angus
Argyll	Argyll and Bute
Bath	Bath and North East Somerset
Bedford	Bedford
Bl Gwent	Blaenau Gwent
Blackburn	Blackburn with Darwen
Blackpool	Blackpool
Bmouth	Bournemouth
Borders	Scottish Borders
Brack	Bracknell
Bridgend	Bridgend
Brighton	City of Brighton and Hove
Bristol	City and County of Bristol
Bucks	Buckinghamshire
C Beds	Central Bedfordshire
Caerph	Caerphilly
Cambs	Cambridgeshire
Cardiff	Cardiff
Carms	Carmarthenshire
Ceredig	Ceredigion
Ches E	Cheshire East
Ches W	Cheshire West and Chester
Clack	Clackmannanshire
Conwy	Conwy
Corn	Cornwall
Cumb	Cumbria
Darl	Darlington
Denb	Denbighshire
Derby	City of Derby
Derbys	Derbyshire
Devon	Devon
Dorset	Dorset
Dumfries	Dumfries and Galloway
Dundee	Dundee City
Durham	Durham
E Ayrs	East Ayrshire
E Dunb	East Dunbartonshire
E Loth	East Lothian
E Renf	East Renfrewshire
E Sus	East Sussex
E Yorks	East Riding of Yorkshire
Edin	City of Edinburgh
Essex	Essex
Falk	Falkirk
Fife	Fife
Flint	Flintshire
Glasgow	City of Glasgow
Glos	Gloucestershire
Gtr Man	Greater Manchester
Guern	Guernsey
Gwyn	Gwynedd
Halton	Halton
Hants	Hampshire
Hereford	Herefordshire
Herts	Hertfordshire
Highld	Highland
Hrtlpl	Hartlepool
Hull	Hull
IoM	Isle of Man
IoW	Isle of Wight
Invclyd	Inverclyde
Jersey	Jersey
Kent	Kent
Lancs	Lancashire
Leicester	City of Leicester
Leics	Leicestershire
Lincs	Lincolnshire
London	Greater London
Luton	Luton
M Keynes	Milton Keynes
M Tydf	Merthyr Tydfil
Mbro	Middlesbrough
Medway	Medway
Mers	Merseyside
Midloth	Midlothian
Mon	Monmouthshire
Moray	Moray
N Ayrs	North Ayrshire
N Lincs	North Lincolnshire
N Lanark	North Lanarkshire
N Som	North Somerset
N Yorks	North Yorkshire
NE Lincs	North East Lincolnshire
Neath	Neath Port Talbot
Newport	City and County of Newport
Norf	Norfolk
Northants	Northamptonshire
Northumb	Northumberland
Nottingham	City of Nottingham
Notts	Nottinghamshire
Orkney	Orkney
Oxon	Oxfordshire
Pboro	Peterborough
Pembs	Pembrokeshire
Perth	Perth and Kinross
Plym	Plymouth
Poole	Poole
Powys	Powys
Ptsmth	Portsmouth
Reading	Reading
Redcar	Redcar and Cleveland
Renfs	Renfrewshire
Rhondda	Rhondda Cynon Taff
Rutland	Rutland
S Ayrs	South Ayrshire
S Glos	South Gloucestershire
S Lanark	South Lanarkshire
S Yorks	South Yorkshire
Scilly	Scilly
Shetland	Shetland
Shrops	Shropshire
Slough	Slough
Som	Somerset
Soton	Southampton
Staffs	Staffordshire
Southend	Southend-on-Sea
Stirling	Stirling
Stockton	Stockton-on-Tees
Stoke	Stoke-on-Trent
Suff	Suffolk
Sur	Surrey
Swansea	Swansea
Swindon	Swindon
T&W	Tyne and Wear
Telford	Telford & Wrekin
Thurrock	Thurrock
Torbay	Torbay
Torf	Torfaen
V Glam	The Vale of Glamorgan
W Berks	West Berkshire
W Dunb	West Dunbartonshire
W Isles	Western Isles
W Loth	West Lothian
W Mid	West Midlands
W Sus	West Sussex
W Yorks	West Yorkshire
Warks	Warwickshire
Warr	Warrington
Wilts	Wiltshire
Windsor	Windsor and Maidenhead
Wokingham	Wokingham
Worcs	Worcestershire
Wrex	Wrexham
York	City of York

How to use the index

Example **Blatherwycke** Northants **137** D9

- grid square
- page number
- county or unitary authority

Aar–Alm

A

Aaron's Hill Sur 50 E3
Aaron's Town Cumb 240 E2
Abbas Combe Som 30 C2
Abberley Worcs 116 D5
Abberton Essex 89 B8
Worcs 117 G9
Abberwick Northumb 264 G4
Abbess End Essex 87 C9
Abbess Roding Essex 87 C9
Abbey Devon 27 E10
Abbeycwmhir Powys 113 C11
Abbey-cwm-hir Powys 113 C11
Abbeydale Glos 80 B5
S Yorks 186 E4
Abbeydale Park S Yorks 186 E4
Abbey Dore Hereford 97 E7
Abbey Field Essex 107 G9
Abbey Gate Kent 53 B9
Abbey Green Shrops 149 C10
Staffs 169 D7
Abbey Hey Gtr Man 184 B5
Abbeyhill Edin 280 G5
Abbey Hulton Stoke 168 F6
Abbey Mead Sur 66 F4
Abbey St Bathans
Borders 272 C5
Abbeystead Lancs 203 C7
Abbey Town Cumb 238 G5
Abbey Village Lancs 194 C6
Abbey Wood London 68 D3
Abbots Bickington Devon 24 E5
Abbots Bromley Staffs 151 E11
Abbotsbury Dorset 17 D7
Abbotsford W Sus 36 C4
Abbotsham Devon 24 B6
Abbotskerswell Devon 9 B7
Abbots Langley Herts 85 E9
Abbotsleigh Devon 8 F6
Abbots Leigh N Som 60 E4
Abbotsley Cambs 122 F4
Abbot's Meads Ches W 166 B5
Abbots Morton Worcs 117 F10
Abbots Ripton Cambs 122 B4
Abbots Salford Warks 117 G11
Abbotstone Hants 48 G5
Abbotswood Hants 32 C5
Sur 50 C4
Abbots Worthy Hants 48 G3
Abbotts Ann Hants 47 E10
Abcott Shrops 115 B7
Abdon Shrops 131 F11
Abdy S Yorks 186 B6
Aber Ceredig 93 B9
Aberaeron Ceredig 111 E9
Aberaman Rhondda 77 E8
Aberangell Gwyn 146 G6
Aber-Arad Carms 92 D6
Aberarder Highld 290 E6
Aberarder House Highld 300 G6
Aberarder Lodge Highld 291 E7
Aberargie Perth 286 F5
Aberarth Ceredig 111 E9
Aberavon Neath 57 C8
Aber-banc Ceredig 93 C7
Aberbargoed Caerph 77 E11
Aberbechan Powys 130 E2
Aberbeeg Bl Gwent 78 E2
Aberbran Powys 95 F9
Abercanaid M Tydf 77 E9
Abercarn Caerph 78 G2
Abercastle Pembs 91 E7
Abercegir Powys 128 C6
Aberchalder Highld 290 C5
Aberchirder Aberds 302 D6
Abercorn W Loth 279 F11
Aber Cowarch Gwyn 147 F7
Abercraf Powys 76 C4
Abercregan Neath 57 B11
Abercrombie Fife 287 G9
Abercwmboi Rhondda 77 F8
Abercych Pembs 92 C4
Abercynafon Powys 77 B9
Abercynffig / Aberkenfig
Bridgend 57 E11
Abercynon Rhondda 77 F9
Aberdalgie Perth 286 E4
Aberdâr / Aberdare
Rhondda 77 E7
Aberdare / Aberdâr
Rhondda 77 E7
Aberdaron Gwyn 144 D3
Aberdeen Aberdeen 293 C11
Aberdesach Gwyn 162 E6
Aberdour Fife 280 D3
Aberdovey / Aberdyfi
Gwyn 128 D2
Aberdulais Neath 76 E3
Aberdyfi / Aberdovey
Gwyn 128 D2
Aberedw Powys 95 B11
Abereiddy Pembs 90 E5
Abererch Gwyn 145 B7
Aberfan M Tydf 77 E9
Aberfeldy Perth 286 C2
Aberffraw Anglesey 162 B5
Aberffrwd Ceredig 112 B3
Mon 78 D5
Aberford W Yorks 206 F4
Aberfoyle Stirl 285 G9
Abergarw Bridgend 58 C2
Abergarwed Neath 76 E4
Abergavenny Mon 78 C3
Abergele Conwy 180 F6
Aber-Giâr Carms 93 C10
Abergorlech Carms 93 E11
Abergwaun / Fishguard
Pembs 91 D9
Abergwesyn Powys 113 G7
Abergwili Carms 93 G8
Abergwynant Gwyn 146 F3
Abergwynfi Neath 57 B11
Aber-gwynfi Neath 57 B11
Abergwyngregyn Gwyn 179 G11
Abergynolwyn Gwyn 128 B3
Aber-Hirnant Gwyn 147 C9
Aberhosan Powys 128 D6
Aberkenfig / Abercynffig
Bridgend 57 E11
Aberlady E Loth 281 E9
Aberlemno Angus 287 B9
Aberlerry Ceredig 128 E2
Aberllefenni Gwyn 128 B5
Aberllydan / Broad Haven
Pembs 72 C5
Aberllynfi / Three Cocks
Powys 96 D3
Abermagwr Ceredig 112 C3
Abermaw / Barmouth
Gwyn 146 F2
Abermeurig Ceredig 111 F11
Aber miwl / Abermule
Powys 130 E3
Abermorddu Flint 166 D4
Abermule / Aber-miwl
Powys 130 E3
Abernaint Powys 148 E2
Abernant Carms 92 G6
Powys 130 D3
Aber-nant Rhondda 77 E8
Abernethy Perth 286 F5
Abernyte Perth 286 D6
Aber-oer Wrex 166 F3
Aberogwr / Ogmore by Sea
V Glam 57 F11
Aberpennar / Mountain Ash
Rhondda 77 F8
Aberporth Ceredig 110 G5
Aber-Rhiwlech Gwyn 147 E8
Aberriw / Berriew
Powys 130 C3
Abersoch Gwyn 144 D6
Abersychan Torf 78 E3
Abertawe / Swansea
Swansea 56 C6
Aberteifi / Cardigan
Ceredig 92 B3
Aberthin V Glam 58 D4
Abertillery Bl Gwent 78 E2
Abertridwr Caerph 58 B6
Powys 147 F10
Abertrinant Gwyn 128 B2
Abertysswg Caerph 77 D10
Aberuchill Castle
Perth 285 E11
Aberuthven Perth 286 F3
Aber-Village Powys 96 G2
Aberyscir Powys 95 F9
Aberystwyth Ceredig 111 A11
Abhainn Suidhe
W Isles 305 H2
Abingdon Oxon 83 F7
Abinger Common Sur 50 D6
Abinger Hammer Sur 50 D5
Abington Northants 120 E5
S Lnrk 259 E10
Abington Pigotts Cambs 104 C6
Abington Vale Northants 120 E5
Abingworth W Sus 35 D10
Ab Kettleby Leics 154 E4
Ab Lench Worcs 117 G10
Ablington Glos 81 D10
Wilts 47 D7
Abney Derbys 185 F11
Aboyne Aberds 293 D7
Abraham Heights Lancs 211 G9
Abram Gtr Man 194 G6
Abriachan Highld 300 F5
Abridge Essex 87 F7
Abronhill N Lnrk 278 F5
Abshot Hants 33 F8
Abson S Glos 61 E8
Abthorpe Northants 102 B2
Abune-the-Hill Orkney 314 D2
Aby Lincs 190 F6
Acaster Malbis York 207 D7
Acaster Selby N Yorks 207 E7
Accrington Lancs 195 B9
Acha Argyll 275 B8
Argyll 288 D3
Achabraid Argyll 275 E9
Achachork Highld 298 E4
Achadh an Eas Highld 308 F6
Achad nan Darach
Highld 284 B4
Achadunan Argyll 284 F5
Achafolla Argyll 275 B8
Achagary Highld 308 D7
Achaglass Argyll 255 C8
Achahoish Argyll 275 F8
Achalader Perth 286 C5
Achallader Argyll 285 C7
Achalone Highld 310 D5
Acha Mor W Isles 304 F5
Achanalt Highld 300 C2
Achanamara Argyll 275 E8
Achandunie Highld 300 B6
Achanelid Argyll 275 E11
Ach'an Todhair Highld 290 F2
Achany Highld 309 J5
Achaphubuil Highld 290 F2
Acharacle Highld 289 C8
Acharn Highld 289 D9
Perth 285 C11
Acharole Highld 310 D6
Acharossan Argyll 275 F10
Acharry Muir Highld 309 K6
Achath Aberds 293 B9
Achavanich Highld 310 E5
Achavelgin Highld 301 D9
Achavraat Highld 301 E9
Achddu Carms 74 E6
Achdregnie Moray 302 G2
Achduart Highld 307 J5
Achentoul Highld 310 F2
Achfary Highld 306 F7
Achfrish Highld 309 H5
Achgarve Highld 307 K3
Achiemore Highld 308 C3
Highld 310 D2
A'Chill Highld 294 E4
Achiltibuie Highld 307 J5
Achina Highld 308 C7
Achinahuagh Highld 308 C5
Achindaul Highld 290 E3
Achindown Highld 301 E8
Achinduich Highld 309 J5
Achinduin Argyll 289 F10
Achingills Highld 310 C5
Achininver Highld 308 C5
Achintee Highld 290 F3
Highld 299 E9
Achintraid Highld 295 B10
Achlaven Argyll 289 F11
Achlean Highld 291 D10
Achleck Argyll 288 E6
Achlorachan Highld 300 D3
Achluachrach Highld 290 E4
Achlyness Highld 306 D7
Achmelvich Highld 307 G5
Achmore Highld 295 B10
Stirl 285 D9
Achnaba Argyll 275 E10
Argyll 289 F11
Achnabat Highld 300 F5
Achnabreck Argyll 275 D9
Achnacarnin Highld 306 F5
Achnacarry Highld 290 E3
Achnacloich Argyll 289 F11
Highld 295 E7
Achnaconeran Highld 290 B6
Achnacraig Argyll 288 E6
Achnacree Argyll 289 F11
Achnacree Bay Argyll 289 F11
Achnacroish Argyll 289 E10
Achnadrish Argyll 288 D6
Achnafalnich Argyll 284 E6
Achnagarron Highld 300 C6
Achnaha Highld 288 C6
Achnahanat Highld 309 K5
Achnahannet Highld 301 G9
Achnahard Argyll 288 G5
Achnairn Highld 309 H5
Achnaluachrach Highld 309 J6
Achnandarach Highld 295 B10
Achnanellan Highld 290 E2
Achnasaul Highld 290 E3
Achnasheen Highld 299 D11
Achnashelloch Argyll 275 D9
Achnavast Highld 310 C4
Achneigie Highld 299 B10
Achormlarie Highld 309 K6
Achorn Highld 310 F5
Achosnich Highld 288 C6
Achranich Highld 289 E9
Achreamie Highld 310 C4
Achriabhach Highld 290 G3
Achriesgill Highld 306 D7
Achrimsdale Highld 311 J3
Achtoty Highld 308 C6
Achurch Northants 137 G10
Achuvoldrach Highld 308 D5
Achvaich Highld 309 K7
Achvarasdal Highld 310 C3
Ackenthwaite Cumb 211 C10
Ackergill Highld 310 D7
Acklam Mbro 225 B9
N Yorks 216 G5
Ackleton Shrops 132 D5
Acklington Northumb 252 C6
Ackton W Yorks 198 C2
Ackworth Moor Top
W Yorks 198 D2
Acle Norf 161 G8
Acock's Green W Mid 134 G2
Acol Kent 71 F10
Acomb Northumb 241 D10
York 207 C7
Acre Gtr Man 196 F2
Lancs 195 C9
Acrefair Wrex 166 G3
Acres Nook Staffs 168 E4
Acre Street W Sus 21 B11
Acton Ches E 167 E10
Dorset 18 F5
London 67 C8
Shrops 130 G6
Staffs 168 G4
Suff 107 C7
Worcs 116 D6
Wrex 166 E4
Acton Beauchamp
Hereford 116 G3
Acton Bridge Ches W 183 F9
Acton Burnell Shrops 131 C10
Acton Green Hereford 116 G3
London 67 D8
Acton Pigott Shrops 131 C10
Acton Place Suff 107 B7
Acton Reynald Shrops 149 E10
Acton Round Shrops 132 D2
Acton Scott Shrops 131 F9
Acton Trussell Staffs 151 F8
Acton Turville S Glos 61 C10
Adabroc W Isles 304 B7
Adambrae W Loth 269 A10
Adam's Green Dorset 29 F8
Adbaston Staffs 150 D5
Adber Dorset 29 C9
Adbolton Notts 154 B2
Adderbury Oxon 101 D9
Adderley Shrops 150 B3
Adderley Green Stoke 168 G6
Adderstone Northumb 264 C4
Addiewell W Loth 269 C9
Addingham W Yorks 205 D7
Addingham Moorside
W Yorks 205 D7
Addington Bucks 102 F4
Corn 6 B5
Kent 53 B7
London 67 G11
Addinston Borders 271 E10
Addiscombe London 67 F10
Addlestone Sur 66 G5
Addlestonemoor Sur 66 F4
Addlethorpe Lincs 175 B8
Adel W Yorks 205 F11
Adeney Telford 150 F4
Adeyfield Herts 85 D9
Adfa Powys 129 C11
Adforton Hereford 115 C8
Adgestone IoW 21 D7
Adisham Kent 55 C8
Adlestrop Glos 100 F4
Adlingfleet E Yorks 199 C10
Adlington Ches E 184 E6
Lancs 194 E6
Adlington Park Lancs 194 E5
Admaston Staffs 151 E10
Telford 150 G2
Admington Warks 100 B4
Adpar Ceredig 92 C6
Adsborough Som 28 B3
Adscombe Som 43 F7
Adstock Bucks 102 E4
Adstone Northants 119 G11
Adswood Gtr Man 184 D5
Adversane W Sus 35 C9
Advie Highld 301 F11
Adwalton W Yorks 197 B8
Adwell Oxon 83 F11
Adwick le Street
S Yorks 198 F4
Adwick upon Dearne
S Yorks 198 G3
Adziel Aberds 303 D9
Ae Dumfries 247 F11
Ae Village Dumfries 247 F11
Affetside Gtr Man 195 E9
Affleck Aberds 303 G8
Affpuddle Dorset 18 C2
Affric Lodge Highld 299 G11
Afon Eitha Wrex 166 F3
Afon-wen Flint 181 G10
Afon Wen Gwyn 145 B8
Afton IoW 20 D2
Agar Nook Leics 153 G9
Agbrigg W Yorks 197 D10
Aggborough Worcs 116 B6
Agglethorpe N Yorks 213 B11
Aglionby Cumb 239 F10
Agneash IoM 192 D5
Aifft Denb 165 B10
Aigburth Mers 182 D5
Aiginis W Isles 304 E6
Aike E Yorks 209 D7
Aikenway Moray 302 E2
Aikerness Orkney 314 A4
Aikers Orkney 314 G4
Aiketgate Cumb 230 B5
Aikton Cumb 239 G7
Ailby Lincs 190 F6
Ailey Hereford 96 B6
Ailstone Warks 118 G4
Ailsworth Pboro 138 D2
Aimes Green Essex 86 E5
Ainderby Quernhow
N Yorks 215 C7
Ainderby Steeple
N Yorks 224 G6
Aingers Green Essex 108 G2
Ainley Top W Yorks 196 D6
Ainsdale Mers 193 E10
Ainsdale-on-Sea Mers 193 E9
Ainstable Cumb 230 B6
Ainsworth Gtr Man 195 E9
Ainthorpe N Yorks 226 D4
Aintree Mers 182 B5
Aird Argyll 275 C8
Dumfries 236 C2
Highld 299 B7
W Isles 296 F3
W Isles 304 E7
Airdachuilinn Highld 306 E7
Aird a Mhachair
W Isles 297 G3
Aird a' Mhulaidh
W Isles 305 G3
Aird Asaig W Isles 305 H3
Aird Dhail W Isles 304 B6
Airdens Highld 309 K6
Airdeny Argyll 289 G11
Aird Mhidhinis W Isles 297 L3
Aird Mhighe W Isles 296 C6
W Isles 305 J3
Aird Mhòr W Isles 297 G4
Aird Mhor W Isles 297 L3
Aird of Sleat Highld 295 E7
Airdrie N Lnrk 268 B5
Airds of Kells Dumfries 237 B8
Aird Thunga W Isles 304 E6
Airdtorrisdale Highld 308 C6
Aird Uig W Isles 304 E2
Airedale W Yorks 198 B3
Aire View N Yorks 204 D5
Airidh a Bhruaich
W Isles 305 G4
Airieland Dumfries 237 D9
Airinis W Isles 304 E6
Airlie Angus 287 B7
Airlies Dumfries 236 D5
Airmyn E Yorks 199 B8
Airntully Perth 286 D4
Airor Highld 295 E9
Airth Falk 279 D7
Airthrey Castle Stirl 278 B6
Airton N Yorks 204 B4
Airyhassen Dumfries 236 E5
Airy Hill N Yorks 227 D7
Airyligg Dumfries 236 C4
Aisby Lincs 155 B10
Lincs 188 C5
Aisgernis W Isles 297 J3
Aish Devon 8 C3
Devon 8 D6
Aisholt Som 43 F7
Aiskew N Yorks 214 B5
Aislaby N Yorks 216 B5
N Yorks 227 D7
Stockton 225 C8
Aisthorpe Lincs 188 E6
Aith Orkney 314 E2
Shetland 312 D8
Shetland 313 H5
Aithnen Powys 148 E4
Aithsetter Shetland 313 K6
Aitkenhead S Ayrs 245 B8
Aitnoch Highld 301 F9
Akeld Northumb 263 D11
Akeley Bucks 102 D4
Akenham Suff 108 B2
Albany T&W 243 F7
Albaston Corn 12 G4
Alberbury Shrops 149 G7
Albert Town Pembs 72 B6
Albert Village Leics 152 F6
Albourne W Sus 36 D3
Albourne Green W Sus 36 D3
Albrighton Shrops 132 C6
Shrops 149 F9
Albro Castle Ceredig 92 B3
Alburgh Norf 142 F5
Albury Herts 105 G8
Sur 50 D5
Albury End Herts 105 G8
Albury Heath Sur 50 D5
Albyfield Cumb 240 G2
Alby Hill Norf 160 C3
Alcaig Highld 300 D5
Alcaston Shrops 131 F9
Alcester Dorset 30 C5
Warks 117 F11
Alcester Lane's End
W Mid 133 G11
Alciston E Sus 23 D8
Alcombe Som 42 D3
Wilts 61 F10
Alconbury Cambs 122 B3
Alconbury Weston
Cambs 122 B3
Aldbar Castle Angus 287 B9
Aldborough Norf 160 C3
N Yorks 215 F8
Aldborough Hatch
London 68 B3
Aldbourne Wilts 63 D9
Aldbrough E Yorks 209 F10
Aldbrough St John
N Yorks 224 C4
Aldbury Herts 85 C7
Aldcliffe Lancs 211 G9
Aldclune Perth 291 G11
Aldeburgh Suff 127 F9
Aldeby Norf 143 E8
Aldenham Herts 85 F10
Alderbrook E Sus 37 B8
Alderbury Wilts 31 B11
Aldercar Derbys 170 F6
Alderford Norf 160 F2
Alder Forest Gtr Man 184 B3
Alderholt Dorset 31 E10
Alderley Glos 80 G3
Alderley Edge Ches E 184 F4
Alderman's Green
W Mid 135 G7
Aldermaston W Berks 64 F5
Aldermaston Soke
W Berks 64 G6
Aldermaston Wharf
W Berks 64 F6
Alderminster Warks 100 B4
Aldermoor Soton 32 D5
Alder Moor Staffs 152 D4
Alderney Poole 18 C6
Alder Row Som 45 E9
Aldersbrook London 68 B2
Alder's End Hereford 98 C2
Aldersey Green Ches W 167 D7
Aldershawe Staffs 134 B2
Aldershot Hants 49 C11
Alderton Glos 99 E10
Northants 102 B4
Shrops 149 E9
Suff 108 C6
Wilts 61 C10
Alderton Fields Glos 99 E10
Alderwasley Derbys 170 E4
Aldfield N Yorks 214 F5
Aldford Ches W 166 D6
Aldgate Rutland 137 C9
Aldham Essex 107 F8
Suff 107 B10
Aldie Highld 309 L7
Aldingbourne W Sus 22 B6
Aldingham Cumb 210 E5
Aldington Kent 54 F5
Worcs 99 C11
Aldington Frith Kent 54 F4
Aldivalloch Moray 302 G3
Aldochlay Argyll 277 C7
Aldon Shrops 115 B8
Aldoth Cumb 229 B8
Aldourie Castle Highld 300 F6
Aldreth Cambs 123 C8
Aldridge W Mid 133 C11
Aldringham Suff 127 E8
Aldrington Brighton 36 F3
Aldsworth Glos 81 C11
Aldunie Moray 302 G3
Aldwark Derbys 170 D2
N Yorks 215 G9
Aldwarke S Yorks 186 C6
Aldwick W Sus 22 D6
Aldwincle Northants 137 G10
Aldworth W Berks 64 D5
Alehouseburn Aberds 302 C6
Alehousehill Aberds 303 G10
Ale Oak Shrops 130 G4
Alexandria W Dunb 277 F7
Aley Som 43 F7
Aley Green C Beds 85 B9
Alfardisworthy Devon 24 E3
Alfington Devon 15 B8
Alfold Sur 50 G4
Alfold Bars W Sus 50 G4
Alfold Crossways Sur 50 F4
Alford Aberds 293 B7
Lincs 191 F7
Som 44 G6
Alfred's Well Worcs 117 C8
Alfreton Derbys 170 D6
Alfrick Worcs 116 G4
Alfrick Pound Worcs 116 G4
Alfriston E Sus 23 E8
Algakirk Lincs 156 B5
Algaltraig Argyll 275 F11
Algarkirk Lincs 156 B5
Alhampton Som 44 G6
Aline Lodge W Isles 305 G3
Alisary Highld 289 B9
Alkborough N Lincs 199 C11
Alkerton Glos 80 D3
Oxon 101 C7
Alkham Kent 55 E9
Alkington Shrops 149 B10
Alkmonton Derbys 152 B3
Alkrington Garden Village
Gtr Man 195 G11
Alladale Lodge Highld 309 L4
Allaleigh Devon 8 E6
Allanaquoich Aberds 292 D3
Allanbank Borders 271 F10
N Lnrk 268 D6
Allangrange Mains
Highld 300 D6
Allanshaugh Borders 271 F8
Allanshaws Borders 271 G9
Allanton Borders 273 E7
N Lnrk 269 D7
S Lnrk 268 E4
Allaston Glos 79 E10
Allathasdal W Isles 297 L2
Allbrook Hants 33 C7
All Cannings Wilts 62 G5
Allendale Town
Northumb 241 F8
Allen End Warks 134 D3
Allenheads Northumb 232 B3
Allensford Durham 242 G3
Allens Green Herts 87 B7
Allensmore Hereford 97 D9
Allenton Derby 153 C7
Allenwood Cumb 239 F11
Aller Devon 9 B7
Devon 27 F9
Dorset 30 G3
Som 28 B6
Allerby Cumb 229 D7
Allerford Som 27 B11
Som 42 D2
Aller Park Devon 9 B7
Allerston N Yorks 217 C7
Allerthorpe E Yorks 207 D11
Allerton Mers 182 D6
W Yorks 205 G8
Allerton Bywater
W Yorks 198 B2
Allerton Mauleverer
N Yorks 206 B4
Allesley W Mid 134 G6
Allestree Derby 152 B6
Allet Corn 4 F5
Allexton Leics 136 C6
Allgreave Ches E 169 B7
Allhallows Medway 69 D10
Allhallows-on-Sea
Medway 69 D10
Alligin Shuas Highld 299 D8
Allimore Green Staffs 151 F7
Allington Kent 53 B8
Lincs 172 G5
Wilts 47 F8
Wilts 61 D11
Wilts 62 G5
Allington Bar Wilts 61 E11
Allithwaite Cumb 211 D7
Alloa Clack 279 C7
Allonby Cumb 229 C7
Allostock Ches W 184 G2
Alloway S Ayrs 257 F8
Allowenshay Som 28 E5
All Saints Devon 28 G4
All Saints South Elmham
Suff 142 G6
Allscot Shrops 132 D4
Allscott Telford 150 G2
All Stretton Shrops 131 D9
Allt Carms 75 E9
Alltami Flint 166 B3
Alltbeithe Highld 290 C2
Alltchaorunn Highld 284 B5
Alltforgan Powys 147 E9
Alltmawr Powys 95 B11
Alltnacaillich Highld 308 E4
Allt-na-giubhsaich
Aberds 292 E4
Allt na h-Airbhe Highld 307 K6
Allt-nan-sùgh Highld 295 C11
Alltrech Argyll 289 F8
Alltsigh Highld 290 B6
Alltwalis Carms 93 E8
Alltwen Neath 76 E2
Alltyblaca Ceredig 93 B10
Allt-yr-yn Newport 59 B9
Allwood Green Suff 125 C10
Alma Notts 171 E7
Almagill Dumfries 238 B3
Almeley Hereford 114 G6

Bleasby Lincs 189 E10
Notts 172 F2
Bleasby Moor Lincs 189 E10
Bleasdale Lancs 203 D7
Bleatarn Cumb 222 C4
Blebocraigs Fife 287 F8
Bleddfa Powys 114 D4
Bledington Glos 100 G4
Bledlow Bucks 84 E3
Bledlow Ridge Bucks 84 F3
Bleet Wilts 45 B11
Blegbie E Loth 271 C9
Blegbury Devon 24 B2
Blencarn Cumb 231 E8
Blencogo Cumb 229 B9
Blendworth Hants 34 E2
Blenheim Oxon 83 D9
Oxon 83 E9
Blenheim Park Norf 158 C6
Blenkinsopp Hall
Northumb 240 E5
Blennerhasset Cumb 229 C9
Blervie Castle Moray 301 D10
Bletchingdon Oxon 83 B8
Bletchingley Sur 51 C10
Bletchley M Keynes 103 E7
Shrops 150 C2
Bletherston Pembs 91 G11
Bletsoe Beds 121 F10
Blewbury Oxon 64 B4
Bliby Kent 54 F4
Blickling Norf 160 D3
Blidworth Notts 171 D9
Blidworth Bottoms
Notts 171 E9
Blidworth Dale Notts 171 E9
Blindburn Northumb 263 G8
Blindcrake Cumb 229 E8
Blindley Heath Sur 51 D11
Blindmoor Som 28 E3
Blingery Highld 310 E7
Blisland Corn 11 G8
Blissford Hants 31 E11
Bliss Gate Worcs 116 C4
Blisworth Northants 120 G4
Blithbury Staffs 151 E11
Blitterlees Cumb 238 G4
Blockley Glos 100 D3
Blofield Norf 142 B6
Blofield Heath Norf 160 G6
Blo' Norton Norf 125 B10
Bloodman's Corner
Suff 143 D10
Bloomfield Bath 45 B7
Bath 61 G8
Borders 262 E3
W Mid 133 E9
Bloomsbury London 67 C10
Blore Staffs 150 C4
Staffs 169 F10
Bloreheath Staffs 150 B4
Blossomfield W Mid 118 B2
Blount's Green Staffs 151 C11
Blowick Mers 193 D11
Blowinghouse Corn 4 E4
Bloxham Oxon 101 D8
Bloxholm Lincs 173 E9
Bloxwich W Mid 133 C9
Bloxworth Dorset 18 C3
Blubberhouses N Yorks 205 B9
Blue Anchor Corn 5 D8
Som 42 E4
Swansea 56 B4
Bluebell Telford 149 G11
Blue Bell Hill Kent 69 G8
Bluecairn Borders 271 G10
Blue Hill Herts 104 G5
Blue Row Essex 89 C8
Bluetown Kent 54 B2
Blue Town Kent 70 D2
Blue Vein Wilts 61 F10
Bluewater Kent 68 E5
Blughasary Highld 307 J6
Blundellsands Mers 182 B4
Blundeston Suff 143 D10
Blundies Staffs 132 F6
Blunham C Beds 122 G3
Blunsdon St Andrew
Swindon 62 B6
Bluntington Worcs 117 C7
Bluntisham Cambs 123 C7
Blunts Corn 6 C6
Blunt's Green Warks 118 D2
Blurton Stoke 168 G5
Blyborough Lincs 188 C6
Blyford Suff 127 B8
Blymhill Staffs 150 G6
Blymhill Lawns Staffs 150 G6
Blyth Borders 270 F2
Northumb 253 G8
Notts 187 D10
Blyth Bridge Borders 270 F2
Blythburgh Suff 127 B9
Blythe Borders 271 F11
Blythe Bridge Staffs 169 G7
Blythe Marsh Staffs 169 G7
Blyth End Warks 134 E4
Blythswood Renfs 267 B10
Blyton Lincs 188 C5
Boarhills Fife 287 F9
Boarhunt Hants 33 F10
Boarsgreave Lancs 195 C10
Boarshead E Sus 52 G4
Boars Hill Oxon 83 E7
Boarstall Bucks 83 C10
Boasley Cross Devon 12 C5
Boath Highld 300 B5
Boat of Garten Highld 291 B11
Bobbing Kent 69 F11
Bobbington Staffs 132 E6
Bobbingworth Essex 87 D8
Bobby Hill Suff 125 C10
Boblainy Highld 300 F4
Bocaddon Corn 6 D3
Bochastle Stirl 285 G10
Bockhanger Kent 54 E4
Bocking Essex 106 G5
Bocking Churchstreet
Essex 106 F5
Bocking's Elm Essex 89 B11
Bockleton Worcs 115 E11
Bockmer End Bucks 65 B10
Bocombe Devon 24 C5
Bodantionail Highld 299 B7
Boddam Aberds 303 E11
Shetland 313 M5
Bodden Som 44 E6
Boddington Glos 99 F7
Bodedern Anglesey 178 E4
Bodellick Corn 10 G5
Bodelva Corn 5 E11
Bodelwyddan Denb 181 F8
Bodenham Hereford 115 G10
Wilts 31 B11
Bodenham Bank Hereford 98 E2
Bodenham Moor
Hereford 115 G10
Bodermid Gwyn 144 D3
Bodewryd Anglesey 178 C5
Bodfari Denb 181 G9
Bodffordd Anglesey 178 F6
Bodham Norf 177 E10
Bodiam E Sus 38 B3
Bodicote Oxon 101 D9
Bodiechell Aberds 303 E7
Bodieve Corn 10 G5
Bodiggo Corn 5 D10
Bodilly Corn 2 C5
Bodinnick Corn 6 E2
Bodle Street Green
E Sus 23 C11
Bodley Devon 41 D7
Bodmin Corn 5 B11
Bodmiscombe Devon 27 F10
Bodney Norf 140 D6
Bodorgan Anglesey 162 B5
Bodsham Kent 54 D6
Boduan Gwyn 144 B6
Boduel Corn 6 C4
Bodwen Corn 5 C10
Bodymoor Heath Warks 134 D4
Bofarnel Corn 6 C2
Bogallan Highld 300 D6
Bogbrae Aberds 303 F10
Bogend Borders 272 F5
Notts 171 F7
S Ayrs 257 C9
Bogentory Aberds 293 C9
Boghall Midloth 270 B4
W Loth 269 B9
Boghead Aberds 293 D8
S Lnrk 268 G5
Bogmoor Moray 302 C3
Bogniebrae Aberds 302 E5
Aberds 302 E6
Bognor Regis W Sus 22 D6
Bograxie Aberds 293 B9
Bogs Aberds 302 G5
Bogs Bank Borders 270 E3
Bogside N Lnrk 268 E6
Bogthorn W Yorks 204 F6
Bogton Aberds 302 D6
Bogtown Aberds 302 C5
Bogue Dumfries 246 G4
Bohemia E Sus 38 E4
Wilts 32 D2
Bohenie Highld 290 E4
Bohetherick Corn 7 B8
Bohortha Corn 3 C9
Bohuntine Highld 290 E4
Bohuntinville Highld 290 E4
Boirseam W Isles 296 C6
Bojewyan Corn 1 C3
Bokiddick Corn 5 C11
Bolahaul Fm Carms 74 B6
Bolam Durham 233 G9
Northumb 252 G3
Bolam West Houses
Northumb 252 G3
Bolas Heath Telford 150 E3
Bolberry Devon 9 G8
Bold Heath Mers 183 D8
Boldmere W Mid 134 E2
Boldon T&W 243 E9
Boldon Colliery T&W 243 E8
Boldre Hants 20 B2
Boldron Durham 223 C10
Bole Notts 188 D3
Bolehall Staffs 134 C4
Bolehill Derbys 170 E3
Derbys 186 G6
S Yorks 186 E5
Bole Hill Derbys 186 G4
Bolenowe Corn 2 B5
Boleside Borders 261 C11
Boley Park Staffs 134 B2
Bolham Devon 27 E7
Notts 188 E2
Bolham Water Devon 27 E11
Bolholt Gtr Man 195 E9
Bolingey Corn 4 E5
Bolitho Corn 2 C5
Bollihope Durham 232 E6
Bollington Ches E 184 F6
Bollington Cross Ches E 184 F6
Bolney W Sus 36 C3
Bolnhurst Beds 121 F11
Bolnore W Sus 36 C4
Bolshan Angus 287 B10
Bolsover Derbys 187 G7
Bolsterstone S Yorks 186 B3
Bolstone Hereford 97 E11
Boltby N Yorks 215 B9
Bolter End Bucks 84 G3
Bolton Cumb 231 G8
E Loth 281 G10
E Yorks 207 C11
Gtr Man 195 F8
Northumb 264 G4
W Yorks 205 F9
Bolton Abbey N Yorks 205 C7
Bolton Bridge N Yorks 205 C7
Bolton-by-Bowland
Lancs 203 D11
Boltonfellend Cumb 239 D11
Boltongate Cumb 229 C10
Bolton Green Lancs 194 D5
Bolton Houses Lancs 202 G4
Bolton-le-Sands Lancs 211 F9
Bolton Low Houses
Cumb 229 C10
Bolton New Houses
Cumb 229 C10
Bolton-on-Swale
N Yorks 224 F5
Bolton Percy N Yorks 206 E6
Bolton Town End Lancs 211 F9
Bolton upon Dearne
S Yorks 198 G3
Bolton Wood Lane
Cumb 229 C11
Bolton Woods W Yorks 205 F9
Boltshope Park Durham 232 B4
Bolventor Corn 11 F9
Bomarsund Northumb 253 G7
Bombie Dumfries 237 D9
Bomby Cumb 221 B10
Bomere Heath Shrops 149 F9
Bonaly Edin 270 B4
Bonar Bridge Highld 309 K6
Bonawe Argyll 284 D4
Bonby N Lincs 200 D4
Boncath Pembs 92 D4
Bonchester Bridge
Borders 262 G3
Bonchurch IoW 21 F7
Bondend Glos 80 B5
Bond End Staffs 152 F2
Bondleigh Devon 25 G11
Bondman Hays Leics 135 B9
Bonds Lancs 202 E5
Bondstones Devon 25 F9
Bonehill Devon 13 F10
Staffs 134 C3
Bo'ness Falk 279 E9
Bonhill W Dunb 277 F7
Boningale Shrops 132 C6
Bonjedward Borders 262 E5
Bonkle N Lnrk 268 D6
Bonnavoulin Highld 289 D7
Bonning Gate Cumb 221 F9
Bonnington Borders 261 B7
Edin 270 B2
Kent 54 F5
Bonnybank Fife 287 G7
Bonnybridge Falk 278 E6
Bonnykelly Aberds 303 D8
Bonnyrigg and Lasswade
Midloth 270 B6
Bonnyton Aberds 302 F6
Angus 287 B10
Angus 287 D7
E Ayrs 257 B10
Bonsall Derbys 170 D3
Bonskeid House Perth 291 G10
Bonson Som 43 E8
Bont Mon 78 B5
Bontddu Gwyn 146 F3
Bont-Dolgadfan Powys 129 C7
Bont Fawr Carms 94 F4
Bont goch / Elerch
Ceredig 128 F3
Bonthorpe Lincs 191 G7
Bontnewydd Ceredig 112 D2
Gwyn 163 D7
Bont-newydd Conwy 181 G8
Bont Newydd Gwyn 146 E5
Gwyn 164 G2
Bontuchel Denb 165 D9
Bonvilston / Tresimwn
V Glam 58 E5
Bon-y-maen Swansea 57 B7
Boode Devon 40 F4
Booker Bucks 84 G4
Bookham Dorset 30 G2
Booleybank Shrops 149 D11
Boon Borders 271 F11
Boon Hill Staffs 168 E4
Boorley Green Hants 33 E8
Boosbeck Redcar 226 B3
Boose's Green Essex 106 E6
Boot Cumb 220 E3
Booth Staffs 151 D10
W Yorks 196 B4
Booth Bank Ches E 184 D2
Booth Bridge Lancs 204 D4
Boothby Graffoe Lincs 173 D7
Boothby Pagnell Lincs 155 C9
Boothen Stoke 168 G5
Boothferry E Yorks 199 B8
Boothgate Derbys 170 F5
Booth Green Ches E 184 E6
Boothroyd W Yorks 197 C8
Boothsdale Ches W 167 B8
Boothstown Gtr Man 195 G8
Boothtown W Yorks 196 B5
Boothville Northants 120 E5
Booth Wood W Yorks 196 D4
Bootle Cumb 210 B2
Mers 182 B4
Booton Norf 160 E2
Boots Green Ches W 184 G3
Boot Street Suff 108 B4
Booze N Yorks 223 E10
Boquhan Stirl 277 D10
Boquio Corn 2 C5
Boraston Shrops 116 D2
Boraston Dale Shrops 116 C2
Borden Kent 69 G11
W Sus 34 C4
Border Cumb 238 G5
Bordesley W Mid 133 F11
Bordesley Green W Mid 134 F2
Bordlands Borders 270 F3
Bordley N Yorks 213 G8
Bordon Hants 49 F10
Bordon Camp Hants 49 F9
Boreham Essex 88 D3
Wilts 45 E11
Boreham Street E Sus 23 C11
Borehamwood Herts 85 F11
Boreland Dumfries 236 C5
Dumfries 248 E5
Fife 280 C6
Stirl 285 D9
Boreland of Southwick
Dumfries 237 C11
Boreley Worcs 116 D6
Borestone Stirl 278 C5
Borgh W Isles 296 C5
W Isles 297 L2
Borghasdal W Isles 296 C6
Borghastan W Isles 304 D4
Borgie Highld 308 D6
Borgue Dumfries 237 E8
Highld 311 G5
Borley Essex 106 C6
Borley Green Essex 106 C6
Suff 125 E9
Bornais W Isles 297 J3
Bornesketaig Highld 298 B3
Borness Dumfries 237 E8
Borough Scilly 1 G3
Boroughbridge N Yorks 215 F7
Borough Green Kent 52 B6
Borough Marsh
Wokingham 65 D9
Borough Park Staffs 134 B4
Borough Post Som 28 C4
Borras Wrex 166 E4
Borras Head Wrex 166 E5
Borreraig Highld 296 F7
Borrobol Lodge Highld 311 G2
Borrodale Highld 297 G7
Borrohill Aberds 303 D9
Borrowash Derbys 153 C8
Borrowby N Yorks 215 B8
N Yorks 226 B5
Borrowdale Cumb 220 C5
Borrowfield Aberds 293 D10
Borrowston Highld 310 E7
Borrowstoun Mains
Falk 279 E9
Borstal Medway 69 F8
Borthwick Midloth 271 D7
Borthwickbrae Borders 261 G10
Borthwickshiels
Borders 261 F10
Borth / Y Borth Ceredig 128 E2
Borth-y-Gest Gwyn 145 B11
Borve Highld 298 E4
Borve Lodge W Isles 305 J2
Borwick Lancs 211 E10
Borwick Rails Cumb 210 D3
Bosavern Corn 1 C3
Bosbury Hereford 98 C3
Boscadjack Corn 2 C5
Boscastle Corn 11 C8
Boscean Corn 1 C3
Boscombe Bmouth 19 C8
Wilts 47 F8
Boscomoor Staffs 151 G8
Boscoppa Corn 5 E10
Boscreege Corn 2 C3
Bosham W Sus 22 C4
Bosham Hoe W Sus 22 C4
Bosherston Pembs 73 G7
Boskednan Corn 1 C4
Boskenna Corn 1 E4
Bosleake Corn 4 G3
Bosley Ches E 168 B6
Boslowick Corn 3 C7
Boslymon Corn 5 C11
Bosoughan Corn 5 C7
Bosporthennis Corn 1 B4
Bossall N Yorks 216 G4
Bossiney Corn 11 D7
Bossingham Kent 54 D6
Bossington Hants 47 G10
Kent 55 B8
Som 41 D11
Bostadh W Isles 304 D3
Bostock Green Ches W 167 B11
Boston Lincs 174 G4
Boston Long Hedges
Lincs 174 F5
Boston Spa W Yorks 206 D4
Boston West Lincs 174 F3
Boswednack Corn 1 B4
Boswin Corn 2 C5
Boswinger Corn 5 G9
Boswyn Corn 2 B5
Botallack Corn 1 C3
Botany Bay London 86 F3
Mon 79 E8
Botcherby Cumb 239 F10
Botcheston Leics 135 B9
Botesdale Suff 125 B10
Bothal Northumb 252 F6
Bothampstead W Berks 64 D4
Bothamsall Notts 187 G11
Bothel Cumb 229 D9
Bothenhampton Dorset 16 C5
Bothwell S Lnrk 268 D4
Bothy Highld 290 F4
Botley Bucks 85 E7
Hants 33 E8
Oxon 83 D7
Botloe's Green Glos 98 F4
Botolph Claydon Bucks 102 G4
Botolphs W Sus 35 F11
Bottacks Highld 300 C4
Botternell Corn 11 G11
Bottesford Leics 154 B6
N Lincs 199 F11
Bottisham Cambs 123 E10
Bottlesford Wilts 46 B6
Bottom Boat W Yorks 197 C11
Bottomcraig Fife 287 E7
Bottom House Staffs 169 E8
Bottomley W Yorks 196 D5
Bottom of Hutton Lancs 194 B3
Bottom o' th' Moor
Gtr Man 195 E7
Bottom Pond Kent 53 B11
Bottoms Corn 1 E3
Botreaux Mill Devon 26 B4
Botrells Close Bucks 85 G7
Botts Green Warks 134 E4
Botusfleming Corn 7 C8
Botwnnog Gwyn 144 C5
Bough Beech Kent 52 D3
Boughrood Powys 96 D2
Boughrood Brest Powys 96 D2
Boughspring Glos 79 F9
Boughton Ches W 166 B6
Lincs 173 F10
Norf 140 C3
Northants 120 D5
Notts 171 B11
Boughton Aluph Kent 54 D4
Boughton Corner Kent 54 D4
Boughton Green Kent 53 C9
Boughton Heath
Ches W 166 B6
Boughton Lees Kent 54 D4
Boughton Malherbe
Kent 53 D11
Boughton Monchelsea
Kent 53 C9
Boughton Street Kent 54 B5
Bougton End C Beds 103 D9
Boulby Redcar 226 B5
Bould Oxon 100 G4
Boulden Shrops 131 F10
Boulder Clough
W Yorks 196 C4
Bouldnor IoW 20 D3
Bouldon Shrops 131 F10
Boulmer Northumb 265 G7
Boulsdon Glos 98 G4
Boulston Pembs 73 C7
Boultenstone Aberds 292 B6
Boultham Lincs 173 B7
Boultham Moor Lincs 173 B7
Boulton Derbys 153 C7
Boulton Moor Derbys 153 C7
Boundary Leics 152 F6
Staffs 169 G7
Boundstone Sur 49 E10
Bountis Thorne Devon 24 D5
Bourn Cambs 122 F6
Bournbrook W Mid 133 G10
Bourne Lincs 155 E11
N Som 44 B3
Bourne End Beds 121 E10
Bucks 65 B11
C Beds 103 C9
Herts 85 D8
Bournemouth Bmouth 19 C7
Bournes Green Glos 80 E6
Sthend 70 B2
Worcs 117 C8
Bourne Vale W Mid 133 D11
Bourne Valley Poole 19 C7
Bournheath Worcs 117 C9
Bournmoor Durham 243 G8
Bournside Glos 99 G8
Bournstream Glos 80 G2
Bournville W Mid 133 G10
Bourton Bucks 102 E4
Dorset 45 G9
N Som 59 G11
Oxon 63 B8
Shrops 131 D11
Wilts 62 G4
Bourton on Dunsmore
Warks 119 C8
Bourton-on-the-Hill
Glos 100 E3
Bourton-on-the-Water
Glos 100 G3
Bourtreehill N Ayrs 257 B8
Bousd Argyll 288 C4
Bousta Shetland 313 H4
Boustead Hill Cumb 239 F7
Bouth Cumb 210 B6
Bouthwaite N Yorks 214 E2
Bouts Worcs 117 F10
Bovain Stirl 285 D9
Boveney Bucks 66 D2
Boveridge Dorset 31 E9
Boverton V Glam 58 F3
Bovey Tracey Devon 14 F2
Bovingdon Herts 85 E8
Bovingdon Green Bucks 65 B10
Herts 85 E8
Bovinger Essex 87 D8
Bovington Camp Dorset 18 D2
Bow Borders 271 G9
Devon 8 D6
Devon 26 G2
Orkney 314 G3
Oxon 82 G4
Bowbank Durham 232 G4
Bowbeck Suff 125 B8
Bow Brickhill M Keynes 103 E8
Bowbridge Glos 80 E5
Bowbrook Shrops 149 G9
Bow Broom S Yorks 187 B7
Bowburn Durham 234 D2
Bowcombe IoW 20 D5
Bow Common London 67 C11
Bowd Devon 15 C8
Bowden Borders 262 C3
Devon 8 F6
Dorset 30 C3
Bowden Hill Wilts 62 F2
Bowdens Som 28 B6
Bowderdale Cumb 222 E3
Bowdon Gtr Man 184 D3
Bower Highld 310 C6
Northumb 251 G7
Bower Ashton Bristol 60 E5
Bowerchalke Wilts 31 C8
Bower Heath Herts 85 B10
Bowerhill Wilts 62 G2
Bower Hinton Som 29 D7
Bowerhope Borders 261 E7
Bower House Tye Suff 107 C9
Bowermadden Highld 310 C6
Bowers Staffs 150 B6
Bowers Gifford Essex 69 B9
Bowershall Fife 279 C11
Bowertower Highld 310 C6
Bowes Durham 223 C9
Bowes Park London 86 G4
Bowgreave Lancs 202 E5
Bowgreen Gtr Man 184 D3
Bowhill Borders 261 D10
Fife 280 B4
Bowhouse Dumfries 238 D2
Bowhousebog or Liquo N
Lnrk 269 D7
Bowing Park Mers 182 D6
Bowismiln Borders 262 E2
Bowithick Corn 11 E9
Bowker's Green Lancs 194 G2
Bowland Bridge Cumb 211 B8
Bowldown Wilts 62 D2
Bowlee Gtr Man 195 F10
Bowlees Durham 232 F4
Bowler's Town E Sus 38 C6
Bowley Hereford 115 G10
Bowley Lane Hereford 98 C3
Bowley Town Hereford 115 G10
Bowlhead Green Sur 50 F2
Bowling W Dunb 277 G9
W Yorks 205 G9
Bowling Alley Hants 49 D9
Bowling Bank Wrex 166 F5
Bowling Green Corn 5 D10
Corn 12 G3
Glos 81 E8
Hants 19 B11
Shrops 150 D2
W Mid 133 F8
Worcs 116 G6
Bowlish Som 44 E6
Bowmans Kent 68 E4
Bowmanstead Cumb 220 F6
Bowmore Argyll 254 B4
Bowness-on-Solway
Cumb 238 E6
Bowness-on-Windermere
Cumb 221 F8
Bow of Fife Fife 287 F7
Bowridge Hill Dorset 30 B4
Bowrie-fauld Angus 287 C9
Bowsden Northumb 273 G9
Bowsey Hill Windsor 65 C10
Bowshank Borders 271 G9
Bowside Lodge Highld 310 C2
Bowston Cumb 221 F9
Bow Street Ceredig 128 G2
Norf 141 D10
Bowthorpe Norf 142 B3
Bowyer's Common Hants 34 B3
Box Glos 80 E5
Wilts 61 F10
Boxbush Glos 80 C2
Glos 98 G3
Box End Beds 103 B10
Boxford Suff 107 C9
W Berks 64 E2
Boxgrove W Sus 22 B6
Box Hill Sur 51 C7
Wilts 61 F10
Boxley Kent 53 B9
Boxmoor Herts 85 D9
Box's Shop Corn 24 G2
Boxted Essex 107 E9
Suff 124 G6
Boxted Cross Essex 107 E10
Boxted Heath Essex 107 E10
Box Trees W Mid 118 C2
Boxwell Glos 80 G4
Boxworth Cambs 122 E6
Boxworth End Cambs 123 D7
Boyatt Wood Hants 32 C6
Boyden End Suff 124 F4
Boyden Gate Kent 71 F8
Boyland Common Norf 141 G11
Boylestone Derbys 152 B3
Boylestonfield Derbys 152 B3
Boyndie Aberds 302 C6
Boyn Hill Windsor 65 C11
Boynton E Yorks 218 F2
Boysack Angus 287 C9
Angus 287 C10
Boys Hill Dorset 29 E11
Boys Village V Glam 58 F4
Boythorpe Derbys 186 G5
Boyton Corn 12 C2
Suff 109 B7
Wilts 46 F3
Boyton Cross Essex 87 D10
Boyton End Essex 106 E2
Suff 106 C4
Bozeat Northants 121 F8
Bozen Green Herts 105 F8
Braaid IoM 192 E4
Braal Castle Highld 310 C5
Brabling Green Suff 126 E5
Brabourne Kent 54 E5
Brabourne Lees Kent 54 E5
Brabster Highld 310 C7
Bracadale Highld 294 B5
Bracara Highld 295 F9
Braceborough Lincs 155 G11
Bracebridge Lincs 173 B7
Bracebridge Heath
Lincs 173 B7
Bracebridge Low Fields
Lincs 173 B7
Braceby Lincs 155 B10
Bracewell Lancs 204 D3
Bracken Bank W Yorks 204 F6
Brackenber Cumb 222 B4
Brackenbottom N Yorks 212 E6
Brackenfield Derbys 170 D5
Brackenhall W Yorks 197 D7
Bracken Hill W Yorks 197 C7
Brackenlands Cumb 229 B11
Bracken Park W Yorks 206 E3
Brackenthwaite Cumb 229 B11
Cumb 229 G9
N Yorks 205 C11
Brackla / Bragle
Bridgend 58 D2
Bracklamore Aberds 303 D8
Bracklesham W Sus 22 D4
Brackletter Highld 290 E3
Brackley Argyll 255 C8
Northants 101 D11
Brackloch Highld 307 G6
Bracknell Brack 65 F11
Braco Perth 286 G2
Bracobrae Moray 302 D5
Braco Castle Perth 286 F2
Bracon N Lincs 199 F9
Bracon Ash Norf 142 D3
Braco Park Aberds 303 C9
Bracorina Highld 295 F9
Bradaford Devon 12 C3
Bradbourne Derbys 170 E2
Bradbury Durham 234 F2
Bradda IoM 192 F2
Bradden Northants 102 B2
Braddock Corn 6 C3
Braddocks Hay Staffs 168 D5
Bradeley Stoke 168 E5
Bradeley Green Ches E 167 G8
Bradenham Bucks 84 F4
Norf 141 B8
Bradenstoke Wilts 62 D4
Brades Village W Mid 133 E9
Bradfield Devon 27 F9
Essex 108 E2
Norf 160 C5
W Berks 64 E6
Bradfield Combust Suff 125 F7
Bradfield Green
Ches E 167 D11
Bradfield Heath Essex 108 F2
Bradfield St Clare Suff 125 F8
Bradfield St George
Suff 125 E8
Bradford Corn 11 F8
Derbys 170 C2
Devon 24 F6
Gtr Man 184 B5
Northumb 264 C5
W Yorks 205 G9
Bradford Abbas Dorset 29 E9
Bradford Leigh Wilts 61 G10
Bradford-on-Avon
Wilts 61 G10
Bradford-on-Tone Som 27 C11
Bradford Peverell Dorset 17 C9
Bradgate S Yorks 186 C6
Bradiford Devon 40 G5
Brading IoW 21 D8
Bradley Derbys 170 F2
Glos 80 G3
Hants 48 E6
NE Lincs 201 F8
Staffs 151 F7
W Mid 133 D8
Wrex 166 E4
W Yorks 197 C7
Bradley Cross Som 44 C3
Bradley Fold Gtr Man 195 F9
Bradley Green Ches W 167 F8
Glos 80 G2
Som 43 F9
Warks 134 C5
Worcs 117 E9
Bradley in the Moors
Staffs 169 G9
Bradley Mills W Yorks 197 D7
Bradley Mount Ches E 184 F6
Bradley Stoke S Glos 60 C6
Bradlow Hereford 98 D4
Bradmore Notts 153 C11
W Mid 133 D7
Bradney Shrops 132 D5
Som 43 F10
Bradninch Devon 27 G8
Bradnock's Marsh
W Mid 118 B4
Bradnop Staffs 169 D8
Bradnor Green Hereford 114 F5
Bradpole Dorset 16 C5
Bradshaw Gtr Man 195 E8
Staffs 168 D6
W Yorks 196 E5
W Yorks 205 G7
Bradstone Devon 12 E3
Bradville M Keynes 102 C6
Bradwall Green Ches E 168 C3
Bradway S Yorks 186 E4
Bradwell Derbys 185 E11
Devon 40 E3
Essex 106 G6
M Keynes 102 D6
Norf 143 C10
Staffs 168 F4
Bradwell Common
M Keynes 102 D6
Bradwell Grove Oxon 82 D2
Bradwell Hills Derbys 185 E11
Bradwell on Sea Essex 89 D8
Bradwell Waterside
Essex 89 D7
Bradworthy Devon 24 E4
Bradworthy Cross Devon 24 E4
Brae Dumfries 237 B10
Highld 307 L3
Highld 309 J4
Shetland 312 G5
Braeantra Highld 300 B5
Braebuster Orkney 314 F5
Braedownie Angus 292 F4
Braeface Falk 278 E5
Braefield Highld 300 F4
Braefindon Highld 300 D6
Braegrum Perth 286 E4
Braehead Dumfries 236 D6
Orkney 314 B4
Orkney 314 F5
S Ayrs 257 E8
S Lnrk 259 C8
S Lnrk 267 D11
S Lnrk 269 E9
Stirl 278 C6
Braehead of Lunan
Angus 287 B10
Braehoulland Shetland 312 F4
Braehour Highld 310 D4
Braehungie Highld 310 F5
Braeintra Highld 295 B10
Braelangwell Lodge
Highld 309 K5
Braemar Aberds 292 D3
Braemore Highld 299 B11
Highld 310 F4
Brae of Achnahaird
Highld 307 H5
Brae of Boquhapple
Stirl 285 G10
Braepark Edin 280 F3
Brae Roy Lodge Highld 290 D5
Braeside Involyd 276 F4
Braes of Enzie Moray 302 D3
Braes of Ullapool Highld 307 K6
Braeswick Orkney 314 C6
Braevallich Argyll 275 C10
Braewick Shetland 312 F4
Shetland 313 H5
Brafferton Darl 233 G11
N Yorks 215 E8
Brafield-on-the-Green
Northants 120 F6
Bragar W Isles 304 D4
Bragbury End Herts 104 G5
Bragenham Bucks 103 F8
Bragle / Brackla
Bridgend 58 D2
Brageenmore Argyll 289 G11
Braichmelyn Gwyn 163 B10
Braichyfedw Powys 129 E7
Braid Edin 280 G4
Braides Lancs 202 C4
Braidfauld Glasgow 268 C2
Braidley N Yorks 213 C10
Braids Argyll 255 C8
Braidwood S Lnrk 268 F6
Braigh Chalasaigh
W Isles 296 D5
Braigo Argyll 274 G3
Brailsford Derbys 170 G3
Brailsford Green Derbys 170 G3
Braingortan Argyll 275 F11
Brain's Green Glos 79 D11
Brainshaugh Northumb 252 C6
Braintree Essex 106 G5
Braiseworth Suff 126 C2
Braishfield Hants 32 B5
Braiswick Essex 107 F9
Braithwaite Cumb 229 G10
S Yorks 198 E6
W Yorks 204 E6
Braithwell S Yorks 187 C8
Brakefield Green Norf 141 B10
Brakenhill W Yorks 198 D2
Bramber W Sus 35 E11
Bramblecombe Dorset 30 G3
Brambridge Hants 33 C7
Bramcote Notts 153 B10
Warks 135 F8
Bramcote Hills Notts 153 B10
Bramcote Mains Warks 135 F8
Bramdean Hants 33 B10
Bramerton Norf 142 C5
Bramfield Herts 86 B3
Suff 127 C7
Bramford Suff 108 B2
W Mid 133 E8
Bramhall Gtr Man 184 D5
Bramhall Moor Gtr Man 184 D6
Bramhall Park Gtr Man 184 D5
Bramham W Yorks 206 E4
Bramhope W Yorks 205 E11
Bramley Derbys 186 F6
Hants 48 B6
Sur 50 D4
S Yorks 187 C7
W Yorks 205 F10
Bramley Corner Hants 48 B6
Bramley Green Hants 49 B7
Bramley Head N Yorks 205 B8
Bramley Vale Derbys 171 B7
Bramling Kent 55 B8
Brampford Speke Devon 14 B4
Brampton Cambs 122 C4
Cumb 231 G9
Cumb 240 E2
Derbys 186 G5
Hereford 97 D8
Lincs 188 F4
Norf 160 E4
Suff 143 G8
S Yorks 198 G2
Brampton Abbotts
Hereford 98 F2
Brampton Ash Northants 136 F5
Brampton Bryan
Hereford 115 C7
Brampton en le Morthen
S Yorks 187 D7
Brampton Park Cambs 122 C4
Brampton Street Suff 143 G8
Bramshall Staffs 151 C11
Bramshaw Hants 32 D3
Bramshill Hants 65 G8
Bramshott Hants 49 G10
Bramwell Som 28 B6
Branatwatt Shetland 313 H4
Branault Highld 289 C7
Branbridges Kent 53 D7
Brancaster Norf 176 E3
Brancaster Staithe Norf 176 E3
Brancepeth Durham 233 D10
Branch End Northumb 242 E3
Branchill Moray 301 D10
Branchton Invclyd 276 F4
Brand End Lincs 174 F5
Branderburgh Moray 302 B2
Brandesburton E Yorks 209 D8
Brandeston Suff 126 E4
Brand Green Glos 98 F4
Hereford 98 C5
Brandhill Shrops 115 B8
Brandis Corner Devon 24 G6
Brandish Street Som 42 D2
Brandiston Norf 160 E2
Brandlingill Cumb 229 F8
Brandon Durham 233 D10
Lincs 172 F6
Northumb 264 F2
Suff 140 F5
Warks 119 B8
Brandon Bank Cambs 140 F2
Brandon Creek Norf 140 E2
Brandon Parva Norf 141 B11
Brandsby N Yorks 215 E11
Brands Hill Windsor 66 D4
Brandwood Shrops 149 D9
Brandwood End
W Mid 117 B11
Brandy Carr W Yorks 197 C10
Brandy Hole Essex 88 F4
Brandyquoy Orkney 314 G4
Brandy Wharf Lincs 189 B8
Brane Corn 1 D4
Bran End Essex 106 F3
Branksome Darl 224 B5
Poole 18 C6
Branksome Park Poole 19 C7
Bransbury Hants 48 E2
Bransby Lincs 188 F5
Branscombe Devon 15 D9
Bransford Worcs 116 G5
Bransgore Hants 19 B9
Branshill Clack 279 C7
Bransholme Hull 209 G8
Branson's Cross Worcs 117 C11
Branston Leics 154 D6
Lincs 173 B8
Staffs 152 E4
Branston Booths Lincs 173 B9
Branstone IoW 21 E7
Bransty Cumb 219 B9
Brant Broughton Lincs 172 E6
Brantham Suff 108 E2
Branthwaite Cumb 229 D11
Cumb 229 G7
Branthwaite Edge Cumb 229 G7
Brantingham E Yorks 200 B2
Branton Northumb 264 F2
S Yorks 198 G6
Branton Green N Yorks 215 G8
Branxholme Borders 261 G11
Branxholm Park
Borders 261 G11
Branxton Northumb 263 B9
Brascote Leics 135 C8
Brassey Green Ches W 167 C8
Brassington Derbys 170 E2
Brasted Kent 52 C3
Brasted Chart Kent 52 C3
Brathens Aberds 293 D8
Bratoft Lincs 175 B7
Brattle Kent 54 G2
Brattleby Lincs 188 E6
Bratton Som 42 D2
Telford 150 G2
Wilts 46 C2
Bratton Clovelly Devon 12 C5
Bratton Fleming Devon 40 F6
Bratton Seymour Som 29 B11
Braughing Herts 105 F7
Braughing Friars Herts 105 G8
Braulen Lodge Highld 300 F2
Braunston Northants 119 D10
Braunstone Leics 135 C11
Braunstone Town
Leicester 135 C11
Braunston-in-Rutland
Rutland 136 B6
Braunton Devon 40 F3
Brawby N Yorks 216 D4
Brawith N Yorks 225 D10
Brawl Highld 310 C2
Brawlbin Highld 310 D4
Bray Windsor 66 D2
Braybrooke Northants 136 G5
Braydon Side Wilts 62 B4
Brayford Devon 41 G7
Brayfordhill Devon 41 G7
Brays Grove Essex 87 D7
Bray Shop Corn 12 G2
Braystones Cumb 219 D10
Brayswick Worcs 98 B6
Braythorn N Yorks 205 D10
Brayton N Yorks 207 G8
Braytown Dorset 18 D2
Bray Wick Windsor 65 D11
Braywoodside Windsor 65 D11
Brazacott Corn 11 C11
Brazenhill Staffs 151 E7
Brea Corn 4 G3
Breach Bath 60 G6
Kent 69 F10
W Sus 22 B3
Breachacha Castle
Argyll 288 D3
Breachwood Green
Herts 104 G2
Breacleit W Isles 304 E3
Breaden Heath Shrops 149 B8
Breadsall Derbys 153 B7
Breadsall Hilltop Derby 153 B7
Breadstone Glos 80 E2
Bread Street Glos 80 D4
Breage Corn 2 D4
Breakachy Highld 300 E4
Brealeys Devon 25 D8
Bream Glos 79 D10
Breamore Hants 31 D11
Bream's Meend Glos 79 D9
Brean Som 43 B9
Breanais W Isles 304 F1
Brearley W Yorks 196 B4
Brearton N Yorks 214 G6
Breascleit W Isles 304 E4
Breaston Derbys 153 C9
Brechfa Carms 93 E10
Brechin Angus 293 G7
Breckan Orkney 314 F2
Breckles Norf 141 E9
Breck of Cruan Orkney 314 E3
Breckrey Highld 298 C5
Brecks S Yorks 187 C7
Brecon Powys 95 F10
Bredbury Gtr Man 184 C6
Bredbury Green
Gtr Man 184 C6
Brede E Sus 38 D4
Bredenbury Hereford 116 F2
Bredfield Suff 126 G5
Bredgar Kent 69 G11
Bredhurst Kent 69 G9
Bredicot Worcs 117 G8
Bredon Worcs 99 D8
Bredon's Hardwick
Worcs 99 D8
Bredon's Norton Worcs 99 D8
Bredwardine Hereford 96 C6
Breedon on the Hill
Leics 153 E8
Breeds Essex 87 C11
Breedy Butts Lancs 202 E2
Breibhig W Isles 297 M2
W Isles 304 E6
Breich W Loth 269 C9
Breightmet Gtr Man 195 F8
Breighton E Yorks 207 G10
Breinton Hereford 97 D9
Breinton Common
Hereford 97 C9
Breiwick Shetland 313 J6
Brelston Green Hereford 97 G11
Bremhill Wilts 62 E3
Bremhill Wick Wilts 62 E3
Bremirehoull Shetland 313 L6
Brenachoile Lodge Stirl 285 G8
Brenchley Kent 53 E7
Brenchoillie Argyll 284 G4
Brendon Devon 24 E5
Devon 24 F5
Devon 41 D9
Brenkley T&W 242 B6
Brent Corn 6 E4
Brent Eleigh Suff 107 B8
Brentford London 67 D7
Brentford End London 67 D7
Brentingby Leics 154 F5
Brent Knoll Som 43 C10
Brent Mill Devon 8 D3
Brent Pelham Herts 105 E8
Brentry Bristol 60 D5
Brentwood Essex 87 G9
Brenzett Kent 39 B8
Brenzett Green Kent 39 B8
Brereton Staffs 151 F11
Brereton Cross Staffs 151 F11
Brereton Green Ches E 168 C3
Brereton Heath Ches E 168 C4
Breretonhill Staffs 151 F11
Bressingham Norf 141 G11
Bressingham Common
Norf 141 G11
Bretby Derbys 152 E5

Carr Vale Derbys 171 B7
Carrville Durham 234 C2
Carry Argyll 275 G10
Carsaig Argyll 275 E8
Argyll 289 G7
Carscreugh Dumfries 236 D4
Carsegowan Dumfries 236 D6
Carse Gray Angus 287 B8
Carse Ho Argyll 275 G8
Carseriggan Dumfries 236 C5
Carsethorn Dumfries 237 D11
Carshalton London 67 G9
Carshalton Beeches
London 67 G9
Carshalton on the Hill
London 67 G9
Carsington Derbys 170 E3
Carskiey Argyll 255 G7
Carsluith Dumfries 236 D6
Carsphairn Dumfries 246 E3
Carstairs S Lnrk 269 F8
Carstairs Junction S
Lnrk 269 F9
Carswell Marsh Oxon 82 F4
Carthridge Sur 50 B4
Carterhaugh Borders 261 D10
Carter Knowle S Yorks 186 E4
Carter's Clay Hants 32 C4
Carter's Green Essex 87 C8
Carter's Hill Wokingham 65 F9
Carterspiece Glos 79 C9
Carterton Oxon 82 D3
Carterway Heads
Northumb 242 G2
Carthamartha Corn 12 F3
Carthew Corn 2 B5
Corn 5 D10
Carthorpe N Yorks 214 C6
Cartington Northumb 252 C2
Cartland S Lnrk 269 F7
Cartledge Derbys 186 F4
Cartmel Cumb 211 D7
Cartmel Fell Cumb 211 B8
Cartsdyke Invclyd 276 F5
Cartworth W Yorks 196 F6
Carty Port Dumfries 236 C6
Carway Carms 75 D7
Carwinley Cumb 239 C10
Carwynnen Corn 2 B5
Cary Fitzpaine Som 29 B9
Carzantic Corn 12 E3
Carzield Dumfries 247 G11
Carzise Corn 2 C3
Cascob Powys 114 D4
Cashes Green Glos 80 D4
Cashlie Perth 285 C8
Cashmoor Dorset 31 E7
Cas Mael / Puncheston
Pembs 91 F10
Cassey Compton Glos 81 C9
Cassington Oxon 83 C7
Cassop Durham 234 D2
Castallack Corn 1 D5
Castell Conwy 164 B3
Denb 165 B10
Castellau Rhondda 58 B5
Castell-Howell Ceredig 93 B8
Castell nedd / Neath
Neath 57 B8
Castell Newydd Emlyn /
Newcastle Emlyn Carms 92 C6
Castell-y-bwch Torf 78 G3
Castell-y-rhingyll Carms 75 C9
Casterton Cumb 212 D2
Castle Devon 28 G4
Som 27 B9
Castle Acre Norf 158 F6
Castle Ashby Northants 121 F7
Castle Bolton N Yorks 223 G10
Castle Bromwich W Mid 134 F2
Castle Bytham Lincs 155 F9
Castlebythe Pembs 91 F10
Castle Caereinion
Powys 130 B3
Castle Camps Cambs 106 C2
Castle Carlton Lincs 190 E5
Castle Carrock Cumb 240 F2
Castlecary N Lnrk 278 F5
Castle Cary Som 44 G6
Castle Combe Wilts 61 D10
Castlecraig Highld 301 C8
Castle Craig Borders 270 G2
Castlecroft Staffs 133 D7
Castle Donington Leics 153 D8
Castle Douglas Dumfries 237 C9
Castle Eaton Swindon 81 F10
Castle Eden Durham 234 D4
Castle End Pboro 138 B2
Castlefairn Dumfries 246 F6
Castlefields Halton 183 E8
Castle Fields Shrops 149 G10
Castle Forbes Aberds 293 B8
Castleford W Yorks 198 B2
Castle Frome Hereford 98 B3
Castle Gate Corn 1 C5
Castlegreen Shrops 130 F6
Castle Green London 68 C3
Sur 66 G3
S Yorks 197 G9
Castle Gresley Derbys 152 F5
Castlehead Renfs 267 C9
Castle Heaton Northumb 273 G8
Castle Hedingham
Essex 106 D5
Castlehill Argyll 254 B4
Borders 260 B6
Highld 310 C5
S Ayrs 257 E9
W Dunb 277 F7
Castle Hill E Sus 37 B9
Gtr Man 184 C6
Kent 53 E7
Suff 108 B3
Worcs 116 F5
Castle Huntly Perth 287 E7
Castle Kennedy
Dumfries 236 D3
Castlemaddy Dumfries 246 F3
Castlemartin Pembs 72 F6
Castlemilk Dumfries 238 B5
Glasgow 268 D2
Castlemorris Pembs 91 E8
Castlemorton Worcs 98 D5
Castle O'er Dumfries 248 E6
Castlerigg Cumb 229 G11
Castle Rising Norf 158 E3
Castleside Durham 233 B7
Castle Street W Yorks 196 C3
Castle Stuart Highld 301 E7
Castlethorpe M Keynes 102 C6
N Lincs 200 F3
Castleton Angus 287 C7
Argyll 275 E9
Derbys 185 E11
Gtr Man 195 E11
Moray 301 G11
Newport 59 C9
N Yorks 226 D3
Castleton Village Highld 300 E6
Castle Toward Argyll 266 B2
Castletown Ches W 166 E6
Cumb 230 E6
Dorset 17 G9
Highld 301 E7
Highld 310 C5
IoM 192 F3
Staffs 151 E8
T&W 243 F9
Castle Town W Sus 36 E2
Castletump Glos 98 F4
Castle-upon-Alun
V Glam 58 E2
Castle Vale W Mid 134 E2
Castleweary Borders 249 C10
Castlewigg Dumfries 236 E6
Castley N Yorks 205 D11
Castling's Heath Suff 107 C9
Caston Norf 141 D9
Castor Pboro 138 D2
Caswell Swansea 56 D5
Catacol N Ayrs 255 C10
Cat Bank Cumb 220 F6
Catbrain S Glos 60 C5
Catbrook Mon 79 E8
Catch Flint 182 G2
Catchall Corn 1 D4
Catchems Corner
W Mid 118 B4
Catchems End Worcs 116 B5
Catchgate Durham 242 G5
Catchory Highld 310 D6
Catcleugh Northumb 250 C6
Catcliffe S Yorks 186 D6
Catcomb Wilts 62 D4
Catcott Som 43 F11
Caterham Sur 51 B10
Catfield Norf 161 E7
Catfirth Shetland 313 H6
Catford London 67 E11
Catforth Lancs 202 F5
Cathays Cardiff 59 D7
Cathays Park Cardiff 59 D7
Cathcart Glasgow 267 C11
Cathedine Powys 96 F2
Catherine-de-Barnes
W Mid 134 G3
Catherine Slack
W Yorks 196 B5
Catherington Hants 33 E11
Catherton Shrops 116 B3
Cat Hill S Yorks 197 F8
Cathiron Warks 119 B9
Catholes Cumb 222 G3
Cathpair Borders 271 F9
Catisfield Hants 33 F8
Catley Lane Head
Gtr Man 195 D11
Catley Southfield
Hereford 98 C3
Catlodge Highld 291 D8
Catlowdy Cumb 239 B11
Catmere End Essex 105 D9
Catmore W Berks 64 C3
Caton Devon 13 G11
Lancs 211 G10
Caton Green Lancs 211 F10
Catrine E Ayrs 258 D2
Cat's Ash Newport 78 G5
Cat's Common Norf 160 E6
Cats Edge Staffs 169 E7
Catsfield E Sus 38 E2
Catsfield Stream E Sus 38 E2
Catsgore Som 29 B8
Catsham Som 44 G5
Catshaw S Yorks 197 G8
Catshill W Mid 133 B11
Worcs 117 C9
Cat's Hill Cross Staffs 150 C6
Catslackburn Borders 261 D8
Catslip Oxon 65 B8
Catstree Shrops 132 D4
Cattadale Argyll 274 G4
Cattal N Yorks 206 C4
Cattawade Suff 108 E2
Cattedown Plym 7 E9
Catterall Lancs 202 E5
Catterick N Yorks 224 F4
Catterick Bridge
N Yorks 224 F4
Catterick Garrison
N Yorks 224 F3
Catterlen Cumb 230 E5
Catterline Aberds 293 F10
Catterton N Yorks 206 D6
Catteshall Sur 50 E3
Catthorpe Leics 119 B11
Cattistock Dorset 17 B7
Cattle End Northants 102 C3
Catton Northumb 241 F8
N Yorks 215 D7
Catwick E Yorks 209 D8
Catworth Cambs 121 C11
Caudle Green Glos 80 C6
Caudlesprings Norf 141 C8
Caulcott C Beds 103 C9
Oxon 101 G10
Cauld Borders 261 G11
Cauldcoats Holdings
Falk 279 F10
Cauldcots Angus 287 C10
Cauldhame Stirl 278 C2
Cauldmill Borders 262 G2
Cauldon Staffs 169 F9
Cauldon Lowe Staffs 169 F9
Cauldwells Aberds 303 D7
Caulkerbush Dumfries 237 D11
Caulside Dumfries 249 G10
Caundle Marsh Dorset 29 E11
Caunsall Worcs 132 G6
Caunton Notts 172 D2
Causeway Hants 33 E11
Hants 34 C2
Mon 60 B2
Causewayend S Lnrk 260 B2
Causeway End Cumb 210 C6
Cumb 211 B9
Dumfries 236 C6
Essex 87 B11
Wilts 62 C4
Causeway Foot W Yorks 197 E7
W Yorks 205 G7
Causeway Green W Mid 133 F9
Causewayhead Cumb 238 G4
Stirl 278 B6
Causewaywood Shrops 131 D10
Causey Durham 242 F6
Causeyend Aberds 293 B11
Causey Park Bridge
Northumb 252 E5
Causeyton Aberds 293 B8
Caute Devon 24 E6
Cautley Cumb 222 G3
Cavendish Suff 106 B6
Cavendish Bridge Leics 153 D8
Cavenham Suff 124 D5
Cavers Carre Borders 262 D3
Caversfield Oxon 101 F11
Caversham Reading 65 E8
Caversham Heights
Reading 65 D8
Caverswall Staffs 169 G7
Cavil E Yorks 207 G11
Cawdor Highld 301 D8
Cawkeld E Yorks 208 C5
Cawkwell Lincs 190 F3
Cawood N Yorks 207 F7
Cawsand Corn 7 E8
Cawston Norf 160 E2
Warks 119 C9
Cawthorne N Yorks 216 B5
S Yorks 197 F9
Cawthorpe Lincs 155 E11
Cawton N Yorks 216 D2
Caxton Cambs 122 F6
Caynham Shrops 115 C11
Caythorpe Lincs 172 F6
Notts 171 F11
Cayton N Yorks 217 C11
Ceallan W Isles 296 F4
Ceann a Bhaigh W Isles 296 E3
Ceann a Bhàigh
W Isles 305 J4
Ceannacroc Lodge
Highld 290 B4
Ceann a Deas Loch
Baghasdail W Isles 297 K3
Ceann Shiphoirt
W Isles 305 G4
Ceann Tarabhaigh
W Isles 305 G4
Cearsiadair W Isles 304 F5
Ceathramh Meadhanach
W Isles 296 D4
Cefn Newport 59 B9
Powys 148 G5
Cefn Berain Conwy 165 B7
Cefn-brith Conwy 164 E6
Cefn-bryn-brain Carms 76 C2
Cefn-bychan Swansea 56 B4
Wrex 166 G3
Cefncaeau Carms 56 B4
Cefn Canol Powys 148 C4
Cefn-coch Conwy 164 B5
Cefn Coch Powys 129 C10
Powys 148 D2
Cefn-coed-y-cymmer
M Tydf 77 D9f
Cefn Cribbwr Bridgend 57 E11
Cefn Cross Bridgend 57 E11
Cefn-ddwysarn Gwyn 147 B9
Cefn Einion Shrops 130 F5
Cefneithin Carms 75 C9
Cefn-eurgain Flint 166 B2
Cefn Fforest Caerph 77 F11
Cefn Glas Bridgend 57 E11
Cefn Golau Bl Gwent 77 D10
Cefn-gorwydd Powys 95 B8
Cefn Hengoed Caerph 77 F10
Cefn-hengoed Swansea 57 B7
Cefn Llwyd Ceredig 128 G2
Cefn-mawr Wrex 166 G3
Cefnpennar Rhondda 77 E8
Cefn Rhigos Rhondda 76 D6
Cefn-y-bedd Flint 166 D4
Cefn-y-Crib Torf 78 F2
Cefn-y-Garth Swansea 76 E2
Cefn-y-pant Carms 92 F3
Cegidfa / Guilsfield
Powys 148 G4
Cei-bach Ceredig 111 F8
Ceinewydd / New Quay
Ceredig 111 F7
Ceint Anglesey 179 F7
Ceinws Powys 128 B5
Cellan Ceredig 94 B2
Cellarhead Staffs 169 F7
Cellarhill Kent 70 G3
Celyn-Mali Flint 165 B11
Cemaes Anglesey 178 C5
Cemmaes Powys 128 B6
Cemmaes Road /
Glantwymyn Powys 128 C6
Cenarth Carms 92 C5
Cenin Gwyn 163 F7
Central Invclyd 276 F5
Central Milton Keynes
M Keynes 102 D6
Ceos W Isles 304 F5
Ceres Fife 287 F8
Ceri / Kerry Powys 130 F2
Cerne Abbas Dorset 29 G11
Cerney Wick Glos 81 F9
Cerrigceinwen Anglesey 178 G6
Cerrig Llwydion Neath 57 C9
Cerrig-mân Anglesey 179 C7
Cerrigydrudion Conwy 165 F7
Cess Norf 161 F8
Cessford Borders 262 E6
Ceunant Gwyn 163 C8
Chaceley Glos 99 E7
Chaceley Hole Glos 98 E6
Chaceley Stock Glos 99 F7
Chacewater Corn 4 G4
Chackmore Bucks 102 D3
Chacombe Northants 101 C9
Chadbury Worcs 99 B10
Chadderton Gtr Man 196 F2
Chadderton Fold
Gtr Man 195 F11
Chaddesden Derby 153 B7
Chaddesley Corbett
Worcs 117 C7
Chaddlehanger Devon 12 F5
Chaddlewood Plym 7 D11
Chaddleworth W Berks 64 D2
Chadkirk Gtr Man 184 D6
Chadlington Oxon 100 G6
Chadshunt Warks 118 G6
Chadsmoor Staffs 151 G9
Chadstone Northants 121 F7
Chad Valley W Mid 133 F10
Chadwell Leics 154 E5
Shrops 150 G5
Chadwell End Beds 121 D11
Chadwell Heath London 68 B3
Chadwell St Mary
Thurrock 68 D6
Chadwick Worcs 116 D6
Chadwick End W Mid 118 C4
Chadwick Green Mers 183 B8
Chaffcombe Som 28 E5
Chafford Hundred
Thurrock 68 D5
Chagford Devon 13 D10
Chailey E Sus 36 D5
Chainbridge Cambs 139 C8
Chain Bridge Lincs 174 G4
Chainhurst Kent 53 D8
Chalbury Dorset 31 F8
Chalbury Common Dorset 31 F8
Chaldon Sur 51 B10
Chaldon Herring or East
Chaldon Dorset 17 E11
Chale IoW 20 F5
Chale Green IoW 20 F5
Chalfont Common Bucks 85 G8
Chalfont Grove Bucks 85 G7
Chalfont St Giles Bucks 85 G7
Chalfont St Peter Bucks 85 G8
Chalford Glos 80 E5
Oxon 84 E2
Wilts 45 C11
Chalford Hill Glos 80 E5
Chalgrave C Beds 103 F10
Chalgrove Oxon 83 F10
Chalk Kent 69 E7
Chalk End Essex 87 C10
Chalkfoot Cumb 230 B2
Chalkhill Norf 141 C7
Chalkhouse Green Oxon 65 D8
Chalkshire Bucks 84 D4
Chalksole Kent 55 E9
Chalkway Som 28 F5
Chalkwell Kent 69 G11
Sthend 69 B11
Challaborough Devon 8 G3
Challacombe Devon 41 E7
Challister Shetland 312 G7
Challoch Dumfries 236 C5
Challock Kent 54 C4
Chalmington Dorset 29 G9
Chalton C Beds 103 F10
Hants 34 D2
Chalvedon Essex 69 B8
Chalvey Slough 66 D3
Chalvington E Sus 23 D8
Chambercombe Devon 40 D4
Chamber's Green Kent 54 E2
Champson Devon 26 B4
Chance Inn Fife 287 F7
Chancery / Rhydgaled
Ceredig 111 B11
Chance's Pitch Hereford 98 C4
Chandler's Cross Herts 85 F9
Worcs 98 D5
Chandler's Ford Hants 32 C6
Chandlers Green Hants 49 B8
Channel's End Beds 122 F2
Channel Tunnel Kent 55 F7
Channerwick Shetland 313 L6
Chantry Devon 25 C9
Som 45 D8
Suff 108 C2
Chapel Corn 4 C6
Cumb 229 E10
Fife 280 C5
Chapel Allerton Som 44 C2
W Yorks 206 F2
Chapel Amble Corn 10 F5
Chapel Brampton
Northants 120 D4
Chapel Chorlton Staffs 150 B6
Chapel Cleeve Som 42 E4
Chapel Cross E Sus 37 C10
Chapel End Beds 103 B11
Beds 122 F2
Cambs 138 G2
C Beds 103 C11
Ches E 167 G11
Essex 105 G11
Northants 138 F2
Warks 134 E6
Chapel-en-le-Frith
Derbys 185 E9
Chapel Field Gtr Man 195 F9
Norf 161 E7
Chapel Fields W Mid 118 B6
York 207 C7
Chapelgate Lincs 157 E8
Chapel Green Herts 104 D6
Warks 119 E9
Warks 134 F5
Chapel Haddlesey
N Yorks 198 B5
Chapelhall N Lnrk 268 C5
Chapel Head Cambs 138 G6
Chapelhill Dumfries 248 E3
Highld 301 B8
N Ayrs 266 G4
Perth 286 D4
Perth 286 E3
Perth 286 E6
Chapel Hill Aberds 303 F10
Glos 79 E10
Lincs 174 E2
Mon 79 F8
N Yorks 206 D2
Chapel House Lancs 194 F3
Chapel Knapp Wilts 61 F11
Chapelknowe Dumfries 239 C8
Chapel Lawn Shrops 114 B6
Chapel-le-Dale
N Yorks 212 D4
Chapel Leigh Som 27 B10
Chapel Mains Borders 271 G11
Chapel Milton Derbys 185 E9
Chapel of Garioch
Aberds 303 G7
Chapel of Stoneywood
Aberdeen 293 B10
Chapel on Leader
Borders 271 G11
Chapel Outon Dumfries 236 E6
Chapel Plaister Wilts 61 F10
Chapel Row Essex 88 E3
E Sus 23 C10
W Berks 64 F5
Chapels Blkburn 195 C7
Cumb 210 C4
Chapel St Leonards
Lincs 191 G9
Chapel Stile Cumb 220 D6
Chapelthorpe W Yorks 197 D10
Chapelton Angus 287 C10
Devon 25 B9
Highld 291 B11
S Lnrk 268 F3
Chapelton Row Dumfries 237 E8
Chapeltown Blkburn 195 D8
Moray 302 G2
S Yorks 186 B5
W Yorks 206 F2
Chapel Town Corn 5 D7
Chapman's Hill Worcs 117 B9
Chapmanslade Wilts 45 D10
Chapman's Town E Sus 23 B10
Chapmans Well Devon 12 C3
Chapmore End Herts 86 B4
Chappel Essex 107 F7
Charaton Cross Corn 6 B6
Charcott Kent 52 D4
Chard Som 28 F4
Chard Junction Dorset 28 G4
Chardleigh Green Som 28 E4
Chardstock Devon 28 G4
Charfield S Glos 80 G2
Charfield Green S Glos 80 G2
Charfield Hill S Glos 80 G2
Charford Worcs 117 D9
Chargrove Glos 80 B6
Charing Kent 54 D3
Charing Cross Dorset 31 E10
Charing Heath Kent 54 D2
Charing Hill Kent 54 C3
Charingworth Glos 100 D4
Charlbury Oxon 82 B5
Charlcombe Bath 61 F8
Charlcutt Wilts 62 D4
Charlecote Warks 118 F5
Charlemont W Mid 133 E10
Charles Devon 41 G7
Charles Bottom Devon 41 G7
Charlesfield Borders 262 D3
Dumfries 238 D5
Charleshill Sur 49 E11
Charleston Angus 287 C7
Renfs 267 C9
Charlestown Aberdeen 293 C11
Corn 5 E10
Derbys 185 C8
Dorset 17 F9
Fife 279 E11
Gtr Man 195 G10
Gtr Man 195 G11
Highld 299 B8
Highld 300 E6
W Yorks 196 B3
W Yorks 205 F9
Charlestown of Aberlour
Moray 302 E2
Charles Tye Suff 125 G10
Charlesworth Derbys 185 C8
Charleton Devon 8 G5
Charlinch Som 43 F8
Charlottetown Fife 286 F6
Charlton Hants 47 D11
Herts 104 F3
London 68 D2
Northants 101 D10
Northumb 251 F8
Oxon 64 B2
Redcar 226 B2
Som 28 B3
Som 44 E6
Som 45 C7
Sur 66 F5
Telford 149 G11
Wilts 30 C6
Wilts 46 B6
Wilts 62 B3
Worcs 99 B10
Worcs 116 C6
W Sus 34 E5
Charlton Abbots Glos 99 G10
Charlton Adam Som 29 B8
Charlton-All-Saints
Wilts 31 C11
Charltonbrook S Yorks 186 B4
Charlton Down Dorset 17 C9
Charlton Horethorne
Som 29 C11
Charlton Kings Glos 99 G9
Charlton Mackrell Som 29 B8
Charlton Marshall Dorset 30 G5
Charlton Musgrove Som 30 B2
Charlton on Otmoor
Oxon 83 B9
Charlton on the Hill
Dorset 30 G5
Charlton Park Glos 99 G9
Charlton St Peter Wilts 46 B6
Charlwood E Sus 51 G11
Hants 49 G7
Sur 51 E8
Charlynch Som 43 F8
Charminster Bmouth 19 C8
Dorset 17 C9
Charmouth Dorset 16 C3
Charnage Wilts 45 G10
Charndon Bucks 102 G3
Charnes Staffs 150 C5
Charney Bassett Oxon 82 G5
Charnock Green Lancs 194 D5
Charnock Hall S Yorks 186 E5
Charnock Richard
Lancs 194 D5
Charsfield Suff 126 F5
Chart Corner Kent 53 C9
Charter Alley Hants 48 B5
Charterhouse Som 44 B3
Chartershall Stirl 278 C6
Charterville Allotments
Oxon 82 C4
Chartham Kent 54 C6
Chartham Hatch Kent 54 B6
Chart Hill Kent 53 D9
Chartridge Bucks 84 E6
Chart Sutton Kent 53 D10
Charvil Wokingham 65 D9
Charwelton Northants 119 F10
Chase Cross London 87 G8
Chase End Street Worcs 98 D5
Chase Hill S Glos 61 B8
Chase Terrace Staffs 133 B10
Chasetown Staffs 133 B10
Chastleton Oxon 100 F4
Chasty Devon 24 G4
Chatburn Lancs 203 E11
Chatcull Staffs 150 C5
Chatford Shrops 131 B9
Chatham Caerph 59 B8
Medway 69 F9
Chatham Green Essex 88 B2
Chathill Northumb 264 D5
Chat Hill W Yorks 205 G8
Chatley Worcs 117 E7
Chattenden Medway 69 E9
Chatter End Essex 105 F9
Chatteris Cambs 139 F7
Chatterley Staffs 168 E4
Chattern Hill Sur 66 E5
Chatterton Lancs 195 D9
Chattisham Suff 107 C11
Chattle Hill Warks 134 E3
Chatto Borders 263 F7
Chatton Northumb 264 D3
Chaulden Herts 85 D8
Chaul End C Beds 103 G11
Chavel Shrops 149 G8
Chavenage Green Glos 80 F5
Chavey Down Brack 65 F11
Chawleigh Devon 26 E2
Chawley Oxon 83 E7
Chawson Worcs 117 E7
Chawston Beds 122 F3
Chawton Hants 49 F8
Chaxhill Glos 80 C2
Chazey Heath Oxon 65 D7
Cheadle Gtr Man 184 D5
Staffs 169 G8
Cheadle Heath Gtr Man 184 D5
Cheadle Hulme Gtr Man 184 D5
Cheadle Park Staffs 169 G8
Cheam London 67 G8
Cheapside Herts 105 E8
Sur 50 B4
Windsor 66 F2
Chearsley Bucks 84 C2
Chebsey Staffs 151 D7
Checkendon Oxon 65 C7
Checkley Ches E 168 F2
Hereford 97 D11
Staffs 151 B10
Checkley Green Ches E 168 F2
Chedburgh Suff 124 F5
Cheddar Som 44 C3
Cheddington Bucks 84 B6
Cheddleton Staffs 169 E7
Cheddleton Heath
Staffs 169 E7
Cheddon Fitzpaine Som 28 B2
Chedglow Wilts 80 G6
Chedgrave Norf 143 D7
Chedington Dorset 29 F7
Chediston Suff 127 B7
Chediston Green Suff 127 B7
Chedworth Glos 81 C9
Chedworth Laines Glos 81 C8
Chedzoy Som 43 F10
Cheeklaw Borders 272 E5
Cheeseman's Green Kent 54 F4
Cheetam Hill Gtr Man 195 G10
Cheglinch Devon 40 E4
Chegworth Kent 53 C10
Cheldon Devon 26 E2
Chelfham Devon 40 F6
Chelford Ches E 184 G4
Chellaston Derby 153 C7
Chell Heath Stoke 168 E5
Chellington Beds 121 F9
Chells Herts 104 F5
Chelmarsh Shrops 132 F4
Chelmer Village Essex 88 D2
Chelmick Shrops 131 E9
Chelmondiston Suff 108 D4
Chelmorton Derbys 169 B10
Chelmsford Essex 88 D2
Chelmsine Som 27 D11
Chelmsley Wood W Mid 134 F3
Chelsea London 67 D9
Chelsfield London 68 G3
Chelsham Sur 51 B11
Chelston Som 27 C11
Torbay 9 C7
Chelston Heathfield
Som 27 C11
Chelsworth Suff 107 B9
Chelsworth Common
Suff 107 B9
Cheltenham Glos 99 G8
Chelveston Northants 121 D9
Chelvey N Som 60 F3
Chelvey Batch N Som 60 F3
Chelwood Bath 60 G6
Chelwood Common
E Sus 36 B6
Chelwood Gate E Sus 36 B6
Chelworth Wilts 81 G7
Chelworth Lower Green
Wilts 81 G9
Chelworth Upper Green
Wilts 81 G9
Chelynch Som 45 E7
Chemistry Shrops 167 G8
Cheney Longville
Shrops 131 G8
Chenhalls Corn 2 B3
Chenies Bucks 85 F8
Cheny Longville Shrops 131 G8
Chepstow Mon 79 G8
Chequerbent Gtr Man 195 F7
Chequerfield W Yorks 198 C3
Chequers Corner Norf 139 B9
Chequertree Kent 54 F4
Cherhill Wilts 62 E4
Cherington Glos 80 F6
Warks 100 D5
Cheristow Devon 24 B3
Cheriton Devon 41 D8
Hants 33 B9
Kent 55 F7
Swansea 56 C3
Cheriton Bishop Devon 13 C11
Cheriton Cross Devon 13 C11
Cheriton Fitzpaine Devon 26 F5
Cheriton or Stackpole Elidor
Pembs 73 F7
Cherrington Telford 150 E3
Cherrybank Perth 286 E5
Cherry Burton E Yorks 208 E5
Cherry Green Essex 105 F11
Herts 105 F7
Cherry Hinton Cambs 123 F9
Cherry Orchard Shrops 149 G9
Worcs 117 G7
Cherry Tree Blkburn 195 B7
Gtr Man 185 C7
Cherrytree Hill Derby 153 B7
Cherry Willingham
Lincs 189 G8
Chertsey Sur 66 F4
Chertsey Meads Sur 66 F5
Cheselbourne Dorset 17 B11
Chesham Bucks 85 E7
Gtr Man 195 E10
Chesham Bois Bucks 85 F7
Cheshunt Herts 86 E5
Chesley Kent 69 G11
Cheslyn Hay Staffs 133 B9
Chessetts Wood Warks 118 C3
Chessington London 67 G7
Chessmount Bucks 85 E7
Chestall Staffs 151 G11
Chester Ches W 166 B6
Chesterblade Som 45 E7
Chesterfield Derbys 186 G5
Staffs 134 B2
Chesterhill Midloth 271 B7
Chesterhope Northumb 251 F9
Chesterknowes Borders 262 D2
Chester-le-Street
Durham 243 G7
Chester Moor Durham 233 B11
Chesters Borders 262 E4
Borders 262 G4
Chesterton Cambs 123 E9
Cambs 138 D2
Glos 81 E8
Oxon 101 G11
Shrops 132 D5
Staffs 168 F4
Warks 118 F6
Chesterton Green
Warks 118 F6
Chesterwood Northumb 241 D8
Chestfield Kent 70 F6
Chestnut Hill Cumb 229 G11
Chestnut Street Kent 69 G11
Cheston Devon 8 D3
Cheswardine Shrops 150 D4
Cheswell Telford 150 F4
Cheswick Northumb 273 F10
Cheswick Buildings
Northumb 273 F10
Cheswick Green W Mid 118 B2
Chetnole Dorset 29 F10
Chettiscombe Devon 27 E7
Chettisham Cambs 139 G10
Chettle Dorset 31 E7
Chetton Shrops 132 E3
Chetwode Bucks 102 F2
Chetwynd Aston Telford 150 F5
Cheveley Cambs 124 E3
Chevening Kent 52 B3
Cheverell's Green Herts 85 B9
Chevin End W Yorks 205 E9
Chevington Suff 124 F5
Chevithorne Devon 27 D7
Chew Magna Bath 60 G5
Chew Moor Gtr Man 195 F7
Chew Stoke Bath 60 G5
Chewton Keynsham Bath 61 F7
Chewton Mendip Som 44 C5
Cheylesmore W Mid 118 B6
Chichacott Devon 13 B8
Chicheley M Keynes 103 B8
Chichester W Sus 22 C5
Chickenley W Yorks 197 C9
Chickerell Dorset 17 E8
Chicklade Wilts 46 G2
Chickney Essex 105 F11
Chicksands C Beds 104 D2
Chicksgrove Wilts 46 G3
Chickward Hereford 114 G5
Chidden Hants 33 D11
Chiddingfold Sur 50 F3
Chiddingly E Sus 23 C8
Chiddingstone Kent 52 D3
Chiddingstone Causeway
Kent 52 D4
Chiddingstone Hoath
Kent 52 E3
Chideock Dorset 16 C4
Chidgley Som 42 F4
Chidham W Sus 22 C3
Chidswell W Yorks 197 C9
Chieveley W Berks 64 E3
Chignall St James
Essex 87 D11
Chignall Smealy Essex 87 C11
Chigwell Essex 86 G6
Chigwell Row Essex 87 G7
Chilbolton Hants 47 F11
Chilbolton Down Hants 48 F2
Chilbridge Dorset 31 G7
Chilcomb Hants 33 B8
Chilcombe Dorset 16 C6
Som 42 F6
Chilcompton Som 44 C6
Chilcote Leics 152 G5
Childerditch Essex 68 B6
Childerley Gate Cambs 123 F7
Childer Thornton
Ches W 182 F5
Child Okeford Dorset 30 E4
Childrey Oxon 63 B11
Childsbridge Kent 52 B5
Child's Ercall Shrops 150 E3
Child's Hill London 67 B8
Childswickham Worcs 99 D11
Childwall Mers 182 D6
Childwick Bury Herts 85 C10
Childwick Green Herts 85 C10
Chilfrome Dorset 17 B7
Chilgrove W Sus 34 E4
Chilham Kent 54 C5
Chilhampton Wilts 46 G5
Chilla Devon 24 G6
Chillaton Devon 12 E4
Chillenden Kent 55 C9
Chillerton IoW 20 E5
Chillesford Suff 127 G7
Chillingham Northumb 264 D3
Chillington Devon 8 G5
Som 28 E5
Chillmill Kent 53 E7
Chilmark Wilts 46 G3
Chilmington Green Kent 54 E3
Chilsham E Sus 23 C10
Chilson Oxon 82 B4
Som 28 G4
Chilson Common Som 28 G4
Chilsworthy Corn 12 G4
Devon 24 F4
Chiltern Green Beds 85 B10
Chilthorne Domer Som 29 D8
Chiltington E Sus 36 D5
Chilton Bucks 83 C11
Durham 233 F11
Kent 71 G11
Oxon 64 B3
Suff 107 C7
Chilton Candover Hants 48 E5
Chilton Cantelo Som 29 C9
Chilton Foliat Wilts 63 E10
Chilton Lane Durham 234 E2
Chilton Moor T&W 234 B2
Chilton Polden Som 43 F11
Chilton Street Suff 106 B5
Chilton Trinity Som 43 F9
Chilvers Coton Warks 135 E7
Chilwell Notts 153 B10
Chilworth Hants 32 D6
Sur 50 D4
Chilworth Old Village
Hants 32 D6
Chimney Oxon 82 E5
Chimney-end Oxon 82 B4
Chimney Street Suff 106 B4
Chineham Hants 49 C7
Chingford London 86 G5
Chingford Green London 86 G5
Chingford Hatch London 86 G5
Chinley Derbys 185 E8
Chinley Head Derbys 185 E9
Chinnor Oxon 84 E3
Chipley Som 27 C10
Chipmans Platt Glos 80 D3
Chipnall Shrops 150 C4
Chippenhall Green Suff 126 B5
Chippenham Cambs 124 D3
Wilts 62 E2
Chipperfield Herts 85 E8
Chipping Herts 105 E7
Lancs 203 E8
Chipping Barnet London 86 F2
Chipping Campden
Glos 100 D3
Chipping Hill Essex 88 B4
Chipping Norton Oxon 100 F6
Chipping Ongar Essex 87 E8
Chipping Sodbury S Glos 61 C8
Chipping Warden
Northants 101 B9
Chipstable Som 27 B8
Chipstead Kent 52 B3
Sur 51 B9
Chirbury Shrops 130 D5
Chirk Bank Shrops 148 B5
Chirk Green Wrex 148 B5
Chirk / Y Waun Wrex 148 B5
Chirmorrie S Ayrs 236 B4
Chirnside Borders 273 D7
Chirnsidebridge
Borders 273 D7
Chirton T&W 243 D8
Wilts 46 B5
Chisbridge Cross Bucks 65 B10
Chisbury Wilts 63 F9
Chiselborough Som 29 E7
Chiseldon Swindon 63 D7
Chiserley W Yorks 196 B4
Chislehampton Oxon 83 F9
Chislehurst London 68 E2
Chislehurst West London 68 E2
Chislet Kent 71 G8
Chislet Forstal Kent 71 G8
Chiswell Dorset 17 G9
Chiswell Green Herts 85 E10
Chiswick London 67 D8
Chiswick End Cambs 105 B7
Chisworth Derbys 185 C7
Chitcombe E Sus 38 C4
Chithurst W Sus 34 C4
Chittering Cambs 123 C9
Chitterley Devon 26 G6
Chitterne Wilts 46 E3
Chittlehamholt Devon 25 C11
Chittlehampton Devon 25 B10
Chittoe Wilts 62 F3
Chitts Hills Essex 107 F9
Chitty Kent 71 G8
Chivelstone Devon 9 G10
Chivenor Devon 40 G4
Chivery Bucks 84 D6
Chobham Sur 66 G3
Choicelee Borders 272 E4
Cholderton Wilts 47 E8
Cholesbury Bucks 84 D6
Chollerford Northumb 241 C10
Chollerton Northumb 241 C10
Cholmondeston
Ches E 167 C10
Cholsey Oxon 64 B5
Cholstrey Hereford 115 F9
Cholwell Bath 44 B6
Chop Gate N Yorks 225 F11
Choppington Northumb 253 G7
Chopwell T&W 242 F4
Chorley Ches E 167 E9
Lancs 194 D5
Shrops 132 G3
Staffs 151 G11
Chorley Common W Sus 34 B4
Chorleywood Herts 85 F8
Chorleywood Bottom
Herts 85 F8
Chorleywood West Herts 85 F8
Chorlton Ches E 168 E2
Chorlton-cum-Hardy
Gtr Man 184 C4
Chorlton Lane Ches W 167 F7
Choulton Shrops 131 F7
Chowdene T&W 243 F7
Chowley Ches W 167 D7
Chownes Mead W Sus 36 C4
Chreagain Highld 289 C10
Chrishall Essex 105 D8
Christchurch Cambs 139 D9
Dorset 19 C9
Glos 79 C9
Newport 59 B10
Christian Malford Wilts 62 D3
Christleton Ches W 166 B6
Christmas Common Oxon 84 G2
Christon N Som 43 B11
Christon Bank Northumb 264 E6
Christow Devon 14 D2
Chryston N Lnrk 278 G3
Chub Tor Devon 7 B10
Chuck Hatch E Sus 52 G3
Chudleigh Devon 14 F3
Chudleigh Knighton
Devon 14 F2
Chulmleigh Devon 25 E11
Chunal Derbys 185 C8
Church Lancs 195 B8
Churcham Glos 80 B3
Church Aston Telford 150 F4
Churchbank Shrops 114 B6
Church Brampton
Northants 120 D4
Churchbridge Corn 6 D4
Staffs 133 B9
Church Brough Cumb 222 C5
Church Broughton
Derbys 152 C4
Church Charwelton
Northants 119 F10
Church Clough Lancs 204 F3
Church Common Hants 34 B2
Church Coombe Corn 4 G3
Church Cove Corn 2 G6
Church Crookham
Hants 49 C10
Churchdown Glos 80 B5
Church Eaton Staffs 150 F6
Churchend Essex 89 G8
Essex 106 G2
Glos 80 D3
Reading 65 E7
S Glos 80 G2
Church End Barnet 86 G2
Beds 121 G12
Beds 122 F2
Brent 67 C8
Bucks 84 B6
Bucks 84 D2
Cambs 121 C11
Cambs 123 C7
Cambs 123 D7
Cambs 138 G4
Cambs 139 B7
C Beds 85 B8
C Beds 103 E9
C Beds 103 G9
C Beds 104 D3
C Beds 122 G3
Essex 88 B2
Essex 105 C11
Essex 105 F11
Essex 106 F4
E Yorks 209 C7
Glos 80 D2
Glos 99 D7
Hants 49 B7
Herts 85 C10
Herts 85 F8
Herts 104 E5
Herts 105 G8
Lincs 156 C4
Lincs 190 B6
Norf 157 F10
Oxon 82 D5
Oxon 100 E6
Suff 108 D4
Sur 50 B5
Warks 134 E4
Warks 134 E5
Wilts 62 D4
W Mid 119 B7
Worcs 98 C6
Church Enstone Oxon 101 G7
Churches Green E Sus 23 B10
Church Fenton N Yorks 206 F6
Churchfield Hereford 98 B4
W Mid 133 E10
Churchfields Wilts 31 B10
Churchgate Herts 86 E4
Churchgate Street Essex 87 C7
Church Green Devon 15 B9
Norf 141 E11
Church Gresley Derbys 152 F5
Church Hanborough
Oxon 82 C6
Church Hill Ches W 167 C10
Pembs 73 C7
Staffs 151 G10
W Mid 133 D9
Worcs 117 D11
Church Hougham Kent 55 E9
Church Houses N Yorks 226 F3
Churchill Devon 28 G4
Devon 40 E5

East Hartford Northumb. 243 B7
East Harting W Sus 34 D3
East Hatch Wilts 30 B6
East Hatley Cambs 122 G5
East Haugh Norf 159 F11
East Hauxwell N Yorks 224 G3
East Haven Angus 287 D9
Eastheath Wokingham 65 F10
East Heckington Lincs 173 G11
East Hedleyhope
Durham 233 C9
East Helmsdale Highld 311 H4
East Hendred Oxon 64 B3
East Herringthorpe
S Yorks 187 C7
East Herrington T&W 243 G9
East Heslerton N Yorks 217 D8
East Hewish N Som 59 G11
East Hill Kent 68 G5
East Hoathly E Sus 23 B8
East Hogaland Shetland 313 K5
East Holme Dorset 18 D3
East Holton Dorset 18 C5
East Holywell Northumb 243 C8
Easthope Shrops 131 D11
Easthopewood Shrops 131 D11
East Horndon Essex 68 B6
Easthorpe Essex 107 G8
Leics 154 B6
Notts 172 E2
East Horrington Som 44 D5
East Horsley Sur 50 C5
East Horton Northumb 264 C2
Easthouse Shetland 313 J5
Easthouses Midloth 270 B6
East Howdon T&W 243 D8
East Howe Bmouth 19 B7
East Huntspill Som 43 E10
East Hyde C Beds 85 B10
East Ilkerton Devon 41 D8
East Ilsley W Berks 64 C3
Easting Orkney 314 A7
Eastington Devon 26 F2
Glos 80 D3
Glos 81 C10
East Keal Lincs 174 C5
East Kennett Wilts 62 F6
East Keswick W Yorks 206 E3
East Kilbride S Lnrk 268 E2
East Kimber Devon 12 B5
East Kingston W Sus 35 G9
East Kirkby Lincs 174 C4
East Knapton N Yorks 217 D7
East Knighton Dorset 18 D2
East Knowstone Devon 26 C4
East Knoyle Wilts 45 G11
East Kyloe Northumb 264 B3
East Kyo Durham 242 G5
East Lambrook Som 28 D6
East Lamington Highld 301 B7
Eastland Gate Hants 33 E11
East Langdon Kent 55 D10
East Langton Leics 136 E4
East Langwell Highld 309 J7
East Lavant W Sus 22 B5
East Lavington W Sus 34 D6
East Law Northumb 242 G3
East Layton N Yorks 224 D3
Eastleach Martin Glos 82 D2
Eastleach Turville Glos 81 D11
East Leake Notts 153 D11
East Learmouth
Northumb 263 B9
Eastleigh Devon 25 B7
Hants 32 D6
East Leigh Devon 8 E3
Devon 25 F11
East Lexham Norf 159 F7
East Lilburn Northumb 264 E2
Eastling Kent 54 B3
East Linton E Loth 281 F11
East Liss Hants 34 B3
East Lockinge Oxon 64 B2
East Loftus Redcar 226 B4
East Looe Corn 6 E5
East Lound N Lincs 188 B3
East Lulworth Dorset 18 E3
East Lutton N Yorks 217 F8
East Lydeard Som 27 B11
East Lydford Som 44 G5
East Lyng Som 28 B4
East Mains Aberds 293 D8
Borders 271 F11
S Lnrk 268 E2
East Malling Kent 53 B8
East Malling Heath Kent 53 B7
East March Angus 287 D8
East Marden W Sus 34 E4
East Markham Notts 188 G2
East Marsh NE Lincs 201 E9
East Martin Hants 31 D9
East Marton N Yorks 204 C4
East Melbury Dorset 30 C5
East Meon Hants 33 C11
East Mere Devon 27 D7
East Mersea Essex 89 C9
East Mey Highld 310 B7
East Molesey Sur 67 F7
Eastmoor Derbys 186 G4
Norf 140 C4
East Moor W Yorks 197 C10
East Moors Cardiff 59 D8
East Morden Dorset 18 B4
East Morton W Yorks 205 E7
East Moulsecoomb
Brighton 36 F4
East Ness N Yorks 216 D3
East Newton E Yorks 209 F11
N Yorks 216 D2
Eastney Ptsmth 21 B9
Eastnor Hereford 98 D4
East Norton Leics 136 C5
East Nynehead Som 27 C11
East Oakley Hants 48 C5
Eastoft N Lincs 199 D10
East Ogwell Devon 14 G2
Eastoke Hants 21 B10
Easton Bristol 60 E6
Cambs 122 C2
Cumb 239 C10
Cumb 239 F7
Devon 8 F3
Devon 13 D10
Dorset 17 G9
Hants 48 G4
IoW 20 D2
Lincs 155 D8
Norf 160 G2
Som 44 D4
Suff 126 F5
W Berks 64 E2
Wilts 61 E11
Easton Grey Wilts 61 B11
Easton in Gordano
N Som 60 D4
Easton Maudit Northants 121 F7
Easton on the Hill
Northants 137 C10
Easton Royal Wilts 63 G8
Easton Town Som 44 G5
Wilts 61 B11
East Orchard Dorset 30 D4
East Ord Northumb 273 E9
Eastover Som 43 F10
East Panson Devon 12 C3
Eastpark Dumfries 238 D2
East Parley Dorset 19 B8
East Peckham Kent 53 D7
East Pennard Som 44 F5
East Perry Cambs 122 D3
East Portholland Corn 5 G9
East Portlemouth Devon 9 G9
East Prawle Devon 9 G10
East Preston W Sus 35 G9
East Pulham Dorset 30 F2
East Putford Devon 24 D5
East Quantoxhead Som 42 E6
East Rainton T&W 234 B2
East Ravendale NE Lincs 190 B2
East Raynham Norf 159 D7
Eastrea Cambs 138 D5
East Rhidorroch Lodge
Highld 307 K7
Eastriggs Dumfries 238 D6
East Rigton W Yorks 206 E3
Eastrington E Yorks 199 B9
Eastrip Wilts 61 E10
East Rolstone N Som 59 G11
Eastrop Hants 48 C6
East Rounton N Yorks 225 E8
East Row N Yorks 227 C7
East Rudham Norf 158 D6
East Runton Norf 177 E11
East Ruston Norf 160 D6
Eastry Kent 55 C10
East Saltoun E Loth 271 B9
East Sheen London 67 D8
East Skelston Dumfries 247 F8
East Sleekburn
Northumb 253 G7
East Somerton Norf 161 F9
East Stanley Durham 242 G6
East Stockwith Lincs 188 C3
East Stoke Dorset 18 D3
Notts 172 F3
Som 29 D7
East Stour Dorset 30 C4
East Stour Common
Dorset 30 C4
East Stourmouth Kent 71 G9
East Stowford Devon 25 B10
East Stratton Hants 48 F4
East Street Kent 55 B10
Som 44 F4
East Studdal Kent 55 D10
East Suisnish Highld 295 B7
East Taphouse Corn 6 C3
East-the-Water Devon 25 B7
East Third Borders 262 B4
East Thirston Northumb 252 D5
East Tilbury Thurrock 69 D7
East Tisted Hants 49 G8
East Torrington Lincs 189 E10
East Town Som 42 G6
Som 44 E6
Wilts 45 B11
East Trewent Pembs 73 F8
East Tuddenham Norf 159 G11
East Tuelmenna Corn 6 B4
East Tytherley Hants 32 B3
East Tytherton Wilts 62 E3
East Village Devon 26 F4
V Glam 58 E3
Eastville Bristol 60 E6
Lincs 174 D6
East Wall Shrops 131 E10
East Walton Norf 158 F4
East Water Som 44 C4
East Week Devon 13 C9
Eastwell Leics 154 D5
East Wellow Hants 32 C4
Eastwell Park Kent 54 D4
East Wemyss Fife 280 B6
East Whitburn W Loth 269 B9
Eastwick Herts 86 C6
Shetland 312 F5
East Wickham London 68 D3
East Williamston Pembs 73 E9
East Winch Norf 158 F3
East Winterslow Wilts 47 G8
East Wittering W Sus 21 B11
East Witton N Yorks 214 B2
Eastwood Hereford 98 C2
Notts 171 F7
Sthend 69 B10
S Yorks 186 C6
W Yorks 196 B3
East Woodburn
Northumb 251 F10
Eastwood End Cambs 139 E8
Eastwood Hall Notts 171 F7
East Woodhay Hants 64 G2
East Woodlands Som 45 E9
East Worldham Hants 49 F8
East Worlington Devon 26 E3
East Worthing W Sus 35 G11
East Wretham Norf 141 E8
East Youlstone Devon 24 D3
Eathorpe Warks 119 D7
Eaton Ches E 168 B5
Ches W 167 C9
Hereford 115 F10
Leics 154 D5
Norf 142 B4
Notts 188 F2
Oxon 82 E6
Shrops 131 F7
Shrops 131 F10
Eaton Bishop Hereford 97 D8
Eaton Bray C Beds 103 G9
Eaton Constantine
Shrops 131 B11
Eaton Ford Cambs 122 E3
Eaton Green C Beds 103 G9
Eaton Hastings Oxon 82 F3
Eaton Mascott Shrops 131 B10
Eaton on Tern Shrops 150 E3
Eaton Socon Cambs 122 F3
Eaton upon Tern Shrops 150 E3
Eau Brink Norf 157 F11
Eau Withington
Hereford 97 C10
Eaves Green W Mid 134 G5
Eavestone N Yorks 214 F4
Ebberly Hill Devon 25 D9
Ebberston N Yorks 217 C7
Ebbesbourne Wake Wilts 31 C7
Ebblake Hants 31 F10
Ebbw Vale Bl Gwent 77 D11
Ebchester Durham 242 F4
Ebdon N Som 59 G11
Ebernoe W Sus 35 B7
Ebford Devon 14 D5
Ebley Glos 80 D4
Ebnal Ches W 167 F7
Ebnall Hereford 115 F9
Ebreywood Shrops 149 F10
Ebrington Glos 100 C3
Ecchinswell Hants 48 B4
Ecclaw Borders 272 B5
Ecclefechan Dumfries 238 C5
Eccle Riggs Cumb 210 B4
Eccles Borders 272 G5
Gtr Man 184 B3
Kent 69 G8
Ecclesall S Yorks 186 E4
Ecclesfield S Yorks 186 C5
Ecclesgreig Aberds 293 G9
Eccleshall Staffs 150 D6
Eccleshill W Yorks 205 F9
Ecclesmachan W Loth 279 G11
Eccles on Sea Norf 161 D8
Eccles Road Norf 141 E10
Eccleston Ches W 166 C6
Lancs 194 D4
Mers 183 B7
Eccleston Park Mers 183 C7
Eccliffe Dorset 30 B3
Eccup W Yorks 205 E11
Echt Aberds 293 C9
Eckford Borders 262 D6
Eckfordmoss Borders 262 D6
Eckington Derbys 186 F6
Worcs 99 C8
Eckington Corner E Sus 23 D8
Ecklands S Yorks 197 G8
Eckworthy Devon 24 D6
Ecton Northants 120 E6
Staffs 169 D9
Ecton Brook Northants 120 E6
Edale Derbys 185 D10
Edale End Derbys 185 D11
Edbrook Som 43 E8
Edburton W Sus 36 E2
Edderside Cumb 229 B7
Edderton Highld 309 L7
Eddington Kent 71 F7
W Berks 63 F10
Eddistone Devon 24 C3
Eddleston Borders 270 F4
Eddlewood S Lnrk 268 E4
Edenbridge Kent 52 D2
Edenfield Lancs 195 D9
Edenhall Cumb 231 E7
Edenham Lincs 155 E11
Eden Mount Cumb 211 D8
Eden Park London 67 F11
Edensor Derbys 170 B2
Edentaggart Argyll 276 C6
Edenthorpe S Yorks 198 F6
Edentown Cumb 239 F9
Eden Vale Durham 234 D4
Wilts 45 C11
Ederline Argyll 275 C9
Edern Gwyn 144 B5
Edford Som 45 D7
Edgarley Som 44 F4
Edgbaston W Mid 133 G11
Edgcote Northants 101 B10
Edgcott Bucks 102 G3
Som 41 F10
Edgcumbe Corn 2 C6
Edge Glos 80 D4
Shrops 131 B7
Edgebolton Shrops 149 E11
Edge End Glos 79 C9
Lancs 203 G10
Edgefield Norf 159 C11
Edgefield Street Norf 159 C11
Edge Fold Blkburn 195 D8
Gtr Man 195 F8
Edge Green Ches W 167 E7
Gtr Man 183 B9
Norf 141 F10
Edgehill Warks 101 B7
Edge Hill Mers 182 C5
Warks 134 D4
Edgeley Gtr Man 184 D5
Edge Mount S Yorks 186 C3
Edgerley Shrops 148 F6
Edgerston Borders 262 G5
Edgerton W Yorks 196 D6
Edgeside Lancs 195 C10
Edgeworth Glos 80 D6
Edginswell Devon 9 B7
Edgiock Worcs 117 E10
Edgmond Telford 150 F4
Edgmond Marsh Telford 150 E4
Edgton Shrops 131 F7
Edgware London 85 G11
Edgwick W Mid 134 G6
Edgworth Blkburn 195 D8
Edham Borders 262 B6
Edial Staffs 133 B11
Edinample Stirl 285 E9
Edinbane Highld 298 D3
Edinburgh Edin 280 G5
Edinchip Stirl 285 E9
Edingale Staffs 152 G4
Edingight Ho Moray 302 D5
Edingley Notts 171 D11
Edingthorpe Norf 160 C6
Edingthorpe Green Norf 160 C6
Edington Som 43 E11
Wilts 46 C2
Edingworth Som 43 C11
Edintore Moray 302 E4
Edistone Devon 24 C2
Edithmead Som 43 D10
Edith Weston Rutland 137 B8
Edlaston Derbys 169 G11
Edlesborough Bucks 85 B7
Edlingham Northumb 252 B4
Edlington Lincs 190 G2
Edmondsham Dorset 31 E9
Edmondsley Durham 233 B10
Edmondthorpe Leics 155 F7
Edmonston S Lnrk 269 G11
Edmonstone Orkney 314 D5
Edmonton Corn 10 G5
London 86 G4
Edmundbyers Durham 242 G2
Ednam Borders 262 B6
Ednaston Derbys 170 G2
Edney Common Essex 87 E11
Edradynate Perth 286 B2
Edrom Borders 272 D6
Edstaston Shrops 149 C10
Edstone Warks 118 E3
Edvin Loach Hereford 116 F3
Edwalton Notts 153 B11
Edwardstone Suff 107 C8
Edwardsville M Tydf 77 F9
Edwinsford Carms 94 E2
Edwinstowe Notts 171 B10
Edworth C Beds 104 C4
Edwyn Ralph Hereford 116 F2
Edzell Angus 293 G7
Efail-fôch Neath 57 B9
Efail Isaf Rhondda 58 C5
Efailnewydd Gwyn 145 B7
Efailwen Carms 92 F2
Efenechtyd Denb 165 D10
Effingham Sur 50 C6
Effirth Shetland 313 H5
Efflinch Staffs 152 F3
Efford Devon 26 G5
Plym 7 D10
Egbury Hants 48 C2
Egdon Worcs 117 G8
Egerton Gtr Man 195 E8
Kent 54 D2
Egerton Forstal Kent 53 D11
Egerton Green Ches E 167 E8
Egford Som 45 D9
Eggbeare Corn 12 D2
Eggborough N Yorks 198 C5
Eggbuckland Plym 7 D10
Eggesford Station
Devon 25 E11
Eggington C Beds 103 F9
Egginton Derbys 152 D5
Egginton Common
Derbys 152 D5
Egglesburn Durham 232 G5
Egglescliffe Stockton 225 C8
Eggleston Durham 232 G5
Egham Sur 66 E4
Egham Hythe Sur 66 E4
Egham Wick Sur 66 E3
Egleton Rutland 137 B7
Eglingham Northumb 264 F4
Egloshayle Corn 10 G5
Egloskerry Corn 11 D11
Eglwysbach Conwy 180 G4
Eglwys-Brewis V Glam 58 F4
Eglwys Cross Wrex 167 G7
Eglwys Fach Ceredig 128 D3
Eglwyswen Pembs 92 D3
Eglwyswrw Pembs 92 D2
Egmanton Notts 172 B2
Egmere Norf 159 B8
Egremont Cumb 219 C10
Mers 182 C4
Egton N Yorks 226 D6
Egton Bridge N Yorks 226 D6
Egypt Bucks 66 B3
Hants 48 E3
W Berks 64 D2
W Yorks 205 G7
Eidon Highld 309 J7
Eight Ash Green Essex 107 F8
Eighton Banks T&W 243 F7
Eignaig Highld 289 E9
Eign Hill Hereford 97 D10
Eil Highld 291 B10
Eilanreach Highld 295 D10
Eildon Borders 262 C3
Eileanach Lodge Highld 300 C5
Eilean Anabaich
W Isles 305 H4
Eilean Darach Highld 307 L6
Eilean Shona Ho Highld 289 B8
Einacleite W Isles 304 F3
Einsiob / Evenjobb
Powys 114 E5
Eisgean W Isles 305 G5
Eisingrug Gwyn 146 C2
Eland Green Northumb 242 C5
Elan Village Powys 113 D8
Elberton S Glos 60 B6
Elborough N Som 43 B11
Elbridge Shrops 149 E7
W Sus 22 C6
Elburton Plym 7 E10
Elcho Perth 286 E5
Elcock's Brook Worcs 117 E10
Elcombe Glos 80 F3
Swindon 62 C6
Elcot W Berks 63 F11
Eldene Swindon 63 C7
Eldernell Cambs 138 D6
Eldersfield Worcs 98 E6
Elderslie Renfs 267 C8
Elder Street Essex 105 E11
Eldon Durham 233 F10
Eldon Lane Durham 233 F10
Eldrick S Ayrs 245 G7
Eldroth N Yorks 212 F5
Eldwick W Yorks 205 E8
Elemore Vale T&W 234 B3
Elerch / Bont-goch
Ceredig 128 F3
Elfhowe Cumb 221 F9
Elford Northumb 264 C5
Staffs 152 G3
Elford Closes Cambs 123 C10
Elgin Moray 302 C2
Elgol Highld 295 D7
Elham Kent 55 E7
Eliburn W Loth 269 B10
Elie Fife 287 G8
Elim Anglesey 178 D5
Eling Hants 32 E5
W Berks 64 D4
Elishader Highld 298 C5
Elishaw Northumb 251 D9
Elizafield Dumfries 238 C2
Elkesley Notts 187 F11
Elkington Northants 120 B2
Elkins Green Essex 87 E10
Elkstone Glos 81 C7
Ellacombe Torbay 9 C8
Ellan Highld 301 G8
Elland W Yorks 196 C6
Elland Lower Edge
W Yorks 196 C6
Elland Upper Edge
W Yorks 196 C6
Ellary Argyll 275 F8
Ellastone Staffs 169 G10
Ellel Lancs 202 B5
Ellemford Borders 272 C4
Ellenborough Cumb 228 D6
Ellenbrook Herts 86 D2
IoM 192 E4
Ellenglaze Corn 4 D5
Ellenhall Staffs 150 D6
Ellen's Green Sur 50 F5
Ellerbeck N Yorks 225 F8
Ellerburn N Yorks 216 C6
Ellerby N Yorks 226 C5
Ellerdine Telford 150 E2
Ellerdine Heath Telford 150 E2
Ellerhayes Devon 27 G7
Elleric Argyll 284 C4
Ellerker E Yorks 200 B2
Ellerton E Yorks 207 F10
N Yorks 224 F5
Shrops 150 D4
Ellesborough Bucks 84 D4
Ellesmere Shrops 149 C8
Ellesmere Park Gtr Man 184 B3
Ellesmere Port Ches W 182 F6
Ellicombe Som 42 E3
Ellingham Hants 31 F10
Norf 143 E7
Northumb 264 D5
Ellingstring N Yorks 214 C3
Ellington Cambs 122 C3
Northumb 253 E7
Ellington Thorpe Cambs 122 C3
Elliot Angus 287 D10
Elliots Green Som 45 D9
Elliot's Town Caerph 77 E10
Ellisfield Hants 48 D6
Elliston Borders 262 D3
Ellistown Leics 153 G8
Ellon Aberds 303 F9
Ellonby Cumb 230 D4
Ellough Suff 143 F8
Elloughton E Yorks 200 B2
Ellwood Glos 79 D9
Elm Cambs 139 B9
Elmbridge Glos 80 B5
Worcs 117 D8
Elm Corner Sur 50 B5
Elm Cross Wilts 62 D6
Elmdon Essex 105 D9
W Mid 134 G3
Elmdon Heath W Mid 134 G3
Elmer W Sus 35 G7
Elmers End London 67 F11
Elmers Green Lancs 194 F3
Elmers Marsh W Sus 34 B5
Elmesthorpe Leics 135 D9
Elmfield IoW 21 C8
Elm Hill Dorset 30 B4
Elmhurst Bucks 84 B4
Staffs 152 G2
Elmley Castle Worcs 99 C9
Elmley Lovett Worcs 117 D7
Elmore Glos 80 B3
Elmore Back Glos 80 B3
Elm Park London 68 B4
Elmscott Devon 24 C2
Elmsett Suff 107 B11
Elms Green Hereford 115 F10
Worcs 116 D4
Elmslack Lancs 211 D9
Elmstead Essex 107 F11
London 68 E2
Elmstead Heath Essex 107 G11
Elmstead Market
Essex 107 G11
Elmsted Kent 54 E6
Elmsthorpe Leics 135 D9
Elmstone Kent 71 G9
Elmstone Hardwicke
Glos 99 F8
Elmswell E Yorks 208 B5
Suff 125 E9
Elmton Derbys 187 G8
Elness Orkney 314 C6
Elphin Highld 307 H7
Elphinstone E Loth 281 G7
Elrick Aberds 293 C10
Elrig Dumfries 236 E5
Elrigbeag Argyll 284 F5
Elrington Northumb 241 E9
Elscar S Yorks 197 G11
Elsdon Hereford 114 G6
Northumb 251 E10
Elsecar S Yorks 186 B5
S Yorks 197 G11
Elsenham Essex 105 F10
Elsenham Sta Essex 105 F10
Elsfield Oxon 83 C8
Elsham N Lincs 200 E4
Elsing Norf 159 F11
Elslack N Yorks 204 D4
Elson Hants 33 G10
Shrops 149 B7
Elsrickle S Lnrk 269 G11
Elstead Sur 50 E2
Elsted W Sus 34 D4
Elsthorpe Lincs 155 E11
Elstob Durham 234 G2
Elston Devon 26 G3
Notts 172 F3
Wilts 46 E5
Elstone Devon 25 D11
Elstow Beds 103 B11
Elstree Herts 85 F11
Elstronwick E Yorks 209 G10
Elswick Lancs 202 F4
T&W 242 E6
Elswick Leys Lancs 202 F4
Elsworth Cambs 122 E6
Elterwater Cumb 220 E6
Eltham London 68 E2
Eltisley Cambs 122 F5
Elton Cambs 137 E11
Ches W 183 F7
Derbys 170 C2
Glos 80 C2
Gtr Man 195 E9
Hereford 115 C9
Notts 154 B5
Stockton 225 B8
Elton Green Ches W 183 G7
Elton's Marsh Hereford 97 C9
Eltringham Northumb 242 E3
Elvanfoot S Lnrk 259 F11
Elvaston Derbys 153 C8
Elveden Suff 124 B6
Elvet Hill Durham 233 C11
Elvingston E Loth 281 G9
Elvington Kent 55 C9
York 207 D9
Elwell Devon 41 G7
Dorset 17 E9
Elwick Hrtlpl 234 E5
Northumb 264 B4
Elworth Ches E 168 C2
Elworthy Som 42 G5
Ely Cambs 139 G10
Cardiff 58 D6
Emberton M Keynes 103 B7
Embleton Cumb 229 E9
Durham 234 F4
Northumb 264 E6
Embo Highld 311 K2
Emborough Som 44 C6
Embo Street Highld 311 K2
Embsay N Yorks 204 C6
Emerson Park London 68 B4
Emerson's Green S Glos 61 D7
Emerson Valley
M Keynes 102 E6
Emery Down Hants 32 F3
Emley W Yorks 197 E8
Emmbrook Wokingham 65 F9
Emmer Green Reading 65 D8
Emmett Carr Derbys 187 F7
Emmington Oxon 84 E2
Emneth Norf 139 B9
Emneth Hungate Norf 139 B10
Emorsgate Norf 157 E10
Empingham Rutland 137 B8
Empshott Hants 49 G9
Empshott Green Hants 49 G8
Emscote Warks 118 D5
Emstrey Shrops 149 G10
Emsworth Hants 22 B2
Enborne W Berks 64 F2
Enborne Row W Berks 64 G2
Enchmarsh Shrops 131 D10
Enderby Leics 135 D10
Endmoor Cumb 211 C10
Endon Staffs 168 E6
Endon Bank Staffs 168 E6
Energlyn Caerph 58 B6
Enfield London 86 F4
Worcs 117 D10
Enfield Highway London 86 F5
Enfield Lock London 86 F5
Enfield Town London 86 F4
Enfield Wash London 86 F5
Enford Wilts 46 C6
Engamoor Shetland 313 H4
Engedi Anglesey 178 F5
Engine Common S Glos 61 C7
Englefield W Berks 64 E6
Englefield Green Sur 66 E3
Englesea-brook Ches E 168 E3
English Bicknor Glos 79 B9
Englishcombe Bath 61 G8
English Frankton
Shrops 149 D9
Engollan Corn 10 G3
Enham Alamein Hants 47 D11
Enis Devon 25 B9
Enisfirth Shetland 312 F5
Enmore Som 43 G8
Enmore Field Hereford 115 E9
Enmore Green Dorset 30 C5
Ennerdale Bridge
Cumb 219 B11
Enniscaven Corn 5 D9
Enoch Dumfries 247 C9
Enochdhu Perth 292 G2
Ensay Argyll 288 E5
Ensbury Bmouth 19 B7
Ensbury Park Bmouth 19 C7
Ensdon Shrops 149 F8
Ensis Devon 25 B9
Enslow Oxon 83 B7
Enstone Oxon 101 G7
Enterkinfoot Dumfries 247 C9
Enterpen N Yorks 225 D9
Enton Green Sur 50 E3
Enville Staffs 132 F6
Eolaigearraidh W Isles 297 L3
Eorabus Argyll 288 G5
Eòropaidh W Isles 304 B7
Epney Glos 80 C3
Epperstone Notts 171 F11
Epping Essex 87 E7
Epping Green Essex 86 D6
Herts 86 D3
Epping Upland Essex 86 E6
Eppleby N Yorks 224 C3
Eppleworth E Yorks 208 G6
Epsom Sur 67 G8
Epwell Oxon 101 C7
Epworth N Lincs 199 G9
Epworth Turbary
N Lincs 199 G9
Erbistock Wrex 166 G5
Erbusaig Highld 295 C9
Erchless Castle Highld 300 E4
Erdington W Mid 134 E2
Eredine Argyll 275 C10
Eriboll Highld 308 D4
Ericstane Dumfries 260 G3
Eridge Green E Sus 52 F5
Erines Argyll 275 F9
Eriswell Suff 124 B4
Erith London 68 D4
Erlestoke Wilts 46 C3
Ermine Lincs 189 G7
Ermington Devon 8 E2
Ernesettle Plym 7 D8
Erpingham Norf 160 C3
Erriottwood Kent 54 B2
Errogie Highld 300 G5
Errol Perth 286 E6
Errol Station Perth 286 E6
Erskine Renfs 277 G9
Erskine Bridge Renfs 277 G9
Ervie Dumfries 236 C2
Erwarton Suff 108 E4
Erwood Powys 95 C11
Eryholme N Yorks 224 D6
Eryrys Denb 166 D2
Escomb Durham 233 E9
Escott Som 42 F5
Escrick N Yorks 207 E8
Esgairdawe Carms 94 C2
Esgairgeiliog Powys 128 B5
Esgyryn Conwy 180 F4
Esh Durham 233 C9
Esher Sur 66 G6
Eshiels Borders 261 B7
Esholt W Yorks 205 E9
Eshott Northumb 252 D6
Eshton N Yorks 204 B4
Esh Winning Durham 233 C9
Eskadale Highld 300 F4
Eskbank Midloth 270 B6
Eskdale Green Cumb 220 E2
Eskdalemuir Dumfries 249 D7
Eske E Yorks 209 E7
Eskham Lincs 190 B5
Eskholme S Yorks 198 D6
Esknish Argyll 274 G4
Esk Valley N Yorks 226 E6
Eslington Park
Northumb 264 G2
Esperley Lane Ends
Durham 233 G8
Esprick Lancs 202 F4
Essendine Rutland 155 G10
Essendon Herts 86 D3
Essich Highld 300 F6
Essington Staffs 133 C9
Esslemont Aberds 303 G9
Eston Redcar 225 B11
Estover Plym 7 D10
Eswick Shetland 313 H6
Etal Northumb 263 B10
Etchilhampton Wilts 62 G4
Etchingham E Sus 38 B2
Etchinghill Kent 55 F7
Staffs 151 F10
Etchingwood E Sus 37 C8
Etherley Dene Durham 233 F9
Ethie Castle Angus 287 C10
Ethie Mains Angus 287 C10
Etling Green Norf 159 G10
Etloe Glos 79 D11
Eton Windsor 66 D3
Eton Wick Windsor 66 D2
Etruria Stoke 168 F5
Etsell Shrops 131 C7
Etterby Cumb 239 F9
Etteridge Highld 291 D8
Ettersgill Durham 232 F3
Ettiley Heath Ches E 168 C2
Ettingshall W Mid 133 D8
Ettingshall Park W Mid 133 D8
Ettington Warks 100 B5
Etton E Yorks 208 E5
Pboro 138 B2
Ettrick Borders 261 G7
Ettrickbridge Borders 261 E9
Ettrickdale Argyll 275 G11
Ettrickhill Borders 261 G7
Etwall Derbys 152 C5
Etwall Common Derbys 152 C5
Eudon Burnell Shrops 132 F3
Eudon George Shrops 132 F3
Euston Suff 125 B7
Euximoor Drove Cambs 139 D9
Euxton Lancs 194 D5
Evanstown Bridgend 58 B3
Evanton Highld 300 C6
Evedon Lincs 173 F9
Eve Hill W Mid 133 E8
Evelix Highld 309 K7
Evendine Hereford 98 C5
Evenjobb / Einsiob
Powys 114 E5
Evenley Northants 101 E11
Evenlode Glos 100 F4
Even Pits Hereford 97 D11
Even Swindon Swindon 62 B6
Evenwood Durham 233 G9
Evenwood Gate Durham 233 G9
Everbay Orkney 314 D6
Evercreech Som 44 F6
Everdon Northants 119 F11
Everingham E Yorks 208 E2
Everland Shetland 312 D8
Everleigh Wilts 47 C8
Everley N Yorks 217 B9
Eversholt C Beds 103 E9
Evershot Dorset 29 G9
Eversley Essex 69 B8
Hants 65 G9
Eversley Centre Hants 65 G9
Eversley Cross Hants 65 G9
Everthorpe E Yorks 208 G4
Everton C Beds 122 G4
Hants 19 C11
Mers 182 C5
Notts 187 C11
Evertown Dumfries 239 B9
Evesbatch Hereford 98 B3
Evesham Worcs 99 C10
Evington Kent 54 D6
Leicester 136 C2
Ewanrigg Cumb 228 D6
Ewden Village S Yorks 186 B3
Ewell Sur 67 G8
Ewell Minnis Kent 55 E9
Ewelme Oxon 83 G10
Ewen Glos 81 F8
Ewenny V Glam 58 D2
Ewerby Lincs 173 F10
Ewerby Thorpe Lincs 173 F10
Ewes Dumfries 249 E9
Ewesley Northumb 252 E3
Ewhurst Sur 50 E5
Ewhurst Green E Sus 38 C3
Sur 50 F5
Ewloe Flint 166 B4
Ewloe Green Flint 166 B3
Ewood Blkburn 195 B7
Ewood Bridge Lancs 195 C9
Eworthy Devon 12 C5
Ewshot Hants 49 D10
Ewyas Harold Hereford 97 F7
Exbourne Devon 25 G10
Exbury Hants 20 B4
Exceat E Sus 23 F8
Exebridge Devon 26 C6
Exelby N Yorks 214 B5
Exeter Devon 14 C4
Exford Som 41 F11
Exfords Green Shrops 131 B9
Exhall Warks 118 F2
Warks 135 F7
Exlade Street Oxon 65 C7
Exley W Yorks 196 C5
Exley Head W Yorks 204 F6
Exminster Devon 14 D4
Exmouth Devon 14 E6
Exnaboe Shetland 313 M5
Exning Suff 124 D2
Exted Kent 55 E7
Exton Devon 14 D5
Hants 33 C10
Rutland 155 G8
Som 42 G2
Exwick Devon 14 C4
Eyam Derbys 186 F2
Eydon Northants 119 G10
Eye Hereford 115 E9
Pboro 138 C4
Suff 126 C2
Eye Green Pboro 138 C4
Eyemouth Borders 273 C8
Eyeworth C Beds 104 B4
Eyhorne Street Kent 53 C10
Eyke Suff 126 G6
Eynesbury Cambs 122 F3
Eynort Highld 294 C5
Eynsford Kent 68 F4
Eynsham Oxon 82 D6
Eype Dorset 16 C5
Eyre Highld 295 B7
Highld 298 D4
Eyres Monsell
Leicester 135 D11
Eythorne Kent 55 D9
Eyton Hereford 115 E9
Shrops 131 F7
Shrops 149 G7
Wrex 166 G4
Eyton on Severn
Shrops 131 B11
Eyton upon the Weald
Moors Telford 150 G3

F

Faberstown Wilts 47 C9
Faccombe Hants 47 B11
Faceby N Yorks 225 E9
Fachell Gwyn 163 B8
Fachwen Gwyn 163 C9
Facit Lancs 195 D11
Fackley Notts 171 C7
Faddiley Ches E 167 E9
Faddonch Highld 295 C11
Fadmoor N Yorks 216 B3
Faerdre Swansea 75 E11
Fagley W Yorks 205 G9
Fagwyr Swansea 75 E11
Faichem Highld 290 C4
Faifley W Dunb 277 G10
Failand N Som 60 E4
Failford S Ayrs 257 D11
Failsworth Gtr Man 195 G11
Fain Highld 299 B11
Faindouran Lodge
Moray 292 C2
Fairbourne Gwyn 146 G2
Fairbourne Heath Kent 53 C11
Fairburn N Yorks 198 B3
Fairburn House Highld 300 D4
Fair Cross London 68 B3
Fairfield Clack 279 C7
Derbys 185 G9
Gtr Man 184 B6
Gtr Man 195 E10
Kent 39 B7
Mers 182 C5
Stockton 225 B8
Worcs 99 C10
Worcs 117 B8
Fairfield Park Bath 61 F9
Fairfields Glos 98 E4
Fairford Glos 81 E11
Fair Green Norf 158 F3
Fairhaven Lancs 193 B10
N Ayrs 255 C10
Fairhill S Lnrk 268 E4
Fair Hill Cumb 230 E6
Fairlands Sur 50 C3
Fairlee IoW 20 C6
Fairlie N Ayrs 266 D4
Fairlight E Sus 38 E5
Fairlight Cove E Sus 38 E5
Fairlop London 87 G7
Fairmile Devon 15 B7
Dorset 19 C9
Sur 66 G6
Fairmilehead Edin 270 B4
Fair Moor Northumb 252 F5
Fairoak Caerph 77 F11
Staffs 150 C5
Fair Oak Hants 33 D7
Hants 64 G5
Lancs 203 D8
Fair Oak Green Hants 65 G7
Fairseat Kent 68 G6
Fairstead Essex 88 B3
Norf 158 F2
Fairview Glos 99 G9
Fairwarp E Sus 37 B7
Fairwater Cardiff 58 D6
Torf 78 G3
Fairwood Wilts 45 C10
Fairy Cottage IoM 192 D5
Fairy Cross Devon 24 C6
Fakenham Norf 159 D8
Fakenham Magna Suff 125 B8
Fala Midloth 271 C8
Fala Dam Midloth 271 C8
Falahill Borders 271 D7
Falcon Hereford 98 E2
Falcon Lodge W Mid 134 D2
Falconwood London 68 D3
Falcutt Northants 101 C11
Faldingworth Lincs 189 E9
Faldonside Borders 262 C2
Falfield Fife 287 G8
S Glos 79 G11
Falkenham Suff 108 D5
Falkenham Sink Suff 108 D5
Falkirk Falk 279 F7
Falkland Fife 286 G6
Falla Borders 262 G6
Fallgate Derbys 170 C5
Fallin Stirl 278 C6
Fallinge Derbys 170 B3
Fallings Heath W Mid 133 D9
Fallowfield Gtr Man 184 C5
Fallside N Lnrk 268 C4
Falmer E Sus 36 F5
Falmouth Corn 3 C8
Falnash Borders 249 B9
Falsgrave N Yorks 217 B10
Falside W Loth 269 B9
Falsidehill Borders 272 G3
Falstone Northumb 250 F6
Fanagmore Highld 306 E6
Fancott C Beds 103 F10
Fangdale Beck
N Yorks 225 G11
Fangfoss E Yorks 207 C11
Fanich Highld 311 J2
Fankerton Falk 278 E5
Fanmore Argyll 288 E6
Fanner's Green Essex 87 C11
Fannich Lodge Highld 300 C2
Fans Borders 272 G2
Fanshowe Ches E 184 G5
Fant Kent 53 B8
Faoilean Highld 295 C7
Far Arnside Cumb 211 D8
Far Bank S Yorks 198 E6
Far Banks Lancs 194 C2
Far Bletchley M Keynes 103 E7
Farcet Cambs 138 E4
Far Coton Leics 135 C7
Far Cotton Northants 120 F4
Farden Shrops 115 B11
Fareham Hants 33 F9
Far End Cumb 220 F6
Farewell Staffs 151 G11
Far Forest Worcs 116 C4
Farforth Lincs 190 F4
Far Green Glos 80 E3
Farhill Derbys 170 C5
Far Hoarcross Staffs 152 E2
Faringdon Oxon 82 F3
Farington Lancs 194 B4
Farington Moss Lancs 194 C4
Farlam Cumb 240 F3
Farlands Booth Derbys 185 D9
Farlary Highld 309 J7
Far Laund Derbys 170 F5
Farleigh N Som 60 F3
Sur 67 G11
Farleigh Court Sur 67 G11
Farleigh Green Kent 53 C8
Farleigh Hungerford
Som 45 B10
Farleigh Wallop Hants 48 D6
Farleigh Wick Wilts 61 G10
Farlesthorpe Lincs 191 G7
Farleton Cumb 211 C10
Lancs 211 F11
Farley Bristol 60 E2
Derbys 170 C3
Shrops 131 B7
Shrops 132 C2
Staffs 169 G9
Wilts 32 B2
Far Ley Staffs 132 D5
Farley Green Suff 124 G4
Sur 50 D5
Farley Hill Luton 103 G11
Wokingham 65 G8
Farleys End Glos 80 B3
Farlington N Yorks 216 F2
Ptsmth 33 F11
Farlow Shrops 132 G2
Farmborough Bath 61 G7
Farmbridge End Essex 87 C10
Farmcote Glos 99 F11
Shrops 132 E5
Farmington Glos 81 B10
Farmoor Oxon 82 D6
Far Moor Gtr Man 194 G4
Farms Common Corn 2 C5
Farmtown Moray 302 D5
Farm Town Leics 153 F7
Farnah Green Derbys 170 F4
Farnborough Hants 49 C11
London 68 G2
Warks 101 B8
W Berks 64 C2
Farnborough Green
Hants 49 B11
Farnborough Park
Hants 49 B11
Farnborough Street
Hants 49 B11
Farncombe Sur 50 E3
Farndish Beds 121 E8
Farndon Ches W 166 E6
Notts 172 E3
Farnell Angus 287 B10
Farnham Dorset 31 D7
Essex 105 G9

Farnham N Yorks 215 G7
Suff 127 E7
Sur 49 D10
Farnham Common Bucks 66 C3
Farnham Green Essex 105 F9
Farnham Park Bucks 66 C3
Farnham Royal Bucks 66 C3
Farnhill N Yorks 204 D6
Farningham Kent 68 F4
Farnley N Yorks 205 D10
W Yorks 205 G11
Farnley Bank W Yorks 197 E7
Farnley Tyas W Yorks 197 E7
Farnsfield Notts 171 D10
Farnworth Gtr Man 195 F8
Halton 183 D8
Far Oakridge Glos 80 E6
Farr Highld 291 C10
Highld 300 F6
Highld 308 C7
Farraline Highld 300 G5
Farr House Highld 300 F6
Farringdon Devon 14 C6
T&W 243 G9
Farrington Dorset 30 D4
Farrington Gurney Bath 44 B6
Far Royds W Yorks 205 G11
Far Sawrey Cumb 221 F7
Farsley W Yorks 205 F10
Farsley Beck Bottom
W Yorks 205 F10
Farther Howegreen
Essex 88 E4
Farthing Corner
Medway 69 G10
Farthing Green Kent 53 D10
Farthinghoe Northants 101 D10
Farthingloe Kent 55 E9
Farthingstone Northants 120 F2
Far Thrupp Glos 80 E5
Fartown W Yorks 196 D6
Farway Devon 15 B9
Farway Marsh Devon 28 G4
Fasach Highld 297 G7
Fasag Highld 299 D8
Fascadale Highld 289 B7
Faslane Port Argyll 276 D4
Fasnacloich Argyll 284 C4
Fasnakyle Ho Highld 300 G3
Fassfern Highld 290 F2
Fatfield T&W 243 G8
Fattahead Aberds 302 D6
Faucheldean W Loth 279 G11
Faugh Cumb 240 G2
Faughill Borders 262 C2
Fauld Staffs 152 D3
Fauldhouse W Loth 269 C8
Fauldiehill Angus 287 D9
Fauldshope Borders 261 D10
Faulkbourne Essex 88 B3
Faulkland Som 45 C8
Fauls Shrops 149 C11
Faverdale Darl 224 B5
Faversham Kent 70 G4
Favillar Moray 302 F2
Fawdington N Yorks 215 E8
Fawdon Northumb 264 F2
T&W 242 D6
Fawfieldhead Staffs 169 C9
Fawkham Green Kent 68 F5
Fawler Oxon 63 B10
Oxon 82 B5
Fawley Bucks 65 B9
Hants 33 G7
W Berks 63 C11
Fawley Bottom Bucks 65 B8
Fawley Chapel Hereford 97 F11
Faxfleet E Yorks 199 C11
Faygate W Sus 51 G8
Fazakerley Mers 182 B5
Fazeley Staffs 134 C4
Feagour Highld 291 D7
Fearby N Yorks 214 C3
Fearn Highld 301 B8
Fearnan Perth 285 C11
Fearnbeg Highld 299 D7
Fearnhead Warr 183 C10
Fearn Lodge Highld 309 L6
Fearnmore Highld 299 C7
Fearn Station Highld 301 B8
Fearnville W Yorks 206 F2
Featherstone Staffs 133 B8
W Yorks 198 C2
Featherwood Northumb 251 C8
Feckenham Worcs 117 E10
Fedw Fawr Anglesey 179 E10
Feering Essex 107 G7
Feetham N Yorks 223 F9
Fegg Hayes Stoke 168 E5
Fèith Mhor Highld 301 G8
Feizor N Yorks 212 F5
Felbridge Sur 51 F11
Felbrigg Norf 160 B4
Felcourt Sur 51 E11
Felden Herts 85 E8
Felderland Kent 55 B10
Feldy Ches E 183 F11
Felhampton Shrops 131 F8
Felin-Crai Powys 95 G7
Felindre Carms 75 C7
Carms 93 D7
Carms 93 G11
Carms 94 E3
Carms 94 F4
Ceredig 111 F10
Powys 96 D3
Powys 96 G3
Powys 130 C3
Powys 130 G3
Rhondda 58 C3
Swansea 75 E10
Felindre Farchog Pembs 92 D2
Felinfach Ceredig 111 F10
Powys 95 E11
Felinfoel Carms 75 E8
Felingwmisaf Carms 93 G10
Felingwmuchaf Carms 93 G10
Felin Newydd Carms 94 D3
Felin-newydd Powys 96 D2
Felin Newydd / New Mills
Powys 129 C11
Felin Puleston Wrex 166 F4
Felin-Wnda Ceredig 92 B6
Felinwynt Ceredig 110 G4
Felixkirk N Yorks 215 C9
Felixstowe Suff 108 E5
Felixstowe Ferry Suff 108 D6
Felkington Northumb 273 G8
Felkirk W Yorks 197 E11
Felldyke Cumb 219 B11
Fell End Cumb 222 F4
Fellgate T&W 243 E8
Felling T&W 243 E7
Felling Shore T&W 243 E7
Fell Lane W Yorks 204 E6
Fellside T&W 242 E5
Fell Side Cumb 230 D2
Felmersham Beds 121 F9
Felmingham Norf 160 D5
Felmore Essex 69 B8
Felpham W Sus 35 H7
Felsham Suff 125 F8
Felsted Essex 106 G3
Feltham London 66 E6
Som 28 D2
Felthamhill London 66 E5
Felthorpe Norf 160 F3
Felton Hereford 97 B11
Northumb 252 C5
N Som 60 F4
Felton Butler Shrops 149 F7
Feltwell Norf 140 E4
Fenay Bridge W Yorks 197 D7
Fence Lancs 204 F2
Fence Houses T&W 243 G8
Fencott Oxon 83 B9
Fen Ditton Cambs 123 E9
Fen Drayton Cambs 122 D6
Fen End Lincs 156 E4
W Mid 118 B4
Fengate Norf 160 E3
Pboro 138 D4
Fenham Northumb 273 G11
T&W 242 D6
Fenhouses Lincs 174 G3
Feniscliffe Blkburn 195 B7
Feniscowles Blkburn 194 B6
Feniton Devon 15 B8
Fenlake Beds 103 B11
Fenn Green Shrops 132 G5
Fennington Som 27 B11
Fenn's Bank Wrex 149 B10
Fenn Street Medway 69 D9
Fenny Bentley Derbys 169 E11
Fenny Bridges Devon 15 B8
Fenny Castle Som 44 E4
Fenny Compton Warks 119 G8
Fenny Drayton Leics 134 D6
Fenny Stratford
M Keynes 103 E7
Fenrother Northumb 252 E5
Fen Side Lincs 174 D4
Fenstanton Cambs 122 D6
Fenstead End Suff 124 G6
Fen Street Norf 141 G11
Suff 125 B9
Suff 125 B11
Fenton Cambs 122 B6
Cumb 240 F2
Lincs 172 E5
Lincs 188 F4
Northumb 263 C11
Stoke 168 G5
Fentonadle Corn 11 F7
Fenton Barns E Loth 281 E10
Fenton Low Stoke 168 F5
Fenton Pits Corn 5 C11
Fenton Town Northumb 263 C11
Fenwick E Ayrs 267 G9
Northumb 242 C3
Northumb 273 G11
S Yorks 198 D5
Feochaig Argyll 255 F8
Feock Corn 3 B8
Feolin Ferry Argyll 274 G5
Ferguslie Park Renfs 267 C9
Ferindonald Highld 295 E8
Feriniquarrie Highld 296 F7
Ferlochan Argyll 289 E11
Fern Angus 292 G6
Bucks 65 B11
Fern Bank Gtr Man 185 B7
Ferndale Kent 52 E5
Rhondda 77 F7
Ferndown Dorset 31 G9
Ferne Wilts 30 C6
Ferness Highld 301 E9
Ferney Green Cumb 221 F8
Fernham Oxon 82 G3
Fernhill Gtr Man 195 E10
Rhondda 77 F8
W Sus 51 E10
Fern Hill Suff 106 B6
Fernhill Gate Gtr Man 195 F7
Fernhill Heath Worcs 117 F7
Fernhurst W Sus 34 B5
Fernie Fife 287 F7
Ferniebrae Aberds 303 D9
Ferniegair S Lnrk 268 E4
Ferniehirst Borders 271 G8
Fernilea Highld 294 B5
Fernilee Derbys 185 F8
Fernsplatt Corn 4 G5
Ferrensby N Yorks 215 G7
Ferring W Sus 35 G9
Ferrybridge W Yorks 198 C3
Ferryden Angus 287 B11
Ferryhill Aberdeen 293 C11
Durham 233 E11
Ferry Hill Cambs 139 G7
Ferryhill Station Durham 234 E2
Ferry Point Highld 309 L7
Ferryside / Glan-y-Ffer
Carms 74 C5
Ferryton Highld 300 C6
Fersfield Norf 141 G11
Fersit Highld 290 F5
Feshiebridge Highld 291 C10
Fetcham Sur 50 B6
Fetterangus Aberds 303 D9
Fettercairn Aberds 293 F8
Fetterdale Fife 287 E8
Fettes Highld 300 D5
Fewcott Oxon 101 F10
Fewston N Yorks 205 C9
Fewston Bents N Yorks 205 C9
Ffairfach Carms 94 G2
Ffair-Rhos Ceredig 112 D4
Ffaldybrenin Carms 94 C2
Ffarmers Carms 94 C3
Ffawyddog Powys 78 B2
Ffodun / Forden Powys 130 C4
Ffont y gari / Font y gary
V Glam 58 F5
Fforddlas Powys 96 D4
Fforddlas Denb 165 C10
Ffordd-y-Gyfraith
Bridgend 57 E11
Fforest Carms 75 E9
Fforest-fach Swansea 56 B6
Fforest Gôch Neath 76 E2
Ffostrasol Ceredig 93 B7
Ffos-y-ffin Ceredig 111 E8
Ffos-y-go Wrex 166 E4
Ffridd Powys 130 D3
Ffrith Wrex 166 D3
Ffrwd Gwyn 163 D7
Ffwl y mwn / Fonmon
V Glam 58 F4
Ffynnon Carms 74 B5
Ffynnon ddrain Carms 93 G8
Ffynnongroes / Crosswell
Pembs 92 D2
Ffynnon Gron Pembs 91 F8
Ffynnongroyw Flint 181 E10
Ffynnon Gynydd Powys 96 C3
Ffynnon-oer Ceredig 111 G10
Fickleshole Sur 67 G11
Fidden Argyll 288 G5
Fiddes Aberds 293 E10
Fiddington Glos 99 E8
Som 43 E8
Fiddington Sands Wilts 46 C4
Fiddleford Dorset 30 E4
Fiddler' Green Norf 141 D10
Fiddler's Ferry Mers 183 C11
Warr 193 D11
Fiddler's Green Glos 99 G8
Hereford 97 D11
Fiddlers Hamlet Essex 87 E7
Field Hereford 114 G6
Som 44 E6
Staffs 151 C10
Field Assarts Oxon 82 C4
Field Broughton Cumb 211 C7
Field Common Sur 66 F6
Field Dalling Norf 159 B10
Field Green Kent 38 B3
Field Head Leics 135 B9
Fields End Herts 85 D8
Field's Place Hereford 115 G8
Fifehead Magdalen
Dorset 30 C3
Fifehead Neville Dorset 30 E3
Fifehead St Quintin
Dorset 30 E3
Fife Keith Moray 302 D4
Fifield Oxon 82 B2
Wilts 46 C6
Windsor 66 D2
Fifield Bavant Wilts 31 B8
Figheldean Wilts 47 D7
Filands Wilts 62 B2
Filby Norf 161 G9
Filby Heath Norf 161 G9
Filchampstead Oxon 83 D7
Filey N Yorks 218 C2
Filgrave M Keynes 103 B7
Filham Devon 8 D2
Filkins Oxon 82 E2
Filleigh Devon 25 B11
Devon 26 E2
Fillingham Lincs 188 D6
Fillongley Warks 134 F5
Filmore Hill Hants 33 B11
Filton S Glos 60 D6
Filwood Park Bristol 60 F5
Fimber E Yorks 217 G7
Finavon Angus 287 B8
Fincastle Ho Perth 291 G10
Finchairn Argyll 275 C10
Fincham Mers 182 C6
Norf 140 B3
Finchampstead
Wokingham 65 G9
Finchdean Hants 34 E2
Finchingfield Essex 106 E3
Finchley London 86 G3
Findern Derbys 152 C6
Findhorn Moray 301 C10
Findhorn Bridge Highld 301 G8
Findochty Moray 302 C4
Findo Gask Perth 286 E4
Findon Aberds 293 D11
W Sus 35 F10
Findon Mains Highld 300 C6
Findon Valley W Sus 35 F10
Findrack Ho Aberds 293 C8
Finedon Northants 121 C8
Fineglen Argyll 275 B10
Fine Street Hereford 96 D6
Fingal Street Suff 126 D4
Fingask Aberds 303 G7
Fingerpost Worcs 116 C4
Fingest Bucks 84 G3
Finghall N Yorks 214 B3
Fingland Cumb 239 F7
Dumfries 259 F7
Finglesham Kent 55 C10
Fingringhoe Essex 107 G10
Finham W Mid 118 B6
Finkle Street S Yorks 186 B4
Finlarig Stirl 285 D9
Finmere Oxon 102 E2
Finnart Perth 285 B9
Finney Green Ches E 184 E5
Staffs 168 F3
Finningham Suff 125 D11
Finningley S Yorks 187 B11
Finnygaud Aberds 302 D5
Finsbury London 67 C10
Finsbury Park London 67 B10
Finstall Worcs 117 D9
Finsthwaite Cumb 211 B7
Finstock Oxon 82 B5
Finstown Orkney 314 E3
Fintry Aberds 303 D7
Dundee 287 D8
Stirl 278 D2
Finwood Warks 118 D3
Finzean Aberds 293 D8
Finzean Ho Aberds 293 D7
Fionnphort Argyll 288 G5
Fionnsbhagh W Isles 296 C6
Firbank Cumb 222 G2
Firbeck S Yorks 187 D9
Firby N Yorks 214 B5
N Yorks 216 F4
Firemore Highld 307 L3
Firgrove Gtr Man 196 E2
Firkin Argyll 285 G7
Firle E Sus 23 D7
Firsby Lincs 175 C7
Firsdown Wilts 47 G8
Firs Lane Gtr Man 194 G6
First Coast Highld 307 K4
Firswood Gtr Man 184 B4
Firth Borders 262 E2
Firth Moor Darl 224 C6
Firth Park S Yorks 186 C5
Fir Toll Kent 54 E2
Fir Tree Durham 233 E8
Fir Vale S Yorks 186 C5
Firwood Fold Gtr Man 195 E8
Fishbourne IoW 21 C7
W Sus 22 C4
Fishburn Durham 234 E3
Fishcross Clack 279 B7
Fisherford Aberds 302 F6
Fishermead M Keynes 103 D7
Fisher Place Cumb 220 B6
Fisherrow E Loth 280 G6
Fishersgate Brighton 36 F3
Fishers Green Herts 104 F4
Fisher's Pond Hants 33 C7
Fisherstreet W Sus 50 G3
Fisherton Highld 301 D7
S Ayrs 257 F7
Fisherton de la Mere
Wilts 46 F4
Fisherwick Staffs 134 B3
Fishery Windsor 65 C11
Fishguard / Abergwaun
Pembs 91 D9
Fishlake S Yorks 199 E7
Fishleigh Devon 25 F8
Fishleigh Barton Devon 25 C9
Fishleigh Castle Devon 25 F8
Fishley Norf 161 G8
W Mid 133 C10
Fishmere End Lincs 156 B5
Fishponds Bristol 60 D6
Fishpool Glos 98 F3
Gtr Man 195 F10
N Yorks 205 D10
Fishpools Powys 114 D3
Fishtoft Lincs 174 G5
Fishtoft Drove Lincs 174 F4
Fishtown of Usan
Angus 287 B11
Fishwick Borders 273 E8
Lancs 194 B5
Fiskavaig Highld 294 B5
Fiskerton Lincs 189 G8
Notts 172 E2
Fitling E Yorks 209 G11
Fittleton Wilts 46 D6
Fittleworth W Sus 35 D8
Fitton End Cambs 157 G8
Fitton Hill Gtr Man 196 G2
Fitz Shrops 149 F8
Fitzhead Som 27 B10
Fitzwilliam W Yorks 198 D2
Fiunary Highld 289 E8
Five Acres Glos 79 C9
Five Ash Down E Sus 37 C7
Five Ashes E Sus 37 C9
Five Bells Som 42 E5
Five Bridges Hereford 98 B3
Fivecrosses Ches W 183 F8
Fivehead Som 28 C5
Five Houses IoW 20 D4
Five Lane Ends Lancs 202 C6
Fivelanes Corn 11 E10
Five Lanes Mon 78 G6
Five Oak Green Kent 52 D6
Five Oaks W Sus 35 B9
Five Roads Carms 75 D7
Five Ways Warks 118 D4
Five Wents Kent 53 C10
Fixby W Yorks 196 C6
Flackley Ash E Sus 38 C5
Flack's Green Essex 88 B3
Flackwell Heath Bucks 65 B11
Fladbury Worcs 99 B9
Fladbury Cross Worcs 99 B9
Fladda Shetland 312 E5
Fladdabister Shetland 313 K6
Flagg Derbys 169 B10
Flaggoners Green
Hereford 116 G2
Flamborough E Yorks 218 E4
Flamstead Herts 85 C9
Flamstead End Herts 86 E4
Flansham W Sus 35 G7
Flanshaw W Yorks 197 C10
Flappit Spring W Yorks 205 F7
Flasby N Yorks 204 B4
Flash Staffs 169 B8
Flashader Highld 298 D3
Flask Inn N Yorks 227 E8
Flathurst W Sus 35 C7
Flaunden Herts 85 E8
Flawborough Notts 172 G3
Flawith N Yorks 215 F9
Flax Bourton N Som 60 F4
Flaxby N Yorks 206 B3
Flaxholme Derbys 170 G4
Flaxlands Norf 142 E2
Flaxley Glos 79 B11
Flax Moss Lancs 195 C9
Flaxpool Som 42 F6
Flaxton N Yorks 216 G3
Fleckney Leics 136 E2
Flecknoe Warks 119 E10
Fledborough Notts 188 G4
Fleet Dorset 17 E8
Hants 22 C2
Hants 49 C10
Lincs 157 E7
Fleet Downs Kent 68 E5
Fleetend Hants 33 F8
Fleet Hargate Lincs 157 E7
Fleetlands Hants 33 G9
Fleets N Yorks 213 G9
Fleetville Herts 85 D11
Fleetwood Lancs 202 D2
Fleggburgh / Burgh St
Margaret Norf 161 G8
Fleming Field Durham 234 C3
Flemings Kent 55 B9
Flemingston V Glam 58 E4
Flemington S Lnrk 268 D3
S Lnrk 268 G4
Flempton Suff 124 D6
Fleoideabhagh W Isles 296 C6
Fletchersbridge Corn 6 B2
Fletcher's Green Kent 52 C4
Fletchertown Cumb 229 C10
Fletching E Sus 36 C6
Fletching Common
E Sus 36 C6
Fleuchary Highld 309 K7
Fleuchlang Dumfries 237 D8
Fleur-de-lis Caerph 77 F11
Flexbury Corn 24 F2
Flexford Hants 32 C6
Sur 50 D2
Flimby Cumb 228 E6
Flimwell E Sus 53 G8
Flint Flint 182 G2
Flint Cross Cambs 105 C8
Flintham Notts 172 F2
Flint Hill Durham 242 G5
Flint Mountain / Mynydd
Fflint Flint 182 G2
Flinton E Yorks 209 F10
Flint's Green W Mid 134 G5
Flintsham Hereford 114 F6
Flishinghurst Kent 53 F9
Flitcham Norf 158 D4
Flitholme Cumb 222 B5
Flitton C Beds 103 D11
Flitwick C Beds 103 D10
Flixborough N Lincs 199 D11
Flixborough Stather
N Lincs 199 E11
Flixton Gtr Man 184 C2
N Yorks 217 D10
Suff 142 F6
Flockton W Yorks 197 E8
Flockton Green
W Yorks 197 D8
Flockton Moor W Yorks 197 E8
Flodaigh W Isles 296 F4
Flodden Northumb 263 B10
Flodigarry Highld 298 B4
Floodgates Hereford 114 F5
Flood's Ferry Cambs 139 E7
Flood Street Hants 31 D10
Flookburgh Cumb 211 D7
Flordon Norf 142 D3
Flore Northants 120 E2
Florence Stoke 168 G6
Flotterton Northumb 251 C11
Flowers Bottom Bucks 84 F4
Flowers Green E Sus 23 C10
Flowery Field Gtr Man 184 B6
Flowton Suff 107 B11
Fluchter E Dunb 277 G11
Flugarth Shetland 313 G6
Flushdyke W Yorks 197 C9
Flush House W Yorks 196 F6
Flushing Aberds 303 E10
Corn 3 C8
Corn 3 D7
Flyford Flavell Worcs 117 G9
Foals Green Suff 126 C5
Fobbing Thurrock 69 C8
Fochabers Moray 302 D3
Fochriw Caerph 77 D10
Fockerby N Lincs 199 D10
Fodderletter Moray 301 G11
Fodderstone Gap Norf 140 B3
Fodderty Highld 300 D5
Foddington Som 29 B9
Foel Powys 147 G9
Foel-gastell Carms 75 C8
Foffarty Angus 287 C8
Foggathorpe E Yorks 207 F11
Foggbrook Gtr Man 184 D6
Fogo Borders 272 F5
Fogorig Borders 272 F5
Fograigarth Shetland 313 H4
Fogwatt Moray 302 D2
Foindle Highld 306 E6
Folda Angus 292 G3
Fold Head Lancs 195 D11
Fold Hill Lincs 175 E7
Foldrings S Yorks 186 C3
Fole Staffs 151 B10
Foleshill W Mid 135 G7
Foley Park Worcs 116 B6
Folke Dorset 29 E11
Folkestone Kent 55 F8
Folkingham Lincs 155 C11
Folkington E Sus 23 E9
Folksworth Cambs 138 F2
Folkton N Yorks 217 D11
Folla Rule Aberds 303 F7
Folley Shrops 132 D5
Follifoot N Yorks 206 C2
Follingsby T&W 243 E8
Folly Dorset 30 G2
Pembs 91 G8
Folly Cross Devon 25 F7
Folly Gate Devon 13 B7
Folly Green Essex 106 F6
Fonmon / Ffwl-y-mwn
V Glam 58 F4
Fonston Corn 11 C10
Fonthill Bishop Wilts 46 G2
Fonthill Gifford Wilts 46 G2
Fontmell Magna Dorset 30 D5
Fontmell Parva Dorset 30 E4
Fontwell W Sus 35 F7
Font-y-gary / Ffont-y-gari
V Glam 58 F5
Foodieash Fife 287 F7
Foolow Derbys 185 F11
Footbridge Glos 99 F10
Footherley Staffs 134 C2
Footrid Worcs 116 C3
Foots Cray London 68 E3
Forbestown Aberds 292 B5
Force Forge Cumb 220 G6
Force Green Kent 52 B2
Force Mills Cumb 220 G6
Forcett N Yorks 224 C3
Ford Argyll 275 C9
Bucks 84 D3
Derbys 186 E6
Devon 8 E2
Devon 8 G5
Devon 24 C6
Devon 28 G2
Glos 99 F11
Hereford 115 F10
Kent 71 F8
Mers 182 B4
Northumb 263 B10
Pembs 91 F9
Plym 7 D9
Shrops 149 G8
Som 27 B9
Som 44 C5
Staffs 169 E9
Wilts 47 G7
Wilts 61 E10
W Sus 35 G7
Forda Devon 12 C6
Devon 40 F3
Fordbridge W Mid 134 F3
Fordcombe Kent 52 E4
Fordell Fife 280 D3
Ford End Essex 87 B11
Essex 105 E9
Forden / Ffodun Powys 130 C4
Forder Corn 7 D8
Forder Green Devon 8 B5
Ford Forge Northumb 263 B10
Fordgate Som 43 G10
Ford Green Lancs 202 D5
Stoke 168 E5
Fordham Cambs 124 C2
Essex 107 F8
Norf 140 D2
Fordham Heath Essex 107 F8
Ford Heath Shrops 149 G8
Ford Hill Northumb 263 B11
Fordhouses W Mid 133 C8
Fordingbridge Hants 31 E10
Fordington Lincs 190 G6
Fordley T&W 243 C7
Fordon E Yorks 217 D10
Fordoun Aberds 293 F9
Ford's Green E Sus 36 B6
Suff 125 D11
Fordstreet Essex 107 F8
Ford Street Som 27 D11
Fordton Devon 14 B2
Fordwater Devon 28 G4
Fordwells Oxon 82 C4
Fordwich Kent 55 B7
Fordyce Aberds 302 C5
Forebridge Staffs 151 E8
Foredale N Yorks 212 F6
Forehill S Ayrs 257 E8
Foreland Fields IoW 21 D9
Foreland Ho Argyll 274 G3
Foremark Derbys 152 D6
Forest Becks Lancs 203 C11
Forestburn Gate
Northumb 252 D3
Forest Coal Pit Mon 96 G5
Forestdale London 67 G11
Foresterseat Moray 301 D11
Forest Gate Hants 33 E10
London 68 C2
Forest Green Glos 80 E4
Sur 50 E6
Forest Hall Cumb 221 E10
T&W 243 D7
Forest Head Cumb 240 F3
Forest Hill London 67 E11
Oxon 83 D9
Wilts 63 F8
Forest Holme Lancs 195 B10
Forest-in-Teesdale
Durham 232 F3
Forest Lane Head
N Yorks 206 B2
Forest Lodge Argyll 284 C6
Highld 292 B2
Perth 291 F11
Forest Mill Clack 279 C9
Forest Moor N Yorks 206 B2
Forestreet Devon 24 E5
Forest Row E Sus 52 G2
Forestside W Sus 34 E3
Forest Side IoW 20 D5
Forest Town Notts 171 C9
Forewoods Common
Wilts 61 G10
Forfar Angus 287 B8
Forgandenny Perth 286 F4
Forge Corn 4 F3
Powys 128 D5
Forge Hammer Torf 78 F3
Forge Side Torf 78 D2
Forgewood N Lnrk 268 D4
Forgie Moray 302 D3
Forglen Ho Aberds 302 D6
Forgue Aberds 302 E6
Forhill Worcs 117 B11
Formby Mers 193 F10
Forncett End Norf 142 E2
Forncett St Mary Norf 142 E3
Forncett St Peter Norf 142 E3
Forneth Perth 286 C4
Fornham All Saints Suff 124 D6
Fornham St Genevieve
Suff 124 D6
Fornham St Martin Suff 125 D7
Fornighty Highld 301 D9
Forrabury Corn 11 C7
Forres Moray 301 D10
Forrestfield N Lnrk 269 B7
Forrest Lodge Dumfries 246 F3
Forry's Green Essex 106 E5
Forsbrook Staffs 169 G7
Forse Highld 310 F6
Forse Ho Highld 310 F6
Forshaw Heath Warks 117 C11
Forsinain Highld 310 E2
Forsinard Highld 310 E2
Forsinard Station Highld 310 E2
Forstal Kent 53 B8
Forston Dorset 17 B9
Fort Augustus Highld 290 C5
Forteviot Perth 286 F4
Fort George Highld 301 D7
Forth S Lnrk 269 E8
Forthampton Glos 99 E7
Forthay Glos 80 F2
Forth Road Bridge Edin 280 F2
Fortingall Perth 285 C11
Fortis Green London 67 B9
Fort Matilda Invclyd 276 F5
Forton Hants 33 G10
Hants 48 E2
Lancs 202 C5
Shrops 149 F8
Som 28 F4
Staffs 150 E5
Forton Heath Shrops 149 F8
Fortrie Aberds 302 E6
Aberds 303 D7
Fortrose Highld 301 D7
Fortuneswell Dorset 17 G9
Fort William Highld 290 F3
Forty Green Bucks 84 E3
Bucks 84 G6
Forty Hill London 86 F4
Forward Green Suff 125 F11
Forwood Glos 80 E5
Fosbury Wilts 47 B10
Foscot Oxon 100 G4
Foscote Bucks 102 D4
Northants 102 B3
Wilts 61 D11
Fosdyke Lincs 156 C6
Fosdyke Bridge Lincs 156 C6
Foss Perth 285 B11
Foss Cross Glos 81 D9
Fossebridge Glos 81 C9
Fostall Kent 70 G5
Fosten Green Kent 53 F10
Fosterhouses S Yorks 199 E7
Foster's Booth
Northants 120 G3
Foster's Green Worcs 117 D9
Foster Street Essex 87 D7
Foston Derbys 152 C3
Leics 136 D2
Lincs 172 G5
N Yorks 216 F3
Foston on the Wolds
E Yorks 209 B8
Fotherby Lincs 190 C4
Fothergill Cumb 228 E6
Fotheringhay Northants 137 E11
Foubister Orkney 314 F5
Foul Anchor Cambs 157 F9
Foulbridge Cumb 230 B4
Foulby W Yorks 197 D11
Foulden Borders 273 D8
Norf 140 D5
Foul End Warks 134 E4
Foulford Hants 31 F11
Foulis Castle Highld 300 C5
Foul Mile E Sus 23 B10
Foulride Green E Sus 23 E9
Foulridge Lancs 204 E3
Foulsham Norf 159 E10
Foundry Corn 2 B3
Foundry Hill Norf 159 D11
Fountain Bridgend 57 E11
Fountainhall Borders 271 F8
Four Ashes Bucks 84 F5
Staffs 132 F6
Staffs 133 B8
Suff 125 C10
W Mid 118 B3
Four Crosses Powys 129 B11
Powys 148 F5
Staffs 133 B9
Wrex 166 E3
Four Elms Devon 28 F3
Kent 52 D3
Four Foot Som 44 G5
Four Forks Som 43 F8
Four Gates Gtr Man 194 F6
Four Gotes Cambs 157 F9
Four Houses Corner
W Berks 64 F6
Four Lane End S Yorks 197 G9
Four Lane Ends Derbys 170 D5
Four Lane Ends Blkburn 195 B7
Ches W 167 C9
Gtr Man 195 E9
W Yorks 205 G8
Four Lanes Corn 2 B5
Fourlanes End Ches E 168 D4
Four Marks Hants 49 G7
Four Mile Bridge
Anglesey 178 F3
Four Mile Elm Glos 80 C4
Four Oaks E Sus 38 C5
Glos 98 F3
Kent 70 G3
W Mid 134 D2
W Mid 134 G4
Four Oaks Park W Mid 134 D2
Fourpenny Highld 311 K2
Four Points W Berks 64 D5
Four Pools Worcs 99 C10
Four Roads Carms 74 D6
IoM 192 F3
Fourstones Northumb 241 D9
Four Throws Kent 38 B3
Four Wantz Essex 87 C10
Four Wents Kent 53 F9
Fovant Wilts 31 B8
Foveran Aberds 303 G9
Fowey Corn 6 E2
Fowler's Plot Som 43 F10
Fowley Common Warr 183 B11
Fowlis Angus 287 D7
Fowlis Wester Perth 286 E3
Fowlmere Cambs 105 B8
Fownhope Hereford 97 E11
Foxash Estate Essex 107 E11
Foxbar Renfs 267 C9
Foxbury London 68 E2
Foxcombe Hill Oxon 83 E7
Fox Corner C Beds 103 F8
Sur 50 C3
Foxcote Glos 81 B8
Som 45 B8
Foxcotte Hants 47 D10
Foxdale IoM 192 E3
Foxdown Hants 48 C4
Foxearth Essex 106 C6
Foxendown Kent 69 F7
Foxfield Cumb 210 B4
Foxford W Mid 135 G7
Foxham Wilts 62 D3
Fox Hatch Essex 87 F9
Fox Hill Bath 61 G9
Hereford 98 B3
Foxhills Hants 32 E4
Foxhole Corn 5 E9
Norf 142 D4
Swansea 57 C7
Fox Hole Swansea 56 D5
Foxholes N Yorks 217 E10
Fox Holes Wilts 45 E11
Foxhunt Green E Sus 23 B8
Fox Lane Hants 49 B11
Foxley Hereford 97 B8
Norf 159 E10
Staffs 168 E3
Wilts 61 B11
Foxlydiate Worcs 117 D10
Fox Royd W Yorks 197 D8
Fox Street Essex 107 F10
Foxt Staffs 169 F8
Foxton Cambs 105 B8
Durham 234 F3
Leics 136 E4
N Yorks 225 F8
Foxup N Yorks 213 D7
Foxwist Green Ches W 167 B10
Foxwood Shrops 116 B2
Foy Hereford 97 F11
Foyers Highld 300 G4
Foynesfield Highld 301 D8
Fraddam Corn 2 C3
Fraddon Corn 5 D8
Fradley Staffs 152 G3
Fradley Junction
Staffs 152 G2
Fradswell Staffs 151 C9
Fraisthorpe E Yorks 218 G3
Framfield E Sus 37 C7
Framingham Earl Norf 142 C5
Framingham Pigot Norf 142 C5
Framlingham Suff 126 E5
Frampton Dorset 17 B8
Lincs 156 B6
Frampton Cotterell
S Glos 61 C7
Frampton Court Glos 99 E10
Frampton End S Glos 61 C7
Frampton Mansell Glos 80 E6
Frampton on Severn
Glos 80 D2
Frampton West End
Lincs 174 G3
Framsden Suff 126 F3
Framwellgate Moor
Durham 233 C11
France Lynch Glos 80 E6
Franche Worcs 116 B6
Frandley Ches W 183 F10
Frankby Mers 182 D2
Frankfort Norf 160 E6
Franklands Gate
Hereford 97 B10
Frankley Worcs 133 G9
Frankley Green Worcs 133 G9
Frankley Hill Worcs 117 B9
Frank's Bridge Powys 114 F2
Frankton Warks 119 C8
Frankwell Shrops 149 G9
Frans Green Norf 160 G2
Frant E Sus 52 F5
Fraserburgh Aberds 303 C9
Frating Essex 107 G11
Frating Green Essex 107 G11
Fratton Ptsmth 21 B9
Freasley Warks 134 D4
Freathy Corn 7 E8
Frecheville S Yorks 186 E5
Freckenham Suff 124 C3
Freckleton Lancs 194 B2
Fredley Sur 51 C7
Freebirch Derbys 186 G4
Freeby Leics 154 E6
Freefolk Hants 48 D3
Freehay Staffs 169 G8
Freeland Oxon 82 C6
Renfs 267 B9
Freeland Corner Norf 160 F3
Freemantle Soton 32 E6
Freester Shetland 313 H6
Freethorpe Norf 143 B8
Free Town Gtr Man 195 E10
Freezy Water London 86 F5
Freiston Lincs 174 G5
Freiston Shore Lincs 174 G5
Fremington Devon 40 G4
N Yorks 223 F10
Frenchay S Glos 60 D6
Frenchbeer Devon 13 D9
Frenches Green Essex 106 G4
Frenchmoor Hants 32 B3
French Street Kent 52 C3
Frenchwood Lancs 194 B4
Frenich Stirl 285 G8
Frensham Sur 49 E10
Frenze Norf 142 G2
Fresgoe Highld 310 C3
Freshbrook Swindon 62 C6
Freshfield Mers 193 F9
Freshford Bath 61 G9
Freshwater IoW 20 D2
Freshwater Bay IoW 20 D2
Freshwater East Pembs 73 F8
Fressingfield Suff 126 B5
Freston Suff 108 D3
Freswick Highld 310 C7
Fretherne Glos 80 D2
Frettenham Norf 160 F4
Freuchie Fife 286 G6
Freuchies Angus 292 G4
Freystrop Pembs 73 C7
Friarn Som 43 F7
Friar Park W Mid 133 E10
Friars Cliff Dorset 19 C9
Friar's Gate E Sus 52 G3
Friar's Hill E Sus 38 E5
Friarton Perth 286 E5
Friday Bridge Cambs 139 C9
Friday Hill London 86 G5
Friday Street E Sus 23 E10
Suff 126 G6
Suff 127 E7
Sur 50 D6
Fridaythorpe E Yorks 208 B3
Friendly W Yorks 196 C5
Friern Barnet London 86 G3
Friesland Argyll 288 D3
Friesthorpe Lincs 189 E9
Frieston Lincs 172 F6
Frieth Bucks 84 G3
Frieze Hill Som 28 B2
Friezeland Notts 171 E7
Frilford Oxon 82 F6
Frilford Heath Oxon 82 F6
Frilsham W Berks 64 E4
Frimley Sur 49 B11
Frimley Green Sur 49 B11
Frimley Ridge Sur 49 B11
Frindsbury Medway 69 E8
Fring Norf 158 C4
Fringford Oxon 102 F2
Friningham Kent 53 B10
Frinkle Green Essex 106 C4
Frinsted Kent 53 B11
Frinton-on-Sea Essex 108 G4
Friockheim Angus 287 C9
Friog Gwyn 146 G2
Frisby Leics 136 C4
Frisby on the Wreake
Leics 154 F3
Friskney Lincs 175 D7
Friskney Eaudyke Lincs 175 D7
Friskney Tofts Lincs 175 E7
Friston E Sus 23 F8
Suff 127 E8
Fritchley Derbys 170 E5
Frith Kent 54 B2
Fritham Hants 32 E2
Frith Bank Lincs 174 F4
Frith Common Worcs 116 D3
Frithelstock Devon 25 D7
Frithelstock Stone Devon 25 D7
Frithend Hants 49 F10
Frith-hill Bucks 84 E6
Frith Hill Sur 50 E3
Frithsden Herts 85 D8
Frithville Lincs 174 E4
Frittenden Kent 53 E10
Frittiscombe Devon 8 G6
Fritton Norf 142 E4
Norf 143 C9
Norf 161 F8
Fritwell Oxon 101 F10
Frizinghall W Yorks 205 F8
Frizington Cumb 219 B10
Frizzeler's Green Suff 124 E5
Frobost W Isles 297 J3
Frocester Glos 80 E3
Frochas Powys 148 G5
Frodesley Shrops 131 C10
Frodingham N Lincs 199 E11
Frodsham Ches W 183 F8
Frogden Borders 263 D7
Frog End Cambs 123 F10
Cambs 123 G8
Froggatt Derbys 186 F2
Froghall Staffs 169 F8
Frogham Hants 31 E11
Kent 55 C9
Froghole Kent 52 C2
Frogholt Kent 55 F7
Frogland Cross S Glos 60 C6
Frog Moor Swansea 56 C3
Frogmore Devon 8 G5
Hants 33 C11
Hants 49 B10
Herts 85 E11
Frognal S Ayrs 257 D8
Frognall Lincs 156 G3
Frogpool Corn 4 G5
Frog Pool Worcs 116 D5
Frogs' Green Essex 105 D11
Frogshail Norf 160 B5
Frogwell Corn 6 B6
Frolesworth Leics 135 E10
Frome Som 45 D9
Frome Bridge Glos 80 D3
Fromefield Som 45 D9
Frome St Quintin Dorset 29 G9
Fromes Hill Hereford 98 B3
Fromington Hereford 97 B10
Fron Denb 165 B9
Gwyn 145 B7
Gwyn 163 D8
Powys 113 D11
Powys 129 C8
Powys 130 C4
Powys 130 D3
Shrops 148 B5
Fron-Bache Denb 166 G2
Froncysyllte Wrex 166 G3
Fron-dêg Wrex 166 F3
Frongoch Gwyn 147 B8
Fron Isaf Wrex 166 G3
Frost Devon 26 F3
Frostenden Suff 143 G9
Frostenden Corner Suff 143 G9
Frosterley Durham 232 D6
Frost Hill N Som 60 G2
Frostlane Hants 32 F6
Frost Row Norf 141 C10
Frotoft Orkney 314 D4
Froxfield C Beds 103 E9
Wilts 63 F9
Froxfield Green Hants 34 B2
Froyle Hants 49 E9
Fryern Hill Hants 32 C6
Fryerning Essex 87 E10
Fryerns Essex 69 B8
Fryton N Yorks 216 E3
Fugglestone St Peter
Wilts 46 G6
Fulbeck Lincs 172 E6
Northumb 252 F5
Fulbourn Cambs 123 F10
Fulbrook Oxon 82 C3
Fulflood Hants 33 B7
Fulford Som 28 B2
Staffs 151 B9
York 207 D8
Fulham London 67 D8
Fulking W Sus 36 E2
Fullabrook Devon 40 E4
Fullarton Glasgow 268 C2
N Ayrs 257 B8
Fuller's End Essex 105 F10
Fuller's Moor Ches W 167 E7
Fuller Street Essex 88 B2

Fullerton Hants......47 F11
Fulletby Lincs......190 G3
Fullshaw S Yorks......197 G8
Full Sutton E Yorks......207 B10
Fullwell Cross London......86 G6
Fullwood E Ayrs......267 E8
Gtr Man......196 F2
Fulmer Bucks......66 B3
Fulmodestone Norf......159 C9
Fulneck W Yorks......205 G10
Fulnetby Lincs......189 F9
Fulney Lincs......156 E5
Fulready Warks......100 B5
Fulshaw Park Ches E......184 E4
Fulstone W Yorks......197 F7
Fulstow Lincs......190 B4
Fulthorpe Stockton......234 G4
Fulwell Oxon......101 G7
T&W......243 F9
Fulwood Lancs......202 G6
Som......28 C2
S Yorks......186 D4
Fundenhall Norf......142 D3
Fundenhall Street Norf......142 D2
Funtington W Sus......22 B3
Funtley Hants......33 F9
Funtullich Perth......285 E11
Funzie Shetland......312 D8
Furley Devon......28 G3
Furnace Argyll......284 G4
Carms......74 E6
Carms......75 E8
Ceredig......128 D3
Highld......299 B9
Furnace End Warks......134 E4
Furnace Green W Sus......51 F9
Furnace Wood W Sus......51 F11
Furneaux Pelham Herts......105 F8
Furner's Green E Sus......36 B6
Furness Vale Derbys......185 E8
Furneux Pelham Herts......105 F8
Furnham Som......28 F4
Further Ford End Essex......105 E9
Further Quarter Kent......53 F11
Furtho Northants......102 C5
Furze Devon......25 B10
Furzebrook Dorset......18 E4
Furzedown Hants......32 B5
London......67 E9
Furzehill Devon......41 D8
Dorset......31 G8
Furze Hill Hants......31 E11
Furzeley Corner Hants......33 E11
Furze Platt Windsor......65 C11
Furzey Lodge Hants......32 G5
Furzley Hants......32 D3
Furzton M Keynes......102 D6
Fyfett Som......28 E2
Fyfield Essex......87 D9
Glos......82 E2
Hants......47 D9
Oxon......82 F6
Wilts......63 F7
Wilts......63 G7
Fylingthorpe N Yorks......227 D8
Fyning W Sus......34 C4
Fyvie Aberds......303 F7

G

Gabalfa Cardiff......59 D7
Gabhsann bho Dheas
W Isles......304 C6
Gabhsann bho Thuath
W Isles......304 C6
Gable Head Hants......21 B10
Gablon Highld......309 K7
Gabroc Hill E Ayrs......267 E9
Gadbrook Sur......51 D8
Gaddesby Leics......154 G3
Gadebridge Herts......85 D8
Gadfa Anglesey......179 D7
Gadfield Elm Worcs......98 E5
Gadlas Shrops......149 B7
Gadlys Rhondda......77 E7
Gadshill Kent......69 E8
Gaer Newport......59 B9
Powys......96 G3
Gaer-fawr Mon......78 F6
Gaerllwyd Mon......78 F6
Gaerwen Anglesey......179 G7
Gagingwell Oxon......101 F8
Gaick Lodge Highld......291 E9
Gailey Staffs......151 G8
Gailey Wharf Staffs......151 G8
Gainfield Oxon......82 F4
Gainford Durham......224 B3
Gain Hill Kent......53 D8
Gainsborough Lincs......188 C4
Suff......108 C3
Gainsford End Essex......106 D4
Gairletter Argyll......276 E3
Gairloch Highld......299 B8
Gairlochy Highld......290 E3
Gairney Bank Perth......280 B2
Gairnshiel Lodge
Aberds......292 C4
Gaisgill Cumb......222 D2
Gaitsgill Cumb......230 B3
Galadean Borders......271 G11
Galashiels Borders......261 B11
Galdlys Flint......182 G2
Gale Gtr Man......196 D2
Galgate Lancs......202 B5
Galhampton Som......29 B10
Gallaberry Dumfries......247 G11
Gallachoille Argyll......275 E8
Gallanach Argyll......288 C4
Argyll......289 G10
Highld......294 G6
Gallantry Bank Ches E......167 E8
Gallatown Fife......280 C5
Galley Common Warks......134 E6
Galleyend Essex......88 E2
Galley Hill Cambs......122 D6
Lincs......190 F6
Galleywood Essex......88 E2
Galligill Cumb......231 B11
Gallin Perth......285 C9
Gallovie Highld......291 E7
Gallowfauld Angus......287 C8
Gallowhill Glasgow......267 D11
Renfs......267 B9
Gallowhills Aberds......303 D10
Gallows Corner London......87 G8
Gallowsgreen Torf......78 D3
Gallows Green Essex......106 F2
Essex......107 F8
Staffs......169 G9
Worcs......117 E8
Gallows Inn Derbys......171 G7
Gallowstree Common
Oxon......65 C7
Galltair Highld......295 C10
Galltegfa Denb......165 D10
Gallt Melyd / Meliden
Denb......181 E9
Gallt-y-foel Gwyn......163 C9
Gallypot Street E Sus......52 F3
Galmington Som......28 C2
Galmisdale Highld......294 G6
Galmpton Devon......8 G3
Torbay......9 D7
Galon Uchaf M Tydf......77 D9
Galphay N Yorks......214 E5
Galston E Ayrs......258 B2
Galtrigill Highld......296 F7
Gam Corn......11 F7
Gamble Hill W Yorks......205 G11
Gamblesby Cumb......231 D8
Gamble's Green Essex......88 C3
Gamelsby Cumb......239 G7
Gamesley Derbys......185 C8
Gamlingay Cambs......122 G4
Gamlingay Cinques
Cambs......122 G4
Gamlingay Great Heath
Cambs......122 G4
Gammaton Devon......25 B7
Gammaton Moor Devon......25 C7
Gammersgill N Yorks......213 C11
Gamston Notts......154 B2
Notts......188 F2
Ganarew Hereford......79 B8
Ganavan Argyll......289 F10
Ganders Green Glos......98 G4
Gang Corn......6 B6
Ganllwyd Gwyn......146 E4
Gannetts Dorset......30 D3
Gannochy Angus......293 F7
Perth......286 E5
Gansclet Highld......310 E7
Ganstead E Yorks......209 G9
Ganthorpe N Yorks......216 E3
Ganton N Yorks......217 D9
Gants Hill London......68 B2
Ganwick Corner Herts......86 F3
Gaodhail Argyll......289 F8
Gappah Devon......14 F3
Garafad Highld......298 C4
Garamor Highld......295 F8
Garbat Highld......300 C4
Garbhallt Argyll......275 D11
Garboldisham Norf......141 G10
Garbole Highld......301 G7
Garden City Bl Gwent......77 D11
Flint......166 B4
Gardeners Green
Wokingham......65 F10
Gardenstown Aberds......303 C7
Garden Village Swansea......56 B5
S Yorks......186 B3
Wrex......166 E4
W Yorks......206 G4
Garderhouse Shetland......313 J5
Gardham E Yorks......208 E5
Gardie Shetland......312 D7
Gardin Shetland......312 G6
Gare Hill Som......45 E9
Garelochhead Argyll......276 C4
Garford Oxon......82 F6
Garforth W Yorks......206 G4
Gargrave N Yorks......204 C4
Gargunnock Stirl......278 C4
Garizim Conwy......179 F11
Garker Corn......5 E10
Garlandhayes Devon......27 D11
Garlands Cumb......239 G10
Garleffin S Ayrs......244 G3
Garlic Street Norf......142 G4
Garlieston Dumfries......236 E6
Garlinge Kent......71 F10
Garlinge Green Kent......54 C6
Garlogie Aberds......293 C9
Garmelow Staffs......150 D5
Garmond Aberds......303 D8
Garmondsway Durham......234 E2
Garmony Argyll......289 E8
Garmouth Moray......302 C3
Garmston Shrops......132 B2
Garn Powys......130 G2
Garnant Carms......75 C11
Garndiffaith Torf......78 E3
Garndolbenmaen Gwyn......163 G7
Garnedd Conwy......164 E2
Garnett Bridge Cumb......221 F10
Garnetts Essex......87 B10
Garnfadryn Gwyn......144 C5
Garnkirk N Lnrk......268 B3
Garnlydan Bl Gwent......77 C11
Garnsgate Lincs......157 E8
Garnswllt Swansea......75 D10
Garn-swllt Swansea......75 D10
Garn-yr-erw Torf......78 C2
Garrabost W Isles......304 E7
Garrachra Argyll......275 E11
Garra Eallabus Argyll......274 F3
Garralburn Moray......302 D4
Garraron Argyll......275 C9
Garras Corn......2 E6
Garreg Flint......181 F10
Gwyn......163 G10
Garrets Green W Mid......134 F2
Garrick Perth......286 F2
Garrigill Cumb......231 C10
Garrison Stirl......285 G7
Garriston N Yorks......224 G3
Garroch Dumfries......246 G3
Garrogie Lodge Highld......291 B7
Garros Highld......298 C4
Garrow Perth......286 C2
Garrowhill Glasgow......268 C3
Garrygualach Highld......290 C3
Garryhorn Dumfries......246 E2
Garsdale Cumb......212 B4
Garsdale Head Cumb......222 G5
Garsdon Wilts......62 B3
Garshall Green Staffs......151 C9
Garsington Oxon......83 E9
Garstang Lancs......202 D5
Garston Herts......85 F10
Mers......182 E6
Garswood Mers......183 B9
Gartachoil Stirl......277 C10
Gartbreck Argyll......254 B3
Gartcosh N Lnrk......268 B3
Garth Bridgend......57 C11
Ceredig......128 G2
Flint......181 E10
Gwyn......179 G9
Newport......59 B9
Newport......78 G4
Perth......285 B11
Powys......95 B9
Powys......114 C5
Shetland......313 H4
Shetland......313 H6
Wrex......166 G3
Garthamlock Glasgow......268 B3
Garthbeg Highld......291 B7
Garthbrengy Powys......95 E10
Garthdee Aberdeen......293 C11
Garthelii Ceredig......111 F11
Garthmyl Powys......130 D3
Garthorpe Leics......154 E6
N Lincs......199 D11
Garth Owen Powys......130 E2
Garth Row Cumb......221 F10
Garthe's Wrex......166 G3
Gartlea N Lnrk......268 C5
Gartloch Glasgow......268 B3
Gartly Aberds......302 F5
Gartmore Stirl......277 B10
Gartmore Ho Stirl......277 B10
Gartnagrenach Argyll......255 B8
Gartness N Lnrk......268 C5
Stirl......277 D10
Gartocharn W Dunb......277 D8
Garton E Yorks......209 F11
Garton-on-the-Wolds
E Yorks......208 B5
Gartsherrie N Lnrk......268 B4
Gartur Stirl......277 B11
Gartymore Highld......311 H4
Garvald E Loth......281 G11
Garvamore Highld......291 D7
Garvard Argyll......274 D4
Garvault Hotel Highld......308 F7
Garve Highld......300 C3
Garvestone Norf......141 B10
Garvock Aberds......293 F9
Invclyd......276 G5
Garvock Hill Fife......280 D2
Garway Hereford......97 G9
Garway Hill Hereford......97 F8
Gaskan Highld......289 B9
Gasper Wilts......45 G9
Gastard Wilts......61 F11
Gasthorpe Norf......141 G9
Gaston Green Essex......87 B7
Gatacre Park Shrops......132 F5
Gatcombe IoW......20 D5
Gateacre Mers......182 D6
Gatebeck Cumb......211 B10
Gate Burton Lincs......188 E4
Gateford Notts......187 E9
Gateford Common
Notts......187 E9
Gateforth N Yorks......198 B5
Gatehead E Ayrs......257 B9
Gate Helmsley N Yorks......207 B9
Gatehouse Northumb......251 F7
Gatehouse of Fleet
Dumfries......237 D8
Gatelawbridge
Dumfries......247 D10
Gateley Norf......159 E9
Gatenby N Yorks......214 B6
Gatesgarth Cumb......220 B3
Gateshead T&W......243 E7
Gatesheath Ches W......167 C7
Gateside Aberds......293 B8
Angus......287 C8
Dumfries......248 E4
E Renf......267 D9
Fife......286 G5
N Ayrs......267 E7
Shetland......312 F4
Gatewen Wrex......166 E4
Gatherley Devon......12 E3
Gathurst Gtr Man......194 F4
Gatlas Newport......78 G4
Gatley End Cambs......104 C5
Gtr Man......184 D4
Gatton Sur......51 C9
Gattonside Borders......262 B2
Gatwick Glos......80 C2
Gatwick Airport W Sus......51 E9
Gaufron Powys......113 D9
Gaulby Leics......136 C3
Gauldry Fife......287 E7
Gaunt's Common Dorset......31 F8
Gaunt's Earthcott S Glos......60 C6
Gaunt's End Essex......105 F10
Gautby Lincs......189 G11
Gavinton Borders......272 E5
Gawber S Yorks......197 F10
Gawcott Bucks......102 E3
Gawsworth Ches E......168 B5
Gawthorpe W Yorks......197 C9
W Yorks......197 D7
Gawthrop Cumb......212 B3
Gawthwaite Cumb......210 C5
Gay Bowers Essex......88 E3
Gaydon Warks......119 G7
Gayfield Orkney......314 A4
Gayhurst M Keynes......103 B7
Gayle N Yorks......213 B7
Gayles N Yorks......224 D2
Gay Street W Sus......35 C9
Gayton Mers......182 E3
Norf......158 F4
Northants......120 G4
Staffs......151 D9
Gayton Engine Lincs......191 D7
Gayton le Marsh Lincs......190 E6
Gayton le Wold Lincs......190 D2
Gayton Thorpe Norf......158 F4
Gaywood Norf......158 E2
Gaza Shetland......312 F5
Gazeley Suff......124 E4
Geanies House Highld......301 B8
Gearraidh Bhailteas
W Isles......297 J3
Gearraidh Bhaird
W Isles......304 F5
Gearraidh Dubh W Isles......296 F4
Gearraidh na h-Aibhne
W Isles......304 E4
Gearraidh na Monadh
W Isles......297 K3
Geàrraidh Sheilidh
W Isles......297 J3
Geary Highld......298 C2
Geat Wolford Warks......100 E4
Geddes House Highld......301 D8
Gedding Suff......125 F9
Geddington Northants......137 G7
Gedgrave Hall Suff......109 B8
Gedintailor Highld......295 B7
Gedling Notts......171 G10
Gedney Lincs......157 E8
Gedney Broadgate Lincs......157 E8
Gedney Drove End
Lincs......157 D9
Gedney Dyke Lincs......157 D8
Gedney Hill Lincs......156 G6
Gee Cross Gtr Man......185 C7
Geeston Rutland......137 C9
Gegin Wrex......166 E3
Geilston Argyll......276 F6
Geinas Denb......165 B9
Geirinis W Isles......297 G3
Geise Highld......310 C5
Geisiadar W Isles......304 E3
Geldeston Norf......143 E7
Gell Conwy......164 B5
Gelli Pembs......73 B9
Rhondda......77 G7
Gellideg M Tydf......77 D8
Gellifor Denb......165 C10
Gelligaer Caerph......77 F10
Gelli-gaer Neath......57 C9
Gelligroes Caerph......77 G11
Gelli-hôf Caerph......77 F11
Gellilydan Gwyn......146 B3
Gellinud Neath......76 E2
Gellinudd Neath......76 E2
Gellyburn Perth......286 D4
Gellygron Neath......76 E2
Gellywen Carms......92 G5
Gelsmoor Leics......153 F8
Gelston Dumfries......237 D9
Lincs......172 G6
Gembling E Yorks......209 B8
Gemini Warr......183 C9
Gendros Swansea......56 B6
Genesis Green Suff......124 F4
Gentleshaw Staffs......151 G11
Geocrab W Isles......305 J3
Georgefield Dumfries......249 E7
George Green Bucks......66 C4
Georgeham Devon......40 F3
George Nympton Devon......26 C2
Georgetown Bl Gwent......77 D10
Georgia Corn......1 B5
Gergask Highld......291 D8
Gerlan Gwyn......163 B10
Germansweek Devon......12 C4
Germiston Glasgow......268 B2
Germoe Corn......2 D3
Gernon Bushes Essex......87 E7
Gerrans Corn......3 B9
Gerrard's Bromley
Staffs......150 C5
Gerrards Cross Bucks......66 B4
Gerrick Redcar......226 C4
Geseilfa Powys......129 E8
Gestingthorpe Essex......106 D6
Gesto Ho Highld......294 B5
Geuffordd Powys......148 G4
Geufron Denb......166 G2
Gibbet Hill Warks......135 G10
W Mid......118 C6
Gibb Hill Ches W......183 F10
Gibbshill Dumfries......237 B9
Gib Heath W Mid......133 F11
Gibraltar Beds......103 B10
Bucks......84 C3
Kent......55 F8
Gibralter Oxon......83 B7
Gibshill Invclyd......276 G6
Gibsmere Notts......172 F2
Giddeahall Wilts......61 E11
Giddy Green Dorset......18 D2
Gidea Park London......68 B4
Gidleigh Devon......13 D9
Giffard Park M Keynes......103 C7
Giffnock E Renf......267 D11
Gifford E Loth......271 B10
Giffordland N Ayrs......266 F5
Giffordtown Fife......286 F6
Gigg Gtr Man......195 F10
Giggetty Staffs......133 E7
Giggleswick N Yorks......212 G6
Giggshill Sur......67 F7
Gignog Pembs......91 G7
Gilberdyke E Yorks......199 B10
Gilbert's Coombe Corn......4 G3
Gilbert's End Worcs......98 C6
Gilbert's Green Warks......118 C2
Gilbertstone W Mid......134 G2
Gilbert Street Hants......49 G7
Gilchriston E Loth......271 B9
Gilcrux Cumb......229 D8
Gildersome W Yorks......197 B8
Gildersome Street
W Yorks......197 B8
Gildingwells S Yorks......187 D9
Gilesgate Durham......233 C11
Gilesgate Moor
Durham......233 C11
Gileston V Glam......58 F4
Gilfach Caerph......77 F11
Hereford......96 E6
Gilfach Goch Rhondda......58 B3
Gilfachrheda Ceredig......111 F8
Gilgarran Cumb......228 G6
Gill N Yorks......204 E5
Gillamoor N Yorks......216 B3
Gillan Corn......3 E7
Gillar's Green Mers......183 B7
Gillbank Cumb......221 F7
Gillbent Gtr Man......184 E5
Gillen Highld......298 D2
Gillesbie Dumfries......248 E5
Gilling East N Yorks......216 D2
Gillingham Dorset......30 B4
Medway......69 F9
Norf......143 E8
Gilling West N Yorks......224 D3
Gillmoss Mers......182 B6
Gillock Highld......310 D6
Gillow Heath Staffs......168 D5
Gills Highld......310 B7
Gill's Green Kent......53 G9
Gillway Staffs......134 C4
Gilmanscleuch Borders......261 E8
Gilmerton Edin......270 B5
Perth......286 E2
Gilmonby Durham......223 C9
Gilmorton Leics......135 F11
Gilmourton S Lnrk......268 G3
Gilnow Gtr Man......195 F8
Gilroyd S Yorks......197 G10
Gilsland Northumb......240 D4
Gilsland Spa Cumb......240 D4
Gilson Warks......134 E3
Gilstead W Yorks......205 F8
Gilston Borders......271 D8
Herts......86 C6
Gilston Park Herts......86 C6
Giltbrook Notts......171 F7
Gilver's Lane Worcs......98 C6
Gilwell Park Essex......86 F5
Gilwern Mon......78 C2
Gimingham Norf......160 B5
Ginclough Ches E......185 F7
Ginger's Green E Sus......23 C10
Giosla W Isles......304 F3
Gipping Suff......125 E11
Gipsey Bridge Lincs......174 F3
Gipsy Row Suff......107 D11
Gipsyville Hull......200 B5
Gipton W Yorks......206 F2
Gipton Wood W Yorks......206 F2
Girdle Toll N Ayrs......266 G6
Girlington W Yorks......205 G8
Girlsta Shetland......313 H6
Girsby Lincs......190 D2
N Yorks......225 D7
Girt Som......29 C10
Girtford C Beds......104 B3
C Beds......122 G3
Girthon Dumfries......237 D8
Girton Cambs......123 E8
Notts......172 B4
Girvan S Ayrs......244 D5
Gisburn Lancs......204 D2
Gisleham Suff......143 F10
Gislingham Suff......125 C11
Gissing Norf......142 F2
Gittisham Devon......15 B8
Givons Grove Sur......51 C7
Glachavoil Argyll......275 F11
Glackmore Highld......300 D6
Glack of Midthird Moray......302 E3
Gladestry Powys......114 F4
Gladsmuir E Loth......281 G9
Glaichbea Highld......300 F5
Glais Swansea......76 E2
Glaisdale N Yorks......226 D5
Glame Highld......298 E5
Glamis Angus......287 C7
Glan Adda Gwyn......179 G9
Glanafon Pembs......73 B7
Glanaman Carms......75 C11
Glan-Conwy Conwy......164 E4
Glandford Norf......177 E8
Glan-Duar Carms......93 C10
Glandwr Caerph......78 E2
Pembs......92 F3
Glan-Dwyfach Gwyn......163 G7
Glandy Cross Carms......92 F2
Glandyfi Ceredig......128 D3
Glan Gors Anglesey......179 F7
Glangrwyney Powys......78 B2
Glanhanog Powys......129 D8
Glanmule Powys......130 E3
Glanrafon Ceredig......128 G2
Glanrhyd Gwyn......144 B5
Pembs......92 C2
Glan-rhyd Gwyn......163 D7
Powys......76 D3
Glantlees Northumb......252 B4
Glanton Northumb......264 G3
Glanton Pike Northumb......264 G3
Glan-traeth Anglesey......178 F3
Glanvilles Wootton
Dorset......29 F11
Glanwern Ceredig......128 F2
Glanwydden Conwy......180 E4
Glan-y-don Flint......181 F11
Glan y Ffer / Ferryside
Carms......74 C5
Glan-y-llyn Rhondda......58 C6
Glan-y-môr Carms......74 C4
Glan-y-nant Caerph......77 F10
Powys......129 G8
Glan-yr-afon Anglesey......179 E10
Flint......181 E10
Gwyn......164 G6
Gwyn......165 G8
Shrops......148 E4
Glan-y-wern Gwyn......146 C2
Glapthorn Northants......137 E10
Glapwell Derbys......171 B7
Glas-allt Shiel Aberds......292 E4
Glasbury Powys......96 D3
Glaschoil Highld......301 F10
Glascoed Denb......181 G7
Mon......78 E4
Powys......129 F11
Powys......148 G2
Wrex......166 E3
Glascorrie Aberds......292 D5
Perth......286 E2
Glascote Staffs......134 C4
Glascwm Powys......114 G3
Glasdir Flint......181 E10
Glasdrum Argyll......284 C4
Glasfryn Conwy......164 E6
Glasgoed Ceredig......92 B6
Glasgoforest Aberds......293 B10
Glasgow Glasgow......267 B11
Glashvin Highld......298 C4
Glasinfryn Gwyn......163 B9
Glasllwch Newport......59 B9
Glasnacardoch Highld......295 F8
Glasnakille Highld......295 D7
Glasphein Highld......297 G7
Glaspwll Powys......128 D4
Glassburn Highld......300 F3
Glassenbury Kent......53 F8
Glasserton Dumfries......236 F6
Glassford S Lnrk......268 F4
Glassgreen Moray......302 C2
Glass Houghton
W Yorks......198 C2
Glasshouse Glos......98 G4
Glasshouse Hill Glos......98 G4
Glasshouses N Yorks......214 G3
Glasslie Fife......286 G6
Glasson Cumb......228 D6
Cumb......239 E7
Lancs......202 B4
Glassonby Cumb......231 D7
Glasterlaw Angus......287 B9
Glaston Rutland......137 C7
Glastonbury Som......44 F4
Glatton Cambs......138 F3
Glazebrook Warr......183 C11
Glazebury Warr......183 B11
Glazeley Shrops......132 F4
Gleadless S Yorks......186 E5
Gleadless Valley
S Yorks......186 E5
Gleadmoss Ches E......168 B4
Gleadsmoss Ches E......168 B4
Gleanhead Dumfries......245 G10
Gleann Tholàstaidh
W Isles......304 D7
Gleaston Cumb......210 E5
Glebe Hants......33 D9
Shetland......313 J6
T&W......243 F8
Glecknabae Argyll......275 G11
Gledhow W Yorks......206 F2
Gledrid Shrops......148 B5
Gleiniant Powys......129 E9
Glemsford Suff......106 B6
Glen Dumfries......237 B10
Dumfries......237 D7
Glenallachie Moray......302 E2
Glenalmond College
Perth......286 E3
Glenalmond Ho Perth......286 E3
Glenamachrie Argyll......289 G11
Glenample Stirl......285 E9
Glenancross Highld......295 F8
Glenapp Castle S Ayrs......244 G3
Glenaros Ho Argyll......289 E7
Glen Auldyn IoM......192 C5
Glenbarr Argyll......255 D7
Glenbeg Highld......289 C7
Highld......301 G10
Glen Bernisdale Highld......298 E4
Glenbervie Aberds......293 E9
Glenboig N Lnrk......268 B4
Glenborrodale Highld......289 C8
Glenbranter Argyll......276 B2
Glenbreck Borders......260 E3
Glenbrein Lodge Highld......290 B6
Glenbrittle House
Highld......294 C6
Glenbrook Edin......270 B2
Glenbuchat Castle
Aberds......292 B5
Glenbuchat Lodge
Aberds......292 B5
Glenbuck E Ayrs......259 D7
Glenburn Renfs......267 C9
Glenbyre Argyll......289 G7
Glencalvie Lodge Highld......309 L4
Glencanisp Lodge
Highld......307 G6
Glencaple Dumfries......237 C11
Glencarron Lodge
Highld......299 D10
Glencarse Perth......286 E5
Glencassley Castle
Highld......309 J4
Glencat Aberds......293 D7
Glenceitlein Highld......284 C5
Glencoe Highld......284 B4
Glencraig Fife......280 B3
Glencripesdale Highld......289 D8
Glencrosh Dumfries......247 F7
Glendavan Ho Aberds......292 C6
Glendearg Borders......262 B2
Glendevon Perth......286 G3
Glendoebeg Highld......290 C6
Glendoe Lodge Highld......290 C6
Glendoick Perth......286 E6
Glendoll Lodge Angus......292 F4
Glendoune S Ayrs......244 D5
Glenduckie Fife......286 F6
Glendye Lodge Aberds......293 E8
Gleneagles Hotel Perth......286 F3
Gleneagles House Perth......286 G3
Glenearn Perth......286 F5
Glenegedale Argyll......254 B4
Glenelg Highld......295 D10
Glenernie Moray......301 E10
Glenfarg Perth......286 F5
Glenfarquhar Lodge
Aberds......293 E9
Glenferness House
Highld......301 E9
Glenfeshie Lodge
Highld......291 D10
Glenfiddich Lodge
Moray......302 F3
Glenfield Leics......135 B10
Glenfinnan Highld......295 G10
Glenfinnan Lodge
Highld......295 G11
Glenfintaig Ho Highld......290 E4
Glenfoot Perth......286 F5
Glenfyne Lodge Argyll......284 F6
Glengap Dumfries......237 D8
Glengarnock N Ayrs......266 E6
Glengolly Highld......310 C5
Glengorm Castle Argyll......288 D6
Glengoulandie Perth......285 B11
Glengrasco Highld......298 E4
Glenhead Farm Angus......292 G4
Glen Ho Borders......261 C7
Glenholt Plym......7 C10
Glenhoul Dumfries......246 F4
Glenhurich Highld......289 C10
Glenkerry Borders......261 G7
Glenkiln Dumfries......237 B10
Glenkindie Aberds......292 B6
Glenlair Dumfries......237 B9
Glenlatterach Moray......301 D11
Glenlee Dumfries......246 G4
Glenleigh Park E Sus......38 F2
Glenleraig Highld......306 F6
Glenlichorn Perth......285 F11
Glenlicht Ho Highld......290 B2
Glenlivet Moray......301 G11
Glenlochar Dumfries......237 C9
Glenlochsie Perth......292 F2
Glenlocksie Lodge
Perth......292 F2
Glenloig N Ayrs......255 D10
Glenlomond Perth......286 G5
Glenluce Dumfries......236 D4
Glenlussa Ho Argyll......255 E8
Glenmallan Argyll......276 B5
Glenmark Angus......292 E6
Glenmarkie Lodge
Angus......292 G4
Glenmarksie Highld......300 D3
Glenmavis N Lnrk......268 B4
W Loth......269 B9
Glenmaye IoM......192 E3
Glenmayne Borders......261 C11
Glenmeanie Highld......300 D2
Glenmidge Dumfries......247 F9
Glenmoidart Ho Highld......289 B9
Glen Mona IoM......192 D5
Glen Mor Highld......295 B10
Glenmore Argyll......275 B9
Argyll......275 G11
Highld......298 E4
Glenmore Lodge
Highld......291 C11
Glenmoy Angus......292 G6
Glen Nevis House Highld......290 F3
Glennoe Argyll......284 D4
Glen of Newmill Moray......302 D4
Glenogil Angus......292 G6
Glenowen Pembs......73 D7
Glen Parva Leics......135 D11
Glenprosen Lodge
Angus......292 G4
Glenprosen Village
Angus......292 G5
Glenquaich Lodge
Perth......286 D2
Glenquiech Angus......292 G6
Glenquithlie Aberds......303 C8
Glenrath Borders......260 C6
Glenrazie Dumfries......236 C5
Glenreasdell Mains
Argyll......255 B9
Glenree N Ayrs......255 E10
Glenridding Cumb......221 B7
Glenrosa N Ayrs......256 B2
Glenrossal Highld......309 J4
Glenrothes Fife......286 G6
Glensanda Highld......289 E10
Glensaugh Aberds......293 F8
Glensburgh Falk......279 E8
Glenshero Lodge Highld......291 D7
Glenshoe Lodge Perth......292 G3
Glen Sluain Argyll......275 D11
Glenstockadale
Dumfries......236 C2
Glenstriven Argyll......275 F11
Glentaggart S Lnrk......259 D8
Glen Tanar House
Aberds......292 D6
Glentarkie Perth......286 F5
Glenternie Borders......260 B6
Glentham Lincs......189 C8
Glentirranmuir Stirl......278 C3
Glenton Aberds......302 G6
Glentress Borders......261 B7
Glentromie Lodge
Highld......291 D9
Glen Trool Lodge
Dumfries......245 G10
Glentrool Village
Dumfries......236 B5
Glentruan IoM......192 B5
Glentruim House Highld......291 D8
Glentworth Lincs......188 D6
Glenuaig Lodge Highld......299 E11
Glenuig Highld......289 B8
Glenure Argyll......284 C4
Glenurquhart Highld......301 C7
Glen Vic Askil Highld......298 E3
Glenview Argyll......284 E5
Glen Village Falk......279 F7
Glen Vine IoM......192 E4
Glespin S Lnrk......259 D8
Gletness Shetland......313 H6
Glewstone Hereford......97 G11
Glinton Pboro......138 B3
Globe Town London......67 C11
Glodwick Gtr Man......196 G2
Glogue Pembs......92 E4
Glooston Leics......136 D4
Glororum Northumb......264 C5
Glossop Derbys......185 C8
Gloster Hill Northumb......253 C7
Gloucester Glos......80 B4
Gloup Shetland......312 C7
Gloweth Corn......4 G5
Glusburn N Yorks......204 E6
Glutt Lodge Highld......310 F3
Glutton Bridge Staffs......169 B9
Gluvian Corn......5 C8
Glympton Oxon......101 G8
Glyn Mon......79 F7
Powys......129 F8
Glynarthen Ceredig......92 B6
Glynbrochan Powys......129 G8
Glyn Castle Neath......76 E4
Glyn-Ceiriog Wrex......148 B4
Glyncoch Rhondda......77 G9
Glyncoed Bl Gwent......77 C11
Glyncorrwg Neath......57 B11
Glyn-cywarch Gwyn......146 C2
Glynde E Sus......23 D7
Glyndebourne E Sus......23 C7
Glyndyfrdwy Denb......165 G10
Glynedd / Glyn neath
Neath......76 D5
Glyne Gap E Sus......38 F3
Glyn Etwy Bl Gwent......77 D11
Glynhafren Powys......129 G7
Glynllan Bridgend......58 B2
Glynmorlas Shrops......148 B6
Glyn-neath / Glynedd
Neath......76 D5
Glynogwr Bridgend......58 B3
Glyntaff Rhondda......58 B5
Glyntawe Powys......76 B4
Gnosall Staffs......150 E6
Gnosall Heath Staffs......150 E6
Goadby Leics......136 D4
Goadby Marwood Leics......154 D5
Goatacre Wilts......62 D4
Goatham Green E Sus......38 C4
Goathill Dorset......29 D11
Goathland N Yorks......226 E6
Goathurst Som......43 G9
Goathurst Common Kent......52 C3
Goat Lees Kent......54 D4
Gobernuisgach Lodge
Highld......308 E4
Gobernuisgeach Highld......310 F3
Gobhaig W Isles......305 H2
Gobley Hole Hants......48 D6
Gobowen Shrops......148 C6
Godalming Sur......50 E3
Goddards Bucks......84 G3
Goddard's Corner Suff......126 D5
Goddard's Green Kent......53 G10
W Berks......65 F7
Goddards' Green W Sus......36 C3
Godden Green Kent......52 B5
Goddington London......68 F3
Godley Gtr Man......185 B7
Godleybrook Staffs......169 G7
Godley Hill Gtr Man......185 C7
Godleys Green E Sus......36 D5
Godmanchester Cambs......122 C4
Godmanstone Dorset......17 B9
Godmersham Kent......54 C5
Godney Som......44 E3
Godolphin Cross Corn......2 C4
Godre'r-graig Neath......76 D3
God's Blessing Green
Dorset......31 G8
Godshill Hants......31 E11
IoW......20 E6
Godstone Sur......51 C10
Godswinscroft Hants......19 B9
Godwell Devon......8 D2
Godwick Norf......159 E8
Godwinscroft Hants......19 B9
Goetre Mon......78 D4
Goferydd Anglesey......178 E2
Goff's Oak Herts......86 E4
Gogar Edin......280 G3
Goginan Ceredig......128 G3
Goirtean a'Chladaich
Highld......290 F2
Golan Gwyn......163 G8
Golant Corn......6 E2
Golberdon Corn......12 G2
Golborne Gtr Man......183 B10
Golcar W Yorks......196 D6
Golch Flint......181 F11
Goldcliff Newport......59 C11
Golden Balls Oxon......83 F9
Golden Cross E Sus......23 C8
E Sus......23 C10
Golden Green Kent......52 D6
Golden Grove Carms......75 B9
Goldenhill Stoke......168 E5
Golden Hill Bristol......60 D5
Hants......19 B11
Pembs......73 E7
Pembs......91 G9
Golden Park Devon......24 C2
Golden Pot Hants......49 E8
Golden Valley Derbys......170 E6
Glos......99 G8
Hereford......98 B3
Golder Field Hereford......115 E11
Golders Green London......67 B9
Goldfinch Bottom
W Berks......64 G4
Goldhanger Essex......88 D6
Gold Hill Dorset......30 E4
Norf......139 E10
Golding Shrops......131 C10
Goldington Beds......121 G11
Goldsborough N Yorks......206 B3
N Yorks......226 C6
Gold's Cross Bath......60 G5
Golds Green W Mid......133 E9
Goldsithney Corn......2 C2
Goldstone Shrops......150 D4
Goldthorn Park W Mid......133 D8
Goldthorpe S Yorks......198 G3
Goldworthy Devon......24 C5
Golford Kent......53 F9
Golftyn Flint......182 G3
Golgotha Kent......55 D9
Gollanfield Highld......301 D8
Gollawater Corn......4 E5
Gollinglith Foot
N Yorks......214 C3
Golly Wrex......166 D4
Golsoncott Som......42 F4
Golspie Highld......311 J2
Golval Highld......310 C2
Golynos Torf......78 E3
Gomeldon Wilts......47 F7
Gomersal W Yorks......197 B8
Gometra Ho Argyll......288 E5
Gomshall Sur......50 D5
Gonalston Notts......171 F11
Gonamena Corn......11 G11
Gonerby Hill Foot Lincs......155 B8
Gonfirth Shetland......313 G5
Good Easter Essex......87 C10
Gooderstone Norf......140 C5
Goodleigh Devon......40 G6
Goodley Stock Kent......52 C2
Goodmanham E Yorks......208 E3
Goodmayes London......68 B3
Goodnestone Kent......55 C9
Kent......70 G4
Goodrich Hereford......79 B9
Goodrington Torbay......9 D7
Good's Green Worcs......132 G5
Goodshaw Lancs......195 B10
Goodshaw Chapel
Lancs......195 B10
Goodshaw Fold Lancs......195 B10
Goodstone Devon......13 G11
Goodwick / Wdig Pembs......91 D8
Goodworth Clatford
Hants......47 E11
Goodyers End Warks......134 F6
Goodyhills Cumb......229 B8
Goole E Yorks......199 C8
Goom's Hill Worcs......117 G10
Goonabarn Corn......5 E9
Goonbell Corn......4 F4
Goon Gumpas Corn......4 G4
Goonhavern Corn......4 E5
Goonhusband Corn......2 D5
Goonlaze Corn......2 B6
Goonown Corn......4 E4
Goon Piper Corn......3 B8
Goonvrea Corn......4 F4
Gooseberry Green Essex......87 F11
Goose Eye W Yorks......204 E6
Gooseford Devon......13 C9
Goose Green Cumb......211 C10
Essex......108 F2
Gtr Man......194 G5
Hants......32 F4
Herts......86 D5
Kent......52 C6
Kent......53 F10
Lancs......194 C3
Norf......142 F2
S Glos......61 C8
W Sus......34 C3
W Sus......35 D10
Gooseham Mill Devon......24 D2
Goosehill W Yorks......197 C11
Goose Hill Hants......64 G4
Goosehill Green Worcs......117 E8
Goosemoor Staffs......150 F6
Goosemoor Green
Staffs......151 G11
Goosenford Som......28 B2
Goose Pool Hereford......97 D9
Goosewell Devon......40 D5
Goosey Oxon......82 G5
Goosnargh Lancs......203 F7
Goostrey Ches E......184 G3
Gorbals Glasgow......267 C11
Gorcott Hill Warks......117 D11
Gord Shetland......313 L6
Gorddinog Conwy......179 G11
Gordon Borders......272 G2
Gordonbush Highld......311 J2
Gordonsburgh Moray......302 C4
Gordonstoun Moray......301 C11
Gordonstown Aberds......302 D5
Aberds......303 F7
Gore Dorset......29 D9
Kent......55 B10
Gorebridge Midloth......270 C6
Gore Cross Wilts......46 C4
Gore End Hants......64 G2
Gorefield Cambs......157 G8
Gorehill W Sus......35 C7
Gore Pit Essex......88 B5
Gore Street Kent......71 F9
Gorgie Edin......280 G4
Gorhambury Herts......85 D10
Goring Oxon......64 C6
Goring-by-Sea W Sus......35 G10
Goring Heath Oxon......65 D7
Gorleston-on-Sea
Norf......143 C10
Gornalwood W Mid......133 E8
Gorrachie Aberds......303 D7
Gorran Churchtown Corn......5 G9
Gorran Haven Corn......5 G10
Gorran High Lanes Corn......5 G9
Gorrenberry Borders......249 D11
Gorrig Ceredig......93 C8
Gorse Covert Warr......183 C11
Gorsedd Flint......181 F11
Gorse Hill Gtr Man......184 B4
Swindon......63 B7
Gorseinon Swansea......56 B5
Gorseness Orkney......314 E4
Gorsethorpe Notts......171 B9
Gorseybank Derbys......170 E3
Gorsgoch Ceredig......111 G9
Gorslas Carms......75 C9
Gorsley Glos......98 F3
Gorsley Common
Hereford......98 F3
Gorsley Ley Staffs......133 B11
Gorstage Ches W......183 G10
Gorstan Highld......300 C3
Gorstanvorran Highld......289 B10
Gorstella Ches W......166 C5
Gorsteyhill Ches E......168 E2
Gorst Hill Worcs......116 C4
Gorstyhill Staffs......168 E2
Gorsty Hill Staffs......151 D11
Gortan Argyll......274 G3
Gortantaoid Argyll......274 F4
Gortenacullish Highld......295 G8
Gorteneorn Highld......289 C8
Gortenfern Highld......289 C8
Gortinanane Argyll......255 C8
Gorton Gtr Man......184 B5
Gortonallister N Ayrs......256 D2
Gosbeck Suff......126 F3
Gosberton Lincs......156 C4
Gosberton Cheal Lincs......156 D4
Gosberton Clough Lincs......156 D3
Goscote W Mid......133 C10
Goseley Dale Derbys......152 E6
Gosfield Essex......106 F5
Gosford Hereford......115 D10
Oxon......83 C7
Gosford Green W Mid......118 B6
Gosforth Cumb......219 E11
T&W......242 D6
Gosforth Valley Derbys......186 F4
Gosland Green Ches W......167 D9
Gosling Green Suff......107 C9
Gosmere Kent......54 B4
Gosmore Herts......104 F3
Gospel Ash Staffs......132 E6
Gospel End Village
Staffs......133 E7
Gospel Green W Sus......50 G2
Gospel Oak London......67 B9
Gosport Hants......21 B8
Hants......32 C5

Gossabrough Shetland 312 E7
Gossard's Green C Beds 103 C9
Gossington Glos 80 E2
Gossops Green W Sus 51 F9
Goswick Northumb 273 F11
Gotham Dorset 31 E9
E Sus 38 F2
Notts 153 C10
Gothelney Green Som 43 F9
Gotherington Glos 99 F9
Gothers Corn 5 D9
Gott Argyll 288 E2
Shetland 313 J6
Gotton Som 28 B2
Goudhurst Kent 53 F8
Goukstone Moray 302 D4
Goulceby Lincs 190 F3
Goulton N Yorks 225 E9
Gourdas Aberds 303 E7
Gourdon Aberds 293 F10
Gourock Invclyd 276 F4
Govan Glasgow 267 B11
Govanhill Glasgow 267 C11
Gover Hill Kent 52 C6
Goverton Notts 172 E2
Goveton Devon 8 F5
Govilon Mon 78 C3
Gowanhill Aberds 303 C10
Gowanwell Aberds 303 E8
Gowdall E Yorks 198 C6
Gowerton / Tre-Gwyr
Swansea 56 B5
Gowhole Derbys 185 E8
Gowkhall Fife 279 D11
Gowkthrapple N Lnrk 268 E5
Gowthorpe E Yorks 207 C11
Goxhill E Yorks 209 E9
N Lincs 200 C6
Goxhill Haven N Lincs 200 B6
Goybre Neath 57 D9
Goytre Neath 57 D9
Gozzard's Ford Oxon 83 F7
Grabhair W Isles 305 G5
Graby Lincs 155 D11
Gracca Corn 5 D10
Gracemount Edin 270 B5
Grade Corn 2 G6
Graffham W Sus 34 D6
Grafham Cambs 122 D3
Sur 50 E4
Grafton Hereford 97 D9
N Yorks 215 G8
Oxon 82 E3
Shrops 149 F8
Worcs 99 D9
Worcs 115 E11
Grafton Flyford Worcs 117 F9
Grafton Regis Northants 102 B5
Grafton Underwood
Northants 137 G8
Grafty Green Kent 53 D11
Grahamston Falk 279 E7
Graianrhyd Denb 166 D2
Graig Carms 74 E6
Conwy 180 G4
Denb 181 G9
Rhondda 58 B5
Wrex 148 B4
Graig-Fawr Swansea 75 E10
Graig-fechan Denb 165 E10
Graig Felen Swansea 75 E11
Graig Penllyn V Glam 58 D3
Graig Trewyddfa Swansea 57 B7
Grain Medway 69 D11
Grains Bar Gtr Man 196 F3
Grainsby Lincs 190 B3
Grainthorpe Lincs 190 B5
Grainthorpe Fen Lincs 190 B5
Graiselound N Lincs 188 B3
Grampound Corn 5 F8
Grampound Road Corn 5 E8
Gramsdal W Isles 296 F4
Granborough Bucks 102 F5
Granby Notts 154 B5
Grandborough Warks 119 D9
Grandpont Oxon 83 D8
Grandtully Perth 286 B3
Grange Cumb 220 B5
Dorset 31 G8
E Ayrs 257 B10
Fife 287 G8
Halton 183 E8
Lancs 203 G7
Medway 69 F9
Mers 182 D2
NE Lincs 201 F9
N Yorks 223 G8
Perth 286 E6
Warr 183 C10
Grange Crossroads
Moray 302 D4
Grange Estate Dorset 31 G10
Grange Hall Moray 301 C10
Grange Hill Durham 233 F10
Essex 86 G6
Grangemill Derbys 170 D2
Grange Moor W Yorks 197 D8
Grangemouth Falk 279 E8
Grangemuir Fife 287 G9
Grange of Cree
Dumfries 236 D6
Grange of Lindores Fife 286 F6
Grange-over-Sands
Cumb 211 D8
Grangepans Falk 279 E10
Grange Park London 86 F4
Mers 183 C7
Northants 120 F5
Swindon 62 C6
Grangetown Cardiff 59 E7
Redcar 235 G7
T&W 243 G10
Grange Villa Durham 242 G6
Grange Village Glos 79 C11
Granish Highld 291 B11
Gransmoor E Yorks 209 B8
Gransmore Green Essex 106 G3
Granston / Treopert
Pembs 91 E7
Grantchester Cambs 123 F8
Grantham Lincs 155 B8
Grantley N Yorks 214 F4
Grantley Hall N Yorks 214 F4
Grantlodge Aberds 293 B9
Granton Dumfries 248 B3
Edin 280 F4
Grantown Aberds 302 D5
Grantown-on-Spey
Highld 301 G10
Grantsfield Hereford 115 E10
Grantshouse Borders 272 B6
Grant Thorold NE Lincs 201 F9
Graplin Dumfries 237 E8
Grappenhall Warr 183 D10
Grasby Lincs 200 G5
Grasmere Cumb 220 D6
Grasscroft Gtr Man 196 G3
Grassendale Mers 182 D5
Grassgarth Cumb 221 F8
Cumb 230 C2
Grass Green Essex 106 D4
Grassholme Durham 232 G4
Grassington N Yorks 213 G10
Grassmoor Derbys 170 B6
Grassthorpe Notts 172 B3
Grasswell T&W 243 G8
Grateley Hants 47 E9
Gratton Devon 24 E5
Gratwich Staffs 151 C10
Gravel Ches W 167 B11
Gravel Castle Kent 55 D8
Graveley Cambs 122 E4
Herts 104 F4
Gravelhill Shrops 149 G9
Gravel Hill Bucks 85 G8
Gravel Hole Gtr Man 196 F2
Shrops 149 B7
Gravelly Hill W Mid 134 E2
Gravels Shrops 130 D6
Gravelsbank Shrops 130 C6
Graven Shetland 312 F6
Graveney Kent 70 G5
Gravenhunger Moss
Shrops 168 G2
Gravesend Herts 105 F8
Kent 68 E6
Grayingham Lincs 188 B6
Grayrigg Cumb 221 F11
Grays Thurrock 68 D6
Grayshott Hants 49 F11
Grayson Green Cumb 228 F5
Grayswood Sur 50 G2
Graythorp Hrtlpl 234 F6
Grazeley Wokingham 65 F7
Grazeley Green W Berks 65 F7
Greagdhubh Lodge
Highld 291 D8
Greamchary Highld 310 F2
Greasbrough S Yorks 186 B6
Greasby Mers 182 D3
Greasley Notts 171 F7
Great Abington Cambs 105 B10
Great Addington
Northants 121 B9
Great Alne Warks 118 F2
Great Altcar Lancs 193 F10
Great Amwell Herts 86 C5
Great Asby Cumb 222 C3
Great Ashfield Suff 125 D9
Great Ashley Wilts 61 G10
Great Ayton N Yorks 225 C11
Great Baddow Essex 88 E2
Great Bardfield Essex 106 E3
Great Barford Beds 122 G2
Great Barrington Glos 82 C2
Great Barrow Ches W 167 B7
Great Barton Suff 125 D7
Great Barugh N Yorks 216 D4
Great Bavington
Northumb 251 G11
Great Bealings Suff 108 B4
Great Bedwyn Wilts 63 G9
Great Bentley Essex 108 G2
Great Berry Essex 69 B7
Great Billing Northants 120 E6
Great Bircham Norf 158 C5
Great Blakenham Suff 126 G2
Great Blencow Cumb 230 E5
Great Bolas Telford 150 E2
Great Bookham Sur 50 C6
Great Bosullow Corn 1 C4
Great Bourton Oxon 101 B9
Great Bowden Leics 136 F4
Great Bower Kent 54 C4
Great Bradley Suff 124 G3
Great Braxted Essex 88 C5
Great Bricett Suff 125 G10
Great Brickhill Bucks 103 E8
Great Bridge W Mid 133 E9
Great Bridgeford Staffs 151 D7
Great Brington
Northants 120 D3
Great Bromley Essex 107 F11
Great Broughton Cumb 229 E7
N Yorks 225 D10
Great Buckland Kent 69 G7
Great Budworth
Ches W 183 F11
Great Burdon Darl 224 B6
Great Burgh Sur 51 B8
Great Burstead Essex 87 G11
Great Busby N Yorks 225 D10
Great Canfield Essex 87 B9
Great Carlton Lincs 190 D6
Great Casterton Rutland 137 B9
Great Cellws Powys 113 E11
Great Chalfield Wilts 61 G11
Great Chart Kent 54 E3
Great Chatwell Staffs 150 G5
Great Chell Stoke 168 E5
Great Chesterford
Essex 105 C10
Great Cheveney Kent 53 E8
Great Cheverell Wilts 46 C3
Great Chilton Durham 233 E11
Great Chishill Cambs 105 D8
Great Clacton Essex 89 B11
Great Claydons Essex 88 E3
Great Cliff W Yorks 197 D10
Great Clifton Cumb 228 F6
Great Coates NE Lincs 201 F8
Great Comberton Worcs 99 C9
Great Common Suff 143 F7
W Sus 35 B8
Great Corby Cumb 239 G11
Great Cornard Suff 107 C7
Great Cowden E Yorks 209 E10
Great Coxwell Oxon 82 G3
Great Crakehall
N Yorks 224 G4
Great Cransley
Northants 120 B6
Great Cressingham
Norf 141 C7
Great Crosby Mers 182 B4
Great Crosthwaite
Cumb 229 G11
Great Cubley Derbys 152 B3
Great Dalby Leics 154 G4
Great Denham Beds 103 B10
Great Doddington
Northants 121 E7
Great Doward Hereford 79 B9
Great Dunham Norf 159 G7
Great Dunmow Essex 106 G2
Great Durnford Wilts 46 F6
Great Easton Essex 106 F2
Leics 136 E6
Great Eccleston Lancs 202 E4
Great Edstone N Yorks 216 C4
Great Ellingham Norf 141 D10
Great Elm Som 45 D8
Great Eppleton T&W 234 B3
Greater Doward Hereford 79 B9
Great Eversden Cambs 123 G7
Great Fencote N Yorks 224 G5
Greatfield Wilts 62 B5
Great Finborough Suff 125 F10
Greatford Lincs 155 G11
Great Fransham Norf 159 G7
Great Gaddesden Herts 85 C8
Greatgap Bucks 84 B6
Greatgate Staffs 169 G9
Great Gate Staffs 169 G9
Great Gidding Cambs 138 G2
Great Givendale
E Yorks 208 C2
Great Glemham Suff 126 E6
Great Glen Leics 136 D3
Great Gonerby Lincs 155 B7
Great Gransden Cambs 122 F5
Great Green Cambs 104 C5
Norf 142 F5
Suff 125 B11
Suff 125 F8
Suff 126 B2
Great Habton N Yorks 216 D5
Great Hale Lincs 173 G10
Great Hallingbury Essex 87 B8
Greatham Hants 49 G9
Hrtlpl 234 F5
W Sus 35 D8
Great Hampden Bucks 84 E4
Great Harrowden
Northants 121 C7
Great Harwood Lancs 203 G10
Great Haseley Oxon 83 E10
Great Hatfield E Yorks 209 E9
Great Haywood Staffs 151 E9
Staffs 151 E10
Great Heath W Mid 134 G6
Great Heck N Yorks 198 C5
Great Henny Essex 107 D7
Great Hinton Wilts 46 B2
Great Hivings Bucks 85 E7
Great Hockham Norf 141 E9
Great Holcombe Oxon 83 F10
Great Holland Essex 89 B12
Great Hollands Brack 65 F11
Great Holm M Keynes 102 D6
Great Honeyborough
Pembs 73 D7
Great Horkesley Essex 107 E9
Great Hormead Herts 105 F7
Great Horton W Yorks 205 G8
Great Horwood Bucks 102 E5
Great Houghton
Northants 120 F5
S Yorks 198 F2
Great Howarth Gtr Man 196 D2
Great Hucklow Derbys 185 F11
Great Job's Cross Kent 38 B4
Great Kelk E Yorks 209 B8
Great Kendale E Yorks 217 G10
Great Kimble Bucks 84 D4
Great Kingshill Bucks 84 F5
Great Langton N Yorks 224 F5
Great Lea Common
Reading 65 F8
Great Leighs Essex 88 B2
Great Lever Gtr Man 195 F8
Great Limber Lincs 200 F6
Great Linford M Keynes 103 C7
Great Livermere Suff 125 C7
Great Longstone Derbys 186 G2
Great Lumley Durham 233 B11
Great Lyth Shrops 131 B9
Great Malgraves Thurrock 69 C7
Great Malvern Worcs 98 B5
Great Maplestead Essex 106 E6
Great Marton Blkpool 202 F2
Great Marton Moss
Blkpool 202 G2
Great Massingham Norf 158 E5
Great Melton Norf 142 B2
Great Milton Oxon 83 E10
Great Missenden Bucks 84 E5
Great Mitton Lancs 203 F10
Great Mongeham Kent 55 C10
Greatmoor Bucks 102 G4
Great Moor Gtr Man 184 D6
Staffs 132 D6
Great Moulton Norf 142 E3
Great Munden Herts 105 G7
Great Musgrave Cumb 222 C5
Greatness Kent 52 B4
Great Ness Shrops 149 F7
Great Notley Essex 106 G4
Great Oak Mon 78 D5
Great Oakley Essex 108 F3
Northants 137 F7
Great Offley Herts 104 F2
Great Ormside Cumb 222 B4
Great Orton Cumb 239 G8
Great Ouseburn
N Yorks 215 G8
Great Oxendon
Northants 136 G4
Great Oxney Green
Essex 87 D11
Great Palgrave Norf 158 G6
Great Parndon Essex 86 D6
Great Pattenden Kent 53 E8
Great Paxton Cambs 122 E4
Great Plumpton Lancs 202 G3
Great Plumstead Norf 160 G6
Great Ponton Lincs 155 C8
Great Preston W Yorks 198 B2
Great Purston
Northants 101 D10
Great Raveley Cambs 138 G5
Great Rissington Glos 81 B11
Great Rollright Oxon 100 E6
Great Ryburgh Norf 159 D9
Great Ryle Northumb 264 G2
Great Ryton Shrops 131 C9
Great Saling Essex 106 F4
Great Salkeld Cumb 231 D7
Great Sampford Essex 106 D2
Great Sankey Warr 183 D9
Great Saredon Staffs 133 B9
Great Saxham Suff 124 E5
Great Shefford W Berks 63 E11
Great Shelford Cambs 123 G9
Great Shoddesden Hants 47 D9
Great Smeaton N Yorks 224 E6
Great Snoring Norf 159 C8
Great Somerford Wilts 62 C3
Great Stainton Darl 234 G2
Great Stambridge Essex 88 G5
Great Staughton Cambs 122 E2
Great Steeping Lincs 174 C6
Great Stoke S Glos 60 C6
Great Stonar Kent 55 B10
Greatstone-on-Sea Kent 39 C9
Great Stretton Leics 136 C3
Great Strickland Cumb 231 G7
Great Stukeley Cambs 122 C4
Great Sturton Lincs 190 F2
Great Sutton Ches W 182 F5
Shrops 131 G10
Great Swinburne
Northumb 241 B10
Great Tew Oxon 101 F7
Great Tey Essex 107 F7
Great Thirkleby N Yorks 215 D9
Great Thurlow Suff 124 G3
Great Torrington Devon 25 D7
Great Tosson Northumb 252 C2
Great Totham Essex 88 C5
Great Tows Lincs 190 C2
Great Tree Corn 6 D5
Great Urswick Cumb 210 E5
Great Wakering Essex 70 B2
Great Waldingfield Suff 107 C8
Great Walsingham Norf 159 B8
Great Waltham Essex 87 C11
Great Warley Essex 87 G9
Great Washbourne Glos 99 E9
Great Weeke Devon 13 D10
Great Weldon Northants 137 F8
Great Welnetham Suff 125 F7
Great Wenham Suff 107 D11
Great Whittington
Northumb 242 C2
Great Wigborough Essex 89 C7
Great Wilbraham
Cambs 123 F10
Great Wilne Derbys 153 C8
Great Wishford Wilts 46 F5
Great Witchingham
Norf 160 E2
Great Witcombe Glos 80 C6
Great Witley Worcs 116 D5
Great Wolford Warks 100 E4
Greatworth Northants 101 C11
Great Wratting Suff 106 B3
Great Wymondley Herts 104 F4
Great Wyrley Staffs 133 B9
Great Wytheford
Shrops 149 F11
Great Yarmouth Norf 143 B10
Great Yeldham Essex 106 D5
Greave Gtr Man 184 C6
Lancs 195 C11
Grebby Lincs 174 B6
Greeba IoM 192 D4
Green Denb 165 B9
Pembs 73 E7
Powys 130 E5
Greenacres Gtr Man 196 F2
Greenan Argyll 275 G11
Greenbank Ches W 183 G10
Falk 279 F7
Shetland 312 C7
Green Bank Cumb 211 C7
Green Bottom Corn 4 F5
Glos 79 B11
Greenburn W Loth 269 C8
Green Close N Yorks 212 F4
Green Clough W Yorks 205 G7
Green Crize Hereford 97 D10
Greencroft Durham 242 G5
Green Cross Sur 49 F11
Greendale Ches E 184 F5
Greendikes Northumb 264 D3
Greendown Som 44 C5
Green Down Devon 28 G3
Greendykes Northumb 264 D3
Greenend N Lnrk 268 C4
Oxon 100 G6
Green End Beds 103 B10
Beds 121 E11
Beds 122 E2
Beds 122 G2
Bucks 84 F4
Bucks 103 E8
Cambs 122 C4
Cambs 123 F7
C Beds 103 D11
Herts 85 D8
Herts 104 E5
Herts 104 E6
Herts 104 G6
Herts 105 F7
Lancs 204 D4
N Yorks 226 E6
Warks 134 F5
Greenfaulds N Lnrk 278 G5
Greenfield C Beds 103 E11
Glasgow 268 C2
Gtr Man 196 G3
Highld 289 D11
Highld 290 C4
Oxon 84 G2
Greenfield / Maes-Glas
Flint 181 F11
Greenfoot N Lnrk 268 B4
Greenford London 66 C6
Greengairs N Lnrk 278 G5
Greengarth Hall Cumb 219 E11
Greengate Gtr Man 196 D2
Norf 159 F10
Green Gate Devon 27 D8
Greengates W Yorks 205 F9
Greengill Cumb 229 D8
Green Hailey Bucks 84 E4
Greenhalgh Lancs 202 F4
Greenhall S Lnrk 268 D3
Greenham Dorset 28 G6
Som 27 C9
W Berks 64 F3
Green Hammerton
N Yorks 206 B5
Greenhaugh Northumb 251 F7
Green Haworth Lancs 195 B9
Greenhead Borders 261 D11
Dumfries 247 D9
N Lnrk 268 E6
Northumb 240 D5
Staffs 169 F7
Green Head Cumb 230 B3
Green Heath Staffs 151 G9
Greenheys Gtr Man 195 G8
Greenhill Dumfries 238 B4
Durham 234 B3
Falk 278 F6
Hereford 98 B4
Kent 71 F7
Leics 153 G8
London 67 B7
S Yorks 186 E4
Worcs 99 B10
Worcs 116 B6
Green Hill Kent 53 C9
Lincs 155 B8
Wilts 62 B5
W Yorks 206 F4
Greenhill Bank Shrops 149 B7
Greenhillocks Derbys 170 F6
Greenhills N Ayrs 267 E7
S Lnrk 268 E2
Greenhithe Kent 68 E5
Greenholm E Ayrs 258 B2
Greenholme Cumb 221 D11
Greenhouse Borders 262 E3
Greenhow N Yorks 214 G2
Greenhow Hill N Yorks 214 G2
Greenigoe Orkney 314 F4
Greenland Highld 310 C6
S Yorks 186 D5
Greenland Mains Highld 310 C6
Greenlands Bucks 65 B9
Worcs 117 D11
Green Lane Devon 13 F11
Hereford 98 B2
Powys 130 D3
Warks 117 E11
Warks 118 B6
Greenlaw Aberds 302 D6
Borders 272 F4
Greenlaw Mains Midloth 270 C4
Greenlea Dumfries 238 B2
Greenley M Keynes 102 C6
Greenloaning Perth 286 G2
Greenlooms Ches W 167 C7
Greenman's Lane Wilts 62 C3
Greenmeadow Swindon 62 B6
Torf 78 F3
Green Moor S Yorks 186 B3
Greenmount Gtr Man 195 E9
Greenmow Shetland 313 L6
Greenoak E Yorks 199 B10
Greenock Invclyd 276 F5
Greenock West Invclyd 276 F5
Greenodd Cumb 210 C6
Green Ore Som 44 C5
Green Parlour Bath 45 C8
Green Quarter Cumb 221 E9
Greenrigg W Loth 269 C8
Greenrow Cumb 238 G4
Greens Borders 249 F11
Green St Green London 68 G3
Greensforge Staffs 133 F7
Greensgate Norf 160 F2
Greenside Cumb 222 E4
Derbys 186 F5
Gtr Man 184 B6
T&W 242 E4
W Yorks 197 D7
Green Side W Yorks 197 E7
W Yorks 205 G11
Greensidehill Northumb 263 F11
Greens Norton
Northants 102 B3
Greensplat Corn 5 D9
Greenstead Essex 107 F10
Greenstead Green Essex 106 F6
Greensted Essex 87 E8
Greensted Green Essex 87 E8
Green Street Essex 87 F10
E Sus 38 E3
Glos 80 B5
Glos 80 E3
Herts 85 F11
Herts 105 G9
Worcs 99 B7
Worcs 99 C7
W Sus 35 C10
Greenstreet Green
Suff 107 B10
Green Street Green Kent 68 E5
London 68 G3
Green Tye Herts 86 B6
Greenway Hereford 98 E4
Pembs 91 E11
Som 27 B11
V Glam 58 E5
Worcs 116 C4
Greenwell Cumb 240 F2
Greenwells Borders 262 C3
Greenwich London 67 D11
Suff 108 C3
Wilts 46 G2
Greenwith Common Corn 4 G5
Greenwoods Essex 87 F11
Greeny Orkney 314 D2
Greep Highld 298 E2
Greet Glos 99 E10
Kent 54 B2
Greete Shrops 115 C11
Greetham Lincs 190 G4
Rutland 155 G8
Greetland W Yorks 196 C5
Greetland Wall Nook
W Yorks 196 C5
Greetwell N Lincs 200 G2
Gregg Hall Cumb 221 G9
Gregson Lane Lancs 194 B5
Gregynog Powys 129 D11
Grèin W Isles 297 L2
Greinetobht W Isles 296 D4
Greinton Som 44 F2
Gremista Shetland 313 J6
Grenaby IoM 192 E3
Grendon Northants 121 E7
Warks 134 C5
Grendon Bishop
Hereford 115 F11
Grendon Common
Warks 134 D5
Grendon Green
Hereford 115 F11
Grendon Underwood
Bucks 102 G3
Grenofen Devon 12 G5
Grenoside S Yorks 186 C4
Greosabhagh W Isles 305 J3
Gresford Wrex 166 E5
Gresham Norf 160 B3
Greshornish Highld 298 D3
Gressenhall Norf 159 F9
Gressingham Lancs 211 F11
Gresty Green Ches E 168 E2
Greta Bridge Durham 223 C11
Gretna Dumfries 239 D8
Gretna Green Dumfries 239 D8
Gretton Glos 99 E10
Northants 137 E7
Shrops 131 D10
Gretton Fields Glos 99 E10
Grewelthorpe N Yorks 214 D4
Greyfield Bath 44 B6
Greygarth N Yorks 214 E3
Grey Green N Lincs 199 F9
Greylake Som 43 G11
Greylake Fosse Som 44 F2
Greynor Carms 75 D9
Greynor-isaf Carms 75 D9
Greyrigg Dumfries 248 F3
Greys Green Oxon 65 C8
Greysouthen Cumb 229 F7
Greystead Northumb 251 F7
Greystoke Cumb 230 E4
Greystoke Gill Cumb 230 F4
Greystone Aberds 292 D6
Aberds 302 F6
Angus 287 C9
Cumb 211 D10
Dumfries 237 B11
Greystonegill N Yorks 212 F3
Greystones S Yorks 186 D4
Warks 99 B11
Greytree Hereford 97 F11
Greywell Hants 49 C8
Griais W Isles 304 D6
Grianan W Isles 304 E6
Gribb Dorset 28 G5
Gribthorpe E Yorks 207 F11
Gridley Corner Devon 12 C3
Griff Warks 135 F7
Griffins Hill W Mid 133 G10
Griffithstown Torf 78 F3
Griffydam Leics 153 F8
Grigg Kent 53 E11
Griggs Green Hants 49 G10
Grillis Corn 2 B5
Grilstone Devon 26 C2
Grimbister Orkney 314 E3
Grimblethorpe Lincs 190 D2
Grimeford Village Lancs 194 E6
Grimes Hill Worcs 117 B11
Grimesthorpe S Yorks 186 C5
Grimethorpe S Yorks 198 F2
Griminis W Isles 296 D3
W Isles 296 F3
Grimister Shetland 312 D6
Grimley Worcs 116 E6
Grimness Orkney 314 G4
Grimoldby Lincs 190 D5
Grimpo Shrops 149 D7
Grimsargh Lancs 203 G7
Grimsbury Oxon 101 C9
Grimsby NE Lincs 201 E9
Grimscote Northants 120 G3
Grimscott Corn 24 F3
Grimshaw Blkburn 195 C8
Grimshaw Green Lancs 194 E3
Grimsthorpe Lincs 155 E10
Grimston E Yorks 209 F11
Leics 154 E3
Norf 158 E4
York 207 C8
Grimstone Dorset 17 C8
Grimstone End Suff 125 D8
Grinacombe Moor Devon 12 C4
Grindale E Yorks 218 E2
Grindigar Orkney 314 F5
Grindiscol Shetland 313 K6
Grindle Shrops 132 C5
Grindleford Derbys 186 F2
Grindleton Lancs 203 D11
Grindley Staffs 151 D10
Grindley Brook Shrops 167 G8
Grindlow Derbys 185 F11
Grindon Northumb 273 G8
Staffs 169 E9
Stockton 234 F3
T&W 243 G9
Grindonmoor Gate
Staffs 169 E9
Grindsbrook Booth
Derbys 185 D10
Gringley on the Hill
Notts 188 C2
Grinsdale Cumb 239 F9
Grinshill Shrops 149 E10
Grinstead Hill Suff 125 G11
Grinton N Yorks 223 F10
Griomasaigh W Isles 297 G4
Griomsidar W Isles 304 F5
Grisdale Cumb 222 G5
Grishipoll Argyll 288 D3
Grisling Common E Sus 36 C6
Gristhorpe N Yorks 217 C11
Griston Norf 141 D8
Gritley Orkney 314 F5
Grittenham Wilts 62 C4
Grittlesend Hereford 98 B4
Grittleton Wilts 61 C11
Grizebeck Cumb 210 C4
Grizedale Cumb 220 G6
Groam Highld 300 E5
Grobister Orkney 314 D6
Grobsness Shetland 313 G5
Groby Leics 135 B10
Groes Conwy 165 C8
Neath 57 D9
Groes Efa Denb 165 B10
Groes-faen Rhondda 58 C5
Groes-fawr Denb 165 B10
Groesffordd Gwyn 144 B5
Powys 95 F11
Groesffordd Marli Denb 181 G8
Groeslon Gwyn 163 C8
Gwyn 163 D7
Groes-lwyd Mon 96 G6
Powys 148 G4
Groespluan Powys 130 B4
Groes-wen Caerph 58 B6
Grogport Argyll 255 C9
Gromford Suff 127 F7
Gronant Flint 181 E9
Gronwen Shrops 148 D5
Groombridge E Sus 52 F4
Grosmont Mon 97 G8
N Yorks 226 D6
Gross Green Warks 119 F7
Grotaig Highld 300 G4
Groton Suff 107 C9
Grotton Gtr Man 196 G3
Grougfoot Falk 279 F10
Grove Bucks 103 G8
Dorset 17 G10
Hereford 98 C2
Kent 71 G8
Notts 188 F2
Oxon 82 G6
Pembs 73 E7
Grove End Kent 69 G11
Warks 100 D6
Warks 134 D3
Grove Green Kent 53 B9
Grovehill E Yorks 208 F6
Herts 85 D9
Grove Hill E Sus 23 C10
Kent 71 G8
Grove Park London 67 D8
London 68 E2
Groves Kent 55 B9
Grovesend Swansea 75 E9
Grove Town W Yorks 198 C3
Grove Vale W Mid 133 E10
Grubb Street Kent 68 F5
Grub Street Staffs 150 D5
Grudie Highld 300 C3
Gruids Highld 309 J5
Gruinard House Highld 307 K4
Gruinards Highld 309 K5
Grula Highld 294 C5
Gruline Argyll 289 E7
Gruline Ho Argyll 289 F7
Grumbeg Highld 308 F6
Grumbla Corn 1 D4
Grunasound Shetland 313 K5
Grundisburgh Suff 126 G4
Grunsagill Lancs 203 C11
Gruting Shetland 313 J4
Grutness Shetland 313 N6
Gryn Goch Gwyn 162 F6
Gualachulain Highld 284 C5
Gualin Ho Highld 308 D3
Guardbridge Fife 287 F8
Guard House W Yorks 204 E6
Guarlford Worcs 98 B6
Guay Perth 286 C4
Gubbion's Green Essex 88 B2
Gubblecote Herts 84 C6
Guesachan Highld 289 B10
Guestling Green E Sus 38 E5
Guestling Thorn E Sus 38 D4
Guestwick Norf 159 D11
Guestwick Green Norf 159 D11
Guide Blkburn 195 B8
Guide Bridge Gtr Man 184 B6
Guide Post Northumb 253 F7
Guilden Morden Cambs 104 C5
Guilden Sutton Ches W 166 B6
Guildford Sur 50 D3
Guildford Park Sur 50 D3
Guildiehaugh W Loth 269 B9
Guildtown Perth 286 D5
Guilford Pembs 73 D7
Guilsborough Northants 120 C3
Guilsfield / Cegidfa
Powys 148 G4
Guilthwaite S Yorks 187 D7
Guilton Kent 55 B9
Guineaford Devon 40 F5
Guisachan Highld 300 G3
Guisborough Redcar 226 B2
Guiseley W Yorks 205 E9
Guist Norf 159 D9
Guith Orkney 314 C5
Guiting Power Glos 99 G11
Gulberwick Shetland 313 K6
Gullane E Loth 281 E9
Guller's End Worcs 99 D7
Gulling Green Suff 124 F6
Gullom Holme Cumb 231 F9
Gulval Corn 1 C5
Gulworthy Devon 12 G4
Gumfreston Pembs 73 E10
Gumley Leics 136 E3
Gummow's Shop Corn 5 D7
Gunby E Yorks 207 F10
Lincs 155 E8
Lincs 175 B7
Gundenham Som 27 C10
Gundleton Hants 48 G6
Gun Green Kent 53 G9
Gun Hill E Sus 23 C9
Gunn Devon 40 G6
Gunnersbury London 67 D7
Gunnerside N Yorks 223 F9
Gunnerton Northumb 241 C10
Gunness N Lincs 199 E10
Gunnislake Corn 12 G4
Gunnista Shetland 313 J7
Gunstone Staffs 133 C7
Guns Village W Mid 133 E9
Gunter's Bridge W Sus 35 C7
Gunthorpe Lincs 188 B4
Norf 159 C10
Notts 171 G11
Pboro 138 C3
Rutland 137 B7
Gunton Suff 143 D10
Gunville IoW 20 D5
Gunwalloe Corn 2 E5
Gunwalloe Fishing Cove
Corn 2 E5
Gupworthy Som 42 F3
Gurnard IoW 20 B5
Gurnett Ches E 184 G6
Gurney Slade Som 44 D6
Gurnos M Tydf 77 D8
Powys 76 D3
Gushmere Kent 54 B4
Gussage All Saints Dorset 31 E8
Gussage St Andrew
Dorset 31 E7
Gussage St Michael
Dorset 31 E7
Gustard Wood Herts 85 B11
Guston Kent 55 E10
Gutcher Shetland 312 D7
Guthram Gowt Lincs 156 E3
Guthrie Angus 287 B9
Guyhirn Cambs 139 C7
Guyhirn Gull Cambs 139 C7
Guy's Cliffe Warks 118 D5
Guy's Head Lincs 157 D9
Guy's Marsh Dorset 30 C4
Guyzance Northumb 252 C6
Gwaelod-y-garth Cardiff 58 C6
Gwaenysgor Flint 181 E9
Gwalchmai Anglesey 178 F5
Gwalchmai Uchaf
Anglesey 178 F5
Gwallon Corn 2 C2
Gwastad Pembs 91 G10
Gwastadgoed Gwyn 145 G11
Gwastadnant Gwyn 163 D10
Gwaun-Cae-Gurwen
Neath 76 C2
Gwaun-Leision Neath 76 C2
Gwavas Corn 2 D5
Corn 2 G6
Gwbert Ceredig 92 B3
Gwedna Corn 2 C4
Gweek Corn 2 D6
Gwehelog Mon 78 E5
Gwenddwr Powys 95 C11
Gwennap Corn 2 B6
Gwenter Corn 2 F6
Gwernaffield-y-Waun
Flint 166 C2
Gwernafon Powys 129 E8
Gwerneirin Powys 129 F10
Powys 130 G3
Gwernesney Mon 78 E6
Gwernogle Carms 93 E10
Gwernol Denb 166 E2
Gwern y brenin Shrops 148 D6
Gwernydd Powys 129 C11
Gwernymynydd Flint 166 C2
Gwern-y-Steeple V Glam 58 D5
Gwersyllt Wrex 166 E4
Gwespyr Flint 181 E10
Gwills Corn 4 D6
Gwinear Corn 2 B3
Gwinear Downs Corn 2 C4
Gwithian Corn 2 A3
Gwredog Anglesey 178 D6
Gwrhay Caerph 77 F11
Gwyddelwern Denb 165 F9
Gwyddgrug Carms 93 D9
Gwynfryn Wrex 166 E3
Gwystre Powys 113 D11
Gwytherin Conwy 164 C5
Gyfelia Wrex 166 F4
Gyffin Conwy 180 F3
Gylen Park Argyll 289 G10
Gyre Orkney 314 F3
Gyrn Denb 165 D11
Gyrn-goch Gwyn 162 F6

H

Habberley Shrops 131 C7
Worcs 116 B6
Habergham Lancs 204 G2
Habertoft Lincs 175 B8
Habin W Sus 34 C4
Habrough NE Lincs 200 E6
Haccombe Devon 14 G3
Haceby Lincs 155 B10
Hacheston Suff 126 F6
Hackbridge London 67 F9
Hackenthorpe S Yorks 186 E6
Hackford Norf 141 C11
Hackforth N Yorks 224 G4
Hack Green Ches E 167 F10
Hackland Orkney 314 D3
Hackleton Northants 120 F6
Hacklinge Kent 55 C10
Hackman's Gate Worcs 117 B7
Hackness N Yorks 227 G9
Orkney 314 G3
Som 43 D10
Hackney London 67 C10
Hackney Wick London 67 C11
Hackthorn Lincs 189 E7
Wilts 47 D7
Hackthorpe Cumb 230 G6
Haclait W Isles 297 G4
Haconby Lincs 156 D2
Hacton London 68 B4
Haddacott Devon 25 C8
Hadden Borders 263 B7
Haddenham Bucks 84 D2
Cambs 123 B9
Haddenham End Field
Cambs 123 B9
Haddington E Loth 281 G10
Lincs 172 C6
Haddiscoe Norf 143 D8
Haddoch Aberds 302 E5
Haddon Cambs 138 E2
Ches E 169 B7
Hade Edge W Yorks 196 F6
Hademore Staffs 134 B3
Haden Cross W Mid 133 F9
Hadfield Derbys 185 B8
Hadham Cross Herts 86 B6
Hadham Ford Herts 105 G8
Hadleigh Essex 69 B10
Suff 107 C10
Hadleigh Heath Suff 107 C9
Hadley London 86 F2
Telford 150 G3
Worcs 117 E7
Hadley Castle Telford 150 G3
Hadley End Staffs 152 E2
Hadley Wood London 86 F3
Hadlow Kent 52 D6
Hadlow Down E Sus 37 C8
Hadlow Stair Kent 52 D6
Hadnall Shrops 149 F10
Hadspen Som 45 G7
Hadstock Essex 105 C11
Hadston Northumb 253 D7
Hady Derbys 186 G5
Hadzor Worcs 117 E8
Haffenden Quarter Kent 53 E11
Hafod Swansea 57 C7
Hafod-Dinbych Conwy 164 E5
Hafod Grove Pembs 92 C2
Hafodiwan Ceredig 111 G7
Hafod-Iom Conwy 180 G5
Hafod-y-Green Denb 181 G8
Hafodyrynys Bl Gwent 78 F2
Hag Fold Gtr Man 195 G7
Haggate Gtr Man 196 F2
Lancs 204 F3
Haggbeck Cumb 239 C11
Haggersta Shetland 313 J5
Haggerston London 67 C10
Northumb 273 G10
Haggington Hill Devon 40 D5
Haggrister Shetland 312 F5
Haggs Falk 278 F5
Haghill Glasgow 268 B2
Hagley Hereford 97 C11
Worcs 133 G8
Hagloe Glos 79 D11
Hagmore Green Suff 107 D9
Hagnaby Lincs 174 C4
Lincs 191 F7
Hagnaby Lock Lincs 174 D4
Hague Bar Derbys 185 D7
Hagworthingham Lincs 174 B4
Haigh Gtr Man 194 F6
S Yorks 197 E9
Haigh Moor W Yorks 197 C9
Haighton Green Lancs 203 G7
Haighton Top Lancs 203 G7
Haile Cumb 219 D10
Hailes Glos 99 E10
Hailey Herts 86 C5
Oxon 64 B6
Oxon 82 C5
Hailsham E Sus 23 D9
Hailstone Hill Wilts 81 G9
Hail Weston Cambs 122 E3
Haimer Highld 310 C5
Haimwood Powys 148 F6
Hainault London 87 G7
Haine Kent 71 F11
Hainford Norf 160 F4
Hains Dorset 30 D3
Hainton Lincs 189 E11
Hainworth W Yorks 205 F7
Hainworth Shaw
W Yorks 205 F7
Hairmyres S Lnrk 268 E2
Haisthorpe E Yorks 218 G2
Hakeford Devon 40 F6
Hakin Pembs 72 D5
Halabezack Corn 2 C6
Halam Notts 171 E11
Halamanning Corn 2 C3
Halbeath Fife 280 D2
Halberton Devon 27 E8
Halcon Som 28 B2
Halcro Highld 310 C6
Haldens Herts 86 C2
Hale Cumb 211 D10
Gtr Man 184 D3
Halton 183 E7
Hants 31 D11
Kent 71 F9
Medway 69 F9
Som 30 B3
Sur 49 D10
Hale Bank Halton 183 E7
Hale Barns Gtr Man 184 D3
Halecommon W Sus 34 C4
Hale Coombe N Som 44 B2
Hale End London 86 G5
Hale Green E Sus 23 C9
Hale Mills Corn 4 G5
Hale Nook Lancs 202 E3
Hales Norf 143 D7
Staffs 150 C4
Hales Bank Hereford 116 G2
Halesfield Telford 132 C4
Halesgate Lincs 156 D6
Hales Green Derbys 169 G11
Norf 143 D7
Halesowen W Mid 133 G9
Hales Park Worcs 116 B5
Hales Place Kent 54 B6
Hales Street Norf 142 F3
Hale Street Kent 53 D7
Hales Wood Hereford 98 E2
Halesworth Suff 127 B7
Halewood Mers 183 D7
Half Moon Village Devon 14 B3
Halford Shrops 131 G8
Warks 100 B5
Halfpenny Cumb 211 B10
Halfpenny Furze Carms 74 C3
Halfpenny Green Staffs 132 E6
Halfway Carms 75 E8
Carms 94 E2
Carms 94 E6
S Yorks 186 E6
W Berks 64 F2
Wilts 45 D11
Halfway Bridge W Sus 34 C6
Halfway House Shrops 148 G6

Halfway Houses
Gtr Man 195 F9
Kent 70 E2
Halfway Street Kent 55 D9
Halgabron Corn 11 D7
Halifax W Yorks 196 B5
Halkburn Borders 271 G9
Halket E Ayrs 267 E8
Halkirk Highld 310 D5
Halkyn / Helygain Flint 182 G2
Halkyn Mountain Flint 182 G2
Hallam Fields Derbys 153 B9
Halland E Sus 23 B8
Hallaton Leics 136 D5
Hallatrow Bath 44 B6
Hallbankgate Cumb 240 F3
Hall Bower W Yorks 196 E6
Hall Broom S Yorks 186 D3
Hall Cross Lancs 202 G4
Hall Dunnerdale Cumb 220 F4
Halleaths Dumfries 248 G3
Hallen S Glos 60 C5
Hallend Warks 118 D2
Hall End Beds 103 B10
C Beds 103 D11
Lincs 174 E6
S Glos 61 B8
Warks 134 C5
Hallew Corn 5 D10
Hallfield Gate Derbys 170 D5
Hall Flat Worcs 117 C9
Hallgarth Durham 234 C2
Hall Garth York 207 C9
Hallglen Falk 279 F7
Hall Green Ches E 168 D4
Essex 106 D5
Lancs 194 C3
Lancs 194 F4
W Mid 133 E10
W Mid 134 G2
W Mid 135 G7
Wrex 167 G7
W Yorks 197 D10
Hall Grove Herts 89 C8
Halliburton Borders 261 B11
Borders 272 F3
Hallin Highld 298 D2
Halling Medway 69 G8
Hallingbury Street Essex 87 B8
Hallington Lincs 190 D4
Northumb 241 B11
Hall i' th' Wood Gtr Man 195 E8
Halliwell Gtr Man 195 E8
Hall of Clestrain Orkney 314 F2
Hall of Tankerness
Orkney 314 F5
Hall of the Forest
Shrops 130 G4
Hallon Shrops 132 D5
Hallonsford Shrops 132 D5
Halloughton Notts 171 E11
Hallow Worcs 116 F6
Hallowes Derbys 186 F5
Hallow Heath Worcs 116 F6
Hallowsgate Ches W 167 B8
Hallrule Borders 262 G3
Halls E Loth 282 G3
Hallsands Devon 9 G11
Hall Santon Cumb 220 E2
Hall's Cross E Sus 23 D11
Hallsford Bridge Essex 87 E9
Halls Green Essex 86 D6
Hall's Green Herts 104 F5
Kent 52 D4
Hallspill Devon 25 C7
Hallthwaites Cumb 210 B3
Hall Waberthwaite
Cumb 220 F2
Hallwood Green Glos 98 E3
Hallworthy Corn 11 D9
Hallyards Borders 260 B6
Hallyburton House
Perth 286 D6
Hallyne Borders 270 G3
Halmer End Staffs 168 F3
Halmond's Frome
Hereford 98 B3
Halmore Glos 79 E11
Halmyre Mains Borders 270 F3
Halnaker W Sus 22 B6
Halsall Lancs 193 E11
Halse Northants 101 C11
Som 27 B10
Halsetown Corn 2 B2
Halsfordwood Devon 14 C3
Halsham E Yorks 201 B9
Halsinger Devon 40 F4
Halstead Essex 106 E6
Kent 68 G3
Leics 136 B4
Halstock Dorset 29 F8
Halsway Som 42 F6
Haltcliff Bridge Cumb 230 D3
Halterworth Hants 32 C5
Haltham Lincs 174 C2
Haltoft End Lincs 174 F5
Halton Bucks 84 C5
Halton 183 E8
Lancs 211 G10
Northumb 241 D11
Wrex 148 B6
W Yorks 206 G2
Halton Barton Corn 7 B8
Halton Brook Halton 183 E8
Halton East N Yorks 204 C6
Halton Fenside Lincs 174 C6
Halton Gill N Yorks 213 D7
Halton Green Lancs 211 F10
Halton Holegate Lincs 174 B6
Halton Lea Gate
Northumb 240 F5
Halton Moor W Yorks 206 G2
Halton Shields
Northumb 242 D2
Halton View Halton 183 D8
Halton West N Yorks 204 C2
Haltwhistle Northumb 240 E6
Halvergate Norf 143 B8
Halvosso Corn 2 C6
Halwell Devon 8 E5
Halwill Devon 12 B4
Halwill Junction Devon 24 G6
Halwin Corn 2 C5
Ham Devon 28 G2
Glos 79 F11
Glos 99 G9
Highld 310 B6
Kent 55 C10
London 67 E7
Plym 7 D9
Shetland 313 K1
Som 27 C11
Som 28 B3
Som 28 E3
Som 45 D7
Wilts 63 G10
Hamar Shetland 312 F5
Hamarhill Orkney 314 C5
Hamars Shetland 313 G6
Hambleden Bucks 65 B9
Hambledon Hants 33 E10
Sur 50 F3
Hamble-le-Rice Hants 33 F7
Hambleton Lancs 202 E3
N Yorks 205 C7
N Yorks 207 G7
Hambleton Moss Side
Lancs 202 E3
Hambridge Som 28 C5
Hambrook S Glos 60 D6
W Sus 22 B3
Ham Common Dorset 30 B4
Hameringham Lincs 174 B4
Hamerton Cambs 122 B2
Hametoun Shetland 313 K1
Ham Green Bucks 83 B11
Hants 48 G2
Hereford 98 C4
Kent 38 B5
Kent 69 F10
N Som 60 D4
Wilts 61 G11
Worcs 117 E10
Ham Hill Kent 69 G8
Hamilton S Lnrk 268 D3
Hamister Shetland 313 G7
Hamlet Dorset 29 F9
Hammer W Sus 49 G11
Hammer Bottom Hants 49 G11
Hammerfield Herts 85 D8
Hammerpot W Sus 35 F9
Hammersmith Derbys 170 E5
London 67 D8
Hammerwich Staffs 133 B11
Hammerwood E Sus 52 F2
Hammill Kent 55 B9
Hammond Street Herts 86 E4
Hammoon Dorset 30 E4
Ham Moor Sur 66 G5
Hamnavoe Shetland 312 E4
Shetland 312 E6
Shetland 312 F6
Shetland 313 K5
Hamnish Clifford
Hereford 115 F10
Hamp Som 43 F10
Hampden Park E Sus 23 E10
Hampen Glos 81 B9
Hamperden End Essex 105 E11
Hamperley Shrops 131 F8
Hampers Green W Sus 35 C7
Hampeth Northumb 252 B5
Hampnett Glos 81 B10
Hampole S Yorks 198 E4
Hampreston Dorset 19 B7
Hampsfield Cumb 211 C8
Hampson Green Lancs 202 C5
Hampstead London 67 B9
Hampstead Garden Suburb
London 67 B9
Hampstead Norreys
W Berks 64 D4
Hampsthwaite N Yorks 205 B11
Hampton Kent 71 F7
London 66 F6
Shrops 132 F4
Swindon 81 G11
Worcs 99 C10
Hampton Bank Shrops 149 C9
Hampton Beech Shrops 130 B6
Hampton Bishop
Hereford 97 D11
Hampton Fields Glos 80 F5
Hampton Gay Oxon 83 B7
Hampton Green Ches W 167 F8
Glos 80 E5
Hampton Hargate Pboro 138 E3
Hampton Heath Ches W 167 F7
Hampton Hill London 66 E6
Hampton in Arden
W Mid 134 G4
Hampton Loade Shrops 132 F5
Hampton Lovett Worcs 117 D7
Hampton Lucy Warks 118 F5
Hampton Magna Warks 118 D5
Hampton on the Hill
Warks 118 E5
Hampton Park Hereford 97 D10
Soton 32 D6
Hampton Poyle Oxon 83 B8
Hamptons Kent 52 C6
Hampton Wick London 67 F7
Hamptworth Wilts 32 D2
Hamrow Norf 159 E8
Hamsey E Sus 36 E6
Hamsey Green London 51 B10
Hamshill Glos 80 E3
Hamstall Ridware Staffs 152 F2
Hamstead IoW 20 C4
W Mid 133 E10
Hamstead Marshall
W Berks 64 F2
Hamsterley Durham 233 E8
Durham 242 F4
Hamstreet Kent 54 G4
Ham Street Som 44 G5
Hamworthy Poole 18 C5
Hanbury Staffs 152 D3
Worcs 117 E9
Hanbury Woodend
Staffs 152 D3
Hanby Lincs 155 C10
Hanchett Village Suff 106 B3
Hanchurch Staffs 168 G4
Handbridge Ches W 166 B6
Handcross W Sus 36 B3
Handforth Ches E 184 E5
Hand Green Ches W 167 C8
Handless Shrops 131 E7
Handley Ches W 167 D7
Derbys 170 C5
Handley Green Essex 87 E11
Handsacre Staffs 151 F11
Handside Herts 86 C2
Handsworth S Yorks 186 D6
W Mid 133 E10
Handsworth Wood
W Mid 133 E11
Handy Cross Bucks 84 G5
Devon 24 B6
Som 42 G6
Hanford Dorset 30 E4
Stoke 168 G5
Hangersley Hants 31 F11
Hanging Bank Kent 52 C3
Hanging Heaton
W Yorks 197 C9
Hanging Houghton
Northants 120 C5
Hanging Langford Wilts 46 F4
Hangingshaw Borders 261 C9
Dumfries 248 F4
Hangleton Brighton 36 F3
W Sus 35 G9
Hangsman Hill S Yorks 199 E7
Hanham S Glos 60 E6
Hanham Green S Glos 60 E6
Hankelow Ches E 167 F11
Hankerton Wilts 81 G7
Hankham E Sus 23 D10
Hanley Stoke 168 F5
Hanley Castle Worcs 98 C6
Hanley Child Worcs 116 E3
Hanley Swan Worcs 98 C6
Hanley William Worcs 116 D3
Hanlith N Yorks 213 G8
Hanmer Wrex 149 B9
Hannaford Devon 25 B10
Hannafore Corn 6 E5
Hannah Lincs 191 F8
Hanningfields Green
Suff 125 G7
Hannington Hants 48 B4
Northants 120 C6
Swindon 81 G11
Hannington Wick
Swindon 81 F11
Hanscombe End C Beds 104 E2
Hansel Devon 8 F6
Hansel Village S Ayrs 257 C9
Hansley Cross Staffs 169 G9
Hanslope M Keynes 102 B6
Hanthorpe Lincs 155 E11
Hanwell London 67 C7
Oxon 101 C8
Hanwood Shrops 131 B8
Hanwood Bank Shrops 149 G8
Hanworth Brack 65 F11
London 66 E6
Norf 160 B3
Happendon S Lnrk 259 C9
Happisburgh Norf 161 C7
Happisburgh Common
Norf 161 D7
Hapsford Ches W 183 G7
Som 45 D9
Hapton Lancs 203 G11
Norf 142 D3
Hararden / Penarlâg
Flint 166 B4
Harberton Devon 8 D5
Harbertonford Devon 8 D5
Harbledown Kent 54 B6
Harborne W Mid 133 G10
Harborough Magna
Warks 119 B9
Harborough Parva
Warks 119 B9
Harbottle Northumb 251 C10
Harbour Heights E Sus 36 G6
Harbourland Kent 53 B9
Harbourneford Devon 8 C4
Harbours Hill Worcs 117 D9
Harbour Village Pembs 91 D8
Harbridge Hants 31 E10
Harbridge Green Hants 31 E10
Harburn W Loth 269 C10
Harbury Warks 119 F7
Harby Leics 154 C4
Notts 188 G5
Harcombe Devon 14 E3
Devon 15 C9
Harcourt Corn 3 B8
Harcourt Hill Oxon 83 E7
Hardbreck Orkney 314 F4
Hardeicke Glos 80 C4
Harden S Yorks 197 G7
W Mid 133 C10
W Yorks 205 F7
Hardendale Cumb 221 C11
Hardenhuish Wilts 62 E2
Harden Park Ches E 184 F4
Hardgate Aberds 293 C9
Dumfries 237 C10
N Yorks 214 G5
W Dunb 277 G10
Hardham W Sus 35 D8
Hardhorn Lancs 202 F3
Hardingham Norf 141 C10
Hardings Booth Staffs 169 C9
Hardingstone Northants 120 F5
Hardings Wood Staffs 168 E4
Hardington Som 45 C8
Hardington Mandeville
Som 29 E8
Hardington Marsh Som 29 F8
Hardington Moor Som 29 E8
Hardiston Perth 279 B11
Hardisworthy Devon 24 C2
Hardley Hants 32 G6
Hardley Street Norf 143 C7
Hardmead M Keynes 103 B8
Hardrow N Yorks 223 G7
Hardstoft Derbys 170 C6
Hardstoft Common
Derbys 170 C6
Hardway Hants 33 G10
Som 45 G8
Hardwick Bucks 84 B4
Cambs 122 D3
Cambs 123 F7
Norf 142 F4
Norf 158 F2
Northants 121 D7
Oxon 82 D5
Oxon 101 C8
Oxon 101 F11
Shrops 131 E7
Stockton 234 G4
S Yorks 187 D7
W Mid 133 D11
Hardwicke Glos 80 C3
Glos 99 F8
Hereford 96 C5
Hardwick Green Worcs 98 E6
Hardwick Village Notts 187 F10
Hardy's Green Essex 107 G8
Hare Som 28 D3
Hare Appletree Lancs 202 B6
Hareby Lincs 174 B4
Harecroft W Yorks 205 F7
Hareden Lancs 203 C8
Hare Edge Derbys 186 G4
Harefield London 85 G9
Soton 33 E7
Harefield Grove London 85 G9
Haregate Staffs 169 D7
Hare Green Essex 107 G11
Hare Hatch Wokingham 65 D10
Harehill Derbys 152 B3
Harehills W Yorks 206 G2
Harehope Borders 270 G4
Northumb 264 E3
Harelaw Durham 242 G5
Hareleeshill S Lnrk 268 E5
Hareplain Kent 53 F10
Harescough Cumb 231 C8
Harescombe Glos 80 C4
Haresfield Glos 80 C4
Swindon 82 G2
Haresfinch Mers 183 B8
Hareshaw N Lnrk 268 C6
Hareshaw Head
Northumb 251 F9
Harestanes E Dunb 278 G3
Harestock Hants 48 G3
Hare Street Essex 86 D6
Herts 104 F6
Herts 105 F7
Harewood W Yorks 206 D2
Harewood End Hereford 97 F10
Harewood Hill W Yorks 204 F6
Harford Carms 94 C2
Devon 8 D2
Devon 40 G6
Hargate Norf 142 E2
Hargate Hill Derbys 185 C8
Hargatewall Derbys 185 F10
Hargrave Ches W 167 C7
Northants 121 C10
Suff 124 F5
Harker Cumb 239 E9
Harker Marsh Cumb 229 E7
Harkland Shetland 312 E6
Harknett's Gate Essex 86 D6
Harkstead Suff 108 E3
Harlaston Staffs 152 G4
Harlaw Ho Aberds 303 G7
Harlaxton Lincs 155 C7
Harlech Gwyn 145 C11
Harlequin Notts 154 B3
Harlescott Shrops 149 F10
Harlesden London 67 C8
Harlesthorpe Derbys 187 F7
Harleston Devon 8 F5
Norf 142 G4
Suff 125 F10
Harlestone Northants 120 E4
Harle Syke Lancs 204 F3
Harley Shrops 131 C11
S Yorks 186 B5
Harleyholm S Lnrk 259 B10
Harley Shute E Sus 38 F3
Harleywood Glos 80 F4
Harling Road Norf 141 F9
Harlington C Beds 103 E10
London 66 D5
S Yorks 198 G3
Harlosh Highld 298 E2
Harlow Essex 86 C6
Harlow Carr N Yorks 205 C11
Harlow Green T&W 243 F7
Harlow Hill Northumb 242 D3
N Yorks 205 C11
Harlthorpe E Yorks 207 F10
Harlton Cambs 123 G7
Harlyn Corn 10 F3
Harman's Corner Kent 69 G11
Harman's Cross Dorset 18 E5
Harmans Water Brack 65 F11
Harmby N Yorks 214 B2
Harmer Green Herts 86 B3
Harmer Hill Shrops 149 E9
Harmondsworth London 66 D5
Harmston Lincs 173 C7
Harnage Shrops 131 C11
Harnham Northumb 242 B3
Wilts 31 B10
Wilts 31 B11
Harnhill Glos 81 E9
Harold Hill London 87 G8
Harold Park London 87 G9
Haroldston West Pembs 72 B5
Haroldswick Shetland 312 B8
Harold Wood London 87 G8
Harome N Yorks 216 C2
Harpenden Herts 85 C10
Harpenden Common
Herts 85 C10
Harper Green Gtr Man 195 F8
Harperley Durham 242 G5
Harper's Gate Staffs 169 D7
Harper's Green Norf 159 E8
Harpford Devon 15 C7
Harpham E Yorks 217 G11
Harpley Norf 158 D5
Worcs 116 E3
Harpole Northants 120 E3
Harpsdale Highld 310 D5
Harpsden Oxon 65 C9
Harpsden Bottom Oxon 65 C9
Harpswell Lincs 188 D6
Harpton Powys 114 F4
Harpurhey Gtr Man 195 G11
Harpur Hill Derbys 185 G9
Harraby Cumb 239 G10
Harracott Devon 25 B9
Harrapool Highld 295 C8
Harras Cumb 219 B9
Harraton T&W 243 G7
Harrier Shetland 313 J1
Harrietfield Perth 286 E3
Harrietsham Kent 53 C11
Harringay London 67 B10
Harrington Cumb 228 F5
Lincs 190 G5
Northants 136 G5
Harringworth Northants 137 D8
Harris Highld 294 F5
Harriseahead Staffs 168 D5
Harriston Cumb 229 C9
Harrogate N Yorks 206 C2
Harrold Beds 121 F8
Harrop Dale Gtr Man 196 F4
Harrow Highld 310 B6
London 67 B7
Harrowbarrow Corn 7 B7
Harrowbeer Devon 7 B10
Harrowby Lincs 155 B8
Harrowden Beds 103 B11
Harrowgate Hill Darl 224 B5
Harrowgate Village
Darl 224 B5
Harrow Green Suff 125 G7
Harrow Hill Glos 79 B10
Harrow on the Hill
London 67 B7
Harrow Street Suff 107 D9
Harrow Weald London 85 G11
Harry Stoke S Glos 60 D6
Harston Cambs 123 G8
Leics 154 C6
Harswell E Yorks 208 E2
Hart Hrtlpl 234 E5
Hartbarrow Cumb 221 G8
Hartburn Northumb 252 F3
Stockton 225 B8
Hartcliffe Bristol 60 F5
Hart Common Gtr Man 194 F6
Hartest Suff 124 G6
Hartest Hill Suff 124 G6
Hartfield E Sus 52 F3
Highld 299 E7
Hartford Cambs 122 C5
Ches W 183 G10
Som 27 B7
Hartfordbeach
Ches W 183 G10
Hartfordbridge Hants 49 B9
Hartford End Essex 87 B11
Hartforth N Yorks 224 D3
Hartgrove Dorset 30 D4
Hartham Herts 86 C4
Harthill Ches W 167 D8
N Lnrk 269 C8
S Yorks 187 E7
Hart Hill Luton 104 G2
Hartington Derbys 169 C10
Hartland Devon 24 C3
Hartle Worcs 117 B8
Hartlebury Shrops 132 D4
Worcs 116 C6
Hartlebury Common
Worcs 116 C6
Hartlepool Hrtlpl 234 E6
Hartley Cumb 222 D5
Kent 53 G9
Kent 68 F6
Northumb 243 B8
Plym 7 D9
Hartley Green Kent 68 F6
Staffs 151 D9
Hartley Mauditt Hants 49 F8
Hartley Westpall Hants 49 B7
Hartley Wintney Hants 49 B9
Hartlington N Yorks 213 G10
Hartlip Kent 69 G10
Hartmoor Dorset 30 C3
Hartmount Highld 301 B7
Hartoft End N Yorks 226 G5
Harton N Yorks 216 G4
Shrops 131 F9
T&W 243 E9
Hartpury Glos 98 F5
Hartsgreen Shrops 132 G5
Hart's Green Suff 125 F7
Hartshead W Yorks 197 C7
Hartshead Green
Gtr Man 196 G3
Hartshead Moor Side
W Yorks 197 C7
Hartshead Moor Top
W Yorks 197 B7
Hartshead Pike
Gtr Man 196 G3
Hartshill Stoke 168 F5
Warks 134 E6
Hart's Hill W Mid 133 F8
Hartshill Green Warks 134 E6
Hartshorne Derbys 152 E6
Hartsop Cumb 221 C8
Hart Station Hrtlpl 234 D5
Hartswell Som 27 B9
Hartwell Northants 120 G5
Staffs 151 B8
Hartwith N Yorks 214 G4
Hartwood Lancs 194 D5
N Lnrk 268 D6
Hartwoodburn Borders 261 D11
Harvel Kent 68 G6
Harvest Hill W Mid 134 G5
Harvieston Stirl 277 D11
Harvills Hawthorn
W Mid 133 E9
Harvington Worcs 99 B11
Worcs 117 C7
Harvington Cross Worcs 99 B11
Harvington Hill Worcs 99 B10
Harwell Notts 187 C11
Oxon 64 B3
Harwich Essex 108 E5
Harwood Durham 232 E2
Gtr Man 195 E8
Harwood Dale N Yorks 227 F9
Harwood Lee Gtr Man 195 E8
Harwood on Teviot
Borders 249 B10
Harworth Notts 187 C10
Hasbury W Mid 133 G9
Hascombe Sur 50 E3
Haselbech Northants 120 B4
Haselbury Plucknett Som 29 E7
Haseley Warks 118 D4
Haseley Green Warks 118 D4
Haseley Knob Warks 118 C4
Haselor Warks 118 F2
Hasfield Glos 98 F6
Hasguard Pembs 72 D5
Haskayne Lancs 193 F11
Hasketon Suff 126 G4
Hasland Derbys 170 B5
Haslemere Sur 50 G2
Haslingbourne W Sus 35 C7
Haslingden Lancs 195 C9
Haslingfield Cambs 123 G8
Haslington Ches E 168 D2
Hasluck's Green W Mid 118 B2
Hassall Ches E 168 D3
Hassall Green Ches E 168 D3
Hassell Street Kent 54 D5
Hassendean Borders 262 E2
Hassingham Norf 143 B7
Hassocks W Sus 36 D3
Hassop Derbys 186 G2
Haster Highld 310 D7
Hasthorpe Lincs 175 B7
Hastigrow Highld 310 C6
Hasting Hill T&W 243 G9
Hastingleigh Kent 54 E5
Hastings E Sus 38 F4
Som 28 D4
Hastingwood Essex 87 D7
Hastoe Herts 84 D6
Haston Shrops 149 E10
Haswell Durham 234 C3
Haswell Moor Durham 234 C3
Haswell Plough Durham 234 C3
Haswellsykes Borders 260 B6
Hatch C Beds 104 B3
Devon 8 F4
Hants 49 C7
Wilts 30 B6
Hatch Beauchamp Som 28 C4
Hatch Bottom Hants 33 E7
Hatch End Beds 121 E11
London 85 G10
Hatchet Gate Hants 32 G5
Hatchet Green Hants 31 D11
Hatch Farm Hill W Sus 34 B6
Hatch Green Som 28 D4
Hatching Green Herts 85 C10
Hatchmere Ches W 183 G9
Hatch Warren Hants 48 D6
Hatcliffe NE Lincs 201 G8
Hateley Heath W Mid 133 E10
Hatfield Hereford 115 F11
Herts 86 D2
S Yorks 199 F7
Worcs 117 G7
Hatfield Broad Oak Essex 87 B8
Hatfield Chase S Yorks 199 E8
Hatfield Garden Village
Herts 86 D2
Hatfield Heath Essex 87 B8
Hatfield Hyde Herts 86 C2
Hatfield Peverel Essex 88 C3
Hatfield Woodhouse
S Yorks 199 F7
Hatford Oxon 82 G4
Hatherden Hants 47 C10
Hatherleigh Devon 25 G8
Hatherley Glos 99 G8
Hathern Leics 153 E9
Hatherop Glos 81 D11
Hathersage Derbys 186 E2
Hathersage Booths
Derbys 186 E2
Hathershaw Gtr Man 196 G2
Hatherton Ches E 167 F11
Staffs 151 G9
Hatley St George Cambs 122 G5
Hatston Orkney 314 E4
Hatt Corn 7 C7
Hatterseat Aberds 303 G9
Hattersley Gtr Man 185 C7
Hatt Hill Hants 32 B4
Hattingley Hants 48 F6
Hatton Aberds 303 F10
Angus 287 D9
Derbys 152 D4
Lincs 189 F11
London 66 D5
Moray 301 D11
Shrops 131 E9
Warks 118 D4
Warr 183 E9
Hattonburn Aberds 293 C9
Hatton Castle Aberds 303 E7
Hattoncrook Aberds 303 G8
Hatton Grange Shrops 132 C5
Hatton Heath Ches W 167 C7
Hatton Hill Sur 66 G2
Hattonknowe Borders 270 F4
Hatton of Fintray
Aberds 293 B10
Hatton Park Northants 121 D7
Haugh E Ayrs 257 D11
Gtr Man 196 E2
Lincs 190 F6
Haugham Lincs 190 E4
Haugh-head Borders 261 B8
Haugh Head Northumb 264 D2
Haughland Orkney 314 E5
Haughley Suff 125 E10
Haughley Green Suff 125 E10
Haughley New Street
Suff 125 E10
Haugh of Glass Moray 302 F4
Haugh of Kilnmaichlie
Moray 301 F11
Haugh of Urr Dumfries 237 C10
Haughs of Clinterty
Aberdeen 293 B10
Haughton Ches E 167 D9
Notts 187 G11
Powys 148 F6
Shrops 132 B4
Shrops 132 D3
Shrops 149 D7
Shrops 149 F11
Staffs 151 E7
Haughton Castle
Northumb 241 C10
Haughton Green
Gtr Man 184 C6
Haughton Le Skerne
Darl 224 B6
Haughurst Hill W Berks 64 G5
Haulkerton Aberds 293 F9
Haultwick Herts 104 G6
Haunn Argyll 288 E5
W Isles 297 K3
Haunton Staffs 152 G4
Hauxton Cambs 123 G8
Havannah Ches E 168 C5
Havant Hants 22 B2
Haven Hereford 97 B11
Hereford 115 G8
Haven Bank Lincs 174 E2
Haven Side E Yorks 201 B7
Havenstreet IoW 21 C7
Havercroft W Yorks 197 E11
Haverfordwest / Hwlffordd
Pembs 73 B7
Haverhill Suff 106 B3
Haverigg Cumb 210 D3
Havering-atte-Bower
London 87 G8
Haveringland Norf 160 E3
Haversham M Keynes 102 C6
Haverthwaite Cumb 210 C6
Haverton Hill Stockton 234 G5
Haviker Street Kent 53 D8
Havyatt Som 44 F4
Havyatt Green N Som 60 G3
Hawarden / Penarlâg
Flint 166 B4
Hawbridge Worcs 99 B8
Hawbush Green Essex 106 G5
Hawcoat Cumb 210 E4
Hawcross Glos 98 E5
Hawddamor Gwyn 146 F3
Hawen Ceredig 92 B6
Hawes N Yorks 213 B7
Hawes' Green Norf 142 D4
Hawes Side Blkpool 202 G2
Hawford Worcs 116 E6
Hawgreen Shrops 150 D2
Hawick Borders 262 F2
Hawkchurch Devon 28 G4
Hawkcombe Som 41 D11
Hawkedon Suff 124 G5
Hawkenbury Kent 52 F5
Kent 53 E10
Hawkeridge Wilts 45 C11
Hawkerland Devon 15 D7
Hawkersland Cross
Hereford 97 B10
Hawkesbury S Glos 61 B9
Warks 135 G7
Hawkesbury Upton
S Glos 61 B9
Hawkes End W Mid 134 G6
Hawkesley W Mid 117 B10
Hawk Green Gtr Man 185 D7
Hawkhill Northumb 264 G6
Hawk Hill Cumb 228 F6
Hawkhope Northumb 250 F6
Hawkhurst Kent 53 G9
Hawkhurst Common
E Sus 23 B8
Hawkinge Kent 55 F8
Hawkin's Hill Essex 106 E3
Hawkley Gtr Man 194 G5
Hants 34 B2
Hawkridge Som 41 G11
Hawksdale Cumb 230 B3
Hawks Green Staffs 151 G9
Hawkshaw Blkburn 195 D9
Hawkshead Cumb 221 F7
Hawkshead Hill Cumb 220 F6
Hawks Hill Bucks 66 B2
Hawk's Hill Sur 51 B7
Hawksland S Lnrk 259 B8
Hawkspur Green Essex 106 E3
Hawks Stones W Yorks 196 B2
Hawkswick N Yorks 213 E9
Hawksworth Notts 172 G3
W Yorks 205 E9
W Yorks 205 F11
Hawkwell Essex 88 G4
Hawley Hants 49 B11
Kent 68 E4
Hawley Bottom Devon 28 G2
Hawley Lane Hants 49 B11
Hawling Glos 99 G11
Hawn Orkney 314 D4
Hawnby N Yorks 215 B10
Hawne W Mid 133 G9
Haworth W Yorks 204 F6
Haws Bank Cumb 220 F6
Hawstead Suff 125 F7
Hawstead Green Suff 125 F7
Hawthorn Durham 234 B4
Hants 49 G7
Rhondda 58 B6
Wilts 61 F11
Hawthorn Corner Kent 71 F8
Hawthorn Hill Brack 65 E11
Lincs 174 D2
Hawthorns Staffs 168 F4
Hawthorpe Lincs 155 D10
Hawton Notts 172 E3
Haxby York 207 B8
Haxey N Lincs 188 B3
N Lincs 199 G9
Haxey Carr N Lincs 199 G9
Haxted Sur 52 D2
Haxton Wilts 46 D6
Hay Corn 10 G5
Haybridge Shrops 116 C2
Som 44 D4
Telford 150 G3
Hayden Glos 99 G8
Haydock Mers 183 B9
Haydon Bath 45 C7
Dorset 29 D11
Som 28 C3
Som 44 D5
Swindon 62 B6
Haydon Bridge
Northumb 241 E8
Haydon Wick Swindon 62 B6
Haye Corn 7 B7
Haye Fm Corn 6 B6
Hayes Bromley 68 F2
Hillingdon 66 C6
Staffs 169 C9
Hayes End London 66 C5
Hayes Knoll Wilts 81 G10
Hayes Town London 66 C6
Hayfield Derbys 185 D8
Fife 280 C5
Hay Field S Yorks 187 B10
Hayfield Green
S Yorks 187 B11
Haygate Telford 150 G2
Haygrass Som 28 C2
Hay Green Essex 87 E10
Herts 104 D6
Norf 157 F10
Hayhill E Ayrs 257 F11
Hayhillock Angus 287 C9
Haylands IoW 21 C7
Hayle Corn 2 B3
Hayley Green W Mid 133 G8
Hay Mills W Mid 134 G2
Haymoor End Som 28 B4
Haymoor Green
Ches E 167 E11
Hayne Devon 26 F5
Haynes C Beds 103 C11
Haynes Church End
C Beds 103 C11
Haynes West End
C Beds 103 C11
Hay-on-Wye Powys 96 C4
Hayscastle Pembs 91 F7
Hayscastle Cross Pembs 91 G8
Haysford Pembs 91 G8
Hayshead Angus 287 C10
Hayston E Dunb 278 G2
Haystoun Borders 261 B7
Hay Street Herts 105 F7
Haythorne Dorset 31 F8
Hayton Aberdeen 293 C11
Cumb 229 C8
Cumb 240 F2
E Yorks 208 D2
Notts 188 E2
Hayton's Bent Shrops 131 G10
Haytor Vale Devon 13 F11
Haytown Devon 24 E5
Haywards Heath W Sus 36 C4
Haywood S Lnrk 269 E9
S Yorks 198 E5
Haywood Oaks Notts 171 D10
Hazard's Green E Sus 23 C11
Hazelbank S Lnrk 268 F6
Hazelbeach Pembs 72 E6
Hazelbury Bryan Dorset 30 F2
Hazeleigh Essex 88 E4
Hazel End Essex 105 G9
Hazeley Hants 49 B8
Hazeley Bottom Hants 49 B9
Hazeley Heath Hants 49 B9
Hazeley Lea Hants 49 B8
Hazelgrove Notts 171 F8
Hazel Grove Gtr Man 184 D6
Hazelhurst Gtr Man 195 D9
Gtr Man 195 G9
Gtr Man 196 G3
Hazelslack Cumb 211 D9
Hazelslade Staffs 151 G10
Hazel Street Kent 53 B11
Kent 53 F7
Hazel Stub Suff 106 C3
Hazelton Glos 81 B9
Hazelton Walls Fife 287 E7
Hazelwood Derbys 170 F4
Devon 8 E4
London 68 G2
Hazlehead S Yorks 197 G7
Hazlemere Bucks 84 F5
Hazler Shrops 131 E9
Hazlerigg T&W 242 C6
Hazles Staffs 169 F8
Hazlescross Staffs 169 F8
Hazleton Glos 81 B9
Hazlewood N Yorks 205 C7
Hazon Northumb 252 C5
Heacham Norf 158 B3
Headbourne Worthy
Hants 48 G3
Headbrook Hereford 114 F6
Headcorn Kent 53 E10
Headingley W Yorks 205 F11
Headington Oxon 83 D8
Headington Hill Oxon 83 D8
Headlam Durham 224 B3
Headless Cross Cumb 211 D7
Worcs 117 D10
Headley Hants 49 F10
Hants 64 G4
Sur 51 C8
Headley Down Hants 49 F10
Headley Heath Worcs 117 B11
Headley Park Bristol 60 F5
Head of Muir Falk 278 E6
Headon Devon 24 G5
Notts 188 F2
Heads S Lnrk 268 F4
Headshaw Borders 261 E11
Heads Nook Cumb 239 F11
Headstone London 66 B6
Headwell Fife 279 D11
Heady Hill Gtr Man 195 E10
Heage Derbys 170 E5
Healaugh N Yorks 206 D5
N Yorks 223 F10
Heald Green Gtr Man 184 D4
Healds Green Gtr Man 195 F11
Heale Devon 40 D6
Som 28 B5
Som 28 D2
Som 45 E7
Healey Gtr Man 195 D11
Northumb 242 F2
N Yorks 214 C3
W Yorks 197 C8
W Yorks 197 D9
Healey Cote Northumb 252 C4
Healeyfield Durham 233 B7
Healey Hall Northumb 242 F2
Healing NE Lincs 201 E8
Heamoor Corn 1 C5
Heaning Cumb 221 F8
Heanish Argyll 288 E2
Heanor Derbys 170 F6
Heanor Gate Derbys 170 F6
Heanton Punchardon
Devon 40 F4
Heap Bridge Gtr Man 195 E10
Heapham Lincs 188 D5
Hearn Hants 49 F10
Hearnden Green Kent 53 D10
Hearthstane Borders 260 D4
Hearthstone Derbys 170 D4
Hearts Delight Kent 69 G11
Heasley Mill Devon 41 G8
Heast Highld 295 D8
Heath Cardiff 59 D7
Derbys 170 B6
Halton 183 E8
Heath and Reach
C Beds 103 F8
Heath Charnock Lancs 194 E5
Heath Common W Sus 35 E10
W Yorks 197 D11
Heathcot Aberds 293 C10
Heathcote Derbys 169 C10
Shrops 150 D3
Warks 118 E6
Heath Cross Devon 13 B10
Devon 14 C2
Heath End Bucks 84 F5
Bucks 85 D7
Derbys 153 E7
Hants 64 G2
Hants 64 G5
S Glos 61 B7
Sur 49 D10
Warks 118 E4
W Mid 133 C10
W Sus 35 D7
Heather Leics 153 G7
Heathercombe Devon 13 E10
Heatherfield Highld 298 E4
Heather Row Hants 49 C8
Heatherside Sur 50 B2
Heatherwood Park
Highld 311 K2
Heatherybanks Aberds 303 E7
Heathfield Cambs 105 B9
Devon 14 F2
E Sus 37 C9
Glos 80 F2
Hants 33 F9
Lincs 189 C10
N Yorks 214 F2
S Ayrs 257 E9
Som 27 B11
Som 43 G7
Heathfield Village Oxon 83 B8
Heath Green Hants 48 F6
Worcs 117 C11
Heathhall Dumfries 237 B11
Heath Hayes Staffs 151 G10
Heath Hill Shrops 150 G5
Heath House Som 44 D2
Heathlands Wokingham 65 F10
Heath Lanes Telford 150 E2
Heath Park London 68 B4
Heathrow Airport London 66 D5
Heath Side Kent 68 E4
Heathstock Devon 28 G2
Heathton Shrops 132 E6
Heathtop Derbys 152 C4
Heath Town W Mid 133 D8
Heathwaite Cumb 221 F8
N Yorks 225 E9
Heatley Staffs 151 D11
Warr 184 D2
Heaton Gtr Man 195 F7
Lancs 211 G8
Staffs 169 C7
T&W 243 D7
W Yorks 205 G8
Heaton Chapel Gtr Man 184 C5
Heaton Mersey Gtr Man 184 C5
Heaton Moor Gtr Man 184 C5
Heaton Norris Gtr Man 184 C5
Heaton Royds W Yorks 205 F8
Heaton's Bridge Lancs 194 E2
Heaton Shay W Yorks 205 F8
Heaven's Door Som 29 C10
Heaverham Kent 52 B5
Heaviley Gtr Man 184 D6
Heavitree Devon 14 C4
Hebburn T&W 243 E8
Hebburn Colliery T&W 243 D8
Hebburn New Town
T&W 243 E8
Hebden N Yorks 213 G10
Hebden Bridge W Yorks 196 B3
Hebden Green Ches W 167 B10
Hebing End Herts 104 G6
Hebron Anglesey 179 E7
Carms 92 F3
Northumb 252 F5
Heck Dumfries 248 G3
Heckdyke N Lincs 188 B3
Heckfield Hants 65 G8
Heckfield Green Suff 126 B3
Heckfordbridge Essex 107 G8
Heckingham Norf 143 D7
Heckington Lincs 173 G10
Heckmondwike
W Yorks 197 C8
Heddington Wilts 62 F3
Heddington Wick Wilts 62 F3
Heddle Orkney 314 E3
Heddon Devon 25 B11
Heddon-on-the-Wall
Northumb 242 D4
Hedenham Norf 142 E6
Hedge End Dorset 30 F4
Hants 33 E7
Hedgehog Bridge Lincs 174 F3
Hedgerley Bucks 66 B3
Hedgerley Green Bucks 66 B3
Hedgerley Hill Bucks 66 B3
Hedging Som 28 B4
Hedley Hill Durham 233 C9
Hedley on the Hill
Northumb 242 F3
Hednesford Staffs 151 G9
Hedon E Yorks 201 B7
Hedsor Bucks 66 B2
Hedworth T&W 243 E8
Heelands M Keynes 102 D6
Heeley S Yorks 186 E5
Hegdon Hill Hereford 115 G11
Heggerscales Cumb 222 C6
Heggle Lane Cumb 230 D3

Heglibister Shetland 313 H5
Heighington Darl 233 G11
Lincs 173 B8
Heighley Staffs 168 F3
Height End Lancs 195 C9
Heightington Worcs 116 C5
Heights Gtr Man 196 F3
Heights of Brae Highld 300 C5
Heights of Kinlochewe Highld 299 C10
Heilam Highld 308 C4
Heiton Borders 262 C6
Helbeck Cumb 222 B5
Hele Devon 12 C2
Devon 13 G10
Devon 27 G7
Devon 40 D4
Som 27 C11
Torbay 9 B8
Helebridge Corn 24 G2
Helensburgh Argyll 276 E5
Helford Corn 3 D7
Helford Passage Corn 3 D7
Helham Green Herts 86 B5
Helhoughton Norf 159 D7
Helions Bumpstead Essex 106 C3
Hellaby S Yorks 187 C8
Helland Corn 11 G7
Som 28 C4
Hellandbridge Corn 11 G7
Hell Corner W Berks 63 G11
Hellesdon Norf 160 G4
Hellesveor Corn 2 A2
Hellidon Northants 119 F10
Hellifield N Yorks 204 B3
Hellifield Green N Yorks 204 B3
Hellingly E Sus 23 C9
Hellington Norf 142 C6
Hellister Shetland 313 J5
Hellman's Cross Essex 87 B9
Helm Northumb 252 D5
N Yorks 223 G8
Helmburn Borders 261 E9
Helmdon Northants 101 C11
Helme W Yorks 196 E5
Helmingham Suff 126 F3
Helmington Row Durham 233 D9
Helmsdale Highld 311 H4
Helmshore Lancs 195 C9
Helmside Cumb 212 B3
Helmsley N Yorks 216 C2
Helperby N Yorks 215 F8
Helperthorpe N Yorks 217 E9
Helpringham Lincs 173 G10
Helpston Pboro 138 B2
Helsby Ches W 183 F7
Helscott Corn 24 G2
Helsey Lincs 191 G8
Helston Corn 2 D5
Helstone Corn 11 E7
Helston Water Corn 4 G5
Helton Cumb 230 G6
Helwith Bridge N Yorks 212 F6
Helygain / Halkyn Flint 182 G2
Hemblington Norf 160 G6
Hemblington Corner Norf 160 G6
Hembridge Som 44 F5
Hemel Hempstead Herts 85 D9
Hemerdon Devon 7 D11
Hemford Shrops 130 C6
Hem Heath Stoke 168 G5
Hemingbrough N Yorks 207 G9
Hemingby Lincs 190 G2
Hemingfield S Yorks 197 G11
Hemingford Abbots Cambs 122 C5
Hemingford Grey Cambs 122 C5
Hemingstone Suff 126 G3
Hemington Leics 153 D9
Northants 137 F11
Som 45 C8
Hemley Suff 108 C5
Hemlington Mbro 225 C10
Hemp Green Suff 127 D7
Hempholme E Yorks 209 C7
Hempnall Norf 142 E4
Hempnall Green Norf 142 E4
Hempriggs House Highld 310 E7
Hemp's Green Essex 107 F8
Hempshill Vale Notts 171 G8
Hempstead Essex 106 D2
Medway 69 G9
Norf 160 B2
Norf 161 D8
Hempsted Glos 80 B4
Hempton Norf 159 D8
Oxon 101 E8
Hempton Wainhill Oxon 84 E3
Hemsby Norf 161 F9
Hemsted Kent 54 E6
Hemswell Lincs 188 C6
Hemswell Cliff Lincs 188 D6
Hemsworth Dorset 31 F7
S Yorks 186 E5
W Yorks 198 E2
Hemyock Devon 27 E10
Henaford Devon 24 D2
Hen Bentref Llandegfan Anglesey 179 G9
Henbrook Worcs 117 D8
Henbury Bristol 60 D5
Ches E 184 G5
Dorset 18 B5
Hendomen Powys 130 D4
Hendon London 67 B8
T&W 243 F10
Hendra Corn 2 B6
Corn 2 C5
Corn 2 D3
Corn 2 F6
Corn 5 C9
Corn 5 D9
Corn 11 E7
Hendrabridge Corn 6 B5
Hendraburnick Corn 11 D8
Hendra Croft Corn 4 D5
Hendre Flint 165 B11
Gwyn 110 B2
Powys 129 D9
Hendre-ddu Conwy 164 B5
Hendredenny Park Caerph 58 B6
Hendreforgan Rhondda 58 B3
Hendrerwydd Denb 165 C10
Hendrewen Swansea 75 D10
Hendy Carms 75 E9
Hendy-Gwyn Carms 74 B2
Hendy Gwyn / Whitland Carms 73 B11
Hên-efail Denb 165 C9
Heneglwys Anglesey 178 F6
Hen-feddau fawr Pembs 92 E4
Henfield S Glos 61 D7
W Sus 36 D2
Henford Devon 12 C3
Henfords Marsh Wilts 45 E11
Henghurst Kent 54 F3
Hengoed Caerph 77 F10
Denb 165 D9
Powys 114 G4
Shrops 148 C5
Hengrave Norf 160 F2
Suff 124 D6
Hengrove Bristol 60 F6
Hengrove Park Bristol 60 F5
Henham Essex 105 F10
Heniarth Powys 130 B2
Henlade Som 28 C3
Henleaze Bristol 60 D5
Henley Dorset 29 G11
Glos 80 B6
Shrops 115 B10
Shrops 131 F9
Som 44 G2
Suff 126 G3
Wilts 47 B10
Wilts 61 F10
W Sus 34 B5
Henley Common W Sus 34 B5
Henley Green W Mid 135 G7
Henley-in-Arden Warks 118 D3
Henley-on-Thames Oxon 65 C9
Henley's Down E Sus 38 E2
Henley Street Kent 69 F7
Henllan Ceredig 93 C7
Denb 165 B8
Henllan Amgoed Carms 92 G3
Henlle Shrops 148 C6
Henllys Torf 78 G3
Henllys Vale Torf 78 G3
Henlow C Beds 104 D3
Hennock Devon 14 E2
Henny Street Essex 107 D7
Henryd Conwy 180 G3
Henry's Moat Pembs 91 F10
Hensall N Yorks 198 C5
Henshaw Northumb 241 E7
W Yorks 205 E10
Hensingham Cumb 219 B9
Hensington Oxon 83 B7
Henstead Suff 143 F9
Hensting Hants 33 C7
Henstridge Devon 40 E5
Som 30 D2
Henstridge Ash Som 30 C2
Henstridge Bowden Som 29 C11
Henstridge Marsh Som 30 C2
Henton Oxon 84 E3
Som 44 D3
Henwood Corn 11 G11
Oxon 83 E7
Henwood Green Kent 52 E6
Heogan Shetland 313 J6
Heol-ddu Carms 75 E7
Swansea 56 B6
Heolgerrig M Tydf 77 D8
Heol-laethog Bridgend 58 C2
Heol-las Bridgend 58 C2
Swansea 57 B7
Heol Senni Powys 95 G8
Heol-y-gaer Powys 96 D3
Heol-y-mynydd V Glam 57 G11
Hepburn Northumb 264 E3
Hepple Northumb 251 C11
Hepscott Northumb 252 G6
Hepthorne Lane Derbys 170 C6
Heptonstall W Yorks 196 B3
Hepworth Suff 125 C9
W Yorks 197 F7
Herbrandston Pembs 72 D5
Hereford Hereford 97 C10
Heribusta Highld 298 B4
Heriot Borders 271 E7
Hermiston Edin 280 G3
Hermitage Borders 250 D2
Dorset 29 F10
W Berks 64 E4
W Sus 22 B3
Hermitage Green Mers 183 C10
Hermit Hill S Yorks 197 G10
Hermit Hole W Yorks 205 F7
Hermon Anglesey 162 B5
Carms 93 E7
Carms 94 F3
Pembs 92 E4
Herne Kent 71 F7
Herne Bay Kent 71 F7
Herne Common Kent 71 F7
Herne Hill London 67 E10
Herne Pound Kent 53 C7
Herner Devon 25 B9
Hernhill Kent 70 G5
Herniss Corn 2 C6
Herodsfoot Corn 6 C4
Heron Cross Stoke 168 G5
Heronden Kent 55 C9
Herongate Essex 87 G10
Heronsford S Ayrs 244 G4
Heronsgate Herts 85 G8
Heron's Ghyll E Sus 37 B7
Herons Green Bath 44 B5
Heronston Bridgend 58 D2
Herra Shetland 312 D8
Herriard Hants 49 D7
Herringfleet Suff 143 D9
Herring's Green Beds 103 C11
Herringswell Suff 124 C4
Herringthorpe S Yorks 186 C6
Hersden Kent 71 G8
Hersham Corn 24 F3
Sur 66 G6
Herstmonceux E Sus 23 C10
Herston Dorset 18 F6
Orkney 314 G4
Hertford Herts 86 C4
Hertford Heath Herts 86 C4
Hertingfordbury Herts 86 C4
Hesketh Bank Lancs 194 C2
Hesketh Lane Lancs 203 E8
Hesketh Moss Lancs 194 C2
Hesket Newmarket Cumb 230 D2
Heskin Green Lancs 194 D4
Hesleden Durham 234 D4
Hesleyside Northumb 251 G8
Heslington York 207 C8
Hessay York 206 C6
Hessenford Corn 6 D6
Hessett Suff 125 E8
Hessle E Yorks 200 B4
W Yorks 198 D2
Hest Bank Lancs 211 F9
Hester's Way Glos 99 G8
Hestinsetter Shetland 313 J4
Heston London 66 D6
Hestwall Orkney 314 E2
Heswall Mers 182 E3
Hethe Oxon 101 F11
Hethel Norf 142 C3
Hethelpit Cross Glos 98 F5
Hethersett Norf 142 C3
Hethersgill Cumb 239 D11
Hetherside Cumb 239 D10
Hetherson Green Ches W 167 F8
Hethpool Northumb 263 D9
Hett Durham 233 D11
Hetton N Yorks 204 B5
Hetton Downs T&W 234 B3
Hetton-le-Hill T&W 234 B3
Hetton-le-Hole T&W 234 B3
Hetton Steads Northumb 264 B2
Heugh Northumb 242 C3
Heugh-head Aberds 292 B5
Heveningham Suff 126 C6
Hever Kent 52 E3
Heversham Cumb 211 C9
Hevingham Norf 160 E3
Hewas Water Corn 5 F9
Hewelsfield Glos 79 E9
Hewelsfield Common Glos 79 E8
Hewer Hill Cumb 230 D3
Hew Green N Yorks 205 B10
Hewish N Som 60 G2
Som 28 F6
Hewood Dorset 28 G5
Heworth T&W 243 E7
York 207 C8
Hexham Northumb 241 E10
Hextable Kent 68 E4
Hexthorpe S Yorks 198 G5
Hexton Herts 104 E2
Hexworthy Devon 13 G9
Hey Lancs 204 E3
Heybridge Essex 87 F10
Essex 88 D5
Heybridge Basin Essex 88 D5
Heybrook Bay Devon 7 F10
Heydon Cambs 105 C8
Norf 160 D2
Heydour Lincs 155 B10
Hey Green W Yorks 196 E4
Heyheads Gtr Man 196 G3
Hey Houses Lancs 193 B10
Heylipol Argyll 288 E1
Heylor Shetland 312 E4
Heyope Powys 114 C4
Heyrod Gtr Man 185 B7
Heysham Lancs 211 G8
Heyshaw N Yorks 214 G3
Heyshott W Sus 34 D5
Heyshott Green W Sus 34 D5
Heyside Gtr Man 196 F2
Heytesbury Wilts 46 E2
Heythrop Oxon 101 F7
Heywood Gtr Man 195 E11
Wilts 45 C11
Hibaldstow N Lincs 200 G3
Hibb's Green Suff 125 G7
Hickford Hill Essex 106 C5
Hickleton S Yorks 198 F3
Hickling Norf 161 E8
Notts 154 D3
Hickling Green Norf 161 E8
Hickling Heath Norf 161 E8
Hickling Pastures Notts 154 D3
Hickmans Green Kent 54 B5
Hicks Forstal Kent 71 G7
Hicks Gate Bath 60 F6
Hick's Mill Corn 4 G5
Hickstead W Sus 36 C3
Hidcote Bartrim Glos 100 C3
Hidcote Boyce Glos 100 C3
Hifnal Shrops 132 D4
Higginshaw Gtr Man 196 F2
High Ackworth W Yorks 198 D2
Higham Derbys 170 D5
Fife 286 F6
Kent 69 E8
Lancs 204 F2
Suff 107 D10
Suff 124 E4
S Yorks 197 F10
Higham Common S Yorks 197 F10
Higham Dykes Northumb 242 B4
Higham Ferrers Northants 121 D9
Higham Gobion C Beds 104 E2
Higham Hill London 86 G5
Higham on the Hill Leics 135 D7
Highampton Devon 25 G7
Highams Park London 86 G5
Higham Wood Kent 52 D5
High Angerton Northumb 252 F3
High Bankhill Cumb 231 C7
High Banton N Lnrk 278 E4
High Barn Lincs 174 C5
High Barnes T&W 243 F9
High Barnet London 86 F2
High Beach Essex 86 F6
High Bentham N Yorks 212 F3
High Bickington Devon 25 C10
High Biggins Cumb 212 D2
High Birkwith N Yorks 212 D5
High Birstwith N Yorks 205 B10
High Blantyre S Lnrk 268 D3
High Bonnybridge Falk 278 F6
High Bradfield S Yorks 186 C3
High Bradley N Yorks 204 D6
High Bray Devon 41 G7
Highbridge Cumb 230 C3
Hants 33 C7
Highld 290 E3
Som 43 D10
W Mid 133 C10
Highbrook W Sus 51 G11
High Brooms Kent 52 E5
High Brotheridge Glos 80 C5
High Bullen Devon 25 C8
Highburton W Yorks 197 E7
Highbury London 67 B10
Ptsmth 33 G11
Som 45 D7
Highbury Vale Nottingham 171 G8
High Buston Northumb 252 B6
High Callerton Northumb 242 C5
High Cark Cumb 211 C7
High Casterton Cumb 212 D2
High Catton E Yorks 207 C10
High Church Northumb 252 F5
Highclere Hants 64 G2
Highcliffe Derbys 186 F2
Dorset 19 C10
High Cogges Oxon 82 D5
High Common Norf 141 B9
High Coniscliffe Darl 224 B4
High Crompton Gtr Man 196 F2
High Cross Cambs 123 F8
Corn 2 D6
E Sus 37 B9
Hants 34 B2
Herts 85 F10
Herts 86 B5
Newport 59 B9
Warks 118 D3
W Sus 36 D2
High Crosshill S Lnrk 268 C2
High Cunsey Cumb 221 G7
High Dubmire T&W 234 B2
High Dyke Durham 232 F5
High Easter Essex 87 C10
High Eggborough N Yorks 198 C5
High Eldrig Dumfries 236 C4
High Ellington N Yorks 214 C3
Higher Alham Som 45 E7
Higher Ansty Dorset 30 G3
Higher Ashton Devon 14 E3
Higher Audley Blkburn 195 B7
Higher Bal Corn 4 E4
Higher Ballam Lancs 202 G3
Higher Bartle Lancs 202 G6
Higher Bebington Mers 182 D4
Higher Berry End C Beds 103 E9
Higher Blackley Gtr Man 195 G10
Higher Boarshaw Gtr Man 195 F11
Higher Bockhampton Dorset 17 C10
Higher Bojewyan Corn 1 C3
Higher Boscaswell Corn 1 C3
Higher Brixham Torbay 9 D8
Higher Broughton Gtr Man 195 G10
Higher Burrow Som 28 C6
Higher Burwardsley Ches W 167 D8
High Ercall Telford 149 F11
Higher Chalmington Dorset 29 G9
Higher Cheriton Devon 27 G10
Higher Chillington Som 28 E5
Higher Chisworth Derbys 185 C7
Highercliff Corn 6 D4
Higher Clovelly Devon 24 C4
Higher Condurrow Corn 2 B5
Higher Crackington Corn 11 B9
Higher Cransworth Corn 5 B9
Higher Croft Blkburn 195 B7
Higher Denham Bucks 66 B4
Higher Dinting Derbys 185 C8
Higher Disley Ches E 185 E7
Higher Downs Corn 2 C3
Higher Durston Som 28 B3
Higher End Gtr Man 194 G4
Higher Folds Gtr Man 195 G7
Higherford Lancs 204 E3
Higher Gabwell Torbay 9 B8
Higher Green Gtr Man 195 G8
Higher Halstock Leigh Dorset 29 F8
Higher Heysham Lancs 211 G8
Higher Hogshead Lancs 195 C11
Higher Holton Som 29 B11
Higher Hurdsfield Ches E 184 G6
Higher Kingcombe Dorset 16 B6
Higher Kinnerton Flint 166 C4
Higher Land Corn 12 G3
Higher Marsh Som 30 C2
Higher Melcombe Dorset 30 G2
Higher Menadew Corn 5 D10
Higher Molland Devon 41 G8
Higher Muddiford Devon 40 F5
Higher Nyland Dorset 30 C2
Higher Penwortham Lancs 194 B4
Higher Pertwood Wilts 45 F11
Higher Porthpean Corn 5 E10
Higher Poynton Ches E 184 E6
Higher Prestacott Devon 12 B3
Higher Rads End C Beds 103 E9
Higher Ridge Shrops 149 C7
Higher Rocombe Barton Devon 9 B8
Higher Row Dorset 31 G8
Higher Runcorn Halton 183 E8
Higher Sandford Dorset 29 C10
Higher Shotton Flint 166 B4
Higher Shurlach Ches W 183 G11
Higher Slade Devon 40 D4
Higher Street Som 42 E6
Higher Tale Devon 27 G9
Higher Tolcarne Corn 5 B7
Higher Totnell Dorset 29 F10
Highertown Corn 4 G6
Corn 11 E8
Higher Town Corn 5 C10
Scilly 1 F4
Som 42 D3
Higher Tremarcoombe Corn 6 B5
Higher Vexford Som 42 F6
Higher Walreddon Devon 12 G5
Higher Walton Lancs 194 B5
Warr 183 D9
Higher Wambrook Som 28 F3
Higher Warcombe Devon 40 D3
Higher Weaver Devon 27 G9
Higher Whatcombe Dorset 30 G4
Higher Wheelton Lancs 194 C6
Higher Whitley Ches W 183 E10
Higher Wincham Ches W 183 F11
Higher Woodsford Dorset 17 D11
Higher Wraxall Dorset 29 G9
Higher Wych Ches W 167 G7
High Etherley Durham 233 F9
High Ferry Lincs 174 F5
Highfield E Yorks 207 F10
Glos 79 E10
Gtr Man 194 G5
Gtr Man 195 F8
Herts 85 D9
N Ayrs 266 E6
Oxon 101 G11
Soton 32 E6
S Yorks 186 D5
T&W 242 F4
High Field Lancs 203 C10
Highfields Cambs 123 F7
Derbys 170 B6
Essex 88 B5
Glos 80 F3
Leicester 136 C2
Northumb 273 E9
Staffs 151 E8
S Yorks 198 F4
High Flatts W Yorks 197 F8
High Forge Durham 242 G6
High Friarside Durham 242 F5
High Gallowhill E Dunb 278 G2
High Garrett Essex 106 F5
Highgate E Sus 52 G2
Kent 53 G9
London 67 B9
Powys 130 D2
S Yorks 198 G3
W Mid 133 F11
High Grange Durham 233 E9
High Grantley N Yorks 214 F4
High Green Cumb 221 E8
Norf 141 B8
Norf 142 B2
Norf 159 G8
Shrops 132 G4
Suff 125 E7
S Yorks 186 B4
Worcs 99 B7
W Yorks 197 E7
High Halden Kent 53 F11
High Halstow Medway 69 D9
High Ham Som 44 G2
High Handenhold Durham 242 G6
High Harrington Cumb 228 F6
High Harrogate N Yorks 206 B2
High Haswell Durham 234 C3
High Hatton Shrops 150 E2
High Hauxley Northumb 253 C7
High Hawsker N Yorks 227 D8
High Heath Shrops 150 D3
W Mid 133 C10
High Hesket Cumb 230 C5
High Hesleden Durham 234 D5
High Hill Cumb 229 G11
High Houses Essex 87 C11
High Hoyland S Yorks 197 E9
High Hunsley E Yorks 208 F4
High Hurstwood E Sus 37 B7
High Hutton N Yorks 216 F5
High Ireby Cumb 229 D10
High Kelling Norf 177 E10
High Kilburn N Yorks 215 D10
High Lands Durham 233 F8
Highlane Ches E 168 B5
Derbys 186 E6
High Lane Gtr Man 185 D7
Worcs 116 E3
Highlanes Corn 10 G4
Staffs 150 C5
High Lanes Corn 2 B3
High Laver Essex 87 D8
Highlaws Cumb 229 B8
Highleadon Glos 98 G5
High Legh Ches E 184 E2
Highleigh W Sus 22 D4
High Leven Stockton 225 C8
Highley Shrops 132 G4
High Littleton Bath 44 B6
High Longthwaite Cumb 229 B11
High Lorton Cumb 229 F9
High Marishes N Yorks 216 D6
High Marnham Notts 188 G4
High Melton S Yorks 198 G4
High Mickley Northumb 242 E3
High Mindork Dumfries 236 D5
Highmoor Cumb 229 B11
Oxon 65 B8
High Moor Derbys 187 E7
Lancs 194 E4
Highmoor Cross Oxon 65 C8
Highmoor Hill Mon 60 B3
High Moorsley T&W 234 B2
Highnam Glos 80 B3
Highnam Green Glos 98 G5
High Nash Glos 79 C9
High Newton Cumb 211 C8
High Newton-by-the-Sea Northumb 264 D6
High Nibthwaite Cumb 210 B5
Highoak Norf 141 C11
High Oaks Cumb 222 G2
High Offley Staffs 150 D5
High Ongar Essex 87 E9
High Onn Staffs 150 F6
High Onn Wharf Staffs 150 F6
High Park Cumb 221 G10
Mers 193 D11
Highridge Bristol 60 F5
High Risby N Lincs 200 E2
Highroad Well Moor W Yorks 196 B5
High Roding Essex 87 B10
High Rougham Suff 125 E8
High Row Cumb 230 D3
Cumb 230 G3
High Salvington W Sus 35 F10
High Scales Cumb 229 B9
High Sellafield Cumb 219 E10
High Shaw N Yorks 223 G7
High Shields T&W 243 D9
High Shincliffe Durham 233 C11
High Side Cumb 229 E10
High Southwick T&W 243 F9
High Spen T&W 242 F4
High Stakesby N Yorks 227 C7
Highstead Kent 71 F8
Highsted Kent 70 G2
High Stoop Durham 233 C8
Highstreet Kent 70 G5
High Street Corn 5 E9
Kent 53 G8
Pembs 73 B11
Suff 107 B7
Suff 127 C8
Suff 127 F8
Suff 143 G7
Highstreet Green Essex 106 E5
Sur 50 F3
High Street Green Suff 125 F10
High Sunderland Borders 261 C11
Hightae Dumfries 238 B3
Highter's Heath W Mid 117 B11
High Throston Hrtlpl 234 E5
High Tirfergus Argyll 255 F7
Hightown Ches E 168 C5
Hants 31 G11
Mers 193 G10
Soton 33 E7
Wrex 166 F4
W Yorks 197 C7
High Town Luton 103 G11
Shrops 132 E4
Staffs 151 G9
Hightown Green Suff 125 F9
Hightown Heights W Yorks 197 C7
High Toynton Lincs 174 B3
High Trewhitt Northumb 252 B2
High Urpeth Durham 242 G6
High Valleyfield Fife 279 D10
High Walton Cumb 219 C9
High Warden Northumb 241 D10
High Water Head Cumb 220 F6
Highway Corn 4 G4
Hereford 97 B9
Som 29 C7
Wilts 62 E4
Windsor 65 C11
Highweek Devon 14 G2
High Westwood Durham 242 F4
High Whinnow Cumb 239 G8
Highwood Devon 27 F10
Dorset 18 D3
Essex 87 E10
Hants 31 F11
Worcs 116 D3
Highwood Hill London 86 G2
High Woolaston Glos 79 F9
High Worsall N Yorks 225 D7
Highworth Swindon 82 G2
Highworthy Devon 24 F6
High Wray Cumb 221 F7
High Wych Herts 87 C7
High Wycombe Bucks 84 G5
Hilborough Norf 140 C6
Hilborough Ho Norf 140 C6
Hilcot Glos 81 B7
Hilcote Derbys 171 D7
Hilcot End Glos 81 E9
Hilcott Wilts 46 B6
Hildenborough Kent 52 D5
Hilden Park Kent 52 D5
Hildersham Cambs 105 B10
Hildersley Hereford 98 G2
Hilderstone Staffs 151 C8
Hilderthorpe E Yorks 218 F3
Hilfield Dorset 29 F10
Hilgay Norf 140 D2
Hill S Glos 79 G10
Warks 119 D9
W Mid 134 D2
Hillam N Yorks 198 B4
Hillbeck Cumb 222 B5
Hillblock Pembs 73 B8
Hillborough Kent 71 F8
Hill Bottom Oxon 64 D6
Hillbourne Poole 18 C6
Hillbrae Aberds 302 E6
Aberds 303 G7
Hill Brow W Sus 34 B3
Hillbutts Dorset 31 G7
Hill Chorlton Staffs 150 B5
Hillcliffe Warr 183 D10
Hillcliffane Derbys 170 F3
Hillcommon Som 27 B11
Hill Common Norf 161 E8
Hill Corner Som 45 D10
Hill Croome Worcs 99 C7
Hillcross Derbys 152 C6
Hill Dale Lancs 194 E3
Hill Deverill Wilts 45 E11
Hilldyke Lincs 174 F4
Hill Dyke Lincs 174 F4
Hillend Fife 280 E2
N Lnrk 268 B6
N Som 43 B11
Shrops 132 E6
Swansea 56 C2
Hill End Durham 232 D6
Fife 279 B10
Glos 99 D8
London 85 G8
N Yorks 205 C7
Som 29 E8
Worcs 117 E8
Hillend Green Glos 98 F4
Hillersland Glos 79 C9
Hillerton Devon 13 B10
Hillesden Bucks 102 F3
Hillesden Hamlet Bucks 102 E3
Hillesley Glos 61 B9
Hillfarance Som 27 C11
Hillfarrance Som 27 C11
Hillfield Devon 8 E6
W Mid 118 B2
Hillfields S Glos 60 D6
W Mid 118 B6
Hillfoot Aberds 303 D9
W Yorks 205 G10
Hillfoot End C Beds 104 E2
Hill Furze Worcs 99 B9
Hill Gate Hereford 97 F9
Hillgreen W Berks 64 D3
Hill Green Essex 105 E9
Kent 69 G10
Hillgrove W Sus 34 B6
Hillhampton Hereford 97 B11
Hillhead Aberds 302 F5
Aberds 303 G8
Corn 5 C11
Devon 9 E8
E Ayrs 257 B10
S Ayrs 257 F10
Hill Head Hants 33 G8
Northumb 241 D10
Hillhead of Auchentumb Aberds 303 D9
Hillhead of Blairy Aberds 302 D6
Hillhead of Cocklaw Aberds 303 E10
Hill Hoath Kent 52 E3
Hill Hook W Mid 134 C2
Hillhouse Borders 271 D10
Hill Houses Shrops 116 B2
Hilliard's Cross Staffs 152 G3
Hilliclay Highld 310 C5
Hillingdon London 66 C5
Hillingdon Heath London 66 C5
Hillington Glasgow 267 C10
Norf 158 D4
Hillis Corner IoW 20 C5
Hillmoor Devon 27 E10
Hillmorton Warks 119 C10
Hill Mountain Pembs 73 D7
Hillockhead Aberds 292 B6
Aberds 292 C5
Hillock Vale Lancs 195 B9
Hill of Beath Fife 280 C3
Hill of Drip Stirl 278 B5
Hill of Fearn Highld 301 B8
Hill of Keillor Angus 286 C6
Hill of Mountblairy Aberds 302 D6
Hill of Overbrae Aberds 303 C8
Hill Park Hants 33 F9
Kent 52 B2
Hillpool Worcs 117 B7
Hillpound Hants 33 D9
Hill Ridware Staffs 151 F11
Hillsborough S Yorks 186 C4
Hillside Aberds 293 D11
Angus 293 G9
Devon 8 C4
Devon 27 F11
Hants 49 C9
Mers 193 E10
Orkney 314 D3
Orkney 314 G4
Shetland 313 G6
Shrops 131 F11
Wilts 81 G9
Hill Side Hants 34 B3
S Yorks 197 G8
Worcs 116 E5
W Yorks 197 D7
Hill Somersal Derbys 152 C2
Hills Town Derbys 171 B7
Hillstreet Hants 32 D4
Hill Street Kent 54 D6
Hillswick Shetland 312 F4
Hilltop Bl Gwent 77 D11
Bucks 85 E7
Derbys 170 C4
Hill Top Derbys 186 F5
Durham 232 G5
Durham 233 C10
Durham 242 G5
Gtr Man 195 G8
Hants 32 G6
Notts 171 F7
N Yorks 214 G3
N Yorks 214 G5
Staffs 133 B7
S Yorks 186 C5
S Yorks 186 D3
S Yorks 187 B7
S Yorks 197 F9
Warks 134 E5
Warks 135 E7
W Mid 133 E9
W Sus 34 C5
W Yorks 196 E5
W Yorks 197 D10
W Yorks 205 G7
W Yorks 205 G11
Hillview T&W 243 G9
Hill View Dorset 18 B5
Hillway IoW 21 D8
Hillwell Shetland 313 M5
Hill Wood W Mid 134 C2
Hill Wootton Warks 118 D6
Hillyfields Hants 32 D5
Hilmarton Wilts 62 D4
Hilperton Wilts 45 B11
Hilperton Marsh Wilts 45 B11
Hilsea Ptsmth 33 G11
Hilston E Yorks 209 G11
Hiltingbury Hants 32 C6
Hilton Aberds 303 F9
Borders 273 E7
Cambs 122 D5
Cumb 231 G10
Derbys 152 C4
Dorset 30 G3
Durham 233 G9
Highld 309 L7
Highld 311 L3
Shrops 132 D5
Staffs 133 B11
Stockton 225 C9
Hilton House Gtr Man 194 F6
Hilton Lodge Highld 300 G2
Hilton of Cadboll Highld 301 B8
Hilton Park Gtr Man 195 G10
Himbleton Worcs 117 F8
Himley Staffs 133 E7
Hincaster Cumb 211 C10
Hinchley Wood Sur 67 F7
Hinchliffe Mill W Yorks 196 F6
Hinchwick Glos 100 E2
Hinckley Leics 135 E8
Hinderclay Suff 125 B10
Hinderton Ches W 182 F4
Hinderwell N Yorks 226 B5
Hindford Shrops 148 C6
Hindhead Sur 49 F11
Hindle Fold Lancs 203 G10
Hindley Gtr Man 194 G6
Northumb 242 F2
Hindley Green Gtr Man 194 G6
Hindlip Worcs 117 F7
Hindolveston Norf 159 D10
Hindon Wilts 46 G2
Hindpool Cumb 210 F3
Hindringham Norf 159 B9
Hindsford Gtr Man 195 G7
Hingham Norf 141 C10
Hinstock Shrops 150 D3
Hintlesham Suff 107 C11
Hinton Glos 79 E11
Hants 19 B10
Hereford 96 D6
Northants 119 G10
S Glos 61 D8
Shrops 131 B8
Som 29 C9
Hinton Ampner Hants 33 B9
Hinton Blewett Bath 44 B5
Hinton Charterhouse Bath 45 B9
Hinton Cross Worcs 99 C10
Hinton-in-the-Hedges Northants 101 D11
Hinton Martell Dorset 31 F8
Hinton on the Green Worcs 99 C10
Hinton Parva Dorset 31 G7
Swindon 63 C8
Hinton St George Som 28 E6
Hinton St Mary Dorset 30 D3
Hinton Waldrist Oxon 82 F5
Hints Shrops 116 C2
Staffs 134 C3
Hinwick Beds 121 E8
Hinwood Shrops 131 B7
Hinxhill Kent 54 E5
Hinxton Cambs 105 B9
Hinxworth Herts 104 C4
Hipperholme W Yorks 196 B6
Hipplecote Worcs 116 F4
Hipsburn Northumb 264 G6
Hipswell N Yorks 224 F3
Hirael Gwyn 179 G9
Hiraeth Carms 92 G3
Hirn Aberds 293 C9
Hirnant Powys 147 E11
Hirst N Lnrk 269 C7
Northumb 253 F7
Hirst Courtney N Yorks 198 C6
Hirwaen Denb 165 C10
Hirwaun Rhondda 77 D7
Hirwaun Common Bridgend 58 C2
Hiscott Devon 25 B8
Hislop Borders 249 C9
Hisomley Wilts 45 D11
Histon Cambs 123 E8
Hitcham Suff 125 G9
Hitchill Dumfries 238 D4
Hitchin Herts 104 F3
Hitchin Hill Herts 104 F3
Hitcombe Bottom Wilts 45 E10
Hither Green London 67 E11
Hittisleigh Devon 13 C10
Hittisleigh Barton Devon 13 B10
Hive E Yorks 208 G2
Hixon Staffs 151 D10
Hoaden Kent 55 B9
Hoar Cross Staffs 152 E2
Hoarwithy Hereford 97 F10
Hoath Kent 71 G8
Hoath Corner Kent 52 E3
Hobarris Shrops 114 B6
Hobbister Orkney 314 F3
Hobble End Staffs 133 B10
Hobbles Green Suff 124 G4
Hobbs Cross Essex 87 C7
Essex 87 F7
Hobbs Wall Bath 61 G7
Hob Hill Ches W 167 E7
Hobkirk Borders 262 G3
Hobroyd Derbys 185 C8
Hobson Durham 242 F5
Hoby Leics 154 F3
Hoccombe Som 27 B10
Hockenden London 68 F3
Hockerill Herts 105 G9
Hockering Norf 159 G11
Hockering Heath Norf 159 G11
Hockerton Notts 172 D2
Hockholler Som 27 C11
Hockholler Green Som 27 C11
Hockley Ches E 184 E6
Essex 88 G4
Kent 54 B3
Staffs 134 C4
W Mid 118 B5
Hockley Heath W Mid 118 C3
Hockliffe C Beds 103 F9
Hockwold cum Wilton Norf 140 F4
Hockworthy Devon 27 D8
Hocombe Hants 32 C6
Hoddesdon Herts 86 D5
Hoddlesden Blkburn 195 C8
Hoddomcross Dumfries 238 C5
Hoddom Mains Dumfries 238 C5
Hoden Worcs 99 B11
Hodgefield Staffs 168 E6
Hodgehill Ches E 168 B4
W Mid 134 F2
Hodgeston Pembs 73 F8
Hodley Powys 130 E3
Hodnet Shrops 150 D2
Hodnetheath Shrops 150 D2
Hodsock Notts 187 D10
Hodsoll Street Kent 68 G6
Hodson Swindon 63 C7
Hodthorpe Derbys 187 F8
Hoe Hants 33 D9
Norf 159 F9
Sur 50 D5
Hoe Benham W Berks 64 F2
Hoe Gate Hants 33 E10
Hoff Cumb 222 B3
Hoffleet Stow Lincs 156 B4
Hogaland Shetland 312 F5
Hogben's Hill Kent 54 B4
Hogganfield Glasgow 268 B2
Hoggard's Green Suff 125 F7
Hoggeston Bucks 102 G6
Hoggington Wilts 45 B10
Hoggrill's End Warks 134 E4
Hogha Gearraidh W Isles 296 D3
Hog Hatch Sur 49 D10
Hoghton Lancs 194 B6
Hoghton Bottoms Lancs 194 B6
Hogley Green W Yorks 196 F6
Hognaston Derbys 170 E2
Hogpits Bottom Herts 85 E8
Hogsthorpe Lincs 191 G8
Hogstock Dorset 31 F7
Holbeach Lincs 157 E7
Holbeach Bank Lincs 157 D7
Holbeach Clough Lincs 156 D6
Holbeach Drove Lincs 156 G6
Holbeache Worcs 116 B5
Holbeach Hurn Lincs 157 D7
Holbeach St Johns Lincs 156 F6
Holbeach St Marks Lincs 157 C7
Holbeach St Matthew Lincs 157 C8
Holbeck Notts 187 G8
W Yorks 205 G11
Holbeck Woodhouse Notts 187 G8
Holberrow Green Worcs 117 F10
Holbeton Devon 8 E2
Holborn London 67 C10
Holborough Kent 69 G8
Holbrook Derbys 170 G5
Suff 108 D3
S Yorks 186 E6
Holbrook Common S Glos 61 E7
Holbrook Moor Derbys 170 F5
Holbrooks W Mid 134 G6
Holburn Northumb 264 B2
Holbury Hants 32 G6
Holcombe Devon 14 G5
Gtr Man 195 D9
Som 45 D7
Holcombe Brook Gtr Man 195 E9
Holcombe Rogus Devon 27 D9
Holcot Northants 120 D5
Holdbrook London 86 F5
Holden Lancs 203 D11
Holdenby Northants 120 D3
Holden Fold Gtr Man 196 F2
Holdenhurst Bmouth 19 B8
Holder's Green Essex 106 F2
Holders Hill London 86 G2
Holdfast Worcs 99 D7
Holdgate Shrops 131 F11
Holdingham Lincs 173 F9
Holditch Dorset 28 G4
Holdsworth W Yorks 196 B5
Holdworth S Yorks 186 C3
Hole Devon 24 D4
W Yorks 204 F6
Hole Bottom W Yorks 196 C2
Holefield Borders 263 C8
Holehills N Lnrk 268 B5
Holehouse Derbys 185 C8
Holehouses Ches E 184 F2
Hole-in-the-Wall Hereford 98 F2
Holemill Aberdeen 293 C10
Holemoor Devon 24 F6
Hole's Hole Devon 7 B8
Holestane Dumfries 247 D9
Holestone Derbys 170 C4
Hole Street W Sus 35 E10
Holewater Devon 41 F8
Holford Som 43 E7
Holgate York 207 C7
Holker Cumb 211 D7
Holkham Norf 176 E5
Hollacombe Devon 24 G5
Devon 26 G4
Hollacombe Hill Devon 7 E10
Holland Orkney 314 A4
Orkney 314 D6
Sur 52 C2
Holland Fen Lincs 174 F2
Holland Lees Lancs 194 F4
Holland-on-Sea Essex 89 B12
Hollands Som 29 D9
Hollandstoun Orkney 314 A7
Hollee Dumfries 239 D7
Hollesley Suff 109 C7
Hollicombe Torbay 9 C7
Hollies Common Staffs 150 E6
Hollinfare Warr 183 C11
Hollingbourne Kent 53 B10
Hollingbury Brighton 36 F4
Hollingdean Brighton 36 F4
Hollingdon Bucks 103 F7
Hollingrove E Sus 37 C11
Hollingthorpe W Yorks 197 D10
Hollington Derbys 152 B4
E Sus 38 E3
Hants 48 B2

Staffs 151 B11
Hollington Cross Hants . . . 48 B2
Hollington Grove
Derbys 152 B4
Hollingwood Derbys 186 G6
Hollingworth Gtr Man . . . 185 B8
Hollin Hall Lancs 204 F4
Hollin Park W Yorks 206 F2
Hollins Cumb 222 G3
Derbys 186 G4
Gtr Man 195 F8
Gtr Man 195 F10
Gtr Man 195 F11
Staffs 168 D6
Staffs 168 E4
Staffs 169 F7
Hollinsclough Staffs . . . 169 B9
Hollins End S Yorks 186 E5
Hollinsgreen Ches E . . . 168 C2
Hollins Green Warr . . . 183 C11
Hollins Lane Lancs 202 C5
Shrops 149 B10
Hollinswood Telford . . . 132 B4
Hollinthorpe W Yorks . . . 206 G3
Hollinwood Gtr Man 196 G2
Shrops 149 B10
Hollis Green Devon 27 F9
Hollis Head Devon 27 G7
Hollocombe Devon 25 E10
Hollocombe Town
Devon 25 E10
Holloway Derbys 170 D4
Wilts 45 G11
Windsor 65 C10
Holloway Hill Sur 50 E3
Hollow Brook Bath 60 G5
Hollowell Northants 120 C3
Hollow Meadows
S Yorks 186 D2
Hollowmoor Heath
Ches W 167 B7
Hollow Oak Dorset 18 C2
Hollows Dumfries 239 B9
Hollow Street Kent 71 G8
Holly Bank W Mid 133 C11
Hollyberry End W Mid . . 134 G5
Holly Brook Som 44 D4
Hollybush Caerph 77 E11
E Ayrs 257 G9
Stoke 168 G5
Torf 78 G3
Worcs 98 D5
Holly Bush Wrex 166 G6
Hollybush Corner Bucks . . 66 B3
Suff 125 F8
Hollybushes Kent 54 B2
Hollybush Hill Bucks 66 C3
Essex 89 B10
Hollycroft Leics 135 E8
Holly Cross Windsor 65 C10
Holly End Norf 139 B9
Holly Green Bucks 84 E3
Worcs 99 C7
Holly Hill N Yorks 224 E3
Hollyhurst Shrops 131 D9
Warks 135 F7
Hollym E Yorks 201 B10
Hollywaste Shrops 116 B2
Hollywater Hants 49 G10
Hollywood Worcs 117 B11
Holmacott Devon 25 B8
Holman Clavel Som 28 D2
Holmbridge W Yorks 196 F6
Holmbury St Mary Sur . . . 50 E6
Holmbush Corn 5 E10
Dorset 28 G5
Holmcroft Staffs 151 D8
Holme Cambs 138 F3
C Beds 104 C3
Cumb 211 D10
N Lincs 200 F2
Notts 172 D4
N Yorks 215 C7
W Yorks 196 F6
W Yorks 205 G9
Holmebridge Dorset 18 D3
Holme Chapel Lancs . . . 195 B11
Holme Green C Beds 104 C3
N Yorks 207 E7
Wokingham 65 F10
Holme Hale Norf 141 B7
Holme Hill NE Lincs 201 F9
Holme Lacy Hereford 97 D11
Holme Lane Notts 154 B2
Holme Marsh Hereford . . . 114 G6
Holme Mills Cumb 211 D10
Holme next the Sea
Norf 176 E2
Holme-on-Spalding-Moor
E Yorks 208 F2
Holme on the Wolds
E Yorks 208 D5
Holme Pierrepont Notts 154 B2
Holmer Hereford 97 C10
Holmer Green Bucks 84 F6
Holmes Lancs 194 D2
Holme St Cuthbert
Cumb 229 B8
Holmes Chapel Ches E . . 168 B3
Holmesdale Derbys 186 F5
Holmesfield Derbys 186 F4
Holme Slack Lancs 203 G7
Holmes's Hill E Sus 23 C8
Holmeswood Lancs 194 D2
Holmethorpe Sur 51 C9
Holmewood Derbys 170 B6
Holme Wood W Yorks . . . 205 G9
Holmfield W Yorks 196 B5
Holmfirth W Yorks 196 F6
Holmhead Angus 293 F7
Dumfries 246 F6
E Ayrs 258 E3
Holmhill Dumfries 247 D9
Holmisdale Highld 297 G7
Holmley Common
Derbys 186 F5
Holmpton E Yorks 201 C11
Holmrook Cumb 219 F11
Holmsgarth Shetland 313 J6
Holmside Durham 233 B10
Holmsleigh Green Devon 28 G2
Holmston S Ayrs 257 E9
Holmwood Corner Sur . . . 51 E7
Holmwrangle Cumb 230 B6
Holne Devon 8 B4
Holnest Dorset 29 E11
Holnicote Som 42 D2
Holsworthy Devon 24 G4
Holsworthy Beacon
Devon 24 F5
Holt Dorset 31 G8
Hants 49 C8
Mers 183 C7
Norf 159 B11
Wilts 61 G11
Worcs 116 E6
Wrex 166 E6
Holtby York 207 C9
Holt End Hants 49 F8
Worcs 117 D11
Holt Fleet Worcs 116 E6
Holt Green Lancs 193 G11
Holt Head W Yorks 196 E5
Holt Heath Dorset 31 G9
Worcs 116 E6
Holt Hill Kent 53 B8
Staffs 152 D2
Holton Oxon 83 D10
Som 29 B11
Suff 127 B7
Holton cum Beckering
Lincs 189 E10
Holton Heath Dorset 18 C4
Holton le Clay Lincs 201 G9
Holton le Moor Lincs . . . 189 B9
Holton St Mary Suff 107 D11
Holt Park W Yorks 205 E11
Holt Pound Hants 49 E10
Holts Gtr Man 196 G3
Holtspur Bucks 84 G6
Holt Wood Dorset 31 F8
Holtye E Sus 52 F3
Holway Dorset 28 G5
Dorset 29 C10
Flint 181 F11
Som 28 C2
Holwell Dorset 30 E2
Herts 104 E3
Leics 154 E4
Oxon 82 D2
Som 45 D8
Holwellbury C Beds 104 E3
Holwick Durham 232 F4
Holworth Dorset 17 E11
Holybourne Hants 49 E8
Holy City Devon 28 G3
Holy Cross T&W 243 D8
Worcs 117 B8
Holyfield Essex 86 E5
Holyhead / Caergybi
Anglesey 178 E2
Holy Island Northumb . . 273 B11
Holylee Borders 261 B9
Holymoorside Derbys . . . 170 B4
Holyport Windsor 65 D11
Holystone Northumb . . . 251 C11
Holytown N Lnrk 268 C5
Holy Vale Scilly 1 G4
Holywell Cambs 122 C6
C Beds 85 B8
Corn 4 D5
Dorset 29 G9
E Sus 23 F9
Glos 80 G3
Hereford 97 C7
Herts 85 F9
Northumb 243 C8
Som 29 E8
Warks 118 D3
Holywell Green
W Yorks 196 D5
Holywell Lake Som 27 C10
Holywell Row Suff 124 B4
Holywell / Treffynnon
Flint 181 F11
Holywood Dumfries 247 G10
Homedowns Glos 99 E8
Homer Shrops 132 C2
Homer Green Mers 193 G10
Homersfield Suff 142 F5
Homerton London 67 B11
Hom Green Hereford 97 G11
Homington Wilts 31 B10
Honeybourne Worcs 100 C2
Honeychurch Devon 25 G10
Honeydon Beds 122 F2
Honey Hall N Som 60 G2
Honeyhill Wokingham . . . 65 F10
Honey Hill Kent 70 G6
Honeystreet Wilts 62 G6
Honey Street Wilts 62 G6
Honey Tye Suff 107 D9
Honeywick C Beds 103 G9
Honicknowle Plym 7 D9
Honiley Warks 118 C4
Honing Norf 160 D6
Honingham Norf 160 G2
Honington Lincs 172 G6
Suff 125 C8
Warks 100 C5
Honiton Devon 27 G11
Honkley Wrex 166 D4
Honley W Yorks 196 E6
Honley Moor W Yorks . . . 196 E6
Honnington Telford 150 F4
Honor Oak London 67 E11
Honor Oak Park London . 67 E11
Honresfeld Gtr Man 196 D2
Hoo Kent 71 G9
Hoober S Yorks 186 B6
Hoobrook Worcs 116 C6
Hood Green S Yorks . . . 197 G10
Hood Hill S Yorks 186 B5
Hood Manor Warr 183 D9
Hooe E Sus 23 D11
Plym 7 E10
Hooe Common E Sus 23 C11
Hoo End Herts 85 B11
Hoofield Ches W 167 C8
Hoo Green Ches E 184 E2
Hoohill Blkpool 202 F2
Hoo Hole W Yorks 196 B4
Hook Cambs 139 E8
Devon 28 F4
E Yorks 199 B9
Hants 33 F8
Hants 49 C8
London 67 G7
Pembs 73 C7
Wilts 62 C5
Hook-a-gate Shrops 131 B9
Hook Bank Worcs 98 C6
Hooke Dorset 16 B6
Hook End Essex 87 F9
Oxon 65 C7
W Mid 134 G4
Hooker Gate T&W 242 F4
Hookgate Staffs 150 B4
Hook Green Kent 53 F7
Kent 68 F6
Hook Heath Sur 50 B3
Hook Norton Oxon 101 E7
Hook Park Hants 33 G7
Hook's Cross Herts 104 G5
Hook Street Glos 79 F11
Wilts 62 C5
Hooksway W Sus 34 D4
Hookway Devon 14 B3
Hookwood Sur 51 E9
Hoole Ches W 166 B6
Hoole Bank Ches W 166 B6
Hooley Sur 51 B9
Hooley Bridge Gtr Man . 195 E11
Hooley Brow Gtr Man . . . 195 E11
Hooley Hill Gtr Man 184 B6
Hoo Meavy Devon 7 B10
Hoop Mon 79 D8
Hoopers Pool Wilts 45 C10
Hoops Devon 24 C5
Hoo St Werburgh
Medway 69 E9
Hooton Ches W 182 F5
Hooton Levitt S Yorks . . . 187 C8
Hooton Pagnell S Yorks . 198 F3
Hooton Roberts S Yorks . 187 B7
Hopcroft's Holt Oxon . . . 101 F9
Hope Derbys 185 E11
Devon 9 G8
Highld 308 D4
Powys 130 B5
Shrops 130 C6
Staffs 169 D10
Hope Bagot Shrops 115 C11
Hopebeck Cumb 229 G9
Hope Bowdler Shrops . . . 131 E9
Hopedale Staffs 169 D10
Hope End Green Essex . 105 G11
Hope Green Ches E 184 E6
Hopeman Moray 301 C11
Hope Mansell Hereford . . 79 B10
Hope Park Shrops 130 C6
Hopesay Shrops 131 G7
Hopesgate Shrops 130 C6
Hope's Green Essex 69 B9
Hope's Rough Hereford . . 98 B2
Hopetown W Yorks 197 C11
Hope under Dinmore
Hereford 115 G10
Hope / Yr Hôb Flint 166 D4
Hopgoods Green
W Berks 64 F4
Hopkinstown Rhondda . . . 77 G9
Hopley's Green Hereford 114 G6
Hopperton N Yorks 206 B4
Hop Pole Lincs 156 G3
Hopsford Warks 135 G8
Hopstone Shrops 132 E5
Hopton Derbys 170 E3
Shrops 149 D11
Shrops 149 E7
Staffs 151 D8
Suff 125 B9
Hoptonbank Shrops 116 B2
Hopton Cangeford
Shrops 131 G10
Hopton Castle Shrops . . . 115 B7
Hoptongate Shrops . . . 131 G10
Hoptonheath Shrops 115 B7
Hopton Heath Staffs 151 D9
Hopton on Sea Norf . . . 143 D10
Hopton Wafers Shrops . . 116 B2
Hopwas Staffs 134 B3
Hopwood Gtr Man 195 F11
Worcs 117 B10
Hopworthy Devon 24 G4
Horam E Sus 23 B9
Horbling Lincs 156 B2
Horbury W Yorks 197 D9
Horbury Bridge
W Yorks 197 D9
Horbury Junction
W Yorks 197 D10
Horcott Glos 81 E11
Horden Durham 234 C4
Horderley Shrops 131 F8
Hordle Hants 19 B11
Hordley Shrops 149 C7
Horeb Carms 75 D7
Carms 93 F10
Ceredig 93 C7
Flint 166 D3
Horfield Bristol 60 D6
Horgabost W Isles 305 J2
Horham Suff 126 C4
Horkesley Heath Essex . 107 F9
Horkstow N Lincs 200 D3
Horkstow Wolds
N Lincs 200 D3
Horley Oxon 101 C8
Sur 51 E9
Horn Ash Dorset 28 G5
Hornblotton Som 44 G5
Hornblotton Green Som . 44 G5
Hornby Lancs 211 F11
N Yorks 224 G4
N Yorks 225 D7
Horncastle Lincs 174 B3
Reading 65 E7
Hornchurch London 68 B4
Horncliffe Northumb 273 F8
Horndean Borders 273 F7
Hants 34 E2
Horndon Devon 12 F6
Horndon on the Hill
Thurrock 69 C7
Horne Sur 51 E10
Horner Som 41 D11
Horne Row Essex 88 E3
Horner's Green Suff 107 C9
Hornestreet Essex 107 E10
Horney Common E Sus . . . 37 B7
Horn Hill Som 43 E8
Hornick Corn 5 E9
Horniehaugh Angus 292 G6
Horning Norf 160 F6
Horninghold Leics 136 D6
Horninglow Staffs 152 D4
Horningsea Cambs 123 E9
Horningsham Wilts 45 E10
Horningtoft Norf 159 E8
Horningtops Corn 6 C5
Hornsbury Som 28 E4
Hornsby Cumb 240 G2
Horns Corner Kent 38 B2
Horns Cross Devon 24 C5
E Sus 38 C4
Hornsea E Yorks 209 D10
Hornsea Bridge
E Yorks 209 D10
Hornsea Burton
E Yorks 209 D10
Hornsey London 67 B10
Hornsey Vale London 67 B10
Horns Green Kent 52 B3
Horn Street Kent 55 F7
Kent 69 G7
Hornton Oxon 101 B7
Horpit Swindon 63 C8
Horrabridge Devon 7 B10
Horringer Suff 124 E6
Horringford IoW 20 D6
Horrocks Fold Gtr Man . 195 E8
Horrocksford Lancs . . . 203 E10
Horsalls Kent 53 C11
Horsebridge Devon 12 G4
Hants 47 G10
Shrops 131 B7
Horse Bridge Staffs 169 E7
Horsebrook Devon 8 D4
Staffs 151 G7
Horsecastle N Som 60 F2
Horsedown Wilts 61 D10
Horsedowns Corn 2 C4
Horsehay Telford 132 B3
Horseheath Cambs 106 B2
Horsehouse N Yorks . . . 213 C10
Horseley Heath W Mid . . 133 E9
Horsell Sur 50 B3
Horsell Birch Sur 50 B3
Horseman's Green
Wrex 166 G6
Horseman Side Essex . . . 87 F8
Horsemere Green W Sus . 35 G7
Horsenden Bucks 84 E3
Horsepools Glos 80 C4
Horseway Cambs 139 F8
Horseway Head
Hereford 114 E6
Horsey Norf 161 E9
Som 43 F10
Horsey Corner Norf 161 E9
Horsey Down Wilts 81 G9
Horsford Norf 160 F3
Horsforth W Yorks 205 F10
Horsforth Woodside
W Yorks 205 F10
Horsham Worcs 116 F4
W Sus 51 G7
Horsham St Faith Norf . . 160 F4
Horshoe Green Kent 52 E3
Horsington Lincs 173 B11
Som 30 C2
Horsley Derbys 170 G5
Glos 80 F4
Northumb 242 D3
Northumb 251 D8
Horsley Cross Essex 108 F2
Horsleycross Street
Essex 108 F2
Horsleyhill Borders 262 F2
Horsley Hill T&W 243 D9
Horsleyhope Durham . . . 233 B7
Horsleys Green Bucks . . . 84 F3
Horsley Woodhouse
Derbys 170 G5
Horsmonden Kent 53 E7
Horspath Oxon 83 E9
Horstead Norf 160 F5
Horsted Green E Sus 23 B7
Horsted Keynes W Sus . . . 36 B5
Horton Bucks 84 B6
Dorset 31 F8
Kent 54 B6
Lancs 204 C3
Northants 120 G6
S Glos 61 C9
Shrops 149 D9
Som 28 E4
Staffs 168 D6
Swansea 56 D3
Telford 150 G3
Wilts 62 G5
Windsor 66 D4
Horton Common Dorset . . 31 F9
Horton Cross Som 28 D4
Horton-cum-Studley
Oxon 83 C9
Horton Green Ches W . . . 167 F7
Horton Heath Dorset 31 F9
Hants 33 D7
Horton in Ribblesdale
N Yorks 212 E6
Horton Kirby Kent 68 F5
Hortonlane Shrops 149 G8
Horton Wharf Bucks 84 B6
Hortonwood Telford 150 G3
Horwich Gtr Man 194 E6
Horwich End Derbys 185 E8
Horwood Devon 25 B8
Horwood Riding S Glos . . . 61 B8
Hoscar Lancs 194 E3
Hose Leics 154 D4
Hoselaw Borders 263 C8
Hoses Cumb 220 G4
Hosey Hill Kent 52 C3
Hosh Perth 286 E2
Hosta W Isles 296 D3
Hoswick Shetland 313 L6
Hotham E Yorks 208 G3
Hothfield Kent 54 D3
Hotley Bottom Bucks 84 E5
Hoton Leics 153 E11
Hotwells Bristol 60 E5
Houbans Shetland 312 F5
Houbie Shetland 312 D8
Houdston S Ayrs 244 D5
Hough Argyll 288 E1
Ches E 168 E2
Ches E 184 F5
Hougham Lincs 172 G5
Hough Green Halton . . . 183 D7
Hough-on-the-Hill
Lincs 172 F6
Hough Side W Yorks . . . 205 G10
Houghton Cambs 122 C5
Cumb 239 F10
Hants 47 G10
Northumb 242 D4
Pembs 73 D7
W Sus 35 E8
Houghton Bank Darl . . . 233 G10
Houghton Conquest
C Beds 103 C10
Houghton Green E Sus . . . 38 C6
Warr 183 C10
Houghton-le-Side
Darl 233 G10
Houghton-le-Spring
T&W 234 B2
Houghton on the Hill
Leics 136 C3
Houghton Regis
C Beds 103 G10
Houghton St Giles Norf . 159 B8
Houghwood Mers 194 G4
Houlland Shetland 312 B7
Shetland 312 F7
Shetland 313 H5
Shetland 313 J6
Houlsyke N Yorks 226 D4
Hound Hants 33 F7
Hound Green Hants 49 B8
Hound Hill Dorset 31 G7
Houndmills Hants 48 C6
Houndscroft Glos 80 E5
Houndslow Borders 272 F2
Houndsmoor Som 27 B10
Houndstone Som 29 D8
Houndwood Borders 272 C6
Hounsdown Hants 32 E5
Hounsley Batch N Som . . . 60 G4
Hounslow London 66 D6
Hounslow Green Essex . . 87 B11
Hounslow West London . . 66 D6
Hourston Orkney 314 E2
Housabister Shetland . . . 313 H6
Housay Shetland 312 F8
Househill Highld 301 D8
House of Daviot Highld . 301 E7
House of Glenmuick
Aberds 292 D5
Houses Hill W Yorks 197 D7
Housetter Shetland 312 E5
Housham Tye Essex 87 C8
Houss Shetland 313 K5
Houston Renfs 267 B8
Houstry Highld 310 F5
Houton Orkney 314 F3
Hove Brighton 36 G3
Hove Edge W Yorks 196 C6
Hoveringham Notts 171 F11
Hoveton Norf 160 F6
Hovingham N Yorks 216 D3
How Cumb 240 F2
Howbeck Bank Ches E . . 167 F11
Howbrook S Yorks 186 B4
How Caple Hereford 98 E2
Howden Borders 262 E5
E Yorks 199 B8
W Loth 269 B11
Howden Clough
W Yorks 197 B8
Howden-le-Wear
Durham 233 E9
Howdon T&W 243 D8
Howdon Pans T&W 243 D8
Howe Highld 310 C7
Norf 142 C5
N Yorks 214 C6
Howe Bridge Gtr Man . . . 195 G7
Howegreen Essex 88 E4
Howe Green Essex 87 B8
Essex 88 E2
Warks 134 F6
Howell Lincs 173 F10
How End C Beds 103 C10
Howe of Teuchar
Aberds 303 E7
Howe Street Essex 87 C11
Essex 106 E3
Howey Powys 113 F11
Howford Borders 261 B8
Borders 261 E9
Howgate Cumb 228 G5
Midloth 270 D4
Howgill Cumb 222 F2
Lancs 204 D2
N Yorks 205 B7
How Green Kent 52 D3
How Hill Norf 161 F7
Howick Mon 79 F8
Northumb 265 F7
Howick Cross Lancs 194 B4
Howle Durham 233 F7
Telford 150 E3
Howleigh Som 28 D2
Howlett End Essex 105 E11
Howley Glos 80 G2
Som 28 F3
Warr 183 D10
Hownam Borders 263 F7
Hownam Mains Borders . 263 E7
Howpasley Borders 249 B8
Howsen Worcs 116 G5
Howsham N Lincs 200 G4
N Yorks 216 G4
Howslack Dumfries 248 B3
Howtel Northumb 263 C9
Howt Green Kent 69 F11
Howton Hereford 97 F8
Howtown Cumb 221 B8
Howwood Renfs 267 C7
How Wood Herts 85 E10
Hoxne Suff 126 B3
Hoxton London 67 C10
Hoy Orkney 314 F2
Hoylake Mers 182 D2
Hoyland S Yorks 197 G11
Hoyland Common
S Yorks 197 G11
Hoylandswaine S Yorks . 197 G9
Hoyle W Sus 34 D6
Hoyle Mill S Yorks 197 F11
Hubbard's Hill Kent 52 C4
Hubberholme N Yorks . . . 213 D8
Hubberston Pembs 72 D5
Hubbersty Head Cumb . . 221 G8
Hubberton Green
W Yorks 196 C4
Hubbert's Bridge Lincs . 174 G3
Huby N Yorks 205 D11
N Yorks 215 F11
Hucclecote Glos 80 B5
Hucking Kent 53 B10
Hucknall Notts 171 F8
Huddersfield W Yorks . . . 196 D6
Huddington Worcs 117 F8
Huddisford Devon 24 D4
Huddlesford Staffs 134 B3
Hud Hey Lancs 195 C9
Hudnall Herts 85 C8
Hudnalls Glos 79 E8
Hudswell N Yorks 224 E3
Wilts 61 F11
Huggate E Yorks 208 B3
Hugglepit Devon 24 C4
Hugglescote Leics 153 G8
Hughenden Valley Bucks . 84 F5
Hughley Shrops 131 D11
Hugh Mill Lancs 195 C10
Hugh Town Scilly 1 G4
Hugus Corn 4 G5
Huish Devon 25 E8
Devon 25 E8
Wilts 62 G6
Huish Champflower Som . 27 B9
Huish Episcopi Som 28 B6
Huisinis W Isles 305 G1
Hulcote C Beds 103 D8
Northants 102 B4
Hulcott Bucks 84 B5
Hulland Derbys 170 F2
Hulland Moss Derbys . . . 170 F3
Hulland Ward Derbys . . . 170 F3
Hullavington Wilts 61 C11
Hullbridge Essex 88 G4
Hull End Derbys 185 E9
Hulme Gtr Man 184 B4
Staffs 168 F6
Warr 183 C10
Hulme End Staffs 169 D10
Hulme Walfield Ches E . . 168 B4
Hulseheath Ches E 184 E2
Hulverstone IoW 20 E3
Hulver Street Suff 143 F9
Humber Devon 14 G3
Hereford 115 F10
Humber Bridge N Lincs . . 200 C4
Humberston NE Lincs . . . 201 F10
Humberstone Leicester . 136 B2
Humberston Fitties
NE Lincs 201 F10
Humbie E Loth 271 C9
Humbledon T&W 243 F9
Humble Green Suff 107 B8
Humbleton E Yorks 209 G10
Northumb 263 D11
Humby Lincs 155 C10
Hume Borders 272 G4
Hummersknott Darl 224 C5
Humshaugh Northumb . . 241 C10
Huna Highld 310 B7
Huncoat Lancs 203 G11
Huncote Leics 135 D10
Hundalee Borders 262 F4
Hundall Derbys 186 F5
Hunderthwaite Durham . 232 G5
Hunderton Hereford 97 D9
Hundleby Lincs 174 B5
Hundle Houses Lincs . . . 174 E3
Hundleshope Borders . . . 260 B6
Hundleton Pembs 73 E7
Hundon Suff 106 B4
Hundred Acres Hants 33 E9
Hundred End Lancs 194 C2
Hundred House Powys . . . 114 G2
Hungarton Leics 136 B3
Hungate W Yorks 197 B11
Hungerford Hants 31 E11
Shrops 131 F10
Som 42 E4
W Berks 63 F10
Windsor 65 E10
Hungerford Green
W Berks 64 D5
Hungerford Newtown
W Berks 63 E11
Hunger Hill Gtr Man 195 F7
Lancs 194 E4
Hungershall Park Kent . . . 52 F5
Hungerstone Hereford . . . 97 D8
Hungerton Lincs 155 D7
Hungladder Highld 298 B3
Hungreyhatton Shrops . . 150 D3
Hunmanby N Yorks 217 D11
Hunmanby Moor
N Yorks 218 D2
Hunningham Warks 119 D7
Hunningham Hill Warks . 119 D7
Hunnington Worcs 133 G9
Hunny Hill IoW 20 D5
Hunsdon Herts 86 C6
Hunsdonbury Herts 86 C6
Hunsingore N Yorks 206 C4
Hunslet W Yorks 206 G2
Hunslet Carr W Yorks . . . 206 G2
Hunsonby Cumb 231 D7
Hunspow Highld 310 B6
Hunstanton Norf 175 G11
Hunstanworth Durham . . 232 B5
Hunsterson Ches E 167 F11
Hunston Suff 125 D9
W Sus 22 C5
Hunston Green Suff 125 D9
Hunstrete Bath 60 G6
Hunsworth W Yorks 197 B7
Hunt End Worcs 117 E10
Huntenhull Green Wilts . 45 D10
Huntercombe End Oxon . . 65 B7
Hunters Forstal Kent 71 F7
Hunter's Quay Argyll 276 F3
Huntham Som 28 B4
Hunthill Lodge Angus . . . 292 F6
Huntingdon Cambs 122 C4
Huntingfield Suff 126 C6
Huntingford Dorset 45 G10
S Glos 80 G2
Huntington Ches W 166 C6
E Loth 281 F9
Hereford 97 C9
Hereford 114 G5
Staffs 151 G9
Telford 132 B3
York 207 B8
Hunting-tower Perth 286 E4
Huntley Glos 80 B2
Staffs 169 G8
Huntly Aberds 302 F5
Huntlywood Borders 272 G2
Hunton Hants 48 F3
Kent 53 D8
N Yorks 224 G3
Hunton Bridge Herts 85 E9
Hunt's Corner Norf 141 F11
Huntscott Som 42 E2
Hunt's Cross Mers 182 D6
Hunts Green Warks 134 D3
Hunt's Green Bucks 84 E5
W Berks 64 E2
Huntsham Devon 27 C8
Huntshaw Devon 25 C8
Huntshaw Water Devon . . 25 C8
Hunt's Hill Bucks 84 F4
Hunt's Lane Leics 135 C9
Huntspill Som 43 D10
Huntstile Som 43 G9
Huntworth Som 43 G10
Hunwick Durham 233 E9
Hunworth Norf 159 B11
Hurcott Som 28 D5
Som 29 B8
Worcs 117 B7
Hurdcott Wilts 47 G7
Hurdley Powys 130 E5
Hurdsfield Ches E 184 G6
Hurgill N Yorks 224 E3
Hurlet Glasgow 267 C10
Hurley Warks 134 D4
Windsor 65 C10
Hurley Bottom Windsor . 65 C10
Hurley Common Warks . . 134 D4
Hurlford E Ayrs 257 B11
Hurliness Orkney 314 H2
Hurlston Lancs 194 E2
Hurlston Green Lancs . . 193 E11
Hurn Dorset 19 B8
E Yorks 208 E6
Hurn's End Lincs 174 F6
Hursey Dorset 28 G6
Hursley Hants 32 B6
Hurst Cumb 230 C4
Dorset 17 C11
Gtr Man 196 G2
N Yorks 223 E10
Som 29 D7
Wokingham 65 E9
Hurstbourne Priors
Hants 48 D2
Hurstbourne Tarrant
Hants 47 C11
Hurstead Gtr Man 196 D2
Hurst Green Essex 89 B9
E Sus 38 B2
Lancs 203 F9
Sur 51 C11
W Mid 133 F9
Hurst Hill W Mid 133 E8
Hurstley Hereford 97 B7
Hurst Park Sur 66 F6
Hurstpierpoint W Sus . . . 36 D3
Hurst Wickham W Sus . . . 36 D3
Hurstwood Lancs 204 G3
Hurtmore Sur 50 D3
Hurworth-on-Tees Darl 224 C6
Hurworth Place Darl . . . 224 D5
Hury Durham 223 B9
Husabost Highld 298 D2
Husbands Bosworth
Leics 136 G2
Husbandtown Angus 287 D8
Husborne Crawley
C Beds 103 D9
Husthwaite N Yorks 215 D10
Hutcherleigh Devon 8 E5
Hutchesontown
Glasgow 267 C11
Hutchwns Bridgend 57 F10
Hut Green N Yorks 198 C5
Huthwaite Notts 171 D7
Hutlerburn Borders 261 E10
Huttock Top Lancs 195 C11
Huttoft Lincs 191 F8
Hutton Borders 273 E9
Cumb 230 F4
Essex 87 F10
E Yorks 208 C6
Lancs 194 B3
N Som 43 B11
Hutton Bonville N Yorks . 224 E6
Hutton Buscel N Yorks . . 217 C9
Hutton Conyers N Yorks . 214 E6
Hutton Cranswick
E Yorks 208 C6
Hutton End Cumb 230 D4
Hutton Gate Redcar 225 B11
Hutton Hang N Yorks . . . 214 B3
Hutton Henry Durham . . . 234 D4
Hutton-le-Hole
N Yorks 226 G4
Hutton Magna Durham . . 224 C2
Hutton Mount Essex 87 G10
Hutton Roof Cumb 211 D11
Cumb 230 E3
Hutton Rudby N Yorks . . 225 D9
Huttons Ambo N Yorks . . 216 F5
Hutton Sessay N Yorks . . 215 D9
Hutton Village Redcar . 225 C11
Hutton Wandesley
N Yorks 206 C6
Huxham Devon 14 B4
Huxham Green Som 44 F5
Huxley Ches W 167 C8
Huxter Shetland 313 G7
Shetland 313 H3
Shetland 313 H5
Huxton Borders 273 B7
Huyton Mers 182 C6
Huyton Park Mers 182 C6
Huyton Quarry Mers 183 C7
Hwlffordd / Haverfordwest
Pembs 73 B7
Hycemoor Cumb 210 B1
Hyde Glos 80 E5
Glos 99 F11
Gtr Man 184 B6
Hants 31 E11
Hants 48 G3
Hereford 115 F9
Hyde Chase Essex 88 E4
Hyde End W Berks 64 G5
Hyde Heath Bucks 84 E6
Hyde Lea Staffs 151 E8
Hyde Park S Yorks 198 G5
Hydestile Sur 50 E3
Hylton Castle T&W 243 F9
Hylton Red House T&W . 243 F9
Hyltons Crossways Norf 160 D4
Hyndburn Bridge
Lancs 203 G10
Hyndford Bridge S Lnrk . 269 G8
Hyndhope Borders 261 E9
Hynish Argyll 288 F1
Hyssington Powys 130 E6
Hystfield Glos 79 F11
Hythe Hants 32 F6
Kent 55 G7
Som 44 C2
Sur 66 E4
Hythe End Windsor 66 E4
Hythie Aberds 303 D10
Hyton Cumb 210 B1

I

Iarsiadar W Isles 304 E3
Ibberton Dorset 30 F3
Ible Derbys 170 D2
Ibsley Hants 31 F11
Ibstock Leics 153 G8
Ibstone Bucks 84 G3
Ibthorpe Hants 47 C11
Iburndale N Yorks 227 D7
Ibworth Hants 48 C5
Icelton N Som 59 F11
Ichrachan Argyll 284 D4
Ickburgh Norf 140 E6
Ickenham London 66 B5
Ickenthwaite Cumb 210 B6
Ickford Bucks 83 D11
Ickham Kent 55 B8
Ickleford Herts 104 E3
Icklesham E Sus 38 D5
Ickleton Cambs 105 C9
Icklingham Suff 124 C5
Ickornshaw N Yorks 204 E5
Ickwell C Beds 104 B3
Ickwell Green C Beds . . . 104 B3
Icomb Glos 100 G4
Icy Park Devon 8 F3
Idbury Oxon 82 B2
Iddesleigh Devon 25 F9
Ide Devon 14 C3
Ideford Devon 14 F3
Ide Hill Kent 52 C3
Iden E Sus 38 C6
Iden Green Kent 53 F8
Kent 53 G10
Idle W Yorks 205 F9
Idle Moor W Yorks 205 F9
Idless Corn 4 F6
Idlicote Warks 100 C5
Idmiston Wilts 47 F7
Idole Carms 74 B6
Idridgehay Derbys 170 F3
Idridgehay Green
Derbys 170 F3
Idrigill Highld 298 C3
Idstone Oxon 63 C9
Idvies Angus 287 C9
Iet-y-bwlch Carms 92 F3
Iffley Oxon 83 E8
Ifield W Sus 51 F8
Ifield Green W Sus 51 F9
Ifieldwood W Sus 51 F8
Ifold W Sus 50 G4
Iford Bmouth 19 C8
E Sus 36 F6
Ifton Heath Shrops 148 B6
Ightfield Shrops 149 B11
Ightfield Heath Shrops . 149 B11
Ightham Kent 52 B5
Igtham Common Kent . . . 52 B5
Iken Suff 127 F8
Ilam Staffs 169 E10
Ilchester Som 29 C8
Ilchester Mead Som 29 C8
Ilderton Northumb 264 E2
Ileden Kent 55 C8
Ilford London 68 B2
Som 28 D5
Ilfracombe Devon 40 D4
Ilkeston Derbys 171 G7
Ilketshall St Andrew
Suff 143 F7
Ilketshall St Lawrence
Suff 143 G7
Ilketshall St Margaret
Suff 142 F6
Ilkley W Yorks 205 D8
Illand Corn 11 F11
Illey W Mid 133 G9
Illidge Green Ches E . . . 168 C3
Illington Norf 141 F8
Illingworth W Yorks 196 B5
Illogan Corn 4 G3
Illogan Highway Corn 4 G3
Illshaw Heath W Mid . . . 118 C2
Illston on the Hill Leics . . 136 D4
Ilmer Bucks 84 D3
Ilmington Warks 100 C4
Ilminster Som 28 E5
Ilsington Devon 13 F11
Ilston Swansea 56 C5
Ilton N Yorks 214 D3
Som 28 D5
Imachar N Ayrs 255 C9
Imber Wilts 46 D3
Imeraval Argyll 254 C4
Immervoulin Stirl 285 F9
Immingham NE Lincs . . . 201 E7
Impington Cambs 123 E8
Ince Ches W 183 F7
Ince Blundell Mers . . . 193 G10
Ince in Makerfield
Gtr Man 194 G5
Inchbae Lodge Highld . . . 300 C4
Inchbare Angus 293 G8
Inchberry Moray 302 D3
Inchbraoch Angus 287 B11
Inchbrook Glos 80 E4
Incheape Highld 309 J6
Incheril Highld 299 C10
Inchgrundle Angus 292 F6
Inchina Highld 307 K4
Inchinnan Renfs 267 B9
Inchkinloch Highld 308 E5
Inchlaggan Highld 290 C3
Inchlumpie Highld 300 B5
Inchmore Highld 300 E3
Highld 300 E5
Inchnacardoch Hotel
Highld 290 B5
Inchnadamph Highld . . . 307 G7
Inchock Angus 287 C10
Inch of Arnhall Aberds . . 293 F8
Inchree Highld 290 G2
Inchrory Moray 292 C3
Inchs Corn 5 C9
Inchture Perth 286 E6
Inchyra Perth 286 E5
Indian Queens Corn 5 D8
Inerval Argyll 254 C4
Ingatestone Essex 87 F11
Ingbirchworth S Yorks . . 197 F8
Ingerthorpe N Yorks 214 F5
Ingestre Staffs 151 E9
Ingham Lincs 188 E6
Norf 161 D7
Suff 125 C7
Ingham Corner Norf 161 D7
Ingleborough Norf 157 F9
Ingleby Derbys 152 D6
Lincs 188 F5
Ingleby Arncliffe
N Yorks 225 E8
Ingleby Barwick
Stockton 225 C9
Ingleby Cross N Yorks . . 225 E9
Ingleby Greenhow
N Yorks 225 D11
Ingleigh Green Devon . . . 25 F10
Inglemire Hull 209 G7
Inglesbatch Bath 61 G8
Inglesham Swindon 82 F2
Ingleton Durham 233 G9
N Yorks 212 E3
Inglewhite Lancs 202 E6
Ingmanthorpe N Yorks . . 206 C4
Ingoe Northumb 242 C2
Ingol Lancs 202 G6
Ingoldisthorpe Norf 158 C3
Ingoldmells Lincs 175 B9
Ingoldsby Lincs 155 C10
Ingon Warks 118 F4
Ingram Northumb 264 F2
Ingrams Green W Sus 34 C4
Ingrave Essex 87 G10
Ingrow W Yorks 205 F7
Ings Cumb 221 F8
Ingst S Glos 60 B5
Ingthorpe Rutland 137 B9
Ingworth Norf 160 D3
Inham's End Cambs 138 D5
Inhurst Hants 64 G5
Inkberrow Worcs 117 F10
Inkerman Durham 233 D8
Inkersall Derbys 186 G6
Inkersall Green Derbys . 186 G6
Inkford Worcs 117 C11
Inkpen W Berks 63 G11
Inkpen Common
W Berks 63 G11
Inkstack Highld 310 B6
Inlands W Sus 22 B3
Inmarsh Wilts 62 G2
Inn Cumb 221 D8
Innellan Argyll 276 G3
Inner Hope Devon 9 G8
Innerleithen Borders . . . 261 B8
Innerleven Fife 287 G7
Innermessan Dumfries . . 236 C2
Innerwick E Loth 282 G4
Perth 285 C9
Innie Argyll 275 B9
Inninbeg Highld 289 E8
Innis Chonain Argyll 284 E5
Innistrynich Argyll 284 E5
Innox Hill Som 45 D9
Innsworth Glos 99 G7
Insch Aberds 302 G6
Insh Highld 291 C10
Inshegra Highld 306 D7
Inshore Highld 308 C3
Inskip Lancs 202 F5
Inskip Moss Side Lancs . 202 F5
Instoneville S Yorks . . . 198 E5
Instow Devon 40 G3
Insworke Corn 7 E8
Intack Blkburn 195 B8
Intake S Yorks 186 E5
S Yorks 198 G5
W Yorks 205 F10
Interfield Worcs 98 B5
Intwood Norf 142 C3
Inver Aberds 292 D4
Highld 311 L2
Perth 286 C4
Inveraliort Highld 295 G9
Inveraldie Angus 287 D8
Inveralivaig Highld 298 E4
Inveralligin Highld 299 D8
Inverallochy Aberds 303 C10
Inveran Highld 299 B8
Highld 309 K5
Inveraray Argyll 284 G4
Inverarish Highld 295 B7
Inverarity Angus 287 C8
Inverarnan Stirl 285 F7
Inverasdale Highld 307 L3
Inverawe Ho Argyll 284 D4
Inverbeg Argyll 276 B6
Inverbervie Aberds 293 F10
Inverboyndie Aberds . . . 302 C6
Inverbroom Highld 307 L6

Invercarron Mains Highld 309 K5
Invercassley Highld 309 J4
Invercauld House Aberds 292 D3
Inverchaolain Argyll 275 F11
Invercharnan Highld 284 C5
Inverchoran Highld 300 D2
Invercreran Argyll 284 C4
Inverdruie Highld 291 B11
Inverebrie Aberds 303 F9
Invereck Argyll 276 E2
Inverernan Ho Aberds 292 B5
Invereshie House Highld 291 C10
Inveresk E Loth 280 G6
Inverey Aberds 292 E2
Inverfarigaig Highld 300 G5
Invergarry Highld 290 C5
Invergelder Aberds 292 D4
Invergeldie Perth 285 E11
Invergordon Highld 301 C7
Invergowrie Perth 287 D7
Inverguseran Highld 295 E9
Inverhadden Perth 285 B10
Inverhaggernie Stirl 285 E7
Inverharroch Moray 302 F3
Inverherive Stirl 285 E7
Inverie Highld 295 F9
Inverinan Argyll 275 B10
Inverinate Highld 295 C11
Inverkeilor Angus 287 C10
Inverkeithing Fife 280 E2
Inverkeithny Aberds 302 E6
Inverkip Invclyd 276 G4
Inverkirkaig Highld 307 H5
Inverlael Highld 307 L6
Inverleith Edin 280 F4
Inverliever Lodge Argyll 275 C9
Inverliver Argyll 284 D4
Inverlochlarig Stirl 285 F8
Inverlochy Argyll 284 E5
Highld 290 F3
Moray 301 G11
Inverlounin Argyll 276 B4
Inverlussa Argyll 275 E7
Inver Mallie Highld 290 E3
Invermark Lodge Angus 292 E6
Invermoidart Highld 289 B8
Invermoriston Highld 290 B6
Invernaver Highld 308 C7
Inverneill Argyll 275 E9
Inverness Highld 300 E6
Invernettie Aberds 303 E11
Invernoaden Argyll 276 B2
Inveronich Argyll 284 G6
Inveroran Hotel Argyll 284 C6
Inverpolly Lodge Highld 307 H5
Inverquharity Angus 287 B8
Inverquhomery Aberds 303 E10
Inverroy Highld 290 E4
Inversanda Highld 289 D11
Invershiel Highld 295 D11
Invershin Highld 309 K5
Invershore Highld 310 F6
Inversnaid Hotel Stirl 285 G7
Invertrossachs Stirl 285 G9
Inverugie Aberds 303 E11
Inveruglas Argyll 285 G7
Inveruglass Highld 291 C10
Inverurie Aberds 303 G7
Invervar Perth 285 C10
Inverythan Aberds 303 E7
Inwardleigh Devon 13 B7
Inwood Shrops 131 D9
Inworth Essex 88 B5
Iochdar W Isles 297 G3
Iping W Sus 34 C5
Ipplepen Devon 8 B6
Ipsden Oxon 64 B6
Ipsley Worcs 117 D11
Ipstones Staffs 169 F8
Ipswich Suff 108 C3
Irby Mers 182 E3
Irby in the Marsh Lincs 175 C7
Irby upon Humber NE Lincs 201 G7
Irchester Northants 121 D8
Ireby Cumb 229 D10
Lancs 212 D3
Ireland C Beds 104 C2
Orkney 314 F3
Shetland 313 L5
Wilts 45 C10
Ireland's Cross Shrops 168 G2
Ireland Wood W Yorks 205 F11
Ireleth Cumb 210 D4
Ireshopeburn Durham 232 D3
Ireton Wood Derbys 170 F3
Irlam Gtr Man 184 C2
Irlams o' th' Height Gtr Man 195 G9
Irnham Lincs 155 D10
Iron Acton S Glos 61 C7
Ironbridge Telford 132 C3
Iron Bridge Cambs 139 D9
Iron Cross Warks 117 G11
Irongray Dumfries 237 B11
Iron Lo Highld 299 G10
Ironmacannie Dumfries 237 B8
Irons Bottom Sur 51 D9
Ironside Aberds 303 D8
Ironville Derbys 170 E6
Irstead Norf 161 E7
Irstead Street Norf 161 F7
Irthington Cumb 239 E11
Irthlingborough Northants 121 C8
Irton N Yorks 217 C10
Irvine N Ayrs 257 B8
Irwell Vale Lancs 195 C9
Isabella Pit Northumb 253 G8
Isallt Bach Anglesey 178 F3
Isauld Highld 310 C3
Isbister Orkney 314 D2
Orkney 314 E3
Shetland 312 D5
Shetland 313 G7
Isel Cumb 229 E9
Isfield E Sus 36 D6
Isham Northants 121 C7
Ishriff Argyll 289 F8
Isington Hants 49 E9
Island Carr N Lincs 200 F3
Islands Common Cambs 122 E3
Islay Ho Argyll 274 G4
Isle Abbotts Som 28 C5
Isle Brewers Som 28 C5
Isleham Cambs 124 C2
Isle of Axholme N Lincs 199 F9
Isle of Dogs London 67 D11
Isle of Man Dumfries 238 B2
Isle of Whithorn Dumfries 236 F6
Isleornsay Highld 295 D9
Islesburgh Shetland 312 G5
Islesteps Dumfries 237 B11
Isleworth London 67 D7
Isley Walton Leics 153 D8
Islibhig W Isles 304 F1
Islington London 67 C10
Telford 150 E4
Islip Northants 121 B9
Oxon 83 C8
Isombridge Telford 150 G2
Istead Rise Kent 68 F6
Isycoed Wrex 166 E6
Itchen Soton 32 E6
Itchen Abbas Hants 48 G4
Itchen Stoke Hants 48 G5
Itchingfield W Sus 35 B10
Itchington S Glos 61 B7
Itteringham Norf 160 C2
Itteringham Common Norf 160 D3
Itton Devon 13 B9
Mon 79 F7
Itton Common Mon 79 F7
Ivegill Cumb 230 C4
Ivelet N Yorks 223 F8
Iver Bucks 66 C4
Iver Heath Bucks 66 C4
Iverley Staffs 133 G7
Iveston Durham 242 G4
Ivinghoe Bucks 84 B6
Ivinghoe Aston Bucks 85 B7
Ivington Hereford 115 F9
Ivington Green Hereford 115 F9
Ivybridge Devon 8 D2
Ivy Chimneys Essex 86 E6
Ivychurch Kent 39 B8
Ivy Cross Dorset 30 C5
Ivy Hatch Kent 52 C5
Ivy Todd Norf 141 B7
Iwade Kent 69 F11
Iwerne Courtney or Shroton Dorset 30 E5
Iwerne Minster Dorset 30 E5
Iwood N Som 60 G3
Ixworth Suff 125 C8
Ixworth Thorpe Suff 125 C8

J

Jackfield Telford 132 C3
Jack Green Lancs 194 B5
Jack Hayes Staffs 168 F6
Jack Hill N Yorks 205 C10
Jack in the Green Devon 14 B6
Jacksdale Notts 170 E6
Jack's Green Essex 105 G11
Glos 80 D5
Jack's Hatch Essex 86 D6
Jackson Bridge W Yorks 197 F7
Jackstown Aberds 303 F7
Jacobstow Corn 11 B9
Jacobstowe Devon 25 G9
Jacobs Well Sur 50 C3
Jagger Green W Yorks 196 D5
Jameston Pembs 73 F9
Jamestown Dumfries 249 D8
Highld 300 D4
W Dunb 277 E7
Jamphlars Fife 280 B4
Janetstown Highld 310 C4
Janke's Green Essex 107 F8
Jarrow T&W 243 D8
Jarvis Brook E Sus 37 B8
Jasper's Green Essex 106 F4
Java Argyll 289 F9
Jawcraig Falk 278 F6
Jaw Hill W Yorks 197 C9
Jaywick Essex 89 C11
Jealott's Hill Brack 65 E11
Jeaniefield Borders 271 G10
Jedburgh Borders 262 E5
Jedurgh Borders 262 F5
Jeffreyston Pembs 73 D9
Jellyhill E Dunb 278 G2
Jemimaville Highld 301 C7
Jennetts Hill W Berks 64 E5
Jennyfield N Yorks 205 B11
Jericho Gtr Man 195 E10
Jersey Farm Herts 85 D11
Jersey Marine Neath 57 C8
Jerviswood S Lnrk 269 F7
Jesmond T&W 243 D7
Jevington E Sus 23 E9
Jewell's Cross Corn 24 G3
Jingle Street Mon 79 C7
Jockey End Herts 85 C8
Jodrell Bank Ches E 184 G3
Johnby Cumb 230 E4
John O'Gaunt Leics 136 B4
John O'Gaunts W Yorks 197 B11
John o'Groats Highld 310 B7
John's Cross E Sus 38 C2
Johnshaven Aberds 293 G9
Johnson Fold Gtr Man 195 E7
Johnson's Hillock Lancs 194 C5
Johnson Street Norf 161 F7
Johnston Pembs 72 C6
Johnstone Renfs 267 C8
Johnstonebridge Dumfries 248 E3
Johnstone Mains Aberds 293 F9
Johnstown Carms 74 B6
Wrex 166 F4
Jolly's Bottom Corn 4 F5
Joppa Corn 2 B3
Edin 280 G6
S Ayrs 257 F10
Jordan Green Norf 159 E11
Jordanhill Glasgow 267 B10
Jordans Bucks 85 G7
Jordanston Pembs 91 E8
Jordanthorpe S Yorks 186 E5
Jordon S Yorks 186 C6
Joyford Glos 79 C9
Joy's Green Glos 79 B10
Jubilee Gtr Man 196 E2
Notts 170 E6
Jugbank Staffs 150 B5
Jump S Yorks 197 G11
Jumpers Common Dorset 19 C8
Jumpers Green Dorset 19 C8
Jumper's Town E Sus 52 G3
Junction N Yorks 204 D6
Juniper Northumb 241 F10
Juniper Green Edin 270 B3
Jurby East IoM 192 C4
Jurby West IoM 192 C4
Jurston Devon 13 E9
Jury's Gap E Sus 39 D7

K

Kaber Cumb 222 C5
Kaimend S Lnrk 269 F9
Kaimes Edin 270 B5
Kaimrig End Borders 269 G11
Kalemouth Borders 262 D6
Kame Fife 287 G7
Kames Argyll 275 B9
Argyll 275 F10
E Ayrs 258 D5
Kates Hill W Mid 133 E9
Kea Corn 4 G6
Keadby N Lincs 199 E10
Keal Cotes Lincs 174 C5
Kearby Town End N Yorks 206 D2
Kearnsey Kent 55 E9
Kearsley Gtr Man 195 F9
Kearstwick Cumb 212 C2
Kearton N Yorks 223 F9
Kearvaig Highld 306 B7
Keasden N Yorks 212 F4
Kebroyd W Yorks 196 C4
Keckwick Halton 183 E9
Keddington Lincs 190 D4
Keddington Corner Lincs 190 D5
Kedington Suff 106 B4
Kedleston Derbys 170 G4
Kedslie Borders 271 G11
Keekle Cumb 219 B10
Keelars Tye Essex 107 G11
Keelby Lincs 201 E7
Keele Staffs 168 F4
Keeley Green Beds 103 B10
Keelham W Yorks 205 G7
Keenley Northumb 241 F7
Keenthorne Som 43 F8
Keeres Green Essex 87 C9
Keeston Pembs 72 B6
Keevil Wilts 46 B2
Kegworth Leics 153 D9
Kehelland Corn 4 G2
Keig Aberds 293 B8
Keighley W Yorks 205 E7
Keil Highld 289 D11
Keilarsbrae Clack 279 C7
Keilhill Aberds 303 D7
Keillmore Argyll 275 E7
Keillor Perth 286 C6
Keillour Perth 286 E3
Keills Argyll 274 G5
Keils Argyll 274 G6
Keinton Mandeville Som 44 G4
Keir Mill Dumfries 247 E9
Keisby Lincs 155 D10
Keiss Highld 310 C7
Keistle Highld 298 D4
Keith Moray 302 D4
Keith Hall Aberds 303 G7
Keith Inch Aberds 303 E11
Keithock Angus 293 G8
Kelbrook Lancs 204 E4
Kelby Lincs 173 G8
Kelcliffe W Yorks 205 E9
Keld Cumb 221 C11
N Yorks 223 E7
Keldholme N Yorks 216 B4
Keld Houses N Yorks 214 G2
Kelfield N Lincs 199 G10
N Yorks 207 F7
Kelham Notts 172 D3
Kelhurn Argyll 276 F6
Kellacott Devon 12 D4
Kellamergh Lancs 194 B2
Kellan Argyll 289 E7
Kellas Angus 287 D8
Moray 301 D11
Kellaton Devon 9 G11
Kellaways Wilts 62 D3
Kelleth Cumb 222 D3
Kelleythorpe E Yorks 208 B5
E Yorks 208 B6
Kelling Norf 177 E9
Kellingley N Yorks 198 C4
Kellington N Yorks 198 C5
Kelloe Durham 234 D2
Kelloholm Dumfries 258 G6
Kells Cumb 219 B9
Kelly Corn 10 G6
Devon 12 E3
Kelly Bray Corn 12 G3
Kelmarsh Northants 120 B4
Kelmscott Oxon 82 F3
Kelsale Suff 127 D7
Kelsall Ches W 167 B8
Kelsall Hill Ches W 167 B8
Kelsay Argyll 254 B2
Kelshall Herts 104 D6
Kelsick Cumb 238 G5
Kelso Borders 262 C6
Kelstedge Derbys 170 C4
Kelstern Lincs 190 C3
Kelsterton Flint 182 G3
Kelston Bath 61 F8
Keltneyburn Perth 285 C11
Kelton Dumfries 237 B11
Durham 232 G4
Kelty Fife 280 C2
Keltybridge Fife 280 B2
Kelvedon Essex 88 B5
Kelvedon Hatch Essex 87 F9
Kelvin S Lnrk 268 E2
Kelvindale Glasgow 267 B11
Kelvinside Glasgow 267 B11
Kelynack Corn 1 D3
Kemacott Devon 41 D7
Kemback Fife 287 F8
Kemberton Shrops 132 C4
Kemble Glos 81 F7
Kemble Wick Glos 81 F7
Kemerton Worcs 99 D8
Kemeys Commander Mon 78 E4
Kemincham Ches E 168 B4
Kemnay Aberds 293 B9
Kempe's Corner Kent 54 D4
Kempie Highld 308 D4
Kempley Glos 98 F3
Kempley Green Glos 98 F3
Kempsey Worcs 99 B7
Kempsford Glos 81 F11
Kemps Green Warks 118 C2
Kempshott Hants 48 C6
Kempston Beds 103 B10
Kempston Church End Beds 103 B10
Kempston Hardwick Beds 103 C10
Kempston West End Beds 103 B9
Kempton Shrops 131 G7
Kemp Town Brighton 36 G4
Kemsing Kent 52 B4
Kemsley Kent 70 F2
Kemsley Street Kent 69 G10
Kenardington Kent 54 G3
Kenchester Hereford 97 C8
Kencot Oxon 82 E3
Kendal Cumb 221 G10
Kendal End Worcs 117 C10
Kendleshire S Glos 61 D7
Kendon Caerph 77 F11
Kendoon Dumfries 246 F4
Kendray S Yorks 197 F11
Kenfig Bridgend 57 E10
Kenfig Hill Bridgend 57 E10
Kengharair Argyll 288 E6
Kenilworth Warks 118 C5
Kenknock Stirl 285 D8
Kenley London 51 B10
Shrops 131 C11
Kenmore Argyll 284 G4
Highld 299 D7
Perth 285 C11
Kenmure Dumfries 237 B8
Kenn Devon 14 D4
N Som 60 F2
Kennacley W Isles 305 J3
Kennacraig Argyll 275 G9
Kennards House Corn 11 E11
Kenneggy Corn 2 D3
Kenneggy Downs Corn 2 D3
Kennerleigh Devon 26 F4
Kennet Clack 279 C8
Kennet End Suff 124 D4
Kennethmont Aberds 302 G5
Kennett Cambs 124 D3
Kennford Devon 14 D4
Kenninghall Norf 141 F10
Kenninghall Heath Norf 141 G10
Kennington Kent 54 E4
London 67 D10
Oxon 83 E8
Kenn Moor Gate N Som 60 F2
Kennoway Fife 287 G7
Kenny Som 28 D4
Kenny Hill Suff 124 B3
Kennythorpe N Yorks 216 F5
Kenovay Argyll 288 E1
Kensaleyre Highld 298 D4
Kensal Green London 67 C8
Kensal Rise London 67 C8
Kensal Town London 67 C8
Kensary Highld 310 E6
Kensington London 67 D9
Mers 182 C5
Kensworth C Beds 85 B8
Kentallen Highld 284 B4
Kentchurch Hereford 97 F8
Kentford Suff 124 D4
Kentisbeare Devon 27 F9
Kentisbury Devon 40 E6
Kentisbury Ford Devon 40 E6
Kentish Town London 67 C9
Kentmere Cumb 221 E9
Kenton Devon 14 E5
London 67 B7
Suff 126 D3
T&W 242 D6
Kenton Bankfoot T&W 242 D6
Kenton Bar T&W 242 D6
Kenton Corner Suff 126 D4
Kenton Green Glos 80 C3
Kentra Highld 289 C8
Kentrigg Cumb 221 G10
Kents Corn 11 B9
Kents Bank Cumb 211 D7
Kent's Green Glos 98 G4
Kents Hill M Keynes 103 D7
Kent's Oak Hants 32 C4
Kent Street E Sus 38 D3
Kent 53 C7
W Sus 36 C2
Kenwick Shrops 149 C8
Kenwick Park Shrops 149 D8
Kenwyn Corn 4 F6
Kenyon Warr 183 B10
Keoldale Highld 308 C3
Keonchulish Ho Highld 307 K6
Kepdowrie Stirl 277 C11
Kepnal Wilts 63 G7
Keppanach Highld 290 G2
Keppoch Highld 295 C11
Keprigan Argyll 255 F7
Kepwick N Yorks 225 G9
Kerchesters Borders 263 B7
Kerdiston Norf 159 E11
Keresforth Hill S Yorks 197 F10
Keresley W Mid 134 G6
Keresley Newlands Warks 134 G6
Kerfield Borders 270 G5
Kerley Downs Corn 4 G5
Kernborough Devon 8 G5
Kerne Bridge Hereford 79 B9
Kernsary Highld 299 B8
Kerridge Ches E 184 F6
Kerridge-end Ches E 184 F6
Kerris Corn 1 D4
Kerry / Ceri Powys 130 F2
Kerrycroy Argyll 266 C2
Kerry Hill Staffs 168 F6
Kerrysdale Highld 299 B8
Kerry's Gate Hereford 97 E7
Kersal Gtr Man 195 G10
Kersall Notts 172 C2
Kersbrook Cross Corn 12 F2
Kerscott Devon 25 B10
Kersey Suff 107 C10
Kersey Tye Suff 107 C9
Kersey Upland Suff 107 C9
Kershopefoot Cumb 249 G11
Kersoe Worcs 99 D9
Kerswell Devon 27 F9
Kerswell Green Worcs 99 B7
Kerthen Wood Corn 2 C3
Kesgrave Suff 108 B4
Kessingland Suff 143 F10
Kessingland Beach Suff 143 F10
Kessington E Dunb 277 G11
Kestle Corn 5 F9
Kestle Mill Corn 5 D7
Keston London 68 G2
Keston Mark London 68 F2
Keswick Cumb 229 G11
Norf 142 C4
Norf 161 C7
Kete Pembs 72 E4
Ketford Glos 98 E4
Ketley Telford 150 G3
Ketley Bank Telford 150 G3
Ketsby Lincs 190 F5
Kettering Northants 121 B7
Ketteringham Norf 142 C3
Kettins Perth 286 D6
Kettlebaston Suff 125 G9
Kettlebridge Fife 287 G7
Kettlebrook Staffs 134 C4
Kettleburgh Suff 126 E5
Kettle Corner Kent 53 C8
Kettle Green Herts 86 B6
Kettlehill Fife 287 G7
Kettleholm Dumfries 238 B4
Kettleness N Yorks 226 B6
Kettleshulme Ches E 185 F7
Kettleshume Ches E 185 F7
Kettlesing N Yorks 205 B10
Kettlesing Bottom N Yorks 205 B10
Kettlesing Head N Yorks 205 B10
Kettlestone Norf 159 C9
Kettlethorpe Lincs 188 F4
W Yorks 197 D10
Kettletoft Orkney 314 C6
Kettlewell N Yorks 213 E9
Ketton Rutland 137 C9
Kevingtown London 68 F3
Kew London 67 D7
Keward Som 44 E4
Kew Bridge London 67 D7
Kewstoke N Som 59 G10
Kexbrough S Yorks 197 F9
Kexby Lincs 188 D5
York 207 C10
Keybridge Corn 11 G7
Keycol Kent 69 G11
Keyford Som 45 D9
Key Green Ches E 168 C5
N Yorks 226 E6
Keyham Leics 136 B3
Keyhaven Hants 20 C2
Keyingham E Yorks 201 B8
Keymer W Sus 36 D4
Keynsham Bath 61 F7
Keysers Estate Essex 86 D5
Key's Green Kent 53 F7
Keysoe Beds 121 E11
Keysoe Row Beds 121 E11
Keyston Cambs 121 B10
Key Street Kent 69 G11
Keyworth Notts 154 C2
Khantore Aberds 292 D4
Kibbear Som 28 C2
Kibblesworth T&W 242 F6
Kibworth Beauchamp Leics 136 E3
Kibworth Harcourt Leics 136 E3
Kidbrooke London 68 D2
Kidburngill Cumb 229 G7
Kiddal Lane End W Yorks 206 F4
Kiddemore Green Staffs 133 B7
Kidderminster Worcs 116 B6
Kiddington Oxon 101 G8
Kidd's Moor Norf 142 C2
Kidlington Oxon 83 C7
Kidmore End Oxon 65 D7
Kidnal Ches W 167 F7
Kidsdale Dumfries 236 F6
Kidsgrove Staffs 168 E4
Kidstones N Yorks 213 C9
Kidwelly / Cydweli Carms 74 D6
Kiel Crofts Argyll 289 F11
Kielder Northumb 250 E4
Kierfiold Ho Orkney 314 E2
Kiff Green W Berks 64 F5
Kilbagie Fife 279 D8
Kilbarchan Renfs 267 C8
Kilbeg Highld 295 E8
Kilberry Argyll 275 G8
Kilbirnie N Ayrs 266 E6
Kilbowie W Dunb 277 G10
Kilbraur Highld 311 H2
Kilbride Argyll 254 C4
Argyll 275 D9
Argyll 289 G10
Argyll 289 G11
Highld 295 C7
Kilbridemore Argyll 275 D11
Kilbryde Castle Stirl 285 G11
Kilburn Angus 292 G5
Derbys 170 F5
London 67 C9
N Yorks 215 D10
Kilby Leics 136 D2
Kilby Bridge Leics 136 D2
Kilchamaig Argyll 275 G9
Kilchattan Argyll 274 D4
Kilchattan Bay Argyll 266 E2
Kilchenzie Argyll 255 E7
Kilcheran Argyll 289 F10
Kilchiaran Argyll 274 G3
Kilchoan Argyll 275 B8
Highld 288 C6
Kilchoman Argyll 274 G3
Kilchrenan Argyll 284 E4
Kilconquhar Fife 287 G8
Kilcot Glos 98 F3
Kilcoy Highld 300 D5
Kilcreggan Argyll 276 E4
Kildale N Yorks 226 D2
Kildalloig Argyll 255 F8
Kildary Highld 301 B7
Kildaton Ho Argyll 254 C5
Kildavanan Argyll 275 G11
Kildermorie Lodge Highld 300 B5
Kildonan Dumfries 236 D2
Highld 298 D3
N Ayrs 256 E2
Kildonan Lodge Highld 311 G3
Kildonnan Highld 294 G6
Kildrum N Lnrk 278 F5
Kildrummy Aberds 292 B6
Kildwick N Yorks 204 D6
Kilfinan Argyll 275 F10
Kilfinnan Highld 290 D4
Kilgetty Pembs 73 D10
Kilgour Fife 286 G6
Kilgrammie S Ayrs 245 C7
Kilgwrrwg Common Mon 79 F7
Kilhallon Corn 5 E11
Kilham E Yorks 217 G11
Northumb 263 C9
Kilkeddan Argyll 255 E8
Kilkenneth Argyll 288 E1
Kilkenny Glos 81 B8
Kilkerran Argyll 255 F8
Kilkhampton Corn 24 E3
Killamarsh Derbys 187 E7
Killaworgey Corn 5 C8
Killay Swansea 56 C6
Killbeg Argyll 289 E8
Killean Argyll 255 C7
Killearn Stirl 277 D10
Killegruer Argyll 255 D7
Killen Highld 300 D6
Killerby Darl 224 B3
Killichonan Perth 285 B9
Killiechoinich Argyll 289 G10
Killiechonate Highld 290 E4
Killiechronan Argyll 289 E7
Killiecrankie Perth 291 G11
Killiemor Argyll 288 F6
Killiemore House Argyll 288 G6
Killilan Highld 295 B11
Killimster Highld 310 D7
Killin Stirl 285 D9
Killinallan Argyll 274 F4
Killingbeck W Yorks 206 G2
Killinghall N Yorks 205 B11
Killington Cumb 212 B2
Devon 41 D7
Killingworth T&W 243 C7
Killingworth Moor T&W 243 C7
Killingworth Village T&W 243 C7
Killin Lodge Highld 291 C7
Killivose Corn 2 B4
Killmahumaig Argyll 275 D8
Killochyett Borders 271 F9
Killocraw Argyll 255 D7
Killundine Highld 289 E7
Killylung Dumfries 247 G11
Kilmacolm Invclyd 267 B7
Kilmaha Argyll 275 C10
Kilmahog Stirl 285 G10
Kilmalieu Highld 289 D10
Kilmaluag Highld 298 B4
Kilmany Fife 287 E7
Kilmarie Highld 295 D7
Kilmarnock E Ayrs 257 B10
Kilmaron Castle Fife 287 F7
Kilmartin Argyll 275 D9
Kilmaurs E Ayrs 267 G8
Kilmelford Argyll 275 B9
Kilmeny Argyll 274 G4
Kilmersdon Som 45 C7
Kilmeston Hants 33 B9
Kilmichael Argyll 255 E7
Argyll 275 F10
Kilmichael Glassary Argyll 275 D9
Kilmichael of Inverlussa Argyll 275 E8
Kilmington Devon 15 B11
Wilts 45 F9
Kilmington Common Wilts 45 F9
Kilmoluaig Argyll 288 E1
Kilmonivaig Highld 290 E3
Kilmorack Highld 300 E4
Kilmore Argyll 289 G10
Highld 295 E8
Kilmory Argyll 275 F8
Highld 289 B7
Highld 294 E5
N Ayrs 255 E10
Kilmory Lodge Argyll 275 C8
Kilmote Highld 311 H3
Kilmuir Highld 298 B3
Highld 298 E2
Highld 300 E6
Highld 301 B7
Kilmun Argyll 275 B10
Argyll 276 E3
Kilnave Argyll 274 F3
Kilncadzow S Lnrk 269 F7
Kilndown Kent 53 G8
Kiln Green Hereford 79 B10
Wokingham 65 D10
Kilnhill Cumb 229 E10
Kilnhurst S Yorks 187 B7
Kilninian Argyll 288 E5
Kilninver Argyll 289 G10
Kiln Pit Hill Northumb 242 G2
Kilnsea E Yorks 201 D12
Kilnsey N Yorks 213 F9
Kilnwick E Yorks 208 D5
Kilnwick Percy E Yorks 208 C2
Kiloran Argyll 274 D4
Kilpatrick N Ayrs 255 E10
Kilpeck Hereford 97 E8
Kilphedir Highld 311 H3
Kilpin E Yorks 199 B9
Kilpin Pike E Yorks 199 B9
Kilrenny Fife 287 G9
Kilsby Northants 119 C11
Kilspindie Perth 286 E6
Kilsyth N Lnrk 278 F4
Kiltarlity Highld 300 E5
Kilton Notts 187 F9
Redcar 226 B4
Som 43 E7
Kilton Thorpe Redcar 226 B3
Kiltyrie Perth 285 D10
Kilvaxter Highld 298 C3
Kilve Som 43 E7
Kilvington Notts 172 G3
Kilwinning N Ayrs 266 G6
Kimberley Norf 141 C11
Notts 171 G8
Kimberworth S Yorks 186 C6
Kimberworth Park S Yorks 186 C6
Kimblesworth Durham 233 B11
Kimble Wick Bucks 84 D4
Kimbolton Cambs 121 D11
Hereford 115 E10
Kimbridge Hants 32 B4
Kimcote Leics 135 F11
Kimmeridge Dorset 18 F4
Kimmerston Northumb 263 B11
Kimpton Hants 47 D9
Herts 85 B11
Kimworthy Devon 24 E4
Kinabus Argyll 254 C3
Kinbeachie Highld 300 C6
Kinbrace Highld 310 F2
Kinbuck Stirl 285 G11
Kincaidston S Ayrs 257 F9
Kincaple Fife 287 F8
Kincardine Fife 279 D8
Highld 309 L6
Kincardine Bridge Falk 279 D8
Kincardine O'Neil Aberds 293 D7
Kinclaven Perth 286 D5
Kincorth Aberdeen 293 C11
Kincorth Ho Moray 301 C10
Kincraig Highld 291 C10
Kincraigie Perth 286 C3
Kindallachan Perth 286 C3
Kine Moor S Yorks 197 G9
Kineton Glos 99 F11
Warks 118 G6
Kineton Green W Mid 134 G2
Kinfauns Perth 286 E5
Kingairloch Highld 289 D10
Kingarth Argyll 255 B11
Kingates IoW 20 F6
Kingbeare Corn 11 G11
Kingcoed Mon 78 D6
Kingdown N Som 60 G4
King Edward Aberds 303 D7
Kingerby Lincs 189 C9
Kingfield Sur 50 B4
Kingford Devon 24 F3
Devon 25 D10
Kingham Oxon 100 G5
Kinghay Wilts 30 B5
Kingholm Quay Dumfries 237 B11
Kinghorn Fife 280 D5
Kingie Highld 290 C3
Kinglassie Fife 280 B4
Kingledores Borders 260 D4
Kingoodie Perth 287 E7
King's Acre Hereford 97 C9
Kingsand Corn 7 E8
Kingsash Bucks 84 D5
Kingsbarns Fife 287 F9
Kingsbridge Devon 8 G4
Som 42 F3
King's Bromley Staffs 152 F2
Kingsburgh Highld 298 D3
Kingsbury London 67 B8
Warks 134 D4
Kingsbury Episcopi Som 28 C6
Kingsbury Regis Som 29 D11
King's Caple Hereford 97 F11
Kingscauseway Highld 301 B7
Kingscavil W Loth 279 F10
Kingsclere Hants 48 B4
Kingsclere Woodlands Hants 64 G4
King's Cliffe Northants 137 D10
Kings Clipstone Notts 171 C10
Kingscote Glos 80 F4
Kingscott Devon 25 D8
King's Coughton Warks 117 F11
Kingscourt Glos 80 E4
Kingscross N Ayrs 256 D2
Kingsditch Glos 99 G8
Kingsdon Som 29 B8
Kingsdown Kent 54 B2
Kent 55 D11
Swindon 63 B7
Wilts 61 F10
King's Dyke Cambs 138 D4
Kingseat Fife 280 C2
Kingseathill Fife 280 D2
King's End Worcs 116 G6
Kingsett Devon 12 E6
Kingsey Bucks 84 D2
Kingsfield Hereford 97 B10
Kingsfold Lancs 194 B4
W Sus 51 F7
Kingsford Aberds 293 B7
E Ayrs 267 F8
Worcs 132 G6
Kingsforth N Lincs 200 D4
King's Furlong Hants 48 C6
Kingsgate Kent 71 E11
King's Green Glos 98 E5
Worcs 116 E5
Kingshall Green Suff 125 E8
Kingshall Street Suff 125 E8
Kingsheanton Devon 40 F5
King's Heath Northants 120 E4
W Mid 133 G11
Kings Hedges Cambs 123 E9
Kingshill Glos 80 F3
Swindon 62 C6
Kings Hill Glos 81 E8
King's Hill Kent 53 C7
W Mid 133 D9
Kingsholm Glos 80 B4
Kingshouse Hotel Highld 284 B6
Kingshurst W Mid 134 F3
Kingside Hill Cumb 238 G5
Kingskerswell Devon 9 B7
Kingskettle Fife 287 G7
Kingsknowe Edin 280 G4
Kingsland Anglesey 178 E2
Hereford 115 E8
London 67 C10
Shrops 149 G9
Kings Langley Herts 85 E9
Kingsley Ches W 183 G9
Hants 49 F9
Staffs 169 F8
Kingsley Green W Sus 49 G11
Kingsley Holt Staffs 169 F8
Kingsley Moor Staffs 169 F7
Kingsley Park Northants 120 E5
Kingslow Shrops 132 D5
King's Lynn Norf 158 E2
King's Meaburn Cumb 231 G8
Kingsmead Hants 33 E9
King's Mills Derbys 153 D8
Wrex 166 F4
Kingsmoor Essex 86 D6
Kings Moss Mers 194 G4
Kingsmuir Angus 287 C8
Fife 287 G9
Kings Muir Borders 261 B7
King's Newnham Warks 119 B9
King's Newton Derbys 153 D7
Kingsnordley Shrops 132 F5
Kingsnorth Kent 54 F4
King's Norton Leics 136 C3
W Mid 117 B11
King's Nympton Devon 25 D11
King's Pyon Hereford 115 G8
Kings Ripton Cambs 122 B5
King's Somborne Hants 47 G11
King's Stag Dorset 30 E2
King's Stanley Glos 80 E4
King's Sutton Northants 101 D9
King's Tamerton Plym 7 D9
Kingstanding W Mid 133 E11
Kingsteignton Devon 14 G3
Kingsteps Highld 301 D9
King Sterndale Derbys 185 G9
King's Thorn Hereford 97 E10
Kingsthorpe Northants 120 E5
Kingsthorpe Hollow Northants 120 E5
Kingston Cambs 122 F6
Devon 8 F2
Devon 9 E8
Dorset 18 F5
Dorset 30 F3
E Loth 281 E10
Gtr Man 184 B6
Hants 31 G11
IoW 20 E5
Kent 55 C7
M Keynes 103 D8
Moray 302 C3
Ptsmth 33 G11
Suff 108 B5
Kingston Bagpuize Oxon 82 F6
Kingston Blount Oxon 84 F2
Kingston by Sea W Sus 36 G2
Kingston Deverill Wilts 45 F10
Kingstone Hereford 97 D8
Hereford 98 G2
Som 28 E5
Staffs 151 D11
S Yorks 197 F10
Kingstone Winslow Oxon 63 B9
Kingston Gorse W Sus 35 G9
Kingston Lisle Oxon 63 B10
Kingston Maurward Dorset 17 C10
Kingston near Lewes E Sus 36 F5
Kingston on Soar Notts 153 D10
Kingston Park T&W 242 D6
Kingston Russell Dorset 17 C7
Kingston St Mary Som 28 B2
Kingston Seymour N Som 60 F2
Kingston Stert Oxon 84 E2
Kingston upon Hull Hull 200 B5
Kingston upon Thames London 67 F7
Kingston Vale London 67 E8
Kingstown Cumb 239 F9
King Street Essex 87 E9
King's Walden Herts 104 G3
Kingsway Bath 61 G8
Halton 183 D8
Kingswear Devon 9 E7
Kingswells Aberdeen 293 C10
Kingswinford W Mid 133 F7
Kingswood Bucks 83 B11
Essex 69 B8
Glos 80 G2
Hereford 114 G5
Herts 85 E10
Kent 53 C10
Powys 130 C4
S Glos 60 E6
Som 42 F6
Sur 51 B8
Warks 118 C3
Warr 183 C9
Kingswood Brook Warks 118 C3
Kingswood Common Staffs 132 C6
Worcs 116 D4
Kings Worthy Hants 48 G3
Kingthorpe Lincs 189 F10
Kington Hereford 114 F5
S Glos 79 G10
Worcs 117 F9
Kington Langley Wilts 62 D2
Kington Magna Dorset 30 C3
Kington St Michael Wilts 62 D2
Kingussie Highld 291 C9
Kingweston Som 44 G4
Kinhrive Highld 301 B7
Kininvie Ho Moray 302 E3
Kinkell Bridge Perth 286 F3
Kinknockie Aberds 303 E10
Aberds 303 G9
Kinkry Hill Cumb 240 B2
Kinlet Shrops 132 G4
Kinloch Fife 286 F6
Highld 289 D8
Highld 294 F5
Highld 295 D8
Highld 308 F3
Perth 286 C5
Perth 286 C6
Kinlochan Highld 289 C10
Kinlochard Stirl 285 G8
Kinlochbeoraid Highld 295 G10
Kinlochbervie Highld 306 D7
Kinloch Damph Highld 299 E8
Kinlocheil Highld 289 B11
Kinlochewe Highld 299 C10
Kinloch Hourn Highld 295 E11
Kinloch Laggan Highld 291 E7
Kinlochleven Highld 290 G3
Kinloch Lodge Highld 308 D5
Kinlochmoidart Highld 289 B9
Kinlochmorar Highld 295 F10
Kinlochmore Highld 290 G3
Kinloch Rannoch Perth 285 B10
Kinlochspelve Argyll 289 G8
Kinloid Highld 295 G8
Kinloss Moray 301 C10
Kinmel Bay / Bae Cinmel Conwy 181 E7
Kinmuck Aberds 293 B10
Kinmundy Aberds 293 B10
Kinnadie Aberds 303 E9
Kinnaird Perth 286 B3
Perth 286 E6
Kinnaird Castle Angus 287 B10
Kinnauld Highld 309 J7
Kinneff Aberds 293 F10
Kinneil Falk 279 E9
Kinnelhead Dumfries 248 C2
Kinnell Angus 287 B10
Kinnerley Shrops 148 E6
Kinnersley Hereford 96 B6
Worcs 99 C7
Kinnerton Powys 114 E4
Kinnerton Green Flint 166 C4
Kinnesswood Perth 286 G5
Kinninvie Durham 233 G7
Kinnordy Angus 287 B7
Kinoulton Notts 154 C3
Kinross Perth 286 G5
Kinrossie Perth 286 D5
Kinsbourne Green Herts 85 B10
Kinsey Heath Ches E 167 G11
Kinsham Hereford 115 E7
Worcs 99 D8
Kinsley W Yorks 198 E2
Kinson Bmouth 19 B7
Kintallan Argyll 275 E8
Kintbury W Berks 63 F11
Kintessack Moray 301 C9
Kintillo Perth 286 F5
Kintocher Aberds 293 C7
Kinton Hereford 115 C8
Shrops 149 F7
Kintore Aberds 293 B9
Kintour Argyll 254 B5
Kintra Argyll 254 C4
Argyll 288 G5
Kintradwell Highld 311 J3
Kintraw Argyll 275 C9
Kinuachdrachd Argyll 275 D8
Kinveachy Highld 291 B11
Kinver Staffs 132 G6
Kinwalsey Warks 134 F5
Kip Hill Durham 242 G6
Kiplin N Yorks 224 F5
Kippax W Yorks 206 G4
Kippen Stirl 278 C3
Kippford or Scaur Dumfries 237 D10
Kippilaw Borders 262 D2
Kippilaw Mains Borders 262 D2
Kipping's Cross Kent 52 F6
Kippington Kent 52 C4
Kirbister Orkney 314 D6
Orkney 314 E2
Orkney 314 F3
Kirbuster Orkney 314 D2
Kirby Bedon Norf 142 B5
Kirby Bellars Leics 154 F4
Kirby Cane Norf 143 E7
Kirby Corner W Mid 118 B5
Kirby Cross Essex 108 G4
Kirby Fields Leics 135 C10
Kirby Green Norf 143 E7
Kirby Grindalythe N Yorks 217 F8
Kirby Hill N Yorks 215 F7
N Yorks 224 D2
Kirby Knowle N Yorks 215 B9
Kirby-le-Soken Essex 108 G4
Kirby Misperton N Yorks 216 D5
Kirby Moor Cumb 240 E2
Kirby Muxloe Leics 135 C10
Kirby Row Norf 143 E7
Kirby Sigston N Yorks 225 G8
Kirby Underdale E Yorks 208 B2
Kirby Wiske N Yorks 215 C7
Kirdford W Sus 35 B8
Kirk Highld 310 D6
Kirkabister Shetland 312 G6
Shetland 313 K6
Kirkandrews Dumfries 237 E8
Kirkandrews-on-Eden Cumb 239 F9
Kirkapol Argyll 288 E2
Kirkbampton Cumb 239 F8
Kirkbean Dumfries 237 D11
Kirkborough Cumb 229 D7
Kirkbrae Orkney 314 B4
Kirk Bramwith S Yorks 198 E6
Kirkbride Cumb 238 F6
Kirkbridge N Yorks 224 G5
Kirkbuddo Angus 287 C9

Kirkburn Borders 261 B7
E Yorks 208 B5
Kirkburton W Yorks 197 E7
Kirkby Lincs 189 C9
Mers 182 B6
N Yorks 225 D10
Kirkby Fenside Lincs 174 C4
Kirkby Fleetham
N Yorks 224 G5
Kirkby Green Lincs 173 D9
Kirkby Hill N Yorks 215 F7
Kirkby in Ashfield Notts 171 D8
Kirkby-in-Furness
Cumb 210 C4
Kirkby la Thorpe Lincs 173 F10
Kirkby Lonsdale Cumb 212 D2
Kirkby Malham N Yorks 213 G7
Kirkby Mallory Leics 135 C9
Kirkby Malzeard
N Yorks 214 E4
Kirkby Mills N Yorks 216 B4
Kirkbymoorside
N Yorks 216 B3
Kirkby on Bain Lincs 174 C2
Kirkby Overblow
N Yorks 206 D2
Kirkby Stephen Cumb 222 D5
Kirkby Thore Cumb 231 F8
Kirkby Underwood
Lincs 155 D11
Kirkby Wharfe N Yorks 206 E6
Kirkby Woodhouse
Notts 171 E7
Kirkcaldy Fife 280 C5
Kirkcambeck Cumb 240 D2
Kirkcarswell Dumfries 237 E9
Kirkcolm Dumfries 236 C2
Kirkconnel Dumfries 258 G6
Kirkconnell Dumfries 237 C11
Kirkcowan Dumfries 236 C5
Kirkcudbright Dumfries 237 D8
Kirkdale Mers 182 C4
Kirk Deighton N Yorks 206 C3
Kirk Ella E Yorks 200 B4
Kirkfieldbank S Lnrk 269 G7
Kirkforthar Feus Fife 286 G6
Kirkgunzeon Dumfries 237 C10
Kirk Hallam Derbys 171 G7
Kirkham Lancs 202 G4
N Yorks 216 F4
Kirkhamgate W Yorks 197 C9
Kirk Hammerton
N Yorks 206 B5
Kirkhams Gtr Man 195 F10
Kirkharle Northumb 252 G2
Kirkheaton Northumb 242 B2
W Yorks 197 D7
Kirkhill Angus 293 G8
E Renf 267 D11
Highld 300 E5
Midloth 270 C4
Moray 302 F2
W Loth 279 G11
Kirkholt Gtr Man 195 E11
Kirkhope Borders 261 E9
Kirkhouse Borders 261 C8
Cumb 240 F3
Kirkiboll Highld 308 D5
Kirkibost Highld 295 D7
Kirkinch Angus 287 C7
Kirkinner Dumfries 236 D6
Kirkintilloch E Dunb 278 G3
Kirk Ireton Derbys 170 E3
Kirkland Cumb 219 B11
Cumb 229 B11
Cumb 231 E8
Dumfries 247 E8
Dumfries 258 G6
S Ayrs 244 E6
Kirkland Guards Cumb 229 C9
Kirk Langley Derbys 152 B5
Kirkleatham Redcar 235 G7
Kirklees Gtr Man 195 E9
Kirklevington Stockton 225 D8
Kirkley Suff 143 E10
Kirklington Notts 171 D11
N Yorks 214 C6
Kirklinton Cumb 239 D10
Kirkliston Edin 280 G2
Kirkmaiden Dumfries 236 F3
Kirk Merrington
Durham 233 E11
Kirkmichael Perth 286 B4
S Ayrs 245 B8
Kirk Michael IoM 192 C4
Kirkmichael Mains
Dumfries 248 F2
Kirkmuirhill S Lnrk 268 G5
Kirknewton Northumb 263 C10
W Loth 270 B2
Kirkney Aberds 302 F5
Kirk of Shotts N Lnrk 268 C6
Kirkoswald Cumb 231 C7
S Ayrs 244 B6
Kirkpatrick Dumfries 247 E10
Kirkpatrick Durham
Dumfries 237 B9
Kirkpatrick-Fleming
Dumfries 239 C7
Kirk Sandall S Yorks 198 F6
Kirksanton Cumb 210 C2
Kirkshaw N Lnrk 268 C4
Kirk Smeaton N Yorks 198 D4
Kirkstall W Yorks 205 F11
Kirkstead Borders 261 E7
Lincs 173 C11
Kirkstile Aberds 302 F5
Kirkstyle Highld 310 B7
Kirkthorpe W Yorks 197 C11
Kirkton Aberds 302 E6
Aberds 302 G6
Angus 286 C6
Angus 287 C8
Angus 287 D8
Argyll 275 C8
Borders 262 G2
Dumfries 247 G11
Fife 280 D4
Fife 287 E7
Highld 295 C10
Highld 299 E9
Highld 301 D7
Highld 309 K7
Perth 286 F3
S Lnrk 259 E10
Stirl 285 G9
W Loth 269 B10
Kirktonhill Borders 271 E9
W Dunb 277 G7
Kirkton Manor Borders 260 B6
Kirkton of Airlie Angus 287 B7
Kirkton of Auchterhouse
Angus 287 D7
Kirkton of Auchterless
Aberds 303 E7
Kirkton of Barevan
Highld 301 E8
Kirkton of Bourtie
Aberds 303 G8
Kirkton of Collace
Perth 286 D5
Kirkton of Craig Angus 287 B11
Kirkton of Culsalmond
Aberds 302 F6
Kirkton of Durris
Aberds 293 D9
Kirkton of Glenbuchat
Aberds 292 B5
Kirkton of Glenisla
Angus 292 G4
Kirkton of Kingoldrum
Angus 287 B7
Kirkton of Largo Fife 287 G8
Kirkton of Lethendy
Perth 286 C5
Kirkton of Logie Buchan
Aberds 303 G9
Kirkton of Maryculter
Aberds 293 D10
Kirkton of Menmuir
Angus 293 G7
Kirkton of Monikie
Angus 287 D9
Kirkton of Oyne Aberds 302 G6
Kirkton of Rayne
Aberds 302 G6
Kirkton of Skene
Aberds 293 C10
Kirkton of Tough
Aberds 293 B8
Kirktoun E Ayrs 267 G8
Kirktown Aberds 303 D10
Kirktown of Alvah
Aberds 302 C6
Kirktown of Deskford
Moray 302 C5
Kirktown of Fetteresso
Aberds 293 E10
Kirktown of Mortlach
Moray 302 F3
Kirktown of Slains
Aberds 303 G10
Kirkurd Borders 270 G2
Kirkwall Orkney 314 E4
Kirkwhelpington
Northumb 251 G11
Kirkwood Dumfries 238 B4
N Lnrk 268 C4
Kirk Yetholm Borders 263 D8
Kirmington N Lincs 200 E6
Kirmond le Mire Lincs 189 C11
Kirn Argyll 276 F3
Kirriemuir Angus 287 B7
Kirstead Green Norf 142 D5
Kirtlebridge Dumfries 238 C6
Kirtleton Dumfries 249 G7
Kirtling Cambs 124 F3
Kirtling Green Cambs 124 F3
Kirtlington Oxon 83 B7
Kirtomy Highld 308 C7
Kirton Lincs 156 B6
Notts 171 B11
Suff 108 D5
Kirton Campus W Loth 269 B10
Kirton End Lincs 174 G3
Kirton Holme Lincs 174 G3
Kirton in Lindsey
N Lincs 188 B6
Kiskin Cumb 210 B1
Kislingbury Northants 120 F3
Kitbridge Devon 28 G4
Kitchenroyd W Yorks 197 F8
Kitebrook Warks 100 E4
Kite Green Warks 118 D3
Kite Hill IoW 21 C7
Kites Hardwick Warks 119 D9
Kit Hill Dorset 30 D4
Kitlye Glos 80 E5
Kit's Coty Kent 69 G8
Kitt Green Gtr Man 194 F5
Kittisford Som 27 C9
Kittle Swansea 56 D5
Kitts End Herts 86 F2
Kitt's Green W Mid 134 F3
Kitt's Moss Gtr Man 184 E5
Kittwhistle Dorset 28 G5
Kittybrewster Aberdeen 293 C11
Kitwell W Mid 133 G9
Kitwood Hants 49 G7
Kivernoll Hereford 97 E9
Kiveton Park S Yorks 187 E7
Knaith Lincs 188 E4
Knaith Park Lincs 188 D4
Knap Corner Dorset 30 C4
Knaphill Sur 50 B3
Knapp Hants 32 C6
Perth 286 D6
Som 28 B4
Wilts 31 B8
Knapp Hill Wilts 30 B5
Knapthorpe Notts 172 D2
Knaptoft Leics 136 F2
Knapton Norf 160 C6
York 207 C7
Knapton Green Hereford 115 G8
Knapwell Cambs 122 E6
Knaresborough N Yorks 206 B3
Knarsdale Northumb 240 G5
Knatts Valley Kent 68 G5
Knauchland Moray 302 D5
Knaven Aberds 303 E8
Knave's Ash Kent 71 G7
Knaves Green Suff 126 D2
Knavesmire York 207 D7
Knayton N Yorks 215 B8
Knebworth Herts 104 G5
Knedlington E Yorks 199 B8
Kneesall Notts 172 C2
Kneesworth Cambs 104 C6
Kneeton Notts 172 F2
Knelston Swansea 56 D3
Knenhall Staffs 151 B8
Knettishall Suff 141 G9
Knightacott Devon 41 F7
Knightcote Warks 119 G7
Knightcott N Som 43 B11
Knightley Staffs 150 D6
Knightley Dale Staffs 150 E6
Knighton Devon 7 F10
Dorset 29 E10
Leicester 135 C11
Oxon 63 B9
Poole 18 B6
Som 43 E7
Staffs 150 D4
Staffs 168 G2
Wilts 63 E9
Worcs 117 F10
Knighton Fields
Leicester 135 C11
Knighton on Teme
Worcs 116 C2
Knighton / Tref-y-Clawdd
Powys 114 C5
Knightor Corn 5 D10
Knightsbridge Glos 99 F7
London 67 D9
Knight's End Cambs 139 E8
Knights Enham Hants 47 D11
Knight's Hill London 67 E10
Knightsmill Corn 11 E7
Knightsridge W Loth 269 B10
Knightswood Glasgow 267 B10
Knightwick Worcs 116 F4
Knill Hereford 114 E5
Knipe Fold Cumb 220 F6
Knipoch Argyll 289 G10
Knipton Leics 154 C6
Knitsley Durham 233 B8
Kniveton Derbys 170 E2
Knocharthur Highld 309 J7
Knock Argyll 289 F7
Cumb 231 F9
Moray 302 D5
Knockally Highld 311 G5
Knockan Highld 307 H7
Knockandhu Moray 302 G2
Knockando Moray 301 E11
Knockando Ho Moray 302 E2
Knockandoo Highld 301 G7
Knockbain Highld 300 D6
Knockbreck Highld 298 C2
Knockbrex Dumfries 237 E7
Knockcarrach Highld 290 B6
Knockdee Highld 310 C5
Knockdolian S Ayrs 244 F4
Knockdow Argyll 276 G2
Knockdown Glos 61 B10
Knockenbaird Aberds 302 G6
Knockenkelly N Ayrs 256 D2
Knockentiber E Ayrs 257 B9
Knockerdown Derbys 170 E2
Knockespock Ho Aberds 302 G5
Knockfarrel Highld 300 D5
Knockglass Dumfries 236 D2
Knockhall Kent 68 E5
Knockhall Castle
Aberds 303 G9
Knockholt Kent 52 B3
Knockholt Pound Kent 52 B3
Knockie Lodge Highld 290 B6
Knockin Shrops 148 E6
Knockin Heath Shrops 149 E7
Knockinlaw E Ayrs 257 B10
Knockinnon Highld 310 F5
Knocklaw Northumb 252 C3
Knocklearn Dumfries 237 B9
Knocklearoch Argyll 274 G4
Knockmill Kent 68 G5
Knocknaha Argyll 255 F7
Knocknain Dumfries 236 C1
Knockothie Aberds 303 F9
Knockrome Argyll 274 F6
Knocksharry IoM 192 D3
Knockstapplemore
Argyll 255 F7
Knockvologan Argyll 274 B4
Knodishall Suff 127 E8
Knokan Argyll 288 G6
Knole Som 29 B7
Knollbury Mon 60 B2
Knoll Green Som 43 F8
Knolls Green Ches E 184 F4
Knoll Top N Yorks 214 F3
Knolton Wrex 149 B7
Knolton Bryn Wrex 149 B7
Knook Wilts 46 E2
Knossington Leics 136 B6
Knotbury Staffs 169 B8
Knott End-on-Sea
Lancs 202 D3
Knotting Beds 121 E10
Knotting Green Beds 121 E10
Knottingley W Yorks 198 C4
Knott Lanes Gtr Man 196 G2
Knott Oak Som 28 E5
Knotts Cumb 230 G4
Lancs 203 C11
Knotty Ash Mers 182 C6
Knotty Corner Devon 24 B6
Knotty Green Bucks 84 G6
Knowbury Shrops 115 C11
Knowe Dumfries 236 B5
Shetland 313 G5
Knowefield Cumb 239 F10
Knowehead Aberds 293 C7
Aberds 302 D5
Dumfries 246 E4
Knowes E Loth 282 F2
Knowesgate Northumb 251 F11
Knowes of Elrick
Aberds 302 D6
Knoweton N Lnrk 268 D5
Knowetop N Lnrk 268 D5
Knowhead Aberds 303 D9
Knowl Bank Staffs 168 F3
Knowle Bristol 60 E6
Devon 15 E7
Devon 26 G3
Devon 27 F8
Devon 40 F3
Hants 33 F9
Shrops 115 C11
Som 43 F10
Wilts 63 G7
W Mid 118 B3
Knowle Fields Worcs 117 F10
Knowlegate Shrops 115 C11
Knowle Green Lancs 203 F8
Sur 66 E4
Knowle Grove W Mid 118 B3
Knowle Hill Sur 66 F3
Knowle Park W Yorks 205 E7
Knowle St Giles Som 28 E4
Knowlesands Shrops 132 E4
Knowles Hill Devon 14 G3
Knowl Green Essex 106 C5
Knowl Hill Windsor 65 D10
Knowlton Dorset 31 E8
Kent 55 C9
Knowl Wall Staffs 151 B7
Knowl Wood W Yorks 196 C2
Knowsley Mers 182 B6
Knowsthorpe W Yorks 206 G2
Knowstone Devon 26 C4
Knox Bridge Kent 53 E9
Knucklas Powys 114 C5
Knuston Northants 121 D8
Knutsford Ches E 184 F3
Knutton Staffs 168 F4
Knuzden Brook Lancs 195 B8
Knypersley Staffs 168 D5
Kraiknish Highld 294 C5
Krumlin W Yorks 196 D5
Kuggar Corn 2 F6
Kyleakin Highld 295 C9
Kyle of Lochalsh Highld 295 C9
Kylepark N Lnrk 268 C3
Kylerhea Highld 295 C9
Kylesknoydart Highld 295 F10
Kylesku Highld 306 F7
Kylesmorar Highld 295 F10
Kylestrome Highld 306 F7
Kyllachy House Highld 301 G7
Kymin Hereford 97 B11
Mon 79 C8
Kynaston Hereford 97 F10
Shrops 149 E7
Kynnersley Telford 150 F3
Kyre Worcs 116 E2
Kyre Green Worcs 116 E2
Kyre Magna Worcs 116 E2
Kyre Park Worcs 116 E2
Kyrewood Worcs 116 D2

L

Labost W Isles 304 D4
Lacasaidh W Isles 304 F5
Lacasdal W Isles 304 E6
Laceby NE Lincs 201 F8
Laceby Acres NE Lincs 201 F8
Lacey Green Bucks 84 F4
Ches E 184 E4
Lach Dennis Ches W 184 G2
Lache Ches W 166 C5
Lackenby Redcar 225 B11
Lackford Suff 124 C5
Lacock Wilts 62 F2
Ladbroke Warks 119 F8
Laddenvean Corn 3 E7
Laddingford Kent 53 D7
Lade Kent 39 C9
Lade Bank Lincs 174 E5
Ladies Riggs N Yorks 214 F2
Ladmanlow Derbys 185 G8
Ladock Corn 5 E7
Ladwell Hants 32 C6
Lady Orkney 314 B6
Ladybank Fife 287 F7
Ladybrook Notts 171 C8
Ladyburn Invclyd 276 F6
Ladycross Corn 12 D2
Ladyes Hill Warks 118 C5
Lady Green Mers 193 G10
Lady Hall Cumb 210 B3
Lady Halton Shrops 115 B9
Lady House Gtr Man 196 E2
Ladykirk Borders 273 F7
Ladyoak Shrops 131 C7
Lady Park T&W 242 F6
Ladyridge Hereford 97 E11
Ladysford Aberds 303 C9
Lady's Green Suff 124 F5
Ladywell London 67 E11
Shrops 149 C9
W Loth 269 B10
Ladywood Telford 132 C3
W Mid 133 F11
Worcs 117 E7
Lady Wood W Yorks 206 F2
Laffak Mers 183 B8
Laga Highld 289 C8
Lagafater Lodge
Dumfries 236 B3
Lagalochan Argyll 275 B9
Lagavulin Argyll 254 C5
Lagg Argyll 274 F6
N Ayrs 255 E10
Laggan Argyll 254 B3
Highld 289 B9
Highld 290 D4
Highld 291 D8
S Ayrs 245 G7
Lagganlia Highld 291 C10
Laggan Lodge Argyll 289 G8
Lagganmullan Dumfries 237 D7
Lagganulva Argyll 288 E6
Lagness W Sus 22 C5
Laide Highld 307 K3
Laig Highld 294 G6
Laigh Carnduff S Lnrk 268 F3
Laigh Fenwick E Ayrs 267 G9
Laigh Glengall S Ayrs 257 F8
Laighmuir E Ayrs 267 F9
Laighstonehall S Lnrk 268 E4
Laindon Essex 69 B7
Lair Highld 299 E10
Perth 292 G3
Laira Plym 7 D10
Lairg Highld 309 J5
Lairg Lodge Highld 309 J5
Lairgmore Highld 300 F5
Lairg Muir Highld 309 J5
Laisterdyke W Yorks 205 G9
Laithes Cumb 230 E5
Laithkirk Durham 232 G5
Laity Moor Corn 4 F3
Lake Devon 12 D6
Devon 24 F6
Devon 40 G5
IoW 21 E7
Poole 18 C5
Wilts 46 F6
Lake End Bucks 66 D2
Lakenham Norf 142 B4
Lakenheath Suff 140 G4
Laker's Green Sur 50 F4
Lakesend Norf 139 D10
Lakeside Cumb 211 B7
Thurrock 68 D5
Worcs 117 D11
Laleham Sur 66 F5
Laleston / Trelales
Bridgend 57 F11
Lamanva Corn 3 C7
Lamarsh Essex 107 D7
Lamas Norf 160 E4
Lamb Corner Essex 107 E10
Lambden Borders 272 G4
Lamberden Kent 38 B4
Lamberhead Green
Gtr Man 194 G4
Lamberhurst Kent 53 F7
Lamberhurst Quarter
Kent 53 F7
Lamberton Borders 273 D9
Lambert's End W Mid 133 E9
Lambeth London 67 D10
Lambfair Green Suff 124 G4
Lambfoot Cumb 229 E9
Lambhill Glasgow 267 B11
Lambley Northumb 240 F5
Notts 171 F10
Lambourn W Berks 63 D10
Lambourne Corn 4 E5
Essex 87 F7
Lambourne End Essex 87 G7
Lambourn Woodlands
W Berks 63 D10
Lambridge Bath 61 F9
Lamb's Cross Kent 53 D9
Lambs Green W Sus 51 F8
Lambs' Green Dorset 18 B5
Lambston Pembs 72 B6
Lambton T&W 243 G7
Lamellion Corn 6 C4
Lamerton Devon 12 F5
Lamesley T&W 243 F7
Laminess Orkney 314 C6
Lamington Highld 301 B7
S Lnrk 259 C11
Lamlash N Ayrs 256 C2
Lamledra Corn 5 G10
Lamloch Dumfries 246 D2
Lammack Blkburn 195 B7
Lamonby Cumb 230 D4
Lamorick Corn 5 C10
Lamorna Corn 1 E4
Lamorran Corn 5 G7
Lampardbrook Suff 126 E5
Lampeter / Llanbedr Pont
Steffan Ceredig 93 B11
Lampeter Velfrey Pembs 73 C11
Lamphey Pembs 73 E8
Lamplugh Cumb 229 G7
Lamport Northants 120 C5
Lampton London 66 D6
Lamyatt Som 45 F7
Lana Devon 12 B2
Devon 24 F4
Lanark S Lnrk 269 G7
Lancaster Lancs 211 G9
Lanchester Durham 233 B9
Lancing W Sus 35 G11
Landbeach Cambs 123 D9
Landcross Devon 25 C7
Landerberry Aberds 293 C9
Landewednack Corn 2 G6
Landford Wilts 32 D3
Landford Manor Wilts 32 C3
Landfordwood Wilts 32 C3
Land Gate Gtr Man 194 G5
Landguard Manor IoW 21 E7
Landhill Devon 12 B4
Landican Mers 182 D3
Landimore Swansea 56 C3
Landkey Devon 40 G5
Landkey Newland Devon 40 G5
Landore Swansea 57 B7
Landport E Sus 36 E6
Ptsmth 33 G10
Landrake Corn 7 C7
Landscove Devon 8 B5
Landshipping Pembs 73 C8
Landshipping Quay
Pembs 73 C8
Landslow Green
Gtr Man 185 B7
Landulph Corn 7 C8
Landwade Suff 124 D2
Landywood Staffs 133 B9
Lane Corn 4 C6
Laneast Corn 11 E10
Lane Bottom Lancs 204 F3
W Yorks 205 F7
Lane End Bucks 84 G4
Lane-end Corn 5 B10
Lane End Cumb 220 G2
Derbys 170 C6
Devon 24 G6
Dorset 18 C3
Flint 166 C3
Glos 79 B10
Hants 33 B9
Hants 33 B11
IoW 21 D9
Kent 68 E5
Lancs 204 D3
Sur 49 E10
S Yorks 186 B5
Wilts 45 D10
W Yorks 204 F6
Lane Ends Ches E 168 D2
Ches E 185 E7
Cumb 210 C6
Derbys 152 C4
Gtr Man 185 C7
Lancs 194 D6
Lancs 203 C11
Lancs 203 G11
N Yorks 204 E5
Stoke 168 E5
W Yorks 205 F10
Lane Green Staffs 133 C7
Laneham Notts 188 F4
Lanehead Durham 232 C2
Northumb 251 F7
Lane Head Derbys 185 F11
Durham 224 C2
Gtr Man 183 B10
Pembs 73 E8
W Mid 133 C9
W Yorks 197 F7
Lane Heads Lancs 202 F4
Lanehouse Dorset 17 F9
Lanercost Cumb 240 E3
Lanescot Corn 5 D11
Lanesend Pembs 73 D9
Lanes End Bucks 84 D6
Lane's End Shrops 132 G2
Lanesfield W Mid 133 D8
Laneshaw Bridge Lancs 204 E4
Lane Side Lancs 195 C9
Laney Green Staffs 133 B9
Lanfach Caerph 78 F2
Langaford Devon 12 B4
Langage Devon 7 E11
Langal Highld 289 C9
Langaller Som 28 B3
Langar Notts 154 C4
Langbank Renfs 277 G7
Langbar N Yorks 205 C7
Langbaurgh N Yorks 225 C11
Langburnshiels Borders 250 C2
Langcliffe N Yorks 212 G6
Langdale Highld 308 E6
Langdale End N Yorks 227 G8
Langdon Corn 12 D2
Langdon Beck Durham 232 E3
Langdon Hills Essex 69 B7
Langdown Hants 32 F6
Langdyke Dumfries 238 C3
Fife 287 G7
Langenhoe Essex 89 B8
Langford C Beds 104 C3
Devon 14 B4
Devon 27 G8
Essex 88 D4
Notts 172 D4
Oxon 82 E2
Som 28 B2
Langford Budville Som 27 C10
Langford Green Devon 27 G8
N Som 44 B3
Langham Dorset 30 B3
Essex 107 E10
Norf 177 E8
Rutland 154 G6
Som 28 E4
Suff 125 C9
Langhaugh Borders 260 C6
Langho Lancs 203 G10
Langholm Dumfries 249 G9
Langholme N Lincs 188 B3
Langhope Borders 261 E10
Langland Swansea 56 D6
Langlee Borders 262 B2
Langleeford Northumb 263 E10
Langlee Mains Borders 262 B2
Langlees Falk 279 E7
Langley Ches E 184 G6
Derbys 170 F6
Essex 105 D8
Glos 99 F10
Gtr Man 195 F11
Hants 32 G6
Herts 104 G4
Kent 53 C10
Northumb 241 E8
Oxon 82 B4
Slough 66 D4
Som 27 B9
Warks 118 E3
W Mid 133 F9
W Sus 34 B4
Langley Burrell Wilts 62 D2
Langleybury Herts 85 E9
Langley Common
Derbys 152 B5
Wokingham 65 F9
Langley Corner Bucks 66 C4
Langley Green Derbys 152 B5
Essex 107 G7
Warks 118 E3
W Mid 133 F9
W Sus 51 F9
Langley Heath Kent 53 C10
Langley Marsh Som 27 B9
Langley Mill Derbys 170 F6
Langley Moor Durham 233 C11
Langley Park Durham 233 C10
Langley Street Norf 143 C7
Langley Vale Sur 51 B8
Langloan N Lnrk 268 C4
Langney E Sus 23 E10
Langold Notts 187 D9
Langore Corn 12 D2
Langport Som 28 B6
Langrick Lincs 174 F3
Langrick Bridge Lincs 174 F3
Langridge Bath 61 F8
Langridge Ford Devon 25 C9
Langrigg Cumb 222 C5
Cumb 229 B9
Langrish Hants 34 C2
Langsett S Yorks 197 G8
Langshaw Borders 262 B2
Langside Glasgow 267 C11
Perth 285 F11
Langskaill Orkney 314 B4
Langstone Devon 13 E10
Hants 22 C2
Newport 78 G5
Langthorne N Yorks 224 G5
Langthorpe N Yorks 215 F7
Langthwaite N Yorks 223 E10
Langtoft E Yorks 217 F10
Lincs 156 G2
Langton Durham 224 B3
Lincs 174 B2
Lincs 190 G5
N Yorks 216 F5
Langton by Wragby
Lincs 189 F11
Langton Green Kent 52 F4
Suff 126 C2
Langton Herring Dorset 17 E8
Langton Long Blandford
Dorset 30 F5
Langton Matravers
Dorset 18 F6
Langtree Devon 25 D7
Langtree Week Devon 25 D7
Langwathby Cumb 231 E7
Langwell Ho Highld 311 G5
Langwell Lodge Highld 307 J6
Langwith Derbys 171 B8
Langwith Junction
Derbys 171 B8
Langworth Lincs 189 F9
Lanham Green Essex 106 G5
Lanivet Corn 5 C10
Lanjeth Corn 5 E9
Lanjew Corn 5 C9
Lank Corn 11 F7
Lanlivery Corn 5 D11
Lanner Corn 2 B6
Lanreath Corn 6 D3
Lanrick Stirl 285 G10
Lansallos Corn 6 E3
Lansbury Park Caerph 59 B7
Lansdown Bath 61 F8
Glos 99 G8
Lanstephan Corn 12 D2
Lanteglos Corn 11 E7
Lanteglos Highway Corn 6 E3
Lanton Borders 262 E4
Northumb 263 C10
Lantuel Corn 5 B9
Lantyan Corn 6 D2
Lapal W Mid 133 G9
Lapford Devon 26 F2
Lapford Cross Devon 26 F2
Laphroaig Argyll 254 C4
Lapley Staffs 151 G7
Lapworth Warks 118 C3
Larachbeg Highld 289 E8
Larbert Falk 279 E7
Larbreck Lancs 202 E4
Larches Lancs 202 G6
Larden Green Ches E 167 E9
Larg Highld 292 B2
Largie Aberds 302 F6
Largiebaan Argyll 255 F7
Largiemore Argyll 275 E10
Largoward Fife 287 G8
Largs N Ayrs 266 D4
Largue Aberds 302 E6
Largybeg N Ayrs 256 E3
Largymeanoch N Ayrs 256 E2
Largymore N Ayrs 256 E2
Larkfield Invclyd 276 F4
Kent 53 B8
W Yorks 205 F10
Larkhall Bath 61 F9
S Lnrk 268 E5
Larkhill Wilts 46 E6
Lark Hill Gtr Man 195 G7
Larklands Derbys 171 G7
Larks' Hill Suff 108 B3
Larling Norf 141 F9
Larport Hereford 97 D11
Larrick Corn 12 F2
Larriston Borders 250 E2
Lartington Durham 223 B10
Lary Aberds 292 C5
Lasborough Glos 80 G4
Lasham Hants 49 E7
Lashenden Kent 53 E10
Lask Edge Staffs 168 D6
Lassington Glos 98 G5
Lassodie Fife 280 C2
Lastingham N Yorks 226 G4
Latcham Som 44 D2
Latchbrook Corn 7 D8
Latchford Herts 105 G7
Oxon 83 E11
Warr 183 D10
Latchingdon Essex 88 E5
Latchley Corn 12 G4
Latchmere Green Hants 64 G6
Latchmore Bank Essex 87 B7
Lately Common Warr 183 B11
Lathallan Mill Fife 287 G8
Lathbury M Keynes 103 B7
Latheron Highld 310 F5
Latheronwheel Highld 310 F5
Latheronwheel Ho
Highld 310 F5
Lathom Lancs 194 E3
Lathones Fife 287 G8
Latimer Bucks 85 F8
Latteridge S Glos 61 C7
Lattiford Som 29 B11
Lattinford Hill Suff 107 D11
Latton Wilts 81 F9
Latton Bush Essex 87 D7
Lauchintilly Aberds 293 B9
Laudale Ho Highld 289 D9
Lauder Borders 271 F10
Lauder Barns Borders 271 F10
Laugharne / Talacharn
Carms 74 C4
Laughern Hill Worcs 116 F5
Laughterton Lincs 188 F4
Laughton E Sus 23 C8
Leics 136 F3
Lincs 155 C11
Lincs 188 B4
Laughton Common
E Sus 23 C7
S Yorks 187 D8
Laughton en le Morthen
S Yorks 187 D8
Launcells Corn 24 F2
Launcells Cross Corn 24 F3
Launceston Corn 12 D2
Launcherley Som 44 E4
Laund Lancs 195 C10
Launton Oxon 102 G2
Laurencekirk Aberds 293 F9
Laurieston Dumfries 237 C8
Falk 279 F8
Lavendon M Keynes 121 G8
Lavenham Suff 107 B8
Laverackloch Moray 301 C11
Laverhay Dumfries 248 D4
Laverlaw Borders 261 B7
Laverley Som 44 F5
Lavernock V Glam 59 F7
Laversdale Cumb 239 E11
Laverstock Wilts 47 G7
Laverstoke Hants 48 D3
Laverton Glos 99 D11
N Yorks 214 E4
Som 45 C9
Lavington Sands Wilts 46 B4
Lavister Wrex 166 D5
Lavrean Corn 5 D10
Lawers Perth 285 D10
Perth 285 E11
Lawford Essex 107 E11
Som 42 F6
Lawford Heath Warks 119 C9
Lawhill Perth 286 F3
Law Hill S Lnrk 268 E6
Lawhitton Corn 12 E3
Lawkland N Yorks 212 F5
Lawkland Green
N Yorks 212 F5
Lawley Telford 132 B3
Lawn Swindon 63 C7
Lawnhead Staffs 150 E6
Lawns W Yorks 197 C10
Lawnswood W Yorks 205 F11
Lawnt Denb 165 B8
Lawrence Hill Newport 59 B10
Lawrence Weston Bristol 60 D4
Lawrenny Pembs 73 D8
Lawrenny Quay Pembs 73 D8
Lawshall Suff 125 G7
Lawshall Green Suff 125 G7
Lawton Hereford 115 F8
Shrops 131 G10
Lawton-gate Ches E 168 D4
Lawton Heath End
Ches E 168 D3
Laxey IoM 192 D5
Laxfield Suff 126 C5
Laxfirth Shetland 313 H6
Shetland 313 J6
Laxford Bridge Highld 306 E7
Laxo Shetland 313 G6
Laxobigging Shetland 312 F6
Laxton E Yorks 199 B9
Northants 137 D8
Notts 172 B2
Laycock W Yorks 204 E6
Layer Breton Essex 88 B6
Layer de la Haye Essex 89 B7
Layer Marney Essex 88 B6
Layerthorpe York 207 C8
Layham Suff 107 C10
Laymore Dorset 28 G5
Layters Green Bucks 85 G7
Laytham E Yorks 207 F10
Layton Blkpool 202 F2
Lazenby Redcar 225 B11
Lazonby Cumb 230 D6
Lea Derbys 170 D4
Hereford 98 G3
Lancs 202 G5
Lincs 188 D4
Shrops 131 B8
Shrops 131 F7
Wilts 62 B3
Lea Bridge London 67 B11
Leabrooks Derbys 170 E6
Lea by Backford
Ches W 182 G5
Leacainn W Isles 305 H3
Leac a Li W Isles 305 J3
Leachkin Highld 300 E6
Leacnasaide Highld 299 B7
Leadburn Midloth 270 D4
Leadendale Staffs 151 B8
Leadenham Lincs 173 E7
Leaden Roding Essex 87 C9
Leadgate Cumb 231 C10
Durham 242 G4
T&W 242 F4
Leadhills S Lnrk 259 G9
Leadingcross Green
Kent 53 C11
Leadmill Derbys 186 E2
Flint 166 C2
Lea End Worcs 117 B10
Leafield Oxon 82 B4
Wilts 61 F11
Lea Forge Ches E 168 F2
Leagrave Luton 103 G10
Leagreen Hants 19 C11
Lea Green Mers 183 C8
Lea Hall W Mid 134 F2
Lea Heath Staffs 151 D10
Leake Lincs 174 F6
N Yorks 225 G8
Leake Commonside
Lincs 174 E5
Leake Fold Hill Lincs 174 E6
Lealholm N Yorks 226 D5
Lealholm Side N Yorks 226 D5
Lea Line Hereford 98 G3
Lealt Argyll 275 D7
Highld 298 C5
Leam Derbys 186 F2
Lea Marston Warks 134 E4
Leamington Hastings
Warks 119 D8
Leamoor Common
Shrops 131 F8
Leamore W Mid 133 C9
Leamside Durham 234 B2
Leanach Argyll 275 D11
Leanachan Highld 290 F4
Leanaig Highld 300 D5
Leapgate Worcs 116 C6
Leargybreck Argyll 274 F6
Lease Rigg N Yorks 226 E6
Leasey Bridge Herts 85 C11
Leasgill Cumb 211 C9
Leasingham Lincs 173 F9
Leasingthorne Durham 233 F11
Leason Swansea 56 C3
Leasowe Mers 182 C3
Leatherhead Sur 51 B7
Leatherhead Common
Sur 51 B7
Leathern Bottle Glos 80 E2
Leathley N Yorks 205 D10
Leaths Dumfries 237 C9
Leaton Shrops 149 F9
Telford 150 G2
Leaton Heath Shrops 149 F9
Lea Town Lancs 202 G5
Lea Valley Herts 85 B11
Leaveland Kent 54 C4
Leavenheath Suff 107 D9
Leavening N Yorks 216 G5
Leavesden Green Herts 85 E9
Leaves Green London 68 G2
Lea Yeat Cumb 212 B5
Leazes Durham 242 F5
Lebberston N Yorks 217 C11
Leburnick Corn 12 E3
Lechlade-on-Thames
Glos 82 F2
Leck Lancs 212 D2
Leckford Hants 47 F11
Leckfurin Highld 308 D7
Leckgruinart Argyll 274 G3
Leckhampstead Bucks 102 D4
W Berks 64 D2
Leckhampstead Thicket
W Berks 64 D2
Leckhampton Glos 80 B6
Leckie Highld 299 C10
Leckmelm Highld 307 K6
Leckuary Argyll 275 D9
Leckwith V Glam 59 E7
Leconfield E Yorks 208 E6
Ledaig Argyll 289 F11
Ledburn Bucks 103 G8
Ledbury Hereford 98 D4
Ledcharrie Stirl 285 E9
Leddington Glos 98 E3
Ledgemoor Hereford 115 G8
Ledgowan Highld 299 D11
Ledicot Hereford 115 E8
Ledmore Angus 293 G7
Highld 307 H7
Lednagullin Highld 308 C7
Ledsham Ches W 182 G5
W Yorks 198 B3
Ledston W Yorks 198 B2
Ledstone Devon 8 F4
Ledston Luck W Yorks 206 G4
Ledwell Oxon 101 F8
Lee Argyll 288 G6
Devon 40 D3
Devon 40 D5
Hants 32 D5
Lancs 203 B7
London 67 E11
Northumb 241 F10
Shrops 149 C8
Leeans Shetland 313 J5
Lee Bank W Mid 133 F11
Leebotten Shetland 313 L6
Leebotwood Shrops 131 D9
Lee Brockhurst Shrops 149 D10
Leece Cumb 210 F4
Lee Chapel Essex 69 B7
Leechpool Mon 60 B4
Lee Clump Bucks 84 E6
Lee Common Bucks 84 E6
Leeds Kent 53 C10
W Yorks 205 G11
Leedstown Corn 2 C4
Leeford Devon 41 D9
Lee Gate Bucks 84 D5
Leegomery Telford 150 G3
Lee Ground Hants 33 F8
Lee Head Derbys 185 C8
Leeholme Durham 233 E10
Leek Staffs 169 D7
Leekbrook Staffs 169 E7
Leek Wootton Warks 118 D5
Lee Mill Devon 8 D2
Leeming N Yorks 214 B5
W Yorks 204 G6
Leeming Bar N Yorks 224 G5
Leemings Lancs 203 D10
Lee Moor Devon 7 C11
W Yorks 197 B10
Lee-on-the-Solent
Hants 33 G9
Lee-over-Sands Essex 89 C10
Lees Derbys 152 B5
Gtr Man 196 G3
W Yorks 204 F6
Leesthorpe Leics 154 G5
Leeswood / Coed-Llai
Flint 166 D3
Leetown Perth 286 E6
Leftwich Ches W 183 G11
Legar Powys 78 B2
Legbourne Lincs 190 E5
Legburthwaite Cumb 220 B6
Legerwood Borders 271 G11
Leggatt Hill W Sus 34 C6
Legsby Lincs 189 D10
Leicester Leicester 135 C11
Leicester Forest East
Leics 135 C10
Leicester Grange Warks 135 E8
Leigh Devon 26 E2
Dorset 18 B6
Dorset 29 F10
Dorset 30 F3
Glos 99 F7
Gtr Man 195 G7
Kent 52 D4
Shrops 130 C6
Sur 51 D8
Wilts 81 G9
Worcs 116 G5
Leigham Plym 7 D10
Leigh Beck Essex 69 C10
Leigh Common Som 30 B2
Leigh Delamere Wilts 61 D11
Leigh Green Kent 54 G2
Leighland Chapel Som 42 F4
Leigh-on-Sea Sthend 69 B10
Leigh Park Hants 22 B2
Leigh Sinton Worcs 116 G5
Leighswood W Mid 133 C11
Leighterton Glos 80 G4
Leighton N Yorks 214 D3
Shrops 132 B2
Som 45 E8
Leighton Bromswold
Cambs 122 B2

Llanfairpwll-gwyngyll
Anglesey 179 G8
Llanfair Talhaiarn
Conwy 180 G6
Llanfair Waterdine
Shrops 114 B4
Llanfairyneubwll
Anglesey 178 F3
Llanfairynghornwy
Anglesey 178 C4
Llanfallteg Carms 73 B11
Llanfallteg West Carms . 73 B10
Llanfaredd Powys 113 G11
Llanfarian Ceredig 111 B11
Llanfechain Powys 148 E3
Llanfechell Anglesey 178 C5
Llanferres Denb 165 C11
Llan Ffestiniog Gwyn 164 G2
Llanfflewyn Anglesey 178 D5
Llanfigael Anglesey 178 E4
Llanfihangel-ar-arth
Carms 93 D9
Llanfihangel-Crucorney
Mon 96 G6
Llanfihangel Glyn Myfyr
Conwy 165 F7
Llanfihangel-helygen
Powys 113 E10
Llanfihangel Nant Bran
Powys 95 E8
Llanfihangel-nant-Melan
Powys 114 F3
Llanfihangel Rhydithon
Powys 114 D3
Llanfihangel Rogiet Mon . 60 B2
Llanfihangel Tal-y-llyn
Powys 96 F2
Llanfihangel Tor y Mynydd
Mon 79 E7
Llanfihangel-uwch-Gwili
Carms 93 G9
Llanfihangel-y-Creuddyn
Ceredig 112 B3
Llanfihangel-yng-Ngwynfa
Powys 147 F11
Llanfihangel yn Nhowyn
Anglesey 178 F4
Llanfihangel-y-pennant
Gwyn 128 B3
Gwyn 163 H8
Llanfilo Powys 96 E2
Llanfleiddan / Llanblethian
V Glam 58 E3
Llanfoist Mon 78 C3
Llanfor Gwyn 147 B8
Llanfrechfa Torf 78 G4
Llanfrothen Gwyn 163 G10
Llanfrynach Powys 95 F11
Llanfwrog Anglesey 178 E4
Denb 165 D10
Llanfyllin Powys 148 F2
Llanfynydd Carms 93 F11
Flint 166 D3
Llanfyrnach Pembs 92 E4
Llangadfan Powys 147 G10
Llangadog Carms 74 D6
Carms 94 F4
Llangadwaladr Anglesey . 162 B5
Powys 148 C3
Llangaffo Anglesey 162 B6
Llangain Carms 74 B6
Llangammarch Wells
Powys 95 B8
Llangan V Glam 58 D3
Llangarron Hereford 97 G10
Llangasty Talyllyn Powys . 96 F2
Llangathen Carms 93 G11
Llangattock Powys 78 B2
Llangattock Lingoed
Mon 97 G7
Llangattock nigh Usk
Mon 78 D4
Llangattock-Vibon-Avel
Mon 79 B7
Llangedwyn Powys 148 E3
Llangefni Anglesey 179 F7
Llangeinor Bridgend 58 B2
Llangeitho Ceredig 112 F2
Llangeler Carms 93 D7
Llangendeirne Carms 75 C7
Llangennech Carms 56 C2
Llangenny Powys 78 B2
Llangernyw Conwy 164 B5
Llangeview Mon 78 E5
Llangewydd Court
Bridgend 57 E11
Llangian Gwyn 144 D5
Llanglydwen Carms 92 F3
Llangoed Anglesey 179 F10
Llangoedmor Ceredig 92 B3
Llangollen Denb 166 G2
Llangolman Pembs 92 F2
Llangors Powys 96 F2
Llangorwen Ceredig 111 A11
Llangovan Mon 79 D7
Llangower Gwyn 147 C8
Llangranog Ceredig 110 G6
Llangristiolus Anglesey .. 178 G6
Llangrove Hereford 79 B8
Llangua Mon 97 F7
Llangunllo Powys 114 C4
Llangunnor Carms 74 B6
Llangurig Powys 113 B8
Llangwm Conwy 165 G7
Mon 78 E5
Pembs 73 D7
Llangwnnadl Gwyn 144 C4
Llangwyfan Denb 165 B10
Llangwyfan-isaf
Anglesey 162 B5
Llangwyllog Anglesey .. 178 F6
Llangwyryfon Ceredig .. 111 C11
Llangybi Ceredig 112 G2
Gwyn 162 G6
Mon 78 F5
Llangyfelach Swansea .. 56 B6
Llangynderyn Carms 75 C7
Llangynhafal Denb 165 C10
Llangynidr Powys 77 B11
Llangyniew Powys 130 B2
Llangynin Carms 74 B2
Llangynog Carms 74 B4
Powys 147 D11
Llangynwyd Bridgend .. 57 D11
Llanhamlach Powys 95 F11
Llanharan Rhondda 58 C4
Llanharry Rhondda 58 C4
Llanhennock Mon 78 G5
Llanhilleth Bl Gwent 78 E2
Llanidloes Powys 129 F8
Llaniestyn Gwyn 144 C5
Llanifyny Powys 129 G1
Llanigon Powys 96 D4
Llanilar Ceredig 112 C2
Llanilid Rhondda 58 C3
Llanilltud Fawr / Llantwit
Major V Glam 58 F3

Llanio Ceredig 112 F2
Llanishen Cardiff 59 C7
Mon 79 E7
Llanllawddog Carms 93 F9
Llanllechid Gwyn 163 B10
Llanllowell Mon 78 F5
Llanllugan Powys 129 C11
Llanllwch Carms 74 B5
Llanllwchaiarn Powys .. 130 E3
Llanllwni Carms 93 D9
Llanllyfni Gwyn 163 E7
Llanmadoc Swansea 56 C2
Llanmaes Cardiff 58 D6
V Glam 58 F3
Llanmartin Newport 59 B11
Llanmerewig Powys 130 E3
Llanmihangel
V Glam 58 E3
Llan-mill Pembs 73 C10
Llanmiloe Carms 74 D3
Llanmorlais Swansea 56 C4
Llannefydd Conwy 181 G7
Llannon Carms 75 D8
Llan-non / Llanon
Ceredig 111 D10
Llannor Gwyn 145 B7
Llanon Pembs 90 E6
Llan-non / Llanon
Ceredig 111 D10
Llanover Mon 78 D4
Llanpumsaint Carms 93 F8
Llanreath Pembs 73 E7
Llanreithan Pembs 91 F7
Llanrhaeadr Denb 165 C9
Llanrhaeadr-ym-Mochnant
Powys 148 D2
Llanrhian Pembs 90 E6
Llanrhidian Swansea 56 C3
Llanrhos Conwy 180 E3
Llanrhyddlad Anglesey .. 178 D4
Llanrhystud Ceredig 111 D10
Llanrosser Hereford 96 D5
Llanrothal Hereford 79 B7
Llanrug Gwyn 163 C8
Llanrumney Cardiff 59 C8
Llanrwst Conwy 164 C4
Llansadurnen Carms 74 C3
Llansadwrn Anglesey 179 F9
Carms 94 E3
Llansaint Carms 74 D5
Llansamlet Swansea 57 B7
Llansanffraid Glan Conwy
Conwy 180 F4
Llansannan Conwy 164 B6
Llansannor V Glam 58 E3
Llansantffraed Ceredig 111 D10
Llansantffraed Cwmdeuddwr
Powys 96 G2
Llansantffraed-in-Elwel
Powys 113 G11
Llansantffraid-ym-Mechain
Powys 148 E4
Llansawel Carms 94 D2
Llansawel / Briton Ferry
Neath 57 C8
Llansilin Powys 148 E4
Llansoy Mon 78 E6
Llanspyddid Powys 95 F10
Llanstadwell Pembs 72 D6
Llansteffan Carms 74 C5
Llanstephan Powys 96 C2
Llantarnam Torf 78 G4
Llanteems Mon 96 G6
Llanteg Pembs 73 C11
Llanthony Mon 96 F6
Llantilio Crossenny Mon . 78 C5
Llantilio Pertholey Mon .. 78 B4
Llantood Pembs 92 C3
Llantrisant Anglesey 178 E5
Mon 78 F5
Rhondda 58 C4
Llantrithyd V Glam 58 E4
Llantwit Neath 57 B9
Llantwit Fardre Rhondda . 58 B5
Llantwit Major / Llanilltud
Fawr V Glam 58 F3
Llanuwchllyn Gwyn 147 C7
Llanvaches Newport 78 G6
Llanvair Discoed Mon 78 G6
Llanvapley Mon 78 C5
Llanvetherine Mon 78 C5
Llanveynoe Hereford 96 E6
Llanvihangel Crucorney
Mon 96 G6
Llanvihangel Gobion
Mon 78 D4
Llanvihangel-Ystern-
Llewern Mon 78 C6
Llanwarne Hereford 97 F10
Llanwddyn Powys 147 F10
Llanwenarth Mon 78 C3
Llanwenog Ceredig 93 B9
Llanwern Newport 59 B11
Llanwinio Carms 92 F5
Llanwnda Gwyn 163 D7
Pembs 91 D8
Llanwnnen Ceredig 93 B10
Llanwnog Powys 129 E10
Llanwrda Carms 94 E4
Llanwrin Powys 128 C5
Llanwrthwl Powys 113 E9
Llanwrtud / Llanwrtyd Wells
Powys 95 B7
Llanwrtyd Wells / Llanwrtud
Powys 95 B7
Llanwyddelan Powys .. 129 C11
Llanyblodwel Shrops 148 E4
Llanybri Carms 74 C4
Llanybydder Carms 93 C10
Llanycefn Pembs 91 G11
Llanychaer Pembs 91 D9
Llanycil Gwyn 147 C8
Llanycrwys Carms 94 C2
Llanymawddwy Gwyn .. 147 F8
Llanymddyfri / Llandovery
Carms 94 E5
Llanymynech Powys 148 E5
Llanynghenedl Anglesey . 178 E4
Llanynys Denb 165 C10
Llan-y-pwll Wrex 166 E5
Llanyrafon Torf 78 G4
Llanyre Powys 113 E10
Llanystumdwy Gwyn .. 145 B9
Llanywern Powys 96 F2
Llawhaden Pembs 73 C8
Llawnt Shrops 148 C5
Llawr Betw / Bettws Bledrws Ceredig 290 G3
Llawr-y-glyn Powys 129 E8
Llay Wrex 166 D4
Llechcynfarwy Anglesey . 178 E5
Llecheiddior Gwyn 163 G7
Llechfaen Powys 95 F11
Llechfraith Gwyn 146 F3
Llechryd Caerph 77 D10
Ceredig 92 C4
Llechrydau Powys 148 C3
Llechwedd Conwy 180 F3
Lledrod Ceredig 112 C2

Llenmerewig Powys 130 E3
Llethrid Swansea 56 C4
Llettyrychen Carms 75 E7
Llidiad Nenog Carms 93 D10
Llidiardau Gwyn 147 B7
Llidiart-y-parc Denb 165 G10
Llithfaen Gwyn 162 G5
Lloc Flint 181 F10
Llong Flint 166 C3
Llowes Powys 96 C3
Lloyney Powys 114 B4
Llugwy Powys 129 C11
Llundain-fach Ceredig .. 111 F11
Llwydarth Bridgend 57 C11
Llwydcoed Rhondda 77 E7
Llwyn Denb 165 C9
Shrops 130 G5
Llwyncelyn Ceredig 111 F8
Llwyndafydd Ceredig .. 111 F7
Llwynderw Powys 130 C4
Llwyn-derw Mon 78 B3
Llwynduris Ceredig 92 C4
Llwyndyrys Gwyn 162 G5
Llwyneinion Wrex 166 F3
Llwyngwril Gwyn 110 B2
Llwyn-hendy Carms 56 B4
Llwyn-hendy Carms 56 B4
Llwynmawr Wrex 148 B4
Llwyn-on Village M Tydf . 77 C8
Llwyn-têg Carms 75 D9
Llwyn-y-brain Carms 73 C11
Llwyn-y-go Shrops 148 E6
Llwyngyog Powys 129 E7
Llwyn-y-groes Ceredig 111 F11
Llwynypia Rhondda 77 G7
Llwyn-yr-hwrdd Pembs .. 92 E4
Llynclys Shrops 148 E5
Llynfaes Anglesey 178 F6
Llysfaen Conwy 180 F5
Llyswen Powys 96 D2
Llysworney V Glam 58 E3
Llys-y-frân Pembs 91 G10
Llywel Powys 95 E7
Llwynypia 77 C10
Loftus Redcar 226 B4
Logan E Ayrs 258 E3
Loganlea W Loth 269 C9
Logan Mains Dumfries. . . 236 E2
Loggerheads Denb 165 C11
Staffs 150 B4
Logie Angus 293 G8
Fife 287 E8
Logie Coldstone Aberds . 292 C6
Logie Hill Highld 301 B7
Logie Newton Aberds 302 F6
Logie Pert Angus 293 G8
Logierait Perth 286 B3
Login Carms 92 G3
Logmore Green Sur 50 D6
Loidse Mhorsgail
W Isles 304 F3
Lolworth Cambs 123 E7
Lonbain Highld 298 D6
Londesborough E Yorks . . 208 D3
London Apprentice Corn .. 5 E10
London Colney Herts 85 E11
Londonderry N Yorks 214 B6
London End Cambs 121 D11
London Fields W Mid 133 E8
London Minstead Hants. . 32 E3
London Beach Kent 53 F11
Londonthorpe Lincs 155 B9
Londubh Highld 307 L3
Lonemore Highld 299 B7
Highld 309 L7
Long Ashton N Som 60 E5
Long Bank Worcs 116 C5
Longbar N Ayrs 266 E6
Longbar Warr 183 C10
Long Bennington Lincs .. 172 G4
Longbenton T&W 243 D7
Longborough Glos 100 F3
Long Bredy Dorset 17 C7
Longbridge Plym 7 D10
Warks 118 E5
W Mid 117 B10
Longbridge Deverill
Wilts 45 E11
Longbridge Hayes Stoke 168 E5
Longbridgemuir
Dumfries. 238 D3
Long Buckby Northants. . 120 D2
Long Buckby Wharf
Northants. 120 D2
Long Clawson Leics 154 D4
Long Common Hants 33 E8
Long Compton Staffs 151 E7
Warks 100 D5
Longcot Oxon 82 G2
Long Crendon Bucks 83 D11
Long Crichel Dorset 31 F7
Longcroft Cumb 238 F7
Falk 278 F5
Longcross Devon 12 F4
Sur 66 F3
Long Cross Wilts 45 G9
Longdale Cumb 222 D2
Longdales Cumb 230 C6
Long Dean Wilts 61 D11
W Yorks 196 D6
Longden Shrops 131 B8
Longden Common
Shrops 131 C8
Long Ditton Sur 67 F7
Longdon Staffs 151 G11
Worcs 98 D6
Longdon Green Staffs .. 151 G11
Longdon on Tern
Telford 150 F2
Longdown Devon 14 C3
Longdowns Corn 2 C3
Long Drax N Yorks 199 B7
Longdrum Angus 292 G4
Long Duckmanton
Derbys 186 G6
Long Eaton Derbys 153 C9
Longfield Kent 68 F6
Shetland 313 M5
Wilts 45 B11
Longfield Hill Kent 68 F6
Longfleet Poole 18 C6
Longford Derbys 152 B4
Glos 98 G6
Kent 68 E5
London 66 D4
Shrops 150 B2
Telford 150 G4
W Mid 135 G7
Longforgan Perth 287 E7
Longformacus Borders .. 272 E4

Lockeridge Wilts 62 F6
Lockeridge Dene Wilts ... 62 F6
Lockerley Hants 32 B3
Lockhills Cumb 230 B6
Locking N Som 43 B11
Locking Stumps Warr. . . 183 C10
Lockington E Yorks 208 D5
Leics 153 D9
Lockleaze Bristol 60 D6
Locklywood Shrops 150 D3
Locksbottom London 68 F2
Locksgreen IoW 20 C4
Locks Heath Hants 33 F8
Lockton N Yorks 226 G6
Loddington Leics 136 C5
Northants. 136 G5
Loddiswell Devon 8 F4
Loddon Norf 143 D7
Loddon Ingloss Norf 142 D6
Lode Cambs 123 E10
Lode Heath W Mid 134 G3
Loders Dorset 16 C5
Lodge Bristol 60 D6
Lodgebank Shrops 149 D11
Lodge Green N Yorks 223 F9
W Mid 134 G5
Lodge Hill Corn 6 C4
W Mid 133 G10
Lodge Lees Kent 55 D8
Lodge Moor S Yorks 186 D3
Lodge Park Worcs 117 D10
Lodsworth W Sus 34 C6
Lodsworth Common
W Sus 34 C6
Lodway Bristol 60 D4
Lofthouse N Yorks 214 E2
W Yorks 197 B10
Lofthouse Gate
W Yorks 197 C10
Loftus Redcar 226 B4
Logan E Ayrs 258 E3
Loganlea W Loth 269 C9
Logan Mains Dumfries. . . 236 E2
Loggerheads Denb 165 C11
Staffs 150 B4
Logie Angus 293 G8
Fife 287 E8
Logie Coldstone Aberds . 292 C6
Logie Hill Highld 301 B7
Logie Newton Aberds 302 F6
Logie Pert Angus 293 G8
Logierait Perth 286 B3
Login Carms 92 G3
Logmore Green Sur 50 D6
Loidse Mhorsgail
W Isles 304 F3
Lolworth Cambs 123 E7
Lonbain Highld 298 D6
Londesborough E Yorks . . 208 D3
London Apprentice Corn .. 5 E10
London Colney Herts 85 E11
Londonderry N Yorks 214 B6
London End Cambs 121 D11
London Fields W Mid 133 E8
London Minstead Hants. . 32 E3
London Beach Kent 53 F11
Londonthorpe Lincs 155 B9
Londubh Highld 307 L3
Lonemore Highld 299 B7
Highld 309 L7

Longframlington
Northumb. 252 C4
Long Gardens Essex 106 D6
Long Green Ches W . 183 G11
Suff 125 B11
Gtr Man. 195 F7
Long Hanborough Oxon .. 82 C6
Longhaven Aberds 303 F11
Longhedge Wilts 45 E10
Longhill Aberds 303 D9
Longhirst Northumb. 252 F6
Longhope Glos 79 B11
Orkney 314 G3
Longhorsley Northumb. . 252 E4
Longhoughton
Northumb. 264 G6
Longlands Bath 61 G8
Cumb. 229 D11
Longlane Derbys 152 B5
W Berks 64 E3
Long Lane Telford 150 F2
Long Lawford Warks 119 B9
Long Lee W Yorks 205 E7
Longlevens Glos 99 G7
Longley W Yorks 196 C5
Longley Estate S Yorks . . 186 C5
Longley Green Worcs 116 G4
Longleys Perth 286 C6
Long Load Som 29 C7
Long Marston Herts 84 B5
N Yorks 206 C6
Warks 100 B3
Long Marton Cumb 231 G9
Long Meadow Cambs .. 123 E10
Long Meadowend
Shrops 131 G8
Long Melford Suff 107 B7
Longmoor Camp Hants .. 49 G9
Longmorn Moray 302 D2
Longmoss Ches E 184 G5
Long Newnton Glos 80 G6
Long Newton Borders .. 262 D3
Stockton 225 B7
Longnewton Borders .. 262 D3
Longney Glos 80 D3
Longniddry E Loth 281 F8
Longnor Shrops 131 C9
Staffs 169 C9
Longnor Park Shrops 131 C9
Long Oak Shrops 149 E7
Longparish Hants 48 E2
Longpark Cumb 239 E10
E Ayrs 257 B10
Long Park Hants 48 G2
Longridge Glos 80 D5
Lancs 203 F8
Staffs 151 F8
W Loth 269 C9
Longridge End Glos 98 G6
Longriggend N Lnrk 278 G6
Long Riston E Yorks 209 E8
Longrock Corn 1 C5
Long Sandall S Yorks .. 198 F6
Longscales N Yorks 205 B10
Longsdon Staffs 169 E7
Longshaw Gtr Man 194 G4
Staffs 169 F9
Longside Aberds 303 E10
Longsight Gtr Man. 184 B5
Long Sight Gtr Man. 196 F2
Longslow Shrops 150 B3
Longsowerby Cumb 239 G9
Longstanton Cambs. 123 D7
Longstock Hants 47 F11
Longstone Corn 2 B11
Longstowe Cambs 122 G6
Long Stratton Norf 142 E3
Long Street M Keynes .. 102 B5
Long Sutton Hants 49 D8
Lincs 157 E8
Som 29 B7
Long Thurlow Suff 125 D10
Longthwaite Cumb 230 G4
Longton Lancs 194 B3
Stoke 168 G6
Longtown Cumb 239 D9
Hereford 96 F6
Longtownmail Orkney . . 314 G4
Longview Mers 182 C6
Longville in the Dale
Shrops 131 E10
Longwell Green S Glos .. 61 E7
Long Whatton Leics 153 E9
Longwick Bucks 84 D3
Long Wittenham Oxon .. 83 G8
Longwood Shrops 132 B2
W Yorks 196 D6
Longwood Edge
W Yorks 196 D6
Longworth Oxon 82 F5
Lon-las Swansea 57 B8
Lonmay Aberds 303 D10
Lonmore Highld 298 E2
Looe Corn 6 E5
Loose Mills Corn 6 C4
Loose Kent 53 C9
Loosebeare Devon 13 B9
Loosegate Lincs 156 D6
Loose Hill Kent 53 C9
Long Bradley W Mid 133 D9
Loosley Row Bucks 84 E4
Loppcombe Corner Wilts .47 F9
Lopen Som 28 E6
Lopen Head Som 28 E6
Loppergarth Cumb. 210 D5
Loppington Shrops 149 D8
Lopwell Devon 7 C9
Lorbottle Northumb. 252 B2
Lorbottle Hall Northumb. 252 B2
Lord's Hill Soton 32 E5
Lord's Wood Medway .. 69 G9
Lornty Perth 286 C5
Loscoe Derbys 170 F6
W Yorks 198 C2
Loscombe Dorset 16 B6
Losgaintir W Isles 305 J2
Lossiemouth Moray 302 B2
Lossit Argyll 254 B2
Lossit Lodge Argyll 274 G4
Lostford Shrops 150 C3
Lostock Gtr Man. 195 F7

Lostock Gralam
Ches W. 183 F11
Lostock Green Ches W . 183 G11
Lostock Hall Lancs 194 B4
Lostock Junction
Gtr Man. 195 F7
Lostwithiel Corn. 6 D2
Loth Orkney 314 C6
Lothbeg Highld 311 H3
Lothersdale N Yorks 204 D5
Lothianbridge Midloth .. 271 B11
Lothmore Highld. 311 H3
Lottisham Som 44 G5
Loudwater Bucks 84 G6
Loughborough Leics 153 F10
Loughor Swansea 56 B5
Loughton Essex 86 F6
M Keynes 102 D6
Shrops 132 G2
Suff 143 D10
Lound Lincs 155 F11
Notts 187 D11
Suff 143 D10
Lount Leics 153 F7
Lour Angus 287 C8
Louth Lincs 190 D4
Lovat Highld 300 E5
Lovatton Devon 7 B10
Love Clough Lancs 195 B10
Lovedean Hants 33 E11
Lover Wilts 32 C2
Loversall S Yorks 187 B9
Loves Green Essex 87 E10
Lovesome Hill N Yorks .. 225 F7
Loveston Pembs 31 E9
Lovington Som 44 G5
Low Ackworth W Yorks . 198 D3
Low Alwinton
Northumb. 251 B10
Low Angerton Northumb 252 G3
Lowbands Glos 98 E5
Low Barlings Lincs 189 G9
Low Barugh S Yorks 197 F10
Low Bentham N Yorks .. 212 F2
Low Biggins Cumb 212 D2
Low Blantyre S Lnrk 268 D3
Low Bradfield S Yorks . 186 C3
Low Bradley N Yorks 204 D6
Low Braithwaite Cumb .. 230 C4
Low Bridge Wilts 46 F5
Low Brunton Northumb . 241 C10
Low Burnham N Lincs . 199 G9
Low Burton N Yorks 214 C4
Low Buston Northumb. . 252 B6
Lowca Cumb 228 G5
Low Catton E Yorks 207 C10
Low Clanyard Dumfries. . 236 F3
Low Common Norf. 142 C2
Low Compton Gtr Man .. 196 F2
Low Coniscliffe Darl. 224 C5
Low Coylton S Ayrs 257 F10
Low Crosby Cumb 239 F10
Low Dalby N Yorks 217 B7
Low Dinsdale Darl 224 C6
Low Ellington N Yorks ... 214 C4
Low Etherley Durham ... 233 F9
Low Fell T&W 243 F7
Low Fremington N Yorks 223 F10
Low Garth N Yorks 226 D4
Low Gate Northumb. 241 D10
Low Grantley N Yorks .. 214 E4
Low Green N Yorks 205 C9
Suff 125 E8
Low Habberley Worcs .. 116 B6
Low Ham Som 29 B7
Low Hauxley Northumb . 253 C7
Low Hawsker N Yorks ... 227 D8
Low Hesket Cumb 230 B5
Low Hesleyhurst
Northumb. 252 D3
Low Hutton N Yorks 216 F5
Lowick Cumb 210 B5
Northants. 137 G9
Northumb. 264 B2
Lowick Bridge Cumb ... 210 B5
Lowick Green Cumb 210 B5
Low Knipe Cumb 230 G6
Low Laithe N Yorks 214 G4
Low Laithes S Yorks 197 G10
Lowlands Torf 78 G3
Low Leighton Derbys ... 185 D8
Low Lorton Cumb. 229 F9
Low Marishes N Yorks .. 216 D6
Low Marnham Notts 172 B4
Low Mill N Yorks 226 F3
Low Moor Lancs 203 E11
W Yorks 197 B7
Low Moorsley T&W 234 B2
Low Moresby Cumb. 228 G5
Low Newton Cumb. 211 C8
Low Newton-by-the-Sea
Northumb. 264 D6
Lownie Moor Angus 287 C8
Low Prudhoe Northumb . 242 E4
Low Risby N Lincs 200 E2
Low Row Cumb 229 C8
Cumb 240 F3
N Yorks 223 F9
Low Salchrie Dumfries. . 236 C2
Low Smerby Argyll 255 E8
Low Street Norf 159 G9
Low Tharston Norf 142 D3
Lowther Cumb 230 G6
Lowthorpe E Yorks 217 G11
Lowton Devon 13 G9
Gtr Man. 183 B10
Som 28 D2
Lowton Common
Gtr Man. 183 B10
Low Toynton Lincs 190 G3
Low Torry Fife 279 D10
Low Valleyfield Fife 279 D10
Low Walton Cumb 219 C9
Low Waters S Lnrk 268 E4
Low Westwood Durham 242 F4
Low Whinnow Cumb 239 G8
Low Whita N Yorks 223 F10
Low Wood Cumb 210 C6
Low Worsall N Yorks ... 225 D7
Low Wray Cumb 221 E7
Loxbeare Devon 27 D7
Loxhill Sur 50 F4
Loxhore Devon 40 F6
Loxhore Cott Devon 40 F6
Loxley S Yorks 186 D4
Warks 118 G4
Loxley Green Staffs 151 C11
Loxton N Som 43 B11
Loxwood W Sus 50 G4

Lower Cadsden Bucks. ... 84 E4
Lower Caldecote
C Beds 104 B3
Lower Cam Glos 80 E2
Lower Canada N Som ... 43 B11
Lower Carden Ches W. .. 167 E7
Lower Catesby
Northants. 119 F10
Lower Caversham
Reading 65 E8
Lower Chapel Powys 95 D10
Lower Chedworth Glos .. 81 C9
Lower Cheriton Devon ... 27 G10
Lower Chicksgrove Wilts . 46 G3
Lower Chute Wilts 47 C10
Lower Clapton London ... 67 B11
Lower Clent Worcs. 117 B8
Lower Clicker Corn 6 C5
Lower Clopton Warks ... 118 E2
Lower Common Hants ... 48 E6
Hants 65 G9
Mon 78 B2
Shrops 131 B9
Lower Copthurst Lancs .. 194 C5
Lower Coberley Glos 81 B7
Lower Coburn Derbys ... 303 D7
Lower Cousley Wood
E Sus 53 G7
Lower Cox Street Kent .. 69 G10
Lower Cragabus Argyll . 254 C4
Lower Creedy Devon 26 G4
Lower Croan Corn 10 G6
Lower Crossings Derbys 185 E8
Lower Cumberworth
W Yorks 197 F8
Lower Cwm-twrch Powys 76 C3
Lower Daggons Hants .. 31 E9
Lower Darwen Blkburn .. 195 B7
Lower Dean Beds 121 D11
Devon 8 C4
Lower Dell Highld 292 B2
Lower Denby W Yorks ... 197 F8
Lower Denzell Corn. 5 B7
Lower Deuchries
Aberds 302 D6
Lower Diabaig Highld ... 299 C7
Lower Dicker E Sus 23 C9
Lower Dinchope Shrops 131 G9
Lower Down Shrops 130 G6
Lower Drift Corn. 1 D4
Lower Dowdeswell Glos . 81 B8
Lower Dunsforth
N Yorks 215 G8
Lower Durston Som 28 B3
Lower Earley Wokingham . 65 E9
Lower East Carleton
Norf. 142 C3
Lower Eastern Green
W Mid 118 B5
Lower Edmonton London 86 G4
Lower Egleton Hereford .. 98 B2
Lower Elkstone Staffs .. 169 D9
Lower Ellastone Staffs .. 169 G10
Lower End Bucks 83 D11
Bucks 102 E4
C Beds 103 D8
C Beds 103 G9
Glos 81 E7
Northants. 120 F6
Northants. 121 E7
Oxon 82 B4
Lower Everleigh Wilts .. 47 C7
Lower Eythorne Kent ... 55 D9
Lower Failand N Som. ... 60 E4
Lower Faintree Shrops .. 132 F3
Lower Falkenham Suff .. 108 D5
Lower Farringdon Hants . 49 F8
Lower Feltham London .. 66 E5
Lower Fittleworth W Sus. 35 D8
Lower Foxdale IoM 192 E3
Lower Frankton Shrops . 149 C7
Lower Freystrop Pembs . 73 C7
Lower Froyle Hants 49 E9
Lower Gabwell Devon ... 9 B8
Lower Gledfield Highld . 309 K5
Lower Godney Som 44 E3
Lower Goldstone Kent ... 71 G9
Lower Gornal W Mid 133 E8
Lower Grange W Yorks . 205 G8
Lower Gravenhurst
C Beds 104 D2
Lower Green Essex 88 E2
Essex 105 E8
Essex 106 E4
Gtr Man. 184 B2
Herts 104 E3
Kent 52 E5
Kent 52 E6
Norf. 159 B9
Staffs 133 B8
Suff 124 D4
Suff 125 D9
Sur 66 F6
Warks 119 D10
W Berks 63 G11
Lower Grove Common
Hereford 97 F11
Lower Hacheston Suff .. 126 F6
Lower Halistra Highld ... 298 D2
Lower Halstock Leigh
Dorset 29 F8
Lower Halstow Kent 69 F11
Lower Hamswell S Glos . 61 E8
Lower Hardres Kent 55 C7
Lower Hardwick
Hereford 115 G9
Lower Harpton Powys .. 114 F5
Lower Hartlip Kent 69 G10
Lower Hartshay Derbys 170 E5
Lower Hawthwaite
Cumb. 210 B4
Lower Haysden Kent 52 D5
Lower Hayton Shrops ... 131 G10
Lower Hazel S Glos 60 B6
Lower Heath Ches E 168 C5
Lower Hempriggs
Moray 301 C11
Lower Heppington Kent . 54 C6
Lower Hergest Hereford. 114 F5
Lower Heyford Oxon 101 G9
Lower Heysham Lancs .. 211 G8
Lower Higham Kent 69 E8
Lower Highmoor Oxon ... 65 B8
Lower Holbrook Suff 108 E3
Lower Holditch Dorset ... 28 G4
Lower Holloway London . 67 B10
Lower Holwell Dorset ... 31 E9
Lower Hook Worcs 98 C6
Lower Hookner Devon ... 13 G10
Lower Hopton Shrops ... 149 E7
Lower Horncroft W Sus . 35 D7

Lower Horsebridge
E Sus 23 C9
Lowerhouse Ches E 184 F6
Lancs 204 G2
Lower House Halton 183 D8
Lower Houses W Yorks . 197 D7
Lower Illey Worcs 133 G9
Lower Island Kent 70 F6
Lower Kersal Gtr Man. . 195 G10
Lower Kilburn Derbys .. 170 G4
Lower Kilcott Glos 61 B9
Lower Killeyan Argyll ... 254 C3
Lower Kingcombe
Dorset 17 B8
Lower Kingswood Sur ... 51 C8
Lower Kinnerton
Ches W. 166 C4
Lower Kinsham
Hereford 115 E7
Lower Knapp Som 28 B4
Lower Knightley Staffs . 150 E6
Lower Knowle Bristol ... 60 E5
Lower Langford N Som .. 60 G3
Lower Largo Fife 287 G8
Lower Layham Suff 107 C10
Lower Ledwyche
Shrops 115 C10
Lower Leigh Staffs 151 B10
Lower Lemington Glos .. 100 E4
Lower Lenie Highld 300 G5
Lower Lode Glos 99 E7
Lower Lovacott Devon ... 25 B8
Lower Loxhore Devon ... 40 F6
Lower Lydbrook Glos ... 79 B9
Lower Lye Hereford 115 D8
Lower Machen Newport . 59 B8
Lower Maes-coed
Hereford 96 E6
Lower Mains Clack 279 B9
Lower Mannington
Dorset 31 F9
Lower Marsh Som 30 C2
Lower Marston Som 45 E9
Lower Meend Glos 79 E9
Lower Menadue Corn ... 5 D10
Lower Merridge Som ... 43 G8
Lower Mickletown
W Yorks 198 B2
Lower Middleton Cheney
Northants. 101 C10
Lower Midway Derbys . 152 E6
Lower Mill Corn 3 B10
Lower Milovaig Highld . 296 F7
Lower Moor Som 44 D4
Wilts 81 G8
Worcs 99 B9
Lower Morton S Glos ... 79 G10
Lower Mountain Flint ... 166 D4
Lower Nazeing Essex ... 86 D5
Lower Netchwood
Shrops 132 E2
Lower Netherton Devon . 14 G3
Lower New Inn Torf 78 E4
Lower Ninnes Corn 1 C5
Lower Nobut Staffs 151 C10
Lower North Dean Bucks. 84 F5
Lower Norton Warks 118 E4
Lower Nyland Dorset ... 30 C3
Lower Ochrwyth Caerph . 59 B8
Lower Odcombe Som ... 29 D8
Lower Oddington Glos .. 100 F4
Lower Ollach Highld 295 B7
Lower Padworth W Berks .64 F6
Lower Penarth V Glam .. 59 E7
Lower Penn Staffs 133 D7
Lower Pennington
Hants 20 C2
Lower Penwortham
Lancs 194 B4
Lower Peover Ches E. ... 184 G2
Lower Pexhill Ches E. .. 184 G5
Lower Pilsley Derbys ... 170 C6
Lower Pitkerrie Highld . 311 L2
Lower Place Gtr Man. .. 196 E2
London 67 C8
Lower Pollicott Bucks ... 84 C2
Lower Porthkerry V Glam .58 F5
Lower Porthpean Corn. .. 5 E10
Lower Quinton Warks ... 100 B3
Lower Rabber Hereford. 114 G5
Lower Race Torf 78 E3
Lower Radley Oxon 83 F8
Lower Rainham Medway . 69 F10
Lower Ratley Hants 32 C4
Lower Raydon Suff 107 D10
Lower Rea Glos 80 B4
Lower Ridge Devon 28 G2
Shrops 148 G6
Lower Roadwater Som .. 42 F4
Lower Rochford Worcs . 116 D2
Lower Rose Corn 4 E5
Lower Row Dorset 31 G8
Lower Sapey Worcs 116 E3
Lower Seagry Wilts 62 C3
Lower Sheering Essex .. 87 C7
Lower Shelton C Beds .. 103 C9
Lower Shiplake Oxon ... 65 D9
Lower Shuckburgh
Warks 119 E9
Lower Sketty Swansea .. 56 C6
Lower Slackstead Hants . 32 B5
Lower Slade Devon 40 D4
Lower Slaughter Glos ... 100 G3
Lower Solva Pembs 87 G11
Lower Soothill W Yorks . 197 C9
Lower Soudley Glos 79 D11
Lower Southfield
Hereford 98 C3
Lower Stanton St Quintin
Wilts 62 C2
Lower Stoke Medway ... 69 D10
Lower Stondon C Beds .. 104 D3
Lower Stonnall Staffs ... 133 C11
Lower Stow Bedon Norf 141 D9
Lower Stratton Som 28 D6
Swindon 63 B7
Lower Street E Sus 38 E2
Norf. 160 C5
Norf. 160 C3
Norf. 160 D6
Suff 108 B3
Suff 124 G5
Lower Strensham Worcs . 99 C8
Lower Stretton Warr 183 E10
Lower Studley Wilts 45 B11
Lower Sundon C Beds .. 103 F10
Lower Swainswick Bath . 61 F9
Lower Swanwick Hants . 33 F7
Lower Swell Glos 100 G3
Lower Sydenham
London 67 G10
Lower Tadmarton Oxon . 101 D8
Lower Tale Devon 27 G10
Lower Tasburgh Norf ... 142 D3
Lower Tean Staffs 151 B10
Lower Thorpe
Northants. 101 B10

384 Low–Mea

Lower Threapwood
Wrex 166 G6
Lower Thurlton Norf 143 D8
Lower Thurnham Lancs 202 C5
Lower Thurvaston
Derbys 152 B4
Lower Todding Hereford 115 B8
Lower Tote Highld 298 C5
Lowertown Corn 2 D5
Corn 5 C11
Devon 12 E5
Lower Town Devon 27 E8
Hereford 98 C2
Pembs 91 D9
Worcs 117 F7
W Yorks 204 G6
Lower Trebullett Corn 12 F2
Lower Tregunnon Corn 11 E10
Lower Treworrick Corn 6 B4
Lower Tuffley Glos 80 C4
Lower Turmer Hants 31 F10
Lower Twitchen Devon 24 D5
Lower Twydall Medway 69 F10
Lower Tysoe Warks 100 B6
Lower Upham Hants 33 D8
Lower Upnor Medway 69 E9
Lower Vexford Som 42 F6
Lower Wainhill Oxon 84 E3
Lower Walton Warr 183 D10
Lower Wanborough
Swindon 63 C8
Lower Weacombe Som 42 E6
Lower Weald M Keynes 102 D5
Lower Wear Devon 14 D4
Lower Weare Som 44 C2
Lower Weedon
Northants 120 F2
Lower Welson Hereford 114 G5
Lower Westholme Som 44 E5
Lower Westhouse
N Yorks 212 E3
Lower Westmancote
Worcs 99 D8
Lower Weston Bath 61 F8
Lower Whatcombe
Dorset 30 G4
Lower Whatley Som 45 D8
Lower Whitley Ches W 183 F10
Lower Wick Glos 80 F2
Worcs 116 G6
Lower Wield Hants 48 E6
Lower Willingdon E Sus 23 E9
Lower Winchendon or
Nether Winchendon
Bucks 84 C2
Lower Withington
Ches E 168 B4
Lower Wolverton Worcs 117 G8
Lower Woodend Aberds 293 B8
Bucks 65 B10
Lower Woodford Wilts 46 G6
Lower Woodley Corn 5 B10
Lower Woodside Herts 86 D2
Lower Woolston Som 29 B11
Lower Woon Corn 5 C10
Lower Wraxall Dorset 29 G9
Som 44 F6
Wilts 61 G10
Lower Wych Ches W 167 G7
Lower Wyche Worcs 98 C5
Lower Wyke W Yorks 197 B7
Lower Yelland Devon 40 G3
Lower Zeals Wilts 45 G9
Lowes Barn Durham 233 C11
Lowesby Leics 136 B4
Lowestoft Suff 143 E10
Loweswater Cumb 229 G8
Low Etherley Durham 233 F9
Low Fell T&W 243 F7
Lowfield S Yorks 186 D5
Lowfield Heath W Sus 51 E9
Low Fold W Yorks 205 F10
Lowford Hants 33 E7
Low Fulney Lincs 156 E5
Low Garth N Yorks 226 D4
Low Gate Northumb 241 E10
N Yorks 214 F5
Low Geltbridge Cumb 240 F2
Lowgill Cumb 222 F2
Lancs 212 G3
Low Grantley N Yorks 214 E4
Low Green N Yorks 205 B10
Suff 125 E7
W Yorks 205 F10
Low Greenside T&W 242 E4
Low Habberley Worcs 116 B6
Low Ham Som 28 B6
Low Hauxley Northumb 253 C7
Low Hawsker N Yorks 227 D8
Low Hesket Cumb 230 B5
Low Hesleyhurst
Northumb 252 D3
Low Hill W Mid 133 C8
Low Hutton N Yorks 216 F5
Lowick Cumb 210 B5
Northants 137 G9
Northumb 264 B2
Lowick Bridge Cumb 210 B5
Lowick Green Cumb 210 B5
Low Knipe Cumb 230 G6
Low Laithe N Yorks 214 G3
Low Laithes S Yorks 197 G11
Lowlands Torf 78 F3
Low Leighton Derbys 185 D8
Low Lorton Cumb 229 F9
Low Marishes N Yorks 216 D6
Low Marnham Notts 172 B4
Low Mill N Yorks 226 F3
Low Moor Lancs 203 E10
W Yorks 197 B7
Lowmoor Row Cumb 231 F8
Low Moorsley T&W 234 B2
Low Moresby Cumb 228 G5
Lowna N Yorks 226 G3
Low Newton Cumb 211 C8
Low Newton-by-the-Sea
Northumb 264 E6
Lownie Moor Angus 287 C8
Lowood Borders 262 B2
Low Prudhoe Northumb 242 E4
Low Risby N Lincs 200 E2
Low Row Cumb 229 C9
Cumb 240 E3
N Yorks 223 F9
Low Salchrie Dumfries 236 C2
Low Smerby Argyll 255 E8
Low Snaygill N Yorks 204 D5
Lowsonford Warks 118 D3
Low Street Norf 141 B10
Thurrock 69 D7
Low Tharston Norf 142 D3
Lowther Cumb 230 G6
Lowthertown Dumfries 238 D6
Lowtherville IoW 21 F7
Low Thornley T&W 242 E5
Lowthorpe E Yorks 217 G11
Lowton Gtr Man 183 B10
Som 27 D11
Lowton Common
Gtr Man 183 B10
Lowton Heath Gtr Man 183 B10
Lowton St Mary's
Gtr Man 183 B10
Low Torry Fife 279 D10
Low Town Shrops 132 E4
Low Toynton Lincs 190 G3
Low Valley S Yorks 198 G2
Low Valleyfield Fife 279 D10
Low Walton Cumb 219 C9
Low Waters S Lnrk 268 E4
Low Westwood Durham 242 F4
Low Whinnow Cumb 239 G8
Low Whita N Yorks 223 F10
Low Wood Cumb 210 C6
Low Worsall N Yorks 225 C7
Low Wray Cumb 221 E7
Loxbeare Devon 26 D6
Loxford London 68 B2
Loxhill Sur 50 F4
Loxhore Devon 40 F6
Loxhore Cott Devon 40 F6
Loxley S Yorks 186 D4
Warks 118 G5
Loxley Green Staffs 151 C11
Loxter Hereford 98 C4
Loxton N Som 43 B11
Loxwood W Sus 50 G4
Loyter's Green Essex 87 C8
Loyterton Kent 70 G3
Lozells W Mid 133 F11
Lubachlaggan Highld 300 B3
Lubachoinnich Highld 309 K4
Lubberland Shrops 116 B2
Lubcroy Highld 309 J3
Lubenham Leics 136 F4
Lubinvullin Highld 308 C5
Lucas End Herts 86 E4
Lucas Green Lancs 194 C5
Sur 50 B2
Luccombe Som 42 E2
Luccombe Village IoW 21 F7
Lucker Northumb 264 C5
Luckett Corn 12 G3
Lucking Street Essex 106 E6
Luckington Wilts 61 C10
Lucklawhill Fife 287 E8
Luckwell Bridge Som 42 F2
Lucton Hereford 115 E8
Ludag W Isles 297 K3
Ludborough Lincs 190 B3
Ludbrook Devon 8 E3
Ludchurch Pembs 73 C10
Luddenden W Yorks 196 B4
Luddenden Foot
W Yorks 196 C4
Ludderburn Cumb 221 G8
Luddesdown Kent 69 F7
Luddington N Lincs 199 D10
Warks 118 G3
Luddington in the Brook
Northants 138 G2
Lude House Perth 291 G10
Ludford Lincs 190 D2
Shrops 115 C10
Ludgershall Bucks 83 B11
Wilts 47 C9
Ludgvan Corn 2 C2
Ludham Norf 161 F7
Ludlow Shrops 115 C10
Ludney Lincs 190 B5
Som 28 E5
Ludstock Hereford 98 D3
Ludstone Shrops 132 E6
Ludwell Wilts 30 C6
Ludworth Durham 234 C3
Luffenhall Herts 104 F5
Luffincott Devon 12 C2
Lufton Som 29 D8
Lugar E Ayrs 258 E3
Lugate Borders 271 G8
Luggate Burn E Loth 282 G2
Lugg Green Hereford 115 E9
Luggiebank N Lnrk 278 G5
Lugsdale Halton 183 D8
Lugton E Ayrs 267 E8
Lugwardine Hereford 97 C11
Luib Highld 295 C7
Luibeilt Highld 290 G4
Lulham Hereford 97 C8
Lullenden Sur 52 E2
Lullington Derbys 152 G5
Som 45 C9
Lulsgate Bottom N Som 60 F4
Lulsley Worcs 116 F4
Lulworth Camp Dorset 18 E2
Lumb Lancs 195 C10
Lancs 195 D9
W Yorks 196 C4
W Yorks 197 E7
Lumb Foot W Yorks 204 F6
Lumburn Devon 12 G5
Lumbutts W Yorks 196 C3
Lumby N Yorks 206 G5
Lumley W Sus 22 B3
Lumley Thicks Durham 243 G8
Lumloch E Dunb 268 B2
Lumphanan Aberds 293 C7
Lumphinnans Fife 280 C3
Lumsdaine Borders 273 B7
Lumsden Aberds 302 G4
Lunan Angus 287 B10
Lunanhead Angus 287 B8
Luncarty Perth 286 E4
Lund E Yorks 208 D5
N Yorks 207 G9
Shetland 312 C7
Lundal W Isles 304 E3
Lundavra Highld 290 G2
Lunderton Aberds 303 E11
Lundie Angus 286 D6
Highld 290 B3
Lundin Links Fife 287 G8
Lundwood S Yorks 197 F11
Lundy Green Norf 142 E4
Lunga Argyll 275 C8
Lunna Shetland 312 G6
Lunning Shetland 312 G7
Lunnister Shetland 312 F5
Lunnon Swansea 56 D4
Lunsford Kent 53 B7
Lunsford's Cross E Sus 38 E2
Lunt Mers 193 G10
Luntley Hereford 115 F7
Lunts Heath Halton 183 D8
Lupin Staffs 152 F2
Luppitt Devon 27 F11
Lupridge Devon 8 E4
Lupset W Yorks 197 D10
Lupton Cumb 211 C11
Lurg Aberds 293 C8
Lurgashall W Sus 34 B6
Lurignich Argyll 289 D11
Lurley Devon 26 E6
Lusby Lincs 174 B4
Lushcott Shrops 131 D11
Luson Devon 8 F2
Luss Argyll 277 C7
Lussagiven Argyll 275 E7
Lusta Highld 298 D2
Lustleigh Devon 13 E11
Lustleigh Cleave Devon 13 E11
Luston Hereford 115 E9
Lusty Som 45 G7
Luthermuir Aberds 293 G8
Luthrie Fife 287 F7
Lutley W Mid 133 G8
Luton Devon 14 F4
Devon 27 G9
Luton 103 G11
Medway 69 F9
Lutsford Devon 24 D3
Lutterworth Leics 135 G10
Lutton Devon 7 D11
Devon 8 C3
Lincs 157 D8
Northants 138 F2
Lutton Gowts Lincs 157 E8
Lutworthy Devon 26 D3
Luxborough Som 42 F3
Luxley Glos 98 G3
Luxted London 68 G2
Luxton Devon 28 E2
Luxulyan Corn 5 D11
Luzley Gtr Man 196 G3
Luzley Brook Gtr Man 196 F2
Lyatts Som 29 E8
Lybster Highld 310 F6
Lydbury North Shrops 131 F7
Lydcott Devon 41 F7
Lydd Kent 39 C8
Lydden Kent 55 D9
Kent 71 F11
Lyddington Rutland 137 D7
Lydd on Sea Kent 39 C9
Lyde Orkney 314 E3
Shrops 130 C6
Lydeard St Lawrence
Som 42 G6
Lyde Cross Hereford 97 C10
Lyde Green Hants 49 B8
S Glos 61 D7
Lydford Devon 12 E6
Lydford Fair Place Som 44 G5
Lydford-on-Fosse Som 44 G5
Lydgate Derbys 186 F4
Gtr Man 196 G3
W Yorks 196 B2
Lydham Shrops 130 E6
Lydiard Green Wilts 62 B5
Lydiard Millicent Wilts 62 B5
Lydiard Plain Wilts 62 B5
Lydiard Tregoze Swindon 62 C6
Lydiate Mers 193 G11
Lydiate Ash Worcs 117 B9
Lydlinch Dorset 30 E2
Lydmarsh Som 28 F5
Lydney Glos 79 E10
Lydstep Pembs 73 F9
Lye W Mid 133 G8
Lye Cross N Som 60 G3
Lye Green Bucks 85 E7
E Sus 52 G4
Warks 118 D3
Wilts 45 B10
Lye Head Worcs 116 C5
Lye Hole N Som 60 G4
Lyewood Common E Sus 52 F4
Lyford Oxon 82 G5
Lymbridge Green Kent 54 E6
Lyme Green Ches E 184 G6
Lyme Regis Dorset 16 C2
Lymiecleuch Borders 249 C9
Lyminge Kent 55 E7
Lymington Hants 20 B2
Lyminster W Sus 35 G8
Lymm Warr 183 D11
Lymore Hants 19 C11
Lympne Kent 54 F6
Lympsham Som 43 C10
Lympstone Devon 14 E5
Lynbridge Devon 41 D8
Lynch Hants 48 D4
Som 42 D2
Lynchat Highld 291 C9
Lynchgate Shrops 131 F7
Lynch Hill Hants 48 D3
Slough 66 C2
Lyndale Ho Highld 298 D3
Lyndhurst Hants 32 F4
Lyndon Rutland 137 C8
Lyndon Green W Mid 134 F2
Lyne Borders 270 G4
Sur 66 F4
Lyneal Shrops 149 C9
Lyneal Mill Shrops 149 C9
Lyneal Wood Shrops 149 C9
Lyne Down Hereford 98 E2
Lyneham Oxon 100 G5
Wilts 62 D4
Lynemore Highld 301 G10
Lynemouth Northumb 253 E7
Lyne of Gorthleck
Highld 300 G5
Lyne of Skene Aberds 293 B9
Lyness Orkney 314 G3
Lyne Station Borders 260 B6
Lynford Norf 140 E6
Lyng Norf 159 F11
Som 28 B4
Lyngate Norf 160 C5
Lyngford Som 28 B2
Lynmore Highld 301 F10
Lynmouth Devon 41 D8
Lynn Staffs 133 C11
Telford 150 F5
Lynnwood Borders 261 G11
Lynsore Bottom Kent 55 D7
Lynsted Kent 70 G2
Lynstone Corn 24 F2
Lynton Devon 41 D8
Lynwilg Highld 291 B10
Lynworth Glos 99 G9
Lyons T&W 234 B3
Lyon's Gate Dorset 29 F11
Lyon's Green Norf 159 G8
Lyonshall Hereford 114 F6
Lyons Hall Essex 88 B2
Lypiatt Glos 80 D6
Lyrabus Argyll 274 G3
Lytchett Matravers
Dorset 18 B4
Lytchett Minster Dorset 18 C5
Lyth Highld 310 C6
Lytham Lancs 193 B11
Lytham St Anne's
Lancs 193 B10
Lythbank Shrops 131 B9
Lythe N Yorks 226 C6
Lythes Orkney 314 H4
Lythmore Highld 310 C4

M

Maam Argyll 284 F5
Mabe Burnthouse Corn 3 C7
Mabie Dumfries 237 B11
Mabledon Kent 52 E5
Mablethorpe Lincs 191 D8
Macclesfield Ches E 184 G6
Macclesfield Forest
Ches E 185 G7
Macduff Aberds 303 C7
Mace Green Suff 108 C2
Machan S Lnrk 268 E5
Macharioch Argyll 255 G8
Machen Caerph 59 B8
Machrie N Ayrs 255 D9
Machrie Hotel Argyll 254 C4
Machrihanish Argyll 255 E7
Machroes Gwyn 144 D6
Machynlleth Powys 128 C4
Machynys Carms 56 B4
Mackerel's Common
W Sus 35 B8
Mackerye End Herts 85 B11
Mackham Devon 27 F11
Mackney Oxon 64 B5
Mackside Borders 262 G4
Mackworth Derbys 152 B6
Macmerry E Loth 281 G8
Madderty Perth 286 E3
Maddington Wilts 46 E5
Maddiston Falk 279 F8
Maddox Moor Pembs 73 C7
Madehurst W Sus 35 E7
Madeley Staffs 168 G3
Telford 132 C3
Madeley Heath Staffs 168 F3
Worcs 117 B9
Madeley Park Staffs 168 G3
Madeleywood Telford 132 C3
Maders Corn 12 G2
Madford Devon 27 E10
Madingley Cambs 123 E7
Madjeston Dorset 30 B4
Madley Hereford 97 D8
Madresfield Worcs 98 B6
Madron Corn 1 C5
Maenaddwyn Anglesey 179 E7
Maenclochog Pembs 91 F11
Maendy V Glam 58 D4
Maenporth Corn 3 D7
Maentwrog Gwyn 163 G11
Maen-y-groes Ceredig 111 F7
Maer Corn 24 F2
Staffs 150 B5
Maerdy Carms 94 G2
Conwy 165 G8
Rhondda 77 F7
Maes-bangor Ceredig 128 G3
Maesbrook Shrops 148 E5
Maesbury Shrops 148 D6
Maesbury Marsh Shrops 148 D6
Maesgeirchen Gwyn 179 G9
Maes-glas Newport 59 B9
Maes Glas / Greenfield
Flint 181 F11
Maesgwyn-Isaf Powys 148 G3
Maeshafn Denb 166 C2
Maesllyn Ceredig 93 C7
Maes llyn Ceredig 93 C7
Maesmynis Powys 95 B10
Maes Pennant Flint 181 F11
Maesteg Bridgend 57 C10
Maes-Treylow Powys 114 D5
Maesybont Carms 75 B9
Maesycoed Rhondda 58 B5
Maesycrugiau Carms 93 C9
Maesycwmmer Caerph 77 G11
Maes-y-dre Flint 166 C2
Maesygwartha Mon 78 C2
Maesymeillion Ceredig 93 B8
Maesypandy Powys 129 D9
Maesyrhandir Powys 129 E11
Magdalen Laver Essex 87 D8
Maggieknockater Moray 302 E3
Maggots End Essex 105 F9
Magham Down E Sus 23 C10
Maghull Mers 193 G11
Magor Mon 60 B2
Magpie Green Suff 125 B11
Mahaar Dumfries 236 B2
Maida Vale London 67 C9
Maidenbower W Sus 51 F9
Maiden Bradley Wilts 45 F10
Maidencombe Torbay 9 B8
Maidenhall Suff 108 C3
Maidenhead Windsor 65 C11
Maiden Head N Som 60 F5
Maidenhead Court
Windsor 66 C2
Maiden Law Durham 233 B9
Maiden Newton Dorset 17 B7
Maidenpark Falk 279 E9
Maidens S Ayrs 244 B6
Maidensgrave Suff 108 B5
Maiden's Green Brack 65 E11
Maidensgrove Oxon 65 B8
Maiden's Hall Northumb 252 D6
Maidenwell Corn 11 G8
Lincs 190 F4
Maiden Wells Pembs 73 F7
Maidford Northants 120 G2
Maids Moreton Bucks 102 D4
Maidstone Kent 53 B9
Maidwell Northants 120 B4
Mail Shetland 313 L6
Mailand Shetland 312 C8
Mailingsland Borders 270 G4
Main Powys 148 F3
Maindee Newport 59 B10
Maindy Cardiff 59 D7
Mainholm S Ayrs 257 E9
Mains Cumb 229 G7
Mainsforth Durham 234 E2
Mains of Airies Dumfries 236 C1
Mains of Allardice
Aberds 293 F10
Mains of Annochie
Aberds 303 E9
Mains of Ardestie
Angus 287 D9
Mains of Arnage Aberds 303 F9
Mains of Auchoynanie
Moray 302 E4
Mains of Baldoon
Dumfries 236 D6
Mains of Balhall Angus 293 G7
Mains of Ballindarg
Angus 287 B8
Mains of Balnakettle
Aberds 293 F8
Mains of Birness Aberds 303 F9
Mains of Blackhall
Aberds 303 G7
Mains of Burgie Moray 301 D10
Mains of Cairnbrogie
Aberds 303 G8
Mains of Cairnty Moray 302 D3
Mains of Clunas Highld 301 E8
Mains of Crichie Aberds 303 E9
Mains of Daltulich
Highld 301 E7
Mains of Dalvey Highld 301 F11
Mains of Dellavaird
Aberds 293 E9
Mains of Drum Aberds 293 D10
Mains of Edingight
Moray 302 D5
Mains of Fedderate
Aberds 303 E8
Mains of Flichity Highld 300 G6
Mains of Hatton Aberds 303 D9
Aberds 303 E7
Mains of Inkhorn Aberds 303 F9
Mains of Innerpeffray
Perth 286 F3
Mains of Kirktonhill
Aberds 293 G8
Mains of Laithers
Aberds 302 E6
Mains of Mayen Moray 302 E5
Mains of Melgund
Angus 287 B9
Mains of Taymouth
Perth 285 C11
Mains of Thornton
Aberds 293 F8
Mains of Towie Aberds 303 E7
Mains of Ulbster Highld 310 E7
Mains of Watten Highld 310 D6
Mainsriddle Dumfries 237 D11
Mainstone Shrops 130 F5
Maisemore Glos 98 G6
Maitland Park London 67 C9
Major's Green W Mid 118 B2
Makeney Derbys 170 G5
Malacleit W Isles 296 D3
Malborough Devon 9 G9
Malcoff Derbys 185 E9
Malden Rushett London 67 G7
Maldon Essex 88 D4
Malehurst Shrops 131 B7
Malham N Yorks 213 G8
Maligar Highld 298 C4
Malinbridge S Yorks 186 D4
Malinslee Telford 132 B3
Malkin's Bank Ches E 168 D3
Mallaig Highld 295 F8
Mallaig Bheag Highld 295 F8
Malleny Mills Edin 270 B3
Malling Stirl 285 G9
Mallows Green Essex 105 F9
Malltraeth Anglesey 162 B6
Mallwyd Gwyn 147 G7
Malmesbury Wilts 62 B2
Malmsmead Devon 41 D9
Malpas Ches W 167 F7
Corn 4 G6
Newport 78 G4
W Berks 64 E6
Malswick Glos 98 F4
Maltby Lincs 190 E4
Stockton 225 C9
S Yorks 187 C8
Maltby le Marsh Lincs 191 E7
Malting End Suff 124 G4
Malting Green Essex 107 G9
Maltings Angus 293 G9
Maltman's Hill Kent 54 E2
Malton N Yorks 216 E5
Malvern Common Worcs 98 C5
Malvern Link Worcs 98 B5
Malvern Wells Worcs 98 C5
Mambeg Argyll 276 D4
Mamble Worcs 116 C3
Mamhilad Mon 78 E4
Manaccan Corn 3 E7
Manadon Plym 7 D9
Manafon Powys 130 C2
Manais W Isles 296 C7
Manar Ho Aberds 303 G7
Manaton Devon 13 E11
Manby Lincs 190 D5
Mancetter Warks 134 D6
Manchester Gtr Man 184 B4
Manchester Airport
Gtr Man 184 D4
Mancot Flint 166 B4
Mancot Royal Flint 166 B4
Mandally Highld 290 C4
Manea Cambs 139 F9
Maney W Mid 134 D2
Manfield N Yorks 224 C4
Mangaster Shetland 312 F5
Mangotsfield S Glos 61 D7
Mangrove Green Herts 104 G2
Mangurstadh W Isles 304 E2
Manhay Corn 2 C5
Manian-fawr Pembs 92 B3
Mankinholes W Yorks 196 C3
Manley Ches W 183 G8
Devon 27 E7
Manley Common
Ches W 183 G8
Manmoel Caerph 77 E11
Man-moel Caerph 77 E11
Mannal Argyll 288 E1
Mannamead Plym 7 D9
Mannerston W Loth 279 F10
Manningford Abbots
Wilts 46 B6
Manningford Bohune
Wilts 46 B6
Manningford Bruce Wilts 46 B6
Manningham W Yorks 205 G9
Mannings Heath W Sus 36 B2
Mannington Dorset 31 F9
Manningtree Essex 107 E11
Mannofield Aberdeen 293 C11
Manor London 68 B2
Manorbier Pembs 73 F9
Manorbier Newton
Pembs 73 F8
Manor Bourne Devon 7 F9
Manordeilo Carms 94 F3
Manor Estate S Yorks 186 D5
Manorhill Borders 262 C5
Manor Hill Corner Lincs 157 F8
Manor House W Mid 135 G7
Manorowen Pembs 91 D8
Manor Park Bucks 84 C4
Ches W 167 B11
E Sus 37 C7
London 68 B2
Notts 153 C11
Slough 66 C3
S Yorks 186 D5
W Yorks 205 D9
Manor Parsley Corn 4 F4
Manor Royal W Sus 51 F9
Man's Cross Essex 106 D5
Mansegate Dumfries 247 G9
Manselfield Swansea 56 D5
Mansel Lacy Hereford 97 B8
Mansell Gamage
Hereford 97 C7
Manselton Swansea 57 B7
Mansergh Cumb 212 C2
Mansewood Glasgow 267 C11
Mansfield E Ayrs 258 G4
Notts 171 C8
Mansfield Woodhouse
Notts 171 C8
Manson Green Norf 141 C10
Mansriggs Cumb 210 C5
Manston Dorset 30 D4
Kent 71 F10
W Yorks 206 F3
Manswood Dorset 31 F7
Manthorpe Lincs 155 B8
Lincs 155 F11
Mantles Green Bucks 85 F7
Manton N Lincs 200 G2
Notts 187 F9
Rutland 137 C7
Wilts 63 F7
Manton Warren N Lincs 200 F2
Manuden Essex 105 F9
Manwood Green Essex 87 C8
Manywells Height
W Yorks 205 F7
Maperton Som 29 B11
Maplebeck Notts 172 C2
Maple Cross Herts 85 G8
Mapledurham Oxon 65 D7
Mapledurwell Hants 49 C7
Maple End Essex 105 D11
Maplehurst W Sus 35 C11
Maplescombe Kent 68 G5
Mapleton Derbys 169 F11
Mapperley Derbys 170 G6
Nottingham 171 G9
Mapperley Park
Nottingham 171 G9
Mapperton Dorset 16 B6
Dorset 18 B4
Mappleborough Green
Warks 117 D11
Mappleton E Yorks 209 E10
Mapplewell S Yorks 197 F10
Mappowder Dorset 30 F2
Maraig W Isles 305 H3
Marazanvose Corn 4 E6
Marazion Corn 2 C2
Marbhig W Isles 305 G6
Marbrack Dumfries 246 E3
Marbury Ches E 167 F9
March Cambs 139 D8
S Lnrk 259 G11
Marcham Oxon 83 F7
Marchamley Shrops 149 D11
Marchamley Wood
Shrops 149 C11
Marchington Staffs 152 C2
Marchington Woodlands
Staffs 152 D2
Marchroes Gwyn 144 D6
Marchwiel Wrex 166 F5
Marchwood Hants 32 E5
Marcross V Glam 58 F2
Marden Hereford 97 B10
Kent 53 E8
T&W 243 C9
Wilts 46 B5
Marden Ash Essex 87 E9
Marden Beech Kent 53 E8
Marden's Hill E Sus 52 G3
Marden Thorn Kent 53 E9
Mardleybury Herts 86 B3
Mardu Shrops 130 G5
Mardy Mon 78 B4
Shrops 148 C5
Marefield Leics 136 B4
Mareham le Fen Lincs 174 C3
Mareham on the Hill
Lincs 174 B3
Marehay Derbys 170 F5
Marehill W Sus 35 D9
Maresfield E Sus 37 C7
Maresfield Park E Sus 37 C7
Marfleet Hull 200 B6
Marford Wrex 166 D5
Margam Neath 57 D9
Margaret Marsh Dorset 30 D4
Margaret Roding Essex 87 C9
Margaretting Essex 87 E11
Margaretting Tye Essex 87 E11
Margate Kent 71 E11
Margery Sur 51 C9
Margnaheglish N Ayrs 256 C2
Margreig Dumfries 237 B10
Margrove Park Redcar 226 B3
Marham Norf 158 G4
Marhamchurch Corn 24 G2
Marholm Pboro 138 C2
Marian Flint 181 F9
Marian Cwm Denb 181 F9
Mariandyrys Anglesey 179 E10
Marianglas Anglesey 179 E8
Marian-glas Anglesey 179 E8
Mariansleigh Devon 26 C2
Marian y de / South Beach
Gwyn 145 C7
Marian y mor / West End
Gwyn 145 C7
Marine Town Kent 70 E2
Marionburgh Aberds 293 C9
Marishader Highld 298 C4
Marjoriebanks Dumfries 248 G3
Mark Dumfries 236 D3
Dumfries 237 C7
S Ayrs 236 B2
Som 43 D11
Markbeech Kent 52 E3
Markby Lincs 191 F7
Mark Causeway Som 43 D11
Mark Cross E Sus 23 C7
E Sus 52 G5
Markeaton Derbys 152 B6
Market Bosworth Leics 135 C8
Market Deeping Lincs 138 B2
Market Drayton Shrops 150 C3
Market Harborough
Leics 136 F4
Markethill Perth 286 D6
Market Lavington Wilts 46 C4
Market Overton Rutland 155 F7
Market Rasen Lincs 189 D10
Market Stainton Lincs 190 F2
Market Warsop Notts 171 B9
Market Weighton
E Yorks 208 E3
Market Weston Suff 125 B9
Markfield Leics 153 G9
Mark Hall North Essex 87 C7
Mark Hall South Essex 87 C7
Markham Caerph 77 E11
Markham Moor Notts 188 G2
Markinch Fife 286 G6
Markington N Yorks 214 F5
Markland Hill Gtr Man 195 F7
Markle E Loth 281 F11
Marksbury Bath 61 G7
Mark's Corner IoW 20 C5
Marks Gate London 87 G7
Marks Tey Essex 107 G8
Markyate Herts 85 B9
Marland Gtr Man 195 E11
Marlas Hereford 97 F8
Marl Bank Worcs 98 C5
Marlborough Wilts 63 F7
Marlbrook Hereford 115 G10
Worcs 117 C9
Marlcliff Warks 117 G11
Marldon Devon 9 C7
Marle Green E Sus 23 B9
Marle Hill Glos 99 G9
Marlesford Suff 126 F6
Marley Kent 55 C7
Kent 55 C10
Marley Green Ches E 167 F9
Marley Heights W Sus 49 G11
Marley Hill T&W 242 F6
Marley Pots T&W 243 F9
Marlingford Norf 142 B2
Mar Lodge Aberds 292 D2
Marloes Pembs 72 D3
Marlow Bucks 65 B10
Hereford 115 B8
Marlow Bottom Bucks 65 B11
Marlow Common Bucks 65 B10
Marlpit Hill Kent 52 D2
Marlpits E Sus 38 E2
Marlpool Derbys 170 F6
Marnhull Dorset 30 D3
Marnoch Aberds 302 D5
Marnock N Lnrk 268 B4
Marple Gtr Man 185 D7
Marple Bridge Gtr Man 185 D7
Marpleridge Gtr Man 185 D7
Marr S Yorks 198 F4
Marrel Highld 311 H4
Marr Green Wilts 63 G8
Marrick N Yorks 223 F11
Marrister Shetland 313 G7
Marros Carms 74 D2
Marsden T&W 243 E9
W Yorks 196 E4
Marsden Height Lancs 204 F3
Marsett N Yorks 213 B8
Marsh Bucks 84 D4
Devon 28 E3
W Yorks 196 D6
W Yorks 204 F6
Marshall Meadows
Northumb 273 D9
Marshall's Cross Mers 183 C8
Marshall's Elm Som 44 G3
Marshall's Heath Herts 85 B11
Marshalsea Dorset 28 G5
Marshalswick Herts 85 D11
Marsham Norf 160 E3
Marshaw Lancs 203 C7
Marsh Baldon Oxon 83 F9
Marsh Benham W Berks 64 F2
Marshborough Kent 55 B10
Marshbrook Shrops 131 F8
Marshchapel Lincs 190 B5
Marsh Common S Glos 60 C5
Marsh End Worcs 98 D6
Marshfield Newport 59 C9
S Glos 61 E9
Marshfield Bank
Ches E 167 D11
Marshgate Corn 11 C9
Marsh Gate W Berks 63 F10
Marsh Gibbon Bucks 102 G2
Marsh Green Ches W 183 F8
Devon 14 C6
Gtr Man 194 F5
Kent 52 E2
Staffs 168 D5
Telford 150 G2
Marsh Houses Lancs 202 C5
Marshland St James
Norf 139 B10
Marsh Lane Derbys 186 F6
Glos 79 D9
Marsh Mills Som 43 F7
Marshmoor Herts 86 D2
Marshside Kent 71 F8
Mers 193 D11
Marsh Side Norf 176 E3
Marsh Street Som 42 E3
Marshwood Dorset 16 B3
Marske N Yorks 224 E2
Marske-by-the-Sea
Redcar 235 G8
Marston Ches W 183 F11
Hereford 115 F7
Lincs 172 G5
Oxon 83 D8
Staffs 150 G6
Staffs 151 D8
Warks 119 B8
Warks 134 E4
Wilts 46 B3
Marston Bigot Som 45 E9
Marston Doles Warks 119 F9
Marston Gate Som 45 D9
Marston Green W Mid 134 F3
Marston Hill Glos 81 F10
Marston Jabbett Warks 135 F7
Marston Magna Som 29 C9
Marston Meysey Wilts 81 F10
Marston Montgomery
Derbys 152 B2
Marston Moretaine
C Beds 103 C9
Marston on Dove
Derbys 152 D4
Marston St Lawrence
Northants 101 C10
Marston Stannett
Hereford 115 F11
Marston Trussell
Northants 136 F3
Marstow Hereford 79 B9
Marsworth Bucks 84 C6
Marten Wilts 47 B9
Marthall Ches E 184 F4
Martham Norf 161 F9
Marthwaite Cumb 222 G2
Martin Hants 31 D9
Kent 55 D10
Lincs 173 D11
Lincs 174 B2
Martindale Cumb 221 B8
Martin Dales Lincs 173 C11
Martin Drove End Hants 31 C9
Martinhoe Devon 41 D7
Martinhoe Cross Devon 41 D7
Martin Hussingtree
Worcs 117 E7
Martin Mill Kent 55 D10
Martin Moor Lincs 174 C2
Martinscroft Warr 183 D11
Martin's Moss Ches E 168 C4
Martinstown Dorset 17 D8
Martinstown or
Winterbourne St Martin
Dorset 17 D8
Martlesham Suff 108 B4
Martlesham Heath Suff 108 B4
Martletwy Pembs 73 C8
Martley Worcs 116 E5
Martock Som 29 D7
Marton Ches E 168 B5
Ches W 167 B10
Cumb 210 D4
E Yorks 209 F9
Lincs 188 E4
Mbro 225 B10
N Yorks 215 G8
N Yorks 216 C4
Shrops 130 C5
Shrops 149 E8
Warks 119 D8
Marton Green Ches W 167 B10
Marton Grove Mbro 225 B9
Marton-in-the-Forest
N Yorks 215 F11
Marton-le-Moor
N Yorks 215 E7
Marton Moor Warks 119 D8
Marton Moss Side
Blkpool 202 G2
Martyr's Green Sur 50 B5
Martyr Worthy Hants 48 G4
Marwick Orkney 314 D2
Marwood Devon 40 F4
Marybank Highld 300 D4
Highld 301 B7
Maryburgh Highld 300 D5
Maryfield Aberds 293 D7
Corn 7 D8
Maryhill Glasgow 267 B11
Marykirk Aberds 293 G8
Maryland Mon 79 D8
Marylebone Gtr Man 194 F5
Marypark Moray 301 F11
Maryport Cumb 228 D6
Dumfries 236 F3
Mary Tavy Devon 12 F6
Maryton Angus 287 B7
Angus 287 B10
Marywell Aberds 293 D7
Aberds 293 D11
Angus 287 C10
Masbrough S Yorks 186 C6
Mascle Bridge Pembs 73 D7
Masham N Yorks 214 C4
Mashbury Essex 87 C11
Masongill N Yorks 212 D3
Masonhill S Ayrs 257 E9
Mastin Moor Derbys 187 F7
Mastrick Aberdeen 293 C10
Matchborough Worcs 117 D11
Matching Essex 87 C8
Matching Green Essex 87 C8
Matching Tye Essex 87 C8
Matfen Northumb 242 C2
Matfield Kent 53 E7
Mathern Mon 79 G8
Mathon Hereford 98 B4
Mathry Pembs 91 E7
Matlaske Norf 160 C3
Matley Gtr Man 185 B7
Matlock Derbys 170 C3
Matlock Bank Derbys 170 C3
Matlock Bath Derbys 170 D3
Matlock Bridge Derbys 170 D3
Matlock Cliff Derbys 170 D4
Matlock Dale Derbys 170 D3
Matshead Lancs 202 E6
Matson Glos 80 B4
Matterdale End Cumb 230 G3
Mattersey Notts 187 D11
Mattersey Thorpe
Notts 187 D11
Matthewsgreen
Wokingham 65 F10
Mattingley Hants 49 B8
Mattishall Norf 159 G11
Mattishall Burgh Norf 159 G11
Mauchline E Ayrs 257 D11
Maud Aberds 303 E9
Maudlin Corn 5 C11
Dorset 28 F5
W Sus 22 B5
Maudlin Cross Dorset 28 F5
Maugersbury Glos 100 F4
Maughold IoM 192 C5
Mauld Highld 300 F4
Maulden C Beds 103 D11
Maulds Meaburn Cumb 222 B2
Maunby N Yorks 215 B7
Maund Bryan Hereford 115 G11
Maundown Som 27 B9
Mauricewood Midloth 270 C4
Mautby Norf 161 G9
Mavesyn Ridware
Staffs 151 F11
Mavis Enderby Lincs 174 B5
Maviston Highld 301 D9
Mawbray Cumb 229 B7
Mawdesley Lancs 194 E3
Mawdlam Bridgend 57 E10
Mawgan Corn 2 D6
Mawgan Porth Corn 5 B7
Maw Green Ches E 168 D2
Mawla Corn 4 F4
Mawnan Corn 3 D7
Mawnan Smith Corn 3 D7
Mawsley Northants 120 B6
Mawson Green S Yorks 198 D6
Mawthorpe Lincs 191 G7
Maxey Pboro 138 B2
Maxstoke Warks 134 F4
Maxted Street Kent 54 E6
Maxton Borders 262 C4
Kent 55 E10
Maxwellheugh Borders 262 C6
Maxwelltown Dumfries 237 B11
Maxworthy Corn 11 C11
Mayals Swansea 56 C6
May Bank Staffs 168 F5
Maybole S Ayrs 257 G8
Maybury Sur 50 B4
Maybush Soton 32 E5
Mayer's Green W Mid 133 E10
Mayes Green Sur 50 F6
Mayeston Pembs 73 E8
Mayfair London 67 C9
Mayfield E Sus 37 B9
Midloth 271 C7
Northumb 243 B7
Staffs 169 F11
W Loth 269 B8
Mayford Sur 50 B3
Mayhill Swansea 56 C6
May Hill Mon 79 C8
May Hill Village Glos 98 G4
Mayland Essex 88 E6
Maylandsea Essex 88 E6
Maynard's Green E Sus 23 B9
Mayne Ho Moray 302 C2
Mayon Corn 1 D3
Maypole Bromley 68 G3
Dartford 68 E4
Kent 71 G7
Mon 79 B7
Scilly 1 G4
Maypole Green Essex 107 G9
Norf 143 D8
Suff 125 F8
Suff 126 D5
Mays Green Oxon 65 C8
May's Green N Som 59 G11
Sur 50 B5
Mayshill S Glos 61 C7
Maythorn S Yorks 197 F7
Maythorne Notts 171 D11
Maywick Shetland 313 L5
Mead Devon 13 G11
Devon 24 D2
Mead End Hants 19 B11
Hants 33 E11
Wilts 31 C8
Meadgate Bath 45 B7
Meadle Bucks 84 D4

Meadowbank Ches W 167 B11
Edin 280 G5
Meadowend Essex 106 C4
Meadowfield Durham 233 D10
Meadowfoot N Ayrs 266 F4
Meadow Green Hereford 116 F4
Meadow Hall S Yorks 186 C5
Meadow Head S Yorks 186 E4
Meadowley Shrops 132 E3
Meadowmill E Loth 281 G8
Meadows Nottingham 153 B11
Meadowtown Shrops 130 C6
Meads E Sus 23 F10
Meadside Oxon 83 G9
Mead Vale Sur 51 D9
Meadwell Devon 12 E4
Meaford Staffs 151 B7
Meagill N Yorks 205 B9
Mealabost W Isles 304 E6
Mealabost Bhuirgh
W Isles 304 C6
Mealasta W Isles 304 F1
Meal Bank Cumb 221 F10
Meal Hill W Yorks 197 F7
Mealrigg Cumb 229 B8
Mealsgate Cumb 229 C10
Meanwood W Yorks 205 F11
Mearbeck N Yorks 212 G6
Meare Som 44 E3
Meare Green Som 28 B4
Som 28 C3
Mearns Bath 45 B7
E Renf 267 D10
Mears Ashby Northants 120 D6
Measborough Dike
S Yorks 197 F11
Measham Leics 152 G6
Meath Green Sur 51 E9
Meathop Cumb 211 C8
Meaux E Yorks 209 F7
Meaver Corn 2 F5
Meavy Devon 7 B10
Medbourne Leics 136 E5
M Keynes 102 D6
Medburn Northumb 242 C4
Meddon Devon 24 D3
Meden Vale Notts 171 B9
Medhurst Row Kent 52 D3
Medlam Lincs 174 D4
Medlar Lancs 202 F4
Medlicott Shrops 131 E8
Medlyn Corn 2 C6
Medmenham Bucks 65 C10
Medomsley Durham 242 G4
Medstead Hants 49 F7
Meerbrook Staffs 169 C7
Meer Common Hereford 115 G7
Meer End W Mid 118 C4
Meerhay Dorset 29 G7
Meers Bridge Lincs 191 D7
Meersbrook S Yorks 186 E5
Meesden Herts 105 E8
Meeson Telford 150 E3
Meeson Heath Telford 150 E3
Meeth Devon 25 F8
Meethe Devon 25 C11
Meeting Green Suff 124 F4
Meeting House Hill
Norf 160 D6
Meggernie Castle Perth 285 C9
Meggethead Borders 260 E5
Meidrim Carms 92 G5
Meifod Denb 165 D8
Powys 148 G3
Meigle N Ayrs 266 B3
Perth 286 C6
Meikle Earnock S Lnrk 268 E4
Meikle Ferry Highld 309 L7
Meikle Forter Angus 292 G3
Meikle Gluich Highld 309 L6
Meikle Obney Perth 286 D4
Meikleour Perth 286 D5
Meikle Pinkerton
E Loth 282 F4
Meikle Strath Aberds 293 F8
Meikle Tarty Aberds 303 G9
Meikle Wartle Aberds 303 F7
Meinciau Carms 75 C7
Meir Stoke 168 G6
Meir Heath Staffs 168 G6
Melbourn Cambs 105 C7
Melbourne Derbys 153 D7
E Yorks 207 E11
S Lnrk 269 G11
Melbury Abbas Dorset 30 D5
Melbury Bubb Dorset 29 F9
Melbury Osmond Dorset 29 F9
Melbury Sampford
Dorset 29 F9
Melby Shetland 313 H3
Melchbourne Beds 121 D10
Melcombe Som 43 G9
Melcombe Bingham
Dorset 30 G3
Melcombe Regis Dorset 17 E9
Meldon Devon 13 C7
Northumb 252 G4
Meldreth Cambs 105 B7
Meldrum Ho Aberds 303 G8
Melfort Argyll 275 B9
Melgarve Highld 290 D6
Meliden / Gallt Melyd
Denb 181 E9
Melinbyrhedyn Powys 128 D6
Melin Caiach Caerph 77 F10
Melincourt Neath 76 E4
Melincryddan Neath 57 B8
Melinsey Corn 3 B10
Melin-y-coed Conwy 164 C4
Melin-y-ddôl Powys 129 B11
Melin-y-grug Powys 129 B11
Melin-y-Wig Denb 165 F8
Melkington Northumb 273 G7
Melkinthorpe Cumb 231 F7
Melkridge Northumb 240 E6
Melksham Wilts 62 G2
Melksham Forest Wilts 62 G2
Mellangaun Highld 307 L3
Mellangoose Corn 2 D5
Melldalloch Argyll 275 F10
Mell Green W Berks 64 D3
Mellguards Cumb 230 B4
Melling Lancs 211 E11
Mers 193 G11
Mellingey Corn 10 G4
Melling Mount Mers 194 G2
Mellis Suff 126 C2
Mellis Green Suff 125 C11
Mellon Charles Highld 307 K3
Mellon Udrigle Highld 307 K3
Mellor Gtr Man 185 D7
Lancs 203 G9
Mellor Brook Lancs 203 G8
Mells Som 45 D8
Suff 127 B8
Mells Green Som 45 D8
Melmerby Cumb 231 D8
N Yorks 213 B11
N Yorks 214 D6
Melon Green Suff 124 F6
Melplash Dorset 16 B5
Melrose Borders 262 C2
Melsetter Orkney 314 H2
Melsonby N Yorks 224 D3
Meltham W Yorks 196 E6
Meltham Mills W Yorks 196 E6
Melton E Yorks 200 B3
Suff 126 G5
Meltonby E Yorks 207 C11
Melton Constable Norf 159 C10
Melton Mowbray Leics 154 F5
Melton Ross N Lincs 200 E5
Melvaig Highld 307 L2
Melverley Shrops 148 F6
Melverley Green Shrops 148 F6
Melvich Highld 310 C2
Membland Devon 7 F11
Membury Devon 28 G3
Memsie Aberds 303 C9
Memus Angus 287 B8
Mena Corn 5 C10
Menabilly Corn 5 E11
Menadarva Corn 4 G2
Menagissey Corn 4 F4
Menai Bridge / Porthaethwy
Anglesey 179 G9
Mendham Suff 142 G5
Mendlesham Suff 126 D2
Mendlesham Green
Suff 125 E11
Menethorpe N Yorks 216 F5
Mengham Hants 21 B10
Menheniot Corn 6 C5
Menherion Corn 2 B6
Menithwood Worcs 116 D4
Menna Corn 5 E8
Mennock Dumfries 247 B8
Menston W Yorks 205 E9
Menstrie Clack 278 B6
Mentmore Bucks 84 B6
Menzion Borders 260 E3
Meoble Highld 295 G9
Meole Brace Shrops 149 G9
Meols Mers 182 C2
Meon Hants 33 G8
Meonstoke Hants 33 D10
Meopham Kent 68 F6
Meopham Green Kent 68 F6
Meopham Station Kent 68 F6
Mepal Cambs 139 G8
Meppershall C Beds 104 D2
Merbach Hereford 96 B6
Mercaston Derbys 170 G3
Merchant Fields
W Yorks 197 B7
Merchiston Edin 280 G4
Mere Ches E 184 E2
Wilts 45 G10
Mere Brow Lancs 194 D2
Mereclough Lancs 204 G3
Mere Green W Mid 134 D2
Worcs 117 E9
Merehead Wrex 149 B9
Mere Heath Ches W 183 G11
Meresborough Medway 69 G10
Mereside Blkpool 202 G2
Meretown Staffs 150 E5
Mereworth Kent 53 C7
Mergie Aberds 293 E9
Meriden Herts 85 F10
W Mid 134 G4
Merkadale Highld 294 B5
Merkland Dumfries 237 B9
N Ayrs 256 B2
S Ayrs 244 E6
Merkland Lodge Highld 309 G4
Merle Common Sur 52 D2
Merley Poole 18 B6
Merlin's Bridge Pembs 72 C6
Merlin's Cross Pembs 73 E7
Merridale W Mid 133 D7
Merridge Som 43 G8
Merrie Gardens IoW 21 E7
Merrifield Devon 8 F6
Devon 24 G3
Merrington Shrops 149 E9
Merrion Pembs 72 F6
Merriott Dorset 16 B6
Som 28 E6
Merriottsford Som 28 E6
Merritown Dorset 19 B8
Merrivale Devon 12 F6
Hereford 98 G2
Merrow Sur 50 C4
Merrybent Darl 224 C4
Merry Field Hill Dorset 31 G8
Merry Hill Herts 85 G10
W Mid 133 D7
Merryhill Green
Wokingham 65 E9
Merrylee E Renf 267 D11
Merry Lees Leics 135 B9
Merrymeet Corn 6 B5
Merry Meeting Corn 11 G7
Merry Oak Soton 32 E6
Mersham Kent 54 F5
Merstham Sur 51 C9
Merston W Sus 22 C5
Merstone IoW 20 E6
Merther Corn 5 G7
Merther Lane Corn 5 G7
Merthyr Carms 93 G7
Merthyr Cynog Powys 95 D9
Merthyr-Dyfan V Glam 58 F6
Merthyr Mawr Bridgend 57 F11
Merthyr Tydfil M Tydf 77 D8
Merthyr Vale M Tydf 77 F9
Merton Devon 25 E8
London 67 E9
Norf 141 D8
Oxon 83 B9
Merton Park London 67 F9
Mervinslaw Borders 262 G5
Meshaw Devon 26 D3
Messing Essex 88 B5
Messingham N Lincs 199 G11
Mesty Croft W Mid 133 E9
Mesur-y-dorth Pembs 87 E11
Metal Bridge Durham 233 E11
Metfield Suff 142 G5
Metherell Corn 7 B8
Metheringham Lincs 173 C9
Methersgate Suff 108 B5
Methil Fife 281 B7
Methilhill Fife 281 B7
Methlem Gwyn 144 C3
Methley W Yorks 197 B11
Methley Junction
W Yorks 197 B11
Methley Lanes
W Yorks 197 B11
Methlick Aberds 303 F8
Methven Perth 286 E4
Methwold Norf 140 E4
Methwold Hythe Norf 140 E4
Mettingham Suff 143 F7
Metton Norf 160 B3
Mevagissey Corn 5 G10
Mewith Head N Yorks 212 F4
Mexborough S Yorks 187 B7
Mey Highld 310 B6
Meyrick Park Bmouth 19 C7
Meysey Hampton Glos 81 F10
Miabhag W Isles 305 H2
W Isles 305 J3
Miabhig W Isles 304 E2
Mial Highld 299 B7
Michaelchurch Hereford 97 F10
Michaelchurch Escley
Hereford 96 E6
Michaelchurch on Arrow
Powys 114 G4
Michaelston-le-Pit
V Glam 59 E7
Michaelston-y-Fedw
Newport 59 C8
Michaelstow Corn 11 F7
Michealston-super-Ely
Cardiff 58 D6
Michelcombe Devon 8 B3
Micheldever Hants 48 F4
Michelmersh Hants 32 B4
Mickfield Suff 126 E2
Micklebring S Yorks 187 C8
Mickleby N Yorks 226 C6
Micklefield Bucks 84 G5
W Yorks 206 G4
Micklefield Green Herts 85 F8
Mickleham Sur 51 C7
Micklehurst Gtr Man 196 G3
Mickleover Derby 152 C6
Micklethwaite Cumb 239 G7
W Yorks 205 E8
Mickleton Durham 232 G5
Glos 100 C3
Mickletown W Yorks 197 B11
Mickle Trafford Ches W 166 B6
Mickley Derbys 186 F4
N Yorks 214 D5
Shrops 150 C2
Mickley Green Suff 124 F6
Mickley Square
Northumb 242 E3
Midanbury Hants 33 E7
Mid Ardlaw Aberds 303 C9
Mid Auchinleck Invclyd 276 G6
Midbea Orkney 314 B4
Mid Beltie Aberds 293 C8
Mid Calder W Loth 269 B11
Mid Cloch Forbie
Aberds 303 D7
Mid Clyth Highld 310 F6
Middle Assendon Oxon 65 B8
Middle Aston Oxon 101 F9
Middle Balnald Perth 286 B4
Middle Barton Oxon 101 F8
Middle Bickenhill
W Mid 134 G4
Middlebie Dumfries 238 B6
Middle Bockhampton
Dorset 19 B9
Middle Bourne Sur 49 E10
Middle Bridge N Som 60 D3
Middle Burnham Som 43 D10
Middle Cairncake
Aberds 303 E8
Middlecave N Yorks 216 E5
Middle Chinnock Som 29 E7
Middle Claydon Bucks 102 F4
Middle Cliff Staffs 169 E8
Middlecliffe S Yorks 198 F2
Middlecott Devon 13 D10
Devon 24 F6
Devon 26 F3
Middle Crackington Corn 11 B9
Middlecroft Derbys 186 G6
Middle Drums Angus 287 B9
Middle Duntisbourne
Glos 81 D7
Middlefield Falk 279 E7
Middleforth Green
Lancs 194 B4
Middle Green Bucks 66 C4
Som 27 D10
Suff 124 D4
Middleham N Yorks 214 B2
Middle Handley Derbys 186 F6
Middle Harling Norf 141 F9
Middle Herrington T&W 243 G9
Middlehill Corn 6 B5
Wilts 61 F10
Middle Hill Pembs 73 C7
Staffs 133 B9
Middlehope Shrops 131 F9
Middle Kames Argyll 275 E10
Middle Littleton Worcs 99 B11
Middle Luxton Devon 28 E2
Middle Madeley Staffs 168 F3
Middle Maes-coed
Hereford 96 E6
Middlemarsh Dorset 29 F11
Middle Marwood Devon 40 F4
Middle Mayfield Staffs 169 G10
Middle Mill Pembs 87 F11
Middlemoor Devon 12 G5
Middlemuir Aberds 303 D9
Aberds 303 E8
Aberds 303 G9
Middleport Stoke 168 F5
Middle Quarter Kent 53 F11
Middle Rainton T&W 234 B2
Middle Rasen Lincs 189 D9
Middlerig Falk 279 F8
Middle Rigg Perth 286 G4
Middle Rocombe Devon 9 B8
Middlesbrough Mbro 234 G5
Middlesceugh Cumb 230 C4
Middleshaw Cumb 211 B11
Middle Side Durham 232 F4
Middlesmoor N Yorks 213 E11
Middle Stoford Som 27 C11
Middle Stoke Devon 13 G9
Medway 69 D10
W Mid 119 B7
Middlestone Durham 233 E11
Middlestone Moor
Durham 233 E10
Middle Stoughton Som 44 D2
Middlestown W Yorks 197 D9
Middle Strath W Loth 279 G8
Middle Street Glos 80 E3
Middle Taphouse Corn 6 C3
Middlethird Borders 272 G3
Middlethorpe York 207 D7
Middleton Aberds 293 B10
Argyll 288 E1
Cumb 212 B2
Derbys 169 C11
Derbys 170 D3
Essex 107 D7
Gtr Man 195 F11
Hants 48 E2
Hereford 115 D10
Hrtlpl 234 E6
IoW 20 D2
Lancs 202 B4
Midloth 271 D7
Norf 158 F3
Northants 136 F6
Northumb 252 F3
Northumb 264 B4
N Yorks 204 E5
N Yorks 205 D8
N Yorks 216 B5
Perth 286 C5
Perth 286 F2
Perth 286 G5
Shrops 115 B10
Shrops 130 D5
Shrops 148 D6
Suff 127 D8
Swansea 56 D2
Warks 134 D3
W Yorks 197 B10
Middleton Baggot
Shrops 132 E2
Middleton Cheney
Northants 101 C9
Middleton Green Staffs 151 B9
Middleton Hall
Northumb 263 D11
Middleton-in-Teesdale
Durham 232 F4
Middleton Junction
Gtr Man 195 G11
Middleton Moor Suff 127 D8
Middleton of Rora
Aberds 303 E10
Middleton One Row
Darl 225 C7
Middleton-on-Leven
N Yorks 225 D9
Middleton-on-Sea
W Sus 35 G7
Middleton on the Hill
Hereford 115 E10
Middleton-on-the-Wolds
E Yorks 208 D4
Middleton Place Cumb 219 G11
Middleton Priors Shrops 132 E2
Middleton Quernhow
N Yorks 214 D6
Middleton St George
Darl 224 C6
Middleton Scriven
Shrops 132 F3
Middleton Stoney
Oxon 101 G10
Middleton Tyas N Yorks 224 D4
Middletown Cumb 219 D9
N Som 60 E3
Powys 148 G6
Warks 117 E11
Middle Town Scilly 1 F4
Middle Tysoe Warks 100 C6
Middle Wallop Hants 47 F9
Middle Weald M Keynes 102 D5
Middlewich Ches E 167 B11
Middlewick Wilts 61 E11
Middle Wick Glos 80 F2
Middle Winterslow Wilts 47 G8
Middlewood Ches E 184 E6
Corn 11 F11
S Yorks 186 C4
Middle Woodford Wilts 46 F6
Middlewood Green
Suff 125 E11
Middleyard Glos 80 E4
Middlezoy Som 43 G11
Middridge Durham 233 F11
Midfield Highld 308 C5
Midford Bath 61 G9
Midgard Borders 262 F3
Mid Garrary Dumfries 237 B7
Midge Hall Lancs 194 C4
Midgehole W Yorks 196 B3
Midgeholme Cumb 240 F4
Midgham W Berks 64 F5
Midgham Green W Berks 64 F5
Midgley W Yorks 196 B4
W Yorks 197 E9
Mid Holmwood Sur 51 D7
Midhopestones S Yorks 186 B2
Midhurst W Sus 34 C5
Mid Lambrook Som 28 D6
Midland Orkney 314 F3
Mid Lavant W Sus 22 B5
Midlem Borders 262 D2
Mid Letter Argyll 284 G4
Midlock S Lnrk 259 E11
Mid Main Highld 300 F4
Midmar Aberds 293 C8
Midmuir Argyll 289 G11
Mid Murthat Dumfries 248 D3
Midpark Argyll 255 B11
Midplaugh Aberds 302 E5
Midsomer Norton Bath 45 C7
Midton Invclyd 276 F4
Midtown Highld 307 L3
Highld 308 C5
Midtown of Buchromb
Moray 302 E3
Midtown of Glass
Aberds 302 E4
Mid Urchany Highld 301 E8
Midville Lincs 174 D5
Mid Walls Shetland 313 H4
Midway Ches E 184 E6
Som 45 D7
Mid Yell Shetland 312 D7
Miekle Toux Aberds 302 D5
Migdale Highld 309 K6
Migvie Aberds 292 C6
Milarrochy Stirl 277 C8
Milber Devon 14 G3
Milborne Port Som 29 D11
Milborne St Andrew
Dorset 18 B2
Milborne Wick Som 29 C11
Milbourne Northumb 242 B4
Wilts 62 B2
Milburn Aberds 302 E5
Aberds 302 F6
Cumb 231 F9
Milbury Heath S Glos 79 G11
Milby N Yorks 215 F8
Milch Hill Essex 106 G4
Milcombe Corn 6 D4
Oxon 101 E8
Milden Suff 107 B9
Mildenhall Suff 124 C4
Wilts 63 F8
Milebrook Powys 114 C6
Milebush Kent 53 D9
Mile Cross Norf 160 G4
Mile Elm Wilts 62 F3
Mile End Cambs 140 G2
Devon 14 G2
Essex 107 F9
Glos 79 C9
London 67 C11
Suff 124 G6
Mileham Norf 159 F8
Mile Oak Brighton 36 F2
Kent 53 E7
Shrops 148 D6
Staffs 134 C3
Miles Green Staffs 168 F4
Sur 50 B3
Miles Hill W Yorks 205 F11
Milesmark Fife 279 D11
Miles Platting Gtr Man 184 B5
Miles's Green W Berks 64 F4
Mile Town Kent 70 E2
Milfield Northumb 263 C10
Milford Derbys 170 F5
Devon 24 C2
Powys 129 E11
Shrops 149 E8
Staffs 151 E9
Sur 50 E2
Wilts 31 B11
Milford Haven Pembs 72 D6
Milford on Sea Hants 19 C11
Milkhouse Water Wilts 63 G7
Milkieston Borders 270 F4
Milkwall Glos 79 D9
Milkwell Wilts 30 C6
Milland W Sus 34 B4
Millarston Renfs 267 C9
Millbank Aberds 303 E11
Highld 310 C5
Kent 71 F8
Mill Bank W Yorks 196 C4
Millbeck Cumb 229 F11
Millbounds Orkney 314 C5
Millbreck Aberds 303 E10
Millbridge Sur 49 E10
Millbrook C Beds 103 D10
Corn 7 E8
Devon 41 G9
Gtr Man 185 B7
Soton 32 E5
Mill Brow Gtr Man 185 D7
Millburn S Ayrs 257 D10
Millcombe Devon 8 F6
Mill Common Norf 142 C6
Suff 143 G8
Mill Corner E Sus 38 C4
Milldale Staffs 169 E10
Mill Dam N Yorks 212 F3
Millden Lodge Angus 293 F7
Milldens Angus 287 B9
Millend Glos 80 D3
Glos 80 F3
Mill End Bucks 65 C9
Cambs 124 F3
Glos 81 C10
Herts 85 G8
Herts 104 E6
Mill End Green Essex 106 F2
Millendreath Corn 6 E5
Millerhill Midloth 270 B6
Miller's Dale Derbys 185 G10
Miller's Green Derbys 170 E3
Essex 87 D9
Millersneuk E Dunb 278 G3
Millerston Glasgow 268 B2
Mill Farm Aberds 303 C8
Millfield Pboro 138 C3
T&W 243 F9
Millgate Lancs 195 D11
Norf 160 D3
Millgillhead Cumb 229 G7
Mill Green Cambs 106 B2
Essex 87 E10
Hants 64 G4
Herts 86 D2
Norf 142 G2
Shrops 150 D3
Suff 107 C9
Suff 125 F9
Suff 126 E2
W Mid 133 C11
Millhalf Hereford 96 B5
Millhall Kent 53 B8
Mill Hall Dumfries 237 E8
Millhayes Devon 27 E10
Devon 28 G2
Millhead Lancs 211 E9
Millheugh S Lnrk 268 E5
Millhill Devon 12 G5
Mill Hill Blkburn 195 B7
Essex 88 G4
E Sus 23 D10
Glos 79 E10
Gtr Man 195 F8
Kent 55 C11
Lincs 175 B8
London 86 G2
Suff 125 G7
Mill Hills Suff 108 B5
Mill Hirst N Yorks 214 G3
Millholme Cumb 221 G11
Millhouse Argyll 275 F10
Cumb 230 D3
Millhousebridge
Dumfries 248 F4
Millhouse Green
S Yorks 197 G8
Millhouses S Yorks 186 E4
S Yorks 198 G2
Millikenpark Renfs 267 C8
Millin Cross Pembs 73 C7
Millington E Yorks 208 C2
Millington Green Derbys 170 F3
Mill Lane Hants 49 C9
Mill Meads London 67 C11
Millmeece Staffs 150 C6
Millmoor Devon 27 E10
Millness Cumb 211 C10
Mill of Brydock Aberds 302 D6
Mill of Chon Stirl 285 G8
Mill of Haldane W Dunb 277 E8
Mill of Kingoodie
Aberds 303 G8
Mill of Lynebain Aberds 302 F4
Mill of Muiresk Aberds 302 E6
Mill of Rango Orkney 314 E2
Mill of Sterin Aberds 292 D5
Mill of Uras Aberds 293 E10
Millom Cumb 210 C3
Millook Corn 11 B9
Millow C Beds 104 C4
Mill Park Argyll 255 G8
Mill Place N Lincs 200 F3
Millpool Corn 2 C3
Corn 11 G8
Millport N Ayrs 266 E3
Millquarter Dumfries 246 G4
Mill Shaw W Yorks 205 G11
Mill Side Cumb 211 C8
Mill Street Kent 53 B7
Norf 159 F11
Suff 107 D9
Milltack Aberds 303 D7
Millthorpe Derbys 186 F4
Lincs 156 C2
Mill Throop Bmouth 19 B8
Millthrop Cumb 222 G3
Milltimber Aberdeen 293 C10
Milltown Aberds 292 C4
Corn 6 B2
Corn 6 D2
Derbys 170 C5
Devon 40 F5
Highld 301 E9
Milltown of Aberdalgie
Perth 286 E4
Milltown of Auchindoun
Moray 302 E3
Milltown of Craigston
Aberds 303 D7
Milltown of Edinvillie
Moray 302 E2
Milltown of Kildrummy
Aberds 292 B6
Milltown of Rothiemay
Moray 302 E5
Milltown of Towie
Aberds 292 B6
Millwall London 67 D11
Milnathort Perth 286 G5
Milner's Heath Ches W 167 C7
Milngavie E Dunb 277 G11
Milnquarter Falk 278 F6
Milnrow Gtr Man 196 E2
Milnsbridge W Yorks 196 D6
Milnshaw Lancs 195 B9
Milnthorpe Cumb 211 C9
W Yorks 197 D10
Milnwood N Lnrk 268 D4
Milo Carms 75 B9
Milson Shrops 116 C2
Milstead Kent 54 B2
Milston Wilts 47 D7
Milthorpe Northants 101 B11
Milton Angus 287 C7
Angus 292 E6
Cambs 123 E9
Cumb 211 C10
Cumb 240 E3
Derbys 152 D6
Dumfries 236 D4
Dumfries 237 B10
Dumfries 247 G8
Fife 287 E8
Glasgow 267 B11
Highld 299 E7
Highld 300 D3
Highld 300 E5
Highld 300 F4
Highld 301 B7
Highld 301 E7
Highld 310 D7
Kent 69 E7
Moray 292 B3
Moray 302 C5
Notts 188 G2
N Som 59 G10
Oxon 83 G7
Oxon 101 E8
Pembs 73 E8
Perth 286 F3
Powys 114 G4
Ptsmth 21 B9
Som 29 C7
Stirl 285 G9
Stoke 168 E6
S Yorks 197 G11
W Dunb 277 G8
Wilts 45 G11
Milton Abbas Dorset 30 G4
Milton Bridge Midloth 270 C4
Milton Bryan C Beds 103 E9
Milton Clevedon Som 45 F7
Milton Coldwells Aberds 303 F9
Milton Combe Devon 7 B9
Milton Common Oxon 83 E11
Milton Coombe Devon 7 B9
Milton Damerel Devon 24 E5
Miltonduff Moray 301 C11
Milton End Glos 80 C2
Glos 81 E10
Milton Ernest Beds 121 F10
Milton Green Ches W 167 D7
Devon 12 F4
Milton Heights Oxon 83 G7
Miltonhill Moray 301 C10
Milton Hill Devon 14 F4
Oxon 83 G7
Miltonise Dumfries 236 B3
Milton Keynes
M Keynes 103 D7
Milton Keynes Village
M Keynes 103 D7
Milton Lilbourne Wilts 63 G7
Milton Malsor Northants 120 F4
Milton Morenish Perth 285 D10
Milton of Auchinhove
Aberds 293 C7
Milton of Balgonie Fife 287 G7
Milton of Buchanan
Stirl 277 C8
Milton of Campfield
Aberds 293 C8
Milton of Campsie
E Dunb 278 F3
Milton of Corsindae
Aberds 293 C8
Milton of Cullerlie
Aberds 293 C9
Milton of Cultoquhey
Perth 286 E2
Milton of Cushnie
Aberds 293 B7
Milton of Dalcapon
Perth 286 B3
Milton of Drimmie
Perth 286 B5
Milton of Edradour
Perth 286 B3
Milton of Gollanfield
Highld 301 D7
Milton of Lesmore
Aberds 302 G4
Milton of Logie Aberds 292 C6
Milton of Machany
Perth 286 F3
Milton of Mathers
Aberds 293 G9
Milton of Murtle
Aberdeen 293 C10
Milton of Noth Aberds 302 G5
Milton of Tullich Aberds 292 D5
Milton on Stour Dorset 30 B3
Milton Regis Kent 70 F2
Milton Street E Sus 23 E8
Milton under Wychwood
Oxon 82 B3
Milverton Som 27 B10
Warks 118 D6
Milwich Staffs 151 C9
Milwr Flint 181 G11
Mimbridge Sur 66 G3
Minard Argyll 275 D10
Minard Castle Argyll 275 D10
Minchington Dorset 31 E7
Minchinhampton Glos 80 E5
Mindrum Northumb 263 C8
Minehead Som 42 D3
Minera Wrex 166 E3
Mineshope Corn 11 B9
Minety Wilts 81 G8
Minffordd Gwyn 145 B11
Gwyn 146 G4
Gwyn 179 G9
Mingarrypark Highld 289 C8
Mingoose Corn 4 F4
Miningsby Lincs 174 C4
Minions Corn 11 G11
Minishant S Ayrs 257 G8
Minllyn Gwyn 147 G7
Minnes Aberds 303 G9
Minngearraidh W Isles 297 J3
Minnigaff Dumfries 236 C6
Minnonie Aberds 303 C7
Minnow End Essex 88 C2
Minnygap Dumfries 248 D2
Minshull Vernon
Ches E 167 C11
Minskip N Yorks 215 G7
Minstead Hants 32 E3
Minsted W Sus 34 C5
Minster Kent 70 E3
Kent 71 G10
Minsterley Shrops 131 C7
Minster Lovell Oxon 82 C4
Minsterworth Glos 80 B3
Minterne Magna Dorset 29 G11
Minterne Parva Dorset 29 G11
Minting Lincs 189 G11
Mintlaw Aberds 303 E10
Minto Borders 262 E3
Minto Kames Borders 262 E3
Minton Shrops 131 E8
Mintsfeet Cumb 221 G10
Minwear Pembs 73 C8
Minworth W Mid 134 E3
Mirbister Orkney 314 E2
Mirehouse Cumb 219 B9
Mireland Highld 310 C7
Mirfield W Yorks 197 D8
Miserden Glos 80 D6
Misery Corner Norf 142 F5
Miskin Rhondda 58 C4
Rhondda 77 F8
Misselfore Wilts 31 C8
Misson Notts 187 C11
Misterton Leics 135 G11
Notts 188 C3
Som 29 F7
Misterton Soss Notts 188 B3
Mistley Essex 108 E2
Mistley Heath Essex 108 E2
Mitcham London 67 F9
Mitcheldean Glos 79 B11
Mitchell Corn 5 E7
Mitchell Hill Borders 260 C3
Mitchellslacks
Dumfries 247 D11
Mitchelston Borders 271 F9
Mitchel Troy Mon 79 C7
Mitcheltroy Common
Mon 79 D7
Mite Houses Cumb 219 F11
Mitford Northumb 252 F5
Mithian Corn 4 E4
Mithian Downs Corn 4 F4
Mitton Staffs 151 F7
Worcs 99 E8
Mixbury Oxon 102 E2
Mixenden W Yorks 196 B5
Mixtow Corn 6 E2
Moat Cumb 239 C10
Moats Tye Suff 125 F10
Mobberley Ches E 184 F3
Staffs 169 G8
Moblake Ches E 167 G11
Mobwell Bucks 84 E5
Moccas Hereford 97 C7
Mochdre Conwy 180 F4
Powys 129 F11
Mochrum Dumfries 236 E5
Mockbeggar Hants 31 F11
Kent 54 E6
Medway 69 E8
Mockerkin Cumb 229 G7
Moclett Orkney 314 B4
Modbury Devon 8 E3
Moddershall Staffs 151 B8
Model Village Derbys 187 G8
Warks 119 E8
Modest Corner Kent 52 E5
Moelfre Anglesey 179 D8
Conwy 181 G7
Powys 148 D3
Moel Tryfan Gwyn 163 D8
Moel-y-crio Flint 165 B11
Moffat Dumfries 248 B3
Moffat Mills N Lnrk 268 C5
Mogador Sur 51 C8
Moggerhanger C Beds 104 B2
Mogworthy Devon 26 D5
Moira Leics 152 F6
Moity Powys 96 C3
Molash Kent 54 C4
Mol-chlach Highld 294 D6
Mold Flint 166 C2
Moldgreen W Yorks 197 D7
Molehill Green Essex 105 G11
Essex 106 G4
Molescroft E Yorks 208 E6
Molesden Northumb 252 G4
Molesworth Cambs 121 B11
Molinnis Corn 5 D10
Moll Highld 295 B7
Molland Devon 26 B4
Mollington Ches W 182 G5
Oxon 101 B8
Mollinsburn N Lnrk 278 G4
Monachty Ceredig 111 E10
Monachylemore Stirl 285 F8
Monar Lodge Highld 300 E2
Monaughty Powys 114 D4
Monboddo House
Aberds 293 F9
Mondaytown Shrops 130 B6
Mondynes Aberds 293 F9
Monemore Stirl 285 D9
Monevechadan Argyll 284 G5
Monewden Suff 126 F4
Moneyacres E Ayrs 267 E8
Moneydie Perth 286 E4
Moneyhill Herts 85 G8
Money Hill Leics 153 F7
Moneyrow Green
Windsor 65 D11
Moneystone Staffs 169 F9
Mongleath Corn 3 C7
Moniaive Dumfries 247 E7
Monifieth Angus 287 D8
Monikie Angus 287 D8
Monimail Fife 286 F6
Monington Pembs 92 C2
Monk Bretton S Yorks 197 F11
Monk End N Yorks 224 D5
Monken Hadley London 86 F3
Monkerton Devon 14 C5
Monk Fryston N Yorks 198 B4
Monk Hesleden Durham 234 D5
Monkhide Hereford 98 C2
Monkhill Cumb 239 F8
W Yorks 198 C3
Monkhopton Shrops 132 E2
Monkland Hereford 115 F9
Monkleigh Devon 25 C7
Monkmoor Shrops 149 G10
Monknash V Glam 58 E2
Monkokehampton Devon 25 F9
Monkscross Corn 12 G3
Monkseaton T&W 243 C8
Monks Eleigh Suff 107 B9
Monk's Gate W Sus 36 B2
Monks Heath Ches E 184 G4
Monk Sherborne Hants 48 B6
Monkshill Aberds 303 E7
Monks Hill Kent 53 E11
Monksilver Som 42 F5
Monks Kirby Warks 135 G9
Monk Soham Suff 126 D4
Monks Orchard London 67 F11
Monk's Park Wilts 61 F11
Monkspath W Mid 118 B2
Monks Risborough Bucks 84 E4
Monksthorpe Lincs 174 B6
Monkston Park
M Keynes 103 D7
Monk Street Essex 106 F2
Monkswood Midloth 270 C6
Mon 78 E4
W Yorks 206 F2
Monkton Devon 27 G11
Kent 71 G9
Pembs 73 E7
S Ayrs 257 D9
T&W 243 E8
V Glam 58 E2
Monkton Combe Bath 61 G9
Monkton Deverill Wilts 45 F11
Monkton Farleigh Wilts 61 F10
Monktonhall E Loth 280 G6
Monkton Heathfield Som 28 B3
Monkton Up Wimborne
Dorset 31 E8
Monkwearmouth T&W 243 F9
Monkwood Hants 49 G7
Monkwood Green
Worcs 116 E6
Monmarsh Hereford 97 B10
Monmore Green W Mid 133 D8
Monmouth / Trefynwy
Mon 79 C8
Monnington on Wye
Hereford 97 C7
Monreith Dumfries 236 E5
Monreith Mains
Dumfries 236 E5
Montacute Som 29 D7
Montcliffe Gtr Man 195 E7
Montcoffer Ho Aberds 302 C6
Montford Argyll 266 C2
Shrops 149 G8
Montford Bridge Shrops 149 F8
Montgarrie Aberds 293 B7
Montgomery Powys 130 D4
Montgomery Lines
Hants 49 C11
Monton Gtr Man 184 B3
Montpelier Bristol 60 E5
Montrave Fife 287 G7
Montrose Angus 287 B11
Montsale Essex 89 F8
Monwode Lea Warks 134 E5
Monxton Hants 47 E10
Monyash Derbys 169 B11
Monymusk Aberds 293 B8
Monzie Perth 286 E2
Monzie Castle Perth 286 E2
Moodiesburn N Lnrk 278 G3
Moolham Som 28 E5
Moon's Green Kent 38 B5
Moon's Moat Worcs 117 D11
Moonzie Fife 287 F7
Moor Som 28 D6
Mooradale Shetland 312 F6
Moor Allerton W Yorks 205 F11
Mooray Wilts 46 G3
Moorby Lincs 174 C3
Moorclose Cumb 228 F5
Gtr Man 195 F11
Moor Common Bucks 84 G4
Moorcot Hereford 115 F7
Moor Crichel Dorset 31 F7
Moor Cross Devon 8 D2
Moordown Bmouth 19 C7
Moore Halton 183 E9
Moor Edge W Yorks 205 F7
Moorend Cumb 239 G8
Derbys 170 F2
Dumfries 239 C7
Glos 80 C5
Glos 80 E2
Gtr Man 185 D7
S Glos 61 D7
Moor End Bucks 84 G4
Cambs 105 B7
C Beds 103 G9
Durham 234 C2
E Yorks 208 F2
Glos 99 G9
Lancs 202 E3
N Yorks 207 F7
N Yorks 215 G7
S Yorks 197 G9
Worcs 117 F8
W Yorks 196 B5
W Yorks 206 D4
York 207 B9
Moorend Cross Hereford 98 B4
Moor End Field N Yorks 215 F8
Moorends S Yorks 199 D7
Moorfield Derbys 185 C8
Moorgate Norf 160 C3
S Yorks 186 C6
Moorgreen Hants 33 D7
Notts 171 F7
Moor Green Herts 104 F6
Staffs 169 G7
Wilts 61 F11
W Mid 133 G11
Moorhaigh Notts 171 C8
Moorhall Derbys 186 G4
Moor Hall W Mid 134 D2
Moorhampton Hereford 97 B7
Moorhaven Village Devon 8 D3
Moorhayne Devon 28 F2
Moorhead W Yorks 205 F8
Moor Head W Yorks 197 B8
W Yorks 197 E8
Moorhey Gtr Man 196 G2
Moorhole S Yorks 186 E6
Moorhouse Cumb 239 F8
Cumb 239 G7
Notts 172 B3
S Yorks 198 E3
Moorhouse Bank Sur 52 C2
Moorhouses Lincs 174 D3
Moorland or Northmoor
Green Som 43 G10
Moorledge Bath 60 G5
Moorlinch Som 43 F11
Moor Monkton N Yorks 206 B6
Moor Monkton Moor
N Yorks 206 B6
Moor of Balvack Aberds 293 B8
Moor of Granary
Moray 301 D10
Moor of Ravenstone
Dumfries 236 E5
Moor Park Cumb 229 D7
Hereford 97 C9

Moor Park Herts 85 G9
Sur 49 D11
Moor Row Cumb 219 C10
Cumb 229 B10
Moorsholm Redcar 226 C3
Moorside Ches W 182 F3
Dorset 30 D3
Durham 233 B7
Gtr Man 195 G9
Gtr Man 196 F3
W Yorks 197 B8
W Yorks 205 F10
Moor Side Lancs 202 F5
Lancs 202 G4
Lincs 174 D2
W Yorks 197 B7
W Yorks 204 F6
Moorstock Kent 54 F6
Moor Street Kent 69 F10
Moorswater Corn 6 C4
Moorthorpe W Yorks 198 E3
Moor Top W Yorks 197 C7
Moortown Devon 12 B2
Devon 12 G6
Devon 25 C8
Hants 31 G11
IoW 20 E4
Lincs 189 B9
Telford 150 F2
W Yorks 206 F2
Morangie Highld 309 L7
Morar Highld 295 F8
Moravian Settlement
Derbys 153 B8
Môrawelon Anglesey 178 E3
Morayhill Highld 301 E7
Morborne Cambs 138 E2
Morchard Bishop Devon 26 F3
Morchard Road Devon 26 G3
Morcombelake Dorset 16 C4
Morcott Rutland 137 C8
Morda Shrops 148 D5
Morden Dorset 18 B4
London 67 F9
Morden Green Cambs 104 C5
Morden Park London 67 F8
Mordiford Hereford 97 D11
Mordington Holdings
Borders 273 D8
Mordon Durham 234 F2
More Shrops 130 E6
Morebath Devon 27 C7
Morebattle Borders 263 E7
Morecambe Lancs 211 G8
More Crichel Dorset 31 F7
Moredon Swindon 62 B6
Moredun Edin 270 B5
Morefield Highld 307 K6
Morehall Kent 55 F8
Moreleggan Argyll 284 G6
Moreleigh Devon 8 E5
Morenish Perth 285 D9
Moresby Cumb 228 G5
Moresby Parks Cumb 219 B9
Morestead Hants 33 B8
Moreton Dorset 18 D2
Essex 87 D8
Hereford 115 E10
Mers 182 C3
Oxon 82 E6
Oxon 83 E11
Staffs 150 F5
Staffs 152 D2
Moreton Corbet
Shrops 149 E11
Moretonhampstead
Devon 13 D11
Moreton-in-Marsh Glos 100 E4
Moreton Jeffries
Hereford 98 B2
Moreton Morrell Warks 118 F6
Moreton on Lugg
Hereford 97 B10
Moreton Paddox Warks 118 G6
Moreton Pinkney
Northants 101 B11
Moreton Say Shrops 150 C2
Moreton Valence Glos 80 D3
Moretonwood Shrops 150 C2
Morfa Carms 56 B4
Carms 75 C9
Ceredig 110 G6
Gwyn 144 C3
Morfa Bach Carms 74 C5
Morfa Bychan Gwyn 145 B10
Morfa Dinlle Gwyn 162 D6
Morfa Glas Neath 76 D5
Morfa Nefyn Gwyn 162 G3
Morfydd Denb 165 F10
Morganstown Cardiff 58 C6
Morgan's Vale Wilts 31 C11
Moriah Ceredig 112 B2
Mork Glos 79 D9
Morland Cumb 231 G7
Morley Ches E 184 E4
Derbys 170 G5
Durham 233 F8
W Yorks 197 B9
Morley Green Ches E 184 E4
Morleymoor Derbys 170 G5
Morley Park Derbys 170 F5
Morley St Botolph
Norf 141 D11
Morley Smithy Derbys 170 G5
Mornick Corn 12 G2
Morningside Edin 280 G3
N Lnrk 268 D6
Morningthorpe Norf 142 E4
Morpeth Northumb 252 F6
Morphie Aberds 293 G9
Morrey Staffs 152 F2
Morridge Side Staffs 169 E8
Morrilow Heath Staffs 151 B9
Morris Green Essex 106 E4
Morriston / Treforys
Swansea 57 B7
Morristown V Glam 59 E7
Morston Norf 177 E8
Mortehoe Devon 40 D3
Morthen S Yorks 187 D7
Mortimer W Berks 65 G7
Mortimer's Cross
Hereford 115 E8
Mortimer West End
Hants 64 G6
Mortlake London 67 D8
Mortomley S Yorks 186 B4
Morton Cumb 230 D4
Cumb 239 G9
Derbys 170 C6
IoW 21 D8
Lincs 155 E11
Lincs 172 C5
Lincs 188 C4
Norf 160 F2
Notts 172 E2
S Glos 79 G10
Shrops 148 E5
Morton Bagot Warks 118 E2
Morton Common Shrops 148 E5
Morton Mains Dumfries 247 D9
Morton Mill Shrops 149 E11
Morton-on-Swale
N Yorks 224 G6
Morton Spirt Warks 117 G10
Morton Tinmouth
Durham 233 G9
Morton Underhill
Worcs 117 F10
Morvah Corn 1 B4
Morval Corn 6 D5
Morven Lodge Aberds 292 C5
Morvich Highld 295 C11
Highld 309 J7
Morville Shrops 132 E3
Morville Heath Shrops 132 E3
Morwellham Quay Devon 7 B8
Morwenstow Corn 24 E2
Mosborough S Yorks 186 E6
Moscow E Ayrs 267 G9
Mose Shrops 132 E5
Mosedale Cumb 230 E3
Moseley W Mid 133 D8
W Mid 133 G11
Worcs 116 F6
Moses Gate Gtr Man 195 F8
Mosley Common
Gtr Man 195 G8
Moss Argyll 288 E1
Highld 289 C8
S Yorks 198 E5
Wrex 166 E4
Mossat Aberds 292 B6
Mossbank Shetland 312 F6
Moss Bank Halton 183 D8
Mers 183 B8
Mossbay Cumb 228 F5
Mossblown S Ayrs 257 E10
Mossbrow Gtr Man 184 D2
Mossburnford Borders 262 F5
Mossdale Dumfries 237 B8
Mossedge Cumb 239 D11
Moss Edge Lancs 202 D4
Lancs 202 E4
Mossend N Lnrk 268 C4
Moss End Brack 65 E11
Ches E 183 F11
Mosser Mains Cumb 229 F8
Mossfield Highld 300 B6
Mossgate Staffs 151 B8
Mossgiel E Ayrs 257 D11
Mosshouses Borders 262 B2
Moss Houses Ches E 184 G5
Mossie Angus 287 B8
Moss Lane Ches E 184 G6
Mossley Ches E 168 C5
Gtr Man 196 G3
Mossley Brow Gtr Man 196 G3
Mossley Hill Mers 182 D5
Moss Nook Gtr Man 184 D4
Mers 183 C8
Moss of Barmuckity
Moray 302 C2
Moss of Meft Moray 302 C2
Mosspark Glasgow 267 C10
Moss Pit Staffs 151 E8
Moss Side Cumb 238 G5
Gtr Man 184 B4
Moss-side Highld 301 D8
Moss Side Lancs 193 G11
Lancs 194 C4
Lancs 202 G3
Mers 182 B6
Moss-side Moray 302 D5
Mosstodloch Moray 302 D3
Mosston Angus 287 C9
Mosstown Aberds 303 C10
Mossy Lea Lancs 194 E4
Mosterton Dorset 29 F7
Moston Ches E 168 C2
Ches W 182 G6
Gtr Man 195 G11
Shrops 149 D11
Moston Green Ches E 168 C2
Mostyn Flint 181 E11
Mostyn Quay Flint 181 E11
Motcombe Dorset 30 B5
Mothecombe Devon 8 F2
Motherby Cumb 230 F4
Motherwell N Lnrk 268 D5
Motspur Park London 67 F8
Mottingham London 68 E2
Mottisfont Hants 32 B4
Mottistone IoW 20 E4
Mottram in Longdendale
Gtr Man 185 B7
Mottram Rise Gtr Man 185 B7
Mottram St Andrew
Ches E 184 F5
Mott's Green Essex 87 B8
Mott's Mill E Sus 52 F4
Mouldsworth Ches W 183 G8
Moulin Perth 286 B3
Moulsecoomb Brighton 36 F4
Moulsford Oxon 64 C5
Moulsham Essex 88 D2
Moulsoe M Keynes 103 C8
Moultavie Highld 300 B6
Moulton Ches W 167 B11
Lincs 156 E6
Northants 120 D5
N Yorks 224 E4
Suff 124 E3
V Glam 58 E5
Moulton Chapel Lincs 156 F5
Moulton Eaugate Lincs 156 F6
Moulton Park Northants 120 E5
Moulton St Mary Norf 143 B7
Moulton Seas End Lincs 156 D6
Moulzie Angus 292 F4
Mounie Castle Aberds 303 G7
Mount Corn 4 D5
Corn 6 B2
Highld 301 E9
W Yorks 196 D5
Mountain Anglesey 178 E2
W Yorks 205 G7
Mountain Air Bl Gwent 77 D11
Mountain Ash / Aberpennar
Rhondda 77 F8
Mountain Bower Wilts 61 D10
Mountain Cross Borders 270 F2
Mountain Street Kent 54 C5
Mountain Water Pembs 91 G8
Mount Ambrose Corn 4 G4
Mount Ballan Mon 60 B3
Mount Batten Plym 7 E9
Mountbenger Borders 261 D8
Mountbengerburn
Borders 261 D8
Mountblow W Dunb 277 G9
Mount Bovers Essex 88 G4
Mount Bures Essex 107 E8
Mount Canisp Highld 301 B7
Mount Charles Corn 5 B10
Corn 5 E10
Mount Cowdown Wilts 47 C9
Mount End Essex 87 E7
Mount Ephraim E Sus 23 B7
Mounters Dorset 30 D3
Mountfield E Sus 38 C2
Mountgerald Highld 300 C5
Mount Gould Plym 7 D9
Mount Hawke Corn 4 F4
Mount Hermon Corn 2 F6
Sur 50 B4
Mount Hill S Glos 61 E7
Mountjoy Corn 5 C7
Mount Lane Devon 12 B3
Mountnessing Essex 87 F10
Mounton Mon 79 G8
Mount Pleasant Bucks 102 E3
Ches E 168 D4
Corn 5 C10
Derbys 152 D6
Derbys 152 F5
Derbys 170 F4
Devon 27 G11
Durham 233 E11
E Sus 23 E7
E Sus 36 D6
Flint 182 G2
Hants 19 B11
Kent 71 F10
London 85 G8
M Tydf 77 F9
Neath 57 B9
Norf 141 E9
Pembs 73 D8
Shrops 149 G9
Stockton 234 G4
Stoke 168 G5
Suff 106 B4
T&W 243 E7
Warks 135 F7
Worcs 99 D10
Worcs 117 E10
W Yorks 197 C8
Mount Sion Wrex 166 E3
Mount Skippett Oxon 82 B5
Mountsolie Aberds 303 D9
Mountsorrel Leics 153 F11
Mount Sorrel Wilts 31 C8
Mount Tabor W Yorks 196 B5
Mount Vernon Glasgow 268 C3
Mount Wise Corn 7 E9
Mousehill Sur 50 E2
Mousehole Corn 1 D5
Mousen Northumb 264 C4
Mousley End Warks 118 D4
Mouswald Dumfries 238 C3
Mouth Mill Devon 24 B3
Mowbreck Lancs 202 G4
Mow Cop Ches E 168 D5
Mowden Darl 224 B5
Essex 88 C3
Mowhaugh Borders 263 E8
Mowmacre Hill
Leicester 135 B11
Mowshurst Kent 52 D3
Mowsley Leics 136 F2
Moxby N Yorks 215 F11
Moxley W Mid 133 D9
Moy Argyll 255 E8
Highld 290 E6
Highld 301 F7
Moy Hall Highld 301 F7
Moy Ho Moray 301 C10
Moyles Court Hants 31 F11
Moylgrove / Trewyddel
Pembs 92 C2
Moy Lodge Highld 290 E6
Muasdale Argyll 255 C7
Muchalls Aberds 293 D11
Much Birch Hereford 97 E10
Much Cowardne Hereford 98 B2
Much Cowarne Hereford 98 B2
Much Dewchurch
Hereford 97 E9
Muchelney Som 28 C6
Muchelney Ham Som 28 C6
Much Hadham Herts 86 B5
Much Hoole Lancs 194 C3
Much Hoole Moss Houses
Lancs 194 C3
Much Hoole Town
Lancs 194 C3
Muchlarnick Corn 6 D4
Much Marcle Hereford 98 E3
Muchrachd Highld 300 F2
Much Wenlock Shrops 132 C2
Muckairn Argyll 289 F11
Muckernich Highld 300 D5
Mucking Thurrock 69 C7
Muckle Breck Shetland 312 G7
Muckleford Dorset 17 C8
Mucklestone Staffs 150 B4
Muckleton Norf 158 B6
Shrops 149 E11
Muckletown Aberds 302 G5
Muckley Shrops 132 D2
Muckley Corner Staffs 133 B11
Muckley Cross Shrops 132 D2
Muckton Lincs 190 E5
Muckton Bottom Lincs 190 E5
Mudale Highld 308 F5
Mudd Gtr Man 185 C7
Muddiford Devon 40 F5
Muddlebridge Devon 40 G4
Muddles Green E Sus 23 C8
Mudeford Dorset 19 C9
Mudford Som 29 D9
Mudford Sock Som 29 D9
Mudgley Som 44 D2
Mugdock Stirl 277 F11
Mugeary Highld 294 B6
Mugginton Derbys 170 G3
Muggintonlane End
Derbys 170 G3
Muggleswick Durham 232 B6
Mugswell Sur 51 C9
Muie Highld 309 J6
Muir Aberds 292 E2
Muircleugh Borders 271 F10
Muirden Aberds 303 D7
Muirdrum Angus 287 D9
Muiredge Fife 281 B7
Muirend Glasgow 267 C11
Muirhead Angus 287 D7
Fife 286 G6
Fife 287 F8
N Lnrk 268 B3
S Ayrs 257 C8
Muirhouse Edin 280 F4
N Lnrk 268 D5
Muirhouselaw Borders 262 D4
Muirhouses Falk 279 E10
Muirkirk E Ayrs 258 D5
Muirmill Stirl 278 E4
Muir of Alford Aberds 293 B7
Muir of Fairburn Highld 300 D4
Muir of Fowlis Aberds 293 B7
Muir of Kinellar
Aberds 293 B10
Muir of Miltonduff
Moray 301 D11
Muir of Ord Highld 300 D5
Muir of Pert Angus 287 D8
Muirshearlich Highld 290 E3
Muirskie Aberds 293 D10
Muirtack Aberds 303 F9
Muirton Aberds 303 D7
Highld 301 C7
Perth 286 E5
Perth 286 F3
Muirton Mains Highld 300 D4
Muirton of Ardblair
Perth 286 C5
Muirton of Ballochy
Angus 293 G8
Muiryfold Aberds 303 D7
Muker N Yorks 223 F8
Mulbarton Norf 142 C3
Mulben Moray 302 D3
Mulberry Corn 5 B10
Mulfra Corn 1 C5
Mulindry Argyll 254 B4
Mulla Shetland 313 G6
Mullardoch House
Highld 300 F2
Mullenspond Hants 47 D9
Mullion Corn 2 F5
Mullion Cove Corn 2 F5
Mumbles Hill Swansea 56 D6
Mumby Lincs 191 G8
Mumps Gtr Man 196 F2
Mundale Moray 301 D10
Munderfield Row
Hereford 116 G2
Munderfield Stocks
Hereford 116 G2
Mundesley Norf 160 B6
Mundford Norf 140 E6
Mundham Norf 142 D6
Mundon Essex 88 E5
Mundurno Aberdeen 293 B11
Mundy Bois Kent 54 D2
Munerigie Highld 290 C4
Muness Shetland 312 C8
Mungasdale Highld 307 K4
Mungrisdale Cumb 230 E3
Munlochy Highld 300 D6
Munsary Cottage Highld 310 E6
Munsley Hereford 98 C3
Munslow Shrops 131 F10
Munstone Hereford 97 C10
Murch V Glam 59 E7
Murchington Devon 13 D9
Murcot Worcs 99 C11
Murcott Oxon 83 B9
Wilts 81 G7
Murdieston Stirl 278 B3
Murdishaw Halton 183 E9
Murieston W Loth 269 C11
Murkle Highld 310 C5
Murlaggan Highld 290 D2
Highld 290 E5
Murra Orkney 314 F2
Murrayfield Edin 280 G4
Murrayshall Perth 286 E5
Murraythwaite Dumfries 238 C4
Murrell Green Hants 49 B8
Murrell's End Glos 98 E4
Glos 98 G5
Murrion Shetland 312 F4
Murrow Cambs 139 B7
Mursley Bucks 102 F6
Murston Kent 70 G2
Murthill Angus 287 B8
Murthly Perth 286 D4
Murton Cumb 231 G10
Durham 234 B3
Northumb 273 F9
Swansea 56 D5
T&W 243 C8
York 207 C8
Murton Grange
N Yorks 215 B10
Murtwell Devon 8 D5
Musbury Devon 15 C11
Muscliff Bmouth 19 B7
Muscoates N Yorks 216 C3
Muscott Northants 120 E2
Musdale Argyll 289 G11
Mushroom Green
W Mid 133 F8
Musselburgh E Loth 280 G6
Musselwick Pembs 72 D4
Mustard Hyrn Norf 161 F8
Muston Leics 154 B6
N Yorks 217 D11
Mustow Green Worcs 117 C7
Muswell Hill London 86 G3
Mutehill Dumfries 237 E8
Mutford Suff 143 F9
Muthill Perth 286 F2
Mutley Plym 7 D9
Mutterton Devon 27 G8
Mutton Hall E Sus 37 C9
Muxton Telford 150 G4
Mwdwl-eithin Flint 181 F11
Mwynbwll Flint 165 B11
Mybster Highld 310 D5
Myddfai Carms 94 F5
Myddle Shrops 149 E9
Myddlewood Shrops 149 E9
Myddyn-fych Carms 75 C10
Mydroilyn Ceredig 111 F9
Myerscough Lancs 202 F5
Myerscough Smithy
Lancs 203 G8
Mylor Bridge Corn 3 B8
Mylor Churchtown Corn 3 B8
Mynachdy Cardiff 59 D7
Rhondda 77 F8
Mynachlog-ddu Pembs 92 E2
Mynd Shrops 115 C7
Myndd Llandegai Gwyn 163 B10
Myndtown Shrops 131 F7
Mynydd Bach Ceredig 112 B4
Mynydd-bach Mon 79 G7
Swansea 57 B7
Mynydd-bach-y-glo
Swansea 56 B6
Mynydd Bodafon
Anglesey 179 D7
Mynydd Fflint / Flint
Mountain Flint 182 G2
Mynydd Gilan Gwyn 144 E5
Mynydd-isa Flint 166 C3
Mynyddislwyn Caerph 77 G11
Mynydd-llan Flint 181 G11
Mynydd Marian Conwy 180 F5
Mynydd Mechell
Anglesey 178 D5
Mynyddygarreg Carms 74 D6
Mynytho Gwyn 144 C6
Myrebird Aberds 293 D9
Myrelandhorn Highld 310 D6
Myreside Perth 286 E6
Myrtle Hill Carms 94 E5
Mytchett Sur 49 B11
Mytchett Place Sur 49 C11
Mytholm W Yorks 196 B3
Mytholmes W Yorks 204 F6
Mytholmroyd W Yorks 196 B4
Mythop Lancs 202 G3
Mytice Aberds 302 F4
Myton Warks 118 E6
Myton Hall N Yorks 215 F8
Myton-on-Swale
N Yorks 215 F8
Mytton Shrops 149 F8

N

Naast Highld 307 L3
Nab Hill W Yorks 197 D7
Nab's Head Lancs 194 B6
Naburn York 207 D7
Nab Wood W Yorks 205 F8
Naccolt Kent 54 E4
Nackington Kent 55 C7
Nacton Suff 108 C4
Nadderwater Devon 14 C3
Nafferton E Yorks 209 B7
Na Gearrannan W Isles 304 D3
Nag's Head Glos 80 F5
Naid-y-march Flint 181 F11
Nailbridge Glos 79 B10
Nailsbourne Som 28 B2
Nailsea N Som 60 D3
Nailstone Leics 135 B8
Nailsworth Glos 80 F5
Nailwell Bath 61 G8
Nairn Highld 301 D8
Nalderswood Sur 51 D8
Nance Corn 4 G3
Nanceddan Corn 2 C2
Nancegollan Corn 2 C4
Nancemellin Corn 4 G2
Nancenoy Corn 2 D6
Nancledra Corn 1 B5
Nangreaves Lancs 195 D10
Nanhoron Gwyn 144 C5
Nanhyfer / Nevern
Pembs 91 D11
Nannau Gwyn 146 E4
Nannerch Flint 165 B11
Nanpantan Leics 153 F10
Nanpean Corn 5 D9
Nanquidno Corn 1 D3
Nanstallon Corn 5 B10
Nant Carms 74 B6
Denb 165 D11
Nant Alyn Flint 165 B11
Nant-ddu Powys 77 B8
Nanternis Ceredig 111 F7
Nantgaredig Carms 93 G9
Nantgarw Rhondda 58 B6
Nant-glas Powys 113 E9
Nantglyn Denb 165 C8
Nantgwyn Powys 113 B9
Nantithet Corn 2 E5
Nantlle Gwyn 163 E8
Nantmawr Shrops 148 E5
Nant Mawr Flint 166 C3
Nantmel Powys 113 D10
Nantmor Gwyn 163 F10
Nant Peris / Old Llanberis
Gwyn 163 D10
Nantserth Powys 113 C9
Nant Uchaf Denb 165 D8
Nantwich Ches E 167 E11
Nant-y-Bai Carms 94 C5
Nant-y-Bwch Bl Gwent 77 C10
Nant-y-cafn Neath 76 D4
Nantycaws Carms 75 B7
Nant y Caws Shrops 148 D5
Nant-y-ceisiad Caerph 59 B8
Nant-y-derry Mon 78 D4
Nant-y-felin Conwy 179 G11
Nant-y-ffin Carms 93 E11
Nantyffyllon Bridgend 57 C11
Nantyglo Bl Gwent 77 C11
Nant-y-gollen Shrops 148 D4
Nant-y-moel Bridgend 76 G6
Nant-y-pandy Conwy 179 G11
Nant-y-Rhiw Conwy 164 D4
Nantyronen Station
Ceredig 112 B3
Napchester Kent 55 D10
Naphill Bucks 84 F4
Napleton Worcs 99 B7
Napley Staffs 150 B4
Napley Heath Staffs 150 B4
Nappa N Yorks 204 C3
Nappa Scar N Yorks 223 G9
Napton on the Hill
Warks 119 E9
Narberth / Arberth
Pembs 73 C10
Narberth Bridge Pembs 73 C10
Narborough Leics 135 D10
Norf 158 G4
Narfords Som 28 F3
Narkurs Corn 6 D6
Narrachan Argyll 275 B10
Narracott Devon 24 D5
Narrowgate Corner
Norf 161 F8
Nasareth Gwyn 163 E7
Naseby Northants 120 B3
Nash Bucks 102 E5
Hereford 114 E6
Kent 55 B9
London 68 G2
Newport 59 C10
Shrops 116 C2
Som 29 E8
Nashend Glos 80 D5
Nash End Worcs 132 G5
Nashes Green Hants 49 D7
Nash Lee Bucks 84 D4
Nash Mills Herts 85 E9
Nash Street E Sus 23 C8
Kent 68 F6
Nassington Northants 137 D11
Nastend Glos 80 D3
Nast Hyde Herts 86 D2
Nasty Herts 105 G7
Natcott Devon 24 C3
Nateby Cumb 222 D5
Lancs 202 E5
Nately Scures Hants 49 C8
Natland Cumb 211 B10
Natton Glos 99 E8
Naughton Suff 107 B10
Naunton Glos 100 G2
Worcs 99 D7
Naunton Beauchamp
Worcs 117 G9
Navant Hill W Sus 34 B6
Navenby Lincs 173 D7
Navestock Heath Essex 87 F8
Navestock Side Essex 87 F9
Navidale Highld 311 H4
Navity Highld 301 C7
Nawton N Yorks 216 C3
Nayland Suff 107 E9
Nazeing Essex 86 D6
Nazeing Gate Essex 86 D6
Nazeing Long Green
Essex 86 E6
Nazeing Mead Essex 86 D5
Neacroft Hants 19 B9
Nealhouse Cumb 239 G8
Neal's Green Warks 134 G6
Neames Forstal Kent 54 B5
Neap Shetland 313 H7
Near Hardcastle
N Yorks 214 F2
Near Sawrey Cumb 221 F7
Nearton End Bucks 102 F6
Neasden London 67 B8
Neasham Darl 224 C6
Neat Enstone Oxon 101 G7
Neath Abbey Neath 57 B8
Neatham Hants 49 E8
Neath / Castell-nedd
Neath 57 B8
Neath Hill M Keynes 103 C7
Neatishead Norf 160 E6
Neat Marsh E Yorks 209 G9
Neaton Norf 141 C8
Nebo Anglesey 179 C7
Ceredig 111 D10
Conwy 164 D4
Gwyn 163 E7
Nebsworth Warks 100 C3
Nechells W Mid 133 F11
Necton Norf 141 B7
Nedd Highld 306 F6
Nedderton Northumb 252 G6
Nedge Hill Som 44 C5
Telford 132 B4
Nedging Suff 107 B9
Nedging Tye Suff 107 B10
Needham Norf 142 G4
Needham Green Essex 87 B9
Needham Market Suff 125 G11
Needham Street Suff 124 D4
Needingworth Cambs 122 C6
Needwood Staffs 152 E3
Neen Savage Shrops 116 B3
Neen Sollars Shrops 116 C3
Neenton Shrops 132 F2
Nefod Shrops 148 B6
Nefyn Gwyn 162 G4
Neighbourne Som 44 D6
Neight Hill Worcs 117 F8
Neilston E Renf 267 D9
Neinthirion Powys 129 B9
Neithrop Oxon 101 C8
Nelly Andrews Green
Powys 130 B5
Nelson Caerph 77 F10
Lancs 204 F3
Nelson Village Northumb 243 B7
Nemphlar S Lnrk 269 G7
Nempnett Thrubwell
N Som 60 G4
Nene Terrace Lincs 138 B5
Nenthall Cumb 231 B11
Nenthead Cumb 231 C11
Nenthorn Borders 262 B5
Neopardy Devon 13 B11
Nepcote W Sus 35 F10
Nepgill Cumb 229 F7
Nep Town W Sus 36 D2
Nerabus Argyll 254 B3
Nercwys Flint 166 C2
Nerston S Lnrk 268 D2
Nesbit Northumb 263 C11
Ness Ches W 182 F4
Orkney 314 C4
Nesscliffe Shrops 149 F7
Nessholt Ches W 182 F4
Nesstoun Orkney 314 A7
Neston Ches W 182 F3
Wilts 61 F11
Netchells Green
W Mid 133 F11
Netham Bristol 60 E6
Nethanfoot S Lnrk 268 F6
Nether Alderley Ches E 184 F4
Netheravon Wilts 46 D6
Nether Blainslie
Borders 271 G10
Nether Booth Derbys 185 D10
Netherbrae Aberds 303 D7
Netherbrough Orkney 314 E3
Nether Broughton Leics 154 D3
Netherburn S Lnrk 268 F6
Nether Burrow Lancs 212 D2
Nether Burrows Derbys 152 B5
Netherbury Dorset 16 B5
Netherby Cumb 239 C9
N Yorks 206 D2
Nether Cassock
Dumfries 248 C6
Nether Cerne Dorset 17 B9
Nether Chanderhill
Derbys 186 G4
Netherclay Som 28 C3
Nether Compton Dorset 29 D9
Nethercote Oxon 101 C9
Warks 119 E10
Nethercott Devon 12 B3
Devon 40 F3
Oxon 101 G9
Som 42 G6
Nether Crimond Aberds 303 G8
Netherdale Shetland 313 H3
Nether Dalgliesh
Borders 249 B7
Nether Dallachy Moray 302 C3
Nether Edge S Yorks 186 E4
Netherend Glos 79 E9
Nether End Derbys 186 G3
Leics 154 G4
W Yorks 197 F8
Nether Exe Devon 26 G6
Netherfield E Sus 38 D2
M Keynes 103 D7
Notts 171 G10
Nethergate Norf 159 D11
Nether Glasslaw Aberds 303 D8
Nether Hall Leicester 136 B2
Netherhampton Wilts 31 B10
Nether Handley Derbys 186 F6
Nether Handwick Angus 287 C7
Nether Haugh S Yorks 186 B6
Nether Headon Notts 188 F2
Nether Heage Derbys 170 E5
Nether Heyford
Northants 120 F3
Nether Hindhope
Borders 263 G7
Nether Horsburgh
Borders 261 B8
Nether Howecleuch S
Lnrk 260 G2
Nether Kellet Lancs 211 F10
Nether Kidston Borders 270 G4
Nether Kinmundy
Aberds 303 E10
Nether Kirton E Renf 267 D9
Netherland Green Staffs 152 C2
Nether Langwith Notts 187 G8
Netherlaw Dumfries 237 E9
Netherlay Dorset 28 F6
Nether Leask Aberds 303 F10
Netherlee E Renf 267 D11
Nether Lenshie Aberds 302 E6
Netherley Aberds 293 D10
Mers 182 D6
W Yorks 196 E4
Nether Loads Derbys 170 B4
Nethermill Dumfries 248 F2
Nethermills Moray 302 D5
Nether Monynut
Borders 272 C4
Nether Moor Derbys 170 B5
Nethermuir Aberds 303 E9
Netherne on-the-Hill
Sur 51 B9
Netheroyd Hill W Yorks 196 D6
Nether Padley Derbys 186 F3
Nether Park Aberds 303 D10
Netherplace E Renf 267 D10
Nether Poppleton York 207 B7
Netherraw Borders 262 E3
Nether Row Cumb 230 D2
Nether Savock Aberds 303 E10
Netherseal Derbys 152 G5
Nether Shiels Borders 271 F8
Nether Silton N Yorks 225 G9
Nether Skyborry Shrops 114 C5
Nether St Suff 125 E8
Netherstoke Dorset 29 F8
Nether Stowe Staffs 152 G2
Nether Stowey Som 43 F7
Nether Street Essex 87 C9
Herts 86 B6
Netherthird E Ayrs 258 F3
Netherthong W Yorks 196 F6
Netherthorpe Derbys 186 G6
S Yorks 187 E8
Netherton Aberds 303 E8
Angus 287 B9
Ches W 183 F8
Corn 11 G11
Cumb 228 D6
Devon 14 G3
Glos 81 E11
Hants 47 B11
Hereford 97 F10
Mers 193 G11
N Lnrk 268 E5
Northumb 251 B11
Oxon 82 F6
Perth 286 B5
Shrops 132 G4
Stirl 277 F11
W Mid 133 F8
Worcs 99 C9
W Yorks 196 E6
W Yorks 197 D9
Netherton of Lonmay
Aberds 303 C10
Nethertown Cumb 219 D9
Highld 310 B7
Lancs 203 F10
Staffs 152 F2
Nether Urquhart Fife 286 G5
Nether Wallop Hants 47 F10
Nether Warden
Northumb 241 D10
Nether Wasdale Cumb 220 E2
Nether Welton Cumb 230 B3
Nether Westcote Glos 100 G4
Nether Whitacre Warks 134 E4
Nether Winchendon or
Lower Winchendon
Bucks 84 C2
Netherwitton Northumb 252 E4
Netherwood E Ayrs 258 D5
Nether Worton Oxon 101 E8
Nether Yeadon
W Yorks 205 E10
Nethy Bridge Highld 301 G10
Netley Hants 33 F7
Netley Hill Soton 33 E7
Netley Marsh Hants 32 E4
Nettacott Devon 14 B4
Netteswell Essex 87 C7
Nettlebed Oxon 65 B8
Nettlebridge Som 44 D6
Nettlecombe Dorset 16 B6
IoW 20 F6
Nettleden Herts 85 C8
Nettleham Lincs 189 F8
Nettlestead Kent 53 C7
Suff 107 B11
Nettlestead Green Kent 53 C7
Nettlestone IoW 21 C8
Nettlesworth Durham 233 B11
Nettleton Glos 80 C6
Lincs 200 G6
Wilts 61 D10
Nettleton Green Wilts 61 D10
Nettleton Hill W Yorks 196 D5
Nettleton Shrub Wilts 61 D10
Nettleton Top Lincs 189 B10
Netton Wilts 46 F6
Neuadd Carms 94 G3
Nevendon Essex 88 G2
Nevern / Nanhyfer
Pembs 91 D11
Nevilles Cross Durham 233 C11
New Abbey Dumfries 237 C11
New Aberdour Aberds 303 C8
New Addington London 67 G11
Newall W Yorks 205 D10
Newall Green Gtr Man 184 D4
New Alresford Hants 48 G5
New Alyth Perth 286 C6
Newark Orkney 314 B7
Pboro 138 C4
Newark-on-Trent Notts 172 E3
New Arley Warks 134 F5
New Arram E Yorks 208 E6
Newarthill N Lnrk 268 D5
New Ash Green Kent 68 F6
New Balderton Notts 172 E4
Newball Lincs 189 F9
Newbarn Kent 55 F7
New Barn Kent 68 F6
New Barnet London 86 F3
New Barnetby N Lincs 200 E5
Newbarns Cumb 210 E4
New Barton Northants 121 E7
New Basford Nottingham 171 G9
Newbattle Midloth 270 B6
New Beaupre V Glam 58 E4
New Beckenham London 67 E11
New Bewick Northumb 264 E3
Newbie Dumfries 238 D5
Newbiggin Cumb 210 F5
Cumb 211 D11
Cumb 219 G11
Cumb 230 F5
Cumb 231 B7
Cumb 231 F8
Durham 232 B5
Durham 232 F4
Durham 233 B8
N Yorks 213 B9
N Yorks 223 G9
Newbiggin-by-the-Sea
Northumb 253 F8
Newbigging Aberds 303 G7
Angus 287 D8
Borders 262 F6
Edin 280 F2
S Lnrk 269 F10
New-bigging Angus 286 C6
Newbiggings Orkney 314 B6
Newbiggin Hall Estate
T&W 242 D6
Newbiggin-on-Lune
Cumb 222 D4
New Bilton Warks 119 B9
Newbold Derbys 186 G5
Gtr Man 196 E2
Leics 136 B5
Leics 153 F8
Newbold Heath Leics 135 B8
Newbold on Avon
Warks 119 B9
Newbold on Stour
Warks 100 B4
Newbold Pacey Warks 118 F5
Newbolds W Mid 133 C8
Newbold Verdon Leics 135 C8
New Bolingbroke Lincs 174 D4
New Bolsover Derbys 187 G7
Newborough Pboro 138 B4
Staffs 152 D2
New Boston Mers 183 B9
New Botley Oxon 83 D7
Newbottle Northants 101 D10
T&W 243 G8
New Boultham Lincs 189 G7
Newbourne Suff 108 C5
New Bradwell M Keynes 102 C6
New Brancepeth
Durham 233 C10
Newbridge Bath 61 F8
Caerph 78 F2
Ceredig 111 F10
Corn 1 C4
Corn 4 G5
Corn 7 B7
Dumfries 237 B11
Edin 280 G2
E Sus 52 G3
Hants 32 D3
IoW 20 D4
Lancs 204 F3
N Yorks 216 B6
Oxon 82 E6
Pembs 91 E8
Shrops 148 D6
W Mid 133 D7
Wrex 166 G3
New Bridge Wrex 166 G3
Newbridge Green Worcs 98 D6
Newbridge-on-Usk Mon 78 G5
Newbridge-on-Wye
Powys 113 F10
New Brighton Flint 166 B3
Mers 182 C4
Wrex 166 E3
W Sus 22 B3
W Yorks 197 B9
W Yorks 205 F8
New Brimington Derbys 186 G6
New Brinsley Notts 171 E7
New Brotton Redcar 235 G9
Newbrough Northumb 241 D9
New Broughton Wrex 166 E4
New Buckenham Norf 141 E11
Newbuildings Devon 26 G3
New Buildings Bath 45 B7
Dorset 18 E5
Newburgh Aberds 303 D9
Aberds 303 G9
Borders 261 F8
Fife 286 F6
Lancs 194 E3
Newburn T&W 242 D5
Newbury Kent 54 B2
W Berks 64 F3
Wilts 45 E10
New Bury Gtr Man 195 F8
Newbury Park London 68 B2
Newby Cumb 231 G7
Lancs 204 D2
N Yorks 205 D11
N Yorks 212 E4
N Yorks 215 F7
N Yorks 225 C10
N Yorks 227 G10
Newby Bridge Cumb 211 B7
Newby Cote N Yorks 212 E4
Newby East Cumb 239 F11
Newby Head Cumb 231 G7
New Byth Aberds 303 D8
Newby West Cumb 239 G9
Newby Wiske N Yorks 215 B7
Newcastle Bridgend 58 D2
Mon 78 B6
Shrops 130 G4
Newcastle Emlyn / Castell
Newydd Emlyn Carms 92 C6
Newcastleton or Copshaw
Holm Borders 249 F11
Newcastle-under-Lyme
Staffs 168 F4
Newcastle upon Tyne
T&W 242 E6
New Catton Norf 160 G4
Newchapel Powys 129 G9
Staffs 168 E5
Sur 51 E11
Newchapel / Capel Newydd
Pembs 92 D4
New Charlton London 68 D2
New Cheltenham S Glos 61 E7
New Cheriton Hants 33 B9
Newchurch Bl Gwent 77 C11
Carms 93 G7
Hereford 115 G7
IoW 21 D7
Kent 54 G5
Lancs 195 C10
Mon 79 F7
Powys 114 G4
Staffs 152 E2
Newchurch in Pendle
Lancs 204 F2
New Clipstone Notts 171 C9
New Costessey Norf 160 G3
Newcott Devon 28 F2
New Coundon Durham 233 E10
New Cowper Cumb 229 B8
Newcraighall Edin 280 G6
New Crofton W Yorks 197 D11
New Cross Ceredig 112 B2
London 67 D11
Oxon 65 D9
Som 28 D6
New Cross Gate London 67 D11
New Cumnock E Ayrs 258 G4
New Deer Aberds 303 E8
New Delaval Northumb 243 B7
New Delph Gtr Man 196 F3
New Denham Bucks 66 C4
Newdigate Sur 51 E7
New Downs Corn 1 C3
Corn 4 E4
New Duston Northants 120 E4
New Earswick York 207 B8
New Eastwood Notts 171 F7
New Edlington S Yorks 187 B8
New Elgin Moray 302 C2
New Ellerby E Yorks 209 F9
Newell Green Brack 65 E11
New Eltham London 68 E2
New End Lincs 190 G2

Norton in Hales Shrops 150 B4
Norton-in-the-Moors
Stoke 168 E5
Norton-Juxta-Twycross
Leics 134 B6
Norton-le-Clay N Yorks 215 E8
Norton Lindsey Warks 118 E4
Norton Little Green
Suff 125 D9
Norton Malreward Bath 60 F6
Norton Mandeville Essex 87 E9
Norton-on-Derwent
N Yorks 216 E5
Norton St Philip Som 45 B9
Norton Subcourse Norf 143 D8
Norton sub Hamdon Som 29 D7
Norton's Wood N Som 60 E2
Norton Woodseats
S Yorks 186 E5
Norwell Notts 172 C3
Norwell Woodhouse
Notts 172 C2
Norwich Norf 142 B4
Norwick Shetland 312 B8
Norwood Derbys 187 E7
Dorset 29 F8
Norwood End Essex 87 D9
Norwood Green London 66 D6
W Yorks 196 B6
Norwood Hill Sur 51 E8
Norwood New Town
London 67 E10
Norwoodside Cambs 139 D8
Noseley Leics 136 D4
Noss Highld 310 D7
Shetland 313 M5
Noss Mayo Devon 7 F11
Nosterfield N Yorks 214 C5
Nosterfield End Cambs 106 C2
Nostie Highld 295 C10
Notgrove Glos 100 G2
Nottage Bridgend 57 F10
Notter Corn 7 C7
Nottingham Nottingham 153 B11
Notting Hill London 67 C8
Nottington Dorset 17 E9
Notton Wilts 62 F2
W Yorks 197 E10
Nounsley Essex 88 C3
Noutard's Green Worcs 116 D5
Novar House Highld 300 C6
Nova Scotia Ches W 167 B10
Novers Park Bristol 60 F5
Noverton Glos 99 G9
Nowton Suff 125 E7
Nox Shrops 149 G8
Noyadd Trefawr Ceredig 92 B5
Noyadd Wilym Ceredig 92 C4
Nuffield Oxon 65 B7
Nun Appleton N Yorks 207 F7
Nunburnholme E Yorks 208 D2
Nuncargate Notts 171 E8
Nunclose Cumb 230 B5
Nuneaton Warks 135 E7
Nuneham Courtenay
Oxon 83 F9
Nuney Green Oxon 65 D7
Nunhead London 67 D11
Nun Hills Lancs 195 C11
Nun Monkton N Yorks 206 B6
Nunney Som 45 D8
Nunney Catch Som 45 E8
Nunnington N Yorks 216 D3
Nunnykirk Northumb 252 E3
Nunsthorpe NE Lincs 201 F9
Nunthorpe Mbro 225 C10
York 207 C8
Nunton Wilts 31 B11
Nunwick N Yorks 214 E6
Nupdown S Glos 79 F10
Nupend Glos 80 D3
Glos 80 F4
Nup End Bucks 84 B5
Herts 86 B2
Nuper's Hatch Essex 87 G8
Nuppend Glos 79 E10
Nuptown Brack 65 E11
Nursling Hants 32 D5
Nursted Hants 34 C3
Nursteed Wilts 62 G4
Nurston V Glam 58 F5
Nurton Staffs 132 D6
Nurton Hill Staffs 132 D6
Nutbourne W Sus 22 B3
W Sus 35 D9
Nutbourne Common
W Sus 35 D9
Nutburn Hants 32 C5
Nutcombe Sur 49 G11
Nutfield Sur 51 C10
Nut Grove Mers 183 C7
Nuthall Notts 171 G8
Nuthampstead Herts 105 E8
Nuthurst Warks 118 C3
W Sus 35 B11
Nutley E Sus 36 B6
Hants 48 E6
Nuttall Gtr Man 195 D9
Nutwell S Yorks 198 G6
Nybster Highld 310 C7
Nye N Som 60 G2
Nyetimber W Sus 22 D5
Nyewood W Sus 34 C4
Nyland Som 44 C3
Nymet Rowland Devon 26 F2
Nymet Tracey Devon 26 G2
Nympsfield Glos 80 E4
Nynehead Som 27 C10
Nythe Som 44 G2
Swindon 63 B7
Nyton W Sus 22 B6

O

Oadby Leics 136 C2
Oad Street Kent 69 G11
Oakall Green Worcs 116 E6
Oakamoor Staffs 169 G9
Oakbank W Loth 269 B11
Oak Bank Gtr Man 195 F10
Oak Cross Devon 12 B6
Oakdale Caerph 77 F11
N Yorks 205 B11
Poole 18 C6
Oake Som 27 B11
Oake Green Som 27 B11
Oaken Staffs 133 C7
Oakenclough Lancs 202 D6
Oakengates Telford 150 G4
Oakenholt Flint 182 G3
Oakenshaw Durham 233 D10
Lancs 203 G10
W Yorks 197 B7
Oakerthorpe Derbys 170 E5
Oakes W Yorks 196 D6
Oakfield Herts 104 F3
IoW 21 C7
Torf 78 G4
Oakford Ceredig 111 F9
Devon 26 C6
Oakfordbridge Devon 26 C6
Oakgrove Ches E 168 B6
M Keynes 103 D7
Oakham Rutland 137 B7
W Mid 133 F9
Oakhanger Ches E 168 E3
Hants 49 F9
Oakhill Som 44 D6
W Sus 51 G7
Oak Hill Stoke 168 G5
Suff 109 B7
Oakhurst Kent 52 C4
Oakington Cambs 123 E8
Oaklands Carms 74 B6
Herts 86 B2
Powys 113 G10
Oakleigh Park London 86 G3
Oakle Street Glos 80 B3
Oakley Beds 121 G10
Bucks 83 C10
Fife 279 D10
Glos 99 G9
Hants 48 C5
Oxon 84 E3
Poole 18 B6
Staffs 150 B4
Suff 126 B3
Oakley Court Oxon 64 B6
Oakley Green Windsor 66 D2
Oakley Park Powys 129 F9
Suff 126 B3
Oakley Wood Oxon 64 B6
Oakmere Ches W 167 B9
Oakridge Glos 80 E6
Hants 48 C6
Oakridge Lynch Glos 80 E6
Oaks Shrops 131 C8
Oaksey Wilts 81 G7
Oaks Green Derbys 152 C3
Oakshaw Ford Cumb 240 B2
Oakshott Hants 34 B2
Oaks in Charnwood
Leics 153 F9
Oakthorpe Leics 152 G6
Oak Tree Darl 225 C7
Oakwell W Yorks 197 B8
Oakwood Derby 153 B7
London 86 F3
Northumb 241 D10
Warr 183 C11
W Yorks 206 F2
Oakwoodhill Sur 50 F6
Oakworth W Yorks 204 F6
Oape Highld 309 J4
Oare Kent 70 G4
Som 41 D10
W Berks 64 E4
Wilts 63 G7
Oareford Som 41 D10
Oasby Lincs 155 B10
Oath Som 28 B5
Oathill Dorset 28 F6
Oathlaw Angus 287 B8
Oatlands Glasgow 267 C11
N Yorks 205 C11
Oatlands Park Sur 66 G5
Oban Argyll 289 G10
Highld 295 G10
W Isles 305 H3
Obley Shrops 114 B6
Oborne Dorset 29 D11
Obthorpe Lincs 155 F11
Obthorpe Lodge Lincs 156 F2
Occlestone Green
Ches W 167 C11
Occold Suff 126 C3
Ocean Village Soton 32 E6
Ochiltree E Ayrs 258 E2
Ochr-y-foel Denb 181 F9
Ochtermuthill Perth 286 F2
Ochtertyre Perth 286 E2
Ochtow Highld 309 J4
Ockbrook Derbys 153 B8
Ocker Hill W Mid 133 E9
Ockeridge Worcs 116 E5
Ockford Ridge Sur 50 E3
Ockham Sur 50 B5
Ockle Highld 289 B7
Ockley Sur 50 F6
Ocle Pychard Hereford 97 B11
Octon E Yorks 217 F10
Octon Cross Roads
E Yorks 217 F10
Odam Barton Devon 26 D2
Odcombe Som 29 D8
Odd Down Bath 61 G8
Oddendale Cumb 221 C11
Odder Lincs 188 G6
Oddingley Worcs 117 F8
Oddington Glos 100 F4
Oxon 83 C9
Odell Beds 121 F9
Odham Devon 25 G7
Odie Orkney 314 D6
Odiham Hants 49 C8
Odsal W Yorks 197 B7
Odsey Cambs 104 D5
Odstock Wilts 31 B10
Odstone Leics 135 B7
Offchurch Warks 119 D7
Offenham Worcs 99 B11
Offenham Cross Worcs 99 B11
Offerton Gtr Man 184 D6
T&W 243 F8
Offerton Green Gtr Man 184 D6
Offham E Sus 36 E5
Kent 53 B7
W Sus 35 F8
Offleyhay Staffs 150 D5
Offleymarsh Staffs 150 D5
Offleyrock Staffs 150 D5
Offord Cluny Cambs 122 D4
Offord D'Arcy Cambs 122 D4
Offton Suff 107 B11
Offwell Devon 15 B9
Ogbourne Maizey Wilts 63 E7
Ogbourne St Andrew
Wilts 63 E7
Ogbourne St George
Wilts 63 E8
Ogden W Yorks 205 G7
Ogdens Hants 31 E11
Ogil Angus 292 G6
Ogle Northumb 242 B4
Ogmore V Glam 57 F11
Ogmore-by-Sea / Aberogwr
V Glam 57 F11
Ogmore Vale Bridgend 76 G6
Okeford Fitzpaine Dorset 30 E4
Okehampton Devon 13 B7
Okehampton Camp
Devon 13 C7
Oker Derbys 170 C3
Okewood Hill Sur 50 F6
Okle Green Glos 98 F5
Okraquoy Shetland 313 K6
Okus Swindon 62 C6
Olchard Devon 14 F3
Old Northants 120 C5
Old Aberdeen
Aberdeen 293 C11
Old Alresford Hants 48 G5
Oldany Highld 306 F6
Old Arley Warks 134 E5
Old Balornock Glasgow 268 B2
Old Basford Nottingham 171 G8
Old Basing Hants 49 C7
Old Belses Borders 262 E3
Oldberrow Warks 118 D2
Old Bewick Northumb 264 E3
Old Bexley London 68 E3
Old Blair Perth 291 G10
Old Bolingbroke Lincs 174 B4
Oldborough Devon 26 F3
Old Boston Mers 183 B9
Old Bramhope
W Yorks 205 E10
Old Brampton Derbys 186 G4
Old Bridge of Tilt
Perth 291 G10
Old Bridge of Urr
Dumfries 237 C9
Oldbrook M Keynes 103 D7
Old Buckenham Norf 141 E11
Old Burdon T&W 243 G9
Old Burghclere Hants 48 B3
Oldbury Kent 52 B5
Shrops 132 E4
Warks 134 E6
W Mid 133 F9
Oldbury Naite S Glos 79 G10
Oldbury-on-Severn
S Glos 79 G10
Oldbury on the Hill Glos 61 B10
Old Byland N Yorks 215 B11
Old Cambus Borders 272 B6
Old Cardinham Castle
Corn 6 B2
Old Carlisle Cumb 229 B11
Old Cassop Durham 234 D2
Oldcastle Mon 96 G6
Oldcastle Heath Ches W 167 F7
Old Castleton Borders 250 E2
Old Catton Norf 160 G4
Old Chalford Oxon 100 F6
Old Church Stoke
Powys 130 E5
Old Clee NE Lincs 201 F9
Old Cleeve Som 42 E4
Old Colwyn Conwy 180 F5
Old Coppice Shrops 131 B9
Old Corry Highld 295 C8
Oldcotes Notts 187 D9
Old Coulsdon London 51 B10
Old Country Hereford 98 C4
Old Craig Aberds 303 G9
Angus 292 G4
Oldcroft Glos 79 D10
Old Crombie Aberds 302 D5
Old Cryals Kent 53 E7
Old Cullen Moray 302 C5
Old Dailly S Ayrs 244 D6
Old Dalby Leics 154 E3
Old Dam Derbys 185 F10
Old Deer Aberds 303 E9
Old Denaby S Yorks 187 B7
Old Ditch Som 44 D4
Old Dolphin W Yorks 205 G8
Old Down S Glos 60 B6
Old Duffus Moray 301 C11
Old Edlington S Yorks 187 B8
Old Eldon Durham 233 F10
Old Ellerby E Yorks 209 F9
Oldend Glos 80 D3
Old Fallings W Mid 133 C8
Oldfallow Staffs 151 G9
Old Farm Park
M Keynes 103 D8
Old Felixstowe Suff 108 D6
Oldfield Cumb 229 F7
Shrops 132 F3
Worcs 116 E6
W Yorks 196 E6
W Yorks 204 F6
Old Field Shrops 115 B9
Oldfield Brow Gtr Man 184 D3
Oldfield Park Bath 61 G8
Old Fletton Pboro 138 D3
Old Fold T&W 243 E7
Oldford Som 45 C9
Old Ford London 67 C11
Old Forge Hereford 79 B9
Oldfurnace Staffs 169 G8
Old Furnace Torf 78 E3
Old Gate Lincs 157 E8
Old Glossop Derbys 185 C8
Old Goginan Ceredig 128 G3
Old Goole E Yorks 199 C8
Old Gore Hereford 98 F2
Old Graitney Dumfries 239 D8
Old Grimsby Scilly 1 F3
Oldhall Renfs 267 C10
Old Hall Powys 129 G8
Oldhall Green Suff 125 F7
Old Hall Green Herts 105 G7
Oldhall Ho Highld 310 D6
Old Hall Street Norf 160 C6
Oldham Gtr Man 196 F2
Oldham Edge Gtr Man 196 F2
Oldhamstocks E Loth 282 G4
Old Harlow Essex 87 C7
Old Hatfield Herts 86 D2
Old Heath Essex 107 G10
Old Heathfield E Sus 37 C9
Old Hill W Mid 133 F9
Old Hills Worcs 98 B6
Old Hunstanton Norf 175 G11
Oldhurst Cambs 122 B6
Old Hurst Cambs 122 B5
Old Hutton Cumb 211 B11
Oldington Shrops 132 D4
Old Johnstone Dumfries 248 D6
Old Kea Corn 4 G6
Old Kilpatrick W Dunb 277 G9
Old Kinnernie Aberds 293 C9
Old Knebworth Herts 104 G4
Oldland S Glos 61 E7
Oldland Common S Glos 61 E7
Old Langho Lancs 203 F10
Old Laxey IoM 192 D5
Old Leake Lincs 174 E6
Old Leckie Stirl 278 C3
Old Lindley W Yorks 196 D5
Old Linslade C Beds 103 F8
Old Llanberis / Nant Peris
Gwyn 163 D10
Old Malden London 67 F8
Old Malton N Yorks 216 E5
Old Marton Shrops 148 C6
Old Mead Essex 105 F10
Oldmeldrum Aberds 303 G8
Old Micklefield
W Yorks 206 G4
Old Mill Corn 12 G3
Old Milton Hants 19 C10
Old Milverton Warks 118 D5
Oldmixon N Som 43 B10
Old Monkland N Lnrk 268 C4
Old Nenthorn Borders 262 B5
Old Netley Hants 33 F7
Old Neuadd Powys 129 F11
Old Newton Suff 125 E11
Old Oak Common London 67 C8
Old Park Corn 6 B4
Telford 132 B3
Old Passage S Glos 60 B5
Old Perton Staffs 133 D7
Old Philpstoun W Loth 279 F11
Old Polmont Falk 279 F8
Old Portsmouth Ptsmth 21 B8
Old Quarrington
Durham 234 D2
Old Radnor Powys 114 F5
Old Rattray Aberds 303 D10
Old Rayne Aberds 302 G6
Old Romney Kent 39 B8
Old Shirley Soton 32 E5
Oldshore Beg Highld 306 D6
Old Shoreham W Sus 36 F2
Oldshoremore Highld 306 D7
Old Snydale W Yorks 198 C2
Old Sodbury S Glos 61 C9
Old Somerby Lincs 155 C9
Oldstead N Yorks 215 C10
Old Stillington Stockton 234 G3
Old Storridge Common
Worcs 116 G4
Old Stratford Northants 102 C5
Old Struan Perth 291 G10
Old Swan Mers 182 C5
Old Swarland Northumb 252 C5
Old Swinford W Mid 133 G8
Old Tame Gtr Man 196 F3
Old Tebay Cumb 222 D2
Old Thirsk N Yorks 215 C8
Old Tinnis Borders 261 D9
Old Toll S Ayrs 257 E9
Oldtown Aberds 293 C7
Aberds 302 G5
Highld 309 L5
Old Town Cumb 211 C11
Cumb 230 C5
Edin 280 G5
E Sus 23 F9
E Sus 38 F2
E Sus 38 F4
E Yorks 218 F3
Herts 104 F4
Scilly 1 G4
Swindon 63 C7
W Yorks 196 B3
Oldtown of Ord Aberds 302 D6
Old Trafford Gtr Man 184 B4
Old Tree Kent 71 G8
Old Tupton Derbys 170 B5
Oldwalls Swansea 56 C3
Old Warden C Beds 104 C2
Old Warren Flint 166 C4
Oldway Swansea 56 D5
Torbay 9 C7
Old Way Som 28 D5
Oldways End Devon 26 B5
Old Weston Cambs 121 B11
Old Wharf Hereford 98 D4
Oldwhat Aberds 303 D8
Old Whittington Derbys 186 G5
Oldwich Lane W Mid 118 C4
Old Wick Highld 310 D7
Old Wimpole Cambs 122 G6
Old Windsor Windsor 66 E3
Old Wingate Durham 234 D3
Old Wives Lees Kent 54 C5
Old Woking Sur 50 B4
Old Wolverton
M Keynes 102 C6
Oldwood Worcs 115 D11
Old Woodhall Lincs 174 B2
Old Woodhouses
Shrops 167 G9
Old Woodstock Oxon 82 B6
Olgrinmore Highld 310 D4
Olive Green Staffs 152 F2
Oliver's Battery Hants 33 B7
Ollaberry Shetland 312 E5
Ollag W Isles 297 G3
Ollerbrook Booth
Derbys 185 D10
Ollerton Ches E 184 F3
Notts 171 B11
Shrops 150 D2
Ollerton Fold Lancs 194 C6
Ollerton Lane Shrops 150 D3
Olmarch Ceredig 112 F2
Olmstead Green Essex 106 C2
Olney M Keynes 121 G7
Olrig Ho Highld 310 C5
Olton W Mid 134 G2
Olveston S Glos 60 B6
Olwen Ceredig 93 B11
Ombersley Worcs 116 E6
Ompton Notts 171 B11
Omunsgarth Shetland 313 J5
Onchan IoM 192 E4
Onecote Staffs 169 D9
Onehouse Suff 125 F10
Onen Mon 78 C6
Onesacre S Yorks 186 C3
Ongar Hill Norf 157 E11
Ongar Street Hereford 115 D7
Onibury Shrops 115 B9
Onich Highld 290 G2
Onllwyn Neath 76 C4
Onneley Staffs 168 G3
Onslow Village Sur 50 D3
Onthank E Ayrs 267 G8
Onziebust Orkney 314 D4
Openshaw Gtr Man 184 B5
Openwoodgate Derbys 170 F5
Opinan Highld 299 B7
Highld 307 K3
Orange Lane Borders 272 G5
Orange Row Norf 157 E10
Orasaigh W Isles 305 G5
Orbiston N Lnrk 268 D4
Orbliston Moray 302 D3
Orbost Highld 298 E2
Orby Lincs 175 B7
Orchard Hill Devon 24 B6
Orchard Leigh Bucks 85 E7
Orchard Portman Som 28 C2
Orcheston Wilts 46 D5
Orcop Hereford 97 F9
Orcop Hill Hereford 97 F9
Ord Highld 295 D8
Ordale Shetland 312 C8
Ordhead Aberds 293 B8
Ordie Aberds 292 C6
Ordiequish Moray 302 D3
Ordiqhill Aberds 302 D5
Ordley Northumb 241 F10
Ordsall Gtr Man 184 B4
Notts 187 E11
Ore E Sus 38 E4
Oreston Plym 7 E10
Oreton Shrops 132 G3
Orford Suff 109 B8
Warr 183 C10
Organford Dorset 18 C4
Orgreave Staffs 152 F3
S Yorks 186 D6
Oridge Street Glos 98 F5
Orlandon Pembs 72 D4
Orlestone Kent 54 G3
Orleton Hereford 115 D9
Worcs 116 D3
Orleton Common
Hereford 115 D9
Orlingbury Northants 121 C7
Ormacleit W Isles 297 H3
Ormathwaite Cumb 229 F11
Ormesby Redcar 225 B10
Ormesby St Margaret
Norf 161 G9
Ormesby St Michael
Norf 161 G9
Ormiclate Castle
W Isles 297 H3
Ormidale Lodge Argyll 275 F11
Ormiscaig Highld 307 K3
Ormiston Borders 262 G2
E Loth 271 B8
Ormsaigbeg Highld 288 C6
Ormsaigmore Highld 288 C6
Ormsary Argyll 275 F8
Ormsgill Cumb 210 E3
Ormskirk Lancs 194 F2
Ornsby Hill Durham 233 B9
Orpington London 68 F3
Orrell Gtr Man 194 F4
Mers 182 B4
Orrell Post Gtr Man 194 G4
Orrisdale IoM 192 C4
Orrock Fife 280 D4
Orroland Dumfries 237 E9
Orsett Thurrock 68 C6
Orsett Heath Thurrock 68 D6
Orslow Staffs 150 F6
Orston Notts 172 G3
Orthwaite Cumb 229 E11
Ortner Lancs 202 C6
Orton Cumb 222 D2
Northants 120 B6
Staffs 133 D7
Orton Brimbles Pboro 138 D3
Orton Goldhay Pboro 138 D3
Orton Longueville
Pboro 138 D3
Orton Malborne Pboro 138 D3
Orton-on-the-Hill Leics 134 C6
Orton Rigg Cumb 239 G8
Orton Southgate Pboro 138 E2
Orton Waterville Pboro 138 D3
Orton Wistow Pboro 138 D2
Orwell Cambs 123 G7
Osbaldeston Lancs 203 G8
Osbaldeston Green
Lancs 203 G8
Osbaldwick York 207 C8
Osbaston Leics 135 C8
Shrops 148 E6
Telford 149 F11
Osbaston Hollow Leics 135 B8
Osbournby Lincs 155 B11
Oscroft Ches W 167 B8
Ose Highld 298 E3
Osea Island Essex 88 D6
Osehill Green Dorset 29 F11
Osgathorpe Leics 153 F8
Osgodby Lincs 189 C9
N Yorks 207 G8
N Yorks 217 C11
Osgodby Common
N Yorks 207 F8
Osidge London 86 G3
Oskaig Highld 295 B7
Oskamull Argyll 288 E6
Osleston Derbys 152 B4
Osmaston Derby 153 C7
Derbys 170 G2
Osmington Dorset 17 E10
Osmington Mills Dorset 17 E10
Osmondthorpe W Yorks 206 G2
Osmotherley N Yorks 225 F9
Osney Oxon 83 D8
Ospisdale Highld 309 L7
Ospringe Kent 70 G4
Ossaborough Devon 40 E3
Ossemsley Hants 19 B10
Osset Spa W Yorks 197 D9
Ossett W Yorks 197 C9
Ossett Street Side
W Yorks 197 C9
Ossington Notts 172 C3
Ostend Essex 88 F6
Norf 161 C7
Osterley London 66 D6
Oswaldkirk N Yorks 216 D2
Oswaldtwistle Lancs 195 B8
Oswestry Shrops 148 D5
Otby Lincs 189 C10
Oteley Shrops 149 C8
Otford Kent 52 B4
Otham Kent 53 C9
Otham Hole Kent 53 C10
Otherton Staffs 151 G8
Othery Som 43 G11
Otley Suff 126 F4
W Yorks 205 D10
Otterbourne Hants 33 C7
Otterburn Northumb 251 E9
N Yorks 204 B3
Otterburn Camp
Northumb 251 D9
Otterden Place Kent 54 C2
Otter Ferry Argyll 275 E10
Otterford Som 28 E2
Otterham Corn 11 C9
Otterhampton Som 43 E8
Otterham Quay Kent 69 F10
Otterham Station Corn 11 D9
Otter Ho Argyll 275 F10
Ottershaw Sur 66 G4
Otterspool Mers 182 D5
Otterswick Shetland 312 E7
Otterton Devon 15 D7
Otterwood Hants 32 G6
Ottery St Mary Devon 15 B8
Ottinge Kent 55 E7
Ottringham E Yorks 201 C9
Oughterby Cumb 239 F7
Oughtershaw N Yorks 213 C7
Oughterside Cumb 229 C8
Oughtibridge S Yorks 186 C4
Oughtrington Warr 183 D11
Oulston N Yorks 215 E10
Oulton Cumb 238 G6
Norf 160 D2
Staffs 150 E5
Staffs 151 B8
Suff 143 D10
W Yorks 197 B11
Oulton Broad Suff 143 E10
Oultoncross Staffs 151 C8
Oulton Grange Staffs 151 B8
Oulton Heath Staffs 151 B8
Oulton Street Norf 160 D3
Oundle Northants 137 F10
Ounsdale Staffs 133 E7
Ousby Cumb 231 E8
Ousdale Highld 311 G4
Ousden Suff 124 F4
Ousefleet E Yorks 199 C10
Ousel Hole W Yorks 205 E8
Ouston Durham 243 G7
Northumb 241 G7
Northumb 242 C3
Outcast Cumb 210 D6
Out Elmstead Kent 55 C8
Outer Hope Devon 8 G3
Outertown Orkney 314 E2
Outgate Cumb 221 F7
Outhgill Cumb 222 E5
Outhill Warks 118 D2
Outhills Aberds 303 D10
Outlands Staffs 150 C5
Outlane W Yorks 196 D5
Outlane Moor W Yorks 196 D5
Outlet Village Ches W 182 G6
Outmarsh Wilts 61 G11
Out Newton E Yorks 201 C11
Out Rawcliffe Lancs 202 E4
Outwell Norf 139 C10
Outwick Hants 31 D10
Outwood Gtr Man 195 F9
Som 28 B4
Sur 51 D10
W Yorks 197 C10
Outwoods Leics 153 F8
Staffs 150 F5
Staffs 152 E4
Warks 134 G4
Ouzlewell Green
W Yorks 197 B10
Ovenden W Yorks 196 B5
Ovenscloss Borders 261 C11
Over Cambs 123 C7
Ches W 167 B10
Glos 80 B4
S Glos 60 C5
Overa Farm Stud Norf 141 F9
Overbister Orkney 314 B6
Over Burrow Lancs 212 D2
Over Burrows Derbys 152 B5
Overbury Worcs 99 D9
Overcombe Dorset 17 E9
Over Compton Dorset 29 D9
Overend W Mid 133 G9
Over End Cambs 137 E11
Derbys 186 G3
Overgreen Derbys 186 G4
Over Green W Mid 134 E3
Over Haddon Derbys 170 B2
Over Hulton Gtr Man 195 F7
Over Kellet Lancs 211 E10
Over Kiddington Oxon 101 G8
Over Knutsford Ches E 184 F3
Over Langshaw
Borders 271 G10
Overleigh Som 44 F3
Overley Staffs 152 F3
Overley Green Warks 117 F11
Over Monnow Mon 79 C8
Overmoor Staffs 169 F7
Over Norton Oxon 100 F6
Over Peover Ches E 184 G3
Overpool Ches W 182 F5
Overs Shrops 131 D7
Overscaig Hotel Highld 309 G4
Overseal Derbys 152 F5
Over Silton N Yorks 225 G9
Oversland Kent 54 B5
Overslade Warks 119 C9
Oversley Green Warks 117 F11
Overstone Northants 120 D6
Over Stowey Som 43 F7
Overstrand Norf 160 A4
Over Stratton Som 28 D6
Over Tabley Ches E 184 E2
Overthorpe Northants 101 C9
W Yorks 197 D8
Overton Aberdeen 293 B10
Aberds 293 B9
Ches W 183 F8
Dumfries 237 C11
Glos 80 C2
Hants 48 D4
Invclyd 276 G5
Lancs 202 B4
N Yorks 207 B7
Shrops 115 C10
Staffs 151 B10
Swansea 56 D3
W Yorks 197 D9
Overton Bridge Wrex 166 G5
Overton / Owrtyn Wrex 166 G5
Overtown Lancs 212 D2
N Lnrk 268 E6
Swindon 63 D7
W Yorks 197 D11
Over Town Lancs 195 B11
Over Wallop Hants 47 F9
Over Whitacre Warks 134 E5
Over Worton Oxon 101 F8
Oving Bucks 102 G5
W Sus 22 C6
Ovingdean Brighton 36 G5
Ovingham Northumb 242 E3
Ovington Durham 224 C2
Essex 106 C5
Hants 48 G5
Norf 141 C8
Northumb 242 E3
Owen's Bank Staffs 152 D4
Ower Hants 32 D4
Owermoigne Dorset 17 D11
Owlbury Shrops 130 E6
Owlcotes Derbys 170 B6
Owl End Cambs 122 B4
Owler Bar Derbys 186 F3
Owlerton S Yorks 186 D4
Owlet W Yorks 205 F9
Owlpen Glos 80 F4
Owl's Green Suff 126 D5
Owlsmoor Brack 65 G11
Owlswick Bucks 84 D3
Owlthorpe S Yorks 186 E6
Owmby Lincs 200 G5
Owmby-by-Spital Lincs 189 D8
Ownham W Berks 64 E2
Owrtyn / Overton Wrex 166 G5
Owslebury Hants 33 C8
Owston Leics 136 B5
S Yorks 198 E5
Owston Ferry N Lincs 199 G10
Owstwick E Yorks 209 G11
Owthorne E Yorks 201 B10
Owthorpe Notts 154 C3
Owton Manor Hrtlpl 234 F5
Oxborough Norf 140 C4
Oxclose S Yorks 186 E6
T&W 243 F7
Oxcombe Lincs 190 F4
Oxcroft Derbys 187 G7
Oxcroft Estate Derbys 187 G7
Oxen End Essex 106 F3
Oxenhall Glos 98 F4
Oxenholme Cumb 211 B10
Oxenhope W Yorks 204 F6
Oxen Park Cumb 210 B6
Oxenpill Som 44 E2
Oxenton Glos 99 E9
Oxenwood Wilts 47 B10
Oxford Oxon 83 D8
Stoke 168 E5
Oxgang E Dunb 278 G3
Oxgangs Edin 270 B4
Oxhey Herts 85 F10
Oxhill Durham 242 G5
Warks 100 B6
Oxlease Herts 86 D2
Oxley W Mid 133 C8
Oxley Green Essex 88 C6
Oxley's Green E Sus 37 C11
Oxlode Cambs 139 F9
Oxnam Borders 262 F5
Oxnead Norf 160 E4
Oxshott Sur 66 G6
Oxspring S Yorks 197 G9
Oxted Sur 51 C11
Oxton Borders 271 E9
Mers 182 D3
Notts 171 E10
N Yorks 206 E6
Oxton Rakes Derbys 186 G4
Oxwich Swansea 56 D3
Oxwich Green Swansea 56 D3
Oxwick Norf 159 D8
Oykel Bridge Highld 309 J3
Oyne Aberds 302 G6
Oystermouth Swansea 56 D6
Ozleworth Glos 80 G3

P

Pabail Iarach W Isles 304 E7
Pabail Uarach W Isles 304 E7
Pabo Conwy 180 F4
Pace Gate N Yorks 205 C8
Pachesham Park Sur 51 B7
Packers Hill Dorset 30 E2
Packington Leics 153 G7
Packmoor Staffs 168 E5
Packmores Warks 118 D5
Packwood W Mid 118 C3
Packwood Gullet
W Mid 118 C3
Padanaram Angus 287 B8
Padbury Bucks 102 E4
Paddington London 67 C9
Warr 183 D10
Paddlesworth Kent 55 F7
Kent 69 G7
Paddock Kent 54 C3
W Yorks 196 D6
Paddockhaugh Moray 302 D2
Paddockhill Ches E 184 F4
Paddockhole Dumfries 248 G6
Paddock Wood Kent 53 E7
Paddolgreen Shrops 149 C10
Padfield Derbys 185 B8
Padgate Warr 183 D10
Padham's Green Essex 87 F10
Padiham Lancs 203 G11
Padney Cambs 123 C10
Padog Conwy 164 E4
Padside N Yorks 205 B9
Padside Green N Yorks 205 B9
Padson Devon 13 B7
Padstow Corn 10 F4
Padworth W Berks 64 F6
Padworth Common
Hants 64 G6
Paganhill Glos 80 D4
Page Bank Durham 233 D10
Page Moss Mers 182 C6
Page's Green Suff 126 D2
Pagham W Sus 22 D5
Paglesham Churchend
Essex 88 G6
Paglesham Eastend
Essex 88 G6
Paibeil W Isles 296 E3
Paible W Isles 305 J2
Paignton Torbay 9 C7
Pailton Warks 135 G9
Painleyhill Staffs 151 C10
Painscastle Powys 96 B3
Painshawfield Northumb 242 E3
Pains Hill Sur 52 C2
Painsthorpe E Yorks 208 B2
Painswick Glos 80 D5
Painter's Forstal Kent 54 B3
Painters Green Wrex 167 G8
Painter's Green Herts 86 B3
Painthorpe W Yorks 197 D10
Paintmoor Som 28 F4
Pairc Shiaboist W Isles 304 D4
Paisley Renfs 267 C9
Pakefield Suff 143 E10
Pakenham Suff 125 D8
Pale Gwyn 147 B9
Pale Green Essex 106 C3
Palehouse Common
E Sus 23 B7
Palestine Hants 47 E9
Paley Street Windsor 65 D11
Palfrey W Mid 133 D10
Palgowan Dumfries 245 G9
Palgrave Suff 126 B2
Pallaflat Cumb 219 C9
Pallington Dorset 17 C11
Pallion T&W 243 F9
Palmarsh Kent 54 G6
Palmer Moor Derbys 152 C2
Palmersbridge Corn 11 F9
Palmers Cross Staffs 133 C7
Sur 50 E4
Palmer's Flat Glos 79 D9
Palmers Green London 86 G4
Palmer's Green Kent 53 E7
Palmerstown V Glam 58 F6
Palmersville T&W 243 C7
Palmstead Kent 55 D7
Palnackie Dumfries 237 D10
Palnure Dumfries 236 C6
Palterton Derbys 171 B7
Pamber End Hants 48 B6
Pamber Green Hants 48 B6
Pamber Heath Hants 64 G6
Pamington Glos 99 E8
Pamphill Dorset 31 G7
Pampisford Cambs 105 B9
Pan IoW 20 D6
Orkney 314 G3
Panborough Som 44 D3
Panbride Angus 287 D9
Pancakehill Glos 81 C9
Pancrasweek Devon 24 F3
Pancross V Glam 58 F4
Pandy Gwyn 128 C2
Gwyn 146 F4
Gwyn 147 D7
Mon 96 G6
Powys 129 C8
Wrex 148 B3
Wrex 166 G6
Pandy'r Capel Denb 165 E9
Pandy Tudur Conwy 164 C5
Panfield Essex 106 F4
Pangbourne W Berks 64 D6
Panhall Fife 280 C6
Panks Bridge Hereford 98 B2
Pannal N Yorks 206 C2
Pannal Ash N Yorks 205 C11
Pannel's Ash Essex 106 C5
Panpunton Powys 114 C5
Panshanger Herts 86 C3
Pant Denb 166 E2
Flint 181 G10
Gwyn 144 C4
M Tydf 77 D9
Powys 129 C11
Shrops 148 E5
Wrex 166 D5
Wrex 166 F3
Pantasaph Flint 181 F11
Pantdu Neath 57 C9
Panteg Ceredig 111 E9
Torf 78 F4
Pantersbridge Corn 6 B3
Pant-glas Gwyn 163 F7
Pant-glâs Powys 128 D5
Pant-glas Shrops 148 C5
Pantgwyn Carms 93 F11
Ceredig 92 B4
Pant-lasau Swansea 57 B7
Pantmawr Cardiff 58 C6
Pant Mawr Powys 129 G7
Panton Lincs 189 F11
Pant-pastynog Denb 165 C8
Pantperthog Gwyn 128 C4
Pantside Caerph 78 F2
Pant-teg Carms 93 F9
Pant-y-Caws Carms 92 F3
Pant-y-crûg Ceredig 112 B3
Pant-y-dwr Powys 113 B9
Powys 113 C9
Pant-y-ffridd Powys 130 C3
Pantyffynnon Carms 75 C10
Pantygasseg Torf 78 F3
Pantymwyn Flint 165 C11
Pant-y-pyllau Bridgend 58 C2
Pant-yr-awel Bridgend 58 B2
Pant-y-Wacco Flint 181 F10
Panxworth Norf 161 G7
Papcastle Cumb 229 E8
Papermill Bank Shrops 149 D11
Papigoe Highld 310 D7
Papil Shetland 313 K5
Papley Northants 138 F2
Orkney 314 G4
Papple E Loth 281 G11
Papplewick Notts 171 E8
Papworth Everard
Cambs 122 E5
Papworth St Agnes
Cambs 122 E5
Papworth Village Settlement
Cambs 122 E5
Par Corn 5 E11
Paradise Glos 80 C5
Paradise Green Hereford 97 B10
Paramoor Corn 5 F9
Paramour Street Kent 71 G9
Parbold Lancs 194 E3
Parbrook Som 44 F5
W Sus 35 B9
Parc Gwyn 147 C7
Parc Erissey Corn 4 G3
Parc-hendy Swansea 56 B4
Parchey Som 43 F10
Parciau Anglesey 179 E7
Parcllyn Ceredig 110 G4
Parc Mawr Caerph 77 G10
Parc-Seymour Newport 78 G6
Parc-y-rhôs Carms 93 B11
Pardown Hants 48 D5
Pardshaw Cumb 229 G7
Pardshaw Hall Cumb 229 F8
Parham Suff 126 E6
Park Corn 10 G6
Devon 14 B2
Dumfries 247 E10
Som 44 G3
Swindon 63 C7
Park Barn Sur 50 C3
Park Bottom Corn 4 G3
Park Bridge Gtr Man 196 G2
Park Broom Cumb 239 F10
Park Close Lancs 204 E3
Park Corner Bath 45 B9
E Sus 23 C8
E Sus 52 F4
Oxon 65 B7
Windsor 65 C11
Parkend Glos 79 D10
Glos 80 C3
Park End Beds 121 G9
Cambs 123 E11
Mbro 225 B10
Northumb 241 B9
Som 43 G7
Staffs 168 E3
Worcs 116 C5
Parkengear Corn 5 F8
Parker's Corner W Berks 64 E6
Parker's Green Herts 104 F6
Kent 52 D6
Parkeston Essex 108 E4
Parkfield Corn 6 B6
S Glos 61 D7
W Mid 133 D8
Parkfoot Falk 278 F6
Parkgate Ches E 184 G3
Ches W 182 F3
Cumb 229 B10
Dumfries 248 F2
Essex 87 B11
Kent 53 G11
Sur 51 E8
S Yorks 186 B6
Park Gate Dorset 30 F2
Hants 33 F8
Kent 55 D7
Suff 124 F4
Worcs 117 C8
W Yorks 197 E8
Park Green Essex 105 F9
Parkhall W Dunb 277 G9
Park Hall Shrops 148 C6
Parkham Devon 24 C5
Parkham Ash Devon 24 C5
Parkhead Cumb 230 C2
Glasgow 268 C2
S Yorks 186 E4
Park Head Cumb 231 C7
Derbys 170 E5
W Yorks 197 F7
Parkhill Aberds 303 E10
Invclyd 277 G7
Park Hill Glos 79 F9
Kent 54 G3
Mers 194 G3
Notts 171 E11
N Yorks 214 F6
S Yorks 186 D5
Parkhill Ho Aberds 293 B10
Parkhouse Mon 79 E7
Parkhouse Green
Derbys 170 G6
Parkhurst IoW 20 C5
Parklands W Yorks 206 F3

Park Lane Staffs 133 B7
Wrex 149 B8
Park Langley London 67 F11
Park Mains Renfs 277 G9
Parkmill Swansea 56 D4
Park Mill W Yorks 197 E9
Parkneuk Aberds 293 F9
Fife 279 D11
Park Royal London 67 C7
Parkside C Beds 103 G10
Cumb 219 B10
Durham 234 B4
N Lnrk 268 D6
Staffs 151 D8
Wrex 166 D5
Parkstone Poole 18 C6
Park Street Herts 85 E10
W Sus 50 G6
Park Town Luton 103 G11
Oxon 83 D8
Park Village Northumb 240 E5
W Mid 133 C8
Park Villas W Yorks 206 F2
Parkway Hereford 98 D4
Som 29 C9
Park Wood Kent 53 C9
Medway 69 G10
Parkwood Springs
S Yorks 186 D4
Parley Cross Dorset 19 B7
Parley Green Dorset 19 B7
Parliament Heath Suff 107 C9
Parlington W Yorks 206 F4
Parmoor Bucks 65 B9
Parnacott Devon 24 F4
Parney Heath Essex 107 E10
Parr Mers 183 C8
Parracombe Devon 41 E7
Parr Brow Gtr Man 195 G8
Parrog Pembs 91 D10
Parsley Hay Derbys 169 C10
Parslow's Hillock Bucks 84 E4
Parsonage Green Essex 88 D2
Parsonby Cumb 229 D8
Parson Cross S Yorks 186 C5
Parson Drove Cambs 139 B7
Parsons Green London 67 D9
Parson's Heath Essex 107 F10
Partick Glasgow 267 B11
Partington Gtr Man 184 C2
Partney Lincs 174 B6
Parton Cumb 228 G5
Cumb 239 G7
Dumfries 237 B8
Glos 99 G7
Hereford 96 B6
Partridge Green W Sus 35 D11
Partrishow Powys 96 G5
Parwich Derbys 169 E11
Pasford Staffs 132 D6
Passenham Northants 102 D5
Passfield Hants 49 G10
Passingford Bridge Essex 87 F8
Passmores Essex 86 D6
Paston Norf 160 C6
Pboro 138 C3
Paston Green Norf 160 C6
Pasturefields Staffs 151 D9
Patchacott Devon 12 B5
Patcham Brighton 36 F4
Patchetts Green Herts 85 F10
Patching W Sus 35 F9
Patchole Devon 40 E6
Patchway S Glos 60 C6
Pategill Cumb 230 F6
Pateley Bridge N Yorks 214 F3
Paternoster Heath Essex 88 C6
Pathe Som 43 G11
Pather N Lnrk 268 E5
Pathfinder Village Devon 14 C2
Pathhead Aberds 293 G9
E Ayrs 258 G4
Fife 280 C5
Midloth 271 C7
Path Head T&W 242 E5
Pathlow Warks 118 F3
Path of Condie Perth 286 F4
Pathstruie Perth 286 F4
Patient End Herts 105 F8
Patmore Heath Herts 105 F8
Patna E Ayrs 257 G10
Patney Wilts 46 B5
Patrick IoM 192 D3
Patrick Brompton
N Yorks 224 G4
Patricroft Gtr Man 184 B3
Patrington E Yorks 201 C10
Patrington Haven
E Yorks 201 C10
Patrixbourne Kent 55 B7
Patsford Devon 40 F4
Patterdale Cumb 221 B7
Pattiesmuir Fife 279 E11
Pattingham Staffs 132 D6
Pattishall Northants 120 G3
Pattiswick Essex 106 G6
Patton Shrops 131 E11
Patton Bridge Cumb 221 F11
Paul Corn 1 D5
Paulerspury Northants 102 B4
Paull E Yorks 201 B7
Paul's Green Corn 2 C4
Paulsgrove Ptsmth 33 F10
Paulton Bath 45 B7
Paulville W Loth 269 B9
Pave Lane Telford 150 F5
Pavenham Beds 121 F9
Pawlett Som 43 E10
Pawlett Hill Som 43 E9
Pawston Northumb 263 C9
Paxford Glos 100 D3
Paxton Borders 273 E8
Payden Street Kent 54 C2
Payhembury Devon 27 G9
Paynes Green Sur 50 F6
Paynter's Cross Corn 7 C7
Paynter's Lane End Corn 4 G3
Paythorne Lancs 204 C2
Payton Som 27 C10
Peacehaven E Sus 36 G6
Peacehaven Heights
E Sus 36 G6
Peacemarsh Dorset 30 B4
Peak Dale Derbys 185 F9
Peak Forest Derbys 185 F10
Peak Hill Lincs 156 F5
Peakirk Pboro 138 B3
Pean Hill Kent 70 G6
Pear Ash Som 45 G9
Pearsie Angus 287 B7
Pearson's Green Kent 53 E7
Peartree Herts 86 C2
Pear Tree Derby 153 C7
Peartree Green Essex 87 F9
Hereford 97 E11
Soton 32 E6
Sur 50 F3
Peas Acre W Yorks 205 E8
Peasedown St John Bath 45 B8
Peasehill Derbys 170 F6
Peaseland Green Norf 159 F11
Peasemore W Berks 64 D3
Peasenhall Suff 127 D7
Pease Pottage W Sus 51 G9
Peas Hill Cambs 139 D8
Peaslake Sur 50 E5
Peasley Cross Mers 183 C8
Peasmarsh E Sus 38 C5
Som 28 E4
Sur 50 D3
Peaston E Loth 271 B8
Peastonbank E Loth 271 B8
Peathill Aberds 303 C9
Peat Inn Fife 287 G8
Peatling Magna Leics 135 E11
Peatling Parva Leics 135 F11
Peaton Shrops 131 G10
Peatonstrand Shrops 131 G10
Peats Corner Suff 126 E3
Pebmarsh Essex 107 E7
Pebsham E Sus 38 F3
Pebworth Worcs 100 B2
Pecket Well W Yorks 196 B3
Peckforton Ches E 167 D8
Peckham London 67 D10
Peckham Bush Kent 53 D7
Peckingell Wilts 62 E2
Pecking Mill Som 44 F6
Peckleton Leics 135 C9
Pedair-ffordd Powys 148 E2
Pedham Norf 160 G6
Pedlars End Essex 87 D8
Pedlar's Rest Shrops 131 G9
Pedlinge Kent 54 F6
Pedmore W Mid 133 G8
Pednor Bottom Bucks 84 E6
Pednormead End Bucks 85 E7
Pedwell Som 44 F2
Peebles Borders 270 G5
Peel Borders 261 B10
IoM 192 D3
Lancs 202 G3
Peel Common Hants 33 G9
Peel Green Gtr Man 184 B2
Peel Hall Gtr Man 184 D4
Peel Hill Lancs 202 G3
Peel Park S Lnrk 268 E2
Peene Kent 55 F7
Peening Quarter Kent 38 B5
Peggs Green Leics 153 F8
Pegsdon C Beds 104 E2
Pegswood Northumb 252 F6
Pegwell Kent 71 G11
Peinaha Highld 298 D4
Peinchorran Highld 295 B7
Peingown Highld 298 B4
Peinlich Highld 298 D4
Peinmore Highld 298 E4
Pelaw T&W 243 E7
Pelcomb Pembs 72 B6
Pelcomb Bridge Pembs 72 B6
Pelcomb Cross Pembs 72 B6
Peldon Essex 89 B7
Pelhamfield IoW 21 C7
Pell Green E Sus 52 G6
Pellon W Yorks 196 B5
Pelsall W Mid 133 C10
Pelsall Wood W Mid 133 C10
Pelton Durham 243 G7
Pelton Fell Durham 243 G7
Pelutho Cumb 229 B8
Pelynt Corn 6 D4
Pemberton Carms 75 E8
Gtr Man 194 G5
Pembles Cross Kent 53 D11
Pembre / Pembrey
Carms 74 E6
Pembrey / Pembre
Carms 74 E6
Pembridge Hereford 115 F7
Pembroke Pembs 73 E7
Pembroke Dock / Doc
Penfro Pembs 73 E7
Pembroke Ferry Pembs 73 E7
Pembury Kent 52 E6
Pempwell Corn 12 F3
Penallt Mon 79 C8
Pen-allt Hereford 97 F11
Penally / Penalun
Pembs 73 F10
Penalt Hereford 97 F11
Penalun / Penally
Pembs 73 F10
Penare Corn 5 G9
Penarlâg / Hawarden
Flint 166 B4
Penarron Powys 130 F2
Penarth V Glam 59 E7
Penarth Moors Cardiff 59 E7
Penbeagle Corn 2 B2
Penbedw Flint 165 B11
Pen-bedw Pembs 92 D4
Penberth Corn 1 E4
Penbidwal Mon 96 G6
Penbodlas Gwyn 144 C5
Pen-bont Rhydybeddau
Ceredig 128 G3
Penboyr Carms 93 D7
Penbryn Ceredig 110 G5
Pencader Carms 93 D8
Pencaenewydd Gwyn 162 G6
Pencaerau Neath 57 B8
Pen-caer-fenny Swansea 56 B4
Pencaitland E Loth 271 B8
Pencarnisiog Anglesey 178 G5
Pencarreg Carms 93 B10
Pencarrow Corn 11 E8
Penceiliogi Carms 75 E8
Pencelli Powys 95 F11
Pen-clawdd Swansea 56 B4
Pencoed Bridgend 58 C3
Pencombe Hereford 115 G11
Pen-common Powys 76 D6
Pencoyd Hereford 97 F10
Pencoys Corn 2 B5
Pencraig Anglesey 179 F7
Hereford 97 G11
Powys 147 D10
Pencroesoped Mon 78 D4
Pencuke Corn 11 C9
Pendas Fields W Yorks 206 F3
Pendeen Corn 1 C3
Pendeford W Mid 133 C7
Penderyn Rhondda 77 D7
Pendine / Pentwyn
Carms 74 D2
Pendlebury Gtr Man 195 G9
Pendleton Gtr Man 184 B4
Lancs 203 F11
Pendock Worcs 98 E5
Pendoggett Corn 10 F6
Pendomer Som 29 E8
Pendoylan V Glam 58 D5
Pendre Bridgend 58 C2
Gwyn 110 C2
Powys 95 F10
Pendrift Corn 11 G8
Penegoes Powys 128 C5
Penelewey Corn 4 G6
Penenden Heath Kent 53 B9
Penffordd Pembs 91 G11
Penffordd Lâs / Staylittle
Powys 129 E7
Pengam Caerph 77 F11
Penge London 67 E11
Pengegon Corn 2 B5
Pengelly Corn 11 E7
Pengenffordd Powys 96 E3
Pengersick Corn 2 D3
Pen-gilfach Gwyn 163 C9
Pengold Corn 11 C8
Pengorffwysfa Anglesey 179 C7
Pengover Green Corn 6 B5
Pen-groes-oped Mon 78 D4
Penguithal Hereford 97 G10
Pengwern Denb 181 F8
Penhale Corn 2 F5
Corn 5 D8
Penhale Jakes Corn 2 D4
Penhallick Corn 3 F7
Corn 4 G3
Penhallow Corn 4 E5
Penhalurick Corn 2 B6
Penhalvean Corn 2 B6
Penhelig Gwyn 128 D2
Penhill Devon 40 G4
Swindon 63 B7
Penhow Newport 78 G6
Penhurst E Sus 23 B11
Peniarth Gwyn 128 B2
Penicuik Midloth 270 C4
Peniel Carms 93 G8
Denb 165 C8
Penifiler Highld 298 E4
Peninver Argyll 255 E8
Penisa'r Waun Gwyn 163 C9
Penistone S Yorks 197 G8
Penjerrick Corn 3 C7
Penketh Warr 183 D9
Penkhull Stoke 168 G5
Penkill S Ayrs 244 D6
Penknap Wilts 45 D11
Penkridge Staffs 151 G8
Pen-lan Swansea 56 B6
Pen-Lan-mabws Pembs 91 F7
Penleigh Wilts 45 C11
Penley Wrex 149 B8
Penllech Gwyn 144 C4
Penllergaer Swansea 56 B6
Penllwyn Caerph 77 F11
Ceredig 128 G3
Penllyn V Glam 58 D3
Pen-llyn Anglesey 178 E4
Pen-lon Anglesey 162 B6
Penmachno Conwy 164 E3
Penmaen Caerph 77 F11
Swansea 56 D4
Penmaenan Conwy 180 F2
Penmaenmawr Conwy 180 F2
Penmaenpool Gwyn 146 F3
Penmaen Rhôs Conwy 180 F5
Penmark V Glam 58 F5
Penmarth Corn 2 B6
Penmayne Corn 10 F4
Pen Mill Som 29 D9
Penmon Anglesey 179 E10
Penmore Mill Argyll 288 D6
Penmorfa Ceredig 110 G6
Gwyn 163 G8
Penmynydd Anglesey 179 G8
Penn Bucks 84 G6
W Mid 133 D7
Pennal Gwyn 128 C4
Pennan Aberds 303 C8
Pennance Corn 4 G4
Pennant Ceredig 111 E10
Conwy 164 D5
Denb 147 C10
Denb 165 E8
Powys 129 D7
Pennant Melangell
Powys 147 D10
Pennar Pembs 73 E7
Pennard Swansea 56 D5
Pennar Park Pembs 72 E6
Penn Bottom Bucks 84 G6
Pennerley Shrops 131 D7
Pennington Cumb 210 D5
Gtr Man 183 B11
Hants 20 C2
Pennington Green
Gtr Man 194 F6
Pennorth Powys 96 F2
Penn Street Bucks 84 F6
Pennsylvania Devon 14 C4
S Glos 61 E8
Penny Bridge Cumb 210 C6
Pennycross Argyll 289 G7
Plym 7 D9
Pennygate Norf 160 E6
Pennygown Argyll 289 E7
Penny Green Derbys 187 F8
Penny Hill Lincs 157 D7
W Yorks 196 D5
Pennylands Lancs 194 F3
Pennymoor Devon 26 E5
Pennypot Kent 54 G6
Penny's Green Norf 142 D3
Pennytinney Corn 10 F6
Pennywell T&W 243 F9
Pen-onn V Glam 58 F5
Penparc Ceredig 92 B4
Pembs 91 E7
Penparcau Ceredig 111 B11
Penpedairheol Caerph 77 F10
Mon 78 E4
Penpergym Mon 78 C4
Penperlleni Mon 78 E4
Penpethy Corn 11 D7
Penpillick Corn 5 D11
Penplas Carms 74 B5
Penpol Corn 3 B8
Penpoll Corn 6 E2
Penponds Corn 2 B4
Penpont Corn 11 G7
Dumfries 247 E8
Powys 95 F9
Penprysg Bridgend 58 C3
Penquit Devon 8 E2
Penrallt Gwyn 145 B7
Powys 129 F9
Penrherber Carms 92 D5
Penrhiw Caerph 78 G2
Penrhiwceiber Rhondda 77 F8
Pen-Rhiw-fawr Neath 76 C2
Penrhiwgarreg Bl Gwent 78 E2
Penrhiw-llan Ceredig 93 C7
Penrhiw-pal Ceredig 92 B6
Penrhiwtyn Neath 57 B8
Penrhos Anglesey 178 E3
Gwyn 144 C6
Hereford 114 F6
Penrhôs Mon 78 C6
Penrhos Mon 78 C6
Powys 76 C3
Pen-rhos Wrex 166 E3
Penrhosfeilw Anglesey 178 E2
Penrhos-garnedd Gwyn 179 G9
Penrhyd Lastra Anglesey 178 C6
Penrhyn Bay / Bae-Penrhyn
Conwy 180 E4
Penrhyn Castle Pembs 92 B2
Penrhyn-coch Ceredig 128 G2
Penrhyndeudraeth
Gwyn 146 B2
Penrhynside Conwy 180 E4
Penrhyn side Conwy 180 E4
Penrhys Rhondda 77 F8
Penrice Swansea 56 D3
Penrith Cumb 230 E6
Penrose Corn 10 G3
Corn 11 F7
Penrose Hill Corn 2 D4
Penruddock Cumb 230 F4
Penryn Corn 3 C7
Pensarn Carms 74 B6
Conwy 181 F7
Pen-sarn Gwyn 145 D11
Gwyn 162 G6
Pensax Worcs 116 D4
Pensby Mers 182 E3
Penselwood Som 45 G9
Pensford Bath 60 G6
Pensham Worcs 99 C8
Penshaw T&W 243 G8
Penshurst Kent 52 E4
Pensilva Corn 6 B5
Pensnett W Mid 133 F8
Penston E Loth 281 G8
Penstone Devon 26 G3
Penstraze Corn 4 F5
Pentewan Corn 5 F10
Pentiken Shrops 130 G4
Pentir Gwyn 163 B9
Pentire Corn 4 C5
Pentirvin Shrops 130 C6
Pentlepoir Pembs 73 D10
Pentlow Essex 106 B6
Pentlow Street Essex 106 B6
Pentney Norf 158 G4
Penton Corner Hants 47 D10
Penton Grafton Hants 47 D10
Penton Mewsey Hants 47 D10
Pentonville London 67 C10
Pentowin Carms 74 B3
Pentraeth Anglesey 179 F8
Pentrapeod Caerph 77 E11
Pentre Carms 75 C8
Denb 165 D10
Flint 165 C11
Flint 166 B4
Flint 166 C2
Flint 166 D2
Powys 129 F11
Powys 130 B4
Powys 130 E5
Powys 147 D11
Powys 148 G3
Rhondda 77 F7
Shrops 148 D4
Shrops 149 F7
Wrex 148 B2
Wrex 166 G3
Pentrebach Carms 94 E6
M Tydf 77 E9
Rhondda 58 B5
Swansea 75 D10
Pentre-bâch Ceredig 93 B11
Pentre-bach Powys 95 E8
Pentrebane Cardiff 58 D6
Pentrebeirdd Powys 148 G3
Pentre Berw Anglesey 179 G7
Pentre-bont Conwy 164 E2
Pentre Broughton Wrex 166 E4
Pentre Bychan Wrex 166 F4
Pentrecagal Carms 92 C6
Pentre-cefn Shrops 148 D4
Pentre-celyn Denb 165 E11
Powys 129 B7
Pentre-chwyth Swansea 57 B7
Pentre Cilgwyn Wrex 148 B4
Pentre-clawdd Shrops 148 C5
Pentre-coed Shrops 149 B7
Pentre-cwrt Carms 93 D7
Pentre Dolau-Honddu
Powys 95 C9
Pentredwr Denb 165 F11
Pentre-dwr Swansea 57 B7
Pentrefelin Anglesey 178 C6
Carms 93 G11
Ceredig 94 B2
Conwy 180 G4
Denb 166 G2
Gwyn 145 B10
Pentre-Ffwrndan Flint 182 G3
Pentrefoelas Conwy 164 E5
Pentref-y-groes Caerph 77 F11
Pentre-galar Pembs 92 E3
Pentregat Ceredig 111 G7
Pentre-Gwenlais Carms 75 B10
Pentre Gwynfryn Gwyn 145 D11
Pentre Halkyn Flint 182 G2
Pentreheyling Shrops 130 E4
Pentre Hodre Shrops 114 B6
Pentre Isaf Conwy 164 B5
Pentre Llanrhaeadr
Denb 165 C9
Pentre Llifior Powys 130 D2
Pentrellwyn Ceredig 93 C8
Pentre-llwyn-llwyd
Powys 113 G9
Pentre-llyn Ceredig 112 C2
Pentre-llyn cymmer
Conwy 165 E7
Pentre Maelor Wrex 166 F5
Pentre Meyrick V Glam 58 D3
Pentre-newydd Shrops 148 B5
Pentre-Piod Torf 78 E3
Pentre-Poeth Carms 75 E8
Newport 59 B9
Pentre'r beirdd Powys 148 G3
Pentre'r Felin Conwy 164 B4
Pentre'r-felin Denb 165 B10
Powys 95 E8
Pentre-rhew Ceredig 112 G3
Pentre-tafarn-y-fedw
Conwy 164 C4
Pentre-ty-gwyn Carms 94 D6
Pentreuchaf Gwyn 145 B7
Pentre-uchaf Conwy 180 F5
Pentrich Derbys 170 E5
Pentridge Dorset 31 D8
Pentrisil Pembs 91 E11
Pentwyn Caerph 77 E10
Cardiff 59 C8
Pen-twyn Caerph 78 E2
Carms 75 C9
Mon 79 D8
Torf 78 E3
Pentwyn Berthlwyd
Caerph 77 F10
Pentwyn-mawr Caerph 77 F11
Pentwyn / Pendine
Carms 74 D2
Pentyrch Cardiff 58 C6
Penuchadre V Glam 57 G11
Pen-Uchar Plwyf Flint 181 G11
Penuwch Ceredig 111 E11
Penwartha Corn 4 E5
Penwartha Coombe Corn 4 E5
Penweathers Corn 4 G6
Penwithick Corn 5 D10
Penwood Hants 64 G2
Penwortham Lane
Lancs 194 B4
Penwyllt Powys 76 B5
Pen-y-Ball Top Flint 181 F11
Penybanc Carms 75 C10
Pen-y-banc Carms 93 G8
Carms 94 G2
Pen-y-bank Caerph 77 E10
Penybedd Carms 74 E6
Penybont Ceredig 128 F2
Powys 114 E2
Pen-y-Bont Bl Gwent 78 D2
Carms 92 F6
Gwyn 128 C4
Gwyn 146 D2
Powys 148 E4
Pen y Bont ar ogwr /
Bridgend Bridgend 58 C2
Penybontfawr Powys 147 E11
Penybryn Caerph 77 F10
Pen-y-Bryn Gwyn 145 B9
Gwyn 146 F3
Pembs 92 C3
Powys 130 C3
Shrops 148 B6
Wrex 166 G3
Penycae Wrex 166 F3
Pen-y-cae Bridgend 58 C2
Neath 57 D9
Powys 76 C4
Pen-y-cae-mawr Mon 78 F6
Penycaerau Gwyn 144 D3
Pen-y-cefn Flint 181 F10
Pen-y-clawdd Mon 79 D7
Pen-y-coed Shrops 148 E5
Pen-y-coedcae Rhondda 58 B5
Penycwm Pembs 90 G6
Pen-y-Darren M Tydf 77 D9
Penydre Swansea 75 E11
Pen-y-fai Bridgend 57 E11
Carms 75 E7
Pen-y-fan Carms 56 B4
Mon 79 D8
Penyfeidr Pembs 91 F7
Pen-y-felin Flint 165 B11
Penyffordd Flint 166 C4
Pen-y-ffordd Denb 181 F8
Flint 181 E10
Penyffridd Gwyn 163 D8
Pen y Foel Shrops 148 E5
Penygarn Torf 78 E3
Pen-y-garn Carms 93 E11
Ceredig 128 F2
Penygarnedd Powys 148 E2
Pen-y-garnedd
Anglesey 179 F8
Penygelli Powys 130 E2
Pen-y-gop Conwy 164 G6
Penygraig Rhondda 77 G7
Pen-y-graig Gwyn 144 C3
Penygraigwen Anglesey 178 D6
Penygroes Gwyn 163 E7
Pembs 92 D3
Pen-y-groes Carms 75 C9
Pen-y-groeslon Gwyn 144 C4
Pen-y-Gwryd Hotel
Gwyn 163 D11
Pen-y-lan Cardiff 59 D7
Newport 59 B9
V Glam 58 D3
Pen-y-maes Flint 181 F11
Pen-y-Myndd Carms 75 E7
Penymynydd Flint 166 C4
Pen-y-Park Hereford 96 C5
Penyraber Pembs 91 D9
Pen-yr-englyn Rhondda 76 F6
Penyrheol Caerph 58 B6
Swansea 56 B5
Torf 78 F3
Pen-yr-heol Bridgend 58 C2
Mon 78 C6
Pen-yr-Heolgerrig
M Tydf 77 D8
Pen-y-rhiw Rhondda 58 B5
Penysarn Anglesey 179 C7
Pen-y-stryt Denb 165 E11
Penywaun Rhondda 77 E7
Pen-y-wern Shrops 114 B6
Penzance Corn 1 C5
Peopleton Worcs 117 G8
Peover Heath Ches E 184 G3
Peper Harow Sur 50 E2
Peppercombe Devon 24 C5
Pepper Hill Som 43 F7
W Yorks 196 B6
Peppermoor Northumb 264 F6
Pepper's Green Essex 87 C10
Pepperstock C Beds 85 B9
Perceton N Ayrs 267 G7
Percie Aberds 293 D7
Percuil Corn 3 C9
Percyhorner Aberds 303 C9
Percy Main T&W 243 D8
Per-ffordd-llan Flint 181 F10
Perham Down Wilts 47 D9
Periton Som 42 D3
Perivale London 67 C7
Perkhill Aberds 293 C7
Perkinsville Durham 243 G7
Perlethorpe Notts 187 G11
Perranarworthal Corn 3 B7
Perrancoombe Corn 4 E5
Perran Downs Corn 2 C3
Perranporth Corn 4 E5
Perranuthnoe Corn 2 D2
Perranwell Corn 3 B7
Corn 4 E5
Perranwell Station Corn 3 B7
Perran Wharf Corn 3 B7
Perranzabuloe Corn 4 E5
Perrott's Brook Glos 81 D8
Perry Devon 26 F5
Kent 55 B9
W Mid 133 E11
Perry Barr W Mid 133 E11
Perry Beeches W Mid 133 E11
Perry Common W Mid 133 E11
Perry Crofts Staffs 134 C4
Perryfields Worcs 117 C8
Perryfoot Derbys 185 E10
Perry Green Essex 106 G6
Herts 86 B6
Som 43 F9
Wilts 62 B3
Perrymead Bath 61 G9
Perrystone Hill Hereford 98 F2
Perry Street Kent 68 E6
Som 28 F4
Perrywood Kent 54 B4
Pershall Staffs 150 C6
Pershore Worcs 99 B8
Pert Angus 293 G8
Pertenhall Beds 121 D11
Perth Perth 286 E5
Perthcelyn Rhondda 77 F9
Perthy Shrops 149 C7
Perton Hereford 97 C11
Staffs 133 D7
Pertwood Wilts 45 F11
Pested Kent 54 C4
Peterborough Pboro 138 D3
Peterburn Highld 307 L2
Peterchurch Hereford 96 D6
Peterculter Aberdeen 293 C10
Peterhead Aberds 303 E11
Peterlee Durham 234 C4
Petersburn N Lnrk 268 C5
Petersfield Hants 34 C2
Peter's Finger Devon 12 D3
Peter's Green Herts 85 B10
Petersham London 67 E7
Peters Marland Devon 25 E7
Peterstone Wentlooge
Newport 59 C9
Peterston-super-Ely
V Glam 58 D5
Peterstow Hereford 97 G11
Peter Tavy Devon 12 F6
Petertown Orkney 314 F3
Peterville Corn 4 E4
Petham Kent 54 C6
Petherwin Gate Corn 11 D11
Petrockstow Devon 25 F8
Petsoe End M Keynes 103 B7
Pett E Sus 38 E5
Pettaugh Suff 126 F3
Pett Bottom Kent 54 E6
Kent 55 C7
Petteridge Kent 53 E7
Pettinain S Lnrk 269 G9
Pettings Kent 68 G6
Pettistree Suff 126 G5
Pett Level E Sus 38 E5
Petton Devon 27 C8
Shrops 149 D8
Petts Wood London 68 F2
Petty Aberds 303 F7
Pettycur Fife 280 D5
Petty France S Glos 61 B9
Pettymuick Aberds 303 G9
Pettywell Norf 159 E11
Petworth W Sus 35 C7
Pevensey E Sus 23 E10
Pevensey Bay E Sus 23 E11
Peverell Plym 7 D9
Pewsey Wilts 63 G7
Pewsey Wharf Wilts 63 G7
Pewterspear Warr 183 E10
Phantassie E Loth 281 F11
Pharisee Green Essex 106 G2
Pheasants Bucks 65 B9
Pheasant's Hill Bucks 65 B9
Pheasey W Mid 133 D11
Pheonix Green Hants 49 B9
Phepson Worcs 117 F8
Philadelphia T&W 243 G8
Philham Devon 24 C3
Philiphaugh Borders 261 D10
Phillack Corn 2 B3
Philleigh Corn 3 B9
Phillip's Town Caerph 77 E10
Philpot End Essex 87 B10
Philpstoun W Loth 279 F10
Phocle Green Hereford 98 F2
Phoenix Green Hants 49 B9
Phoenix Row Durham 233 F9
Phorp Moray 301 D10
Pibsbury Som 28 B6
Pibwrlwyd Carms 74 B6
Pica Cumb 228 G6
Piccadilly S Yorks 187 B7
Warks 134 D4
Piccadilly Corner Norf 142 F5
Piccotts End Herts 85 D9
Pickburn S Yorks 198 F4
Picken End Worcs 98 C6
Pickering N Yorks 216 C5
Pickering Nook Durham 242 F5
Picket Hill Hants 31 F11
Picket Piece Hants 47 D11
Picket Post Hants 31 F11
Pickford W Mid 134 G5
Pickford Green W Mid 134 G5
Pickhill N Yorks 214 C6
Picklenash Glos 98 F4
Picklescott Shrops 131 D8
Pickles Hill W Yorks 204 F6
Pickletillem Fife 287 E8
Pickley Green Gtr Man 195 G7
Pickmere Ches E 183 F11
Pickney Som 27 B11
Pickstock Telford 150 E4
Pickup Bank Blkburn 195 C8
Pickwell Devon 40 E3
Leics 154 G5
Pickwick Wilts 61 E11
Pickwood Scar W Yorks 196 C5
Pickworth Lincs 155 C10
Rutland 155 G9
Picton Ches W 182 G6
Flint 181 E10
N Yorks 225 D8
Pict's Hill Som 28 B6
Piddinghoe E Sus 36 G6
Piddington Bucks 84 G4
Northants 120 G6
Oxon 83 B10
Piddlehinton Dorset 17 B10
Piddletrenthide Dorset 17 B10
Pidley Cambs 122 B6
Pidney Dorset 30 F2
Piece Corn 2 B5
Piercebridge Darl 224 B4
Piercing Hill Essex 86 F6
Pierowall Orkney 314 B4
Piff's Elm Glos 99 F8
Pigdon Northumb 252 F5
Pightley Som 43 F8
Pig Oak Dorset 31 G8
Pigstye Green Essex 87 D10
Pike End W Yorks 196 D4
Pikehall Derbys 169 D11
Pike Hill Lancs 204 G3
Pike Law W Yorks 196 D4
Pikeshill Hants 32 F3
Pikestye Hereford 97 B10
Pilford Dorset 31 G8
Pilgrims Hatch Essex 87 F9
Pilham Lincs 188 C5
Pilhough Derbys 170 C3
Pill N Som 60 D4
Pembs 72 D6
Pillaton Corn 7 C7
Staffs 151 G8
Pillerton Hersey Warks 100 B6
Pillerton Priors Warks 100 B5
Pilleth Powys 114 D5
Pilley Glos 81 B7
Hants 20 B2
S Yorks 197 G10
Pilley Bailey Hants 20 B2
Pillgwenlly Newport 59 B10
Pilling Lancs 202 D4
Pilling Lane Lancs 202 D3
Pillmouth Devon 25 C7
Pillowell Glos 79 D10
Pillows Green Glos 98 F5
Pillwell Dorset 30 D3
Pilmuir Borders 261 G11
Pilning S Glos 60 B5
Pilrig Edin 280 F5
Pilsbury Derbys 169 C10
Pilsdon Dorset 16 B4
Pilsgate Pboro 137 B11
Pilsley Derbys 170 C6
Derbys 186 G2
Pilsley Green Derbys 170 C6
Pilson Green Norf 161 G7
Piltdown E Sus 36 C6
Pilton Devon 40 G5
Edin 280 F4
Northants 137 G10
Rutland 137 C8
Som 44 E5
Pilton Green Swansea 56 D2
Piltown Som 44 F5
Pimhole Gtr Man 195 E10
Pimlico Herts 85 D9
Lancs 203 E10
London 67 D9
Northants 102 C2
Pimperne Dorset 29 F9
Dorset 30 F6
Pinchbeck Lincs 156 D4
Pinchbeck Bars Lincs 156 D3
Pinchbeck West Lincs 156 E4
Pincheon Green
S Yorks 199 D7
Pinckney Green Wilts 61 G10
Pincock Lancs 194 D5
Pineham Kent 55 D10
M Keynes 103 C7
Pinehurst Swindon 63 B7
Pinfarthings Glos 80 E5
Pinfold Lancs 193 E11
Pinfold Hill S Yorks 197 G9
Pinfoldpond C Beds 103 E8
Pinford End Suff 124 F6
Pinged Carms 74 E6
Pingewood W Berks 65 F7
Pin Green Herts 104 F4
Pinhoe Devon 14 C5
Pinkett's Booth W Mid 134 G5
Pink Green Worcs 117 D11
Pinkie Braes E Loth 281 G7
Pinkney Wilts 61 B11
Pinkneys Green Windsor 65 C11
Pinksmoor Som 27 D10
Pinley W Mid 119 B7
Pinley Green Warks 118 D4
Pin Mill Suff 108 D4
Pinminnoch Dumfries 236 D2
S Ayrs 244 E5
Pinmore S Ayrs 244 E6
Pinmore Mains S Ayrs 244 E6
Pinnacles Essex 86 D6
Pinner London 66 B6
Pinner Green London 85 G10
Pinnerwood Park
London 85 G10
Pin's Green Worcs 98 B6
Pinsley Green Ches E 167 F9
Pinstones Shrops 131 F9
Pinvin Worcs 99 B9
Pinwall Leics 134 C6
Pinwherry S Ayrs 244 F5
Pinxton Derbys 171 E7
Pipe and Lyde Hereford 97 C10
Pipe Aston Hereford 115 C9
Pipe Gate Shrops 168 G2
Pipehill Staffs 133 B11
Pipehouse Bath 45 B9
Piperhall Argyll 266 D2
Piperhill Highld 301 D8
Pipe Ridware Staffs 151 F11
Piper's Ash Ches W 166 B6
Piper's End Worcs 98 E6
Piper's Hill Worcs 117 D9
Piper's Pool Corn 11 E11
Pipewell Northants 136 F6
Pippacott Devon 40 F4
Pippin Street Lancs 194 C5
Pipps Hill Essex 69 B7
Pipsden Kent 53 G9
Pipton Powys 96 D3
Pirbright Sur 50 B2
Pirbright Camp Sur 50 B2
Pirnmill N Ayrs 255 C9
Pirton Herts 104 E2
Worcs 99 B7
Pisgah Ceredig 112 B3
Stirl 285 G11
Pishill Oxon 65 B8
Pishill Bank Oxon 84 G2
Pismire Hill S Yorks 186 C5
Pistyll Gwyn 162 G4
Pit Mon 78 D5
Pitagowan Perth 291 G10
Pitblae Aberds 303 C9
Pitcairngreen Perth 286 E4
Pitcalnie Highld 301 B8
Pitcaple Aberds 303 G7
Pitchcombe Glos 80 D5
Pitchcott Bucks 102 G5
Pitcher's Green Suff 125 F8
Pitchford Shrops 131 C10
Pitch Green Bucks 84 E3
Pitch Place Sur 49 F11
Sur 50 C3
Pitcombe Som 45 G7
Pitcorthie Fife 280 D2
Fife 287 G9
Pitcot Som 45 D7
V Glam 57 G11
Pitcox E Loth 282 F2
Pitcur Perth 286 D6
Pitfancy Aberds 302 E5
Pitfichie Aberds 293 B8
Pitforthie Aberds 293 F10
Pitgair Aberds 303 D7
Pitgrudy Highld 309 K7
Pithmaduthy Highld 301 B7
Pitkennedy Angus 287 B9
Pitkevy Fife 286 G6
Pitkierie Fife 287 G9
Pitlessie Fife 287 G7
Pitlochry Perth 286 B3
Pitmachie Aberds 302 G6
Pitmain Highld 291 C9
Pitmedden Aberds 303 G8
Pitminster Som 28 D2
Pitmuies Angus 287 C9
Pitmunie Aberds 293 B8
Pitney Som 29 B7
Pitrocknie Perth 286 C6
Pitscottie Fife 287 F8
Pitsea Essex 69 B8
Pitses Gtr Man 196 G2
Pitsford Northants 120 D5
Pitsford Hill Som 42 G6
Pitsmoor S Yorks 186 D5
Pitstone Bucks 84 B6
Pitstone Green Bucks 84 B6
Pitstone Hill Bucks 85 C7
Pitt Hants 33 B7
Pittachar Perth 286 E2
Pitt Court Glos 80 F3
Pittendreich Moray 301 C11
Pittentrail Highld 309 J7
Pittenweem Fife 287 G9
Pitteuchar Fife 280 B5
Pittington Durham 234 C2
Pittodrie Aberds 302 G6
Pitton Swansea 56 D2
Wilts 47 G8
Pitts Hill Stoke 168 E5
Pittswood Kent 52 D6
Pittulie Aberds 303 C9
Pittville Glos 99 G9
Pityme Corn 10 F5
Pity Me Durham 233 B11
Pityoulish Highld 291 B11
Pixey Green Suff 126 B4
Pixham Sur 51 C7
Worcs 98 B6
Pixley Hereford 98 D3
Shrops 150 D3
Pizien Well Kent 53 C7
Place Newton N Yorks 217 E7
Plaidy Aberds 303 D7
Corn 6 E5
Plain-an-Gwarry Corn 4 G3
Plain Dealings Pembs 73 B9
Plains N Lnrk 268 B5
Plainsfield Som 43 F7
Plain Spot Notts 171 E7
Plain Street Corn 10 F5
Plaish Shrops 131 D10
Plaistow Bromley 68 E2
Newham 68 C2
W Sus 50 G4
Plaistow Green Essex 106 F6
Plaitford Wilts 32 D3
Plaitford Green Hants 32 C3
Plank Lane Gtr Man 194 G6
Plans Dumfries 238 D3
Plantation Bridge Cumb 221 F9
Plantationfoot Dumfries 248 E4
Plardiwick Staffs 150 E6
Plasau Shrops 149 E7
Plâs Berwyn Denb 165 G11
Plas-canol Gwyn 145 F11
Plas Coch Wrex 166 E4
Plas Dinam Powys 129 F10
Plas Gogerddan Ceredig 128 G2
Plashet London 68 C2
Plashett Carms 74 D3
Plasiolyn Powys 129 C11
Plas Llwyngwern Powys 128 C5
Plas Meredydd Powys 130 D3
Plas Nantyr Wrex 148 B3
Plasnewydd Powys 129 D9
Plaster's Green Bath 60 G4
Plastow Green Hants 64 G4
Plas-yn-Cefn Denb 181 G8
Platt Kent 52 B6
Platt Bridge Gtr Man 194 G6
Platt Lane Shrops 149 B10
Platts Common
S Yorks 197 G11
Platt's Heath Kent 53 C11
Plawsworth Durham 233 B11
Plaxtol Kent 52 C6
Playden E Sus 38 C6
Playford Suff 108 B4
Play Hatch Oxon 65 D8
Playing Place Corn 4 G6
Playley Green Glos 98 E5
Plealey Shrops 131 B8
Pleamore Cross Som 27 D10
Plean Stirl 278 D6
Pleasant Valley Pembs 73 D10
Pleasington Blkburn 194 B6
Pleasley Derbys 171 C8
Pleasleyhill Notts 171 C8
Pleck Dorset 30 D3
Dorset 30 E2
W Mid 133 D9
Pleckgate Blkburn 203 G9
Pleck or Little Ansty
Dorset 30 G3
Pledgdon Green Essex 105 F11
Pledwick W Yorks 197 D10
Plemstall Ches W 183 G7
Plenmeller Northumb 240 E6
Pleshey Essex 87 C11
Plockton Highld 295 B10
Plocrapol W Isles 305 J3
Plot Gate Som 44 G4
Plot Street Som 44 F5
Ploughfield Hereford 97 C7
Plough Hill Warks 134 E6
Plowden Shrops 131 F7
Ploxgreen Shrops 131 C7
Pluckley Kent 54 D2
Pluckley Thorne Kent 54 E2
Plucks Gutter Kent 71 G9
Plumbland Cumb 229 D9
Plumbley S Yorks 186 E6
Plumford Kent 54 B4
Plumley Ches E 184 F2
Plump Hill Glos 79 B11
Plumpton Cumb 230 D5
E Sus 36 E5
Northants 101 B11
Plumpton End Northants 102 B4
Plumpton Foot Cumb 230 D5
Plumpton Green E Sus 36 D5
Plumpton Head Cumb 230 E6
Plumstead London 68 D3
Norf 160 C2
Plumstead Common
London 68 D3
Plumstead Green Norf 160 C2
Plumtree Notts 154 C2
Plumtree Green Kent 53 D10
Plumtree Park Notts 154 C2
Plungar Leics 154 C5
Plush Dorset 30 G2
Plusha Corn 11 E11
Plushabridge Corn 12 G2
Plusterwine Glos 79 F9
Plwmp Ceredig 111 G7
Plymouth Plym 7 E9
Plympton Plym 7 D10
Plymstock Plym 7 E10
Plymtree Devon 27 G9
Pobgreen Gtr Man 196 F4
Pochin Houses Caerph 77 E11
Pocket Nook Gtr Man 183 B10
Pockley N Yorks 216 B2
Pocklington E Yorks 208 D2
Pockthorpe Norf 141 D8
Norf 158 D6
Norf 159 E10
Norf 159 F11
Pode Hole Lincs 156 E4
Podimore Som 29 C8
Podington Beds 121 E8
Podmoor Worcs 117 C7
Podmore Norf 159 G9
Staffs 150 B5
Podsmead Glos 80 B4
Poffley End Oxon 82 C5
Pogmoor S Yorks 197 F10
Point Corn 3 B8
Point Clear Essex 89 C9
Pointon Lincs 156 C2
Pokesdown Bmouth 19 C8
Pol a Charra W Isles 297 K3
Polbae Dumfries 236 B4

Polbain Highld 307 H4
Polbathic Corn 7 D7
Polbeth W Loth 269 C10
Polborder Corn 7 C7
Polbrock Corn 5 B10
Polchar Highld 291 C10
Polebrook Northants 137 F11
Pole Elm Worcs 98 B6
Polegate E Sus 23 D9
Pole Moor W Yorks 196 D5
Poles Highld 309 K7
Polesden Lacey Sur 50 C6
Poleshill Som 27 C9
Pole's Hole Wilts 45 C10
Polesworth Warks 134 C5
Polgear Corn 2 B5
Polgigga Corn 1 E3
Polglass Highld 307 J5
Polgooth Corn 5 E9
Poling W Sus 35 G8
Poling Corner W Sus 35 F8
Polkerris Corn 5 E11
Polla Highld 308 D3
Polladras Corn 2 C4
Pollard Street Norf 160 C6
Pollhill Kent 53 C11
Poll Hill Mers 182 E3
Pollie Highld 309 H7
Pollington E Yorks 198 D6
Polliwilline Argyll 255 G8
Polloch Highld 289 C9
Pollok Glasgow 267 C10
Pollokshields Glasgow 267 C11
Polmadie Glasgow 267 C11
Polmarth Corn 2 B6
Polmassick Corn 5 F9
Polmear Corn 5 E11
Polmont Falk 279 F8
Polmorla Corn 10 G5
Polnessan E Ayrs 257 G10
Polnish Highld 295 G9
Polopit Northants 121 B10
Polpenwith Corn 2 D6
Polpeor Corn 2 B2
Polperro Corn 6 E4
Polruan Corn 6 E2
Polsham Som 44 E4
Polsloe Devon 14 C4
Polstead Suff 107 D9
Polstead Heath Suff 107 C9
Poltalloch Argyll 275 D9
Poltesco Corn 2 F6
Poltimore Devon 14 B5
Polton Midloth 270 C5
Polwarth Borders 272 E4
Polwheveral Corn 2 D6
Polyphant Corn 11 E11
Polzeath Corn 10 F4
Pomeroy Derbys 169 B10
Pomphlett Plym 7 E10
Ponciau Wrex 166 F3
Pond Close Som 27 B10
Ponde Powys 96 D2
Pondersbridge Cambs 138 E5
Ponders End London 86 F5
Pond Park Bucks 85 E7
Pond Street Essex 105 D9
Pondtail Hants 49 C10
Pondwell IoW 21 C8
Poniou Corn 1 B4
Ponjeravah Corn 2 D6
Ponsanooth Corn 3 B7
Ponsford Devon 27 F8
Ponsonby Cumb 219 D11
Ponsongath Corn 3 F7
Ponsworthy Devon 13 G10
Pont Corn 6 E2
Pont Aber Carms 94 G4
Pont Aber-Geirw Gwyn 146 D5
Pontamman Carms 75 C10
Pontantwn Carms 74 C6
Pontardawe Neath 76 E2
Pontarddulais Swansea 75 E9
Pontarfynach / Devils Bridge Ceredig 112 B4
Pont-ar-gothi Carms 93 G10
Pont ar Hydfer Powys 95 F7
Pont-ar-llechau Carms 94 G4
Pontarsais Carms 93 F8
Pontblyddyn Flint 166 C3
Pontbren Araeth Carms 94 G3
Pontbren Llwyd Rhondda 76 D6
Pontcanna Cardiff 59 D7
Pont Cyfyng Conwy 164 D2
Pont Cysyllte Wrex 166 G3
Pontdolgoch Powys 129 E10
Pont Dolydd Prysor Gwyn 146 B4
Pontefract W Yorks 198 C3
Ponteland Northumb 242 C5
Ponterwyd Ceredig 128 G4
Pontesbury Shrops 131 B7
Pontesbury Hill Shrops 131 B7
Pontesford Shrops 131 B8
Pontfadog Wrex 148 B4
Pontfaen Pembs 91 E10
Pont-faen Powys 95 E9
Shrops 148 B5
Pont Fronwydd Gwyn 146 E6
Pont-gareg Pembs 92 C2
Pontgarreg Ceredig 110 G6
Ponthen Shrops 148 F6
Pont-Henri Carms 75 D7
Ponthir Torf 78 G4
Ponthirwaun Ceredig 92 B5
Pont Hwfa Anglesey 178 E2
Pontiago Pembs 91 D8
Pont iets / Pontyates Carms 75 D7
Pontithel Powys 96 D3
Pontllanfraith Caerph 77 F11
Pontlliw Swansea 75 E10
Pont-Llogel Powys 147 F10
Pontllyfni Gwyn 162 E6
Pontlottyn Caerph 77 D10
Pontneddfechan Powys 76 D6
Pontnewydd Torf 78 F3
Pont-newydd Carms 74 D6
Flint 165 B11
Pontnewynydd Torf 78 E3
Pont Pen-y-benglog Gwyn 163 C10
Pontrhydfendigaid Ceredig 112 D4
Pont Rhydgaled Powys 128 G6
Pont Rhyd-goch Conwy 163 C11
Pont-Rhyd-sarn Gwyn 147 D7
Pont Rhyd-y-berry Powys 95 D9
Pont Rhyd-y-cyff Bridgend 57 D11
Pontrhydyfen Neath 57 C9
Pont-rhyd-y-groes Ceredig 112 C4
Pontrhydyrun Torf 78 F3
Pont-Rhythallt Gwyn 163 C8
Pontrilas Hereford 97 F7
Pontrobert Powys 148 G2
Pont-rug Gwyn 163 C8
Pont Senni / Sennybridge Powys 95 F8
Ponts Green E Sus 23 B11
Pontshill Hereford 98 G2
Pont-siân Ceredig 93 B8
Pont Siôn Norton Rhondda 77 G9
Pontsticill M Tydf 77 C9
Pont-Walby Neath 76 D5
Pontwgan Conwy 180 G3
Pontyates / Pont-iets Carms 75 D7
Pontyberem Carms 75 C8
Pont-y-blew Shrops 148 B6
Pontyclun Rhondda 58 C4
Pontycymer Bridgend 76 G6
Pontyglasier Pembs 92 D2
Pont-y-gwaith Rhondda 77 G8
Pontymister Caerph 78 G2
Pontymoel Torf 78 E3
Pont-y-pant Conwy 164 E3
Pont y Pennant Gwyn 147 E8
Pontypool Torf 78 E3
Pontypridd Rhondda 58 B5
Pont yr Afon-Gam Gwyn 164 G2
Pont-yr-hafod Pembs 91 F8
Pont-y-rhyl Bridgend 58 B2
Pont-Ystrad Denb 165 C9
Pont-y-wal Powys 96 E2
Pontywaun Caerph 78 G2
Pooksgreen Hants 32 E5
Pool Corn 4 G3
W Yorks 205 D10
Poolbrook Worcs 98 C5
Poole N Yorks 198 B3
Poole 18 C6
Som 27 C10
Poole Keynes Glos 81 F8
Poolend Staffs 169 D7
Poolestown Dorset 30 D2
Poolewe Highld 307 L3
Pooley Bridge Cumb 230 G5
Pooley Street Norf 141 G11
Poolfold Staffs 168 D5
Poolhead Shrops 149 C9
Pool Head Hereford 115 G11
Pool Hey Lancs 193 D11
Poolhill Glos 98 F4
Poolmill Hereford 97 G11
Pool o' Muckhart Clack 286 G4
Pool Quay Powys 148 G5
Poolsbrook Derbys 186 G6
Poolside Moray 302 E4
Poolstock Gtr Man 194 G5
Pooltown Som 42 F3
Pootings Kent 52 D3
Pope Hill Pembs 72 C6
Pope's Hill Glos 79 C11
Popeswood Brack 65 F10
Popham Devon 41 G8
Hants 48 E5
Poplar London 67 C11
Poplar Grove Lincs 190 B6
Poplars Herts 104 G5
Popley Hants 48 C6
Porchester Nottingham 171 G9
Porchfield IoW 20 C4
Porin Highld 300 D3
Poringland Norf 142 C5
Porkellis Corn 2 C5
Porlock Som 41 D11
Porlockford Som 41 D11
Porlock Weir Som 41 D11
Portachoillan Argyll 255 B8
Port Allen Perth 286 E6
Port Ann Argyll 275 E10
Port Appin Argyll 289 E11
Port Arthur Shetland 313 K5
Portash Wilts 46 G3
Port Askaig Argyll 274 G5
Portavadie Argyll 275 G10
Port Bannatyne Argyll 275 G11
Port Brae Fife 280 C5
Port Bridge Devon 9 D7
Portbury N Som 60 D4
Port Carlisle Cumb 238 E6
Port Charlotte Argyll 254 B3
Portchester Hants 33 F10
Portclair Highld 290 B6
Port Clarence Stockton 234 G5
Port Dinorwic / Y Felinheli Gwyn 163 B8
Port Driseach Argyll 275 F10
Port Dundas Glasgow 267 B11
Port Edgar Edin 280 F2
Port Ellen Argyll 254 C4
Port Elphinstone Aberds 293 B9
Portencalzie Dumfries 236 B2
Portencross N Ayrs 266 F3
Porterfield Renfs 267 B9
Port Erin IoM 192 F2
Port Erroll Aberds 303 F10
Porter's End Herts 85 B11
Portesham Dorset 17 D8
Portessie Moray 302 C4
Port e Vullen IoM 192 C5
Port-Eynon Swansea 56 D3
Portfield Argyll 289 G9
Som 28 B6
W Sus 22 B5
Portfield Gate Pembs 72 B6
Portgate Devon 12 D4
Port Gaverne Corn 10 E6
Port Glasgow Invclyd 276 G6
Portgordon Moray 302 C3
Portgower Highld 311 H4
Porth Corn 4 C6
Rhondda 77 G8
Porthallow Corn 3 E7
Corn 6 E4
Porthcawl Bridgend 57 F10
Porth Colmon Gwyn 144 C3
Porthcothan Corn 10 G3
Porthcurno Corn 1 E3
Portheiddy Pembs 90 E6
Port Henderson Highld 299 B7
Porthgain Pembs 90 E6
Porthgwarra Corn 1 E3
Porthhallow Corn 3 E7
Porthill Shrops 149 G9
Staffs 168 F5
Port Hill Oxon 65 B7
Porthilly Corn 10 F4
Porth Kea Corn 4 G6
Porthkerry V Glam 58 F5
Porthleven Corn 2 D4
Porthllechog / Bull Bay Anglesey 178 C6
Porthloo Scilly 1 G4
Porthmadog Gwyn 145 B11
Porthmeor Corn 1 B4
Porth Navas Corn 3 D7
Porthoustock Corn 3 E8
Porthpean Corn 5 E10
Porthtowan Corn 4 F3
Porth Tywyn / Burry Port Carms 74 E6
Porth-y-felin Anglesey 178 E2
Porthyrhyd Carms 75 B8
Carms 94 D4
Porth-y-waen Shrops 148 E5
Portico Mers 183 C7
Portincaple Argyll 276 C4
Portington Devon 12 F4
E Yorks 207 G11
Portinnisherrich Argyll 275 B10
Portinscale Cumb 229 G11
Port Isaac Corn 10 E5
Portishead N Som 60 D3
Portkil Argyll 276 E5
Portknockie Moray 302 C4
Port Lamont Argyll 275 F11
Portland Som 44 F3
Portlethen Aberds 293 D11
Portlethen Village Aberds 293 D11
Portlevorchy Highld 306 D7
Portling Dumfries 237 D10
Port Lion Pembs 73 D7
Portloe Corn 3 B10
Port Logan Dumfries 236 E2
Portlooe Corn 6 E4
Portmahomack Highld 311 L3
Port Mead Swansea 56 B6
Portmeirion Gwyn 145 B11
Portmellon Corn 5 G10
Port Mholair W Isles 304 E7
Port Mor Highld 288 B6
Portmore Hants 20 B2
Port Mulgrave N Yorks 226 B5
Portnacroish Argyll 289 E11
Portnahaven Argyll 254 B2
Portnalong Highld 294 B5
Portnaluchaig Highld 295 G8
Portnancon Highld 308 C4
Port Nan Giùran W Isles 304 E7
Port nan Long W Isles 296 D4
Portnellan Stirl 285 E8
Stirl 285 F8
Port Nis W Isles 304 B7
Portobello Edin 280 G6
T&W 243 F7
W Mid 133 D9
W Yorks 197 D10
Port of Menteith Stirl 285 G9
Porton Wilts 47 F7
Portpatrick Dumfries 236 D2
Port Quin Corn 10 E5
Portrack Stockton 225 B9
Port Ramsay Argyll 289 E10
Portreath Corn 4 F3
Portree Highld 298 E4
Port St Mary IoM 192 F3
Portscatho Corn 3 B9
Portsea Ptsmth 33 G10
Portsea Island Ptsmth 33 G11
Portskerra Highld 310 C2
Portskewett Mon 60 B4
Portslade Brighton 36 F3
Portslade-by-Sea Brighton 36 G3
Portslade Village Brighton 36 F3
Portsmouth Ptsmth 21 B9
W Yorks 196 B2
Port Solent Ptsmth 33 F10
Portsonachan Argyll 284 E4
Portsoy Aberds 302 C5
Port Sunlight Mers 182 E4
Port Sutton Bridge Lincs 157 E9
Portswood Soton 32 E6
Port Talbot Neath 57 D9
Porttanachy Moray 302 C3
Port Tennant Swansea 57 C7
Portuairk Highld 288 C6
Portvasgo Highld 308 C5
Portway Dorset 18 D2
Glos 98 E5
Hereford 97 B9
Hereford 97 D9
Som 28 B6
Som 44 F3
W Mid 133 F9
Worcs 117 C11
Port Wemyss Argyll 254 B2
Port William Dumfries 236 E5
Portwood Gtr Man 184 C6
Portwrinkle Corn 7 E7
Posenhall Shrops 132 C3
Poslingford Suff 106 B5
Posso Borders 260 C6
Postbridge Devon 13 F9
Postcombe Oxon 84 F2
Post Green Dorset 18 C5
Postling Kent 54 F6
Postlip Glos 99 F10
Post Mawr / Synod Inn Ceredig 111 G8
Postwick Norf 142 B5
Potarch Aberds 293 D8
Potash Suff 108 D2
Potbridge Hants 49 C8
Pot Common Sur 50 E2
Potholm Dumfries 249 F9
Potmaily Highld 300 F4
Potman's Heath Kent 38 B5
Potsgrove C Beds 103 F9
Potten End Herts 85 D8
Potten Street Kent 71 F9
Potter Brompton N Yorks 217 D9
Pottergate Street Norf 142 E3
Potterhanworth Lincs 173 B9
Potterhanworth Booths Lincs 173 B9
Potter Heigham Norf 161 F8
Potter Hill Leics 154 E4
S Yorks 186 B4
Potterne Wilts 46 B3
Potterne Wick Wilts 46 B4
Potternewton W Yorks 206 F2
Potters Bar Herts 86 E3
Potters Brook Lancs 202 C5
Potters Corner Kent 54 E3
Potter's Cross Staffs 132 G6
Potters Crouch Herts 85 D10
Potter's Forstal Kent 53 D11
Potter's Green E Sus 37 C8
W Mid 135 G7
Pottersheath Herts 86 B2
Potters Hill N Som 60 F4
Potters Marston Leics 135 D9
Potter Somersal Derbys 152 B2
Potterspury Northants 102 C5
Potter Street Essex 87 D7
Potterton Aberds 293 B11
W Yorks 206 F4
Pottery Field W Yorks 206 G2
Potthorpe Norf 159 E8
Pottington Devon 40 G5
Potto N Yorks 225 E9
Potton C Beds 104 B4
Pott Row Norf 158 E4
Pott Shrigley Ches E 184 F6
Pouchen End Herts 85 D8
Poughill Corn 24 F2
Devon 26 F5
Poulner Hants 31 F11
Poulshot Wilts 46 B3
Poulton Ches W 166 D5
Glos 81 E10
Mers 182 C4
Mers 182 E4
Poulton-le-Fylde Lancs 202 F2
Pound Som 28 D6
Pound Bank Worcs 98 B5
Worcs 116 C4
Poundbury Dorset 17 C9
Poundffald Swansea 56 C5
Poundfield E Sus 52 G4
Poundford E Sus 37 C9
Poundgate E Sus 37 B7
Poundgreen Wokingham 65 F7
Pound Green E Sus 37 C8
Hants 48 B5
IoW 20 D2
Suff 124 G4
Worcs 116 B5
Pound Hill W Sus 51 F9
Poundland S Ayrs 244 F5
Poundon Bucks 102 F2
Poundsbridge Kent 52 E4
Poundsgate Devon 13 G10
Poundstock Corn 11 B10
Pound Street Hants 64 G3
Pounsley E Sus 37 C8
Poverest London 68 F3
Povey Cross Sur 51 E9
Powburn Northumb 264 F3
Powderham Devon 14 E5
Powder Mills Kent 52 D5
Powers Hall End Essex 88 B4
Powerstock Dorset 16 B6
Powfoot Dumfries 238 D4
Pow Green Hereford 98 C4
Powhill Cumb 238 F6
Powick Worcs 116 G6
Powler's Piece Devon 24 D5
Powmill Perth 279 B10
Pownall Park Ches E 184 E4
Powntley Copse Hants 49 E8
Poxwell Dorset 17 E10
Poyle Slough 66 D4
Poynings W Sus 36 E3
Poyntington Dorset 29 D11
Poynton Ches E 184 E6
Telford 149 F11
Poynton Green Telford 149 F11
Poyntzfield Highld 301 C7
Poyston Pembs 73 B7
Poyston Cross Pembs 73 B7
Poystreet Green Suff 125 F9
Praa Sands Corn 2 D3
Pratling Street Kent 53 B8
Pratt's Bottom London 68 G3
Praze Corn 2 B3
Praze-an-Beeble Corn 2 B4
Predannack Wollas Corn 2 F5
Prees Shrops 149 C11
Preesall Lancs 202 D3
Preesall Park Lancs 202 D3
Prees Green Shrops 149 C11
Preesgweene Shrops 148 B5
Prees Heath Shrops 149 B11
Preeshenlle Shrops 148 C6
Prees Higher Heath Shrops 149 B11
Prees Lower Heath Shrops 149 C11
Prees Wood Shrops 149 C11
Prenbrigog Flint 166 C3
Prendergast Pembs 73 B7
Pembs 90 G6
Prenderguest Borders 273 D8
Prendwick Northumb 264 G2
Pren-gwyn Ceredig 93 C8
Prenteg Gwyn 163 G9
Prenton Mers 182 D4
Prescot Mers 183 C7
Prescott Devon 27 E9
Glos 99 F9
Shrops 132 G3
Shrops 149 E8
Presdales Herts 86 C5
Preshome Moray 302 C4
Press Derbys 170 B5
Pressen Northumb 263 B8
Prestatyn Denb 181 E9
Prestbury Ches E 184 F6
Glos 99 G9
Presteigne Powys 114 E6
Presthope Shrops 131 D11
Prestleigh Som 44 E6
Prestolee Gtr Man 195 F9
Preston Borders 272 D5
Brighton 36 F4
Devon 14 G3
Dorset 17 E10
E Loth 281 F11
E Loth 281 G7
E Yorks 209 G9
Glos 81 E8
Glos 98 E3
Herts 104 G3
Kent 70 G4
Kent 71 G8
Lancs 194 B4
London 67 B7
Northumb 264 D5
Rutland 137 C7
Shrops 149 G10
Torbay 9 C7
T&W 243 D8
Wilts 62 D4
Wilts 63 E9
Preston Bagot Warks 118 D3
Preston Bissett Bucks 102 F3
Preston Bowyer Som 27 B10
Preston Brockhurst Shrops 149 E10
Preston Brook Halton 183 E9
Preston Candover Hants 48 E6
Preston Capes Northants 119 G11
Preston Crowmarsh Oxon 83 G10
Preston Deanery Northants 120 F5
Prestonfield Edin 280 G5
Preston Fields Warks 118 D3
Preston Grange T&W 243 C8
Preston Green Warks 118 D3
Preston Gubbals Shrops 149 F9
Preston-le-Skerne Durham 234 G2
Preston Marsh Hereford 97 B11
Prestonmill Dumfries 237 D11
Preston Montford Shrops 149 G8
Preston on Stour Warks 118 G4
Preston-on-Tees Stockton 225 B8
Preston on the Hill Halton 183 E9
Preston on Wye Hereford 97 C7
Prestonpans E Loth 281 G7
Preston Pastures Worcs 100 B3
Preston Plucknett Som 29 D8
Preston St Mary Suff 125 G8
Preston-under-Scar N Yorks 223 G11
Preston upon the Weald Moors Telford 150 F3
Preston Wynne Hereford 97 B11
Prestwich Gtr Man 195 G10
Prestwick Northumb 242 C5
S Ayrs 257 D9
Prestwold Leics 153 E11
Prestwood Bucks 84 E5
Staffs 133 F7
Staffs 169 G10
Prey Heath Sur 50 B3
Price Town Bridgend 76 G6
Prickwillow Cambs 139 G11
Priddy Som 44 C4
Pride Park Derbys 153 B7
Priestacott Devon 24 F6
Priestcliffe Derbys 185 G10
Priestcliffe Ditch Derbys 185 G10
Priest Down Bath 60 G6
Priestfield W Mid 133 D8
Worcs 98 C6
Priesthaugh Borders 249 C11
Priesthill Glasgow 267 C10
Priesthorpe W Yorks 205 F10
Priest Hutton Lancs 211 E10
Priestley Green W Yorks 196 B6
Prieston Borders 262 D2
Priestside Dumfries 238 D4
Priestthorpe W Yorks 205 F8
Priest Weston Shrops 130 D5
Priestwood Brack 65 F11
Kent 69 G7
Priestwood Green Kent 69 G7
Primethorpe Leics 135 E10
Primrose T&W 243 E8
Primrose Corner Norf 160 G6
Primrose Green Norf 159 F11
Primrosehill Herts 85 E9
Primrose Hill Bath 61 F8
Lancs 193 F11
London 67 C9
W Mid 133 F8
Primrose Valley N Yorks 218 D2
Primsland Worcs 117 E8
Prince Hill Ches E 168 G2
Prince Royd W Yorks 196 D6
Princes End W Mid 133 E9
Princes Gate Pembs 73 C10
Prince's Marsh Hants 34 B3
Princes Park Mers 182 D5
Princes Risborough Bucks 84 E4
Princethorpe Warks 119 C8
Princetown Caerph 77 C10
Devon 13 G7
Prinsted W Sus 22 B3
Printstile Kent 52 E5
Prion Denb 165 C9
Prior Muir Fife 287 F9
Prior Park Northumb 273 E9
Prior Rigg Cumb 239 D11
Priors Frome Hereford 97 D11
Priors Halton Shrops 115 B9
Priors Hardwick Warks 119 F9
Priorslee Telford 150 G4
Priors Marston Warks 119 F9
Prior's Norton Glos 99 G7
Priors Park Glos 99 E7
Priorswood Som 28 B2
Priory Pembs 72 D6
Priory Green Suff 107 C8
Priory Heath Suff 108 C3
Priory Wood Hereford 96 B5
Prisk V Glam 58 D4
Pristacott Devon 25 B8
Priston Bath 61 G7
Pristow Green Norf 142 F2
Prittlewell Sthend 69 B11
Privett Hants 21 B7
Hants 33 B11
Prixford Devon 40 F4
Probus Corn 5 F7
Proncy Highld 309 K7
Prospect Cumb 229 C8
Prospect Village Staffs 151 G10
Prospidnick Corn 2 C4
Provanmill Glasgow 268 B2
Prowse Devon 26 F4
Prudhoe Northumb 242 E3
Prussia Cove Corn 2 D3
Ptarmigan Lodge Stirl 285 G7
Pubil Perth 285 C8
Publow Bath 60 G6
Puckeridge Herts 105 G7
Puckington Som 28 D5
Pucklechurch S Glos 61 D7
Pucknall Hants 32 B5
Puckrup Glos 99 D7
Puckshole Glos 80 D4
Puddaven Devon 8 C5
Puddinglake Ches W 168 B2
Pudding Pie Nook Lancs 202 F6
Puddington Ches W 182 G4
Devon 26 E4
Puddle Corn 5 D11
Puddlebridge Som 28 E4
Puddledock Hextable 68 E4
Norf 141 E11
Westerham 52 C3
Puddletown Dorset 17 C11
Pudleigh Som 28 E4
Pudleston Hereford 115 F11
Pudsey W Yorks 196 B2
W Yorks 205 G10
Pulborough W Sus 35 D8
Pulcree Dumfries 237 D7
Pule Hill W Yorks 196 B5
Puleston Telford 150 E4
Pulford Ches W 166 D5
Pulham Dorset 30 F2
Pulham Market Norf 142 F3
Pulham St Mary Norf 142 F4
Pullens Green S Glos 79 G10
Pulley Shrops 131 B9
Pullington Kent 53 G10
Pulloxhill C Beds 103 E11
Pulverbatch Shrops 131 C8
Pumpherston W Loth 269 B11
Pumsaint Carms 94 C3
Puncheston / Cas-Mael Pembs 91 F10
Puncknowle Dorset 16 D6
Punnett's Town E Sus 37 C10
Purbrook Hants 33 F11
Purewell Dorset 19 C9
Purfleet Thurrock 68 D5
Puriton Som 43 E10
Purleigh Essex 88 E4
Purley London 67 G10
Purley on Thames W Berks 65 D7
Purlogue Shrops 114 B5
Purlpit Wilts 61 F11
Purls Bridge Cambs 139 F9
Purn N Som 43 B10
Purse Caundle Dorset 29 D11
Purslow Shrops 131 G7
Purston Jaglin W Yorks 198 D2
Purtington Som 28 F5
Purton Glos 79 E11
W Berks 64 D3
Wilts 62 B5
Purton Common Wilts 62 B5
Purton Stoke Wilts 81 G9
Purwell Herts 104 F4
Pury End Northants 102 B4
Pusey Oxon 82 F5
Putley Hereford 98 D2
Putley Common Hereford 98 D2
Putley Green Hereford 98 D3
Putloe Glos 80 D3
Putney London 67 D8
Putney Heath London 67 E8
Putney Vale London 67 E8
Putnoe Beds 121 G11
Putsborough Devon 40 E3
Putson Hereford 97 D10
Puttenham Herts 84 C5
Sur 50 D2
Puttock End Essex 106 C6
Puttock's End Essex 87 B9
Putton Dorset 17 E9
Puxey Dorset 30 E3
Puxley Northants 102 C5
Puxton N Som 60 G2
Pwll Carms 75 E7
Powys 130 C3
Pwll-clai Flint 181 G11
Pwllcrochan Pembs 72 E6
Pwll-glas Denb 165 E10
Pwllgloyw Powys 95 E10
Pwllheli Gwyn 145 B7
Pwll-Mawr Cardiff 59 D8
Pwll-melyn Flint 181 G11
Pwllmeyric Mon 79 G8
Pwll-trap Carms 74 B3
Pwll-y-glaw Neath 57 C9
Pwllypant Caerph 59 B7
Pye Bridge Derbys 170 E6
Pyecombe W Sus 36 E3
Pye Corner Devon 14 B4
Kent 53 D11
Newport 59 B9
S Glos 60 D6
Pye Green Staffs 151 G9
Pye Hill Notts 170 E6
Pyewipe NE Lincs 201 E9
Pyle IoW 20 F5
Swansea 56 D5
Pylehill Hants 33 D7
Pyle Hill Sur 50 B3
Pyleigh Som 42 G6
Pyle / Y Pîl Bridgend 57 E10
Pylle Som 44 F6
Pymore or Pymoor Cambs 139 F9
Pype Hayes W Mid 134 E2
Pyrford Sur 50 B4
Pyrford Green Sur 50 B4
Pyrford Village Sur 50 B4
Pyrland Som 28 B2
Pyrton Oxon 83 F11
Pytchley Northants 121 C7
Pyworthy Devon 24 G4

Q

Quabbs Shrops 130 G4
Quabrook E Sus 52 G2
Quadring Lincs 156 C4
Quadring Eaudike Lincs 156 C4
Quags Corner W Sus 34 C5
Quainton Bucks 84 B2
Quaker's Yard M Tydf 77 F9
Quaking Houses Durham 242 G5
Quality Corner Cumb 219 B9
Quarhouse Glos 80 E5
Quarley Hants 47 E9
Quarmby W Yorks 196 D6
Quarndon Derbys 170 G4
Quarndon Common Derbys 170 G4
Quarrelton Renfs 267 C8
Quarrendon Bucks 84 B4
Quarr Hill IoW 21 C7
Quarriers Village Invclyd 267 B7
Quarrington Lincs 173 G9
Quarrington Hill Durham 234 D2
Quarrybank Ches W 167 B8
Quarry Bank W Mid 133 F8
Quarryford E Loth 271 B11
Quarryhead Aberds 303 C9
Quarry Heath Staffs 151 G8
Quarry Hill Highld 309 L7
Quarry Hill Staffs 134 C4
Quarrywood Moray 301 C11
Quarter S Lnrk 268 E4
Quartley Devon 27 B7
Quatford Shrops 132 E4
Quatquoy Orkney 314 E3
Quatt Shrops 132 F5
Quebec Durham 233 C9
W Sus 34 C3
Quedgeley Glos 80 C4
Queen Adelaide Cambs 139 G11
Queenborough Kent 70 E2
Queen Camel Som 29 C9
Queen Charlton Bath 60 F6
Queen Dart Devon 26 D4
Queenhill Worcs 99 D7
Queen Oak Dorset 45 G9
Queen's Bower IoW 21 E7
Queensbury London 67 B7
W Yorks 205 G8
Queen's Corner W Sus 34 B5
Queensferry Edin 280 F2
Flint 166 B4
Queen's Head Shrops 148 D6
Queenslie Glasgow 268 B3
Queen's Park Beds 103 B10
Blkburn 195 B7
Ches W 166 B6
Essex 87 F11
Northants 120 E5
Queenstown Blkpool 202 F2
Queen Street Kent 53 D7
Wilts 62 B4
Queensville Staffs 151 E8
Queenzieburn N Lnrk 278 F3
Quemerford Wilts 62 F4
Quendale Shetland 313 M5
Quendon Essex 105 E10
Queniborough Leics 154 G2
Quenington Glos 81 E10
Quernmore Lancs 202 B6
Queslett W Mid 133 E11
Quethiock Corn 6 C6
Quhamm Shetland 312 G6
Quholm Orkney 314 E2
Quick Gtr Man 196 G3
Quick Edge Gtr Man 196 G3
Quicks Green W Berks 64 D5
Quidenham Norf 141 F10
Quidhampton Hants 48 C4
Wilts 46 G6
Quilquox Aberds 303 F9
Quina Brook Shrops 149 C10
Quinbury End Northants 120 G2
Quindry Orkney 314 G4
Quinton Northants 120 G5
W Mid 133 G9
Quintrell Downs Corn 5 C7
Quixhill Staffs 169 G10
Quoditch Devon 12 B4
Quoig Perth 286 E2
Quoisley Ches E 167 F8
Quoit Corn 5 C8
Quorndon or Quorn Leics 153 F11
Quothquan S Lnrk 259 B11
Quoyloo Orkney 314 D2
Quoynee Highld 310 D6
Quoyness Orkney 314 F2
Quoys Shetland 312 B8
Shetland 313 G6

R

Raasay Ho Highld 295 B7
Rabbit's Cross Kent 53 D9
Rableyheath Herts 86 B2
Raby Cumb 238 G5
Mers 182 F4
Racecourse Suff 108 C3
Racedown Hants 47 E9
Rachan Mill Borders 260 C4
Rachub Gwyn 163 B10
Rack End Oxon 82 E6
Rackenford Devon 26 D5
Rackham W Sus 35 E9
Rackheath Norf 160 G5
Rackley Som 43 C11
Racks Dumfries 238 C2
Rackwick Orkney 314 B4
Orkney 314 G2
Radbourne Derbys 152 B5
Radcliffe Gtr Man 195 F9
Northumb 253 C7
Radcliffe on Trent Notts 154 B2
Radclive Bucks 102 E3
Radcot Oxon 82 F3
Raddery Highld 301 D7
Raddington Som 27 B8
Raddon Devon 26 G6
Radernie Fife 287 G8
Radfall Kent 70 G6
Radfield Kent 70 G2
Radford Bath 45 B7
Nottingham 171 G9
Oxon 101 G8
W Mid 134 G6
Worcs 117 F10
Radfordbridge Oxon 101 G8
Radford Semele Warks 118 E6
Radipole Dorset 17 E9
Radlet Som 43 F8
Radlett Herts 85 F11
Radley Oxon 83 F8
Radley Green Essex 87 D10
Radley Park Oxon 83 F8
Radlith Shrops 131 B8
Radmanthwaite Notts 171 C8
Radmoor Shrops 150 E2
Radmore Green Ches E 167 D9
Radmore Wood Staffs 151 D11
Radnage Bucks 84 F3
Radnor Corn 4 G4
Radnor Park W Dunb 277 G9
Radstock Bath 45 C7
Radstone Northants 101 C11
Radway Warks 101 B7
Radway Green Ches E 168 E3
Radwell Beds 121 F10
Herts 104 D4
Radwinter Essex 106 D2
Radwinter End Essex 106 D2
Radyr Cardiff 58 C6
Raera Argyll 289 G10
Rafborough Hants 49 B11
Rafford Moray 301 D10
Raga Shetland 312 D6
Ragdale Leics 154 F3
Ragdon Shrops 131 E9
Raggalds W Yorks 205 G7
Ragged Appleshaw Hants 47 D10
Raginnis Corn 1 D5
Raglan Mon 78 D6
Ragmere Norf 141 E11
Ragnall Notts 188 G4
Rahane Argyll 276 D4
Rahoy Highld 289 D8
Raigbeg Highld 301 G8
Rails S Yorks 186 D3
Rainbow Hill Worcs 117 F7
Rainford Mers 194 G3
Rainford Junction Mers 194 G3
Rainham London 68 C4
Medway 69 F10
Rainhill Mers 183 C7
Rainhill Stoops Mers 183 C8
Rainow Ches E 185 F7
Rainowlow Ches E 185 F7
Rain Shore Gtr Man 195 D11
Rainsough Gtr Man 195 G10
Rainton Dumfries 237 D8
N Yorks 215 D7
Rainton Bridge T&W 234 B2
Rainton Gate Durham 234 B2
Rainworth Notts 171 D9
Raisbeck Cumb 222 D2
Raise Cumb 231 B10
Rait Perth 286 E6
Raithby Lincs 190 E4
Raithby by Spilsby Lincs 174 B5
Rake W Sus 34 B4
Rake Common Hants 34 B3
Rake End Staffs 151 F11
Rake Head Lancs 195 C10
Rakes Dale Staffs 169 G9
Rakeway Staffs 169 G8
Rakewood Gtr Man 196 E2
Raleigh Devon 40 G5
Ralia Lodge Highld 291 D9
Rallt Swansea 56 C4
Ram Carms 93 B11
Ram Alley Wilts 63 G8
Ramasaig Highld 297 G7
Rame Corn 2 C6
Corn 7 F8
Rameldry Mill Bank Fife 287 G7
Ram Hill S Glos 61 D7
Ram Lane Kent 54 D3
Ramnageo Shetland 312 C8
Rampisham Dorset 29 G9
Rampside Cumb 210 F4
Rampton Cambs 123 D8
Notts 188 F3
Ramsbottom Gtr Man 195 D9
Ramsburn Moray 302 D5
Ramsbury Wilts 63 E9
Ramscraigs Highld 311 G5
Ramsdean Hants 34 C2
Ramsdell Hants 48 B5
Ramsden London 68 F3
Oxon 82 B5
Worcs 99 B8
Ramsden Bellhouse Essex 88 G2
Ramsden Heath Essex 88 F2
Ramsden Wood W Yorks 196 C2
Ramsey Cambs 138 F5
Essex 108 E4
IoM 192 C5
Ramseycleuch Borders 261 G7
Ramsey Forty Foot Cambs 138 F6
Ramsey Heights Cambs 138 F5
Ramsey Island Essex 89 D7
Ramsey Mereside Cambs 138 F5
Ramsey St Mary's Cambs 138 F5
Ramsgate Kent 71 G11
Ramsgill N Yorks 214 E2
Ramshaw Durham 233 B7
Durham 233 F8
Ramsholt Suff 108 C6
Ramshorn Staffs 169 F9
Ramsley Devon 13 C8
Ramslye Kent 52 F5
Ramsnest Common Sur 50 G2
Ranais W Isles 304 F6
Ranby Lincs 190 F2
Notts 187 E11
Rand Lincs 189 F10
Randwick Glos 80 D4
Ranfurly Renfs 267 C7
Rangag Highld 310 E5
Rangemore Staffs 152 E3
Rangeworthy S Glos 61 B7
Rankinston E Ayrs 257 G11
Rank's Green Essex 88 B3
Ranmoor S Yorks 186 D4
Ranmore Common Sur 50 C6
Rannerdale Cumb 220 B3
Rannoch Lodge Perth 285 B9
Rannoch Station Perth 285 B8
Ranochan Highld 295 G10
Ranskill Notts 187 D11
Ranton Staffs 151 E7
Ranton Green Staffs 150 E6
Ranworth Norf 161 G7
Rapkyns W Sus 50 G6
Raploch Stirl 278 C5
Rapness Orkney 314 B5
Rapps Som 28 D4
Rascal Moor E Yorks 208 F2
Rascarrel Dumfries 237 E9
Rashielee Renfs 277 G9
Rashiereive Aberds 303 G9
Rashwood Worcs 117 D8
Raskelf N Yorks 215 E9
Rassal Highld 299 E8
Rassau Bl Gwent 77 C11
Rastrick W Yorks 196 C6
Ratagan Highld 295 D11
Ratby Leics 135 B10
Ratcliff London 67 C11
Ratcliffe Culey Leics 134 D6
Ratcliffe on Soar Leics 153 D9
Ratcliffe on the Wreake Leics 154 G2
Ratford Wilts 62 E3
Ratfyn Wilts 47 E7
Rathen Aberds 303 C10
Rathillet Fife 287 E7
Rathmell N Yorks 204 B2
Ratho Edin 280 G2
Ratho Station Edin 280 G2
Rathven Moray 302 C4
Ratlake Hants 32 C6
Ratley Warks 101 B7
Ratling Kent 55 C8
Ratlinghope Shrops 131 D8
Ratsloe Devon 14 B5
Rattar Highld 310 B6
Ratten Row Cumb 230 B3
Cumb 230 C2
Lancs 202 E4
Norf 157 G10
Rattery Devon 8 C4
Rattlesden Suff 125 F9
Rattray Perth 286 C5
Raughton Cumb 230 B3
Raughton Head Cumb 230 B3
Raunds Northants 121 C9
Ravelston Edin 280 G4
Ravenfield S Yorks 187 B7
Ravenglass Cumb 219 F11
Ravenhead Mers 183 C8
Ravenhills Green Worcs 116 G4
Raveningham Norf 143 D7
Ravenscar N Yorks 227 E9
Ravenscliffe Stoke 168 E4
W Yorks 205 F9
Ravenscraig Invclyd 276 F5
Ravensdale IoM 192 C4
Ravensden Beds 121 G11
Ravenseat N Yorks 223 E7
Raven's Green Essex 108 G2
Ravenshall Staffs 168 F3
Ravenshead Notts 171 E9
Ravensmoor Ches E 167 E10
Ravensthorpe Northants 120 C3
Pboro 138 C3
W Yorks 197 C8
Ravenstone Leics 153 G8
M Keynes 120 G6
Ravenstonedale Cumb 222 E4
Ravenstown Cumb 211 D7
Ravenstruther S Lnrk 269 F8
Ravenswood Village Settlement Wokingham 65 G10
Ravensworth N Yorks 224 D2
Raw N Yorks 227 D8
Rawcliffe E Yorks 199 C7
York 207 C7
Rawcliffe Bridge E Yorks 199 C7
Rawdon W Yorks 205 F10
Rawdon Carrs W Yorks 205 F10
Rawfolds W Yorks 197 C7
Rawgreen Northumb 241 F10
Raw Green S Yorks 197 F9
Rawmarsh S Yorks 186 B6
Rawnsley Staffs 151 G10
Rawreth Essex 88 G3
Rawreth Shot Essex 88 G3
Rawridge Devon 28 F2
Rawson Green Derbys 170 F5
Rawtenstall Lancs 195 C10
Rawthorpe W Yorks 197 D7
Rawyards N Lnrk 268 B5
Raxton Aberds 303 F8
Raydon Suff 107 D11
Raygill N Yorks 204 D4
Raylees Northumb 251 E10

Sevenhampton Glos 99 G10
Swindon 82 G2
Seven Kings London 68 B3
Sevenoaks Kent 52 C4
Sevenoaks Common
Kent 52 C4
Sevenoaks Weald Kent 52 C4
Seven Sisters / Blaendulais
Neath 76 D4
Seven Springs Glos 81 B7
Seven Star Green Essex 107 F8
Severn Beach S Glos 60 B4
Severnhampton Swindon 82 G2
Severn Stoke Worcs 99 C7
Sevick End Beds 121 G11
Sevington Kent 54 E4
Sewards End Essex 105 D11
Sewardstone Essex 86 F5
Sewardstonebury Essex 86 F5
Sewell C Beds 103 G9
Sewerby E Yorks 218 F3
Seworgan Corn 2 C6
Sewstern Leics 155 E7
Sexhow N Yorks 225 D9
Sezincote Glos 100 E3
Sgarasta Mhor W Isles 305 J2
Sgiogarstaigh W Isles 304 B7
Sgiwen / Skewen Neath 57 B8
Shabbington Bucks 83 D11
Shab Hill Glos 80 B6
Shackerley Shrops 132 B6
Shackerstone Leics 135 B7
Shacklecross Derbys 153 C8
Shackleford Sur 50 D2
Shackleton W Yorks 196 B3
Shacklewell London 67 B10
Shacklford Sur 50 D2
Shade W Yorks 196 C2
Shadforth Durham 234 C2
Shadingfield Suff 143 G8
Shadoxhurst Kent 54 F3
Shadsworth Blkburn 195 B8
Shadwell Glos 80 F3
London 67 C11
Norf 141 G8
W Yorks 206 F2
Shaffalong Staffs 169 E7
Shaftenhoe End Herts 105 D8
Shaftesbury Dorset 30 C5
Shafton S Yorks 197 E11
Shafton Two Gates
S Yorks 197 E11
Shaggs Dorset 18 E3
Shakeford Shrops 150 D3
Shakerley Gtr Man 195 G7
Shakesfield Glos 98 E3
Shalbourne Wilts 63 G10
Shalcombe IoW 20 D3
Shalden Hants 49 E7
Shalden Green Hants 49 E7
Shaldon Devon 14 G4
Shalfleet IoW 20 D4
Shalford Essex 106 F4
Som 45 G8
Sur 50 D4
Shalford Green Essex 106 F4
Shalloch Moray 302 D3
Shallowford Devon 25 B11
Devon 41 E8
Staffs 151 D7
Shalmsford Street Kent 54 C5
Shalstone Bucks 102 D2
Shamley Green Sur 50 E4
Shandon Argyll 276 D5
Shandwick Highld 301 B8
Shangton Leics 136 D4
Shankhouse Northumb 243 B7
Shanklin IoW 21 E7
Shannochie N Ayrs 255 E10
Shannochill Stirl 277 B10
Shanquhar Aberds 302 F5
Shanwell Fife 287 E8
Shanzie Perth 286 B6
Shap Cumb 221 B11
Shapridge Glos 79 B11
Shapwick Dorset 30 G6
Som 44 F2
Sharcott Wilts 46 B6
Shard End W Mid 134 F3
Shardlow Derbys 153 C8
Shareshill Staffs 133 B8
Sharlston W Yorks 197 D11
Sharlston Common
W Yorks 197 D11
Sharmans Cross W Mid 118 B2
Sharnal Street Medway 69 E9
Sharnbrook Beds 121 F9
Sharneyford Lancs 195 C11
Sharnford Leics 135 E9
Sharnhill Green Dorset 30 F2
Sharoe Green Lancs 202 G6
Sharow N Yorks 214 E6
Sharpenhoe C Beds 103 E11
Sharperton Northumb 251 C11
Sharples Gtr Man 195 E8
Sharpley Heath Staffs 151 B9
Sharpness Glos 79 E11
Sharpsbridge E Sus 36 C6
Sharp's Corner E Sus 23 B9
Sharpstone Bath 45 B9
Sharp Street Norf 161 E7
Sharpthorne W Sus 51 G11
Sharptor Corn 11 G11
Sharpway Gate Worcs 117 D9
Sharrington Norf 159 B10
Sharrow S Yorks 186 D4
Sharston Gtr Man 184 D4
Shatterford Worcs 132 G5
Shatterling Kent 55 B9
Shatton Derbys 185 E11
Shaugh Prior Devon 7 C10
Shavington Ches E 168 E2
Shaw Gtr Man 196 F2
Swindon 62 B6
W Berks 64 F3
Wilts 61 F11
W Yorks 204 F6
Shawbank Shrops 131 G9
Shawbirch Telford 150 G2
Shawbury Shrops 149 E11
Shawclough Gtr Man 195 E11
Shaw Common Glos 98 F3
Shawdon Hall Northumb 264 G3
Shawell Leics 135 G10
Shawfield Gtr Man 195 E11
Staffs 169 C9
Shawfield Head
N Yorks 205 C11
Shawford Hants 33 C7
Som 45 C9
Shawforth Lancs 195 C11
Shaw Green Herts 104 E5
Lancs 194 D4
N Yorks 205 C11
Shawhead Dumfries 237 B10
N Lnrk 268 C4
Shaw Heath Ches E 184 F3
Gtr Man 184 D5
Shawhill Dumfries 238 D6
Shawlands Glasgow 267 C11
Shaw Lands S Yorks 197 F10
Shaw Mills N Yorks 214 G5
Shawsburn S Lnrk 268 E5
Shaw Side Gtr Man 196 F2
Shawton S Lnrk 268 F3
Shawtonhill S Lnrk 268 F3
Shay Gate W Yorks 205 F8
Sheandow Moray 302 F2
Shear Cross Wilts 45 E11
Shearington Dumfries 238 D2
Shearsby Leics 136 E2
Shearston Som 43 G9
Shebbear Devon 24 F6
Shebdon Staffs 150 D5
Shebster Highld 310 C4
Sheddens E Renf 267 D11
Shedfield Hants 33 E9
Sheen Staffs 169 C10
Sheepbridge Derbys 186 G5
Sheepdrove W Berks 63 D10
Sheep Hill Durham 242 F5
Sheeplane C Beds 103 E8
Sheepridge Bucks 65 B11
W Yorks 197 D7
Sheepscar W Yorks 206 G2
Sheepscombe Glos 80 C5
Sheepstor Devon 7 B11
Sheepwash Devon 25 F7
Northumb 253 F7
Sheepway N Som 60 D3
Sheepy Magna Leics 134 C6
Sheepy Parva Leics 134 C6
Sheering Essex 87 C8
Sheerness Kent 70 E2
Sheerwater Sur 66 G4
Sheet Hants 34 C3
Shrops 115 C10
Sheets Heath Sur 50 B2
Sheffield Corn 1 D5
S Yorks 186 D5
Sheffield Bottom
W Berks 65 F7
Sheffield Green E Sus 36 C6
Sheffield Park S Yorks 186 D5
Shefford C Beds 104 D2
Shefford Woodlands
W Berks 63 E11
Sheigra Highld 306 C6
Sheildmuir N Lnrk 268 D5
Sheinton Shrops 132 C2
Shelderton Shrops 115 B8
Sheldon Derbys 169 B11
Devon 27 F10
W Mid 134 G3
Sheldwich Kent 54 B4
Sheldwich Lees Kent 54 B4
Shelf Bridgend 58 C2
W Yorks 196 B6
Shelfanger Norf 142 G2
Shelfield Warks 118 E2
W Mid 133 C10
Shelfield Green Warks 118 E2
Shelfleys Northants 120 F4
Shelford Notts 171 G11
Warks 135 F8
Shell Worcs 117 F9
Shelland Suff 125 E10
Shellbrook Leics 152 F6
Shelley Essex 87 E9
Suff 107 D10
W Yorks 197 E8
Shelley Woodhouse
W Yorks 197 E8
Shell Green Halton 183 D8
Shellingford Oxon 82 G4
Shellow Bowells Essex 87 D10
Shellwood Cross Sur 51 D8
Shelsley Beauchamp
Worcs 116 E4
Shelsley Walsh Worcs 116 E4
Shelthorpe Leics 153 F10
Shelton Beds 121 D10
Norf 142 E4
Notts 172 G3
Shrops 149 G9
Stoke 168 F5
Shelton Green Norf 142 E4
Shelton Lock Derby 153 C7
Shelton under Harley
Staffs 150 B6
Shelve Shrops 130 D6
Shelvin Devon 27 G11
Shelvingford Kent 71 F8
Shelwick Hereford 97 C10
Shelwick Green
Hereford 97 C10
Shenfield Essex 87 G10
Shenington Oxon 101 C7
Shenley Herts 85 E11
Shenley Brook End
M Keynes 102 D6
Shenleybury Herts 85 E11
Shenley Church End
M Keynes 102 D6
Shenley Fields W Mid 133 G10
Shenley Lodge
M Keynes 102 D6
Shenley Wood
M Keynes 102 D6
Shenmore Hereford 97 D7
Shennanton Dumfries 236 C5
Shennanton Ho
Dumfries 236 C5
Shenstone Staffs 134 C2
Worcs 117 C7
Shenstone Woodend
Staffs 134 C2
Shenton Leics 135 C7
Shenval Highld 300 G4
Moray 302 G2
Shenvault Moray 301 E10
Shepeau Stow Lincs 156 G6
Shephall Herts 104 G5
Shepherd Hill W Yorks 197 C9
Shepherd's Bush London 67 C8
Shepherd's Gate Norf 157 F11
Shepherd's Green Oxon 65 C8
Shepherd's Hill Sur 50 G2
Shepherd's Patch Glos 80 E2
Shepherd's Port Norf 158 C3
Shepherdswell or
Sibertswold Kent 55 D9
Shepley W Yorks 197 F7
Shepperdine S Glos 79 F10
Shepperton Sur 66 F5
Shepperton Green Sur 66 F5
Shepreth Cambs 105 B7
Shepshed Leics 153 F9
Shepton Beauchamp
Som 28 D6
Shepton Mallet Som 44 E6
Shepton Montague Som 45 G7
Shepway Kent 53 C9
Sheraton Durham 234 D4
Sherberton Devon 13 G8
Sherborne Bath 44 B5
Dorset 29 D10
Glos 81 C11
Sherborne St John Hants 48 B6
Sherbourne Warks 118 E5
Sherbourne Street Suff 107 C9
Sherburn Durham 234 C2
N Yorks 217 D9
Sherburn Grange
Durham 234 C2
Sherburn Hill Durham 234 C2
Sherburn in Elmet
N Yorks 206 G5
Shere Sur 50 D5
Shereford Norf 159 D7
Sherfield English Hants 32 C3
Sherfield on Loddon
Hants 49 B7
Sherfin Lancs 195 B9
Sherford Devon 8 G5
Dorset 18 C4
Som 28 C2
Sheriffhales Shrops 150 G5
Sheriff Hill T&W 243 E7
Sheriff Hutton N Yorks 216 F3
Sheriff's Lench Worcs 99 B10
Sheringham Norf 177 E11
Sherington M Keynes 103 B7
Sheringwood Norf 177 E11
Shermanbury W Sus 36 D2
Shernal Green Worcs 117 E8
Shernborne Norf 158 C4
Sherrard's Green Worcs 98 B5
Sherrardspark Herts 86 C2
Sherriffhales Shrops 150 G5
Sherrington Wilts 46 F3
Sherston Wilts 61 B11
Sherwood Nottingham 171 G9
Sherwood Green Devon 25 C9
Sherwood Park Kent 52 E6
Shettleston Glasgow 268 C2
Shevington Gtr Man 194 F4
Shevington Moor
Gtr Man 194 E4
Shevington Vale
Gtr Man 194 F4
Sheviock Corn 7 D7
Shewalton N Ayrs 257 B8
Shibden Head W Yorks 196 B5
Shide IoW 20 D5
Shiel Aberds 292 B4
Shiel Bridge Highld 295 D11
Shieldaig Highld 299 B8
Highld 299 D8
Shieldhall Glasgow 267 B10
Shieldhill Dumfries 248 F2
Falk 279 F7
S Lnrk 269 G10
Shield Row Durham 242 G6
Shielfoot Highld 289 C8
Shielhill Angus 287 B8
Invclyd 276 G4
Shifford Oxon 82 E5
Shifnal Shrops 132 B4
Shilbottle Northumb 252 B5
Shilbottle Grange
Northumb 252 B6
Shildon Durham 233 F10
Shillford E Renf 267 D8
Shillingford Devon 27 C7
Oxon 83 G9
Shillingford Abbot Devon 14 D4
Shillingford St George
Devon 14 D4
Shillingstone Dorset 30 E4
Shillington C Beds 104 E2
Shillmoor Northumb 251 B9
Shilton Oxon 82 D3
Warks 135 G8
Shilvington Northumb 252 G5
Shimpling Norf 142 G3
Suff 125 G7
Shimpling Street Suff 125 G7
Shincliffe Durham 233 C11
Shiney Row T&W 243 G8
Shinfield Wokingham 65 F8
Shingay Cambs 104 B6
Shingham Norf 140 C5
Shingle Street Suff 109 C7
Shinner's Bridge Devon 8 C5
Shinness Highld 309 H5
Shipbourne Kent 52 C5
Shipdham Norf 141 B9
Shipdham Airfield Norf 141 B9
Shipham Som 44 B2
Shiphay Torbay 9 B7
Shiplake Oxon 65 D9
Shiplake Bottom Oxon 65 C8
Shiplake Row Oxon 65 D9
Shiplate N Som 43 B11
Shiplaw Borders 270 F4
Shipley Derbys 170 G6
Northumb 264 F4
Shrops 132 D6
W Sus 35 C10
W Yorks 205 F8
Shipley Bridge Sur 51 E10
Shipley Common
Derbys 171 G7
Shipley Shiels Northumb 251 E7
Shipmeadow Suff 143 F7
Shipping Pembs 73 D10
Shippon Oxon 83 F7
Shipston-on-Stour
Warks 100 C5
Shipton Bucks 102 F5
Glos 81 B8
N Yorks 207 B7
Shrops 131 E11
Shipton Bellinger Hants 47 D8
Shipton Gorge Dorset 16 C5
Shipton Green W Sus 22 C4
Shipton Lee Bucks 102 G4
Shipton Moyne Glos 61 B11
Shipton Oliffe Glos 81 B8
Shipton on Cherwell
Oxon 83 B7
Shipton Solers Glos 81 B8
Shiptonthorpe E Yorks 208 E3
Shipton-under-Wychwood
Oxon 82 B3
Shirburn Oxon 83 F11
Shirdley Hill Lancs 193 E11
Shirebrook Derbys 171 B8
Shirecliffe S Yorks 186 C4
Shiregreen S Yorks 186 C5
Shirehampton Bristol 60 D4
Shiremoor T&W 243 C8
Shirenewton Mon 79 G7
Shire Oak W Mid 133 C11
Shireoaks Derbys 185 E9
Notts 187 E9
Shires Mill Fife 279 D10
Shirkoak Kent 54 F2
Shirland Derbys 170 D6
Shirlett Shrops 132 D3
Shirley Derbys 170 G2
Hants 19 B9
London 67 F11
Soton 32 E6
W Mid 118 B2
Shirley Heath W Mid 118 B2
Shirley holms Hants 19 B11
Shirley Warren Soton 32 E5
Shirl Heath Hereford 115 F8
Shirrell Heath Hants 33 E9
Shirwell Devon 40 F5
Shirwell Cross Devon 40 F5
Shiskine N Ayrs 255 E10
Shitterton Dorset 18 C2
Shobdon Hereford 115 E8
Shobley Hants 31 F11
Shobnall Staffs 152 E4
Shobrooke Devon 26 G5
Shoby Leics 154 F3
Shocklach Ches W 166 F6
Shocklach Green
Ches W 166 F6
Shoeburyness Sthend 70 C2
Sholden Kent 55 C11
Sholing Soton 32 E6
Sholing Common Soton 33 E7
Sholver Gtr Man 196 F3
Shootash Hants 32 C4
Shooters Hill London 68 D2
Shootersway Herts 85 D7
Shoot Hill Shrops 149 G8
Shop Corn 10 G3
Corn 24 E2
Devon 24 E5
Shop Corner Suff 108 E4
Shopford Cumb 240 C3
Shopnoller Som 43 G7
Shop Hill W Sus 34 B6
Shopwyke W Sus 22 B5
Shore Gtr Man 196 D2
W Yorks 196 B2
Shore Bottom Devon 28 G2
Shoreditch London 67 C10
Som 28 C2
Shoregill Cumb 222 E5
Shoreham Kent 68 G4
Shoreham Beach W Sus 36 G2
Shoreham-by-Sea
W Sus 36 F2
Shore Mill Highld 301 C7
Shoresdean Northumb 273 F9
Shores Green Oxon 82 D5
Shoreside Shetland 313 J4
Shoreswood Northumb 273 F8
Shoreton Highld 300 C6
Shorley Hants 33 B9
Shorncliffe Camp Kent 55 F7
Shorncote Glos 81 F8
Shorne Kent 69 E7
Shorne Ridgeway Kent 69 E7
Shorne West Kent 69 E7
Shortacombe Devon 12 D6
Shortacross Corn 6 D5
Shortbridge E Sus 37 C7
Short Cross W Mid 133 G9
Shortfield Common Sur 49 E10
Shortgate E Sus 23 B7
Short Green Norf 141 F11
Shorthampton Oxon 100 G6
Shortheath Hants 49 F9
Sur 49 E10
Short Heath Derbys 152 G6
W Mid 133 C9
W Mid 133 E11
Shorthill Shrops 131 B8
Shortlands London 67 F11
Shortlanesend Corn 4 F6
Shortlees E Ayrs 257 B10
Shortmoor Devon 28 G2
Dorset 29 G7
Shorton Torbay 9 C7
Shortroods Renfs 267 B9
Shortstanding Glos 79 C9
Shortstown Beds 103 B11
Short Street Wilts 45 D10
Shortwood Glos 80 F4
S Glos 61 D7
Shorwell IoW 20 E5
Shoscombe Bath 45 B8
Shoscombe Vale Bath 45 B8
Shotatton Shrops 149 E7
Shotesham Norf 142 D5
Shotgate Essex 88 G3
Shotley Northants 137 D8
Suff 108 D4
Shotley Bridge Durham 242 G3
Shotleyfield Northumb 242 G3
Shotley Gate Suff 108 E4
Shottenden Kent 54 C4
Shottermill Sur 49 G11
Shottery Warks 118 G3
Shotteswell Warks 101 B8
Shottisham Suff 108 C6
Shottle Derbys 170 F4
Shottlegate Derbys 170 F4
Shotton Durham 234 D4
Durham 234 F3
Flint 166 B4
Northumb 242 B6
Northumb 263 C8
Shotton Colliery
Durham 234 C3
Shotts N Lnrk 269 C7
Shotwick Ches W 182 G4
Shouldham Norf 140 B3
Shouldham Thorpe Norf 140 B3
Shoulton Worcs 116 F6
Shover's Green E Sus 53 G7
Shraleybrook Staffs 168 F3
Shrawardine Shrops 149 F8
Shrawley Worcs 116 E6
Shreding Green Bucks 66 C4
Shrewley Warks 118 D4
Shrewley Common
Warks 118 D4
Shrewsbury Shrops 149 G9
Shrewton Wilts 46 E5
Shripney W Sus 22 C6
Shrivenham Oxon 63 B8
Shropham Norf 141 E9
Shroton or Iwerne Courtney
Dorset 30 E5
Shrub End Essex 107 G9
Shrubs Hill Sur 66 F3
Shrutherhill S Lnrk 268 F5
Shucknall Hereford 97 C11
Shudy Camps Cambs 106 C2
Shulishadermor Highld 298 E4
Shulista Highld 298 B4
Shuna Ho Argyll 275 C8
Shurdington Glos 80 B6
Shurlock Row Windsor 65 E10
Shurnock Worcs 117 E10
Shurrery Highld 310 D4
Shurrery Lodge Highld 310 D4
Shurton Som 43 E8
Shustoke Warks 134 E4
Shute Devon 15 B11
Devon 26 G5
Shute End Wilts 31 B11
Shutford Oxon 101 C7
Shut Heath Staffs 151 E7
Shuthonger Glos 99 D7
Shutlanger Northants 120 G4
Shutta Corn 6 E5
Shutt Green Staffs 133 B7
Shuttington Warks 134 B5
Shuttlesfield Kent 55 E7
Shuttlewood Derbys 187 G7
Shuttleworth Gtr Man 195 D10
Shutton Hereford 98 F3
Shwt Bridgend 57 D11
Siabost bho Dheas
W Isles 304 D4
Siabost bho Thuath
W Isles 304 D4
Siadar W Isles 304 C5
Siadar Iarach W Isles 304 C5
Siadar Uarach W Isles 304 C5
Sibbaldbie Dumfries 248 F4
Sibbertoft Northants 136 G3
Sibdon Carwood Shrops 131 G8
Sibford Ferris Oxon 101 D7
Sibford Gower Oxon 101 D7
Sible Hedingham Essex 106 E5
Sibley's Green Essex 106 F2
Sibsey Lincs 174 E5
Sibsey Fen Side Lincs 174 E4
Sibson Cambs 137 D11
Leics 135 C7
Sibster Highld 310 D7
Sibthorpe Notts 172 F3
Notts 188 G2
Sibton Suff 127 D7
Sibton Green Suff 127 C7
Sicklesmere Suff 125 E7
Sicklinghall N Yorks 206 D3
Sid Devon 15 D8
Sidbrook Som 28 B3
Sidbury Devon 15 C8
Shrops 132 F3
Sidcot N Som 44 B2
Sidcup London 68 E3
Siddal W Yorks 196 C6
Siddick Cumb 228 E6
Siddington Ches E 184 G4
Glos 81 F8
Siddington Heath
Ches E 184 G4
Sidemoor Worcs 117 C9
Side of the Moor
Gtr Man 195 E8
Sidestrand Norf 160 B5
Sideway Stoke 168 G5
Sidford Devon 15 C8
Sidlesham W Sus 22 D5
Sidlesham Common
W Sus 22 C5
Sidley E Sus 38 F2
Sidlow Sur 51 D9
Sidmouth Devon 15 D8
Sidway Staffs 150 B5
Sigford Devon 13 G11
Sighthill Edin 280 G3
Glasgow 268 B2
Sigingstone / Tresigin
V Glam 58 E3
Signet Oxon 82 C2
Sigwells Som 29 C10
Silchester Hants 64 G6
Sildinis W Isles 305 G4
Sileby Leics 153 F11
Silecroft Cumb 210 C2
Silfield Norf 142 D2
Silford Devon 24 B6
Silian Ceredig 111 G11
Silkstead Hants 32 C6
Silkstone S Yorks 197 F9
Silkstone Common
S Yorks 197 G9
Silk Willoughby Lincs 173 G9
Silloth Cumb 238 G4
Sills Northumb 251 C8
Sillyearn Moray 302 D5
Siloh Carms 94 D4
Silpho N Yorks 227 G9
Silsden W Yorks 204 D6
Silsoe C Beds 103 D11
Silton Dorset 30 B3
Silverburn Midloth 270 C4
Silverdale Lancs 211 E9
Staffs 168 F4
Silverdale Green Lancs 211 E9
Silver End Essex 88 B4
W Mid 133 F8
Silvergate Norf 160 D3
Silver Green Norf 142 E5
Silverhill E Sus 38 E3
Silver Hill E Sus 38 B2
Silverhill Park E Sus 38 E4
Silver Knap Som 29 C11
Silverknowes Edin 280 F4
Silverley's Green Suff 126 B5
Silvermuir S Lnrk 269 F8
Silverstone Northants 102 C3
Silver Street Glos 80 E3
Kent 69 G11
Som 27 C11
Som 44 G4
Worcs 117 B11
Silverton Devon 27 G7
W Dunb 277 F8
Silvertonhill S Lnrk 268 E4
Silvertown London 68 D2
Silverwell Corn 4 F4
Silvington Shrops 116 B2
Silwick Shetland 313 J4
Sim Hill S Yorks 197 G9
Simister Gtr Man 195 F10
Simmondley Derbys 185 C8
Simm's Cross Halton 183 D8
Simm's Lane End Mers 194 G4
Simonburn Northumb 241 C9
Simonsbath Som 41 F9
Simonsburrow Devon 27 D10
Simonside T&W 243 E8
Simonstone Lancs 203 G11
N Yorks 223 G7
Simprim Borders 272 F6
Simpson M Keynes 103 D7
Pembs 72 B5
Simpson Cross Pembs 72 B5
Simpson Green W Yorks 205 F9
Sinclair's Hill Borders 272 E6
Sinclairston E Ayrs 257 F11
Sinclairtown Fife 280 C5
Sinderby N Yorks 214 C6
Sinderhope Northumb 241 G8
Sinderland Green
Gtr Man 184 C2
Sindlesham Wokingham 65 F9
Sinfin Derby 152 C6
Sinfin Moor Derby 153 C7
Singdean Borders 250 C3
Singlebrough Bucks 102 E5
Singlehill Bath 45 B8
Singleton Lancs 202 F3
W Sus 34 E5
Singlewell Kent 69 E7
Singret Wrex 166 D4
Sinkhurst Green Kent 53 E10
Sinnahard Aberds 292 B6
Sinnington N Yorks 216 B4
Sinton Worcs 116 E6
Sinton Green Worcs 116 E6
Sion Hill Bath 61 F8
Sipson London 66 D5
Sirhowy Bl Gwent 77 C11
Sisland Norf 142 D6
Sissinghurst Kent 53 F9
Sisterpath Borders 272 F5
Siston S Glos 61 D7
Sithney Corn 2 D4
Sithney Common Corn 2 D4
Sithney Green Corn 2 D4
Sittingbourne Kent 70 G2
Six Ashes Staffs 132 F5
Six Bells Bl Gwent 78 E2
Sixhills Lincs 189 D11
Six Hills Leics 154 E2
Sixmile Kent 54 E6
Six Mile Bottom Cambs 123 F11
Sixpenny Handley Dorset 31 D7
Sizewell Suff 127 E9
Skaigh Devon 13 C8
Skail Highld 308 E7
Skaill Orkney 314 C4
Orkney 314 E2
Orkney 314 F5
Skares E Ayrs 258 F2
Skateraw E Loth 282 F4
Skaw Shetland 312 B8
Shetland 312 G7
Skeabost Highld 298 E4
Skeabrae Orkney 314 D2
Skeeby N Yorks 224 E4
Skeete Kent 54 E6
Skeffington Leics 136 C4
Skeffling E Yorks 201 D11
Skegby Notts 171 C7
Notts 188 G3
Skegness Lincs 175 C9
Skelberry Shetland 313 G6
Shetland 313 M5
Skelbo Highld 309 K7
Skelbo Street Highld 309 K7
Skelbrooke S Yorks 198 E4
Skeldyke Lincs 156 B6
Skelfhill Borders 249 C11
Skellingthorpe Lincs 188 G6
Skellister Shetland 313 H6
Skellorn Green Ches E 184 E6
Skellow S Yorks 198 E4
Skelmanthorpe W Yorks 197 E8
Skelmersdale Lancs 194 F3
Skelmonae Aberds 303 F8
Skelmorlie N Ayrs 266 B3
Skelmuir Aberds 303 E9
Skelpick Highld 308 D7
Skelton Cumb 230 D4
E Yorks 199 B9
N Yorks 223 E11
Redcar 226 B3
York 207 B7
Skelton-on-Ure
N Yorks 215 F7
Skelwick Orkney 314 B4
Skelwith Bridge Cumb 220 E6
Skendleby Lincs 174 B6
Skendleby Psalter Lincs 190 G6
Skene Ho Aberds 293 C9
Skenfrith Mon 97 G9
Skerne E Yorks 208 B6
Skerne Park Darl 224 C5
Skeroblingarry Argyll 255 E8
Skerray Highld 308 C6
Skerricha Highld 306 D7
Skerryford Pembs 72 C6
Skerton Lancs 211 G9
Sketchley Leics 135 E8
Sketty Swansea 56 C6
Skewen / Sgiwen Neath 57 B8
Skewes Corn 5 B9
Skewsby N Yorks 216 E2
Skeyton Norf 160 D4
Skeyton Corner Norf 160 D5
Skiag Bridge Highld 307 G7
Skibo Castle Highld 309 L7
Skidbrooke Lincs 190 C6
Skidbrooke North End
Lincs 190 B6
Skidby E Yorks 208 G6
Skilgate Som 27 B7
Skillington Lincs 155 D7
Skinburness Cumb 238 F4
Skinflats Falk 279 E8
Skinidin Highld 298 E2
Skinner's Bottom Corn 4 F4
Skinners Green W Berks 64 F2
Skinnet Highld 308 C5
Skinningrove Redcar 226 B4
Skipness Argyll 255 B9
Skippool Lancs 202 E3
Skiprigg Cumb 230 B3
Skipsea E Yorks 209 B9
Skipsea Brough E Yorks 209 C9
Skipton N Yorks 204 C5
Skipton-on-Swale
N Yorks 215 D7
Skipwith N Yorks 207 F9
Skirbeck Lincs 174 G4
Skirbeck Quarter Lincs 174 G4
Skirethorns N Yorks 213 G9
Skirlaugh E Yorks 209 F8
Skirling Borders 260 B3
Skirmett Bucks 65 B9
Skirpenbeck E Yorks 207 B10
Skirwith Cumb 231 E8
Skirza Highld 310 C7
Skitby Cumb 239 D10
Skitham Lancs 202 E4
Skittle Green Bucks 84 E3
Skulamus Highld 295 C8
Skullomie Highld 308 C6
Skyborry Green Shrops 114 C5
Skye Green Essex 107 G7
Skye of Curr Highld 301 G9
Skyfog Pembs 90 F6
Skyreholme N Yorks 213 G11
Slack Derbys 170 C4
W Yorks 196 B3
W Yorks 196 D5
Slackcote Gtr Man 196 F3
Slackhall Derbys 185 E9
Slackhead Moray 302 C4
Slack Head Cumb 211 D9
Slackholme End Lincs 191 G8
Slacks of Cairnbanno
Aberds 303 E8
Slad Glos 80 D5
Sladbrook Glos 98 F5
Slade Devon 27 F10
Devon 40 D4
Kent 54 C2
Pembs 72 B6
Slade End Oxon 83 G9
Slade Green London 68 D4
Slade Heath Staffs 133 B8
Slade Hooton S Yorks 187 D8
Sladen Green Hants 48 C2
Sladesbridge Corn 10 G6
Slades Green Worcs 99 E7
Slaggyford Northumb 240 G5
Slaidburn Lancs 203 C10
Slaithwaite W Yorks 196 E5
Slaley Derbys 170 D3
Northumb 241 F11
Slamannan Falk 279 G7
Slape Cross Som 43 F10
Slapewath Redcar 226 B2
Slapton Bucks 103 G8
Devon 8 G6
Northants 102 B2
Slateford Edin 280 G4
Slate Haugh Moray 302 C4
Slatepit Dale Derbys 170 B4
Slattocks Gtr Man 195 F11
Slaugham W Sus 36 B3
Slaughterbridge Corn 11 D8
Slaughterford Wilts 61 E10
Slaughter Hill Ches E 168 D2
Slawston Leics 136 E5
Slay Pits S Yorks 199 F7
Sleaford Hants 49 F10
Lincs 173 F9
Sleagill Cumb 221 B11
Sleap Shrops 149 D9
Sleapford Telford 150 F2
Sleapshyde Herts 86 D2
Sleastary Highld 309 K6
Slebech Pembs 73 B8
Sledge Green Worcs 98 E6
Sledmere E Yorks 217 G8
Sleeches Cross E Sus 52 G5
Sleepers Hill Hants 33 B7
Sleetbeck Cumb 240 B2
Sleet Moor Derbys 170 E6
Sleight Dorset 18 B5
Sleights N Yorks 227 D7
Slepe Dorset 18 C4
Sliabhna h-Airde
W Isles 296 F3
Slickly Highld 310 C6
Sliddery N Ayrs 255 E10
Slideslow Worcs 117 C9
Sligachan Hotel Highld 294 C6
Sligneach Argyll 288 G4
Sligrachan Argyll 276 C3
Slimbridge Glos 80 E2
Slindon Staffs 150 C6
W Sus 35 F7
Slinfold W Sus 50 G6
Sling Glos 79 D9
Gwyn 163 B10
Slingsby N Yorks 216 E3
Slioch Aberds 302 F5
Slip End C Beds 85 B9
Herts 104 D5
Slippery Ford W Yorks 204 E6
Slipton Northants 121 B9
Slitting Mill Staffs 151 F10
Slochd Highld 301 G8
Slockavullin Argyll 275 D9
Slogan Moray 302 E3
Sloley Norf 160 E5
Sloncombe Devon 13 D10
Sloothby Lincs 191 G7
Slough Slough 66 D3
Slough Green Som 28 C3
W Sus 36 B3
Slough Hill Suff 125 G7
Sluggan Highld 301 G8
Sluggans Highld 298 E4
Slumbay Highld 295 B10
Sly Corner Kent 54 G3
Slyfield Sur 50 C3
Slyne Lancs 211 F9
Smailholm Borders 262 B4
Smallbridge Gtr Man 196 D2
Smallbrook Devon 14 B3
Glos 79 E9
Smallburgh Norf 160 E6
Smallburn Aberds 303 E10
E Ayrs 258 D5
Smalldale Derbys 185 E11
Derbys 185 F9
Small Dole W Sus 36 E2
Small End Lincs 174 D6
Smalley Derbys 170 G6
Smalley Common
Derbys 170 G6
Smalley Green Derbys 170 G6
Smallfield Sur 51 E10
Smallford Herts 85 D11
Small Heath W Mid 134 F2
Smallholm Dumfries 238 B4
Small Hythe Kent 53 G11
Smallmarsh Devon 25 C10
Smallrice Staffs 151 C9
Smallridge Devon 28 G4
Smallshaw Gtr Man 196 G2
Smallthorne Stoke 168 E5
Small Way Som 44 G6
Smallwood Ches E 168 C4
Worcs 117 D10
Smallwood Green Suff 125 F8
Smallwood Hey Lancs 202 D3
Smallworth Norf 141 G10
Smannell Hants 47 D11
Smardale Cumb 222 D4
Smarden Kent 53 E11
Smarden Bell Kent 53 E11
Smart's Hill Kent 52 E4
Smaull Argyll 274 G3
Smeatharpe Devon 27 E11
Smeaton Fife 280 C5
Smeeth Kent 54 F5
Smeeton Westerby
Leics 136 E3
Smelthouses N Yorks 214 G3
Smercleit W Isles 297 K3
Smerral Highld 310 F5
Smestow Staffs 133 E7
Smethcott Shrops 131 D9
Smethwick W Mid 133 F10
Smethwick Green
Ches E 168 C4
Smirisary Highld 289 B8
Smisby Derbys 152 F6
Smite Hill Worcs 117 F7
Smithaleigh Devon 7 D11
Smithbrook W Sus 34 C6
Smith End Green Worcs 116 G5
Smithfield Cumb 239 D10
Smith Green Lancs 202 C5
Smithies S Yorks 197 F11
Smithincott Devon 27 E9
Smithley S Yorks 197 G11
Smith's End Herts 105 D8
Smiths Green Ches E 184 G4
Smith's Green Ches E 168 E3
Essex 105 G11
Essex 106 C3
Smithston Aberds 302 G5
Smithstown Highld 299 B7
Smithton Highld 301 E7
Smithwood Green Suff 125 G8
Smithy Bridge Gtr Man 196 D2
Smithy Gate Flint 181 F11
Smithy Green Ches E 184 G2
Gtr Man 184 D5
Smithy Houses Derbys 170 F5
Smithy Lane Ends Lancs 194 E2
Smock Alley W Sus 35 D9
Smockington Leics 135 F9
Smoky Row Bucks 84 D4
Smoogro Orkney 314 F3
Smug Oak Herts 85 E10
Smyrton S Ayrs 244 G4
Smythe's Green Essex 88 B6
Snagshall E Sus 38 C3
Snaigow House Perth 286 C4
Snailbeach Shrops 131 C7
Snails Hill Som 29 E7
Snailswell Herts 104 E3
Snailwell Cambs 124 D2
Snainton N Yorks 217 C8
Snaisgill Durham 232 F5
Snaith E Yorks 198 C6
Snape N Yorks 214 C5
Suff 127 F7
Snape Green Lancs 193 E11
Snape Hill Derbys 186 F5
S Yorks 198 G2
Snapper Devon 40 G5
Snaresbrook London 67 B11
Snarestone Leics 134 B6
Snarford Lincs 189 E9
Snargate Kent 39 B7
Snarraness Shetland 313 H4
Snatchwood Torf 78 E3
Snave Kent 39 B8
Sneachill Worcs 117 G8
Snead Powys 130 E6
Snead Common Worcs 116 D4
Sneads Green Worcs 117 D7
Sneath Common Norf 142 F3
Sneaton N Yorks 227 D7
Sneatonthorpe N Yorks 227 D8
Snedshill Telford 132 B4
Sneinton Nottingham 153 B11
Snelland Lincs 189 E9
Snelston Derbys 169 G11
Snetterton Norf 141 E9
Snettisham Norf 158 C3
Sneyd Green Stoke 168 F5
Sneyd Park Bristol 60 D5
Snibston Leics 153 G8
Snig's End Glos 98 F5
Snipeshill Kent 70 G2
Sniseabhal W Isles 297 H3
Snitter Northumb 252 C2
Snitterby Lincs 189 C7
Snitterfield Warks 118 F4
Snitterton Derbys 170 C3
Snitton Shrops 115 B11
Snittongate Shrops 115 B11
Snodhill Hereford 96 C6
Snodland Kent 69 G7
Snods Edge Northumb 242 G3
Snowden Hill S Yorks 197 G9
Snowdown Kent 55 C8
Snow End Herts 105 E8
Snow Hill Ches E 167 E10
W Yorks 197 C10
Snow Lea W Yorks 196 D5
Snowshill Glos 99 E11
Snow Street Norf 141 G11
Snydale W Yorks 198 D2
Soake Hants 33 E11
Soar Anglesey 178 G5
Carms 94 F2
Devon 9 G9
Gwyn 146 B2
Powys 95 E9
Soar-y-Mynydd Ceredig 112 G5
Soberton Hants 33 D10
Soberton Heath Hants 33 E10
Sockbridge Cumb 230 F6
Sockburn Darl 224 D6
Sockety Dorset 29 F7
Sodom Denb 181 G9
Shetland 313 G7
Wilts 62 C4
Sodylt Bank Shrops 148 B6
Soham Cambs 123 C11
Soham Cotes Cambs 123 B11
Soho London 67 C9
Som 45 D7
W Mid 133 F10
Solas W Isles 296 D4
Soldon Cross Devon 24 E4
Soldridge Hants 49 G7
Sole Street Kent 54 D5
Kent 69 F7
Solfach / Solva Pembs 90 G5
Solihull W Mid 118 B2
Solihull Lodge W Mid 117 B11
Sollers Dilwyn Hereford 115 F8
Sollers Hope Hereford 98 E2
Sollom Lancs 194 D3
Solva / Solfach Pembs 90 G5
Somerby Leics 154 G5
Lincs 200 F5
Somercotes Derbys 170 E6
Somerdale Bath 61 F7
Somerford Ches E 168 B4
Dorset 19 C9
Staffs 133 B7
Somerford Keynes Glos 81 G8
Somerley W Sus 22 D4
Somerleyton Suff 143 D9
Somersal Herbert
Derbys 152 B2
Somersby Lincs 190 G4
Somersham Cambs 123 B7
Suff 107 B11
Somers Town London 67 C9
Ptsmth 21 B8
Somerton Newport 59 B10
Oxon 101 F9
Som 29 B7
Suff 124 G6
Somerton Hill Som 29 B7
Somerwood Shrops 149 G11
Sompting W Sus 35 G11
Sompting Abbotts
W Sus 35 F11
Sonning Wokingham 65 D9
Sonning Common Oxon 65 C8
Sonning Eye Oxon 65 D9
Sontley Wrex 166 F4
Sookholme Notts 171 B8
Sopley Hants 19 B9
Sopwell Herts 85 D11
Sopworth Wilts 61 B10
Sorbie Dumfries 236 E6
Sordale Highld 310 C5
Sorisdale Argyll 288 C4
Sorley Devon 8 F4
Sorn E Ayrs 258 D3
Sornhill E Ayrs 258 C2
Sortat Highld 310 C6
Sotby Lincs 190 F2
Sothall S Yorks 186 E6
Sots Hole Lincs 173 C10
Sotterley Suff 143 G9
Soudley Shrops 131 E9
Shrops 150 D4
Soughley S Yorks 197 G7
Soughton / Sychdyn
Flint 166 B2
Soulbury Bucks 103 F7
Soulby Cumb 222 C4
Cumb 230 F5
Souldern Oxon 101 E10
Souldrop Beds 121 E9
Sound Ches E 167 F10
Shetland 313 H5
Shetland 313 J6
Sound Heath Ches E 167 F10
Soundwell S Glos 60 D6

394 Sou–Sto

Sourhope Borders 263 E8
Sourin Orkney 314 C4
Sourlie N Ayrs 266 G6
Sour Nook Cumb 230 C3
Sourton Devon 12 C6
Soutergate Cumb 210 C4
South Acre Norf 158 G6
South Acton London 67 D7
South Alkham Kent 55 E8
Southall London 66 C6
South Allington Devon 9 G10
South Alloa Falk 279 C7
Southam Cumb 219 C9
Glos 99 F9
Warks 119 E8
South Ambersham
W Sus 34 C6
Southampton Soton 32 E6
South Anston S Yorks 187 E8
South Ascot Windsor 66 F2
South Ashford Kent 54 E4
South Auchmachar
Aberds 303 E9
Southay Som 28 D6
South Baddesley Hants 20 B3
South Ballachulish
Highld 284 B4
South Balloch S Ayrs 245 D8
South Bank Redcar 234 G6
York 207 C7
South Barrow Som 29 B10
South Beach Northumb 243 B8
South Beach / Marian-y-de
Gwyn 145 C7
South Beddington
London 67 G9
South Benfleet Essex 69 B9
South Bents T&W 243 E10
South Bersted W Sus 22 C6
South Blainslie
Borders 271 G10
South Bockhampton
Dorset 19 B9
Southborough Bromley 68 F2
Kent 52 E5
Kingston-upon-Thames 67 F7
Southbourne Bmouth 19 C8
W Sus 22 B3
South Bramwith
S Yorks 198 E6
South Brent Devon 8 D3
South Brewham Som 45 F8
South Bromley London 67 C11
Southbrook Wilts 45 G10
South Broomage Falk 279 E7
South Broomhill
Northumb 252 D6
Southburgh Norf 141 C9
South Burlingham Norf 143 B7
Southburn E Yorks 208 C5
South Cadbury Som 29 B10
South Cairn Dumfries 236 C1
South Carlton Lincs 189 F7
Notts 187 E9
South Carne Corn 11 E10
South Cave E Yorks 208 G4
South Cerney Glos 81 F8
South Chailey E Sus 36 D5
South Chard Som 28 F4
South Charlton
Northumb 264 E5
South Cheriton Som 29 C11
Southchurch Sthend 70 B2
South Church Durham 233 F10
South Cliffe E Yorks 208 F3
South Clifton Notts 188 G4
South Clunes Highld 300 E5
South Cockerington
Lincs 190 D5
South Common Devon 28 G4
Southcoombe Oxon 100 F6
South Cornelly Bridgend 57 E10
South Corriegills
N Ayrs 256 C2
South Corrielaw
Dumfries 248 G5
Southcote Reading 65 E7
Southcott Corn 11 B9
Devon 24 D6
Wilts 47 B7
Southcourt Bucks 84 C4
South Cove Suff 143 G9
South Creagan Argyll 289 E11
South Creake Norf 159 B7
Southcrest Worcs 117 D10
South Crosland
W Yorks 196 E6
South Croxton Leics 154 G3
South Croydon London 67 G10
South Cuil Highld 298 C3
South Dalton E Yorks 208 D5
South Darenth Kent 68 F5
Southdean Borders 250 B4
Southdene Mers 182 B6
South Denes Norf 143 C10
Southdown Bath 61 G8
Corn 7 E8
South Down Hants 33 C7
Som 28 E2
South Duffield N Yorks 207 G9
South Dunn Highld 310 D5
South Earlswood Sur 51 D9
Southease E Sus 36 F6
South Elkington Lincs 190 D3
South Elmsall W Yorks 198 E3
South Elphinstone
E Loth 281 G7
Southend Argyll 255 G7
Bucks 65 B9
Glos 80 F2
London 67 E11
Oxon 83 E9
W Berks 64 D2
W Berks 64 E5
Wilts 63 E7
South End Beds 103 B10
Bucks 103 F7
Cumb 210 G4
E Yorks 209 E9
Hants 31 D10
South-end Herts 86 B6
South End N Lincs 200 C6
Norf 141 E9
Southend-on-Sea
Sthend 69 B11
Southerhouse Shetland 313 K5
Southerly Devon 12 D6
Southernby Cumb 230 D3
Southern Cross Brighton 36 F3
Southernden Kent 53 D11
Southerndown V Glam 57 G11
Southerness Dumfries 237 D11
Southern Green Herts 104 E6
South Erradale Highld 299 B7
Southery Norf 140 E2
Southey Green Essex 106 E5
South Fambridge Essex 88 F5
South Farnborough
Hants 49 C11
South Fawley W Berks 63 C11
South Ferriby N Lincs 200 C3
Southfield Northumb 243 B7
South Field E Yorks 200 B4
Windsor 66 D3
Southfields London 67 E9
Thurrock 69 C7
Southfleet Kent 68 E6
South Flobbets Aberds 303 F7
Southford IoW 20 F6
South Garth Shetland 312 D7
South Garvan Highld 289 B11
Southgate Ceredig 111 A11
London 86 G3
Norf 159 C7
Norf 160 E2
Swansea 56 D5
W Sus 51 F9
South Glendale W Isles 297 K3
South Gluss Shetland 312 F5
South Godstone Sur 51 D11
South Gorley Hants 31 E11
South Gosforth T&W 242 D6
South Green Essex 87 G11
Essex 89 B8
Kent 69 G11
Norf 157 F10
Norf 159 G11
Suff 126 B3
South Gyle Edin 280 G3
South-haa Shetland 312 E5
South Hackney London 67 C11
South Ham Hants 48 C6
South Hampstead London 67 C9
South Hanningfield Essex 88 F2
South Harefield London 66 B5
South Harrow London 66 B6
South Harting W Sus 34 D3
South Hatfield Herts 86 D2
South Hayling Hants 21 B10
South Hazelrigg
Northumb 264 C3
South Heath Bucks 84 E6
Essex 89 B10
South Heighton E Sus 23 E7
South-heog Shetland 312 E5
South Hetton Durham 234 B3
South Hiendley
W Yorks 197 E11
South Hill Corn 12 G2
N Som 43 B10
Pembs 72 C4
South Hinksey Oxon 83 E8
South Hole Devon 24 C2
South Holme N Yorks 216 D3
South Holmwood Sur 51 D7
South Hornchurch
London 68 C4
South Huish Devon 8 G3
South Hykeham Lincs 172 C6
South Hylton T&W 243 F9
Southill C Beds 104 C3
Dorset 17 E9
Southington Hants 48 D4
South Kelsey Lincs 189 B8
South Kensington London 67 D9
South Kessock Highld 300 E6
South Killingholme
N Lincs 201 D7
South Kilvington
N Yorks 215 C8
South Kilworth Leics 136 G2
South Kirkby W Yorks 198 E2
South Kirkton Aberds 293 C9
South Kiscadale N Ayrs 256 D2
South Knighton Devon 14 G2
Leicester 136 C2
South Kyme Lincs 173 F11
South Lambeth London 67 D10
South Lancing W Sus 35 G11
Southlands Dorset 17 F9
South Lane S Yorks 197 F9
Southleigh Devon 15 C10
South Leigh Oxon 82 D5
South Leverton Notts 188 E3
South Littleton Worcs 99 B11
South Lopham Norf 141 G10
South Luffenham
Rutland 137 C8
South Malling E Sus 36 E6
Southmarsh Som 45 G8
South Marston Swindon 63 B7
Southmead Bristol 60 D5
South Merstham Sur 51 C9
South Middleton
Northumb 263 E11
South Milford N Yorks 206 G5
South Millbrex Aberds 303 E8
South Milton Devon 8 G4
South Mimms Herts 86 E2
Southminster Essex 89 F7
South Molton Devon 26 B2
Southmoor Oxon 82 F5
South Moor Durham 242 G5
South Moreton Oxon 64 B5
South Mundham W Sus 22 C5
South Muskham Notts 172 D3
South Newbald E Yorks 208 F4
South Newbarns Cumb 210 F4
South Newington Oxon 101 E8
South Newsham
Northumb 243 B8
South Newton Wilts 46 G5
South Normanton
Derbys 170 D6
South Norwood London 67 F10
South Nutfield Sur 51 D10
South Ockendon Thurrock 68 C5
Southoe Cambs 122 E3
Southolt Suff 126 D3
South Ormsby Lincs 190 F5
Southorpe Pboro 137 C11
South Ossett W Yorks 197 D9
South Otterington
N Yorks 215 B7
Southover Dorset 17 C8
E Sus 36 F6
E Sus 37 B11
South Owersby Lincs 189 C9
Southowram W Yorks 196 C6
South Oxhey Herts 85 G10
South Park Sur 51 D8
South Pelaw Durham 243 G7
South Perrott Dorset 29 F7
South Petherton Som 28 D6
South Petherwin Corn 12 E2
South Pickenham Norf 141 C7
South Pill Corn 7 D8
South Pool Devon 8 G5
South Poorton Dorset 16 B6
Southport Mers 193 D10
South Port Argyll 284 E4
Southpunds Shetland 313 L6
South Quilquox Aberds 303 F8
South Radworthy Devon 41 G9
South Rauceby Lincs 173 F8
South Raynham Norf 159 E7
South Reddish Gtr Man 184 C5
Southrepps Norf 160 B5
South Reston Lincs 190 E6
Southrey Lincs 173 B10
Southrop Glos 81 E11
Oxon 101 E7
Southrope Hants 49 E7
South Ruislip London 66 B6
South Runcton Norf 140 B2
South Scarle Notts 172 C4
Southsea Ptsmth 21 B8
Wrex 166 E4
South Shian Argyll 289 E11
South Shields T&W 243 D9
South Shore Blkpool 202 G2
South Side Durham 233 F8
Orkney 314 D5
South Somercotes Lincs 190 C6
South Stainley N Yorks 214 G6
South Stainmore Cumb 222 C6
South Stanley Durham 242 G5
South Stifford Thurrock 68 D6
Southstoke Bath 61 G8
South Stoke Oxon 64 C6
W Sus 35 F8
South Stour Kent 54 F4
South Street E Sus 36 D5
Kent 54 B5
Kent 68 G6
Kent 69 G10
Kent 70 F6
London 52 B2
South Tawton Devon 13 C9
South Tehidy Corn 4 G3
South Thoresby Lincs 190 F6
South Tidworth Wilts 47 D8
South Tottenham
London 67 B10
Southtown Norf 143 B10
Orkney 314 G4
Som 28 D4
Som 44 F5
South Town Devon 14 E5
Hants 49 F7
South Twerton Bath 61 G8
South Ulverston Cumb 210 D6
South View Hants 48 C6
Southville Devon 8 G4
Torf 78 F3
South Voxter Shetland 313 G5
Southwaite Cumb 230 C4
South Walsham Norf 161 G7
Southwark London 67 D10
South Warnborough
Hants 49 D8
Southwater W Sus 35 B11
Southwater Street
W Sus 35 B11
Southway Plym 7 C9
Som 44 E4
South Weald Essex 87 G9
South Weirs Hants 32 G3
Southwell Dorset 17 G9
Notts 172 E2
South Weston Oxon 84 F2
South Wheatley Corn 11 C10
Notts 188 D3
South Whiteness
Shetland 313 J5
Southwick Hants 33 F10
Northants 137 E10
Som 43 D11
T&W 243 F9
Wilts 45 B10
W Sus 36 F2
South Widcombe Bath 44 B5
South Wigston Leics 135 D11
South Willesborough
Kent 54 E4
South Willingham
Lincs 189 E11
South Wimbledon London 67 E9
South Wingate Durham 234 E4
South Wingfield Derbys 170 D5
South Witham Lincs 155 F8
Southwold Suff 127 B10
South Wonford Devon 24 F5
South Wonston Hants 48 F3
Southwood Derbys 153 E7
Hants 49 B10
Norf 143 B7
Som 44 G5
Worcs 116 E4
South Woodford London 86 G6
South Woodham Ferrers
Essex 88 F4
South Wootton Norf 158 E2
South Wraxall Wilts 61 G10
South Yardley W Mid 134 G2
South Yarrows Highld 310 E7
South Yeo Devon 25 G8
South Zeal Devon 13 C9
Soval Lodge W Isles 304 F5
Sowber Gate N Yorks 215 B7
Sowerby N Yorks 215 C8
W Yorks 196 C4
Sowerby Bridge
W Yorks 196 C5
Sowerby Row Cumb 230 D3
Sower Carr Lancs 202 E3
Sowley Green Suff 124 G4
Sowood W Yorks 196 D5
Sowood Green W Yorks 196 D5
Sowton Devon 14 C5
Sowton Barton Devon 14 D2
Soyal Highld 309 K5
Soyland Town W Yorks 196 C4
Spacey Houses N Yorks 206 C2
Spa Common Norf 160 C5
Spalding Lincs 156 E4
Spaldington E Yorks 207 G11
Spaldwick Cambs 122 C2
Spalford Notts 172 B4
Spanby Lincs 155 B11
Spango Inverclyd 276 G4
Spanish Green Hants 49 B7
Sparham Norf 159 F11
Sparhamhill Norf 159 F11
Spark Bridge Cumb 210 C6
Sparkbrook W Mid 133 G11
Sparkford Som 29 B10
Sparkhill W Mid 133 G11
Sparkwell Devon 7 D11
Sparl Shetland 312 G5
Sparnon Corn 1 E3
Sparnon Gate Corn 4 G3
Sparrow Green Norf 159 G9
Sparrow Hill Som 44 C2
Sparrowpit Derbys 185 E9
Sparrow's Green E Sus 52 G6
Sparsholt Hants 48 G2
Oxon 63 B10
Spartylea Northumb 232 B3
Spath Staffs 151 B11
Spaunton N Yorks 226 G4
Spaxton Som 43 F8
Spean Bridge Highld 290 E4
Spear Hill W Sus 35 D10
Spearywell Hants 32 B4
Speckington Som 29 C9
Speed Gate Kent 68 F5
Speedwell Bristol 60 E6
Speen Bucks 84 F4
W Berks 64 F3
Speeton N Yorks 218 E2
Speke Mers 182 E6
Speldhurst Kent 52 E5
Spellbrook Herts 87 B7
Spelsbury Oxon 101 G7
Spelter Bridgend 57 C11
Spen W Yorks 197 B7
Spencers Wood
Wokingham 65 F8
Spen Green Ches E 168 C4
Spennells Worcs 116 C6
Spennithorne N Yorks 214 B2
Spennymoor Durham 233 E11
Spernall Warks 117 E11
Spetchley Worcs 117 G7
Spetisbury Dorset 30 G6
Spexhall Suff 143 G7
Speybank Highld 291 C10
Spey Bay Moray 302 C3
Speybridge Highld 301 G10
Speyview Moray 302 E2
Spillardsford Aberds 303 D10
Spilsby Lincs 174 B6
Spindlestone Northumb 264 C5
Spinkhill Derbys 187 F7
Spinney Hill Northants 120 E5
Spinney Hills Leicester 136 C2
Spinningdale Highld 309 L6
Spion Kop Notts 171 B9
Spirthill Wilts 62 D3
Spital Mers 182 E4
Windsor 66 D3
Spitalbrook Herts 86 D5
Spitalfields London 67 C10
Spitalhill Derbys 169 F11
Spital Hill S Yorks 187 C10
Spital in the Street
Lincs 189 D7
Spital Tongues T&W 242 D6
Spithurst E Sus 36 D6
Spittal Dumfries 236 D5
E Loth 281 F9
E Yorks 207 C11
Highld 310 D5
Northumb 273 E10
Pembs 91 G9
Stirl 277 D10
Spittalfield Perth 286 C5
Spittal Houses S Yorks 186 B5
Spittal of Glenmuick
Aberds 292 E5
Spittal of Glenshee
Perth 292 F3
Spittlegate Lincs 155 C8
Spixworth Norf 160 F4
Splatt Corn 10 F4
Corn 11 D10
Devon 25 F10
Som 43 F8
Splayne's Green E Sus 36 C6
Splott Cardiff 59 D7
Spofforth N Yorks 206 C3
Spondon Derby 153 B8
Spon End W Mid 118 B6
Spon Green Flint 166 C3
Spooner Row Norf 141 D11
Spoonleygate Shrops 132 D6
Sporle Norf 158 G6
Spotland Bridge
Gtr Man 195 E11
Spott E Loth 282 F3
Spratton Northants 120 C4
Spreakley Sur 49 E10
Spreyton Devon 13 B9
Spriddlestone Devon 7 E10
Spridlington Lincs 189 E8
Sprig's Alley Oxon 84 F3
Springbank Glos 99 G8
Spring Bank Cumb 229 G10
Springboig Glasgow 268 C3
Springbourne Bmouth 19 C8
Springburn Glasgow 268 B2
Spring Cottage Leics 152 F6
Spring End N Yorks 223 F9
Springfield Argyll 275 F11
Caerph 77 F11
Dumfries 239 D8
Essex 88 D2
Fife 287 F7
Gtr Man 194 F5
Highld 300 C6
M Keynes 103 D7
Moray 301 D10
W Mid 133 D8
W Mid 133 F9
W Mid 133 G11
Springfields Stoke 168 G5
Spring Gardens Som 45 D9
Spring Green Lancs 204 E4
Spring Grove London 67 D7
Springhead Gtr Man 196 G3
Springhill E Renf 267 D10
IoW 20 B6
N Lnrk 269 D7
Staffs 133 B11
Staffs 133 C9
Spring Hill Gtr Man 196 F2
Lancs 195 B8
W Mid 133 D7
Springholm Dumfries 237 C10
Springkell Dumfries 239 B7
Spring Park London 67 F11
Springside N Ayrs 257 B9
Springthorpe Lincs 188 D5
Spring Vale S Yorks 197 G9
Spring Valley IoM 192 E4
Springwell Essex 105 C10
T&W 243 F7
T&W 243 F9
Springwells Dumfries 248 E3
Sproatley E Yorks 209 G9
Sproston Green Ches W 168 B2
Sprotbrough S Yorks 198 G4
Sproughton Suff 108 C2
Sprouston Borders 263 B7
Sprowston Norf 160 G4
Sproxton Leics 155 E7
N Yorks 216 C2
Sprunston Cumb 230 B3
Spunhill Shrops 149 C8
Spurlands End Bucks 84 F5
Spurstow Ches E 167 D9
Spurtree Shrops 116 D2
Spynie Moray 302 C2
Spyway Dorset 16 C6
Square and Compass
Pembs 91 E7
Squires Gate Blkpool 202 G2
Sraid Ruadh Argyll 288 E1
Srannda W Isles 296 C6
Sronphadruig Lodge
Perth 291 F9
Stableford Shrops 132 D5
Staffs 150 B6
Stacey Bank S Yorks 186 C3
Stackhouse N Yorks 212 F6
Stackpole Pembs 73 F7
Stackpole Quay Pembs 73 F7
Stacksford Norf 141 E11
Stacksteads Lancs 195 C10
Stackyard Green Suff 107 B9
Staddiscombe Plym 7 E10
Staddlethorpe E Yorks 199 B10
Staddon Devon 24 C3
Devon 24 G5
Staden Derbys 185 G9
Stadhampton Oxon 83 F10
Stadhlaigearraidh
W Isles 297 H3
Stadmorslow Staffs 168 D5
Staffield Cumb 230 C6
Staffin Highld 298 C4
Stafford Staffs 151 E8
Stafford Park Telford 132 B4
Stafford's Corner Essex 89 B7
Stafford's Green Dorset 29 C10
Stagbatch Hereford 115 F9
Stagden Cross Essex 87 C10
Stagehall Borders 271 G9
Stagsden Beds 103 B9
Stagsden West End
Beds 103 B9
Stag's Head Devon 25 B11
Stain Highld 310 C7
Stainburn Cumb 228 F6
N Yorks 205 D10
Stainby Lincs 155 E8
Staincliffe W Yorks 197 C8
Staincross S Yorks 197 E10
Staindrop Durham 233 G8
Staines Green Herts 86 C3
Staines-upon-Thames
Sur 66 E4
Stainfield Lincs 155 D11
Lincs 189 G10
Stainforth N Yorks 212 F6
S Yorks 198 E6
Staining Lancs 202 F3
Stainland W Yorks 196 D5
Stainsacre N Yorks 227 D8
Stainsby Derbys 170 B6
Lincs 190 G4
Stainton Cumb 211 B10
Cumb 230 F5
Cumb 239 F9
Durham 223 B11
Mbro 225 C9
N Yorks 224 F2
S Yorks 187 C9
Stainton by Langworth
Lincs 189 F9
Staintondale N Yorks 227 F9
Stainton le Vale Lincs 189 C11
Stainton with Adgarley
Cumb 210 E5
Stair Cumb 229 G10
E Ayrs 257 E10
Stairfoot S Yorks 197 F11
Stairhaven Dumfries 236 D4
Staithes N Yorks 226 B5
Stakeford Northumb 253 F7
Stake Hill Gtr Man 195 F11
Stakenbridge Worcs 117 B7
Stake Pool Lancs 202 D4
Stalbridge Dorset 30 D2
Stalbridge Weston
Dorset 30 D2
Stalham Norf 161 D7
Stalham Green Norf 161 E7
Stalisfield Green Kent 54 C3
Stallen Dorset 29 D10
Stallingborough
NE Lincs 201 E7
Stalling Busk N Yorks 213 B8
Stallington Staffs 151 B8
Stalmine Lancs 202 D3
Stalmine Moss Side
Lancs 202 D3
Stalybridge Gtr Man 185 B7
Stambermill W Mid 133 G8
Stamborough Som 42 F4
Stambourne Essex 106 D4
Stambourne Green
Essex 106 D4
Stamford Lincs 137 B10
Stamford Bridge
Ches W 167 B7
E Yorks 207 B10
Stamfordham Northumb 242 C3
Stamford Hill London 67 B10
Stamperland E Renf 267 D11
Stamshaw Ptsmth 33 G10
Stanah Cumb 220 B6
Lancs 202 E3
Stanborough Herts 86 C2
Stanbridge C Beds 103 G9
Dorset 31 G8
Stanbridgeford C Beds 103 G9
Stanbrook Essex 106 F2
Worcs 98 B6
Stanbury W Yorks 204 F6
Stand Gtr Man 195 F9
N Lnrk 268 B5
Standburn Falk 279 G8
Standeford Staffs 133 B8
Standen Kent 53 E11
Standen Hall Lancs 203 E10
Standen Street Kent 53 G10
Standerwick Som 45 C10
Standford Hants 49 G10
Standford Bridge
Telford 150 E4
Standingstone Cumb 229 B11
Cumb 229 E7
Standish Glos 80 D4
Gtr Man 194 E5
Standish Lower Ground
Gtr Man 194 F5
Standlake Oxon 82 E5
Standon Hants 32 B6
Herts 105 G7
Staffs 150 B6
Standon Green End Herts 86 B5
Stane N Lnrk 269 D7
Stanecastle N Ayrs 257 B8
Stanfield Norf 159 E8
Stoke 168 E5
Stanford C Beds 104 C3
Kent 54 F6
Norf 141 E7
Shrops 148 G6
Stanford Bishop
Hereford 116 G3
Stanford Bridge Worcs 116 D4
Stanford Dingley
W Berks 64 E5
Stanford End Wokingham 65 G8
Stanford Hills Notts 153 E10
Stanford in the Vale
Oxon 82 G4
Stanford-le-Hope
Thurrock 69 C7
Stanford on Avon
Northants 119 B11
Stanford on Soar Notts 153 E10
Stanford on Teme
Worcs 116 D4
Stanford Rivers Essex 87 E8
Stanfree Derbys 187 G7
Stanground Pboro 138 D4
Stanhill Lancs 195 B8
Stanhoe Norf 158 B6
Stanhope Borders 260 D4
Durham 232 D5
Kent 54 E3
Stanion Northants 137 F8
Stank Cumb 210 E4
Stanklyn Worcs 117 C7
Stanks W Yorks 206 F3
Stanley Derbys 170 G6
Durham 242 G5
Lancs 194 F3
Notts 171 C7
Perth 286 D5
Shrops 132 G3
Shrops 132 G5
Staffs 168 E6
Wilts 62 E3
W Yorks 197 C10
Stanley Common
Derbys 170 G6
Stanley Crook Durham 233 D9
Stanley Downton Glos 80 E4
Stanley Ferry W Yorks 197 C11
Stanley Gate Lancs 194 G2
Stanley Green Ches E 184 E5
Poole 18 C6
Shrops 149 B10
Stanley Hill Hereford 98 C3
Stanley Moor Staffs 168 E6
Stanley Pontlarge Glos 99 E9
Stanleytown Rhondda 77 G8
Stanlow Ches W 182 F6
Staffs 132 D5
Stanmer Brighton 36 F4
Stanmore Hants 33 B7
London 85 G11
Shrops 132 E4
W Berks 64 D3
Stanner Powys 114 F5
Stannergate Dundee 287 D8
Stannersburn Northumb 250 F6
Stanners Hill Sur 66 G3
Stanningfield Suff 125 F7
Stanningley W Yorks 205 G10
Stannington Northumb 242 B6
S Yorks 186 D4
Stanpit Dorset 19 C9
Stansbatch Hereford 114 E6
Stansfield Suff 124 G5
Stanshope Staffs 169 E10
Stanstead Suff 106 B6
Stanstead Abbotts Herts 86 C5
Stansted Kent 68 G6
Stansted Airport Essex 105 G11
Stansted Mountfitchet
Essex 105 G10
Stanthorne Ches W 167 B11
Stanton Glos 99 E11
Mon 96 G6
Northumb 252 F4
Staffs 169 F10
Suff 125 C9
Stantonbury M Keynes 102 C6
Stanton by Bridge
Derbys 153 D7
Stanton-by-Dale Derbys 153 B9
Stanton Chare Suff 125 C9
Stanton Drew Bath 60 G5
Stanton Fitzwarren
Swindon 81 G11
Stanton Gate Notts 153 B9
Stanton Harcourt Oxon 82 D6
Stanton Hill Notts 171 C7
Stanton in Peak Derbys 170 C2
Stanton Lacy Shrops 115 B9
Stanton Lees Derbys 170 C3
Stanton Long Shrops 131 E11
Stanton-on-the-Wolds
Notts 154 C2
Stanton Prior Bath 61 G7
Stanton St Bernard Wilts 62 G5
Stanton St John Oxon 83 D9
Stanton St Quintin Wilts 62 D2
Stanton Street Suff 125 D9
Stanton under Bardon
Leics 153 G9
Stanton upon Hine Heath
Shrops 149 E11
Stanton Wick Bath 60 G6
Stantway Glos 80 C2
Stanwardine in the Fields
Shrops 149 E8
Stanwardine in the Wood
Shrops 149 D8
Stanway Essex 107 G8
Glos 99 E11
Stanway Green Essex 107 G9
Suff 126 C4
Stanwell Sur 66 E5
Stanwell Moor Sur 66 E4
Stanwick Northants 121 C9
Stanwick-St-John
N Yorks 224 C3
Stanwix Cumb 239 F10
Stanycliffe Gtr Man 195 F11
Stanydale Shetland 313 H4
Staoinebrig W Isles 297 H3
Stape N Yorks 226 G5
Stapehill Dorset 31 G9
Stapeley Ches E 167 F11
Stapenhill Staffs 152 E5
Staple Kent 55 B9
Som 42 E6
Staplecross E Sus 38 C3
Staple Cross Devon 27 C8
Staplefield W Sus 36 B3
Staple Fitzpaine Som 28 D3
Stapleford Cambs 123 G9
Herts 86 B4
Leics 154 F6
Lincs 172 D5
Notts 153 B9
Wilts 46 F5
Stapleford Abbotts Essex 87 G8
Stapleford Tawney Essex 87 F8
Staplegrove Som 28 B2
Staplehay Som 28 C2
Staple Hill S Glos 61 D7
Worcs 117 C9
Staplehurst Kent 53 E9
Staple Lawns Som 28 D3
Staplers IoW 20 D6
Staples Hill W Sus 35 B8
Staplestreet Kent 70 G5
Stapleton Bristol 60 D6
Cumb 240 C2
Hereford 114 D6
Leics 135 D8
N Yorks 198 D4
N Yorks 224 C5
Shrops 131 C9
Som 29 C7
Stapley Som 27 E11
Staploe Beds 122 E2
Staplow Hereford 98 C3
Stapness Shetland 313 J4
Star Fife 287 G7
Pembs 92 E4
Som 44 B2
Stara Orkney 314 D2
Starbeck N Yorks 206 B2
Starbotton N Yorks 213 E9
Starcross Devon 14 E5
Stareton Warks 118 C6
Stargate T&W 242 E5
Star Hill Mon 79 E7
Starkholmes Derbys 170 D4
Starling Gtr Man 195 E9
Starlings Green Essex 105 E9
Starr's Green E Sus 38 D3
Starston Norf 142 G4
Start Devon 8 G6
Startforth Durham 223 B10
Start Hill Essex 105 G10
Startley Wilts 62 C2
Startop's End Bucks 84 C6
Starveall S Glos 61 B9
Starvecrow Kent 52 D5
Statenborough Kent 55 B10
Statford St Andrew Suff 127 E7
Statham Warr 183 D11
Stathe Som 28 B5
Stathern Leics 154 C5
Station Hill Cumb 229 B11
Station Town Durham 234 D4
Statland Common
Norf 141 D10
Staughton Green Cambs 122 D2
Staughton Highway
Cambs 122 E2
Staughton Moor Beds 122 E2
Staunton Glos 79 C8
Glos 98 F5
Staunton in the Vale
Notts 172 G4
Staunton on Arrow
Hereford 115 E7
Staunton on Wye
Hereford 97 B7
Staupes N Yorks 205 B10
Staveley Cumb 211 B7
Cumb 221 F9
Derbys 186 G6
N Yorks 215 G7
Staveley-in-Cartmel
Cumb 211 B7
Staverton Devon 8 C5
Glos 99 G7
Northants 119 E10
Wilts 61 G11
Staverton Bridge Glos 99 G7
Stawell Som 43 F11
Stawley Som 27 C9
Staxigoe Highld 310 D7
Staxton N Yorks 217 D10
Staylittle Ceredig 128 F2
Staylittle / Penffordd-Lâs
Powys 129 E7
Staynall Lancs 202 E3
Staythorpe Notts 172 E3
Stead W Yorks 205 D8
Steam Mills Glos 79 B10
Stean N Yorks 213 E11
Steanbow Som 44 F5
Stearsby N Yorks 216 E2
Steart Som 29 B9
Som 43 D9
Stebbing Essex 106 G3
Stebbing Green Essex 106 G3
Stechford W Mid 134 F2
Stede Quarter Kent 53 F11
Stedham W Sus 34 C5
Steel Northumb 241 F10
Northumb 251 G9
Steel Bank S Yorks 186 D4
Steel Cross E Sus 52 G4
Steelend Fife 279 C10
Steele Road Borders 250 E2
Steeleroad-end Borders 250 E2
Steel Green Cumb 210 D3
Steel Heath Shrops 149 B10
Steen's Bridge
Hereford 115 F11
Steep Hants 34 B2
Steephill IoW 21 F7
Steep Lane W Yorks 196 C4
Steeple Dorset 18 E4
Essex 88 E6
Steeple Ashton Wilts 46 B2
Steeple Aston Oxon 101 F9
Steeple Barton Oxon 101 G8
Steeple Bumpstead
Essex 106 C3
Steeple Claydon Bucks 102 F3
Steeple Gidding Cambs 138 G2
Steeple Langford Wilts 46 F4
Steeple Morden Cambs 104 C5
Steep Marsh Hants 34 B3
Steeraway Telford 132 B3
Steeton W Yorks 204 E6
Stein Highld 298 D2
Steinmanhill Aberds 303 E7
Stella T&W 242 E5
Stelling Minnis Kent 54 D6
Stelvio Newport 59 B9
Stembridge Som 28 C6
Swansea 56 C3
Stemster Highld 310 C5
Stemster Ho Highld 310 C5
Stenalees Corn 5 D10
Stenaquoy Orkney 314 C5
Stencoose Corn 4 F4
Stenhill Devon 27 E9
Stenhouse Dumfries 247 E8
Edin 280 G4
Stenhousemuir Falk 279 E7
Stenigot Lincs 190 E3
Stennack Corn 2 B5
Stenness Shetland 312 F4
Stenscholl Highld 298 C4
Stenso Orkney 314 D3
Stenson Derbys 152 D6
Stenton E Loth 282 G2
Fife 280 B5
Stentwood Devon 27 F10
Stenwith Lincs 154 B6
Stepaside Corn 5 F9
Pembs 73 D10
Powys 129 F11
Stepping Hill Gtr Man 184 D6
Steppingley C Beds 103 D10
Stepps N Lnrk 268 B3
Sterndale Moor Derbys 169 B10
Sternfield Suff 127 E7
Sterridge Devon 40 D5
Stert Wilts 46 B4
Sterte Poole 18 C6
Stetchworth Cambs 124 F2
Stevenage Herts 104 G4
Steven's Crouch E Sus 38 D2
Stevenston N Ayrs 266 G5
Stevenstone Devon 25 D8
Steventon Hants 48 D4
Oxon 83 G7
Shrops 115 C10
Steventon End Essex 105 C11
Stevington Beds 121 G9
Stewards Essex 87 D7
Steward's Green Essex 87 E7
Stewartby Beds 103 C10
Stewarton Argyll 255 F7
E Ayrs 267 F8
Stewkley Bucks 103 F7
Stewkley Dean Bucks 102 F6
Stewley Som 28 D4
Stewton Lincs 190 D5
Steyne Cross IoW 21 D8
Steyning W Sus 35 E11
Steynton Pembs 72 D6
Stibb Corn 24 E2
Stibbard Norf 159 D9
Stibb Cross Devon 24 E6
Stibb Green Wilts 63 G8
Stibbington Cambs 137 D11
Stichill Borders 262 B6
Sticker Corn 5 E9
Stickford Lincs 174 D5
Stick Hill Kent 52 E3
Sticklepath Devon 13 C8
Devon 40 G5
Som 28 E4
Som 42 F4
Sticklinch Som 44 F5
Stickling Green Essex 105 E9
Stickney Lincs 174 D4
Stiffkey Norf 177 E7
Stifford's Bridge Hereford 98 B4
Stiff Street Kent 69 G11
Stileway Som 44 E3
Stillingfleet N Yorks 207 E7
Stillington N Yorks 215 F11
Stockton 234 G3
Stilton Cambs 138 F3
Stinchcombe Glos 80 F2
Stinsford Dorset 17 C10
Stiperstones Shrops 131 C7
Stirchley Telford 132 B4
W Mid 133 G11
Stirkoke Ho Highld 310 D7
Stirling Aberds 303 E11
Stirl 278 C5
Stirtloe Cambs 122 D3
Stirton N Yorks 204 C5
Stisted Essex 106 G5
Stitchcombe Wilts 63 F8
Stitchin's Hill Worcs 116 G5
Stithians Corn 2 B6
Stittenham Highld 300 B6
Stivichall W Mid 118 B6
Stixwould Lincs 173 B11
Stoak Ches W 182 G6
Stobhill Northumb 252 G6
Stobhillgate Northumb 252 F6
Stobieside S Lnrk 258 B4
Stobo Borders 260 B5
Stoborough Dorset 18 D4
Stoborough Green
Dorset 18 D4
Stobs Castle Borders 250 B2
Stobshiel E Loth 271 C9
Stobswood Northumb 252 E6
Stock Essex 87 F11
Lancs 204 D3
N Som 60 G3
Stockbridge Hants 47 G11
S Yorks 198 F5
W Sus 22 C5
W Yorks 205 E7
Stockbridge Village
Mers 182 C6
Stockbury Kent 69 G10
Stockcross W Berks 64 F2
Stockend Glos 80 D4
Stocker's Head Kent 54 C3
Stockerston Leics 136 D6
Stockfield W Mid 134 G2
Stock Green Worcs 117 F9
Stockheath Hants 22 B2
Stock Hill Suff 125 D9
Stockholes Turbary
N Lincs 199 F9
Stockiemuir Stirl 277 E10
Stocking Hereford 98 E2
Stockingford Warks 134 E6
Stocking Green Essex 105 D11
Stocking Pelham Herts 105 F9
Stockland Devon 28 G2
Stockland Bristol Som 43 E8
Stockland Green Kent 52 E5
W Mid 133 E11
Stockleigh English Devon 26 F5
Stockleigh Pomeroy
Devon 26 G5
Stockley Wilts 62 F4
Stocklinch Som 28 D5
Stockport Gtr Man 184 C5
Stocksbridge S Yorks 186 B3
Stocksfield Northumb 242 E3
Stocks Green Kent 52 D5
Stockstreet Essex 106 G6
Stockton Hereford 115 E10
Norf 143 E7
Shrops 130 C5
Shrops 132 D4
Telford 150 F5
Warks 119 E8
Wilts 46 F3
Stockton Brook Staffs 168 E6
Stockton Heath Warr 183 D10
Stockton-on-Tees
Stockton 225 B8
Stockton on Teme
Worcs 116 D4
Stockton on the Forest
York 207 B9
Stocktonwood Shrops 130 C5
Stockwell Devon 27 G7
Glos 80 C6
London 67 D10
Stockwell End W Mid 133 C7
Stockwell Heath Staffs 151 E11
Stockwitch Cross Som 29 C9
Stockwood Bristol 60 F6
Dorset 29 F9
Stock Wood Worcs 117 F10
Stockwood Vale Bath 60 F6
Stodday Lancs 202 B5
Stodmarsh Kent 71 G8
Stody Norf 159 C11
Stoer Highld 307 G5
Stoford Som 29 E9
Wilts 46 F5
Stoford Water Devon 27 F9
Stogumber Som 42 F5
Stogursey Som 43 E8
Stoke Devon 24 C2
Hants 22 C2
Hants 48 C2
Medway 69 D10
Plym 7 D9
Suff 108 C3
W Mid 119 B7
Stoke Abbott Dorset 29 G7
Stoke Albany Northants 136 F6
Stoke Aldermoor
W Mid 119 B7
Stoke Ash Suff 126 C2
Stoke Bardolph Notts 171 G10
Stoke Bishop Bristol 60 D5
Stoke Bliss Worcs 116 E3
Stoke Bruerne Northants 102 B4
Stoke by Clare Suff 106 C4
Stoke-by-Nayland Suff 107 D9

Durham 233 E10
Todlachie Aberds 293 B8
Todmorden W Yorks 196 C2
Todpool Corn 4 G4
Todrig Borders 261 F10
Todwick S Yorks 187 E7
Toft Cambs 123 F7
Lincs 155 F11
Shetland 312 F6
Warks 119 C9
Toft Hill Durham 233 F9
Lincs 174 C2
Toft Monks Norf 143 E8
Toft next Newton Lincs 189 D8
Toftrees Norf 159 D7
Tofts Highld 310 C7
Toftshaw W Yorks 197 B7
Toftwood Norf 159 G9
Togston Northumb 252 C6
Tokavaig Highld 295 D8
Tokers Green Oxon 65 D8
Tokyngton London 67 C7
Tolastadh a Chaolais
W Isles 304 E3
Tolastadh bho Thuath
W Isles 304 D7
Tolborough Corn 11 F9
Tolcarne Corn 2 B5
Corn 2 C5
Tolcarne Wartha Corn 2 B5
Toldish Corn 5 D8
Tolgus Mount Corn 4 G3
Tolhurst E Sus 53 G7
Tolladine Worcs 117 F7
Tolland Som 42 G6
Tollard Farnham Dorset 30 D6
Tollard Royal Wilts 30 D6
Toll Bar Mers 183 C7
Rutland 137 B10
S Yorks 198 F5
Tollbar End W Mid 119 B7
Toll End W Mid 133 E9
Tollerford Dorset 17 B7
Toller Fratrum Dorset 17 B7
Toller Porcorum Dorset 17 B7
Tollerton Notts 154 C2
N Yorks 215 G10
Toller Whelme Dorset 29 G8
Tollesbury Essex 89 C7
Tollesby Mbro 225 B10
Tolleshunt D'Arcy Essex 88 C6
Tolleshunt Knights Essex 88 C6
Tolleshunt Major Essex 88 C5
Tollie Highld 300 D5
Toll of Birness Aberds 303 F10
Tolm W Isles 304 E6
Tolmers Herts 86 E4
Tolpuddle Dorset 17 C11
Tolskithy Corn 4 G3
Tolvaddon Downs Corn 4 G3
Tolvah Highld 291 D10
Tolworth London 67 F7
Tomaknock Perth 286 E2
Tom an Fhuadain
W Isles 305 G5
Tomatin Highld 301 G8
Tombreck Highld 300 F6
Tombui Perth 286 B2
Tomchrasky Highld 290 B4
Tomdoun Highld 290 C3
Tomich Highld 300 B6
Highld 300 G3
Tomich House Highld 300 E5
Tomintoul Aberds 292 D3
Moray 292 B3
Tomlow Warks 119 E9
Tomnaven Moray 302 F4
Tomnavoulin Moray 302 G2
Tomperrow Corn 4 G5
Tompkin Staffs 168 E6
Tompset's Bank E Sus 52 G2
Tomsleibhe Argyll 289 F8
Tomthorn Derbys 185 F9
Ton Mon 78 F5
Ton Breigam V Glam 58 D3
Tonbridge Kent 52 D5
Tonderghie Dumfries 236 F6
Tondu Bridgend 57 E11
Tone Som 27 C10
Tonedale Som 27 C10
Tone Green Som 27 C11
Tong Kent 53 D10
Shrops 132 B5
W Yorks 205 G10
Tonge Leics 153 E8
Tonge Corner Kent 70 F2
Tonge Fold Gtr Man 195 F8
Tonge Moor Gtr Man 195 E8
Tong Forge Shrops 132 B5
Tong Green Kent 54 C3
Tongham Sur 49 D11
Tongland Dumfries 237 D8
Tong Norton Shrops 132 B5
Tong Park W Yorks 205 F9
Tong Street W Yorks 205 G9
Tongue Highld 308 D5
Tongue End Lincs 156 F3
Tongwell M Keynes 103 C7
Tongwynlais Cardiff 58 C6
Tonmawr Neath 57 B10
Tonna / Tonnau Neath 57 B9
Tonnau / Tonna Neath 57 B9
Ton-Pentre Rhondda 77 F7
Ton-teg Rhondda 58 B5
Tontine Lancs 194 G4
Tonwell Herts 86 B4
Tonypandy Rhondda 77 G7
Ton-y-pistyll Caerph 77 F11
Tonyrefail Rhondda 58 B4
Toot Baldon Oxon 83 E9
Toothill Hants 32 D5
Swindon 62 C6
W Yorks 196 C6
Toot Hill Essex 87 E8
Staffs 169 G9
Tooting Graveney London 67 E9
Topcliffe N Yorks 215 D8
W Yorks 197 B9
Topcroft Norf 142 E5
Topcroft Street Norf 142 E5
Top End Beds 121 E10
Top Green Notts 172 F3
Topham S Yorks 198 D6
Topleigh W Sus 34 D6
Top Lock Gtr Man 194 F6
Top of Hebers Gtr Man 195 F11
Top o' th' Lane Lancs 194 C5
Top o' th' Meadows
Gtr Man 196 F3
Toppesfield Essex 106 D4
Toppings Gtr Man 195 E8
Toprow Norf 142 D3
Topsham Devon 14 D5
Top Valley Nottingham 171 F9
Torbeg N Ayrs 255 E10
Torboll Farm Highld 309 K7
Torbothie N Lnrk 269 D7
Torbreck Highld 309 J7
Torbrex Stirl 278 C5
Torbryan Devon 8 B6
Torbush N Lnrk 268 D6
Torcross Devon 8 G6
Torcroy Highld 291 D9
Tore Highld 300 D6
Torfrey Corn 6 E2
Torgyle Highld 290 B5
Torinturk Argyll 275 G9
Torkington Gtr Man 184 D6
Torksey Lincs 188 F4
Torlum W Isles 296 F3
Torlundy Highld 290 F3
Tormarton S Glos 61 D9
Tormisdale Argyll 254 B2
Tormitchell S Ayrs 244 E6
Tormore Highld 295 E8
N Ayrs 255 D9
Tornagrain Highld 301 E7
Tornahaish Aberds 292 C4
Tornapress Highld 299 E8
Tornaveen Aberds 293 C8
Torness Highld 300 G5
Toronto Durham 233 E9
Torpenhow Cumb 229 D10
Torphichen W Loth 279 G9
Torphin Edin 270 B4
Torphins Aberds 293 C8
Torpoint Corn 7 E8
Torquay Torbay 9 C8
Torquhan Borders 271 F8
Torr Devon 7 E11
Devon 8 C2
Torra Argyll 254 B4
Torran Argyll 275 C9
Highld 298 E5
Highld 301 B7
Torrance E Dunb 278 G2
Torrans Argyll 288 G6
Torranyard N Ayrs 267 G7
Torre Som 42 E4
Torbay 9 C8
Torridon Highld 299 D9
Torridon Ho Highld 299 D8
Torries Aberds 293 B8
Torrin Highld 295 C7
Torrisdale Highld 308 C6
Torrisdale Castle Argyll 255 D8
Torrisdale-Square
Argyll 255 D8
Torrish Highld 311 H3
Torrisholme Lancs 211 G9
Torroble Highld 309 J5
Torroy Highld 309 K5
Torrpark Corn 11 D10
Torry Aberdeen 293 C11
Aberds 302 F4
Torryburn Fife 279 D10
Torsonce Borders 271 G9
Torsonce Mains Borders 271 G9
Torterston Aberds 303 E10
Torthorwald Dumfries 238 B2
Tortington W Sus 35 F8
Torton Worcs 116 C6
Tortworth S Glos 80 G2
Torvaig Highld 298 E4
Torver Cumb 220 G5
Torwood Falk 278 E6
Torwoodlee Mains
Borders 261 B11
Torworth Notts 187 D11
Tosberry Devon 24 C3
Toscaig Highld 295 B9
Toseland Cambs 122 E4
Tosside N Yorks 203 B11
Tostock Suff 125 E9
Totaig Highld 295 C10
Highld 298 D2
Totardor Highld 294 B5
Tote Highld 298 E4
Totegan Highld 310 C2
Tote Hill Hants 32 C4
W Sus 34 C5
Totford Hants 48 F5
Totham Hill Essex 88 C5
Totham Plains Essex 88 C5
Tothill Lincs 190 E6
Tot Hill Hants 64 G3
Totland IoW 20 D2
Totley S Yorks 186 F4
Totley Brook S Yorks 186 E4
Totley Rise S Yorks 186 E4
Totmonslow Staffs 151 B9
Totnell Dorset 29 F10
Totnes Devon 8 C6
Totnor Hereford 97 E11
Toton Notts 153 C10
Totronald Argyll 288 D3
Totscore Highld 298 C3
Tottenham London 86 G4
Tottenham Hale London 67 B10
Tottenhill Norf 158 G2
Tottenhill Row Norf 158 G2
Totteridge Bucks 84 G5
London 86 G2
Totternhoe C Beds 103 G9
Totteroak S Glos 61 C8
Totterton Shrops 131 F7
Totties W Yorks 197 F7
Tottington Gtr Man 195 E9
Norf 141 D7
Tottlebank Cumb 210 C6
Tottleworth Lancs 203 G10
Totton Hants 32 E5
Touchen End Windsor 65 D11
Toulston N Yorks 206 E5
Toulton Som 43 G7
Toulvaddie Highld 311 L2
Tournaig Highld 307 L3
Toux Aberds 303 D9
Tovil Kent 53 C9
Towan Corn 10 G3
Towan Cross Corn 4 F4
Toward Argyll 266 B2
Towcester Northants 102 B3
Towednack Corn 1 B5
Towerage Bucks 84 G4
Tower End Norf 158 F3
Tower Hamlets Kent 55 E10
Towerhead N Som 44 B2
Tower Hill Ches E 184 F6
Devon 12 C3
Essex 108 E5
Herts 85 E8
Mers 194 G2
Sur 51 D7
W Mid 133 E11
W Sus 35 B11
Towersey Oxon 84 D2
Tow House Northumb 241 E7
Towie Aberds 292 B6
Aberds 302 G5
Aberds 303 C8
Towiemore Moray 302 E3
Tow Law Durham 233 D8
Town Barton Devon 14 C2
Townend Derbys 185 E9
Staffs 151 B9
W Dunb 277 F8
Town End Bucks 84 F3
Cambs 139 D8
Cumb 211 B7
Cumb 211 C8
Cumb 212 C2
Cumb 220 D6
Cumb 221 E8
Cumb 221 F7
Cumb 231 F8
Derbys 185 F11
E Yorks 207 C10
Mers 183 D7
W Yorks 196 D5
Townfield Durham 232 B5
Town Fields Ches W 167 B10
Towngate Cumb 230 B6
Lincs 156 G2
Town Green Gtr Man 183 B9
Lancs 194 F2
Norf 161 G7
Townhead Argyll 275 G11
Cumb 229 D7
Cumb 230 D6
Cumb 231 E8
Dumfries 237 E8
N Lnrk 268 B4
Northumb 251 E9
S Ayrs 244 C6
S Yorks 186 E4
S Yorks 197 G7
Town Head Cumb 220 D6
Cumb 221 E8
Cumb 222 C2
Cumb 222 C3
Cumb 231 F7
Cumb 231 F8
Cumb 231 G8
Cumb 231 G9
Derbys 185 F11
N Yorks 204 B2
N Yorks 212 F5
Staffs 169 F8
W Yorks 204 D6
Townhead of Greenlaw
Dumfries 237 C9
Townhill Fife 280 D2
Swansea 56 C6
Townhill Park Hants 33 E7
Town Kelloe Durham 234 D3
Townlake Devon 12 G4
Townland Green Kent 54 G2
Town Lane Gtr Man 183 B11
Town Littleworth E Sus 36 D6
Town of Lowton Mers 183 B10
Town Park Telford 132 B3
Town Row E Sus 52 G5
Townsend Bath 44 B5
Bucks 84 D2
Devon 25 B10
Herts 85 D10
Oxon 63 B11
Pembs 72 D4
Som 44 C4
Stoke 168 F6
Wilts 46 B3
Wilts 46 B4
Towns End Hants 48 B5
Som 30 D2
Town's End Bucks 102 G2
Dorset 18 B3
Dorset 18 E5
Dorset 29 F9
Som 45 D7
Townsend Fold Lancs 195 C10
Townshend Corn 2 C3
Town Street Glos 98 F6
Townwell S Glos 79 G11
Town Yetholm Borders 263 D8
Towthorpe E Yorks 217 G8
York 207 B8
Towton N Yorks 206 F5
Towyn Conwy 181 F7
Toxteth Mers 182 D5
Toynton All Saints Lincs 174 C5
Toynton Fen Side Lincs 174 C5
Toynton St Peter Lincs 174 C6
Toy's Hill Kent 52 C3
Trabboch E Ayrs 257 E10
Traboe Corn 2 E6
Trabrown Borders 271 F10
Tracebridge Som 27 C9
Tradespark Highld 301 D8
Orkney 314 F4
Trafford Park Gtr Man 184 B3
Traigh Ho Highld 295 F8
Trallong Powys 95 F9
Trallwn Rhondda 77 G9
Swansea 57 B7
Tramagenna Corn 11 E7
Tram Inn Hereford 97 E9
Tranch Torf 78 E3
Tranent E Loth 281 G8
Tranmere Mers 182 D4
Trantlebeg Highld 310 D2
Trantlemore Highld 310 D2
Tranwell Northumb 252 G5
Trapp Carms 75 B11
Traprain E Loth 281 F11
Trap's Green Warks 118 D2
Trapshill W Berks 63 G11
Traquair Borders 261 C8
Trash Green W Berks 65 F7
Travellers' Rest Carms 74 B5
Trawden Lancs 204 F4
Trawscoed Powys 95 E11
Trawsfynydd Gwyn 146 B4
Trawsnant Ceredig 111 D11
Treadam Mon 78 B5
Treaddow Hereford 97 G10
Treal Corn 2 F6
Trealaw Rhondda 77 G8
Treales Lancs 202 G4
Trearddur Anglesey 178 F3
Treaslane Highld 298 D3
Treath Corn 3 D7
Treator Corn 10 F4
Tre-Aubrey V Glam 58 E4
Trebanog Rhondda 77 G8
Trebanos Neath 76 E2
Trebarber Corn 5 C7
Trebartha Corn 11 F11
Trebarwith Corn 11 D7
Trebarwith Strand Corn 10 D6
Trebeath Corn 11 D11
Tre-Beferad V Glam 58 F3
Trebell Green Corn 5 C11
Treberfydd Powys 96 F2
Trebetherick Corn 10 F4
Trebilcock Corn 5 C9
Treble's Holford Som 43 G7
Tre-boeth Swansea 57 B7
Treborough Som 42 F4
Trebudannon Corn 5 C7
Trebullett Corn 12 F2
Treburgett Corn 11 F7
Treburgie Corn 6 C4
Treburley Corn 12 F3
Treburrick Corn 10 G3
Trebyan Corn 5 C11
Trecastle Powys 95 F7
Trecenydd Caerph 58 B6
Trecott Devon 25 G10
Trecwn Pembs 91 E9
Trecynon Rhondda 77 E7
Tredannick Corn 10 G6
Tredaule Corn 11 E10
Tredavoe Corn 1 D5
Treddiog Pembs 91 F7
Tredegar Bl Gwent 77 D10
Trederwen Powys 148 F5
Tre-derwen Powys 148 F4
Tredethy Corn 11 G7
Tredington Glos 99 F8
Warks 100 C5
Tredinnick Corn 1 C4
Corn 5 D10
Corn 6 B3
Corn 6 D4
Corn 10 G4
Tredogan V Glam 58 F5
Tredomen Caerph 77 G10
Powys 96 E2
Tredown Devon 24 D2
Tredrizzick Corn 10 F5
Tredunnock Mon 78 G5
Tredustan Powys 96 E2
Tredworth Glos 80 B4
Treen Corn 1 B4
Corn 1 E3
Treesmill Corn 5 D11
Treeton S Yorks 186 D6
Trefaes Gwyn 144 C5
Trefanny Hill Corn 6 D4
Trefasser Pembs 91 D7
Trefdraeth Anglesey 178 G6
Trefdraeth / Newport
Pembs 91 D11
Trefecca Powys 96 E2
Trefechan Ceredig 111 A11
M Tydf 77 D8
Wrex 166 F3
Trefeglwys Powys 129 E9
Trefeitha Powys 96 E2
Trefenter Ceredig 112 D2
Treffgarne Pembs 91 G9
Treffynnon Pembs 90 F6
Treffynnon / Holywell
Flint 181 F11
Trefgarn Owen Pembs 91 F7
Trefil Bl Gwent 77 C10
Trefilan Ceredig 111 F11
Trefin / Trevine Pembs 90 E6
Treflach Shrops 148 D5
Trefnanney Powys 148 F4
Trefnant Denb 181 G9
Trefonen Shrops 148 D5
Trefor Anglesey 178 E5
Gwyn 162 F5
Treforda Corn 11 E7
Treforest Rhondda 58 B5
Treforgan Ceredig 92 B4
Tre-Forgan Neath 76 D3
Treforys / Morriston
Swansea 57 B7
Trefriw Conwy 164 C3
Trefrize Corn 12 F2
Tref y Clawdd / Knighton
Powys 114 C5
Trefynwy / Monmouth
Mon 79 C8
Tregada Corn 12 E2
Tregadgwith Corn 1 D4
Tregadillett Corn 12 E2
Tre-gagle Mon 79 D8
Tregaian Anglesey 178 F6
Tregajorran Corn 4 G3
Tregamere Corn 5 C8
Tregardock Corn 10 E6
Tregare Mon 78 C6
Tregarland Corn 6 D5
Tregarlandbridge Corn 6 D4
Tregarne Corn 3 E7
Tregaron Ceredig 112 F3
Tregarrick Mill Corn 6 D4
Tregarth Gwyn 163 B10
Tregath Gwyn 163 B10
Tregatillian Corn 5 C8
Tregatta Corn 11 D7
Tregavarah Corn 1 D4
Tregear Corn 2 E5
Tregeare Corn 11 D10
Tregeiriog Wrex 148 C3
Tregele Anglesey 178 C5
Tregellist Corn 10 F6
Tregeseal Corn 1 C3
Tregew Corn 3 C8
Tre-Gibbon Rhondda 77 E7
Tregidden Corn 3 E7
Treginnis Pembs 90 G4
Treglemais Pembs 90 F6
Tregole Corn 11 B9
Tregolls Corn 2 B6
Tregolwyn / Colwinston
V Glam 58 D2
Tregona Corn 5 B7
Tregonce Corn 10 G4
Tregonetha Corn 5 C9
Tregonna Corn 10 G4
Tregonning Corn 5 D7
Tregony Corn 5 G8
Tregoodwell Corn 11 E8
Tregorden Corn 10 G6
Tregorrick Corn 5 E10
Tregoss Corn 5 C9
Tregoyd Powys 96 D4
Tregoyd Mill Powys 96 D3
Tregreenwell Corn 11 E7
Tregrehan Mills Corn 5 E10
Tregroes Ceredig 93 C8
Tregullon Corn 5 C11
Tregunna Corn 10 G5
Tregurrian Corn 5 B7
Tregurtha Downs Corn 2 C2
Tre Gwyr / Gowerton
Swansea 56 B5
Tregyddulan Pembs 91 D7
Tregynon Powys 129 D11
Trehafod Rhondda 77 G8
Trehafren Powys 129 E11
Trehan Corn 7 D8
Treharris M Tydf 77 F9
Trehemborne Corn 10 G3
Treherbert Rhondda 76 F6
Tre-hill V Glam 58 E5
Trehunist Corn 6 C6
Tre-Ifor Rhondda 77 D7
Trekeivesteps Corn 11 G10
Trekenner Corn 12 F2
Trekenning Corn 5 C8
Treknow Corn 11 D7
Trelales / Laleston
Bridgend 57 F11
Trelan Corn 2 F6
Tre-lan Flint 165 B11
Trelash Corn 11 C9
Trelassick Corn 5 E7
Trelawnyd Flint 181 F9
Treleddyd-fawr Pembs 90 F5
Treleigh Corn 4 G4
Treletert / Letterston
Pembs 91 F8
Trelew Corn 3 B8
Trelewis M Tydf 77 F10
Treligga Corn 11 E7
Trelights Corn 10 F5
Trelill Corn 10 F6
Trelion Corn 5 E8
Treliske Corn 4 F6
Trelissick Corn 3 B8
Treliver Corn 5 B9
Trellech Mon 79 D8
Trelleck Grange Mon 79 E7
Trelogan Flint 181 E10
Treloquithack Corn 2 D5
Trelowia Corn 6 D5
Trelowth Corn 5 E9
Trelystan Powys 130 C5
Tremadog Gwyn 163 G9
Tremail Corn 11 D9
Tremain Ceredig 92 B4
Tremaine Corn 11 D10
Tremains Bridgend 58 D2
Tremar Corn 6 B5
Trematon Corn 7 D7
Trematon Castle Corn 7 D8
Tremayne Corn 2 B4
Trembraze Corn 6 B5
Tremedda Corn 1 B5
Tremeirchion Denb 181 G9
Tremethick Cross Corn 1 C4
Tremore Corn 5 C10
Tremorebridge Corn 5 C10
Tremorfa Cardiff 59 D8
Tre-Mostyn Flint 181 F10
Trenance Corn 4 C6
Corn 5 B7
Corn 5 C9
Corn 10 G4
Trenant Corn 6 B4
Corn 10 G5
Trenarren Corn 5 F10
Trenay Corn 6 B3
Trench Telford 150 G3
Trench Green Oxon 65 D7
Trench Wood Kent 52 D5
Trencreek Corn 4 C6
Trencrom Corn 2 B2
Trendeal Corn 5 E7
Trenear Corn 2 C5
Treneglos Corn 11 D10
Trenerth Corn 2 B4
Trenewan Corn 6 E3
Trengune Corn 11 C9
Trenhorne Corn 11 F11
Treningle Corn 5 B10
Treninnick Corn 4 C6
Trenoon Corn 2 F6
Trenoweth Corn 3 C7
Trent Dorset 29 D9
Trentham Stoke 168 G5
Trentishoe Devon 40 D6
Trentlock Derbys 153 C9
Trent Vale Stoke 168 G5
Trenwheal Corn 2 C4
Treoes V Glam 58 D2
Treopert / Granston
Pembs 91 E7
Treorchy / Treorci
Rhondda 77 F7
Treorci / Treorchy
Rhondda 77 F7
Treowen Caerph 78 F2
Powys 130 E2
Tre-pit V Glam 58 E2
Trequite Corn 10 F6
Tre'r-ddôl Ceredig 128 E3
Trerhyngyll V Glam 58 D4
Trerise Corn 2 F6
Trer llai / Leighton
Powys 130 B4
Trerose Corn 3 D7
Trerulefoot Corn 6 D6
Tresaith Ceredig 110 G5
Tresamble Corn 3 B7
Tresarrett Corn 11 G7
Tresavean Corn 2 B6
Tresawle Corn 5 F7
Tresawsen Corn 4 F5
Trescoll Corn 5 C10
Trescott Staffs 132 D6
Trescowe Corn 2 C3
Tresean Corn 4 D5
Tresevern Croft Corn 2 B6
Tresham Glos 80 G3
Tresigin / Sigingstone
V Glam 58 E3
Tresillian Corn 5 F7
Tresimwn / Bonvilston
V Glam 58 E5
Tresinney Corn 11 E8
Tresinwen Pembs 91 C7
Treskerby Corn 4 G4
Treskillard Corn 2 B5
Treskilling Corn 5 D10
Treskinnick Cross Corn 11 B10
Treslothan Corn 2 B5
Tresmeer Corn 11 D10
Tresowes Green Corn 2 D3
Tresoweshill Corn 2 D4
Tresparrett Corn 11 C8
Tresparrett Posts Corn 11 C8
Tressady Highld 309 J7
Tressait Perth 291 G10
Tresta Shetland 312 D8
Shetland 313 H5
Treswell Notts 188 F3
Treswithian Corn 4 G2
Treswithian Downs Corn 4 G2
Tre-Taliesin Ceredig 128 E3
Trethellan Water Corn 2 B6
Trethevy Corn 11 D7
Trethewell Corn 3 B9
Trethewey Corn 1 E3
Trethillick Corn 10 F4
Trethomas Caerph 59 B7
Trethosa Corn 5 E8
Trethowel Corn 5 E10
Trethurgy Corn 5 D10
Tretio Pembs 90 F5
Tretire Hereford 97 G10
Tretower Powys 96 G3
Treuddyn Flint 166 D3
Trevadlock Corn 11 F11
Trevalga Corn 11 D7
Trevalgan Corn 1 A5
Trevalyn Wrex 166 D5
Trevance Corn 10 G4
Trevanger Corn 10 F5
Trevanson Corn 10 G5
Trevarrack Corn 1 C5
Trevarren Corn 5 C8
Trevarrian Corn 4 B6
Trevarrick Corn 5 G9
Trevarth Corn 4 G4
Trevaughan Carms 73 B11
Carms 93 G7
Tre-vaughan Carms 93 G8
Treveal Corn 1 A5
Trevegean Corn 1 D3
Treveighan Corn 11 F7
Trevellas Corn 4 E4
Trevelmond Corn 6 C4
Trevelver Corn 10 G5
Trevemper Corn 4 D6
Treven Corn 11 D7
Trevena Corn 2 D4
Trevenen Corn 2 D5
Trevenen Bal Corn 2 D5
Trevenning Corn 11 F7
Treveor Corn 5 G9
Treverbyn Corn 5 D10
Corn 6 B4
Treverva Corn 3 C7
Trevescan Corn 1 E3
Trevethin Torf 78 E3
Trevia Corn 11 E7
Trevigro Corn 6 B6
Trevilder Corn 10 G6
Trevilla Corn 3 B8
Trevilson Corn 4 D6
Trevine Corn 10 F5
Trevine / Trefin Pembs 90 E6
Treviscoe Corn 5 D8
Treviskey Corn 2 B6
Trevithal Corn 1 D5
Trevoll Corn 4 D6
Trevone Corn 10 F3
Trevor Wrex 166 G3
Trevorrick Corn 10 G4
Trevor Uchaf Denb 166 G2
Trevowah Corn 4 D5
Trevowhan Corn 1 B4
Trew Corn 2 D4
Trewalder Corn 11 E7
Trewarmett Corn 11 D7
Trewartha Corn 2 B2
Corn 3 B10
Trewassa Corn 11 D8
Treween Corn 11 E10
Trewellard Corn 1 C3
Trewen Corn 11 E7
Corn 11 E11
Mon 79 G7
Trewennack Corn 2 D5
Trewennan Corn 11 E7
Trewern Powys 148 G5
Trewetha Corn 10 E6
Trewethen Corn 10 F6
Trewethern Corn 10 F6
Trewey Corn 1 B5
Trewidland Corn 6 D5
Trewindle Corn 6 C2
Trewint Corn 6 C5
Corn 11 B9
Corn 11 E10
Trewithian Corn 3 B9
Trewithick Corn 11 D11
Trewollock Corn 5 G10
Trewoodloe Corn 12 G2
Trewoofe Corn 1 D4
Trewoon Corn 2 F5
Corn 5 E9
Treworga Corn 5 G7
Treworgan Common
Mon 78 D6
Treworlas Corn 3 B9
Treworld Corn 11 C8
Trewornan Corn 10 G5
Treworrick Corn 6 B4
Treworthal Corn 3 B9
Trewyddel / Moylgrove
Pembs 92 C2
Trewyn Devon 24 G4
Tre-wyn Mon 96 G6
Treyarnon Corn 10 G3
Treyford W Sus 34 D4
Trezaise Corn 5 D9
Trezelah Corn 1 C5
Triangle Glos 79 E8
Staffs 133 B11
W Yorks 196 C4
Trickett's Cross Dorset 31 G9
Triffleton Pembs 91 G9
Trillacott Corn 11 D11
Trimdon Durham 234 E3
Trimdon Colliery
Durham 234 D3
Trimdon Grange
Durham 234 D3
Trimingham Norf 160 B5
Trimley Lower Street
Suff 108 D5
Trimley St Martin Suff 108 D5
Trimley St Mary Suff 108 D5
Trimpley Worcs 116 B5
Trimsaran Carms 75 E7
Trims Green Herts 87 B7
Trimstone Devon 40 E3
Trinafour Perth 291 G9
Trinant Caerph 78 E2
Tring Herts 84 C6
Tringford Herts 84 C6
Tring Wharf Herts 84 C6
Trinity Angus 293 G8
Devon 27 F7
Edin 280 F4
Trinity Fields Staffs 151 D8
Trisant Ceredig 112 B4
Triscombe Som 43 F7
Trislaig Highld 290 F2
Trispen Corn 4 E6
Tritlington Northumb 252 E6
Troan Corn 5 D7
Trochry Perth 286 C3
Trodigal Argyll 255 E7
Troedrhiwdalar Powys 113 G9
Troedrhiwffenyd Ceredig 93 C8
Troedrhiwfuwch Caerph 77 E10
Troedyraur Ceredig 92 B6
Troedyrhiw M Tydf 77 E9
Trofarth Conwy 180 G5
Trolliloes E Sus 23 C10
Tromode IoM 192 E4
Trondavoe Shetland 312 F5
Troon Corn 2 B5
S Ayrs 257 C8
Trooper's Inn Pembs 73 C7
Trosaraidh W Isles 297 K3
Trossachs Hotel Stirl 285 G9
Troston Suff 125 C7
Trostre Carms 56 B4
Trostrey Common Mon 78 E5
Troswell Corn 11 C11
Trotshill Worcs 117 F7
Trotten Marsh W Sus 34 B4
Trottiscliffe Kent 68 G6
Trotton W Sus 34 C4
Trough Gate Lancs 195 C11
Troutbeck Cumb 221 E8
Cumb 230 F3
Troutbeck Bridge Cumb 221 F8
Troway Derbys 186 F5
Trowbridge Cardiff 59 C8
Wilts 45 B11
Trowell Notts 153 B9
Trow Green Glos 79 D9
Trowle Common Wilts 45 B10
Trowley Bottom Herts 85 C9
Trows Borders 262 C5
Trowse Newton Norf 142 B4
Troydale W Yorks 205 G10
Troy Town Kent 52 D2
Kent 54 E5
Medway 69 F8
Truas Corn 11 D7
Trub Gtr Man 195 F11
Trudoxhill Som 45 E8
Trueman's Heath
Worcs 117 B11
True Street Devon 8 C6
Trull Som 28 C2
Trumaisgearraidh
W Isles 296 D4
Trumfleet S Yorks 198 E6
Trumpan Highld 298 C2
Trumpet Hereford 98 D3
Trumpington Cambs 123 F8
Trumpsgreen Sur 66 F3
Trunch Norf 160 C5
Trunnah Lancs 202 E2
Truro Corn 4 G6
Truscott Corn 12 D2
Trusham Devon 14 E3
Trusley Derbys 152 B5
Trussall Corn 2 D5
Trussell Corn 11 D10
Trusthorpe Lincs 191 E8
Truthan Corn 4 E6
Truthwall Corn 2 C2
Trwstllewelyn Powys 130 D3
Tryfil Anglesey 178 E6
Trysull Staffs 133 E7
Trythogga Corn 1 C5
Tubbs Mill Corn 5 G9
Tubney Oxon 82 F6
Tubslake Kent 53 G9
Tuckenhay Devon 8 D6
Tuckermarsh Devon 7 B8
Tuckerton Som 28 B3
Tuckhill Shrops 132 F5
Tuckingmill Corn 4 G3
Corn 11 F7
Wilts 30 B6
Tucking Mill Bath 61 G9
Tuckton Bmouth 19 C8
Tuddenham Suff 108 B3
Suff 124 C4
Tuddenham St Martin
Suff 108 B3
Tudeley Kent 52 D6
Tudeley Hale Kent 52 D6
Tudhay Devon 28 G4
Tudhoe Durham 233 D11
Tudhoe Grange
Durham 233 E11
Tudor Hill W Mid 134 D2
Tudorville Hereford 97 G11
Tudweiliog Gwyn 144 B4
Tuebrook Mers 182 C5
Tuesley Sur 50 E3
Tuesnoad Kent 54 E2
Tuffley Glos 80 C4
Tufnell Park London 67 B9
Tufton Hants 48 D3
Pembs 91 F10
Tugby Leics 136 C5
Tugford Shrops 131 F11
Tughall Northumb 264 D6
Tulchan Lodge Angus 292 F3
Tullecombe W Sus 34 B4
Tullibardine Perth 286 F3
Tullibody Clack 279 B7
Tullich Argyll 284 F4
Highld 299 E9
Highld 300 G6
Tullich Muir Highld 301 B7
Tulliemet Perth 286 B3
Tulloch Aberds 293 F9
Aberds 303 F8
Highld 290 E5
Perth 286 E4
Tulloch Castle Highld 300 C5
Tullochgorm Argyll 275 D10
Tulloch-gribban Highld 301 G9
Tullochroisk Perth 285 B11
Tullochvenus Aberds 293 C7
Tulloes Angus 287 C9
Tullybannocher Perth 285 E11
Tullybelton Perth 286 D4
Tullycross Stirl 277 D9
Tullyfergus Perth 286 C6
Tullymurdoch Perth 286 B5
Tullynessle Aberds 293 B7
Tulse Hill London 67 E10
Tumbler's Green Essex 106 F6
Tumble / Y Tymbl Carms 75 C8
Tumby Lincs 174 D2
Tumby Woodside Lincs 174 D3
Tummel Bridge Perth 285 B11
Tumpy Green Glos 80 E2
Tumpy Lakes Hereford 97 B10
Tunbridge Hill Medway 69 E10
Tunbridge Wells / Royal
Tunbridge Wells Kent 52 F5
Tunga W Isles 304 E6
Tungate Norf 160 D5
Tunley Bath 45 B7
Glos 80 E6
Tunnel Hill Worcs 98 C6
Tunnel Pits N Lincs 199 G8
Tunshill Gtr Man 196 E2
Tunstall E Yorks 209 G12
Kent 69 G11
Lancs 212 E2
Norf 143 B8
N Yorks 224 F4
Staffs 150 D5
Stoke 168 E5
Suff 127 G7
T&W 243 G9
Tunstead Derbys 185 G10
Gtr Man 196 G4
Norf 160 E5
Tunworth Hants 49 D7
Tupsley Hereford 97 C10
Tupton Derbys 170 B5
Turbary Common Poole 19 C7
Turfdown Corn 5 B11
Turf Hill Gtr Man 196 E2
Turfholm S Lnrk 259 B8
Turfmoor Devon 28 G3
Shrops 149 F7
Turgis Green Hants 49 B7
Turin Angus 287 B9
Turkdean Glos 81 B10
Turkey Island Hants 33 E9
W Sus 34 D3
Turkey Tump Hereford 97 F10
Tur Langton Leics 136 E4
Turleigh Wilts 61 G10
Turleygreen Shrops 132 F5
Turlin Moor Poole 18 C5
Turmer Hants 31 F10
Turn Lancs 195 D10
Turnalt Argyll 275 C9
Turnastone Hereford 97 D7
Turnberry S Ayrs 244 B6
Turnchapel Plym 7 E9
Turnditch Derbys 170 F3
Turner Green Lancs 203 G8
Turner's Green E Sus 23 B10
E Sus 52 G6
Warks 118 D3
W Berks 64 F4
Turners Hill W Sus 51 F10
Turners Puddle Dorset 18 C2
Turnerwood S Yorks 187 E8
Turnford Herts 86 E5
Turnhouse Edin 280 G3
Turnhurst Stoke 168 E5
Turnstead Milton
Derbys 185 E8
Turnworth Dorset 30 F4
Turrerich Perth 286 D2
Turriff Aberds 303 D7
Tursdale Durham 234 D2
Turton Bottoms Blkburn 195 D8
Turves Cambs 138 D6
Turves Green W Mid 117 B10
Turvey Beds 121 G8
Turville Bucks 84 G3
Turville Heath Bucks 84 G2
Turweston Bucks 102 D2
Tushielaw Borders 261 F8
Tutbury Staffs 152 D4
Tutnall Worcs 117 C9
Tutnalls Glos 79 E10
Tutshill Glos 79 G8
Tutt Hill Kent 54 D3
Tuttington Norf 160 D4
Tutts Clump W Berks 64 E5
Tutwell Corn 12 F3
Tuxford Notts 188 G2
Twatt Orkney 314 D2
Shetland 313 H5
Twechar E Dunb 278 F4
Tweedale Telford 132 C4
Tweeddaleburn Borders 270 E5
Tweedmouth Northumb 273 E9
Tweedsmuir Borders 260 E3
Twelve Heads Corn 4 G5
Twelve Oaks E Sus 37 C11
Twelvewoods Corn 6 B4
Twemlow Green Ches E 168 B3
Twenties Kent 71 F10
Twenty Lincs 156 E3
Twerton Bath 61 G8
Twickenham London 67 E7
Twigworth Glos 98 G6
Twineham W Sus 36 D3
Twineham Green W Sus 36 C3
Twinhoe Bath 45 B8
Twinstead Essex 107 D7
Twinstead Green Essex 106 D6
Twiss Green Warr 183 B11
Twist Devon 28 G3
Twiston Lancs 204 E2
Twitchen Devon 41 G9
Shrops 115 B7
Twitchen Mill Devon 41 G9
Twitham Kent 55 B9
Twitton Kent 52 B4
Two Bridges Devon 13 G8
Glos 79 D11
Two Burrows Corn 4 F4
Two Dales Derbys 170 C3
Two Gates Staffs 134 C4
Two Mile Ash M Keynes 102 D6
W Sus 35 B10
Two Mile Hill Bristol 60 E6
Two Mile Oak Cross Devon 8 B6
Two Mills Ches W 182 G5
Two Pots Devon 40 E4
Two Waters Herts 85 D9
Twr Anglesey 178 E2
Twycross Leics 134 C6
Twydall Medway 69 F9
Twyford Bucks 102 F3
Derbys 152 D6
Dorset 30 D5
Hants 33 C7
Leics 154 G4
Lincs 155 E8
Norf 159 E10
Oxon 101 D9
Shrops 148 D6
Wokingham 65 D9
Worcs 99 B10
Twyford Common
Hereford 97 D10
Twyn-Allws Mon 78 C3
Twynholm Dumfries 237 D8
Twyning Glos 99 D7
Twyning Green Glos 99 D8
Twynllanan Carms 94 G5
Twynmynydd Carms 75 C11
Twyn Shôn-Ifan Caerph 77 G11
Twynyrodyn M Tydf 77 D9
Twyn-yr-odyn V Glam 58 E6
Twyn-y-Sheriff Mon 78 D6
Twywell Northants 121 B9
Tyberton Hereford 97 D7
Tyburn W Mid 134 E2
Tyby Norf 159 D11
Ty-coch Swansea 56 C6
Tycroes Carms 75 C10
Tycrwyn Powys 148 F2
Tyddewi / St Davids
Pembs 90 F5
Tydd Gote Lincs 157 F9
Tydd St Giles Cambs 157 F8
Tydd St Mary Lincs 157 F8
Tyddyn Powys 129 F9
Tyddyn Angharad Denb 165 F9
Tyddyn Dai Anglesey 178 C6
Tyddyn-mawr Gwyn 163 G9
Ty-draw Conwy 164 D5
Swansea 57 C7
Tye Hants 22 C2
Tye Common Essex 87 G11
Tyegate Green Norf 161 G7
Tye Green Essex 87 C10
Essex 87 D7
Essex 87 F11
Essex 105 D11
Essex 105 G10
Essex 106 G5
Tyersal W Yorks 205 G9
Ty-fry Mon 78 F6
Tyganol V Glam 58 E4
Ty-hen Carms 92 G6
Gwyn 144 C3
Ty-isaf Carms 56 B4
Tyla Mon 78 C2
Tylagwyn Bridgend 58 B2
Tyldesley Gtr Man 195 G7
Tyle Carms 94 F3
Tyle-garw Rhondda 58 C4
Tyler Hill Kent 70 G6
Tylers Causeway Herts 86 D3
Tylers Green Bucks 84 G6
Tyler's Green Essex 87 D8
Sur 51 C11
Tyler's Hill Bucks 85 E7
Ty Llwyn Bl Gwent 77 D11
Tylorstown Rhondda 77 F8
Tylwch Powys 129 G9
Ty-mawr Anglesey 179 D7
Ty Mawr Carms 93 C10
Ty-mawr Conwy 181 F7
Ty Mawr Cwm Conwy 164 F6
Tynant Rhondda 58 B5
Ty-nant Conwy 165 G7
Gwyn 147 D8

Tyncelyn Ceredig 112 E2
Tyndrum Stirl. 285 D7
Tyne Dock T&W 243 D9
Tyneham Dorset 18 E3
Tynehead Midloth 271 D7
Tynemouth T&W 243 D9
Tyne Tunnel T&W 243 D8
Tynewydd Ceredig 92 B4
Neath 76 D4
Rhondda 76 F6
Ty-Newydd Ceredig 111 D10
Tyning Bath 45 B7
Tyninghame E Loth 282 F2
Tyn-lon Gwyn 163 D7
Tynron Dumfries 247 E8
Tyntesfield N Som 60 E4
Tyntetown Rhondda 77 F9
Ty'n-y-bryn Rhondda 58 B4
Ty'n-y-celyn Wrex 148 B3
Tyn-y-coed Shrops 148 D4
Ty'n-y-coedcae Caerph 59 B7
Ty'n-y-cwm Swansea 75 E10
Tynyfedw Conwy 165 B7
Tyn-y-fedwen Powys 148 C2
Ty'n-y-ffordd Denb 181 G8
Tyn-y-ffridd Powys 148 C2
Ty'n-y-garn Bridgend 57 E11
Tynygongl Anglesey 179 E8
Tynygraig Ceredig 112 D3
Tyn-y-graig Powys 113 G10
Ty'n-y-groes Conwy 180 G3
Ty'n-y-maes Gwyn 163 C10
Tyn-y-pwll Anglesey 178 D6
Ty'n-yr-eithin Ceredig 112 E3
Tynyrwtra Powys 129 F7
Tyrells End C Beds 103 E9
Tyrell's Wood Sur 51 B7
Ty'r-felin-isaf Conwy 164 C5
Ty Rhiw Rhondda 58 C6
Tyrie Aberds 303 C9
Tyringham M Keynes 103 B7
Tyseley W Mid 134 G2
Ty-Sign Caerph 78 G2
Tythecott Devon 24 D6
Tythegston Bridgend 57 F11
Tytherington Ches E 184 F6
S Glos 61 B7
Som 45 D9
Wilts 46 E2
Tytherleigh Devon 28 G4
Tytherton Lucas Wilts 62 E2
Tyttenhanger Herts 85 D11
Ty-uchaf Powys 147 E10
Tywardreath Corn 5 E11
Tywardreath Highway
Corn 5 D11
Tywyn Conwy 180 F3
Gwyn 110 C2

U

Uachdar W Isles 296 F3
Uags Highld 295 B9
Ubbeston Green Suff 126 C6
Ubley Bath 44 B4
Uckerby N Yorks 224 E4
Uckfield E Sus 37 C7
Uckinghall Worcs 99 D7
Uckington Glos 99 G8
Shrops 131 B11
Uddingston S Lnrk 268 C3
Uddington S Lnrk 259 C9
Udimore E Sus 38 D5
Udley N Som 60 G3
Udny Green Aberds 303 G8
Udny Station Aberds 303 G9
Udston S Lnrk 268 D3
Udstonhead S Lnrk 268 F4
Uffcott Wilts 62 D6
Uffculme Devon 27 E9
Uffington Lincs 137 B11
Oxon 63 B10
Shrops 149 G10
Ufford Pboro 137 C11
Suff 126 G5
Ufton Warks 119 E7
Ufton Green W Berks 64 F6
Ufton Nervet W Berks 64 F6
Ugadale Argyll 255 E8
Ugborough Devon 8 D3
Ugford Wilts 46 G5
Uggeshall Suff 143 G8
Ugglebarnby N Yorks 227 D7
Ughill S Yorks 186 C3
Ugley Essex 105 F10
Ugley Green Essex 105 F10
Ugthorpe N Yorks 226 C5
Uidh W Isles 297 M2
Uig Argyll 276 E2
Argyll 288 D3
Highld 296 F7
Highld 298 C3
Uigen W Isles 304 E2
Uigshader Highld 298 E4
Uisken Argyll 274 B4
Ulaw Aberds 303 G9
Ulbster Highld 310 E7
Ulcat Row Cumb 230 G4
Ulceby Lincs 190 G6
N Lincs 200 E6
Ulceby Skitter N Lincs 200 E6
Ulcombe Kent 53 D10
Uldale Cumb 229 D10
Uley Glos 80 F3
Ulgham Northumb 252 E6
Ullapool Highld 307 K6
Ullcombe Devon 28 F2
Ullenhall Warks 118 D2
Ullenwood Glos 80 B6
Ulleskelf N Yorks 206 E6
Ullesthorpe Leics 135 F10
Ulley S Yorks 187 D7
Ullingswick Hereford 97 B11
Ullington Worcs 100 B2
Ullinish Highld 294 B5
Ullock Cumb 229 G7
Cumb 229 G10
Ulnes Walton Lancs 194 D4
Ulpha Cumb 220 G3
Ulrome E Yorks 209 B9
Ulshaw N Yorks 214 B2
Ulsta Shetland 312 E6
Ulva House Argyll 288 F6
Ulverley Green W Mid 134 G2
Ulverston Cumb 210 D5
Ulwell Dorset 18 E6
Umberleigh Devon 25 C10
Unapool Highld 306 F7
Unasary W Isles 297 J3
Under Bank W Yorks 196 F6
Underbarrow Cumb 221 G9
Undercliffe W Yorks 205 G9
Underdale Shrops 149 G10
Underdown Devon 14 D3
Underhill London 86 F3
Wilts 45 G11
Underhoull Shetland 312 C7
Underling Green Kent 53 D9
Underriver Kent 52 C5
Underriver Ho Kent 52 C5
Under the Wood Kent 71 F8
Under Tofts S Yorks 186 D4
Underton Shrops 132 E3
Underwood Newport 59 B11
Notts 171 E7
Pembs 73 C7
Plym 7 D10
Undley Suff 140 G3
Undy Mon 60 B2
Ungisiadar W Isles 304 F3
Unifirth Shetland 313 H4
Union Cottage Aberds 293 D10
Union Mills IoM 192 E4
Union Street E Sus 53 G8
United Downs Corn 4 G4
Unstone Derbys 186 F5
Unstone Green Derbys 186 F5
Unsworth Gtr Man 195 F10
Unthank Cumb 230 B3
Cumb 230 D5
Cumb 231 C8
Derbys 186 F4
Unthank End Cumb 230 D5
Upavon Wilts 46 C6
Up Cerne Dorset 29 G11
Upchurch Kent 69 F10
Upcott Devon 24 D2
Devon 25 F9
Devon 25 F11
Devon 40 F3
Hereford 114 G6
Som 27 C11
Upend Cambs 124 F3
Up End M Keynes 103 B8
Up Exe Devon 26 G6
Upgate Norf 160 F2
Upgate Street Norf 141 E11
Norf 142 E5
Up Green Hants 65 G9
Uphall Dorset 29 G9
W Loth 279 G11
Uphall Station W Loth 279 G11
Upham Devon 26 F5
Hants 33 C8
Uphampton Hereford 115 E7
Worcs 116 E6
Up Hatherley Glos 99 G8
Uphempston Devon 8 C6
Uphill N Som 43 B10
Uphill Manor N Som 43 B10
Up Holland Lancs 194 F4
Uplands Glos 80 D5
Swansea 56 C6
Uplawmoor E Renf 267 D8
Upleadon Glos 98 F5
Upleadon Court Glos 98 F5
Upleatham Redcar 226 B2
Uplees Kent 70 G3
Uploders Dorset 16 C6
Uplowman Devon 27 D8
Uplyme Devon 16 C2
Up Marden W Sus 34 E3
Upminster London 68 B5
Up Mudford Som 29 D9
Up Nately Hants 49 C7
Upnor Medway 69 E9
Upottery Devon 28 F2
Uppacott Devon 25 B9
Uppat Highld 311 J2
Uppend Essex 105 F9
Upper Affcot Shrops 131 F8
Upper Ardchronie
Highld 309 L6
Upper Ardgrain Aberds 303 F9
Upper Ardroscadale
Argyll 275 G11
Upper Arley Worcs 132 G5
Upper Armley W Yorks 205 G11
Upper Arncott Oxon 83 B10
Upper Astley Shrops 149 F10
Upper Aston Shrops 132 E6
Upper Astrop
Northants 101 D10
Upper Badcall Highld 306 E6
Upper Bangor Gwyn 179 G9
Upper Basildon W Berks 64 D5
Upper Batley W Yorks 197 B8
Upper Battlefield
Shrops 149 F10
Upper Beeding W Sus 35 E11
Upper Benefield
Northants 137 F9
Upper Bentley Worcs 117 D9
Upper Bighouse Highld 310 D2
Upper Birchwood
Derbys 170 E6
Upper Blainslie
Borders 271 G10
Upper Boat Rhondda 58 B6
Upper Boddam Aberds 302 F6
Upper Boddington
Northants 119 G9
Upper Bogrow Highld 309 L7
Upper Bogside Moray 302 D2
Upper Bonchurch IoW 21 F7
Upper Booth Derbys 185 D10
Upper Borth Ceredig 128 F2
Upper Boyndlie Aberds 303 C9
Upper Brailes Warks 100 D6
Upper Brandon Parva
Norf 141 B10
Upper Breakish Highld 295 C8
Upper Breinton Hereford 97 C9
Upper Broadheath
Worcs 116 F6
Upper Brockholes
W Yorks 196 B5
Upper Broughton Notts 154 D3
Upper Broxwood
Hereford 115 G7
Upper Bruntingthorpe
Leics 136 F2
Upper Brynamman
Carms 76 C2
Upper Buckenhill
Hereford 97 E11
Upper Bucklebury
W Berks 64 F4
Upper Bullington Hants 48 E3
Upper Burgate Hants 31 D11
Upper Burnhaugh
Aberds 293 D10
Upper Bush Medway 69 F7
Upperby Cumb 239 G10
Upper Caldecote
C Beds 104 B3
Upper Cam Glos 80 F3
Upper Canada N Som 43 B11
Upper Canterton Hants 32 E3
Upper Catesby
Northants 119 F10
Upper Catshill Worcs 117 C9
Upper Chapel Powys 95 C10
Upper Cheddon Som 28 B2
Upper Chicksgrove Wilts 31 B7
Upper Church Village
Rhondda 58 B5
Upper Chute Wilts 47 C9
Upper Clapton London 67 B10
Upper Clatford Hants 47 E11
Upper Coberley Glos 81 B7
Upper College Shrops 149 C11
Upper Colwall Hereford 98 C5
Upper Common Hants 48 D6
Upper Cotburn Aberds 303 D7
Upper Cotton Staffs 169 F9
Upper Coullie Aberds 293 B9
Upper Cound Shrops 131 C11
Upper Coxley Som 44 E4
Upper Cudworth
S Yorks 197 F11
Upper Culphin Aberds 302 D6
Upper Cumberworth
W Yorks 197 F8
Upper Cwmbran Torf 78 F3
Upper Cwm-twrch Powys 76 C3
Upperdale Derbys 185 G11
Upper Dallachy Moray 302 C3
Upper Deal Kent 55 C11
Upper Dean Beds 121 D10
Devon 8 C4
Upper Denby W Yorks 197 D8
W Yorks 197 F8
Upper Denton Cumb 240 D4
Upper Derraid Highld 301 F10
Upper Diabaig Highld 299 C8
Upper Dicker E Sus 23 D9
Upper Dinchope Shrops 131 G9
Upper Dormington
Hereford 97 D11
Upper Dounreay Highld 310 C4
Upper Dovercourt Essex 108 E4
Upper Dowdeswell Glos 81 B8
Upper Druimfin Argyll 289 D7
Upper Dunsforth
N Yorks 215 G8
Upper Dunsley Herts 84 C6
Upper Eashing Sur 50 E3
Upper Eastern Green
W Mid 134 G5
Upper Eathie Highld 301 C7
Upper Edmonton London 86 G4
Upper Egleton Hereford 98 C2
Upper Elkstone Staffs 169 D9
Upper Ellastone Staffs 169 G10
Upper Elmers End
London 67 F11
Upper End Derbys 185 F9
Glos 81 C10
Glos 81 D8
Leics 154 G4
Upper Enham Hants 47 D11
Upper Farmcote Shrops 132 E5
Upper Farringdon Hants 49 F8
Upper Feorlig Highld 298 E2
Upper Fivehead Som 28 C4
Upper Forge Shrops 132 F4
Upper Framilode Glos 80 C3
Upper Froyle Hants 49 E9
Upper Gambolds Worcs 117 D9
Upper Gills Highld 310 B7
Upper Glenfintaig
Highld 290 E4
Upper Godney Som 44 E3
Upper Goldstone Kent 71 G9
Upper Gornal W Mid 133 E8
Upper Gravenhurst
C Beds 104 D2
Upper Green Essex 105 E8
Mon 78 B5
Suff 124 E4
W Berks 63 G11
W Yorks 197 B9
Upper Grove Common
Hereford 97 F11
Upper Guist Norf 159 D10
Upper Hackney Derbys 170 C3
Upper Hale Sur 49 D10
Upper Halistra Highld 298 D2
Upper Halliford Sur 66 F5
Upper Halling Medway 69 G7
Upper Ham Worcs 99 D7
Upper Hambleton
Rutland 137 B8
Upper Hamnish
Hereford 115 F10
Upper Harbledown Kent 54 B6
Upper Hardres Court
Kent 55 C7
Upper Hardwick
Hereford 115 F8
Upper Hartfield E Sus 52 G3
Upper Hartshay Derbys 170 E5
Upper Haselor Worcs 99 C10
Upper Hatton Staffs 150 B6
Upper Haugh S Yorks 186 B6
Upper Hawkhillock
Aberds 303 F10
Upper Hayesden Kent 52 E5
Upper Hayton Shrops 131 G10
Upper Heath Shrops 131 F11
Upper Heaton W Yorks 197 D7
Upper Hellesdon Norf 160 G4
Upper Helmsley
N Yorks 207 B9
Upper Hengoed Shrops 148 C5
Upper Hergest Hereford 114 G5
Upper Heyford
Northants 120 F3
Oxon 101 F9
Upper Hill Glos 79 F11
Hereford 115 G9
Upper Hindhope
Borders 251 B7
Upper Holloway London 67 B9
Upper Holton Suff 127 B8
Upper Hopton W Yorks 197 D7
Upper Horsebridge
E Sus 23 C9
Upper Howsell Worcs 98 B5
Upper Hoyland
S Yorks 197 G11
Upper Hulme Staffs 169 C8
Upper Hyde IoW 21 E7
Upper Ifold Sur 50 G4
Upper Inglesham Swindon 82 F2
Upper Inverbrough
Highld 301 F8
Upper Kergord Shetland 313 H6
Upper Kidston Borders 270 G4
Upper Kilcott Glos 61 B9
Upper Killay Swansea 56 C5
Upper Killeyan Argyll 254 C3
Upper Kinsham
Hereford 115 D7
Upper Knockando
Moray 301 E11
Upper Lambourn
W Berks 63 C10
Upper Landywood
Staffs 133 B9
Upper Langford N Som 44 B3
Upper Langwith Derbys 171 B8
Upper Layham Suff 107 C10
Upper Leigh Staffs 151 B10
Upper Lenie Highld 300 G5
Upper Littleton N Som 60 G5
Upper Loads Derbys 170 B4
Upper Lochton Aberds 293 D8
Upper Lode Worcs 99 E7
Upper Longdon Staffs 151 G11
Upper Longwood
Shrops 132 B2
Upper Ludstone Shrops 132 D6
Upper Lybster Highld 310 F6
Upper Lydbrook Glos 79 B10
Upper Lyde Hereford 97 C9
Upper Lye Hereford 115 D7
Upper Maes-coed
Hereford 96 D6
Upper Marsh W Yorks 204 F6
Upper Midhope S Yorks 186 B2
Upper Midway Derbys 152 E5
Uppermill Gtr Man 196 F3
Upper Milovaig Highld 297 G7
Upper Milton Oxon 82 B3
Som 44 D4
Upper Minety Wilts 81 G8
Upper Mitton Worcs 116 C6
Upper Moor Worcs 99 B9
Upper Moor Side
W Yorks 205 G10
Upper Morton S Glos 79 G11
Upper Nash Pembs 73 E8
Upper Netchwood
Shrops 132 E2
Upper Newbold Derbys 186 G5
Upper Nobut Staffs 151 B10
Upper North Dean Bucks 84 F4
Upper Norwood London 67 F10
W Sus 34 D6
Upper Obney Perth 286 D4
Upper Ochrwyth Caerph 59 B8
Upper Oddington Glos 100 F4
Upper Ollach Highld 295 B7
Upper Padley Derbys 186 F2
Upper Pickwick Wilts 61 E11
Upper Pollicott Bucks 84 C2
Upper Poppleton York 207 C7
Upper Port Highld 301 G10
Upper Postern Kent 52 D6
Upper Quinton Warks 100 B3
Upper Race Torf 78 F3
Upper Ratley Hants 32 C4
Upper Ridinghill
Aberds 303 D10
Upper Rissington Glos 82 B2
Upper Rochford Worcs 116 D2
Upper Rodmersham Kent 70 G2
Upper Sandaig Highld 295 D9
Upper Sanday Orkney 314 F5
Upper Sapey Hereford 116 E3
Upper Saxondale Notts 154 B3
Upper Seagry Wilts 62 C2
Upper Shelton C Beds 103 C9
Upper Sheringham
Norf 177 E10
Upper Shirley London 67 G11
Soton 32 E6
Upper Siddington Glos 81 F8
Upper Skelmorlie
N Ayrs 266 B4
Upper Slackstead Hants 32 B5
Upper Slaughter Glos 100 G3
Upper Solva Pembs 90 G5
Upper Soudley Glos 79 C11
Uppersound Shetland 313 J6
Upper Stanton Drew
Bath 60 G6
Upper Staploe Beds 122 F2
Upper Stoke Norf 142 C5
W Mid 135 G7
Upper Stondon C Beds 104 D2
Upper Stowe Northants 120 F2
Upper Stratton Swindon 63 B7
Upper Street Hants 31 D11
Norf 142 G3
Norf 160 B5
Norf 160 E6
Norf 160 F6
Norf 161 F7
Suff 108 E2
Suff 124 G5
Suff 126 G2
Upper Strensham Worcs 99 D8
Upper Studley Wilts 45 B10
Upper Sundon C Beds 103 F10
Upper Swainswick Bath 61 F9
Upper Swanmore Hants 33 D9
Upper Swell Glos 100 F3
Upper Sydenham
London 67 E10
Upper Tankersley
S Yorks 186 B4
Upper Tean Staffs 151 B10
Upperthong W Yorks 196 F6
Upperthorpe Derbys 187 E7
N Lincs 199 G9
Upper Threapwood
Ches W 166 F6
Upper Thurnham Lancs 202 C5
Upper Tillyrie Perth 286 G5
Upperton E Sus 23 E10
Oxon 83 G11
W Sus 35 C7
Upper Tooting London 67 E9
Upper Tote Highld 298 D5
Uppertown Derbys 170 C4
Highld 300 F4
Highld 310 B7
Northumb 241 C9
Orkney 314 G4
Upper Town Derbys 170 D3
Derbys 170 E2
Durham 233 D7
Hereford 97 B11
N Som 60 F4
Suff 125 D8
Wilts 62 D3
W Yorks 204 G6
Upper Treverward
Shrops 114 B5
Upper Tysoe Warks 100 C6
Upper Up Glos 81 F8
Upper Upham Wilts 63 D8
Upper Upnor Medway 69 E9
Upper Vobster Som 45 D8
Upper Walthamstow
London 67 B11
Upper Wardington Oxon 101 B9
Upper Wardley W Sus 34 B4
Upper Weald M Keynes 102 D5
Upper Weedon
Northants 120 F2
Upper Welland Worcs 98 C5
Upper Wellingham E Sus 36 E6
Upper Welson Hereford 114 G5
Upper Westholme Som 44 E5
Upper Weston Bath 61 F8
Upper Weybread Suff 126 B4
Upper Whiston S Yorks 187 D7
Upper Wick Glos 80 F2
Worcs 116 G6
Upper Wield Hants 48 F6
Upper Wigginton
Shrops 148 B6
Upper Winchendon
Bucks 84 C2
Upper Witton W Mid 133 E11
Upper Wolvercote Oxon 83 D7
Upper Wolverton Worcs 117 G8
Upperwood Derbys 170 D3
Upper Woodend Aberds 293 B8
Upper Woodford Wilts 46 F6
Upper Woolhampton
W Berks 64 F5
Upper Wootton Hants 48 C5
Upper Wraxall Wilts 61 E10
Upper Wyche Hereford 98 C5
Uppincott Devon 26 G5
Uppingham Rutland 137 D7
Uppington Dorset 31 F8
Shrops 132 B2
Upsall N Yorks 215 B9
Upsher Green Suff 107 C8
Upshire Essex 86 E6
Up Somborne Hants 47 G11
Upstreet Kent 71 G8
Up Sydling Dorset 29 G10
Upthorpe Glos 80 E3
Suff 125 C9
Upton Bucks 84 C3
Cambs 122 B3
Ches W 166 B6
Corn 11 G11
Corn 24 G2
Cumb 230 D2
Devon 8 G4
Devon 27 G9
Dorset 17 E10
Dorset 18 C5
E Yorks 209 C8
Hants 32 D5
Hants 47 B11
IoW 21 C7
Kent 71 F11
Leics 135 D7
Lincs 188 D5
London 68 C2
Mers 182 D3
Mers 183 D7
Norf 161 G7
Northants 120 E4
Notts 172 E2
Notts 188 F2
Oxon 64 B4
Oxon 82 C2
Pboro 138 C2
Slough 66 D3
Som 27 B7
Som 29 B7
Warks 118 F2
Wilts 45 G11
W Yorks 198 E3
Upton Bishop Hereford 98 F2
Upton Cheyney S Glos 61 F7
Upton Cressett Shrops 132 E3
Upton Crews Hereford 98 F2
Upton Cross Corn 11 G11
Upton End C Beds 104 E2
Upton Field Notts 172 E2
Upton Green Norf 161 G7
Upton Grey Hants 49 D7
Upton Heath Ches W 166 B6
Upton Hellions Devon 26 G4
Upton Lea Bucks 66 C3
Upton Lovell Wilts 46 E2
Upton Magna Shrops 149 G11
Upton Noble Som 45 F8
Upton Park London 68 C2
Upton Pyne Devon 14 B4
Upton Rocks Halton 183 D8
Upton St Leonards Glos 80 C5
Upton Scudamore Wilts 45 D11
Upton Snodsbury Worcs 117 G8
Upton upon Severn
Worcs 99 C7
Upton Warren Worcs 117 D8
Upwaltham W Sus 34 E6
Upware Cambs 123 C10
Upwell Norf 139 C9
Upwey Dorset 17 E9
Upwick Green Herts 105 G9
Upwood Cambs 138 G5
Uradale Shetland 313 K6
Urafirth Shetland 312 F5
Uragaig Argyll 274 D4
Urchfont Wilts 46 B4
Urdimarsh Hereford 97 B10
Ure Shetland 312 F4
Ure Bank N Yorks 214 E6
Urgashay Som 29 C9
Urgha W Isles 305 J3
Urgha Beag W Isles 305 H3
Urishay Common
Hereford 96 D6
Urlar Perth 286 C2
Urlay Nook Stockton 225 C7
Urmston Gtr Man 184 C3
Urpeth Durham 242 G6
Urquhart Highld 300 D5
Moray 302 C2
Urra N Yorks 225 E11
Urray Highld 300 D5
Ushaw Moor Durham 233 C10
Usk Mon 78 E5
Usselby Lincs 189 C9
Usworth T&W 243 F8
Utkinton Ches W 167 B8
Utley W Yorks 204 E6
Uton Devon 14 B2
Utterby Lincs 190 C4
Uttoxeter Staffs 151 C11
Uwchmynydd Gwyn 144 D3
Uxbridge London 66 C5
Uxbridge Moor London 66 C5
Uyea Shetland 312 D5
Uyeasound Shetland 312 C7
Uzmaston Pembs 73 C7

V

Vachelich Pembs 90 F5
Vadlure Shetland 313 J4
Vagg Som 29 D8
Vaila Hall Shetland 313 J4
Vaivoe Shetland 312 G7
Vale W Yorks 196 B2
Vale Down Devon 12 D6
Vale of Health London 67 B9
Valeswood Shrops 149 E7
Valleyfield Dumfries 237 D8
Valley Park Hants 32 C6
Valley Truckle Corn 11 E7
Valley / Y Fali Anglesey 178 F3
Valsgarth Shetland 312 B8
Valtos Highld 298 C5
Van Caerph 59 B7
Powys 129 F9
Vange Essex 69 B8
Vanlop Shetland 313 M5
Varchoel Powys 148 G4
Varfell Corn 2 C2
Varteg Torf 78 D3
Vassa Shetland 313 H6
Vastern Wilts 62 C5
Vatsetter Shetland 312 E7
Shetland 313 L5
Vatten Highld 298 E2
Vaul Argyll 288 E2
Vauxhall London 67 D10
Mers 182 C4
W Mid 133 F11
Vaynol Hall Gwyn 163 B8
Vaynor M Tydf 77 C8
Veensgarth Shetland 313 J6
Velator Devon 40 F3
Veldo Hereford 97 C11
Velindre Powys 96 D3
Vellanoweth Corn 2 C2
Vellow Som 42 F5
Velly Devon 24 C3
Veness Orkney 314 D5
Venn Devon 8 F4
Venngreen Devon 24 E5
Vennington Shrops 130 B6
Venn Ottery Devon 15 C7
Venn's Green Hereford 97 B10
Venny Tedburn Devon 14 B2
Venterdon Corn 12 G3
Vention Devon 40 E3
Ventnor IoW 21 F7
Venton Devon 7 D11
Ventongimps Corn 4 E5
Ventonleague Corn 2 B3
Venus Hill Herts 85 E8
Veraby Devon 26 B3
Vermentry Shetland 313 H5
Vernham Bank Hants 47 B10
Vernham Dean Hants 47 B10
Vernham Row Hants 47 B10
Vernham Street Hants 47 B11
Vernolds Common
Shrops 131 G9
Verwood Dorset 31 F9
Veryan Corn 3 B10
Veryan Green Corn 5 G8
Vicarage Devon 15 D10
Vicarscross Ches W 166 B6
Vickerstown Cumb 210 F3
Victoria Corn 5 C9
S Yorks 197 F7
Victoria Dock Village
Hull 200 B6
Victoria Park Bucks 84 C4
Victory Gardens Renfs 267 B10
Vidlin Shetland 312 G6
Viewpark N Lnrk 268 C4
Vigo W Mid 133 C10
Vigo Village Kent 68 G6
Vinegar Hill Mon 60 B2
Vinehall Street E Sus 38 C3
Vines Cross E Sus 23 B9
Viney Hill Glos 79 D11
Vinney Green S Glos 61 D7
Virginia Water Sur 66 F3
Virginstow Devon 12 C3
Viscar Corn 2 C6
Vobster Som 45 D8
Voe Shetland 312 E5
Shetland 313 G6
Vogue Corn 4 G4
Vole Som 43 D11
Vowchurch Hereford 97 D7
Vowchurch Common
Hereford 97 D7
Voxmoor Som 27 D10
Voxter Shetland 312 F5
Voy Orkney 314 E2
Vron Gate Shrops 130 B6
Vulcan Village Mers 183 C9

W

Waberthwaite Cumb 220 G2
Wackerfield Durham 233 G9
Wacton Hereford 116 F2
Norf 142 E3
Wacton Common Norf 142 F3
Wadbister Shetland 313 J6
Wadborough Worcs 99 B8
Wadbrook Devon 28 G4
Waddesdon Bucks 84 B2
Waddeton Devon 9 D7
Waddicar Mers 182 B5
Waddicombe Devon 26 B5
Waddingham Lincs 189 B7
Waddington Lancs 203 E10
Lincs 173 C7
Waddingworth Lincs 189 G11
Waddon Devon 14 F3
London 67 G10
Wadebridge Corn 10 G5
Wadeford Som 28 E4
Wade Hall Lancs 194 C4
Wadenhoe Northants 137 G10
Wades Green Ches E 167 C11
Wadesmill Herts 86 B5
Wadhurst E Sus 52 G6
Wadshelf Derbys 186 G4
Wadsley S Yorks 186 C4
Wadsley Bridge S Yorks 186 C4
Wadswick Wilts 61 F10
Wadwick Hants 48 C2
Wadworth S Yorks 187 B9
Waen Denb 165 B10
Denb 165 C7
Flint 181 G11
Powys 129 E9
Waen Aberwheeler
Denb 165 B9
Waen-fâch Powys 148 F4
Waen Goleugoed Denb 181 G9
Waen-pentir Gwyn 163 B9
Waen-wen Gwyn 163 B9
Wag Highld 311 G4
Wagbeach Shrops 131 C7
Wagg Som 28 B6
Waggersley Staffs 151 B7
Waggs Plot Devon 28 G4
Wainfelin Torf 78 E3
Wainfleet All Saints
Lincs 175 D7
Wainfleet Bank Lincs 175 D7
Wainfleet St Mary Lincs 175 D8
Wainfleet Tofts Lincs 175 D7
Wainford Norf 142 E6
Waingroves Derbys 170 F6
Wainhouse Corner Corn 11 B9
Wain Lee Staffs 168 D5
Wainscott Medway 69 E8
Wainstalls W Yorks 196 B4
Waitby Cumb 222 D5
Waithe Lincs 201 G9
Wakefield W Yorks 197 C10
Wake Green W Mid 133 G11
Wake Hill N Yorks 214 E3
Wake Lady Green
N Yorks 226 F3
Wakeley Herts 104 F6
Wakerley Northants 137 D9
Wakes Colne Essex 107 F7
Wakes Colne Green
Essex 107 E7
Walberswick Suff 127 C9
Walberton W Sus 35 F7
Walbottle T&W 242 D5
Walby Cumb 239 E10
Walcombe Som 44 D5
Walcot Bath 61 F9
Lincs 155 B11
N Lincs 199 C11
Oxon 82 B4
Shrops 130 F6
Swindon 63 C7
Telford 149 G11
Worcs 99 B8
Walcote Leics 135 G11
Warks 118 F2
Walcot Green Norf 142 G2
Walcott Lincs 173 D10
Norf 161 C7
Walden N Yorks 213 C10
Walden Head N Yorks 213 C9
Walden Stubbs N Yorks 198 D5
Waldersey Cambs 139 C8
Waldershaigh S Yorks 186 B3
Walderslade Medway 69 G9
Walderton W Sus 34 E3
Walditch Dorset 16 C5
Waldley Derbys 152 B2
Waldridge Durham 243 G7
Waldringfield Suff 108 C5
Waldringfield Heath
Suff 108 B5
Waldron E Sus 23 B8
Waldron Down E Sus 37 C8
Wales Som 29 C9
S Yorks 187 E7
Wales Bar S Yorks 187 E7
Walesby Lincs 189 C10
Notts 187 G11
Walesby Grange Lincs 189 C10
Wales End Suff 106 B5
Waleswood S Yorks 187 E7
Walford Hereford 97 G11
Hereford 115 C7
Shrops 149 E8
Som 28 B3
Staffs 150 C6
Walford Heath Shrops 149 F8
Walgherton Ches E 167 F11
Walgrave Northants 120 C6
Walham Glos 98 G6
Walham Green London 67 D9
Walhampton Hants 20 B2
Walkden Gtr Man 195 G8
Walker T&W 243 E7
Walker Barn Ches E 185 G7
Walkerburn Borders 261 B9
Walker Fold Lancs 203 E9
Walkeringham Notts 188 C3
Walkerith Lincs 188 C3
Walkern Herts 104 F5
Walker's Green Hereford 97 B10
Walker's Heath W Mid 117 B11
Walkerville N Yorks 224 F4
Walkford Dorset 19 C10
Walkhampton Devon 7 B10
Walkington E Yorks 208 F5
Walkley S Yorks 186 D4
Walkmill Shrops 131 E7
Walk Mill Lancs 204 G3
Walkmills Shrops 131 D9
Wall Corn 2 B4
Northumb 241 D10
Staffs 134 B2
Wallacestone Falk 279 F8
Wallaceton Dumfries 247 F8
Wallacetown S Ayrs 245 C7
S Ayrs 257 E8
Shetland 313 H5
Wallands Park E Sus 36 E6
Wallasey Mers 182 C4
Wallbank Lancs 195 D11
Wall Bank Shrops 131 E10
Wallbrook W Mid 133 E8
Wallcrouch E Sus 53 G7
Wallend London 68 C2
Wall End Cumb 210 C4
Kent 71 G8
Waller's Green Hereford 98 D3
Walley's Green Ches E 167 C11
Wall Heath W Mid 133 F7
Wall Hill Gtr Man 196 F3
Wallingford Oxon 64 B6
Wallington Hants 33 F9
Herts 104 E5
London 67 G9
Wallington Heath
W Mid 133 C9
Wallingwells Notts 187 E9
Wallis Pembs 91 F10
Wallisdown Poole 19 C7
Walliswood Sur 50 F6
Wall Mead Bath 45 B7
Wall Nook Durham 233 B10
Wallow Green Glos 80 F4
Wallridge Northumb 242 B3
Walls Shetland 313 J4
Wallsend T&W 243 D7
Wallston V Glam 58 E6
Wallsuches Gtr Man 195 E7
Wallsworth Glos 98 G6
Wall under Heywood
Shrops 131 E10
Wallyford E Loth 281 G7
Walmer Kent 55 C11
Walmer Bridge Lancs 194 C3
Walmersley Gtr Man 195 E10
Walmgate Stray York 207 C8
Walmley W Mid 134 E2
Walmsgate Lincs 190 F5
Walnut Grove Perth 286 E5
Walnut Tree M Keynes 103 D7
Walnuttree Green Herts 105 G9
Walpole Som 43 E10
Suff 127 C7
Walpole Cross Keys
Norf 157 F10
Walpole Highway Norf 157 G10
Walpole Marsh Norf 157 F9
Walpole St Andrew
Norf 157 F10
Walpole St Peter Norf 157 F9
Walrow Som 43 D10
Walsal End W Mid 118 B4
Walsall W Mid 133 D10
Walsall Wood W Mid 133 C10
Walsden W Yorks 196 C2
Walsgrave on Sowe
W Mid 135 G7
Walsham le Willows
Suff 125 C9
Walshaw Gtr Man 195 E9
Walshford N Yorks 206 C4
Walsoken Cambs 157 G9
Walson Mon 97 G8
Walston S Lnrk 269 F11
Walsworth Herts 104 E4
Walters Ash Bucks 84 F4
Walter's Green Kent 52 E4
Walterston V Glam 58 E5
Walterstone Hereford 96 F6
Waltham Kent 54 D6
NE Lincs 201 G9
Waltham Abbey Essex 86 E5
Waltham Chase Hants 33 D9
Waltham Cross Herts 86 E5
Waltham on the Wolds
Leics 154 D6
Waltham St Lawrence
Windsor 65 D10
Waltham's Cross Essex 106 E3
Walthamstow London 67 B11
Walton Bucks 84 C4
Cumb 240 E2
Derbys 170 B5
Leics 135 F11
Mers 182 C5
M Keynes 103 D7
Pboro 138 C3
Powys 114 F5
Shrops 115 B9
Som 44 F3
Staffs 151 C7
Staffs 151 D7
Suff 108 D5
Telford 149 F11
Warks 118 G5
W Yorks 197 D11
W Yorks 206 D4
Walton Cardiff Glos 99 E8
Walton Court Bucks 84 C4
Walton East Pembs 91 G10
Walton Elm Dorset 30 D3
Walton Grounds
Northants 101 E10
Walton Heath Hants 33 F10
Walton Highway Norf 157 G9
Walton in Gordano
N Som 60 E2
Walton-le-Dale Lancs 194 B5
Walton Manor Oxon 83 D8
Walton-on-Thames Sur 66 F6
Walton on the Hill
Staffs 151 E9
Sur 51 B8
Walton-on-the-Naze
Essex 108 G5
Walton on the Wolds
Leics 153 F11
Walton-on-Trent
Derbys 152 F4
Walton Pool Worcs 117 B8
Walton St Mary N Som 60 E2
Walton Summit Lancs 194 B5
Walton Warren Norf 158 F4
Walton West Pembs 72 C5
Walwen Flint 181 F10
Flint 181 G11
Flint 182 F2
Walwick Northumb 241 C10
Walworth Darl 224 B4
London 67 D10
Walworth Gate Darl 233 G10
Walwyn's Castle Pembs 72 C5
Wambrook Som 28 F3
Wampool Cumb 238 G6
Wanborough Sur 50 D2
Swindon 63 C8
Wandel Dyke S Lnrk 259 D11
Wandle Park London 67 F10
Wandon End Herts 104 G2
Wandsworth London 67 E9
Wangford Suff 127 B9
Wanlip Leics 154 G2
Wanlockhead Dumfries 259 G9
Wannock E Sus 23 E9
Wansford E Yorks 209 B7
Pboro 137 D11
Wanshurst Green Kent 53 D9
Wanson Corn 24 G1
Wanstead London 68 B2
Wanstrow Som 45 E8
Wanswell Glos 79 E11
Wantage Oxon 63 B11
Wants Green Worcs 116 F5
Wapley S Glos 61 D8
Wappenbury Warks 119 D7
Wappenham Northants 102 B2
Wapping London 67 C10
Warbleton E Sus 23 B10
Warblington Hants 22 B2
Warborough Oxon 83 G9
Warboys Cambs 138 G6
Warbreck Blkpool 202 F2
Warbstow Corn 11 C10
Warbstow Cross Corn 11 C10
Warburton Gtr Man 184 D2
Warburton Green
Gtr Man 184 E3
Warcop Cumb 222 B4
Warden Kent 70 E4
Northumb 241 D10
Powys 114 E6
Ward End W Mid 134 F2
Warden Hill Glos 99 G8
Warden Point IoW 20 D2
Warden Street C Beds 104 C2
Ward Green Suff 125 E10
S Yorks 197 G10
Ward Green Cross
Lancs 203 F8
Wardhedges C Beds 103 D11
Wardhill Orkney 314 D6
Wardington Oxon 101 B9
Wardlaw Borders 261 F7
Wardle Ches E 167 D10
Gtr Man 196 D2
Wardle Bank Ches E 167 D10
Wardley Gtr Man 195 G9
Rutland 136 C6
T&W 243 E7
W Sus 34 B4
Wardlow Derbys 185 G11
Wardour Wilts 30 B6
Wardpark N Lnrk 278 F5
Wardrobes Bucks 84 E4
Wardsend Ches E 184 E6
Wardy Hill Cambs 139 G9
Ware Herts 86 C5
Kent 71 G9
Wareham Dorset 18 D4
Warehorne Kent 54 G3
Warenford Northumb 264 D4
Waren Mill Northumb 264 C4
Warenton Northumb 264 C4
Wareside Herts 86 B5
Waresley Cambs 122 G4
Worcs 116 C6
Ware Street Kent 53 B9
Warfield Brack 65 E11
Warfleet Devon 9 E7
Wargate Lincs 156 C4
Wargrave Mers 183 C9
Wokingham 65 D9
Warham Hereford 97 D9
Norf 176 E6
Warhill Gtr Man 185 B7
Waring's Green W Mid 118 C2
Wark Northumb 241 B9
Northumb 263 B8
Warkleigh Devon 25 C10
Warkton Northants 121 B7

Wispington Lincs 190 G2
Wissenden Kent 54 E2
Wissett Suff 127 B7
Wistanstow Shrops 131 F8
Wistanswick Shrops 150 D3
Wistaston Ches E 167 E11
Wistaston Green
Ches E 167 E11
Wiston Pembs 73 B8
S Lnrk 259 C11
W Sus 35 E10
Wiston Mains S Lnrk 259 C11
Wistow Cambs 138 G5
Leics 136 D2
N Yorks 207 F7
Wiswell Lancs 203 F10
Witcham Cambs 139 G9
Witchampton Dorset 31 F7
Witchford Cambs 123 B10
Witcombe Som 29 C7
Withacott Devon 24 D6
Witham Essex 88 C4
Witham Friary Som 45 E8
Witham on the Hill
Lincs 155 F11
Witham St Hughs Lincs 172 C5
Withcall Lincs 190 E3
Withdean Brighton 36 F4
Witherenden Hill E Sus 37 B10
Withergate Norf 160 D5
Witheridge Devon 26 E4
Witheridge Hill Oxon 65 C7
Witherley Leics 134 D6
Withermarsh Green
Suff 107 D10
Withern Lincs 190 E6
Withernsea E Yorks 201 B10
Withernwick E Yorks 209 E9
Withersdale Street Suff 142 G5
Withersdane Kent 54 D5
Withersfield Suff 106 B3
Witherslack Cumb 211 C8
Witherwack T&W 243 F9
Withial Som 44 F5
Withiel Corn 5 B9
Withiel Florey Som 42 G3
Withielgoose Corn 5 B10
Withielgoose Mills Corn 5 B10
Withington Glos 81 B8
Gtr Man 184 C5
Hereford 97 C11
Shrops 149 G11
Staffs 151 B10
Withington Green
Ches E 184 G4
Withington Marsh
Hereford 97 C11
Withleigh Devon 26 E6
Withnell Lancs 194 C6
Withnell Fold Lancs 194 C6
Withybed Green Worcs 117 C10
Withybrook Som 45 D7
Warks 135 G8
Withybush Pembs 73 B7
Withycombe Som 41 F11
Som 42 E4
Withycombe Raleigh
Devon 14 E6
Withyditch Bath 45 B8
Withyham E Sus 52 F3
Withy Mills Bath 45 B7
Withymoor Village
W Mid 133 F8
Withypool Som 41 F10
Withystakes Staffs 169 F7
Withywood Bristol 60 F5
Witley Sur 50 F2
Witnells End Worcs 132 G5
Witnesham Suff 126 G3
Witney Oxon 82 C5
Wittensford Hants 32 E3
Wittering Pboro 137 C11
Wittersham Kent 38 B5
Witton Angus 293 F7
Norf 142 B6
W Mid 133 E11
Worcs 117 E7
Witton Bridge Norf 160 C6
Witton Gilbert Durham 233 B10
Witton Hill Worcs 116 E5
Witton-le-Wear Durham 233 E8
Witton Park Durham 233 E9
Wiveliscombe Som 27 B9
Wivelrod Hants 49 F7
Wivelsfield E Sus 36 C4
Wivelsfield Green E Sus 36 C5
Wivenhoe Essex 107 G10
Wivenhoe Cross Essex 107 G10
Wiveton Norf 177 E8
Wix Essex 108 F3
Wixams Beds 103 C10
Wixford Warks 117 G11
Wixhill Shrops 149 D11
Wixoe Suff 106 C4
Woburn C Beds 103 E8
Woburn Sands
M Keynes 103 D8
Wofferwood Common
Hereford 116 G3
Wokefield Park W Berks 65 F7
Woking Sur 50 B4
Wokingham Wokingham 65 F10
Wolborough Devon 14 G3
Woldhurst W Sus 22 C5
Woldingham Sur 51 B11
Woldingham Garden Village
Sur 51 B11
Wold Newton E Yorks 217 E10
NE Lincs 190 B2
Wolfclyde S Lnrk 260 B2
Wolferd Green Norf 142 D5
Wolferlow Hereford 116 E3
Wolferton Norf 158 D3
Wolfhampcote Warks 119 D10
Wolfhill Perth 286 D5
Wolf's Castle Pembs 91 F9
Wolfsdale Pembs 91 G8
Wolfsdale Hill Pembs 91 G8
Woll Borders 261 E11
Wollaston Northants 121 E8
Shrops 148 G6
W Mid 133 G7
Wollaton Nottingham 153 B10
Wollerton Shrops 150 C2
Wollerton Wood Shrops 150 C2
Wollescote W Mid 133 G8
Wollrig Borders 261 E11
Wolsingham Durham 233 D7
Wolstanton Staffs 168 F5
Wolstenholme
Gtr Man 195 D11
Wolston Warks 119 B8
Wolsty Cumb 238 G4
Wolterton Norf 160 C3
Wolvercote Oxon 83 D7
Wolverham Ches W 182 F6
Wolverhampton W Mid 133 D8
Wolverley Shrops 149 C9
Worcs 116 B6
Wolverstone Devon 27 G10
Wolverton Hants 48 B5
Kent 55 E9
M Keynes 102 C6
Shrops 131 F9
Warks 118 E4
Wilts 45 G9
Wolverton Common
Hants 48 B5
Wolvesnewton Mon 79 F7
Wolvey Warks 135 F8
Wolvey Heath Warks 135 F8
Wolviston Stockton 234 F5
Womaston Powys 114 E5
Wombleton N Yorks 216 C3
Wombourne Staffs 133 E7
Wombridge Telford 150 G3
Wombwell S Yorks 197 G11
Womenswold Kent 55 C8
Womersley N Yorks 198 D4
Wonastow Mon 79 C7
Wonderstone N Som 43 B10
Wonersh Sur 50 D4
Wonford Devon 14 C4
Wonson Devon 13 D9
Wonston Dorset 30 F2
Hants 48 F3
Wooburn Bucks 66 B2
Wooburn Green Bucks 66 B2
Wood Pembs 91 G7
Som 28 D4
Woodacott Devon 24 F5
Woodacott Cross Devon 24 F5
Woodale N Yorks 213 D10
Woodbank Argyll 255 F7
Ches W 182 G5
Shrops 131 F11
Woodbastwick Norf 160 F6
Woodbeck Notts 188 F3
Wood Bevington
Warks 117 G11
Woodborough Notts 171 F10
Wilts 46 B6
Woodbridge Dorset 30 D5
Dorset 30 E2
Glos 81 C8
Northumb 253 F7
Suff 108 B5
Woodbridge Hill Sur 50 C3
Woodbridge Walk Suff 109 B7
Wood Burcote Northants 102 B3
Woodburn Common
Bucks 66 B2
Woodburn Moor Bucks 84 G6
Woodbury Devon 14 D6
Woodbury Salterton
Devon 14 D6
Woodchester Glos 80 E4
Woodchurch Kent 54 G2
Mers 182 D3
Woodcock Wilts 45 E11
Woodcock Heath
Staffs 151 D11
Woodcock Hill Herts 85 G9
W Mid 133 G10
Woodcombe Som 42 D3
Woodcot Hants 33 G9
Woodcote London 67 G10
Oxon 64 C6
Sur 51 B8
Telford 150 F5
Woodcote Green London 67 G9
Worcs 117 C8
Woodcott Hants 48 C2
Woodcroft Glos 79 F8
Woodcutts Dorset 31 D7
Wood Dalling Norf 159 D11
Woodditton Cambs 124 F3
Woodeaton Oxon 83 C8
Wood Eaton Staffs 150 F6
Wooden Pembs 73 D10
Woodend Ches E 185 D7
Cumb 219 C10
Cumb 220 F3
Cumb 229 F10
Cumb 229 G7
Essex 87 C9
Fife 280 B4
Northants 102 B2
Notts 171 C7
Staffs 152 D3
W Loth 279 F11
W Sus 22 B4
Wood End Beds 103 B10
Beds 121 D11
Beds 121 F11
Bucks 102 E5
C Beds 103 C9
Gtr Man 196 F2
Hereford 98 C2
Herts 104 F6
Warks 134 D4
Warks 134 F5
Windsor 66 E2
W Mid 133 C8
W Mid 135 G7
Wood Enderby Lincs 174 C3
Woodend Green Essex 105 F11
Northants 102 B2
Wood End Green London 66 C5
Woodend Ho Argyll 275 G11
Woodfalls Wilts 31 C11
Woodfield Glos 80 F2
Oxon 101 G11
S Ayrs 257 E8
Wood Field Sur 51 B7
Woodford Corn 24 E2
Devon 8 E5
Glos 79 F11
Gtr Man 184 E5
London 86 G6
Northants 121 B9
Plym 7 D10
Som 42 F5
Som 44 E4
Woodford Bridge London 86 G6
Woodford Green London 86 G6
Woodford Halse
Northants 119 G10
Woodford Wells London 86 G6
Woodgate Devon 27 D10
Norf 159 F10
W Mid 133 G9
Worcs 117 D9
W Sus 22 C6
Wood Gate Staffs 152 D3
Woodgate Hill Gtr Man 195 E10
Woodgates End Essex 105 F11
Woodgates Green
Worcs 116 C2
Woodgate Valley
W Mid 133 G10
Woodgreen Hants 31 D11
Oxon 82 C5
Wood Green Essex 86 E6
London 86 G4
Norf 142 E4
W Mid 133 D9
Worcs 116 D6
Woodhall Herts 86 C2
Invclyd 276 G6
N Yorks 207 G9
N Yorks 223 G9
Wood Hall Essex 105 E9
Woodhall Hills
W Yorks 205 F10
Woodhall Spa Lincs 173 C11
Woodham Bucks 84 B2
Durham 233 F11
Sur 66 G4
Woodham Ferrers Essex 88 F3
Woodham Mortimer
Essex 88 E4
Woodham Walter Essex 88 D4
Woodhatch Sur 51 D9
Woodhaven Fife 287 E8
Wood Hayes W Mid 133 C8
Woodhead Aberds 303 F7
Woodheads Borders 271 F10
Woodhey Gtr Man 195 D9
Mers 182 D4
Woodhey Green Ches E 167 E9
Woodhill Essex 88 E3
N Som 60 D3
Shrops 132 G4
Som 28 B5
Woodhorn Northumb 253 F7
Woodhouse Cumb 211 C10
Cumb 219 B9
Hants 47 D11
Leics 153 F10
N Lincs 199 F9
S Yorks 186 D6
W Yorks 196 C6
W Yorks 197 C11
W Yorks 205 F7
W Yorks 205 F11
Wood House Lancs 203 C10
Woodhouse Down S Glos 60 B6
Woodhouse Eaves
Leics 153 G10
Woodhouse Green
Staffs 168 C6
Woodhouselee Midloth 270 C4
Woodhouselees
Dumfries 239 C9
Woodhouse Mill
S Yorks 186 D6
Woodhouse Park
Gtr Man 184 D4
Woodhouses Ches W 183 F8
Cumb 239 G8
Gtr Man 184 C3
Gtr Man 196 G2
Staffs 133 B11
Staffs 152 F3
Woodhurst Cambs 122 B6
Woodingdean Brighton 36 F5
Woodington Hants 32 C4
Woodkirk W Yorks 197 C9
Woodlake Dorset 18 C3
Woodland Cumb 210 B4
Devon 8 B5
Devon 8 D2
Durham 233 F7
Kent 54 E6
Woodland Head Devon 13 B11
Woodlands Aberdeen 293 B10
Aberds 293 D9
Aberds 303 G8
Dorset 31 F9
Dumfries 238 B3
Gtr Man 185 B7
Hants 32 E4
Highld 300 C5
Kent 68 G5
London 67 D7
N Yorks 206 C2
Som 43 E7
Som 44 F4
S Yorks 198 F4
Wokingham 65 C9
W Yorks 196 B5
Woodlands Common
Dorset 31 F9
Woodlands Park
Windsor 65 D11
Woodlands St Mary
W Berks 63 E10
Woodlane Shrops 150 D3
Staffs 152 E2
Wood Lane Shrops 149 C8
Staffs 168 E4
Wood Lanes Ches E 184 E6
Woodleigh Devon 8 F4
Woodlesford W Yorks 197 B11
Woodley Gtr Man 184 C6
Hants 32 C5
Wokingham 65 E9
Woodley Green
Wokingham 65 E9
Woodleys Oxon 82 B6
Woodlinkin Derbys 170 F6
Woodloes Park Warks 118 D5
Woodmancote Glos 80 F3
Glos 81 D8
Glos 99 F9
Worcs 99 C8
W Sus 22 B3
W Sus 36 E2
Woodmancott Hants 48 E5
Woodmansey E Yorks 209 F7
Woodmansgreen W Sus 34 B5
Woodmans Green E Sus 38 D3
Woodmansterne Sur 51 B9
Woodmill Staffs 152 E2
Woodminton Wilts 31 C8
Woodnesborough Kent 55 B10
Woodnewton Northants 137 E10
Woodnook Lancs 195 B9
Lincs 155 C8
Wood Norton Norf 159 D10
Worcs 99 B10
Woodplumpton Lancs 202 G6
Woodram Som 28 D2
Woodrising Norf 141 C9
Wood Road Gtr Man 195 E9
Woodrow Bucks 84 F6
Cumb 229 B10
Dorset 30 E3
Dorset 30 F2
Worcs 117 B7
Worcs 117 D11
Wood Row W Yorks 197 B11
Woods Hereford 96 B5
Woods Bank W Mid 133 D9
Woodsden Kent 53 G9
Woodseats Derbys 185 C7
Wood Seats S Yorks 186 B4
Woodseaves Shrops 150 C3
Staffs 150 D5
Woodsend Pembs 72 C5
Wilts 63 D8
Woods End Gtr Man 184 B2
Woodsetton W Mid 133 E8
Woodsetts S Yorks 187 E9
Woodsfield Worcs 98 B6
Woodsfold Lancs 202 F5
Woodsford Dorset 17 C11
Wood's Green E Sus 52 G6
Woodside Aberdeen 293 C11
Aberds 303 E10
Beds 121 G11
Brack 66 E2
C Beds 85 B9
Ches E 167 C10
Ches W 183 G8
Derbys 170 G5
Derbys 187 G7
Dumfries 238 B2
Durham 233 F9
Essex 87 E7
Fife 287 G8
Hants 20 C2
Herts 85 E10
Herts 86 D3
IoW 20 C6
London 67 F10
N Lincs 199 G8
Perth 286 D6
Shrops 130 G6
Telford 132 C3
W Mid 133 F8
W Yorks 196 B6
Woodside Green Essex 87 B8
Kent 54 C2
Woodside of Arbeadie
Aberds 293 D9
Woodside Park London 86 G3
Woods Moor Gtr Man 184 D6
Woodspeen W Berks 64 F2
Woodspring Priory
N Som 59 F10
Wood Stanway Glos 99 E11
Woodstock Kent 70 G2
Oxon 82 B6
Pembs 91 F10
Woodston Pboro 138 D3
Wood Street Norf 161 E7
Sur 50 C3
Wood Street Village Sur 50 C3
Woodthorpe Derbys 187 G7
Leics 153 F10
Lincs 190 E6
Notts 171 G9
York 207 D7
Woodton Norf 142 E5
Woodtown Devon 24 C6
Devon 25 B7
Woodvale Mers 193 E10
Woodville Derbys 152 F6
Dorset 30 C4
Woodville Feus Angus 287 C10
Woodwall Green Staffs 150 C5
Wood Walton Cambs 138 G4
Woodway Oxon 64 C4
Woodway Park W Mid 135 G7
Woodwell Northants 121 B9
Woodwick Orkney 314 D3
Woodworth Green
Ches E 167 D9
Woodyates Dorset 31 D8
Woody Bay Devon 41 D7
Woofferton Shrops 115 D10
Wookey Som 44 D4
Wookey Hole Som 44 D4
Wool Dorset 18 D2
Woolacombe Devon 40 E3
Woolage Green Kent 55 D8
Woolage Village Kent 55 C8
Woolaston Glos 79 F9
Woolaston Common Glos 79 E9
Woolaston Slade Glos 79 E9
Woolaston Woodside
Glos 79 E9
Woolavington Som 43 E10
Woolbeding W Sus 34 C5
Wooldale W Yorks 197 F7
Wooler Northumb 263 D11
Woolfall Heath Mers 182 C6
Woolfardisworthy Devon 26 F4
Woolfardisworthy or
Woolsery Devon 24 C4
Woolfold Gtr Man 195 E9
Woolfords Cottages S
Lnrk 269 D10
Woolford's Water Dorset 29 F11
Woolgarston Dorset 18 E5
Woolgreaves W Yorks 197 D10
Woolhampton W Berks 64 F5
Woolhope Hereford 98 D2
Woolhope Cockshoot
Hereford 98 D2
Woolland Dorset 30 F3
Woollard Bath 60 G6
Woollaston Staffs 151 F7
Woollaton Devon 25 E7
Woollensbrook Herts 86 C5
Woolley Bath 61 F8
Cambs 122 C3
Corn 24 D3
Derbys 170 C5
Wilts 61 G10
W Yorks 197 E10
Woolley Bridge Gtr Man 185 B8
Woolley Green Wilts 61 G10
Windsor 65 C11
Woolmere Green Worcs 117 E9
Woolmer Green Herts 86 B3
Woolmer Hill Sur 49 G11
Woolmersdon Som 43 G9
Woolminstone Som 28 F6
Woolpack Corner Kent 53 F11
Woolpit Suff 125 E9
Woolpit Green Suff 125 E9
Woolpit Heath Suff 125 E9
Woolridge Glos 98 G6
Woolsbridge Dorset 31 F9
Woolscott Warks 119 D9
Woolsery or
Woolfardisworthy
Devon 24 C4
Woolsgrove Devon 26 G3
Woolsington T&W 242 D5
Woolstanwood Ches E 167 D11
Woolstaston Shrops 131 D9
Woolsthorpe Lincs 155 E8
Woolsthorpe by Belvoir
Lincs 154 C6
Woolsthorpe-by-
Colsterworth Lincs 155 E8
Woolston Corn 6 B5
Devon 8 G4
Shrops 131 F8
Shrops 148 E6
Som 29 B10
Som 42 F5
Soton 32 E6
Warr 183 D10
Woolstone Glos 99 E9
M Keynes 103 D7
Oxon 63 B9
Woolston Green Devon 8 B5
Woolton Mers 182 D6
Woolton Hill Hants 64 G2
Woolvers Hill N Som 59 G11
Woolverstone Suff 108 D3
Woolverton Som 45 C9
Woolwell Devon 7 C10
Woolwich London 68 D2
Woolwich Ferry London 68 D2
Woon Corn 5 D10
Woonton Hereford 115 E10
Hereford 115 G7
Wooperton Northumb 264 E2
Wooplaw Borders 271 G9
Woore Shrops 168 G2
Wooton Shrops 115 C11
Shrops 132 F5
Wootten Green Suff 126 C4
Wootton Beds 103 B10
Hants 19 B10
Hereford 97 D11
Hereford 114 G6
IoW 20 C6
Kent 55 D8
N Lincs 200 D5
Northants 120 F5
Oxon 82 B6
Oxon 83 E7
Shrops 115 B9
Shrops 148 D6
Staffs 150 D6
Staffs 169 F10
Wootton Bourne End
Beds 103 B9
Wootton Bridge IoW 20 C6
Wootton Broadmead
Beds 103 C10
Wootton Common IoW 20 C6
Wootton Courtenay Som 42 E2
Wootton Fitzpaine Dorset 16 B3
Wootton Green Beds 103 C9
W Mid 118 B4
Wootton Rivers Wilts 63 G7
Woottons Staffs 151 B11
Wootton St Lawrence
Hants 48 C5
Wootton Wawen Warks 118 E3
Worbarrow Dorset 18 F3
Worcester Worcs 117 F7
Worcester Park London 67 F8
Wordsley W Mid 133 F7
Wordwell Suff 124 C6
Worfield Shrops 132 D5
Worgret Dorset 18 D4
Work Orkney 314 E4
Workhouse Common
Norf 161 E7
Workhouse End Beds 122 G2
Workhouse Green Suff 107 D8
Workhouse Hill Essex 107 E9
Workington Cumb 228 F5
Worksop Notts 187 F9
Worlaby Lincs 190 F4
N Lincs 200 E4
Worlds End Hants 33 E10
W Mid 134 G2
World's End Bucks 84 D5
London 86 F4
Suff 125 F9
W Berks 64 D3
W Sus 36 D4
Worle N Som 59 G11
Worlebury N Som 59 G10
Worleston Ches E 167 D11
Worley Glos 80 F4
Worlingham Suff 143 F8
Worlington Devon 40 G3
Suff 124 C3
Worlingworth Suff 126 D4
Wormadale Shetland 313 J5
Wormald Green
N Yorks 214 G6
Wormbridge Hereford 97 E8
Wormbridge Common
Hereford 97 E8
Wormegay Norf 158 G3
Wormelow Tump
Hereford 97 E9
Wormhill Derbys 185 G10
Wormingford Essex 107 E8
Worminghall Bucks 83 D10
Wormington Glos 99 D10
Worminster Som 44 E5
Wormiston Ho Fife 287 G10
Wormit Fife 287 E7
Wormleighton Warks 119 G8
Wormley Herts 86 D5
Sur 50 F2
Wormleybury Herts 86 D5
Wormley West End Herts 86 D4
Worms Ash Worcs 117 C8
Wormshill Kent 53 B11
Worms Hill Kent 53 F8
Wormsley Hereford 97 B8
Wornish Nook Ches E 168 B4
Worplesdon Sur 50 C3
Worrall S Yorks 186 C4
Worrall Hill Glos 79 C10
Worsbrough S Yorks 197 G11
Worsbrough Bridge
S Yorks 197 G11
Worsbrough Common
S Yorks 197 F10
Worsbrough Dale
S Yorks 197 G11
Worsham Oxon 82 C3
Worsley Gtr Man 195 G8
Worsley Hall Gtr Man 194 F5
Worsley Mesnes
Gtr Man 194 G5
Worstead Norf 160 D6
Worsthorne Lancs 204 G3
Worston Devon 7 E11
Lancs 203 E11
Worswell Devon 7 F10
Worten Kent 54 E3
Worth Kent 55 B10
Som 44 D4
W Sus 51 F9
Worth Abbey W Sus 51 G10
Wortham Suff 125 B11
Worthen Shrops 130 C6
Worthenbury Wrex 166 F6
Worthing Norf 159 F9
W Sus 35 G10
Worthington Leics 153 E8
Worth Matravers Dorset 18 F5
Worthy Som 41 D11
Worthybrook Mon 79 C7
Worting Hants 48 C6
Wortley Glos 80 G3
S Yorks 186 B4
W Yorks 205 G11
Worton N Yorks 223 G9
Oxon 83 C7
Wilts 46 B3
Wortwell Norf 142 G5
Wotherton Shrops 130 C5
Wothorpe Pboro 137 B10
Wotter Devon 7 C11
Wotton Glos 80 B4
Sur 50 D6
Wotton-under-Edge
Glos 80 G3
Wotton Underwood
Bucks 83 B11
Woughton on the Green
M Keynes 103 D7
Woughton Park
M Keynes 103 D7
Wouldham Kent 69 G8
Woundale Shrops 132 E5
Wrabness Essex 108 E3
Wraes Aberds 302 F5
Wrafton Devon 40 F3
Wragby Lincs 189 F10
W Yorks 198 D2
Wragholme Lincs 190 B5
Wramplingham Norf 142 B2
Wrangaton Devon 8 D3
Wrangbrook W Yorks 198 E3
Wrangham Aberds 302 F6
Wrangle Lincs 174 E6
Wrangle Bank Lincs 174 E6
Wrangle Lowgate Lincs 174 E6
Wrangle Low Ground
Lincs 174 E6
Wrangway Som 27 D10
Wrantage Som 28 C4
Wrawby N Lincs 200 F4
Wraxall Dorset 29 G9
N Som 60 E3
Som 44 F6
Wray Lancs 212 F2
Wray Common Sur 51 C9
Wraysbury Windsor 66 E4
Wrayton Lancs 212 E2
Wrea Green Lancs 202 G3
Wreaks End Cumb 210 B4
Wreath Som 28 F4
Wreay Cumb 230 B4
Cumb 230 G4
Wrecclesham Sur 49 D10
Wrekenton T&W 243 F7
Wrelton N Yorks 216 B5
Wrenbury Ches E 167 F9
Wrenbury cum Frith
Ches E 167 F9
Wrench Green N Yorks 217 B9
Wreningham Norf 142 D3
Wrentham Suff 143 G9
Wrenthorpe W Yorks 197 C10
Wrentnall Shrops 131 C8
Wressle E Yorks 207 G10
N Lincs 200 F3
Wrestlingworth C Beds 104 B5
Wretham Norf 141 F8
Wretton Norf 140 D3
Wrexham Wrex 166 E4
Wreyland Devon 13 E11
Wribbenhall Worcs 116 B5
Wrickton Shrops 132 F2
Wrightington Bar Lancs 194 E4
Wright's Green Essex 87 B8
Wrinehill Staffs 168 F3
Wringsdown Corn 12 D2
Wrington N Som 60 G3
Wrinkleberry Devon 24 C4
Writhlington Bath 45 C8
Writtle Essex 87 D11
Wrockwardine Telford 150 G2
Wrockwardine Wood
Telford 150 G4
Wroot N Lincs 199 G8
Wrose W Yorks 205 F9
Wrotham Kent 52 B6
Wrotham Heath Kent 52 B6
Wroughton Swindon 62 C6
Wroxall IoW 21 F7
Warks 118 C4
Wroxeter Shrops 131 B11
Wroxhall Warks 118 C4
Wroxham Norf 160 F6
Wroxton Oxon 101 C8
Wyaston Derbys 169 G11
Wyatt's Green Essex 87 F9
Wybers Wood NE Lincs 201 F8
Wyberton Lincs 174 G4
Wyboston Beds 122 F3
Wybunbury Ches E 168 F2
Wychbold Worcs 117 D8
Wych Cross E Sus 52 G2
Wychnor Staffs 152 F3
Wychnor Bridges Staffs 152 F3
Wyck Hants 49 F9
Wyck Rissington Glos 100 G3
Wycliffe Durham 224 C2
Wycoller Lancs 204 F4
Wycomb Leics 154 E5
Wycombe Marsh Bucks 84 G5
Wyddial Herts 105 E7
Wydra N Yorks 205 C10
Wye Kent 54 D5
Wyebanks Kent 54 C2
Wyegate Green Glos 79 D9
Wyesham Mon 79 C8
Wyfordby Leics 154 F5
Wyke Dorset 30 B3
Shrops 132 C2
Sur 50 C2
W Yorks 197 B7
Wyke Champflower Som 45 G7
Wykeham Lincs 156 D5
N Yorks 216 D6
N Yorks 217 C9
Wyken Shrops 132 E5
W Mid 135 G7
Wyke Regis Dorset 17 F9
Wykey Shrops 149 E7
Wykin Leics 135 D8
Wylam Northumb 242 E4
Wylde Hereford 115 D9
Wylde Green W Mid 134 E2
Wyllie Caerph 77 G11
Wylye Wilts 46 F4
Wymans Brook Glos 99 G8
Wymbush M Keynes 102 D6
Wymering Ptsmth 33 F10
Wymeswold Leics 154 E2
Wymington Beds 121 E9
Wymondham Leics 155 F7
Norf 142 C2
Wymondley Bury Herts 104 F4
Wymott Lancs 194 C4
Wyndham Bridgend 76 G6
Wyndham Park V Glam 58 D5
Wynds Point Hereford 98 C5
Wynford Eagle Dorset 17 B7
Wyng Orkney 314 G3
Wynn's Green Hereford 98 B2
Wynyard Village
Stockton 234 F4
Wyre Piddle Worcs 99 B9
Wysall Notts 154 D2
Wyson Hereford 115 D10
Wythall Worcs 117 B11
Wytham Oxon 83 D7
Wythburn Cumb 220 C6
Wythenshawe Gtr Man 184 D4
Wythop Mill Cumb 229 F9
Wyton Cambs 122 C5
E Yorks 209 G9
Wyverstone Suff 125 D10
Wyverstone Green
Suff 125 D10
Wyverstone Street
Suff 125 D10
Wyville Lincs 155 D7
Wyvis Lodge Highld 300 B4

Y

Yaddlethorpe N Lincs 199 F11
Yafford IoW 20 E4
Yafforth N Yorks 224 G6
Yair Borders 261 C11
Yalberton Torbay 9 D7
Yalding Kent 53 C7
Yanley N Som 60 F5
Yanworth Glos 81 C9
Yapham E Yorks 207 C11
Yapton W Sus 35 G7
Yarberry N Som 43 B11
Yarborough NE Lincs 201 F9
Yarbridge IoW 21 D8
Yarburgh Lincs 190 C5
Yarcombe Devon 28 F2
Yard Som 42 F5
Yarde Som 42 F5
Yardhurst Kent 54 E3
Yardley W Mid 134 F2
Yardley Gobion
Northants 102 C5
Yardley Hastings
Northants 121 F7
Yardley Wood W Mid 118 B2
Yardro Powys 114 F4
Yarford Som 28 B2
Yarhampton Worcs 116 D5
Yarhampton Cross
Worcs 116 D5
Yarkhill Hereford 98 C2
Yarlet Staffs 151 D8
Yarley Som 44 D4
Yarlington Som 29 B11
Yarlside Cumb 210 F4
Yarm Stockton 225 C8
Yarmouth IoW 20 D3
Yarnacott Devon 40 G6
Yarnbrook Wilts 45 C11
Yarnfield Staffs 151 C7
Yarningale Common
Warks 118 D3
Yarnscombe Devon 25 C9
Yarnton Oxon 83 C7
Yarpole Hereford 115 E9
Yarrow Borders 261 D9
Northumb 250 F6
Som 43 D11
Yarrow Feus Borders 261 D8
Yarrowford Borders 261 C10
Yarsop Hereford 97 B8
Yarwell Northants 137 D11
Yate S Glos 61 C8
Yateley Hants 65 G10
Yate Rocks S Glos 61 C8
Yatesbury Wilts 62 E5
Yattendon W Berks 64 E5
Yatton Hereford 115 D8
N Som 60 F2
Yatton Keynell Wilts 61 D11
Yaverland IoW 21 D8
Yawthorpe Lincs 188 C5
Yaxham Norf 159 G10
Yaxley Cambs 138 E3
Suff 126 C2
Yazor Hereford 97 B8
Y Bala / Bala Gwyn 147 B8
Y Bont Faen / Cowbridge
V Glam 58 E3
Y Borth / Borth Ceredig 128 E2
Yeabridge Som 28 D6
Yeading London 66 C6
Yeadon W Yorks 205 E10
Yealand Conyers Lancs 211 E10
Yealand Redmayne
Lancs 211 D10
Yealand Storrs Lancs 211 D9
Yealmbridge Devon 7 E11
Yealmpton Devon 7 E11
Yearby Redcar 235 G8
Yearngill Cumb 229 C8
Yearsley N Yorks 215 E11
Yeaton Shrops 149 F8
Yeaveley Derbys 169 G11
Yedingham N Yorks 217 D7
Yelden Beds 121 D10
Yeldersley Hollies
Derbys 170 G2
Yeldon Beds 121 D10
Yelford Oxon 82 E5
Yelland Devon 40 G3
Yelling Cambs 122 E5
Yelsted Kent 69 G10
Yelvertoft Northants 119 B11
Yelverton Devon 7 B10
Norf 142 C5
Yenston Som 30 C2
Yeoford Devon 13 B11
Yeolmbridge Corn 12 D2
Yeo Mill Devon 26 B4
Yeo Vale Devon 24 C6
Yeovil Som 29 D9
Yeovil Marsh Som 29 D8
Yeovilton Som 29 C8
Yerbeston Pembs 73 D9
Yesnaby Orkney 314 E2
Yetlington Northumb 252 B2
Yetminster Dorset 29 E9
Yett N Lnrk 268 D5
Yettington Devon 15 D7
Yetts o' Muckhart Clack 286 G4
Yew Green Warks 118 D4
Yewhedges Kent 54 B3
Yew Tree Gtr Man 185 B7
W Mid 133 D10
Yewtree Cross Kent 55 E7
Y Fali / Valley Anglesey 178 F3
Y Felinheli / Port Dinorwic
Gwyn 163 B8
Y Ferwig Ceredig 92 B3
Y Ffôr Gwyn 145 B7
Y-Ffrith Denb 181 E8
Y Gors Ceredig 112 B2
Y Gribyn Powys 129 E8
Yieldshields S Lnrk 269 E7
Yiewsley London 66 C5
Yinstay Orkney 314 E5
Y Mwmbwls / The Mumbles
Swansea 56 D6
Ynus-tawelog Swansea 75 D10
Ynys Gwyn 145 B11
Ynysboeth Rhondda 77 F9
Ynysddu Caerph 77 G11
Ynysforgan Swansea 57 B7
Ynysgyfflog Gwyn 146 G2
Ynyshir Rhondda 77 G8
Ynys-isaf Powys 76 C3
Ynyslas Ceredig 128 E2
Ynysmaerdy Neath 57 B8
Rhondda 58 C4
Ynysmeudwy Neath 76 D2
Neath 76 D2
Ynys Tachwedd Ceredig 128 E2
Ynystawe Swansea 75 E11
Ynyswen Powys 76 C4
Rhondda 77 F7
Ynysybwl Rhondda 77 G9
Ynysygwas Neath 57 C9
Yockenthwaite N Yorks 213 D8
Yockleton Shrops 149 G7
Yodercott Devon 27 E9
Yokefleet E Yorks 199 C10
Yoker W Dunb 267 B10
Yonder Bognie Aberds 302 E5
Yondertown Devon 7 D11
Yopps Green Kent 52 C6
York Lancs 203 G10
York 207 C7
Yorkletts Kent 70 G5
Yorkley Glos 79 D10
Yorkley Slade Glos 79 D10
York Town Sur 65 G11
Yorton Shrops 149 E10
Yorton Heath Shrops 149 E10
Yottenfews Cumb 219 D10
Youlgrave Derbys 170 C2
Youlstone Devon 24 D3
Youlthorpe E Yorks 207 B11
Youlton N Yorks 215 G9
Youngsbury Herts 86 B5
Young's End Essex 88 B2
Young Wood Lincs 189 G10
Yoxall Staffs 152 F2
Yoxford Suff 127 D7
Y Pîl / Pyle Bridgend 57 E10
Yr Hôb / Hope Flint 166 D4
Ysbyty Cynfyn Ceredig 112 B4
Ysbyty Ifan Conwy 164 F4
Ysbyty Ystwyth Ceredig 112 D4
Ysceifiog Flint 181 G11
Ysgeibion Denb 165 D9
Yspitty Carms 56 B5
Ystalyfera Neath 76 D3
Ystrad Rhondda 77 F7
Ystrad Aeron Ceredig 111 F10
Ystradfellte Powys 76 C6
Ystradffin Carms 94 B5
Ystradgynlais Powys 76 C3
Ystradmeurig Ceredig 112 D4
Ystrad-mynach Caerph 77 G10
Ystradowen Carms 76 C2
V Glam 58 D4
Ystrad Uchaf Powys 129 C11
Ystumtuen Ceredig 112 B4
Ythanbank Aberds 303 F9
Ythanwells Aberds 302 F6
Ythsie Aberds 303 F8
Y Tumble / Tumble Carms 75 C8
Y Waun / Chirk Wrex 148 B5

Z

Zeal Monachorum Devon 26 G2
Zeals Wilts 45 G9
Zelah Corn 4 E6
Zennor Corn 1 B5
Zoar Corn 3 F7
Zouch Notts 153 E10

County and unitary authority boundaries

Ordnance Survey National Grid

The blue lines which divide the Navigator map pages into squares for indexing match the Ordnance Survey National Grid and correspond to the small squares on the boundary map below. Each side of a grid square measures 10km on the ground.

The National Grid 100-km square letters and kilometre values are indicated for the grid intersection at the outer corners of each page. For example, the intersection SE6090 at the upper right corner of page 215 is 60km East and 90km North of the south-west corner of National Grid square SE.

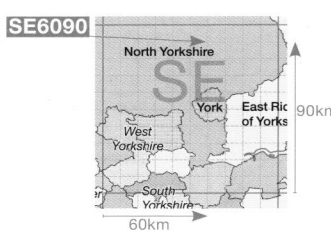

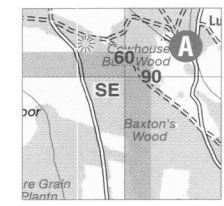

Using GPS with Navigator mapping

Since Navigator Britain is based on Ordnance Survey mapping, and rectified to the National Grid, it can be used with in-car or handheld GPS for locating identifiable waypoints such as road junctions, bridges, railways and farms, or assessing your position in relation to any of the features shown on the map.

On your receiver, choose British Grid as the location format and for map datum select Ordnance Survey (this may be described as Ord Srvy GB or similar, or more specifically as OSGB36). Your receiver will automatically convert the latitude/longitude co-ordinates transmitted by GPS into compatible National Grid data.

Positional accuracy of any particular feature is limited to 50–100m, due to the limitations of the original survey and the scale of Navigator mapping.

For further information see www.gps.gov.uk

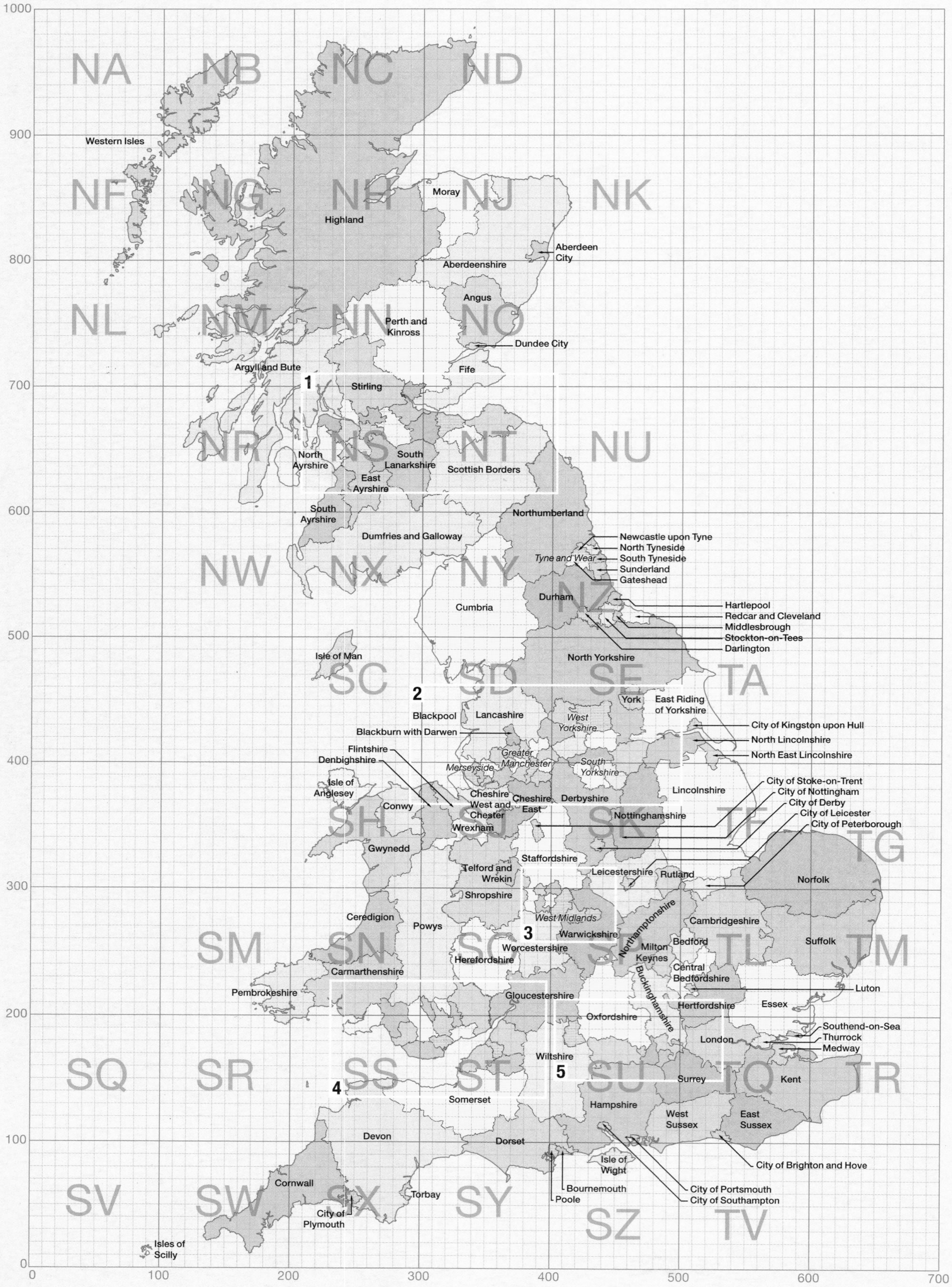

Greater London

1 City and County of the City of London
2 Hackney
3 Tower Hamlets
4 Southwark
5 Lambeth
6 Wandsworth
7 Hammersmith and Fulham
8 Royal Borough of Kensington and Chelsea
9 City of Westminster
10 Camden
11 Islington
12 Haringey
13 Waltham Forest
14 Newham
15 Greenwich
16 Lewisham
17 Merton
18 Richmond upon Thames
19 Hounslow
20 Ealing
21 Brent
22 Barnet
23 Enfield
24 Redbridge
25 Barking and Dagenham
26 Havering
27 Bexley
28 Bromley
29 Croydon
30 Sutton
31 Kingston upon Thames
32 Hillingdon
33 Harrow

1 Central Scotland

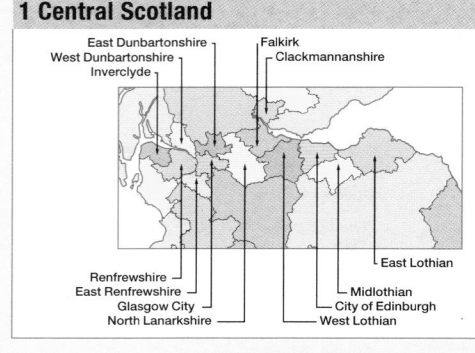

2 Northern England

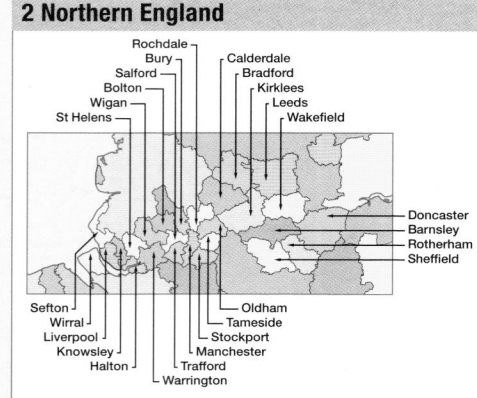

3 West Midlands

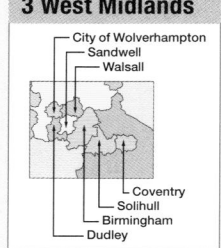

4 South Wales and Bristol area

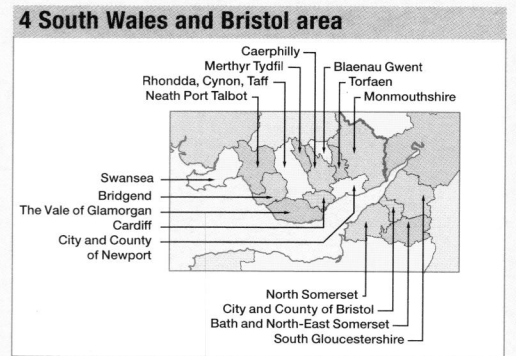

5 Thames Valley

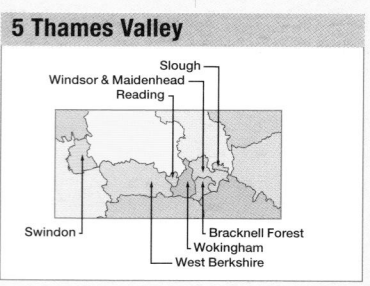